D1314573

The IEBM Handbook of Human Resource Management

The IEBM Handbook of Human Resource Management

Edited by
Michael Poole and Malcolm Warner

INTERNATIONAL THOMSON BUSINESS PRESS
I(T)P® An International Thomson Publishing Company

London • Bonn • Boston • Johannesburg • Madrid • Melbourne • Mexico City • New York • Paris •
Singapore • Tokyo • Toronto • Albany, NY • Belmont, CA • Cincinnati, OH • Detroit, MI

The IEBM Handbook of Human Resource Management

Copyright ©1998 International Thomson Business Press

First published by International Thomson Business Press

I⊤P®   A division of International Thomson Publishing Inc.
The ITP logo is a trademark under licence

British Library Cataloguing-in-Publication Data
A catalogue record for this book is available from the British Library

First edition 1998

Typeset by Hodgson Williams Associates, Cambridge
Printed in England by Clays Ltd, St Ives plc

ISBN 1-86152 -166-9

International Thomson Business Press   International Thomson Business Press
Berkshire House   20 Park Plaza
168–173 High Holborn   13th Floor
London WC1V 7AA   Boston MA 02116
UK   USA

http://www.itbp.com

Contents

Contents

List of Contributors

Professor Roy J. Adams
Emeritus Professor of Industrial Relations
DeGroote School of Business
McMaster University
Hamilton
Ontario
Canada

Dr Alan Arthurs
School of Management
University of Bath
Avon
England

Professor Greg J. Bamber
Director, Graduate School of Management
Griffith University
Brisbane
Queensland
Australia

Professor Miryam Barad
Department of Industrial Engineering
Tel Aviv University
Israel

Professor Philippe Bernoux
Directeur de Recherches
Groupe Lyonnais de Sociologie Industrielle
Centre National de la Recherche
Scientifique
Université Lumiére Lyon II
France

Professor Paul Blyton
Professor of Industrial Relations and
Industrial Sociology
Cardiff Business School
University of Wales, Cardiff
Wales

Professor Chris Brewster
Director, Centre for European Human
Resource Management
Cranfield School of Management
Cranfield University
Bedford
England

Professor William Brown
Montague Burton Professor of Industrial
Relations
Faculty of Economics and Politics
University of Cambridge
England

Professor Dr André Büssing
Chair of Psychology
Faculty of Economics and Social Science
Technical University of Munich
Munich
Germany

Professor Richard Butler
Professor of Organizational Analysis, and
Chair of Graduate School of Social Sciences
and Humanities
Management Centre
University of Bradford
England

Professor Kim S. Cameron
Marriott School of Management
Brigham Young University
Provo
Utah
USA

Professor Robert F. Conti
Associate Professor
Bryant College
Rhode Island
USA

Mrs Jane Cranwell-Ward
Director, Henley Learning Partnership
Henley Management College
Henley-on-Thames
England

Professor David Cray
School of Business
Carleton University
Ottawa
Canada

Professor Colin Crouch
*European University Institute, Florence,
Italy
and Fellow, Trinity College
University of Oxford
England*

Professor Anne Cummings
*Department of Management
The Wharton School
University of Pennsylvania
Philadelphia, PA
USA*

Dr Anne Daly
*School of Economics and Marketing
University of Canberra
Belconnen
Australia*

Dr Helen De Cieri
*Department of Human Resource Studies
Cornell University
Ithaca, NY
USA*

Peter J. Dowling
*Department of Management
University of Tasmania
Launceston
Australia*

Professor Paul K. Edwards
*Industrial Relations Research Unit (IRRU)
Warwick Business School
University of Warwick
Coventry
England*

Professor J.E.T. Eldridge
*Department of Sociology
University of Glasgow
Scotland*

Professor Ellen Fagenson-Eland
*Associate Professor
George Mason University
Fairfax
Virginia
USA*

Professor Robert J. Flanagan
*Konosuke Matsushita Professor of
International Labor Economics and Policy
Analysis
Graduate School of Business
Stanford University
Stanford
California
USA*

Professor Gary W. Florkowski
*Joseph M. Katz Graduate School of
Business
University of Pittsburgh
Pennsylvania
USA*

Professor Yitzhak Fried
*Department of Management and
Organization Science
School of Business Administration
Wayne State University
Detroit
Michigan
USA*

Professor Sally Riggs Fuller
*Department of Management and
Organization
School of Business Administration
University of Washington
Seattle
USA*

Colin Gill
*Lecturer in Management Studies
The Judge Institute of Management Studies
University of Cambridge
England*

Dr Richard Gillespie
*Museum of Victoria
Melbourne
Australia*

Dr Ian Glover
*Lecturer
Department of Management and
Organization
University of Stirling
Scotland*

Dr Pauline Graham
Research Fellow
Department of Engineering
University of Bradford
England

Professor Wyn Grant
Professor of Politics
University of Warwick
Coventry
England

Professor Justin Greenwood
School of Public Administration and Law
The Robert Gordon University
Aberdeen
Scotland

Professor David Guest
Department of Organizational Psychology
Birkbeck College
University of London
England

Professor Tove Helland Hammer
Department of Organizational Behavior
New York State School of Industrial and
Labor Relations
Cornell University
Ithaca, NY
USA

Dr Charles Hampden-Turner
Judge Institute of Management Studies
University of Cambridge
England

Professor John Hayes
Leeds University Business School
University of Leeds
England

Dr Frank Heller
The Tavistock Institute
London
England

Professor Peter Herriot
Associate Director
Institute for Employment Studies
and Visiting Professor
City University Business School
and University of Surrey

Professor Dr Friso den Hertog
Professor of Innovation Management
Maastricht Economic Research Institute on
Innovation and Technology
The University of Maastricht
The Netherlands

Dr Martin Hilb
Professor of Business Administration
Director of the Institute for Leadership and
Human Resource Management
University of St Gallen
Switzerland
and Adjunct Professor of International
Human Resource Management
University of Dallas
Texas
USA

Dr Geert Hofstede
Emeritus Professor of Organizational
Anthropology and
International Management
Maastricht University
The Netherlands

Professor Vandra L. Huber
Department of Management and
Organization
School of Business Administration
University of Washington
Seattle
USA

John M. Jermier
College of Business
University of South Florida
Tampa
USA

Dr Ian Kessler
Fellow
Templeton College
and School of Management Studies
University of Oxford
England

Dr Robin J. Kramar
Senior Lecturer
Graduate School of Management
Macquarie University
Sydney
Australia

Professor Karen Legge
Warwick Business School
University of Warwick
Coventry
England

Professor Richard J. Long
Professor, College of Commerce
University of Saskatchewan
Saskatoon
Canada

Professor Craig Lundberg
School of Hotel Administration
Cornell University
Ithaca
NY
USA

Sara McGaughey
Department of Management
University of Tasmania
Launceston
Australia

Professor Gerald Mars
Management Centre
University of Bradford
England

Dr Segun Matanmi
Senior Lecturer
Department of Sociology
Lagos State University
Nigeria

Jennifer M. Myatt
Goizueta Business School
Emory University
Atlanta
Georgia
USA

Professor Walter Nord
Professor of Organizational Theory
College of Business
University of South Florida
Tampa
USA

L.I. Okazaki-Ward
Senior Research Fellow
Cranfield School of Management
Cranfield University
Bedford
England

Professor Koji Okubayashi
School of Business Administration
Kobe University
Kobe
Japan

Professor Greg R. Oldham
C. Clinton Spivey Professor
University of Illinois at Urbana-Champaign
USA

Dr Nick Oliver
Reader, Judge Institute of Management
Studies
University of Cambridge
England

Professor Barbara Parker
Albers School of Business and Economics
Seattle University
Washington
USA

Lisa Hope Pelled
Assistant Professor
Management and Organization
University of Southern California
Marshall School of Business
Los Angeles
USA

Professor Michael Poole
Professor of Human Resource Management
Cardiff Business School
University of Wales, Cardiff
Wales

Professor Betty Jane Punnett
Mona Institute of Business
University of the West Indies
and University of Windsor, Canada

Professor John Purcell
Work and Employment Research Centre
(WERC)
School of Management
University of Bath
Avon
England

W. David Rees
Independent Consultant
and Visiting Lecturer
University of Westminster
England

Dr Chris Rowley
Lecturer
School of Management
Royal Holloway College
University of London
England

Professor Dr S. Antonio Ruiz-Quintanilla
Visiting Associate Professor
New York State School of Industrial and
Labor Relations
Cornell University
Ithaca, NY
USA

Dr Paul Ryan
Institute of Industrial Relations
University of California at Berkeley
USA
and
King's College
University of Cambridge
England

Professor Yoko Sano
Faculty of Business and Commerce
Tokyo International University
Japan

Professor Randall S. Schuler
Stern School of Business
New York University
USA

David E. Simmons
Australian Centre in Strategic Management
Queensland University of Technology
Brisbane
Australia

Bob Simpson
Reader in Law
London School of Economics and Political
Science
England

Professor Chris Smith
School of Management
Royal Holloway College
University of London
Egham, Surrey
England

Dr Ian G. Smith
Senior Lecturer
Cardiff Business School
University of Wales, Cardiff
Wales

Professor Jeffrey Sonnenfeld
Goizueta Business School
Emory University
Atlanta
Georgia
USA

Professor Arndt Sorge
Scientific Director of WORC (Work and
Organization Research Centre)
Tilburg University
The Netherlands

Dr Gillian Stamp
Director of the Brunel Institute of
Organisation & Social Studies (BIOSS)
Brunel University
Uxbridge
England

Dr Rosemary Stewart
Emeritus Fellow in Organizational
Behaviour
Director of Oxford Health Care
Management Institute
Templeton College
University of Oxford
England

Professor John Storey
Open University Business School
The Open University
Milton Keynes
England

Professor George Strauss
Emeritus Professor of Business
Administration
Institute of Industrial Relations
University of California at Berkeley
USA

Dr Joo-Seng Tan
Nanyang Business School
Nanyang Technological University
Singapore

Dr Paul Taylor
Senior Lecturer
Department of Psychology
The University of Waikato
Hamilton
New Zealand

Professor George Thomason
Emeritus Professor
University of Wales, Cardiff
Wales

Thera Tolner
Research Fellow
Maastricht Economic Research Institute on
Innovation and Technology
University of Maastricht
The Netherlands

Professor Derek P. Torrington
Emeritus Professor of Human Resource
Management
Manchester School of Management
University of Manchester Institute of
Science and Technology (UMIST)
England

Professor Rosalie L. Tung
Ming and Stella Wong Professor of
International Business
Faculty of Business Administration
Simon Fraser University
Burnaby
British Columbia
Canada

Dr Terry Wallace
Lecturer in Industrial Sociology and
Industrial Relations
Cardiff Business School
University of Wales, Cardiff
Wales

Professor Malcolm Warner
Fellow
Wolfson College
and Judge Institute of Management Studies
University of Cambridge
England

Professor Hoyt N. Wheeler
College of Business Administration
University of South Carolina
Columbia
USA

Professor William Foote Whyte
New York State School of Industrial and
Labor Relations
Cornell University
Ithaca, NY
USA

Dr Adrian Wilkinson
Manchester School of Management
University of Manchester Institute of
Science and Technology (UMIST)
England

Morgen Witzel
London Business School
and Durham University Business School
England

Professor Mohamed Zairi
SABIC Chair in Best Practice Management
The European Centre for Total Quality
Management
University of Bradford
England

Professor Milan Zeleny
Graduate School of Business
Fordham University at Lincoln Center
New York
USA

Acknowledgements

The publishers would like to thank the following for permission to use copyright material:

Culture, cross-national
Country clusters
S. Ronen and O. Shenkar (1985) 'Clustering countries on attitudinal dimensions: a review any synthesis', *Academy of Management Review.*

Cultural values: levels of individualism in alpha and beta
Reproduced from M. Mendenhall, B. J. Punnett and D. A. Ricks (1995), *Global Management,* by permission of Blackwell Publishers.

Employee relations, management of
The management style matrix in Purcell and Ahlstrand, *Human Resource Management in the Multi-divisional Company* (1994), by permission of Oxford University Press.

Human capital
Average returns to education by country type and level (per cent per year)
G. Psacharopoulos, Returns to education: a further international update and implications, from the *Journal of Human Resources* 20 (4) 1985. Reprinted by permission of the University of Wisconsin Press.

Human resource flows
Inter-regional labour migration networks J. Salt (1989) 'A comparative overview of international trends and types, 1950–80' *International Migration Review* 23: 431–56;
J. Salt (1992) 'The future of international labor migration', *International Migration Review* 26 (4): 1077–111. Reprinted permission granted by the Center for Migration Studies.

Human resource flows
Evolution of human resource planning in the USA; Human resource forecasting approaches
Material reproduced with permission of The McGraw-Hill Companies.

Human resource management, international
Flow chart of the selection–decision process
Permission granted by Columbia University, New York City.

Human resource management in Europe
Legal regulation and the practice of employee participation in the EC
Reproduced by permission of European Foundation for the Improvement of Living and Working Conditions.

Industrial and labour relations
Strategic choices of the actors; Action, power and structure
Reproduced from R.J. Adams and N.M. Meltz (eds) (1993) *Industrial Relations Theory: Its Nature, Scope and Pedagogy,* by permission of
Scarecrow Press Inc.

Industrial relations in Japan
Percentage of unions according to subjects to be covered by works councils (WC) or collective bargaining (CB) Ministry of Labour, Japan, 1989

Industrial relations in Japan
Subjects discussed in *shokuba knodankai* (round table at workshop); Degree of participation according to subject (management decisions); Degree of participation according to subject (working conditions)
Ministry of Labour, Japan, 1990

Industrial relations in the United States of America
Originally published in G.J. Bamber and R.D. Lansbury (eds) (1993) *International Comparative Industrial Relations: A Study of Industrialized Economies*, 2nd edn, London: International Thomson Business Press

Job design
The job characteristics model; Hackman's model of self-directed work teams Hackman/Oldham, *Work Redesign*, ©1980 by Addison-Wesley Publishing Co., Inc.

Job design
Summary of expected costs and benefits from the four job design approaches, reprinted, by permission of the publisher, from *Organizational Dynamics*, Winter 1987 © 1987. American Management Association, New York. All rights reserved.

Motivation and satisfaction
Different forms of work satisfaction from A. Bruggemann, P. Groskurth and E. Ulich (1975) *Arbeitszufriedenheit,* by permission of Hans Huber.

Negotiation skills
The prisoner's dilemma
Reproduced from A. Rapoport and A.M. Chammah (1965) *Prisoner's Dilemma: A Study of Conflict and Cooperation,* by permission of the University of Michigan Press.

Problem solving
The fish bone technique
Reproduced from S. Majaro (1988) *Managing Ideas for Profit: The Creative Gap*, by permission of Professor Simon Majoro.

Stress
The relationship between stress and performance
Reproduced from *Executive Health* (1978), by permission of Dr A. Melhuish.

Total quality management
Baldridge Award criterial framework
Figure taken from the *1993 Award Criteria*, p. 33, National Institute of Standards and Technology, Office of Quality Programs, Gaithersburg, MD 20899, USA.

Training
The performance analysis approach to identifying training needs
Copyright ©1984 by Lake Publishing Company, Belmont, CA, USA.

Introducing Human Resource Management

The origins of this Handbook may be traced to the growing interest in human resource management and the consequent recognition of the importance of a contemporary reference volume for encompassing the key themes, issues and major thinkers in this field. The areas covered are designed to provide a comprehensive and international set of up-to-date materials, written by the leading world scholars and for an audience that includes academics, students of business and management and, of course, the managers of business activities that are increasingly organized along multinational lines in the increasingly globalized competitive economy.

Human resource management has developed in recent years as a broad encompassing field of study that incorporates and synthesizes elements from personnel management, organizational behaviour and industrial and labour relations, building on broader concepts and insights from a variety of cognate disciplines including economics, law, psychology and sociology, amongst others. It has become integral to degrees in Business Administration and, above all, to Masters in Business Administration (MBAs) following the decision at Harvard University to incorporate the subject into the core of its 'flagship' programme. Moreover, the 'Harvard School' developed arguably the most commonly accepted definition of the term to include management decisions that shape the nature of the relationship between the organization and employees namely, its human resources. It is likely to become integral to managing organizations in the twenty-first century.

In much of the growing body of international literature in the field, there is a recognition that human resource management differs, in certain fundamental respects, from the earlier themes of personnel management and, in its organization, from personnel departments. Above all, it is viewed as being linked closely to the emergent strategies, especially of large organizations, both public as well as private. It also involves all managerial personnel (and especially general managers). It regards people as the most important single asset of the organization. It seeks to enhance not only company performance but also individual and societal well-being. But within human resource management, there are two main strands of thinking. The first (often referred to as the 'hard' variant of HRM) focuses on the links with strategy and the role of HRM in furthering the competitive advantage of the firm. The second (typically labelled 'soft' HRM) builds on human relations traditions and stresses the importance of the subject as a means of furthering employee satisfaction and a range of related 'humanistic' objectives that are achievable from the insights of systematic studies within HRM. The two levels of philosophy and practice here are inextricably linked in much of the writing on the subject, although the reader must be careful to distinguish the 'analytical' from the 'normative' dimensions.

Turning more specifically, then, to the structure of this comprehensive volume, the main areas have been classified into (1) general categories covering the main concerns of the discipline; (2) global items incorporating the world's key regions; (3) the focal policy-areas of HRM; (4) the central themes within industrial and labour relations; and (5) the key thinkers in the broad HRM field itself.

To begin with, then, there are major overviews of the area including entries on human resource management, personnel management, managerial behaviour, the work ethic and work systems. In each case, there is a scholarly overview of the main emergent themes set against a genuinely international backcloth of research, ideas and writings. Each contribution also sets out to provide a basis for defining a range of further specific areas for more detailed analysis in other entries.

The global compass of the volume is also enhanced by selecting key nations and regions for further detailed study. There are thus entries on international human resource management, human resource management in Europe as well as in Japan. Moreover, from the concerns of industrial relations, there are specific entries to cover both the advanced economies and developing countries. These contributions help greatly to understand some of the main variations in practices that stem from diverse cultures and histories of nations and their different political and economic environments.

The main policy areas of human resource management include employee influence, human resource flows, work systems and reward systems. Under employee influence, in addition to a major overview on industrial democracy, there are more specific entries on communications and empowerment. For human resource flows, the specific 'inflow' areas of recruitment and selection are included. Performance appraisal and careers also feature strongly. Furthermore, the importance of human resource development for the advance of organizations and nations is fully acknowledged with the entries on management development and training. Discipline, dismissals and relocation are also major issues emerging from the literature on human resource flows and hence they are incorporated in the Handbook. Modern understandings of work systems stress the importance of designing work roles for greater employee satisfaction and commitment. Hence, in addition to entries on commitment and motivation and satisfaction, there are specific authoritative studies on job design and job evaluation. Modern HRM approaches also stress that reward systems should be more sophisticated and be linked with organizational performance. These emergent concerns are reflected in entries not only on payment systems but also on profit sharing and employee shareholding and financial incentives.

A fourth set of entries are designed to encompass the field of industrial and labour relations. This area of study is defined to encompass all aspects of the employment relationship. The three main 'parties' or 'actors' are thus, as is to be expected, analysed in detail. From the concerns of management, there are overviews of the management of employee relations and of employers' associations. Trade unions and the processes of collective bargaining deservedly feature strongly. The role of governments in the sphere of industrial (and labour) relations is additionally fully recognized in the entries on corporatism and third party intervention. The applied themes of this subject arose principally from concern over the so-called 'problem of conflict'. To reflect this issue, a major entry on industrial conflict is included alongside one on negotiation skills.

But human resource management and industrial (and labour) relations must also be seen as both interdisciplinary and multidisciplinary subjects. Thus, it is scarcely surprising that it was felt to be fitting to include a range of issues stemming from cognate discipline and fields of study. Human capital and human relations are thus major relevant entries. Key themes from organizational behaviour and occupational psychology including leadership and organizational culture are incorporated. From economics, the study of labour markets, for example, finds a natural place in a Handbook of this type, as well as other themes such as employment and unemployment and the economics of training. The role of culture is vital for human resource management and hence there are relevant entries here including the theme of Japanization. Studies recognizing the saliency of gender have multiplied rapidly in recent years and, to reflect this quickening of attention, equal employment opportunities and women managers in organizations comprise significant entries. Moreover, employment law, deconstruction analysis and management and work and leisure impact on the concerns of HRM and therefore are encompassed.

Finally, the origins and development of any discipline depend greatly on key thinkers who have illuminated the field. Amongst the main world scholars and inventors who have enhanced the emergence of this broadly defined field of study include Chris Argyris,

Charles E. Bedaux, Harry Braverman, Hugh Armstrong Clegg, John Thomas Dunlop, Allan Flanders, Mary Parker Follett, Henry Ford, Frank Bunker Gilbreth, Lillian Evelyn Moller Gilbreth, Alvin W. Gouldner, Frederick Herzberg, Kaoru Ishikawa, George Elton Mayo, Taiichi Ohno, Thomas J. Peters, Robert M. Reich, Randall S. Schuler, Frederick Winslow Taylor and Yoichi Ueno. Others could have been included in the roll of honour but those chosen seemed to the editors to be amongst the core of critical international formative thinkers – constraints of space alone led exclusions from the potential list.

The upshot therefore is an authoritative, inclusive and informed volume that we hope will provide a valuable reference base for an increasingly international audience. World businesses and their human resource systems are becoming ever more multi-national in their structure and operations. The issues encompassed in this Handbook are thus likely to become ever more relevant and vital for management and business as we progress towards and into the new millennium.

We should like to thank everyone who offered advice and encouragement throughout the development of the *IEBM* project. We would especially like to thank the authors, advisers and in-house publishing team who helped create this title.

Michael Poole and Malcolm Warner,
September 1997

Human resource management

Culture

Overview

For a concept so central to organizational behaviour, the meaning of organizational culture continues to be vague, diverse and contradictory. In part this conceptual confusion was imported with the basic analytical framework from anthropology. To some extent, however, the original ambiguity of the term has been exacerbated by the wide range of uses that organizational theorists and practitioners have made out of it.

The vagueness and diversity of the concept have been a hindrance to the development of a theory of culture as it makes comparison and accumulation of results extremely difficult. On the other hand the lack of a paradigmatic definition has meant that theorists have been free to apply the concept of culture and its derivatives to a wide variety of settings.

Exactly when and where the concept of culture entered organization research has been the subject of some debate and conjecture. What is clear is that its early use was nearly coincidental with widespread interest in the way that national culture affected the operation and efficiency of organizations, specifically Japanese organizations. Thus the term 'culture' has always had two major, closely related meanings within organization theory. First, it has stood for the body of values, myths, symbols, stories and artefacts that are held in common by members of an organization. Second, it has represented the value-based commonalities that exist within a nation (or some other large political unit). Despite the early influence of the comparative approach to the study of organization culture and the commonality of methodological tools, the two areas have remained largely separate.

I The components of culture

In her early analysis of the field Smircich (1983) outlined five basic meanings for culture within the literature. Alvesson and Melin (1987) outlined two contrasting perspectives while Frost *et al.* (1991) presents three. Ott (1989) argues that organizational culture is not amenable to consistent definition due to its polemical nature.

Schein provides a definition of organizational culture encompassing many of its central elements:

> Culture is a pattern of shared basic assumptions, invented, discovered or developed by a given group, as it learns to cope with its problems of external adaptation and internal integration, that has worked well enough to be considered valid, and, therefore, is to be taught to new members of the group as the correct way to perceive, think, and feel in relation to those problems.
>
> (Schein 1991: 247)

This definition, however, does not directly include the shared values of the individuals in organizations, which are often seen as the basis of culture.

In the absence of a clear definition of organization culture, there has been a great deal of emphasis on its indicators and components. In general the culture of an organization is thought to be found in the common values that its members hold. There have been attempts to divine which values are most important for a specific organization. This effort occasionally links values to some organization outcome such as success, productivity or openness to change. More often empirical research has focused on simply identifying the values which are present in the organization and the strength with which they are held. The link between values and action is more often assumed than investigated.

While values provide the basis for culture, they are difficult to access directly. Both researchers and practitioners have concentrated on the more apparent manifestations of culture in organizations. These can be placed in three general categories. First, the myths and stories that are current in organizations illustrate those values which are predominant in an organization (Wilkins 1983). Such stories do not necessarily illustrate positive achievements; for example, stories may emphasize the ambiguity that organizational members feel. For some researchers the factuality of stories has been an issue while for others the assumption has been that all such tales are to some extent fabricated. An additional issue in the investigation of myths and stories has been the degree to which they are spontaneous manifestations of the culture of the organization. Stories and myths have been treated both as upwellings of the collective subconscious and as purposeful creations of dominant groups in the organization.

Symbols in organizations have also been investigated as important markers of organizational culture (Dandridge 1993). Logos, product design, office arrangement, the presence or absence of personal items and office art have all been objects of scrutiny. Not all symbols are material. The use of certain verbal expressions, even non-verbal cues, are seen to have importance for expressing organization culture. As with stories and myths there have been questions raised as to the source and purpose of symbols. Some are identified as attempts by managers/owners to establish or support a specific culture. Others are seen as more spontaneous and less controllable.

Partly as a result of the emphasis on verbal symbols the study of organization culture has moved to the study of language in organizations. The recent interest in this area has numerous roots, but the manifestation of values and cultural norms in patterns of speech, common usages and discourse styles is seen as a powerful tool for the study of culture. This line of enquiry has developed quickly from a number of sources so that there is no clear research agenda as yet. This is complicated by the fact that a variety of techniques used to study language have been imported into the field, each with its own particular bias and approach. At this point virtually all one can say is that this part of the field is still in considerable ferment and it is likely to be some time before clear lines of discussion emerge.

Levels within organizations

One of the key issues in the study of culture has been its consistency through the organization. Top-level managers may repeat the story of a super-salesperson (a common myth in commercial organizations) with approbation. Those lower in the organization may regard it with disdain as an attempt to encourage harder work or to justify unfair or harsh treatment. Should researchers be looking for distinct cultures at different levels within the organization? Is there a managerial culture and a shop-floor culture? Are there different cultures for different occupational specialties? These issues have received relatively little attention within the field.

Besides looking at the different levels within an organization one may also consider that cultures may exist at levels outside the organization. Industrial-level cultures may be enhanced by a common set of competitive conditions, management problems and government regulation. Occupational or professional cultures which spread across organizations may exist when work conditions are similar, when there is frequent movement among organizations and when professional groups exist which promote identification with others in similar occupational niches (Bloor and Dawson 1994). The culture of the society or societies in which an organization exists will also have an effect on the organizational culture although Hofstede and his colleagues (1990; 1993) have argued that the cultural effects at the organizational and individual levels are distinct (see CULTURE, CROSS-NATIONAL). The daunting methodological and logistical problems inherent in disentangling the effects of these levels have limited research in this area.

2 Subcultures and countercultures

The possibility that organization culture exists in modified form at different levels and that it may be differentially perceived by various groups in the organization raises yet another question of uniformity. What is the importance of subcultures and countercultures within the organization? Subcultures may form around the natural divisions of an organization, the occupational specialties, the geographical sub-units, the product specializations, the functional departments. Each may espouse its own values, have its own symbols and heroes. These subcultures may provide an important source of variation within a firm with a strong culture. At the same time they may foster strong subcultures the values of which take precedence over more general organizational values.

While there has been some investigation into subcultures in organizations there has been little into countercultures in which organization members adopt values that are not simply different but contrary to those of the overall organization. For example, the possible functions of countercultures in strong culture organizations and the conditions which give rise to organization countercultures have yet to be investigated.

3 Culture as control

One of the underlying issues in the study of organization culture is its function in the organization. The concerns reflected in Ouchi's (1981) discussion of successful organization cultures and their similarity to Japanese management techniques laid considerable emphasis on the use of organization culture as a means of control. In this, and a number of studies that followed, the advantages of culture-based control were promoted. In a strong organization culture individuals and teams will control themselves. This is not only highly efficient but it contributes to the smooth functioning of the organization since adherence to a coherent set of shared values decreases conflict and confusion. While there have been some acknowledgements of the possible costs and limitations of using culture as a control mechanism in that it may make the organization less adaptive or that it may disadvantage parts of the organization not central to the culture, culture has generally been seen as a positive, relatively cheap means of control.

The positive view of culture as control, which is predominantly a North American view, has been challenged by European writers, especially those from the UK. They see the management of culture not as a humanistic means for harnessing human capabilities, but as a cynical, manipulative strategy which appeals to managers because it is cheap and insidious (Wilmott 1993) (see DECONSTRUCTION ANALYSIS AND MANAGEMENT). These writers point to the emphasis on leaders and founders as the sources of organization culture as opposed to culture arising from mutual interaction throughout the organization.

This point of view raises two related questions. First, what are the sources of culture? This is, of course, partly a definitional problem, but it also addresses the fundamental question as to where the origins of culture lie. As Smircich (1983) put it, culture may be something that an organization is or something that an organization has. If the organization is to be regarded as a society with a culture, then the culture stems from the interactions of those within the organization; culture derives from all levels and all sectors. Leaders are then the caretakers of culture but not its source. If, on the other hand, one regards culture as something that an organization has, then its source may be located in any number of places, including some external to the organization. It also carries the implication that a new or modified culture may be imposed.

The second issue, which has received relatively little attention in the literature, is the ownership of culture. If culture derives from all segments of the organization, then ownership is presumably vested in all those who participate, which may include some who are nominally external to the organization. If culture is seen only as an attribute then the articulation of culture is the perquisite of top managers or owners.

4 Changing culture

Whichever view is taken, one of the tasks that faces any manager is the changing of culture. The different points of view concerning culture are reflected in the attitudes towards changing culture. One stream of thought sees the changing (or maintenance) of culture as a key managerial task. To some extent this might be viewed as a contingency theory of culture. As the external environment of the organization changes, the culture of the organization must be changed to meet it. While there is general consensus that changing organization culture may be a difficult undertaking (Deal 1985), there is considerable disagreement about the tools to be used and the rapidity with which change may be executed; there is also considerable controversy over the effectiveness of cultural change. This stems in part from the difficulty of linking culture to organization effectiveness or success.

If culture is viewed not as an attribute of the organization but an essential part of its self-definition, the process of cultural change is seen differently. The time-scale slows dramatically. Culture can only change through slow evolution or through violent reaction to crisis or external threat. At best cultural change is mediated by the leaders of the organization. At worst there is a constant tension between the culture which those at the top wish to impose and the culture which is stubbornly maintained by the remainder of the organization. In this view culture becomes both a battleground and an asset which both sides wish to control.

Thick and thin

Questions of cultural effectiveness and cultural change depend on the strength of the culture; how deeply rooted it is within the organization and how closely it is tied to individual and group behaviours. Thick cultures provide values which are shared by a large percentage of the organization's members (Geertz 1973). These values have a direct and visible connection to the behaviours of individuals and groups within the organization. Thin cultures have poorly articulated value systems which have little effect on behaviour.

While it is easy to understand the thickness concept, it is less easy to measure. In any investigation of organization culture there is a problem in linking the surface manifestations of culture to the values that underlie the culture. The visible (or audible) presence of the culture may not necessarily mean that the underlying values are consistently held. One of the often-cited examples of a myth is that of the wild ducks at IBM. Wild ducks are those employees who choose to act in other than accepted ways. They are held to be necessary to the creative spirit of the organization. It is one of the more enduring (and promoted) myths of the firm. However, there is considerable evidence that this myth is held in disdain by many of IBM's employees who observe that the common fate for wild ducks is to be shot down (Martin and Powers 1983). Observing many surface manifestations of a culture does not necessarily mean that the culture is thick.

5 Themes in the study of culture

Within the study of organization culture there are a number of themes that can be seen through much of the literature. The first theme is the degree to which organization culture is an intentional outcome. The study of organization culture has drawn on a number of methodological and theoretical traditions. Part of this diversity has stemmed from divergent views of how culture is produced. If culture is seen as an integral and fundamental part of the organization society, then both its study and its management can be seen as tasks which require great insight and little manipulation. If culture is seen as the exercise of ideological hegemony, then clearly it can be understood through linking managerial and ownership goals to cultural manifestations. Altering the culture depends on applying the appropriate tools to the problem. Similarly, understanding organization culture becomes less of a task of understanding deeply rooted values than of analysing the utility of surface manifestations.

Implicit in the intentionality debate is the focus on the control of culture. This debate is occasionally explicit but more often implicit. Many of those writing about strategies for changing organization culture assume that culture can be controlled. Assumptions about who controls culture in an organization often accompany this point of view. Other authors assert that culture may be controlled but that who controls it is either unclear or subject to internal struggle. Finally, there are researchers who believe that culture is only slightly amenable to control. It may be utilized or modified but it is too basic a part of the organization to allow easy modification. In a sense, these authors believe that no one controls organization culture.

Finally, there is the theme of organization persistence. To some extent this is the obverse of the concern with cultural change, but it is not the same as the question about how difficult it is to effect cultural change. To what extent do the features of organization culture continue even though external and even internal conditions may change? All three of these themes are linked and none of them has given rise to a clear-cut answer. It may be that clear answers wait upon a clarification of the very definition of organization culture. In that case the wait may be a long one.

DAVID CRAY
CARLETON UNIVERSITY SCHOOL OF
BUSINESS

Further reading

(References cited in the text marked *)

Alvesson, M. (1994) 'Talking in organizations: managing identity and impressions in an advertising agency', *Organization Studies* 15: 535–63. (An interesting example of language use in organizations.)

* Alvesson, M. and Melin, L. (1987) 'Major discrepancies and contradictions in organizational culture', paper presented at the 3rd International Conference on Organizational Symbolism and Corporate Culture, Milan, July. (A thorough discussion of the conceptual difficulties inherent in organizational culture.)

* Bloor, G. and Dawson, P. (1994) 'Understanding professional culture in organizational context', *Organization Studies* 15: 275–95. (Examines the interaction between organizational culture and professional subcultures.)

* Dandridge, T.C. (1993) 'Symbols' function and use', in L.R. Pondy, P.J. Frost, G. Morgan and T.C. Dandridge (eds), *Organizational Symbolism,* Greenwich, CT: JAI Press Inc. (Considers the role of symbols in organizational culture.)

* Deal, T.E. (1985) 'Cultural change: opportunity, silent killer or metamorphosis?', in R.H. Kilmann *et al.* (eds), *Gaining Control of the Corporate Culture*, San Francisco, CA: Jossey Bass. (An early discussion of the managerialist view of cultural change.)

* Frost, P.J., Moore, L.F., Louis, M.R., Lundberg, C.C. and Martin, J. (1991) 'Introduction: ten empirical studies of culture', in P.J. Frost, L.F. Moore, M.R. Louis, C.C. Lundberg and J. Martin (eds), *Reframing Organizational Culture*, Newbury Park, CA: Sage Publications. (A useful introduction to contemporary approaches to organizational culture.)

* Geertz, C. (1973) *The Interpretation of Cultures*, New York: Basic Books. (A classic discussion of the meaning and study of culture from the anthropological point of view.)

* Hofstede, G., Bond, M.H. and Luk, C. (1993) 'Individual perceptions of organizational cultures: a methodological treatise on levels of analysis', *Organization Studies* 14: 483–503. (Looks at the methodological difficulties of studying culture at various levels.)

* Hofstede, G., Neuyen, B., Ohayv, D.D. and Sanders, G. (1990) 'Measuring organizational cultures: a qualitative and quantitative study across twenty cases', *Administrative Science Quarterly* 35: 286–316. (An attempt to disentangle the effects of organizational and national culture.)

* Martin, J. and Powers, M.E. (1983) 'Truth or corporate propaganda: the value of a good war story', in L.R. Pondy, P.J. Frost, G. Morgan and T.C. Dandridge (eds), *Organizational Symbolism*, Greenwich, CT: JAI Press Inc. (An early examination of the role of stories in organizational culture.)

* Ott, J.S. (1989) *The Organizational Culture Perspective*, Pacific Grove, CA: Brooks/Cole. (A useful view of the application of organizational culture concepts to managerial tasks.)

* Ouchi, W.G. (1981) *Theory Z: How American Business Can Meet the Japanese Challenge,*

Reading, MA: Addison-Wesley. (This classic book, which outlines the connection between elements of Japanese national culture and organizational success, is more often cited than understood.)

* Schein, E.H. (1991) 'What is culture?', in P.J. Frost, L.F. Moore, M.R. Louis, C.C. Lundberg and J. Martin (eds), *Reframing Organizational Culture*, Newbury Park, CA: Sage Publications. (One point of view on the definitional debate by a well-known author in the field.)

* Smircich, L. (1983) 'Concepts of culture and organizational analysis', *Administrative Science Quarterly* 28: 339–58. (One of the earliest and most influential treatments of the conceptual confusion surrounding culture.)

Turner, B.A. (1986) 'The sociological aspects of organizational symbolism', *Organization studies* 7: 101—15. (A very useful summary and discussion of organizational culture from an astute commentator with a point of view that contrasts strongly with much mainstream writing on the subject.)

Weick, K.E. (1987) 'Organizational culture as a sign of high reliability', *California Management Review* 29: 11227. (An unusual discussion of the functions and disfunctions of organizational culture.)

* Wilkins, A.L. (1983) 'Organizational stories as symbols which control the organization', in L.R. Pondy, P.J. Frost, G. Morgan and T.C. Dandridge (eds), *Organizational Symbolism*, Greenwich, CT: JAI Press Inc. (Investigates how stories and myths are used to control behaviour in organizations.)

* Wilmott, H. (1993) 'Strength is ignorance; slavery is freedom: managing culture in modern organizations', *Journal of Management Studies* 30: 515–51. (A strong statement on the managerial use of culture for control, manipulation and the exercise of power.)

See also: ORGANIZATION BEHAVIOUR; ORGANIZATION CULTURE

Related topics in the IEBM: BUSINESS CULTURE, JAPANESE; BUSINESS CULTURE, NORTH AMERICAN; BUSINESS CULTURES, EUROPEAN; COORDINATION AND CONTROL; MANAGEMENT IN JAPAN; MANAGEMENT IN THE UNITED KINGDOM; ORGANIZATION PARADIGMS; POWER

Culture, cross-national

Overview

This entry discusses firms doing business across national borders, and the role of culture in effective management of these firms. Figure 1 outlines relationships between a variety of variables and organizational effectiveness. The major focus here are the four central items identified as *cross-national culture* (national culture, for short), *cultural values*, *individual and group needs, attitudes, norms*, and *organizational effectiveness*.

Figure 1 identifies national culture as emanating from *societal* variables (not necessarily restricted by national boundaries) such as language, religion and history, as well as *national* variables (which are clearly associated with national boundaries) such as government, laws and regulations, geography and economic conditions. This national culture is also seen as being influenced by current events both within the country and in the world at large. National culture is, thus, relatively stable but does change in response to circumstances.

National culture is depicted as playing a fundamental role in forming cultural values. In turn, these values interact with the needs, attitudes and norms of individuals and groups and result in behaviours which contribute to organizational effectiveness, or lack thereof. Additional influences are the values derived from the corporate culture and the individual's professional culture; thus individuals and groups within an organization can be

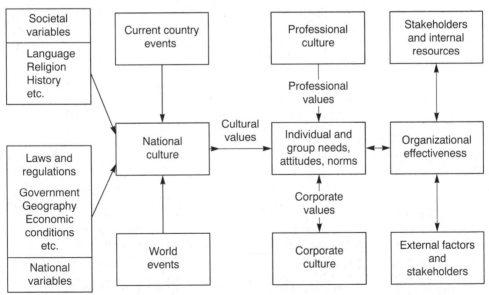

Figure 1 Culture and international management

expected to share some values, but they can also be expected to differ with respect to others.

The organization's effectiveness will increase to the extent that the factors influencing behaviour are understood by managers. An international firm's performance is likely to be enhanced when systems are in place that are congruent with the various influences that determine behaviours. While it is clearly impossible to understand all of the factors influencing behaviour, national cultures and attendant values appear to be an important starting point. A focus on national culture has been questioned by some scholars. Their concern is that the idea that nations and cultures may be coterminous is incorrect and, thus, thinking in these terms is misleading. It is certainly the case that nations and cultures are not the same; nevertheless, it seems appropriate from an international organization's viewpoint to consider national cultures, as the following illustrates.

An organization's activities are legally constrained by national requirements, rather than cultural ones. This results in international firms identifying with national boundaries. Human resource considerations encourage firms to take a national perspective. The workforce in a particular location is predominantly a national workforce – labour mobility within a country is often greater than between countries. This means that management systems need to be designed with the national character of the workforce in mind. Governments encourage this through legislation; usually, laws and regulations regarding employees encompass all citizens of a country and do not apply differentially to different cultural groups. In contrast, laws and regulations may differ quite dramatically from country to country. The firm has to function within this system; therefore, it is appropriate to begin its cultural analysis at the national culture level.

Figure 1 serves as a guide for this entry, which is divided into four main sections. The first considers the importance of cultural values for international managers and discusses why national cultures are expected to vary; it explores the relationship of societal culture and national culture to behaviour. The second

section focuses on the meaning of cultural values; it defines various terms and looks at their associations. The third examines three cultural value models that can be applied at the national level and their impact on effective management and the last considers a variety of additional issues – stereotyping, variation within nations, overlapping cultures and environmental forces leading to convergence or divergence of cultures in different national locations.

1 The importance of cultural values for international managers

Managers in international businesses need to understand and appreciate a variety of differences among nations. Among other differences, nations exhibit varying cultural profiles; thus, understanding the cultural environment is a component of the international manager's task. Managers who have worked in foreign locations acknowledge that understanding the culture in those locations is necessary if one is to manage effectively (see HUMAN RESOURCE MANAGEMENT, INTERNATIONAL). Virtually all of the activities undertaken by managers are affected, at least to some degree, by the cultural environment. Consider some examples which show the importance of culture in the management process:

(1) International firms need to negotiate with various foreign constituencies. Success in these negotiations rests on understanding the cultural background of the negotiators.
(2) Strategic alliances are becoming more and more common between firms with different strategies and objectives. To succeed, managers may need to understand the cultural factors that influence organizational strategies and objectives.
(3) Managers in foreign locations frequently find that employees behave in ways that are quite different from these managers' expectations.
(4) Expatriates (employees working outside their home country) find culture shock affects their general ability to function well in foreign

locations (see HUMAN RESOURCE MANAGE-MENT, INTERNATIONAL). Cultural understanding and adaptability have been identified as contributing to better expatriation.

(5) Various functional aspects of organizations, such as accounting, finance, and marketing can differ markedly from one location to another. For an organization to be effective overseas, these functional aspects must fit the local culture.

2 The meaning of culture

Culture is a concept that is familiar to most people. It is difficult, however, to specify what is meant by the concept. For example, two anthropologists (Kroeber and Kluckhohn 1952) catalogued 164 separate and distinct definitions of the word 'culture'. This issue is further complicated by the fact that the word culture has several quite different meanings. Culture can refer to a shared, commonly-held body of general beliefs and values that define what is right for one group (Kluckhohn and Strodtbeck 1961; Lane and DiStefano 1988), or to socially elitist concepts, including refinement of mind, tastes and manners (Heller 1988).

The word apparently originates with the Latin *cultura*, which is related to *cultus*, which can be translated as cult or worship. Members of a cult believe in specific ways of doing things, and thus develop a culture which enshrines those beliefs. Culture here is used in this sense. The following definition, proposed by Terpstra and David, delineates what is meant by the word culture in the international management context:

> Culture is a learned, shared, compelling, interrelated set of symbols whose meaning provides a set of orientations for members of a society. These orientations, taken together, provide solutions to problems that all societies must solve if they are to remain viable.
>
> (Terpstra and David 1985: 5)

There are several elements of this definition which are important to gain an understanding of the relationship of cultural issues and international management (Punnett and Ricks 1992):

(1) Culture is learned – this means that it is not innate; people are socialized from childhood to learn the rules and norms of their culture. It also means that when one goes to another culture, it is possible to learn the new culture.

(2) Culture is shared – this means that the focus is on those things that are shared by members of a particular group rather than on individual differences; as such, it means that it is possible to study and identify group patterns.

(3) Culture is compelling – this means that specific behaviour is determined by culture without individuals being aware of the influence of their culture; as such, it means that it is important to understand culture in order to understand behaviour.

(4) Culture is interrelated – this means that while various facets of culture can be examined in isolation, these should be understood in context of the whole; as such, it means that a culture needs to be studied as a complete entity.

(5) Culture provides orientation to people – this means that a particular group reacts in general in the same way to a given stimulus; as such, it means that understanding a culture can help in determining how group members might react in various situations.

Because culture is so fundamental to society, it influences people's behaviours in critical ways. Effective management depends, at least in part, on ensuring that people behave in ways that are appropriate for the organization. This means that understanding culture is important for managers. Where cultural differences exist they should be accommodated to achieve desired behaviour and results. This is easier in theory than it is in reality. Each of us is influenced by our own culture, and people are inevitably somewhat ethnocentric as the following section explains.

3 Ethnocentrism and parochialism

Anthropologists believe that cultural attributes develop as a response to the environment and become a preferred way of behaving for a group of people because they help the people survive. It is not surprising, then, that cultural preferences are associated with right and correct ways of behaving. Consequently, different ways of behaving are seen as bad and incorrect. If 'our way' somehow contributed to our survival, it is hard to accept that 'their way' can also be acceptable. This view of the world is referred to as an ethnocentric view. Ethnocentric means that the view of our own and other cultures is centred on our own, and the belief that our own culture is superior to others.

Adler (1986) described a similar view of one's own culture as best in terms of parochialism. Parochial people also assume that the home culture is superior but the assumption arises for different reasons. The assumption of superiority arises not because cultures are compared but because differences are not recognized. This often arises where someone simply lacks knowledge about other cultures.

Ethnocentrism implies that the belief in the home culture's superiority is conscious, while parochialism implies only that the home culture is believed to be superior because little is known of other cultures. Both ethnocentrism and parochialism are common among managers who have to deal with people in foreign locations. Managers need not feel guilty about ethnocentrism or parochialism, given its frequent occurrence. Managers do need, however, to recognize that they are likely to exhibit either or both of these attitudes, and that these attitudes will inhibit their ability to work effectively in other cultures. The first step is to recognize the prevalence of these attitudes. Once recognized, one can begin to change them. Changing these attitudes begins with developing a better understanding of one's home culture.

4 Defining and understanding cultural values

Values are useful in explaining and understanding cultural similarities and differences in behaviour; thus, understanding values and their cultural basis is helpful to international

managers. If international managers understand how values can vary from culture to culture, they are more likely to accept and interpret correctly behavioural differences. This acceptance and correct interpretation, in turn, enable managers to interact effectively with others whose values and behaviours are unfamiliar.

It is helpful to define the concept as well as to distinguish it from, and relate it to, others. This serves to delineate the domain of cultural values, and to underscore their importance to international managers. The following discussion begins with cultural values, then examines needs, attitudes and norms. These latter concepts are all similar to that of cultural values, but each contributes somewhat differently to behaviour.

Values

Values have been described as enduring beliefs that specific modes of conduct or end states of existence are socially preferable to their opposites (Rokeach 1973); a value system is seen as a relatively permanent perceptual framework which influences an individual's behaviour (England 1978). Values establish the standards by which the importance of everything in society is judged. Throughout these definitions, the important issue for international management appears to be the role of social values in behaviour.

In a general sense, values and norms are societal, while needs and attitudes are individual. Values interact with needs, attributes and norms as the following discussion explains.

Needs

Needs are described as forces motivating an individual to act in a certain way; once satisfied, needs no longer have an impact on behaviour (see MOTIVATION AND SATISFACTION). For example, a need for food motivates people to seek food; once people have eaten, they normally no longer seek food (unless motivated by other needs). Cultural values interact with individual needs because they influence how people choose to satisfy their needs (see HERZBERG, F.).

It is generally accepted that two of the most basic and universal human needs are the need for food and the need for sex, yet satisfaction of these needs differs because of societal values. In most societies a value of human life precludes cannibalism to satisfy a need for food. Societies often have accepted times for eating, and even when people are hungry, they observe these timeframes. Similarly, social customs regarding sexual partners limit satisfaction of sexual needs.

Many societies practice restrictions regarding food, often associated with religious rituals. During Lent, Christians may forgo favourite foods or limit their intake of meat. During the month of Ramadan, Muslims fast completely during daylight hours. Some sects eat no meat, some do not allow beef, others prohibit shellfish or pork, and still others do not allow certain combinations of foods. Individual needs are put aside to observe these restrictions.

Many societies also have customs regarding the timing and selection of sexual partners. Some societies allow men to have multiple wives, others have group marriages where any partner may have sex with any other. In some locations marriages are arranged for girls at birth and they must remain virgins until marriage, in others men and women select their own sexual and marriage partners. As with food, individual needs are put aside to observe these restrictions.

Attitudes

Attitudes are described as a tendency to respond favourably or unfavourably to objects or situations, based on beliefs about them. Societal values influence what we respond favourably to and what we view with disfavour.

In a business setting dress can mean quite different things depending on what the society values, and how different types of dress are interpreted. If wearing a suit and tie indicates a conservative business perspective and conservatism is valued, this would result in a favourable attitude to someone in this attire. Elsewhere, if innovation in business was more highly valued, and wearing a brightly coloured T-shirt and jeans was seen as indicating an innovative perspective, this might be viewed positively. Similarly, in some societies males with long hair are seen negatively, while in others long hair represents virtue.

Norms

Norms prescribe or proscribe specific behaviours in specific situations and result in standardized, distinctive ways of behaving. They are seen as normal (thus the word 'norms') and appropriate behaviour. A typical US norm involves eating with the fork in the right hand and this seems acceptable and normal to people who have lived in the USA for extended periods. People in many other countries hold their forks in the left hand, and in other places forks are not used at all. For those accustomed to using the right hand for a fork, the reverse can be quite uncomfortable and using chopsticks in place of a fork almost impossible. Similarly, for those used to a fork in the left hand or chopsticks, the US norm is uncomfortable.

Norms probably originated from values but they no longer clearly represent these. The US norm of eating with the fork in the right hand would not be described as a 'societal value'; it is simply the accepted way of behaving in the USA.

5 Cultural value models

There are a variety of cultural value models that have been developed by scholars in different fields. Three have been selected to give a sense of the models available for managers. These particular models were identified because they have been presented widely in the international management literature. Each model is described and its limitations noted, then the model is related to some aspect of management. This discussion is very simplistic and in no way comprehensive. It is intended only to illustrate the potential for practical applications of cultural models in the international business setting.

Country clusters

Examining clusters of countries that share similar values can be a useful approach for international managers. One of the most extensive studies resulting in country clusters was carried out by Ronen and Shenkar (1985). This was a synthesis of previous research and identified eight clusters of countries. A number of countries which did not fall into one of the clusters were identified as independent. These clusters are illustrated in Figure 2.

The countries included in the diagram in Figure 2 reflected the available research. The clusters can be helpful to managers who have to decide on the degree to which cultural adaptation is needed when moving cross-culturally. A manager interacting with colleagues from within the home cluster can expect relatively similar values and easy adaptation – Australians interacting with Canadians will be on somewhat familiar territory. Moving outside the home cluster can be relatively more difficult because of the likely diversity of values and greater need for adaptation – a Mexican going to Saudi Arabia is likely to be faced with more cultural adaptation than the Australian working in Canada.

The countries included in the list are only those where appropriate research has occurred. Sometimes it is possible to make informed judgements regarding the likely

---

Cluster 1 - Anglo
   Australia, Canada, New Zealand, UK, USA

Cluster 2 - Germanic
   Austria, Germany, Switzerland

Cluster 3 - Latin European
   Belgium, France, Italy, Portugal, Spain

Cluster 4 - Nordic
   Denmark, Finland, Norway, Sweden

Cluster 5 - Latin American
   Argentina, Chile, Columbia, Mexico, Peru, Venezuela

Cluster 6 - Near Eastern
   Greece, Iran, Turkey

Cluster 7 - Far Eastern
   Hong Kong, Indonesia, Malaysia, Philippines, Singapore, South Vietnam, Taiwan

Cluster 8 - Arab
   Bahrain, Kuwait, Saudi Arabia, United Arab Emirates

Independent (not closely related to other countries)
   Japan, India, Israel

Note Countries within a cluster are considered similar with regard to their cultural values. Clusters are arranged in an approximate order of cluster similarity; that is, the Anglo cluster is more similar to the European clusters (Germanic, Latin European and Nordic) than it is to the Latin American, Near Eastern, Far Eastern and Arab clusters. A major limitation of these clusters is that they are based on empirical studies which, at that time, did not include Africa, much of Asia, and eastern Europe. Asia has received more attention recently (see Hofstede 1991), but Africa and eastern Europe still have not been studied extensively.

Figure 2 Country clusters
Source: Punnett (1989: 17)

position of countries which are not represented, based on information about their cultural antecedents and neighbours.

Limitations of country cluster information

These clusters can help international managers but there are some limitations to consider. For example:

1 Geographic regions such as Africa and eastern Europe are not represented, and within clusters, major countries are missing (for example, Brazil in Latin America and the People's Republic of China in the Far East). Managers may be particularly interested in one of these countries or regions.
2 The clusters are based on variables studied in the past; it is possible that different clusters would emerge if studying different variables.
3 These clusters do not identify the relative similarity among clusters; this may be an important consideration for international managers.
4 The clusters may overemphasize similarity within a cluster or dissimilarity among clusters. Countries within a cluster do differ and those in different clusters can exhibit some similarities.

The role of country clusters in international decisions

Grouping countries into culturally similar clusters is helpful to international managers in a number of ways. If we consider some typical concerns of international managers we can see how country clusters might be used. The following examples are by no means inclusive, there are many additional ways in which country cluster information can be used by international managers. These examples should, however, give a sense of how this information may be factored into international management decisions.

(1) Members of a cluster can be expected to share basic cultural values, and people in all the countries in a cluster are likely to behave in relatively similar ways. Managers with experience in one country (say, Norway) can then move relatively easily to another country in the same cluster (say, Finland). This does not mean that everything in Finland will be the same as in Norway. Rather, it means that the experience gained in Norway is likely to be helpful in adjusting to Finland.

(2) Managers in one country in a cluster can move to others in the same cluster with a minimum of culture shock and with relatively little need for adaptation. Movement from one cultural cluster to another can be expected to be somewhat difficult. Managers in one cluster moving to another cluster need to be particularly aware of the effect of cultural differences. They need to expect culture shock and be prepared to adapt to the new cultural experience.

(3) Countries in different clusters are likely to exhibit different cultural values and the people to behave in relatively dissimilar ways. Managers moving from a country in one cluster (say, Singapore) to a country in a different cluster (say, Argentina) can expect to encounter substantial differences. They can be prepared for this and adapt their management style as needed.

(4) Decisions regarding locations for international subsidiaries can take advantage of information provided by country clusters. A firm seeking to expand internationally might initially want to gain experience in culturally similar locations. For example, a Canadian firm might expand to other countries in the Anglo cluster. Alternatively an international firm with substantial experience may feel there is potential benefit in expanding to countries that are culturally different. In this case, the Canadian firm could consider places like Saudi Arabia, Portugal or Indonesia.

(5) International staffing decisions can benefit from a consideration of country clusters. Allocating personnel to relatively similar cultures (for example, moving French personnel to Belgium) minimizes the culture shock they should experience. Such a move can be relatively easy, and extensive cross-cultural training and support are not needed. In contrast, a move to a country in a different cluster (for example, French personnel to the USA) may present a greater challenge. In this move a greater degree of culture shock is likely and, therefore, appropriate training and support

have to be provided (see HUMAN RESOURCE MANAGEMENT, INTERNATIONAL).

(6) International managers can consider country clusters in relation to joint ventures and strategic alliances. Many alliances fail because of the differing objectives of the parties involved, and to some extent these objectives reflect the national culture (for example, Japanese managers are generally believed to take a longer-term view than US managers). Firms entering alliances within a familiar cluster may be able to reach agreement on objectives more easily than in an unfamiliar cluster. When entering an alliance in an unfamiliar cluster, it is important to allow adequate time to discuss objectives in detail and it may be necessary to consider innovative proposals.

(7) Managers may find negotiations follow similar procedures within clusters but can change quite dramatically between clusters. Managers who are aware of this are likely to be better negotiators because they will prepare for and use the similarities and differences that exist.

(8) Managers need to consider whether management practices and approaches can be transferred from one country to another. Management practices are more likely to be generalizable within cultural clusters. Managers who have successfully worked in one country can have some confidence that they can be effective in other countries in the same cluster.

(9) International managers often have to make decisions about expanding to new locations. Given a choice of expanding to two locations which are equally attractive in other ways, cultural similarities and differences may be a deciding factor. Expansion to new locations within a familiar cluster is likely to involve fewer unexpected occurrences than expanding to an unfamiliar cluster. In contrast, the differences that are inherent in a new cluster may provide opportunities that do not exist in culturally similar locations.

(10) Subsidiaries of international firms are often grouped based on similarities of activities, and regional groupings are fairly common. Country clusters provide one basis for deciding on regional groupings. Countries within a cluster can be expected to share some characteristics such as language, religion, etc. and to express relatively similar values. These similarities suggest that taking a common approach to countries within a cluster may be appropriate.

(11) Marketing in different countries can be a major challenge for international managers. A major concern for marketers is taking advantage of efficiencies offered by standardized marketing approaches while adapting to cultural differences. Country clusters provide input into decisions regarding marketing standardization and adaptation. The relative similarity of countries within a cluster suggests that greater standardization may be appropriate while differences between clusters highlight the need for adaptation.

Kluckhohn and Strodtbeck's value orientation model

The anthropologists Kluckhohn and Strodtbeck (1961) explained cultural similarities and differences in terms of basic problems which all human societies face. Cultural differences are explained by varying ways of coping with these problems – different societies adopt different solutions. This model has been used by a number of international management authors and provides a means of assessing national culture that many people find helpful.

Consider the various solutions that societies have developed for the five problem areas identified by these two anthropologists.

Relationship to nature – subjugation, harmony and mastery

Societies which view themselves as subjugated to nature view life as essentially preordained; people are not masters of their own destinies, and trying to change the inevitable is futile. Societies which view themselves as living in harmony with nature believe that people must alter their behaviour to accommodate nature. Societies that view themselves as able to master nature think in terms of the supremacy of the human race, and harnessing the forces of nature.

Time orientation – past, present and future

Societies which are orientated towards the past look for solutions in the past; what would our forefathers have done? Societies which are present-orientated consider the immediate effects of their actions; what will happen if I do this? Societies which are future-orientated look to the long-term results of today's events; what will happen to future generations if we do these things today?

Basic human nature – evil, good, mixed

Societies which believe that people are primarily evil focus on controlling the behaviour of people through specified codes of conduct and sanctions for wrongdoing. Societies that believe that people are essentially good would exhibit trust and rely on verbal agreements. Societies that see people as mixed probably also see people as changeable and would focus on means to modify behaviour, to encourage desired behaviour and discourage behaviours that are not desirable.

Activity orientation – being, containing and controlling, doing

Societies which are primarily 'being'-orientated are emotional; people react spontaneously based on what they feel at the time. Those which are 'doing'-orientated are constantly striving to achieve; people are driven by a need to accomplish difficult tasks. Those concerned with containing and controlling focus on moderation and orderliness; people seek to achieve a balance in life and in society.

Human relationships – individual, lineal, co-lineal

Societies which are primarily individual believe that individuals should be independent, and take responsibility for their own actions. Those that are lineal are concerned with the family line and the power structure that underlies a hierarchy. Those that are co-lineal are group-orientated and emphasize group interactions and actions.

The Kluckhohn and Strodtbeck model in international management

These value orientations can be related to effective management practices in different locations. The following suggestions illustrate how these orientations may be related to management.

1   In a society that believes humans are subjugated by nature, planning would be futile, because the future is preordained.
2   In a society that is present-orientated, rewards would be closely tied to current performance.
3   In a society that believes in the basic goodness of humans, participative management is likely to be the normal approach.
4   In a society that is primarily being-orientated, decisions are likely to be intuitive with less concern for logic.
5   In a society that is hierarchical, the organization structure might reflect this in a formal, authority-based hierarchy.

Understanding these dimensions of culture can provide international managers with insights into people's behaviour in foreign locations, and allow these managers to adapt their own style and adjust their organization's practices to accommodate the differences (see LEADERSHIP). Consider the following possibilities:

(1) In a society that thinks in terms of mastery over nature, technology is likely to be admired and people willing to work towards production goals and objectives set by management. In a society that emphasizes harmony with nature, technology may be accepted but there will be concern over the impact of technology on nature, and goals and objectives will be acceptable if they relate both to productivity and the environment. In a society that sees itself as subject to nature, mastery of technology may be viewed with caution and specific goals and objectives disliked.

(2) In a past-orientated society, market research would focus on the past and customer tastes would not be expected to change dramatically or quickly. Sales efforts would emphasize past quality, performance, etc.,

and would use familiar approaches. In a present-orientated society, market research would focus on what is current, and identify products and services with immediate practical benefits. Sales efforts would emphasize these immediate benefits and use topical references and up-to-date approaches. In a future-orientated society, market research would be concerned with expectations of the future and would try to identify tomorrow's tastes and needs. Sales efforts will emphasize the long-term benefits of products and services and use futuristic references and images.

(3) If the society believes that all people are basically good then managers will expect that people working for a firm intend to do their best and contribute to the organization's effectiveness. If errors occur they will be explained as occurring in spite of people's efforts. If people are believed to be basically evil, managers will not expect people to work hard on their own. Errors will be explained in terms of individual human error and disassociated from the firm. If people are seen as mixed, the selection of the best people to work in the firm might be emphasized. Errors can be admitted readily and the actions taken to correct and avoid them in the future explained.

(4) In a being-orientated society people are spontaneous and react emotionally. Accounting and financial systems would need to be relatively flexible allowing for alternative ways of carrying out necessary activities. Policies and procedures would be general and provide guidelines rather than specific and detailed instructions. In a containing and controlling society the emphasis would be on logic. Systems would be rationally designed and explained assuming that people will comply with logical systems. Policies and procedures will be complex and include both qualitative and quantitative guidelines and instructions. In a doing-orientated society the concern is for activity and accomplishment. Systems will be pragmatic, emphasizing expected results. Policies and procedures will be relatively simple and described in operational, active terms.

(5) In a society that is primarily individual the individual person will be the focus of management activities. This will be true of decision making, leadership, work design, rewards, etc. In a society that is lineal, the hierarchy of power and authority will be important in all management activities. Leadership is associated with level in the organization which is accompanied by power and authority (see LEADERSHIP). Vertical differentiation will be stressed, and decisions, work design and rewards will conform to the hierarchical structure. In a society that is co-lineal, group activities are normal and preferred. The group becomes the focus in terms of decisions, leadership, work design and rewards.

Hofstede's value survey model

The value survey model (VSM) has been widely discussed in international management literature and it appears to provide information of relevance from a managerial point of view. The Hofstede (1980) model proposed four dimensions of culture (a fifth dimension was added based on research in the Far East – Chinese Culture Connection, 1987 – but is not discussed here).

Individualism
Individualism (IDV) is the degree to which individual decision making and action is accepted and encouraged by the society (see DECISION MAKING). Where IDV is high, the society emphasizes the role of the individual; where IDV is low, the society emphasizes the role of the group. Some societies view individualism positively and see it as the basis for creativity and achievement; others view it with disapproval and see it as disruptive to group harmony and cooperation.

Uncertainty avoidance
Uncertainty avoidance (UAI) is the degree to which the society is willing to accept and deal with uncertainty. Where UAI is high, the society is concerned with certainty and security, and seeks to avoid uncertainty; where UAI is low, the society is comfortable with a high degree of uncertainty and is open to the unknown. Some societies view certainty as necessary, so that people can function without worrying about the consequences of

uncertainty; others view uncertainty as providing excitement and opportunities for innovation and change.

Power distance

Power distance (PDI) is the degree to which power differences are accepted and sanctioned by society. Where PDI is high, the society believes that there should be a well-defined order of inequality in which everyone has a rightful place; where PDI is low, the prevalent belief is that all people should have equal rights and the opportunity to change their position in the society. Some societies view a well-ordered distribution of power as contributing to a well-managed society because each person knows what their position is, and people are, in fact, protected by this order. Others view power as corrupting, and believe that those with less power will inevitably suffer at the hands of those with more.

Masculinity

Masculinity (MAS) is the degree to which traditional male values are important to a society. Traditional male values incorporate assertiveness, performance, ambition, achievement and material possessions, while traditional female values focus on the quality of life, the environment, nurturing and concern for the less fortunate (see WOMEN MANAGERS IN ORGANIZATIONS). In societies that are high on MAS, sex roles are clearly differentiated and men are dominant; if MAS is low, sex roles are more fluid and feminine values predominate throughout. Some societies see the traditional male values as being necessary for survival; that is, men must be aggressive and women must be protected. Others view both sexes as equal contributors to society and believe that a dominance by traditional male values is destructive. The extremes of each of these indices have been described. Most countries are not at the extreme, but may be moderately high or moderately low; thus, effective management practices will not usually reflect an extreme tendency. An examination of profiles of different countries shows the variety that is possible considering these four dimensions. Some examples illustrate how these might influence management practices.

(1) New Zealand as a society is individualistic, does not avoid uncertainty and believes in equality and traditional male values. This would suggest that organizational structures will be relatively flat, with individuals making decisions on their own and competing for scarce resources.

(2) Italy as a society is individualistic, avoids uncertainty and believes in equality (within the confines of sex distinctions) and traditional male values. This would suggest a similar structure, but a reliance on gathering information for decisions and an emphasis on job security and seniority are important components of the management system.

(3) Singapore as a society is collectivist, does not avoid uncertainty, believes in power distinctions and is relatively low on masculinity. This suggests a paternalistic leadership system, with the leader expressing concern for subordinates and the quality of life, but without undue concern for job security.

(4) Japan as a society is collectivist but also high on uncertainty avoidance as well as masculinity, and relatively high on power distance. This would suggest a system that seeks consensus among group members but is competitive and has clear distinctions in terms of power; job security would be stressed and jobs allocated on the basis of sex.

Limitations of the value survey model

The scores reported by Hofstede are based on employees within one organization, a large US multinational company. Certain types of individuals will be attracted to such an organization, and this will be reflected in these scores. These scores should not, therefore, be interpreted as an accurate description of the national culture as a whole; rather, they should be seen as an indication of the similarities and differences that one might expect to find among employees in this type of organization in different countries.

In addition, these scores represent a central tendency in a particular population, but there is likely to be a wide array of values in any country; organizations and industries will attract and retain individuals with value systems that fit into the organizational culture. For example, a study of fast food restaurant managers in Canada and the USA revealed a very low level of individualism, combined with no uncertainty avoidance and high power distance and masculinity (Punnett and Withane 1990). This is quite dissimilar from the Canadian and US value profile presented by Hofstede; but, it appears to match the needs of an industry where people must work in close coordination, where there is little job security and where there are clear distinctions of power and a great deal of competition.

Researchers have also expressed concerns regarding the survey instrument used in Hofstede's research, and the validity of the measure has been questioned. Researchers question whether the country scores provided are representative of the normal population and whether the important cultural variables are the ones being measured. These concerns should all be kept in mind when interpreting the results of Hofstede's study. From a practical perspective, the cultural variables described by the model are intuitively appealing because of their apparent relationship to the management process.

Using the value survey model in international management

The management process is often described as consisting of planning, organizing, staffing, directing and controlling. These aspects of the management process probably occur in some form in all businesses, but the form may differ depending on the environment. In particular, the cultural values that are typical of a particular society can influence what is effective in terms of the management process. Consider some extremes of the Hofstede dimensions as they might relate to aspects of the management process.

Where individualism is high, individual input is sought from those individuals who have particular knowledge or expertise. Superiors are expected to make day-to-day decisions and communicate these to subordinates who are expected to carry them out. Input may be sought from subordinates, or others, who will

be affected by decisions, or who have particular knowledge or expertise. Individuals may disagree with particular decisions, but will generally go along with them if the majority agree, or if the decision has been made by a person in a position of power.

Individuals are given specific responsibility for completing tasks and achieving goals and objectives. The individual is expected to make the necessary decisions to carry through a given assignment. Management by objectives (MBO) is a popular approach, because MBO incorporates the idea of top management setting strategic directions, lower levels developing action plans to achieve these, and individuals accepting and working towards individual goals.

Where collectivism is high, organizational plans are formulated on the basis of the larger societal direction, and with input from all organizational members. The overall direction of the organization is discussed and agreed to throughout the organization. Decisions are made collectively, with all affected participating in the process. Disagreements are dealt with throughout the process, and consensus from all members is sought. Tasks and assignments are carried out by groups. There is pressure from the group for conformance to acceptable standards. When decisions need to be made, they are made by the group as a whole. The quality circle approach is popular, because it incorporates the idea of bottom-up decision making, consensus among members and group involvement.

Where uncertainty avoidance is high, uncertainty can be avoided by having group members share responsibility for planning and decisions, or, alternatively, by having one person in a position of power take responsibility. The advice of experts is likely to be important in formulating plans and making decisions. Planning provides security and is well accepted. Plans are likely to be detailed and complex, incorporating priorities and contingencies. Specific plans provide direction and little ambiguity. Strategic planning is as long-term as it is practical. Checks and balances ensure that performance is at the planned level, and allow for correction before a major departure occurs. Decisions are reached slowly. If responsibility is shared, then group agreement is important to the planning process. If a powerful individual makes the decisions, then these are imparted to subordinates as absolutes. In any case, disagreement is discouraged.

Where uncertainty avoidance is low, planning is flexible and relatively short-term. Uncertainty is seen as inevitable, and therefore the organization must be able to change direction quickly. Planning is accepted as providing guidance but not constraints. Formal planning is most likely to take place at top levels and be, at least partially, based on a subjective evaluation of opportunities. Personal preferences are likely to be evident in strategic directions. A certain amount of risk taking will be encouraged. Individuals are likely to accept the risk of individual decision making, and the need for making quick decisions will be stressed.

Where power distance is high, planning and decision making is done at the top. Input is accepted from those in powerful positions, but no input is expected from those at lower levels. Long-term plans are kept secret. Operational decisions are made on a daily basis by superiors, and work assigned to subordinates. All decisions are referred to the superior, and subordinates are discouraged from taking the initiative and making decisions. Subordinates accept assigned work and carry out tasks as instructed. Those in positions of power are respected; those in inferior positions expect that more powerful individuals will take responsibility for decision making.

Where power distance is low, everyone is seen as being capable of contributing to the planning process, and input from a variety of organizational levels is sought in developing strategic plans. Decision making in general is participative, and long-term plans are likely to be shared among organizational members. Operational decisions incorporate the views of those who must carry them out. The people involved in particular tasks are expected to make the routine decisions necessary to complete the task, and decisions are only referred to the superior when they involve unusual circumstances. Power differences exist, but are minimized, and friendly relationships between superiors and subordinates are normal.

Where traditional masculine values predominate, strategic plans emphasize specific, measurable advances by the organization (for example, increases in market share, profitability, etc.); these are difficult but believed to be achievable, and results are observable. Strategic choices are made at the top level. Operational decisions will focus on task accomplishment and tasks will be undertaken by those people most likely to perform at the desired level. Certain tasks will be seen as more suitable for males, others as more suitable for females. In some cases, responsibility for different types of decisions will be on the basis of sex. Outside of their traditional decision making roles, each sex will tend to emulate the other.

Where traditional feminine values predominate, strategic plans will take into account the environment, the quality of working life, and concern for the less fortunate. Profitability and market share, for example, will be defined within this context. Operational decisions will focus on satisfaction with work and development of a congenial and nurturing work environment. Task accomplishment will be within this framework. Work will be seen as generally suitable for either sex, with more concern for assigning work according to individual abilities and preferences. Decision making will be shared between the sexes. Decision making responsibility will depend on ability and preferences rather than sex. Male values of achievement, money and performance will rank equally with female values of nurturing, quality of life and caring for the less fortunate.

6 Variation within cultures

Models of cultural values are helpful in understanding cultural similarities and differences. In essence, however, they are stereotypes. Any culture is far more complex than such models would suggest, and it is important that this complexity is recognized. One can think of these cultural stereotypes as describing the values of a typical member of a particular culture, but must acknowledge that any culture is made up of individuals, many of whom will not share the typical values. In working with people from other cultures, both of these aspects need to be considered (Mendenhall *et al.* 1995). To illustrate both cultural preference and individual variation, consider two cultures, Alpha and Beta; Alpha might be a culture described as valuing personal initiative, and Beta as valuing group harmony (the USA and Japan, respectively, would fit these descriptions to some degree). These values are measured on an individualism scale.

If these preferences are considered as describing the average in these two societies, these cultural values can be pictured graphically as normal curves. In Figure 3, the y axis represents the relative frequency of occurrence of individualism in society, and the x

axis represents a continuum from low individualism to high individualism. The individualism preferences of the two cultures, Alpha and Beta, are pictured on the graph. As Graph A illustrates, there are some Alphans who are quite concerned with group harmony (contrary to their average) and there are some Betans who are quite concerned with personal initiative (contrary to their average). It is possible to talk of the Alphans as generally being high on individualism and concerned with personal initiative, and the Betans as generally being low on individualism and concerned with group harmony. At the same time, individuals within both the Alpha and Beta cultures can vary from this general preference. In contrast, it is possible, although unlikely, that there could be virtually no overlap between two cultures as in Graph B. Two cultures can also be very similar and yet reflect a subtle difference in preferences. This would be the case in Canada and the USA, two countries often seen as holding similar values, yet with some differences in their cultural values. This is illustrated in Graph C; here, there is a great deal of overlap between the cultures, yet the norm structures for each country are slightly different.

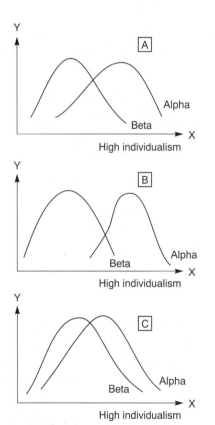

Figure 3 Cultural values: levels of individualism in alpha and beta
Source: Mendenhall *et al.* (1995: 292)

7 Going beyond national culture

A focus simply on national culture can be somewhat misleading if one limits consideration to this level. There are clear cases where cultures transcend national boundaries (for example, the British culture in many former colonies) and other cases where several cultures are evident in one nation (for example, multiculturalism in Canada). Equally, because cultures change in response to the environment, they may become more similar or more different over time. On the whole, as discussed earlier, from the organization's viewpoint, a focus on national cultures is an appropriate beginning. Within this framework, subcultures, overlapping cultures, and forces for convergence and divergence need to be considered.

Understanding subcultures

Identifying subcultures and their values is necessary in some situations and can be particularly useful to international managers; for example:

(1) A subculture may hold values which are in sharp contrast to those of the broader national culture. If a manager is interacting substantially with members of such a subculture, he or she will need to appreciate and accommodate these differences. Sikh immigrants to Canada still maintain their cultural heritage and believe in the importance of wearing turbans. The Royal Canadian Mounted Police – Canada's famed Mounties – found it was necessary to accommodate this cultural custom in order to attract and retain Sikhs in the force.

(2) The values of a subculture can be more similar to a foreign manager's own cultural values than those of the broader national culture. A manager might want to seek out members of this subculture in situations where similar values are desired. A manager from a largely Christian country such as the United Kingdom might find some similarity of values with the Christian minority in Japan, and might seek out this group at certain times, particularly in times of grief.

(3) Members of a subculture whose values are in conflict with the broader national culture may not be integrated into the workforce easily. Contrasting values may cause personal conflicts among employees from different groups. A manager must be sensitive to these potential conflicts and identify ways of dealing with them. The indigenous Malays and the Chinese in Malaysia have been described as exhibiting sometimes radically different values that can lead to conflicts at work. These are partially due to conflicting religious practices – the Malays, for the most part, are Muslims while the Chinese are Confucian and Buddhists – and partially due to attitudes towards work – the Malays are seen as easygoing and working to live, while the Chinese are described as concerned with getting ahead and work is more central to their lives.

(4) Synergy can develop where employees with different values work together because they may view the same situation from varying perspectives. Managers who can effectively control interactions among employees with different values can benefit from the development of new and innovative ways of thinking. The Bata Shoe Company has subsidiaries throughout the world and finds that by bringing its diverse marketing managers together in Canada, new ideas for products and marketing approaches can be developed (see BATA'S SYSTEM).

(5) Working with a variety of subcultures within one national location provides many of the same experiences as working in a new national culture. Managers can increase their cross-cultural sensitivity by seeking out members of different cultural minorities and interacting and working with them on an ongoing basis. The USA is made up of many groups which maintain their cultural heritage in spite of being Americans. Some companies have made a virtue of this cultural diversity; for example, Monsanto is reported to have developed programmes to ensure that all employees are culturally aware.

Understanding overlapping cultures

Subcultures are often encountered and cannot be ignored by international managers. The same is true of cultures that overlap national boundaries. There are many situations where groups in different countries share similar values. In fact, the subcultures identified previously (for example, the Sikhs) can be found in many countries and their values will be somewhat similar in each location. The similarities in values are often attributable to shared ethnicity or religion; some examples illustrate this potential overlap:

(1) Rastafarians (members of a religious sect originating in Jamaica) can be found throughout the Caribbean and in Canada, the UK and the USA. Those values and customs associated with their religious beliefs remain similar even when they have been integrated into societies outside Jamaica.

(2) The Jewish people often exhibit similar values no matter where in the world they have settled. To some extent this is because of shared religious beliefs, but even non-practising Jews feel a kinship with other Jews

in different parts of the world, and many Jews see this as a shared cultural heritage, not simply a religious similarity.

(3) The British left a clear mark on many of their colonies, and the governing class in former British colonies retain many British characteristics.

(4) The boundaries of many nations have been identified so that cultural groups have been divided. These groups often share more culture with their counterparts in other countries that with the nation in which they live. The Kurdish people of Iran, Iraq and Turkey provide a good example of this division of a culture. Ethnic Russians living in many of the new states formed from the USSR are in a similar situation.

It can also be helpful for international managers to identify overlapping cultural values that may be found in different locations. Familiarity with the cultural values of a group in one location can then be useful in identifying values of a counterpart group elsewhere.

Forces for convergence and divergence

Whether cultures are converging or diverging is a further issue of interest to international managers. Some people argue that there are many forces in the world which encourage countries to become more alike and to share common values. For example, the ease of global communication and travel means that people are often exposed to foreigners and foreign media. People in the USA can watch French television, listen to radio broadcasts from the People's Republic of China and attend Indian movies. Without ever leaving home, they can meet Japanese tourists, talk with Saudi business people, and have dinner with African students in Balinese restaurants. Similarly, around the world, products that originated in the USA are sought – Levi's jeans, Coca-Cola, Elvis Presley records and Rambo movies, among other things. The British rock group 'the Beatles' have been popular in countries as diverse as the USA, Russia and Japan. Over time, it would seem that if people are exposed to similar experiences, and interact with others from different

cultures, there might be a convergence of values.

The current worldwide concern with the environment also suggests a potential converging of values. If cultural values develop in response to perceived survival needs, then global concerns that are not defined by national boundaries may lead to global solutions and shared values. Similarly, regional economic integration, as exemplified by the European Union, is also a force for convergence of values. These regions seek to standardize a variety of practices, and this standardization, in turn, is likely to influence cultural values.

In addition, the existence of multinational and global companies has been seen as contributing to the convergence of cultures. These organizations inevitably take aspects of the home culture with them to foreign locations, and subsidiaries will share, to some extent, a corporate culture and perhaps a professional culture. At the same time, as the firm draws its leaders from around the world there is a sharing of values. Over time, this would suggest an increasing importance of the corporate influence and some convergence of values.

In contrast, there are arguments that cultural values are not converging, but may be diverging. The ease of communication and travel may have this latter effect. Extensive exposure to foreigners and foreign media may increase awareness of the home values, which may be seen as particularly 'good' in contrast to foreign values. A sense of domination by foreigners can result in a determination to maintain one's own value system. Canadians, for example, feel that they are very influenced by the USA and react by being more Canadian; some people in the USA are concerned about the Japanese influence and react by perceiving Japanese ways as negative.

Events in the late 1980s and early 1990s, such as the collapse of the Soviet Union, suggest that strong cultural value differences have been maintained by groups within the union in spite of efforts to eliminate these differences. Similarly, French Canadians wish to be recognized as a distinct society and native American groups' arguments for self-government focus around cultural uniqueness and suggest divergence rather than convergence.

It could also be argued that the activities of multinational and global companies can contribute to divergence. Some of these companies provide products or services specifically developed for particular countries or regions and they adapt their decisions to fit the needs of different locations. This sensitivity to cultural differences can in effect perpetuate the differences.

Arguments for both convergence and divergence are quite reasonable. Perhaps one can conclude that convergence will occur in some aspects of culture and divergence in others. International managers should be aware of the forces leading to both, and in specific situations consider their likely impact.

8 Conclusion

The relationship of national culture and international management is an extremely complex one. The discussion in this entry is necessarily limited in scope and depth. It should, however, provide the reader with a basic understanding of the issues associated with developing and using cultural understanding to enhance international operations.

There are western biases inherent in these discussions of culture and management. For example, the management process – consisting of planning, organizing, staffing, directing and controlling – is familiar to most readers because that is how business and management is usually approached in North America and Europe, but consider the following.

1 Is planning a necessary part of management? If events are pre-determined, planning may at best be a waste of time, and at worst a questioning of a higher power.
2 Should firms be formally organized? If personal influence is important in day-to-day activities, it may not be appropriate to identify positions within the firm.
3 Can people be allocated to fill positions within the firm? If people prefer to work at tasks as they arise, it may not be helpful to allocate them to specific slots.

4 Does management actively seek to direct and motivate subordinates? If people believe that they should work hard only for personal achievement, it may be counterproductive for management actively to direct and motivate them.

This inherent western bias to thinking about management illustrates a major challenge for international cross-cultural management. Effective managers should not take anything for granted. Openness to the possibility that the world is not the world you know and accept is constantly necessary.

BETTY JANE PUNNETT
UNIVERSITY OF THE WEST INDIES

Further reading

(References cited in the text marked *)

* Adler, N.J. (1986) *International Dimensions of Organizational Behavior*, Boston, MA: PWS-KENT Publishing Company. (An excellent overview of the topic intended as a companion text for courses in organizational behaviour.)

Bhagat, R. and McQuaid, S.J. (1982) 'The role of subjective culture in organizations: a review and direction for future research', *Journal of Applied Psychology – Monograph* 67 (5): 61–74. (A comprehensive, scholarly review of the relationship between culture and organizations.)

* England, G. (1978) 'Managers and their value systems: A five country comparative study', *Columbia Journal of World Business*, 13 (2): 35–44. (A relatively early study of differences in national culture as they relate to managers, which identifies both similarities and differences in managerial values across national boundaries.)

* Heller, F.A. (1988) 'Cost benefits of multinational research on organizations', *International Studies of Management and Organization* 18 (3): 5-18. A discussion of the need for international management research, including a better understanding of the role of culture in international management.)

* Hofstede, G. (1980) *Culture's Consequences*, Beverley Hills, CA: Sage Publications. (An extensive study of the differences in values across cultures around the world, which gives substantial insight into the relationship of culture, values and behaviour.)

Hofstede, G. (1991) *Cultures and Organizations – Software of the Mind*, London: McGraw-Hill. (An extension of the 1980 work, incorporating Confucian dynamism to the model, and further discussing the role of culture in organizations.)

* Kluckhohn, A. and Strodtbeck, F. (1961) *Variations in Value Orientations*, Westport, CT: Greenwood Press. (A well-recognized anthropological assessment of variations in values that has been adopted by some management scholars.)

* Kroeber, A. and Kluckhohn, C. (1952) *Culture: A Critical Review of Concepts and Definitions*, Cambridge, MA: Papers of the Peabody Museum, Harvard University. (A classic discussion of the meaning of culture, its development and its implications.)

* Lane, H. and DiStefano, J. (1988) *International Management Behavior – From Policy to Practice*, Scarborough, Ont: Nelson Canada. (A text of cases, readings and conceptual discussion which examines behaviour in the context of international management.)

* Mendenhall, M., Punnett, B.J. and Ricks, D.A. (1995) *Global Management*, Boston, MA: Blackwell. (A comprehensive text on all aspects of international management.)

* Punnett, B.J. (1989) *Experiencing International Business and Management*, Boston, MA: PWS-KENT Publishing Company. (A unique collection of experiential exercises, projects and profiles pertaining to international business and management.)

Punnett, B.J. (1997) 'Towards effective management of expatriate spouses', *Journal of World Business*. (A discussion of the challenges faced by expatriate spouses with suggestions for managing these challenges.)

* Punnett, B.J. and Ricks, D.A. (1992) *International Business*, Boston, MA: PWS-KENT Publishing Company. (A comprehensive introduction to the field of international business.)

* Punnett, B.J. and Withane, S. (1990) 'Hofstede's value survey model: to embrace or abandon?', in S.B. Prasad (ed.), *Advances in International Comparative Management*, vol. 5: 69–90. (An application of Hofstede's model in different industries and with different ethnic groups.)

Ricks, D.A. (1983) *Big Business Blunders – Mistakes in Multinational Marketing*, Homewood, IL: Dow-Jones Irwin. (A wonderful and humorous compilation of mistakes that companies have made around the world.)

* Rokeach, J. (1973) *The Nature of Human Values*, New York: Free Press. (Fundamental to the understanding of values and their impact on human behaviour.)

* Ronen, S. and Shenkar, O. (1985) 'Clustering countries on attitudinal dimensions: A review and synthesis', *Academy of Management Review* 10 (3): 435–54. (A comprehensive review of previous studies to identify clusters of countries exhibiting similar national cultures.)

* Terpstra, V. and David, K. (1985) *The Cultural Environment of International Business*, Cincinnati, OH: Southwestern Publishing. (An excellent text reviewing many aspects of culture and their relationship to international business.)

Related topics in the IEBM: GLOBAL STRATEGIC ALLIANCES; GLOBALIZATION; GLOBALIZATION AND CORPORATE NATIONALITY; GLOBALIZATION AND SOCIETY; INTERNATIONAL BUSINESS ELITES; INTERNATIONAL BUSINESS NEGOTIATIONS; INTERNATIONAL MARKETING; MANAGEMENT IN AUSTRALIA; MANAGEMENT IN ITALY; MANAGEMENT IN JAPAN; MANAGEMENT IN MEXICO; MANAGEMENT IN NORTH AMERICA; MANAGEMENT IN SCANDINAVIA; MANAGEMENT IN SINGAPORE; MANAGEMENT IN THE ARAB WORLD; MARKETING MANAGEMENT, INTERNATIONAL; MARKETING RESEARCH; MIGRANT MANAGERS; MULTINATIONAL CORPORATIONS; ORGANIZATION CULTURE; ORGANIZATION STRUCTURE; ORGANIZING, PROCESS OF; POWER

Decision making

Overview

Decision making has long been seen as a central managerial activity. At the centre of this activity is the problem of choosing a course of action under conditions of uncertainty and ambiguity. A number of different strategies for making a choice are outlined. Underlying these strategies is a dualism between programmed, routine decisions which, given intendedly rational decision makers, would use a computational strategy, and unprogrammed, non-routine decisions which would use an iterative process involving interaction and mutual adjustment between decision makers.

Decision making takes place within an organizational context, setting a timeframe for the definition of problems, solutions and participants. Within this timeframe preceding decisions have already set constraints for choices made in the present which will, in turn, affect succeeding decisions. Concurrent decisions also compete for the attention of decision makers.

Coping with uncertainty forms the nub of decision making. Without uncertainty as to which course of action to take there would be no decision to be made. The dominant paradigm of organizational decision making assumes that decision makers are intendedly rational but that rationality is 'bounded' by lack of knowledge about preferences and any associated instrumentalitites.

Uncertainty involves the interpretation of problems and possible solutions through an interplay between a number of psychological and sociological processes. Psychological approaches to decision making tend to emphasize the inherent biases resulting from information assymetry and framing effects. Sociological approaches tend to be more descriptive and to emphasize the use of power and the interplay between different interests.

Much of the empirical research into organizational decision making has been concerned with finding patterns between variables that attempt to describe the processes found in real-life situations. This research, more by implication than by empirical measurement, has been concerned with discovering appropriate decision patterns for particular situations and types of decision. The general conclusion is that what has been called a 'sporadic' or 'muddling through' process is effective under conditions of high uncertainty while the more orderly 'constricted' process is appropriate for routine, relatively clear-cut decisions. In this respect, the general well-established thesis of the distinction between routine and non-routine decision making is supported.

There is increasing interest in finding linkages between decision-making processes and aspects of the general organizational culture and institutional framework within which an organization exists. According to this approach managerial decision making is seens as being severely constrained both by the cultural limitations upon the way in which problems and solutions are defined and by the external institutional forces acting on an organization, requiring it to demonstrate its worthiness for support through adopting certain structures and procedures.

I Understanding decision making

The study of decision making has attracted continual interest in the literature on business and management. This is so especially since the publication in 1938 of *The Functions of the Executive* by Chester Barnard, a book which put decision making and the associated processes of communication and cooperation at the centre of managerial work.

Prior to Barnard's book writing on business and management emphasized the rational processes of decision making: the good manager was a 'rational economic man' (March and Simon 1958) who carefully planned and organized. Barnard, however, observed that the practice of management is very different to this, a point developed further by Simon (1947). In Simon's theory decision making under uncertainty is seen to be far removed from utility maximization because decision makers do not possess enough information about end preferences and the means to reach them. The reality for decision makers is scarcity of information and lack of ability to determine all possible outcomes. In this condition of 'bounded rationality' decision makers tend to 'satisfice' by using simple rules of thumb, selecting the first satisfactory solution to a problem.

This emphasis upon how decision makers behave opened up the idea that the highly rational image of business decision makers presented by classic economic theory is limited to a quite restricted set of conditions. As conditions get more complex a different type of decision process begins to take over. A behavioural view pushed consideration of decision beyond simply examining the outcomes of decisions to examining the processes by which decisions are made.

The Behavioural Theory of the Firm (Cyert and March 1963) was another landmark book linking a psychological theory of the decision maker to an economic and organizational theory of how organizations, as opposed to individuals, learn and adapt to changing conditions (see ORGANIZATION BEHAVIOUR). Although only partially achieved, the ambition of linking individual utilities to organizational needs for cooperative behaviour remains a vital item on the research agenda through cultural or institutional perspectives (Douglas 1987).

More recent writings investigating the nature of managerial work (Mintzberg 1975; Hickson *et al.* 1986; Butler *et al.* 1993) have emphasized the centrality of decision making and how managers take action upon intuitive and political factors in addition to using computational procedures (see MANAGERIAL BEHAVIOUR).

The decision maker: visions of rationality

Any theory of decision making must include consideration of human nature and how people make choices. Personality, risk-taking propensity and the need for achievement are all factors which have been proposed as having an effect upon decision making, as have Jung's psychological types (Nutt 1993). Any number of human characteristics exist but we limit our discussion to those characteristics which are related to human problem solving and, in particular, the notion of rationality.

Rationality is the reason for doing something and to judge a behaviour as reasonable is to be able to say that the behaviour is understandable within a given frame of reference. That behaviour may, however, appear as rational to the actors in a situation but irrational to an observer. Behaviour inconsistent with the actor's frame of reference may be deemed irrational, as may behaviour for which an observer can find no explanation. Even 'abnormal' behaviour may be explicable as, for instance, when Freud sought explanations for neuroses and psychoses.

Two terms that are also at the centre of a behavioural theory of decision making are risk and uncertainty. Although closely related a distinction can usefully be made. When utilities and probabilities can be attached to a number of different outcomes decision making can be said to take place under risk whereas decision making under uncertainty does not even allow complete knowledge of all possible outcomes and their associated probabilities and payoffs (March and Simon 1958: 137). Most theories of risk assume that decision makers prefer smaller risks to larger ones although there are exceptions to this.

There are many ways in which the term rationality has been used in the decision-making literature. Classic economic theory assumes a perfectly informed decision maker and a rational decision maker would successfully optimize outcomes. The ability to map out a complete decision tree was called by Lindblom (1959) 'synoptic' decision making. However, other than as a point of reference, such a notion does not get us far in considering decision making under uncertainty in complex organizations.

Intended rationality is the most useful starting point for thinking about the decision maker since we must assume that: a choice is to be made, even if it means doing nothing; there are decision makers who are aware of the possibility of choice; and their behaviour will be orientated towards the achievement of a goal or an improvement in their condition, but without necessarily achieving that goal. Intended rationality may be seen as consisting of two component rationalities to which the literature sometimes refers: (1) substantive rationality, which describes the primary orientation of economics whereby decision makers use the available information to increase their position on a given utility function; and (2) procedural rationality, which refers to an acceptance on the part of decision makers that their computational power is limited and that they are not in possession of complete information about options.

Bounded rationality is a general term referring to the limits of both substantive and procedural rationality. When there is uncertainty as to what is wanted and how to achieve it we can say that bounded rationality exists. *Cognitive limits to rationality* refers to the idea that bounded rationality is a result of the cognitive constraints of decision makers to understand their utility function and their powers of computation. *Local rationality* takes into account the notion that behaviour in decision making, which might appear irrational from an organizational perspective, can be explicable in

terms of the interests of individuals, groups or organizational sub-units.

Studying decision making

Decision making has attracted the attention of a wide spectrum of social scientists, particularly since the Second World War when it was seemingly given an impetus by the needs of the US Military searching for ways to manage large complex organizations. March's *The Handbook of Organizations* (1965) with its two articles on decision theory also shows the importance of the topic at this time. The term 'behavioural decision theory' was also coined at this time to distinguish a broader social science approach from economic theories of decision making which traditionally emphasized the goal of utility maximization.

This entry concentrates upon theories of decision making that are especially relevant to the understanding of organizational and managerial problems. It is useful to summarize the many key approaches, concerns and orientations that have been used to study organizational decision making as follows.

Case studies have been used to investigate particularly complex or difficult decisions such as the purchase of a new computer. Case studies aim to give richness of detail especially about the political problems of making and implementing a decision (Pettigrew 1973).

Laboratory experimentation has typically attracted psychologists concentrating upon issues such as the extent to which bias occurs in the way in which information is used in decision making (Hogarth 1980).

Game theory came to prominence during the Cold War due to a particular interest in military application (the notion of 'winning' and 'losing' providing an attractive analogy). It remains a useful way of thinking about decision making.

Simulation can be used in decision-making research using computers (Kleindorfer *et al.* 1993) or other techniques, such as case vignettes upon which participants pronounce a choice, or 'synthetic' investment decisions where scores on a limited number of variables are provided and decision makers have to decide whether to accept or reject a proposal (Butler *et al.* 1993).

Comparative field studies have become an increasingly common way of investigating organizational decision making as a way of overcoming the lack of generalizability of single cases, and the lack of real-life feel of laboratory experiments and game theory. Typically, these studies create types of decision out of patterns in the associated processes and draw conclusions as to the likely conditions under which each type is best suited (Mintzberg *et al.* 1976; Hickson *et al.* 1986; Butler *et al.* 1993).

Descriptive, normative and *prescriptive orientations*. Research on decision making either aims to describe what happens in particular situations (descriptive), to develop a more explanatory theory whereby propositions can be tested with a view to defining norms as to how certain aspects of decision making can be changed (normative) or to develop heuristics (Bazerman 1993) to act as simplifying strategies to guide judgement (prescriptive).

Psychological and *sociological orientations*. Decision making may be studied in terms of the psychological characteristics of individuals through, for instance, variables concerned with Jung's personality types (Kleindorfer *et al.* 1993) or as sociological studies where the aim is to identify key powerful individuals in an organization and to discover interrelationships between them to explain how they manage to influence the outcomes of major decisions (Pettigrew 1973).

Information and its use is a major concept in decision theory: an information processing approach to decision making sees information as central to the process of coping with uncertainty and hence many studies of decision making have investigated the use of information.

Studies of power and politics help mitigate the problem of a sole reliance upon information processing by focusing on the strategic use of information; it can be withheld, used opportunistically or distorted, while the use of power opens up a political dimension to decision making (Hickson *et al.* 1986).

Programmed and unprogrammed decisions

Programmed decisions are those which are routine, repetitive and have clearly defined ends and means. Unprogrammed decisions are those which are non-routine, one-off and badly structured. As already implied, the bounded rational model is appropriate for unprogrammed decisions whereas the computational rational model is appropriate for programmed decisions.

The processes involved in each type of decision differ (Simon 1960). The computational rationality of the programmed decisions leads to the use of extensive search procedures to explore all possible options and, after application of appropriate algorithms, an optimal choice can be made. The bounded rationality of unprogrammed decisions will tend to involve problematic searches, with the need for alternatives prompted by a crisis or the availability of a solution and the use of satisficing to make a choice. Implementation will tend to be disjointed and incremental.

Table 1 Programmed and unprogrammed decisions compared

Decision type	Programmed	Unprogrammed
	Routine, repetitive	Novel, badly structured
Rationality	Intended, synoptic	Intended, bounded
Process	Computational methods	Heuristic
	Extensive search	Problemistic search
	Optimizing	Satisficing
		Disjointed and incremental

Conceptual framework

The great diversity of approaches to the study of organizational decision making makes it necessary here to delimit the subject by means of a conceptual framework.

The core of the framework draws upon the 'garbage can' model of decision making (March 1988) by proposing that decision making involves streams of activities which serve to cope with uncertainty over time, specifically, problem definition, solution building, choosing, influencing and implementing.

Essentially, a decision is constrained by the performance of preceding decisions and will, in turn, affect succeeding decisions by its own performance. A decision can also involve sub-decisions, and concurrent decisions taking place elsewhere in the organization may also affect a decision. This network of decisions exists within an organization which, in turn, exists within a task and institutional environment (see Figure 1).

2 Strategies for choosing

The activity of choosing is central to decision making. Thompson (1967) notes that decision making involves two kinds of uncertainty. There can be uncertainty over outcome preferences (the ends) due to disagreements among managers, or there can be uncertainty concerning the means to reach the ends. Combining these two dimensions gives four

decision strategies – computation, judgement, negotiation, inspiration (Figure 2) – each of which can be associated with a particular organizational type – bureaucratic, collegiate, political, charismatic.

When there is agreement over ends and clear means to reach those ends the appropriate choice strategy is computation, implying the existence of an algorithm into which the appropriate data can be fed and a number of known steps followed to calculate the optimal choice. Providing participants see the procedure as legitimate, the answer comes out of the calculations, even though those calculations may be complex. This is the kind of rational–legal authority identified by Weber as belonging to bureaucracy.

If there is a high degree of means uncertainty due to ambiguous beliefs about causation decision makers will no longer have faith in their algorithms to give an optimal choice. Bounded rationality rules and the decision strategy needs to accomodate this by satisficing methods. This does not mean that computations are not needed; they may provide a

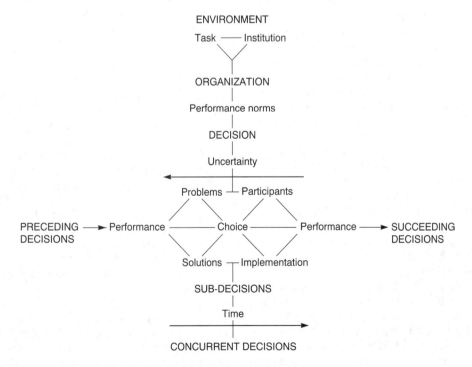

Figure 1 Framework for the study of managerial and organizational decision making

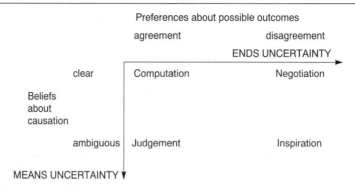

Figure 2 Strategies for choosing

useful heuristic or a symbolic function to show that procedural rationality is being adhered to. This strategy rests upon a collegial view of organization whereby a self-governing college group will talk, opinionate and strive to reach a view on a solution. At the minimum, sufficient agreement over a step forward would be made to allow action to be taken.

If there is a high degree of ends uncertainty due to disagreements over preferences about possible outcomes decision makers will have to negotiate and bargain to clarify their objectives. This strategy rests upon the notion of decision making as a political process in which trade-offs and deals are made, and coalitions built. The outcome of this political process, if a decision is to be made, will at the minimum be a sufficient agreement on ends to allow action to be taken (Cyert and March 1963).

When ends and means uncertainty is high, decision makers would seem to have an almost impossible task of choosing any course of action. Inspiration is the only way forward with individual decision makers acting on hunches and, in extreme cases, on a belief in divine intervention. Under these conditions errors would be accepted as a possibility and the problem becomes one of correcting those errors in further decisions. This image of decision making puts emphasis upon decision making as a stream of choices whereas the computational strategy emphasizes the independence of each decision. The notion of inspiration connects with theories of leadership and charisma since under conditions of very

high uncertainty trust in the characteristics of an individual replaces trust in procedures. The charismatic leader is seen by the followers to have solutions, or at least to possess the wisdom to find solutions, and may offer a new set of preferences to shift attention away from old conflicts.

The kind of organization surrounding this process is obviously the most difficult to define having been described as organized anarchy, as pertaining to chaos theory, or as a garbage can, into which various odds and ends are thrown and sorted.

Patterns of decision making

In practice, mixtures of processes are used and various comparative studies have attempted to discover patterns in these decision-making processes.

From a study of seventeen investment decisions and fifty-five participating managers Butler *et al.* (1993) found that computation provides a necessary but not sufficient condition for effective decision making. Those decisions which manage to achieve an interaction between computation, bargaining, judgement and inspiration are the most effective in terms of objectives attainment and learning.

Mintzberg *et al.* (1976) examined the processes of decision making used in a range of decisions by comparing twenty-five decision cases in a variety of organizations. Data was collected concerning the extent to which various phases of decision making were used and concerning other factors such as the duration of each decision, the extent to which interruptions occurred and the number of branches and recycles in the sequence suggested by the model. From analysis of the data six generalized types of decision were identifiable.

1 *Simple interrupt.* Stimulus by problem, solution given, recognition and diagnosis stages used with a lot of interruptions. These were the non-complex decisions with given solutions which got blocked.
2 *Political design process.* Given solutions or modifications to ready-made solutions were used in these decisions but interruptions were more extensive due to intensive political activity.
3 *Basic search.* This type of decision would appear to come nearest to the rational type in that there were few interruptions and the emphasis was upon rational search processes and finding solutions in accordance with organizational procedure.
4 *Modified search.* Represents a rather more complex basic search type in which ready-made solutions are modified to a particular decision.
5,6 *Basic* and *dynamic designs.* These two decision types appear to move towards the bounded rational type in that custom-made solutions are found following considerable design and evaluation effort.

Hickson *et al.* (1986) also provided a systematic attempt to observe the processes of strategic decision making across a large number of decision issues in many different types of organization. These studies examined 150 strategic decisions in thirty organizations of many different types ranging across a spectrum of manufacturing and service, and public and private organizations. Detailed observations and interviews were carried out concerning the processes used in a range of decisions within each organization and covering a range of topics. Generally these were high-level or 'top decisions', involving the long-term strategy of the organization and covering a range of issues dealing with matters such as the introduction of new products, closing down facilities and factories, reorganizations, mergers or acquisitions, personnel matters or

investment in new equipment. Observations were made concerning a number of specific variables of the processes. *Scrutiny* is the basic process of searching, designing and evaluating solutions using various information sources. Also included in scrutiny is the degree of effort that goes into preparing reports, such as test markets or engineering development tests. *Interaction* is the degree of social interaction between participants which may be formal, whereby a decision is processed through committees and procedures, or informal involving discussions over lunch, in corridors or elsewhere. *Negotiation* is the degree of bargaining over preferences ranging from the decision being not open to negotiation, through negotiation occurring only in the final stages, to negotiation resulting in limited consensus. *Delays* are the number of impediments and interruptions in the smooth flow of a decision which may occur for a number of reasons ranging from problems of sequencing, through awaiting priority in the order of attention, solving and awaiting further investigations, to awaiting to overcome resistance to change. *Duration* is measured by the time between an issue being deliberately considered in the organization to final authorization. *Centrality*, or the extent to which a decision is centralized or decentralized, is usually considered to be a major variable of decision making in an organization.

Data was subjected to a cluster analysis to establish patterns of decision making. Three distinct patterns or clusters emerged. The first, the sporadic cluster, consisted of a group of fifty-three decisions with above average delays, impediments, scrutiny (on all subvariables), informal interaction and duration, and were authorized at the highest level in the organization following some negotiation. Overall these decisions may be described as informally spasmodic and protracted.

As a means of making decisions, in a wide range of British organizations, the sporadic method was used in about one-third of the decisions studied. This sporadic cluster may be contrasted to the fluid cluster, which also accounted for about one-third of the decisions. With these, there were less delays, impediments, scrutiny and duration, some negotiation and more formal interaction, but all decisions were still authorized at the highest level. Overall, these decisions may be described as steadily paced, quick and formally channelled.

The third group, the constricted decision cluster, is characterized by less scrutiny, negotiation and formal interaction than the other decision types. Decisions were authorized below the highest level but, paradoxically, used more sources of information during scrutiny than did the fluid decisions. Overall these may be seen as narrowly channelled decisions.

The complexity and political nature of the various decision issues were also assessed and, in general, the most complex and politically sensitive decisions were treated in a sporadic way; hence, sporadic issues were found to be those involving many diverse interests, were serious in their potential consequences, contentious and externally influenced.

Those decisions which scored slightly less on complexity and least of all on political sensitivity tended to be treated in a fluid manner. The distinguishing feature here with regard to the sporadically-treated issues was that the fluid issues were less serious but rarer (more unusual). It appears that top management wanted direct control over these decisions and permitted only that degree of delegation that could be formally managed.

Decision issues with the least complexity and political sensitivity were handled by the constricted process, the distinguishing feature being that the issues were familiar (programmed), involving internal interests only and were non-contentious.

3 Performance

The question of performance and effectiveness of organizational decision making has been somewhat neglected but is obviously of concern to managers. The problem is, however, to find appropriate dimensions upon which to assess performance.

A field study of investment decisions indicated two dimensions of decision effectiveness (Butler *et al.* 1993). The first, objectives attainment, is the extent to which prior objectives, financial and non-financial, are reached.

One feature found to have a strong effect upon increasing objectives attainment involved clarity over who was providing leadership for the decision. The second is the extent to which a decision and its associated processes lead to learning. Decision processes that involved a high degree of negotiation taking place over time, and a high degree of inspiration, tended to have high levels of learning. The distinction between the two views of performance pinpoints two different but pervasive aspects of organizational decision making; decision making as a rational process of meeting objectives or as an adaptive process.

Bias in information use

Much of the research carried out within a psychological paradigm has concerned itself with possible sources of bias in the way in which information gets used in decision making (Tversky and Kahneman 1981; Hogarth 1980; Bazerman 1993).

Following are some key biases which have been noted:

Availability of information. There is a tendency for people to pay attention to information that is readily available in the immediate environment, for example, by drawing upon well-publicized or frequently occurring events.

Selective perception. People will come to a problem with a bias according to existing group organizational or cultural memberships. Information is then sought which is consistent with prior ideas or first impressions, rather than information to falsify a hypothesis.

Concrete information. A view which is supported by received, statistical or verifiable information tends to get more weight than a view about which there is scant, ambiguous or more subjective information.

Illusory correlation. A belief that two variables co-vary when they are, in fact, unrelated in any causal connection, can lead to a spurious analysis of a situation.

Inconsistency of judgements. There may be an inability to apply a given set of criteria consistently, such as when selecting students for admission to a university.

Conservatism. There can be a failure to revise opinions if new information comes to light. This is discussed below under Bayes' theorem.

Order effects of data presentation. Sometimes the first items in a presentation can assume undue importance – primacy – sometimes the last items can be considered more important – recency.

Incorrect extrapolations. Past trends are often used to estimate the future by assuming a linear growth. In practice growths can be exponential, like the growth of an epidemic, as can declines.

Use of heuristics to reduce mental effort. Habit and rules of thumb are part of a satisficing approach to decision making. They can be a source of bias and lead to lazy decision making when, in fact, more complete information is available.

Apparent representativeness. Judging the likelihood of an event by estimating the degree of similarity to a class of event, for example selecting a manager for a job because he exhibits characteristics typical of a good manager in terms of dress, speech, etc.

Law of small numbers. (A small sample is taken as representative of a population.)

Justifiability. Data is selected to support a preconceived argument. The converse would be falsifiability whereby decision makers deliberately set out to find data to refute an argument.

In order to help overcome some of these biases Neustadt and May (1986: 37) recommend that decision makers should identify clearly the historical analogues they are using, suggesting that an elementary procedure is to break these analogues down into information which is known, presumed or unclear. Positive action can be taken upon known information whereas further search or cautious action only should be taken on the presumed or clear.

Error coping

The notion of bias suggests that there is a correct answer to a problem and that a decision process can be subjected to the same kind of analysis as statistical hypothesis testing, which identifies two types of error. A Type I error leads to rejection of a true hypothesis: an example of this would be management neglecting to use basic cost accounting methods to assess the worthiness of a cost-reduction proposal where the information and techniques are available with great precision. This kind of error is an error of lack of precision in the process. A Type II error leads to acceptance of a false hypothesis: an example of this would be management making a major investment decision based entirely upon a rate of return calculation but where the data fed into that calculation is highly dubious with regard to what is meant. This kind of error is an error of spurious precision. The garbage can model suggests that sometimes accepting errors can be rational since the costs of making a possible mistake can be outweighed by the possible advantages to be gained from making an inspirational type of decision.

Risk and disasters

Another approach to decision effectiveness comes from the burgeoning literature upon disaster and risk management given impetus by a number of well-publicized incidents such as the Chernobyl reactor failure (Royal Society 1992).

This literature points to a difference between an engineering and a social science view of risk. The engineering definition follows a computational approach to decision making and defines risk in terms of the probability of an adverse event, whereas the social science definition follows a judgemental perspective and emphasizes the perception and interpretation of the risk by participants in a given social situation. A kind of 'institutional blindness' can be used to explain how signals of forthcoming problems can be ignored, sometimes through a process of 'defensive avoidance' (Janis and Mann 1977). The literature serves to reinforce the idea that both what is perceived as a disaster and what are then perceived as the causes of that disaster are socially as well as technically induced.

On a less dramatic scale investigations of the management of large projects (Morris and Haugh 1987) show that cost overruns between 40 and 200 per cent are the norm, with higher levels in defence. It is particularly at the early stages of a project that the incubation of later disasters can be laid through a combination of internal and external management problems.

4 Defining problems

Literature on decision making emphasizes that a problem is perceived when there is a gap between the expectation and the reality of performance. There is also an assumption that problems tend to start as ill defined but get less uncertain with the process, which may be generally true although many problems which initially appear simple may become more complex as the decision proceeds.

The problem stream

Problems are constantly being recognized, defined and labelled by organizational participants. Labels can get attached to these problems or topics according to their relevance for organizational sub-systems. Hickson et al. (1986) identified ten such problems or topics; technology, reorganizations, control, domain, services, products, personnel, boundary, inputs and location. Topic type was found to affect some aspects of decision processes; for example, reorganization decisions are the most rare and are amongst the most contentious.

Psychological research uses the term 'framing' to describe the parameters by which problems become defined, especially through the way in which information about choices and their possible effects is interpreted (Tversky and Kahneman 1981). For example, in public policy issues the manner in which information about possible risks of a disease, diet or not wearing seatbelts in cars is presented can make a vital difference to how people respond.

Interest

Problems can involve the interests of a wide range of diverse organizational groups each with their different motivations for getting involved in decisions. Organizations can provide financial incentives for managers to raise new capital investment project proposals although it has been found that managers do not generally admit to any great amount of career interest in raising such proposals (Butler et al. 1993). More usually the rewards for involvement in decisions is less clear cut and may range from a simple desire to be 'in on things', or to gain information that may be of use, or at a later stage be identified as the champion of a successful project (Butler et al. 1993: chapter 6). People sometimes fight for the right to participate without necessarily pursuing that right (March 1988: 396).

The ability of individuals to set the agenda of discussions about a topic has an important part to play in defining a problem. A distinction needs to be made between power exerted by someone directly taking part in decision making and the power exerted by someone who manages to suppress the discussion of certain issues while surreptitiously allowing discussion of other issues; this is the power of non-decision making (Hickson et al. 1986).

Chairing committees and other formal bodies in an organization gives an ability to control admission of topics on an agenda and to control the order in which topics are discussed; topics which are placed at the end of a long agenda tend to get less attention (Pfeffer 1981).

Avoidance of problems

Rather than actively seeking to identify possible problems decision makers can indulge in defensive avoidance, a process whereby decision makers filter out information which does not conform to an existing point of view. This condition is encouraged by 'groupthink' whereby strong group norms can give group members an illusion of invulnerability, make it difficult for individual dissent to emerge, or top management can filter out information which does not fit existing policy (Janis and Mann 1977).

If information systems are too precisely engineered to current organizational needs organizational problems will be defined more and more within the same parameters. Ambiguity will, therefore, be weeded out when the need is to increase ambiguity (March 1988).

Aspects of problem definition

Comparative research into organizational decision making generally assesses the nature of the problem that is being considered, many of the ideas being related to the concept of decision framing used in the psychological paradigm of decision research. Sociological studies of decision making tend to search for one or two summarizing descriptors of the overall process of decision making. For example, the nature of the problem under consideration can be described in terms of the associated technical complexity and political sensitivity (Hickson *et al.* 1986).

Consequentiality captures an aspect of complexity, giving the idea of decision makers looking forward to assess the future impact of a decision, such as the seriousness for the organization if things go wrong. Certain problems can also be seen to set precedents or to be particularly radical for the organization and therefore need to be considered more carefully. These aspects tend to be related to the comparative rarity of a decision within an organization. The greater the rarity the less likely there will be well-established procedures for solution building. Reorganization decisions were found to be the most rare, whereas decisions about products and supplies (inputs) were the least rare. Although such measures vary according to conditions there appears to be little doubt that reorganization decisions are one of the most difficult for an organization to cope with due to their rule-setting nature.

5 Solution building

The computational model of decision making requires that solutions are designed and evaluated in response to a problem. The inspirational model suggests that solutions form a stream of action relatively independent from problems, that solutions are more abundant than problems and can provide the impetus to a choice rather than vice versa (March 1988).

Professionals and members of skill groups have an in-built bias towards producing solutions in accordance with the ideology of that profession; engineers may suggest a product design solution to a problem of declining sales while a marketing person may see a solution more in terms of improvement in service.

Capital budgeting theory and practice provides an example of the tension between the computational and inspirational ways of building solutions. The theory is particularly concerned with methods of appraising the worthiness of projects, with the concept of risk playing a key role. Surveys have shown how techniques such as discounted cash flow (DCF), internal rate of return (IRR) and net present value (NPV) are increasingly being used in industry. Case studies of actual decisions, however, show how frequently such techniques are abused, either by figures being manipulated to support a particular interest or by calculations being conducted after a choice has been made. Managers consistently show a satisficing behaviour by preferring 'naive' methods of appraisal, such as payback period, to more sophisticated and theoretically more rational methods, such as DCF (Butler *et al.* 1993).

Assimilating new information

The computational strategy relies upon the ability of decision makers to scan the environment for as many alternative solutions as possible and to evaluate their likely outcomes. One problem with formal methods of appraisal is that new information may come to light as a decision proceeds through the implementation phase, thus providing decision makers with the chance to alter their original prediction.

Bayes' theorem provides an analytical method to take into account the effect of new information upon an initial probability estimate of a particular outcome. Assume fairly rational decision makers in a company wish to assess the national market success of a new product line and they have an initial probability estimate of product success based upon the best available information at that time. They decide to carry out a test market before a full-scale launch (a sub-decision in terms of the organizational model of decision making) but they know that test markets are not infallible and can only be relied upon with a limited degree of confidence.

There are two aspects to the confidence that can be placed in a test market: (1) the likelihood that the test market will indicate a success and that the product will be successful nationwide; (2) the likelihood that the test market will indicate a success and that the product will be unsuccessful nationwide. The question is: How can an original estimate of a successful national product launch be amended in the light of a subsequent test market? Bayes' theorem gives a method for computing the answer based upon the assumption of rational decision makers. An original estimate of the probability of success is increased by a test market indicating a success given that the product has been successful but is decreased by an estimate that the test market will indicate a success even if the product has not been successful in the market. Put in more formal terms, Bayes' theorem states that when two hypotheses are being considered the posterior odds (the ratio of the two probabilities after the information) are proportional to the product of the prior odds and the likelihood ratio.

The significant aspect of Bayes' theorem for a theory of organizational decision making is that it represents a move away from a pure computational strategy by recognizing the importance of subjective probabilities. Investigations of the actual information processing behaviour of decision makers shows a tendency towards conservatism, meaning that individuals do not make as much revision to initial probability estimates as the theorem suggests they should. Explanations for this have been sought in terms of how the new information may be misperceived or misused; the discovery of a conservative bias accords with case studies of decision making

whereby, once a decision is being implemented, it requires a large body of contrary evidence to alter that action.

Intuition

Case studies of managerial decision making generally support the idea that decision makers are prepared to act on what they see as incomplete information (Hickson *et al.* 1986). Intuition and judgement are central to the process of solution building, a topic that has been attracting an increasing amount of research. Isenberg (1984) found a number of key characteristics concerning the thought processes of senior managers:

- a feel for inconsistencies in information
- ability to build upon well-learned patterns of behaviour
- synthesis of isolated pieces of information
- intuition to check on formal analysis
- an understanding of the importance of interpersonal and organizational processes

At the individual level techniques are suggested to develop lateral thinking and improve intuition but these characteristics should not be ignored. Managers need to develop a 'map' or framework for linking together the myriad problems with which they have to cope. Such a framework may offer a number of specific suggestions:

- bolster intuition with rational thinking
- offset tendencies to be overly rational by imagination and learning to act with incomplete information
- learn to 'map' unfamiliar territory
- use 'rules of thumb'
- spend time understanding a problem
- look for connections between diverse problems
- recognize thinking as a critical asset

Most models of judgement and intuition can be seen as ways of trying to push the process as far as possible towards the computational strategy by systematizing the intuitive processes of judgement and bargaining.

Hogarth (1980) identified a number of models for the improvement of judgement which go beyond the linear model of giving each outcome a weight according to the product of an outcome and its probability. One way is to use a conjunctive model whereby cut-off points are selected such that any alternative falling below this point is rejected; this can be seen as a systematized form of satisficing.

Janis and Mann (1977) present a method for resolving psychological conflicts in decision making involving a 'decisional balance sheet'. The process encourages vigilance (but not hypervigilance) and overtly develops alternatives in order to ensure that groupthink does not force decision makers into agreeing to a choice which they are against.

The architecture of complexity
Simon (1962) argues that the processes of intuition can be analysed in terms of a hierarchical arrangement of assemblies and sub-assemblies, illustrating this point by the parable of two watchmakers, Hora and Tempus.

Hora learned to assemble watches by building a series of sub-assemblies and then assembling the sub-assemblies. If Hora was interrupted during assembly, work already put into a partly finished sub-assembly could be lost, but this would be the limit of the loss. The other sub-assemblies would remain intact and, providing there was a set of rules for assembling the sub-assemblies, the watch could be completed. Tempus, on the other hand, assembled watches in one big leap which meant simultaneously holding many parts in a state of suspension. If everything meshed the watch could be assembled very quickly. If there was an interruption, however, all the work done to that point on a particular watch could be lost and Tempus would have to start again.

The two methods of assembling complex bits of machinery can be compared to different methods of learning. Simon argues that mystical processes called intuition or experience can be decomposed into architectures of sub-assemblies. In this way experienced practitioners in many fields, such as chess, can hold in their heads the solutions to many standard moves to be fitted together into a pattern during a match.

Formal planning systems lay down procedures for strategic decision making. Such procedures attempt to identify systematic ways of defining problems and building solutions. If, however, they do not sufficiently reflect the reality of decision making within an organization such procedures may come to be carried out primarily for symbolic reasons (Langley 1989).

6 Participating and influencing

The way in which power and influence are exerted in decision making is a major feature of most descriptions of decision making. One approach to the measurement of influence has been through the use of a 'control graph' (Tannenbaum 1968). By dividing an organization into different levels (lower, middle and upper) of management it is possible to map the extent to which each level has influence over decisions, the slope and the shape of the graph portraying the distribution of influence. A straight line sloping upwards from left to right (that is, influence increases as levels are ascended) gives a 'normal' bureaucratic type of organization whereby higher management has more influence than lower management (see INDUSTRIAL DEMOCRACY).

Some organizations, notably democratic ones in which a total membership can vote on an issue, tend to show a horizontal graph. It is also possible to have an inverted graph whereby influence decreases as the hierarchy is ascended, a situation approximated by some professional organizations whereby the higher levels are mainly administrators for autonomous professional workers. However, the 'iron law' of oligarchy suggests that this could be an unstable situation and that higher echelons would tend to accumulate power by virtue of being at the centre of an information network.

Other studies (Butler *et al.* 1993; Hickson *et al.* 1986) have assessed the extent to which participants from different functional groups and external organizations get involved and exert influence over decisions. In general, the involvement and influence of external participants is much less than for internal participants. Liaison positions, followed closely by marketing and sales departments, were found to exert the most influence in decision making, the least influential internal departments being purchasing departments, and the least influential of all participants to be trade unions.

Power

The degree of influence exerted by participants will vary according to their power in the organization. The strategic contingencies theory of power predicts that the influence exerted by managers over a range of decision topics is a result of the strategic position of the particular department to which they belong.

The strategic position of a department with regard to exerting influence is increased by its centrality in the workflow and by the extent to which it is non-substitutable by other departments or outsiders. In particular, managers' power is increased if their departments can show that they are able to cope with critical uncertainties for the organization (see MANAGERIAL BEHAVIOUR).

The strategic contingencies theory of power gives us a useful way of thinking about connections between problems and solutions. Making the connection requires action by participants in the organization and relies upon the ability of that participant to activate both a problem and a solution.

Other approaches to power emphasize the ability of powerful people to make the rules concerning who can participate in decision making and the kinds of procedures that have to be followed. It is this rule-making ability that is at the heart of the institutional effects upon decision making.

Individual versus group decision making

An important question underlying the issue of participation in decision making concerns the question of whether groups are more effective decision makers than individuals. A number of factors are likely to favour groups over individuals:

1 as the need for acceptance increases it becomes more necessary to involve those af-

fected by the decision to enable implementation and legitimate outcomes;
2 as complexity increases it becomes necessary to include other individuals for reasons of expertise;
3 defining, solving and choosing are likely to be slower, but implementing to be quicker, in groups;
4 where creating ideas or remembering information is needed a group increases the probability of task success;
5 when the task gains from duplication of effort and/or the division of labour groups gain over individuals; no one individual can comprehend the entirety of the task and there needs to be selection of individuals according to ability.

Brainstorming is a technique to facilitate the generation of creative alternatives by encouraging free expression and by avoiding the evaluation of options until all ideas are assembled. The following three rules are generally used: (1) ideas are freely expressed without considering their quality; (2) group members are encouraged to modify and combine previously stated ideas; and (3) there is a moratorium upon evaluation until all ideas have been stated. The Delphi technique (developed at the Rand Corporation) is a similar but rather more formalized technique involving physically separating participants during idea generation and then collating judgements on topics (Kleindorfer *et al.* 1993).

Devil's advocates are one way in which new ideas can be injected and conflict deliberately engendered to counteract the effects of groupthink. This necessitates someone deliberately presenting an opposite viewpoint to any prevailing or emerging consensus. The process works by getting people to think again before committing themselves to a course of action (Schwenk 1984).

Risky shift deals with a question that has long been a focus of controversy: whether groups are more likely to take risky decisions than individuals. Under certain conditions there is a shift towards riskier decisions when an individual rather than a group makes a decision, although if a group shows particularly innovative values it can show more risk than the individuals (Kleindorfer *et al.* 1993).

Centralization/decentralization

A major dimension of organizational decision making concerns the extent to which the process is centralized or decentralized. Some decisions require authorization at a level above the highest internal level (usually chief executive or board) by being authorized outside the organization, at a headquarters or some equivalent location (Butler *et al.* 1993).

Centralized decision making is generally associated with low levels of innovation but helps implementation when minimal commitment is required from other organizational participants. As decisions get more complex centralization becomes a less effective method since high-level decision makers do not have enough information to make effective choices and are liable to be overloaded with decision making. Centralization can occur either by top management directly making a decision or by laying down some general parameters and policies but delegating actual operating decisions to a lower-level authority.

Leadership

Leadership is a feature of decision making that is often noted (see LEADERSHIP). 'Great man' theories of politics, business and organization tend to explain decisions in terms of the individual characteristics of someone who is particularly adept at guiding the processes. The four choice strategies suggest four types of leadership ability: for the computational strategy a good administrator would be needed; for the judgemental a person who can build consensus; for the negotiation strategy an organizational politician is needed; and for the inspirational a charismatic leader. If during the decision process ends and/or means uncertainty shifts, the nature of the required leadership may change. For instance, a decision may start off as highly uncertain on both dimensions and be driven by a charismatic leader but as it shifts towards implementation a good administrator is needed.

Transactional and transformational leadership

Two types of leadership, the transactional and the transformational have been referred to by Burns (Butler 1991). The transactional leader is comparable to the administrator or bureaucrat who sets up a system intervening only on a management by exception basis and providing rewards proportional to effect. Transformational leadership, related to inspirational decision making, is characterized by charisma (exuding enthusiasm, encouraging expression of opinions, exciting a vision), individual attention to subordinates and intellectual stimulation.

Game theory

Game theory is a method for analysing decision making under conditions of conflict when the payoff to a participant depends upon the behaviour of others in the game. A game requires: (1) participants or players; (2) rules; (3) payoffs and associated values; (4) controllable moves which each player can make; and (5) information availability. Early writings emphasized two-player, zero-sum competitive games but developments have led to a theory of n-person cooperative games holding promise of greater validity for the theory of organizational decision making (Kreps 1990; Kleindorfer *et al.* 1993). The essence of the cooperative game is the need for equal payoffs to players if they cooperate but large punishments for betrayal of trust. Games can also be strategic, laying out possible moves in a matrix of payoffs, or games can be extensive, laying out a decision tree of moves giving payoffs based upon previous moves made thereby introducing time as a variable (Kreps 1990: 9).

As the available moves and associated payoffs are predetermined by the rules of the game the essence of game theory is to determine the extent to which players choose the most rational route. It provides a way of thinking forward in a series of 'what if' thought experiments but in so doing makes simplifications as to how the rules of the game and payoffs are set. The past is compressed into these rules and payoffs which represent experience of past behaviour.

Decision makers do not necessarily behave as in the crisp moves of game theory, as shown by the much analysed Cuban Missile Crisis (Allison 1971) during which the USA and the former Soviet Union stood face to face on the brink of nuclear war. In setting up missile bases in Cuba the Soviet leadership assumed that the Americans would not seriously challenge their move; game theory predicted a step-by-step military escalation whereas President Kennedy threatened a 'complete one-shot annihilation' of the Soviet Union.

7 Time

Speed in managerial decision making is often thought to be a virtue but evidence indicates that the speed of analysing and choosing is less important than getting commitment so that implementation can proceed quickly. Evidence also shows that the duration of strategic decision making as assessed by the time from the inception of an issue to its authorization varies greatly, ranging from three weeks to nine years with a mean of one to two years (Hickson *et al.* 1986; Butler *et al.* 1993). The image of managerial decisiveness is further eroded when it is also seen that various forms of discontinuities are normal.

Discontinuities in the process is one of the most troublesome aspects for decision makers. Two of the most common reasons for delays concern awaiting further investigation and awaiting the outcome of external resistance to a proposal. The least common cause of delay concerns searching for further information, followed by sequencing delays due to awaiting priority in the order of attention (Hickson *et al.* 1986). Another aspect of time found to concern managers is if the decision is perceived to be of too slow a pace. Nevertheless there is evidence to show that slow, deliberate decision making increases learning (Butler *et al.* 1993).

Preceding the more overt problem-defining and solution-building phases of decision making may be an extensive gestation period during which an idea is conceived. Gestation times have been found to vary widely, from a matter of days to fifteen years, with a mean approximating to two years. Gestation time is found to be uncorrelated with duration (Hickson *et al.* 1986).

The value of time

Cultures valuing individualism (the English-speaking nations) could be expected to value quick decisions, whereas a culture valuing collectivism (Japan) could be expected to value a more deliberate participative process especially during problem defining and solution building (Hofstede 1980) (see ORGANIZATION CULTURE).

Organizations inevitably put a money value on time and the kinds of rules an organization uses for appraising capital projects can be critical in determining the way in which time is conceived. Using the more popular payback period rather than the more sophisticated DCF calculation tends to encourage a shorter time horizon (Marsh 1990), with attendant concerns over the propensity for managers to take an overly short-term view of business strategy. Capital appraisal methods generally ignore the managerial cost of making the decision – the managerial time spent on the process. Managerial time comprises the sum of the time spent by participants over the decision and an organization 'spends' this in anticipation of a future return (Butler *et al.* 1993).

The timeframe

Decision making is located within a timeframe of preceding, succeeding and concurrent other decisions. Topics arise in part out of preceding decisions which set constraints for a current decision. The more frequently a given topic occurs the greater the ability to develop routines and procedures, these procedures in turn setting constraints for succeeding decisions.

If decision makers' attention is involved with concurrent decisions their attention may be drawn away from a focal decision. Hence the greater the degree of interdependence between other decisions in an organization the greater the urgency and pacing of decision making. The Bay of Pigs débâcle that haunted President Kennedy in the 1960s, when

American troops were forced to make a hasty exit from Cuba after mounting an invasion, has been attributed to the idea that the President and his advisors were never able to spend more than forty-five minutes at a time in consultation prior to making the decision to invade (Neustadt and May 1986).

As decision making proceeds sub-decisions are often made on the way; for example, a sub-decision for an investment decision might be to set up a project team. The membership of such a team and its terms of reference can critically affect the progress of the focal decision issue. Thus, sub-decisions also set constraints (Simon 1947; Butler *et al.* 1993).

Timeframes are useful for thinking about the question of timing in decision making. For example, the ability of an aspiring chief executive to bring himself to the attention of the board of directors by appropriately timing the raising of the particular issue of electricity generation in a chemical company was critical to the achievement of that ambition (Hickson *et al.* 1986). To be too early or too late in raising problems or proposing solutions can lose or fail to gain support for an issue. Bringing people in, or leaving them out, or choosing a decision strategy at the right moment can make the difference to a solution's acceptance and implementation.

8 Implementation

We can identify two opposing ideas as to how choices are implemented. First, planned implementation is a dominant idea in the strategic planning literature and clearly related to the computational choice strategy whereby the process of choosing by policy makers is largely separated from the process of implementation which is carried out by different people.

Incremental implementation is a different process and clearly more related to inspirationally produced decisions. The emphasis now turns upon the process of feedback between policy makers and implementers during implementation. At the extreme, the distinction between the two sets of people disappears and in extreme cases implementation can be initiated prior to completion of other decision activities (Butler *et al.* 1993).

Much has been written about how to formulate formal strategic planning but assessment of whether these systems improve the effectiveness of strategic decisions is inconclusive. However, planning systems are usually seen to: increase problem awareness; identify organizational strengths and weaknesses; provide information and communications; allocate resources; provide quantification of objectives and resources; and provide a moral framework for decision making. Research has also shown that well-developed formal planning systems increase lateral communications in an organization (Bazzaz and Grinyer 1981).

Knee-deep in the big muddy

As implementation of a choice proceeds, commitment to that choice grows, making it difficult to withdraw, a phenomenom called 'knee-deep in the big muddy'. Experiments show how decision makers who have made an initial investment in phase one of a project are more likely to spend larger amounts in a subsequent phase two investment when phase one shows signs of going wrong than when phase one is showing signs of success. This escalating commitment is amplified if the decision makers are held personally responsible for the consequences of a decision (Bazerman 1993).

This phenomenon is alarming from a managerial perspective but is illustrated by cases as varied as a government sinking more troops into a war that cannot be won, to individuals sinking more money into a repairing an unrepairable used car. The implication is that decision makers need to gather strength as evidence accumulates to indicate that a mistake has been made and to quickly withdraw.

Project implementation

There is a well-established literature on project management which gives us an opportunity to investigate the relationships between different decision-making activities in order to achieve success. It is an axiom of project management that implementation can be eased if a number of factors are present, in particular thorough early planning involving the client.

There is also evidence to show that when efficiency is the measure of project success planning factors are emphasized in the early stages but give way to political factors as the implementation proceeds. When, however, external success measures, such as client satisfaction, are more important planning factors dominate throughout the life of a project (Pinto and Prescott 1990).

9 Organization and decision making

Central to the model of organizational decision making presented here is the notion of norms as applied to the performance of organizations and of decisions made therein. To understand the source of these norms we need to see an organization as a technical system, as a natural system and as an institutionalized system.

The ideal for the technical system perspective is to remove uncertainty by perfecting ideologies and structures aimed at fulfilling instrumental objectives. Decision making thereby becomes more routinized and computational as internal structures are developed. A natural system perspective sees an organization as open to an inherently uncertain task environment. Decision making involves steering a course between the efficiency logic of improving technical methods and the adaptability logic of responding to competitive changes and demands in the task environment. This established perspective is well summarized in prescriptions about the need for fuzzy organizational structures and satisficing/inspirational decision making as environmental and technical uncertainty increases (Thompson 1967; Butler 1991). Managerial ideology also needs to match structure and context; in a stable task environment with well-defined technology ideology tends to focus upon efficiency but as the environment gets more uncertain a 'robust' ideology becomes necessary, meaning

that decision makers need to hold among themselves a broad set of beliefs about aims and methods and that most importantly there should be an over-arching understanding of what the organization as a whole stands for and is trying to achieve. Structures to enhance robustness include use of group rather than individual decision making and organizational mission statements.

The institutional environment

A criticism of the natural system perspective is that it presents a too intentionally rational view of decision making. An essential aspect of the institutional approach to organizational decision making emphasizes the limitations upon choice for both individuals and organizations imposed by social norms (Douglas 1987). Four types of norm constraining action have been suggested: economic; instrumental; referent (or social) and moral (Butler 1991). Norms are carried into an organization, forming individual and group preferences as regards particular decisions. For example, strong economic norms as a result of a competitive environment will tend to filter through to the evaluation of investments as an emphasis upon financial measures such as IRR.

Whatever typology may be suggested, norms act as standards of desirability and vary across different sectors of the environment and over time, and in this respect an organization has to make choices as to which norms are most important (Butler 1991; Thompson 1967). Here the notion of sector (or industry) helps us to identify the set of interrelated organizations to which a focal organization belongs and provides norms concerning appropriate technologies and structures (Butler 1991). For example, if funding decisions are centralized within an institutional sector, funding decisions within an organization also tend to be more centralized, whereas a more complex fragmented sector will involve organizations in complex linkages. It is under these more complex conditions that organizations anxious to demonstrate conformity with institutional procedures tend to stress symbolic aspects in their decision making (Meyer and Scott 1983).

As organizations have become increasingly international, national cultures have gathered great significance in theories of decision making (Hofstede 1980) (see ORGANIZATION CULTURE). For example, a comparison of Brazilian and UK managers finds that UK managers tend towards more individualistic, methodical and slow decision making (Oliveira and Hickson 1991).

One way in which the institutional environment defines organizations is by ownership (private versus public); whether they are commercial in the degree to which revenues are raised by selling a product direct to customers or whether they are service rather than manufacturing organizations. Hickson *et al.* (1986) found that there was a slight tendency for public organizations to display more sporadic processes, while the degree of commercialism made little difference to the decision processes, but it was found that manufacturing organizations had a slightly greater tendency towards sporadic decision making.

The classification of external interest units by Hickson *et al.* (1986: 63) further illuminates the importance of institutional forces upon organizational decision making. Transactions with suppliers, customers and clients take place in the task environment and these units were the most involved and the most influential of all external units. However, units concerned with private institutional norms, such as auditors, trade associates and shareholders also were quite involved and influential in decision making. Units concerned with public institutional norms such as government departments and agencies (for example, health and safety regulators) were also quite highly involved. Both public and private standards enforcement is a factor that is taken into account in strategic decisions but these enforcers do not exert much direct influence.

Decision topics over which private standard units had most influence concerned topics about inputs, location and personnel, whereas public standard units had most influence over domain and location topics. Public standard units exhibited a very high degree of influence over decisions concerning mergers, alliances and various forms of cooperative ventures where the need for public regulation necessarily appears very high. There is also evidence to indicate that a high number and diversity of external interest units over decision making leads to the sporadic type of decision process. Regulations create their own uncertainties and dependencies. The extent to which there is agreement or disparity over the impact of regulation upon a particular issue can therefore be important to the effectiveness of a decision. There is evidence that disparity about the impact of regulations upon an organization increases learning during decision making (Butler *et al.* 1993).

10 Conclusions

This entry has approached the examination of managerial decision making using an organizational model of decision making which sees decisions as involving a number of activities, with participants in the process acting with intentional rationality but constrained by a number of factors. It is well established within the literature on organizational decision making that uncertainty poses a major constraint due to lack of information about the means to achieve certain ends and lack of agreement over outcome preferences.

More recent theorizing about organizational decision making is emphasising the importance of institutional factors, which also impose constraints upon decision makers. These institutional factors are historically determined and set performance norms for organizations which are then translated into norms to assess the performance of decisions and also the means by which decisions are made.

RICHARD BUTLER
UNIVERSITY OF BRADFORD
MANAGEMENT CENTRE

Further reading

(References cited in the text marked *)

* Allison, G.T. (1971) *The Essence of Decision: Explaining the Cuban Missile Crisis*, Boston, MA: Little Brown & Co. (A classic case highlighting the importance of political factors in decision making.)

* Barnard, C.I. (1938) *The Functions of the Executive*, Cambridge, MA: Harvard University Press. (A foundation book in modern management theory, written by a practising manager, which indicates the importance of decision making.)

* Bazerman, M. (1993) *Judgment in Managerial Decision Making*, 3rd edn, New York: Wiley. (A practical book from a psychological perspective; includes exercises.)

* Bazzaz, S. and Grinyer, P.H. (1981) 'Corporate planning in the U.K.: the state of the art in the 70's', *Strategic Management Journal* 2: 151–68. (Helps to link the strategic planning and decision-making literatures.)

* Butler, R.J. (1991) *Designing Organizations: A Decision Making Perspective*, London: Routledge. (Sees organizational design in terms of the need to provide structures that enable effective decision making.)

* Butler, R.J., Davies, L., Pike, R. and Sharp, J. (1993) *Strategic Investment Decisions: Theory, Practice and Process*, London: Routledge. (A study of fifty-five managers making seventeen strategic investments. Uses case studies and a survey.)

* Cyert, R. and March, J.G. (1963) *The Behavioural Theory of the Firm*, Englewood Cliffs, NJ: Prentice Hall. (A pathbreaking book indicating the need to see the actions taken by firms in terms of the limits to rationality in managerial decision making.)

* Douglas, M. (1987) *How Institutions Think*, London: Routledge & Kegan Paul. (Introduces us to the neglected anthropological view of decision making in institutions.)

* Hickson, D., Butler, R.J., Cray, D., Mallory, G. and Wilson, D.C. (1986) *Top Decisions: Strategic Decision Making in Organizations*, Oxford: Basil Blackwell. (The theory of organizational decision making based upon an extensive study of 150 decisions in thirty highly varied organizations.)

* Hofstede, G. (1980) *Culture's Consequences: International Differences in Work-related Values*, Beverly Hills, CA: Sage Publications. (Study across forty countries, introducing the four dimensions of national culture.)

* Hogarth, R.M. (1980) *Judgment and Choice: The Psychology of Decision*, Chichester: Wiley. (An extensive discussion of the psychological perspective on decision making.)

* Isenberg, D.J. (1984) 'How senior managers think', *Harvard Business Review* 62 (November–December): 80–90. (A practical introduction to intuition.)

* Janis, I.L. and Mann, L. (1977) *Decision Making: A Psychological Anaylsis of Conflict: Choice and Commitment*, New York: The Free Press. (Incorporates the influential notions of 'groupthink' and 'defensive avoidance' into an overall framework.)

* Kleindorfer, P.R, Kunreuther, H.C. and Schoemaker, P.J.H. (1993) *Decision Sciences: An Integrative Perspective,* Cambridge: Cambridge University Press. (Integrates the managerial science and psychological perspectives on decision making.)

* Kreps, D. (1990) *Game Theory and Economic Modelling*, Oxford: Clarendon Press. (An introduction to game theory.)

* Langley, A. (1989) 'In search of rationality: the purposes behind the use of formal analysis in organizations', *Administrative Science Quarterly* 34 (4): 598–631. (Emphasizes the symbolic nature of formal analysis.)

* Lindblom, C. (1959) 'The science of muddling through', *Public Administration Review* 19: 79–88. (Colourfully points to the limits of rationality in decision making.)

* March, J.G. (1965) *The Handbook of Organizations*, Chicago, IL: Rand McNally. (Gives the 'state of the art' in the 1960s. Many things have not changed.)

* March, J.G. (1988) *Decisions and Organizations*, London: Blackwell. (Contains a number of papers on the anarchic theme of decision making.)

* March, J.G. and Simon, H.A. (1958) *Organizations*, New York: Wiley. (A classic book in part concerned with building a model of organizations from the microprocesses of decision making.)

* Marsh, P. (1990) *Short Termism*, London: Institutional Fund Managers Association. (Introduces us to the importance of time horizons with special reference to financial decisions.)

* Meyer, J.W. and Scott, W.R. (1983) *Organizational Environments: Ritual and Rationality*, Beverly Hills, CA: Sage Publications. (A view on the effect of institutional environments upon organizational decision making.)

* Mintzberg, H. (1975) *The Nature of Managerial Work*, New York: Harper Row. (Emphasizes the interrupted nature of managerial decision making.)

* Mintzberg, H., Raisinghai, D. and Theoret, A. (1976) 'The structure of unstructured decision processes', *Administrative Science Quarterly* 21 (2): 246–75. (A study of twenty-five decisions in terms of a number of basic routines. Most decisions illustrate a discontinuous circular process.)

* Morris, P.W.G. and Haugh, G. H. (1987) *The Anatomy of Major Projects: A Study of the Reality of Project Management*, Chichester: Wiley. (Illustrates the implementation aspect of decision making.)
* Neustadt, R.E. and May, E.R. (1986) *Thinking in Time: The Uses of History for Decision Makers*, New York: The Free Press. (Emphasizes the importance of time.)
* Nutt, P. (1993) 'Flexible decision styles and the choices of top executives', *Journal of Management Studies* 30 (5): 695–721. (Looks at the effect of Jung's personality types upon decision making.)
* Oliveira, B. and Hickson, D.J. (1991) 'Cultural bases of strategic decision making: a Brazilian and English comparison', paper presented at the European Group for Organization Studies (EGOS) 10th colloquium, Vienna, July 15–17. (A cross-cultural study of decision making.)
* Pettigrew, A. (1973) *The Politics of Organizational Decision Making*, London: Tavistock Publications. (The case that injected the vital political dimension into the study of decision making.)
* Pfeffer, J. (1981) *Power in Organizations*, Marshfield, MA: Pittman Co. (A useful treatment of organizational power with implications for decision making.)
* Pinto, J.K. and Prescott, J.E. (1990) 'Planning and tactical factors in the project implementation process', *Journal of Management Studies* 27 (3): 305–27. (An investigation of the balance between planning and political factors.)
* Royal Society (1992) *Risk: Analysis, Perception and Management*, London: Royal Society. (A presentation of the differences between an engineering and a social science perspective on risk.)
* Schwenk, C.R. (1984) 'Devil's advocacy in managerial decision making', *Journal of Management Studies* 21 (2): 153–68. (Argues that an organization needs someone to speak out against prevailing assumptions.)
* Simon, H.A. (1960) *The New Science of Management Decision*, New York: Harper Row. (A presentation of the bounded rational critique of the rational model of decision making.)
* Simon, H.A. (1962) 'The architecture of complexity', *Proceedings of the American Philosophical Society* 106: 467–82. (A stalwart attempt to reduce the processes of intuition and judgement to a hierarchy of learned routines.)
* Simon, H.A. (1976) *Administrative Behaviour: A Study of Decision Making Process in Administrative Organizations*, 3rd edn, New York: The Free Press. (First published in 1947, this book built upon Barnard's *The Functions of the Executive* to emphasize the shift from classic to modern management theory.)
* Tannenbaum, A.S. (1968) *Control in Organizations*, New York: McGraw-Hill. (Provides a simple and effective way of mapping the influence of different organizational functions on decision making.)
* Thompson, J.D. (1967) *Organizations in Action*, New York: McGraw-Hill. (This enduring classic allows us to put decision making in an organizational context.)
* Tversky, A. and Kahneman, A. (1981) 'The framing of decisions and the psychology of choice', *Science* 211: 453–8. Also in G. Wright (ed.) *Behavioural Decision Making*, London: Plenum Press, chapter 2. (A sample paper from these key authors writing within the psychological paradigm.)

See also: DECISION MAKING

Related topics in the IEBM: ACCOUNTING; ACCOUNTING AND ORGANIZATIONS; BARNARD, C.I.; BUSINESS SYSTEMS; COGNITION; CONFLICT AND POLITICS; COORDINATION AND CONTROL; GAME THEORY AND GAMING; HABITUAL DOMAINS IN; INFORMATION AND KNOWLEDGE INDUSTRY; INSTITUTIONAL ECONOMICS; JUNG, C.G. MANAGEMENT SCIENCE; MARCH, J.G. AND CYERT, R.M.; MARKETING RESEARCH; MULTINATIONAL CORPORATIONS, ORGANIZATION STRUCTURE IN; OPERATIONS RESEARCH; ORGANIZATION PARADIGMS; ORGANIZATION TYPES; ORGANIZATIONAL EVOLUTION; ORGANIZATIONAL PERFORMANCE; ORGANIZING, PROCESS OF; POWER; PUBLIC SECTOR ORGANIZATIONS; SHORT-TERMISM; SIMON, H.A.; WEBER, M.

Deconstruction analysis and management

1 The philosophy of deconstruction
2 Deconstruction and management
3 Deconstructing human resource management

Overview

This entry applies a form of postmodernist epistemology – deconstruction analysis – to analysing management's concern with issues of performativity and to evaluating the discourse of human resource management. At first sight, deconstruction analysis, originally an approach to literary criticism exemplifying postmodern epistemology, may appear irrelevant to understanding management and organizations. Such an assumption, however, would be mistaken. By facilitating subversive readings of texts, deconstruction analysis offers useful tools for a critique of human resource management rhetoric.

1 The philosophy of deconstruction

At its simplest, deconstruction may be seen as a mode of discourse or textual analysis that uses reversals, inversions and paradoxes to call into question the orthodox interpretations derived from conventional forms of analysis. A starting point is the work of the French philosopher Jacques Derrida. He argues that modern Western thought has attempted to establish grounds of certainty and truth by repressing the limitless instability of language. This logocentrism pivots social action upon the idea of an original 'logos' or predetermined metaphysical structure (for example, a rational agent with mind and soul) that validates and gives meaning to social action, privileging unity and identity over separation and difference. In contrast, for Derrida, language and text are not so much a means of communicating pre-existing facts or thoughts, but a set of sounds and marks upon which meaning is imposed. That meaning is ultimately undecidable, because not only are texts structured around binary oppositions ('good'/'bad', 'formal'/'informal', 'nature'/'culture'), in which one term dominates the other ('male'/'female'), but the relationship between opposing terms is one of mutual definition ('black'/'white'). Hence, to quote Norris (1987: 35), individual terms 'give way to a process where opposites merge in a constant undecidable exchange of attributes'. Derrida shows, for example, how the ancient Greek term *pharmakon* is intrinsically undecidable since it can mean both 'remedy' and 'poison' and 'good' and 'bad' simultaneously (Derrida 1978). A managerially relevant example might be 'cost-cutting', which simultaneously contains notions of 'efficiency' (good) and 'job loss' (bad).

Meaning is made more undecidable by the deconstructive reading of text. Note first the literal meaning of deconstruction, that is, taking a text apart word by word, not destroying its arguments or premises. Its aim is to deconstruct, not destruct. Modernism would assert just one reading of a text, the one intended by the author, that is, the subject of the writing. In contrast, a Derridean, deconstructive position would 'decentre' the subject and assert the primacy of the reader. Rather than assuming that the structure of a text has a unifying centre, providing an overarching signification, what each reader understands the text to be is equally valid. Decentring aims to disperse meaning, not to integrate it. Implicit meanings are often exposed by discovering gaps or absences in the text ('aporias') or by concentrating on minor details or peripheral aspects of the text ('margins'). Margins include such things as footnotes or digressions, where it is argued that significant meanings are often obscured or hidden. Further, in reading a text a reader might choose to deconstruct or overturn hierarchies within it (for example, that implied by the 'her'/'his' opposition), bringing about a reversal of the overt and official meanings of a text in favour of a subversive reading – for example, a feminist reading. Reversal is achieved by identifying and then reorganizing the explicit contrasts or differences of a text ('profit'/'loss', 'conflict'/'cooperation'). But the reflexive logic of deconstruction does not allow this reversal to result in a new, permanent, if opposite, hierarchy. This would be merely another instance of prioritizing structures over process, in which opposing terms are kept separate and discrete rather than inhabiting each other. The process of deconstruction must be continuous, a process Derrida terms 'metaphorization'.

Finally, Derrida's concept of *différance* gives further insight into the idea of a text's undecidability. Derrida proposes that the meaning of any word or phrase is derived from a process of deferral to other words that differ from itself (that is, *différance* embodies ideas of deferral or postponement in time and difference in space). Hence, *différance* should be understood as the continuous absence of a deferred meaning as well as the difference of opposed meanings.

The nature of *différance* as an undecidable movement that cannot be pinned down is well caught by Gergen's analysis of the words 'let's be logical about this; the bottom line would be the closing of the Portsmouth division' (1992: 219). He shows that the meaning of such words is not transparent, but rests on the meanings we attribute to words like 'logical', 'bottom line' and so forth. But this in turn requires that we defer to other words. To answer what 'logical' means, for example, we have to consider other terms like 'rational', 'systematic' and 'coherent'. But we could have chosen other terms and, even for the terms we have chosen, there are multiple meanings bearing the 'trace' (to use Derrida's term) or connotations of many other words and contexts in an ever-expanding network of significations. 'What seemed on the surface to be a simple, straightforward piece of wise advice, on closer inspection can mean virtually anything' (Gergen 1992: 219). Hence the essence of undecidability is the existence of contradictory, if postponed or marginalized,

meanings within a single term, meanings that can be brought to the surface and prioritized at the reader's volition. Hence the true meaning of a text can never be known and nothing can be said about it that is anything other than temporary or provisional. The project of deconstruction, then, is to reveal and celebrate the ambivalence of all texts, which can only be understood in relation to other texts ('intertextuality') and not in relation to any literal meaning or normative truth. As Derrida famously put it, 'there is nothing outside the text'.

2 Deconstruction and management

The relevance of deconstruction analysis to management is that it queries the certainties of taken-for-granted managerial assumptions and allows for subversive readings of the 'text' of organizational life. The text of organizational life, taken in its widest sense, comprises enactments that may be read for symbolic meaning, such as artefacts, actions or words themselves (see ORGANIZATION BEHAVIOUR). Organizational life in this sense may be seen as a discourse – a text of symbolic representations open to the reader's interpretation, an interpretation that involves reading between the lines for what remains unspoken or taken-for-granted, such as evasions or unwritten assumptions (aporias, margins). Focusing on the written or spoken word, such discourse analysis deals crucially with issues of representation. That is, it starts with the premise that words do not merely reflect what is being talked about, but they actually construct and even constitute what is being talked about. Feminist writers, for example, show how the structure of language literally constructs a 'man-made' patriarchal world (Spender 1980). Hence a further aspect of a subversive reading of the text is to consider how managers create rhetorics as part of their role as transformational leaders, engaged in moulding the mind-sets of employees (or, as it might be described in management-speak, 'developing a vision of the organization's unique contribution and winning the hearts and minds of employees to wholeheartedly share in that vision') (see LEADERSHIP).

To illustrate how deconstruction analysis may be used to develop a subversive reading of organizational life, the concept of 'performativity' and the rhetoric of human resource management may be considered (see HUMAN RESOURCE MANAGEMENT). As conventionally understood, management epitomizes the epistemology of systematic modernism. In other words, it involves the application of positivistic, deductive reasoning in order to accumulate greater knowledge of and control over the material world and, through resultant increases in efficiency, to achieve continuous material progress. Given competing alternatives in a world of uncertainty, constraints and opportunities, this instrumental rationality will facilitate the choice of actions that will yield preferred outcomes. The preferred outcome is usually that of 'performativity', or the optimization of input/output relationships. Resting as it does on a hypothetico-deductive knowledge base, performativity crucially assumes the existence of linear cause-and-effect relationships. This is expressed in many normative models of managerial action, from models of determinants and consequences for the performance of human resource management policies (Beer *et al.* 1985; Devanna *et al.* 1984) to Peters and Waterman's famous eight rules for achieving excellence (1982) (see PETERS, T.J.).

A deconstructive analysis of such texts might begin by using Nietzsche's deconstruction of causality. In undertaking most actions in organizations, managers work on the taken-for-granted assumption that their actions have causes and effects. Implicit in this assumption is that such causes have a logical and temporal priority to their effects. But as Nietzsche argues, the assumption rests on a chronological reversal. Imagine one feels a sudden pain. This may cause one to look for its causes and, noticing, perhaps, a pin, one may posit a link and reverse the perceptual order (pain then pin) to produce a causal sequence (pin then pain). As Nietzsche succinctly puts it:

The fragment of the outside world of which we become conscious comes after the effect that has been produced on us and is projected *a posteriori* as its 'cause'. In the phenomenalism of the 'inner world' we invent the chronology of cause and effect. The basic fact of 'inner experience' is that cause gets imagined after the effect has occurred.

(Nietzsche 1966: 804)

Yet as Culler (1983) points out – and here we have the essence of deconstruction – this does not lead to the conclusion that the notion of causality should be abandoned. For this act of deconstructing the nature of causality, this uncovering of the paradox of causation, itself relies on the notion of cause: the experience of pain causes us to discover the pin and thus causes the production of a cause. Similarly, the contradiction emerges that engagement with the outer 'objective' world (the discovery of the pin), the taken-for-granted determinant of action, is caused by prioritizing the inner world, where the chronology of cause and effect is invented.

Finally, deconstruction reverses the traditionally held hierarchical oppositions implicit in the notion of causality. The distinction between cause and effect posits cause as coming first, both logically and temporally. But deconstruction upsets this hierarchy by allowing an exchange of properties. In other words, if effect is what causes the cause to become a cause, the effect, not the cause, should be privileged as the origin. In other words, if either cause or effect can be the origin of the other, the concept of origin loses the meaning it requires in the causal scheme and hence contradicts it.

This reversal, while retaining ideas of cause and effect, is evident in the work of commentators such as March and Brunsson, who speak of management engaging with 'technologies of foolishness' (March 1981), management whose 'rational decision-making' may, in fact, constitute 'action irrationality' (Brunsson 1982). Both assert that in an uncertain but politically charged organizational world, seeking the best ('most rational') solution to a problem (the logic of performativity and the assumption of linear causality) is unrealistic. A safer strategy is to engage in a course of action (a solution) to which one can generate some commitment and then to invent a problem that it solves. Such a deconstructive analysis alerts the reader to the possibility that management is not about deciding goals and then developing strategies to achieve them, as in Peters and Waterman (1982), but rather that achievable courses of action that have support in the organization for whatever – possibly contradictory – reasons are enacted and then their consequences are identified and justified as legitimate goals. As March (1981: 569) notes, the contradiction exists that 'when a major stimulus for change comes from a sense of competence, problems are created in order to solve them, and solutions and opportunities stimulate awareness of previously unsalient or unnoticed problems or preferences.' In these circumstances, the rhetoric of justification may become the official reality rather than the prior actions that stimulate the temporally subsequent but privileged (and hence logically prior) rhetoric.

3 Deconstructing human resource management

In the last decade, human resource management in the USA and the UK has been presented by mainstream academics and management alike as a key to achieving competitive advantage (Beer and Spector 1985; Walton 1985; Guest 1987). A conventional mode of analysing human resource management is then to identify why it has arisen (global competition, Japanization, enterprise culture, etc.), its similarities and differences as compared to personnel management, the extent to which it is implemented in practice and its outcomes (see JAPANIZATION). Such analysis is essentially positivistic and concerned with issues of performativity.

An analysis of human resource management grounded in deconstruction asks different questions, which centre on the multiple and potentially contradictory readings of the human resource management text that render it 'undecidable' and on the construction of this text. Who are the authors/readers of the human resource management text and what are they trying to construct/deconstruct?

A starting point in deconstructing the text of human resource management is to focus on what has been termed the 'brilliant ambiguity' (Keenoy 1990a) of the very term *human resource management*. One reading of this term is to foreground what has been termed its 'hard', 'utilitarian instrumentalism' meaning, a reading that emphasizes the quantitative, calculating and strategic aspects of managing the human resource in as rational a way as any other economic factor. This focus is on human *resource management*. But another reading, the 'soft', 'developmental humanism' one, while still emphasizing the importance of integrating human resource management policies with business objectives, sees this as involving treating employees as valued assets, as resourceful humans, a source of competitive advantage through their commitment, adaptability and high quality skills, performance, and so on. Human resource management in this reading puts *resource management* in the background and highlights *human resource*, a reversal of the previous reading (Storey 1987; Hendry and Pettigrew 1990).

A deconstruction analysis of human resource management would focus on how frequently its commentators have recourse to colourful and memorable imagery and metaphor, a process that in itself extends and juxtaposes readings of a text. Armstrong (1987), for example, invited readers to consider whether human resource management was a case of the 'emperor's new clothes' or of 'old [personnel] wine in new [human resource management] bottles'. Keenoy (1990b) questioned whether human resource management was a case of 'the wolf in sheep's clothing'. Guest (1990) analysed human resource management in terms of the 'American Dream'. Keenoy and Anthony (1992) likened human resource managers to 'shamans [who] cannot be expected to do the chores'. In deconstructing this imagery, the reader may be struck by two aspects. First, the extent to which it is biblically derived or has religious overtones and second, the recurring theme that human resource management presents itself in a deceptive but new packaging. Putting these two ideas together and applying Derrida's ideas about the trace of many other terms ('networks of signification' according to Gergen (1992: 219)), the reader can interpret this imagery as implying that human resource management involves supernatural/magical/divine intervention, packaged in a consumer-friendly but glitzy form – the antithesis of the hard-nosed rationalism of *resource management*. Keenoy and Anthony come close to another postmodernist's – Baudrillard's – ideas about the ready consumption of the hyperreal (human resource management) in preference to the more mundane, real (personnel management) when they write:

> There should be little wonder. . . . . that there are parts of the organization that personnel management cannot reach, because its engagement in practical control makes it impossible to avoid the contradictions between apparent and espoused values that aspirations to cultural change reveal. Human resource management is not so disadvantaged. It is concerned with the management of beliefs, with the manufacture of acquiescence in corporate values, with the production of images. . . . . it is the business of human resource management to shift perceptions of reality.
>
> (Keenoy and Anthony 1992: 138–9)

Reading the margins here, it is interesting to note that the authors themselves revert to the representational world of the media – in this case advertising – in their adaptation of the famous slogan about the beer that 'refreshes the parts other beers cannot reach'. This sub-text can then be read as human resource management asserting the values of consumption over those of production – itself a postmodern theme.

In looking at the language used to represent human resource management from a deconstructive position, one is struck by the degree, as in much rhetoric, to which binary oppositions are employed. In the examples cited above, we have 'old' and 'new', 'wolf' and 'sheep', 'wine' (a liquid to be contained) and 'bottle' (a container). Human resource

management has also been identified with the use of 'tough love' (Legge 1989). Above all, we have the oft- – and already – cited opposition between hard and soft models of human resource management.

This latter example is particularly interesting because it has structured much of the academic discourse about human resource management in the UK. In a sense, a process of 'metaphorization', to use Derrida's term, has been gradually reversing the hierarchy contained in this discourse. A starting point is the idea that in a patriarchy 'hard' (a masculine characteristic) is likely to take precedence over 'soft' (a feminine characteristic), certainly in the external world of work. And this was how the discourse was read – with 'standard modern' styles of employee relations in the majority of UK companies backgrounding readings of softer, 'sophisticated paternalist' employee relations styles (associated with industries where female staff or knowledge workers were prevalent, such as Marks & Spencer and IBM) (Purcell and Sisson 1983). Partly inspired by the Japanese icon, itself something of a culture shock, the soft model of human resource management was then talked up, backgrounding the hard model, which superficially resembled discredited standard modern practices. Now, in the light of empirical work and critiques of the soft model and in the context of extended economic recession, the hard model of human resource management is receiving more attention (Guest 1995).

A final deconstructive reading of the human resource management text is to overthrow the conventional reading of senior managers as transformational leaders, managing their organization's culture to obtain employee commitment to a shared vision of the route to competitive advantage. A deconstructive reading of this text would see managers not as presenting or clarifying a vision in which all can participate to mutual advantage, but as using rhetoric to cloak the harsh reality of management prerogative in the service of capitalism, thereby facilitating an intensification of work and a commodification of labour (see LABOUR PROCESS). Many commentators, of a Marxist as well as a postmodern stance, have identified how human resource management rhetoric masks the reality of organizational life: 'rightsizing' = mass redundancies; 'customer care' = market forces are supreme; 'lean production' = mean production; 'empowerment' = making someone else take the risk and responsibility (Sisson 1994). But deconstructive analysis does not allow this prioritizing of rhetoric over reality to rest here. Rather, as Keenoy and Anthony (1992) assert, this binary opposition must itself be undermined and reversed. Rhetoric is not apart or separate from the 'real' world: rhetoric *is* the real world. 'Once it was deemed sufficient to redesign the organization so as to make it fit for human capacity and understanding: now it is better to redesign human understanding to fit the organization's purpose' (Keenoy and Anthony 1992: 239).

Deconstruction allows the managerial reader to take apart the texts and stories of the advocates of human resource management as a positive message, a gospel to achieve competitive advantage. A critical reader might search for the paradoxes, contradictions and absences in the human resource management text and come up with a totally different, negative reading. Meaning is undecidable: both readings are valid if they give meaning to the reader.

KAREN LEGGE
UNIVERSITY OF WARWICK

Further reading

(References cited in the text marked *)

* Armstrong, M. (1987) 'Human resource management: a case of the emperor's new clothes?', *Personnel Management* 19 (8): 30–35. (A critical look at the subject.)

Baudrillard, J. (1990) *The Revenge of the Crystal: A Baudrillard Reader*, P. Foss and J. Pefanis (eds), London: Pluto Press. (A useful selection of readings from a major postmodern theorist.)

* Beer, M. and Spector, B. (1985) 'Corporate-wide transformations in human resource management', in R.E. Walton and P.R Lawrence (eds), *Human Resource Management, Trends and Challenges*, Boston, MA: Harvard Business School Press. (A favourable analysis of human resource management.)

* Beer, M., Spector, B., Lawrence, P., Quinn Mills, D. and Walton, R. (1985) *Human Resource Management: A General Manager's Perspective*, Glencoe, IL: Free Press. (Provides examples of human resource management in action.)

* Brunsson, N. (1982) 'The irrationality of action and action rationality: decisions, ideologies and organizational actions', *Journal of Management Studies* 19 (1): 29–44. (A critical view of the way organizations operate.)

* Culler, J. (1983) *On Deconstruction*, London: Routledge & Kegan Paul. (A wide-ranging study of the subject.)

Derrida, J. (1978) *Writing and Difference*, London: Routledge & Kegan Paul. (A collection of essays that provides a valuable introduction to Derrida's work.)

* Devanna, M.A., Fombrun, C.J. and Tichy, N.M. (1984) 'A framework for strategic human resource management', in C.J. Fombrun, N.M. Tichy and M.A. Devanna (eds), *Strategic Human Resource Management*, New York: Wiley. (A model for human resource management operations.)

* Gergen, K.J. (1992) 'Organization theory in the postmodern era', in M. Reed and M. Hughes (eds), *Rethinking Organization*, London: Sage Publications. (Discusses the ambiguity of management-speak.)

* Guest, D.E. (1987) 'Human resource management and industrial relations', *Journal of Management Studies* 24 (5): 503–21. (Looks at ways of achieving competitive advantage through human resource management techniques.

* Guest, D.E. (1990) 'Human resource management and the American Dream', *Journal of Management Studies* 27 (4): 378–97. (Analyses what differentiates human resource management in the USA from that in the rest of the world.)

* Guest, D.E. (1995) 'Human resource management, industrial relations and trade unions', in J. Storey (ed.), *Human Resource Management: A Critical Text*, London: Routledge. (Examines strategic issues in the field of industrial relations.)

* Hendry, C. and Pettigrew, A. (1990) 'Human resource management: an agenda for the 1990s', *International Journal of Human Resource Management* 1 (1): 17–44. (A 'soft' approach to human resource management.)

* Keenoy, T. (1990a) 'HRM: rhetoric, reality and contradiction', *International Journal of Human Resource Management* 1 (3): 363–84. (A criti-

cal look at the language of human resource management.)

* Keenoy, T. (1990b) 'HRM: a case of the wolf in sheep's clothing', *Personnel Review* 19 (2): 3–9. (Challenges conventional analyses of human resource management.)

* Keenoy, T. and Anthony, P. (1992) 'HRM: metaphor, meaning and morality', in P. Blyton and P. Turnbull (eds), *Reassessing Human Resource Management*, London: Sage Publications. (Discusses how rhetoric is used in the construction of organizational beliefs.)

* Legge, K. (1989) 'Human resource management – a critical analysis', in J. Storey (ed.), *New Perspectives on Human Resource Management*, London: Routledge. (A theoretical critique.)

* March, J.G. (1981) 'Footnotes to organizational change', *Administrative Science Quarterly* 26: 563–77. (Examines the relation between goals, rhetoric and competence.)

* Nietzsche, F. (1966) *Werke*, vols 1–3, ed. K. Schelechta, Munich. (The works of a major modern philosopher.)

* Norris, C. (1987) *Derrida*, London: Fontana. (A useful introduction to a difficult philosopher.)

* Peters, T.J. and Waterman, R.H., Jr (1982) *In Search of Excellence: Lessons from America's Best-Run Companies*, New York: Harper & Row. (Lessons in the art of management derived from leading companies.)

* Purcell, J. and Sisson, K. (1983) 'Strategies and practice in the management of industrial relations', in G.S. Bain (ed.), *Industrial Relations in Britain*, Oxford: Blackwell. (An analysis of different styles of employee relations.)

* Sisson, K. (1994) 'Personnel management: paradigms, practice and prospects', in K. Sisson (ed.), *Personnel Management*, 2nd edn, Oxford: Blackwell. (A look at the jargon of management.)

* Spender, D. (1980) *Man-Made Language*, London: Routledge. (A look at how language constructs and affirms a patriarchal culture.)

* Storey, J. (1987) *Developments in the Management of Human Resources: An Interim Report*, Warwick Papers in Industrial Relations 17, Warwick: Industrial Relations Research Unit, University of Warwick School of Industrial and Business Studies. (A theoretical account of different ways of understanding human resource management.)

* Walton, R.E. (1985) 'Toward a strategy of eliciting employee commitment based on policies of mutuality', in R.E. Walton and P.R Lawrence (eds), *Human Resource Management, Trends and Challenges*, Boston, MA: Harvard Business School Press. (A mainstream account of human resource management strategy.)

See also: BRAVERMAN, H.; HUMAN RESOURCE MANAGEMENT; HUMAN RESOURCE MANAGEMENT, INTERNATIONAL; ORGANIZATION BEHAVIOUR

Related topics in the IEBM: GLOBALIZATION; MARCH, J.G. AND CYERT, R.M.; ORGANIZATION BEHAVIOUR, HISTORY OF; ORGANIZATIONAL INFORMATION AND KNOWLEDGE; ORGANIZING, PROCESS OF; POWER

Downsizing

Overview

Downsizing is a pervasive activity that has been undertaken by a majority of organizations in the industrialized world in the last two decades. The long-term impact on organizational performance and individual well-being, however, has been largely negative. Research has demonstrated that the way downsizing is implemented is more important than the fact that it is implemented. Of the three approaches available to downsize, systemic strategies (including organizational renewal) are significantly more effective than workforce reduction or organizational redesign strategies. Organizations whose performance improves as a result of downsizing have managed the process as a renewal, revitalization and culture change effort, not just as a strategy to reduce expenses or organization size.

1 The prevalence of downsizing

Despite the fact that downsizing has been ubiquitous for nearly two decades, it still remains the most pervasive yet unsuccessful phenomena in the business world. Downsizing has become the norm rather than an exception among modern organizations – both in the profit sector and the non-profit sector. It is still rare to go a week without reading about one more organization's massive layoff or downsizing effort somewhere in Europe, North America and, increasingly, Asia. Almost no firm, especially those of medium and large size, has avoided downsizing in the last ten years. Non-profit organizations such as government, health care, and educational institutions have followed suit. The transition from command to capitalistic economies in eastern Europe and the former Soviet bloc has led to massive consolidation and downsizing, and unremitting global competition has kept the pressure on almost everyone to lower costs, increase efficiencies, and do more with less. For example, a recent survey of 2,000 corporate executives in Canada, France, Germany, Japan, the UK and the USA found that 94 per cent of companies surveyed had engaged in downsizing between 1993 and 1995. Between one third and one half of the medium and large firms in the USA have downsized every year since 1988. Nearly three-quarters of US households have had a close encounter with lay-offs since 1980.

2 What is downsizing?

Organizational downsizing refers to a set of voluntary activities, undertaken on the part of the management of an organization, designed to reduce costs. The focus may be monetary costs, time costs, or technological costs. Downsizing is usually, but not exclusively, accomplished by reducing the size of the workforce. That is, downsizing is a term used to encompass a whole range of activities from personnel layoffs and hiring freezes to consolidations and mergers of organization units.

The concept of organizational downsizing has arisen out of popular usage, not precise theoretical construction. In fact, identifying the definition and conceptual boundaries of downsizing is more relevant for theoretical purposes than for practical ones. Cameron (1994; 1995a) and Cameron et al. (1993) found, for example, that the terminology used to describe downsizing strategies was quite unimportant to practising managers. In studies of several hundred organizations, they found that the term used to describe downsizing activities did not matter much. An array of alternative terms are used as substitutes for downsizing by practitioners such as building-down, compressing, consolidating,

55

contracting, de-hiring, demassing, dismantling, downshifting, functionalizing, rationalizing, reallocating, reassigning, rebalancing, redeploying, redesigning, redirecting, reduction-in-force, re-engineering, renewing, reorganizing, reshaping, resizing, restructuring, retrenching, revitalizing, rightsizing, slimming down, streamlining, transferring, or even leaning up. All of these terms were found by Cameron *et al.* to be used interchangeably, even though each may have a different connotation.

Although practising managers care little about the precise definition of downsizing, for scholarly purposes a carefully constructed conceptual meaning is required in order for cumulative and comparative research to occur. For example, on the surface downsizing can be interpreted as a mere reduction in organizational size. However, when this is the case downsizing is often confused with the concept of organizational decline, which also can be interpreted as reduction in organizational size. Yet important differences exist that make downsizing and decline separate phenomena conceptually and empirically. Several important attributes of downsizing also make it distinct from other related concepts such as those listed above. These attributes of downsizing refer to intent, personnel, efficiency, and work processes.

(1) *Intent.* Downsizing is not something that happens to an organization, but it is something that managers and organization members undertake purposively. This implies, first of all, that downsizing is an intentional set of activities. This differentiates downsizing from loss of market share, loss of revenues, or the unwitting loss of human resources that are associated with organizational decline. Downsizing is distinct from mere encroachment by the environment on performance or resources because it implies organizational action.

(2) *Personnel.* Downsizing usually involves reductions in personnel, although it is not limited solely to personnel reductions (see HUMAN RESOURCE MANAGEMENT; PERSONNEL MANAGEMENT). A variety of personnel reduction strategies are associated with downsizing such as transfers, outplacement,

retirement incentives, buyout packages, layoffs, attrition and so on. These reductions in personnel may occur in one part of an organization but not in other parts (for example, in the production function but not in the engineering function), but still be labelled organizational downsizing. However, downsizing does not always involve reductions in personnel because some instances occur in which new products are added, new sources of revenue opened up, or additional work acquired without a commensurate number of employees being added. Fewer numbers of workers are then employed per unit of output compared to some previous level of employment.

(3) *Efficiency.* Downsizing is focused on improving the efficiency of the organization and occurs either proactively or reactively in order to contain costs, enhance revenue or bolster competitiveness. That is, downsizing may be implemented as a defensive reaction to decline or as a proactive strategy to enhance organizational performance. In either case, it represents a set of activities targeted at organizational improvement. By and large, downsizing in most firms has been implemented as a defensive reaction to financial crisis, loss of competitiveness, or inefficiency. Proactive and anticipatory downsizing has been rare, although recently re-engineering and restructuring, coupled with downsizing, have become common proactive strategies.

(4) *Work processes.* Downsizing affects work processes, wittingly or unwittingly. When the workforce contracts, for example, fewer employees are left to do the same amount of work and this has an impact on what work gets done and how it gets done. Overload, burnout, inefficiency, conflict and low morale are possible consequences, or more positive outcomes may occur such as improved productivity, efficiency or speed (see Cameron 1994). Moreover, when downsizing activities include restructuring, re-engineering, or eliminating work (such as discontinuing functions, abolishing hierarchical levels, merging units or redesigning tasks), work processes are usually altered substantially. Regardless of whether or not the work is the focus of downsizing activities, work

processes are always influenced one way or another by downsizing.

In the case of each of these attributes, the level of analysis for downsizing is the organization itself, not the individual or the industry. For example, a substantial literature exists on the psychological reactions individuals may have to layoffs and job loss. Impacts on psychological health, financial well-being, propensity toward illness and accidents, personal attitudes, family relationships, and other personal factors have been investigated by a number of researchers (for example, Kozlowski *et al.* 1993). However, whereas by far the most common action taken by organizations engaging in downsizing is laying off workers, downsizing entails a much broader set of actions and connotations.

At the industry level of analysis, a large literature also exists on divestitures, mergers and industry realignments. Market segmentation, divestitures of unrelated businesses, reconfiguring competitive positions, reinforcing core competencies and consolidating industry structures are among the topics addressed. The definition of organizational downsizing being described here, however, may or may not involve selling off, transferring out, merging businesses or altering the industry structure. Much less research has investigated the organization level of analysis than the individual and industry levels of analysis. That is, strategies for approaching downsizing, processes for implementing downsizing and impacts on organizational performance seem to have been under-investigated in the scholarly literature.

To summarize, organizational downsizing refers to an intentionally instituted set of activities designed to improve organizational efficiency and performance which affects the size of the organization's workforce, costs and work processes. It is implied that downsizing is usually undertaken in order to improve organizational performance. Downsizing, therefore, may be reactive and defensive or it may be proactive and anticipatory. Ineffectiveness or impending failure are the most common motivations for downsizing, but they are not prerequisites.

Downsizing may be undertaken when no threat or financial crisis exists at all.

3 The trouble with downsizing

The trouble with downsizing is that as a strategy for improvement it is, by and large, a failure. Admittedly, downsizing announcements usually lead to positive reactions among the financial community. Almost universally favourable reactions have occurred because of the promise of cost savings, reduced expenses and increased competitiveness. For example, the average increase in stock price the day after a downsizing announcement was made in seven major firms in 1993 (IBM, Sears, Xerox, US West, McDonnell Douglas, RJR Nabisco and DuPont) was 5.5 per cent.

However, two-thirds of companies that downsize end up doing it again a year later, and the stock prices of firms that downsized during the 1980s actually lagged behind the industry average in the 1990s. One survey found that 74 per cent of senior managers in downsized companies said that morale, trust and productivity suffered after downsizing, and half of the 1,468 firms in another survey indicated that productivity deteriorated after downsizing. A majority of organizations that downsized in a third survey failed to achieved desired results, with only 9 per cent reporting an improvement in quality. These outcomes led to much criticism in the popular press, with organizations being accused of 'dumbsizing' rather than downsizing.

By way of example, in a review of the scholarly literature on the effects of layoffs, turnover and job rotation policies, Cole (1993) identified a variety of problems associated with job loss resulting from downsizing:

1 loss of personal relationships between employees and customers;
2 destruction of employee and customer trust and loyalty;
3 disruption of smooth, predictable routines in the firm;
4 increases in formalization (rules), standardization and rigidity;

5 loss of cross-unit and cross-level knowledge resulting from longevity and from interpersonal interactions over time;

6 loss of knowledge of how to respond to non-routine challenges faced by the firm;

7 less documentation and, therefore, less sharing of information about changes;

8 loss of employee productivity;

9 loss of a common organizational culture.

Cameron *et al.* (1993) reported still another set of negative outcomes uncovered in a study of organizations in the car industry. Effects of downsizing included:

1 increased centralization of decision making;

2 the adoption of a short-term, crisis mentality;

3 loss of innovativeness;

4 increased resistance to change;

5 decreasing employee morale, commitment and loyalty;

6 the escalation of politicized special interest groups and political infighting;

7 risk-aversion and conservatism in decision making;

8 loss of trust among customers and employees;

9 increasing interpersonal conflict;

10 restricted communication flows and less information sharing;

11 lack of teamwork;

12 loss of accessible, forward-thinking, aggressive leaders.

The negative effects of downsizing on individual well-being, physical and emotional health, personal attributes, family relationships, and personal economic factors have been no less disconcerting. Research has shown that in a variety of types of organizations and with a variety of types of employees, downsizing has produced negative rather than positive results (Kozlowski *et al.* 1993; Brockner 1988).

Despite this track record, downsizing remains a strategy of choice for organizations faced with excess capacity, bloated employee ranks, sky-high costs and declining efficiency. Most observers simply see no other choice available, plus the fact that downsizing

does seem to produce some positive outcomes. Tomasko (1987), for example, identifies ways in which downsizing has had positive impact on the performance of organizations in adapting to change, and Richardson (1988) argued that downsizing provides an 'ultimate advantage' in containing costs. Consequently, downsizing is normally the first alternative selected by organizations under pressure to cut expenses and improve efficiency.

4 Approaches to downsizing

In several empirical investigations of downsizing, three different approaches to downsizing have been identified (see Cameron *et al.* 1993). These three approaches summarize the kinds of strategies available to organizations as they implement downsizing. They also differ in their effectiveness and impact on organizational performance. The three approaches can be labelled (1) workforce reduction strategies; (2) organization redesign strategies; and (3) systemic strategies.

Workforce reduction strategy

By far the most common downsizing strategy implemented by organizations is a workforce reduction strategy. This strategy focuses mainly on eliminating headcount or reducing the number of employees in the workforce (see INDUSTRIAL AND LABOUR RELATIONS). This includes early retirements, transfers and outplacement, buy-out packages, golden parachutes, attrition, job banks, and layoffs or firings. Such actions are usually executed immediately via top-down directives and they are almost always implemented across the entire organization or a major sub-unit.

The disadvantages of workforce reduction strategies are illustrated by comparing them to throwing a grenade into a crowded room, closing the door and expecting the explosion to eliminate a certain percentage of the workforce. It is difficult to predict exactly who will be eliminated and who will remain. Which employees will take advantage of an early retirement offer or buy-out package, for example, often cannot be predicted. It is also impossible to determine what relevant knowledge, what institutional memory and what critical skills will be lost to the organization when employees leave. What is certain is that critical skills, knowledge, memory and relationships *will be lost or damaged.*

The main advantages of this kind of strategy, in addition to providing an immediate shrinkage and economic cost savings, are to capture the attention of members of the organization to the serious condition that may exist, to motivate resource reductions in day-to-day work and to create readiness in the organization for further change. Quick-hit, across-the-board cuts get attention. Workforce reduction can create the crisis consciousness needed to initiate other kinds of dramatic change.

On the other hand, the harm caused by a workforce reduction strategy may offset the positive effects of unfreezing the organization. Because this strategy approaches downsizing as a temporary activity to be finished and abandoned, it mitigates against continuous and long-term improvement, involving and empowering employees, human resources as the most valuable asset, and bettering processes. When implemented in the absence of other strategies, 'grenade-type' approaches to downsizing were rarely positive and generally negative in their consequences.

Organizational redesign strategy

The second type of downsizing strategy, organization redesign, aims at cutting out work in addition to or in place of workers. Studies have shown that around half of the downsizing organizations implement this strategy (for example, Cameron 1994). This includes eliminating functions, hierarchical levels, divisions or products; consolidating and merging units; reconfiguring work processes; and reducing work hours. Reengineering or restructuring are frequently used substitute words. This strategy is difficult to implement quickly because some changing of the organizational architecture is required. It is, by and large, a medium-term strategy in that it requires some advanced analysis of the areas to be consolidated or redesigned, followed by eliminating or repositioning sub-units within the organization to reduce required tasks.

A redesign strategy helps avoid the problem of overloading fewer workers with the same amount of work for the organization to perform. Instead, an organization redesign strategy helps ensure that changes are targeted at the magnitude of work and organizational arrangements. The downsized organization can achieve a greater degree of efficiency because of its simplified structure. It also focuses on work reduction as a priority over human resource reduction. It adopts a longer time horizon in terms of desired impact and it has less adverse effect on employee commitment, morale and loyalty.

On the other hand, a redesign strategy is focused exclusively on the internal workings of the organization and it still defines downsizing as a finite programme with a beginning and an end. It ignores continuous redesign of work processes, dissemination of an overriding philosophy of never-ending improvement and holding everyone in the organization responsible for advancement, all key attributes of high performing organizations (Cameron 1995b). The organization's relationships with customers as well as upstream and downstream coordination may be damaged or destroyed, and the ultimate target of change remains exclusively with profitability.

Systemic strategy

The third type of downsizing strategy, which, research suggests, is implemented by less than a third of the organizations, is fundamentally different from the other two. It focuses on changing the organization's systems, culture, and the attitudes and values of employees, not just the size of the workforce, the configuration of the architecture or the magnitude of the work. It is *systemic* (that is, focused on systems) in two ways: internal systems (for example, values, communication, production and human resource systems) and external systems (for example, the production chain including upstream suppliers and downstream customers).

This type of strategy involves redefining downsizing as a way of life, as an ongoing process, as a basis for continuous improvement, rather than as a programme or target. Its main goal is renewal and revitalization as much as cost reduction. Downsizing is equated with simplification of all aspects of the organization, including suppliers, inventories, design processes, production methods, customer relations, marketing and sales support, and so on. Costs all along the customer chain, especially invisible and unmeasured costs, are the main targets. Examples of downsizing targets include reducing wait time, response time, rework, paper, incompatibilities in data and information systems, number of suppliers, rules and regulations, unused training, excessive audits, and so on.

Instead of being the first target for elimination, employees are defined as resources to help generate and implement downsizing ideas in other areas. All employees are held accountable for reducing costs and for finding improvements. A continuous improvement ethic is applied to the task of downsizing and cost savings throughout the entire system of inter-organizational relationships are pursued as an ongoing objective. Downsizing is not an activity that reaches an end point, but it continues indefinitely as a general philosophy for doing business.

Since this third type of strategy requires a long-term perspective, it may not generate the immediate improvement in bottom-line numbers that workforce reduction strategies sometimes generate. Along with redesign strategies, systemic strategies often require up-front investment in employee training, system diagnosis and team formation. On the other hand, they avoid the need to continually implement grenade-type strategies each time cost savings are needed. In empirical analyses of downsizing strategies and organizational performance, a systemic strategy has been found to be significantly more effective than the other two strategies (Cameron *et al.* 1993; Cameron 1995b).

The three downsizing strategies are not mutually exclusive, of course. Most organizations implement several alternatives in a single type of strategy (for example, layoffs, early retirements, buyouts – all workforce reduction strategies). That is, they relied on one overall strategy type (usually workforce reduction) but used multiple examples of it. On the other hand, the most effective firms implement all three types of strategies and the effects on performance when all three strategies are applied have been found to be significantly different than when workforce reduction strategies or organization redesign strategies were used alone.

KIM CAMERON
BRIGHAM YOUNG UNIVERSITY

Further reading

(References cited in the text marked *)

* Brockner, J. (1988) 'The effects of work layoff on survivors', in B.M. Staw and L.L. Cummings (eds), *Research in Organizational Behavior*, vol. 10, Greenwich, CT: JAI Press Inc. (Provides a summary of research on 'survivor guilt' and other problematic effects of worker layoffs.)
* Cameron, K.S. (1994) 'Strategies for successful organizational downsizing', *Human Resource Management Journal* 33: 189–212. (The lead article in a special issue on organizational downsizing that reports empirical research results on effective downsizing.)
* Cameron, K.S. (1995a) *Strategic Downsizing: The Case of a US Army Command*, Washington, DC: US Army Research Institute. (Reports the results of a study of the impact of downsizing on the US army.)
* Cameron, K.S. (1995b) 'Downsizing, quality, and performance', in R.E. Cole (ed.), *The Fall and Rise of the American Quality Movement*, New York: Oxford University Press. (An empirical investigation of the relationship between total quality management and downsizing.)
* Cameron, K.S., Freeman, S.J., and Mishra, A.K. (1993) 'Downsizing and redesigning organizations' in Huber, G.P. and Glick, W.H. (eds) *Organizational Change and Redesign*, New York: Oxford University Press. (A literature review and report of research on the implementation and effects of downsizing.)
* Cole, R.E. (1993) 'Learning from learning theory: implications for quality improvements of turnover, use of contingent workers, and job rotation policies', *Quality Management Journal* 1: 9–25. (A discussion of the negative effects of

layoffs and job loss based on principles from learning theory.)

* Kozlowski, S.W.J., Chao, G.T., Smith, E.M., and Hedlund, J. (1993) 'Organizational downsizing: strategies, interventions, and research implications', in C.L. Cooper and I.T. Robertson (eds), *International Review of Industrial and Organizational Psychology*, New York: Wiley. (An extensive summary of the literature on downsizing, mainly from the psychological perspective.)

* Richardson, P.R. (1988) *Cost Containment: The Ultimate Advantage*, New York: The Free Press. (A discussion of strategy formulation and implementation regarding cost containment in organizations.)

* Tomasko, R.M. (1987) *Downsizing: Reshaping the Corporation for the Future*, New York: AMACOM Books. (A discussion of how to implement downsizing so as to produce positive organizational effects.)

See also: HUMAN RESOURCE MANAGEMENT; HUMAN RESOURCE MANAGEMENT, INTERNATIONAL

Related topics in the IEBM: ORGANIZATION DEVELOPMENT; ORGANIZATIONAL DECLINE AND FAILURE; ORGANIZATIONAL PERFORMANCE; RE-ENGINEERING; STRATEGY, IMPLEMENTATION OF

Groups and teams

Overview

Many organizations are involved with the introduction of teamwork. A team can be considered as a number of people (a group) organized around a set of objectives. Teamwork can be regarded as a remedy for the dysfunctions of bureaucratic structures which are still dominant in organizations. The main characteristic of bureaucracy in organizations is segmentation: large problems are being cut into sub-problems and sub-sub-problems. These sub- and sub-sub-problems are allocated to sub-units and sub-sub-units. In the end the solutions offered by these units must be assembled again to form a meaningful whole. Today, bureaucracies must operate in a far more complex and uncertain environment than ever before. They threaten to be destroyed by the burden of activities created by themselves to control and coordinate the segmented organization. In order to survive they must invest in new control strategies. Two of these strategies imply the introduction of team concepts in the design of the organization. One strategy involves the introduction of 'lateral linkages'. These are groups that horizontally cut across the existing boundaries of functions. A special form of this is the management team. The creation of self-contained units is the second team-based strategy. With this alternative the functions are integrated around a certain order flow; complete little firms are created within the walls of a bigger firm. The autonomous production team is an important example of this.

The creation of a teamwork organization is to be approached from a double perspective. The team is both the result of organization design choices and of a development process by which the team members learn from their experiences. Organization design and organization development are to be viewed as two sides of the same coin. The introduction of teamwork in organizations is a matter of careful design. The team is an organization in itself, but at the same time is part of a larger system. Tasks must be allocated between and within teams. Systems must be introduced to control the work process. A number of important structural criteria apply to both the lateral and the production teams: a complete task to be carried out independently; a good link with other groups in the organization; sufficient instruments to steer the group's own process; and a good internal organization.

A sound structure does not necessarily imply an effective organization. Managers and workers alike must learn to work in such a new structure. Important in this respect is that there exists a balance between task-orientated activities and the maintenance activities focused on the group atmosphere, that is, keeping good social relationships and a general state of well-being in the group. An effective team is a result of group development.

1 Definitions

Groups and teams are key subjects both in modern management literature and in management practice. The words 'groups' and 'teams' are often used as substitutes. In other cases we attach quite different meanings to them. Theorists tend to use the word 'group' predominantly in a descriptive sense, and use a variety of definitions according to their own theoretical perspective. A well-accepted broad definition of a group is: 'two or more individuals in face-to-face interaction, each aware of his or her membership in the group, each aware of the others who belong to the group, and each aware of their positive interdependence as they strive to achieve mutual goals' (Johnson and Johnson 1991). Such groups can be found almost anywhere: in families, schools, sports clubs and work organizations (see ORGANIZATION BEHAVIOUR). This entry focuses on groups in work organizations.

In everyday language the word 'team' is often used in a normative sense as a special sort of group with positive traits. Like a sports team, it is associated in daily life with 'cooperation', 'cohesion' and 'teamwork'. 'This group is not a team yet' is a frequently used sentence which expresses the difference in meaning in everyday language. A set of individuals has to be tied together for a certain purpose. The word 'team' is used here as an instrument to fulfil a set of objectives. This is reflected in a well-accepted definition of a team: 'a set of interpersonal relationships structured to achieve established goals' (Johnson and Johnson 1991). However, this formal definition is not so very different from that of a group. This might be the reason why both words are often used as synonyms in the literature. Here we stay closer to the meaning of the terms 'groups' and 'teams' as they are used in daily life and everyday language: the group and the team are regarded as poles of a continuum (Tyson 1989). Any team is to be regarded as a group. The group turns into a team once it gets organized well enough to fulfil a purpose. This implies a process of *organization design* by which effective patterns of task allocation, decision making and communication emerge. The transition of groups into teams is in this respect the result of a learning process or, in other words, the result of *organization development*. The group becomes an effective team by using its experience in following and improving organizational patterns. This represents the double perspective.

2 Teamwork as a cure for bureaucracy

Whereas groups as social entities is probably as old as mankind, organizational interest in groups and teams is more recent. One of the main reasons is that up until now teamwork has often been viewed as a cure for bureaucracy. The main characteristic of bureaucracy is 'segmentation' (Kanter 1983). Large problems are being cut into sub-problems and sub-sub-problems. These sub- and sub-sub-problems are allocated to sub-units and sub-sub-units. In the end the solutions offered by these units must be assembled again to form a meaningful whole. Segmentation is based on the concentration of functions in the firm; tasks, skills and processes of the same kind are allocated to specialized units. This functional concentration takes place at all levels in the organization. At the top level, the traditional main functions are marketing, research and development, production and finance. The main functions are in their turn divided into partial functions. In a marketing department one usually finds groups such as product planning, sales planning, sales, sales promotion and customer services. Finally, one finds functional concentration as an organizing principle on the shop floor. For example, in a traditional tool workshop one finds drillers working with drillers and turners with turners. On the 'shop floor' of an insurance company (see Example 1), tasks are frequently split up according to both the type of insurance and the type of operational task, such as the processing of a policy and the assessment of claims. A characteristic of bureaucracy is the distinction between 'doing' and 'thinking'. The operational or production tasks carried out on the shop floor are carefully stripped from 'indirect' tasks by which the production process is controlled and improved. These tasks (planning, work preparation, maintenance, quality control) are allocated to staff departments, which are functionally concentrated. In this way the functions all become part of a complex machine. Mintzberg (1979) refers in this respect to organizations as 'machine bureaucracies'. Such machine bureaucracies must carry a heavy control load because the strong division of parts requires extensive coordination. Within the bureaucracy coordination demands a steep hierarchy and a complex system of rules and procedures. In this set-up there is no place for teams. Teams are even regarded as a negative element of the organization. Their initiatives might disturb the functioning of the fine-tuned machinery and groups might hide themselves from management control. Frederick Winslow Taylor (Braverman 1974), the father of scientific management, even regarded the group (especially the informal group) as a threat to productivity (see TAYLOR, F.W.). In his view workers only want to do as little work as possible for the highest possible pay. He referred to this attitude as 'soldiering'. In a group individuals are given the chance to hide themselves from organizational controls. To him group development was synonymous with 'systematic soldiering'. In a traditional bureaucracy one might make an exception in this respect for groups which are outside the organization and in highly unpredictable situations, like the service or installation unit, the crew of a submarine or a sales group in Africa.

Machine bureaucracy has been very effective for decades. It was the 'era of mass production' in which economy of scale was the leading and compelling guideline: a product was produced for as long as possible in batches as large as possible. However, the dysfunctions of bureaucracy became manifest the moment the organization had to act in a flexible and adaptable way. This was the case when: life cycles of products and services were drastically shortened; smaller batches of customized products had to be delivered; the pace of technological innovation was accelerating and technologies were increasingly melting and integrating into hybrids and systems; competition was taking place in global rather than local markets; and quality requirements of customers became increasingly strict.

At this point the bureaucracy threatens to be destroyed by its own control burden and must invest in new strategies. Galbraith (1973) distinguishes four main strategies. First, the organization simply accepts that it is not effective; for example, it accepts 'slack' in the form of overcapacity or stock. As a second strategy the control system is reinforced by the introduction of 'vertical control systems'. The third and the fourth strategies imply an introduction of team concepts in the design of the organization; the third involves the

introduction of *lateral linkages*, or groups that horizontally cut across the existing boundaries of functions (a special form of this is the *management team*); the fourth is the creation of self-contained units in which the functions are integrated around a certain underflow and complete little firms are created within the walls of a bigger firm (the autonomous *production team* is an important example).

Management teams

A characteristic of 'machine bureaucracy' is that the functions which make up the organization do not come together until the top of the firm. Management solves the problems between the functions of the organization; the classic problems between productions and sales and between product development and process development. The management of a factory, division or corporation is confronted with a large variety of interface problems which cannot be solved at a lower level in classic bureaucracy simply because of the lack of horizontal and lateral linkages (see MANAGERIAL BEHAVIOUR). It is no surprise that the communication and decision-making channels to the top can be heavily clogged up. In the 1970s such interface problems became increasingly frequent because more and more subjects came into existence that could not be demarcated within the boundaries of the organizational functions: logistics, quality, innovation. Thus, there was a manifest need to act together as a team in the top echelon of the firm, the division or the plant, rather than as representatives of functional sub-interests in the firm. For this purpose 'team-building programmes' were set up, focused on promoting trust and open communication within teams. This was subsequently extended to the lower echelons of the organization. Each manager can be considered in this view as the chairman of his own team. This process is referred to as organization development.

Lateral teams

The establishment of a task force or project group is frequently used when a problem arises that cannot be solved within the normal organization. In cases like these a temporary group is created, composed of the different organizational functions, with the task of solving such a problem. The problem may be related to the development of a product, a new system for job classification or a sales campaign in a new market. Such groups may vary greatly as regards life span, degree of organization, degree of participation, influence and resources. Sometimes such a group has a very short life; for example, members of an *ad hoc* group charged with the internal relocation within an office will cooperate intensively with one another for a limited number of weeks in order to finish a concrete job. A group that must prepare a merger with another firm is similar, but possesses substantially more power. Some groups have a permanent character; for example, the users' councils representing information technology users from various plants. These meet on a regular basis to communicate about different subjects. They often have a representative and advisory character. The time invested by the members in such a team is mostly limited.

In innovation projects the time invested by team members may be the larger part of their working time. The project group may be important to the extent that it becomes the core of the work organization. The functional departments then become suppliers of manpower to a multi-functional or multidisciplinary team. The project manager is really the boss, or a 'heavyweight project manager' (Clark and Wheelwright 1992), who controls the resources and is responsible for the result. The managers of the functional departments are responsible for updating the functional know-how and clearly play an inferior role. In groups with a 'lightweight project manager' the functional managers are the ones that possess most power. This leads to the classic field of tension of the matrix organization: the members of the project team are pushed back and forth by both their functional and their project managers.

Production teams

The team concept is also frequently applied in the primary process of production of service organizations. These groups are labelled semi-autonomous groups, self-managing groups or production cells. By introducing these groups organizations distance themselves from the Taylorist production organization. The teams are given the responsibility for a whole product or a whole service package, or for a meaningful part of the product or service package. Team members learn to perform all tasks or an important part of the tasks. Jobs are being integrated and/or there is a possibility of job rotation. Teams are also given the responsibility for indirect tasks, for example, work scheduling, quality control, maintenance and ordering supplies. Sometimes they even hire new members. Example 1, taken from den Hertog (1994), gives an example of such a group.

Example 1: a large Dutch general insurance company redesigned one its major divisions. In the old situation the work was organized in product units (fire, cars, and so on). Within the product groups the work was split into two main domains: acceptance of risk (processing policies) and assessment of damage claims. The market called for an integration and improvement of services towards the customers. Product units were replaced by regional units responsible for the service of a set of customers (in this case, independent insurance intermediaries). Within each unit insurance teams were introduced which handled the whole range of insurances, both in acceptance and assessment. In the following phase acceptance and assessment will also be integrated in the insurance.

Such groups have a number of advantages (Agurén and Edgren 1980; Roberts 1993). First, the control burden can be strongly reduced. A great number of operations can be taken care of close to their execution, which means that problems can be solved directly where they arise without the intervention of a staff department. The size of the staff services thus can be strongly reduced. Flexibility has increased because it is much easier to introduce a new product variant in a single team than to rebuild a whole production line. The waiting times between functions and operations can also be strongly reduced, so that the throughput time of an order is also decreased. In addition, small batches can be run more rapidly. Thus, not only is the client served quicker, but the stock can also be reduced. Finally, the process is more motivating because the simple jobs that are fragmented in the machine bureaucracy can be combined into meaningful and more complex tasks. The shift of responsibilities to the shop floor and the integration of thinking and doing offers a perspective on a more participative style of decision making within the organization, which better matches the democratic values outside the organization (see DECISION MAKING; INDUSTRIAL DEMOCRACY).

3 Organization design

The introduction of teamwork in organizations is a matter of careful design. When looking for an alternative to an assembly line, it does not suffice to take a pair of scissors and cut the larger system into pieces before pasting them together. A number of important structural criteria apply both to the lateral and the production teams:

1 a complete task to be carried out independently;
2 a good link with other groups in the organization;
3 sufficient instruments to steer the group's own process;
4 a good internal organization.

The team is an organization in itself, but at the same time it is also part of a larger system. If one does not take this into account sooner or later the team threatens to be rejected by the surrounding organization as an alien body. This is one of the most essential lessons learned from the introduction of semi-autonomous groups in the 1960s and 1970s (van Eijnatten 1993). In this respect the introduction of team concepts into an organization is a matter of organization design. Tasks must be allocated between and within teams. Systems must be introduced to control the work process. Since 1980 the development of such design strategies for teamwork has made much progress, not only on paper but in the

design practice as well (for example, Agurén and Edgren 1980; van Eijnatten 1993; Roberts 1993; Warnecke 1993). The approaches described in this literature share the following similarities:

1 the organization is approached as an entity;
2 the design focuses on production flows;
3 responsibilities are pushed down in the organization as low as possible;
4 formal design rules and design instruments are used in a clear sequence of design steps.

The basic logic on which these approaches are based becomes visible in three main design stages. These stages are outlined using the terminology of the Dutch version of the sociotechnical systems approach (van Eijnatten 1993).

Stage 1: functional requirements

The redesign must enable the organization to better meet the external demands, both current and future, which are placed upon the firm or institution. A strategic analysis of strengths and weaknesses, opportunities and threats is the basis for a list of functional requirements. In design practice this analysis involves a large group of managers and workers, with the purpose of obtaining both a better starting point and support in the organization for the redesign process. Functional requirements may be related to all facets of business, for example: it must be possible to deliver an order within three weeks; stocks cannot constitute more than 10 per cent of total capital; the call rate from the market must be reduced to less than 1 per cent; the quality of work must be matched with the qualifications of the workforce.

Stage 2: the production structure

The focus of the redesign is on the production process: the chain of activities by which material and information is transformed into a product or service. This is also referred to as the production structure. The redesign concentrates on creating parallel production flows – a coherent flow of more or less similar orders. In a machine plant this may concern orders for machine parts that undergo a similar pattern of operations and that are of similar size. In an insurance company (see Example 1) this may be the flow of services performed for a certain part of its clients. When formulating the parallel flows it is important that there exist as few interfaces between the flows as possible. It must be possible to solve the larger part of the problems within the parallel flows. The effect of parallelization is that it radically decreases internal variance of possible operation patterns. The large complex system is rebuilt into a set of smaller, orderly production units that are responsible for a part of the order flow (Figure 1). Production teams are accountable for a whole product or a meaningful, completed part of it. In the case of a highly complex product, such as an automobile or a large information system, it is often necessary to form modules or segments. Segmentation here does not mean the splitting up of tasks but the assembling of meaningful parts of the whole process. The production structure is designed from the top down: the global structures are filled in first, followed by the task structure at group and individual level (Figure 1). This is quite logical because the global structures (main flows and segments) determine the degrees of freedom for the design at detail level rather than the other way around.

Stage 3: the control structure

In this approach the control structure is derived from the production structure. One must first establish what must be controlled before one can determine how the production system can be controlled. If the production structure can be simplified, the control structure can be simplified also. The control structure is designed the opposite way around from the production structure: from the bottom up. As a basic rule, everything that can be controlled locally on the shop floor, within and between teams, must be controlled there. The decisions that remain to be made are subsequently controlled at the following level. In this way only the most essential (strategic) matters are left for the management team. In the design of the control structure the greatest part of staff activities (planning, maintenance, quality control) are brought to the production flows as closely as possible. These activities are performed for the most part within the production teams themselves.

Thus, more or less complete firms come into existence that are able to control a maximum set of operations and decisions within the greater whole. The same organizational logic is followed at each level of the firm. Warnecke (1993) speaks of the 'fractal company' in this respect, because the properties of

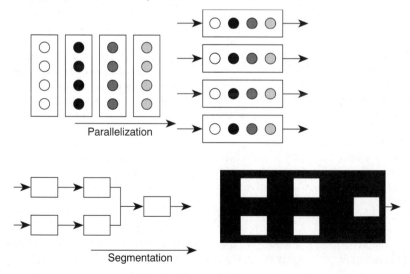

Figure 1 Parallelization and segmentation

the whole can be found at each system level. This type of approach has been applied in a large variety of firms: automobile assembly, insurance companies, machine plants, maintenance workshops of air carriers, banks, post offices, chemical plants and oil refineries. Following a sound design strategy with a clear design sequence is crucial to prevent design faults from being ingrained, which are difficult to repair later.

4 Group development

A sound structure does not necessarily imply an effective organization. Managers and workers alike must learn to work in such a new structure. For many people the step from the old to the new situation is a big one. One has often unlearned to carry responsibility and work together in a tightly knit group. This is illustrated by Example 2. The example shows that tasks are broadened. The team members are about to perform the most important operations for all types of insurance. They have much closer contact with clients and must also use a new computer system. The group must be given time to get used to and deal with this much broader task, but equally important is that they must learn what it is like to work closely together in a team. This often becomes clear as soon as a teamwork organization is implemented.

Example 2: on 1st September, the insurance company relocates to a brand new building. This is also the date of the implementation of the new teamwork organization. Anne goes to work with mixed feelings combining curiosity, uneasiness and eagerness. She has to find her way in the new building. Last weekend Anne had a goodbye dinner with her old room-mates. She now shares a room with two new colleagues whom she hardly knows. She feels uncomfortable about the whole situation. She only knows three of the twelve colleagues in the team and decides to make a fresh start and be nice to everyone, not knowing what to expect from them. After some time she begins to feel more secure as a member of the group. Everybody is trying to make the best of the given situation. Only Johan, one of her room-mates, has been irritating her from the

start. He is always late for work and to the group meetings and he always has an excuse. Some of Anne's colleagues remain strangers in her eyes. Avoiding them seems to be the practical solution. They are just colleagues and have no authority over her. This goes on for some time.

Suddenly, during a team meeting one day, there is an outburst of anger. The group leader is irritated that more and more people are late for the group meeting. Other members mention the heavy workload and complain about the rather authoritarian way the group leader reacts. Two other team members complain about the way work is divided over group members and about the way the information system functions; they have to ask their colleagues for missing information again and again. Too much client-related information is still not covered by the system. A special meeting is convened after this one, to discuss the work process, make new appointments and discuss responsibilities and procedures. The meeting goes fine, and Anne is quite relieved. Irritations are finally expressed. All agree on the goals they want to achieve as a team. During the meetings following this one the atmosphere has really changed. At last Anne and her colleagues can get their jobs properly done. Missing information is not such a problem any more. There is always a colleague who can help out. Anne, by now, begins to like the new working conditions and her colleagues. When someone is late the group deals with this with lots of humour but with a clear message. Sometimes somebody is grouchy or there is a chaotic discussion about procedures. Some people have more knowhow than others and have more to say sometimes during meetings. But in general, Anne, as well as her colleagues, seems to have found a balance between the group goals and the way they work together.

Looking at the group described in Example 2, several observations can be made of what working in groups is all about. First, it may be clear that group work is not automatically a pleasure, or at least is not always a pleasure. Negative feelings may rise, but, fortunately, positive feelings may arise as well. The question is: what keeps groups together, despite the negative feelings? Second, the changes obviously take place over time. One might wonder whether there is some sort of basic pattern for groups to develop into effective teams.

What keeps groups together?

Basically, the processes that underlie group development fall into two realms that constantly seek to co-exist. A group engages in goal-oriented or task activities as well as maintenance-oriented activities. The first activities (task roles) are aimed at achieving goals, getting the job done. The maintenance roles focus on the group atmosphere, keeping good social relationships and a general state of well-being within the group. Over-emphasis on one realm at the expense of the other leads to frustration, discontent or withdrawal. In order to be an effective team there must be a reasonable balance between both realms. A structure will evolve out of the task realm that is appropriate to the task group, while out of the maintenance realm a structure will develop appropriate to the emotional needs of group members. Combining the two realms results in group development, in which compromises are sought to balance task and maintenance needs and behaviours (Crawley 1978).

Is there some sort of standard pattern for group development?

In the research on group behaviour, the life cycle metaphor is often used to describe group development as a 'biological' process, starting with birth and ending with old age or death (departure). A good example is Tuckman's five-stage model – forming, storming, norming, performing and adjourning – which has proved its value in training and consultancy (Tuckman and Jensen 1977). In Tuckman's theory group structure is the result of simultaneous task activities and group-relating (maintenance or social–emotional) activities. The assumption is that a group must go through one stage before being able to go to the next, and every transition holds the risk of regression to an earlier stage.

Forming. As group members come together for the first time they are all looking for reasons to be there. There is insecurity about tasks and about personal interest in the group. Normally group members are polite and somewhat distant, waiting for what is to come. Social contacts per group member are mostly limited to one or two others. There is a great need for clarity and the group leader is expected to offer this. Dependency is high at this stage.

Storming. In this phase individual search takes place. Personal conflicts about roles and responsibilities are common. Often group members compete over positions and status within the group. The atmosphere can be very hostile, not accepting individual differences. A group leader can be heavily attacked at this stage. However, the group still depends on this person – while showing counterdependency. Facilitating group conflict, leading/coaching the group to dialogue and understanding, should be the leader's major concern in order to reach the next stage.

Norming. Contrasts and differences between group members facilitate them to become more understanding. Acceptance of differences of opinions and views arises. Information is shared with group members, and a sense of shared responsibility grows. Cooperation is central to the group and cooperative patterns emerge that are broadly accepted. Decisions are made on a basis of consensus. Group cohesion grows and the group is enchanted, being freed from previous tensions. At the end of this stage a feeling of disenchantment may occur, as a reaction to the enchantment and as a reaction toward authority. The group needs the fight with the group leader, to become independent and to set its own norms. A group leader should not go into counterattack, but should stimulate the group to set standards (within reasonable limits), facilitating the group to the transition to the next stage.

Performing. High performance can be reached at this stage of group development. Group performance is continuously brought up in discussions. The group is looking for improvement to increase performance. We might speak of consensual validation in the sense that group members are positively valued for their own specific talents and limits. Group members are honest in their feedback and accountable for their own behaviour. They have settled for the role each member has, including the group leader.

Adjourning. The existence of groups is limited by time. Over time group members leave and are replaced by others. Changing group composition often implies regression to an earlier stage. The rate of transition will depend on the extent of change. Group departure is often accompanied by rituals, such as having a drink or a last conversation. Some group members tend to look back, others to look forward. Change in group composition enables a group to remain open-minded. New group members can be very 'refreshing' as they do not stick to the norms and routines developed by the former group. They offer the group the opportunity to reconsider its unquestioned, old routines and thus give the group a chance to keep learning.

In the practice of organization redesign there are a number of strategies by which group development can be effectively supported:

Participative design. Members of the future teamwork organization are given an active role in the redesign of their own organization. They become committed at an early stage to the new way of working. Furthermore, they can express their own preferences and the problems they foresee.

Training team leaders. Team leaders are prepared for their new roles as coach, stimulator and decision maker. They exchange experiences during the start-up phase and learn from their colleagues.

Group feedback. At regular intervals the teams reflect on their progress in becoming a 'real team'. In meetings they do not discuss only task-related issues but also maintenance issues.

Introduction of new members. A relative stability of group membership is important, but from time to time 'new blood' must be brought in to avoid the team from becoming rooted in its own behavioural patterns.

5 Conclusions

The main conclusion one can draw from the arguments presented here is that organization design and organization development are two sides of the same coin. New structures will not help when the members of the team stick to old behavioural patterns and when they do not make any progress in the development of satisfying social relationships. The effectiveness and efficiency of a team are dependent on the learning process the team undergoes by passing through successive developmental stages. These stages or phases are facilitated by group leaders, adopting a style contingent on the stage the group is in. The group can then develop its own task and maintenance structure. The group should be autonomous enough to develop itself toward effective and efficient routines and norms, with feedback from group members as the dominant learning vehicle.

However, the design of effective structures is also vital. The group can only develop itself as a self-managing team when it is given a self-contained and meaningful task. Furthermore, the team must be embedded in an organizational environment with enough degrees of freedom to realize its own potential. When the surrounding functions remain untouched and act along the same centralistic and bureaucratic patterns sooner or later the team will relapse into frustration, rebellion or apathy. The team cannot develop itself without the right amount of capacity to control its own processes. The design and development of teams must always be an integrated part of the redesign and development of the organization as a whole.

FRISO DEN HERTOG
THERA TOLNER
MERIT, UNIVERSITY OF MAASTRICHT

Further reading

(References cited in the text marked *)

* Agurén, S. and Edgren, J. (1980) *New Factories: Job Design through Factory Planning in Sweden*, Stockholm: Swedish Employers' Confederation (SAF). (A compilation of practical

experiences from the Swedish programme for job reform.)

* Braverman, H. (1974) *Labor and Monopoly Capital: The Degradation of Work in the Twentieth Century*, New York: Review Press. (A Marxist interpretation of the development of work organization from the rise of mass production until the present revolution in information technologies.)

* Clark, K.B. and Wheelwright, S.C. (1992) *Revolutionizing Product Development: Quantum Leaps in Speed, Efficiency and Quality*, New York: The Free Press. (This influential book provides a good insight into the different strategies to improve the organization of product design process in practice.)

* Crawley, J. (1978) 'The lifecycle of the group', *Small Groups Newsletter* 1 (2): 39–44. (A brief but illuminating article on goal orientation and maintenance tasks needed to fulfil group needs.)

* Eijnatten, F.M. van (1993) *The Paradigm that Changed the Work Place*, Assen: Van Gorcum. (A historical sketch of the development of human-centred strategies for job design: 'sociotechnical systems design'.)

* Galbraith, J.R. (1973) *Designing Complex Organisations*, Reading: Addison-Wesley. (This small and very readable book is a classic introduction to organization design and still relevant today.)

* Hertog, J.F. den (1994) 'Entrepreneurship at the shopfloor: Nationale Nederlanden', in L.E. Andreasen, B. Coriat, J.F. den Hertog and R. Kaplinsky (eds), *Europe's Next Step: Organisational Innovation, Competition and Employment*, London: Frank Cass Publishers. (A case description which illustrates the introduction of a teamwork organization in a large Dutch insurance firm.)

* Johnson, D.W. and Johnson, F.P. (1991) *Joining Together: Group Theory and Group Skills*, Englewood Cliffs, NJ: Prentice Hall. (An up-to-date US textbook on group theory. Uses experiential learning throughout the book as a learning tool to students.)

* Kanter, R.M. (1983) *The Change Masters: Innovation for Productivity in the American Corporation*, New York: Simon & Schuster. (This book reports on a research project in which the strategies of successfully innovating US firms are compared with those of less successful firms.)

* Mintzberg, H. (1979) *The Structuring of Organisations: A Synthesis of Research*, Englewood Cliffs, NJ: Prentice Hall. (In this book the author presents a typology of organizational structures, dividing them into simple structure, machine bureaucracy, professional bureaucracy and adhocracy. This book is a must for the interested reader.)

* Roberts, H.J.E. (1993) *Accountability and Responsibility; The Influence of Organisation Design on Management Accounting*, Maastricht: Datawyse/University of Maastricht. (The report of a research project in three medium-sized Dutch firms. The study shows how the management accounting systems could be simplified and made more effective after the introduction of teamwork.)

Tjosfold, D. (1991) *Team Organisation: An Enduring Competitive Advantage*, Chichester: Wiley. (An accessible book with a strong belief in the power of teams and teamwork to gain competitive advantage. Each theme starts with a short case illustrating everyday organizational experience.)

* Tuckman, B.W. and Jensen, M.A. (1977) 'Stages of small group development revisited', *Group and Organisation Studies* 2 (4): 419–27. (One of the many articles providing a model for group development. Its main distinction from other models is the focus on increased efficiency as an outcome of group development.)

* Tyson, B.T. (1989) *Working with Groups*, South Melbourne: Macmillan. (A comprehensive booklet primarily orientated towards bringing theory into practice. Very handy to look up themes, theories and authors.)

* Warnecke, H.J. (1993) *The Fractal Company: A Revolution in Corporate Culture*, Berlin: Springer. (This rather practical book offers an organization design theory for the future firm, with teamwork being one of the main issues.)

See also: FOLLETT, M.P.; HUMAN RELATIONS; TOTAL QUALITY MANAGEMENT

Related topics in the IEBM: CONFLICT AND POLITICS; COORDINATION AND CONTROL; INNOVATION AND CHANGE; LEWIN, K.; MANUFACTURING SYSTEMS, DESIGN OF; ORGANIZATION BEHAVIOUR, HISTORY OF; ORGANIZATION DEVELOPMENT; ORGANIZATION STRUCTURE; ORGANIZATION TYPES; ORGANIZATIONAL PERFORMANCE; PRODUCT DEVELOPMENT; TRIST, E.L.

Hawthorne experiments

Overview

The Hawthorne studies, initially undertaken to investigate the relationship between workplace conditions and worker productivity, introduced a wide range of topics to the field of management study. Investigators found no strong relationship between workplace conditions and productivity but reached several conclusions: individual work behaviour is driven by a complex set of factors; work groups develop norms which mediate between the needs of the individual and institution; employees should not be considered appendages of machinery; awareness of employee sentiments and participation can reduce resistance to change; the workplace is an interlocking social system, not simply a production system; social structure maintained through symbols of prestige and power. These findings opened the door to the study of client-centred therapy, small group behaviour, organization theory and research methodology.

1 Introduction

That the worker is more than an appendage to the machine is hardly a groundbreaking concept today. It is common knowledge that the social system or culture of the workplace is as important as the physical production system. Leadership patterns and the group dynamics of work teams are recognized as core variables in effective management (see LEADERSHIP; GROUPS AND TEAMS). As commonplace as these ideas are today, such thinking was revolutionary seventy years ago, before the Hawthorne studies were conducted.

The Hawthorne studies represented groundbreaking work in the field of management when they were undertaken in 1924. While the original intention of the studies was to determine the effect of workplace conditions on employee productivity, in line with the Taylorist view of management of that day (see TAYLOR, F.W.), their findings addressed topics far afield from physical work conditions. These findings opened the doors to a wide range of topics in the study of management. Focus eventually shifted away from the time and motion studies made popular by Taylor to the influence of management style and worker motivation (see MOTIVATION AND SATISFACTION). The move away from scientific management represented a paradigm shift. While the Hawthorne studies were not undertaken with the intention of developing new areas of management theory, and as such did not provide definitive evidence on the factors they uncovered, they were still revolutionary for their time. Expecting to find evidence to support the idea of an optimal physical work environment, Hawthorne researchers instead discovered that the physical work environment was only one of many factors, including managerial style and group context, which influence employee productivity. This pioneering, exploratory research fundamentally altered the field of management research.

2 Origins and context

The initial agenda for the Hawthorne studies was to investigate the relationship between the illumination intensity on the shop floor of manual work sites and employee productivity. The Hawthorne research is so named because the studies were conducted by Western Electric at the company's Hawthorne Works, a large plant outside Chicago, IL, where at the time literally every phone and switch in the USA was manufactured. There were six studies, which ran for the duration of several months to several years between the years of 1924 and 1933. The research findings were first reported in Roethlisberger and Dickson (1939), Whitehead (1938) and Homans (1941, 1950).

At the time, Frederick Taylor's scientific management was the currently accepted management doctrine. Taylor's work, although not viewed so in retrospect, was undertaken with the intention of improving conditions for workers by scientifically engineering their work tasks. Scientific management improved the safety of the workplace and protected workers from unfair supervision while increasing their productivity. The mills of the late 1800s were often chaotic, unpredictably dangerous places to work, characterized by frequent accidental mutilation and death. The Progressive social movement in US culture embraced this triumph of the engineer as a triumph for a humane, efficient and more just workplace. Unfortunately, the passions of the workers were seen as variables that it was necessary to control. The sense of craftsmanship and ownership of the task were reduced as centralized engineering departments broke down workers' assignments into highly regimented, mechanistic tasks paced by the schedule of the machine.

Within this context, the Hawthorne studies were undertaken to investigate the effect of work conditions on employee productivity. The earliest of the six studies, a joint effort between Hawthorne researchers and the National Research Council of the National Academy of Sciences, addressed the effect of light intensity. The results of these studies showed an unexpected relationship between the level of illumination and worker productivity. In fact, the test group, which was subjected to continually reduced lighting, showed an increase in productivity up to the point where the equipment was barely visible. In the final experiment of this stage, when experimenters only pretended to increase and decrease light intensity, workers commented that the supposedly brighter light was much more pleasant. Researchers concluded that uncontrolled factors played a much stronger role in productivity than lighting.

This work led to further studies which attempted to account for the unexpected findings by controlling other factors related to productivity. At this point, the National Research Council withdrew from the studies and Western Electric, with the later collaboration of Harvard University researchers, redefined the research purpose from a study of illumination to a study of the physical factors causing fatigue and monotony.

This phase, the Relay Assembly Test Room, was based around a group of five young women who were isolated from the shop floor and subjected to varied work conditions. The study continued for five years through thirteen experimental treatments which involved variations in the number and duration of rest breaks, and the length of the working day and working week. As conditions of work were progressively relaxed, production steadily rose, and when the original, more demanding work conditions were reintroduced, the workers' productivity dropped only slightly (still 30 per cent above initial levels). Absenteeism also dropped to one-third of the prior record for these workers and one-third of the average absenteeism of the workers on the main shop floor. Evidence to support hypotheses about the relief from fatigue or from monotony was inconclusive.

In the midst of the Relay Assembly Test Room research, two related studies were launched to test for other possible explanations of prior findings on productivity increases. In the initial illumination study, investigators had altered incentive systems due to the ability to control incentives more directly in a small group. Hypothesizing that the incentive system may have been the driver of productivity increases, two studies were undertaken which altered the incentive system but not the working conditions of test groups. While these groups showed some initial increase in productivity (15 per cent), the magnitude of the increase did not match the increase demonstrated in the illumination studies.

In response to findings, management promptly instituted rest breaks more widely in the company, but did not see any significant signs of increased productivity. In fact, it was concluded that the chief result had been to demonstrate the importance of employee attitudes and preoccupations. The friendlier, more participative style of supervision and the freedom from tight quotas and harsh discipline seemed to correspond with increases in both morale and productivity.

Investigators were impressed with the ability to improve productivity through work conditions, but were not certain about what conditions were superior. To shed light on the topic, they decided to interview employees directly. From 1928 to 1930, 21,000 employees were interviewed. Although management acted on many of the complaints, interview analysts found that the complaints were misleading when not considered in light of their context – the personal family and economic background of the workers. Empathetic listening and the recognition of the spillover between the employees' work and non-work sectors of life were found to be important management skills. Furthermore, the interview programme suggested that directly soliciting the opinions and perceptions of workers was a strong motivator.

Hawthorne investigators, noting social stratification between different job holders, concluded that another factor affecting productivity might have been social relations in the workplace. A final test was initiated which examined the relationship between a group of fourteen workers holding three different jobs who worked together to produce a single output. An unanticipated worker culture was revealed through group norms and activities such as the restriction of output, informal leadership patterns, friendships, job trading, cooperation and group discipline (see WORK SYSTEMS).

3 Analysis

The general conclusions which the researchers distilled from these six phases of investigation were:

1 individual work behaviour is rarely a pure consequence of simple cause and effect relationships, but rather is determined by a complex set of factors;

2 the informal or primary work group develops its own set of norms which mediates between the needs of the individuals and the institution;

3 the social structure of these informal groups is maintained through job-related symbols of prestige and power;

4 employees could no longer be considered a simple appendage of machinery, and the more a supervisor could learn about an individual worker's personal context, the better;

5 an awareness of employee sentiments and employee participation can reduce resistance to change;

6 and of most importance, the workplace is an interlocking social system, not simply a production system.

While these findings do not appear to be breakthrough discoveries when reflected upon from 70 years later, they represented a fundamental break with the management literature of that day. Investigators were solely concerned with the creation of the optimal method and physical setting for accomplishing a task. Their unit of analysis was initially the task, and later the worker, but never extended beyond to the interrelationship between workers or between workers and management.

The Hawthorne studies have been credited as the father of such far-ranging social science topics as client-centred therapy (Rogers 1942), small group behaviour (Homans 1941, 1950; Whyte 1943; Blau 1955; Cartwright and Zander 1968), organization theory (Barnard 1938; Simon 1945; Parsons 1960) and research methodology (Selltiz *et al.* 1959; Perrow 1972). Even today they still serve to enlighten management theorists interested in topics such as work teams and employee empowerment. While few consider scientific management to be a topic which currently provides any insight into management, the Hawthorne studies have withstood the test of time. While their findings have been enhanced and developed, they have not been replaced (see INDUSTRIAL DEMOCRACY).

Beyond the contributions to our understanding of workplace dynamics, the

Hawthorne studies also pioneered advances in methodology. Hawthorne investigators utilized field-based research, talking to practitioners rather than relying on the library and laboratory. They viewed matters from an interdisciplinary perspective. They focused on systemic issues, analysing the interrelationship between organization and environment. Finally, the studies demonstrated the merit of theory-generating as well as hypothesis-testing research.

The discovery of the so-called 'Hawthorne Effect' is another contribution of this work. While neither this term, nor the specific phenomenon it describes, were discussed by the original investigators, it is the most well-known contribution of the studies. The Hawthorne Effect refers to a temporary increase in employee productivity in response to personal attention by supervisors and the opportunity to participate in a new programme. The term is often misused to describe an improvement in productivity resulting from any type of change, rather than specifically from special attention to employees.

With regard to theory development, the Hawthorne Effect also highlighted a potential methodology problem in study design:

A second significant contribution of the Hawthorne experiments was the insight they provided into the reactivity of human subjects in experiments. The observation that measurements of behaviour in a controlled study were altered by subjects' knowledge that they were in an experiment later to be call the Hawthorne Effect, 'caused some consternation in both academic and industrial circles' at the time (Dickson and Roethlisberger, 1966, p.220).

(Adair 1984: 334)

As might be expected with any groundbreaking research, the Hawthorne studies are not without their critics. Ideological critics contend that the studies showed a pro-management bias in favour of manipulating the workforce (Bell 1947; Dunlop 1950). Yet the central view of management at the time was Taylorism, a theory completely ignoring the human element. The Hawthorne studies pushed far beyond the creation of the most efficient task to consider group context and supervisor attention to workers.

Methodological critics (Argyle 1953; Carey 1967; Parsons 1974, 1978; Franke and Kaul 1978; Bramel and Friend 1981) contend that the lack of adequate controls in the study, the changes in incentive plans and the changes in the number of participants during the study undermine the validity of the findings. Yet, the Hawthorne investigators never suggested that their findings were replicable. They never denied the important contributions of pay and physical qualities of work. They merely increased the list of factors contributing to performance by adding the human social dimension.

Most important, these findings should be considered in light of the circumstances in which they were undertaken. The intent of the investigators was not to run a carefully controlled study to confirm their hypotheses concerning the effect of various factors upon worker productivity. The studies were exploratory in nature. Their goal was to generate hypotheses to be tested by future investigators (and on that count they were very successful). Under the guidance of Harvard's Elton Mayo (see MAYO, G.E.), such an approach led to the creation of the field of applied social anthropology, with such protégés as George Homans, Lloyd Warner and Fritz Roethlisberger.

Likewise, it should be remembered that investigators unearthed determinants of productivity which they had no expectation of finding when they undertook the studies. It would have been impossible to design studies that carefully controlled for factors which no one considered to have bearing upon productivity. While the studies were not methodologically perfect, this fact should not decrease the importance of their findings. Future work stimulated by the Hawthorne studies confirms their findings, and stands in defence of their initial worth. Criticisms of the studies are also plagued by a reliance on an inaccurate history of work conditions, misquotes and interpretation of original data and a general thirst to denigrate the revolutionary work which these studies represent.

According to Adair: 'In the first 15 experimental psychology textbooks I examined with reference to Hawthorne, not one had described the studies accurately' (1984: 335). Several misrepresentations of the circumstances of the studies have perpetuated unfounded criticisms of the studies over the years. Critics have proposed alternative explanations for productivity increases based on their misunderstanding of the environment.

(1) *Discipline*. Some have claimed that discipline was a cause of the improved productivity of the relay test room, citing as evidence that two workers were replaced in the test room during the period of study. Yet any who left the studies did so voluntarily, not at the request of supervisors. In addition, it has been documented that participation in the studies was a welcome reprieve from autocratic supervision on the main floor (Carey 1967; Franke and Kaul 1978).

(2) *Fear of job loss*. Fear of job loss is cited as another reason that productivity increased, particularly in light of the Great Crash. In point of fact, the late 1920s and early 1930s were a tremendous boom time in the US economy despite the Great Crash. It was not until a few years later that the general economy felt the repercussions. This was also a particularly successful period for Western Electric (Franke and Kaul 1978).

(3) *Worker learning due to enhanced feedback*. Critics claim that test room employees received more feedback on their results than other workers. However, the tasks assigned were a simple fifty movements with which the workers were already familiar. Feedback on performance was always ample, even prior to the test room. Workers knew at the start of the day how many blank relay blocks they had to build and knew through the day how many remained in front of them awaiting complete assembly; feedback was thus instantaneous (Parsons 1974).

In final defence of the studies, interviews conducted with Hawthorne participants some fifty years later support the original investigators' conclusions. Participants suggested that management style, group dynamics and the prestige of being chosen for the assignment all contributed to their satisfaction in participating in the studies. They discounted factors such as heightened awareness of productivity levels and others suggested by critics. Overall, participants' recollections validate the contribution of the studies.

In support of group dynamics, the workers reported: 'We had a lot of fun there in that test room.... We all became close. You know, we'd go out together... meet at each other's houses and have dinner. We were a group' (Sonnenfeld 1985: 124). Concerning productivity levels, supervisor Donald Chipman commented: 'Each girl [study participants were teenagers at the time of the field experiments] knew at the end of the day or the following morning, first thing the next morning, what her output had been for the day before... and they knew what the norm was and they knew what the top output was, and what poor performance was... everybody knew what the day's output was' (Sonnenfeld 1985: 124).

4 Evaluation

In light of both criticism and support of the Hawthorne studies, several conclusions can be drawn concerning their contribution to the field of management. Their most significant contribution was to redefine the field of management research. The Hawthorne investigators were the first behavioural scientists to go into industry. They actually observed the phenomenon under study. Their close interaction with the field allowed them to generate new hypotheses when their initial concern over physical work conditions was not supported. The use of interviews to determine worker perceptions of physical conditions uncovered the importance of management concern for employee welfare. The studies highlighted the potential contribution of anthropological techniques such as ethnography to the study of management science.

Beyond contributions to the methodology of management study, the Hawthorne tests fostered the development of theoretical concepts as well. The studies recognized alternative management styles to the command and control style which was popular at the time. The realization that individual work behaviour is determined by a complex set of factors broadened the horizons of researchers beyond the narrowly prescribed set of factors discussed at that time.

The most significant contribution of the Hawthorne studies was to break the boundaries of scientific management and pioneer a new paradigm in management research. The discovery that physical work conditions were not of primary importance to worker productivity forced researchers to shift their focus from the individual unit of analysis to other contextual factors which affect the work environment.

5 Conclusions

What is revolutionary? Consider the contributions of Nobel Prize winning novelist Sinclair Lewis in *Mainstreet* for his now dated glimpse into small town life, or sociologist Max Weber's *On Bureaucracy* for his appreciation of the institutionalization of charismatic leadership into orderly delegated hierarchy and fairness in decision making. Each of these men pioneered breakthroughs in his respective field which opened a door to a new paradigm. Subsequently, contributions of their revolutionary work are often downplayed as the work is interpreted in the light of modern innovations. What is ignored is the fact that their fields would not have made such progress were it not for their initial contributions in defining the trajectory of the field. Such is the case of the Hawthorne studies. Discounted by some for their methodological imperfections, their detractors fail to realize their contributions to redefining the field of management. These studies were the first visit of behavioural scientists into the workplace. Their methods were the ethnographic tools of anthropologists – nonjudgemental participant observation. The Hawthorne studies opened the door to study of the effects of social context and managerial style in the workplace. Contemporary management approaches such as team leadership, total quality management, group dynamics, quality of working life and job enrichment, corporate cultures, and the like, all share strong indebtedness to the Hawthorne studies.

JEFFREY A. SONNENFELD
EMORY UNIVERSITY

JENNIFER M. MYATT
EMORY UNIVERSITY

Further reading

(References cited in the text marked *)

* Adair, J.G. (1984) 'The Hawthorne effect: a reconsideration of the methodological artifact', *Journal of Applied Psychology* 69 (2): 334–5. (Discusses the methodological implications of the Hawthorne Effect.)
* Argyle, M. (1953) 'The relay Assembly Test Room in retrospect', *Occupational Psychology* 27: 98–103. (Retrospective methodological study of the Hawthorne experiments.)
* Barnard, C.I. (1938) *The Function of the Executive*, Cambridge, MA: Harvard University Press. (Classic text analysing the nature and purpose of executive management, and that of organization behaviour.)
* Bell, D. (1947) 'Adjust men to machines', *Commentary* 3: 79–88. (Critical assessment of the Hawthorne experiments arguing against the Taylorist trend.)
* Blau, P.M. (1955) *The Dynamics of Bureaucracy*, Chicago, IL: University of Chicago Press. (Text analysing interpersonal relations within government agencies.)
* Bramel, D. and Friend, R. (1981) 'Hawthorne: the myth of the docile worker and class bias in psychology', *American Psychologist* 36: 867–78. (Presents a strong argument against the validity of the Hawthorne findings.)
* Carey, A. (1967) 'The Hawthorne studies as radical criticism', *American Sociological Review* 32: 403–16. (First major critical analysis; based on official accounts.)
* Cartwright, D. and Zander, A. (1968) *Group Dynamics*, 3rd edn, New York: Harper & Row. (Useful text on the dynamics of small groups.)
* Dunlop, J.T. (1950) 'Framework for the analysis of industrial relations: two views', *Industrial and Labor Relations Review* 3: 383–93. (Interesting argument against Taylorism and its effects on the workforce.)
* Franke, R.H. and Kaul, J.D. (1978) 'The Hawthorne experiments: first statistical interpretation', *American Sociology Review* 43: 623–43.

(Statistical reworking of the Relay Assembly Test Room data.)

* Homans, G.C. (1941) *'The Western Electric Researchers'*, National Research Council Report, New York: Reinhold. (One of the first studies of the data emerging from the Hawthorne studies. Covers work and industry fatigue and its relation to industrial production.)

* Homans, G.C. (1950) *The Human Group*, New York: Harcourt, Brace and World. (Classic social anthropological text on group behaviour.)

Landsberger, H.A. (1958) *Hawthorne Revisited, Management and the Worker, Its Critics and Developments in Human Relations and Industry*, Ithaca, NY: Cornell University Press. (First response to early sociological critics.)

Mayo, E. (1933) *The Human Problems of an Industrial Civilization*, New York: Macmillan. (Published version of Mayo's Lowell Lecture Series describing the Hawthorne studies.)

* Parsons, H.M. (1974) 'What happened at Hawthorne?', *Science* 183: 922–32. A well-balanced critical analysis of the Hawthorne findings.)

* Parsons, H.M. (1978) 'What caused the Hawthorne effect?', *Administration and Society* 10: 259–82. (Methodological critique.)

* Parsons, T. (1960) *Structure and Process in Modern Societies*, Glencoe, IL: Illinois Free Press. (Describes the Hawthorne experiments within the larger context of organizational theory.)

* Perrow, C. (1972) *Complex Organizations*, Glenview, IL: Scott Foresman & Co. (Critical essay on the nature and workings of complex organizations.)

* Roethlisberger, F.J. and Dickson, W.J. (1939) *Management and the Worker*, Cambridge, MA: Harvard University Press. (Initial report presenting the results of the field experiments.)

* Rogers, C.R. (1942) *Counseling and Psychotherapy: Newer Concepts in Practice*, Boston: Houghton Mifflin. (The pioneer of modern counselling cites the Hawthorne studies as an important influence.)

* Selltiz, C., Deutsch, M. and Cook, S.W. (1959) *Research Methods in Social Relations*, New York: Holt, Rinehart & Winston. (Useful text on research methodology which stresses the importance of the Hawthorne studies.)

* Simon, H.A. (1945) *Administrative Behavior*, New York: The Free Press. (Studies the process of decision making in administrative organizations)

Sonnenfeld, J.A. (1982) 'Clarifying critical confusion in the Hawthorne hysteria', *American Psychologist* 37: 1397–9. (Response to a critique of the Hawthorne studies published by Bramel and Friend in 1981.)

Sonnenfeld, J.A. (1983) 'Academic learning, worker learning, and the Hawthorne studies', *Social Forces* 61 (3): 904–9. (Review of the official Hawthorne records and conversations which sheds light on erroneous interpretations of findings.)

* Sonnenfeld, J.A. (1985) 'Shedding light on the Hawthorne studies', *Journal of Occupational Behavior* 6 (1): 111–30. (An in-depth description of the six stages of the studies and review of the various critics and defenders of the work.)

* Whitehead, T.N. (1938) *The Industrial Worker*, vols 1 and 2, Cambridge, MA: Harvard University Press. (Ethnographic chronicling of the logs of the Hawthorne observers.)

* Whyte, W.F. (1943) *Street Corner Society*, Chicago, IL: University of Chicago Press. (Outlines the social structure of an Italian slum.)

See also: GROUPS AND TEAMS; HUMAN RELATIONS; HUMAN RESOURCE MANAGEMENT; INDUSTRIAL DEMOCRACY; LEADERSHIP; MAYO, G.E.; MOTIVATION AND SATISFACTION; OCCUPATIONAL PSYCHOLOGY; ORGANIZATION BEHAVIOUR; PRODUCTIVITY; TAYLOR, F.W.; WORK AND ORGANIZATION SYSTEMS

Related topics in the IEBM: ORGANIZATION BEHAVIOUR, HISTORY OF; WEBER, M.

Human capital

Overview

The idea that expenditure on such things as education, on-the-job training and healthcare can be thought of as an investment in an individual's future ability to generate income is not a new one. An early statement of the concept of human capital can be found in Adam Smith's *Wealth of Nations*:

> When any expensive machine is erected, the extraordinary work to be performed by it before it is worn out, it must be expected, will replace the capital laid out upon it, with at least the ordinary profits. A man educated at the expence of much labour and time to any of those employments which require extraordinary dexterity and skill, may be compared to one of those expensive machines. The work which he learns to perform, it must be expected, over and above the usual wages of common labour, will replace to him the whole expence of his education, with at least the ordinary profits of an equally valuable capital. It must do this too in a reasonable time, regard being had to the very uncertain duration of human life, in the same manner as to the more certain duration of the machine. The difference between the wages of skilled labour and those of common labour is founded upon this principle.
>
> (Smith [1776] 1976: 118)

While human capital theory has been developed and expanded over the last two centuries, a number of its basic ideas are contained in the above quotation from Adam Smith. First, expenditure on the productivity-enhancing skills of people has similarities with investment in physical capital which can be expected to generate income in the future. Second, expenditure on education, on-the-job training, healthcare or migration to areas with greater employment opportunities, can all be thought of as investments which are normally rewarded in the future by higher income. Third, differing levels of investment in human capital can explain productivity differences between individuals and therefore differences in their rates of pay. Fourth, it is in the individual's interests to invest in human capital when the net benefits exceed the net benefits of investing in an alternative asset.

It is not only private individuals who make decisions to invest in human capital but also in most countries, the state undertakes considerable investment in this area, for example in education and health. One rationale for this intervention is that benefits from investment in human capital accrue not only to the individuals directly involved but to society at large; for example, a more educated and informed community should make better political decisions and raising public health standards reduces the incidence of disease to everyone.

The calculation of private and social rates of return to investment in human capital is the subject of the next section. We will then consider the decision to invest in different forms of on-the-job training, and look at the estimation of earnings functions as a method for calculating rates of return to education and training. Finally, we will outline some of the criticisms which have been made of the human capital model.

1 The costs and benefits of investment in human capital

The private calculation

The individual's problem is to maximize their utility over their lifetime given the costs and benefits associated with investment in human capital. These can take either a direct monetary form or involve foregone opportunities or non-pecuniary costs and benefits. As much of the literature focuses on education as a form of human capital investment, it will be used here as an example.

An individual deciding whether to undertake a university course at the end of secondary education needs to compare the costs and benefits of continuing in education. There are both direct and indirect costs. Direct costs include tuition fees, books, equipment and any additional living costs perhaps of moving to another town. Indirect costs include what is usually the largest cost of continuing in education, the foregone earnings from employment while undertaking full-time study. There may also be other non-pecuniary costs such as separation from family and friends.

Against these costs, the individual must weigh the potential benefits from education. On average, more educated people earn higher incomes than less educated people. There may also be non-pecuniary benefits from investment in education; for example, it may increase the choice of occupations and create the opportunities for more congenial employment. There are also the consumption benefits of learning and knowledge for its own sake (see TRAINING, ECONOMICS OF).

The choice facing the individual deciding whether or not to continue on to university education is summarized in Figure 1. The line marked 'university' represents the expected income stream of the individual who decides to continue on to university. It shows that initially the costs of this strategy exceed the benefits but with the completion of education,

there is a substantial increase in income. The line marked 'secondary' illustrates the expected income stream of the person if they do not enter university, but rather go straight into employment. In this case the individual will have a higher initial income than as a university student but at an older age, can expect a lower income than a university graduate. A comparison of these two income streams shows whether further education is a worthwhile investment.

However, in order to compare the true benefits and costs of education, it is necessary to take into account the fact that they accrue to the individual at different stages of their life. There are two methods commonly used in these types of calculations; comparing the net present values (NPV) of each option and second, estimating the internal rate of return.

The NPV of a university education is the difference between the discounted future earnings of a university graduate and the discounted costs incurred in undertaking that education (including the opportunity cost of foregone earnings while studying). If this is positive, university education is worthwhile. Putting this more formally:

$$NPV = \sum_{i=21}^{60} \Delta \frac{income_i}{(1+r)^{i-21}} - \sum_{j=18}^{21} \frac{costs}{(1+r)^{j-18}} \quad (1)$$

Where r is the interest rate and it is assumed the student is aged 18 years, would spend four years at university and retire at age 60 years.

An alternative approach is to calculate the internal rate of return to the investment. This is the rate of discount ρ which will equate the income benefits from additional education with the costs associated with acquiring that education. This can then be compared with the rate of return on alternative investments to see whether to invest in education or not.

$$\sum_{i=21}^{60} \Delta \frac{income}{(1+\rho)^{i-21}} = \sum_{j=18}^{21} \frac{costs_i}{(1+\rho)^{j-18}} \quad (2)$$

While potential students may not make these detailed calculations formally, there is evidence from the fluctuating numbers of students in tertiary education, that people do make some rough calculations of the returns

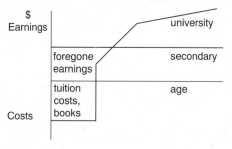

Figure 1 The expected income streams from alternative education decisions

to education before undertaking further study (see for example, Freeman 1976). A range of factors will determine the numbers who decide to undertake university education. For example, those who place a very high value on income now rather than income in the future are less likely to continue with university education. These people who give little weight to the future, are called present-orientated. Other factors that will influence the decision on continuing in education are any changes in the private costs of education (both direct and indirect) or in the income differential between those with a university degree and those without.

The social calculation

As already noted, in most countries, the state spends considerable amounts on investment in human capital. This raises the question, from a social point of view, is this investment worthwhile or should the funds be put to alternative uses? Calculations such as those described above for the private individual, can be undertaken for the social return to education. These need to include, in addition to the costs and benefits outlined for the individual, any additional costs associated with public subsidies to education and the additional social benefits of having a more highly educated population. While the private benefits of education include post-tax income, the social benefits include pre-tax income.

Table 1 reproduces some broad summary statistics on the estimated private and social rates of return to education (Psacharopoulos 1985). As these figures represent a summary across a broad range of countries, they should be only taken as a rough indication of the rates of return to education in particular countries. There are a number of interesting features of this table. In each country group, the rate of return to investment in primary education was higher than for the higher education levels. There was also a pattern of lower rates of return in the higher income country groups where human capital resources were in more plentiful supply. A final notable feature of the table is that the social rate is well above the private rate of return.

There has been considerable controversy over the calculation of both private and social rates of return to education, particularly with respect to which costs and benefits should be included. It is also difficult to disentangle the 'pure' effects of education from the combined effects of ability, motivation and education on income.

2 General and specific training

Investment in productivity-enhancing skills not only takes place in a formal classroom environment but also while on the job (see TRAINING). Becker (1975) distinguished two polar cases of on-the-job training, general and specific. General training is defined as training which will raise productivity in many firms, not just in the firm providing it. Some examples are secretarial, computing and plumbing skills. 'Employees pay for general

Table 1 Average returns to education by country type and level (per cent per year)

Region/country type	Private			Social		
	Primary	*Secondary*	*Higher*	*Primary*	*Secondary*	*Higher*
Africa	26	17	13	45	26	32
Asia	27	15	13	31	15	18
Latin America	26	18	16	32	23	23
Intermediate	13	10	8	17	13	13
Advanced	n.a.	11	9	n.a.	12	12

Source: Psacharopoulos (1985)

on-the-job training by receiving wages below what they would receive elsewhere' (Becker 1975: 21). Firms will only provide this type of training in transferable skills if the wage paid to the trainee equals their contribution to output. Apprenticeship schemes are one example of a means by which firms do provide general training for a range of skilled occupations such as plumbers, electricians and hairdressers.

In contrast, specific training only raises productivity in the firm where the training takes place and has little or no effect on productivity elsewhere (see PRODUCTIVITY). Examples include training in a particular firm's computer or library system, learning to operate a telephone exchange where telephone services are supplied by a monopoly and training with a sophisticated piece of army equipment. These skills cannot be readily transferred to other firms. The costs and benefits of specific training are shared by the firm and the employee. 'The shares of each depend on the relations between quit rates and wages, layoff rates and profits, and on other factors not discussed here, such as the cost of funds, attitude toward risk and desires for liquidity' (Becker 1975: 30). The employee will be reluctant to invest in firm-specific skills if there is a high probability of losing this job and the firm will be reluctant to invest where there is a high quit rate.

The potential income streams for an individual choosing whether to undertake no training (the line marked W0), some general training (Wg) or some specific training (Ws) are illustrated in Figure 2. Both sorts of training make the experience earnings profile steeper than in the case of no training. The rate of increase in earnings with age declines as in the case of formal education, it is assumed that there is some depreciation of human capital with time. There is also a reduced amount of investment with rising experience as the time remaining to reap the benefits of such investment becomes shorter and the opportunity cost of foregone earnings rises. Initially, the income of an employee engaging in firm-specific training is above that of an employee undertaking general training because the firm bears some of the costs of the firm-specific training, but the income gains to the employee

from this type of training are not so great at higher levels of experience. In a competitive labour market the rate of return on each form of investment in training should be equalized at the margin.

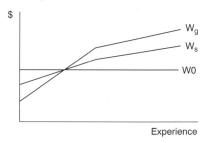

Figure 2 General and specific training

3 The earnings function

A technique which has been extensively applied to the calculation of the rate of return to both education and on-the-job training is regression analysis (see PAYMENT SYSTEMS). As it is very difficult to observe a monetary measure of investment in human capital, Mincer (1974) proposed a time equivalent measure of investment in both education (formal schooling) and on-the-job training. An individual's investment in formal schooling, under certain assumptions can be approximated by the years spent in education. Similarly, investment in on-the-job training can be approximated by years of working experience. Where detailed work histories have been unavailable, researchers have used potential work experience, that is the difference between the current age of the individual and their age on leaving school. Mincer proposed two functional forms for the inclusion of working experience in the earnings regression but the most widely applied form is the quadratic (see also Murphy and Welch 1990). The quadratic form allows for the fact that individuals reduce their investment in training as their experience increases and that there is some depreciation in the existing investments. Earnings functions based on this work by Mincer have been estimated across a wide range of countries and time periods. The following equation presents the general form:

$$LnY = \alpha + \beta S + \gamma E + \delta E^2 + \varepsilon Z + u \qquad (3)$$

where LnY is the natural logarithm of earnings or income, S is the years of schooling, E is working experience, Z a vector of measured control characteristics, α, β, γ, δ, ε are estimated coefficients and u is a normally distributed error term assumed independent of the other variables in the regression. The use of the semi-logarithmic functional form means that the coefficients on each variable measure the percentage increase in earnings with an additional year of schooling or experience holding all other variables included in the regression constant.

Mincer's original results are presented as an example of this methodology. They are derived from data on annual earnings of 31,093 white non-farm, non-student males in the USA in 1959 (Mincer 1974: 92). He estimated the following regression equation:

$$LnY = 6.20 + 0.107S + 0.81E - 0.0012E^2$$
$$(72.3) \quad (75.5) \quad (-55.8)$$
$$= R^2 = 0.285 \qquad (4)$$

where the figures in brackets are the t statistics on each coefficient and R^2 is the coefficient of determination which shows how much of the variation in earnings is explained by the variables on the right hand side of the equation. Schooling and experience explain about a quarter of the variation in earnings between individuals included in this equation; that is most of the earnings differential cannot be explained by these measured human capital variables.

According to these results, US males in 1959 on average increased their income by 10.7 per cent for each additional year spent in school. The first year of working experience added 8.1 per cent to earnings. Additional experience raised earnings further for the first 33.75 years of experience, taking into account both the experience and experienced squared terms. For males with over 33.75 years of experience, additional experience reduced earnings as the effects of declining

investment and depreciation of existing investments came to dominate.

This methodology has been used to address a wide range of economic questions, but one of the major focuses of researchers estimating earnings regressions has been the explanation of earnings differentials between different groups in society. These include male/female, immigrant/native born, and racial earnings differentials (see Borjas 1994; Elliott 1991; Gunderson 1989; Sloane 1985 for surveys of studies in these areas). A typical approach, following the work of Blinder (1973), has been to estimate earnings regressions for the two groups the researcher wishes to compare; for example males and females. The question is then asked, how much of the observed earnings differential can be explained by differences in human capital endowments (the Ss and Es in equation (3)), and how much by differences between males and females in the rewards for these endowments as measured by the coefficient differences (the α, β, γ, δ, ε)? Different returns to investment in human capital may reflect factors on either the supply or demand side of the labour market. On the supply side of the labour market, for example, females may decide to concentrate on non-market work and therefore not invest in skills which would raise their productivity and earnings in the labour market (Mincer and Polachek 1974). On the demand side of the labour market, discrimination against individuals on the basis of sex or race may reduce the rewards for any given investment (Elliott 1991; Sloane 1985).

Results for countries such as the USA, Great Britain and Australia suggest the measured human capital endowments of males and females are very similar, what differs is the reward for these endowments in the labour market. Estimates for these countries, however, suggest that different levels of education and working experience are more important in determining differences in earnings between racial and ethnic groups.

4 General criticisms of the human capital approach

The human capital model outlined above postulates that people's earnings will reflect their contribution to output and that this contribution is influenced greatly by the extent to which they have invested in human capital to raise their productivity. The main criticisms of the theory relate to whether education and training do in fact, raise productivity. There has been little research done into comparing the human capital approach with theories from outside economics. Blaug (1976), for example, argued that any psychological theory of learning curves could account for rising earnings profiles.

One alternative explanation of the higher earnings of educated people is offered by the screening hypothesis which argues that education does not raise productivity but rather acts as a signalling device for pre-existing abilities (Arrow 1973). If the most able and highly motivated people continue with education, it will be in the employers' interests to use educational attainment as a method for selecting employees and fixing earnings even if the education adds nothing to employees' productivity. However, if education acts as an efficient screening device, it may still perform the socially productive role of placing the right people in the right jobs. Against the screening hypothesis it is argued that while it offers an explanation of why starting salaries may differ by education level, it has more difficulty in explaining why these differences persist once the employer has knowledge of a worker's productivity. It also has difficulty in explaining why there is a positive association between higher levels of national income and more educated populations.

Other criticisms of human capital theory have focused on issues such as the neglect of the role of innate abilities, motivation and family background in determining earnings and employment outcomes (see MOTIVATION AND SATISFACTION). Where studies have been able to take such factors into account, they generally still find a role for education and training in raising incomes. In fact, Ashenfelter and Krueger's (1994) study of the rate of return to education for identical twins in the USA, found that following adjustments for measurement error, the rate of return was actually higher than previously estimated.

5 Conclusion

Modern developments in human capital theory have made a considerable contribution to our knowledge of how labour markets work and have offered guidance to education policy makers throughout the world. The growing collection of household-based data sets and access to computing facilities have made the calculation of rates of return to education and training much easier in a wide variety of circumstances. There are still major outstanding issues, such as understanding the relationship between education, pre-existing abilities and earnings, which require further investigation. It is also important that the results of these studies are widely available to education policy makers.

A major issue for the future includes better estimation of the differences between the private and social rates of return to education and training. In a period where governments are looking more closely at public investments and the value of maintaining public provision of certain services, education expenditure is likely to be subject to more stringent review. A clear idea of the costs and benefits associated with public subsidies to education should improve decision making.

Further research on the determinants of earnings of various groups within society should increase our understanding of the effects over time of policies directed at affirmative action and anti-discrimination. Research on the role of human capital in explaining earnings differentials remains important.

ANNE DALY
UNIVERSITY OF CANBERRA

Further reading

(References cited in the text marked *)

* Arrow, K. (1973) 'Higher education as a filter', *Journal of Public Economics* 2: 193–216. (This article presents the screening hypothesis as an

alternative to the human capital explanation of the earnings differential between people with different levels of education.)

* Ashenfelter, O. and Krueger, A. (1994) 'Estimates of the economic return to schooling from a new sample of twins', *American Economic Review* 85 (5): 1157–73. (This article estimates the rate of return to additional schooling for a sample of genetically identical twins in the USA.)

* Becker, G. (1975) *Human Capital: A Theoretical and Empirical Analysis*, 2nd edn, New York: NBER. (This book presents the general arguments of the human capital approach and some empirical estimates using data from the USA.)

* Blaug, M. (1976) 'The empirical status of human capital theory: a slightly jaundice survey', *Journal of Economic Literature* 14 (3): 827–55. (This article outlines some of the major arguments against human capital theory.)

* Blinder, A. (1973) 'Wage discrimination: reduced form and structural estimates', *Journal of Human Resources* 8 (4): 436–55. (This article presents the methodology for separating the difference in earnings into that part which is due to differences in human capital endowments and that part which is due to differences in the rewards for these endowments.)

* Borjas, G. (1994) 'The economics of immigration', *Journal of Economic Literature* 32 (4): 1667–717. (This article surveys the empirical estimates of the costs and benefits of immigration.)

* Elliott, R. (1991) *Labor Economics, A Comparative Text*, London: McGraw-Hill. (This textbook contains a discussion of both theoretical and empirical aspects of the human capital approach with examples from a range of countries.)

* Freeman, R. (1976) *The Overeducated American*, New York: Academic Press. (This book examines the effects of the arrival of the post-Second World War baby boom in the labour market on the returns to college education in the USA and the effects on people's decisions to undertake further education.)

* Gunderson, M. (1989) 'Male–female wage differentials and policy responses', *Journal of Economic Literature* 27 (1): 46–72. (This article surveys the estimates of the sources of male/female earnings differentials and considers how successful policies have been in changing outcomes.)

* Mincer, J. (1974) *Schooling, Experience and Earnings*, New York: NBER. (This book presents both a theoretical and empirical discussion of the human capital model. It sets out the theoretical justification for the estimation of earnings functions.)

* Mincer, J. and Polachek, S. (1974) 'Family investments in human capital: earnings of women', *Journal of Political Economy* 82 (2): 76–108. (This article argues that the lower earnings for women compared with men can in large part be explained by a rational decision not to invest in skills which raise market productivity and earnings when women do not anticipate spending much of their lives in paid employment.)

* Murphy, K. and Welch, F. (1990) 'Empirical age-earnings profiles', *Journal of Labor Economics* 8 (2). (This article focuses on one technical aspect estimating earnings functions, namely the functional form for experience.)

* Psacharopoulos, G. (1985) 'Returns to education: a further international update and implications', *Journal of Human Resources* 20 (4): 583–97. (An international survey of estimates of the private and social rates of return to education following earlier studies by the author.)

* Sloane, P. (1985) 'Discrimination in the labour market', in Carline, D., Pissarides, C., Siebert, S. and Sloane, P. (eds), *Labour Economics*, London: Longman. (This book contains detailed chapters on human capital and discrimination including both theoretical and empirical results.)

* Smith, A. (1776) *The Wealth of Nations*, Harmondsworth: Penguin, 1982. (Smith's classic work, in which he explains how an economy operates and how it can grow.)

See also: COLLECTIVE BARGAINING; EMPLOYMENT AND UNEMPLOYMENT, ECONOMICS OF; HUMAN RESOURCE DEVELOPMENT; HUMAN RESOURCE MANAGEMENT; INDUSTRIAL AND LABOUR RELATIONS; MANAGEMENT DEVELOPMENT; PERSONNEL MANAGEMENT

Related topics in the IEBM: SMITH, A.

Human relations

1 **Historical background**
2 **Evolving trends**
3 **Evaluation and conclusions**

Overview

Broadly speaking, the two major strands in modern management are recognized to be *scientific management*, based on the logic of economic man and efficiency, and *human relations*, based on that of the social individual and sentiment. The human relations movement, as an academic discipline, grew out of scientific management in the 1930s. Both sides aimed at achieving high productivity, but scientific management sought to adapt worker to task whereas human relations veered towards adjusting task to worker. Since its academic accreditation, the human relations movement has developed through various schools: mainly group dynamics and industrial relations, to organizational humanism, through to individualism and systemic interdependence. The evolving trend is towards the growth of mutually accountable, self-managing teams (against hierarchical relationships) working in the flexible organization which sees itself an integral part of the overall ecosystem.

1 Historical background

In the second half of the eighteenth century, industrialization and the emergence of factories broke the direct relationship between employer and employee. The new ways of working introduced the supervisor/manager as intermediary and required different methods to direct workers. In tune with the generally accepted mores of the time ('the hungriest worker is the best worker'), and with labour supply outpacing demand, factory wages were kept very low and women and children were engaged to supplement the workforce at minimal cost.

Not everyone held the same opinions as the factory-owners, however. In the vanguard of those who saw things differently was the Welshman Robert Owen (1771–1858). He is perhaps the first exemplar of modern personnel management (see PERSONNEL MANAGEMENT). In charge of textile mills in the north of England, he introduced many reforms during his years there between 1800 and 1828. Owen *inter alia* stopped employing children under 12 years of age, a very radical measure at the time; created good working conditions; and provided proper meal facilities in the workplace. Ahead of his time, he also introduced the right of appeal: 'If anyone thought that the superintendent did not do justice, he or she had a right to complain to me or, in my absence, to the master of the mills' (Urwick and Brech 1946: 51). Seeing the factory as central to the community, he arranged for the paving of streets, organized the collection of refuse, built better houses for the people and opened evening centres for education and recreation. All this, he insisted, was not 'welfare' but, related to the good profits the mills were making, evidence that 'personnel management pays'.

In the USA the Social Gospel emerged in the late nineteenth century as a counterpoint to Social Darwinism. Essentially welfarist and aiming at industrial betterment, it asked employers to improve working conditions. Direct managerial involvement was one of its tenets. Whiting Williams (1878–1975), a keen follower, went out as a worker to study first-hand industrial relations in coal mines, steel mills and elsewhere. He arrived at some startlingly modern views on the value of work to the individual. All persons, whether workers or managers, measured their individual worth and value to society in terms of their jobs. Jobs influenced their standing, as without them people were isolated both economically and from their community: 'the worker's vision of himself, his friends, his employer and the whole of his world to come is circumscribed by his job' (Williams 1920: 299). Whiting Williams thus placed the individual firmly in the context of the groups to which he or she belonged.

Another pioneer was Mary Parker Follett (1868–1933) (see FOLLETT, M.P.). A political scientist who lectured on business management in the late 1920s, Follett went further in emphasizing the importance of the group. For her the basic unit of society was the group individual. Using elements of the then new Gestalt psychology, Follett saw a business as both a social institution and an economic unit and developed insights into conflict, leadership, power and authority which were to underpin the thinking of Rensis Likert and Douglas McGregor.

In the early decades of the twentieth century, there were some enlightened employers who appreciated the value of a committed workforce. The majority, however, followed the precepts of scientific management propagated by Frederick W. Taylor (1856–1915) (see TAYLOR, F.W.), based on the strict division of labour: managers commanded and workers as 'hands' carried out the orders. The scientific method was to find the ablest workers and create the right working conditions to maximize production. Workers received their appropriate reward exclusively through their piecework pay packet. Little regard was paid to human relations.

The 1930s: the Hawthorne experiments and the human relations school

In late 1924 the Council of Industrial Lighting commissioned the Massachusetts Institute of Technology to research the effect of workplace illumination on worker productivity at the Hawthorne plant of Western Electric. By April 1927 the experimenters still could not establish any direct relationship between lighting and productivity. The tests were therefore abandoned, but one of the researchers was allowed to continue in the Relay Assembly Test Room. He established that the upward trend in output continued irrespective of changes in working conditions, and even

when the lighting in the room was reduced to the level of moonlight.

Elton Mayo (1880–1949) (see MAYO, G.E.), an Australian who had studied logic, philosophy and medicine, was at this time a professor at Harvard University. He had also been consulted by the Council of Industrial Lighting in 1927 but became more closely involved only when he visited the plant in 1929. The remarkable change in mental attitude in the group, Mayo felt, was due to the more considerate approach of the researcher. This factor, he thought, was the key to solving the problem. He therefore arranged for the experiments specifically to follow this more cooperative approach: the supervisor was to be open and friendly and the researcher nondirective in interviews. In the freer environment, the women talked more. The earlier interview of thirty minutes now grew to ninety minutes. They became more friendly and developed personal relationships with one another both in and out of work. Morale improved and productivity increased. This result, Mayo concluded, was due to the personal interest being paid to the workers and the more cooperative supervision (Mayo 1933). Thus, in his eyes, the link between supervision, morale and productivity was established, and soon became the keystone of the human relations movement.

Other experiments in group behaviour also took place at the Hawthorne plant. In the Bank Wiring Room, where the supervisory role remained unchanged, the men worked as teams. An analysis of social relations revealed informal groupings within the formal structure. The workers had a clear-cut idea of what constituted a fair day's work and doctored the production reports to conform to this standard. They also used their own devices to discipline those who violated the group norm. The researchers found that the workers restricted output during both good and bad times. They concluded that sentiment affected the workers as much as economic return. Accordingly, to get the best out of the workers, management had to take account of the 'logic of sentiments' as well as the 'logic of efficiency'. Balancing both required a different mix of managerial skills: managers had to understand human behaviour and learn how best to communicate with and motivate the workers. Technical skills alone were not enough to deal with behaviour examined at the Hawthorne plant (see HAWTHORNE EXPERIMENTS; WORK AND ORGANIZATION SYSTEMS).

Over time Mayo changed his interpretation, almost completely removing the logic of efficiency from the equation. For Mayo the problem was that managers thought the answers to industrial problems resided in technical efficiency when in fact the problems were social and human ones. Authority, he concluded, had to be based on social skills in securing cooperation rather than on technical skills or expertise.

Mayo's detractors claim he interpreted the results to corroborate with his own view: that of the organization as a social system, with workers being dealt with through 'the psychology of the total situation'. Fritz Roethlisberger, the co-author of the Hawthorne official results, recalled: 'Mayo was an adventurer in the realm of ideas. . . the [Hawthorne] data were not his; the results were not his; but the interpretations of what the results meant and the new questions and hypotheses that emerged from them were his' (Roethlisberger 1977: 50–1). Controversy over the Hawthorne experiments was still ongoing in the late 1990s.

The 1940s and 1950s: group dynamics and industrial relations

At the same time in the 1920s as Whiting Williams and Mary Parker Follett were emphasizing the importance of the group, the sociologist, Eduard Lindeman, was developing ways of observing and categorizing group interactions and classifying attitudes of group members (see GROUPS AND TEAMS). The Hawthorne experiments and their Mayoist interpretation now confirmed the group, rather than the individual, as the central subject of study.

In the 1940s, Jacob L. Moreno (1892–1974), a medical doctor specializing in psychiatry, developed sociometry, psychodrama and sociodrama. Sociometry was an analytical technique 'to bring individuals together who are capable of harmonious interpersonal relationships and so create a social group which can function at the maximum efficiency' (Moreno 1934: 11); psychodrama and sociodrama were role-playing techniques used to analyse interpersonal relations.

Kurt Lewin (1890–1947), who studied Gestalt psychology in Berlin, was also working on groups at this time. He observed how group members interacted with one another and how group behaviour modified their own. Following this line of research, Lewin investigated family food habits during the Second World War. He established the fact that changes were easier to introduce through group discussion and participation than through directional talks. This new insight on how best to introduce change provided the basis for future action research on organizational change.

The Tavistock Institute of Human Relations in London was also carrying out work in the same field, its researchers, Trist and Bamforth, investigating the effects of new technology on the social system and work organization in coal mining (Trist and Bamforth 1951: 6–38). In 1947 the Institute set up the journal *Human Relations*, with its motto 'Towards the Integration of the Social Sciences'. Towards the new millennium, the journal continues to flourish.

In 1945, Kurt Lewin founded the Research Center for Group Dynamics. The Center later moved to the University of Michigan where Norman Maier, one of the foremost advocates of 'group-in-action' training techniques, investigated the extent to which group decision making was more effective than the command/order direction. His findings were that the group controlled through leadership rather than force; ensured discipline through internal pressure; pooled thinking; respected the individual; and allowed all its members to participate in deciding on things that directly affected them in their work.

Also during this period, human relations studies began to move towards industrial relations, including for the first time trade unions (see INDUSTRIAL AND LABOUR RELATIONS). The industrial sociologists of the 1950s held that the answer to industrial conflict was not domination by management or workers but finding mutual accommodation through collective bargaining and the use of professional industrial relations experts. In the universities and elsewhere, the human relations units were renamed industrial relations departments. Case studies and role playing became the most-used teaching techniques. Training developed from two sources: research into teamwork and leadership and into trade unions and industrial relations (see TRAINING).

The 1960s and 1970s: organizational humanism

The humanist philosophy was slow to penetrate business organizations, which continued to be managed on hierarchical and conflictual capital/labour lines. It was not until the upheavals of the Second World War that the need for change became urgent. The war had brought about greater social and political democracy. Workers, by the 1960s, had grown in self-assurance and expectations, and trade unions had become more militant in their demands (see INDUSTRIAL DEMOCRACY). In this new climate, the behavioural scientists developed a different perspective on motivation, advocating industrial democracy in the workplace. The Mayoists had believed workers were actuated by 'the logic of sentiments' and managers by 'the logic of efficiency'. In this more democratic age, the organizational humanists combined the two logics into the democratic theory, which applied to both groups.

Abraham Maslow (1908–70), an early humanist psychologist, offered what became one of the best-known theories on motivation (see MOTIVATION AND SATISFACTION). People were motivated, he suggested, by a dynamic hierarchy of needs: physiological, safety, love, esteem and self-actualization. Once a need was satisfied, people moved up the ladder to the next, but moved back if gratification of the lower order need was threatened or removed. The theory applied to societies as well as individuals. In a subsistence-level economy, physiological needs would predominate. As the economy moved forward, its other needs would become more important. In

Western industrial societies the physiological and safety needs of people were generally cared for. Accordingly, in the workplace, individuals had to be motivated through their need for self-esteem: having their work recognized as valuable and being made to feel needed.

On similar lines, Frederick Herzberg (1923–) (see HERZBERG, F.) distinguished between what he called the 'hygiene factors', which, like the principles of medical hygiene, were preventive rather than curative, and the 'motivators', relating to job content, which led to job satisfaction and positive attitudes. Thus, to be effectively motivated, workers had to have a job which was challenging and brought responsibility, recognition and opportunities for growth.

Chris Argyris (1923–) (see ARGYRIS, C.) was interested essentially in the dichotomy between individual and organization. According to him, the normal individual progresses along a continuum: from infancy to adulthood, from immaturity to maturity, from dependence to independence. The organization, through specialization of labour, the command/obey direction and the strict control of activity, prevents the individual from attaining his or her self-actualizing potential. Argyris concentrated on reducing the conflict and promoting integration between individual and organization.

Douglas McGregor (1906–64), who taught psychology at the Massachusetts Institute of Technology, is another important figure among industrial psychologists. Against the then standard theory, which he labelled Theory X, that 'the average human being has an inherent dislike of work and will avoid it if he can', he developed Theory Y, that 'the average human being does not inherently dislike work' (McGregor 1960: 33–4). McGregor held that 'man will exercise self-direction and self-control in the service of objectives to which he is committed' and 'the capacity to exercise a relatively high degree of imagination, ingenuity and creativity in the solution of organizational problems is widely, not narrowly, distributed in the population' (1960: 48).

Rensis Likert (1903–81), at the University of Michigan, identified four types of leadership behaviour: (1) exploitative; (2) benevolent; (3) consultative; and (4) participative. Following McGregor, Likert favoured the fourth method, that which involved supportive relationships and group decision making.

These ideas on motivation, leadership and group decision making were not new. Indeed, McGregor and Likert acknowledged Follett's influence on their thinking. But, although not new, they were ripe for acceptance. It was now widely recognized that the strict division of labour was dysfunctional and assembly-line work alienating. Jobs had to be enlarged, enriched and rotated. In Sweden for example, Volvo, the car manufacturer, assigned engine assembly to work groups where the workers themselves could share or trade off tasks, check quality and be directly responsible for the entire assembly of the car. This proved very successful at the time.

A new way of looking at people was emerging. Edward W. Bakke at the Yale Labor-Management Center had already referred in 1958 to the people in the organization as a resource, similar to money or materials. He did so not to dehumanize the personnel function but, on the contrary, to emphasize the importance of the human factor. Later, Wendell French used the words 'human resources administration' as a subtitle to a personnel management text (French 1964). Over time, human resource management became an integral part of the mission and strategy of every organization. Much of the earlier work on human and industrial relations was consolidated and a vast amount of new thought and experimentation developed. All this was passed on, through the business schools which had proliferated, to the new generation of managers who would implement it in industry and business.

The 1980s and 1990s: individualism and systemic interdependence

The 1980s witnessed a change in the political climate, with a move away from the collectivism of previous decades. In the UK the trend towards state intervention began to reverse, with privatization of public utilities being the most visible sign. In its place was a move towards individualism: a celebration of the entrepreneur as the basic creator of wealth. On the other hand, the effects of global environmental deterioration emphasized the need for joint action and brought systemic thinking to the fore. Nature, peoples and industries were all part of the same ecosystem, interdependent with one another. Nature could not be consistently maltreated. When abused, it retaliated. Cooperation, not domination, was the watchword. Individual action, while useful, was not sufficient.

International policing was required and could only be achieved through cooperation between states and across frontiers. The growth of microelectronics in both factory and office introduced immediate availability of information to all, redistributed power and authority and took decision making down the organizational hierarchy. Many layers of middle management were eliminated. The resulting structural unemployment led to a move towards self-employment and the growth of the small business.

2 Evolving trends

The 1990s have been dubbed the 'caring decade'. Communitarianism, propounded by the sociologist Amitai Etzioni as the new faith to safeguard the family and the community against violence, crime and drugs has been finding general acceptance. It is likely therefore that the business organization will finally accept itself as an economic unit and social institution.

Although hierarchy cannot be eliminated completely from any form of structure, the indications are that the framework of the organization of the future will be looser, with networks of self-managing teams, mutually self-controlling and joined by commitment to the overall vision. Yet another factor that will undoubtedly affect the running of organizations is the influx of women at top managerial levels. They will increasingly bring their own ways of looking at things – more inclusive, more holistic, essentially systemic – into managing organizations (see WOMEN MANAGERS IN ORGANIZATIONS).

3 Evaluation and conclusions

Schools of thought run into each other and can never be neatly divided into periods. This is particularly so in the case of human relations. The growth of management studies in universities and business schools since the 1950s has meant an inevitable profusion of theories, with not a little resulting confusion. Harold Koontz (1908–84) christened the phenomenon 'the management theory jungle' (Koontz 1961). The proliferation continued. Twenty years later, viewing the literature, he was surprised:

> some people are discovering what we've known for years. For example, I found some things like this... that the actual management depends on the situation. I thought, my gosh, there must be something new there. Only to find, after spending a lot of time reading, that there wasn't anything, and I don't know any practicing manager who doesn't manage in the light of the situation'.
>
> (Greenwood 1984)

In the USA, the main provider of management thinking in the latter part of the twentieth century, the indiscriminate search for the new has ignored and discarded, to some extent, the past. None the less, into the 1990s, there is some evidence of a return to the past. Europe, Japan and other countries in the Pacific Rim, no longer so subservient to American management thinking, are beginning to question its given universalism and ways of achieving effective modes of behaviour at work. Meanwhile, amidst the proliferation of academic journals on every aspect of management, has come a new journal, the *Journal of Management History*. The study of human relations will be enriched through this reconnection with its past and with the work of its early European and other pioneers. It will gain in depth as it integrates the basic virtues of the cultures of an emerging widely varied working population, spread across frontiers and continents.

PAULINE GRAHAM
UNIVERSITY OF BRADFORD

Further reading

(References cited in the text marked *)

Argyris, C. (1957) *Personality and Organization: The Conflict Between the System and the Individual*, New York: Harper & Row. (An investigation of the dichotomy between the needs of the individual and those of the organization).

Bakke, E.W. (1958) *The Human Resources Function*, New Haven, CN: Yale Labor-Management Center. (The first treatment of the workforce as a resource, such as money or materials, and its function as such.)

Follett, M.P. (1918) *The New State – Group Organization: The Solution for Popular Government*, New York: Longmans Green. (An exploration of the place of the individual in society and how to organize for democratic governance.)

* French, W. (1964) *The Personal Management Process: Human Resources Administration*, Boston, MA: Houghton Mifflin. (An analysis of the personnel function as human resource management.)

* Greenwood, R.G. (1984) 'Koontz: a reminiscence', address presented at the meetings of the Academy of Management, Boston, MA, August. (A description of Koontz' continuing interest in the 'management theory jungle'.)

* Koontz H. (1961) 'The management theory jungle', *Journal of the Academy of Management* 4 (3): 182–6. (The first comprehensive analysis of the differences between different management theories.)

Likert, R. (1961) *New Patterns of Management*, New York: McGraw-Hill. (An exposition of his four different types of leadership behaviour.)

Likert, R. (1967) *The Human Organization: Its Management and Value*, New York: McGraw-Hill.

Lindeman, E. (1924) *Social Discovery: An Approach to the Study of Functional Groups*, New York: Republic Publishing Co. (A study of how groups work.)

* McGregor, D. (1960) *The Human Side of Enterprise*, New York: McGraw-Hill. (How people view their work and McGregor's concepts of Theories X and Y.)

Maslow, A. (1954) *Motivation and Personality*, New York: Harper & Row. (A theory of motivation and of the different categories of human needs in their hierarchical relationships.)

* Mayo, E. (1933) *The Human Problems of an Industrial Civilization*, New York: Macmillan.

(Mayo's account of the Hawthorne experiments and his conclusions.)

* Moreno, J.L. (1934) *Who Shall Survive?: A New Approach to Human Interrelations*, Washington, DC: Nervous & Mental Disease Publishing Co. (How to group people for effective and harmonious work.)

* Roethlisberger, F.J. (1977) *The Elusive Phenomena*, G.F.F. Lombard (ed.), Cambridge, MA: Harvard University Press. (A discussion on the Hawthorne experiments.)

Roethlisberger, F.J. and Dickson, W.J. (1939) *Management and the Worker*, Cambridge, MA: Harvard University Press. (The detailed analysis of the Hawthorne experiments which promoted the human relations school.)

* Trist, E.L. and Bamforth, K.W. (1951) 'Some social and psychological consequences of the longwall method of coal-getting', *Human Relations* 4: 3–38.(A longitudinal study in coal mining of the effects of new technology on work organization and the social system of the workers.)

* Urwick, L. and Brech, E.F.L. (1946) *The Making of Scientific Management*, vol. 2, London: Management Publications Trust. (An overview of management in British industry, with a chapter on Robert Owen.)

* Williams, W. (1920) *What's on the Worker's Mind? By One Who Put on Overalls to Find Out*, New York: Charles Scribner's Sons. (A pioneering study of the social meaning of jobs.)

Wren, D.A. (1994) *The Evolution of Management Thought*, New York: John Wiley. (An excellent treatise on the history of management thought.)

See also: ARGYRIS, C.; FOLLETT, M.P.; GROUPS AND TEAMS; HUMAN RESOURCE MANAGEMENT; INDUSTRIAL AND LABOUR RELATIONS; INDUSTRIAL DEMOCRACY; LEADERSHIP; MAYO, G.E.; MOTIVATION AND SATISFACTION; ORGANIZATION BEHAVIOUR; PERSONNEL MANAGEMENT; TAYLOR, F.W.; TRAINING

Related topics in the IEBM: BUSINESS SCHOOLS; ENVIRONMENTAL MANAGEMENT; INFORMATION TECHNOLOGY AND SOCIETY; LEWIN, K.; ORGANIZATION BEHAVIOUR, HISTORY OF; ORGANIZATION NETWORKS; POWER; TRIST, E.L.

Human resource development

Overview

This entry presents an overall summary of the state and future trends of employee development, raising a series of issues which will affect companies in the future.

Employee development is still an underdeveloped area in terms of both research and practice. Although there is no shortage of textbooks which prescribe best practice, there is still lacking a credible analytical framework which can be used by either students or practitioners. In the practitioner sphere, employee development tends to lack strategic orientation; in particular it is often not properly integrated with systems for selection, appraisal and reward of employees, neither are there systems for the objective evaluation of the success of development activities.

The entry looks at employee development in a systematic way, beginning with objectives, responsibilities and target groups and then surveying paths for employee development and the strategies and activities which can be used to achieve employee development. The final section of the entry looks at future trends in employee development and how greater emphasis on this issue will be necessary in the years to come.

1 The objectives of employee development

The primary objective of human resource development is that all employees have positions which include purpose, satisfaction and freedom to act (see HUMAN RESOURCE MANAGEMENT). Furthermore, employee development should foster the capability of employees to find a lifelong balance (Bolles 1991) between learning, working and leisure time. Employees' needs for development should always correspond with the development needs of the company, its customers and the public.

The concept of employee development focuses on self-development which ideally takes place on three levels:

1 the individual level (employees of all levels are developed to become associates, or intrapreneurs, who behave as if the company is their own);
2 the group level (instead of teams of stars, star teams of humanistic intrapreneurs are developed in all areas of the organization);
3 the organization level (the company is developed to become a learning and vision-driven organization).

2 The distribution of roles

The distribution of roles for employee development should follow the principle of subsidiarity, as shown in Figure 1. Primary responsibility for employee development is delegated to each employee: this is fundamental to self-development. Secondary responsibility is executed by the employee's direct superior, ideally operating as a coach; the superior on the next level above, acting as a mentor; and the managing director, operating as a promoter. The human resource management representative is responsible for the participative development, introduction, coordination and evaluation of development concepts, acting as an internal consultant (see HUMAN RESOURCE MANAGEMENT).

Target groups

Many companies still provide development opportunities to only a cadre of employees, in the form of management development (see MANAGEMENT DEVELOPMENT). However,

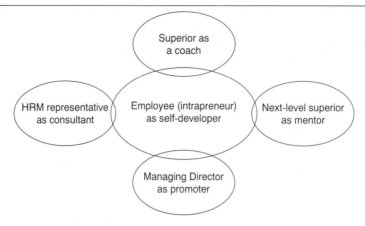

Figure 1 The distribution of roles for employee development

this approach fails to utilize the rich non-managerial talents possessed by many employees. The fact that there are so many 'head-hunters' operating throughout the industrialized world indicates that most companies have failed in developing their own human resources, to the detriment of both employees and organization.

Recognition of this fact means that more and more companies are likely to move away from the short-term view ('these days you can't afford to wait for someone to grow into the job') towards a long-term 80:20 policy ('it is our policy to fill job vacancies by the promotion or rotation of motivated and qualified employees within our company'). Only in exceptional cases (less than 20 per cent), such as lowest level jobs or when entering a new business field where the properly qualified individual is not available within the company, should the company go outside the organization for hiring. It should be stressed that such a policy helps employees at all levels of the organization to develop to their greatest potential and thus make the best use of all their abilities in the interests of both the individuals themselves and the company.

3 Paths of employee development

The traditional definition of employee development is still career development (promotion) (see CAREERS). However, evidence shows that in many large corporations more and more executives no longer value promotion as a career incentive: 'higher is not always nicer!' When third- and fourth-level executives working in large corporate HQs of multinational companies are asked what was the best job of their career, many cite posts such as general managers of subsidiaries, where the managers felt that they had control and were able to influence results. At head office, these same managers feel alienated from the company's customers and products and separated from the 'action'.

The flattening of organizational structures and change in corporate values means the definition of employee development needs to be broadened. Therefore, in addition to promotion, companies have to offer other on-the-job-development strategies. As illustrated in Figure 2, such strategies include: (1) functional and/or international job rotation (unilateral or bilateral, internal or external, to or from customers and/or suppliers); (2) job enrichment activities; (3) participation in multi-functional and/or multi-cultural project teams; (4) professional and/or managerial promotions; (5) realignment (the possibility of returning to former positions if the employee desires); (6) preventive outplacement activities (see RELOCATION); (7) outsourcing of non-strategic corporate functions (intrapreneurs develop into entrepreneurs); and (8) the development of 'tent managers' into 'camping managers', as formerly large and

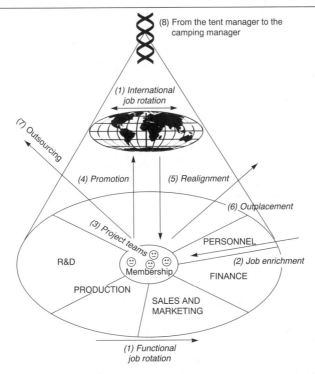

Figure 2 Several career paths

centralized 'tower organizations' become decentralized vision-driven 'confederations of tents' where all associates know the company's customers, employees, shareholders and environment (the 'tent managers' at the top of each company try to develop new 'tent managers' within their area and thus become 'camping managers').

Such strategies have to be integrated into long-term employee development plans and must be supported by targeted near-the-job and off-the-job activities as well as coaching and mentoring concepts.

Strategies of employee development

All employee development activities should be based on equal opportunities, without any discrimination on the grounds of irrelevant social data such as age, sex or nationality. Pepsi-Cola, for example, has as its motto: 'We only discriminate based upon ability' (see EQUAL EMPLOYMENT OPPORTUNITIES).

Using the portfolio concept (Odiorne 1985), four employee development phases can be distinguished, as shown in Figure 3.

The *introductory phase* consists of hiring employees with development potential and making them rapidly familiar with their new tasks and the new working environment. This phase should last as short a time as possible. In contrast, employees should remain in the *growth phase* as long as possible. This can be

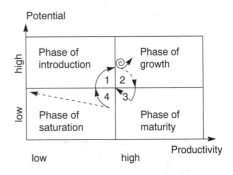

Figure 3 Employee development instruments based on a portfolio concept

achieved by offering employees tasks which provide purpose and fun and allow freedom to act.

The *maturity phase* includes employees who demonstrate high performance but low potential for growth; eventually, these employees may end up in the *saturation phase* as performance begins to decline as well. In order to avoid this happening, employees can be offered two options. They can take up a new position with which they can re-identify, thus returning to the introductory phase. Alternatively, a preventive outplacement can be undertaken, usually with the help of a consulting company, to help the employee find a suitable position outside the organization.

Activities in employee development

All activities in employee development have to serve both the needs of the employee and those of the company. Schein (1978) divided actions into six phases, corresponding with the professional life cycle of the employee:

1 initial entry into the organization;
2 transition from being a specialist to a generalist;
3 transition from technical work to managerial work;
4 transition from fully work-involved to being more accommodating to family concerns;
5 transition from being 'on the way up' to 'levelling off';
6 transition from being fully employed to being partly employed and retiring.

In all of these critical career transitions, employees can use the 'personal career coach of the 1990s' described by Hollander (1991). Hollander sees employees as moving through phases; in the first phase they like their job but have yet to master its skills; in the second phase they both like the job and do it well; in the third phase they begin to drift into a situation where the formerly ideal job becomes 'the velvet handcuffs of expertise without enthusiasm'.

4 Development in the future

As stated above, employee development is still handled at a very low level in most companies. However, there are many opportunities for management to change this situation. The following are three examples of changes which companies need to make in order to integrate employee development more fully into their organizations and capitalize on the skills and abilities their employees possess.

From operational employee training to strategic employee development

Employee training and development are worthless unless there is a clear strategic company vision of the role and goals of development (see TRAINING). Strategic employee development has to be based on a holistic company mission, which must be developed by the entire management team (including the HR director) in consensus. The employee development concept must not only be based on the company mission, but must also be linked to other key human resource management instruments such as selection, appraisal and reward (see HUMAN RESOURCE FLOWS; HUMAN RESOURCE MANAGEMENT).

From an ethnocentric approach to a geocentric approach

With regard to career development policies, a multinational company can choose from four options: (1) ethnocentric, where all key positions abroad are filled by home country nationals; (2) polycentric, where all key positions are filled by local nationals; (3) regiocentric, where all key positions abroad are filled by a national from within a region; and (4) geocentric where all key positions abroad are filled by the foremost talented individual within the worldwide operation, regardless of nationality. Figure 4 illustrates that the most advanced policy is the geocentric development approach.

Despite high transfer costs and the potential problems of repatriation of expatriates back to their home country at the end of their careers, the geocentric approach has many

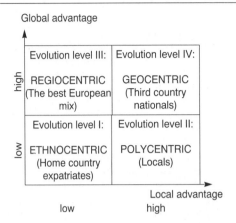

Figure 4 Evolution levels of international employee development

advantages. It exploits the richness of worldwide human resources instead of concentrating only on local or home country resources (see HUMAN RESOURCE MANAGEMENT, INTERNATIONAL). It enables a better identification by subsidiary employees with corporate worldwide strategies, and creates a well-rounded global company culture which can benefit from the transferable comparative advantages of all cultures where the company operates. It enables employees in various locations to have greater career possibilities.

From the company's point of view, one of the most useful aspects of the geocentric approach is that it develops transnational capabilities in managers, meaning that they can manage across national boundaries. Global integration is achieved without loss of local flexibility. More than anything else, this policy allows greater linkage of local operations to each other and, in so doing, provides better leveraging local and central capabilities.

From a single-male-orientated to a dual career and family-orientated development

In most countries, increasing numbers of women are likely to work during most stages of their lives. The dual income (and dual development) household is well on its way to becoming the norm of the future, creating a need for new relations between home and work and thus demanding changes in both areas. Multinational companies have to offer dual career possibilities (including appropriate extensive cross-cultural training for the whole family) by assisting partners who are not employees in finding attractive work near their new locations, and assisting in finding appropriate education programmes for the children of expatriates (see EQUAL EMPLOYMENT OPPORTUNITIES; RELOCATION).

The change of the traditional 'work ethic' includes key trends including a reduced emphasis on the importance of material wealth as a motivator of work activity, pressure for resistance to authority, desire to realize the balance between work and other aspects of life and increased concern with finding intrinsically interesting and personally rewarding work. Most employees expect a fair compensation and benefits package, employment security and a pleasant working environment. However, if companies wish to motivate the new generation of young, individual, freedom-minded employees ('Yiffies') they will have to provide in addition: (1) jobs which include purpose, joy and freedom to act; (2) superiors who act as exemplary coaches; and (3) permanent useful learning experiences on the job. It is the responsibility of top managers within each company to decide whether they want to become the masters of change rather than its victims.

MARTIN HILB
UNIVERSITY OF ST GALLEN
UNIVERSITY OF DALLAS

Further reading

(References cited in the text marked *)

* Bolles, R.N. (1991) *The Three Boxes of Life*, Berkeley, CA: Ten Speed Press. (A rich and rewarding guidebook on life/work planning written in a light tone.)

Boxall, P.F. (1992) 'Strategic HRD: beginning of a new theoretical sophistication', *Human Resource Journal* 2 (3): 60–74. (Illustrates the fact that the future academic strength of HRM will depend on how effectively scholars dedicate themselves to building credible analytical frameworks.)

Brewster, C. and Larsen, H.H. (1992) 'Human resource management in Europe: evidence from ten countries', *International Journal of Human Resources Management* 3 (3): 409–34. (Provides a distinct picture of differences in human resource management practices in ten European countries.)

*   Hollander, D. (1991) *The Doom Loop System*, New York: Penguin. (Displays a profound sensitivity to the complexities of career-minded individuals.)

*   Odiorne, G.S. (1985) *Strategic Management of Human Resources*, San Francisco, CA: Pitman. (Uses for the first time the portfolio concept developed by the Boston Consulting Group in the area of human resources management, interrelating performance with the political dimension of human resources.)

Perlmutter, H.V. and Heenan, D.A. (1974) 'How multinational should your top manager be?', *Harvard Business Review* 6: 121–31. (Describes various attitudes of executives regarding their reaction towards foreign ideas and persons.)

*   Schein, E. (1978) *Career Dynamics*, Reading, MA: Addison-Wesley. (Presents a three-dimensional model of career dynamics including various phases of critical career paths.)

United Nations (1993) *Human Development Report 1993*, New York: United Nations. (Illustrates that the future academic strengths of human resource management will depend on the commitment of scholars and their dedication to building credible analytical frameworks.)

See also: CAREERS; EQUAL EMPLOYMENT OPPORTUNITIES; HUMAN RESOURCE FLOWS; HUMAN RESOURCE MANAGEMENT; HUMAN RESOURCE MANAGEMENT, INTERNATIONAL; MANAGEMENT DEVELOPMENT; OCCUPATIONAL PSYCHOLOGY; ORGANIZATION BEHAVIOUR; RELOCATION; TRAINING; TRAINING, ECONOMICS OF; WOMEN MANAGERS IN ORGANIZATIONS

Related topics in the IEBM: EXECUTIVE TRAINING; ORGANIZATION DEVELOPMENT; ORGANIZATION STRUCTURE

Human resource flows

Overview

Employers can staff vacancies from a wide array of sources. External labour markets may be tapped for new organizational members when there is a need for expertise that is cost-prohibitive to develop internally; for an infusion of new perspectives that might improve business processes; for compliance with equal employment opportunity mandates; or for additional manpower to redress shortages in semi-skilled and unskilled labour. How far afield a firm must go to satisfy its demand for qualified persons varies greatly across countries and over time. The skill mix within a given nation can be quite dynamic, affected by demographic shifts (for example, altered labour force participation rates among key population subgroups), migration flows (for example, brain drains from emigration, skill booms from in-migration), government policies for human-capital formation (for example, magnitude and targeting of expenditures on education, vocational training initiatives) and large-scale technology transfers. Even when skills are abundant in the indigenous population, strong norms about the acceptability of certain types of work may create artificial shortages that necessitate importing labour. For example, menial or dangerous jobs in the manufacturing, construction and service sectors of industrialized economies are often filled by individuals from less developed countries. All of these factors must be considered when establishing the appropriate geographic scope for external searches.

Alternatively, employers may seek full exploitation of their internal labour markets when vacancies arise within business units. There are numerous advantages in doing so for domestic firms, such as providing incentives for employee retention, extending the returns on company-specific skills or knowledge, or simply decreasing recruitment and selection costs. However, this strategy assumes that the firm has sufficient human resource slack to be stockpiling skills for creative deployment internally. Major downsizing trends in western economies have made it more difficult to rely heavily on such sourcing in recent decades. It is increasingly the case that firms are shrinking to a smaller permanent core of key employees and drawing upon a large flexible pool of contingent workers from the outside as demand dictates. Multinational enterprises (MNEs) appear to be in a better position in this regard, having bigger internal labour markets that transcend the skill constraints associated with any single national labour force. Yet, as will be discussed below, they seldom utilize the wide range of talents available within their far-flung operations.

In addition to designating the preferred configuration of labour markets, firms must decide how pro-active they want to be in managing human resource flows. American firms, in particular, have a long history of operating in a crisis management mode after labour surpluses or shortages have occurred. The lag period for an effective response usually proves costly in financial and psychological terms. Shortages normally translate into increased work intensity for those already employed. The pressure to acquire additional human resources may also promote higher compensation costs for newcomers or less stringent screening. Surpluses raise the spectre of terminations or layoffs, jeopardizing the economic security of those affected. Employers only accept some of the separation costs through severance pay or supplemental unemployment benefits. Those who retain their jobs may become demoralized and less productive, wondering whether their departure is imminent.

Table 1 displays a steady evolution in the sophistication of human resource planning activities since the turn of the century. Scientific management principles laid the groundwork for employment planning in two ways. First, time-and-motion studies fostered the measurement and simplification of tasks. Second, manning tables and payroll budgeting were emphasized to establish how many employees were needed and to outline labour cost constraints. From 1940 until 1960, human resource planning improved, with the widespread introduction of organizational charts, replacement charting and regression-based forecasting. In the 1970s, state-of-the-art planning utilized computer-based information systems, affirmative action models and cost–benefit assessments. Some large firms even created formal human resource planning sub-units within the human resource

Table 1 Evolution of human resource planning in the USA

Period	Planning concerns	Segment targeted	Emerging patterns
1900–40	Work engineering	Hourly employees	• Formal job analysis • Workload manning tables (engineered standards) • Payroll budgeting and control
1940–60	Staffing continuity	Hourly and managerial employees	• Organizational charting • Replacement planning • Workload forecasting (ratios, regression)
1960s	Employment stabilization (balancing supply and demand)	Managerial, professional and technical employees	• Skills inventories • Formalized forecasting activities • Experimentation with mathematical models in forecasting

1970s	Affirmative action
	
	More cost-effective HR utilization
		Managerial, professional and technical employees	• Affirmative action modelling
			
			• Computer-based HR information
			  systems
			• HR cost-benefit analyses
			• HR planning units formalized
			• HR analysis formally linked to
			  business planning and budgeting

1980s	Career management
	
	Increasing the profit contribution from human resources
		All employees	• Career planning and development
			  programmes
			
			• Process analyses for the job redesign
			  and organizational re-engineering

1990s and beyond	Contingent/just-in-time staffing;
	Making permanent employees strategic assets
	
	Globalization
		All employees	• HR auditing as part of
			  management accounting
			• HR benchmarking/ competitor
			  intelligence
			
			• Transnational competencies targeted
			  in HR planning

Source: Rows 1–5 adapted from Walker (1980)

management department. By the 1980s, human resource management practitioners had also intensified efforts to have human resource supply and demand analyses incorporated into business strategy formulation. Thus, firms that repeatedly experience human resource flow imbalances may not be taking full advantage of the planning technologies at their disposal.

The remainder of this entry will be devoted to recent trends in human resource flows and the utilization of forecasting methodologies to capitalize on their occurrence. Ultimately, the objective is to assess the implications of these developments for competition between firms.

I Typology of human resource flows

Country-to-country flows

Long before capital markets and communication systems achieved a truly global scale, large human resource flows were commonplace among nations. The International Labour Office (1987) reported that between 19.7 and 21.7 million migrants were economically active worldwide in 1980, and all signs point to a continued expansion of their ranks since then. The long-term relocation of individuals outside of their country of origin can be the result of non-economic forces (for example, political persecution, family reunification) or economic ones (such as higher compensation or expanded work opportunities) (see RELOCATION). Whatever the intended destination, the national trade-offs associated with their departure remain hotly debated. Proponents of unrestricted exit argue that sender countries can benefit substantially due to ongoing remittances from overseas employment, a reduction in domestic unemployment during *emigrés'* absence and the local investment of accrued savings following re-migration. To illustrate, Martin (1991) disclosed that Turkey secured US$1.5–2 billion per year in remittances between 1979 and 1988. Many Asian nations also realize substantial financial gains in this manner. During the early to mid-1980s, Pakistan obtained over US$2 billion per annum on average from its migrant workers, South Korea US$1.3 billion, Bangladesh US$400 million, Sri Lanka US$250 million and India US$1.6 billion (1980 figure only) (Appleyard 1989).

Critics of these labour exchanges counter that 'brain drain' migration of highly skilled manpower imposes serious financial losses and hinders the advancement of key economic sectors within labour-exporting societies. Indigenous investments in human capital never yield adequate returns because developing nations have to purchase more expensive, replacement expertise from outside their borders, and because educated migrants are prone to utilizing overseas savings to entrench themselves abroad rather than enhance their return status (see HUMAN CAPITAL). Numerous proposals have been forwarded to restore equity in these situations, such as imposing a tax on receiver nations to fund development projects in migrants' homeland or enforcing the pre-departure reimbursement of educational expenses incurred by the State, as in Romania. Contrary to popular belief though, advanced industrialized economies (AIEs) no longer attract the vast majority of international migrants. A recent United Nations Population Report documented that most migration entails, instead, movement from one developing country to another that is less poor (Lederer 1993).

Against such a backdrop, this entry will examine the different forms of migration, how flow patterns have changed over time and pertinent research on immigration to assess their implications for employers around the globe.

Types of migration

Migration activity can be distinguished both in terms of its temporal nature and legality. *Settlement migration* refers to foreigners who lawfully immigrate to a target country and maintain a long-term, legal residence therein. Prospects for host citizenship, if desired, may be daunting if eligibility for naturalization is contingent on satisfying an excessively long waiting period (for example, Bahrain has a twenty-five year residency requirement).

Even when the time lag is less onerous, potential *emigrés* are confronted with admissions criteria that have changed dramatically in recent decades. Beginning in the 1960s, several AIEs revoked country-of-origin quotas or restrictions, replacing them with criteria designed to reunite families. The USA did so in 1965 when its Immigration and Nationality Act was amended, making family ties the key variable in the visa allocation system. Although Canadian legislation had favoured the admission of close relatives of citizens and residents for years, the 1976 Immigration Act identified family reunification as a major goal. Australia altered its entry policies along similar lines during the early 1980s. Consistent with this pattern, two-thirds of the immigrants granted settlement rights by the UK in 1986 gained access due to family considerations (Salt 1989).

The most recent wave of immigration reform has directed attention away from family units to domestic labour market needs by conferring paramount importance upon foreigners who are highly skilled or wealthy business investors. In 1990, the USA adopted legislation that nearly tripled the number of available visas for employment-based immigration. Up to 140,000 visas can be issued annually now, all but 10,000 of which are reserved for persons with extraordinary ability, outstanding academics and researchers, executives and select managers of MNEs, skilled workers and investors capable of investing at least US$1 million and creating ten or more domestic jobs. Similarly, in 1994 Canada unveiled a plan designed to encourage immigration by those who can start businesses or fill specialized jobs and to cut back on the number of persons entering for family-based reasons. The latter would be achieved by requiring previously admitted immigrants to post a cash bond for incoming relatives guaranteeing that they will not use social assistance programmes after their arrival. Even Japan, which traditionally shuns immigration, enacted the Revised Immigration Control Law in 1990 in part to simplify immigration procedures for highly qualified foreigners.

Despite withholding naturalization, several countries have been troubled by *de facto* settlement migration over the last twenty-five years. The problem is most acute in western Europe, where legions of foreign 'guestworkers' were imported from southern Europe, Turkey and west Africa to capitalize on the region's post-war, economic revitalization (see MANAGEMENT IN EUROPE). Family reunifications, which were tolerated by host governments, subsequently increased foreign population stocks to 4.4 million in West Germany, 3.7 million in France and another 1.5 million in Belgium, Switzerland and The Netherlands combined (Salt 1989). The original premises justifying the use of guestworkers were that citizenship would not be extended and that such persons would elect to return home after short employment stints. However, about one-third of guestworkers entering West Germany between 1961 and 1976 have not returned (International Labour Office 1987), and there are no indications that neighbouring countries have fared any differently on this issue. Japan grapples with similar challenges in dealing with the approximately 700,000 Koreans residing within its borders (Salt 1992).

Settlement migration can be reversible of course. To illustrate, 31 per cent of the 15.7 million immigrants coming to the USA over the period 1908–57 re-migrated, as did 18 per cent of the 3.4 million entering during the 1960s (International Labour Office 1987). Australia also witnessed substantial re-migration among settlers arriving in the 1960s (23 per cent) and 1970s (41 per cent). In western Europe, guestworker return has been promoted through various incentive schemes. Host countries like France and West Germany experimented briefly with modest return bonuses and training programmes, while sender nations have instituted such measures as permitting migrants to open foreign currency accounts with preferential interest rates, awarding migrants customs exemptions for imports designed to increase income opportunities, assisting their job search efforts and creating housing incentives. However, it remains unclear whether these initiatives have had a meaningful impact on decisions to leave the country.

Contract migration exhibits markedly different features. Here, countries permit foreigners to fill specific job vacancies in the labour market by issuing individual or group visas for their employment. Visa recipients must reapply periodically for extensions when the nature of the services provided is open-ended (for example, domestic servants, factory workers). *Laissez-faire* government policies with respect to renewals can lead to *de facto* settlement migration as noted above. Block visas typically occur when the jobs in question will cease to exist upon completion of a predefined project. For example, a foreign employer might seek this visa mode to bring in managers and construction workers after winning a bid on a local infrastructure project. Contract migrants are normally prohibited from changing organizations without prior consent from the employer-sponsor and host government. They may also be required to leave the country for a lengthy period before undertaking their new responsibilities (Saudi Arabia, for example, insists on a two-year absence before re-entry).

Block visa migration tends to be associated with oil-rich Arab states, which have displayed mounting interest in contractors based in South Korea, Japan, China, Singapore, the Philippines and Turkey. Over 600,000 Asian contract migrants were present in the Middle East in the late 1980s (Shadid *et al.* 1992). Resort to block visa migration is growing elsewhere as well. West Germany, which employed 20,000–30,000 contract migrants from central and eastern Europe throughout the 1980s, subsequently increased its quota ceiling to 100,000 (Bohning 1991). Hoping to reduce the utilization of illegal foreign labour, Taiwan developed formal guidelines in 1991 permitting the recruitment of young, unmarried persons through pre-approved employment agencies in Indonesia, Thailand, Malaysia and the Philippines. Taiwanese employers have been slow to respond however, objecting to requirements that sponsoring firms post a per capita cash bond equal to five months' compensation and agree to one-year employment contracts that can only be renewed once (Baum 1992).

Illegal (irregular) migration is the last major facet of migration activity examined. It can arise by way of illegal host country entry or by a person remaining within the host in an unauthorized economic capacity. The USA has had a major problem with the former, with approximately five million unlawful entries during the 1980s and early 1990s (Nelan 1993). In western Europe and Japan, there is considered to be a more pressing need to enforce the time and activity restrictions that define lawful entry for aliens. By the beginning of the 1990s, 14 per cent (2.6 million) of the foreign population stock in western Europe could be classified as 'irregulars' working outside the limitations of their visas or remaining in-country after having been denied refugee status (Bohning 1991). Legal status may be forthcoming for some migrants in France, where foreign workers and their dependents are legalized *ex post facto* if they would have been approved prior to their arrival. Japan still has between 300,000 and 500,000 illegal 'guestworkers' whose employment is inconsistent with their visa restrictions, most coming from Thailand, South Korea, Malaysia, China, and the Philippines (Salt 1992).

The profiling of AIEs is not meant to infer that developing nations are immune to this problem: Shadid *et al.* (1992) suggest a 1980 figure of 88,000 unlawful migrants for Saudi Arabia and as many as 38,000 for Kuwait. In southeast Asia, Taiwan has long been a haven for illegal foreign workers, with numbers that may approach 200,000 (Moore 1990). Hong Kong has been an even bigger magnet for such migration, particularly from China. From 1976 to 1980, approximately 400,000 persons illegally entered the colony from the mainland (Appleyard 1989). Singapore had an estimated 120,000 irregulars in 1981, and Malaysia another 450,000, with some sources suggesting that the actual figure may be as high as one million (Tasker 1990; Appleyard 1989).

Geographical migration systems

Salt (1989) proposed that global migration is best understood in terms of a series of spatial networks that form an interactive whole.

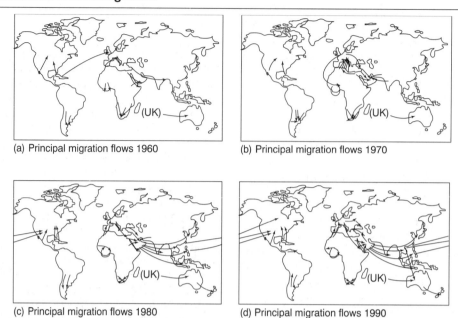

(a) Principal migration flows 1960

(b) Principal migration flows 1970

(c) Principal migration flows 1980

(d) Principal migration flows 1990

Figure 1 Inter-regional labour migration flows
Note: These flow patterns do not document movement involving less than 20,000 migrants per annum or inter-regional movements such as those between the USA and Canada or those within the European Union
Source: Salt (1989, 1992)

Within each region, substantial changes are evident with respect to the volume of migrants and the primary feeder nations over time (see Figure 1). The North American, western European, and Asia Pacific networks are reviewed briefly below.

Since the mid-twentieth century, there has been a precipitous decline in the proportion of US immigration that can be traced to Europe. Of the immigrant pool, 15 per cent listed a European point-of-origin in 1992, compared with 70 per cent in 1940 (Nelan 1993). During the 1960s and 1970s, Mexico and the Caribbean region played an increased role in in-migration fuelled by expanded opportunities to utilize visas to reunite families once close relatives became legally established in the receiving host country. Substantial trans-Pacific and Central American migration over the last fifteen years has further diversified the flow of people into the USA – so that by 1992 Latin American/Caribbean and Asian *emigrés* accounted for 44 per cent and 37 per cent of the immigration influx, respectively.

Although the USA has the largest population of economically active foreigners of any nation, Canada takes in the highest number of immigrants per capita among AIEs. Like the USA, the geographic mix of entrants has shifted decidedly away from Europe with a much greater influence from Pacific Basin countries in recent decades. Unlike the USA which has long legislated ceilings on annual immigration, Canada has allowed the inflow to vary based on domestic labour market conditions. There was a decided break with this policy in 1994, however, when the Canadian government announced its intent to cap immigration at about 200,000 per annum, starting in 1995. This target reinforced a downward trend in permitted entries during the mid-1990s.

Starting slowly in the 1950s with post-war resettlement, migration into western Europe peaked in the early 1970s when guestworker importation was at its high-water mark. By 1980, there were two million Turks living in western Europe with about 800,000 linked to the workforce (Martin 1991). Migration into the area remained robust thereafter despite bans on new guestworker entries. Between 1980 and 1992, the twelve European Community nations absorbed eight million migrants, approximately 50 per cent of whom were from North Africa, Turkey and the former Yugoslavia (Lederer 1993). Central and eastern Europe may take on greater significance as a feeder source if market reforms there falter in the future. Emigration from central and eastern Europe jumped from approximately 125,000 persons a year from 1980–87 to 1.5 million per annum from 1988–90, and has been forecast to remain as high as 800,000 per year until at least 1996 (Lockhart and Brewster 1992).

Asia Pacific emerged as a major immigration hub in the late 1980s, capitalizing on local reserves of migratory labour. By 1990, 800,000 Asians were working legally in the region outside of their home countries (Tasker 1990), with hundreds of thousands more employed unlawfully. Newly industrializing economies (NIEs) like South Korea, Taiwan, Malaysia and Indonesia began aggressive measures to import employees to alleviate chronic labour shortages in the construction, manufacturing and financial services sectors (Salt 1992). Japan also experienced a substantial increase in worker migration, most of the irregulars coming from elsewhere in Asia while legal migrants increasingly hailed from South America. The latter phenomenon can be attributed to immigration law reforms in 1990 that exempted the descendants of former Japanese nationals from a general requirement that foreigners must possess specialist skills or know-how to gain lawful entry. By 1991, 148,000 South Americans of Japanese descent had taken advantage of this provision and migrated to Japan to work (Shimada 1994). The number of less skilled entrants may increase dramatically due to a new programme administered by the Japanese International Training Cooperation Organization (JITCO). JITCO is authorized to admit 100,000 foreign workers per annum from NIEs for one-year training stints in select industries, with a small subset eligible to remain for twelve months of supplemental on-the-job training.

Research

Thorough empirical studies of international migration are surprisingly scarce. Martin (1991) reported that guestworkers had restrained wage increases in Germany and had increased labour productivity in some industries by prompting firms to shift to more flexible staffing policies instead of stockpiling workers to guard against periodic labour shortages. However, no econometric analyses were presented to corroborate these observations. Borjas' (1992) review of US immigration research prompted the following conclusions about its character and impacts: (1) the relative skill levels of successive immigrant waves have been deteriorating in the post-war era, a decline that accelerated during the 1970s; (2) it is unlikely that recent immigrants will reach earnings parity with natives with regard to their worklives; (3) a strong inter-generational link exists between the skills entering immigrants possess and those held by second-generation Americans; and (4) immigration has a minimal impact on the earnings of natives even in small labour markets that have assimilated large immigrant flows. An updated analysis of immigrants who arrived in the USA after 1980 determined that although skill levels rose over the decade they still were low by historical standards (Funkhouser and Trejo 1995). Given that 25 per cent of the new workers entering the US labour market during the 1980s were immigrants, the previously discussed policy shift regarding admissions (particularly the 1990 Immigration Act) is not surprising.

Existing research also shows that migrants tend to reside in highly concentrated pockets within receiving nations. Not surprisingly, the dominant pattern across countries is for foreign workers to cluster in urban labour markets which are heavily industrialized (Evers-Koelman et al. 1987; Martin and Miller 1980). One major exception would be the directed segregation of contract migrants assigned to infrastructure projects, which is not uncommon in the Middle East and is increasingly practised in southeast Asia. Where segregation is not mandated by the host government, the potential geographic diffusion of migrants over time looms as an issue. Bartel and Koch (1991) studied the mobility patterns of Asian, Latin American and European immigrants arriving in the USA after 1964 and found no systematic evidence that these populations become more dispersed over time. Relocations did occur, but typically involved cities that already had sizeable ethnic communities in common (see RELOCATION).

Country-to-firm flows

Outside of the Middle East, where foreign workers can comprise a majority of the resident population, international migration tends to be a minor, albeit important, component of labour market dynamics (see LABOUR MARKETS). For example, legal and illegal migration accounted for, at best, about 25 per cent of all new workers in the USA in the 1980s (Borjas 1988). Therefore, one needs to assess how broader demographic changes within host societies impact on human resource supply.

The global workforce will have grown by 600 million persons from 1985–2000, 95 per cent of this growth registered in the labour markets of developing countries (Johnston 1991). Some nations (like Mexico and Pakistan) will witness a robust annual growth rate of 3 per cent. The prospects for growth are much more modest among AIEs – 1 per cent per annum in the USA, Canada and Australia; 0.5 per cent per annum in Japan and France; 0.2 per cent per annum in the UK and Italy; negative growth in Germany. Besides growing faster, NIEs increasingly will be able to draw highly educated workers from local labour markets. It is estimated that, by the year 2000, 60 per cent of the matriculated college students worldwide will come from developing countries (Johnston 1991). Gender and age-related shifts in labour force participation will create independent pressures for innovative human resource management as highlighted below.

Of particular note, all of these changes will occur during a time when companies in developed economies will be seeking to maximize

gains from massive internal restructuring. The USA's highly publicized wave of corporate downsizing and de-layering should not obfuscate similar patterns occurring throughout Europe and Japan.

Supply-side changes

Having grown for decades, the global female labour force participation rate (LFPR) reached approximately 59 per cent in 1987 (Johnston 1991) (see EQUAL EMPLOYMENT OPPORTUNITIES). While there was a tendency for developed economies to have higher LFPRs, substantial differences did exist among these countries. Sweden ranked the highest at 75 per cent, followed by the USA, Canada and the UK in the 61–70 per cent range, Germany, France, Japan and Australia in the 51–60 per cent range, with Italy at 44 per cent. With the exception of Thailand and China, where LFPRs exceeded 70 per cent, participation levels were lower for women in developing economies. To illustrate: the corresponding rates for South Korea and Turkey fell between 41–50 per cent, while those in India, Indonesia, Brazil, Mexico and the Philippines did not exceed 40 per cent.

Educational gains, expanded cultural latitude to work outside of the home and public policy initiatives will make women increasingly eligible sources of labour supply in the decades ahead. For example, Japan passed a law in 1986 requiring firms to introduce systems to re-hire women who leave for reasons associated with childbirth or childcare. Sasajima (1993) reported that 17 per cent of firms with at least thirty employees had implemented such a programme, often containing stipulations for a probationary period of part-time work before re-employment, a maximum return age (such as 40) or assurances of a minimum period of work after returning (such as five years). Other Japanese firms have sought to increase career choice by adopting dual career tracks (one precluding out-of-area transfers), with allocation based on ability and employee wishes. Survey research suggested that 25 per cent of the companies with 1,000–4,999 workers had done so, as had 42 per cent of those organizations with a labour force of 5,000 or more (Sasajima 1993). Singapore, meanwhile, has adopted more aggressive public policies to increase female LFPR, such as offering free transportation to and from work, tax incentives to locate factories close to residential areas and the establishment of childcare centres (Organization for Economic Cooperation and Development 1991). (See Adler and Izaraeli's (1994) compilation of works on the supply and demand forces affecting women managers in twenty-one countries for a more comprehensive treatment of this subject.)

Ageing trends present another supply-side challenge to overcome with different short- and long-term repercussions for human resource management practice. Rapidly expanding NIEs in Asia are confronted with major labour shortages that, if left unresolved, will hinder further economic growth. While birth rates remain high by Western standards, LFPRs among persons under the age of 20 have dropped considerably as a greater proportion of this group lengthens their education prior to labour market entry. The decrease has been most notable in South Korea, Taiwan, Singapore and Hong Kong (Chiu and Levin 1993; Organization for Economic Cooperation and Development 1991). Singapore has responded to this situation by creating incentives for firms to employ individuals beyond the age of 55 (such as lowering the employers' contribution to the government-administered pension system), and has contemplated legislation postponing mandatory retirement until 60.

In contrast, the primary obstacle for AIEs is a rapidly 'greying' workforce over the next few decades. By the year 2000, individuals under the age of 34 will comprise less than 40 per cent of the labour force in the USA, Canada, Germany, the UK and Japan (Johnston 1991). The corresponding percentage for developing countries is 54.9 per cent. The problem is most acute in Japan, where the age 65+ cohort is projected to reach 24 per cent of the total population by 2020 (Sasajima 1993). The USA faces a similar situation in which nearly 40 per cent of its population could be age 55 or older by 2020. As more and more firms engage in corporate restructuring and implement high-performance work systems

(such as empowered teams, flexible organization and job designs, effectiveness-driven reward systems), employees will be called upon increasingly to be adaptable and continuous learners. Despite this, a recent survey of large US firms found that older employees were rated below average in terms of their flexibility and suitability for training (Hall and Mirvis 1994). To be competitive, firms will be required to devise effective development strategies to reach this group and successfully integrate them. Low birth rates will make it increasingly important to gain better access to retired workers. Already, some US companies are positioning themselves well in this regard: McDonald's Corporation and Days Inn have established hiring programmes for senior citizens, and the Travelers financial services company has instituted a retiree job bank whereby registrants designate their availability for work.

Demand-side changes

Organizational downsizing during the 1980s and early 1990s restructured the nature of human resource demand in most AIEs (see CAREERS). In its aftermath, firms have exhibited strong interest in retaining a streamlined, 'permanent' human resource base that can be enlarged through flexible staffing arrangements whenever customer demand escalates (see HUMAN RESOURCE MANAGEMENT; HUMAN RESOURCE MANAGEMENT, INTERNATIONAL). A growing number of firms have formalized their commitment to contingent workers by articulating a human resource strategy that specifies the percentage of staffing needs that will be satisfied from their ranks (see, for example, Flynn 1995). This complementary, contingent workforce can be assembled from many sources. Some companies, like AT&T Universal Card Services, have sought to create in-house pools of employees interested in *ad hoc* assignments in different departments. A cross-training policy allows interested employees to rotate into target units when the respective departments are slow, in order to learn skills that can be redeployed in future, temporary transfers. One multi-industry survey found that 25–35 per cent of firms with over 250 employees maintained such pools (Mangum *et al.* 1985).

Other means of orchestrating a contingent workforce include the use of part-timers, independent contractors, leased workers and temporary employees ('temps') (see FLEXI-BILITY). The number of leased employees has rocketed in the United States, expanding from about 10,000 persons in 1984 to 1.6 million in 1993 (Pandya 1995). Temporary services has also emerged as a large growth sector in the USA, encompassing 1.8 million workers by the mid-1990s (Flynn 1995). Forecasts indicate that 95 per cent of US companies will be using temporary employees by the end of the twentieth century (Kanter 1994). The proliferation of temps outside clerical support roles is particularly noteworthy, as professionals now comprise about 20 per cent of the temporary employees utilized in the USA. In addition, the US temporary services industry continues to diversify its offerings to businesses to decrease clients' staffing and development costs even further. Many agencies now focus exclusively on specialists (such as engineers, healthcare specialists, human resource executives), and, as Kelly Services has done in a creative partnership with the Sentry Group, may agree to coordinate all sourcing from temp vendors. Temporary agencies are also undertaking more pre-assignment training to minimize the productivity lags that normally accompany new placements. One survey found that 29 per cent of the respondents had experienced at least 20 hours of training from their temp agency (Paik Sunoo 1994) (see FLEXIBILITY).

Temporary workers also are a well-established labour force segment in Europe outside of Italy and Spain. Much of this growth occurred during the 1980s, when the number of temps more than doubled in West Germany and the UK, and more than quadrupled in The Netherlands (Bronstein 1991). In 1989, French temporary work agencies reported being unable to meet approximately 30 per cent of users' demand due to talent shortages. The demographic characteristics and workplace entitlements of these employees bear little resemblance to those prevailing in the USA, however. Only 30 per cent provide

clerical support; the remainder are assigned to industrial jobs. In addition, men outnumber women in this employment category in every country except for the UK. Approximately 60 per cent of the temps are male in Switzerland, The Netherlands, and Belgium, 74 per cent in France, and 80 per cent in Germany (Bronstein 1991). Men represent just 28 per cent of the US temporary workforce by comparison (Paik Sunoo 1994). The same sources also indicate that European temps are, on average, much younger.

European nations have also imposed more stringent standards on temporary employment practices. Unlike the USA where assignment duration can be open-ended, Denmark restricts assignments to a maximum of three months, Germany to six months with limited possibilities for an extension, and France to 18 months counting extensions (Bronstein 1991). Moreover, France mandates that temps receive the same rate of pay as permanent employees *plus* a wage premium, while Denmark awards five weeks' vacation time to temporary workers (Overman 1993). Some 'progressive' temporary agencies in the USA are experimenting with benefits packages to improve worker retention (see for example, Diesenhouse 1993), but it is unclear whether this development signals a trend.

Project-based contract migration is the closest equivalent to this phenomenon in emerging economies. As noted above, foreign contractors utilize block visas to bring in workers for a finite period, after which they return home rather than merging into the host labour market.

Interested readers should consult Evers-Koelman *et al.* (1987) for additional idiosyncratic details of fifteen selected labour markets in Europe, Asia and North America. This source summarizes the major changes which are evident within each market, its dominant problems and significant labour market policy measures that have been instituted by government in the post-1970 period.

Intra-firm flows

Internal labour markets (ILMs) provide another forum within which human resource flows can occur (see HUMAN RESOURCE MAN-AGEMENT). Normally associated with medium- to large-sized firms, these phenomena are characterized by limited ports of organizational entry (that is external hiring is confined to low-level jobs), systematic movement along career ladders, pay gradients which reflect that higher-level positions require more firm-specific competencies, seniority or merit-based criteria for advancement or downsizing, and a strong preference for filling vacancies through in-house promotions. These criteria collectively constrain human resource inflows from the external labour market *and* channel internal human resource flows along predetermined lines of progression or mobility clusters. When multiple ILMs exist within a given firm (such as non-salaried blue- and white-collar, lower-level salaried and senior-level salaried), the opportunities to cross labour force segments are limited also. Besides improving job security, these employment systems arguably supply an impetus for more extensive training in firm-specific skills and heightened employee motivation to learn and exhibit them.

Country-level trends

The larger question here is whether the extensive restructuring described earlier has all but obliterated the value of ILMs in developed countries. Available evidence is sketchy at best. Osterman (1992) concluded that these markets have remained fairly robust in the USA. Job tenure continues to be quite lengthy for most middle-aged men, and has grown considerably among female employees since the late 1970s. In addition, there appears to have been a sizeable inertia hindering a widespread redefinition of ILM rules that would place greater emphasis on flexible job design and flexible pay systems based on their level of diffusion.

Given the diversity of industrial relations systems in Europe, it would be unrealistic to expect that ILMs have moved in unison throughout the region (see INDUSTRIAL RELATIONS IN EUROPE). This is borne out by juxtaposing recent patterns in the French and

British manufacturing sectors. While France has long nurtured ILMs in industry, these have not played a very prominent role in the UK given the dominance of external recruitment for skilled positions, a weak relationship between length of service and employee competencies, and low pay differentiation for seniority (Eyraud *et al.* 1990). These researchers contend that ILMs gained a wider following in the UK during the 1980s, as evidenced by the decline of its traditional apprenticeship system and concomitant rise in popularity of the Youth Training Scheme which allows for more employer-specific training. France, on the other hand, has displayed signs of making vocational training more portable across companies, thereby loosening ILMs' grip on staffing decisions.

ILMs have exhibited their widest scope in Japan, extending beyond the boundaries of a single large firm to encompass its tightly interwoven network of suppliers and related organizations. Japanese companies have actively utilized this network in the past to avert high unemployment during recession periods – they simply transfer workers with quasi-lifetime employment to affiliated smaller firms who in turn release more 'peripheral' segments of the workforce (in particular, women and older workers) (Sasajima 1993; Standing 1988). A new trend seems to be materializing in the use of these extended ILMs, one in which temporary transfers to related organizations (referred to as *shukko*) become a means of developing new areas of business and forging new alliance linkages. These flows ordinarily sweep transferees from manufacturing units into the wholesale, retail or service sectors, and from large to smaller firms (Sano 1993) (see INDUSTRIAL RELATIONS IN JAPAN).

Multinational enterprises

MNEs can staff their international operations with three types of employees: parent-country nationals (PCNs), host-country nationals (HCNs) and third-country nationals (TCNs). The mix and distribution of these groups worldwide provides valuable insight into how multinationals configure their ILMs.

Ethnocentric staffing policies are evident when PCNs occupy most of a multinational's key overseas positions. During its early stages of internationalization, the domestic parent firm may use this approach to facilitate the acquisition of foreign market expertise or to transfer skills that are perceived to be unavailable in host countries. In later organizational life stages, home-country management may justify this pattern as the best means of insuring strategic control over its geographically remote units.

The root issue here focuses on how prevalent this human resource flow pattern is across MNEs. Tung (1982) uncovered systematic variations in ethnocentric staffing based on the location of headquarters and whether the host unit was situated in an AIE or NIE. Japanese MNEs tended to expatriate PCNs much more frequently when filling senior- and middle-management positions in AIEs than did European or US firms. The staffing approach for lower managerial positions was decidedly polycentric (that is, a high reliance on HCNs) in AIEs regardless of the MNE's home country, although Japanese multinationals displayed levels considerably below those for their western-based counterparts. European and Japanese firms behaved very similarly in NIEs, often reporting that 40–50 per cent of host managerial positions were occupied by PCNs. In general, US companies were least likely to staff management vacancies in NIEs with PCNs (see RELOCATION).

Interesting differences also arise in the distribution of foreign experience among home-country executives. In one survey, European- and Pacific-based MNEs were much more inclined to have chief executive officers, board members and individuals heading strategic business units with international backgrounds than were US multinationals (Conference Board 1992). The reverse held true for functional heads, although the edge was slight. Other research corroborates the limited overseas experience of top management in Canadian and American MNEs. (See Adler and Bartholomew (1992).

Rotating HCNs and TCNs through home operations for training or short-term assignments could reduce the dysfunctional aspects of ethnocentric staffing practices (such as high labour costs, adjustment problems, local workforce alienation) (see TRAINING). However, the normal rationale for doing so among North American and European firms is to assimilate HCNs and TCNs into the culture which predominates at headquarters, not to evolve that culture (Copp 1977; Desatnick and Bennett 1978; International Labour Office 1981). If managed properly, these supplemental human resource flows would not only enhance the prospects for regiocentric or geocentric staffing, but also could create transnational managerial competencies that enable the MNE to capitalize on untapped cultural synergies within its structure. Firms in other regions are experimenting more actively with this concept. To illustrate, Matsushita has instituted a programme which will annually place 100 managers from overseas subsidiaries into its Japanese offices and factories with the express intent of forcing home-country managers to deal with foreign colleagues and issues (*The Economist* 1991).

2 Implications for practice

To derive competitive advantage from the flow patterns outlined above, firms must have an accurate assessment of their human resource needs over the planning horizon envisaged (see HUMAN RESOURCE MANAGEMENT). This necessitates a careful comparison of labour demand and supply conditions to determine whether there will be net surpluses or shortages within individual business units or the entire organization. Enduring shortages signal that the internal labour market is being overtaxed, substantiating a need to canvass the external labour market more effectively or to broaden its territorial scope. Permanent, large-scale surpluses not only suggest that external hiring initiatives should be curtailed, but also may foreshadow the financial desirability of permanently scaling down operations in the afflicted areas. It may even be the impetus for creating a contingent workforce that services the needs of external customers, thereby generating new opportunities for economic growth.

Accordingly, the next few paragraphs provide a brief review of human resource forecasting as it is practised in contemporary organizations. Several recommendations will then be made regarding ways to forge better linkages between human resource flow analyses and strategic planning.

Forecasting human resource flows

Approaches

Table 2 lists numerous methods that can be used to determine the supply and demand for human resources within domestic or international firms. On the supply side, practitioners may engage in replacement planning, Markov analysis or goal programming (see PERSONNEL MANAGEMENT). Replacement planning seeks to identify an internal supply pool for every position in the firm. The process commences with a thorough human resource audit amassing performance and potential appraisals for the existing workforce. Next, a modified version of the organizational chart is prepared to locate candidates for particular job vacancies should they arise. Employees are considered viable replacements if their current jobs are structurally linked to the 'vacant' position and predefined appraisal criteria are met. This static approach can seriously underestimate supply because it fails to account for qualified persons who are not structurally linked to the positions being evaluated and for stock depletion attributable to turnover and retirement. Some companies practise a specialized version of this activity, called succession planning, for key executive and technical members of the organization. While the basic objectives are shared, succession planning tends to emphasize longer time horizons (between one and three years rather than twelve months or less) and incorporates inputs from multiple assessors, articulates detailed development plans for each subject and specifies contingency placements over a range of positions.

Markov analysis is anchored in a more dynamic view of human resource supply, tracing aggregate movements of workers over time. A transition probability matrix is constructed reflecting historical patterns of internal job changes and exits from the firm. Each vector of probability estimates is derived from studying how many job incumbents remained

Table 2 Human resource forecasting approaches

Model orientation	Techniques
Simple forecasting	• Judgemental (expert) estimates • Delphi • Position ratios (e.g., staff, employees) • Regression analysis • Time-series extrapolation
Organizational change	• Replacement/succession charting • Markov/Stochastic analysis
Optimization	• Linear/nonlinear programming (single-stage optimization) • Dynamic programming (multi-stage optimization) • Goal programming

Integrated simulations	• Integrated 'top-down' and 'bottom-up' judgemental estimation
	• Joint external–internal labour market simulation
	   (e.g., AVAIL & NAVDYN models used by the US Navy)
	• Joint business–labour market simulation
	   (e.g., integrated model developed by AT&T)

Note: For more detailed applications of the foregoing techniques, interested readers should consult Grinhold and Marshall (1977) and Niehaus (1979)
Source: Adapted from Walker (1980) and Niehaus (1988)

in their jobs over a set interval (such as twelve months), how many moved laterally or vertically within the organization and how many left due to turnover and retirement. It should be apparent that this approach captures more of the potential influences on staffing levels than replacement charting. However, a few caveats are in order as well. First, sample size is a critical concern. Unless the number of persons in each job state is large, the transition probabilities will be very unstable. Second, all individuals in a job state are assumed to have the same probability of movement. Performance and seniority differences are ignored. As a result, Markov analysis does not reveal which workers will move, nor does it decipher the exact job state they will occupy at a later date.

Goal programming represents a hybrid planning technique that combines Markov analysis with linear programming, mapping how employees can be redistributed to maximize the attainment of predetermined objectives. When incompatible goals co-exist, decision makers can indicate a priority scheme that should be followed, generating minimally acceptable solutions that satisfy the imposed constraints. For example, a firm may have budgeting, promotion and equal employment opportunities policies that cannot be accommodated or it may want to place upper limits on the number of persons who can be shifted from one unit to another or can be recruited from the external labour market. The fact that goal programming is a comprehensive, highly adaptive forecasting approach can be a two-edged sword. To experience its advantages, one must be willing to commit extensive resources in order to formulate the full range of desired parameters – as an illustration: a relatively 'routine' application incorporated over 1,200 variables and more than 1,100 constraints (Draper and Merchant 1978).

Judgemental (expert estimate) approaches are a popular, qualitative means of forecasting human resource demand among US firms. Here, a panel of senior executives, functional specialists and, possibly, external consultants, collectively deliberate over the human resource implications of such items as pre-

existing business strategy, company or unit sales, planned capital expenditures, industry sales, interest rates, gross domestic product (GDP) levels, etc. Consensus is sought in a series of meetings that vary in duration, frequency and spacing across companies. Concerns about the lack of standardization in weighting data and the vagaries of small-group dynamics have prompted many firms to adopt a 'Delphi' system instead. Unlike the expert estimate format, Delphi participants are secluded at the outset, with information flows throughout the forecasting process being tightly regulated by designated intermediaries. Ideally, each expert generates an independent series of updated projections based on new data (which may include peer forecasts) periodically forwarded by support staff. Delphi proponents contend that this framework nurtures more comprehensive analyses and supplies better documentation of the factors underlying the participants' estimates.

Some organizations favour more quantitative methods of divining manpower demand. Linear regression (that is, $Y = a + bX$) bases projections on the historical bivariate correlation between employment levels and a business-related criterion like sales. Since no single factor can account fully for staffing needs, such forecasts have little chance of being accurate other than for small firms in very static environments. Accordingly, an expanded set of predictor variables may be added providing the impetus for multiple regression analysis (that is, $Y = b_0 + b_1 \times x_1 + b_2 \times x_2 + b_3 \times x_3 + b_4 \times x_4 + ...$) to compute future demand states. In both regression scenarios, beta-coefficients are calculated to isolate the direction and magnitude of impact that each independent variable has on human resource needs. Once this has been done, estimated values for the independent variables are inserted into the equation to generate demand figures.

In a related fashion, time series analysis seeks to filter out cyclical trends and random variations in employment so that long-term trends can be estimated. Once these anomalies have been removed, past staffing levels are extrapolated using moving average or exponential smoothing techniques. The obvious limitation of this approach is its failure to consider future changes in business policies or economic conditions.

Research

Virtually all of the reported research on human resource forecasting has focused on the domestic practices of American firms, raising concerns about whether the findings described below can be extrapolated. Bearing this caveat in mind, three kinds of studies have been performed examining the prevalence of individual techniques, the determinants of method choice and the predictive accuracy of select forecasting approaches. Surveys conducted during the 1970s and 1980s revealed that most practitioners were more inclined to utilize qualitative methods which de-emphasized mathematical analyses. Expert estimates and replacement charts were used to forecast human resource demand far more often than were time series and computer simulations. The use of skills inventories and succession planning/replacement charts likewise dwarfed flow models, simulations and operations management methods as means of forecasting supply regardless of the planning horizon being evaluated.

It is difficult to account for the predominance of qualitative forecasting. One possibility is that human resource management units generally lack staff with the experience or academic training to apply complex quantitative models (see HUMAN RESOURCE MANAGEMENT). Alternatively, top management may not attach enough significance to human resource planning to allocate the funds needed for expensive forecasting approaches. Fiorito *et al.* (1985) found that organizational size was positively correlated with forecasting sophistication in two of the four industries studied. This is broadly consistent with the argument that technique adoption is influenced by resource availability. In addition, planners with economics degrees were more likely to employ rigorous quantitative techniques than those with degrees in human resource management, business administration, industrial engineering or other disciplines. More research is clearly needed in this area to pinpoint the determinants of forecasting practices.

Craft (1980, 1988) argued that environmental characteristics should be a pivotal consideration in the choice of forecasting methods. Assume that the firm's external environment can be classified on the basis of its unpredictability (that is, stable versus dynamic) and the breadth and depth of information needed to understand it at a particular moment (simple versus complex). Craft suggested that qualitative forecasting based on historical data (such as replacement charting and skills inventories) is most appropriate in stable–simple environments. Although they were not mentioned, quantitative approaches like linear regression and time series analysis also seem very appropriate in this type of setting. Subjective and intuitive procedures (such as expert estimate and Delphi) were paired with dynamic–complex environments. Stable–complex environments seem tailor-made for multiple regression, Markov analysis and goal programming, while those characterized as dynamic–simple may be more conducive to judgmental, qualitative methods.

Surprisingly little attention has been devoted to the accuracy of human resource forecasting. Milkovich *et al.* (1972) reported a higher level of agreement between a Delphi estimate of the demand for buyers and the actual number that were hired than was apparent for an estimate based on regression analysis. Gillespie *et al.* (1976) found that their Markov model of job movements in a large accounting firm predicted annual staffing levels within 4 per cent of the true distribution. In contrast, Gascoigne (1968) discussed several unsuccessful attempts to forecast accurate manpower levels in a British company. Regression analysis failed to explain much of the variance in employment levels, leading to forecasting errors as large as 20 per cent over a two-year period. Wikstrom (1971) recorded widely different forecasting experiences among the eighty-four firms surveyed. Differences in accuracy were associated with: (1) predictability of the industry; (2) time horizon of the forecast; (3) quality of human resource data utilized; (4) extent to which manpower planning was integrated with other planning; and (5) organizational experience with planning in general. Reviewing this body of research, it becomes apparent that no single approach has been investigated enough to draw firm conclusions about relative superiority.

Table 3 presents subjective ratings for a representative cross-section of the forecasting designs that have been discussed. This evaluation achieves two aims. First, it acknowledges that a given design may be highly effective for one kind of forecast yet ill-suited for another. Reading across the rows, one also can pinpoint the inherent strengths and weaknesses of a particular design. This emphasizes the need to match carefully the design with the setting. More realistic expectations and judgements of forecasting might result if practitioners and academics embraced this diagnostic framework.

Other reforms might bolster the credibility of human resource forecasting efforts. Practitioners may be inadvertently conveying a false sense of precision when they transmit forecasts with single point estimates. A preferred approach would be the submission of interval estimates which also state the probability of possible outcomes contained therein (Craft 1980; Yelsey 1982). Next, better integration of qualitative and quantitative forecasting methods is sorely needed. The two are not mutually exclusive, notwithstanding the tendencies of planners and researchers to act as though they were. Some strides have been made in uniting both forecasting orientations. Drandell (1975) developed an innovative procedure that combined time series analysis, managerial (expert) estimates and regression analysis. This composite design surpassed both of the first two techniques in predicting one government agency's human resource levels one year in advance. Causal cross-impact analysis may also hold some promise (Gatewood and Gatewood 1983). This approach asks a group of experts for a subjective development of two data sets: one featuring events/trends having a high expected impact on the dependent variable, and another containing estimates of the future consequences arising from their occurrence or alteration. All of the data later serve as inputs for interactive computer simulations.

Linking human resource flow analyses to strategic planning

The strategic planning process can benefit substantially from various human resource analyses including: (1) the internal and external availability of personnel; (2) impending changes in the legal and socio-economic dimensions of labour markets; (3) human resource competitor intelligence detailing the competencies and capabilities of industry rivals; and (4) the feasibility and impact of proposed strategic alternatives (Craft 1988) (see HUMAN RESOURCE MANAGEMENT; PERSONNEL MANAGEMENT). The later in the planning process these factors are considered, the less likely it is that an organization will maximize whatever competitive advantage can be derived from its workforce. European firms tend to be much more aggressive in incorporating the human resource management function into strategic planning than are US companies. Brewster and Larsen (1992) reported that at least 40 per cent of the firms surveyed directly involved human resource management staff in strategy formulation in nine of the ten western European countries studied. Such participation was the majority practice among Swedish, Norwegian and German companies. In contrast, the human resource management function is much more likely to be involved *post hoc* during strategy implementation in US firms (see, for example, Burack and Gutteridge 1978; Butensky and Harari 1983) (see HUMAN RESOURCE MANAGEMENT IN EUROPE).

US multinationals appear to follow the lead of most domestic businesses. The Bureau of National Affairs (1993) disclosed that 62 per cent of respondent firms held the human resource management department solely responsible for ensuring that international personnel administration coincided with strategic planning, while another 31 per cent assigned that unit partial responsibility. However, nothing in the data suggested that these departments participated in goal *development*. Miller *et al.* (1986) similarly found that

	Captures historical trends and patterns	Takes HR flows over time into account	Changes in predictive factors can be addressed on a regular basis	Assumptions about the future can be designed into the forecast	Useful in assessing the quality of human capital available
Judgemental estimates	Sometimes valid	Fully invalid	Fully valid	Sometimes valid	Fully invalid
Delphi	Fully valid	Often valid	Sometimes valid	Fully valid	Often valid
Ratios/relationships derived from regression or comparative analysis	Fully valid	Sometimes valid	Fully invalid	Fully invalid	Fully invalid
Markov modelling/ Cross-impact analysis	Fully valid	Fully valid	Sometimes valid	Fully invalid	Sometimes valid
Optimization models	Fully invalid	Sometimes valid	Sometimes valid	Fully valid	Often valid

Table 3 Validity of human resource forecasting designs
Source: Adapted from Yesley (1982)

the human resource function was largely ignored in the formulation of global strategic plans, relegated instead to an oversight role in its implementation. It therefore is not surprising to learn that senior executives in US-based firms devote no more than 10 per cent of their time on average to international human resource management strategy (Reynolds 1992). Yet available evidence indicates that global competitiveness will hinge increasingly on building timely, comprehensive human resource flow analyses into strategic planning. A recent international survey revealed that Latin American, European, North American and Asian companies awarded a high priority to strengthening the linkage between human resource and business strategies by the year 2000 (Towers Perrin 1992). A majority of the respondents in eleven out of twelve nations also felt that issue identification/strategic studies would be a high-priority human resource activity by the end of the decade.

Accordingly, organizations should institute measures to increase the likelihood that human resource flow analyses discussed in this chapter find their way into the strategic planning process. If immediate inclusion of human resource executives on the strategic planning team constitutes too large a departure from the existing corporate culture, incremental strides toward greater human resource management involvement could include:

1 preparing/purchasing environmental scanning reports of domestic and international labour markets that are distributed to the strategic planning group or management generally;
2 incorporating guidelines and forms for human resource data into the materials managers are to complete in preparation for business planning;
3 charging human resource executives to perform SWOT (strengths, weaknesses, opportunities and threats) analyses that are circulated within top management;
4 opening up the human resource planning process to line management to increase their sense of ownership in the human resource management function; and

5 adding human resource executives to the set of managers that must approve strategic business plans before they can be implemented.

In an increasingly global economy, these kinds of initiatives will greatly enhance a firm's ability to identify the external and internal labour market initiatives which will promote and sustain competitive advantage in a given industry.

3 Conclusion

The foregoing discussion sought to highlight changing patterns of human resource flows across nations and the state of business practice in predicting such phenomena. First, there is a strong indication that workforce diversity will become a more prominent management challenge in AIEs and NIEs alike in the decades ahead. The ongoing diversification of sender countries in international migration flows already has altered significantly the ethnic mix of host labour markets in receiver countries in North America and western Europe. Highly restrictive immigration criteria have not insulated the more prosperous Asian countries from similar forces for change given the magnitude of illegal immigration activity. Other contributing factors in most societies are the growing labour force participation rates of women and individuals whose age exceeds cultural norms for retirement. All of these groups bring different expectations and needs to the workplace, suggesting that organizational cultures will need to be modified to appeal to a broader set of internal stakeholders. Firms that respond effectively should have access to a larger external labour-supply pool *vis-à-vis* competitors who cling to traditional labour market practices. Second, there is likely to be increased experimentation with contingent employment by businesses and governments around the world. Pervasive corporate restructuring in developed countries has placed a premium on utilizing labour-market segments that are amenable to more flexible work relationships, be they in the form of temporary assignments, longer-term leasing of services, or more widespread use of part-time employment. Locating and motivating individuals to be productive and committed to organizations offering such arrangements remain critical supply-side challenges to overcome for interested firms. The continued growth of contract migration as a means of expanding local infrastructure further underscores this metamorphosis in the nature of employment. Third, and perhaps most important, emerging economies will contribute increasingly, over time, to the world's net growth in highly-skilled labour. This development argues strongly for a shift away from ethnocentric staffing policies within multinational enterprises, and for a greater willingness by domestic firms to creatively draw upon the talents of legal aliens who are studying/training within their national borders. For many firms, the biggest obstacles to capitalizing on these opportunities are the lack of sophistication in human resource planning and ambivalence toward aggressively incorporating such data into the strategic planning process. Both constraints can be remedied with the appropriate vision and support from the executive management team.

GARY FLORKOWSKI
UNIVERSITY OF PITTSBURGH

Further reading

(References cited in the text marked *)

* Adler, N.J. and Bartholomew, S. (1992) 'Managing globally competent people', *Academy of Management Executive* 6 (3): 52–65. (Makes a case for the creation of human resource management systems that are transnational in scope, representation and process, as well as the gap that North American firms must bridge to achieve this outcome.)

* Adler, N.J. and Izraeli, D.N. (eds) (1994) *Competitive Frontiers: Women Managers in a Global Economy*, Cambridge, MA: Blackwell. (An extensive compilation of international commentaries on the changing status of women.)

* Appleyard, R. (1989) 'International migration and developing countries', in R. Appleyard (ed.), *The Impact of International Migration on Developing Countries*, Paris: Organization for Economic Cooperation and Development. (A brief overview of the economic plight of developing economies that service the skilled labour needs of developed countries.)

* Bartel, A.P. and Koch, M.J. (1991) 'Internal migration of U.S. immigrants', in J.M. Abowd and R.B. Freeman (eds), *Immigration, Trade, and the Labor Market*, Chicago, IL: University of Chicago Press. (An empirical study investigating the internal mobility patterns of Asian, central and South American, and European immigrants who entered the USA after 1964.)

* Baum (1992) 'Hiring and firing: labour shortage spurs rethink on foreign workers', *Far Eastern Economic Review* 155 (15): 15. (A brief note summarizing new labour guidelines issued by the Taiwanese government to ease restrictions on the use of foreign labour.)

* Bohning, W.R. (1991) 'Integration and immigration pressures in western Europe', *International Labour Review* 130 (4): 445–58. (An interesting commentary on the public policy options available to western European nations to cope with immigration pressures.)

* Borjas, G.J. (1988) *International Differences in the Labor Market Performance of Immigrants*, Kalamazoo, MI: W.E. Upjohn Institute for Employment Research. (Reviews immigration trends in the USA, Canada and Australia, and conducts an empirical study of the determinants of immigrant-stock quality.)

* Borjas, G.J. (1992) 'Immigration research in the 1980s: a turbulent decade', in D. Lewin, O.S. Mitchell and P.D. Sherer (eds), *Research Frontiers in Industrial Relations and Human Resources*, Madison, WI: Industrial Relations Research Association. (An excellent summary of US immigration trends before 1980 and the accompanying studies of their labour market effects.)

* Brewster, C. and Larsen, H.H. (1992) 'Human resource management in Europe: evidence from ten countries', *International Journal of Human Resource Management* 3: 409–34. (A groundbreaking study detailing systematic variation across countries in the diffusion of human resource responsibilities within firms and the human resource management function's role in business strategy.)

* Bronstein, A.S. (1991) 'Temporary work in western Europe: threat or complement to permanent employment?', *International Labour Review* 130 (3): 291–310. (An account of temporary employment practices and policies in the region.)

* Burack, E.H. and Gutteridge, T.G. (1978) 'Institutional manpower planning: rhetoric versus reality', *California Management Review* 20 (3):

13–22. (A field study of the attributes of employment planning systems in the United States.)

* Bureau of National Affairs (1993) *Human Resources Activities, Budgets and Staff: 1992–93*, SHRM–BNA survey no 58, Washington, DC: Bureau of National Affairs. (Describes the resources and activities of human resource management departments for a sample of large US firms.)

* Butensky, C.F. and Harari, O. (1983) 'Models versus reality: an analysis of twelve human resource planning systems', *Human Resource Planning* 6 (1): 11–24. (An empirical study assessing the extent to which human resource management planning systems in a sample of large US corporations incorporated features advocated by planning professionals.)

* Chiu, S. and Levin, D.A. (1993) 'From a labour-surplus to a labour-scarce economy: challenges to human resource management in Hong Kong', *International Journal of Human Resource Management* 4 (1): 159–88. (A discussion of the socioeconomic underpinnings of Hong Kong's prevailing labour-market problems and the need for more responsive governmental and corporate initiatives.)

* Conference Board (1992) *Recruiting and Selecting International Managers*, report no. 998, New York: Conference Board. (Survey findings are reported regarding the staffing practices of a large sample of American-based multinational enterprises and a small comparison group of European and Asian MNEs.)

* Copp, R. (1977) 'Locus of industrial relations decision making in multinationals', in R.F. Banks and J. Stieber (eds), *Multinationals, Unions, and Labor Relations in Industrialized Countries*, Ithaca, NY: Cornell University. (Describes one US multinational's approach to structuring and managing industrial-relations decisions on an international scale.)

* Craft, J.A. (1980) 'A critical perspective on human resource planning', *Human Resource Planning* 3 (1): 39–52. (The author presents an excellent critique of human resource management planning activities in American firms.)

* Craft, J.A. (1988) 'Human resource planning and strategy', in L. Dyer (ed.), *Human Resource Management: Evolving Roles and Responsibilities*, Washington, DC: Bureau of National Affairs. (This work develops a compelling framework for engineering more effective linkages between human resource management planning efforts and the larger strategic planning process.)

* Desatnick, R.L. and Bennett, M.L. (1978) *Human Resource Management in the Multinational Company*, New York: Nichols Publishing. (An in-depth discussion of the human resource management challenges encountered in multinational firms.)

* Diesenhouse, S. (1993) 'A temp firm with a difference', *New York Times* 26 December: F3. (This article profiles how one US temporary agency is trying to improve workforce retention.)

* Drandell, M. (1975) 'A composite forecasting methodology for manpower planning utilizing objective and subjective criteria', *Academy of Management Journal* 18: 510–19. (A field study assessing the predictive power of pre-existing and hybrid employment forecasting methods.)

* Draper, J. and Merchant, J.R. (1978) 'Selecting the most appropriate manpower model', in D.T. Bryant and R.J. Niehaus (eds), *Manpower Planning and Organizational Design*, New York: Plenum Press. (Essential decision-making criteria are reviewed to guide the selection of planning models.)

* *The Economist* (1991) 'The glamour of Gaijins', 21 September: 78. (A brief note about one Japanese company's plan to assign large numbers of foreign managers to home-country business units.)

* Evers-Koelman, I., Fischer, M.M. and Nijkamp, P. (1987) 'Results of cross-national comparisons of regional labour markets in 15 countries', in M.M. Fischer and P. Nijkamp (eds), *Regional Labour Markets*, New York: Elsevier Science Publishers B.V. (The authors identify major labour market changes which are evident within fifteen select countries and review significant public-policy measures that have been instituted as a result.)

* Eyraud, F., Marsden, D. and Silvestre, J. (1990) 'Occupational and internal labour markets in Britain and France', *International Labour Review* 129 (4): 501–17. (Compares evolving staffing and development trends among British and French employers.)

Feuer, M.J., Niehaus, R.J. and Sheridan, J.A. (1984) 'Human resource forecasting: a survey of practice and potential', *Human Resource Planning* 7 (2): 85–98. (A field study surveying the structural features of human resource management forecasting efforts in US companies.)

* Fiorito, J., Stone, T.H. and Greer, C.R. (1985) 'Factors affecting the choice of human resource forecasting techniques', *Human Resource Planning* 8 (1): 1–24. (An empirical analysis of

the determinants of planning-method choice in American firms.)

* Flynn, G. (1995) 'Contingent staffing requires serious strategy', *Personnel Journal* 74 (4): 50–8. (Highlights the experiences of several American companies that have increased their reliance on flexible staffing approaches.)

* Funkhouser, E. and Trejo, S.J. (1995) 'The labor market skills of recent male immigrants: evidence from the current population survey', *Industrial and Labor Relations Review* 48 (4): 792–811. (An interesting empirical study updating the labour-market performance of groups that immigrated to the United States in the late 1980s.)

* Gascoigne, I.M. (1968) 'Manpower forecasting at the enterprise level: a case study', *British Journal of Industrial Relations* 6: 94–106. (Reports the results of a British field study of employment forecasting accuracy.)

* Gatewood, R.D. and Gatewood, E.J. (1983) 'The use of expert data in human resource planning: guidelines from strategic forecasting', *Human Resource Planning* 6 (2): 83–94. (The authors discuss several innovative attempts to strengthen the value of qualitatively oriented forecasting techniques.)

* Gillespie, J.F., Leininger, W.E. and Kahalas, H. (1976) 'A human resource planning and valuation model', *Academy of Management Journal* 19: 650–6. (A case study evaluating the accuracy employment-supply forecasts generated via Markov analysis.)

* Grinold, R.C. and Marshall, K.T. (1977) *Manpower Planning Models*, New York: Elsevier North-Holland. (An expanded discussion of alternative planning models for employment.)

* Hall, D.T. and Mervis, P.H. (1994) 'The new workplace and older workers', in J.A. Auerbach and J.C. Welch (eds), *Aging and Competition: Rebuilding the U.S. Workforce*, Washington, DC: National Planning Association. (Articulates an agenda for organizational change to increase firms' ability to derive competitive advantage from an aging workforce.)

Heneman, H.G., Jr and Seltzer, G. (1970) *Employer Manpower Planning and Forecasting*, Manpower Research Monograph No. 19, United States Department of Labor, Washington, DC: US Government Printing Office. (Survey results depicting the state of manpower planning practices in the United States.)

* International Labour Office (1981) *Multinationals' Training Practices and Development*, Geneva: International Labour Office. (A study of the training commitment that MNEs exhibit in

developing countries and how these programmes are administered.)

* International Labour Office (1987) *World Labour Report 1–2*, Oxford: Oxford University Press. (This report identifies a typology of international migration movements and presents comprehensive statistics of such activity during the 1970s.)

* Johnston, W.B. (1991) 'Global work force 2000: the new world labor market', *Harvard Business Review* 69 (3): 115–27. (Summarizes recent and projected labour market trends in emerging and advanced industrialized economies.)

* Kanter, R.M. (1994) 'U.S. competitiveness and the aging workforce: toward organizational and institutional change', in J.A. Auerbach and J.C. Welch (eds), *Aging and Competition: Rebuilding the U.S. Workforce*, Washington, DC: National Planning Association. (An appraisal of how corporate restructuring has impacted American's aging workforce and its global competitiveness.)

* Lederer, E.M. (1993) 'Migration creating crisis for all nations', *Pittsburgh Post-Gazette* 7 July: 3. (A brief note documenting mounting pressures on receiver countries to accommodate increased immigration.)

Lockhart, T. and Brewster, C. (1992) 'Human resource management in the European Community', in C. Brewster, A. Hegewishch T. Lockhart and L. Holden (eds), *The European Human Resource Management Guide*, New York: Academic Press (A review of prominent social-policy issues pertaining to labour within the European Union.)

* Mangum, G., Mayhill, D. and Nelson, K. (1985) 'The temporary help market: a response to the dual internal labor market', *Industrial and Labor Relations Review* 38 (4): 599–611. (An empirical study of the use of temporary employees and their organizational impact.)

* Martin, P.L. (1991) *The Unfinished Story: Turkish Labour Migration to Western Europe*, Geneva: International Labour Office. (An illuminating investigation of the effects that Turkish guestworkers have had on the economies of western Europe and Turkey.)

* Martin, P.L. and Miller, M.J. (1980) 'Guestworkers: lessons from western Europe', *Industrial and Labor Relations Review* 33 (3): 315–30. (Evaluates the desirability of a guestworker policy for the United States based on French, Swiss and German experiences with foreign-sourced employees.)

* Milkovich, G.T., Annoni, A. and Mahoney, T. (1972) 'The use of Delphi procedures in man-

power forecasting', *Management Science* 19 (4): 381–8. (A field study evaluating the predictive power of alternative employment forecasting methods.)

* Miller, E.L., Beechler, S., Bhatt, B. and Nath, R. (1986) 'The relationship between the global strategic planning process and the human resource management function', *Human Resource Management* 9: 9–23. (An enlightening case study of how a small sample of US multinationals link the human resource management function to strategic planning and its implementation.)

* Moore, J. (1990) 'Taiwan does little to stem tide of alien workers', *Far Eastern Economic Review* 148 (14): 20. (A short synopsis of Taiwan's illegal alien problem.)

* Nelan, B.W. (1993) 'Not quite so welcome anymore', *Time* 142 (21): 14. (Part of a special issue examining America's struggle with immigration-linked pressures for extensive social change in an economically constrained environment.)

* Niehaus, R.J. (1979) *Computer-Assisted Human Resources Planning*, New York: Wiley. (Discusses numerous, innovative computer applications pertaining to human resource management planning.)

* Niehaus, R.J. (1988) 'Models for human resource decisions', *Human Resource Planning* 11 (2): 95–107. (Describes models of human resource forecasting designs.)

* Organization for Economic Cooperation and Development (1991) *The OECD Employment Outlook*, Paris: Organization for Economic Cooperation and Development. (The most pertinent section of this report profiles major labour market trends for the region's newly industrializing economies.)

* Osterman, P. (1992) 'Internal labor markets in a changing environment: models and evidence', in D. Lewin, O.S. Mitchell and P.D. Sherer (eds), *Research Frontiers in Industrial Relations and Human Resources*, Madison, WI: Industrial Relations Research Association. (The author combines quantitative and qualitative data to assess the fate of internal labour markets in American companies.)

* Overman, S. (1993) 'Temporary services go global', *HR Magazine* 38 (8): 72–4. (Summarizes the stage of development of the temporary-services industry in select countries.)

* Paik Sunoo, B. (1994) 'Temporary services create employment opportunities', *Personnel Journal* 73 (7): 56. (Survey statistics are excerpted to document the prevalence of temporary employment relationships in the United States.)

* Pandya, M. (1995) 'Employee leasing: the risks of swimming in a big pool', *New York Times* 11 June: F10. (The author presents a brief exposé of this form of contingent employment in the United States.)

* Reynolds, C. (1992) 'Are you ready to make IHR a global function', *HR News: International HR*, February: C1–C3. (Survey results are reported concerning the structure and activities of the international human resource management function in US-based multinational firms.)

* Salt, J. (1989) 'A comparative overview of international trends and types, 1950–1980', *International Migration Review* 23: 431–56. (Discusses how the volume and character of international migration has shifted during the post-World War II era.)

* Salt, J. (1992) 'The future of international labor migration', *International Migration Review* 26 (4): 1077–111. (Updates the changing character of existing and emerging regional migration networks.)

* Sano, Y. (1993) 'Changes and continued stability in Japanese HRM systems: choice in the share economy', *International Journal of Human Resources Management* 4 (1): 11–27. (Examines the fundamental restructuring of Japanese human resource management practices in large, contemporary organizations.)

* Sasajima, Y. (1993) 'Changes in labour supply and their impacts on human resource management: the case of Japan', *International Journal of Human Resource Management* 4 (1): 29–44. (The author assesses how Japanese human resource management practices have been modified to deal with significant demographic changes in that nation's labour market.)

* Shadid, W.A., Spaan, E.J.A.M. and Speckmann, J.D. (1992) 'Labour migration and the policy of the Gulf States', in F. Eelens, T. Schampers and J.D. Speckmann (eds), *Labour Migration to the Middle East: From Sri Lanka to the Gulf*, London: Kegan Paul International. (An account of migration activity in the region and the public policies that seek to regulate it.)

* Shimada, H. (1994) *Japan's 'Guest Workers': Issues and Public Policies*, Tokyo: University of Tokyo Press. (The role of foreign workers in the Japanese economy and possible public policy responses by the host nation are profiled.)

* Standing, G. (1988) 'Would revenue-sharing pay cure unemployment?', *International Labour Review* 127: 1–18. (The author develops an argument that contests the macroeconomic em-

ployment benefits that have been attributed to profit sharing by its proponents.)

* Tasker, R. (1990) 'A rising wage of illegal immigrants: the lure of jobs', *Far Eastern Economic Review* 148 (14): 18–19. (A discussion of illegal immigration levels in east and southeast Asia.)

* Towers Perrin (1992) *Priorities for Competitive Advantage: A Worldwide Human Resource Study*, Chicago, IL: Towers Perrin. (A global study of the human resource management priorities and initiatives that will influence global competitiveness in the twenty-first century.)

* Tung, R.L. (1982) 'Selection and training procedures of U.S., European, and Japanese multinationals', *California Management Review* 25: 57–71. (A comparative study of the staffing and development practices that characterize MNEs based in different regions.)

* Walker, J.W. (1980) *Human Resource Planning*, New York: McGraw-Hill. (Describes the evolution of human resource planning in the USA until 1980.)

* Wikstrom, W.S. (1971) *Manpower Planning: Evolving Systems*, report no. 521, New York: Conference Board. (Survey results characterizing the state of manpower planning practices among large American companies.)

* Yelsey, A. (1982) 'Validity of human resources forecast designs', *Human Resource Planning* 5 (4): 217–21. (Presents an overarching framework to evaluate the strengths and weaknesses of select forecasting techniques.)

See also: COMMITMENT, EMPLOYMENT AND UNEMPLOYMENT, ECONOMICS OF; FLEXIBILITY; HUMAN RESOURCE MANAGEMENT, INTERNATIONAL; ORGANIZATION BEHAVIOUR; RELOCATION; TRAINING

Related topics in the IEBM: COMMITMENT IN JAPAN; ECONOMICS OF DEVELOPING COUNTRIES; ECONOMIES OF EAST ASIA; MANAGEMENT IN JAPAN; MANAGEMENT IN NORTH AMERICA; MANAGEMENT IN PACIFIC ASIA; MARKOV PROCESSES AND APPLICATIONS; MIGRANT MANAGERS; MODELLING AND FORECASTING

Human resource management

1 Human resource management and
   its importance
2 Goals of human resource
   management
3 Activities and roles
4 Managing the human resource
   function
5 Trends in human resource
   management
6 Conclusions

Overview

Managing human resources effectively has
become vital to organizations of the twenty-
first century. The heightened levels of global
competitiveness has alerted all firms to the
fact that all their resources must be utilized
better than ever before. Human resource management has received much attention recently
because of the recognition that much more
could be gained from a better handling of the
field. Consequently academics have begun to
devote more attention to the topic.

Academics and human resource management professionals together have identified
several human resource activities that are
critical for organizational survival. Survival is
enhanced because of the ability of effective
human resource management to attract, retain, motivate and retrain employees. These
goals have become particularly important
over the past decade because of the rapidly
changing environmental forces such as global
competition. For human resources to be effective, however, requires that not only do the
several human resource activities need to be
performed effectively, but also that the human
resource departments in organizations need to
play several roles and that those in these departments need to have a broader and deeper
range of competencies than previously
required.

1 Human resource management and its importance

Human resource management is the use of
several activities to ensure that human resources are managed effectively for the
benefit of the individual, society and the
business.

(Schuler 1995: 5)

Now more than ever, human resource management is recognized as being critical to the
survival and success of organizations. In 1991
the IBM Corporation and the human resource
consulting firm of Towers Perrin conducted
jointly a worldwide study of nearly 3,000 senior human resource managers and chief
executive officers (CEOs). Results indicate
that about 70 per cent of human resource managers see the human resource function as critical to the success of organizations: by the year
2000 more than 90 per cent expect the human
resource department to be critical. While the
human resource respondents were perhaps
slightly more positive about this trend, the
CEOs were very similar in their level of
agreement (Towers Perrin 1992). Before
defining human resource management and its
importance, however, it might be informative
to step back for a moment and establish the
historical context of where we are today.

The early years

As with many disciplines, the study of managing people has changed rather dramatically
during this century. Beginning with the works
of Taylor (see TAYLOR, F.W.) around the turn
of the century, the focus of managing people
in organizations was on developing precise
analytical schemes to select and reward an
individual. This focus was typically for the
purposes of motivating, controlling and
improving the productivity of entry-level
employees. During the 1920s work on these
analytical schemes expanded to encompass

issues of appraising and training individuals, essentially for the same purposes.

While the focus during the first quarter century was on the individual employee, the second quarter was to see it shift to the group. Mayo's work at the Hawthorne plant focused on improving the productivity of individuals by experimenting with groups. His efforts included changing the group composition and incentive schemes. They also included changing environmental conditions, namely lighting and the physical arrangements. Knowledge of groups and the impact of group on individuals advanced with the work of Lewin and Sherif and Sherif during the 1930s and into the 1940s. Yet with few notable exceptions, such as the work of Barnard on CEOs, this work was focused primarily on the people doing the work.

During the 1950s and 1960s much of the work concerned with managing individuals in organizations highlighted individual needs and motivation. Advances were being made in selection and development: the Second World War work with assessment centres expanded to the private sector and the development of tests for selection and placement continued. Work in performance appraisal and training progressed. Yet, again, most of the work focused, explicitly or implicitly, on improving the performance of the individuals doing the work in the organization. At this time, however, the more applied work in these areas related to managing and motivating individuals became the domain of those identifying primarily with personnel psychology and industrial and organizational psychology. The more theoretical work came under the new domain of organizational behaviourists.

Enter human resource management

During the 1970s another discipline evolved under the name of human resource management. Encompassing the methodological tradition of the personnel and industrial and organizational psychologists and the theoretical frameworks of the organizational behaviourists, human resource management took on a broader focus than earlier work. This focus included concerns for the safety and health of the worker as well as individual satisfaction and performance. Industrial relations and planning for personnel needs also came within the domain of human resource management. Yet throughout the work on all the human resource management topics, the primary focus of attention remained on the entry-level employee (see INDUSTRIAL AND LABOUR RELATIONS; ORGANIZATION BEHAVIOUR).

In the late 1970s and 1980s, the discipline of organizational strategy started to make an impact upon human resource management. Environmental forces, namely more intense international and domestic competition for companies, also began to make an impact. This dual blow reflected the continued theoretical and applied sides of human resource management. The result of this within human resource management was recognition that a substantial number of organizational characteristics not generally addressed actually had/have substantial impact upon managing human resources. Thus, organizational characteristics such as structure, strategy, size, culture, and product and organizational life cycle began to be incorporated into the work under the human resource management label.

Today, forces of global competition, worldwide labour availability, business ethics and the environment are winning the attention of human resource management. Of course, this does not mean that the issues of the 1970s and 1980s can be forgotten. To the contrary, these are all carried forward, making the job of human resource management challenging, rewarding and exciting.

Collectively, all these events, until the late 1970s and early 1980s, described the discipline and study of 'personnel management' (see PERSONNEL MANAGEMENT). Then the discipline and study began to change (some say that practice was actually leading theory here) and gradually assume the label of 'personnel and human resource management' or just 'human resource management'. Was the change in terminology a reflection of real change? Without a doubt much of the activity in strategic human resource management SHRM and SIHRM, described later in this chapter, addressed new areas of activities.

The questions are then: did this change in labels really change the thrust and focus of the core personnel activities, namely staffing, appraisal and evaluation, compensation, training, safety and industrial relations?; and if so, how?

Providing affirmative answers to both these questions is the insightful characterization offered by Storey (1992). Storey offers 27 points of difference between personnel/industrial relations and human resource management. In turn, these 27 points are grouped into three categories: beliefs and assumptions; strategic aspects; and key levers. As a complement to Storey's characterization, Figure 1 offers a scheme to differentiate between personnel and human resource management.

While exceptions can certainly be found, human resource management has moved from a domestic focus to a more multinational and global focus. There is more concern now for the environment, including ecological issues, and for healthcare and illiteracy. Organizationally, human resource management has gone from being concerned only with the operational issues of personnel to include the

Environmental

  Domestic - - - - - - - - - - - - - Global
  Internal - - - - - - - - - - - - - External

Organizational

  Operational - - - - - - - - - - Strategic
  Attract, retain - - - - - - - - - Bottom line
   and motivate

Managerial

  Functional - - - - - - - - - - - Partner

Self-HR department

  Specialists - - - - - - - - - - - Generalists

Workers

  Conflict - - - - - - - - - - - - - Harmony

HRM practices

  Individual focused - - - - - - - Team focused
  Narrowly developed - - - - - Broadly
           developed

Figure 1 Areas of differences between personnel and human resource management

more strategic, business level concerns of the organization itself. Human resource departments might also be concerned about the operations of key suppliers and customers! Managerially, human resource professionals are working more closely with the line, to some extent a customer of the human resource department. As the human resource profession has become more involved in the global, external and strategic issues of the organization, so has its critical goals changed. Whereas the goals in personnel are attracting, retaining and motivating workers, the goals of human resource management are concerned with the bottom line: competitiveness, profitability, survival, competitive advantage and workforce flexibility. While the goals of attracting, retaining and motivating are still important, they are critical primarily as a means by which to reach and improve the bottom line goals.

This is a move away from a functional orientation where the concern was with developing human resource products and services rather than understanding the human resource implications of the business and the managers. Concurrently, human resource professionals have become more generalist. This trend is articulated at the individual level (each human resource professional becoming multi-skilled) and at the departmental level (teams of different specialists work together to serve the customer). In relation to the employees, the human resource department and the professionals have moved from a philosophical orientation of conflict and differentiation to one of harmony and egalitarianism. In the area of human resource *practices*, whereas personnel management is associated with practices that are narrowly targeted and individually focused, human resource management is associated with practices that are more broadly conceived and team-focused.

This rather brief history is meant to provide the reader with a supplemental perspective to that developed by Storey (1992) in describing the general differences between personnel management and human resource management. While the characterizations in Figure 1 provide relatively clear differences, in practice it is not surprising to find something less than these pure types. Accordingly, these characterizations are presented in Figure 1 not as either/or choices but rather end points on several continua. In fact, this has also reflected the evolution of the discipline with academia. Articles and books evolved from being titled 'personnel/industrial relations management' to 'personnel and human resource management' to 'human resource management'. It is suggested here that this evolution represented movement along the continua presented in Figure 1.

Debates today

As this evolution and transformation of the field of studying and managing human resources have taken place, debates in the field have also evolved. The worthy debates are many, but the ones offered here reflect the six areas given in Figure 1. While there may be differences in the debates depending on which side of the Atlantic one stands, these differences are perhaps more of degree than kind (Brewster and Tyson 1991; Sparrow and Hiltrop 1994).

In terms of the environmental area, debate revolves around the extent to which the human resource community should be involved in greater social problems outside the organization. Perhaps the best contribution human resource management can make to the community is to make its own organization as effective and efficient as possible. Others say, of course, that it is impossible not to be concerned about the impact of the organization upon the environment and its dependence for supplies, such as skilled individuals.

Some would also debate the appropriateness and the ability of human resource management to become more strategic. There are many problems such as healthcare and literacy that are critical to the organization and rightly fall to the human resource department. Responsibility for these areas, some would suggest, is right and appropriate for human resource management. Expanding beyond this operational domain of personnel is thus unnecessary. Furthermore, as human resource practitioners are not trained to be

knowledgeable in the business, they lack the ability to be strategic.

Continuing with the same line of reasoning then, the human resource manager probably best serves the line manager by acting as the behind-the-scenes supplier of materials and lines rather than as in equal partnership on centre stage.

If the personnel profession is really one requiring training and the possession of a technical body of knowledge, is the personnel professional likely to be more effective if focused on a limited number of topics or practices? Can the compensation specialist really be expected to develop valid selection tests? Within academia a similar debate is heard: should business schools be left to teach only the general, more strategically focused human resource management, thereby leaving the psychology departments to teach the traditional personnel management specialities?

Is the harmony model possible between workers and managers? Are these two groups really of the same cloth? Will there always be conflict between the owners and their representatives and the workers? Is the human resource professional, perhaps by playing the role of partner, subverting the true interests of the workers? Of course, the defending position here says that the partnership role for human resource management implies not carrying out what is in the interests of the managers, but rather what is in the best interests of the business. Is it reasonable to assume that the manager acts in the interests of the business better than others, including the human resource manager? Here it can be argued that the expression of partnership means the human resource manager working with managers and the workers in the best interests of the business and the best interests of the community.

In countries described as being individualistic by Hofstede (1980), is it appropriate, indeed ethical, to impose team-focused human resource practices on the workers? Regardless of whether workers are working effectively in teams to improve quality today, will they be able to continue this type of activity? In the short run workers can adapt, but is this in their best interests in the long term?

Similarly, is it fair for superior workers to accept an average wage for the group's productivity? Or, is it fair and reasonable to ask workers to evaluate each other (indeed, is this consistent with the model of harmony?) or to make decisions about employing and dismissing? In this process is the organization asking the workers to represent themselves rather than asking a formal union organization to represent them? The debate can continue by focusing on the real role of teams and harmony. Is it really to improve efficiency and the lot of the workers, or is it to remove the force of the union from the workplace? As human resource practices move from being more narrowly developed to more broadly developed, are organizations making themselves more attractive and unions less attractive to the workers? Are workers more empowered and involved less likely to seek power through third-party representation? And even if workers do respond favourably and this serves the organization well in doing battle with global competition, who guarantees that these conditions will last?

In summary, the discipline of managing human resources (see ORGANIZATION BEHAVIOUR) in organizations has transformed itself tremendously throughout the twentieth century. Today what organizations and the human resource/personnel professional have is a range of alternatives for managing human resources. Similarly, academics have an equally vast set of topics to address. It appears that no group has all the answers. Indeed, as the review of some of debate topics suggests, for any answer exists a question, or even a challenge. Perhaps an additional duty of the academics and the practitioners is to provide an understanding of these topics as well as the substantive content of the many areas of the profession itself. While it is far beyond the scope of this entry to provide greater insight into these debate topics, it is possible to address the substantive content of the many areas of the profession. But even with this focus, it is only possible to provide a brief review. Certainly many excellent books and articles offer much greater description of them all. What follows is a description of the discipline that is intended to represent a composite view

of personnel and human resource management. While it is certainly more heavily weighted to the right-hand side of Figure 1, it gives credence to the left-hand side as well. This seems consistent with practice and academia. This begins with the goals of managing human resources.

2 Goals of human resource management

While serving the very success of the business can certainly be regarded as an important goal of human resource management, it is a rather broad conception. Several specific goals help lead to this overall achievement of success and importance. The three general goals or purposes traditionally associated with human resource management are attracting applicants, retaining desirable employees and motivating employees. Increasingly, another goal is being added: retraining employees.

The heightened attention paid to how a firm manages its human resources is attributed to the recognition that effective management of human resources has a positive impact on the firm's overall success and, ultimately, its bottom line. This term refers to the organization's survival, growth, profitability, competitiveness and flexibility in adapting to changing conditions. Human resource departments positively affect the bottom line through: (1) improving productivity; (2) improving quality of worklife; (3) increasing the firm's legal compliance; (4) gaining competitive advantage; and (5) assuring workforce flexibility – the more specific goals of managing human resources (Schuler and Huber 1993). These specific goals and their relationship with human resource activities and the environment described below are shown in Figure 2.

3 Activities and roles

Human resource management activities

The activities performed by the human resource department include: (1) scanning and analysing the environment; (2) planning for human resource needs; (3) staffing the human resource needs of the organization; (4) appraising employee behaviour; (5) compensating employee behaviour; (6) improving the work environment; and (7) establishing and maintaining effective work relationships. Not all human resource departments of organizations currently perform all these activities, but the trend is clearly in that direction. Certainly, they are performed in the most effective firms in highly competitive environments today (Towers Perrin 1992) (see CAREERS; HUMAN RESOURCE DEVELOPMENT; PAYMENT SYSTEMS; TRAINING).

Scanning, analysing and planning
Increasingly, the success in managing human resources depends upon scanning and

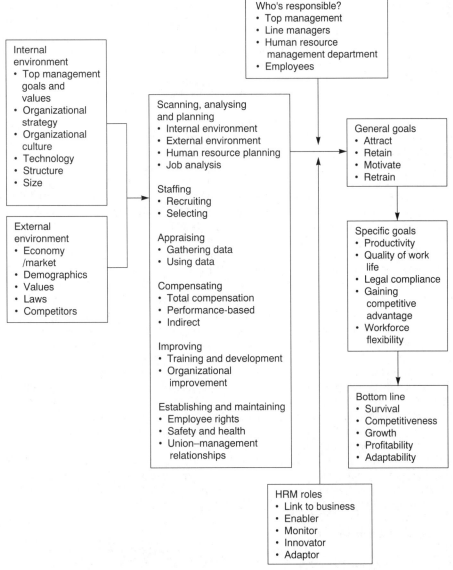

Figure 2 Human resource management goals and environment
Source: Adapted from Schuler and Huber (1993: 32)

analysing the environment, both internal and external, and human resource planning. A particularly important aspect of the external environment is the extensive set of legal considerations. These legal considerations affect virtually all human resource activities. Other aspects of the external environment that are important to scan and analyse include levels of domestic and international competition, workforce and demographic changes, and general economic and organizational trends. Important aspects of the internal environment include the strategy of the firm, its technology, the goals and values of top management, the size of the firm, its culture and its structure. Understanding these internal and external environments and scanning them constantly ensures that the needs of the business are being served and that the demands of the environment are being considered in human resource management decisions.

Planning for human resource needs
Human resource planning involves two major components: planning and forecasting the organization's short-term and long-term human resource requirements (the macro component); and analysing the jobs in the organization to determine the skills and abilities needed (the micro component). These two components are essential if the other human resource management activities are to be performed effectively. They indicate: (1) what types of employees (namely, what competencies) and how many of them are needed today, as well as tomorrow; (2) how employees will be obtained (for example, from outside recruiting or by internal transfers and promotions); and (3) the training and development programmes the organization may need. In fact, these two components of planning can be viewed as the major factors influencing the staffing and training and development activities of the entire organization (see HUMAN RESOURCE DEVELOPMENT; TRAINING).

Staffing the organization's human resource needs
Once the organization's human resource needs have been determined, they are filled by the staffing activities. These activities include

recruiting job candidates; and selecting the most appropriate job applicants for the available jobs. Both activities must be carried out in accordance with legally mandated fair employment practices, and with attention to how they can affect the overall direction of an organization.

The organization must cast a wide net in recruiting potential employees in order to ensure a full and fair search for job candidates. After the candidates have been identified, they must be selected. Common procedures used in selection include obtaining completed application forms or résumés; interviewing the candidates; checking education, background, experience and references; and administering various forms of tests (see RECRUITMENT AND SELECTION).

Appraising employee behaviour
The performance of employees must be appraised (see PERFORMANCE APPRAISAL). If they are not doing well it is necessary to diagnose the reasons. It may show that employee training is necessary or that some type of motivation should be provided, such as more rewards, feedback or a redesigned job. All of this is accomplished often by the human resource department cooperating with line managers in gathering performance appraisal information and utilizing performance appraisal information.

Not all employees are 'good' ones. Some may be continually absent, some may be alcoholics or some may be late to work all the time. With the rise of employee rights, the greater concern for social responsibility and the increasing cost of replacing employees, however, some organizations find it preferable to retain employees and improve their performance rather than dismiss them. This means that employees should be told when they are not doing well and offered help to improve. Performance appraisal can be helpful also in identifying training needs and determining employee compensation.

Compensating employee behaviour
Employees are generally rewarded on the basis of the value of the job, their personal contributions and their performance.

Although providing rewards based on level of performance can increase an employee's motivation to perform, rewards are often given only according to the value of the job. Other rewards (namely, indirect fringe benefits) are provided just for being a member of the organization. The compensating activity includes: (1) administering direct compensation; (2) providing performance-based pay; and (3) administering indirect benefits (see PAYMENT SYSTEMS).

Improving the work environment

Improving the work environment is a crucial activity of human resource management. As domestic and international competition increase, organizations have to improve their competitiveness. This may mean implementing organization improvement programmes: (1) to train employees and provide management development opportunities; (2) to raise the level of product or service quality; (3) to enhance innovation; or (4) to reduce costs. This may also mean redesigning jobs and improving communications with employees. All these programmes come under the activity of organization improvement. Making these available to employees can result in higher employee satisfaction and better retention rates. They can also ensure that the firm has the necessary employee competencies and flexibility (see WORK AND ORGANIZATION SYSTEMS).

Establishing and maintaining effective work relationships

This function is composed of the following sets of activities: (1) respecting employee rights; (2) providing a safe and healthy workplace; (3) understanding the reasons and methods used by employees when organizing; and (4) bargaining and settling grievances with employees and the organizations representing them. A crucial activity here is improving the physical and sociopsychological workplace to maximize employee safety and health. Failure to improve conditions for health and safety can be illegal and very costly.

Increasingly, employees are gaining more rights. Consequently, employment decisions such as dismissals, layoffs and demotions must be made with care and evidence provided. It is important that the managers of the organization be aware of all employee rights. The human resource manager is in an excellent position to inform line managers of these rights.

This activity is particularly important for organizations that have unions. For example, unions can be instrumental in developing new programmes for the improvement of human resources (which result from joint union-management programmes) (Kochan *et al.* 1992).

Roles of the human resource department

Human resource departments in effective firms in highly competitive environments today must play many roles in the organization. The more roles they play, the more likely they will be effective in improving the organization's productivity, enhancing the quality of worklife in the organization, complying with all the necessary laws and regulations related to managing human resources effectively, gaining competitive advantage and enhancing workforce flexibility.

Linking human resource management to the business role

Traditionally, many human resource departments had a relatively limited involvement in the total organization's affairs and goals. Human resource managers were often concerned only with making staffing plans, providing specific job training programmes or running annual performance appraisal programmes. Consequently, these human resource managers were concerned only with the short-term, operational and managerial – perhaps day-to-day – human resource needs.

With the growing importance of human resource management to the success of the firm, human resource managers and their departments are getting more involved in the organization, and establishing a *partnership* with line managers. They are getting to know the needs of the business, where it is going, where it should be going – and are helping it to get there. As a consequence they and their departments are playing many more roles; linking human resource management to the business role is one of the newest and most important of these.

Enabler role

In reality, human resource programmes succeed because line managers make them succeed. The human resource department's fundamental job, therefore, is to enable line managers to make things happen. Thus, in the more traditional human resource activities – such as selecting, interviewing, training, evaluating, rewarding, counselling, promoting and dismissing – the human resource manager is basically providing a service to line managers. In addition, the human resource department administers direct and indirect compensation programmes. It can also assist line managers by providing information about, and interpretation of, fair employment legislation, and safety and health standards.

To fulfil these responsibilities, the human resource department must be accessible or it will lose touch with the line managers' needs. The human resource staff should be as close as possible to the people. A trend in this role of being accessible and of providing services and products to others (customers) is called *customerization*. Customerization means viewing everybody as a customer, whether internal or external to the organization, and then putting that customer first (Schuler and Jackson 1988). For human resource departments, customers are typically other line and staff managers. Increasingly, customers include other organizations and even the non-managerial employees. Another important part of customerization is *benchmarking*. Benchmarking is a structured approach for looking outside an organization by studying other organizations and adapting the best outside practices to complement internal operations with creative, new ideas. One of the greatest values of benchmarking that firms find is learning about the practices that are used by competitors and other companies to achieve their results. As such, benchmarking provides insights into new ways of carrying out human resource management and challenges 'business as usual' methods.

Monitoring role

Although the human resource department may delegate much of the implementation of human resource activities to line managers, it is still responsible for seeing that activities are implemented fairly and consistently. This is especially true today because of the complex set of legal regulations. Responses to these regulations can best be made by a central group supplied with accurate information, the necessary expertise and the support of top management.

Expertise is also needed for implementing human resource activities such as distributing employee benefits. Since employing human resource management experts is costly, organizations hire as few as possible and centralize them. Their expertise then filters through to other areas of the organization (Carroll 1991).

In organizations with several locations and several divisions or units, tension often exists between the need to decentralize and the need for centralizing the expertise necessary to comply with complex regulations. A major trend in this role of monitoring and coordinating development is the use of computer technology and human resource information systems.

Innovator role

Important and ever-expanding roles for the human resource department include providing up-to-date application of current techniques and developing and exploring innovative approaches to human resource problems and concerns. Benchmarking certainly helps in this innovator role.

Today, organizations are asking their human resource departments for innovative approaches and solutions on how to improve productivity and quality of worklife while complying with the law in an environment of high uncertainty, energy conservation and intense international competition. They are also demanding approaches and solutions that can be justified in economic terms. To achieve this and to better manage the organization's human resources, human resource management utilizes a contribution assessment.

The human resource department can demonstrate its contribution to the organization in many ways. As human resource departments seek to become partners with the rest of the organization in providing strategic direction, they are being pro-active in providing evidence of their contributions.

While the contributions of human resource departments can be assessed using many criteria or standards, these contributions can be grouped into two categories: (1) doing the right thing; and (2) doing things right.

Doing the right thing means the human resource department does things which are needed by the organizations to be successful. In essence, assessors ask if the department is helping the organization be more successful in areas such as competitiveness, profitability, adaptability and strategy implementation. Is it facilitating the work of line managers and employees in their efforts to contribute to the maximum of their potential?

Doing things right means that the human resource department does the right things as efficiently as possible. Of course, the organization wants to employ the best people, but they want to do it at the least cost per employee possible. The human resource department wants to facilitate the work of the line managers, but they want to do it in a way that maximizes the benefit and minimizes the cost.

Adaptor role

It is increasingly necessary that organizations adapt new technologies, structures, processes, cultures, and procedures to meet the demands of stiffer competition. Organizations look to the human resource department for the skills to facilitate organizational change and to maintain organizational flexibility and adaptability. One consequence of this adaptor role is the need to be more future-orientated. For example, as external environments and organizational strategies change, new skills and competencies are needed. To help ensure the right skills and competencies are available at the appropriate time, human resource departments need to correctly anticipate these changes and train employees. Fostering a mind-set of continuous change and offering education

programmes help foster a flexible and adaptable workforce (Walker 1988, 1989).

4 Managing the human resource function

Who is responsible for managing human resources?

Everyone should be responsible for managing human resources; and, as organizations demonstrate more openness and mutuality in their human resource policies and practices, everyone is.

Managing human resources effectively is the task of individuals who have specialized in and are primarily responsible for human resource management – human resource managers and staff and line managers (those in charge of the employees who are producing the products and delivering the services of the company). These two managers are interdependent in the management of human resources. Increasingly they will work together. Thus, CEOs, human resource managers and all levels of senior management will be involved in managing human resources. While this is already happening in some firms, in the recent IBM/Towers Perrin worldwide human resource survey, both CEOs and senior human resource managers agreed that partnership should be occurring to a much greater extent by the year 2000. In this scenario, the human resource department's leader will be counted among senior executives and will play significant roles in acquiring, deploying and utilizing the firm's most vital resources.

Amidst other senior executives, the human resource leader will be indistinguishable from others in concern for and understanding of the needs of the business. Likewise the staff of the human resource department will appear indistinguishable from their counterparts in the firm. Sharing in the human resource function, line managers, human resource staff and non-managerial employees together will forge and implement human resource activities, structure, roles, policies, goals and practices.

Employees are also taking a part in human resource management. For example, employees are to appraise their own performance or that of their colleagues. It is no longer uncommon for employees to write their own job descriptions. Perhaps most significantly, employees are taking a more active role in managing their own careers, assessing their own needs and values and designing their own jobs. None the less, the human resource department must help guide this process. To these ends, the human resource department must be staffed with qualified individuals.

Staffing the human resource department

To perform all those roles effectively the top human resource leaders and staff members need to be functional experts, capable administrators, business consultants and problem solvers with global awareness. Management expects the human resource staff 'to have it all'. Administrative skills are also essential for efficiency. Specialized human resource expertise is also important, but particularly in combination with business knowledge and perspective. In flexible organizations, problem-solving and consulting skills are vital in guiding and supporting new management practices.

Managers would like human resource staff to work closely with them to help solve their people-related business challenges as efficiently and promptly as possible. While line managers may best understand their own people, many desire help in handling their people-related business problems. As the human resource staff becomes more capable and effective, managers find it easier to work with them as partners in dealing with these problems.

Being at the top of the organization, reporting directly to the CEO and possessing business skills allow the human resource leader to play a part in human resource management policy formulation and provide them with the power necessary to ensure fair and consistent implementation.

How effectively an organization's human resources are managed depends for the large part upon the knowledge, skills and abilities of the people in the human resource department, particularly the human resource leader, the human resource generalists and the human resource specialists (collectively referred to as human resource professionals).

The human resource leader
Perhaps the most effective person who can head the human resource department is an outstanding performer in the organization who possesses human resource management expertise and line-management experience. Line experience gives the human resource manager an understanding of the needs of the business and the needs of the department's customers. To accomplish this, human resource professionals rotate through various line positions over the course of a few years. Short of actually serving as a line manager, the individual could serve as a special assistant to the line manager or head a special task force handling a company-wide project.

For decentralized organizations the human resource leader of the business unit is similar in some respects to the corporate human resource leader. With smaller corporate staffs, however, the corporate person may actually manage a much smaller operation than human resource leaders in the business units. Never the less, the route to the corporate human resource position should include rotation through the various businesses. A drawback to this method is that the same human resource ideas and concepts will be carried around the organization; injecting new ideas may require the employment of an outside person.

Whether in corporate or business units, for the human resource leader to be effective in playing the human resource roles described, the leader needs the following knowledge, skills and abilities (competencies):

- problem-solving skills
- business knowledge/organization sensitivity
- knowledge of compensation techniques to reinforce business plans
- strategic and conceptual skills

- knowledge of succession/career-planning systems
- established relationships and acknowledged leadership skills
- ability to analyse and plan from data
- computer literacy
- competence in human resource management functional areas
- awareness of the financial impacts in the human resource function as well as to the organization, particularly in areas such as pension costs, healthcare and compensation

While this list of competencies is rather extensive, these are the ones that effective human resource leaders in firms in highly competitive environments need. Some firms are now adopting procedures to identify the systematically required qualities necessary for their human resource staff (Walker 1990).

Human resource generalists

Line positions are one important source for human resource generalists. A brief period in a human resource position by a line supervisor, usually as a human resource generalist, can bring to the human resource department the knowledge, language, needs and requirements of the line. As a result, the human resource department can fill more effectively its service role. Another source of human resource talent is current non-managerial employees. Like line managers, these people bring with them information about employee needs and attitudes.

Some companies have a policy of assigning line managers to work in the corporate human resource department for two or three years as a part of their career development. Indeed, in the IBM/Towers Perrin worldwide human resource survey, having experience in human resources is seen as critical for the careers of line managers – or this is what the results indicate for the year 2000. Currently the situation is slightly different: in 1991 only 25 per cent of the CEOs and line managers said the human resource experience was critical for a line manager; however, 65 per cent said it would be critical in the year 2000. This latter

result certainly fits the needs of CEOs in the year 2000: according to a major worldwide survey conducted by the Korn/Ferry consulting firm and the Columbia Business School, knowledge and skill in human resource management is seen as second in importance, right behind skill and knowledge in strategy formulation in the year 2000 for CEOs (Korn/Ferry International and Columbia University 1989).

Human resource generalists should possess many of the same qualities as human resource specialists, but the level of expertise in a human resource speciality generally need not be of the same depth. After serving as a non-managerial human resource generalist, the next move could be to the position of manager of a human resource activity or even the manager of one of the firm's field locations. Whereas the former may result in specialization, moving to the field is likely to result in a broadening of human resource experience.

Human resource specialists

Human resource staff specialists should have skills related to the speciality, an awareness of the relationship of the speciality to other human resource activities, and a knowledge of the organization and where the specialized function fits. Individuals joining an organization for the first time should also have an appreciation of the political realities of organizations. Since specialists may work at almost any human resource activity, qualified applicants may come from specialized programmes in law, organizational and industrial psychology, labour and industrial relations, human resource management, counselling, organizational development, and medical and health sciences. In addition to current specialities, human resource management will need specialists in total quality management, in the new service technologies, in behaviour performance improvement systems and in organizational change and design.

With the increase in regulatory requirements for the use of human resources and the increased expertise necessary to deal with complex human resource activity, some organizations have moved away from using human resource generalists towards human resource specialists. However, with pressure to serve the customer better, some organizations are returning to the human resource generalists. In fact, many organizations have both human resource generalists and human resource specialists. Both are valuable, and both reflect an increasing level of professionalism.

Professionalism in human resource management

Like any profession, human resource management follows a code of professional ethics (Turnow 1984). All professions share the code of ethics that human resource management follows (see PERSONNEL MANAGEMENT).

1   Practitioners must regard the obligation to implement public objectives and to protect the public interest as more important than blind loyalty to an employer's preferences.
2   In daily practice professionals must understand thoroughly the problems assigned and must undertake whatever study and research are required to ensure continuing competence and the best of professional attention.
3   Practitioners must maintain a high standard of personal honesty and integrity in every phase of daily practice.
4   Professionals must give thoughtful consideration to the personal interest, welfare and dignity of all employees who are affected by their directions, recommendations and actions.
5   Professionals must make very sure that the organizations that represent them maintain a high regard and respect for the public interest and that they never overlook the importance of the personal interest and dignity of employees.

Ethical human resource issues in organizations
Increasingly, human resource professionals are becoming involved in more ethical issues. Some of the most serious issues involve differences in the way people are treated based on favouritism or relation to top management. In a recent survey, conducted by the US-based Society for Human Resource Management (SHRM) and the Commerce Case Clearing House (CCCH), human resource professionals identified more than forty ethical incidents, events and situations relevant to human resource activities (Applebaum 1991). The ten 'most serious' ethical situations reported by human resource managers are listed below:

*   employment, training or promotion based on favouritism (friendships or relatives)
*   allowing differences in pay, discipline, promotion, etc. due to friendships with top management
*   sexual harassment
*   sex discrimination in promotion
*   using discipline for managerial and non-managerial personnel inconsistently
*   not maintaining confidentiality
*   sex discrimination in compensation
*   non-performance factors used in appraisals
*   arrangements with vendors or consulting agencies leading to personal gain
*   sex discrimination in recruitment or employing

5   Trends in human resource management

What is happening today in the field of human resource management is nothing short of revolutionary. The organizational function of human resource management is becoming more important than ever. Line managers are getting involved in human resource management, and human resource managers are becoming members of the management team. Also, because human resource management is seen as critical to the success of organizations, virtually everyone in the organization can make a contribution to the management of people and the success of the organization at the same time.

In comparison with the past, today's and tomorrow's characterizations of human resource management reflect the more intense levels of national, regional and global competition, projected demographic and workforce figures, anticipated legal and regulatory changes, and significant technological developments. Translated through major changes in organizational strategy, structure, shape and technology, these environmental forces require speed, quality, innovation and globalization for firms wishing to survive the battlefield of international competition. These environmental forces are giving rise to *strategic* human resource management (SHRM) and *strategic international* human resource management (SIHRM).

Strategic human resource management

Strategic human resource management (SHRM) is largely about integration and adaptation. Its concern is to ensure that: (1) human resource management is fully integrated with the strategy and the strategic needs of the firm; (2) human resource policies are consistent both across policy areas and across hierarchies; and (3) human resource practices are adjusted, accepted and used by

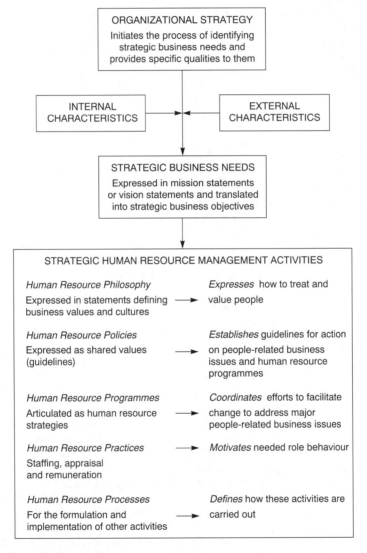

Figure 3 The 5-P Model – Linking strategic business needs and strategic human resource management activities
Source: Adapted from Schuler (1992)

line managers and employees as part of their everyday work.

Together, these viewpoints suggest that SHRM has many different components, including philosophies, policies, programmes, practices and processes. The various statements also imply what SHRM does: it links, it integrates and it connects across levels in organizations. Implicitly or explicitly, its purpose is to more effectively utilize human resources *vis-à-vis the strategic needs of the organization*. The key components of SHRM are illustrated in Figure 3.

Typically, organizations define (or redefine) their strategic business needs during times of turbulence. As such, these needs reflect management's overall plan for survival, growth, adaptability and profitability. Internal characteristics (such as culture and the nature of the business) as well as external characteristics (such as the state of the economy and critical success factors in the industry) may well influence the definition of needs. The biggest factor affecting SHRM, however, is not a particular characteristic so much as it is experience with this mode of planning. Human resource managers who have never before been asked to meld human resource activities with strategic needs will find that the process takes time, persistence and a detailed understanding of the needs that have been defined. In fact, linkages between human resource activities and business needs tend to be the exception even during non-turbulent times. When such linkages do occur, they are usually driven by the organization's efforts to formulate and implement a particular strategy.

To trigger specific actions, the business needs are generally translated into more actionable statements, which might be called 'strategic business objectives'. For other organizations, these might be called 'business vision statements'. By calling them strategic business objectives, firms believe that the statement conveys a more specific action element, starting with an influence on human resource philosophy (Schuler 1992).

Human resource philosophy

This is a statement of how the organization regards its human resources, what role the resources play in the overall success of the business, and how they are to be treated and managed. This statement is typically very general, thus allowing interpretation at more specific levels of action within an organization. The human resource philosophy provides guidelines for action on people-related business issues and for the development of human resource programmes and practices based on strategic needs.

Human resource policies

The term human resource policy, as used here, does not mean human resource policy manual. While a policy manual may contain statements of general guidelines, employees often perceive the manual as a 'rule book' prescribing very specific actions permitted in very specific situations. Human resource policy here means general guidelines that aid the development of more specific human resource programmes and practices. Human resource policies can be written for each of the several human resource activities like compensation and training. Using a policy such as pay for performance, local units can then craft specific human resource practices consistent with the policy.

Human resource programmes

Shaped by human resource policies, human resource programmes represent coordinated human resource efforts specifically intended to initiate, disseminate and sustain efforts towards strategic organizational change necessitated by the strategic business needs. These efforts may begin at the top of the organization and filter down or they may begin elsewhere.

Human resource programmes can be initiated, disseminated and sustained for many types of strategic organizational change efforts. These efforts, however, have several elements in common. First, they receive their impetus from the firm's strategic intentions and directions. Second, they involve human resource management issues, that is to say they represent major people-related business issues that require a major organizational change effort to address. They also share the reality of having strategic goals against which a programme's effectiveness can be measured.

Human resource practices
One useful way to approach this component of human resource strategy is from the framework of roles. Generally speaking, the roles that individuals assume in organizations fall into three categories: (1) leadership; (2) managerial, and (3) operational. In each case, behaviours associated with a given role should support strategic needs.

Leadership roles include establishing direction, aligning people, motivating and inspiring individuals, and causing dramatic and useful change. Managerial roles are the traditional roles of planning, directing, delegating, organizing and coordinating. Operational roles are the roles needed to deliver services or to make products. In essence, they are 'doing' roles, and as such their content is far more specific than for the other roles. In a service setting a role statement might be 'greets customers as they enter the sales area'. In a manufacturing organization a role might be 'reads blueprints accurately' or 'performs soldering operations consistent with quality standards'.

Although these three roles are labelled leadership, managerial and operational, this does not necessarily mean that only non-managers perform the operational roles or only managers perform the managerial and leadership roles. In the process of formulating and implementing new strategic objectives, organizations typically evaluate the 'who does what' question. In some cases this results in a shift of role responsibilities. For example, at the Nissan Motor Manufacturing Plant in the UK and the Honda Manufacturing Plant in Marysville, Ohio, an analysis of roles and responsibilities performed by first-level supervisors led to a more effective allocation of work. Many of these activities, it was discovered, could be distributed to non-managerial employees.

Once the role behaviours, whether leadership, managerial or operational, are identified, human resource practices can be developed to cue and reinforce role behaviour performance. While many human resource practices are used in organizations without regard to organizational strategy, some practices tie role behaviour directly to strategic needs. Consider, for example, a company that has defined a need to improve quality. Human resource practices might provide cues for topics such as group participation in problem solving and training in statistical measures of quality control (Schuler and Jackson 1987).

Human resource processes
This area deals with exactly how all the other human resource activities are identified, formulated and implemented. Thus, it is a significant SHRM activity. Human resource processes vary along a continuum of extensive participation by all employees or no participation by any employees. Two continua could be used to differentiate between the formulation and implementation stages: for example, high participation/involvement and implementation. However, it appears that there is a need for consistency across these two process dimensions.

The need for consistency becomes evident across all the SHRM activities. This need arises because all such activities influence individual behaviour. If they are not consistent with each other, that is, if they are not sending the same messages about what is expected and rewarded, it hardly provides a situation for the successful implementation of strategic business needs. Recognizing this need for consistency is an important component. This need, along with an awareness of the other aspects of SHRM, translates into a greater need to be systematic. Strategic human resource management requires consistency and a systematic orientation.

Strategic international human resource management

The world has become more competitive, dynamic, uncertain and volatile than ever before (Kanter 1991; Kobrin 1992). To be successful, many firms have to compete on the global playing field because the costs associated with the development and marketing of new products are too great to be amortized only over one market, even a large one such as the USA or Europe (Bartlett and Ghoshal 1991). Yet there are some products and services that demand accommodation to location customs, tastes, habits and regulations. Thus for many multinational enterprises (MNEs) the likelihood of operating in diverse environments has never been greater. While these scenarios suggest paths that MNEs have indeed taken to being internationally competitive, they are being superseded by the need both to manage globally, as if the world were one vast market, and simultaneously to manage locally, as if the world were a vast number of separate and loosely connected markets (Bartlett and Ghoshal 1991). The trend is creating a great deal of challenge and opportunity in understanding and conceptualizing exactly how MNEs can compete effectively.

With the concern for being global and the concern about the transfer of learning and being multi-domestic and therefore simultaneously being sensitive to local conditions several strategic concerns relevant to international human resource management arise. For example, can and how do MNEs link their globally dispersed units through human resource policies and practices? Can and how do MNEs facilitate a multi-domestic response that is simultaneously consistent with the need for global coordination and the transfer of learning and innovation across units through human resource policies and practices?

SIHRM is defined as 'human resource management issues, functions, and policies and practices that result from the strategic activities of multinational enterprises and that impact the international concerns and goals of those enterprises' (Schuler *et al.* 1993).

While this definition is certainly consistent with the definition of human resource management presented within a single country or domestic context (for examples see Schuler and Huber 1993 and Boam and Sparrow 1992), it facilitates the inclusion of a significant number of factors discussed in the international literature, both in the areas of international management and business, and international human resource management (Dowling *et al.* 1994; Phatak 1992).

Strategic multinational enterprise components
There are two major strategic components of MNEs that give rise to and influence SIHRM. These are the inter-unit linkages and internal operations (Hennart 1982; Phatak 1992). These are illustrated in Figure 4.

Inter-unit linkages
MNEs are concerned with operating effectively in several different countries. Consequently, MNEs are continually discussing how to manage their various operating units. In particular, they are interested in how these units are to be differentiated and then how they are to be integrated, controlled and coordinated (Ghoshal 1987; Galbraith 1992). Differentiation and integration questions are important because they influence the effectiveness of the firm (Lawrence and Lorsch 1967). In addition to this importance is the challenge that tends to be associated with selecting from among the several choices and alternatives that exist in differentiating and integrating an MNE (Phatak 1992; Prahalad and Doz 1987). Because of this importance and the challenge associated with them, general questions about differentiating and integrating the units of the firm are regarded as strategic ones (Hambrick and Snow 1989). Thus, for international human resource management they are also strategic. In fact, for SIHRM the issues associated with differentiating and integrating the units of an MNE represent a major influence on SIHRM issues, functions, and policies and practices (Schuler *et al.* 1991; Fulkerson and Schuler 1992). Depicted in Figure 4, issues and questions associated with differentiation and integration are covered by the term 'Inter-unit linkages' under the general heading 'IHRM issues'.

Internal operations
MNEs are also concerned about strategic issues other than those dealing with the linkages of the units. They are concerned about the internal operations of those units. In addition to working together, each unit has to work within the confines of its local environment, its laws, politics, culture, economy and society. Each unit also has to be operated as

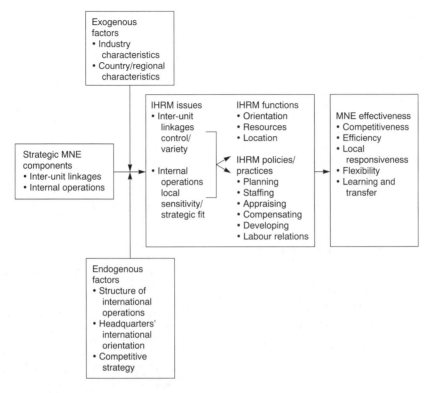

Figure 4 Integrative framework of international human resource management in multinational enterprises (MNEs)
Source: Adaoted from Schuler *et al.* (1993)

effectively as possible relative to the competitive strategy of the MNE and the unit itself. Thus, for MNEs these concerns regarding the internal operations of the units are also strategic (Prahalad and Doz 1987). They can influence the level of effectiveness of the MNE and SIHRM in significant ways. Consequently, internal operations are also included in Figure 4 under the heading 'IHRM issues'. How these internal operations and the inter-unit linkages of MNEs influence SIHRM is described in more detail in Schuler *et al.* (1993).

6 Conclusions

This section describes six activities of human resource management, defines what is human resource management, and examines its goals. Because of the increasing complexity of human resource management, nearly all organizations have established a human resource department. Not all of these departments, however, perform all the activities discussed. A department's activities – and the way it performs them – greatly depend upon the roles the department plays in the organization. Organizations that are most concerned with human resource management allow their departments to perform the roles to link human resource management to the business, provider, auditor, innovator and adaptor. When this occurs the departments are able to link their human resource activities to the business and demonstrate their value to the organizations by showing how their human resource activities influence productivity, quality of worklife, competitive advantage, flexibility and legal compliance – all specific goals associated with the organization's bottom-line criteria.

For each of the human resource activities described above, departments can choose from many human resource practices. For example, in performance-based pay, human resource departments may choose to use a merit pay plan or profit-sharing plan. In addition to being familiar with all the human resource practices, human resource departments need to know which ones to use depending upon the needs of the business. When human resource departments begin to coordinate their human resource activities with the business they start to identify and select specific practices. They also begin to involve line managers and employees in the formulation and implementation of the practices. Thus, human resource departments need to be staffed with individuals who are aware of all the human resource activities and practices and have a knowledge and appreciation of the business. They should also be knowledgeable about the goals and roles of human resource management in organizations. When done well human resource management can attain the specific and general human resource goals and the bottom-line indicators of company performance shown in Figure 2.

Two major trends in human resource management are SHRM and SIHRM. The development of these will reflect and enhance the value of managing human resources in the global organizations of the twenty-first century.

RANDALL S. SCHULER
NEW YORK UNIVERSITY

Further reading

(References cited in the text marked *)

* Applebaum, F.H. (1991) '1991 SHRM/CCH Survey', *APD* 26 June. (Ethics are becoming important in all areas of business. Issues relevant to human resource management are discussed.)
* Bartlett, C.A. and Ghoshal, S. (1991) *Managing Across Borders: The Transnational Solution*, London: London Business School. (Excellent description of the strategic business issues facing firms wishing to be global.)
* Boam, R. and Sparrow, P. (1992) *Designing and Achieving Competency*, London: McGraw-Hill. (Excellent description of the methodology to identify and train for needed competencies and skills.)
* Brewster, C. and Hegewisch, A. (1994) *Policy and Practice in European Human Resource Management*, London: Routledge. (Provides extensive analysis of survey data collected throughout European nations.)
* Brewster, C. and Tyson, S. (1991) *International Comparisons in Human Resource Management*, London: Pitman. (Text providing excellent material to illustrate similarities and differences in human resource management in many countries.)
* Carroll, S. (1991) 'HRM roles and structures in the information age', in R.S. Schuler (ed.), *HRM in the Information Age*, Washington, DC: SHRM/BNA. (Discusses centralization and decentralization in human resource departments and what the important contingencies are.)
* Dowling, P.J., Schuler, R.S. and DeCieri, H. (1994) *International Dimensions of Human Resource Management*, 2nd edn, Belmont, CA: Wadsworth Inc. (A short treatise introducing the reader to dimensions of international human resource management.)
* Fulkerson, J.R. and Schuler, R.S. (1992) 'Managing worldwide diversity at Pepsi-Cola International', in S.E. Jackson (ed.), *Diversity in the Workplace*, New York: Guilford Press. (Worldwide diversity can be integrated in global firms by using flexible human resource policies and practices as illustrated in this case study.)
* Galbraith, J.R. (1992) *The Value Adding Corporation*, CEO Publication, Los Angeles, CA: University of Southern California. (Detailed presentation of how organizations are designed to add value to a business for the twenty-first century.)
* Ghoshal, S. (1987) 'Global strategy: an organizing framework', *Strategic Management Journal* (8): 425–40. (An excellent article describing how global firms can think about and conceptualize strategy at the global level.)
* Hambrick, D.C. and Snow, C.C. (1989) 'Strategic reward systems', in C.C. Snow (ed.), *Strategy, Organization Design and Human Resource Management*, Greenwich, CT: JAI Press Inc. (Linking compensation to the strategies of firms described in some detail at the managerial level.)
* Hennart, J.F. (1982) *A Theory of the Multinational Enterprise*, Ann Arbor, MI: University of Michigan Press. (Good theoretical treatise on the essence and meaning of what it is to be an MNE.)

* Hofstede, G. (1980) *Culture's Consequences: International Differences in Work-related Values*, Beverly Hills, CA: Sage Publications. (Classic text on the four dimensions of culture that are referred to by many researchers.)
* Kanter, R.M. (1991) 'Transcending business boundaries: 12,000 world managers view change', *Harvard Business Review* May–June: 151–64. (Excellent article reporting on how managers around the world see the environment of business.)
* Kobrin, S.J. (1992) 'Multinational strategy and international human resource management policy', unpublished paper, The Wharton School, University of Pennsylvania. (Good conceptual and empirical study of the relationship between various multinational strategies and international human resource policies.)
* Kochan, T.A., Batt, R. and Dyer, L. (1992) 'International human resource studies: a framework for future research', in D. Lavin, O.S. Mitchael and P.D. Sheren (eds), *Research Frontiers in IR and IR*, Madison, WI: IRRA. (Position paper on the growth of strategic HR within the IR community.)
* Korn/Ferry International and Columbia University (1989) *Reinventing the CEO*, Korn/Ferry International and Columbia University. (Jointly conducted study surveyed 1,000 senior managers in 1988 and reported interesting results.)
* Lawrence, P.R. and Lorsch, J.W. (1967) *Organization and Environment*, Boston, MA: Harvard University Press. (Classic study on organizational design, specifically on integration and differentiation.)
* Phatak, A.V. (1992) *International Dimensions of Management*, 3rd edn, Boston, MA: PWS–KENT Publishing Co. (A small book nicely describing all the key aspects of international management.)
* Prahalad, C.K. and Doz, Y. (1987) *The Multinational Mission: Balancing Local Demands and Global Vision*, New York: The Free Press. (Excellent presentation of the importance of acting locally and thinking globally.)
* Schuler, R.S. (1992) 'Strategic human resource management: linking the people with the strategic needs of the business', *Organizational Dynamics*, Summer: 18–31. (Conceptual and empirical article describing strategic human resource management and introducing the 5-P Model.)
* Schuler, R.S. (1995) *Managing Human Resources*, 5th edn, St Paul, MN: West Publishing Co. (Text providing extensive detail of all human resource activities and numerous examples of what companies in the USA are doing to manage their people.)
* Schuler, R.S., Dowling, P. and DeCieri, H. (1993) 'An integrative framework of strategic international human resource management', *International Journal of Human Resource Management*, December: 717–64. (Conceptual article describing, for the first time, SIHRM and offering several testable propositions.)
* Schuler, R.S., Fulkerson, J.R. and Dowling, P.J. (1991) 'Strategic performance measurement and management in multinational corporations', *Human Resource Management*, 30: 365–92. (Conceptual and empirical description of how firms can tie together global operations using performance measurement systems.)
* Schuler, R.S. and Huber, V.L. (1993) *Personnel and Human Resource Management*, 5th edn, St Paul, MN: West Publishing Co. (Text providing extensive detail and numerous examples of all human resource activities and issues, both domestic and global.)
* Schuler, R.S. and Jackson, S.E. (1987) 'Linking competitive strategy and human resource management practices', *Academy of Management Executive*, 3: 207–19. (Classic article describing the contingency between human resource practices and Porter's competitive strategies.)
* Schuler, R.S. and Jackson, S.E. (1988) 'Customerizing the HR department', *Personnel Journal* June: 36–44. (Discusses the importance of and the techniques of getting the human resource department closer to the customer (the line manager).)
  Schuler, R.S. and Jackson, S.E. (1996) *Human Resource Mangement: Positioning for the 21st Century*, 6th edn, St Paul, MN: West Publishing Co. (Text providing extensive coverage of all human resource management activities; numerous examples of actual firms.)
* Sparrow, P. and Hiltrop, J.-M. (1994) *European Human Resource Management in Transition*, Hemel Hempstead: Prentice Hall. (Excellent text presenting human resource management in European. Some comparisons with the USA.)
* Storey, J. (1992) *Developments in the Management of Human Resources*, London: Blackwell. (An excellent description of how 'personnel' differs from today's 'human resource management' approach to managing human resources.)
* Towers Perrin (1992) 'Priorities for gaining competitive advantage', Towers Perrin. (Important worldwide survey for human resource professionals and academics: likely to have major impact on human resource management.)

* Turnow, W.W. (1984) 'The codifications project and its importance to professionalism', *Personnel Administrator*, June: 84–100. (What it means to be a human resource professional and the implications for human resource professionals.)
* Walker, J. (1988) 'Managing human resources in flat, lean and flexible organizations: trends for the 1990s', *Human Resource Planning*, 11 (2): 129. (The trends in these organizations are for human resource management to be more decentralized and adaptable to change.)
* Walker, J. (1989) 'Human resource notes for the 90s', *Human Resource Planning* 12 (3): 55. (Description of trends in human resource management entering the 1990s.)
* Walker, J. (1990) 'What's new in HR development?', *Personnel*, July: 41. (As human resource departments must change, so must the human resource leader and staff. Key ways for human resource development are described.)

See also: CAREERS; EMPLOYEE RELATIONS, MANAGEMENT OF; HUMAN RESOURCE DEVELOPMENT; HUMAN RESOURCE FLOWS; HUMAN RESOURCE MANAGEMENT, INTERNATIONAL; HUMAN RESOURCE MANAGEMENT IN EUROPE; INDUSTRIAL AND LABOUR RELATIONS; OCCUPATIONAL PSYCHOLOGY; ORGANIZATION BEHAVIOUR; PAYMENT SYSTEMS; PERFORMANCE APPRAISAL; PERSONNEL MANAGEMENT; RECRUITMENT AND SELECTION; TAYLOR, F.W.; TRAINING; WORK AND ORGANIZATION SYSTEMS

Related topics in the IEBM: GLOBAL STRATEGIC PLANNING; GLOBALIZATION; MULTINATIONAL CORPORATIONS

Industrial democracy

Overview

The term 'industrial democracy' refers to the structures and institutional mechanisms that give workers or their representatives the opportunity to influence organizational decision making in their places of employment. Programmes vary in the amount of involvement they allow workers in the decision-making process and the degree of influence workers have over decision outcomes. There has been some debate over whether mere worker involvement, or participation, in decision making was a sufficient condition for industrial democracy, or whether joint decision making, or power sharing, between workers and management was necessary before one could speak of democracy in the workplace. There is, in practice, a large range of programmes and institutions that enable labour's voice to be heard in a formal way within the enterprise. These differ in the scope of decisions they include, the amount of power workers can exercise *vis-à-vis* management, and the organizational level at which the decisions are made. Some are purposefully designed to give workers a very modest role in decision making while others are intended to give the workforce a substantial amount of power in organizational governance.

Industrial democracy, or worker participation in management as it is usually called in the USA, can be direct or indirect (through representatives), and prescribed by law, established through contracts or granted by the employer. It is convenient to place the different models or forms of participation in two categories based on their origins – legal statutes and employer grants. Legally based or prescribed structures such as worker representation on corporate boards of directors, works councils or trade union representation (collective bargaining) are formal systems with written rules and regulations that provide uniform guidelines for involving workers in decision making in all organizations that come under the jurisdiction of the law or contract. Employer-granted or employer-initiated participation usually does not specify employees' legal rights to be involved in decision making. To the extent that formal written agreements exist in granted programmes, they are specific to a given enterprise. Examples of granted participation are shop floor employee involvement programmes, labour–management committees, like those found in productivity gainsharing plans, and autonomous work teams.

This entry contains a brief description of the theoretical models used to justify industrial democracy, descriptions of major types, an account of historical developments, as well as developments since 1990, and an evaluation of the different forms of worker participation.

1 Theoretical foundations

In traditional capitalist economies, control over the use of capital, labour and profits belongs to the capital owners, or their management representatives. Within industrial democracy, some of the rights of ownership are transferred to non-owning workers (see PROFIT SHARING AND EMPLOYEE SHAREHOLDING SCHEMES). Four sets of theoretical arguments, or bases, have been used to legitimate this transfer: democratic theory, socialist theory, human growth and development theory, and a productivity and efficiency rationale (Dachler and Wilpert 1978).

(1) *Democratic theory* states that the individual's capacity for acting as a responsible, intelligent, informed and cooperative citizen is inherent, but can and should be further developed through experience with the democratic process in the family, in school, at work and in political activities. Because participatory democracy at the political level alone is not sufficient to sustain a democratic system, people need to experience democracy in the workplace as well (Pateman 1970).

(2) *Socialist theory* has as its goal the economic liberation of the working class, which means the abolition of wage labour and the capitalist system of production. Worker participation serves this goal by gradually increasing workers' control of the production process, and by providing the education and development of workers enabling them to manage and govern the enterprises (Blumberg 1968).

(3) *Human growth and development theories* suggest that people have a psychological need to develop to their full potential and become independent, active, self-controlled individuals engaged in continuous learning. This need can be met, in part, at work, in jobs that are intrinsically interesting and challenging and give the worker autonomy and responsibility. Direct worker participation will satisfy growth needs and, by doing so, increase worker motivation and job performance (Likert 1961).

(4) *The productivity and efficiency rationale* is an assumption that worker involvement in decision making will increase individual productivity and job satisfaction, and decrease absenteeism and turnover, because workers will develop a commitment to organizational goals and feel that they have a stake in the organization's future (Coch and French 1948).

The human growth and development and the productivity and efficiency models share the basic assumption that workers have untapped energy and talent that will be released in the employer's service when opportunities for participation are available. This 'untapped reservoir' hypothesis is largely untested,

except for inferences made about its veracity when participation programmes succeed in producing the expected results (see HUMAN RELATIONS).

2 Types of industrial democracy

No classification scheme for industrial democracy structures and programmes is completely satisfactory because the boundaries between the different types are not always clear, and there are new forms of worker participation evolving that do not fit neatly into a single category. With this caveat in mind, four main types are identified here: (1) co-determination, or supervisory board representation; (2) works councils and similar bodies, such as labour–management committees; (3) trade union representation; and (4) shop-floor programmes (see INDUSTRIAL AND LABOUR RELATIONS).

In some countries, particularly those with co-determination laws such as Germany, all four types operate and play different, but overlapping, roles in a coordinated and integrated system (Streeck 1984). In other countries, years of experience with formal participative structures have transformed participation into an informal co-management process, where the union or employee representatives are unofficial members of the management team. Examples of such collaboration exist under the Norwegian model (Hammer *et al.* 1994). There is no specific structure into which one can classify the latter, but it is emerging as an effective way of ensuring that workers' interests are included in managerial decision making. There are also programmes or structures that once belonged in these classification schemes, but are no longer viable forms of participation. This type of transformation has taken place as the workers' councils or workers' assemblies that were prevalent in the former socialist countries of eastern Europe have faded. Finally, there is the unique form of worker participation based on ownership of capital found in producers' cooperatives, which is described later in this entry.

'Co-determination' refers to worker representation on boards of directors. In countries that have two-tiered management structures for large enterprises, such as Germany, Austria and The Netherlands, worker directors sit on the supervisory board which sets corporate policy, approves major investments, mergers, expansions and plant closures, and also appoints members to a management board that actually manages the enterprise. In one-tier board systems, the worker representatives serve on the management board, or board of directors. Legally mandated co-determination exists in Austria, Germany, Luxembourg, Denmark, Norway and Sweden. The Netherlands has a modified system of board representation, in the sense that Dutch workers do not elect board representatives directly, but their enterprise works councils have the right to veto nominees to the supervisory board.

One controversial issue has been specifying the required number of worker representatives to serve on a board. Some trade unions have argued for, and attained, parity representation (Germany), while others have agreed to one-third representation (Austria, Luxembourg and Norway), or less (Sweden). Usually, but not always, worker directors are union officials or members of enterprise works councils (see INDUSTRIAL RELATIONS IN EUROPE).

Limited attempts with co-determination initiated by governments, or negotiated between employers and their unions in the absence of legislation, are documented in the UK, Ireland, Australia and the USA. The number of worker representatives, and the method of selecting or appointing them, have differed across countries and enterprises (Stern 1988).

Works councils are plant-level bodies of elected employees which regularly meet with management to discuss a wide variety of personnel issues, such as work and leave schedules, pay schemes, employee selection and training, safety, technological changes that affect the nature and pace of work and the work environment, and social welfare issues. Works councils are covered by law in most of Europe, but in some countries they are established by union–employer agreements. Both the legislation and the agreements differ with respect to: (1) the minimum workforce size

required for establishing works councils; (2) membership composition – whether they are joint labour–management bodies (Belgium and Denmark), consist of workers only but with a management director presiding at meetings (France), or comprise workers only (Germany, Austria, The Netherlands); (3) the number and types of issues they are involved in; and (4) how much power they have *vis-à-vis* management. In general, works councils have three kinds of rights: the right to information, the right of consultation in economic and financial matters, and the right of consent in social and personnel affairs. Technically, works council members are elected by the workers, not appointed by the unions, but in practice, the members usually have close union ties.

It is useful to distinguish between works councils and joint consultative committees. The latter are found in a large number of countries, from the UK and the USA to the newly industrialized countries in the Asia-Pacific region, as well as in Third World countries (Frenkel 1993). Joint consultative committees have more open-ended mandates to deal with issues of common interest to labour and management. Even where they are prescribed by law, their power is quite limited.

Trade union representation and collective bargaining models differ across and within countries (see COLLECTIVE BARGAINING; TRADE UNIONS). In corporatist societies, such as Austria and Scandinavia, negotiations are cooperative ventures between the state and the central union and employer confederations (see CORPORATISM). There is usually very little room for local deviations from contract terms once an agreement has been reached at central level. In pluralist societies, such as the UK and the USA, bargaining is adversarial (although it can be integrative), more decentralized, and results in a wider variety of contracts that have room for local idiosyncrasies (see COLLECTIVE BARGAINING).

In countries such as the UK, the USA and Canada, plant-level union representation through shop steward committees serves much the same functions as works councils. In the USA, in particular, a number of the issues dealt with by the European works councils are subject to collective bargaining.

Enterprise, or company, unions play a substantial role in the extensive form of consultative participation used in Japanese firms. The role of Japanese unions is to represent worker interests in the workplace, but they are, by their very nature, not independent labour voice mechanisms. They negotiate with management over wages and employment conditions, but serve primarily to adapt worker interests to employer goals.

Shop-floor programmes provide opportunities for direct workplace participation by large numbers of workers over a small number of issues immediately connected with the labour process. These programmes come in a variety of forms, many tailor-made to suit the production technologies and management philosophies of the employer. Common labels, such as employee involvement or job redesign, can mean very different participation experiences in different enterprises. Most of these programmes are created on the employer's initiative and have no legislative mandate. Their adoption is motivated primarily by a concern for productivity and efficiency. Where a workforce is unionized, the programmes are usually negotiated and are often covered by local supplements to a collective bargaining agreement. Shop-floor programmes have also originated in co-determination legislation, such as the Norwegian Work Environment Act of 1977, which prohibits the employer from using work processes that are psychologically debilitating, and recommends that worker autonomy and decision-making rights be designed into the job.

3 Economic democracy

When workers are capital owners, they often play a prominent role in enterprise governance, and employee ownership has therefore been defined as an example of industrial democracy. However, it is important to distinguish between industrial and economic democracy, because the former confers the decision-making rights of ownership on non-owning workers for purely political, social or pragmatic economic reasons (see PROFIT SHARING AND EMPLOYEE SHAREHOLDING SCHEMES).

The two major forms of employee ownership are producers' cooperatives and employee stock-ownership plans (ESOPs). Producers' cooperatives are industrial firms that are owned, managed and operated by workers. A few have originated in their founders' political and philosophical commitment to worker ownership and control, but most were formed for practical economic reasons – to create jobs and provide job security in periods of economic distress and industrial conflict. The large majority of cooperatives have profit maximization (financial returns to owners) as the primary goal. The cooperatives are characterized by equality of ownership and decision making rights. Each worker-owner usually owns one share, all shares are held within the firm, and owners are required to sell their shares back to the company when they resign or retire. Usually, a company charter specifies that differences between worker-owners in compensation and influence be minimized, and dictates that the firm be democratically run. The most impressive collection of producers' cooperatives, from a financial returns and a job creation perspective, are in Mondragón, Spain (Thomas and Logan 1982).

ESOPs are used mostly in the USA, where the common form is a benefit plan through which employees receive company stock. In most plans, the employer contributes stock (or cash to purchase stock) to a special trust for distribution to individual accounts of participating workers. The logic behind an ESOP, when used as a benefit or incentive plan, is to give workers a financial and psychological interest in ownership and company growth. ESOPs have also been established because employers have had a philosophical commitment to widespread share ownership and worker participation.

In the USA, by the end of 1993, employee ownership through ESOPs and similar plans existed in some 9,500 firms, and covered approximately ten million workers. The popularity of ESOPs has derived in large measure from their immediate financial utility to the employer: they are used to raise capital, to lower corporate taxes, to avoid costly pension plan obligations, and as barter in concession bargaining with unions to lower labour costs (see PROFIT SHARING AND EMPLOYEE SHARE-HOLDING SCHEMES).

The link between stock ownership and industrial democracy is clearest in those enterprises where ESOPs are used as a mechanism to spread worker participation, where the employer has sold the firm to the workforce rather than to an outside buyer by using an ESOP, or where local unions have obtained seats on corporate supervisory boards, in addition to share ownership, in exchange for wage and benefit concessions (Hammer *et al.* 1991).

4 Historical background

With the exception of trade union representation, which began to cover the mass of industrial workers by the early part of the twentieth century both in Europe and the USA, the existing legally based forms of industrial democracy date primarily from 1945, when they were introduced in Europe to contain labour–management conflict as part of the post-war reconstruction effort. In addition, worker participation in enterprise governance and policy setting was imposed on German employers by the Allied powers, with support from the German trade unions, as an alternative to nationalization of the industries that had been heavily involved in wartime production.

In the USA, worker participation became a topic of heated and value-laden debate with the early demonstration experiments of the Human Relations School (Coch and French 1948) (see HUMAN RELATIONS). At the time, the arguments for involving workers in decision making were a mixture of the pragmatic and economic, the moral and ideological. Both employers and employees would benefit, it was argued, if workers were allowed to grow and develop psychologically through participation, which would channel workers' creative energies towards the attainment of organizational goals (Likert 1961) (see WORK AND ORGANIZATION SYSTEMS).

During the late 1950s and the 1960s, workplace democracy was not an important issue in European industrial relations, although experiments in shop-floor participation in the form of autonomous work groups received considerable attention in Scandinavia (Emery and Thorsrud 1976).

However, by the 1970s, worker participation was seen as a mechanism for the redistribution of power within enterprises, and ultimately, within the broader society (Pateman 1970). Several European countries enacted co-determination laws which placed non-managerial workers, or their representatives, on corporate boards of directors, to participate in decision making at the policy making and strategic level of the enterprise. The laws also established works councils to involve workers in the management of social and personnel affairs at the workplace level. The wave of legislation that was passed in northern Europe, in spite of substantial employer opposition, was made possible by the close working relationships between ruling social democratic governments and trade unions. Although employers and trade unions resisted efforts to legislate worker participation in the UK, the Labour government experimented with worker representation on the boards of the then nationalized British Steel Corporation and the Post Office (Batstone *et al.* 1983).

In the USA, concern over declining industrial productivity and quality in the face of foreign competition, and workers' unwillingness to accept physically and psychologically debilitating work, stimulated a pragmatic interest in worker participation by academicians, employers, some trade unionists, and branches of the Federal government. A series of joint union–management Quality of Working Life experiments with shop-floor participation started in private industry and were assisted by modest government funding.

During the 1980s, there was a general shift to the political right, with the increasing number of conservative governments in Western countries being less hospitable towards both trade unions and legislation to protect and strengthen workplace democracy. The public interest in industrial democracy as a political or ideological movement faded as well. Structural changes in national economic life during this decade made governments, employers and trade unions turn their attention to the social problem of increased unemployment and the employment effects of new technologies. Policies began to address the practical problems of improving productivity, flexibility and innovation in the enterprise. The social and economic pressures came from increased international competition which had created a shift in manufacturing philosophy from mass production and standardization to flexible, specialized, customer demand-driven production. There was a growth in multinational firms, a general de-industrialization of western Europe and the USA, and with it a shift from manufacturing to service-sector employment. There was still considerable interest in worker participation at the workplace level, but it was driven primarily by employer initiative, and based on the practical goals of increasing enterprise productivity and profitability.

Employer-initiated participation programmes became an important component of human resource management in US firms during the late 1970s and 1980s. Participation was part of a long-term business strategy to create a non-union industrial relations system. The transformation of US industrial relations began with the development of non-union sectors within traditionally unionized industries. Corporations closed, or stopped investing in, older unionized plants while starting up new non-union manufacturing facilities. Management of these greenfield sites introduced innovative programmes of employee involvement, job redesign, productivity gain-sharing and employee stock ownership, with the dual purpose of building commitment and motivation among employees while preventing unionization (Kochan *et al.* 1986).

5 Developments from 1990

The political upheaval in eastern Europe during the late 1980s and early 1990s, with the fall of communism, reunification of Germany and breakup of the former Yugoslavia, had some effect on the policies and practices of industrial democracy. Workers' self-management, an extreme form of industrial democracy in which the workforce's authority to govern the firm exceeds the management's (exemplified by Yugoslav workers' councils), was no longer seen as a practical and desirable way to manage enterprises in the market-driven economy that the former socialist states strove to attain. The demise of communism in eastern Europe also reduced the power of the trade unions in France and Italy, where the union movement traditionally has had a strong communist political base, and lessened the prospects for industrial democracy in those countries (Slomp 1995).

The move by the European Union (EU) towards a single market in 1992 breathed new life into an old and stormy debate about equalizing worker participation rights in member countries. In September 1994, a directive on European Works Councils, specifying the introduction of works councils in large companies with branches in at least two member states, was accepted by all EU members except the UK (see INDUSTRIAL RELATIONS IN EUROPE).

Decentralization of collective bargaining, from the national to the sector or industrial branch level in Europe, and from the industry to the local union level in the USA, served to strengthen the employers' power in collective bargaining, and contributed to the increasing variety of granted worker participation programmes designed to integrate, or merge, worker and employer interests. Sharp declines in union membership, particularly in the US private sector, but also in some European countries, further eroded unions' power. The corporatist model of collaboration between the state and the central trade union and employers' organizations, which was instrumental in the passage of the industrial democracy legislation during the 1970s, was largely abandoned in the Nordic countries, and declined in importance in other countries as well (Slomp 1995).

The low level of unionization in the USA (less than 12 per cent of private sector workers and 35 per cent of public sector workers were union members in 1995), and the increasing opposition and hostility from employers to the prospect of unionization, left a large number of workers with minimal, or no, participation rights. In 1994, a presidential commission on the future of worker–management relations recommended a number of changes in US labour laws to enable workers to unionize more easily, and to have available, at the employer's discretion, alternative mechanisms for participation in decision making, such as a modified form of the German works council. The latter proposal met with strong opposition from the central union organization (AFL-CIO), because works councils deal with issues that are normally covered by collective bargaining. Their possible adoption by US employers was seen by labour as the introduction of company unions. At the end of 1995, there were no prospects for labour law reform in the USA (see TRADE UNIONS).

6 Evaluation of industrial democracy legislation and practice

How the effectiveness of industrial democracy legislation and workplace participation programmes is evaluated depends on the reason why the laws were passed and the programmes instituted. The European co-determination legislation had two broad goals: the integration of labour's interests into the decision making of the enterprise and the redistribution of power across organizational hierarchies. The over-arching goal of the legislation was industrial peace deriving from the convergence of labour, management and stockholder interests occurring when power is more widely shared between hierarchies and social classes.

Industrial relations in countries with strong co-determination laws have, in fact, been peaceful, but industrial democracy cannot be given sole credit for this situation. Strong corporatism and tripartism ensured an accommodation to worker interests at the national policy level, through labour legislation, social security, employment policies and industrial policy. The fact that the social partnership between the trade unions and employers extended beyond the industrial arena to encompass the social conditions under which people live also contributed to industrial harmony.

An evaluation of laws and programmes must be based on an assessment of how well they attain their more immediate goals. Research has attempted to answer two questions: (1) Do the laws and contractual agreements that dictate worker participation in enterprise decision making lead to actual worker involvement and, if so, does this involvement increase workers' influence over decision outcomes? (2) Does worker participation lead to increased organizational effectiveness by increasing worker motivation and job performance?

There are a number of country-specific studies evaluating the effectiveness of either single legislative acts or an entire system of participation. Among these, the German system has received by far the most attention. However, there are also comparative cross-country evaluations. The largest of these studies examined the impact of the rules and regulations for participation written down in laws, contracts or management policies (*de jure* participation), on the actual involvement and influence experienced by different groups (*de facto* participation), in twelve European countries, in 1977 and 1987 (IDE International Research Group 1981, 1993). The results from 1977 showed a high degree of formalized participation in most countries, except the UK, for both worker and management representatives. Nevertheless, a surprising amount of legal and contractual power over all kinds of decisions was concentrated in the hands of top management and supervisory bodies. The effect of hierarchy was even stronger on *de facto* participation. Across countries and enterprises, workers had the least and top management the most influence in all areas of decision making, and the more strategic the decisions, the larger the influence gap between hierarchical levels. Workers participated in the execution rather than in the formulation of organizational goals and policies. Worker influence, although modest, was none the less enhanced by the existence of formal prescriptions.

Ten years later, the real formal power was still in the hands of top management, although the power prescribed for works councils was also large in a few countries (Germany, The Netherlands, Denmark). With respect to influence, the findings were strikingly similar from one decade to the next: while workers' influence increased as a function of their formal power, it was still low in all the European countries. In addition, unemployment levels, which were becoming substantial in many countries during the late 1980s, served to increase the influence of top management, particularly in those firms where labour's power had been fairly strong in 1977; management took advantage of a deteriorating labour market to reassert its authority and control over decision making.

The conclusion that can be drawn from the research on legally or contractually based participation is that even the modest amount of influence workers have over decision making requires formal structures, either at the national or the enterprise level.

The evaluation of voluntary participation, primarily shop-floor programmes, seldom includes an independent assessment of worker influence because the plans focus on organizational effectiveness. There is a plethora of single-firm studies of both traditional and innovative participation programmes in the USA, Europe and Japan. The studies are difficult to compare because the programmes and outcomes differ across firms. In many enterprises, participation is just one component of a whole package of high-involvement management practices which also include technological changes, job redesign, and performance contingent compensation. It is impossible to untangle the effects of participation from the other programme components.

Large-scale, comparative case studies of union–management cooperation, however, have shown that employee involvement programmes combining direct participation on the shop floor with representative participation on labour–management committees (some also include union representation and collective bargaining), have been successful in boosting enterprise productivity (Appelbaum and Batt 1994; Kochan *et al.* 1986).

What is not successful, at least not in the USA, is the adoption of single pieces of integrated multi-structure participation programmes, such as worker representation on boards of directors, without works council and trade union representation.

A number of explanations have been offered for the gaps between expectations and reality with respect to a redistribution of power within enterprises. Blame has been placed on inadequacies in the participative structures and programmes, lack of trade union power, market forces, technology, and organizational structure, as well the absence of appropriate skills and values in worker representatives. However, one of the strongest obstacles to the diffusion of workplace democracy may be management ideology and values. Where management opposes worker participation and holds on to the traditional managerial prerogative of governing the enterprise with minimal or no interference from labour, turning prescriptions for worker involvement into worker influence has been very difficult. Such opposition has increased in the last decade. On the other hand, where management sees the long-term economic value, and perhaps also the social and political value, of worker involvement for attaining organizational effectiveness and competitive advantage, modest, and sometimes substantial, worker participation has been possible.

7 Conclusion

A more conservative political environment and the pragmatic demands of market pressures at the state, trade union and enterprise levels have supplanted a political and ideological drive to democratize the workplace from top to bottom. Human resource management practices aimed at increasing workers' commitment to the employer's goals of productivity improvement and quality enhancement have become more sophisticated, and have served to focus worker participation on shop-floor issues (see HUMAN RESOURCE MANAGEMENT). Although labour–management power sharing and joint decision making is close to the reality experienced by the workforce in many enterprises, industrial democracy is nevertheless far from reaching its potential in most organizations, and it is unlikely to do so any time soon.

TOVE HELLAND HAMMER
CORNELL UNIVERSITY

Further reading

(References cited in the text marked *)

* Appelbaum, E. and Batt, R. (1994) *The New American Workplace: Transforming Work Systems in the United States*, Ithaca, NY: ILR Press. (Description and evaluation of recent workplace innovations in US firms, based on large cross-sectional surveys and 185 case studies.)
* Batstone, E., Ferner, A. and Terry, M. (1983) *Unions on the Board: An Experiment in Industrial Democracy*, Oxford: Blackwell. (An empirical study of the 1978–9 experiment in industrial democracy in the British Post Office, which gave union representatives parity representation with management on the corporate board.)
* Blumberg, P. (1968) *Industrial Democracy: The Sociology of Participation*, London: Constable. (Theoretical treatise on how and why direct worker participation will reduce alienation from work and how labour and socialist political movements can further the idea and practice of workers' management.)
* Coch, L. and French, J.R.P., Jr (1948) 'Overcoming resistance to change', *Human Relations* 1 (4): 512–33. (Classic study of experimentation with limited shop-floor participation in a US apparel manufacturing plant.)
* Dachler, P.H. and Wilpert, B. (1978) 'Conceptual dimensions and boundaries of participation in organizations: a critical evaluation', *Administrative Science Quarterly* 23 (1): 1–39. (Description of the dimensions along which worker participation programmes differ, and the theoretical and political origins of workplace participation.)
* Emery, F. and Thorsrud, E. (1976) *Democracy at Work*, Leiden: Martinus Nijhoff Publishers. (Description and evaluation of the Norwegian Industrial Democracy Programme, which entailed experiments with autonomous work groups in several Norwegian firms.)
* Frenkel, S. (ed.) (1993) *Organized Labor in the Asia-Pacific Region: A Comparative Study of Trade Unionism in Nine Countries*, Ithaca, NY: ILR Press. (Chapters describe the current state of trade unionism in China, Thailand, Malaysia, Korea, Taiwan, Hong Kong, Singapore, Australia and New Zealand.)
* Hammer, T.H., Currall, S.C. and Stern, R.N. (1991) 'Worker representation on boards of directors: a study of competing roles', *Industrial and Labor Relations Review* 44 (4): 661–80. (Empirical study of the effectiveness of worker directors as a voice for labour on the corporate boards of fourteen US firms in the early 1980s.)
* Hammer, T.H., Ingebrigtsen,B., Karlsen, J.I. and Svarva, A. (1994) 'Organizational renewal: the management of large scale organizational change in Norwegian firms', paper presented at the Conference on Transformation of European Industrial Relations, Helsinki. (Cross-sectional study of worker involvement in decision making in 225 private and public sector firms during organizational change projects.)
* IDE International Research Group (1981) *Industrial Democracy in Europe*, Oxford: Clarendon Press. (A comparative study of the written rules and regulations prescribing participation in decision making and the amounts of actual involvement experienced in 134 firms in twelve European countries.)
* IDE International Research Group (1993) *Industrial Democracy in Europe Revisited*, New York: Oxford University Press. (Re-examination of formalized and actual participation in ten of the original twelve European countries, and initial studies of participation patterns in Poland and Japan.)
* Kochan, T.A., Katz, H.C. and McKersie, R.B. (1986) *The Transformation of American Industrial Relations*, New York: Basic Books. (Account of how and why the US industrial relation system, institutionalized in the 1950s, underwent a radical change in the early 1980s.)
* Likert, R. (1961) *New Patterns of Management*, New York: McGraw-Hill. (Classic theoretical treatise on the utility of worker participation for employers and employees.)
* Pateman, C. (1970) *Participation and Democratic Theory*, Cambridge: Cambridge University Press. (Theoretical treatise on how political and socially experienced democracy educates and develops the individual to function in a democratic society.)
* Slomp, H. (1995) 'National variations in worker participation', in A.W. Harzing and J. Van Ruysseveldt (eds), *International Human Resource Management: An Integrated Approach*, London: Sage Publications. (Very useful chapter describing the historical development and present functions of different participation structures in western Europe.)

* Stern, R.N. (1988) 'Participation by representation: workers on boards of directors in the United States and abroad', *Work and Occupations* 15 (4): 396–422. (Evaluation of different countries' experiences with worker directorships, based on analyses of case studies.)
* Streeck, W. (1984) 'Co-determination: the fourth decade', in B. Wilpert and A. Sorge (eds), *International Yearbook of Industrial Democracy*, vol. 2, London: Wiley. (Assesses the effectiveness of the German co-determination legislation and its worker participation structures.)
* Thomas, H. and Logan, C. (1982) *Mondragón: An Economic Analysis*, London: Allen & Unwin. (Excellent evaluation of the economic performance of the Mondragón cooperatives. Includes a history of Mondragón and descriptions of the structures developed to sustain the economic and industrial democracy of the producers' cooperatives.)

See also: COLLECTIVE BARGAINING; HUMAN RELATIONS; HUMAN RESOURCE MANAGEMENT; INDUSTRIAL AND LABOUR RELATIONS; INDUSTRIAL RELATIONS IN EUROPE; MONDRAGÓN; ORGANIZATION BEHAVIOUR; PROFIT SHARING AND EMPLOYEE SHAREHOLDING SCHEMES; TRADE UNIONS; WORK AND ORGANIZATION SYSTEMS

Related topics in the IEBM: COMMITMENT IN JAPAN; MANAGEMENT IN EUROPE; REGIONAL ENTRIES LISTED UNDER MANAGEMENT

Interest groups

Overview

Interest groups represent one way for organizations such as firms to manage their external political environments, although in practice many organizations use formal groups as one among a range of strategies with which to influence public affairs. Interest groups range from private groups organizing firms through to public groups open to individuals wishing to join. Organizations are significantly easier to organize than individuals.

The influence of an interest in public affairs depends mainly upon its ability to make itself indispensable by bringing key resources which governments need. Interests in possession of a sufficient quality of these become 'insider' groups with government, and form closed policy-making communities, whereas others find themselves excluded. 'Insider interests' enjoy monopolistic access over public policies, particularly in 'low politics' fields involving relatively technical issues, whereas in 'high politics' fields involving politicized issues they operate on more of a 'level playing field' with other types of interests. 'Outsider' interests therefore seek to disrupt closed 'policy communities' by seeking to politicize issues. A further factor governing the influence of interest representation concerns the extent of crowding, so that in Brussels, for instance, there is now one person working in the 'lobbying' sector for every European Commission official. There are now increasing signs of public authorities seeking to manage their interactions with outside interests.

1 The external political environment of business

The study of interest groups has largely been left to political scientists, although it is a key management concept because interest groups offer firms the means to help manage their external political environments.

Political action by firms can occur individually, or in some form of collective action, whether by formal interest groups, or in relatively informal, and sometimes *ad hoc* alliances that can be as unstructured as an occasional lunch club. For this reason, political science has adopted the more generic terminology of 'interest representation' to embrace the activities involved where organizations seek to manage their external environments.

Typically, the smallest of small firms, faced with basic survival issues, do not have the resources to either act collectively or engage their external political environments. Conversely, no large firm could afford to remain one if it ignored political conditions that may well determine its future prosperity. A tobacco firm, for instance, might find its core product market eroded by public legislation; a pulp manufacturer could face intolerable pressures on profit margins as a result of environmental legislation; an industry in decline could find time to diversify in the presence of supportive public policies; while a whole range of industries could discover new horizons by public policy initiatives such as the decision to create a single market in Europe from 1992. Consequently, every large firm invests resources in public affairs management, often through the use of dedicated departments, sometimes by retaining a public affairs firm, and, more often than not, in forums of collective action.

The largest of firms in the most concentrated sectors may find that its sectoral affairs are best managed alone, although there can

153

hardly be a single large firm without interest group affiliation of some kind, even if this is restricted to general organizations of business. Even in these conditions, firms may have to act collectively in sectoral groups for the purpose of pleasing public authorities who prefer to speak with 'one voice' fora. Thus, the European Association of Consumer Electronics Manufacturers Association is essentially a cloak for the large European firms in the sector (particularly Philips and Thomson), formed in part to satisfy the wishes of the European Commission (Cawson 1992). There are signs that public authorities are becoming increasingly active in demanding the organization of business interests into collective fora, because it simplifies the needs of consultation for them. In Britain, a recent President of the Board of Trade asked industrial domains to create one voice structures where these were absent, while in Brussels the Commission has publicly criticized those business groups it finds ineffective.

Firms engage in interest group activities as a means of promoting, and defending, their interests, primarily in public policies, where these could either be significantly threatened or advanced; to satisfy the needs of public authorities to simplify public policy making and implementation; as a means of intelligence gathering about political and economic conditions; and, sometimes, to gain access to a range of goods and services at preferential terms. For all but the smallest firms, the costs of non-participation in collective fora are likely to significantly outweigh those of participation. Thus, the French car manufacturer PSA (Peugeot/Citroën) found in March 1994 that it was unable any longer to stay outside the European automobiles manufacturers association, ACEA, if it wished to continue to prosper. Similarly, American firms, often with a reputation as 'free booters' (Jacek 1995), in reality find it essential to act in collective fora, first and foremost as a means of defending and promoting their interests in public policies. Not to belong to a relevant association would be to jeopardize the firm by risking competitors taking collective decisions which could be highly damaging to the excluded firm's interests. As Jordan and McLaughlin (1993: 155) wryly comment: 'the free rider cannot expect to steer the vehicle'.

2 Resources with which to influence public policies

The spectrum of interest groups range from those that are private collections of organizations and closed to outsiders, such as an industrial trade association, to those that are open to any individual to join. Firms are significantly easier to organize than are individuals, and have greater resources to contribute to defending and promoting themselves than do other types of interests. Consequently, they also enjoy more coherent patterns of collective action than do public interest groups, and workers (see ORGANIZATION BEHAVIOUR).

The key to understanding the influence of interests in public policy making and implementation lies in the possession or absence of 'bargaining chips' (Greenwood 1997). Firms and sectors with the greatest intensity of these can make themselves indispensable, and significantly influence the character of public policy making and implementation. These resources have the greatest effect when they are organized properly.

Information and expertise

Public policies are shaped around information. Firms and industrial associations may well have greater collective expertise than will public officials. The European Commission, for instance, has one person responsible for Europe's multi-billion ECU insurance industry. It is a severely overloaded bureaucracy that has become dependent upon the expertise private interests can bring. One official commented that:

> At the beginning (the Commission official) is a very lonely official with a blank piece of paper, wondering what to put on it. Lobbying at this very early stage offers the greatest opportunity to shape thinking and ultimately to shape policy. The drafter is usually in need of ideas and information and a lobbyist who is recognized as being

trustworthy and a provider of good information can have an important impact at this stage.

(Hull 1993: 83)

Some Commission reports are therefore written by trade associations or firms, or heavily reliant upon their statistics because it does not have the resources to collect the information itself. Business interests often have a monopoly over information and expertise that gives them exclusive and unrivalled access to public policies. Public policies that are technically unsound are unworkable, and the possession of vital information can guarantee influence over policy formulation.

Economic muscle

Some companies have greater resources at their disposal than do individual countries; the Ford motor corporation, for instance, has greater wealth than the gross domestic product of the Republic of Ireland. They are therefore bound to be significant political actors. Public policy makers are dependent upon businesses to perform. Key factors such as employment, balance of trade, and wealth creation, and indeed the popularity of public institutions, including ruling parties, count on business activities.

Some business sectors and firms are so powerful that to be taken account of, they do not even have to flex their muscles. In local politics, a town's prosperity may be wholly dependent upon a single employer, and its interests will therefore automatically be taken into account; while in some countries the major wealth creators will enjoy similar influence. Business, as Lindblom comments, has a privileged position in public affairs at the outset (Lindblom 1977).

Prestige value

Status resources also influence access to public policies. Public bureaucracies are keen to promote high technology producer domains that provide the foundations for tomorrow's prosperity. The use of public policy instruments to promote such industries smacks of vision, and may reflect to a country a desired self-image of steadily increasing importance. Similarly, established industrial 'names', such as Rolls Royce and Mercedes, are strongly connected with international identities and therefore command a privileged place in public policies.

Power in implementation

Producer groups such as farmers are powerful actors because they own significant land resources. It would be inconceivable for a national or regional ministry to adopt policies on land use without negotiating with farmers first, because these actors have the ability to make or break a policy as a function of the position as the key actors responsible for implementation.

The ability to help public organizations carry out policies

Public authorities have increasingly had to do more for less in recent years. They are inevitably overloaded, and any interest that can help by performing public interest functions can make itself indispensable. Self-regulatory instruments are the most common form of these, particularly in areas where the state would otherwise inevitably be drawn into regulation. Industrial self-regulation has a chequered history, although in its most successful forms it can provide governments with a virtually cost-free, responsive, flexible and effective way of balancing industrial and public interests while at the same time partly relieving them of responsibilities. For industry, self-regulation provides the means to retain control over affairs; while for consumers, such instruments can provide reassurance and a speedy, cost-free method of redress. In tourism, for instance, both governmental, industry and consumer interests are met by mutual industry assurance schemes guaranteeing to rescue holiday-makers whose tour operator has gone into liquidation. Self-regulation also meets an ideological preference among some parties for withdrawing from 'big government', and among like-minded governments they have become a favoured mechanism of policy implementation. In turn, this represents a key opportunity for private interests to exert influence. Their popularity is underlined by the fact that they are now increasingly being used by transnational authorities and the best organized groups in the governance of industrial affairs. EFPIA, for instance, the European pharmaceutical industry federation, successfully headed off a Commission proposal to regulate the marketing of medicines to doctors by creating and administering a self-regulatory code, and ensuring compliance among its members across Europe for its provisions. The 'parcelling' out of public functions to private interests has in some cases made the dividing line between public and private interests wafer thin. Business groups capable of acting in such a disciplined way can make themselves indispensable to public authorities.

There are forms of assistance with governmental overload other than self-regulatory schemes. For instance, Philips has developed broadcasting technologies through research that are strategically important for Europe, and seconded personnel to the Commission service concerned with information technologies known as DG XIII (Cawson 1995). Such an example is further illustration of the dependence by public authorities on private interests, to be able to compete in global markets in key technologies. Firms such as these, therefore, have a 'reserved seat' at the policy-making table in this domain.

The organization of the interest into a non-competitive format

Interests organized into competitive groupings are unlikely to be successful because public policies will either be unable to arbitrate between the factions, or will favour one type of interest at the expense of others. Any bureaucracy will find it extremely difficult to deal with competitive groupings, and indeed, many have devoted resources to assist with the organization of interests into single formats, ranging from grant giving through to public criticism. There are things that interests can do to ensure that competitive formats do not emerge, such as to ensure that the largest firms have the most say in the policies of the trade association, while at the same time not squeezing out the interests of the smaller players. In Europe, for instance, the Senior Advisory Group Biotechnology (SAGB) is essentially a 'rich firm only' club, and, although effective, laid the conditions for a rival, competitive organization to emerge specializing in organizing the excluded, smaller players. Only in the most concentrated of sectors, such as European consumer electronics where there are only three firms of importance, is there no need for a trade association.

Coherent organization of the interest and decision-making power given to representative outlets

Some interest groups are so cumbersome that they are ineffective, while there are examples of groups collapsing on coherence grounds. Among the factors essential to the ability to work well is the capacity for speedy decision making, that requires the delegation of powers to the secretariat to take action without the need for constant prior referral to the membership constituency beforehand. Members might be willing to endorse retrospective action, but to engage in prior consultation might also result in disagreement and conflict.

Unquestionably the most influential contribution to understanding collective action was that provided by Mancur Olson (1965). Olson suggested that the most rational behaviour of firms would be not to pay membership fees but to 'free ride' on the benefits obtained by others in collective action. Groups would, therefore, need to provide incentives beyond the prospect of political action to survive, such as access to discounted goods and services. Debate since has questioned whether firms do act in such a rational, utility maximizing fashion, and some groups appear to attract and maintain members without providing material incentives. Jordan and McLaughlin (1993), drawing on earlier work by Cyert and March (1963), propose the presence of a softer, or 'bounded' version of rationality where firms join because the costs of non-membership exceed those of membership. These costs include loss of access to intelligence, particularly in uncertain business environments, and to networking opportunities; conversely, the benefit concerns the need to manage through minimizing surprises. More mundane factors may also be applicable, such as the prospect of social and career opportunities for company public affairs officials who recommend trade association membership to their employers.

The ability to influence members

An interest group able to deliver authoritative opinion on behalf of its members, negotiate policy agreements with governments, and then make the deal stick with its constituency will be invaluable to public policy makers. The most advanced form of this is where a group can deliver self-regulation among its members that works.

3 Interest representation in public policies

Interests who are rich in 'bargaining chips' will enjoy influence in public affairs. In many cases, these are required in combination; thus, an economically powerful interest may find its influence severely curtailed if it is badly organized and incoherent in its interest group behaviour. Sufficiently resource-rich interests have the ability to become 'insider groups' with public authorities, because they are indispensable to public policy making and implementation. Those without such resources become 'outsider interests', although some groups might decide to become 'outsider' groups by choice, because they wish to remain independent from governments. Indeed, governments have themselves sometimes sought to bring groups in as a strategy of control. There is also a 'grey area', where groups can be insiders where technical issues are concerned by virtue of their specialist knowledge, or those who are peripheral to insider status by virtue of certain weaknesses (Jordan *et al.* 1995). In general, a measure of an interest's influence is the extent to which it makes its affairs visible to the

wider public. Those whose needs and demands are met by public policies do not have to appeal for public support, whereas those who do, do so because they have invariably lost their case with government. As Jordan and Richardson remark (1987: 193): 'campaigns are the currency of the unsuccessful'.

Private interests interact with public policies through 'policy networks' (Rhodes 1988). At one end of the continuum are 'policy communities', relatively settled coalitions of permanent officials in public authorities, together with the representatives of the 'insider' interest. The stability of these mechanisms make them excellent vehicles for the negotiation of policies and resolution of conflicts. On the other extreme are the 'here today, gone tomorrow' 'issue networks', that are unstable alliances of interests thrown together by circumstance. Policy communities tend to operate as governance mechanisms for the interest with which they are concerned. They are particularly likely where the issues at hand are 'low politics', that is, relatively uncontroversial, often technical, issues that might be restricted to a particular sector of business. 'High politics', on the other hand, involve the 'big issue', politicized affairs to which no single interest can enjoy monopolistic access by virtue of its entry into the public domain. In these affairs, business groups operate on much more of a 'level playing field' with public interest groups. For these latter groups, politicizing issues represents a deliberate strategy to break up the monopoly of influence with which business interests can enjoy. One example of this concerns the issue of 'bio patenting', where an industry inspired draft directive from the European Commission aimed at protecting copyright of inventions involving biotechnological processes was voted down by the European Parliament after heavy campaigning by public interest groups. Business interest influence in public affairs is therefore by no means as automatic as a simple reading of the 'bargaining chips' list might suggest. Similarly, some public institutions are by design more immune than others to pressures from private interests, such as the US Federal Reserve, the Bundesbank, and the Bank of England.

In most developed countries the quantity of interest representation that public authorities face has reached overload proportions. In Europe, for instance, there is now one person working in the interest representation sector for every Commission official (excluding linguists and secretaries) (Grant 1995), and there are now moves to manage the problem. The management of interest representation by public authorities appears to have three purposes. One is to ensure that the good information gets through from the crowd of voices; a second is to address concerns about an imbalance between business and other types of interests, amid concerns that business groups enjoy privileged access; while a third is to prevent abuses and enhance standards in public life. Some authorities have now developed statutory regulation, while others encourage 'lobbyists' to develop self-regulation through codes of good practice. Looking to the future, these are issues that private interests will have to address in order to maintain the ability to influence public policies.

JUSTIN GREENWOOD
THE ROBERT GORDON UNIVERSITY

Further reading

(References cited in the text marked *)

Cawson, A. (ed.) (1985) *Organized Interests and the State*, London: Sage Publications. (One of the first applications of corporatist ideas to sub-national levels by focusing on business sectors.)

* Cawson, A. (1992) 'Interest groups and public policy making: the case of the European consumer electronics industry', in J. Greenwood, J. Grote and K. Ronit (eds), *Organized Interests and the European Community*, London: Sage Publications. (A case study of interest representation in the consumer electronics domain at the European level that illustrates many of the wider issues beyond the sector concerned.)

* Cawson, A. (1995) 'Public policies and private interests: the role of business interests in determining Europe's future television system', in J. Greenwood (ed.), *European Casebook on Business Alliances*, Hemel Hempstead: Prentice Hall. (A case study of European broadcasting

public policy making and the influences of private interests.)

Cigler, A.J. and Loomis, B.A. (eds) (1995) *Interest Group Politics* (5th edn), Washington, DC: CQ Press. (American focus examining group techniques and practices.)

* Cyert, R.M. and March, J.G. (1963) *A Behavioural Theory of the Firm*, Englewood Cliffs, NJ: Prentice Hall. (A classic work in organization theory, looking inside the firm to develop theoretical ideas about economic behaviour.)

* Grant, W. (1995) *Pressure Groups, Politics and Democracy in Britain*, 2nd edn, Hemel Hempstead: Prentice Hall. (A textbook with a British/European focus providing an in-depth introduction to all of the issues concerning interest groups and their involvement in public affairs.)

Greenwood, J. (ed.) (1995) *European Casebook on Business Alliances*, Hemel Hempstead: Prentice Hall. (A collection of nineteen cases examining the capacity of business interests to work together and influence public policies at the European level.)

* Greenwood, J. (1997) *Representing Interests in the European Union*, London: Macmillan. (A textbook with an in-depth and comprehensive examination of interest representation and collective action throughout the range of private and public interests, and the contribution made by interests to the building of the European Union).

* Hull, R. (1993) 'Lobbying Brussels: a view from within', in S. Mazey and J.J. Richardson (eds), *Lobbying in the European Community*, Oxford: Oxford University Press. (A first hand view of 'lobbying' from a Commission official.)

* Jacek, H. (1995) 'The American organisation of firms', in J. Greenwood (ed.), *European Casebook on Business Alliances*, Hemel Hempstead: Prentice Hall. (A case study of the American organization of firms at the European level for the purpose of interest representation.)

* Jordan, A.G. and McLaughlin, A.M. (1993) 'The rationality of lobbying in Europe: why are Euro groups so numerous and so weak?', in S. Mazey and J.J. Richardson (eds), *Lobbying in the European Community, Oxford: Oxford University Press*. (A study of the organization of European car manufacturers at the European level and analysing why firms join groups.)

* Jordan, A.G. and Richardson, J.J. (1987) *British Politics and the Policy Process*, London: Allen & Unwin. (An introduction to the workings of the British political process, showing how pub-

lic policies are made inside and out with Parliament.)

* Jordan, A.G., Maloney, W.A. and McLaughlin, A.M. (1995) 'Interest groups and public policy: the insider/outsider model revisited', *Journal of Public Policy* 14: 17–38. (An article giving precision to different types of insider and outsider groups.)

* Lindblom, C (1977) *Politics and Markets*, New York: Basic Books. (A citation classic analysing the relationship between government and business in the world's political economic systems.)

Lowi, T.J. (1964) 'American business, public policy, case studies and political theory', *World Politics*, 16: 677–715. (A theoretical classic which suggests that the type of policy under consideration influences the underlying politics, and focusing upon consequent methodological issues in case study research of interest group influence.)

* Olson, M. (1965) *The Logic of Collective Action*, Cambridge, MA: Harvard University Press. (The definitive study of collective action that questions whether associability is automatic, and whether collective action can be examined using economic theory.)

* Rhodes, R.A.W. (1988) *Beyond Whitehall and Westminster*, London: Unwin Hyman. (Develops the idea of policy networks ranging from policy communities through to issue networks.)

Richardson, J.J. (1993) *Pressure Groups, Politics and Democracy in Britain*, Oxford: Oxford University Press. (A collection of readings from a variety of authors focusing on the key concepts developed in the study of pressure groups, with a focus on selected countries.)

Streeck, W. and Schmitter, P.C. (eds) (1985) *Private Interest Government*, London: Sage Publications. (Examines the parcelling-out of public functions by public authorities to private interests by evaluating a number of sectors across ten western countries.)

Wilson, G.K. (1990) *Interest Groups*, Oxford: Blackwell. (A summary of the key controversies in the study of interest groups and a survey of interest group systems in a variety of countries.)

See also: ORGANIZATION BEHAVIOUR

Related topics in the IEBM: BIG BUSINESS AND CORPORATE CONTROL; BUSINESS ETHICS; BUSINESS AND SOCIETY; CONTEXTS AND ENVIRONMENTS; CORPORATE GOVERNANCE; ENVIRONMENTAL MANAGEMENT; ENVIRONMENTAL REPORTING; GOVERNMENT, INDUSTRY AND THE PUBLIC SECTOR; INFORMATION REVOLUTION; INFORMATION TECHNOLOGY; MANAGEMENT IN EUROPE; MANAGEMENT IN THE UK; MULTINATIONAL CORPORATIONS; ORGANIZATIONAL INFORMATION AND KNOWLEDGE

Interpersonal skills

Overview

Some approaches to the study of social interaction are only concerned with observable behaviour, what interactors actually say and do, whereas others are also concerned with the cognitive processes that guide behaviour. Training can improve the interactors' ability to relate effectively with others. While the focus of most training interventions tends to be observable behaviour, the beliefs that interactors hold about themselves and others also deserve attention. These beliefs can influence both the way interactors interpret circumstances and the way in which they decide to behave in the light of these interpretations.

Interpersonal skills have a hierarchical structure which has provided a basis for a micro-skills approach to the development of interpersonal competence. This involves isolating and practising sub-skills and then synthesizing them into larger units of behaviour.

1 The importance of interpersonal skills

One of the most widely used definitions of management is getting things done through people. Managers and others spend a considerable part of their working day relating with others. One of the findings of the early work activity studies is that managers consistently underestimate the amount of time they spend in face to face contact. There are also indications that they underestimate seriously the effect that their behaviour has on the way others behave and, therefore, on the achievement of personal and organizational goals (see ORGANIZATION BEHAVIOUR).

Definitions

Hayes (1991) defines interpersonal skills as goal-directed behaviours used in face to face interactions, in order to bring about a desired state of affairs. Interpersonal skills is just one of a number of broadly similar terms such as interactive skills, people skills, face to face skills, social skills and social competence. Argyle (1984) defines social competence in terms of the successful attainment of goals. Socially competent people are those who possess the skills necessary to produce desired effects on other people in social situations. These desired effects might include persuading somebody to make a purchase, to learn, to make a concession in a negotiation, to be impressed with the actor's expertise or to support them in a crisis. Honey (1988) offers a similar definition. He refers to interactive skills as the skills people use in face to face encounters to arrange their behaviour so that it is in step with their objectives. He emphasizes the point that interactive skills have very little to do with being nice or winning friends, unless these sorts of outcomes are encapsulated in the individual's objectives. The common theme in all of these definitions is the ability to behave in ways that increase the probability of achieving desired outcomes.

2 The study of interpersonal interactions

Some investigators, like Duncan and Fiske (1977), focus their attention on specific, immediately observable behaviours, such as head nods and eyebrow flashes, of which the larger actions are composed. They argue that when human conduct is characterized at this relatively low level of abstraction there is the advantage that observers are only required to use the minimum of inferring. This contrasts with an alternative approach, such as that adopted by Bales (1950) and Honey (1988), which pays attention to the intention that lies behind the behaviour and therefore requires more interpretation on the part of the observer.

Some investigators limit their concern to how people behave, and they fail to pay attention to what is going on in the actors' heads, to what they are thinking. Mangham (1978) argues that if we are to understand better the conduct of people in organizations we need to address what it is they appear to think and feel about themselves and others. Exchange theorists such as Thibaut and Kelley (1959) emphasize the costs and benefits of interaction, and symbolic interactionists such as Mangham (1986) emphasize the way situations are defined and the actors' ability to think through (rehearse) how the interaction might unfold before deciding what to do. Both are examples of approaches to the study of social interaction which place heavy emphasis on cognition as a guide to behaviour.

Argyle's social skill model

Argyle's (1969) social skill model of social interaction provides a conceptual framework which has been widely used as a basis for research and practice. He argues that the

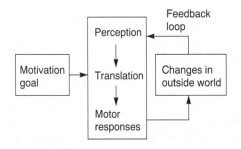

Figure 1 The motor skill model
Source: Argyle (1969)

sequences of behaviour that occur in social interaction can be looked at as a kind of motor skill.

In any social encounter each individual has plans or goals which they attempt to realize through the continuous correction of their social performance in the light of the reactions of others. Social performance involves a set of motor responses. Just as a driver can take corrective action by moving the steering wheel, the interviewer can take corrective action when the respondent is talking too much by interrupting, asking closed questions or looking less interested in what the respondent is saying. This model draws attention to the importance of feedback and the perception of appropriate cues, and to the ability to identify effective corrective action (referred to as translation in the model). Not everyone knows that open-ended questions make people talk more and that closed questions make them talk less. Argyle recognizes that there are some aspects of social behaviour that have no immediate parallel in motor skills, such as seeing the other person's point of view and projecting a self image.

3 A transactional approach to social interaction

Social interaction can be viewed as a transaction in which each interactor is seeking a satisfactory outcome. Leary (1957) advances the notion that people are motivated to behave towards others in ways that elicit from them desirable kinds of behaviour that are complementary to their own. For example, those who favour managerial–autocratic behaviours (see MANAGERIAL BEHAVIOUR) interact with others in ways that invite them to be obedient and respectful. When others respond with the desired complementary behaviour the interaction is perceived to be rewarding, whereas if they respond with non-complementary behaviour it is experienced as unpleasant and costly.

Thibaut and Kelley (1959) also adopt a transactional approach, and argue that people voluntarily enter and stay in a relationship only so long as it is adequately satisfactory in terms of reward and cost. One widely held view is that the secret of human exchange is to give to the other person behaviour that is more valuable to him than it is costly to you, and to get from the other behaviour that is more valuable to you than it is costly to him.

4 Viewing social interaction as a skilled performance

Goffman (1959), Mangham (1978) and others have used drama as a metaphor for describing and explaining a wide range of interactions. Goffman talks about putting on a performance for an audience and argues that a person's portrayal of action will be determined by his or her assessment of the audience. He also notes that actors use mirrors so that they can practice and become an object to themselves, backstage, before going 'on-stage' and becoming an object to others. Problems can arise if an interactor interprets what they observe as being a true reflection of the other person, when in reality the appraisee's behaviour may well be a performance, a reaction to the situation. Problems can also arise for all interactors if their ability to manage their behaviour, 'to put on a performance', is impaired.

Goffman and other symbolic interactionists agree that each person tries to control others by attempting to influence the way they define the situation. The interactor influences the others' definition by expressing themselves (performing) in such a way as to give the others the kind of impression that will lead them to act voluntarily in accordance with the interactor's own plan. But, knowing this, the others may pay attention to the signals that the interactor gives off (such as non-verbal signals) to check the validity of their performance.

5 Beliefs about interpersonal competence

Morgan (1971) suggests that some people are more successful in the way that they relate with others because they are more skilled, that is because they either do certain things that

others do not do, or they do them better (see OCCUPATIONAL PSYCHOLOGY). While he recognizes that other variables can influence the outcome of social interactions he postulates that skills, which are learnable, are the most important contributor to differences in the facility to deal with people.

Gahagan (1984) accepts the importance of skills, but she also believes that there are other factors which deserve attention. She defines talk and action as the visible front line element of daily encounters, but notes that behind this front line are what she refers to as the supply lines of values, beliefs and feelings about self and others. She argues that helping people to improve their encounters and relationships with others involves attending to both the front and supply lines.

One approach to improving interpersonal competence that focuses on what Gahagan refers to as the supply lines is concerned with modifying beliefs about oneself. Anxiety can undermine performance in a wide range of social situations and anxious people often experience difficulty relating with others. One reason is that they fail to focus sufficient attention on their performance because they are too preoccupied with the consequences of an inadequate performance.

Another self-defeating belief that can undermine interpersonal competence is the conviction that there is nothing that one can do to control outcomes in a relationship. People who believe this may engage in what is often referred to as disabling self-talk, and may tell themselves that they cannot cope. This can create a set of circumstances in which a person fails to take any voluntary action to improve the relationship. Training can help by challenging self-defeating beliefs and promoting a sense of self-efficacy.

Modifying beliefs about others can also lead to improved interpersonal competence. In order to respond effectively it is necessary to perceive the other person's intentions and behaviour correctly. A number of factors affect the ability to do this. One is selective attention. Another is attribution. Not only do people attend to different things or relationship events, they also interpret the information they receive in different ways. People often make what is referred to as the fundamental attribution error. This involves a tendency to pay too little attention to the extent to which situational or external factors constrain behaviour, and to attribute too much importance to internal factors such as a person's intentions and character, thus leading to the development of inaccurate beliefs about others.

A number of training interventions can be used to improve one's ability to interpret the behaviour of others and to monitor their reactions to one's own behaviour. One of these is sensitivity training, another is role playing, which provides an opportunity for trainees to take the role of another and to experience a relationship from a different perspective. Alban Metcalf and Wright (1986) refer to several approaches to perceptual training including a number which are designed to increase the trainee's sensitivity to non-verbal clues, such as the facial expression of emotion.

6 The hierarchical structure of interpersonal skills

Argyle's social skills model presents the interactor as someone who pursues goals by emitting motor responses which are modified in the light of continuous feedback. Social skill is seen to have a hierarchical structure in which the larger, high-level units consist of integrated sequences and groupings of lower level units. Argyle illustrates this with the example of the interview which has a number of phases, each with a certain sequence of questions, each consisting of a number of words and accompanying non-verbal signals.

Wright and Taylor (1994) adopt a similar hierarchical approach in their discussion of interpersonal behaviour. At the lowest level they identify what they term the *primary components*, what interactors actually say and do, their verbal and non-verbal behaviour. An interpersonally skilled person is someone who, at this level, has a wide range of components at her disposal and is able to select the one most appropriate to the situation and purpose at hand, and perform it well. Wright and Taylor see the next level as being concerned

with *structure* and the way in which the components are sequenced, while the third level is the *overall approach*. They suggest that the components used in an interaction and the way in which they are structured will depend, at least in part, on the type of interaction the interactors wish to have.

Thinking about interpersonal skills in terms of a hierarchy draws attention to the fact that it is not enough for the skilled performer to know how to ask open questions or provide constructive feedback. They need to know when, and in what combination, these primary components should be used if, in the light of the other's response, they wish to maintain a particular type of relationship, for example to maintain a participative relationship with an appraisee who is reluctant to engage in conversation.

Hargie (1986), Hayes (1991), Wright and Taylor (1994) and others take the view that an effective approach to developing interpersonal competence is to isolate and practise important sub-skills (sometimes referred to as micro-skills) and then to synthesize these into larger units of behaviour. An example might further illustrate the hierarchical organization of interpersonal skills. The *accent*, a one or two word restatement that focuses attention on what somebody has just said, is one of several behaviours that can be grouped together under the broad heading of following skills. *Following skills* are behaviours that help a person to encourage somebody else to talk and help the listener to concentrate on what the speaker has to say. Following skills are one of a number of sets of behaviours which, at another level, are referred to collectively as listening skills. *Listening skills*, which involve an active search for a full and accurate understanding of the meaning of another's message, are, in their turn, just one of the sets of behaviour which comprise *helping skills*. A person's approach to helping will be reflected in the way in which these various micro-skills are sequenced and structured. (Listening skills are also an important element of other complex interpersonal skills such as interviewing and negotiating.) All of the above mentioned authors focus attention on what they believe to be important micro-skills.

Hargie describes the micro-skills approach to interpersonal skills training as one of homing in and honing up. Once trainees have identified and practised the micro-skills they can be helped to use them appropriately in an integrated fashion.

Interpersonal skills can make an important contribution to personal effectiveness in work settings. These skills can be learned, and training interventions that focus on both observable behaviours and the beliefs that interactors hold about themselves and others can facilitate the development of interpersonal competence (see TRAINING).

JOHN HAYES
LEEDS UNIVERSITY BUSINESS SCHOOL

Further reading

* Alban Metcalf, B.M. and Wright, P. (1986) 'Social skills training for managers', in C.R. Hollin and P. Trower, *Handbook of Social Skills Training*, vol. 1, *Applications Across the Life Span*, Oxford: Pergamon Press. (A thorough review of many methods of interpersonal skills training, with an extensive set of references.)
* Argyle, M. (1969) *Social Interaction*, London: Methuen. (A book which made an important theoretical contribution to the study of this subject.)
* Argyle, M. (1984) 'Social behaviour', in C.L. Cooper and P. Makin (eds), *Psychology for Managers*, London: British Psychological Society and Macmillan. (Provides a brief introduction to Argyle's social skill model.)
* Bales, F.G. (1950) *Interaction Process Analysis: A Method for the Study of Small Groups*, Reading, MA: Addison-Wesley. (The reader is referred to a useful summary in D.S. Sills, *Encyclopedia of the Social Sciences*, vol. 8, New York: Crowell Collier and Macmillan, 465–71.)
* Duncan, S. and Fiske, D.W. (1977) *Face-to-Face Interaction: Research, Methods and Theory*, Hillsdale, NJ: Lawrence Erlbaum. (Provides a discussion of how to do research on face to face interaction.)
* Gahagan, J. (1984) *Social Interaction and its Management*, London: Methuen. (Provides a broad perspective on purposeful interaction.)
* Goffman, E. (1959) *The Presentation of Self in Everyday Life*, Garden City, NJ: Anchor Books. (Based on careful observations of everyday life, this book examines the structures of social encounters from the perspective of the dramatic performance.)
* Hargie, O. (1986) *A Handbook of Communication Skills*, London: Croom Helm. (Many of the skill elements mentioned here are also elaborated in O. Hargie, S. Saunders and D. Dickson (1987) *Social Skills in Interpersonal Communication*, London: Croom Helm.)
* Hayes, J. (1991) *Interpersonal Skills: Goal Directed Behaviour at Work*, London: Routledge. (Provides an overview of some of the most important skill elements.)
* Honey, P. (1988) *Face to Face Skills*, Aldershot: Gower. (Presents a practical approach to shaping the behaviour of others.)
* Leary, T. (1957) *Interpersonal Diagnosis of Personality*, New York: Ronald. (The essentials of Leary's model are also presented in Chapter 4 of R.C. Carson (1970) *Interaction Concepts of Psychology*, London: George Allen & Unwin.)
* Mangham, I.L. (1978) *Interactions and Interventions in Organizations*, Chichester: Wiley. (Considers how individuals construct their performances on the basis of their interpretation of their circumstances.)
* Mangham, I.L. (1986) *Power and Performance in Organisations: An Exploration of Executive Process*, Oxford: Blackwell. (Mangham takes the stage as his organizing metaphor and offers a good insight to the interactionist perspective.)
* Morgan, T. (1971) 'A critical survey of training in interactive skills', in N. Rackham, P. Honey and M. Colbert (eds), *Developing Interactive Skills*, Guilsborough: Wellens. (Highlights a number of key issues related to the efficacy of interpersonal skills training.)
* Thibaut, J.W. and Kelley, H.H. (1959) *The Social Psychology of Groups*, Chicester: Wiley. (Offers a theoretical analysis of interpersonal relations based upon an exchange or bargaining view of human interaction.)
* Wright, P.L. and Taylor, D.L. (1994) *Improving Leadership Performance*, London: Prentice Hall. (Discusses leadership from a skills perspective.)

See also: HUMAN CAPITAL; HUMAN RESOURCE MANAGEMENT; JOB EVALUATION; MOTIVATION AND SATISFACTION; OCCUPATIONAL PSYCHOLOGY; ORGANIZATION BEHAVIOUR

Labour process

Overview

The concept of the labour process is taken from Marx's political economy and refers to purposeful activity in which a natural object or raw material is transformed into a useful product which satisfies a human need. The elements of which the process consists are human labour, the object upon which work is performed, instruments or tools and a purpose or goal. Different class regimes or modes of production create different labour processes, involving distinct ways of combining human producers, instruments, raw materials and purposes. Tools and raw materials can be owned in common or privately; producers can be free or enslaved, skilled or dedicated to one process in a complex production system. The intention of production can be cooperative, to create useful goods for a whole group or society to share. It can equally be personal, producing for oneself or one's family's subsistence. Or, as in the case of capitalism, it can be organized for private need, to satisfy the owner of the instruments of production, raw material and finished product.

1 Introduction

Marx was primarily concerned with analysing the capitalist labour process. The objective of this is profitable production, not production for the purpose of creating use values for all to share in. The capitalist seeks to get a financial return on investments and generate more value from workers than is returned in the form of wages. The main methods to increase the amount of labour going to capital is to extend workers' time at work or to increase or intensify their productivity within the same time, by using machinery, applying science to production, or using organizational strategies to change the balance of returns on the labour process. A fragmented or 'detailed' division of labour appeared with the movement of workers into factories from the putting-out or cottage system, where the labour process was under the direct control of the worker. For Marx the factory system brought workers and the labour process under the direct control of the industrial capitalist, and facilitated a more rapid accumulation of capital, by permitting a systematic, self-conscious and scientific analysis of the labour process and ways and means of enhancing labour productivity for capital. It allowed the reconstitution of handicrafts into discrete tasks coordinated and controlled by the capitalist, not the craft worker. The worker was 'de-skilled', the price of labour power cheapened, and the worker became 'a mere living appendage' to the machine (Marx 1867: 548).

Marx's writings on the labour process were recovered by Braverman (1922–1976), and his hugely influential *Labor and Monopoly Capital* can be said to have created the current interest in the perspective. Braverman, an American Marxist who spent some of his life working as a craft worker, developed Marx's analysis of the worker in industrial capitalism and applied this, through a reinterpretation of Taylorism and scientific management, to work within productive and non-productive spheres of advanced, corporate capitalism. Braverman is credited with systematizing industrial sociology, giving it an overarching theory and rigorous historical perspective on the central dynamic of contemporary capitalism (Littler 1982; Thompson 1989). A central theme of his approach is capital's attempt to gain power over the labour process by controlling the skill levels of workers. For

Braverman, Taylorism was not an engineering ideology or incentive system as criticized by human relations theory, but the core practice of management within large-scale or monopoly capitalism, the highest stage of capitalist control over the labour process.

Braverman suggested that there was an inherent tendency to 'de-skill' and 'degrade' labour from a skilled or craft form to a routine or standard form, and this was a pervasive tendency affecting productive and non-productive work, manual, clerical and technical-scientific work in monopoly or corporate capitalism. Craftsmen – they are typically male – command, through their technical knowledge, not only higher wages, but also more control over their daily work and its performance. Braverman argued that monopoly capitalism by using scientific management had systematically reduced craft control and cheapened and degraded labour in the process. This was a central drive or purpose of the system, creating mass labour markets, mass production and mass consumption. It was through the 'massification' of labour that capital dominated, and Braverman's 'objective' account of this process is pessimistic about the prospect for an alternative system, for worker resistance or divergent ways of organizing work which use or enhance workers' skills and knowledge.

The post-Braverman labour process debate has remained concerned with the question of control in the employment relationship and the impact of technology and management strategy on skill levels. Within industrial sociology, organizational behaviour, employee relations and labour history, the 'labour process' perspective is firmly entrenched. It has given a radical or critical edge to management studies, even though many of Braverman's ideas have been challenged and criticized.

2 Labour and labour power

Marx distinguished between a labourer's work (labour) and their capacity to work (labour power). In the capitalist employment relationship the capitalist or owner purchases the mere capacity to work, for a fixed time, but as this ability only exists as an endowment of a living individual, the capitalist must devise ways of acquiring this potential. This means engaging the individual worker to release/realize their capacity to work.

Under certain conditions, such as an external danger which threatens both workers and capitalists equally – a war, for example – there may be accord between workers and employers over what constitutes labour – what amount of use value should be generated. But under normal capitalist relations of production no such unanimity exists. There is permanent conflict over the precise share of the value which goes to workers in the form of wages and is retained by owners in the form of revenue. Labour's share, in Marxist terms, is determined by the time necessary to reproduce and maintain the worker as a commodity ready to work. But as this varies historically and culturally between societies, and is not an economic law, it only points to the need to examine precise patterns of conflict and exchange between the two classes. This labour theory of value is a baggage which has been largely abandoned in contemporary labour process analysis. Relations of reciprocity between owners and producers also vary, and definitions of what constitutes a 'fair day's work' cannot be determined mathematically, but must be constituted through the practical social interchange between workers and employers in the production process. Calculation is accomplished partly through customary definitions of hours and wages, but mainly through modern methods of organizing worker and employer interests at the level of the workplace, through institutions of interest group representation, such as trade unions and employers' organizations, and at the level of State, through enacting laws and regulations which attempt in various ways to codify the exchange relations between capital and labour.

The labour process perspective following Braverman rests on the idea of the indeterminacy of labour. The exchange of wages for time at work does not guarantee a return to the purchaser. Through the interchange between the worker and employer, established wage norms, the going rate or labour market rate operate to prescribed standards. In many occupations custom and practice, rules and regulations may define hours of work, training requirements, etc. However such agreements are mercurial, unsustainable over even the short term due to the incessant pressures of competition, which create the conditions for ever more regular re-negotiation of the effort bargain and incentive system. It is a central element in labour process analysis that concrete relations in production, rather than interchange through markets, actually define the share of labour going to workers and employers. This is the indeterminacy of labour.

So despite attempts to institutionalize reward and output targets, the exchange through the employment relationship does not finalize a guaranteed output of labour. It is the responsibility of the employer as temporary 'owner' of labour power to maximize return. Historically, this was achieved through ruthless coercion, rigid supervision and prison-like controls over workers. Employers in many countries had unlimited contractual rights over 'their' workers, the State reinforcing their domination of the employment relationship. Through trade union and political organization by workers, through the action of 'progressive' employers, and through the spread of more sophisticated methods of maximizing the return on labour power using insights of social science and engineering, the organization of the labour process in production became more complicated, specialized and less reliant on coercion and crude control by employers. Nevertheless, the core elements of the capitalist labour process remain the same: antagonism between the two classes, indeterminacy of labour, and therefore the permanent struggle between capital and labour over the 'effort bargain'.

Friedman (1977) usefully distinguishes between employers' strategies to maximize their return based on treating labour as an *object* – a commodity to be tightly controlled – and a *subject*, an intelligence and will to be purposefully engaged. Taylorism and human relations theory reflect this dichotomy. His 'direct control' and 'responsible autonomy' differentiation of employers' strategies towards labour control reflect the fact that labour is the possession of the individual owner, who rents or temporarily loans himself or herself to the owner of capital for use.

Employers seeking to maximize labour can do so through payment systems tied to output or work quotas; it can be achieved through designing tasks which are technologically driven, via assembly lines, mechanical pacing or types of organization where the division of labour is accentuated. Alternatively, output can be increased by seeking to get the worker to identify with his or her work – something which is normal in non-capitalist labour processes where the fruits and tools of labour belong to the producer, and the time taken to work are within their control. However, under capitalism these are all alienated from the direct producer; their labour effort is objectified in the commodities they produce but do not own. The organization of work is not decided cooperatively, with shared output goals and performance standards, but through a managerial command structure in which producers have a limited input. Because of these material, ownership differences, any attempt to enact identification between worker and capitalist work relies on a purely symbolic, rhetorical or ideological appeal; it is an artifice, something which contradicts both legal claims on the outcome of labour, and the daily practice of the labour process which reinforces the separation and estrangement of the worker from work. Because waged labour is the dominant form of engagement with capital, managers and non-producers may also experience alienation, or claim equivalence with workers, which may be part of their appeal to corporate or collective goals which are above everyone – reified in Marxist terms. Work therefore takes on an estranged form.

The above description may appear arcane, but this is only because the commodification of labour has been normalized. Through habituation, through the spread of capitalist values throughout society and through the elimination of all other forms of work except waged labour, these values assume the weight of custom and are internalized into the workforce as normal. The pre-conditions for the capitalist labour process are the creation of 'free' wage labour, a class who are free from ownership of the means of existence other than as owners of their labour power, and free to sell this labour power through market transaction rather than be tied to one employer or geographical area. The transition to capitalism in all countries necessitates creating the conditions in which free wage labour becomes normalized, which usually means destroying other forms of subsistence.

3 Braverman's legacy

From the appearance of *Labor and Monopoly Capital* there has been an ongoing 'debate' on the labour process. Taylorism for Braverman encapsulates employers' attempt to de-skill and directly remove workers' intelligence from the labour process (see TAYLOR, F.W.). Braverman interpreted Taylorism as completing the dissociation of the labour process from the skills of the worker, separating the 'conception' of work from its 'execution', polarizing skills between a small category of specialists and a mass of unskilled workers. It has been both this reading of Taylorism and its alleged continued significance which has most animated contemporary debate.

Initially writers responded to Braverman's agenda. We can classify reactions in terms of those stressing how Braverman neglected certain themes, such as: subjectivity (see chapters in Knights and Willmott 1990 for a review); consciousness (Burawoy 1979); resistance (Edwards 1986); gender (see chapters in Wood 1989; Thompson 1989); managerial strategy and national diversity (Littler 1982; Burawoy 1985). In terms of the empirical shortcomings of his work, especially the so-called 'de-skilling' thesis, which writers have explored historically, sectorally, occupationally and nationally to test whether deskilling has occurred as a universal tendency (see Brown 1992 for a review of the evidence on de-skilling). Braverman drew on his own experience and the writings of others, but did not engage in empirical validation of his ideas in the conventional sense. Many reactions to his work have applied conventional methodological 'tests' through surveys, but especially case studies, to explore the direction of skill acquisition, distribution and social construction.

Reactions have also challenged the theoretical basis of Braverman's work – his determinism in judging scientific management the 'one best way' of capitalist practice and his historical chronology – in the transition from contracting relations to employment relations and Taylorism (Clawson 1980; Littler 1982; Burawoy 1985; Knights and Willmott 1990) (see ORGANIZATION BEHAVIOUR).

Braverman's death shortly after the publication of *Labor and Monopoly Capital* gave the debate around the labour process a slightly unreal inflection. The text was artificially frozen, providing a target that could not answer back and an icon for the faithful to worship. *Labor and Monopoly Capital* was codified into a few catchphrases, such as the 'de-skilling thesis', for an army of PhD students to examine. We can examine this legacy through a number of key themes.

4 Control, compliance and consent

All labour processes except the most simple require coordination, the administration or organization of the interrelated tasks which combine together to produce useful products. Coordination is a neutral activity. Inside the capitalist firm however, coordination becomes externalized and specialized, saturated with authority through the formal hierarchy of command, the parcelization of tasks into routine and non-routine elements and the separation between workers and managers. Compulsion and control are necessary where labour is non-voluntary, this is particularly evident in the employment relation where employers' prerogatives over the deployment of labour, and discipline, supervision and scrutiny of workers' movements and actions are deemed the responsibilities of management. However, even the most controlled working environment requires consent from workers. Labour, because it is tied to the individual, cannot be alienated or objectified without the individual in some way agreeing to this process, albeit due to economic compulsion, promise of rewards or satisfaction.

Control is a major theme in the labour process literature. Whether through a catalogue of the various 'means' of management control or the historical evolution of employer's control strategies (Edwards 1979), it is argued that management is synonymous with labour control. Taylorism had as its *raison d'être* managerial control over workers' movement, thought and skill. Fordism, through the assembly line, introduces a technology aimed at pacing and controlling the action of workers. Control in the labour process directs attention to working environments in which there is low trust, coercion, limited worker responsibility and a generally directed and regulated working environment. Braverman, as noted above, assumed this was the primary arena of social relations within all societies in the era of monopoly capitalism. However, post-Braverman labour process writing focused on the themes of both compliance and consent, suggesting that employers may more productively use labour power by engaging with it rather than controlling it. Groups of relatively autonomous workers, who are increasing as manual labour declines, either cannot, will not or do not need to be tightly controlled. Indeed rigid control is expensive and can be counterproductive. Rather, appeals to professional values, career chances, goodwill or trust are deemed more suitable methods of translating the capacity of skilled and professional workers into labour effort and value.

Consent may be projected as the ideal of some management philosophies – Japanese management systems, for example – but research within a labour process framework on Japanese companies and those adopting Japanese methods reveals that labour compliance rather than consent is the perceived experience of workers. Such management philosophies as human resource management have been interpreted as projecting a rhetoric of consent within a strongly unitarian and compliant labour regulation system. Attention to management interest in employee participation, involvement, the benefits of high trust, team working and flexibility indicate that instead of controlling employees within a Taylorist mode, competitive edge in management-labour relations has in the last decade come from a stress on gaining worker commitment through shared norms and values, or increasing the ideological, and sometimes material (through share schemes) interest of workers in their labour process (see GROUPS AND TEAMS). This reflects several processes:

1 the generic decline of the Taylorist-Fordist control apparatus;
2 the spread of Japanese management ideas, especially team working;
3 the influence of new industry management systems, especially North American computer companies;
4 the influence of neo-human relations theory, which has researched the link between satisfaction, commitment and greater productivity.

Critical labour process theory seeks to uncover the tension between the control ambitions of management within an emergent culture and ideology where it is unfashionable or problematic to have direct control rather than employee empowerment, cultural control and commitment. Tensions between management proclamation and action is central to Braverman's discussion of the actual levels of skills in the US labour force compared with official statistics. In this sense it is part of a labour process perspective to look beyond rhetoric and into the workings of the labour process as practised.

5 Resistance

Braverman's analysis implied that Taylorism completed the alienation of the worker from the labour process. That the objective forces of capitalism, managerial power and monopoly knowledge were in some way omnipotent. Careful reading of Braverman indicates that he actually saw labour resistance as normal due to the lack of agreement on work effort, and the inability of management to treat labour as a passive player (see INDUSTRIAL CONFLICT). Braverman noted: 'the fact that workers are rebellious, and that the average pace of production is decided in a practice which largely assumes the form of a struggle, whether organized or not' (1974: 180).

However, the dynamic in his book reinforces a view of workers as passive and capital as dominant within the labour process.

A stress on the role of resistance has therefore featured as a critique of Braverman. Resistance is seen as influencing management strategy towards work organization (Edwards 1979). Worker organization into trade unions contributes to labour market segmentation, which in turn conditions employers' bargaining ability and power in controlling the labour process (see TRADE UNIONS). Trade unions as organized opposition to employers restructuring of the labour process feature in Littler's (1982) account of the spread of Taylorism into British industry in the 1930s. Strikes and other forms of organized opposition checked or limited employers' strategies. While trade unions also segment the labour market into more manageable divisions, and resistance can be overplayed, it is fair to say that contestation, organized, collective and individual, is an inherent part of labour process dynamics. For a useful comparative discussion see Edwards (1986).

Much reaction to Braverman has sought to stress the role of worker resistance and consciousness in the labour process, both as organized efforts to limit collectively the prerogatives of management and gain control and autonomy for labour, and as individual refusal to work according to the strictures of capital. But this could equally be seen as putting too much emphasis on the significance of labour to determine the effort bargain, rather than technology or managerial capability. These extremes – passive labour and active labour – are unhelpful. What is required is a careful empirical assessment of the weighting of the different forces shaping the labour process in each particular setting.

6 Stages, phases and national systems

Capitalism in Marx's work evolves as a system from manufacture to machinofacture and modern industry. His chronology and analysis has a technological imperative, with the incorporation of science into production technology subordinating workers. Drawing off the work of Babbage and Ure, Marx overstated the power of technology in modern industry, and understated the role of agency and managerial organization. Lazonick (1990), through detailed historical examination of the impact of machinery on craft work in the British textile mills which Marx ([1867] 1976) used for his discussion of the labour process, reveals the persistence of craft controls over recruitment, training, supervision of other workers, repair and maintenance of machines and the shop floor division of labour.

In fact, the factory system did not immediately transfer the control of the labour process to the industrial capitalist, as initially internal contractor systems operated, which off loaded responsibility for organizing work onto a male skilled worker and inhibited the growth of the managerial hierarchy (Littler 1982; Clawson 1980; Lazonick 1990). It was really with the decay of insider contracting and the growth of direct employment of labour and supervisors that organizational capabilities for restructuring the labour process developed. This change was organizational not technological or spatial (the appearance of the factory), as Marx suggested. Taylorism theorized and legitimated the growth of managerial and related staff responsible for separating the labour process from the labourer, and transferring planning, purpose and design aspects of work into management and its allied agents. Scientific management developed in the USA for a variety of reasons – scarcity of skilled labour, abundance of immigrant labour, mass markets, larger enterprises – but in the course of the twentieth century spread across Europe and into Japan. The significance of Taylorism as a system is central to the creation of labour process analysis in the USA in the 1970s.

In Braverman, there is a more definite chronological system shift from private, small-scale capital under craft worker control, to large-scale, monopoly capital under scientific management as the pinnacle of labour process control. Post-Braverman writers have stressed post-Taylorist stages or phases of the labour process, and highlighted two things.

First, the continued evolution of labour process organization within capitalism beyond the possibilities for accumulation afforded by classical scientific management. Control through culture, values and various neo-human relations policies seeks to engage, not simply coerce the worker (see ORGANIZATION CULTURE). Second, the role of new national and regional centres of accumulation which offer a synthesis of classical scientific management within different cultural contexts and class accords, which allow for post-Taylorist practices to be embedded in unique ways. The organization of the labour process in Japan and the transfer of the Japanese system to the West is central here (see Elger and Smith 1994 for an overview). However, the European, especially the German experience of post- and neo-Taylorism is also important (Altmann *et al.* 1992).

Marx's analysis of the nature of the capitalist labour process uses England as its historical laboratory. England, the most economically advanced and dominant capitalist economy represented the future that all other societies would mirror. Braverman wrote through the experience of the USA as the dominant capitalist economy of the twentieth century, originator of scientific management and therefore the common model for all other societies. In fact both were wrong to associate the most advanced with a single future. If we interject country differences into this picture, as cross-national studies of labour process organization have done, then we see that the norm is for there to be *both* national pluralism in work organization as well as pressure to find a 'one best way' to organize. National differences are not infinite, and dominant economies remain important sources of 'best practice' which are used in many societies. Japan has assumed this new ascendant role and has provided, through the way the labour process is organized in Japanese companies, the manner of their 'transplantation' in the West, and through the emulation of Japanese-style management organization, new models, techniques and ideas, which have flowed into the discourse on the labour process from the mid-1980s.

7 Future developments

The labour process debate will develop at two levels, the macro and micro. At the macro level there will continue to be a profusion of models and labels to describe or capture through a single paradigm the step changes in the contemporary workplace. These are most likely to be informed by aspects of the Japanese case, as this rising economy has dominated discussion of new working arrangements. These models project 'one best way' for labour process organization, and therefore follow the path pioneered by classical scientific management.

In direct contradistinction, other writers will argue the case for greater pluralism and diversity in the organization of the labour process, especially between the Western welfare capitalist economies and Eastern developmental economies, where the integration of the worker into society, the firm and production process is so different.

Arising from the internationalization of capital and decline in the nation-state, there will be more attention to 'hybrid' forms of labour process organization, with the stress on borrowing and adapting methods and 'best practices' from range of country, sector and leading company models. There will be closer attention paid to the relationship between national institutional arrangements and particular production regimes. Finally, there will be more attention paid to the relationship between labour process and labour market analysis, between the more detailed segmentation of labour contracts, the growth of contingent, atypical and 'flexible' employment, and the effects of this on worker interest group representation, resistance and organization.

At the micro level there will be closer attention paid to how the social composition of labour inputs into the labour process influences the shape of work. Most obviously, how the gendering of tasks and occupations structures work experience, but also the impact of race and ethnicity on the structuring of work. More detailed analysis will be devoted to the management of meaning, consent, subjectivity and individuality, and the drift in favour of cultural or normative managerial control which taps worker commitment and uses values not rules to intensify labour productivity.

CHRIS SMITH
ROYAL HOLLOWAY UNIVERSITY OF LONDON

Further reading

(References cited in the text marked *)

* Altmann, N., Kohler, C. and Meil, P. (eds) (1992) *Technology and Work in German Industry*, London: Routledge. (A useful account of the theoretical and practical critique of Taylorism from one branch of German industrial sociology. Revealing for its more pragmatic and theoretically broader engagement with work relative to US and British academic interventions.)

Belanger, J., Edwards, P. and Haiven, L. (eds) (1994) *Workplace Industrial Relations and the Global Challenge*, Ithaca, New York: ILR Press. (Despite the focus on industrial relations in the title, this volume makes a genuine effort to present cross-national research on workplace restructuring, the majority of chapters having country comparative data from within the workplace, and seeking, imaginatively to link shop floor developments to wider national and international trends.)

* Braverman, H. (1974) *Labor and Monopoly Capital: The Degradation of Work in the Twentieth Century*, New York: Monthly Review Press. (The main reference for contemporary debates on the labour process. Although heavily criticized and limited by reliance on US capitalism, the breadth and quality of the writing and analysis make the book a modern classic.)

* Brown, R.K. (1992) *Understanding Industrial Organisations: Theoretical Perspectives in Industrial Sociology*, London: Routledge. (A clear essay on approaches to industrial sociology. Chapter 5 explores debates around the labour process and offers the most succinct and accessible account of the main ideas and trends.)

* Burawoy, M. (1979) *Manufacturing Consent*, Chicago, IL: University of Chicago Press. (Participant observation study of piece working on the shop floor, building on classical studies of piece working culture and patterns of managerial indulgence towards workplace informality; rich in detail and interpretation.)

* Burawoy, M. (1985) *The Politics of Production*, London: Verso. (Examines the character of management controls under different political and economic systems – nineteenth-century capitalism, advanced monopoly capitalism, state socialism and underdeveloped Africa. Not an easy read, but important for linking the nature of work and managerial or 'factory regimes' to wider economic, political and institutional forces and contexts.)

* Clawson, D. (1980) *Bureaucracy and the Labor Process*, New York: Monthly Review Press. (A useful supplement to Braverman's account of labour process organization in the USA in the nineteenth and twentieth centuries; highlights the limitations of craft control and its domination by white male workers.)

* Edwards, R. (1979) *Contested Terrain: The Transformation of the Workplace in the Twentieth Century*, London: Heinemann. (A useful integration of labour process and labour market theory, which overviews the evolution of different management control techniques – personal, bureaucratic and technical – in US industry in the twentieth century. Stresses the manner in which control evolves through contradiction brought about by worker resistance.)

* Edwards, P. (1986) *Conflict at Work*, Oxford: Blackwell. (A materialist, non-Marxist interpretation of conflict within the workplace, with an interesting discussion on the institutional structuring of work, the comparative formation of work cultures and their impact on labour process struggles.)

* Elger, T. and Smith, C. (eds) (1994) *Global Japanization? Transnational Transformation in the Labour Process*, London: Routledge. (Offers a deconstruction of the ideology of the 'Japanese model' of work organization, highlighting the impact of globalization on labour process theory and practice within a more internationally integrated workplace.)

Jurgens, U., Malsch, T. and Dohse, K. (1993) *Breaking from Taylorism: Changing Forms of Work in the Automobile Industry*, Cambridge: Cambridge University Press. (Debates on the alleged shift away from Taylorism and Fordism towards 'new production paradigms' have largely come from analysis of the auto industry. This book compares car plants in different countries and companies during the 1980s under the impact of Japanese production methods and competition. It seriously qualifies the more dramatic claims of the 'lean production' model of the future of work.)

Kenney, M. and Florida, R. (1993) *Beyond Mass Production: the Japanese System and its Transfer to the US*, Oxford: Oxford University Press. (With an explicit commitment to the idea of Japanese production methods as a new and systematic development, 'innovation mediated production', the book charts the 'transfer' of this paradigm to the US via sector analysis of Japanese firms in the US. Qualification is required for the model being promoted, but the data collected is comprehensive and the analysis worth reading.)

* Knights, D. and Willmott, H. (eds) (1990) *Labour Process Theory*, London: Macmillan. (The best collection of essays on theoretical developments, which, while missing the debates on flexibility and Japan, nevertheless contains excellent alternative models and re-statements of aspects of Braverman's legacy.)

Knights, D., Willmott, H. and Collinson, D. (eds) (1985) *Job Redesign: Critical Perspectives on the Labour Process*, Aldershot: Gower. (The first of many collections to come out of the Aston/UMIST Organization and Control of Labour Process Conference – now the International Labour Process Conference – with several essential readings, especially those by Littler, Kelly, Child and Manwaring and Wood.)

* Lazonick, W. (1990) *Competitive Advantage on the Shop Floor*, Cambridge: Cambridge University Press. (A collection of path-breaking essays which deconstruct Marx's reading of the genealogy of labour process organization, together with managerial analysis of different forms of managerial shop floor control systems in the UK, the USA and Japan.)

* Littler, C.R. (1982) *The Development of the Labour Process in Capitalist Societies*, London: Heinemann. (Useful for advancing labour process theory, especially by separating the procedures and processes around the systematization of the recruitment and selection of labour and its bureaucratic organization in production; and in highlighting the national peculiarities to the evolution of managerial regimes in the USA, Britain and Japan.)

* Marx, K. (1867) *Capital*, vol. 1, Harmondsworth: Penguin, 1976. (Marx's theory of the labour process is explained here in specific chapters, and is embedded in others which explore the structure of social relations in modern industry, the role of machinery and struggles during the working day.)

Penn, R., Rose, M. and Rubery, J. (eds.) (1994) *Skill and Occupational Change*, Oxford: Oxford University Press. (Based upon survey data from a large scale British research programme under the Social Change and Economic Life Initiative (SCELI). The authors present evidence which counters Braverman's claim for a *general* tendency towards deskilling, in favour of a contradictory process of 'up-skilling' for certain groups – 'service class' employees – and skill degradation and polarization for others, especially female part-time manual workers. Despite all the limitations of surveys as a method for adequately exploring the extent and meaning of skill changes, the book contains useful chapters on skill trends, gender and technical change, and provides an important macro contribution to one theme in the labour process debate.)

* Thompson, P. (1989) *The Nature of Work: An Introduction to Debates on the Labour Process*, 2nd edn, London: Macmillan. (Thompson examines key themes which Braverman neglected or understated, such as resistance at work, consent in the employment relation and gender relations. This second edition also evaluates post-Taylorist debates which hinge around the idea of flexible manufacturing and working.)

* Wood, S. (ed.) (1989) *The Transformation of Work? Skill, Flexibility and the Labour Process*, London: Unwin Hyman. (Ostensibly a new edition of Wood's earlier collection, this reader indicates the pace of change within the debate, revealing more attention to diverse internationalization projects, through attention to Japan and Sweden, and the new theme of flexibility which emerged in the mid-1980s.)

See also: HUMAN RESOURCE MANAGEMENT; INDUSTRIAL AND LABOUR RELATIONS; ORGANIZATION BEHAVIOUR; PAYMENT SYSTEMS; PERSONNEL MANAGEMENT

Related topics in the IEBM: GLOBALIZATION; MANAGEMENT IN GERMANY; MANAGEMENT IN JAPAN; MARX, K.H.; ORGANIZATION PARADIGMS; ORGANIZATION TYPES; TECHNOLOGY AND ORGANIZATIONS

Leadership

Overview

It has been claimed that in 1896 in the USA, the Library of Congress had no book on leadership, but within one person's lifetime, eighty-five years later, over 5,000 entries on leadership were reviewed by Bass in 1981. This explosion of interest has included an enormous diversity of activity by people known as leaders. Fiedler and Garcia in 1987 listed as examples of leadership Henry V's victory at Agincourt against overwhelming odds; George Washington, who defeated better-equipped English forces; and Lee Iacocca, who produced the dramatic turnaround of the Chrysler Corporation. They then went on to show the macabre side of leadership by including Hitler, and the Reverend Jim Jones, who induced 800 of his followers to commit suicide. Looking at more recent events, one could add successful business tycoons like Robert Maxwell in the UK, Alan Bond in Australia, and Ivan Boësky in the USA, who all allegedly defrauded millions of people who had fallen under their leadership spell.

With such a wide range of examples to illustrate a phenomenon described in a single word, one has to ask oneself whether the leadership concept has practical utility for understanding organizational behaviour. The answer is a qualified 'yes'. The qualification implies that some usefulness can be extracted from the available evidence, but great care has to be taken not to overstate the explanatory thrust of a term which has given rise to thousands of different definitions and a variety of *post hoc* explanations covering both good and evil.

The literature will be divided into two main streams: universalist approaches and situational approaches. The former include great person theories, personality theories, psychoanalytic theories, charismatic, transformational and transactional theories, organizational economics, grid theory and popular descriptive theories. Situational approaches are, in general, of more recent origin and are based on the assumption that different styles of behaviour, including leadership, are appropriate for contrasting varieties of real-life situations. These approaches are sometimes called contingency theories because they attempt to specify the effect of contingent situations on different behavioural responses. Psychologically orientated theories tend to concentrate on intra-organizational contingencies, like the nature of the task, while sociological theories tend to stress the effect of factors external to the organization, like turbulence of the environment.

The contrast between generalistic and contingency approaches is important and it will be argued that the thrust of evidence in support of the latter lends itself to a more realistic prescriptive approach to leadership. At the same time it must be recognized that there is often a degree of overlap between the two schemata.

1 Universalist approaches

Perhaps the oldest and best-known literature on leadership uses examples of great persons. It extracts from the description of their personality and behaviour some alleged essential characteristics which are assumed to have universal validity. Using Field Marshall Sir William Slim, one early writer extracts five hallmarks of leadership: courage, willpower, flexibility of mind, knowledge and integrity. The terms vary from analyst to analyst although some, like integrity, have a hallowed place in most historic–descriptive lists.

One of several problems with this approach is that the lists do not critically distinguish between good and evil, between, say, George Washington and Benito Mussolini. Integrity, for instance, can be defined as 'the thing that makes people trust you' and this, like most of the other characteristics listed earlier, would apply to all the people mentioned so far as well as to many people all around us who do not fall into the 'great person' category.

Even if these personal attributes could be validly applied to all leaders, the theory would not be useful for management because, with few exceptions, they are not easily assessable for selection nor can they be trained. Moreover, personality theories of leadership have shown no consistent identification of traits and have now been largely abandoned. This does not mean that personality is unimportant, only that in most cases it is a peripheral rather than a major explanatory factor (Smith and Peterson 1988) (see MOTIVATION AND SATISFACTION).

Psychoanalytic explanations of leadership also examine personality using a number of universal concepts. There is a long tradition of applying psychoanalytic theories of personality development and categories of maladjustment to biographical data of famous people. Freud, for instance, enquired into the life of Leonardo da Vinci to trace his variations in artistic output and his later interests in biology and engineering to the inhibitions of his sexual drive. More recently the use of psychoanalytic theory has been applied to assess leader motivation and preoccupations. The 'royal road' to understand senior managers' preoccupations is thought to be through the mechanism called transference, which describes the:

interface between therapist and patient and . . . derive from the kind of relationships which develop between parents and children . . . It can be described as the projection or displacement upon another person of unconscious wishes and feelings originally directed towards important individuals in childhood.

(Kets de Vries *et al.* 1993: 10)

In the de Vries *et al.* schema, 'transference is the determining factor in understanding an individual's style' and is therefore presumably invariant with situations.

Sociological theories have also used broad classifications, for instance Max Weber's famous categorization of charismatic leadership which has developed into a description of leaders who are able to change the needs and aspirations of their followers to agree with the leader's own requirements. This type was later called transformational leadership and can be contrasted with the less dynamic, more traditional transactional leader who uses rewards and disciplinary methods to achieve organizational effectiveness more or less around the status quo. In terms of organizational change, the transactional leader will favour incrementalism while the transformational leadership is characterized by fairly fundamental and substantial leaps into new domains without necessarily achieving success, but nevertheless imprinting his or her personality on the process (Bass 1992).

Bass used and developed the charismatic transformational concept by relating it to stress. For instance, it is held that under conditions when a charismatic leader's life is threatened, he tends to remain cool and composed while non-charismatic leaders suffer the effects of stress. Bass gives the examples of Mahatma Gandhi, Franklin D. Roosevelt, Benito Mussolini and Ronald Reagan. He produces evidence to suggest that 'to be effective under stress, the leader must be transformational – able to rise above what the group sees as its immediate needs' (Bass 1992: 144–5).

The problem with typologies described so far is that when internal organizational needs or external pressures change, a given leadership type may suddenly become dysfunctional. Since environmental and competitive pressures, changes in technology and other factors often follow distinct cyclical patterns, it would be necessary to change managers quite frequently. But Japan, which, over many decades, has pursued a permanent secure employment policy in large organizations has demonstrated that this is not necessary.

An alternative approach, but still within the universalist framework is to discover a leadership style which is superior in all situations. A popular approach used in consultancy and management training postulates a two-dimensional grid: concern for production and concern for people (Blake and Mouton 1964). Maximizing both gives the best leader style and this is assumed to apply in more or less all situations. One consultant even claims that concentration on only one of the two dimensions is associated with 'a range of severe mental and physical illness'. This extreme recommendation for a single, best style was originally derived from research at Ohio University in the early 1950s, but quite soon their findings were superseded by evidence that concern for people and consideration are particularly important. For instance, it was found that grievances and labour turnover were highest when the leader showed low concern for people. Later, as shall be seen, even this generalization had to be encompassed within a more situationally oriented model.

The Blake and Mouton grid approach provides an easily remembered prescription and consequently it is still widely used in organizational training, but its validity can be seriously questioned (Yukl 1994). Another fairly simple concept, at least to begin with, is the idea that leaders can be divided into a stratification depending on their 'time-span of discretion'. This is 'the maximum time-span during which people are required to exercise discretion' in their managerial work (Jaques 1976: 99). Simple tasks often have a short time span; a repetitive television set assembly operation, for instance, may have a time span of less than a minute, while a member of a large company board will be expected to produce five-year plans. Jaques developed this type of general theory over seven strata which relate time span to organizational function and level and also account for differences in pay.

An extension of the great person theory of leadership is the great company theory, which has also produced an enormous literature and is subject to similar limitations. A particularly well-known example of this approach is the series of books starting with *In Search of Excellence: A Lesson from America's Best Run Companies* by Peters and Waterman (1982). The book was an outstanding success; it was translated into most major languages and is thought to have sold over five million copies. The authors' eight attributes of excellence are:

- managing ambiguity and paradox
- a bias for action
- close to the customer
- autonomy and entrepreneurship
- productivity through people
- hands-on, value-driven
- 'stick to the knitting'
- simple form, lean staff

However, some of the companies used to construct these attributes have failed the test of time. The most telling example is of a company which the authors described as passing 'all hurdles for excellent performance 1961–1980' (Peters and Waterman 1982: 20). This was International Business Machines or IBM which nearly collapsed under the weight of enormous debts in the early 1990s. A similar success–failure cycle can be traced in many other attempts to extract universal wisdom from descriptions of case examples.

Microeconomic theories tend to generalize about human nature and build these (usually untested) generalizations into their theoretical models. The roots of organizational economics go back to the 1930s but it took half a century for its theories to enter the organizational literature with two concepts: agency theory and transactional cost theory. Both can be interpreted to relate to managerial leadership. They concentrate on analyses of what goes on inside and between organizations and the role of individual managers in these processes. Although the level of analysis is new, the traditional notion of the economic person and his/her motivation remain. There are owners seeking to maximize the net return of their investment. They are called principals. Then there are agents, that is to say managers, who operate on behalf of owners but will try to maximize their own equally self-centred interests. Since both act egotistically, conflict is inevitable. Consequently it becomes necessary for principals to distrust and constrain agents. Agents in turn will use ingenuity to defeat or circumvent the constraints to achieve their ends.

The term 'the dismal science' as a description of economics is in fact partly due to its assumption that the economic person is selfishly individualistic and will, given the opportunity, act deceitfully to maximize personal gains. Therefore, the economic person cannot be trusted, may shirk responsibilities, and in general has to be constrained or at least carefully monitored by the principal. In transaction cost theory, the lack of trust of individual actors is extended to the problem of dealing with other firms that may not deliver the appropriate goods or services at the best quality or lowest cost. Under such conditions vertical integration may produce economic benefits.

These theories about people in leadership positions have been compared to McGregor's Theory X and Y (McGregor 1967). Theory X describes managerial strategies quite close to the assumptions of economics, while Theory Y has a positive, humanistic message about people's sense of responsibility, and their willingness to work purposefully in groups towards common ends. Management theories, in contrast to organizational economics, tend to support McGregor's Theory Y and have accumulated empirical evidence in its support. To stress the difference between these two opposing sets of assumptions, a stewardship theory about corporate governance, that is to say leadership, has been proposed. Under stewardship theory 'there is no conflict of interest between managers and owners. . .managers are team players. . .that will act in the best interest of owners. Managers are not opportunistic agents. . .but good stewards' (Donaldson 1990). Both models start off in a generalistic format but can also be cast into a situational framework (see MANAGERIAL BEHAVIOUR).

2 Situational leadership

McGregor's (1967) posthumous publication develops a situational approach by describing a number of situational constraints which can be described by a simple formula: $P = f(I, a, b, c, . . .E, m, n, o)$. A person's leadership behaviour (P) is a function specified by certain characteristics of the individual (I, a, b, c,), for instance his knowledge, skill, motivation and attitudes as well as certain aspects of the environment (E, m, n, o) which can include the nature of the person's job and reward system. Situational theories spurn simplistic generalization and instead attempt to identify certain leadership characteristics or behaviour that match the complexities of real life. Fiedler pioneered this approach by showing that effectiveness depends on the interaction between a leader's personality or motivation on the one hand, and the favourable or unfavourable conditions in which he or she is expected to operate. Favourable conditions apply, for instance, when a leader is supported by followers, knows how to carry out specific tasks, and is given sufficient power to handle subordinates. Vroom and others have developed situational leadership models which take account of different contingencies which determine which decision procedure (from autocratic to participative) will be most effective in the specified conditions. Such models have been found useful for training managers to think and act flexibly and to recognize that leaders have choices which they can use in diverse situations (Vroom 1977). Vroom, following previous US work on leadership, sees participative decision making as an ideal, or at least as the democratic style at which organizations should aim in order to achieve effectiveness. Most writing on leadership favours participative methods to increase flexibility and competitiveness in modern industry (Lawler 1986; Rooney 1993) (see MOTIVATION AND SATISFACTION).

If one thinks of leadership–subordinate interaction as a range of sharing influence and power, then there are one or two positions beyond participation and consensus that have to be explored and may be more suitable, and even more effective than participation in some circumstances. For instance, there are various ways of decentralizing authority and responsibility by delegation to individuals or groups and by forming units with degrees of semi-autonomy. These decentralized organizational patterns have become important in relation to new forms of technology which facilitate such an approach. Several examples of these sociotechnical developments have been successfully developed in different parts of the world. They have been supported by two five-year action projects in Norway and Sweden to further democratize organizational life.

Another way of looking at contingencies is to ask why leaders are successful in some situations but not in others. Little systematic research has been done on this, but collecting newspaper cuttings over time brings up many examples. One of the most widely reported recent cases concerns John Akers, IBM's Chief Executive who, at the age of 58, was fired on 26 January 1993, after a spectacularly successful business career during which he had been Chief Executive at IBM since 1985. It seems he was unable to cope with the rapid technological and market changes that engulfed the computer industry from the late 1980s.

Heinz Schimmelbush, the charismatic 49-year-old Chief Executive of the German Metallgesellschaft was ousted on 17 December 1993. He had been described as the darling of German management circles and had in 1991 been elected German Manager of the Year. He had been with his company for twenty years and rose rapidly through the ranks to become Chief Executive in 1988. He was fired for alleged mismanagement and for not keeping his board properly informed of serious financial problems which he attempted to cover up with creative accounting.

On 1 December 1993, the *Financial Times* described in great detail the spectacular rise and fall of Roy Ashman, the co-founder and Chief Executive of Harland Simon, a company engaged in the manufacture of process control equipment. Shares had collapsed from 590 pence to 253 pence. For a while the company had outperformed the All Share Index by 200 per cent and in 1992 London's financial centre, the City, had expected a profit of £12.5 million, rather than the announced loss of £6.3 million.

These three almost random recent examples illustrate the vulnerability of the 'great man' theory applied to business leadership. In addition to examples where failure is due to inappropriate or faulty decisions by leaders who could not cope with changing technical

or economic circumstances, there are as many examples where previously successful leaders failed through alleged dishonesty or fraud; Milken (with junk bonds) in the USA, Saunders (of the Guinness drinks company), and Nadir (the Polly Peck fruit and textile conglomerate), both in the UK, are among the better known cases (see DECISION MAKING).

3 Limits to free choice

Even in small, face-to-face groups, leaders have been shown to be influenced by the composition of the group, their values and skills. Smith and Peterson (1988) review the very extensive field of group processes and leadership and come to the conclusion that the leader does not usually have the power to determine the culture of the group without the support of historical, economic and structural circumstances (see GROUPS AND TEAMS).

Leadership, almost by definition, is a voluntary activity but there are limits to free choice. Many companies run executive development programmes, which, like the teaching based on Blake and Mouton's grid (1964), train employees to use or conform with the organization's 'house style' rather than their own leadership inclination. This limitation of choice also applies to situational theories like Vroom's which are normative, by specifying the 'best method' that corresponds to a clearly identified set of situations. Consultancy-based managerial training methods are usually not based on published research, but prescribe preferred leadership styles all the same.

Furthermore, western European countries, with the exception of the UK and Italy, have industrial relations legislation which requires organizations to establish certain representative committees to consult their employees on specified issues, like changes of ownership and large-scale redundancies. These legal requirementsstarted in West Germany in 1951 with a co-determination law giving workers or their chosen representatives half the places on the supervisory board of the coal, iron and steel industries. Later legislation extended similar provision to the rest of German industry (now also in the former East Germany). The harmonization aims of the European

Union will provide minimum legislative support for a variety of social charter measures which limit managerial decision influence in countries that had not previously provided such measures. In the USA, collective bargaining agreements often incorporate provisions which constrain managerial decision making for the duration of the contract and can be enforced through legal action. The law or its interpretation is also important in deciding the leadership objectives of senior management and the role of Boards of Directors. Does company law support the conventional assumption that it is the objective of private enterprise companies to maximize the returns to shareholders? Or is long-term survival and prosperity more easily achieved by having regard to a wider constituency of stakeholders? The German codetermination model, which has influenced most company legislation in Continental Europe, gives employees a limited stake in some aspects of organizational decision making. There is now much discussion of extending the stakeholder model to include customers, suppliers and perhaps banks. Such a dispersal of influence complicates the role of leadership by converting it into something like Trusteeship (Kay 1997). However, creating the conditions for trust (as we argue in the next section) has always been seen as a central responsibility for leaders in all walks of life, although it may reduce the scope for centralized leadership.

Other problems with free choice result from a lack of success of certain leadership methods which make it difficult to perseverate with them once the failure becomes known. Two examples are worth mentioning. One revolves around the issue of inauthentic democracy. The advocacy of a participative house style has already been mentioned. Participation is often regarded as a panacea for many organizational problems, including overcoming resistance to change. At least one well-known social scientist who carried out important work in this area (Likert 1967), thought that joint decision making and consensus management was universally valid. A well-known social scientist tells the story of a conversation with Rensis Likert over dinner. He asked 'Would System 4 [joint decision making] work equally well in all cultures?' Likert, pointing to his attaché case plastered with hotel stickers, replied 'I've been to dozens of countries throughout the world. System 4 works everywhere I have been. Sometime I may find some Hottentot tribe where it isn't appropriate. But I haven't found it yet.'

Since the 1970s, with the acceptance of contingency theory, such conclusions have been shown to be quite unwarranted but the notion lingers on and is probably responsible for the occurrence of examples of pseudo or inauthentic participation in different parts of the world. It sanctions the practice of appearing to consult or involve employees, when the decision has already been taken, or when there is no intention of making use of the suggestions received during the consultative process. Inauthentic leadership methods lead to frustration and opposition, for instance from trade unions, to more genuine attempts to democratize organizational life.

Another limitation is based on the widespread belief that participative leadership can function irrespective of competence, that is to say, relevant experience and skill among subordinates. This belief is based on an inappropriate analogy with political participation, where universal adult voting rights are successfully practised in all democracies. However, working with a highly specialized vocabulary and complex modern technical issues, participation requires training and experience to reach the necessary level of competence (Heller 1992). Without this competence, democratic leadership will not succeed. The undervaluation of the essential role which training and competence play in democratic leadership practices almost certainly contributes to inauthentic participation.

In the literature on organization, the major constraints on leadership are seen to derive from a variety of theories and supporting evidence which attribute organizational change and adaptation of structures to the type and complexity of technology or to various ecological/environmental pressures. One review of the literature (Leavy and Wilson 1994) argues that these deterministic theories, which virtually eliminate the role of leadership, and the opposite voluntaristic view, which pays no attention to constraints on leadership, can be reconciled. This will be dealt with in the section on strategy below.

4 Leadership and strategy

Since the 1950s, the literature on leadership has covered three phases. It started with an analysis of individual characteristics of skill and performance and expanded to include wider considerations of followers and groups, as well as the necessary antecedent conditions that helped or hindered the emergence of leaders. More recently, as management became more firmly established as an intellectual discipline in its own right, the leadership role is seen as a central aspect of the formation of organizational policy and strategy. This trend links leadership into the decision process of the top layers of the power structure and consequently reduces the attention given to the role of lower levels.

Three examples of this approach will be given. The first is the fourfold strategy classification of Miles and Snow (1978). 'Defenders' devise and, as far as possible, maintain an environment which favours a stable form of organization. Such organizations concentrate on high-quality engineering to produce and distribute goods using mechanistic cost-control structures. By contrast, 'prospectors' favour a dynamic environment where they can discover and work with new, preferably innovative, products for which risks and failure rates are high. This type of organization requires flexibility in its administration and technology, and consequently invests in human resources by favouring decentralized unit operations within an organic structure. Third, 'analyser' organizations combine characteristics of Defenders and Prospectors by minimizing risks and maximizing entrepreneurial profit objectives. Their technology has to contain a stable as well as flexible orientation and their administrations favour a matrix-type human resources system. Finally, Miles and Snow have observed unstable organizations that react inconsistently to their environment and consequently have an erratic and poor performance record; they are called 'reactors'.

In describing these four organizational strategies in terms of structures and administrative processes, Miles and Snow also describe, although indirectly, the leadership behaviour at senior levels which characterize firms pursuing the three viable strategies. The names they have chosen to describe these typologies – defenders, prospectors, analysers and reactors – characterize a set of leadership adaptations to environmental conditions.

A different leadership–strategy connection is developed by Dunphy and Stace (1990) but is not inconsistent with Miles and Snow. Their point of departure is a critique of the prevalent organization development (OD) view of leadership, in particular in relation to achieving change. The OD model favours slow, incremental change achieved through leadership that involves employees in the process of building up an organic, flexible and cohesive organization.

Dunphy and Stace have produced evidence to suggest that the OD method is suitable only in a limited number of circumstances. They argue that strategic considerations derived from an assessment of the socio-economic and political environment may require different strategies. More autocratic and radical alternatives are in part a consequence of the rapidity of external changes or the emergence of new competition. Coercive measures may become necessary if employees are unwilling to respond to the external signals so that the viability of the enterprise is put at risk. Structural changes, like diversification or mergers, may have a similar effect.

These considerations produce a 2 × 2 typology; vertically it differentiates between (1) collaborative versus (2) coercive modes; and horizontally between (3) incremental versus (4) transformative change strategies. Testing the model in a sample of Australian industry which they grouped into high, medium and low performers, they report that none of the 450 managers interviewed rated their executives as using a collaborative change style. High and medium-high performers used a variety of approaches, but the directive, tough method was predominant. Low performers preferred careful, timid fine tuning.

They conclude that the OD tender-minded participative incremental approach is not a universal or even a preferred solution for Australian industry at the time of their research, although several companies used variants of the 'soft' style in earlier years. They conclude that businesses should, and usually do, select the most situationally valid business strategy to fit environmental circumstances. A policy based on a tough, fast-moving leadership style received support from an advocacy which owes more to consultancy experience than research; it is called 're-engineering' from a book with that name by Hammer and Champy (1994). The authors argue that salvation for modern business does not lie in adaptation or incremental change, but in grasping the nettle of revolution by redesigning and 'starting all over, starting from scratch' (1994: 2).

These strategic management models relate to leadership indirectly and assign it a peripheral or subsidiary role. Leavy and Wilson (1994), however, attempt to integrate technology–environmental determinism with psychological approaches that give primary consideration to human agency and leadership. Their bridge-building is based on an extensive review of the literature and a longitudinal field research in a small number of firms in Ireland. Their description of leaders as 'tenants of time and context' stresses the interaction between leadership competence, historic circumstances and specific contextual elements like technology. Historic circumstances include the national political climate, which is capable of influencing the ideology and behaviour of leaders and enterprises. Leavy and Wilson single out the post-1979 period during which the leaders were subject to a more constraining context, based on economic–political circumstances which made them more reactive and defensive than in the previous two decades. Even so, during the same period and subject to similar contextual pressures, some firms grew while others failed, and this could be traced back to aggressive and imaginative leadership.

Leavy and Wilson conclude that the industrial environment is not an adequate explanation of organizational strategy, although it acts as a significant constraint. The available range of choice allows elements of leadership to generate 'organizational actions and outcomes of strategic significance' (1994: 184).

A simple schema extracting the core requirements from the very extensive literature and experience of leadership, has been put forward by Zand (1997) who sees successful leaders as integrators of three critical forces: knowledge, trust, and power. The triadic leader who knows how to handle these three forces will be effective but not always popular. By facing a variety of different contingencies she/he will need to adjust the relationship between the triad and the priority given to knowledge, trust, and power. Trust is possibly the most elusive element in this triangle; it is not the same as amiability or popularity. The key elements are disclosing information, sharing influence and exercising appropriate control. Unpredictability is the enemy of trust. A critical requirement for the triadic leader is the constant encouragement of knowledge acquisition and the creation of a climate which facilitates the utilization of competence, whereas more traditional autocratic leaders tend to obstruct the utilization of competence (a point also made in the section on free choice above). However, by specifying power as one of the core requirements, Zand accepts that triadic leaders have to exercise legitimate and sanctioned decision choices over goals, structure, and strategy. Team working is an important means towards implementing the triadic strategy.

5 Conclusion

It has been seen that the complexity of this subject and its undoubted importance in the political economy has led to many interpretations. Some commentators have attempted to eliminate leadership as a significant explanatory force and substitute impersonal explanations, like competition and survival of the fit; others continue to find charisma and personal attributes to override the situational environmental context. Situational or contingency leadership theories tend to account for more of the available evidence than the 'one best style' theories but consultants and popular books are still beguiled by their simplicity.

One way of reducing the excessive randomness in the field of leadership theories is to concentrate attention on certain core activities and characteristics, for instance by singling out decision making and/or the distribution of power as major attributes of leadership or by concentrating on Zand's three basic leadership requirements: knowledge, trust, and power (see DECISION MAKING).

It is clear that no paradigm has emerged in the diverse constituencies of social science. This could mean that the jury is still out, but with more time and effort, an acceptable evidence-based role for organizational leadership will emerge. Alternatively, it is possible that organizational behaviour and, in particular, changes in organizations over time, require a broader explanation in which personal leadership will remain a molecular constituent in a molar concept that has yet to evolve (see MANAGERIAL BEHAVIOUR).

FRANK HELLER
THE TAVISTOCK INSTITUTE, LONDON

Further reading

(References cited in the text marked *)

Bass, B.M. (1981) *Stogdill's Handbook of Leadership*. New York: Free Press. (This is the standard reference book on the leadership research literature.)

* Bass, B.M. (1992) 'Stress and leadership', in F. Heller (ed.) *Decision making and Leadership*, Cambridge: Cambridge University Press. (Describes the literature which links the theory of transformational leadership with stress.)

* Blake, R. and Mouton, J. (1964) *The Managerial Grid*, Houston, TX: Gulf Publishing Company. (An old classic describing the consultancy package which attempts to train the ideal leader; still used but overtaken by events.)

* Donaldson, L. (1990) 'The ethereal hand: organizational economics and management theory', *Academy of Management Review* 15 (3): 369–81.

* Dunphy, Dexter and Stace, Doug (1990) *Under New Management*, Sydney: McGraw-Hill. (An important theoretical analysis of different approaches to organizational change, including coercive strategies.)

Fiedler, F. and Garcia, J. (1987) *New Approaches to Effective Leadership*. New York: John Wiley & Sons. (Fiedler pioneered a contingency theory of leadership, now developed to apply to competence.)

* Hammer, M. and Champy, J. (1994) *Re-engineering the Corporation: A Manifesto for Business Revolution*, London: Nicholas Brealey Publishing. (Hotly debated consultancy advice for radical, decisive global change to achieve competitiveness.)

* Heller, F.A. (1992) (ed.) *Decision Making and Leadership*, Cambridge: Cambridge University Press. (Heller's chapter reviews evidence and builds up a model of human resources based on the need for competence allied to participation.)

* Jaques, E. (1976) *A General Theory of Bureaucracy*, London: Heinemann. (Part 3 describes the time-span approach to measuring the appropriate position of people in the hierarchy.)

* Kay, J. (1997) The stakeholder corporation. In: G. Kelly, D. Kelly and A. Gamble (eds.) Stakeholder Capitalism, University of Sheffield in Association with Political & Economic Research Centre. (This article by Kay is in a book which discusses new theoretical developments in political, economic and management theories in support of extending top management's responsibilities for long-term organizational success by considering the interests of stakeholders other than owners of shares.)

* Kets de Vries, M.F.R., Miller, D. and Noĺl, A. (1993) 'Understanding the leader–strategy interface: application of the strategic relationship interview method', *Human Relations* 46 (1): 1–120. (Describes a psychoanalytic approach to leadership.)

* Lawler, E. (1986) *High Involvement Management: Participative Strategies for Improving Organizational Performance*, San Francisco, CA: Jossey Bass. (Puts forward strong arguments for participative leadership now necessary for US companies in order to compete with the Far East.)

* Leavy, B. and Wilson, D. (1994) *Strategy and Leadership*, London: Routledge. (Extensive review of the literature and research evidence in support of a strategic leader model.)

* Likert, R. (1967) *The Human Organization*, New York: McGraw-Hill. (Classic book summarizing a decade of important leadership-relevant research.)

* McGregor, D. (1967) *The Professional Manager*, New York: McGraw-Hill. (A classic exposition of Theories X and Y as well as a contingency approach to leadership.)

* Miles, R. and Snow, C. (1978) *Organization Strategy, Structure And Process*, New York:

McGraw-Hill. (Research-based typology of organizations with leadership implications.)

* Peters, T. and Waterman, R., Jr (1982) *In Search of Excellence: Lessons from America's Best Run Companies*, New York: Harper & Row. (A best seller because of its smooth style and broad, easily memorable generalizations, but poor on methodology and hence unreliable.)

* Rooney, P.M. (1993) 'Effects of worker participation in the USA: managers' perceptions vs. empirical measures', in W. Lafferty and E. Rosenstein (eds), *International Handbook of Participation in Organizations*, vol. 3, Oxford: Oxford University Press. (Summarizes data from large-scale survey of employee-owned firms in the USA where leaders share power with other employees.)

* Smith, P. and Peterson, M. (1988) *Leadership, Organizations and Culture*, London: Sage Publications. (An authoritative review of evidence and theories on leadership with attempted synthesis.)

* Vroom, V. (1977) 'Leadership revisited', in B. Staw (ed.), *Psychological Foundation of Organizational Behavior*, Santa Monica, CA: Goodyear Publishing Co. (Vroom and colleagues have built up an important contingency model of leadership useful for management development.)

* Yukl, G. (1994) *Leadership in Organizations*, 3rd edn, Englewood Cliffs, NJ: Prentice Hall. (The standard comprehensive review of all major research data and theory on the psychology of leadership.)

* Zand, D.E. (1997) *The Leadership Triad: Knowledge, Trust and Power*. New York: Oxford University Press. (Zand has developed this synthesis of three core ingredients of leadership: knowledge, trust, and power from the research literature as well as from a large number of well known case examples.)

See also: DECISION MAKING; GROUPS AND TEAMS; MANAGERIAL BEHAVIOUR; MOTIVATION AND SATISFACTION; ORGANIZATION BEHAVIOUR; ORGANIZATION CULTURE

Related topics in the IEBM: AGENCY, MARKETS AND HIERARCHIES; COGNITION; CONTEXTS AND ENVIRONMENTS; ORGANIZATION BEHAVIOUR, HISTORY OF; ORGANIZATION DEVELOPMENT; POWER; RE-ENGINEERING; STRATEGIC CHOICE; STRATEGY; WEBER, M.

Managerial behaviour

Overview

Studies of managerial behaviour have been made since the early 1950s. Two major aspects of this area of research should be noted. One is the confusion of terminology and the other its complexities. There has been confusion between managerial behaviour, managerial work and managerial jobs so that inappropriate generalizations about one of these have been made from a study of another one.

The methods and findings of the main researchers, starting with Sune Carlson in Sweden in the early 1950s, who have done most to develop our understanding of managerial behaviour and managerial jobs are summarized. From these we have learnt that the managers who were studied – and that wording is significant because of the dangers of generalizing to managers in other cultural settings – acted in a more reactive way than Fayol's analysis of managerial functions would imply. Their working pattern was fragmented. The social aspects of management were highlighted in a number of studies. The managers spent the majority of their time talking and listening. They were part of a social system and sought to secure the cooperation of others through networking, trading and negotiating. These are just some of the generalizations made.

Studies of differences in behaviour have taught us that there are wide variations both for the same manager from one week to another and, more importantly, between managers in similar jobs. There are also wide differences between managers' jobs even in the same country. These differences are greater when comparisons are made across countries. Much of the literature reflects an Anglo-American bias.

The complexities of studying managerial behaviour have gradually been revealed. First, we have not been able to define what is distinctively 'managerial' about managerial work. Second, how researchers seek to answer the question 'what do managers do?' depends upon their perspective. Managers can be thought of as working in the organizational interest and/or in their own interest. They may also be seen as developing an ideology of management and acting as the agents of capitalism. Third, recording managerial activities poses considerable methodological problems, which may not be recognized, including the fact that the categories used for work content reflect the researchers' perception of management tasks. Fourth, the potential area of study is very wide: a diagram is presented to summarize some of the complexities and the different areas of study. This can also be used as a guide to potential topics for research. Future studies should take account of these complexities, but what is most needed is imaginative thinking and attention to the nature of the context within which the managers are working.

The main practical implications of studies of managerial behaviour are to improve our ability to select and train managers appropriately and to recognize the differences in job requirements. Most researchers have also drawn conclusions for improving managerial effectiveness.

The early research into managerial behaviour arose partly from simple curiosity: What are all those managers actually doing? There had been a long history of studies of workers' behaviour and of the nature of workers' jobs, but not of managerial behaviour or managerial jobs. There were, of course, also more specifically academic concerns in studying managerial behaviour, such as identifying common managerial activities or distinguishing the differences in managerial jobs. There were, too, practical interests such as offering guidance for management selection and training, and suggestions for improving managerial effectiveness. These practical concerns are still a reason for seeking a better understanding of managerial jobs and of managerial behaviour.

1 Definitions

The term 'managerial behaviour' is often used ambiguously in academic writing. It is used, sometimes without explanation, for one or more of the following: behaviour itself, often described as 'what managers do'; managerial jobs; and/or managerial work. Because of this confusion it is important to note in what sense an author is using the term and in doing research to be clear which of these one is planning to study. In this article 'managerial behaviour' will be used to embrace all three, namely, jobs, work and behaviour, because the research to be described has often embraced more than one. However, the distinctive meanings of each should be remembered in order to prevent inappropriate generalizations:

1 managerial behaviour is the behaviour that can be reported, whether from observation by others or by self-reports;
2 managerial work refers to theories about its nature;
3 managerial jobs are the jobs that managers occupy.

The first problem that needs recognizing in a discussion of managerial behaviour is that there is no agreed definition of 'manager'. Nor have all researchers into managerial behaviour acknowledged the problem, as (Hales 1986) pointed out. The definitional problem arises from the difficulties in defining the distinctive character of managerial work, for example, is a housewife a manager? The two simplest, and least ambiguous,

definitions of 'manager' are: anyone who is responsible for the work of other people; and the definition that Stewart (1976) used: 'all those above a certain level in the hierarchy, usually those above foreman level on the works side and those above the first level of supervision in the offices' (Stewart 1976: 2). There are more complex definitions that may refer to the manager's responsibility for resources or for securing the achievement of goals, but one of the two simpler definitions is more suitable for determining who to include in studies of managerial behaviour. The problem of deciding what is distinctively managerial about managerial work remains unsolved (Hales 1986). Hence the practical argument for taking those whom an organization grades as managers as managers for research purposes (see ORGANIZATION BEHAVIOUR).

Whitley (1989) has probably made the best attempt to distinguish what is managerial about managerial work. He suggests that there are five major characteristics of managerial tasks:

1 they are highly interdependent, contextual and systemic;
2 they are relatively unstandardized;
3 they are changeable and developing;
4 they combine both the maintenance of administrative structures and their changes;
5 they rarely generate visible and separate outputs which can be directly connected to individual inputs.

Another source of terminological confusion, particularly in the USA, is the tendency to use the term 'leadership studies' in so general a sense as to embrace managerial behaviour. This confusion is made easier by the fact that there is no agreed definition for either 'manager' or 'leader'. A separate article discusses leadership studies so that all that is necessary here is to distinguish their areas of interest (see LEADERSHIP). The core question that these two fields of study have sought to answer is different: for leadership researchers it has been 'what makes a good leader?'; for researchers in managerial behaviour it has been 'what are managers doing?' Both fields have evolved so that the questions have become more complex. There is an overlap between the two fields because some leadership researchers have also been interested, though to a much lesser extent, in what leaders are doing; and managerial behaviour researchers have often also been interested in drawing lessons for effective management and more rarely in identifying behavioural differences between effective and ineffective managers. Both groups of researchers have been interested in whether, and if so the extent to which, it is possible to give general answers as distinct from contingent ones.

2 History of studies

The interest in the nature of managerial behaviour started in the 1950s. It was part of the general move by social scientists to try and find out what actually happened in organizations. Before then writers had theorized about organizational principles or the functions of management, but had not studied managers at work. The summary below will highlight the main developments but is not intended to be a review of all the research that has been done.

The major early theorist of managerial work was Henri Fayol who drew on his own experience. He wrote in 1916, but his work did not become widely available in English until 1949. His description of the functions of management is still quoted today with minor modifications. He gave them as: planning, organization, command (now modified to motivation), coordination and control. Their longevity has shown that they have proved useful as a way of conceptualizing managerial work, but they are abstract categories which tell us little about managerial behaviour. Hence the reason for the studies described below.

The early studies were usefully described as the Work Activity School (Mintzberg 1973). The main method used in the early studies was recording the work activities of managers using simple categories. The first major study was by Sune Carlson in Sweden in the early 1950s. He organized a diary analysis of the activities of nine managing directors, seven Swedish and two French, for four weeks. The discussion of research methods, particularly of the problems of recording

activities, and the practical focus of the study remain pertinent to researchers today. This study grew out of a long-standing group of Swedish managing directors who met with Professor Carlson to discuss top management problems. They decided that a study of their own work could be a way of improving selection and training procedures for top management posts.

Unlike all subsequent studies Carlson used a variety of people to record the data, including the chief executive, his secretary (they were all men), telephone operators and porters. The diary analysis was supplemented by extensive interviews and by considerable background knowledge of the individual and the firm. Despite all the subsequent research, Carlson's book remains a study that any researcher interested in recording work activities, by whatever methods, should read carefully.

Mintzberg (1973) and Stewart (1967) briefly describe other diary studies conducted in the 1950s and 1960s. Stewart (1967, 1988) is the other major study using the diary method. It was based on a specially designed diary which 160 middle and senior private sector managers kept for four weeks. They were given the figures for their month compared with those of other participants and invited to suggest reasons why theirs differed: these explanations were used to help in explaining the variations between managers. It was the analysis of the variations in activities that is the most distinctive feature of this study. For each category, such as percentage of working time spent alone, the mean and range of differences were shown. Variations were analysed from one week to another for each participant and across the sample. The variations were shown to be very large for each type of analysis. Such an analysis contrasts with studies that have sought to generalize across sample members ignoring variations.

A major limitation of the diary studies is that they cannot reliably seek to compare categories of *what* managers are doing as distinct from where, when and with whom they are working together with simple analyses of how they are doing it, such as telephoning, formal meetings or working alone. Even the reliability of comparisons of the simple categories is limited by how reliably activities are recorded.

Yet these relatively simple categories produced some interesting findings that are common across the early studies. They show that, with a few exceptions, managers studied spent the majority of their time talking and listening; for some managers this accounted for more than 90 per cent of their time. One of the more surprising findings, which Carlson first noticed, was that most of a manager's activities were brief, apart from formal meetings, and were often interrupted. Although many brief contacts will not be picked up in a diary record, the diary studies still showed that most managers rarely had as much as half an hour alone and uninterrupted. Later observational studies showed just how fragmented it could be, with more than a hundred different activities in a day.

Studies of *what* managers are doing was clearly the next stage. Three US studies have each contributed a distinctive conceptual analysis to generalizing about managerial behaviour and managerial work. The first was by Leonard Sayles (1964). It was based on a study of seventy-five lower and middle level managers in one division of a large US company manufacturing technically sophisticated capital equipment. The study was an ethnological one over several years and included observations, interviews and feedback of findings. The study emphasized that it was the system of relationships that mattered more for work efficiency than the individual assignments and motivation. Unlike the subsequent studies which focused on the individual manager, Sayles described managerial work as part of a social system. He highlighted the dynamics of social relationships: 'Enormous personality energy is required to interact in as diverse and multiple roles as those encompassed by the typical executive position' (Sayles 1964: 260). He stressed the importance of lateral relationships; identified different types which he called trading, workflow, service, advisory, auditing, stabilization and innovation; and discussed their particular difficulties.

Sayles stressed the mundaneness and frustration of much managerial work and its dependence upon building and maintaining a predictable, reciprocating system of relationships. The emphasis that he placed on the latter may reflect both the kind of managers that he studied, all of whom were embedded in an organization that required such cooperative relationships as compared with managers in charge of small distinct units, and their cultural background.

The second study chronologically was by Henry Mintzberg (1973). This, more than the other three studies, provided an overview of previous work before reporting Mintzberg's own observational study of a week for each of five chief executives in different kinds of organizations. The best known aspect of his study is his classification of ten managerial roles into three main headings: interpersonal, informational and decisional. He described the manager as a nerve centre for the monitoring and dissemination of information. It was this stress on the informational role of a manager which was his most distinctive contribution. He also usefully distinguished different interpersonal roles: figurehead, leader and liaison. Two other roles, though not classified as interpersonal, involved interpersonal relationships: spokesman and negotiator. Perhaps because his analysis was simpler than that of Sayles, his work generated more related studies, which sought to test or just to use his roles as a research framework. Mintzberg emphasized the manager's preference for live action: a generalization that it is easy to forget was only based on the observation of five US Chief Executive Officers (CEOs).

The next major US contributor to the study of managerial behaviour was John Kotter (1982). His was a wider study than Mintzberg's 1973 study in that it covered fifteen general managers in different companies and in addition to documentary material, questionnaire, observation and lengthy, usually repeat, interviews he interviewed key contacts of the general managers. The study also included the managers' personal and background characteristics and the context of the company within which they worked. Kotter was concerned with the general and the differential characteristics of the fifteen managers. One of his important conclusions was that they worked in very contextually specific settings and were unlikely to be able to move successfully to a general manager job in a different setting.

Kotter contributed two key concepts to the study of managerial behaviour: agendas and networks. He argued that the managers developed an agenda during the first six months to a year in the job. The agenda was composed of loosely connected goals and plans. To achieve their agendas they developed a network of contacts who could be of help and took time keeping this network up-to-date and, hopefully, supportive. Agendas tended to cover a longer time period than most formal plans, were less numerical and more strategic in nature. Like the findings of the diary studies, he noted that the general managers' time was characterized by brief and disjointed conversations and that almost all of their time was spent with other people. He stressed, as Sayles had done, the importance of relationships outside the straight line hierarchy. Like previous researchers he was concerned to spell out the implications of his study for improving general managers' performance.

The main aim of the studies described so far, apart from Stewart (1967), was to generalize about managerial work from studying managerial behaviour and to discuss the implications for managerial effectiveness, although all, except Carlson, also briefly discussed differences between managerial jobs. Stewart (1967, 1976, 1982; *et al.* 1994) was primarily interested in the differences between managers' jobs because such differences have implications for managerial selection, training, careers and effectiveness. Like Kotter she argued that the differences between managerial jobs can make it hard, and sometimes impossible, for managers to move to very different kinds of jobs, particularly if they are in different contexts.

Differences between managerial jobs were first studied by Hemphill (1960) who used a lengthy questionnaire with 575 items and asked 93 business executives to rate the extent to which each was part of their job. The limitations of such a methodology were later

discovered by Stewart who tested a questionnaire on managers in similar jobs and found that their ratings varied the whole length of a seven-point scale. The reasons for this finding were later found to be the differences in jobholders' perception and behaviour.

Stewart (1976) failed in its original aim of developing a meaningful overall categorization of differences in managerial jobs. Instead it identified some individual categories of differences: the nature and difficulty of the contacts required in the job; whether the job was a boss-dependent one where the scope of the job was partially dependent upon the boss; and whether the job was an exposed one where the jobholders' mistakes were personally identifiable.

Stewart (1982) developed her main conceptual contribution to the study of managerial behaviour: the demands, constraints and choices model, which is a way of expressing the flexibility that exists in jobs for different jobholders to behave differently not just in their management style but also in the nature of the work that they choose to do. Demands are defined as the work that any jobholder must do. Constraints are the factors that limit what a jobholder can do. Choices are the opportunities in a job for different jobholders to choose to emphasize or to select different work, for example, coaching subordinates. This model was used in Stewart *et al.* (1994).

So far, the studies described have broadly adopted a similar approach to studying managerial behaviour, even though they have used different methods for doing so. It has been based on a detailed analysis of managers' activities. In this sense all the studies described so far could still be seen as belonging to the Work Activity School. They all adopted a managerial perspective. They were not seeking to look more broadly at the question 'what *are* managers doing?' nor at the *why* behind managerial actions.

Jane Hannaway (1989) differs from the studies described so far because, although she used work activity type methods, she sought to suggest 'realistic interpretations of behaviour' in organizations. She was interested in how managers behave in 'a hierarchical social system that is characterized by uncertain tasks, ambiguous outcomes, and biased feedback' (Hannaway 1989: 141).

Hannaway's material was 29,640 random samples of the work activities of fifty-two managers over six weeks. The managers, who were divided into three hierarchical levels, all worked in the central office of a large US school district. The sample was about two-thirds of the managers in the central office. Each was supplied with a random beeper. On the beep they were asked to punch in their answers to ten questions. Her study is the most ambitious of the studies that have used a random beep. But what is interesting about it are the conclusions that she drew. She describes her book as more an interpretative essay than the report of an empirical study.

Hannaway was interested in the why of managerial actions and in the necessarily bounded rationality of managers' attempts to make sense of their working situation. She suggested that two sets of objectives underlie much of what managers do: (1) most want to do a good job for the organization; and (2) they want to get ahead or at least not to be the one who is blamed when things go badly. So she distinguished between behaviour that is in the interest of the organization and behaviour that is in the interest of the manager and pointed out that they do not necessarily coincide. Any observer of organizations would know that this is true, but yet it is not discussed in most studies of managerial behaviour – those writing about politics in management being the major exception.

Hannaway described managers' reactions to the dilemma that faces many of them, and which was certainly true for the managers whom she studied, that 'the connections between managerial actions and outcomes are not tight'. Many managers would say that that statement underrates the difficulty that they face. How do they know that they are doing a good job? Further, how can they persuade others that they are doing so? This dilemma was well expressed by a dentist who became a general manager in charge of a group of hospitals. He said: 'When I was a dentist I knew what I had done during a day, now that I am a manager I cannot tell what I achieve'. Hannaway argued that managers seek to protect

themselves from the ambiguity of managerial work by signalling their worth to others. They also try to reduce the chance that negative signals are sent about them. It is much easier, she suggested, for a manager's failure to be well known than for good work to be heralded, so managers – at least in the administrative bureaucracy that she was studying – sought to protect themselves by involving others in any potentially risky decision.

The study of politics in management has been a separate area of research. Yet the classic study, Dalton's *Men Who Manage* (1959), is a study of an aspect of managerial behaviour, which described and explained how a group of middle managers distorted the information that they gave to head office to forward their own political goals. The fact that people behave politically in organizations is now widely accepted, that is they present slanted information so as to win arguments, to gain resources or to forward their career and they form alliances to try to achieve the goals that they favour.

Managers have more opportunity for such political behaviour than other employees and more need for it as Hannaway's analysis suggests. It is a reminder of the truth of Hannaway's distinction between activities that are in the interest of the organization and those that are in the interest of the manager. Of course, the distinction is often blurred. Managers may, for example, present a biased argument for taking a particular decision because they believe that it is in the organization's interest. But they may also be motivated by more self-seeking reasons, such as the desire to do down a colleague, or to be noticed by top management.

So far managers have been described as acting in the interest of the organization as well as in their own interest. Another group of writers have seen managerial behaviour in a quite different light, and so have given a different answer than the writers cited so far to the question, 'what are managers doing?' Their approach can be called the radical interpretation of managerial behaviour.

Hugh Willmott (1984) illustrates this approach in his critique of studies of managerial behaviour. It is a much more radical criticism than that of Hales and others who have written from within the managerial perspective. Willmott's main criticism is that 'the work of managers is widely (mis)represented and idealized as a technical, politically neutral activity' (1984: 350). He describes a manager as someone who is 'institutionally empowered to determine and/or regulate certain aspects of the actions of others' (1984: 350). He criticizes the view of managers as functionaries or professionals who apply technical expertise to get things done. The radical critique's answer to the question, 'what are managers doing?' is 'preserving the capitalist structure of production relations', that is they are agents of capital. Willmott suggests that managers need to recognize the conflict of interest between labour and capital and its implications for their role.

Reinhard Bendix (1956) in his comparisons of work and authority in the West and in Russia argued that the conflict was not between capital and labour but between the managers and the managed in any large organization. Managers in large organizations, he said, whether capitalist or socialist, develop ideologies to justify their exercise of authority.

Gowler and Legge (1983) make a similar point when they suggest that, from the viewpoint of social anthropology, managers are managing meaning. The rhetoric of management is used, they say, to justify the role of managers. The managing of meaning is yet another way of thinking about what managers are doing.

Gowler and Legge give four examples of what they call the rhetoric of management. One is to eulogize 'plain speaking', while often adopting speech that is highly ambiguous. Two is to justify hierarchy by giving a techno-social justification for delegation and downward looking relations. Three is the rhetoric of accounting which serves to simplify and clarify inherent ambiguities. The fourth is the idealization of achievement.

3 Stages in managerial jobs

So far, no reference has been made to the fact that in any complex job it takes time for the jobholder to understand the job and to learn

how best to tackle it. Hence a jobholder's perception of the job may be different in the early period from what it is after some time in the job. John Gabarro (1987) is the main example of a study that described managerial actions over time. He made a longitudinal study of seventeen top and senior managers for three to three and a half years from first taking up the job. He concluded that the managers went through five different stages, during that time, which alternated between learning and action. He gives descriptive names to each of the stages. These are: first, *taking hold*, lasting three to six months; second, *immersion*, lasting four to eleven months and during which time the manager makes few changes; third, *reshaping*, usually a period of intense change lasting three to six months; fourth, *consolidation*, for three to nine months; and finally *refinement*. It will be noticed that the time spans are quite broad for each stage, so that there is considerable individual variation. The reshaping period could be seen, using Kotter's concepts, as the time when the manager understands enough about the new job to formulate a change agenda and has developed the necessary supportive network to implement it.

The paucity of interest in studying stages in jobs may be at least partly explained by the growth of shorter-term studies of transitions. Gabarro was also studying a transition but his interest was over a longer period as he analysed managers' actions over time. Another study of a transition that also has relevance for studies of managerial behaviour is Linda Hill's (1992) study of nineteen newly appointed sales managers. Her focus was on the problems that they experienced, but its relevance for managerial behaviour is that it highlights problems that may be distinctive to newly appointed junior managers. 'May be' because we do not have suitable comparative studies of middle and top managers.

4 Cultural and organizational differences in management

Until very recently studies of managerial behaviour, as distinct from studies of managerial attitudes, have been limited to managers in one country. The authors, almost wholly US and British, have often written as if their findings can be generalized to all managerial behaviour and all managerial jobs. This is despite the long-term interest in cultural differences in managerial attitudes and the use of questionnaires to make cross cultural comparisons of managers' views of their work.

One objective of the cross-cultural studies of managerial attitudes and values has been to identify differences. Hofstede (1984) is a widely quoted example of such research (see ORGANIZATION CULTURE). His work and that of others offers evidence for differences in managerial attitudes and values, but it does not tell us how far, nor in what ways, these influence managerial behaviour.

We have seen that research into managerial behaviour has mainly emphasized the similarities, but that differences have also been studied. Both approaches are worthwhile because we need to understand the similarities and the differences. The same dichotomy exists in considering the impact of cultural factors upon managerial behaviour. In some senses it can be argued that management is management anywhere in the world. This view underlies the rationale for mixing managers from different countries in the same management programmes.

Management is an occupation which has common features in any part of the world. Hence Fayol's categories, despite their abstraction, can be seen as applying to managers anywhere. It is the circumstances within which managers plan, coordinate, control, organize and motivate that differ and hence the ways in which these functions can be performed effectively. It can also be argued that managers anywhere have, as Bendix (1956) suggested, to seek to overcome resistance to their exercise of authority, that is to determine or regulate the behaviour of others; though the task may be easier in some cultures than others. In the more fluid knowledge-based organizations the task may also be easier because there is less managing to be done as individuals manage more of their own activities.

A study by Stewart *et al.* (1994) is unusual in being a comparative study of managerial behaviour in two countries, the UK and Germany. It compared middle managers' behaviour and perceptions of their jobs in three companies in different industries. The jobs and companies were selected to be as comparable as possible. The research methods included the collection of background material on the companies by interviews and documentary material, interviews with ten managers and their bosses in each of the three companies in each country, and, uniquely, joint observation by a British and German researcher of some managers in each company. This study had four unusual features. One was the use of joint observation to reduce cultural bias. Two was the findings of the very different ways in which the British and German managers both perceived and performed their role. Three was the information provided about the nature of middle management work in the companies studied and how this differs from top management. Four was the analysis of the contextual factors affecting the jobs, particularly the organizational differences which made it impossible to compare, as had been intended, similar jobs even in companies selected for their similarities.

The study shows the dangers of a domination of management writing by an Anglo-American viewpoint which presents as 'management' a view of its nature that makes no mention of its cultural limitations. We know that Japanese managerial behaviour is different, though unfortunately we do not have comparable studies of behaviour, but that there should be major differences between the behaviour of managers in two western European countries is perhaps even more striking.

5 Complexities of managerial behaviour

The history of research into managerial behaviour is similar to that of most, if not all, behavioural studies in that there has been a growing awareness of the complexities of the area of study. It has gradually become evident, from the experience of researchers and from the criticisms made of their work, that there are some major complexities to studying this area. There are also, as has been pointed out above, ambiguities about what is being studied.

The fragmentation of the manager's working day is one example of the unexpected complications that can underlie even what looks like a very simple finding. The fragmentation of managers' work was a characteristic highlighted in a number of studies. One of the lessons drawn from it was that the classic picture of a manager as a planner was misleading. Mintzberg argued that 'the manager works in an environment of stimulus-response' (1973: 38). Yet, as in so much social research, the picture is not as simple as it first appeared. Three reasons for this have been highlighted – and more may yet appear. First, the amount of fragmentation may be in part at the manager's discretion and the exercise of this discretion may be influenced by personal, organizational and cultural factors. A study that included observation concluded that 'the amount of fragmentation was, for some of the managers, more a reflection of their personal style than of the demands of the job' (Stewart 1976: 38). Second, it may be misleading to describe a work pattern as fragmented as it may merely be a methodological artefact caused by the way activities are coded: the manager may be pursuing the same topic although with different people and using different methods (Stewart *et al.* 1994). Third, a fragmented work pattern may be a reflection of national culture rather than an intrinsic characteristic of managerial work (see CULTURE, CROSS-NATIONAL). We should always remember, when tempted to generalize about managerial behaviour, how narrow is the range of countries where studies have been made. We need studies of managerial behaviour in very different cultures to know whether fragmentation is common. A small study by Robert Doktor (1990) found that Japanese and Korean chief executives had a much less fragmented pattern than US ones. He suggested two reasons for this: hurried contacts would be considered impolite and Japanese managers have fewer and longer meetings.

There are complexities in studying managerial behaviour that are common to many other fields of social research.

1 What methodologies should be used to provide valid and reliable information?
2 What conceptual framework or paradigm should be used to study managerial behaviour?
3 Behaviour is multi-dimensional – what aspects of behaviour should be studied?
4 How far can one generalize about managerial work and managerial behaviour?
5 What factors are relevant in considering differences in managerial jobs? In managerial behaviour?

We have already referred to some of the methodological problems and to good discussions of the subject. So the main point to be made here is the inadequate attention that has often been paid to validity. It has been too readily assumed that managers' answers to questionnaire items can be equated with behaviour or with a valid description of the nature of their job. The extent to which individuals perceive jobs differently, do them differently both in what they do and how they do it, and also the extent to which managers' jobs themselves differ have often been ignored. If, for example, managers are asked to answer questions about their job, how should the answers be interpreted? Are they a factual description of the job? The individual's perception of the job? What the individual thinks it is politic to say? Is what is said likely to be a stable view or affected by particular events or moods? Such questions pose well-known problems in social research. Yet it is easy to forget – as reports on many questionnaire studies especially have shown – that what a respondent says about the job is a personal statement. The recognition of this is a major reason why researchers have increasingly used a number of different methodologies and sources to collect data.

One of the complexities of studying managerial actions is knowing how to categorize the data collected. The usual practice for an observer is to keep a record of the subject, people and method of each activity. Simple analyses of these are not difficult, but it becomes much harder when conceptual categories are applied. If, for example, either the Fayol or the Mintzberg categories are used, it

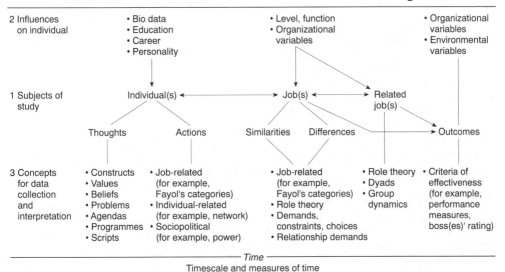

Figure 1 Potential field of studies of managerial jobs and behaviour
Source: Stewart (1989)
Note: 'Jobs' is used rather than 'work' as the former is a specific subject for study whereas 'managerial work' is a more ambiguous concept

is often hard to know to which category an activity belongs or, if it belongs to several, how to divide the activity between the different headings. Even if that problem can be overcome, such categorizations still leave untouched much of what could come under the heading: what a manager is doing.

The danger is as Marples pointed out as long ago as 1967 – but his comments remain applicable today – that the collection of data has been guided more by what is operationally possible than by what is theoretically desirable. His main objection was to analysis by episodes and of aggregated episodes – an objection similar to that mentioned above during the discussion of fragmentation. He suggested a concept to get away from analysis by episodes, that of a manager's 'problem portfolios'. He said that this was a way of getting at the managers' output, which could be seen as problem solving and decision making. Analysis of time spent, he criticized, could be viewed as only analysing the input.

Some of the other complexities can be discussed with the help of the diagram shown in

Figure 1, which provides a map of the field of study and can be used as a guide either to identifying what to study or to understand the focus of a particular study. Further methodological decisions are indicated by the two lines at the bottom of the diagram, for time and range. There may, depending on the aims of the research, be decisions to be made about both or any of the subjects shown in the diagram. For example, in analysing activities, however they are categorized, should they be measured and if so should the measure be frequency or duration or both? How long should the study last? Should all the working time be studied, or samples of time and if the latter should it be random sampling? What should be the definition of working time? Then there are other aspects of time that may be relevant to a study of managerial behaviour: time in the job and the time the job has been in existence.

There are also often decisions to be made about the range of the study, as distinct from the number to be studied. The researcher's view of the nature of managerial work will help to determine what decisions are required.

If the similarities across functions, levels, types of organizations, and possibly countries, are seen as more important than the differences, then no decisions have to be made about range in terms of type of managerial job. The only range decisions required are about how comprehensive, or how specific is to be the focus of the research: a study, say, of one aspect of behaviour, or one aspect of managerial work or an attempt to embrace all aspects within the perspective adopted.

One aspect of the complexity of studying managerial behaviour, and of seeking to understand it, is evident from even a casual glance at the diagram: it is the variety of relevant topics and concepts. The problem starts with a potential ambiguity about who or what is being studied, which is shown in the central group in the diagram. Is it the individual and/or the job? If the latter, is it a single job or related jobs? When can the individual and the job be considered separately? An example may be found in identifying the individual's qualifications for the job and in writing a job description. When should the interaction between the individual and the job be taken into account? For example, the individual may shape the job so that when he or she leaves it may be seen to be a somewhat different job, or the job may be so stressful for the individual that he or she ceases to perform adequately. Very bureaucratic jobs exist more independently of the jobholder than do jobs in more fluid organizations. Similarly, established jobs are likely to offer less scope for the individual to shape than will a new job.

Further choices are shown in the lines below the individual and the job: is it the individual's thought and/or actions that are to be studied? The word 'thought' is chosen as the most all-embracing, including attitudes, values and opinions. But there are problems of interpretation, as we described above.

If the focus of the research is on the job, a decision will have to be made about the primary aim of the study. The possibilities include to: make an in-depth study of individual jobs; generalize about the characteristics of managerial jobs; identify differences between managerial jobs; understand the relationship between two or more jobs.

A problem still more difficult than those discussed so far is deciding what concepts to use as a guide to data collection and analysis. In part the answer will lie in the focus of the study and in whether the researcher believes that suitable concepts already exist.

Looking at the bottom line of the diagram, the first set of concepts is for thoughts. The suggestions show that the first problem in research design will be in deciding what is the purpose of the study and hence what aspects of thoughts will be of interest. For example, one of the potentially interesting conceptual suggestions for a researcher who is seeking to understand the rationale behind managerial actions is that managers use mental programmes or scripts to guide them in familiar problem solving. Another concept which has been used by a number of researchers is that people develop their own personal constructs to interpret the world. This has been operationalized in a technique called Repertory Grid, which is a way of getting at the nature of the constructs that an individual is using. Either concept could provide a starting point for trying to understand the 'why' behind some managerial actions. A different perspective would be provided by research which sought to identify the values underlying managerial actions. Here, Gordon England's (1975) cross-cultural study of managerial values provides some helpful distinctions between operative, intended and adopted values.

Turning to the concepts for studying managers' actions, the earlier discussion of different perspectives on what managers are doing is relevant. If, for example, managers are seen as primarily motivated by furthering the organizational goals then the search will be for concepts that are relevant to that. But if the perspective is a political one then other concepts will be appropriate. Of course, in grounded research the researcher will be alert to concepts that emerge from the data. Hannaway's concept of managers signalling their value to others is an example. The concepts that emerge will be constrained by the types of data collected, which in turn will reflect the researcher's prior decisions/assumptions about what data is relevant.

Role theory provides an obvious set of concepts that can be useful in studies of managerial work, as Marples (1967) originally and Hales (1986) later pointed out. Stewart's demands, constraints and choices model is related to role theory. Hales suggests that using role theory to study managerial behaviour has a number of advantages. It is especially useful in highlighting the importance of studying both the structural expectations of what the jobholder will do and the effect of individual perceptions and choices. It highlights the dynamic interplay between the individual jobholder and those who have expectations of how the role will be performed. It is particularly useful in the study of managerial behaviour because managers have more choice in their interpretation of the role than holders of more clearly defined jobs and because the nature of their job is dependent upon the expectations of their role set. The less bureaucratic the organization the more true that is.

The next heading under 'Subjects of study' in the diagram is 'Related jobs'. This has had very little attention in studies of managerial behaviour, perhaps because of the difficulties in doing so. There is a small early study by Hodgson *et al.* (1965) which pointed out that there is both functional and psychosocial work to be done among people who have to work closely together. A study by Stewart (1991) of twenty district general managers and their chairmen discussed the nature of their relationship and its importance for the general manager. Chairmen were found to have very different perceptions of their role, which in turn affected the nature of the role that their general manager was able to play. It was suggested that a complementary relationship would strengthen the top leadership of the organization.

The last heading under 'Subjects of study' in the diagram is 'Outcomes'. Like the previous heading, very little research has been done. This is true even within the limited definition of outcomes as managerial effectiveness in organizational terms. One, possibly the major, reason for this neglect is the difficulty of doing such research. There is the considerable problem of defining effectiveness, but that can be reduced for research purposes

by selecting one or more criterion of effectiveness, despite its limitations. There is also the problem of comparing the behaviour of managers who are rated as effective or less effective. Such comparison raises both practical and ethical problems. There are yet greater problems. The general one in all studies of managerial behaviour of deciding what aspects to study is at its most acute in studies of effectiveness. This is due to the problem of being able to say with any confidence that it is the particular behaviours studied which are relevant to distinguishing differences in effectiveness.

Researchers have correctly been criticized for ignoring the context within which managers are acting or the personal characteristics which could influence behaviour. Hence the top line in the diagram summarizes some of the potential influences on managerial behaviour.

There are the individual influences such as gender, age, ethnic background, education, career and personality (see EQUAL EMPLOYMENT OPPORTUNITIES; WOMEN MANAGERES IN ORGANIZATIONS). Studies that sought to study the effects of any one of these individual variables would be trying to find out whether they affected managers' behaviour. The main one that has been of interest to researchers is whether there are differences in the behaviour of men and women managers. But it is not clear from the conclusions of a wide variety of studies whether women managers do behave differently.

Remarkably little research has been done into the contextual variables affecting managerial work. Earlier we discussed cross-cultural variables, but even within the same country there are a number of other potentially important contextual variables. Each of these poses two different questions. First, what effect does the variable have on the nature of the managers' jobs? Second, does the variable affect managerial behaviour? To take an example, if a comparison is being made between chief executive jobs in different organizations, one can ask: In what ways are these jobs similar and in what ways are they different? One can also ask the same dual question about behaviour. Unless the research is very carefully designed it will be difficult to distinguish the differences in jobs from those in behaviour. An awareness of the distinction should at least prevent mistaken deductions. To take another example, if a comparison is being made between middle and top management jobs then the research should seek to hold constant other variables like function and organization.

One of the organizational variables is whether the jobs being studied are new jobs or well established ones. New jobs are usually less well defined than established jobs. The expectations of the role set have not been formed by their experience of previous incumbents. Hence new jobs usually offer more scope for the jobholder to interpret the job as they wish. But we have no studies that compare new and well established jobs. We also have, as noted above, little research that looks at behaviour over time in a job.

6 The ways forward

In a meeting in Sweden to celebrate the fortieth anniversary of the publication of Carlson's *Executive Behaviour* Mintzberg (1991) asked why we had failed to come to grips with managerial work – the fact that we have failed should be obvious from the discussion so far – though the answer may be to cease being so concerned with generalizing about managerial work, and more with understanding managerial behaviour. The diagram shows that there are plenty of subjects for study and different ways of studying them. So the problem is not a paucity of interesting areas for research, but rather a failure to recognize the complexities of the research mapped in the diagram. It is a failure too, as Mintzberg (1991) suggested, to apply sufficient imaginative effort to the study of managerial work. That is another way of saying that we have not thought sufficiently imaginatively about managerial behaviour. One problem may be the desire to put it into neat categories. Hannaway's study, quoted earlier, is an unusual example of such imaginative thinking when she conceived that some of the managers' activities could be interpreted as signalling their worth to others.

Some of the studies of managerial behaviour made by political scientists, (e.g. Kaufman (1981) and Hargrove and Glidewell (1990)) which are usually ignored by the writers discussed here, could provide a stimulus to new ways of thinking about what managers do. Political scientists have usually had different interests in designing their research: they have been more interested in the effects of the context upon behaviour and have noticed other aspects of behaviour than researchers who follow Mintzberg (1973) or a development of the traditional functional roles.

If the prime need is more imaginative thinking, as suggested above, then it requires more thinking about the meaning of the data. It also requires research designs that stimulate, indeed necessitate, such thinking. This is more likely to mean qualitative research or at least a qualitative aspect to the research. Researchers will be inclined to use the methods with which they are comfortable, but a mix of methods is likely to yield best results.

7 Practical implications

Most researchers of managerial behaviour have spelt out the practical implications of their work for improving managerial effectiveness and management selection and training. The main lessons are summarized by author, but it should be remembered that many, though not all, are judgemental rather than proven because of the problems described earlier of assessing the relation between managerial effectiveness and managerial behaviour. Despite this uncertainty most writers have been clear what lessons they believe their studies have for managerial effectiveness and have been keen to share these with their readers.

It may be remembered that Sune Carlson's (1951) study originated in a seminar of chief executives whose members were interested in improving their own effectiveness and that of the selection and training for top management. Carlson stressed the value for the chief executives of knowing what they were doing because of the gap that often existed between what they believed they did and what they actually did. He pointed to the distinction between what may be suspected, for example that the chief executives spent much time outside their own companies, and having a record of behaviour which shows whether and to what extent the suspicions are confirmed. Similarly, Carlson pointed out the difference between chief executives feeling that they do not have enough time to work alone or to discuss development with their subordinates and knowing how much time was spent during the last month.

Carlson used a phrase 'administrative pathologies' which has not been utilized by later writers, but still seems of value. He meant deviations from admittedly more efficient procedures and the causes of these deviations. He gave as examples being overloaded with details or neglecting work, such as personal inspection tours, which the executive judged to be important. Carlson suggested that the existence of such pathologies was the main lesson for executive training from his study. He also criticized the chief executives for having a 'diary complex', so that their work was too tied to what was in their diary, which was too often determined by other people. If they really think that personal visits are important then they should be written into the diary if they are to get done.

Stewart (1967) similarly found that managers thought that they benefited from keeping a diary record of their time. The mere act of keeping such a record stimulated reflection about how they worked and the analysis of the time record often startled them and led to plans for changing the way that they worked. She illustrated different kinds of diaries that could be used to check on one's work and the kinds of questions that could usefully be asked. She argued that there was a danger of being so immersed in activity – the pleasures of being busy – that it was all too easy not to review the effectiveness or efficiency of one's work.

One of Marples' concerns, which remains valid today, was that managers may have so little control over the sources of their problems that they have little opportunity to acquire the desirable habit of being able to perceive problems. He suggested that management development needs to try to ensure that managers have the opportunity to exercise the skills of perceiving problems not initiated by others.

Mintzberg (1973) also advocated that managers should analyse their own work, perhaps using a diary to do so. He suggested ten points for more effective managing. Since Mintzberg had emphasized the manager as a nerve centre for information, his advice included giving conscious attention to passing on information to subordinates. He suggested that superficiality was the prime occupational hazard of the manager, because of the variety and brevity of activities. The danger is of dealing with all issues at a superficial level and not taking the time to concentrate on those that require more attention. Later, Mintzberg (1991) said that the problem of superficiality had become worse because increasingly managers find themselves in charge of organizations that they do not or cannot understand. He suggested two reasons for this: the organizations themselves which have become too diversified; or managers brought in from outside without an adequate understanding of the business.

Kotter (1982) devoted his last chapter to the implications for increasing the performance of general managers. He, unlike Mintzberg, was not seeking to generalize from the group he studied to managers generally. Because one of the findings of his study was the specificity of general management jobs, he urged selectors and general managers who are seeking a move to realize that different types of general management situations may require different types of people. Both the knowledge required and the kind of person needed can differ. An alternative he suggests is designing jobs that fit the characteristics of available candidates for them. Some jobs, particularly heading large conglomerates may be impossibly big.

Kotter points to the problems that new general managers may face in adapting to their new job, particularly if they have previously only worked in a functional role. He suggests that they may need help in setting their agenda and in network building and that in the early months their attention should not be diverted elsewhere. For experienced general managers the development problem may be to prevent them from developing tunnel vision. This requires mixing with people from different businesses and being exposed to a variety of perspectives and issues. Therefore, Kotter argues for the value of longer executive programmes which provide such a mix and challenge.

Stewart (1976, 1982) offers similar but more detailed advice about the importance of matching individuals to jobs. She emphasizes the importance of understanding the characteristics of different types of jobs in the organization. She offers the demands, constraints and choices approach as a way of doing so, together with a recognition of the nature of the relationship demands. Such an understanding, she argues, is valuable for those applying for a job, for selectors and for all those concerned with management development, since varied job experience provides one of the best forms of development.

Drawing together these different views one can ask what contribution studies of managerial behaviour have made to practitioners? Questions of this type are always hard to answer. Perhaps the most important, though hardest to identify, is the way in which the findings are conveyed through the business schools, management trainers and publications and gradually help to change how managers think about their own effectiveness. It may be that the management trainers, who use the researchers' different models, do most to convey the lessons spelt out by the researchers. It is in management education and training rather than in management selection and appraisal that there seems to be more evidence of the lessons being applied.

The research described in this article influences management education by the way that it changes the descriptions that are presented of the nature of management and of managerial work and hence how potential managers are taught to think about the managerial role. This is a very general statement about the application of research. Fortunately, in management training it is easier to be more specific about some of the programmes that have been developed to apply the research lessons. The recognition of the frenetic character of much

managerial behaviour and of the very personal ways in which managers see and do their jobs has led to the development of short courses that seek to help managers learn to manage both their jobs and themselves. Similarly, the research lessons about the social and negotiated nature of managerial work have been applied in programmes that aim to teach managers to understand themselves as well as others.

ROSEMARY STEWART
TEMPLETON COLLEGE, OXFORD

Further reading

(References cited in the text marked *)

Barnard, C. (1938) *The Functions of the Executive*, Cambridge, MA: Harvard University Press. (An insightful classic by a CEO, with a psychosocial view of organizations; not easy reading.)

* Bendix, R. (1956) *Work and Authority in Industry*, New York: Wiley. (Highlights the development of managerial ideologies in the UK, the USA and Russia.)

Campbell, J.R., Dunnette, M.D., Lawler, E.E. III and Weick, K.E., Jr (1970) *Managerial Behaviour, Performance and Effectiveness*, New York: McGraw-Hill. (A critical synthesis of research to that date, still worth reading.)

* Carlson, S. (1951) *Executive Behaviour: A Study of the Workload and Working Methods of Managing Directors*, Stockholm: Strömbergs. (The first major study of managerial behaviour which researchers should still read.)

Carroll, S.J. and Gillen, D.J. (1987) 'Are the classical management functions useful in describing work?', *Academy of Management Review* 12(1): 38–51. (A good defence of the continued utility of Fayol's functions of management.)

* Dalton, M. (1959) *Men Who Manage*, New York: McGraw-Hill. (The pioneering study of the political games that managers play.)

* Doktor, R. (1990) 'Asian and American CEOs: a comparative study', *Organizational Dynamics* 18 (3): 46–56. (A small-scale comparative study of work patterns; a warning against generalizations of fragmentation.)

* Fayol, G.H. (1949) *General and Industrial Management*, London: Pitman. (Observations of a top French industrialist and classic writer on management theory.)

* Gabarro, J.H. (1987) *The Dynamics of Taking Charge*, Boston, MA: Harvard Business

School. (A longitudinal study of the different stages of taking up a top management job.)

* Gowler, D. and Legge, K. (1983) 'The meaning of management and the management of meaning: a view from social anthropology', in M.J. Earl (ed.), *Perspectives on Management: A Multi-disciplinary Analysis*, Oxford: Oxford University Press. (Illustrates the ways in which managers seek to develop a managerial ideology.)

* Hales, C.P. (1986) 'What do managers do? A critical review of the evidence', *Journal of Management Studies* 23: 88–115. (Much the best critique of studies of managerial behaviour with suggestions for improvement.)

* Hannaway, J. (1989) *Managers Managing*, New York: Oxford University Press. (A perceptive study which points to the self-promoting aspects of managerial behaviour.)

* Hargrove, E. C. and Glidewell, J. F. (eds.) (1990) *Impossible Jobs in Public Management*, Lawrence: University Press of Kansas. (A series of papers probing the difficulties of selected managerial jobs. It is of interest for highlighting an under researched aspect of managerial jobs and some of the differences in public sector jobs from those in the private sector.)

* Hemphill, J.K. (1960) *Dimensions of Executive Positions*, Columbus, OH: Bureau of Business Research, Ohio State University. (The findings of Hemphill's study, which identified ten dimensions in managerial jobs.)

* Hill, L.A. (1992) *Becoming a New Manager: Mastery of a New Identity*, Cambridge, MA: Harvard Business School Press. (An attractive account of a repeat, multi-interview study of nineteen new junior sales managers.)

* Hodgson, R.C., Levinson, D.J. and Zaleznik, A. (1965) *The Executive Role Constellation*, Boston, MA: Harvard Business School Press. (A study of role sharing among three executives in a hospital.)

* Hofstede, G. (1984) *Culture's Consequences: International Differences in Work-related Values*, Beverly Hills, CA: Sage Publications. (An analysis of four cross-cultural dimensions and their effects on organizational structures and behaviour.)

* Kaufman, H. (1981) *The Administrative Behavior of Federal Bureau Chiefs*, Washington: Brookings. (An interesting example of the different approach of a political scientist to the study of managerial behaviour. He made an indepth study of six federal bureau chiefs over a year and was primarily interested in how influential they are.)

* Kotter, J. (1982) *The General Managers*, New York: The Free Press. (An illuminating multi-method study of fifteen US general managers; stresses their distinctive context.)

Luthans, F., Rosenkrantz, S. A. and Hennessey, H. W. (1985) 'What do successful managers really do? An observational study of managerial activities', *Journal of Applied Behavioral Science*, 3: 255–270. (Makes two useful contributions: developing a methodology for training observers to make similar recordings of managerial activities; seeking to distinguish what successful managers do differently. However, it assumes that we know what activities should be recorded, so makes no conceptual contribution.)

* Marples, D. (1967) 'Studies of managers – a fresh start?', *Journal of Management Studies* 4 (3): 282–99. (An early critique of activity studies, still useful for research ideas.)

* Mintzberg, H. (1973) *The Nature of Managerial Work*, London: Harper & Row. (Most famous of the studies, this observational study of five US chief executives contains stimulating over-generalizations.)

* Mintzberg, H. (1991) 'Managerial work forty years later', in S. Carlson (ed), *Executive Behaviour: Reprinted with Contributions by Henry Mintzberg and Rosemary Stewart*, Uppsala: Acta Universitatis Upsaliensis. (A reflection on Carlson's work forty years later and comments on progress since.)

* Sayles, L. (1964) *Managerial Behaviour*, New York: McGraw-Hill. (Unjustly partially neglected, an early ethnological study of managers in an engineering factory.)

* Stewart, R. (1967; 2nd edn 1988) *Managers and their Jobs*, Maidenhead: McGraw-Hill. (Large-scale diary-study, emphasizing variations in managers' activities over a month. The second edition includes a new chapter that brings the lessons from research up to date.)

* Stewart, R. (1976) *Contrasts in Management*, Maidenhead: McGraw-Hill. (A multi-method, large-scale study highlighting differences in managerial jobs.)

* Stewart, R. (1982) *Choices for the Manager*, Maidenhead: McGraw-Hill. (Multi-method large empirical study describing the flexibility in managerial jobs; developed demands, constraints and choices model.)

* Stewart, R. (1991) 'Chairmen and chief executives: an exploration of their relationship', *Journal of Management Studies* 28 (5): 511–28. (A study of different forms of role sharing between twenty pairs of chairmen and CEOs.)

* Stewart, R., Barsoux, J-L., Kieser, A., Ganter, H. and Walgenbach, P. (1994) *Managing in Britain and Germany*, Basingstoke: Macmillan. (A comparative study of middle managers' perceptions and behaviour in the two countries.)

Watson, T. (1996) 'How do managers think? Identity, morality and pragmatism in managerial theory and practice', *Management Learning*, 3: 323–341. (An observational, ethnographic study in a manufacturing and development plant, which aimed at understanding the ways in which managers think and act.)

* Whitley, R. (1989) 'On the nature of managerial tasks and skills: their distinguishing characteristics and organization', *Journal of Management Studies* 26 (3): 209–24. (Identifies distinctive nature of managerial skills and their implications for management education and research.)

* Willmott, H.C. (1984) 'Images and ideals of managerial work: a critical examination of conceptual and empirical accounts', *Journal of Management Studies* 21 (3): 349–68. (A useful critique of the managerial bias in studies of managerial behaviour.)

See also: ORGANIZATION BEHAVIOUR

Related topics in the IEBM: DIVERSITY; FAYOL, H.; GENDER AND ACCOUNTING; MANAGEMENT IN GERMANY; MANAGEMENT IN JAPAN; MANAGEMENT IN NORTH AMERICA; MANAGEMENT IN RUSSIA; MANAGEMENT IN SOUTH KOREA; MANAGEMENT IN THE UK; MANAGERIAL THEORIES OF THE FIRM; MINTZBERG, H.; OPERATIONS MANAGEMENT; ORGANIZATION BEHAVIOUR, HISTORY OF

Occupational psychology

Overview

Occupational psychology is a British term used to describe the study of the behaviour of people at work. Different terms are used in other countries, so a first step is to outline the boundaries of the field and to set it in its international context. A psychological perspective on work behaviour offers distinctive insights and perspectives and these are identified. Since occupational psychology offers an expanding range of career opportunities, the scope for its application is also outlined.

The domain of occupational psychology encompasses the following: selection and assessment, careers and career counselling, training and development, design of work and working environment, motivation and performance, individual–organizational linkages, well-being and the quality of working life, and change and transition. A final section considers how far occupational psychology has been able to contribute to its dual goals of worker well-being and organizational effectiveness. It also explores some of the challenges currently faced by occupational psychologists. These include the tension between science and application; the pressure to develop and pursue fads and fashions; and the need for a more international perspective.

1 Introduction

Occupational psychology is concerned with the behaviour of people at work. The term 'occupational psychology' is peculiarly British and reflects an early concern with vocational and career guidance. In the USA, the closest term is *industrial psychology* or *organizational psychology* and, increasingly, industrial and organizational (I/O) psychology, while in much of Europe it is *work and organizational psychology*. The domain overlaps the field of organizational behaviour which has broader connotations through a concern with the organizational context of work behaviour (see ORGANIZATION BEHAVIOUR). As such, it has a broader disciplinary base than occupational psychology, drawing on sociological and economic theory as well as the newer fields of management, business and organization theory.

Psychologists in Europe have attempted to delineate the field by distinguishing between work psychology, personnel psychology and organizational psychology.

(1) *Work psychology* covers the nature of tasks, the way they are arranged and the consequences for work in terms of effort, fatigue and performance. It embraces task design and ergonomics, the term for human–machine interaction. It can extend to include aspects of working hours and the physical work environment.

(2) *Personnel psychology*, which is increasingly referred to as human resource management, views people as employees. It is therefore concerned with selection, training, reward systems, careers and appraisal. It also touches on commitment and a range of questions about employment relations.

(3) *Organizational psychology* is concerned with arrangements which apply to a group or larger collection of individuals. It therefore covers topics like decision making, communication, leadership, power, culture and organizational change. This is familiar

territory for those working in the field of organizational behaviour.

Whether one accepts this European perspective or not, it is helpful in highlighting the range of issues that psychologists are concerned with in the workplace. Despite the limited international use of the term, this entry in the encyclopedia will continue to refer to the field of occupational psychology and to the work of occupational psychologists.

2 Distinctive characteristics

There are a number of features that help to make occupational psychology distinctive. The first is its strong link to the discipline of psychology. Much of psychology is concerned with individual behaviour; occupational psychology is concerned with the behaviour of individuals in the workplace. This means that much of the intellectual stimulus and new theory is drawn from psychology. So, too, is much of the distinctive methodology. Therefore, as mainstream psychology has become increasingly dominated by a cognitive perspective, focusing on how people process and store information about the world, so this approach has spilled over into occupational psychology, with research on, for example, how people judge success or failure and its implications for the promotion of women (see WOMEN MANAGERS IN ORGANIZATIONS).

Traditionally, the methods of psychology have been modelled on those used in the physical sciences. Ideally research is conducted under controlled conditions with carefully validated and precise measures, often repeated over time while some sort of experiment takes place. The results are then carefully measured and analysed using sophisticated statistical techniques. In work settings such rigour is often impossible to achieve. This has led to a number of responses. One is to create simulated conditions and samples in controlled conditions. The outcome of this is that there are research papers on, for example, wage negotiations and bargaining using first-year psychology students in the psychology department laboratory acting out the roles of management and union

representatives. Such research, which holds many attractions for those educated in mainstream psychology, is often viewed scathingly by those from outside the discipline who believe that the context and prior experience are vital ingredients in the reality of bargaining. As a result, there is a flourishing literature on the relevance of laboratory studies to organizational settings. While this debate has not been resolved, it is possible to accept that there is room for such research as a basis for developing and testing theory. However, it is equally important that it is subsequently tested in work settings if it is to have credibility beyond the discipline of psychology.

The link to the discipline of psychology is reflected in the background of occupational psychologists. In the USA, Division Fourteen of the American Psychological Association is devoted to I/O psychology and is widely known as the Society for Industrial and Organizational Psychology. Its members will have majored in psychology and retain their links to the core profession through membership of this division. In the UK, the Division of Occupational Psychology is one of the largest divisions of the British Psychological Society. As a chartered body, the Society, through the Division, offers chartered status, which is in effect a licence of competence to practise, to those who have undertaken an accredited training programme and have obtained sufficient supervised work experience. One unstated aim of this professionalization is to ensure the link between mainstream and occupational psychology as a guarantee of competence in what is becoming a popular, crowded and sometimes controversial field.

However, it is important not to take the narrow link with psychology too far. While major research in occupational psychology is often published in journals such as the *Journal of Applied Psychology* and the *Psychological Bulletin*, both of which cover other areas of psychology, there is a range of more narrowly focused journals such as *Personnel Psychology* and the *Journal of Occupational and Organizational Psychology*. Other journals in which the work of occupational psychologists is published have titles which reflect the broad, inter-disciplinary nature of much of the work in occupational psychology. These include *Organizational Behaviour and Human Decision Processes, Human Relations,* the *Journal of Organizational Behaviour,* the various human resource management journals and the Academy of Management Journals. Psychology provides the focus and perspective, but a broader interdisciplinary framework informs many of the issues that occupational psychologists address.

A further distinctive feature of occupational psychology is its focus on the individual level of analysis as a point of departure. Whereas sociology might be concerned at its core with society or, in work settings, with the organization and economics with the workings of the macroeconomic and microeconomic institutions, psychology is concerned with individual behaviour. It therefore places people at the centre of its agenda and inevitably the feelings, concerns and aspirations of people at work figure strongly (see WORK AND ORGANIZATION SYSTEMS). Of course, individuals at work rarely operate in isolation; their behaviour is influenced by others and they often work in groups. Therefore, while the individual provides the initial focus, an understanding of individual behaviour at work requires an analysis of the social context and of social influences on behaviour. Social psychology, a major area within psychology, has concentrated on this, studying issues such as leadership, group processes, communication and social perception which readily translate into topics of concern to occupational psychologists.

A focus on the worker as an individual has the potential to offer a radical perspective on work behaviour by posing the question 'what about the concerns of the worker?'. Alternatively, it can lead psychologists to ignore structural issues of power and control which some would argue ultimately determine what happens to the worker (see EMPLOYEE RELATIONS, MANAGEMENT OF; INDUSTRIAL AND LABOUR RELATIONS; TRADE UNIONS). Therefore, although a psychological perspective implies a potentially pluralist view, setting the priorities of workers alongside and possibly against those of the organization, in practice this perspective has sometimes been crowded out by the dominance of 'science' or the demand from organizations for help in the area of personnel psychology. This demand for help and the ready response of many occupational psychologists resulted, many years ago, in the claim that occupational psychologists were little more than 'servants of power'. For many psychologists this was an unfair gibe. However, it is a reminder of the pitfalls as well as the potential of adopting an individual perspective on people at work.

3 Occupational psychology as an occupation

Occupational psychology provides a major source of employment to those who have studied psychology at university. It is, of course, only one area of employment for psychologists; others include clinical, educational, counselling and forensic psychology. Like all these areas, occupational psychology requires further specialist training and education to acquire the necessary knowledge and skills. Occupational psychologists work in three main domains. First, they work as academics. They are to be found in psychology departments of universities, in business schools, in departments of organizational behaviour and occasionally in research units and research institutions. While there are departments of applied psychology, in the UK the only department devoted exclusively to occupational psychology, and the leading centre for the education and training of occupational psychologists, is the department of organizational (formerly occupational) psychology at Birkbeck College, University of London. Most but not all of the research bodies are closely linked to universities. In the USA, one of the best known is the Michigan Institute of Social Research, while in the UK the leading centre for research has been the Social and Applied Psychology unit, recently re-titled the Institute of Work Psychology, based at Sheffield University. There are similar units in a number of European countries. Another of the best-known research institutes in the UK is the Tavistock Institute of Human Relations, which has been a source of important research and theory, and has always operated as an independent organization, providing consultancy through action research.

A second major form of work for occupational psychologists exists in commercial and governmental organizations. Traditionally, the government and its agencies has been a major employer of occupational psychologists working especially in the defence and employment fields. In defence, the work, often with a strong research orientation, has covered almost all aspects of occupational psychology with major interest in selection and training, human–machine interaction and occupational stress. In employment departments, activities have focused on those who have employment problems, ranging from the unemployed to those seeking rehabilitation and counselling following accidents and illness. In both government and commercial organizations, occupational psychologists are likely to devote a significant amount of their time to processes of assessment, counselling and training (see TRAINING). Although many posts will carry the specific title of occupational psychologist, even more occupational psychologists are likely to be employed in human resource departments working as human resource professionals but providing distinctive expertise based on their background and training in occupational psychology.

The third main area of work is in consultancy. There is a heavy demand for the services of occupational psychologists by organizations that do not have a sufficient amount of work to employ a full-time specialist or who need distinctive types of help and expertise for a short period. There can also be advantages in using outside experts to provide a dispassionate diagnosis and analysis of the need for change. Outsiders may also have an important part to play in individual assessment, in assisting in the achievement of organizational change and in providing training and counselling. In practice, psychological testing and assessment probably constitute the largest area of work for consultant occupational psychologists.

There has been a rapid growth in the demand for occupational psychology consultancy, a demand exacerbated by changing employment patterns that have sometimes led organizations to dispense with some of the activities they do not regard as central to their operations. These non-central activities may include occupational psychology or even parts of the human resource management function; paradoxically, however, it has sometimes required the help of occupational psychologists to manage the process of reducing numbers and the consequences of placing ever-increasing demands on those who remain.

From this brief outline of the main types of employment for occupational psychologists, it can be seen that a range of knowledge and skills are required. For those in academic employment, the need is for up-to-date knowledge of research and theory and the skills to conduct research. For those working in organizations or as consultants, a good knowledge base is important but more emphasis may be placed on applied skills. There are a number of key skills. The first fall into the areas of assessment and diagnosis of individuals but also of organizations. They may therefore range from use of psychometric tests or observation of people at work to identify training needs to development, application and interpretation of attitude surveys.

A second area can be described as provision of counselling and advice. Again, this may be counselling at the individual level for those uncertain about their career direction or experiencing harassment at work or advice to a team about how well it is working. There may also be advice to an organization about all aspects of behaviour at work. Finally, there are more explicit types of intervention. These can range from provision of training to conciliation in disputes or facilitation of major organizational change (see ARGYRIS, C.). The important point to note is that a key to effectiveness is likely to be the possession of a range of skills which may result in change at the individual, group or organizational level.

The goals of occupational psychology are seldom made explicit. However, they are important. Broadly speaking, they can be defined as seeking to achieve improved individual well-being at work and improved organizational effectiveness. The challenge is to keep these aims in balance and to seek both. The risk is that one gets emphasized at the expense of the other.

Since employers are generally the paymasters of occupational psychologists and typically they give more weight to increased organizational effectiveness, there is a risk that this is emphasized at the expense of individual well-being. As a result, one of the potentially distinctive features of occupational psychology, the focus on the individual, and by implication on the concerns and well-being of the individual, may become submerged. This entry will explore the success of occupational psychologists in achieving their dual objectives. First, however, it is necessary to examine more closely some of the main topics within the field.

4 The domain of occupational psychology

In the foregoing sections, occupational psychology has been described from the European perspective, in terms of a number of levels. The Division of Occupational Psychology of the British Psychological Society has identified several of areas of knowledge that must be covered in any accredited course. These are: personnel selection and assessment; training; human–machine interaction; design of environments and work, including health and safety; counselling and personal development; employee relations and motivation; and organizational development and change. This list, which has remained largely unchanged for a number of years, lacks the conceptual integrity of the European model and neglects the organizational context within which much of the work of occupational psychologists takes place. However, it does capture some of the areas of activity in which occupational psychologists, rather than experts in organizational behaviour, have tended to apply their specialist skills.

This section examines briefly eight areas recognized internationally as important aspects of the field. Each offers distinctive issues for both academic and practising occupational psychologists.

Selection and assessment

Assessment, and in particular selection of staff into an organization or for promotion or accelerated development, is the most widely carried out activity among occupational psychologists. One reason for this is that psychology and psychologists are attributed particular expertise in assessment. Another is that psychometric tests and other techniques sometimes used in assessment require some expertise to administer and interpret. Both test developers and national psychological associations have had some success in restricting their use to psychologists or those with specialist training provided by psychologists.

All organizations undertake selection and most selection is not conducted by specialists. One way of looking at selection is to consider it as a series of decisions (see RECRUITMENT AND SELECTION). Non-specialists often ignore some of the steps and take poor decisions. The role of occupational psychologists has been to identify the key steps, seek to understand what constitutes a good decision and how this can be demonstrated, develop and advise on methods to improve selection decisions and sometimes participate in the process at some or all of the stages.

Underpinning their work on selection and assessment, occupational psychologists draw upon theories about the nature of individual abilities and about the role of abilities, personality and motivation in shaping performance at work (see MOTIVATION AND SATISFACTION). They also require a clear view of the nature and importance of individual differences and therefore about management of diversity at work. At a deeper level of analysis, the approach adopted may also reflect a view about the sources of abilities and the debate which, simplistically, poses questions about the role of heredity and environment in shaping abilities. Inevitably, this kind of debate leads to moral and ethical questions for the practising occupational psychologist which cannot easily be evaded by hiding behind a smokescreen of 'science' or 'scientific method'.

The major steps and therefore the major decisions in selection start with identification of a vacancy, often because someone has moved on but sometimes because of expansion or re-organization, and a decision about whether or not to fill it. Decisions must then be taken about the nature of the job and about the qualities required in a person who will perform the job effectively. A process of recruitment is then required to create a pool of applicants and this entails decisions about whether to look inside or outside the organization, where to advertise and what sort of pay, terms and conditions to offer to attract a high-quality pool of applicants. There are then decisions about the methods of selection and who will be involved. Finally, the actual decision about who to select and what terms to offer must be taken.

There are two particularly difficult areas in the selection process where the occupational psychologist can make a distinctive contribution. One is the assessment of what is required for effective performance; the other is assessment of whether applicants possess the qualities necessary to perform effectively. In the 1990s, much of the debate has centred around the identification of *competences* and *competencies*. The distinction may seem confusing but is potentially important. Competences relate to that early stage in the selection process where the requirements to perform the job effectively are identified. They are derived from analysis of the job and are therefore likely to be common requirements for anyone who is to perform the job. At a simple level, a typist must be able to type. At a more complex level, a doctor must possess a range of knowledge and skills but also, perhaps, certain attitudes, including professional ethics and a degree of resilience in order to be able to face long hours and harrowing experiences. Occupational psychologists can contribute to the process of detailed job analysis to identify the job competences. For training purposes, these might be placed in some sort of hierarchy of complexity based on an understanding of processes of acquisition of knowledge and skills. Occupational psychologists can help to identify what might be clustered at the various levels.

Analysis of job competences can identify what is required to perform the job. Those individuals who possess these requirements, through training and experience, may be expected to perform the job adequately. What it can not do, especially for complex jobs such as those in management, is demonstrate who will perform the job particularly well. In a competitive organizational world, companies want outstanding, rather than merely adequate, performance. They therefore need information about the qualities of individuals. This consideration gives rise to the following question: what are the individual competencies that are associated with superior performance in a given job? Therefore, while competences are associated with a particular job, competencies are qualities of individuals.

If an employer wishes to distinguish between those employees who are merely adequate and those who are outstanding in the job, he or she must, as a first step, choose some way of measuring job performance. In the typist's job, such measurement might be straightforward; in the case of doctors, comparisons will be much more difficult because there will be multiple-performance criteria; and similar difficulties will arise in relation to most managerial jobs.

The conventional method of measuring job performance has been to use some form of performance appraisal (see PERFORMANCE APPRAISAL). Performance appraisal is a process of arriving at judgements of an individual's performance based on a number of agreed criteria. These might be judgements by the superior on a number of dimensions; or they might be achievement against jointly agreed performance targets. Usually, some scope for judgement is permitted, providing leeway to take into account particular circumstances such as a difficult market, a cutback in resources or a refocusing of priorities. Such flexibility is a strength, but also a weakness, since judgements may be made partly subjectively. In response, occupational psychologists have devoted much research to ways of developing appraisal techniques that minimize various forms of bias. These include particular types of rating scales, a focus on objective criteria such as sales or quality rejects, the use of self-appraisal, subordinate appraisal or even '360-degree appraisal', which may involve all interested parties.

While occupational psychology can help increase the reliability of performance appraisals, inevitably there is almost always an element of judgement and therefore potential bias. Bias becomes particularly apparent in those situations where some sort of ranking of individuals is required, perhaps for selection, promotion or pay awards. In identifying competencies, one of the simpler, albeit cruder, indicators that might be used in large companies is rate of promotion. Those who have advanced further and faster appear to possess qualities that are valued in the organization. They can be compared with their counterparts who have made slower progress.

Once individuals have been ranked according to their performance, the next challenge is to identify what it is that differentiates them and then to devise ways of measuring these qualities at the point of selection. This provides the second major challenge and area of distinctive contribution for occupational psychologists. One of the added complications is that those embarking on their careers will have little or no work experience and the need is therefore to assess the potential to demonstrate these qualities.

The methods used in assessment – and especially at the point of selection to determine potential and sometimes experience – include various psychometric and performance tests, interviews, biodata and application forms. Biodata consist of an assessment of past activities, which are combined and weighted in some way, and is based on the plausible assumption that past performance, even in some areas of life that may not seem directly relevant, predicts future performance. For example, it might be thought that evidence of leadership at school and in sports activities is an indication of leadership potential in a business career.

The most controversial method of assessment is probably the psychometric test, and in particular the personality test (assuming that methods such as graphology, the assessment of handwriting and astrology are ignored, since these have no demonstrated ability to predict future performance at work). There are many types of psychometric tests, including: those used to assess general ability; tests of what is often described as general intelligence; and tests of specific abilities and aptitudes, which refer to components of intelligence such as verbal or numerical ability or mechanical aptitude. Psychometric tests also measure personality or disposition, including concepts ranging from introversion and extraversion to the need for achievement or power. Usually, these tests have been carefully developed by psychologists and are presented in the form of batteries, measuring several things at once. They must be presented carefully and interpreted even more carefully. It is in the interpretation and use of the information from tests that the expertise of occupational psychologists may be particularly valuable.

Employers concerned about using tests may prefer to interview applicants. However, the evidence suggests that interviews are generally less effective than many tests, particularly tests of ability in predicting performance. This is because it is all too easy for bias to creep in. Equally, the evidence shows that a good interview, well-structured and geared to the specific situation, can be effective; unfortunately, however, good interviewers are relatively rare.

There has been extensive research over many years to identify the best means of predicting future performance at work. From this it seems that the best methods to use are performance tests for those who claim particular performance abilities, tests of specific aptitudes and assessment centres that use a combination of methods. Biodata can also be effective. However, all of these require psychological expertise to design and interpret and, since such expertise is expensive, many firms prefer to fall back on the more familiar combination of application form and interview. This sometimes also reflects anxiety on the part of some selectors about using psychological methods which they feel they do not fully understand.

One important reason why it makes sense to use sound techniques for selection is that recent developments in utility analysis, a form of cost-benefit analysis to determine the financial impact of using different methods, shows that there are considerable financial payoffs from using the better techniques. Even allowing some leeway for error, the benefits to the organization are impressive, suggesting that it makes sense to use the expertise of occupational psychologists in the selection and assessment of candidates at work.

Careers and career counselling

Many of the techniques used for assessment during selection can also be applied to career counselling. Indeed, the early days of vocational guidance, when much of the effort was directed toward the occupational choice of school-leavers, gave rise to the title 'occupational psychology'. Whereas there is inevitably an adversarial element in selection, in career assessment the process is a collaborative one. Similar tests and other forms of assessment might be used, together with additional tests of occupational preferences. Taken together, traditionally these have formed the basis of an assessment and of guidance about suitable occupations, usually defined as those occupations in which an individual would perform well and find job satisfaction (see CAREERS).

Psychologists have been particularly interested in the influences on career choice. At one level, these can be considered in terms of factors such as class and parental background and educational experience. At a more personal level, consideration can be given to career preferences. Schein (1978) describes these as career anchors and identifies at least eight, including security, competence and challenge. Sociologists have undertaken similar work, using labels such as 'orientations' to describe these relatively stable preferences for features of work. These orientations, or anchors, derive from social contexts and experiences and, although relatively stable, they can be altered through further experiences. They help to explain preferences for certain types of work and career and are therefore of interest to occupational psychologists when offering advice about career choices.

The traditional field of vocational guidance was based on a rather static model, seeking a fit or match between person and job that would be sustainable over a lifetime of work. In a rapidly changing world, an approach of this type is inappropriate. Furthermore, it did not really fit with models drawn from developmental psychology, which viewed individuals as evolving over the life span. A number of developmental models have influenced models of career development over the working life. For example, Levinson *et al.* (1978) offered a model in which there are three main stages of adult life, but within each there are periods of transition and stability. By implication, career change may occur during periods of transition. A more focused four-stage model of adult careers, presented by Super and his colleagues, includes exploration, establishment, maintenance and disengagement.

While assessment remains central to career advice, the focus of advice and counselling has tended to shift towards models that give greater emphasis to personal competence and self-assessment. The goal of career counselling then becomes the development of an awareness of one's own strengths and limitations, as well as interests and circumstances, and how these might change.

The pace of change, which has rendered any static view of careers guidance inappropriate, has also presented a serious challenge to the traditional concept of the career. According to the traditional view, the career was a progression of jobs which implied movement up an organizational hierarchy. As such, the view was always elitist and male-dominated. Change makes it less easy to predict that specific areas of expertise at work, specific organizations and traditional hierarchies in general will remain over the long term. This perspective calls for a redefinition of the career. As a first step, it might be redefined as a sequence of jobs, possibly related in some way. Alternatively, in an attempt to remove some of the gender bias, it might be seen as a series of activities over the lifespan which include periods of work, development and other activities.

As the concept of the career changes, shifting the focus to a sequence of jobs, so occupational psychologists have shifted their attention from processes for providing advice about careers to a concern for job choice, job entry and job transition. Some have concentrated on the type of information that can usefully be provided in advance – realistic job previews – and the impact this has on acceptance of and tenure in a job or the type of information most valued at the start of a new job. Nicholson and West (1988) have gone further, developing a four-stage model of job change and transition involving preparation, encounter, adjustment and stabilization.

As occupational psychologists have been developing new theories and concepts of the career, they are giving increasing attention to the concept of the 'psychological contract' between individuals and employees. The argument is that the traditional 'contract' between individuals and their employers of job security for loyalty will be replaced. The alternative is as yet unclear, but may involve high intrinsic and extrinsic rewards (see HERZBERG, F.) and the prospect of opportunities for self-development in return for commitment and high performance over a relatively fixed period. Changing career patterns also present new challenges for career management, including the need to develop opportunities for self-development, to consider ideas such as mentoring and to expand the scope for career counselling. Movement in and out of organizations and the growth of more dynamic and unpredictable careers also increases the demand from individuals for forms of career counselling which might be needed at any point in working life.

Training and development

Learning theory has always been a central element in psychology and it has provided many insights for application in the fields of education and training. The main contribution to training lies in the design and delivery of learning. This has formed the core of what has sometimes been described as the systematic approach to training (see TRAINING). The systematic approach consists of a series of steps: analyse the job and the trainees; identify training needs as the gap between what the individual can do and what the job requires; set training objectives; design the content, methods and media of training; implement the training; and evaluate its impact (Goldstein 1993).

Contributions to training form one of the core activities of occupational psychologists. Psychological knowledge can contribute to each of the stages outlined above. This knowledge goes beyond learning theory, which traditionally has leant heavily on the behaviourist school of psychology, but which now co-exists alongside more cognitive perspectives. For example, goal-setting theory, which is concerned with the impact of the nature of goals and the way they are set on subsequent motivation and performance, can help to focus learning objectives and shape what has to be learned. The concept of self-efficacy – the confidence someone has to undertake a specific task – is likely to influence the learning process and therefore needs to be built into training activities.

There is much to commend in this systematic approach. It forces one to think carefully about training and to organize it according to sound principles. However, it tends to view training as something that is done to someone; it may be more sensible to adopt a perspective of learning, which is a more active self-directed activity. Also, the reality of organizational life is rather different to the systematic model. When asked how they learn, people tend to cite informal rather than formally organized experiences. They might learn more from an informal mentoring process or from being 'thrown in at the deep end' in a crisis than through formal training. As organizations become more dynamic in response to change and innovation, the idea of training as something that occurs at the start of employment, as a kind of apprenticeship or professional training for life, becomes untenable. The knowledge of a graduate engineer, for example, becomes obsolete in a few years. This calls for constant learning and for the creation of an organizational context that supports learning.

Another problem with the systematic approach is that it tends to favour formal, off-the-job conditions for learning, giving rise to problems of *transfer*. Occupational psychologists may be highly skilled at designing learning conditions; they are not always so effective at ensuring conditions for the implementation and performance of the new learning back in the workplace. The problem of transfer can be organizational and political rather than purely technical, raising questions about the value of even the most superb training if transfer is not feasible.

Often, the problem of transfer is not recognized because only limited evaluation has been conducted. Approaches to systematic evaluation have been developed. Typically, these involve a number of levels, from reactions to the experience and evidence of learning in the context of the training programme to performance improvement and its impact back in the work environment.

The separation of training/learning and everyday work is a cultural one. In Japanese organizations, the distinction may be blurred with development of subordinates accepted as an integral part of the job of a supervisor or manager. In a country such as Germany, the initial apprenticeship system, predominantly within the workplace, is widely accepted as the norm.

One potential solution to both the problem of transfer and to the tendency of rapid change to produce skill obsolescence that has attracted the attention of psychologists is the concept of the 'learning organization' (Senge 1990). This rather nebulous concept means, in effect, creating a culture in which continual learning is the norm. By focusing on organizational culture, occupational psychologists depart from their familiar territory. Nevertheless, this solution builds on earlier ideas of 'organization development', an approach that draws attention to the way in which organizational processes operate. For example, it might focus on how decisions are reached or how teams work and seek ways of improving them by combining some off-the-job training activity with conscious efforts to operate differently in the workplace.

Organization development (OD) is a deliberate attempt to achieve improvements in organizational processes such as decision making, problem-solving and communication through learning, and through the use of the behavioural sciences, especially psychological knowledge and theory (see COMMUNICATION; DECISION MAKING). The model of OD derives in part from ideas about how to bring about effective change. It seeks to alter knowledge, beliefs and behaviour within the workplace and to reinforce this through the social and structural context on the assumption that such an approach is more likely to bring about long-term change in performance than context-free learning.

Training and development represents another area of activity where rapid change has increased the demand for the skills of the occupational psychologist. Training is no longer a one-off activity at the start of employment but rather a continual process for which each individual must take some responsibility. Occupational psychologists are helping to structure this more complex form of learning and (moving out of their traditional domain) to contribute to the design of effective learning environments.

Design of work and the working environment

One of the ways in which occupational psychology has sought to achieve the twin objectives of high worker well-being and high performance is through theory, research and practice with regard to the design of work (see JOB DESIGN). Starting with motivation theory and ideas about individual needs, a case has been made for job enrichment, which is the process of building opportunities for responsibility, autonomy and achievement into the job. The argument is that when jobs are designed in this way – as opposed to the traditional Taylorist way in which they tended to be as simple as possible – the results are higher motivation, performance and satisfaction. An alternative view, based initially on the work of psychologists at the Tavistock Institute of Human Relations (Trist *et al.* 1963), suggested that it was more useful to design work for groups rather than individuals and advocated design based on autonomous work groups (see GROUPS

AND TEAMS). Sociotechnical systems theory, the theory underlying this kind of job design, went well beyond motivation and indeed beyond the traditional boundaries of psychology.

There have been several well-known cases of job redesign on the basis of autonomous work groups. One of the best-known occurred at one of the Volvo factories in Sweden, where a purpose-built plant enabled work-groups to construct major parts of a car. Evaluations of this approach show that it can result in increased satisfaction among the workforce and indirect benefits through lower absence and labour turnover. However, it has rarely had the anticipated effect of a direct impact on motivation and performance.

Sociotechnical systems theory, by its very nature, considers the social and technical context of work (see WORK SYSTEMS). However, it has sometimes been vague in its ways of operationalizing the environment. The environment can be conceptualized variously to include factors at the level of the workplace, the organization and the wider economic and social environment. The traditional approach of psychologists has been to try to control the environment, ideally by conducting studies in the controlled conditions of a laboratory. In field settings, the ideal is to conduct some form of controlled experiment in which the environment is the same for both the experimental and control groups while some other variable is manipulated. An exception to this is the field of ergonomics, or human machine interaction, where aspects of the environment become the specific object of psychological study, largely because of their potential impact on the individual.

Incorporating elements of engineering and physiology as well as psychology, ergonomics has contributed to areas such as design of computer displays and user-friendly instructions for the assembly of household goods. It has also made a major contribution to the understanding of workload, effort, attention and fatigue in the context of inspection, and boredom at work. Many of these issues are low profile and lacking in glamour, only catching attention when an incident occurs or public concern grows about an issue such as

repetitive strain injury (RSI), which sensible ergonomic design can help prevent.

The physical environment includes the layout of offices, heating, lighting, noise levels and arrangements of working hours, including shift work. All these issues can have a crucial bearing on the health and safety of workers. Recent advances in the study of human error (Reason 1990) and accidents, which adopt a systems perspective, have moved the conventional analysis of safety and accidents beyond the simplistic view of 'victim as guilty', in which the person having an accident is usually to blame, to one where those who design and manage the work and safety system accept greater responsibility. One problem is that there can sometimes appear to be a conflict between financial priorities and the need for a safe and healthy work environment. This key area of the work of occupational psychologists therefore often lacks sufficient investment from companies.

Motivation and performance

Psychology has a long tradition of research into motivation, which is often closely allied to theories of learning and of personality (see MOTIVATION AND SATISFACTION). Personality theory has contributed to the content of motivation by helping to identify what are often described as needs. In the 1930s, Henry A. Murray produced a long list of needs (Murray 1938); in the 1940s, Abraham Maslow described five needs, organized in a hierarchy of importance, in which the peak of motivation was to achieve 'self-actualization', or continuing self-fulfilment. More recently, McClelland has focused on three needs – for achievement, power and affiliation. The first two have particular appeal to management. The implicit theory is that if opportunities to satisfy these needs are provided in the workplace, then workers will be motivated to perform more effectively. These needs can be extended into a set of values, as reflected in Douglas McGregor's distinction between Theory X, based on a limited view of the motives of workers, and Theory Y, based on a more optimistic view, which parallels the ideas of Maslow and suggests essentially that workers seek self-fulfilment at work (McGregor 1960). Theory X implies a need for tight management control of the workforce; Theory Y points to the case for providing challenge and autonomy (see HUMAN RELATIONS).

The contemporary approach to motivation developed from roots in learning theory, but it contains a strong cognitive perspective and is therefore more pragmatic and more concerned with the process of motivation or the conditions under which highly motivated behaviour is likely to occur. Expectancy theory, one of the best-known approaches of this type, suggests that motivation will be highest when workers perceive that there is a strong link between their effort, performance and rewards. This leaves open the question of what rewards are going to be attractive. In the 1990s, much attention has been focused on the role of pay as an incentive. It is far from clear that pay is a key incentive or, if it is potentially important, that the conditions under which it can operate as an incentive can be met. The emphasis in expectancy theory is on the individual's perceptions rather than on what management or anyone else may regard as objective reality, locating it clearly within a cognitive approach. Another influential cognitive approach to motivation, goal-setting theory, proposes that motivation will be higher when individuals have clear, demanding goals to which they are committed and on which regular feedback about progress is given.

Motivation and its causes and consequences has been one of the main areas of research among academic occupational psychologists for many years. One reason for this is that the prizes for companies who can tap worker motivation appear to be high. Need theories have had a disappointing track record, but some of the cognitive theories, including expectancy theory and goal-setting theory, have a more impressive record of positive association with higher performance (Kleinbeck et al. 1990).

Individual–organization linkages

Both psychologists and sociologists have long been interested in the question of whether work is a central life interest. Insights into the important role of work have been obtained by psychologists exploring the impact of unemployment on well-being (see EMPLOYMENT AND UNEMPLOYMENT, ECONOMICS OF). Studies of the impact of unemployment represent a long-standing research tradition from work in Austria in the 1930s (Jahoda 1982) to, for example, recent comprehensive studies in Australia. This research has revealed the hidden functions of work, for example in structuring time, in providing meaning in life and in providing social contacts. Furthermore, those who report high levels of job involvement, a relatively persistent characteristic, feel the effects of unemployment more.

In the 1980s, there was growing interest in the concept of organizational commitment (see HUMAN RESOURCE MANAGEMENT). One reason for this was concern among a number of organizations about their ability to attract and retain the most talented workers. Another was the growth of human resource management with its emphasis on the benefits of a committed, high quality-workforce (Walton 1985). Occupational psychologists have contributed to the conceptualization of organizational commitment (Mowday et al. 1982) and pointed out possible steps for improving organizational commitment among employees. Research has shown that key predictors of commitment to organizations include the degree to which employee expectations are met, fairness and responsibility in the job. Where such measures are implemented effectively, the consequences include lower labour turnover and absenteeism. It is also plausible to expect higher performance, but this generally has not been forthcoming.

Interest in promoting commitment to the organization opens up the possibility of competing commitments. Occupational psychologists have been particularly interested in exploring the dual commitment to company and trade union. However, the profession, leisure interests and the family provide additional and potentially competing commitments. Increasingly, companies have looked to the role of the work group and work team, and to leadership to enhance commitment to the organization. These are areas in which social psychologists have a rich tradition of research, often conducted in controlled laboratory conditions. Occupational psychologists have taken a lead in applying these theories in the workplace and they have a long history of research and application.

The concept of organizational commitment tends to assume a unitarist framework of shared interest in the success of the organization. As such, it ignores any structural basis for conflict. Indeed, in considering conflict, occupational psychologists have focused most readily on individual manifestations, such as labour turnover and absenteeism, and have tended to view conflict as an avoidable aberration. This is a limiting perspective, heavily criticized by occupational psychologists interested in industrial relations, who have paid more attention to inter- and intragroup conflict (Walton and McKersie 1965) (see INDUSTRIAL CONFLICT). They have also made a major contribution to the understanding of processes of bargaining, negotiation and conciliation, starting from a pluralist perspective within which differences of interest are seen as legitimate. Some of this work draws on general psychology and can be applied to interpersonal conflict and negotiation within the family, the community, in schools and even in international relations.

Well-being and quality of working life

One of the distinctions made in psychology has been between: the behaviourist school, with its emphasis on manifest behaviour; the Freudian psychoanalytic tradition, with its concern for the often unconscious neuroses and psychoses believed to dominate human behaviour; and the cognitive perspective with its concern for the way in which individuals actively perceive and interpret their world. However, some attention has also been given to what was at one point termed 'third force' psychology, an off-shoot from the Freudian tradition, heavily influenced by Carl Gustav Jung and more concerned with positive mental health. (The term 'third force' reflects a failure at the time to recognize the cognitive perspective as a distinctive approach.) Representatives of this group include a number of well-known writers such as Erich Fromm, Abraham Maslow, Karen Horney and Carl Rogers.

The tradition of concern for the 'problem' of mental health has spilt over into the work setting and is most manifest in a long-standing tradition of work on occupational stress (see STRESS). Occupational stress can be broadly defined as an inability to cope with the real or anticipated demands of the job. The demands may include an excessive quantity of work, excessive difficulty or mental load and conflicting or ambiguous roles. One of the problems in this area is that stress can act as a stimulus, providing challenge and excitement. Considerable individual differences make it difficult to point to a particular job and say it is inherently stressful. Nevertheless, there is some consensus in the research that perceived stress is greatest in those jobs which combine a high demand with a low level of personal control. Such conditions are found much more in blue-collar jobs (for example, on the production line) than in managerial and professional positions. Although extensive research has confirmed the feelings of discomfort or stress associated with jobs that are overdemanding in some way, a direct link to illnesses such as heart disease has not been shown. Any link to illness is mediated by other factors, such as diet, smoking and a resilience related to heredity. Concern for the 'problems' of the workplace extends to the study of alcoholism and drug abuse in the workplace and to the development of programmes of treatment.

One of the difficulties with a predominantly individualistic perspective on problems such as stress or alcoholism at work is that there is the temptation, noted previously with reference to accidents at work, to blame the victim. The problem of stress thus lies with the individual experiencing stress and the solution is perhaps to send that person on a course to learn how to cope with stress and manage his or her work life more effectively. The problem with such an approach is that it fails to take into account the conditions that gave rise to the stress in the first place. If they have not been tackled, then courses of treatments are unlikely to have any effect. Once again, it is necessary to extend the focus beyond the traditional level of psychological analysis to consider structural factors. The problem then becomes not the individual on the production line but the production line itself and, beyond that, the imperatives that give rise to the need for a production line. While a wider perspective may not solve the problem – in this case capitalism cannot be ignored – it helps to shift the focus of the analysis and the 'blame'.

Another outcome of a broader perspective is to shift thinking away from how to deal with the problems of stress and toward policies and practices designed to improve the well-being of the workforce. This builds on the perspective of the 'third force' psychologists by focusing on positive mental health. In the USA, this is termed 'wellness'. The idea of wellness or well-being at work is concerned with both positive physical and mental health. It therefore embraces exercise and diet but also job design and workload. The idea of well-being extends beyond satisfaction to embrace the more active concept of positive mental health, and the assumption is that mental health is influenced by a range of policies and practices over which the organization has some choice.

The possibility of using the research findings of occupational psychology to develop a set of positive policy proposals has found its clearest expression in the principles underlying the quality of working life movement, which rose to prominence internationally in the 1970s. The essential argument is that there is now sufficient evidence about the impact of good practices in a range of areas – such as working hours, health and safety, education of the workforce, job design, equal opportunity and employee participation – to justify a legislative programme. In many cases, the claims have been overwhelmed by more pressing economic concerns, but strong elements of the approach survive in the European Social Chapter, a set of policies to promote the quality of working life through a legislative framework (see HUMAN RESOURCE MANAGEMENT IN EUROPE; INDUSTRIAL RELATIONS IN EUROPE).

Change and transition

In much of what has been described above, change is implicit. Organizational change is a complex, multi-faceted concept which has often proved elusive to researchers but rewarding to consultants. Occupational psychologists have contributed by assisting in the process of change and by dealing with the consequences, and more particularly the negative consequences, of change. Some of the key issues include the extent to which employees should participate in change that affects them; the predictable resistance that occurs when people are threatened with loss of control over issues that matter to them; and the sense of 'learned helplessness' that arises when the loss of control resulting from imposed change causes people to become passive and to lose initiative. Once again, some of the more interesting work in this has been undertaken in studies of the unemployed and particularly the long-term unemployed (see DOWNSIZING).

Change can be an opportunity as much as a threat. One of the key requirements for change is a positive approach to new technology and a great deal of attention has been devoted to ways of ensuring a positive response to new technology and associated innovation. Once again, most studies emphasize the importance of a participative approach and of careful communication. Occupational psychologists have a particular interest in the process of change rather than its content. In typical organizational contexts, where rapid change is increasingly the norm, they have a vital role to play in ensuring that the changes are effective for all parties.

5 Achieving the goals of occupational psychology

It was suggested in section three that the broad goals of occupational psychology could be defined in terms of the twin objectives of seeking high worker well-being and high organizational effectiveness. To what degree have these objectives been achieved? Thousands of studies of job satisfaction in many countries show that the great majority of workers are, generally, fairly satisfied with their jobs. In other words, their jobs at least provide them with an acceptable minimum of satisfaction. On the other hand, there is relatively little highly enthusiastic endorsement of jobs, more particularly at lower levels in organizations. These studies suggest, therefore, that many people experience a basic level of satisfaction rather than the more active concept of well-being.

Many research studies have examined the impact of interventions intended to alter behaviour in organizations. Their impact has been equivocal. While there are some instances of performance improvements – and there certainly is evidence to show that careful selection results in better selection decisions, well-designed training produces more effective learning, and so on – the interventions have often been somewhat piecemeal and any impact often marginal and short-lived. One reason for the failure of some changes is that they occur at a level in the organization where they fail to become firmly embedded. Another reason is that it has often proved difficult to be specific about measuring individual and group performance and identifying specific causal factors.

If, when taken separately, the evidence demonstrating the relationship between well-being and performance is somewhat weak, then it is seldom to be expected that improvements in both will occur or even that they can co-exist. Using the data on job satisfaction, research carried out over many years shows that the correlation between job satisfaction and performance averages about 0.14. In other words, there is a small positive, but weak, association. There are a number of plausible reasons why this might be so; for example, satisfaction and performance might be caused by different factors. Certainly, one should guard against an assumption that high satisfaction leads to high performance or vice versa (see PRODUCTIVITY). Nevertheless, a major challenge for occupational psychologists is to identify and create conditions under which the two can be achieved jointly.

So far, the kind of interventions advocated by occupational psychologists to improve well-being and organizational performance have often been poorly implemented or largely ignored. As a result, for certain issues where the impact on the well-being of all or part of the workforce is unambiguous, it has sometimes been necessary to legislate to change managerial behaviour. It would seem that companies are eager to use occupational psychologists to help in decisions about individuals and to tackle specific problems, including how to handle problem employees; however, they are less enthusiastic about interventions at the broader policy level, which require sustained management commitment and some financial investment. These may include safety programmes, educational programmes and job redesign. For some of these, and indeed for areas such as equal opportunity and industrial democracy, legislation has been necessary to induce action by management, even in the more socially enlightened countries (see EQUAL EMPLOYMENT OPPORTUNITIES; INDUSTRIAL DEMOCRACY).

Science versus application

Many psychologists claim that theirs is a young science. A large proportion of them prefer to devote their energies to theory testing in laboratories, taking the view that careful development is necessary before application is possible. While this is understandable, and while the developments emanating from the laboratories provide many helpful insights, others would argue that the applied problems that need solving today are so urgent that they cannot wait for laboratory testing. As a result, occupational psychology has provided leading-edge applied work, sometimes in advance of the evidence that it will have the impact intended. On the one hand, this has raised doubts in some minds about the efficacy of occupational psychology; on the other hand, psychologists would argue that if they did not tackle the problems with their partial knowledge, others with even less understanding would volunteer their services. The argument raises complex ethical and professional dilemmas which each occupational psychologist must solve in his or her own way. It also provides part of the rationale for professional chartered status and a proper registration system.

Occupational psychology as fad and fashion

In an era when effective management of human resources promises to provide the key basis for competitive advantage, the search for new solutions to complex human problems has led to a steady flow of fads and fashions based on ideas derived from occupational psychology. At different times, these have included: the human relations movement; participative and, more recently, charismatic or transformational leadership; need for achievement; need for power; job enrichment; management by objectives; the Managerial Grid; stress management programmes, and so on (see LEADERSHIP). The list is seemingly endless. Many of these ideas are simplified versions of original theory and research, packaged and sometimes oversold to a management audience. One consequence of the preponderance of such fads and fashions is a cynicism among other academics about the contribution made by occupational psychology.

On a few occasions, occupational psychologists have shown the confidence to market a fuller package of techniques, believing they had something distinctive to offer. This entry has already referred to two such contributions. One occasion was the organization development (OD) movement, which focused on ways of managing change. By concerning itself with the process rather than the content of change, OD promised to have relevance to all organizations. In practice, it often reflected values which preferred a particular non-coercive approach to change and, revealing its academic roots, gave much weight to careful diagnosis. It was therefore limited by the threat of 'analysis paralysis', being weak on power and ultimately offering no solutions, just a perspective and a set of process packages. A second approach that offered more than just a single idea has been the 'quality of working life' movement. Despite its initial promise, it has often been treated with suspicion by both management and trade unions. In

contrast to OD, it was strong on content but rather naive about implementation. In the end, legislation has been necessary to implement it. Finally, there are hints of an emerging approach, derived largely from occupational psychology, in the ideas underpinning a 'full utilization' model of human resource management. The subject matter of occupational psychology – the behaviour of people at work – means that more fads and fashions and more prescriptive approaches are likely to arise as an ever more urgent search continues for new ideas to gain competitive advantage through management of human resources.

North America, Europe and an international occupational psychology

The field of occupational, or I/O, psychology is dominated by the USA. The sheer mass of work, the number of academic departments, the control of many of the key journals and the great emphasis on journal publications and the methodology associated with them in the American academic institutions means that most new ideas come from North America. However, even within the broad church of American ideas, there is a certain standardization of approach, reflecting the influence of the most prestigious journals. This leaves less room for a more critical, more abstract, more reflective and less managerial perspective, which is sometimes, although not exclusively, associated with European academics (see COMMUNICATION, CROSS-CULTURAL). Occupational psychology in western Europe, however, is more disparate and suffers from some language barriers. Furthermore, in the context of information overload, the complex reflective analysis will invariably be crowded out by the short, sharp journal piece with its clear hypotheses, sophisticated statistics and unambiguous conclusions.

Occupational psychology, at both national and international levels, needs to celebrate diversity and ensure that many voices are heard. Beyond North America and western Europe, there is an emerging south-east Asian voice, impressive work in eastern Europe and lively communities in South America and southern Africa. These will serve as an antidote to western hegemony. On the other hand, the basis on which the subject often flourishes is managerial interest, managerial sponsorship and implicit acceptance of managerial definitions of the key issues in question.

6 Occupational psychology – coming of age?

Occupational psychology is a subject full of tensions and challenges. It has promised much and continues to carry high expectations from many in employment. In one sense, all big organizational issues are, at least in part, human resource issues; and all human resource issues are partly occupational psychology issues. If one follows this line of reasoning, it is to be expected that occupational psychology will increasingly be in demand. This entry noted at the outset that psychology provides both a point of departure and a specific opportunity to focus on the concerns of the worker. A cursory analysis reveals the importance of continuing to draw upon ideas from mainstream psychology but also of adopting a broader level of analysis; what happens at the individual level depends on what happens elsewhere. That same cursory analysis reveals that the concern for the worker is often overwhelmed by the management agenda. A confident occupational psychology will need to move out of its narrow domain, embrace a more pluralist perspective and embrace some of the frameworks of organizational behaviour if it is to achieve its potential contribution to employee well-being and organizational effectiveness.

DAVID GUEST
BIRKBECK COLLEGE, UNIVERSITY OF
LONDON

Further reading

(References cited in the text marked *)

Arthur, M.B., Hall, D.T. and Lawrence, B.S. (eds) (1989) *Handbook of Career Theory*, Cambridge: Cambridge University Press. (One of the best overviews of the range of approaches to all aspects of the career concept.)

Campbell, J.P. and Campbell, R.J. (eds) (1988) *Productivity in Organizations*, San Francisco, CA: Jossey Bass. (Review of research in occupational psychology and organizational behaviour into the impact of a range of interventions on performance and productivity.)

Cranny, C.J., Smith, P.C. and Stone, E.F. (1992) *Job Satisfaction*, New York: Lexington Books. (Comprehensive set of writings about the nature, causes and consequences of job satisfaction.)

Drenth, P. J-D., Thierry, H.K., Willems, P.J. and de Wolff, C.J. (1984) *Handbook of Work and Organizational Psychology*, Chichester: Wiley. (One of the most authoritative European textbooks of occupational psychology.)

Dunnette, M.D., and Hough, L.M. (1991) *Handbook of Industrial and Organizational Psychology*, 2nd edn, Palo Alto, CA: Consulting Psychologists Press Inc. (Major authoritative review of the state of the field both in North America and internationally by a range of leading experts.)

* Goldstein, I.L. (1993) *Training in Organizations*, Pacific Grove, CA: Brooks/Cole. (One of the leading textbooks and overviews of training in organizations.)

Herriot, P. (ed.) (1989) *Assessment and Selection in Organizations: Method and Practice for Recruitment and Appraisal*, Chichester: Wiley. (Thorough and wide-ranging overview of assessment and selection, providing a distinctively European perspective. An update, jointly edited by N. Anderson and P. Herriot, was published in 1994.)

* Jahoda, M. (1982) *Employment and Unemployment: A Social-Psychological Analysis*, Cambridge: Cambridge University Press. (The presentation of a distinctive and influential approach to the analysis of unemployment which reflects a long tradition of research from the early Austrian work at Marienthal.)

Karasek, R. and Theorell, T. (1990) *Healthy Work: Stress, Productivity and the Reconstruction of Working Life*, New York: Basic Books. (This book takes the core findings on stress at work as the starting point for outlining the case for a positive approach to health and well-being at work.)

* Kleinbeck, U., Quast, H-H., Thierry, H. and Hacker, H. (1990) *Work Motivation*, Hillsdown, NJ.: Lawrence Erlbaum. (Predominantly European perspective on motivation at work.)

* Levinson, D.J., Darrow, D.N., Klein, E.B., Levinson, M.H. and McKee, B. (1978) *The Seasons of a Man's Life*, New York: A.A. Knopf. (Pre-

sents a view about life stages which has implications for careers in organizations.)

* McGregor, D. (1960) *The Human Side of Enterprise*, New York: McGraw-Hill. (Includes McGregor's discussion of worker motivation, which suggests that people seek self-fulfilment at work.)

* Mowday, R.T., Porter, L.W. and Steers, R.M. (1982) *Employee–Organization Linkages: The Psychology of Commitment, Absenteeism and Labour Turnover*, New York: Academic Press. (This book presents the research and theoretical basis for taking organizational commitment seriously.)

* Murray, H.A. (1938) *Explorations in Personality*, New York: Harper & Row, 1954. (Contains Murray's description of needs which play an important role in human motivation.)

* Nicholson, N. and West, M. (1988) *Managerial Job Change: Men and Women in Transition*, Cambridge: Cambridge University Press. (Empirically based analysis of the nature and impact of transitions at work and particularly within careers.)

* Reason, J. (1990) *Human Error*, Cambridge: Cambridge University Press. (Authoritative overview of the research on error and approaches to minimizing error and accidents at work.)

* Schein, E.H. (1978) *Career Dynamics: Matching Individual and Organizational Needs*, Reading, MA: Addison-Wesley. (One of the classic approaches to the analysis of careers and career preferences.)

* Senge, P.M. (1990) *The Fifth Discipline*, New York: Doubleday/Currency. (This influential book makes a case for taking the concept of the 'learning organization' seriously.)

Steers, R.M. and Porter, L.W. (1991) *Motivation and Work Behavior*, 5th edn, New York: McGraw-Hill. (Regularly updated set of the best readings which provides an excellent overview of current issues in motivation and performance at work.)

* Trist, E.L., Higgin, G.W., Murray, H. and Pollock, A.B. (1963) *Organizational Choice*, London: Tavistock Publications. (Overview of some of the key work on sociotechnical systems and a comprehensive statement about its implications.)

* Walton, R.E. (1985) 'From control to commitment', *Harvard Business Review* 63 (March–April): 76–84. (Classic article which makes the case for a new approach to the management of people at work.)

* Walton, R.E. and McKersie, R.B. (1965) *A Behavioral Theory of Labour Negotiations* New York: McGraw-Hill. (Influential book outlining a psychological approach to the theory of bargaining behaviour in the context of industrial relations.)

Warr, P.B. (1995) *Psychology at Work*, 4th edn, Harmondsworth: Penguin. (Accessible set of chapters providing an overview of some of the main areas of occupational psychology, written within a European, and particularly British, perspective.)

See also: FOLLETT, M.P.; HUMAN RELATIONS; HUMAN RESOURCE DEVELOPMENT; HUMAN RESOURCE MANAGEMENT, INTERNATIONAL; INTERPERSONAL SKILLS; MANAGERIAL BEHAVIOUR; STRESS

Related topics in the IEBM: BUSINESS ETHICS; COGNITION; GURU CONCEPT; INFORMATION TECHNOLOGY; JUNG, C.G.; MANAGEMENT IN NORTH AMERICA; MANAGEMENT IN SCANDINAVIA; MANAGEMENT IN THE UK; MCCLELLAND, D.C.; ORGANIZATION BEHAVIOUR, HISTORY OF; ORGANIZATION DEVELOPMENT; ORGANIZATION PARADIGMS; ORGANIZATION STRUCTURE; ORGANIZATIONAL LEARNING; ORGANIZATIONAL PERFORMANCE; ORGANIZING, PROCESS OF; TECHNOLOGY AND ORGANIZATIONS; TRIST, E.L.

Organization behaviour

Overview

This entry provides conceptual and methodological pointers and a guide through the field of organization behaviour. It is an extremely complex and broad-ranging area, and there are references to other organization behaviour entries and an attempt to show how they all fit into a larger concept.

Organization behaviour has to be seen as both a practical and an academic field. A discipline in itself, it is also a cross-disciplinary endeavour. Essentially the word 'organization' has two different meanings: one refers to a particular social collectivity and the other to organizational properties of collectivities. The field of organization behaviour is subdivided into specialist topics according to various criteria. The main ones are: the level of aggregation and analysis; specific aspects of organizational life; goal-, product- or service-related specificities; criteria of performance in organizational domains; particular approaches to theory-building; synchronic or diachronic perspectives.

Subdivisions cannot be broken up into separate compartments. A satisfactory treatment of one specific topic usually requires reference to other fields. This requirement can be described by reciprocal 'predication', whereby a specific organizational insight emerges on the basis of different insights from other sub-fields.

Despite the co-existence of different theoretical and research traditions, a coherent body of organization behaviour theory can be summarized. Dominant explanatory factors are utilitarian, culturalist and institutionalist approaches. There are also different types of theory distinguished by their epistemological foundations: nomothetic, idiographic and dialectic approaches. Such approaches compete with one another, but they can also be intertwined. Academic advance and innovation in organization behaviour proceeds through the mutual competition and cross-fertilization of distinct approaches. It can be argued that more satisfactory accounts and explanations result when students are competent in different approaches and in combining these to create new fields.

This is also the basis for an effective cross-fertilization between theory, research and practice. A pragmatic, undogmatic handling of theoretical approaches leads to more useful practical recipes, and organization behaviour theory and research thrive where practical organizational experience is systematically integrated into a more properly academic treatment.

1 The differing meanings of organization

Although most people think that they have an idea of what 'organization' means, in the more rigorous field of scientific terminology things are much less simple (Morgan 1986). Essentially the word is used in two different ways which must be carefully distinguished. The distinction is important in order to understand further notions and propositions of organization theory. Also, it is important to distinguish the more scholarly usage of 'organization' (in its two meanings) from the more everyday usage. For instance, in shops you may see a notice which reads: 'Closed during reorganization'. You are likely to see that the shop is empty, that there are ladders standing about and workmen painting the walls and the ceiling or doing the floor. Evidently the shop owners have used the term 'reorganization' to glorify the more mundane activities of redecoration. Similarly, people say that they have to 'get organized', which means they want to have more order in their working or private life.

Likewise, natural scientists have become accustomed to discussing the organization of things like molecular structures. This is not so far removed in meaning from the shop being reorganized, and it is arguably further from the meanings of the word that are implied here because human action is more visible in the shop than in most molecular structures. However, they obviously have something in common because they are all metaphorically related to each other, metaphorical relations making the understanding of meanings much easier. But metaphor is also a danger because it can make meanings exchangeable which, under rigorous scrutiny, should not be so.

The first meaning of organization, within the body of theory and findings covered here, is a particular *social unit* or *collectivity*. Not all social units and collectivities are organizations; neither a tribe, nor a family, nor a complete society can be depicted as such. What defines an organization in this particular sense will be discussed below but, for the moment, it is important to remember that organizations are social units which can be demarcated on the basis of the people who belong to them. Thus, with this approach organizations may include the Methodist Church, a multinational enterprise, a local construction firm, a hospital and a tank battalion.

The second meaning of the word refers to *organizational properties*, both structures and processes, within a social unit or collectivity. Units and collectivities are, in this sense, 'organized' in specific ways. They have types of management, authority relationships, numbers of supervisors per worker, definitions of rights and obligations, modes of decision making and other aspects which are used to characterize them.

An organization in the first sense – a social collectivity – not only is an organization but also has an organization in the second sense. This is not sophistry. The literature discusses organizational properties of collectivities which are not typified as organizations. For

example, complete societies are described as organized in particular ways; but, although they have organizational properties they are not in themselves organizations! For the purposes here, however, organization behaviour will largely disregard the organization of entities that are not organizations. This is something for the wider disciplines of sociology and social anthropology. Here, it is crucial to be precise: the organization as a collectivity or the organizational properties which it has.

The difference between the two meanings is best realized when we acknowledge that organizations (in the first sense) not only have organizational properties but many other things in addition. They have goals: specific targets towards which action in the organization is orientated. The Methodist Church aims at the spiritual and religious well-being of people that belong to the Church; a multinational enterprise like General Motors has as its goal the manufacture of cars; a construction firm aims to build houses; a hospital has the aim of curing people of illnesses; and a tank battalion has the goal of exerting physical force and violence against enemies, with the aid of battle tanks. Organizational goals immediately imply specific products such as motor cars, but products can also be services, including church services, medical treatment and military services.

Organizations – as collectivities – also have techniques, technologies, physical capital (buildings, machines, offices) and strategies to achieve their goals. Whereas the techniques and technologies of a motor manufacturer consist of things such as transfer lines, robots and metal-working machines, the technique of a church includes sermons, prayer, singing, confession, holy communion and group meetings, and the technique of the tank battalion is rooted in the design and operating principles of battle tanks. There are also specific techniques for accounting and control, such as double-entry book-keeping, budgeting systems, hospital management systems, military administration, tactics, strategy and command principles. Furthermore, organizations make use of typical inputs like human resources, raw materials and information to achieve their goals. Having members that help to achieve these goals, organization size is also a feature – members are necessary to help attain goals, thus numbers are important. Then there are the stakeholders, with a more or less controlling interest in the organization. These include shareholders, governments, employees and public action groups.

Such properties can be extremely important, although they are not necessarily counted as part of the organizational properties of the collectivity. In organization theory, they are grouped under the notion of *organizational context*. In terms of our two notions of organization, context embraces precisely those properties of the organization (the collectivity) which are not properly organizational, i.e. which do not directly include organization structures and processes. Context is something that is, at least in part, integral to the organization, situated on the side of the fence which separates everything that belongs to the organization from that which does not belong to it. In this sense all assets and liabilities – whether financial, human or technical – stakeholder structures and organization size are the central ingredients of the context of an organization.

Human resources and personnel management practices are naturally very important elements of the organizational context. The skills and knowledge of employees, their professional competence, posture and attitudes, their obligations, performance and aspirations, the socialization and career they follow in an organization and beyond, and the employment relation and industrial relations in which they are engaged, are all very much related to organizational structures and practices. Hence, the relations between human resources theory and research and organizational behaviour have been intense, and there has been substantial overlap between these fields. Organizational phenomena can usually only be explained if human resources are included in the explanation, and vice versa.

Organizational environment is also important. This lies outside the organization itself, situated on the opposite side of the fence to context. It includes banks and financial institutions, and all kinds of other organizations (suppliers, clients, governmental authorities, industrial federations, trade unions) and persons. For the Methodist Church it would include other Christian denominations, agnostics, Jews, Muslims, Buddhists and other spiritual world views, depending on the country in which it is situated. For the tank battalion it would include all other units and levels of command in the army and, of course, enemy and allied forces, plus the local environment in which it is located. The environment of General Motors meanwhile includes all competitors, clients and suppliers, plus many institutions that provide it with all kinds of personnel, regulations and information.

It is customary to make a distinction between the *task environment* and the *general environment*. The task environment relates to everything that bears on the immediate achievement of the organizational goal, for example state-of-the-art technology, competitors, market structures, sales networks and sources of finance. The general environment, however, is less specific with regard to the task or goal of the organization; it includes the law of the land, general governmental policies, public attitudes, education systems, political affairs, social stratification and everything else which may indirectly affect organizational life. For instance, national holidays have been instituted without a direct regard for what they imply for a motor car manufacturer but they do affect its operations in that they are part of a general scheme to structure the rhythm and pace of working activities in the society at large.

Human resources also are a powerful environmental factor. They have to be apprehended as governed by societally specific institutions, dispositions, preferences, values and other endowments. As such, they cannot simply be governed by enterprise personnel management, or even top management, for that matter. Societally specific types of socialization into roles, careers, labour markets and occupations are interdependent with organizational structures and practices. This interdependence very much gives organizing a societal, and therefore also environmental, flavour.

The difference between contexts and environments is better understood if the difference between the two meanings of organization is borne in mind. Contexts are located on the inside of organizations as collectivities, or on their boundaries, but outside the ambit of organizational properties. Environments, however, are located outside the organization as a collectivity.

The essence of organization theories lies primarily in the relationships between organization structures and processes on the one hand and contexts and environments on the other. Certain structures and processes thrive in specific contexts and environments, and others in different ones. Specifically, well-matched contexts, environments and organizational properties are often considered to be a prime condition of success (Mintzberg 1983). The selection of specific contexts and environments basically constitutes an enterprise *strategy*.

Whether you reduce or increase the size of an organization appreciably, or change its products, technology or controlling interests (contextual changes), or enter new markets, or create subsidiaries elsewhere (environmental changes), you do in most of these cases make strategic moves. To a large extent, the literature on strategy is an outgrowth of the organizational literature. Basically, strategy making and implementation has come to be identified as the central link between the organization, its organizational properties and contexts and environments.

After these clarifications, it is easier to explain what is particular about organizations and what distinguishes them from entities like families and complete societies. First, organizations, as collectivities, have reasonably clear boundaries; one can distinguish non-members from members and things within the domain of the organization from those without. They distinguish internal forms of capital, machines, buildings, information and types of behaviour from external forms. Where blurred boundaries occur, as in the 'open systems' mentioned by Scott (1981: 22–3), it may be that the membership role is poorly defined: membership fluctuates and it is not always clear which types of behaviour belong within the organizational domain. Civic action groups are an example of this.

Nevertheless, where boundaries are drawn too generously, there is a strong sensitivity. Members of such characteristically open and ambiguous organizations do not mind the openness as long as the organization does not encroach on the rest of their life. In modern societies with pluralist political systems, most of the time and with regard to most of their members, organizations only care about what happens inside their domain. They do not care about their members' leisure, family life and political persuasion. However, the contrary may apply in societies with pre-modern or totalitarian patterns.

Sensitivity with regard to organizational boundaries is related to another characteristic of modern organizations: their goals and purposes. The domain that is defined in this way usually is specific rather than encompassing. Neither an employee of General Motors, nor a minister in the Methodist Church, nor a nurse in a hospital, nor a corporal in a tank battalion have to ask their superior's permission before marrying, for example. In past decades, however, the contrary was evident in most societies. On the other hand, many organizations do provide marriage counselling, help against drug abuse, kindergartens, sporting or other facilities that are not directly related to the organization's goal. Asian firms are often styled as 'family firms'. Yet, even there, when the employee is encouraged to consider the firm as a type of family and relations at work are very much personalized, it is still true that working life is separated from private life, maybe precisely because the family acts as a cushion for the demands of working life.

Where enterprises, or armies or hospitals, in whichever modern society, take on wider responsibilities, these are usually organized in functionally specific forms. Counselling in the case of alcohol abuse is offered by specialized social workers rather than supervisors regardless of whether it is offered by the firm or the community. Childcare is provided by a kindergarten rather than directly in the office or the factory, and so on. The fact that something is organized overwhelmingly implies that it is imposed on functions and people that become specialized through the very act of organizing. Of course, not everything happens in organizations in the societies we live in, but a very great deal does. Sometimes organizations imply a more encompassing, rather than specific, involvement. Owner-manager families, for example, may be involved in the enterprise to such an extent that the difference between working and family life is minimal. Religious ministers' and battalion commanders' partners are often still expected to furnish services for the community or the battalion free of charge. The social closure of some milieux often goes against the grain of modern organization.

The clear demarcation of an organizational domain is linked to the definition of membership in organizations. This is embodied in personnel rosters, identity cards or similar documents. Members are all those who are officially acknowledged as employed or who are contributing towards the purpose of the organization. Clubs have members that are not employed, but most of the time members contribute work for a wage and are involved in the labour process. Hospitals and educational institutions have patients who are not members but are part of the 'throughput', which is 'processed' to become more healthy, sane or educated, and who leave the organization as a 'product'. Likewise, inmates in prisons should not be counted as members but as throughput and final products, leaving the organization equipped with improved civic virtues or criminal skills. (The latter illustrates that the declared goal of an organization may radically diverge from its factual, or latent, result.)

Our notion of modern organization is very much an 'ideal type' which is found in reality to a limited extent. The partners of many managers, or ministers of religion, or military officers, or nurses and doctors, may become jealous of the organizational involvement of the partner. Companies may examine the private life of managers before giving them promotion or a foreign posting. Unsupportive partners are often considered a career obstacle. Methodist ministers with changing sexual partners arouse conflict in most church communities. But note that such conflict is overwhelmingly due to the expectation that some people ought to define a specific organizational goal as their central interest in life. Even

where there are strong drives to accommodate non-work roles in the organization, there are also strong drives to eliminate sexual harassment and preferential treatment. Watchdogs are increasingly appointed to counteract such tendencies which were the rule in pre-modern or early modern enterprises or other institutions.

As an ideal, but also in reality, organizations have specific goals, members that help achieve them and are most of the time only partially involved, and a reasonably clear demarcation of their own physical, human and financial resources. Specificity of goals is linked to the deployment of overt, visible and formalized organization structures, all of which are linked to the spread of rationality. In principle, rational organization is only possible where a goal is clearly and specifically defined, and other goals are, within the organizational domain, subordinated to it or relegated to other organizations or to other spheres of life. There are, of course, different types of organizations.

Scott (1981) has conceptualized organizations as implying three kinds of systemic properties. Systems are, generally speaking, integrated sets of elements that are both differentiated and linked by strong interrelationships. They are, therefore, reasonably complex internally and demarcated from their environment. But they also sustain themselves through the interrelationships which they have with their environment. Systems are found in nature, technology and human life. There are economic, social and political systems. In organizational life, specific and stable goals imply 'rational systems'; specific and shifting or changeable goals imply 'natural systems'; ambiguous goals and membership involvement imply 'open systems'. These tend to have different sets of organization structures and processes.

2 Characteristics of organization behaviour

After clarifying the meanings of organization, it is possible to sketch what organization behaviour is all about as an academic subject and a field of study. This consists of the behaviour of organizations and of people in organizations. Behaviour for this purpose includes mental behaviour, such as thinking, feeling or imagining. While the notion of behaviour is usually restricted to living species, it is also used with regard to organizations, without implying that these behave in the same way as humans or animals. Of course, there would not be any organization behaviour without human behaviour.

Organization behaviour looks at the following manifestations of behaviour:

- the mental attitudes, values, preferences and inclinations of individuals;
- the behaviour of individuals in the way they handle physical objects, information and social encounters;
- the behaviour of groups, teams and other face-to-face groupings such as cliques of friends;
- the behaviour of organized units such as departments, divisions, firms or larger concerns;
- the behaviour of networks of sets of organizations;
- the behaviour of organizational contexts and environments, for example, the evolution of technology, markets, competition, governmental regulation, etc.

We cannot simply reduce organization behaviour to individual human behaviour. The outcome of conflict between individuals in organizations, for example, may be decided by distributions of power, information or other resources, or by contextual or environmental structures. Such factors are not reducible to individual behaviour. They refer to arrangements and processes at a supra-individual level which may, naturally, have implications at the level of individuals. To some extent seemingly objective arrangements or distributions depend on subjective and inter-subjective 'enactment'. But even in this case individual behaviour is rooted in structures which refer to supra-individual levels (Giddens 1986). Furthermore, organization behaviour is in no way meant to have a 'behaviouristic' prejudice, although that may

well have been so at the beginning, when the term started to be used.

The term came into existence in the beginning of the 1960s when several sub-disciplines that were relevant for the explanation of what happens in and between organizations and between organizations and their contexts and environments were grouped together. A historical treatment of the field makes it abundantly clear that organization behaviour has been derived from disciplines such as industrial engineering, the sociology of work and organization, social psychology, business studies, administrative science and law. In addition, some of these disciplines have arisen in different forms under specific national constellations. The resulting complexity of organization behaviour as an international field is daunting. Some pioneers, who are defined more by their practical experience and autodidactic insights, are hard to slot into an academic discipline.

Using this historical approach, the subject unusually appears as cross-, trans- or multi-disciplinary. It is marked by human and social sciences, engineering, economics, business studies and law, all wrapped into one. Such a basis makes one wonder whether it is at all possible to provide a fairly coherent treatment of the field. The answer is 'yes', despite many impressions to the contrary. Conceptually, and in comparison to most other specialities in human and social sciences, organization behaviour is probably one of the most integrated subjects, having a strong empirical foundation. This was probably helped by the fact that pioneers of the field, such as Max Weber, Henri Fayol, Frederick W. Taylor and Chester Barnard (see TAYLOR, F.W.), or of the socio-technical school, such as Fred Emery, Eric Trist, E.J. Miller and A.K. Rice, were very keen systematizers (Pugh and Hickson 1989: 210–17). In addition, the orientation of the problem and the focus which this provided helped to erase the disciplinary differences which earlier academic training and specialization tended to bring about. The writings of Hofstede, Mintzberg (1983), Tannenbaum or Heller, for example, do not suggest immediately that they are engineers by training and, in part, job experience (see LEADERSHIP).

As might be expected in any field that is concerned with evolving, living and – worst of all – human phenomena, there is no absence of controversy and conflicting approaches. Organization behaviour is certainly under tension from the pull that is being exerted in different directions. Yet there is increasing agreement regarding the legitimacy of some countervailing forces and conceptual differences. The subject has moved beyond the point where proponents of countervailing approaches have thought it desirable to attack the opposition.

Organization behaviour is a subject which branches out in many different directions. On the one hand, through its psychological and sociological foundations, it is keen to explain organizational phenomena, as is any other 'basic' discipline. As such, it is concerned with the way in which the organizational world actually is, rather than the way it ought to be. On the other hand, the subject is, through inspiration from both practising engineers and managers from humanistically concerned scholars, decidedly normative, or keen to pronounce on the way organization ought to be fashioned and improved. However, criteria for evaluating what is best or better may differ. Efficiency, effectiveness, profits, added value, market growth, employee satisfaction and use and development of human capacities (personal growth) are all used in different combinations and accentuations. Add to this the differences between organization paradigms, and the result is a fairly complex set of approaches.

The way such different approaches relate to each other, and the ways in which they may even be intertwined despite conceptual differences, is now understood better and may be debated without acrimony. Despite the differences which will always exist between scholarly theory and everyday practice, it is fair to say that a good level of applicability of organization behaviour has been maintained despite the increasing academicization. This conflicts with the image that is frequently projected by many practitioners. Businessmen scoffed for decades at concepts like work in groups (see GROUPS AND TEAMS) and job enrichment until they started to be sold by consultants under a new trend called 'lean production'. They earlier derided discussion of organization culture (see ORGANIZATION CULTURE), but adopted the theories when consultants started selling 'organizational excellence'.

It is a frequent experience in the history of organization behaviour that practitioners may be particularly gullible victims of organizational fashions, to the extent that they have not previously read or understood sound organization behaviour theory and research. For instance, the enthusiasm about 'excellent organizations' largely meant that people had not bothered to grasp and apply standard organization behaviour concepts which had been known for up to thirty years. To learn from this experience requires a continuous two-way dialogue between theory/research and practice.

3 Subdivisions of organization behaviour

The overall field of organization behaviour is often broken down into two parts: organization theory and organization behaviour. This is slightly confusing because organization behaviour is also used to refer to the whole field. In the more narrow sense, it refers to the behaviour of people in organizations. Organization theory refers to theory and findings about the behaviour of complete organizations. This distinction indicates that the level of analysis can be used to subdivide the whole field. Theories and findings can be specialized according to the analytical level, which is a level of aggregation. Throughout organizational life there is this vertical dimension which stretches from the single individual to aggregations of complete organizations. Somewhere in the middle we have what is called the 'focal organization': a more or less self-contained organized unit with a reasonable measure of autonomy and a collective identity which makes it the primary reference point for all its members.

To give an example, a tank battalion, a medium-sized owner-managed firm or a local hospital may be salient focal organizations. Their members may conceive themselves, in the first instance, as belonging to this unit, and they will expect the unit to maintain its identity, boundaries and autonomy in the face of its environment. The matter is much less clear in the case of a larger concern like General Motors. This larger industrial group has big local sub-organizations in countries outside the USA, such as Vauxhall in the UK and Opel in Germany. The latter operate under their own company and brand names and have different plants with individual identities. These are all tied into the international group via a complex hierarchy of subdivisions. In this case there is no immediately visible focal organization. There are competing sets of boundaries and identities in the shape of the brand name, the locality or a national subsidiary. The larger an organization is, the more there is a tendency for the focal organization to be blurred.

Sometimes management tries to shift the focus and identity of organizations. It may try to get hospitals to see themselves as more independent and responsible, rather than as dependent units of a larger health service (a tendency which can be seen in Europe). Or it may try to unite the identities of car workers in the bigger concern, by emphasizing the 'GM' label next to divisional (Oldsmobile, Chevrolet, etc.) and subsidiary (Vauxhall, Opel) labels. Sometimes both tendencies occur parallel with one other. Military forces in many countries have seen a proliferation of unit or service badges, berets, caps, etc., after the onslaught of standardization of rules and dress. This adds to the difficulty of defining empirically exactly what is the focal organization identity.

In many cases it is better to speak of complex sets of organizations that are hierarchically and laterally intertwined (Aldrich and Whetten 1981). In such an arrangement most organizational units have different measures of autonomy, self-containment and a collective sense of identity. A discussion of the vertical or hierarchical dimensions of such organizational sets helps to demonstrate the implications of such interlocking for organization behaviour analysis.

At the lowest level, that of the working individual, we find that organization behaviour is the study and explanation of work attitudes, motivation and satisfaction, cognition or perception in work roles and beyond (see MOTIVATION AND SATISFACTION). To some extent the individual brings such properties with his or herself when entering the organization, but they also evolve with the experience of working in, or contributing to, the organization. Individual factors interact with the situation in which the individual finds his or herself, in which they become socialized and try to adapt the situation to suit personal tastes and requirements. Matching individual and work context is one of the primary concerns of personnel/human resource management (see PERSONNEL MANAGEMENT; HUMAN RESOURCE MANAGEMENT).

The next analytical level is that of face-to-face groups. In groups and teams organization members meet, cooperate, quarrel and build personal friendships or allegiances (see GROUPS AND TEAMS). They have a dynamic of their own and evolve properties that are not simply the average of individual properties. Individuals influence group and team life but they themselves also become modified by the dynamics that develop in face-to-face groupings. Groups and teams are central ingredients in the coordination and control of organization processes. They are important both in informal and formal organization structures. Management both encourages and obstructs the formation of groups and teams, depending on different contexts, perceptions and policies.

Above the aggregation and analytical level of face-to-face groups things are more complicated. A small hospital may consist of a few interlocking groups, above which a clearly identifiable focal organization is the next and most important unit. However, in a company like General Motors or in a large military service there is instead a complicated web of sub-components which is hard to typify according to a generally applicable scheme. Terms like department, shop, site, establishment, battalion, regiment, brigade, division, business unit, faculty or others are used depending on the line of activity an organization is in and the level of aggregation.

Sometimes it is hard to say whether we are dealing with inter-organizational relations or organization networks, or with sub-components of a self-contained organization. As suggested above this is due to the difficulty in identifying a truly focal organization. Where the focal organization evaporates, it is appropriate to analyse organizational sets, inter-organizational relations and networks. Sometimes these are controlled from a centre and, where this happens, a common organizational goal and identity can be said to exist. But, even in industrial groups, business units or divisions or subsidiaries may compete with each other rather than cooperate.

Some subdivisions include various levels of aggregation and specialize in thematic aspects of organizational life. Managerial behaviour, leadership, labour process, cognition, organizational learning and decision making are clear examples. For some purposes such a distinction is impractical.

Organizational sets may feature different amounts of common goal orientation, coordination and control of activities and different identities. 'Industrial districts' are an example of interlinked firms that are formally independent of one another but which may share a number of pooled functions, such as research and development, marketing, education, training or maintenance; or they are inter-linked firms in the industrial chain. The linkages between organizations in the set may be strongly competitive, cooperative or quasi-absent. Where focal organizations share at least a product market, the term 'organizational populations' increasingly has come to be used: societies and economies become populated by organizations and types of organizations in the same way that the earth becomes populated by biological species. Note, however, that different focal organizations may well compete fiercely in their task environment (in the same market) while cooperating in their general environment, for example by setting up a common training scheme. But they may also cooperate in their task environment; oil companies that compete nevertheless tend to set up and operate common pipeline systems.

Organizations tend to spawn other organizations. Part of this phenomenon is the formation of interest associations by various firms and public corporations. Examples are employers' associations, industry and professional organizations, chambers of industry and commerce, guilds and other more specific organizations dedicated to particular missions and purposes. Private individuals also set up organizations. These do not produce or sell anything but are intimately involved in economic organizational life and constitute an important part of the environment for industrial and service firms. Trade unions are the most obvious example (see TRADE UNIONS). Furthermore, organizations set up 'daughter' organizations. Ours are organizational societies where, even if you want to work against organizations, you are likely to set up another organization. More recently, some people have tried to counteract this trend by setting up social movements, more 'open systems' with more ambiguous goals, less demarcated boundaries, unhierarchical structures, more free-floating coordination and less formally circumscribed responsibilities. Even these tend to be subject to modern organizational drift.

The high organization of organizational environments leads us to the phenomenon of institutionalization. Organizational sets and populations are part of, and embedded in, institutionalized relationships with other organized actors. For the purposes of economic life, the world of such institutionalized relationships and sets is captured by the literature on business systems. Organizing, in the sense of endowing social behaviour with organizational properties, implies institutionalization. Sellers encounter organized customers and organized patterns of demand. Recruiting firms face institutionalized producers of skills and knowledge such as schools and colleges. Product and service markets are often highly regulated. Even de-regulated airlines have to succumb to safety regulations and air traffic control.

This demonstrates that, as well as vertically integrated organization sets, at each level of aggregation, there are institutions which are part of the task and the general environment of units. They extend right into the context of organization. For example, work safety regulations imposed by governments have to be internalized and implemented. This has led to the visualization of organization itself as institutionalized. It is filled with institutions that are specific not to focal organizations but to local, regional or societal entities. Institutionalization is a highly salient concept in the literature on the process of organizing. This sets a counterpoint to theories that have been highlighted above. The idea is that goals, structures, boundaries and other patterns are not as fixed as mainstream organization theory pretends. They are modified and developed in an unending process whereby individuals and systems interact to bring forth fluctuating and evolving patterns.

Institutionalization therefore is not only linked with rigidity of patterns but with their ambiguity and constant modification. Where the literature on structure emphasizes neat systems and predictable actors, the literature on the process of organizing stresses unpredictable actors and unruly systems. Institutionalization brings in conflict, contradictions, power, ideology and politics as very important traits of organizational life. Blurred, fluctuating goals imply power, conflict and politics. Again, this applies to analyses at all the levels of aggregation. Essentially this means that organizations are only imperfectly explained as 'systems'. The systems aspect of organizations emphasizes that behaviour is informed by clear system goals. This is only partially true. Actors in organizations have, in addition, goals such as furthering their own well-being or career, or those of friends and specific colleagues, or the well-being of interests outside the organization. Hence, actors are not simply like wheels in an organizational machine; they are also to some extent likely to 'throw a spanner in the works'. This is why organizations have to be considered as entities in which opposing parties wrangle for power and influence and strike compromises. This aspect indicates that organizational life may be orientated by goals different from the systemic goals (Lammers 1993: 24–32).

The political character of organizational life extends across all levels of analysis. Individuals operate politically in groups and other face-to-face contacts, to accommodate their interests and further their personal aims. Groups wrangle and form coalitions with other groups. Departmentally, divisionally or professionally specific segments do likewise. Organizational units, in addition, have reference points in the organizational context or environment. They are dedicated or opposed to specific strategies, stakeholders, customers and markets. They maintain certain professional, industrial or industrial relations standards. They may be linked to interests in the governmental sphere. The analytically sharp boundary between the organizational unit and its environment is, in everyday life, more like a revolving door than a wall and many transfers and transactions occur across this boundary; of people with their preferences and values, of various sorts of information and of behavioural and institutional routines. Such routines are anchored in collectivities which cross-cut the organized unit in question. However, such units do not passively absorb influences from outside the organization but interact with actors and systems within their own environment, helping to fashion it in a more active way.

Interaction between contexts, environments and organization structure and process is endemic to subdivisions such as business systems, organization culture, organization development, innovation and change, managerial behaviour, decision making, cognition, agency, markets and hierarchies, organization types, technology, labour process, information and knowledge and organizational learning. Current research in organization theory can be described as imbued with a drive to identify and analyse intense interaction and correspondence between contextual, environmental and organizational properties.

Whichever way organizational units are demarcated (large or small), and whichever side of organizational life is considered, analysis of such *correspondences* is a widespread and powerful tool. Theories elaborating on this are usually called contingency theories. A lot may be learned about the functioning of groups by looking at their tasks, technology, product range and variation, size, and control and management systems. There are also contingency theories for leadership and decision making (see LEADERSHIP; DECISION MAKING). Focal organizations are shown to be designed in conjunction with contingencies such as size, task structures, technology and environmental variables (Mintzberg 1983). One of the most important series of research studies has brought forth a theory on general relationships between organization structure, its context and environment (Pugh and Hickson 1989: 16–23). Contingency arguments are also applicable to the design of conglomerates or networks but the importance attached to market structures and external institutions tends to be greater if the analytical focus is moved from the individual to sets of organizations.

On the other hand, correspondences of these types are not uncontroversial. There is a great deal of empirical proof for the opposing principle, functional *equivalence* or *equifinality* (Child 1972). This quite simply means that different sorts of internal arrangements are perfectly compatible with identical contextual or environmental states. This principle goes against the idea of a quasi-ideal 'match', which is inherent to the principle of correspondence. Whereas correspondence theory suggests that rigid and bureaucratic structures are not a good match for volatile and shifting product markets, equifinality theorists claim that it may very well turn out to be a good match, but only if the level and diversity of competence in the workforce is large and organization culture produces motivated and flexible actors.

The diligent reader, scholar and practitioner is well advised to make judicious and eclectic use of both, opposed, perspectives. To some extent and in specific situations correspondence works well, and for other problems and questions, equifinality is the better one. The literature on performance emphasizes correspondence theory, explaining performance by tight matching, or the 'fit', of environments, contexts, structures and processes. Against that, the consideration of poor performance shows that organizations survive very well, notwithstanding poor fit.

A subdivision of increasing importance, that of organizational populations, is concerned with the way environmental 'niches' get populated by organization types. This terminology has been transferred from population ecology, a speciality within biology. At the centre of this field of study are larger sets of organizations, the focal organization being more peripheral. Furthermore, it is often assumed, in line with the literature on decline and failure, that organizations are typically inelastic, not really capable of achieving fit by their own actions, whether this is pro-active or reactive. However, to date there is not much organizational population research of sufficient depth in matters of organization forms and processes. Yet, this approach rightly highlights the role played by environmental 'selection', whereby 'fit' between environmental and organizational characteristics may indeed emerge.

Again, two perspectives have to be combined. On the one hand, all organizations are inelastic, clinging to established ways of doing things. Their identity would be blurred if everything was in flux all the time. Organizations need stable routines, otherwise goal-directed coordination would be impossible. But they can achieve good performance despite this inelasticity, and for a very simple reason: according to the equifinality principle one can make do, under varying circumstances, with basically similar organizational tools. On the other hand, there is, in organizational as in biological life, a persistent random variation of the genetic – in our case socioeconomic – heritage. Thus the environment can be imagined to select those variations that show acceptable or good fit and weed out those that do not.

Such considerations get us involved at levels of analysis above the focal organization. Subdivisions in organization behaviour cannot only be divided up on the basis of criteria like the level of aggregation or the substance of organizational life covered. In addition, there are subdivisions of the field due to the type of theoretical approach put forward.

Another criterion for demarcating subdivisions relates to the specific goals or products of organizations. Much of current general organization behaviour theory has been derived from evidence from industrial, service, financial or commercial organizations. Such organizations are often exposed to competition and particular criteria of performance. The latter usually consist of profitability, efficiency, productiveness, effectiveness, product quality, added value, market share, growth and returns on invested capital in various combinations. Alongside such criteria and their consequences for theory and findings are fields with different or quasi-absent performance criteria. A notable field is that of public sector organization, which has differing mixes of performance criteria.

Such organizations often hold protected monopolies and are instruments of the body politic. Therefore, criteria like political conformity, predictability, standardization of behaviour and transparency may be more important than performance in the commercial and economic sense. However, it has also become clear that the ossification of larger enterprises has reduced the difference with regard to public organization practice; more recently, there has also been a drive in many countries to make public organizations operate according to competitive and commercial criteria and to change their structures and behaviour accordingly. Thus, there is a lot of to-and-fro between the different domains, which increases the salience of organization behaviour theory in the public administration domain.

A classic theorist, Max Weber, underlined the importance of military and bureaucratic patterns in setting the organizational tone for commerce, finance and industry. This has taken place to an extent which is often unknown. For example, the doctrine of 'management by objectives', which became a buzzword in industrial and commercial management in the 1960s, dates back to the principle of *Auftragstaktik* (tactical operations by objectives) that was introduced into the Prussian Army in the first half of the last century. In return, evidence shows that officers in the military are encouraged by their education

and training to adopt methods and postures from management and organizational experiences outside the military.

Some fields emphasize the investigation of different organizations at one point in time whereas others emphasize the study of organization over time. This latter view is very much concentrated in fields such as organizational populations, organizational evolution, organization development, innovation and change, the process of organizing, decision making and organizational learning. Other fields are more likely to feature the former, but the distinction is far from clear-cut. Appeals to increase the number of studies that are diachronic are a feature of much of the literature.

Taking an overview of the topic, it can be seen that the entire field of organization behaviour is subdivided by criteria stressing:

• the level of aggregation and analysis
• specific aspects of organizational life
• goal-, product- or service-related specificities
• criteria of performance in organizational domains
• particular approaches to theory-building
• synchronic or diachronic perspectives

Chapter headings of standard textbooks are mostly rather untidy combinations of such criteria. However, it is impossible to arrange organization behaviour in a fashion which is as tidy as the organizational chart of a tank battalion. Here, we have tried to make the systematization as tidy as possible but, in reality, the picture of the discipline is more akin to that of a software consultancy, with a messy division of labour. There still exist ambiguities, overlaps and inconsistencies but this has made it possible to preserve the closeness of organization behaviour to real organizational life.

4 Types of theory

The paradoxical nature of organization behaviour has already been mentioned. Attempts to augment the logical consistency of a theory which is endemic to all scientific activity leads to a reduction, or covering up, of paradox. Hence, a counter-theory to any existing theory is a logical necessity in any regime which simultaneously has to come to grips with paradox and to expel it. This conflict may even be described as the methodologically necessary climax to paradox.

The simple but important consequence is that knowledge and mastery of different organization paradigms are central. Paradigms are one-sided views of the real world. The necessity for conflicting paradigms to exist is a consequence of simultaneous attempts to take account of and to expel – under the ruling norms of scholarly discourse – the pervasive phenomenon of paradoxicality. However, even conflicting paradigms can be predicated upon another in a novel form, such that new paradigms emerge that displace older ones. Seen in this way the co-existence of paradigms is not as bewildering as it may appear at first sight. It is a normal ingredient of reasonable discourse, research and theory-building.

In different paradigms different types of theory are represented and combined. Types of organization behaviour theory can be distinguished according to two criteria. The first criterion is the *substantive foundation of explanations*. Theories aim to explain reasons for events, forms and developments. They can be distinguished according to the kinds of reasons they provide; that is, which groups of substantive factors they refer to. According to this first criterion, the first class of theories in organization behaviour consists of *utilitarian theories* (Mintzberg 1983). These explain organizational life with reference to the usefulness of events, forms and developments. This is the case where organization is explained through its potential to meet requirements or opportunities in the organizational context or in the environment. Every time that organizational properties are explained by their match with goals, contexts, environments, and strategies, and by their profitability, efficiency or effectiveness under such contexts and environments, this is utilitarian theory. Such a theory is invariably founded upon a type of behaviour that rationally (by the conscious evaluation of different outcomes and courses of action) or by trial and error is geared to maximize or satisfy utilitarian

ambitions. The type of utility may differ however. Such conflict is underlined by the *behavioural theory of the firm* (Cyert and March 1963), which is one of the cornerstones of organization behaviour.

The second class of theories are *institutional theories*. Institutions are relatively stable and typified patterns in the social fabric of society or in networks of social interaction. With institutional theories the usefulness of organizational arrangements is secondary. Things are done a certain way because institutionalized norms or rules suggest courses of action, either explicitly or implicitly. The legitimacy of a specific institution, including all institutionalized patterns of behaviour, may be separate from its relative utilitarian value (Meyer and Rowan 1977). To paraphrase Abraham Lincoln: some people manage to be utilitarian all of the time, most people are utilitarian some of the time, but not all people can be utilitarian all of the time. Usually, utilitarian orientations can survive to the extent that they are embedded in a context which is thick with institutions.

Third is *culturalist theory* (see ORGANIZATION CULTURE). This is concerned with values, preferences, meaningful symbols and mental programmes in the widest sense. It is the mental programming of acting individuals that matters. Under such an approach usefulness is also secondary, but it crops up as a function of the mentioned preferences and values. Culturalist theorists stress the fact that utilities differ according to classes of actors and that such classes of actors are differentiated by different processes of socialization. Culturalists also tend to look at institutions as reducible to individual mental programmes. While they do not go against notions of utility and institutionalization in principle, they do reiterate their cultural relativity.

Utilitarian theories tend to have a strong economic or business administration element. Institutionalist theories have strong sociological, social anthropological or political science roots. Culturalist theories are bound up with psychology or anthropology. However, such distinctions are far from clear-cut. Organization behaviour theorizing tends to combine foundations of the utilitarian, institutionalist and culturalist kinds. Accents are placed differently in each theoretical approach. Theories which explain organizational life with reference to the characteristics of a capitalist or socialist order feature a blend of utilitarian and institutionalist approaches. There may also be a blend of institutionalist and culturalist arguments, such as in the explanation for the commitment of employees in Japanese organizations (Lincoln and Kalleberg 1992). Last but not least, there is a blend of utilitarian and culturalist approaches, for instance in the links established between Calvinist or Buddhist beliefs, entrepreneurship and economic success (see ORGANIZATION CULTURE).

Note that utilitarian, institutionalist and culturalist theories are not simply alternatives. They do not compete only with one another but are systematically intertwined – or can be. All human behaviour, including organization behaviour, is impossible to imagine as guided by utilitarian, institutionalist or culturalist considerations only. Economic research and theory show that utilitarian considerations are shaped by mentalities and social institutions. This was the basic idea behind the groundbreaking contribution of Cyert and March (1963) when they conceived the behavioural theory of the firm. Sociological research and theory has shown that institutions, although at least partly autonomous with regard to utilitarian criteria, are also legitimated or created because of their utility in maintaining the coherence and survival of larger collectivities. This is the essence of the structural–functionalist school in the social sciences. Such reflections essentially tell us that these three theory types are predicated upon one another.

In simple terms this means the following. Institutions and mentalities are very utilitarian (useful) things. A specific institution may exist without being concerned about its utility, but utility cannot be achieved without institutions. Unbridled and one-sided emphasis of utilitarian motives is ruinous for the achievement of a utility as it leads to disorientation and anarchy. Utilitarian considerations themselves need institutions and mentalities to be cultivated. Cultural mentalities interact with institutions, and they are similarly useful in guiding human action through an overly complex world. An artificial behavioural repertoire of cultural attitudes and institutions limits purely utilitarian behavioural choice, but the restriction of behavioural choice which is thereby achieved also makes utilitarian action possible. We try to arrive at 'satisficing' solutions which, although not necessarily the best, are satisfactory within cultural and institutional bounds, and such bounds are not only restrictive but also 'enabling'. In the wake of the classic work by March and Simon (1958) the emergent idea was that rationality is always 'bounded', that is, confined to a more narrowly circumscribed area; unbounded rationality would quite simply amount to irrationality.

There is another class of theory types based on epistemological criteria. *Epistemology* is concerned with the theory of knowledge, providing an explanation of the background from which systems of knowledge, particularly scientific systems, emerge. One school has argued that the highlight of science is the construction of *nomothetic theories*. Such theories posit generally valid statements about relations between independent phenomena. The logic of such statements implies propositions in the form: 'if A happens, this will be associated with B', or 'if A happens, this will lead to B'. Mainstream organization theory, for example, argues that environmental and contextual properties, such as the variability of the task environment, and organizational characteristics, are interdependent. Another central finding is that the increasing size of an organization is associated with greater hierarchical, departmental and professional differentiation. Such nomothetic theories, usually conceived according to the epistemology of natural sciences, are easier to construct if the emphasis is placed on a specific class of substantive factors, whether utilitarian, institutional or cultural.

There also exists a tradition of *idiographic theory*. Idiography means the depiction of what is specific to individual things or people, and it illuminates phenomena that deviate from generally established theories. It focuses on phenomena that are specific to industrial sectors, products, societies or enterprises.

Note that idiographic treatments may again construct arguments that are utilitarian, institutionalist or culturalist. All these perspectives may provide reasons for deviations from generally established patterns. High organizational simplicity in a large organizational unit, as an exemplary deviant phenomenon, can be explained by the attitudes of ruling elites in the organization (culture), professional roles rooted in training systems and labour markets (institutions), or overhead cost-cutting (utilitarian considerations).

Both of these theory types aim at statements which are, ideally, free from contradictions. This kind of logical streamlining and empirical corroboration are the idealistic goals of what is often called 'positivistic' theory-building. Positivism has come to be a word with a derogatory meaning through its usage by opponents of such methodological currents but, unfortunately, there is no other convenient neutral word available for use.

Lammers (1978) put forward nomothetic and idiographic theory as the two basic variants of theory-building in comparative organization theory. Other scholars argue that this classification is not exhaustive or complete. Reality usually discounts a single-minded reference to one class of substantive factors only and forces theorists to employ approaches that at least partly contradict each other. Thus, nomothetic theories with the same epistemological foundation, but stressing different explanations, cannot be reconciled under a theory programme which stresses logical consistency. In addition, the tension between nomothetic and idiographic accounts of reality generates inconsistencies in the larger body of theory.

There is a necessity for a third epistemological type, *dialectical theory*. Essentially this is the acknowledgement, rather than avoidance, of conflicting and contradictory statements. In a positivistic statement a phenomenon may only be classed as A or non-A: a third possibility is ruled out. In dialectical theory, the opposite applies: a phenomenon may be classed as both A and non-A.

Consider a simple example. There are different approaches to explaining Japanese organization and employment practices

(Lincoln and Kalleberg 1992). One school argues that these have grown out of societally specific values and institutions that predate the modernization and industrialization of Japan and that such practices cannot be explained by the task environment, only by the cultural and institutional environment of organizing, entrepreneurship and industrial relations.

Other scholars argue that such practices are, in fact, perfectly rational and utilitarian responses to the industrial and labour market situation of that country. They represent solutions which can also be found elsewhere and which increasingly are being propagated in many countries. These conflicting views can be simplified as one of the importance of task environmental versus cultural and institutional factors. It can be seen how such a conflict is linked to the prevalence of positivistic theory-building. Within a dialectical approach it would be possible to argue that organization and employment practices are, in fact, the conjoint result of task, cultural and institutional factors: although such environments must be looked at independently of each other, the effect of a particular environment has to be explained by its predication upon another type of environment. Thus, the admission that both non-A (independence) and A (reciprocal interdependence) apply. Dialectic theorists would be particularly prevalent in fields such as the process of organizing, power, conflict and politics, and cognition.

Positivistic theorists, however, would counter this view by arguing that logical contradictions are impossible to sustain, and they would try to find out under which conditions precisely factors are independent and under which other conditions they are interdependent. This would be an attempt to suspend contradictions by advancing nomothetic theory-building. Stalwarts of both nomothetic and dialectical theory-building would look at such an attempt by the 'opposite' side to extend its domain with strong misgivings. The sharpness of some academic debates can only be explained by feelings of being threatened, on your own substantive 'patch', by the encroachment of people who lay claim to this patch or part of it: academics are able to live with the plurality of epistemological approaches only if no-one trespasses.

Students should remember that competition between different organization paradigms and approaches is the central ingredient of academic innovation. There is no harm in trying to 'dialecticize' a nomothetic theory or in trying to 'nomotheticize' a theory framed in dialectical terms. Where there is no one single valid dogma students should be prepared to live with different paradigms and epistemological foundations. Besides, in the last instance the reconciliation of opposing approaches happens pragmatically rather than dogmatically, research, instruction and discourse in actual practice being a very pragmatic affair. This works because we operate without one single and lasting epistemological foundation. In the same way that people in organizations have 'tacit' (not formally and coherently expressed) knowledge, so does the coherence of academic discourse arise from a tacit understanding rather than the application of a formally laid-down and logically consistent theory of scientific activity.

As a consequence, students and practitioners are not well advised to absorb and try to apply theory as if it was a dogma. Organizational practice is not a technocratic affair where a received wisdom can be monopolized by specialists in the field. Organization behaviour practitioners will have to select, specify, recombine and modify theories which they find in the literature in an active way. The evaluation of organizational experimentation bears out the fact that practice has always been to a large extent autonomous with regard to organization behaviour theory. There is an important element of trial and error and adaptation to locally specific ambitions and perceived requirements involved (Warner 1981). This means that practitioners who demand intellectual grounding and the refinement of what they do will have to be theory-builders and researchers themselves, at least to some extent, if they are to expound a rationale.

Some of the leading theorists and researchers of organization behaviour have been eminent practitioners themselves. Obvious examples are Frederick W. Taylor, Henri Fayol and Chester Barnard, to name some pioneers. In return, parts of organizational practice such as organization development, team or group work, quality circles and lean production, which have become available in very practical easy to follow forms, rest on eminent theoretical and research foundations, such as the social psychology of Kurt Lewin or the sociotechnical school.

Most organization behaviour authors and practitioners will not realistically see themselves as a business leader and pioneering scholar rolled into one. But they may all realistically aspire to a tentative emulation, on a more modest scale, of an ideal: an ideal that aspires to the closest possible integration of practice, theory and research. However, this must be followed in a way which does not confuse and compromise business and academic goals: scholarly rectitude is not the only thing that makes organization behaviour theories useful. The practical value of theories may be founded not on their factual corroboration and logical consistency, but on their ideology, short-sightedness and manipulative character. A differentiation between practical and scholarly roles is, therefore, a necessity.

ARNDT SORGE
TILBURG UNIVERSITY

Further reading

(References cited in the text marked *)

* Aldrich, H. and Whetten, D.A. (1981) 'Organization-sets, action-sets, and networks: making the most of simplicity', in P.C. Nystrom and W.H. Starbuck (eds), *Handbook of Organizational Design*, vol. 1, Oxford: Oxford University Press. (Fundamental conceptualization of sets of organizations and their interrelations.)

* Child, J. (1972) 'Organizational structure, environment and performance: the role of strategic choice', *Sociology* 6 (1): 1–22. (Important article about the difference between contingency theory and functional equivalence principles linked with strategic choice.)

Crozier, M. and Friedberg, E. (1977) *L'acteur et le système* (Actors and Systems), Paris: Editions du Seuil. (A central conceptualization of organization theory, with reciprocal interaction of actor and system constructions as an important ingredient.)

* Cyert, R.M. and March, J.G. (1963) *A Behavioral Theory of the Firm*, Englewood Cliffs, NJ: Prentice Hall. (A classic and still informative work that argues that business behaviour is governed by the normal principles of human behaviour.)

Daft, R.L. (1992) *Organization Theory and Design*, 4th edn, St Paul, MN: West Publishing Co. (Probably the best basic textbook in the field, with an emphasis on structure and design and featuring many examples and exercises.)

* Giddens, A. (1986) *The Constitution of Society*, Berkeley, CA: University of California Press. (A general social theory text which intertwines individualistic and structuralist perspectives under 'structuration theory'.)

Hackman, J.R., Lawler, E.E. and Porter, L.W. (eds) (1983) *Perspectives on Behavior in Organizations*, 2nd edn, New York: McGraw-Hill. (A volume with fifty-seven important readings from the whole field of organization behaviour. Probably the best edited volume of its kind; very useful at intermediate levels of instruction.)

Hellriegel, D., Slocum, J.W. and Woodman, R.W. (1992) *Organizational Behaviour*, 6th edn, St Paul, MN: West Publishing Co. (A well-known introductory text which is particularly strong on the psychological and socio-psychological aspects of organization behaviour. Includes cases and exercises.)

* Lammers, C. (1978) 'The comparative sociology of organizations', *Annual Review of Sociology* 4: 458–510. (Derives nomothetic and idiographic approaches in organization behaviour from the philosophy of the social sciences.)

* Lammers, C. (1993) *Organiseren van bovenop en van onderop. Een beknopte inleiding in de organisatiesociologie*, Utrecht: Het spectrum. (A stimulating introduction to the sociology of organization. Strong on nationally different streams in organization behaviour and a source for an important typology.)

* Lincoln, J.A. and Kalleberg, A.L. (1992) *Culture, Control and Commitment: A Study of Work Organization and Work Attitudes in the United States and Japan*, Cambridge: Cambridge University Press. (A methodologically intriguing comparison which goes against stereotypes of how and why attitudes and behaviour are different between Japan and other countries.)

* March, J.G. and Simon, H.A. (1958) *Organizations*, New York: Wiley. (A classic conceptualization of organization behaviour.)

* Meyer, J.W. and Rowan, B. (1977) 'Institutionalized organizations: formal structure as myth and ceremony', *American Journal of Sociology* 83: 340–63. (Sketches an institutionalist programme as opposed to systemic and contingency approaches.)

* Mintzberg, H. (1983) *Structure in Fives: Designing Effective Organizations*, Englewood Cliffs, NJ: Prentice Hall. (An original statement of contingency theory in structure and design.)

* Morgan, G. (1986) *Images of Organization*, Newbury Park, CA: Sage Publications. (Presents a whole range of different perspectives on organizations, stressing paradigmatic and conceptual pluralism, and is eminently readable.)

Mullins, L.J. (1989) *Management and Organisational Behaviour*, 2nd edn, London: Pitman. (A good basic textbook with an emphasis on the management and 'behaviour within organizations' aspects of organization behaviour.)

Nystrom, P.C. and Starbuck, W.H. (1981) *Handbook of Organizational Design*, 2 vols, Oxford: Oxford University Press. (Probably the best advanced-level handbook in organization behaviour.)

Perrow, C. (1986) *Complex Organizations: A Critical Essay*, 3rd edn, New York: McGraw-Hill. (A well-written and vivid overview, with an emphasis on the presentation and critique of different approaches in organization structure and design; theoretically committed but balanced, and rich in facts.)

* Pugh, D.S. and Hickson, D.J. (1989) *Writers on Organizations*, 4th edn, Newbury Park, CA: Sage Publications. (Contains the biographies and the main ideas, findings and publications of thirty-six important authors in organization behaviour.)

* Scott, W.R. (1981) *Organizations: Rational, Natural and Open Systems*, Englewood Cliffs, NJ: Prentice Hall. (An important conceptualization of organization theory, stressing the plurality of organization models.)

Thompson, J.D. (1976) *Organization in Action*, New York: McGraw-Hill. (A pioneering statement of organization and administration theory which has been influential and can suggest even today new insights and hypotheses.)

* Warner, M. (1981) 'Organizational experiments and social innovations', in P.C. Nystrom and W.H. Starbuck (eds), *Handbook of Organizational Design*, vol. 1, Oxford: Oxford University Press. (Summarizes the lessons from experiments in the history of organizational design and experimentation.)

See also: DECISION MAKING; GROUPS AND TEAMS; ORGANIZATION CULTURE; TAYLOR, F.W..

Related topics in the IEBM: BARNARD, C.I.; BUSINESS CULTURE, JAPANESE; BUSINESS SYSTEMS; COGNITION; CONFLICT AND POLITICS; CONTEXTS AND ENVIRONMENTS; CO-ORDINATION AND CONTROL; FAYOL, H.; INNOVATION AND CHANGE; INTER-ORGANIZATIONAL RELATIONS; LEWIN, K.; MARCH, J.G. AND CYERT, R.M.; MINTZBERG, H.; ORGANIZATION BEHAVIOUR, HISTORY OF; ORGANIZATION DEVELOPMENT; ORGANIZATION NETWORKS; ORGANIZATION PARADIGMS; ORGANIZATION TYPES; ORGANIZATIONAL DECLINE AND FAILURE; ORGANIZATIONAL EVOLUTION; ORGANIZATIONAL LEARNING; ORGANIZATIONAL PERFORMANCE;ORGANIZATIONAL POPULATIONS;ORGANIZING, PROCESS OF; POWER; PUBLIC SECTOR ORGANIZATIONS; TECHNOLOGY AND ORGANIZATIONS; TRIST, E.L.; WEBER, M.

Organization culture

Overview

The concept of 'organization culture' has become popular since the early 1980s. There is no consensus about its definition but most authors will agree that it is something holistic, historically determined, related to the things anthropologists study, socially constructed, soft and difficult to change. It is something an organization has, but can also be seen as something an organization is.

Organization cultures should be distinguished from national cultures. Cultures manifest themselves, from superficial to deep, in symbols, heroes, rituals and values. National cultures differ mostly on the values level; organization cultures at the levels of symbols, heroes and rituals, together labelled 'practices'.

Differences in national cultures have been studied for over fifty countries. They show five independent dimensions of values: power distance; individualism versus collectivism; masculinity versus femininity; uncertainty avoidance; and long-term versus short-term orientation. National culture differences are reflected in solutions to organization problems in different countries, but also in the validity of management theories in these countries. Different national cultures have different preferred ways of structuring organizations and different patterns of employee motivation. For example, they limit the options for performance appraisal, management by objectives, strategic management and humanization of work.

Research into organization cultures identified six independent dimensions of practices: process-orientated versus results-orientated; job-orientated versus employee-orientated; professional versus parochial; open systems versus closed systems; tightly versus loosely controlled; and pragmatic versus normative. The position of an organization on these dimensions is determined in part by the business or industry the organization is in. Scores on the dimensions are also related to a number of other 'hard' characteristics of the organizations. These lead to conclusions about how organization cultures can be and cannot be managed.

Managing international business means handling both national and organization culture differences at the same time. Organization cultures are somewhat manageable while national cultures are given facts for management; common organization cultures across borders are what keeps multinationals together.

1 The concept of organization culture

The term 'organization culture' (in the USA generally 'organization*al* culture') became popular in the English language around 1980 (Pettigrew 1979; Schein 1985). In the management literature the term '*corporate* culture' is common (Deal and Kennedy 1982). An earlier concept, in use since the 1950s, is 'organization climate'. The difference between 'culture' and 'climate' is a matter of

definition; there is no consensus in the literature. 'Culture' tends to be treated as a long-
range, stable characteristic of an organization
and 'climate' as a shorter range, more changeable characteristic (see ORGANIZATION
BEHAVIOUR).

Since the early 1980s an extensive literature has developed on organization culture
which has also spread to other language areas.
'Culture' has become a fad, among managers,
among consultants and among academics,
with somewhat different concerns. An important role in its popularization was played by a
book by Peters and Waterman (1982), *In
Search of Excellence*. The authors claimed
that excellent US companies were characterized by strong, dominant, coherent cultures in
which 'people way down the line know what
they are supposed to do in most situations because the handful of guiding values is crystal
clear' (1982: 76).

Because of the faddish nature of the concept, the literature on organization culture
consists of a remarkable collection of pep
talks, war stories and some insightful in-depth
case studies. Systematic research is rare; Peters and Waterman's study of 'excellent companies', for example, does not meet academic
standards.

Nevertheless, organization culture has
proven to be more than just a fad. It has gained
its place in organization theory. Organiza-
tion(al)/corporate culture has acquired a
status similar to structure, strategy and
control.

There is no consensus about its definition,
but most authors will probably agree that the
organization(al)/corporate culture concept refers to something that is:

1 holistic (describing a whole which is more
than the sum of its parts);
2 historically determined (reflecting the history of the organization);
3 related to the things anthropologists study
(like rituals and symbols);
4 socially constructed (created and preserved by the group of people who together
form the organization);
5 soft (although Peters and Waterman assure
their readers that 'soft is hard');

6 difficult to change (although authors disagree on how difficult).

All of these characteristics of organizations
had been separately recognized in the literature of the previous decades; what is new
about organization culture is their integration
into one single concept.

A distinction can be made between authors
who see organization culture as something an
organization *has*, and those who see it as
something an organization *is* (Smircich
1983). The former leads to an analytical approach and a concern with change. It predominates among managers and management
consultants. The latter supports a synthetic
approach and a concern with understanding
and is almost exclusively found among pure
academics. Discussion here is from the first
perspective (has), while accepting some insights from the second – especially that culture should be treated as an integrated whole.

2 Organization cultures and national cultures

The organization culture literature has been
influenced by reports of differences among
national cultures that affect organizations and
management, sometimes labelled 'comparative management' (Farmer and Richman
1965; Haire *et al.* 1966; Negandhi and Prasad
1971; Lammers and Hickson 1979; Hofstede
1980). The evident competitive success of
Japanese organizations in the 1960s and
1970s led to a recognition that national culture
mattered (Ouchi 1981; Pascale and Athos
1981).

'Culture' in general has been defined as:
'the collective programming of the mind
which distinguishes the members of one
group or category of people from another'
(Hofstede 1991: 5). Consequently 'organization culture' can be defined as: 'the collective programming of the mind which
distinguishes the members of one organization from another'. Next to organization and
national cultures, one can distinguish occupational cultures, business cultures, gender cultures, age group cultures (like youth culture),
and so on. However, the use of the word

culture, for all these categories, does not mean that they are identical phenomena. For different kinds of social systems, their cultures may well be of a different nature. This is particularly the case for organization cultures versus national cultures, if only because membership of an organization is usually partial and voluntary while 'membership' of a nation is permanent and involuntary.

Culture as collective programming of the mind manifests itself in several ways (see CULTURE, CROSS-NATIONAL). From the many terms used to describe manifestations of culture the following four together cover the total concept rather neatly: symbols, heroes, rituals and values. These can be imagined as the skins of an onion, symbols representing the most superficial and values the deepest manifestations of culture, with heroes and rituals in between.

Symbols are words, gestures, pictures or objects which carry a particular meaning only recognized as such by those who share the culture. The words in a language or jargon belong to this category, as do dress, hairstyle, Coca-Cola, flags and status symbols. New symbols are easily developed and old ones disappear; symbols from one cultural group are regularly copied by others. This is why symbols represent the outer, most superficial layer of culture.

Heroes are persons, alive or dead, real or imaginary, who possess characteristics which are highly prized in a culture, and thus serve as models for behaviour. Founders of companies often become cultural heroes. In this age of television outward appearances have become more important in the choice of heroes than ever before.

Rituals are collective activities, technically superfluous to reach desired ends but which within a culture are considered socially essential: thus, they are carried out for their own sake. Ways of greeting and paying respect to others and social and religious ceremonies are examples. Business and political meetings organized for seemingly rational reasons often serve mainly ritual purposes, like allowing the leaders to assert themselves.

Symbols, heroes and rituals together can be labelled '*practices*'. As such they are visible to an outside observer; their cultural meaning, however, is invisible and lies precisely and only in the way these practices are interpreted by insiders.

The core of culture is formed by *values*. Values are broad tendencies to prefer certain states of affairs over others. Values are feelings with a plus and a minus side. They deal with:

- evil versus good
- dirty versus clean
- ugly versus beautiful
- unnatural versus natural
- abnormal versus normal
- paradoxical versus logical
- irrational versus rational

Values are among the first things children learn – not consciously, but implicitly. Development psychologists believe that by the age of ten most children have their basic value system firmly in place, and after that age changes are difficult to obtain. Because they were acquired so early in our lives, many values remain unconscious to those who hold them. Therefore they cannot be discussed, nor can they be directly observed by outsiders. They can only be inferred from the way people act under various circumstances.

Two large research projects, one into national (Hofstede 1991) and one into organization culture (Hofstede *et al.* 1990) differences showed that national cultures differ mostly at the level of values, while organization cultures differ mostly at the level of the more superficial practices: symbols, heroes and rituals.

Figure 1 illustrates the different mixes of values and practices for the national and the organization levels of culture, as well as for gender, (social) class, occupation and business. These differences can be explained by the different places of socialization (learning) for values and for practices; these have been listed at the right side of the diagram. Values are acquired in one's early youth, mainly in the family and in the neighbourhood and later at school. The two characteristics present at birth are gender and nationality. By the time a child is ten years old most of its basic values

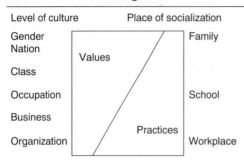

Level of culture		Place of socialization
Gender		Family
Nation	Values	
Class		
Occupation		School
Business		
	Practices	
Organization		Workplace

Figure 1 The mix of values and practices in culture for different social systems

have been programmed into its mind. The school as a socializing place relates to the student's future occupation. Organization cultures are only learned through socialization at the workplace, which most people enter as adults – that is, with the bulk of their values firmly in place. A business culture level (like the culture of banking or of tourism) is placed somewhere between occupation and organization.

Figure 1 illustrates that national cultures and organization cultures are phenomena of a different order. Using the same term 'cultures' for both can be misleading.

In the popular management literature organization cultures have often been presented as a matter of values (see for example Peters and Waterman 1982). The confusion arises because this literature does not distinguish between the values of the founders and leaders and those of the ordinary employees. Founders and leaders create the symbols, the heroes and the rituals that constitute the daily practices of the organization's members. Members do not have to adapt their personal values to the organization's needs. A work organization, as a rule, is not a 'total institution' like a prison or a mental hospital.

Members' values depend primarily on criteria other than membership in the organization: examples are gender, nationality, class and occupation. The way these values enter the organization is through the hiring process: an organization recruits people of a certain gender, nationality, class, education or age. Their subsequent socialization in the organization is a matter of learning the practices:

symbols, heroes and rituals. Personnel officers who pre-select the people to be hired play an important role in maintaining an organization's values (for better or for worse).

The fact that organization cultures are composed of practices rather than values makes them *somewhat* manageable: they can be managed by changing the practices. The values of employees, once hired, can hardly be changed by an employer, because they were acquired when the employees were children. Sometimes an employer can activate latent values which employees possess but were not allowed to show earlier, like a desire for initiative and creativity, by allowing practices which previously were forbidden.

3 Dimensions of national cultures

The large research project into national culture differences referred to took place across subsidiaries of a multinational corporation (IBM) in sixty-four countries. Subsequent studies covered students in ten and twenty-three countries, respectively, and elites in nineteen countries (Hofstede 1991; Hofstede and Bond 1988; Hoppe 1990). These studies together identified five independent dimensions of national culture differences:

(1) *Power distance*, that is the extent to which the less powerful members of organizations and institutions (like the family) accept and expect that power is distributed unequally. This represents inequality (more versus less), but defined from below, not from above. It suggests that a society's level of inequality is endorsed by the followers as much as by the leaders. Power and inequality, of course, are fundamental facts of any society and anybody with some international experience will be aware that 'all societies are unequal, but some are more unequal than others'.

Figure 2 lists some of the differences in the workplace between small and large power distance cultures. The statements refer to extremes; actual situations may be found anywhere in between the extremes. People's behaviour in the work situation is strongly affected by their previous experiences in the

Small power distance societies	Large power distance societies
Hierarchy means an inequality of roles, established for convenience	Hierarchy means existential inequality
Subordinates expect to be consulted	Subordinates expect to be told what to do
Ideal boss is resourceful democrat	Ideal boss is benevolent autocrat (good father)
Collectivist societies	**Individualist societies**
Value standards differ for in-group and out-groups: *particularism*	Same value standards apply to all: *universalism*
Other people are seen as members of their group	Other people seen as potential resources
Relationship prevails over task	Task prevails over relationship
Moral model of employer–employee relationship	Calculative model of employer–employee relationship
Feminine societies	**Masculine societies**
Assertiveness ridiculed	Assertiveness appreciated
Undersell yourself	Oversell yourself
Stress on life quality	Stress on careers
Intuition	Decisiveness
Weak uncertainty avoidance societies	**Strong uncertainty avoidance societies**
Dislike of rules – written or unwritten	Emotional need for rules – written or unwritten
Less formalization and standardization	More formalization and standardization
Tolerance of deviant persons and ideas	Intolerance of deviant persons and ideas

Figure 2 Consequences for the workplace of differences in national cultures

family and in the school: the expectations and fears about the boss are projections of the experiences with the father – or mother – and the teachers. In order to understand superiors, colleagues and subordinates in another country we have to know something about families and schools in that country.

(2) *Individualism* on the one side versus its opposite, *collectivism*, that is the degree to which individuals are integrated into groups. On the individualist side we find societies in which the ties between individuals are loose: everyone is expected to look after him/herself and his/her immediate family. On the collectivist side we find societies in which people from birth onwards are integrated into strong, cohesive in-groups, often extended families (with uncles, aunts and grandparents) which

continue protecting them in exchange for unquestioning loyalty. The word 'collectivism' in this sense has no political meaning: it refers to the group, not to the state. Again, the issue addressed by this dimension is an extremely fundamental one, regarding all societies in the world.

Figure 2 also shows some differences in the workplace between collectivist and individualist cultures; most real cultures will be somewhere in between these extremes. The words 'particularism' and 'universalism' are common sociological categories. Particularism is a way of thinking in which the standards for the way a person should be treated depend on the group or category to which this person belongs. Universalism is a way of thinking in which the standards for the way a person should be treated are the same for everybody.

(3) *Masculinity* versus its opposite, *femininity*, refers to the distribution of roles between the sexes which is another fundamental issue for any society to which a range of solutions are found. The IBM studies revealed that women's values differ less among societies than men's values and that men's values from one country to another contain a dimension from very assertive and competitive and maximally different from women's values on the one side, to modest and caring and similar to women's values on the other. The assertive pole has been called 'masculine' and the modest, caring pole 'feminine'. The women in feminine countries have the same modest, caring values as the men; in the masculine countries they are somewhat assertive and competitive, but not as much as the men, so that these countries show a gap between men's values and women's values. Figure 2 also lists some of the differences at the work place between feminine and masculine cultures.

(4) *Uncertainty avoidance* deals with a society's tolerance for uncertainty and ambiguity; it ultimately refers to man's search for Truth. It indicates to what extent a culture programmes its members to feel either uncomfortable or comfortable in unstructured situations. Unstructured situations are novel, unknown, surprising, different from usual. Uncertainty avoiding cultures try to minimize the possibility of such situations by strict laws and rules, safety and security measures, and on the philosophical and religious level by a belief in absolute Truth; 'there can only be one Truth and we have it'. People in uncertainty avoiding countries are also more emotional and are motivated by inner nervous energy. The opposite type, uncertainty accepting cultures, are more tolerant of opinions different from what they are used to; they try to have as few rules as possible, and on the philosophical and religious level they are relativist and allow many currents to flow side by side. People within these cultures are more phlegmatic and contemplative and are not expected by their environment to express emotions. Figure 2 lists some of the differences in the workplace between weak and strong uncertainty avoidance cultures.

(5) *Long-term orientation* versus *short-term orientation*, the fifth dimension, was found in a study among students in twenty-three countries around the world, using a questionnaire designed by Chinese scholars (Hofstede and Bond 1988). It can be said to deal with Virtue regardless of Truth. Values associated with long-term orientation are thrift and perseverance; values associated with short-term orientation are respect for tradition, fulfilment of social obligations and protection of one's 'face'. Both the positive and negative rated values of this dimension are found in the teachings of Confucius, the most influential Chinese philosopher who lived around 500 BC; however, the dimension also applies to countries without a Confucian heritage. There has been insufficient research as yet on the implications of differences along this dimension to allow composing a table of differences like those for the other four dimensions given in Figure 2.

Scores on the first four dimensions were obtained for fifty countries and three regions on the basis of the IBM study, and on the fifth dimension for twenty-three countries on the basis of student data collected by Bond. For score values see Hofstede (1991). Power distance scores are high for Latin, Asian and African countries and smaller for Germanic countries. Individualism prevails in developed and western countries, while collectivism prevails in less developed and eastern countries; Japan takes a middle position on this dimension. Masculinity is high in Japan, in some European countries like Germany, Austria and Switzerland, and moderately high in English-speaking countries; it is low in Nordic countries and in The Netherlands and moderately low in some Latin and Asian countries like France, Spain and Thailand. Uncertainty avoidance scores are higher in Latin countries, in Japan and in German-speaking countries, and lower in English-speaking, Nordic, and Chinese culture countries. A long-term orientation is mostly found in east Asian countries, in particular in China, Hong Kong, Taiwan, Japan and South Korea.

The grouping of country scores points to some of the roots of cultural differences. These should be sought in the common history of similarly scoring countries. All Latin countries, for example, score relatively high on both power distance and uncertainty avoidance. Latin countries (those today speaking a Romance language, namely Spanish, Portuguese, French or Italian) have inherited at least part of their civilization from the Roman empire. The Roman empire in its days was characterized by the existence of a central authority in Rome and a system of law applicable to citizens anywhere. This established in its citizens' minds the value complex which we still recognize today: centralization fostered large power distance and a stress on laws fostered strong uncertainty avoidance. The Chinese empire also knew centralization, but it lacked a fixed system of laws, being governed by men rather than by laws. In present-day countries once under Chinese rule, the mind-set fostered by the empire is reflected in large power distance but medium to weak uncertainty avoidance. The Germanic part of Europe, including the UK, never succeeded in establishing an enduring common central authority and countries which inherited its civilizations show smaller power distance. Assumptions about historical roots of cultural differences always remain speculative but in the given examples they are quite plausible. In other cases roots remain hidden.

The country scores on the five dimensions are statistically correlated with a multitude of other data about the countries. For example, power distance is correlated with the use of violence in domestic politics and with income inequality in a country. Individualism is correlated with national wealth (per capita gross national product) and with mobility between social classes from one generation to the next. Masculinity is correlated negatively with the share of their gross national product that governments of the wealthy countries spend on development assistance to the Third World. Uncertainty avoidance is associated with Roman Catholicism and with the legal obligation in developed countries for citizens to carry identity cards. Long-term orientation is correlated with national economic growth during the past twenty-five years, showing that what led to the economic success of the east Asian economies in this period is their populations' cultural stress on the future-orientated values of thrift and perseverance.

4 National cultures and the functioning of organizations

Organization structure

The national culture of a country affects its parents and its children, teachers and students, labour union leaders and members, politicians and citizens, journalists and readers, managers and subordinates. Therefore management practices in a country are culturally dependent, and what works in one country does not necessarily work in another. Not only the managers and subordinates are human and children of their culture: also the management teachers, the people who wrote and still write theories and create management concepts, are human and constrained by the cultural environment in which they grew up and which they know. Such theories and concepts cannot without further proof be applied in another country; if they are applicable at all, it is often only after considerable adaptation.

The structuring of organizations is primarily influenced by the two dimensions of power distance and uncertainty avoidance. This is because organizing always demands the answering of two questions: (1) who should have the power to decide what? and (2) what rules or procedures will be followed to attain the desired ends? The answer to the first question is influenced by cultural norms of power distance; the answer to the second question, by cultural norms about uncertainty avoidance. Individualism and masculinity affect primarily the functioning of the people within the organizations. Long-term orientation affects the economic performance of organizations.

Research into the *formal* structures of organizations carried out by British researchers from the University of Aston in Birmingham in the 1960s and early 1970s (the 'Aston studies': Pugh and Hickson 1976) already concluded that the two major dimensions along which structures of organizations differ are 'concentration of authority' and 'structuring of activities'. The first is affected by power distance, the second by uncertainty avoidance. Power distance and uncertainty avoidance indices measure the *informal*, subjective mental programming of the people within a country. The fact that these vary systematically between countries explains why the formal structures of organizations also vary: formal structures serve to meet informal cultural needs.

Differences in implicit models of organizations were proven for the case of France, Germany and the UK by a study among IN-SEAD (Institut européen d'administration) business students in Fontainebleau, France (Hofstede 1991: 140–3). In dealing with a case study of organizational conflict French students, coming from a country with large power distance and strong uncertainty avoidance, treated the organization like a 'pyramid of people' and advocated measures to concentrate the authority and also structure the activities. Germans, coming from a country with strong uncertainty avoidance but small power distance, treated the organization as a 'well-oiled machine' and wanted to structure the activities without concentrating the authority. British students with a national culture characterized by small power distance and weak uncertainty avoidance treated the organization as a 'village market' and advocated neither concentrating authority nor structuring activities but developing the managers' negotiation skills. Each of these models dealt with the same case study. All things being equal, French organizations do concentrate authority more, German organizations do prefer more structure and people in British organizations do believe more in resolving problems *ad hoc* (Maurice *et al.* 1980). A fourth combination, large power distance with weak uncertainty avoidance, is found in Asia and Africa and leads to an implicit model of an organization as an (extended) 'family', in which the owner–manager is the omnipotent (grand)father.

Mintzberg (1983) has provided a well-known typology of organization structures. Organizations in general contain up to five distinct parts – an operating core; a strategic apex; a middle line; a technostructure; and support staff – and they use one or more of five mechanisms for coordinating activities – mutual adjustment; direct supervision; standardization of work processes; standardization of outputs; and standardization of skills. Most organizations show one of five typical configurations: (1) the simple structure, in which the key part is the strategic apex and the coordinating mechanism is direct supervision; (2) the machine bureaucracy, in which the key part is the technostructure and the coordinating mechanism is standardization of work processes; (3) the professional bureaucracy, in which the key part is the operating core and the coordinating mechanism is standardization of skills; (4) the divisionalized form, in which the key part is the middle line and the coordinating mechanism is standardization of outputs; and (5) the adhocracy, in which the key part is the support staff and the coordinating mechanism is mutual adjustment.

Mintzberg did not account for national culture in his typology but the link between the five configurations and the quadrants of the power distance × uncertainty avoidance matrix is easy to make. The adhocracy corresponds with the village market implicit organization model; the professional bureaucracy with the well-oiled machine model; the full (machine) bureaucracy with the pyramid model; and the simple structure with the family model. The divisionalized form, meanwhile, takes a middle position on both culture dimensions, containing elements of all four models. Other things being equal, organizers in a particular country will favour a particular configuration because it fits their implicit mental model of what an organization should be.

Motivation

The power distance × uncertainty avoidance mix also affects the motivation of employees within an organization. Herzberg *et al.* (1959)

argued that the work situation contains elements with a positive motivation potential (the real motivators) and elements with a negative potential (the hygiene factors) (see HERZBERG, F.). The motivators were the work itself, achievement, recognition, responsibility and advancement. These are often labelled 'intrinsic' elements of the job. The hygiene factors, which had to be present in order to prevent demotivation but which could not motivate by themselves, were company policy and administration, supervision, salary and working conditions. These are the 'extrinsic' elements of the job. Herzberg assumed this distinction to be a universal characteristic of human motivation. According to him it is the job content which makes people act, not the job context (see MOTIVATION AND SATISFACTION).

Long before Herzberg the issue of human motivation was raised by Sigmund Freud (1856–1939), one of the founding fathers of present-day psychology. According to Freud we are impelled to act by unconscious forces inside us which he calls our 'id'. Our conscious conception of ourselves, our 'ego' tries to control these forces. The ego in its turn is influenced by an inner pilot, again unconscious, our 'superego'. The superego criticizes the thoughts and acts of the ego and causes feelings of guilt and anxiety when the ego is felt to be giving in to the id. The superego is developed in the young child, primarily by the influence of the parents.

Freud (see FREUD, S.) was an Austrian and he conceived his ideas in the Austrian intellectual environment of his day. Austria in the power distance × uncertainty avoidance matrix takes an extreme position: small power distance but strong uncertainty avoidance. The latter stands for a strong psychological need for rules; the former for psychological independence from a flesh-and-blood boss to enforce these rules. The superego can be interpreted as an interiorized boss/father, who controls the individual through self-imposed guilt feelings. In Austria and other small power distance, strong uncertainty avoidance countries like Germany, rules as part of what Herzberg called 'company policy and administration'

should not be seen as 'hygiene'; they can be real motivators.

In a similar way, when power distances are large supervision should not be seen as a hygiene factor. In large power distance countries dependence on more powerful people is a basic need which can be a real motivator. When, in addition, uncertainty avoidance is strong, as in most Latin countries, the motivator is the boss in the sense of the formally appointed superior. When uncertainty avoidance is weaker, as in Asian and African countries, the motivator should rather be labelled the master. The master differs from the boss in that the power of the former is based on tradition and charisma more than on formal position.

A cultural analysis thus shows that Herzberg's theory of motivation is culturally constrained; like all management theories it reflects the culture of the environment in which its author grew up and carried out research. The same holds for another US theory of motivation: Maslow's (1970) 'hierarchy of human needs'. In Maslow's hierarchy self-actualization is seen as the supreme need. However, this assumes an individualist culture in which the self prevails over the group. In collectivist cultures harmony with the group will rather be the supreme need. Maslow also ranks esteem over 'belongingness'. This assumes a masculine culture; in feminine cultures belongingness will prevail over esteem as a motivator.

A third culturally constrained motivation theory is McClelland's (1961) 'achievement motive'. McClelland predicted that countries for which he found a stronger achievement motive would show faster economic growth. This prediction did not come true. Hofstede (1980: 170–1) showed that McClelland's achievement motive corresponds to weak uncertainty avoidance plus strong masculinity; a combination found in all English-speaking countries. However, in the years following McClelland's study some stronger uncertainty avoidance countries like Japan and Germany grew faster economically than the English-speaking countries. McClelland had presented a culture pattern specific to his home society (the USA) as a universal norm.

Performance appraisal and management by objectives

Performance appraisal systems (see PER-FORMANCE APPRAISAL) are recommended in the North American and western European management literature. They assume that employees' performance will be improved if the employees receive direct feedback about what their superior thinks of them, which may well be the case in individualist cultures. However, in collectivist countries such direct feedback destroys the harmony which is expected to govern interpersonal relationships. It may cause irreparable damage to the employee's 'face' and ruin his or her loyalty to the organization. In such cultures, including all east Asian and Third World countries, feedback instead should be given indirectly, for example through the withdrawing of a favour, or via an intermediary person trusted by both superior and employee.

Management by objectives as a management technique was developed in the USA (see MANAGERIAL BEHAVIOUR). Under a system of management by objectives subordinates have to negotiate about their objectives with their superiors. The system therefore assumes a cultural environment in which issues can be settled by negotiation rather than by authority and rules, which means a medium to low power distance and a not too high uncertainty avoidance. In a large power distance environment subordinates and superiors will be unable to function in the ways the system prescribes. In a stronger uncertainty avoidance environment the system needs a more elaborate formal structure with norms and examples; this is the case in Germany.

Strategic management

Strategic management as a concept was also developed in the USA. It assumes a weak uncertainty avoidance environment in which deviant strategic ideas are encouraged. Although it is taught in countries with a stronger uncertainty avoidance, like Germany or France, its recommendations are followed there only rarely, because in these cultures it is seen as the role of top managers to remain involved in daily operations (Horovitz 1980).

Humanization of work

This is a general term for a number of approaches in different countries which try to make work more interesting and rewarding for the people who carry it out. In the USA, which is a masculine and individualist society, the prevailing form of humanization of work has been 'job enrichment': giving individual tasks more intrinsic content. In Sweden which is feminine and less individualist, the prevailing form has been the forming of semi-autonomous work groups, in which members exchange tasks and help each other (see GROUPS AND TEAMS). In Germany and German-speaking Switzerland the introduction of flexible working hours has been a popular way of adapting the job to the worker. Flexible working hours however have never become as common in other countries; their popularity in German-speaking countries can be understood by the combination of a small power distance (acceptance of responsibility by the worker) with a relatively strong uncertainty avoidance (internalization of rules).

5 National cultures: convergence or divergence?

Do national cultures in the modern world become more similar? The evidence cited is usually taken from the level of practices: people dress the same, buy the same products and use the same fashionable words (symbols), they see the same TV shows and movies (heroes), they perform the same sports and leisure activities (rituals). These rather superficial manifestations of culture are sometimes mistaken for all there is; the deeper, underlying level of values, which moreover determine the meaning to people of their practices, is overlooked.

Value differences between nations described by authors centuries ago are still present today, in spite of continued close contacts. Studies at the values level continue to show impressive differences among nations; after the IBM studies from around 1970 (Hofstede 1980) this was also the case for the European Value Systems Study (Harding and Phillips 1986; Ester *et al.* 1993). The only convergence is on the dimension of individualism, with countries that have become richer moving towards greater individualism. But even here pre-existing differences between countries survive. On average the Japanese have become richer than Americans and there is evidence of an increase in individualism in Japan, but traditional elements of Japanese collectivism survive as well. Because the process of organizing is affected by national cultural values, the nationality component in the structure and functioning of organizations is unlikely to disappear for decades or even centuries to come. International organizations will continue to have to take this component into account.

6 Dimensions of organization cultures

A research project similar to the IBM studies but focusing on organization rather than national cultures was carried out by IRIC (the Institute for Research on Intercultural Cooperation, The Netherlands) in the 1980s (Hofstede *et al.* 1990). Qualitative and quantitative data were collected for twenty work organizations or parts of organizations in The Netherlands and Denmark. The units studied varied from a toy manufacturing company to two municipal police corps. As mentioned above, this study found large differences among units in practices (symbols, heroes, rituals) but only modest differences in values, beyond those due to such basic facts as nationality, education, gender and age group.

Six independent dimensions permit description of the larger part of the variety in organization practices. These six dimensions can be used as a framework to describe organization cultures, but their research base in twenty units from two countries is too narrow to consider them universally valid. For describing organization cultures in other countries and/or in other types of organizations additional

dimensions may be necessary or some of the six may be less useful. The six dimensions of organization cultures, discussed below, are listed in Figure 3, together with some of the ways in which they manifest themselves.

(1) *Process-oriented versus results-oriented cultures.* The former are dominated by technical and bureaucratic routines, the latter by a common concern for outcomes. This dimension is associated with a culture's degree of homogeneity: in results-orientated units, everybody perceives their practices in about the same way; in process-orientated units, there are vast differences in perception among different levels and parts of the unit. The degree of homogeneity of a culture is a measure of its 'strength': the study confirmed that strong cultures are more results-orientated than weak ones, and vice versa (Peters and Waterman 1982)

(2) *Job-oriented versus employee-oriented cultures.* The former assume responsibility for the employees' job performance only, nothing more; employee-orientated cultures assume a broad responsibility for their members' well-being. At the level of individual managers the distinction between job orientation and employee orientation has been popularized by Blake and Mouton's Managerial Grid (1964). The IRIC study shows that job versus employee orientation is part of a culture and not (only) a choice for an individual manager. A unit's position on this dimension seems to be largely the result of historical factors, like the philosophy of its founder(s) and the presence or absence in its recent history of economic crises with collective layoffs.

(3) *Professional versus parochial cultures.* In the former the (usually highly educated) members identify primarily with their profession; in the latter the members derive their identity from the organization for which they work. Sociology has long known this dimension as 'local' versus 'cosmopolitan', the contrast between an internal and an external frame of reference.

(4) *Open systems versus closed systems cultures.* This dimension refers to the common style of internal and external communication and to the ease with which outsiders and

1 Process-orientated	Results-orientated
People avoid taking risks	Comfortable in unfamiliar situations
People spend little effort	People spend maximal effort
Each day is the same	Each day presents new challenges
2 Job-orientated	**Employee-orientated**
Pressure for getting job done	Attention to personal problems
Important decisions by individuals	Important decisions by groups
Organization only interested in work people do	Organization concerned with welfare of employees and their families
3 Professional	**Parochial**
Think years ahead	Do not think far ahead
Employees' private life is considered their business	Norms of organization cover behaviour on job and at home
Only competence plays a role in recruiting	Family, social class and school play a role in recruiting
4 Open system	**Closed system**
Organization and people transparent to newcomers and outsiders	Organization and people closed and secretive, even to insiders
Almost anyone fits into the organization	Only very special people fit into the organization
New employees need only a few days to feel at home	New employees need more than a year to feel at home
5 Tight control	**Loose control**
Everybody cost-conscious	Nobody cost-conscious
Meeting times kept punctually	Meeting times only kept approximately
Lots of jokes about job and organization	Always serious about job and organization
6 Pragmatic	**Normative**
Emphasis on meeting needs of customers	Emphasis on correctly following procedures
Results more important than procedures	Correct procedures more important than results
Pragmatic not dogmatic in matters of ethics	High standard of ethics, even at expense of results

Figure 3 Manifestations at the workplace of different organization cultures

newcomers are admitted. This dimension is the only one of the six for which there is a systematic difference between Danish and Dutch units. It seems that organizational openness is a societal characteristic of Denmark more than of The Netherlands. This shows that organization cultures also contain elements that reflect national culture differences.

(5) *Tightly versus loosely controlled cultures.* This dimension deals with the degree of formality and punctuality within the organization. It is partly a function of the unit's technology: banks and pharmaceutical

companies can be expected to show tight control, research laboratories and advertising agencies loose control. However, even when possessing the same technology, units still differ on this dimension.

(6) *Pragmatic versus normative cultures*. This last dimension describes the prevailing way (flexible or rigid) of dealing with the environment, in particular with customers. Units selling services are likely to be found towards the pragmatic (flexible) side; units involved in the application of legal rules towards the normative (rigid) side. This dimension measures the degree of 'customer orientation', which is a popular topic in the management literature.

7 Determinants of organization cultures

Inspection of the scoring profiles of the twenty units on the six dimensions shows that dimensions 1, 3, 5 and 6 (process versus results, professional versus parochial, tight versus loose and pragmatic versus normative) are affected by the type of work the organization does and by the type of market in which it operates. In fact, these four dimensions partly reflect the *business* or *industry culture*. In Figure 1 it was located between the occupational and the organizational level because a given industry employs specific occupations and also maintains specific organizational practices, both for logical or traditional reasons. On dimension 1 most manufacturing and large office units scored process-orientated; research and development and service units scored more results-orientated. On dimension 3 units with a traditional technology scored parochial; high-tech units scored professional. On dimension 5 units delivering precision or risky products or services (such as pharmaceuticals or money transactions) scored tight, those with innovative or unpredictable activities scored loose. Surprisingly the two municipal police corps studied scored on the loose side: the work of a policeman is unpredictable and police personnel have considerable discretion in the way they carry out their task. On dimension 6 service units and those operating in competitive markets scored pragmatic; units involved in the implementation of laws and those operating under a monopoly scored normative.

While the task and market environment thus affect dimension scores, the IRIC study also identified distinctive elements in each organization's culture, even compared to other organizations in the same industry. These represent competitive advantages or disadvantages.

The remaining two dimensions, 2 and 4 (job versus employee and open versus closed), seem to be less constrained by task and market but rather based on historical factors like the philosophy of the founder(s) and recent crises. In the case of dimension 4, as shown above, the national cultural environment was proved to play an important role.

Although organization cultures are primarily composed of practices, they do have a modest values component. The organizations in the IRIC study differed somewhat on three clusters of values. The first resembles the cross-national dimension of uncertainty avoidance. A cross-organizational uncertainty avoidance measure is correlated with dimension 4 (open versus closed), with weak uncertainty avoidance obviously on the side of an open communication climate. A second cluster of cross-organizational values bears some resemblance to power distance. It is correlated with dimension 1 (process versus results orientated), larger power distances being associated with process orientation and smaller ones with results orientation.

Clusters of cross-organizational value differences associated with individualism and masculinity were not found in the IRIC study. Questions which in the cross-national study composed the individualism and masculinity dimensions formed a different configuration in the cross-organizational study labelled 'work centrality' (strong or weak): namely, the importance of work in one's total life pattern. It was correlated with dimension 3: professional versus parochial. Obviously work centrality is stronger in professional organization cultures. In parochial cultures people do not take their work problems home with them.

For the other three dimensions, 2, 5 and 6, no link with values was found at all. These

249

dimensions merely describe practices to which people have been socialized without their basic values being involved.

In the cross-national IBM study the country scores on the five dimensions were statistically correlated with a multitude of other data about the countries. The IRIC cross-organizational study included a similar 'validation' of the dimensions against external data. This time, of course, the data used consisted of information about the organizational units obtained in other ways and from other sources.

Besides interviews and an employee survey the IRIC study included the collection of quantifiable data about the units as wholes. Examples of such information (labelled 'structural data') are total employee strength, budget composition, economic results and the ages of key managers.

There was a strong correlation between the scores on dimension 1 (process versus results orientation) and the balance of labour versus material cost in the operating budget. Labour-intensive organizations (holding the number of employees constant) scored more results-orientated, while material-intensive organizations scored more process-orientated. Results-orientated units had lower absenteeism. They also had flatter structures (larger spans of control) and less specialization and formalization. Also, in results-orientated units union membership tended to be lower.

The strongest correlation with dimension 2 (job versus employee orientation) was with the way the organizational unit was controlled from above. If the top manager was evaluated on profits and other financial performance measures the members scored the unit culture as job-orientated; if they were evaluated on performance versus a budget members scored the unit culture as employee-orientated. Where the top managers stated they allowed controversial news to be published in the employee journal members felt the unit to be more employee-orientated. Job orientation was also correlated with the employees' average seniority and age and negatively with the education level of the top management team.

On dimension 3 (professional versus parochial) organizational units with a traditional technology tended to score parochial; high-tech units scored professional. The strongest correlations of this dimension were with various measures of size: larger organizations fostered more professional cultures. Professional cultures had less labour union membership. Their managers had a higher level of education and age. Their organization structures showed more specialization. An interesting correlation was with the way the top managers claimed to spend their time. In the units with a professional culture the top managers spent a larger share of their time in meetings and person-to-person discussions. Finally, the privately owned organizations studied tended to score more professional than the public ones.

Dimension 4 (open versus closed systems) was responsible for the single strongest correlation with external data; that between the percentage of women among the employees and the openness of the communication climate. The percentage of women among managers and the presence of at least one woman in the top management team were also correlated with openness. Openness was negatively associated with formalization and positively with higher average seniority of employees.

The strongest correlation on dimension 5 (tight versus loose control) was with an item in the self-reported time budget of the top managers where they affirmed spending a relatively large part of their time reading and writing reports and memos from inside the organization, control was tighter. Also, material-intensive units had more tightly controlled cultures. In units in which the number of employees had recently increased control was felt to be looser; where the number of employees had been reduced control was perceived as tighter. Finally, absenteeism among employees was lower where control was perceived to be less tight. Absenteeism is evidently one way of escaping from the pressure of a tight control system.

For dimension 6 (pragmatic versus normative) only one meaningful correlation with external data was found: privately owned organizations in the sample were more pragmatic, public units (such as the police corps) more normative.

Missing from the list of external data correlated with culture are measures of the organizations' performance. This does not mean that culture is not related to performance, only that it is extremely difficult to find valid yardsticks for comparing performance across different organizations.

8 Individual perceptions of organization cultures

Different individuals within the same organization will not necessarily perceive the culture of their organization in the same way. Hofstede, Bond and Luk (1993) re-analysed the data of Hofstede *et al.*'s Organization Culture study. This time, they focused on the variance of answers within the organizations studied. They did this by deducting from every individual's answer on a question the mean score of that question for the organizational unit. Thus, they only retained the within-unit variance, eliminating the between-unit variance that had been the basis of the dimensions of organizational culture found. After elimination of the between-unit variance, the data from the individuals within the twenty units were combined into one matrix of within-unit variance.

Study of this matrix showed that individuals within-unit showed large differences in values, but smaller differences in (perceptions of) organizational practices. This is the opposite of what was found at the between-organizational level. It is obvious, because value differences rest in differences of individual personality, whereas perceptions of practices are still based on the same objective practices.

A further (factor-) analysis of the individual answers showed that individual answers varied along six dimensions

1 integration (in the organization)
2 active involvement
3 orderliness
4 need for achievement
5 machismo
6 authoritarianism

The first five correspond closely to the five basic dimensions of personality ('the Big Five') recognized by modern personality theory: Neuroticism (with a negative sign), Extraversion, Conscientiousness, Openness, and Agreeableness (again with a negative sign). The sixth reminds usof the 'Authoritarian Personality' studies by Adorno *et al.* (1950).

In conclusion, differences among individuals in their perceptions of the culture of their organizations were shown to be a matter of the individual's personality. Agreeable individuals perceive the organizations as agreeable; conscientious individuals perceive the organizations as conscientious, etc.

9 Managing (with) organization cultures

In spite of their relatively superficial nature, organization cultures are hard to change because they have developed into collective habits. Changing them is a top management task which cannot be delegated. Some kind of culture assessment by an independent party is usually necessary, which includes the identification of different sub-cultures which may need quite different approaches. The top management's major strategic choice is either to accept and optimally use the existing culture or to try to change it. If an attempt at change is made it should be preceded by a cost–benefit analysis. A particular concern is whether the manpower necessary for a culture change is available.

Turning around an organization culture demands visible leadership which appeals to the employees' feelings as much as to their intellect (see LEADERSHIP). The leader or leaders should assure themselves of sufficient support from key persons at different levels in the organization. Subsequently, they can change the practices by adapting the organization's structure (its functions, departments, locations and tasks) matching tasks with employee talents. After the structure, controls may have to be changed, based on a decision on what aspects of the work have to be coordinated – how and by whom at what level. At the same time it is usually necessary to change certain personnel policies relating to recruitment, training and promotion. Finally, turning around a culture is a lengthy process. It takes sustained attention from top management, persistence for several years, and new culture assessments to see whether the intended changes have, in reality, been attained, as well as what other changes occurred in the meantime.

In the case of mergers and acquisitions a diagnosis is needed for identifying the potential areas of culture conflict between partners. Decisions on mergers are traditionally made from a financial point of view only: mergers are part of a big money power game and seen as a defence against (real or imaginary) threats by competitors. Those making the decision rarely imagine the operating problems which arise inside the newly formed hybrid organizations. A diagnosis of the cultures involved should be input when deciding whether or not to merge and after the decision has been made; it should also be input when planning for managing the post-merger integration so as to minimize friction losses and preserve unique cultural capital.

The six dimensions discussed above describe the culture of an organization, but they are not prescriptive: no position on one of the six dimensions is intrinsically good or bad. Peters and Waterman (1982) have presented eight maxims as norms for excellence. The results of the IRIC study suggest that what is good or bad depends in each case on where one wants the organization to go, and a cultural feature that is an asset for one purpose is unavoidably a liability for another. Labelling positions on the dimension scales as more or less desirable is a matter of strategic choice, and this will vary from one organization to another. In particular, the popular stress on customer orientation (becoming more pragmatic on dimension 6) is highly relevant for organizations engaged in services and the manufacturing of custom-made quality products, but it may be unnecessary or even harmful for, for example, the manufacturing of standard products in a competitive price market.

10 Managing culture differences in multinationals

Most multinational corporations do not only operate in different countries but also in different lines of business or at least in different product/market divisions. Different business lines and/or divisions often have different organization cultures. By offering common practices strong cross-national organization cultures within a business line or division can bridge national differences in values among organization members. Common practices, not common values, are what keep multinationals together.

Like all organizations multinationals are held together by people. The best structure at a given moment depends primarily on the availability of suitable people. Two roles are particularly crucial: country business unit managers who form the link between the culture of the business unit and the corporate culture which is usually heavily affected by the nationality of origin of the corporation; and 'corporate diplomats', home country or other nationals impregnated with the corporate culture, multilingual, from various occupational backgrounds and experienced in living and functioning in various foreign cultures. They are essential to make multinational structures work, either as liaison persons in the various head offices or as temporary managers for new ventures.

The availability of suitable people at the right moment is the main task of multinational personnel management. This means the timely recruiting of future managerial talent from different nationalities and career moves through planned transfers where these people will absorb the corporate culture. Multinational personnel departments have to find their way between uniformity and diversity in personnel policies. Too much uniformity is unwarranted because people's mental programmes are not uniform. It leads to corporate-wide policies being imposed on subsidiaries where they will not work (or only receive lip service from obedient but puzzled locals). On the other side, the assumption that everybody is different and that people in subsidiaries therefore always know best and should be allowed to go their own ways is unwarranted also. In this case an opportunity is lost to build a corporate culture with unique features which keep the organization together and provide it with a distinct and competitive psychological advantage.

Mergers and takeovers within countries have a dubious success record, but cross-national ventures are even less likely to succeed. They have to bridge both national and organization culture gaps. Even more than in the case of national ventures, they call for a cultural map of the prospective partner as an input into the decision making on whether to merge or not.

Structure should follow culture: the purpose of an organization structure is the coordination of activities. For the design of the structure of a multinational, multi-business corporation, three questions have to be answered for each business unit (a business unit represents one business line in one country). The three questions are: (1) which of the unit's inputs and outputs should be coordinated from elsewhere in the corporation? (2) where and at what level should the coordination take place? and (3) how tight or loose should the coordination be? In every case there is a basic choice between coordination along geographical lines and coordination along business lines. The decisive factor is whether business know-how or national cultural know-how is more crucial for the success of the operation.

Matrix structures are a possible solution but they are costly, often meaning a doubling of the management ranks, and their actual functioning may raise more problems than it resolves. A single structural principle (geographic or business) is unlikely to fit for an entire corporation. Joint ventures further complicate the structuring problem. The optimal solution is nearly always a patchwork structure that in some cases follows business and in others geographical lines. This may lack beauty, but it does follow the needs of markets and business unit cultures. Variety within the environment in which a corporation operates should be matched with appropriate internal variety. Optimal solutions will also change over time, so that the periodic

reshufflings which any large organization knows should be seen as functional.

GEERT HOFSTEDE
INSTITUTE FOR RESEARCH ON
INTERCULTURAL COOPERATION
MAASTRICHT UNIVERSITY
THE NETHERLANDS

Further reading

(References cited in the text marked *)

* Adorno, T.W., Frenkel-Brunswick, E., Levinson, D.J. and Sanford, R.N. (1950) *The Authoritarian Personality*, Nrew York: Harper and Row.
* Blake, R.R. and Mouton, J.S. (1964) *The Managerial Grid*, Houston, TX: Gulf. (A classic US management theory arguing that the behaviour of individual managers can be classified along two independent dimensions: concern for people and concern for production.)

Czarniawska-Joerges, B. and Guillet de Monthoux, P. (1994) *Good Novels, Better Management: Reading Organizational Realities*, Chur: Harwood Academic Publishers. (Descriptions and analyses of famous nineteenth- and early twentieth-century novels from nine countries, considered as case studies of management.)

* Deal, T.E. and Kennedy, A.A. (1982) *Corporate Cultures: The Rites and Rituals of Corporate Life*, Reading, MA: Addison-Wesley. (An introduction to the subject, demonstrating how anthropological concepts can be used in the study of organizations.)
* Ester, P., Halman, L. and De Moor, R. (1993) *The Individualizing Society: Value Change in Europe and North America*, Tilburg: Tilburg University Press. (Results of a series of surveys measuring personal values among the populations of twenty-two countries.)
* Farmer, R.N. and Richman, B.M. (1965) *Comparative Management and Economic Progress*, Homewood, IL: Irwin. (A pioneer book on comparative management, now dated.)

Frost, P.J., Moore, L.F., Louis, M.R., Lundberg, C.C. and Martin, J. (eds) (1985) *Organizational Culture*, Beverly Hills, CA: Sage Publications. (A collection of twenty-two readings, inspired by academic rather than practical interest.)

Frost, P.J., Moore, L.F., Louis, M.R., Lundberg, C.C. and Martin, J. (eds) (1991) *Reframing Organizational Culture*, Newbury Park, CA: Sage Publications. (Another collection of readings, even more esoteric than the previous one, which focuses more on the persons studying the organizations than on the organizations themselves.)

* Haire, M., Ghiselli, E.E. and Porter, L.W. (1966) *Managerial Thinking: An International Study*, New York: Wiley. (First international survey study of values in organizations.)

* Harding, S. and Phillips, D. (1986) *Contrasting Values in Western Europe*, London: Macmillan. (An earlier report on the survey study also covered by Ester *et al.*, see above.)

* Herzberg, F., Mausner, B. and Snyderman, B.B. (1959) *The Motivation to Work*, New York: Wiley. (A well-known American management theory distinguishing 'motivators' from 'hygiene factors'.)

* Hofstede, G. (1980) *Culture's Consequences: International Differences in Work-related Values*, Beverly Hills, CA: Sage Publications. (The first presentation of the first four dimensions of national culture across forty countries, written for a scholarly readership and with extensive validation against data from other sources.)

Hofstede, G. (ed.) (1986) *Organizational culture and control*, special issue of *Journal of Management Studies* 23 (3). (Links two central concepts in management: five papers on the relationship of culture with information, control and meaning; two on empirical studies of organization culture.)

* Hofstede, G. (1991) *Cultures and Organizations: Software of the Mind*, London: McGraw-Hill. (A popular overview of the author's and related research; deals with national as well as organization cultures. Translated into Chinese, Danish, Dutch, Finnish, French, German, Japanese, Korean, Norwegian and Swedish.)

* Hofstede, G. and Bond, M.H. (1988) 'The Confucius connection: from cultural roots to economic growth', *Organizational Dynamics* 16 (4): 4–21. (Using the results of the Chinese Values Survey, introduces the fifth dimension of national culture differences and argues that it explains national economic growth over the past twenty-five years.)

* Hofstede, G., Bond, M.H. and Luk, C.L. (1993) Individual perceptions of organizational cultures: a methodological treatise on levels of analysis, *Organization Studies*, 14: 483–503.

* Hofstede, G., Neuijen, B., Ohayv, D.D. and Sanders, G. (1990) 'Measuring organizational cultures', *Administrative Science Quarterly* 35: 286–316. (An account of the results of the IRIC survey of organization cultures across twenty units in Denmark and Holland.)

* Hoppe, M.H. (1990) 'A comparative study of country elites', PhD thesis, University of North Carolina at Chapel Hill. (A replication of the Hofstede survey with elites from nineteen countries.)

* Horovitz, J.H. (1980) *Top Management Control in Europe*, London: Macmillan. (A comparison between the UK, France and Germany.)

Jaques, E. (1951) *The Changing Culture of a Factory*, London: Tavistock Publications. (A classic; the story of social change at the Glacier Metal Company in London.)

* Lammers, C.J. and Hickson, D.J. (1979) *Organizations Alike and Unlike: International and Inter-institutional Studies in the Sociology of Organizations*, London: Routledge & Kegan Paul. (A sociological overview of the relationship between societies and their institutions.)

* McClelland, D.C. (1961) *The Achieving Society*, Princeton, NJ: Van Nostrand Reinhold. (A US theory arguing that the strength of the 'need for achievement' is the determining factor in the economic development of societies.)

* Maslow, A.H. (1970) *Motivation and Personality*, 2nd edn, New York: Harper & Row. (The popular US theory of motivation, arguing that needs can be ordered in a pyramid.)

* Maurice, M., Sorge, A. and Warner, M. (1980) 'Societal differences in organizing manufacturing units: a comparison of France, West Germany and Great Britain', *Organization Studies* 1: 59–86. (A three-nation study showing the relationship between the larger society and the way work is organized.)

* Mintzberg, H. (1983) *Structure in Fives: Designing Effective Organizations*, Englewood Cliffs, NJ: Prentice Hall. (A well-known North American theory distinguishing five typical ways of structuring organizations.)

* Negandhi, A.R. and Prasad, S.B. (1971) *Comparative Management*, New York: Appleton-Century-Crofts. (An early introduction to the field.)

* Ouchi, W.G. (1981) *Theory Z*, Reading, MA: Addison-Wesley. (Describes how US management can use Japanese methods.)

* Pascale, R.T. and Athos, A.G. (1981) *The Art of Japanese Management*, New York: Simon & Schuster. (Japanese management described for US readers.)

* Peters, T.J. and Waterman, R.H. (1982) *In Search of Excellence: Lessons from America's Best-Run Companies*, New York: Harper & Row. (Best-selling missionary document prescribing eight maxims for companies to become excellent.)

* Pettigrew, A.M. (1979) 'On studying organizational cultures', *Administrative Science Quarterly* 24: 570–81. (Early introduction to the 'organization culture' concept.)
* Pugh, D.S. and Hickson, D.J. (1976) *Organizational Structure in its Context: The Aston Programme I*, London: Saxon House. (An overview of the 'Aston studies' on organization structure.)
* Schein, E.H. (1985) *Organizational Culture and Leadership*, San Francisco, CA: Jossey Bass. (A boardroom consultant's view of organization culture and change; thorough discussion of the concept of organization culture but surprisingly blind to the influences of nationality and industry.)
* Smircich, L. (1983) 'Concepts of culture and organizational analysis', *Organizational Culture*, a special issue of *Administrative Science Quarterly* 28: 339–58. (A clear guide in the conceptual jungle; the whole issue is recommended as an overview of the state of the art at that time.)
  Weinshall, T.D. (ed.) (1993) *Societal Culture and Management*, Berlin: Walter de Gruyter. (Reader reprinting some of forty articles that appeared in the 1970s and 1980s.)

See also: CULTURE, CROSS-NATIONAL; MANAGERIAL BEHAVIOUR; MOTIVATION AND SATISFACTION; ORGANIZATION BEHAVIOUR

Related topics in the IEBM: AGENCY, MARKETS AND HIERARCHIES; ASTON GROUP; BUSINESS STRATEGIES, EAST ASIAN; BUSINESS SYSTEMS; COGNITION; CONTEXTS AND ENVIRONMENTS; COORDINATION AND CONTROL; ECONOMIES OF EAST ASIA; MCCLELLAND, D.C.; MINTZBERG, H.; ORGANIZATION BEHAVIOUR, HISTORY OF; ORGANIZATION PARADIGMS; ORGANIZATION STRUCTURE; ORGANIZATION TYPES; ORGANIZATIONAL CONVERGENCE; ORGANIZATIONAL PERFORMANCE; ORGANIZING, PROCESS OF; POWER; STRATEGY, CONCEPT OF

Personnel management

Overview

This entry describes and analyses the origins of personnel management in the development of mass production industry and its growth over the course of the twentieth century.

It locates personnel management as the strategic approach to the human resourcing task which was thought to suit the mass producer best. Beginning as a support to the supervisory function, it developed in some countries (but not others) to the point where it made some claim to being influential on strategic thinking and decision taking.

It also illustrates the diversity of form taken by the function in different cultures and suggests that the extent to which general management is prepared to accept that law has a significant part to play in regulating its own behaviour may exert a strong influence on the way personnel management develops.

The entry identifies the management tasks to which personnel specialists are expected to contribute and attempts to establish where the function's main contribution to management thinking and practice has been. It concludes that the function has contributed most to increasing the validity and reliability of managerial judgements and to improving the ways in which organizations seek to control the behaviour of semi-skilled employees.

The underlying philosophy of the mass production organization is seen to be such as to encourage the personnel specialists to emphasize the value of, and to develop methods for, relying on a body of rules as a foundation for achieving stability in productive performance and relations. In some countries advocates of personnel management have become

closely bound up with this strategy, possibly to the extent that they are seen to be incapable of switching to other strategies when the underlying market conditions change. However, it is concluded here that personnel functionaries, however designated, are likely to continue to adapt their approaches to the strategies that emerge from current rethinking of organizational objectives and strategies.

1 Definition and context

The term 'personnel management' is used to encompass those managerial actions concerned with the acquisition and utilization of labour services by any organization which pursues an economic purpose. The terms 'labour management' or 'human resource management' are sometimes used as substitutes, although they may be assigned subtly different meanings in some contexts. Nevertheless, the characteristic which distinguishes this management function from others is that it focuses squarely on the value of human resources to organizational activity (see HUMAN RESOURCE MANAGEMENT; INDUSTRIAL AND LABOUR RELATIONS).

Personnel management, like the management of any other resource, forms an element of all managerial activity because, by definition, all managers achieve their role objectives by organizing, directing and controlling the activities of other people, usually those of their subordinates in a hierarchy of roles. All managers must ensure therefore that the personnel needed are both procured from the external labour market and used effectively in the service of the organization's purpose.

Acquisition and utilization may be broken down into the particular tasks of recruiting, selecting, deploying, using, assessing, developing and rewarding the labour services necessary to achieving the goals of the organization and its management. These

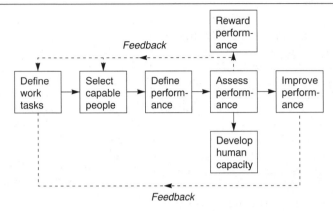

Figure 1 The sequence of human resourcing tasks

tasks, charted in Figure 1, are inescapable requirements in all organizations and are, therefore, similar in content wherever they are found although their mix and strategic contexts are not. They may be both conceived and organized into a function and assigned to officers of the organization in different ways. The characterization of the activities and the manner in which they are composed in the particular case are seen to be the product of a strategic underpinning, namely whether they fall within a conception of personnel management or of human resource management. However, the business strategies to which they relate differ: personnel management has developed within the context of a mass-production-fora-mass-market strategy and human resource management within that of a flexibleproduction-for-the-customized-market strategy, whether in the USA, Europe or Japan.

This distinction defines for personnel management the underlying and unchallengeable objectives and values which its exponents must necessarily accept, and for most of the twentieth century these have formed the foundations for their actions. These values are rarely made explicit in individual organizations and have to be inferred from the way managers, as agents of the organization, conduct themselves. In general the relevant values flow from the typical mass production strategy which emphasizes that the best way to achieve profitability in the mass market is:

1　to maintain a constant downward pressure on labour and other costs in order to main

tain or increase its competitiveness in terms of price, and;
2　to maintain a steady supply of products or services in line with the fluctuations in demand in the product market and free from disruption from any other cause.

Where these aims are pursued in labour markets in which appropriately skilled and motivated labour is relatively scarce, they produce business and human resource strategies which presume that:

(a) labour will be hired in from the external labour market and discharged back to it in line with the demand in the product market and little expenditure will be incurred in improving the labour supply;
(b) labour with the required skills and competencies either will be hired in (by poaching if necessary) or the work to be done de-skilled in order to enlarge the pool from which it can be drawn;
(c) labour is then required to apply these skills and competencies to the work offered by the employer and to perform to standards which meet the cost–benefit criteria established by the employer;
(d) labour is also expected to work to the rules and procedures laid down by the employer as guaranteeing that the work will be done in the best, cheapest and most orderly way;
(e) labour is subject to disciplinary action (and ultimately to discharge) in the event that the rules are not complied with in making the contribution required.

These form the parameters of the situation into which, from the end of last century onwards, the novel concept of labour or personnel management was introduced.

The following sections deal with a number of issues regarding the concept of personnel management.

- how has it developed?
- what have been the problems generated by its development and what are its achievements?
- why is there talk of it now being eclipsed by a new concept, that of human resource management?

Discussion draws heavily on the experience of the UK and the USA and also on a number of countries with different approaches to defining and allocating the roles associated with personnel management.

Although there is some basic similarity in approach, countries and cultures, as well as individual organizations, differ in the way they divide, define and assign the people-related tasks within organizations as they attempt to maintain integrity of purpose while securing the benefits of specialization. Tasks may be divided vertically, between those concerned with strategic and tactical decisions and those concerned with execution or implementation. Or they may be segregated horizontally, to achieve greater expertise in, for example, any of the areas separately identified in Figure 1.

Definition and allocation tends to follow where the basic division leads. The effect therefore may be to assign broadly defined personnel-orientated tasks to managers with broad operational responsibility (the generalists) or narrowly defined tasks to technicians or managers with narrow functional responsibility (the specialists). In either case the assignment may be given to managers/technicians who are relatively high or relatively low in the hierarchy of roles which makes up the modern (bureaucratic) organization. Individual organizations and cultures exercise choices on these dimensions with the result that personnel management may assume a variable character.

2 Origins and growth

The origins of personnel management lie in the adjustments made in the course of the industrial rationalizations which occurred in the UK and the USA at the end of the nineteenth century and elsewhere at other times. These developments were designed to address the mass market and resulted in the development of a technology usually referred to as mass production. Facilitated by new technologies they resulted in a new division of labour (typically identified with simplified and standardized tasks) and a new approach to the control of human work (usually identified with scientific management or Taylorism (see TAYLOR, F.W.)).

The central position of the skilled craftsmen, no longer in adequate supply, in the production process was taken over by the semi-skilled worker and this change necessitated a corresponding change in the way work and workers were managed. The craftsman's training had equipped him with sufficient skills and motivation to perform a range of work tasks to an acceptable standard with little direct and immediate supervision. Control of their performance had been secured by following a strategy of *selection* – carefully choosing the best craftsmen available from the pool.

This strategy was not appropriate to semi-skilled workers whose lower levels of skill and motivation called for a more direct and immediate supervision to inject the skills needed to carry out short-cycle tasks and to ensure that they performed them throughout the work period. A new cadre of supervisors became the key figures in the new regime and gave the name, *supervision*, to the new labour control strategy. As tasks were fragmented and human interest in work was reduced, control in accordance with detailed rules of work replaced the relationship of trust in the integrity of reliable workers which had served previously.

In addition to coping with the many technical and logistical tasks which production required, supervisors sought to maintain an adequate supply of compliant workers for the organization. This involved them in recruiting, inducting, allocating, motivating, assessing, remunerating and disciplining employees. They injected a limited amount of induction training but then relied on discipline and monetary incentives to sustain performance at the required level.

The number and complexity of their combined technical and human tasks increased as the size of the workplace increased and as the workers organized themselves into general labour unions which challenged management on a wider range of issues than the pay and apprenticeship ratios that the earlier craft unions had been concerned with.

On both sides of the Atlantic the response to the resultant overload was to appoint specialist functionaries to relieve the supervisor of some of the burden. Labour officers (mainly concerned with recruitment and selection activities) and welfare workers (expected to increase workers' loyalty by demonstrating to them that the employer cared) were therefore appointed at this time (Eilbirt 1959; Niven 1967). Work study engineers took responsibility for establishing work procedures and standards and for aligning these with bonus payments. At this stage, however, the first-line supervisors remained highly esteemed generalists and retained the 'final say' in these matters. The new lower status functionaries were there to help, support and service them, not to act on their own authority.

In the UK the burgeoning trade unions quickly challenged the extent of the welfare officers' concern for worker welfare. In the USA the timing was different because semi-skilled worker unionism was effectively resisted by employers until the 1930s. The 'social secretaries' were less strongly challenged in the USA than the welfare officers in the UK, although their impact was probably no greater because workers in both countries recognized that 'welfarism' was often motivated by the employer's desire to exploit them more effectively.

In both countries, however, the recruitment and selection activities of the labour officers were quickly augmented by the need to shape and administer employment contracts and to draw up compendia of works rules and disciplinary procedures to be applied in the event of their breach. The administration of pay became more complex as incentive (bonus) schemes replaced time-related rates as the main determinants of reward and as the unions sought to influence pay through collective bargaining (see COLLECTIVE BARGAINING; RECRUITMENT AND SELECTION).

The number and status of the labour and welfare officers both increased in the UK during the First World War, which put the new production systems to an urgent test. The general 'mobilization' of non-industrial workers for the war effort, and the subsequent pressure on employers to maintain production in the many 'munitions' industries, created new strains in the employment relationship as the attempt was made to secure worker compliance with the demands for war production.

This had two broad effects. First, it stimulated research by industrial psychologists, into the human, social and physical conditions affecting the workers' productive performance. This was to continue at a reduced rate after the war, but it supplied some of the theoretical underpinning for personnel management methods and techniques. In the USA the development of personnel management rested more singularly on the development of research-derived methods of improving human resourcing and utilization and many of the ideas adopted in the UK derived from this source.

Second, it established work and works rules as the main foundation for achieving control of labour. The workers' unions were then drawn into the process of both agreeing and policing them in the belief that agreed rules would be more effective than imposed rules in creating the conditions necessary to achieve greater worker compliance and productivity.

By the 1930s, therefore, the characteristic features of personnel management were already in place, although elaboration continued over later years. Labour officers were firmly established as technicians concerned with six broad areas of human resourcing activity:

1 Employment procedures (relating to labour supply and the determination of conditions and regulations of employment);
2 Personal relationships (including personal consultation and individual guidance, where required, on employees' problems);
3 Organizational relationships (including definition of responsibilities and duties, the notification of appointments, transfers, etc., and organization-wide mechanisms for joint consultation and the dissemination of information);
4 Education and training (of operative staff, both factory and administrative, supervisors and executives);
5 Physical working conditions (including matters of health, convenience and safety);
6 Social services and amenities (internal and external to the firm: physical, educational, social or recreational).

At this time these specialist executant roles remained sharply segregated from the planning and policy-making roles of general and operational managers. Subsequently, in the UK, the organizational status of the occupation set was to rise, but in other countries, typically in Germany and to a lesser extent in the USA, the segregation was to persist in its sharper form. They also tended to retain their 'original' associations and definitions – being primarily welfare, recruitment or training roles – and rarely were these generalized into a broad personnel function. It was this absence of coalescence within organizations at this time which denied personnel managers the conditions in which a broad-based professional association might develop.

Professionalization

In the UK the Second World War (which had similar consequences for personnel management as the First World War) was the catalyst which changed these conditions. By the end of it, personnel managers were able to describe themselves as performing a professional function, with a significant advisory and service role (Niven 1967; Crichton 1968). Its scope was as wide as 'people at work', its methods were informed by the findings of industrial

psychological research, and a body of relevant theoretical and technical knowledge had been assembled for transmission to students of the art (Northcott 1955). The occupational association was able to claim that its objectives contributed to the public good and to seek general support for its aspirations to be regarded as a professional body.

Part of this process involved separating personnel concerns from those of supervision, and giving them a clearer management connotation. To this end, personnel management was described as:

1 'an extension of general management', concerned with management's 'second responsibility' of 'prompting and stimulating every employee to make his fullest contribution to the purpose of the business...'
2 'an advisory function' and 'a staff activity' carrying 'no obvious authority except that which arises from its terms of reference and the knowledge and skill of the adviser'.
3 an organized function, 'that is, a body of duties brought together as the responsibilities of one person and carried out wherever they occur in the organization' (Northcott 1955: 12).

It was also claimed that each of its component elements – employment, wages, joint consultation, health and safety, welfare (employee services) and education and training – formed a distinct division of the personnel function (Moxon 1946).

The creation of a specialist function which might properly be referred to in the round as personnel management and the gradual establishment of a group of persons with a relevant professional expertise opened up opportunities for pursuing vertical careers entirely within the function, with access to the boardroom as a possible apex. This meant that, in principle at least, the occupational group could become involved in strategic or planning decisions and that those who did so might be internally differentiated from those members whose roles were confined to the executive activities associated with their implementation.

This view of the occupation remains less relevant to the position attained by it in a number of other countries. In Germany, for example, the personnel manager tends to be assigned lower order executant roles, often as a support to the kinds of activity associated now with the Works Councils, and is denied the status normally assigned to the technical managers: the opportunity to become a major player in the game of strategy or policy formation is correspondingly less.

This is to some extent a reflection of Germany's greater reliance on external, judicial, evaluation of managerial conduct which denies internal functionaries scope for influencing the values brought to bear by management in its human resource decisions. The effect is that the work role of the German personnel manager is less pro-active than that of his or her British colleague (Lawrence 1991) (see HUMAN RESOURCE MANAGEMENT IN EUROPE).

This view of a role subordinate to that of the line management is not absent in the USA or the UK, where doubts about the claims to professional integrity exist and criticisms are voiced about its piecemeal growth. It has been described as an assemblage of remnants (a 'rag-bag') or unconsidered trifles which mainstream managers were too preoccupied or simply unwilling to handle for themselves (Crichton 1968). In the USA Drucker condemned it on the grounds that personnel management 'puts together and calls personnel management all those things that do not deal with people and that are not management' (Drucker 1961: 243). But this focuses on what personnel specialists do and reflects the perspective which regards the management of personnel as an inseparable element of the general responsibility of the general and operations managers.

This highlights one of the two distinct conceptions of the management of personnel which have guided the development of practice emerging from these different approaches to handling people issues: namely, that which sees the function as an inescapable part of the ordinary management process and tends to emphasize the need to reserve strategic decisions for the organization's central, general management cadre, and to confine executive action in support of line management to technicians with a clearly subordinate status and role.

Although in the past central management may not have discharged their strategic decision-making function in respect of personnel very consciously or effectively, it has usually succeeded in excluding personnel specialists from this territory. This has been the case in the UK where the professional Institute of Personnel Management (IPM) has, with only limited success, maintained pressure to secure a specialist contribution to strategy formation at this level.

At the executant level organizations may choose between two alternative ways of lightening line managers' workloads and taking advantage of the benefits of specialization:

1 either to assign responsibility for action to the operational managers along with the freedom to seek advice or help from any source;
2 or to allocate some part of the general responsibility to specialist officers working with operations managers. This attempt to capitalize on the benefits of specialization can, however, take one of three forms:

a) rotation of generalist managers through specialist personnel roles for limited periods as part of their career development (as in the larger Japanese companies and increasingly often in the larger European companies);
b) appointment of specialist personnel managers on permanent contracts to supply expertise by way of advice or execution wherever and whenever it is needed;
c) hiring of commercial consultancy organizations to provide advice or service as required to allow the organization to avoid incurring a continuing burden of overhead costs.

All options involve a division of labour which leaves control in the hands of operations managers but offers scope to tap sources of advice and support: the main difference lies in whether these sources are incorporated into the bureaucratic organization or purchased from outside the organization as necessary.

The option chosen carries implications for control and for the development of an occupational identity and career paths. They vary in the opportunity they provide for challenges to general management values to be externally powered. They offer practitioners spiralist, bureaucratic or commercial careers and differential scope for forming an occupational association (see CAREERS).

A mediating role

The creation of an independent professional association implies that it will develop its own set of values of relevance to its members' activities. The possibility that these values will be different (at least to some extent) from those adopted by the host organizations which employ the members must always exist, but in the context of personnel management it assumes greater significance because personnel practitioners are involved in the containment of conflict arising from attempts by stakeholders to secure adoption or maintenance of their values in all managerial decisions.

In the UK this became a significant issue because of one long-standing perception of the personnel officer's function as one concerned with mediation. This might be between either: the worker and the harsher consequences of scientific management as implicit in the original welfare officers' and social secretaries' roles; or management and the trade unions once the conflict of interests and values between these stakeholders was institutionalized in collective bargaining (see COLLECTIVE BARGAINING).

The issue remains alive within the profession in the UK fostered partly by the IPM's attempt in 1963 to define the function in compromise terms, concerned with achieving both efficiency and justice in organizations (IPM 1963).

The eclecticism inherent in this statement has hindered attempts by members of the occupation to enhance their status, both within organizations and generally. Internally it fuelled line managers' doubts about where the specialists' loyalties lay and prevented them from accepting the legitimacy of any advice

that they might offer. More generally, since the welfare orientation was often seen by workers as a managerial sleight of hand to divert their attention from their exploited condition, and mediation as an attempt to contain conflict in management's interest, they found it difficult to accord legitimacy to their role. Both parties were led to question whether an effective mediating role could exist when the mediators are on the employer's payroll.

This stems from the inherent conflicts of interest of stakeholders in modern organizations, but it only becomes a problem when the aim of containing conflict by rule is adopted and someone has to establish whether the rules have been properly applied and properly obeyed.

In those economies in which many of these rules are determined 'voluntarily' (as the term has it) by the parties themselves, there must always be a presumption that they will then carry out all the assessments necessary. British experience suggests that an internal policing or mediating agency is likely to attract mistrust and suspicion from both parties.

These suspicions or distrusts are often exacerbated (although not created) by the enactment of labour or industrial relations legislation, and when the guardians of the internal rules assume responsibility for ensuring that the organization conforms to the requirements thus imposed. In a number of countries, such as the USA from the 1930s onwards and the UK during the 1960s and 1970s, the grafting of new legislation onto an already well-developed body of voluntary rules administered by internal agencies tended to increase role ambiguity. By subjecting employers' actions in respect of employees to greater external regulation than before, this legislation tended to increase the number of rules which personnel specialists were called upon to administer. It also emphasized that organizations had to deal with people issues not only to suit their own business interests but also to conform to social norms as expressed in legislation.

Thus, in the UK, individual workers were given greater statutory protection from employer decisions and, for part of the time, the trade unions were given support for their efforts to extend their control through collective bargaining. The personnel practitioners fell heir to policing these new rules.

Because they already had a role in devising and policing works rules and collective agreements the task of monitoring the organization's conformity to external rules, regulations and procedures seemed complementary. Their assumption of this wider mediation role had the effect of augmenting their power in dealings with operational management and increasing the tensions which existed between them as they came to be seen as defenders of industrial relations rules (and their associated values) for their own sake, even when this operated against the immediate economic interests of the host organization.

These tensions are not unknown in other countries but they appear to be muted where managements have learned over a longer period the advantage to be derived from placing as many as possible of the processes of rule-making and rule-enforcement outside the organization, even when this entails compliance with externally imposed laws. For example, in Germany general and operations management demonstrate considerable confidence in their system of formal regulation and orient their behaviours accordingly, in the belief that it frees local managers from many of the issues which otherwise might impede their attempts to sustain efficient operations.

In that context legislation establishes many of the rules to be applied to the employment relationship and the external labour courts supervise their application. Sectoral collective bargaining over rates of pay and hours of work segregate these issues from works council negotiations on work organization and performance standards, allowing much of the 'personnel activity' to be undertaken by technicians rather than senior managers. The interest of both management and workers in the internal mediation role is met in some circumstances by making the appointment of the labour (personnel) director by law subject to agreement between the main stakeholders.

In those countries which subject the employment relationship to closer control by law, members of the legal profession often play a bigger part in these issues than personnel practitioners themselves. The legal enforceability of collective agreements in the USA and a number of other industrialized countries has resulted in more lawyers being put on the payroll or drawn into the rule-making and -enforcing processes than, for example, would be true of the UK. As a consequence, the role of the personnel officer is very often subordinated to that of the labour relations manager, who is primarily concerned with (collective) contract negotiation. An incidental consequence of this is, however, that the occupation of personnel management *per se* risks less contamination from association with rule making, mediation and enforcement. Unfortunately it might also make human resource management as a strategy more appealing due to its enhanced status (see HUMAN RESOURCE MANAGEMENT; INDUSTRIAL AND LABOUR RELATIONS).

In the UK, however, the association of the personnel management function with internal rules and external laws hindered the profession's attempts to maintain credibility when, in the 1980s, government took steps to deregulate business and curb the power and influence of the trade unions. The contemporaneous actions taken by businesses to increase flexibility in their dealings with customers led some to seek more direct methods of modifying worker behaviour than securing orientation to rule. This, in turn, led them to form coalitions with trainers rather than with personnel managers for whom training had been regarded as a less significant mode of control than rule-based discipline.

From this point onwards the history of personnel management becomes entwined with the growth of human resource development and human resource management. This does not mark the demise of personnel management, but it does change the emphasis from reliance on rules to reliance on values and the replacement of traditional selection and supervision strategies with those of development and partnership.

There is no more reason to suppose that either human resource development or human resource management will become universal strategies than there was to expect personnel management to become relevant to all organizational settings. Personnel management had its typical host organization and human resource management and human resource development are likely to follow suit in this respect at least. For the future, it is likely that the personnel management function will be more closely integrated at the strategic level with more general business considerations; that the hierarchical career path for practitioners will be replaced by a spiralist path for general managers; that the opportunities to specialize in personnel activities will be offered on a temporary basis; and that personalized contracts of employment and individualized programmes of training, development and reward will replace the standardized practices which were previously upheld by a body of imposed or agreed rules (Fletcher 1993).

Models of personnel management

It may be concluded that personnel management is a concept associated with a particular phase in the evolution of both market relationships (being associated with supplying mass markets within a framework of price competition) and work organization (associated with a high level of specialization within bureaucratic structures). The typical host organization is the company which employs relatively large numbers of semi-skilled workers on routine tasks to produce standardized products for a mass market.

It is not normally found in all of these, nor in smaller private undertakings (in which people issues continue to be handled by general or line managers), nor in public sector organizations (which control labour through an establishment office, often linked to the financial control function). This alone (and without any benefits of hindsight provided by the arrival of human resource development and human resource management) supports the view that personnel management is only one of a number of possible approaches to dealing with people issues in organizations.

It may also be concluded that personnel management is in itself not homogeneous in character. The tasks to be performed and the

skills required to perform them combine in diverse ways.

At least four models of personnel management organization can be identified, both within and between economies (in the sense that different economies use different approaches but also demonstrate preferences for one model rather than another). The four may be summarized as:

(1) *The 'integrated' model*, in which personnel issues are handled within the responsibility of the general and line manager, and little or no internal segregation is permitted (even if external agencies may be used or listened to from time to time or for particular purposes).

(2) *The 'delegated service' model*, in which the routine tasks associated with personnel processes are segregated and allocated to lower status technicians, although the general and line managers and supervisors retain final authority to decide on the issues raised.

(3) *The 'advice and support' model*, in which the organization equips itself with specialized personnel management expertise at a relatively senior managerial level and creates a presumption that although operations managers retain ultimate authority, it is incumbent on them to consider the advice offered before deciding on the issues.

(4) *The 'external reference' model*, in which the managers take decisions and act on personnel issues as best they may, using such resources of information and expertise as may be available to them, and accepting that they will be subject to external assessment, either by judges or arbitrators, whenever the need for this is shown to arise.

What is normally identified as 'personnel management' is found in models 2 and 3. Model 1 is identified more with 'managing personnel' in the non-specialist mode and now with human resource management.

Model 4 has less claim to be considered a model of personnel management, but it is assuming relevance to the process in many countries, particularly in western Europe, and may exist alongside any of the other three. As its prominence increases, it may create a situation in which organizations make less use of 'generalist' personnel practitioners (that is, of persons capable of handling the whole range of tasks subsumed in Figure 1 above) and rely more on mono-skilled experts such as lawyers, psychologists or remuneration specialists (who may be put on the payroll or engaged temporarily as consultants).

3 Evaluation

It is not easy to separate the impact of 'personnel management' on either management practice or the treatment accorded to workers from the influence of other institutions on them.

On the one hand, general and operations managers have influenced them, both directly through their determination of strategy and policy and indirectly through the appointment of the personnel practitioners themselves. Central management normally determines strategies and policies in the light of operating conditions, not personnel management considerations, regardless of the way these are presented (by rotating generalists, by personnel specialists or by external advocates).

On the other, the trade unions have achieved some success by a sustained pressure on management to adopt alternative values and practices. This is a method especially effective when backed by sanctions. Personnel practitioners do not have the opportunity to impose sanctions, and although they may have served as organizational receptors for values and ideas initiated elsewhere, identifying their unique contribution to the introduction of such values and practices remains difficult. Every category of actor has access to ideas generated and personnel practitioners can claim no particular advantage in this respect other than that they keep up with such developments.

Their influence must also be restricted by the very nature of the goals and authority assigned by the host organization. It is to be presumed that employers who place personnel management on their agenda or personnel managers on their payroll expect to obtain value for the time or money spent and will continue to employ them only if their expectations are realized.

Precisely what employers expect or obtain will vary from case to case, but more efficient performance of the tasks listed in Figure 1 is likely to figure prominently in their motivation and experience. They no doubt also expect personnel managers to uphold, rather than challenge, the core values of the business and to use their best endeavours to ensure that such values are accepted without serious challenge by the workers.

The authority assigned to personnel managers for this purpose frequently restricts their scope for effecting significant change. Their authority is essentially theoretical (rather than managerial or administrative) and they succeed or otherwise to the extent that they can secure acceptance of their advice by rational argument. Ultimate authority to decide is usually left with the general and operations managers and specialists must act on their authority when providing their services.

It is not surprising therefore that personnel practitioners have had little impact on organizational values or strategies. In the first place, they are not appointed for this purpose; only rarely have personnel specialists been admitted to the boardroom, while generalists on rotation are unlikely to seek to challenge existing values. Where specialists are restricted to lower level technical tasks (whether as personnel officer, psychologist or trainer) their orientation is more likely to be towards improving methods and techniques and not towards modifying the management approach to people issues.

In the second place, their 'staff' positions in line-and-staff organization provides them with a weak power base from which to exert influence. The final choice is rarely left to personnel specialists and when their expertise enables them to influence decisions their success in this respect often creates a tension between those holding the line-and-staff positions.

This may be exacerbated when the specialist practitioners are enabled to establish either a separate (specialist) career structure within organizations or an independent occupational association outside them. The former fosters the growth of in-practice values and ideas and insulates them from challenge by other managers with different interests and orientations. The latter creates the possibility that the practitioners may be empowered as a consequence to advocate the adoption by organizations of alternative values. This is likely to be a greater potential threat to the unitary enterprise than an actual one. The history of the IPM demonstrates that while alternative sets of values may be identified, neither can be selected as a foundation for good practice to the exclusion of the other. The IPM's 1963 Statement recognized the choice as one of treating people as resources to the organization and treating them as inherently valuable persons capable of making a contribution to that process. Its compromise rejected the 'rabble hypothesis' as unacceptable on both efficiency and humanitarian grounds and advocated respect for personal integrity and the treatment of people at work equitably and humanely in order to achieve efficiency.

This suggests that personnel management, no matter how it might be organized in different contexts, is itself a creature of the mass production organization and in no position to challenge the assumptions on which it is based. Even where (as in the UK) it developed an independent association to propagate its own professional values, the resultant rhetoric rarely brought about any fundamental change in practice or the values which underpinned it. Recent experience suggests that it is when senior management sees a need to alter the business strategy to relieve a commercial problem that the assumptions on which personnel policies are based are questioned. But when this happens the existing personnel function may disappear along with some of the older values.

Improving practice

The main impact of personnel management as a distinct function is, as might be expected, upon the choice of methods and techniques applied to recruiting, selecting, developing, rewarding, etc., within a strategic framework decided by the more senior management.

Even here it has not usually been permitted to deal with all aspects of the labour control process, which must limit its potential impact.

The definition of work tasks and expected standards of performance, a key feature in the employment relationship, is carried out by the industrial engineers or management services staff. Definition and control of the rewarding and disciplining processes are retained by supervisors and line managers. Personnel specialists are restricted to advising improvements in the methods and techniques of resourcing organizations, improving performance at work and containing conflict between stakeholders with different interests.

At best, therefore, they may have some opportunity to effect marginal changes of practice when recommending or applying methods and techniques intended to uphold central values. Cumulatively, over time, this may produce a significant shift, but it is likely to be a slow process. This may smooth some of the rougher and less humane edges of management practices which flow from the central values but not modify the values themselves.

The generation of new practical ideas is not the exclusive preserve of personnel specialists, being a process shared with social scientists. The role of the practitioner, whether generalist or specialist, is usually that of the experimenter – who pragmatically identifies a problem and attempts to solve it by the most immediate or expedient means. That of the social scientist is often to refine these problem definitions and attempted solutions to the point where the latter acquire greater validity and reliability and become capable of more general application. The existence of a cadre of specialist practitioners may then help to ensure that the refined methods are taken up and applied.

Independent research in the social sciences has produced a body of knowledge which has been absorbed and used to inform recruiting, selecting, inducting, training, developing and rewarding activities. This has sometimes been melded with professional or practitioner concerns to yield a set of 'professional' principles and practices which increase the coherence of actions taken in the personnel management area. Consequently, what personnel managers do is seen to be rooted in social science-based 'theories of management practice', and personnel management to be concerned only with techniques for achieving ends that are defined for, and not challenged by, it. The long-standing supervisor link is not yet broken.

This set of principles focuses on three main contexts of managerial action.

(1) That of accessing the labour market to ensure a supply of appropriately skilled or malleable workers and choosing which workers to employ or discharge. (Improvements are seen in refined techniques of recruiting applicants and selecting those to be engaged or disengaged. They relate to establishing the appropriate criteria to be used in selection and the procedures for validly and reliably assessing applicants.) (See RECRUITMENT AND SELECTION.)

(2) That of structuring the workplace to ensure that the human resources engaged are utilized both effectively and efficiently and in a way which contributes to the achievement of the low-price competition goal of the host. (Improvements are concerned with increasing the compliance of workers with the rules of work appropriate to this type of business organization, with refining the disciplinary and remuneration systems and with redefining the rules themselves, but not usually by using the training mechanism for this purpose.) (See DISCIPLINE AND DISMISSALS; TRAINING.)

(3) That of containing potentially disruptive conflicts that might develop as trade unions challenge management decisions over an increasingly wide area of work activity. (Improvements have been sought by securing agreement to a reliance on negotiating procedures instead of, or prior to, breaching the employment relationship in order to bring about a change in industrial relations policy or practice.) (See COLLECTIVE BARGAINING.)

In developing methods and techniques for these purposes considerable use has been made of research findings and theory, but the main contribution of the personnel specialist has probably been to legitimate their application in actual workplaces.

Whether, in their turn, these applications have improved performance or raised levels of productivity and profitability is one of those questions which it is impossible to answer. Certainly they proved acceptable to those directly charged with achieving these ends, at least until changes in global markets threatened the foundations of the mass production system.

Challenging management

Reservations and tensions surround the acceptance of such principles for three reasons:

1 although the personnel function is usually subordinate to the central management cadre, the advocacy of more refined methods tends to threaten the line managers' self-conceptions by implying deficiencies in their technical knowledge and skills;
2 the combined efforts of the line managers and the personnel functionaries to improve efficiency have often been insufficient to sustain profitability in increasingly competitive markets and it is easy, and natural, for each to blame the other for the failure;
3 the contribution of the personnel management function under both of these heads usually results in behaviours being controlled more closely by rules and procedures, a situation which the specialists can justify but the managers and workers usually find irksome.

These, and the specific techniques associated with them, are a largely unavoidable concomitant of any attempt to increase the sophistication or professionalism of management and supervision which, arguably, has been the main contribution which personnel management has made to organizational functioning.

The controls directed at management behaviour attempt to improve the quality of the judgements involved in the decision-taking processes, particularly those relating to the selecting, deploying, developing, promoting, rewarding, disciplining or discharging of personnel. Success depends on the determination of relevant data and its generation as a spin-off from central production activities.

Those controls directed at (non-managerial) employees attempt to inculcate both values and behaviours which are considered to be appropriate to the achievement of the organization's production and performance ends. This process highlights the necessity for ensuring that direct and indirect communications between organization and employees are both effective in themselves and consistent with one another.

In both cases the controls are normally enshrined in a set of rules that have to be followed in order that certain desired outcomes will be achieved. These outcomes may be 'improved performance' in the managerial case or 'enhanced remuneration' in the employee case. Because these are desired by the people concerned, it is not necessary to enshrine the rules in formal statements of policy: the technique provides its own legitimacy. It is sufficient to indicate the rules necessary to achieve outcomes and rely on the desire to achieve them to do the rest.

Controlling judgements

Attempts to improve management judgements rest on a set of methods and techniques designed to inform management's decisions relating to all aspects of hiring, repositioning or discharging people and to reduce the effects of natural bias in the exercise of judgement in these situations. They are concerned with measuring or assessing two aspects of human beings; some features of their personality and their potential for performing work tasks to the standards considered necessary. Controls are necessary to prevent bias although most people have an inflated view of their own ability to make such judgements.

Personnel practitioners, despite their position of functional subordination, have challenged the common self-conception by increasing the sophistication of the instruments used to control the gathering, assembly and consideration of information needed for purposes of selecting, placing, promoting, training, rewarding and discharging employees. This in itself intrudes upon the generalists' preserves but the construction of instruments intended to control the exercise of judgement (as in plans used in interviewing, performance appraisal or disciplinary hearings) intrudes even further by implying that

managers cannot otherwise make unbiased judgements.

Motivating performance

Attempts to increase profitability have involved a set of techniques concerned with increasing the quantity and quality of workers' contributions to the organization's overall performance. Those associated with selection and performance appraisal fall within this category, but another class of techniques is more directly concerned with directing or steering employee behaviour rather than with assessing it either prospectively or retrospectively.

This technique is concerned with communication in the broad sense, which occurs in a multitude of contexts, such as instruction, persuasion, suggestion, negotiation, training and development and motivation. It is another human activity in which most people, and certainly most managers, consider themselves to be naturally proficient, so any suggestion that the way they approach communicating needs to be improved and controlled can be perceived as equally threatening to the self-image.

The need to improve communications has been present for a long time, although more recently the pressure to do so has probably increased. The traditional solution to the problem adopted in British organizations was that of selecting managers and supervisors with a demonstrable competence in communicating so that specific training in the skills of communicating could be dispensed with as unnecessary. The idea that non-managers might also need training in communication has also been given little credibility. Consequently, little progress has been made in improving communication by this direct, training method.

Personnel practitioners in the UK have often displayed reluctance to use direct methods of changing behaviours, such as training and development, as a strategy. They have played a part in training managerial and craft apprentices and trainees, as well as staff categories in short supply, but training has not been accorded high priority in their general approach to control or change. In fact, they have tended to accept the view commonly found in their host organizations that education and training are appropriately pursued at the employee's expense, namely off-the-job.

Consistent with this approach, structural solutions to the communications problem attracted greater interest and higher priority. In order to improve communications additional channels were constructed (such as line and staff channels or briefing groups) and others replaced when they became ineffective (as when trade union representatives 'captured' them and introduced 'noise' into the communication). This was intended to reinforce messages communicated via one channel by transmitting similar messages through another, in the manner that messages passed through the chain of command can be reinforced by adding team briefing. This admitted the possibility that messages passing along a number of different channels might, in fact, become non-reinforcing – might in fact increase confusion.

The same might be said of the traditional reliance in this situation on communicating through the pay packet. This stemmed from the belief that monetary incentives could tap human motivation sufficiently strongly and precisely to meet the needs of the mass production organization. The pay packet does indeed convey a message, but it communicates only a very broad and blunt one: like budgetary control, it requires supplementation by messages with a more specific content if it is not to give rise to conflicting interpretations of what is required. This outmoded form of communication has, however, tended to persist in the form of performance-related pay, which now fits badly with changed systems of work organization. The failure of the pay system to motivate provides line management with another reason for criticizing the performance of the personnel practitioners (see PAYMENT SYSTEMS).

The fact that messages are conveyed through a wide variety of media (channels) within organizations (the individual manager, the pay system, the system of work organization and allocation, for example) makes it necessary or desirable to check that the messages they transmit are consistent with one another. Personnel practitioners have attempted this at a structural level, but it is probably true to say

that their influence in this respect has been minimal for the reason already cited – that they have access to control of only some of the main media involved.

Containing conflict
Personnel management has also contributed to the development of methods of containing conflict in organizations which need to prevent disruption of the production of standardized products that have to be made available in volume in order to protect markets and profitability. This is yet another imperative of the host organization that personnel managers have accepted as their own.

In the UK and some other European countries this activity became a priority concern of personnel managers, although in Germany and the USA the law and lawyers were drawn into it more closely than personnel practitioners *per se*. Where it became linked with the personnel function it tended to identify it with reliance on rules and procedures (some developed from legal prescriptions and some developed in collective bargaining). Personnel practitioners are therefore seen to have a strong traditional involvement in consultation and negotiation with employee representatives (see COLLECTIVE BARGAINING; TRADE UNIONS).

The underlying theory is that behaviours may be controlled by securing the orientation of employees' behaviours to rules. They may be controlled more effectively if the necessary rules and procedures are established by agreement and not simply imposed. Since neither orientation nor agreement are automatic, it is necessary to devote time and resources to creating them; personnel managers consequently spend a great deal of their time on negotiations and on utilizing the grievance and disciplinary procedures through which the sovereignty of the rules is established and sustained.

The game of rule making by negotiation can, as in the UK in the 1970s, take over the role of the personnel officer. It may be seen as a response to a situation in which the whole employment relationship is forced to pivot on the outmoded concept of a purposive employment contract. This is a contract which establishes very limited obligations and undertakings, but it has to apply to a relationship which is in fact replete with extensive obligations and undertakings.

The terms of the contract are minimal: employees warrant that they can perform the work on offer and undertake to do it to the employer's order; employers warrant that they can provide opportunities for work and undertake to remunerate the employees for carrying it out. The employment relationship is, however, both more extensive in terms of mutual undertakings and their duration than the legal definition of the contract implies and the purposes which it is required by both parties to serve are wider than those that the lawyers are able to attach to it. For this reason collective bargaining – whether or not it is concluded with a legally enforceable agreement – may be regarded as an extension of the process of employment contracting which is necessary to fill out the minimal contractual undertakings. If trade unions had not sought to engage the employers in collective bargaining the employers might, in their own interests, have found it necessary to invent something very much like it.

This is, therefore, an area of activity where the personnel practitioners have come closest to injecting new values into managerial practice. The values in question are not necessarily those advanced by trade unions, but those which are related to the very concept of the employment contract itself. Attempts are being made to accommodate modern realities by introducing 'personal contracts', but for the most part these do not rise above the level of expediency and pragmatism and the need to consider more fundamental changes is not often recognized. In addition, government deregulation programmes begun in the 1980s have effectively retarded the process of redesigning institutions to make them fit the new economic and social realities.

4 The personnel management contribution

This evidence leads us to the conclusion that what we identify as personnel management

has never been expected to revolutionize the approach to the human resourcing tasks of the mass production/large-scale bureaucratic organization which has been its usual host and, therefore, cannot be castigated for failing to do what the host organization neither expected nor allowed it to do.

The function is introduced to ensure that semi-skilled workers able and willing to perform short-cycle tasks are recruited and maintained in an essentially compliant condition, but its particular form and emphasis is likely to vary with the circumstances surrounding its introduction.

The function is more often than not established as a service of help and advice to operations and general management, and assigned a status within the organization which reinforces this; only rarely is it drawn as an equal partner into deciding about strategies and policies, even on the few occasions when these are placed on the host organization's agenda.

It has developed a guiding philosophy, appropriate to the mass production organization and incorporated within its body of relevant knowledge, which emphasizes the long-term benefits to be obtained by securing employee orientation to and compliance with the rules by which work and the relationships surrounding it are to be ordered; the manner in which this is used to affect practice varies, but generally it has characterized the approach of the specialist to his/her task and role. It has been as little involved in creating the cultures now associated with human resource management and human resource development as it was in creating those which preceded them. What it has achieved, in association with external pressure groups and research organizations, is a distinct improvement in the methods and techniques applied by management in general to the human resourcing of organizations; its particular role has been to increase organizational receptivity to new ideas and theories of practice.

The association of the function with a characteristic philosophy and approach has meant that it often came to be seen as outmoded when the global shift from a mass to a customized market forced organizations to rethink their business and human resourcing strategies. This led general and operations managers to reassert their authority in the personnel area and to seek an alliance with those who claimed to have expertise in effecting behavioural modification by more direct methods (as in training).

But none of this, despite the predictions of the 1980s, has eclipsed the personnel specialists. They continue to demonstrate what their historical evolution shows them to be well capable of: accommodating themselves, their philosophies and their mix of practices to the conditions emerging in their host organizations. Nevertheless, for reasons which may have little to do with the capacity of personnel practitioners to achieve, any future consideration of personnel management may well take place under the title of human resource management if the desire to get rid of old associations and images were to triumph.

GEORGE F. THOMASON
UNIVERSITY OF WALES, CARDIFF

Further reading

(References cited in the text marked *)

* Crichton, A. (1968) *Personnel Management in Context*, London: Batsford. (Analyses the validity of the claim to increasing professionalization made by personnel managers in the wake of the Second World War.)

Department of Employment (1972) *Training for the Management of Human Resources*, The Hayes Committee Report, London: Department of Employment. (An analysis of the problem of training for work in the UK in the light of experience of the first Industrial Training Act, which paved the way for the development of a more pro-active approach to training within the framework of human resource development.)

* Drucker, P. (1961) *The Practice of Management*, London: Mercury Books. (Classic text outlining the seven tasks of the manager of the future.)

* Eilbirt, H. (1959) 'The development of personnel management in the United States', *Business History Review* 33 (3): 345–64. (A succinct account of the development of the employment management function in the USA including an indication of the functions with which managers were involved.)

Flanders, A. (1965) *Industrial Relations: What's Wrong with the System*, London: IPM. (A classic statement of the view that the personnel strategy is one concerned with control through rules and that collective bargaining is a process whereby rules can be developed jointly by management and unions to the advantage of both.)

* Fletcher, C. (1993) *Appraisal: Routes to Improved Performance*, London: IPM. (A review of current practice in an area which has assumed greater significance with the development of new contractual conditions in work organizations. It points to the limitations of existing contractual forms as mechanisms for containing the employment relationship.)

* IPM (1963) 'Statement on personnel management and personnel policies', *Personnel Management* March: 11–15. (Document outlining the necessity for personnel managers to compromise between treating employees purely as resources and recognizing their personal rights.)

* Lawrence, P. (1991) 'The personnel function: an Anglo-German comparison', in C. Brewster and S. Tyson (eds), *International Comparisons in Human Resource Management*, London: Pitman. (A comparison of the nature and organization of the function in the two countries, with more detail on the German position.)

Legge, K. (1988) 'Personnel management in recession and recovery', *Personnel Review* 17 (2): 1–72. (An analysis of then current developments in personnel management in the face of recession and subsequent recovery.)

* Moxon, G.R. (1946) *The Functions of a Personnel Department*, London: IPM. (Argues that personnel management can be split into separate and distinct areas.)

* Niven, M.M. (1967) *The Institute of Personnel Management, 1913–63*, London: IPM. (A history of the Institute of Personnel Management, indicating origins and the main milestones in its progress.)

* Northcott, C.H. (1955) *Personnel Management*, London: Pitman. (Textbook outline of the new professional role of personnel managers. Attempts to separate personnel management from supervision.)

Thomason, G. (1988) *A Textbook of Human Resource Management*, London: IPM. (A standard text indicating the main components of specialist personnel management as practised in the UK.)

See also: CAREERS; COLLECTIVE BARGAINING; EMPLOYEE RELATIONS, MANAGEMENT OF; HUMAN RESOURCE

DEVELOPMENT; HUMAN RESOURCE FLOWS; HUMAN RESOURCE MANAGEMENT; HUMAN RESOURCE MANAGEMENT IN EUROPE; INDUSTRIAL AND LABOUR RELATIONS; PAYMENT SYSTEMS; PRODUC-TIVITY; RECRUITMENT AND SELECTION; TAYLOR, F.W.; TRADE UNIONS

Related topics in the IEBM: MANAGEMENT IN JAPAN; MANAGEMENT IN NORTH AMERICA; ORGANIZATIONAL PERFORMANCE

Problem solving

Overview

Problem solving is an important part of the managerial role. Few writers have written exclusively on the topic. Those who have, broadly agree on the key stages of a systematic approach required to take effective decisions. There are different types of problems which will be outlined and these require different approaches to reaching a solution. The stages of problem solving will be described followed by techniques which can be used to solve the problem more effectively. In recent years more and more attention has been focused on problem solving in teams. Issues relevant to team-based problem solving will be discussed. There is also a growing need to help others solve problems and relevant skills for this process will be outlined. Problem-solving processes are at the heart of total quality management, project management and continuous improvement programmes. Recent writers have also drawn attention to the need to create the right organization culture and climate for problems to be solved innovatively, particularly when the organization is undergoing dramatic change.

1 Types of problem

Kepner and Tregoe (1981) defined a problem as the deviation that occurs as a result of some unanticipated change which produces an unwanted effect in place of the desired effect. This may in turn impact on performance and result in substandard quality of work. Francis (1990) emphasizes the need to be more specific when describing a problem. His classification gives an indication of the different types of problem which need to be solved.

1 *Mystery* – an unexplained deviation from what is expected, the emphasis is on the lack of explanation for something happening which does not match expectations and has an unknown cause.
2 *Assignment* – this happens when an individual is given a task to do by someone else. It is a kind of contract between the boss and the subordinate. The contract needs to be understood, explicit, achievable and agreed.
3 *Difficulty* – something which is difficult to achieve due to lack of awareness of how to manage the situation or the lack of resources.
4 *Opportunity* – a situation which offers a potential benefit.
5 *Puzzle* – which has a correct answer and wrong answers. To find the correct answer complexities and uncertainties must be unravelled. Some puzzles may never be solved.
6 *Dilemma* – there are at least two options for action which are equally attractive or unattractive and judgement is required to make a decision.

Depending on the type of problem, different stages in the problem-solving process assume different degrees of importance.

2 Stages of problem solving

Most companies require their managers to be competent problem solvers (see MANAGERIAL BEHAVIOUR). The difference between a good and a poor problem solver often lies in the extent to which the managers adopt a systematic approach to problem solving. Wilson (1993) provides a useful comparison between the different models which have been developed. All the models are based on the need to identify and clarify the problem, use the right hand side of one's brain to think divergently to gather information and ideas. There is then a phase of convergent thinking to analyse the data collected and decide on the best course of action. Wilson points out that different cultures devote different amounts of time to the different stages (see CULTURE, CROSS-NATIONAL; ORGANIZATION CULTURE). In the East, for example in Japan, much longer is spent generating creative ideas than in Western cultures where the solution is arrived at much quicker but where longer is spent putting ideas into practice. Most models emphasize a number of key steps.

1 *Analysing the problem* – at this stage information is gathered to identify the real problem and its causes and to assess its importance.
2 *Objective setting and establishing criteria for success* – this involves having a clear view of the end goal and of how success at achieving the objective will be measured.
3 *Information gathering* – this step requires data to be collected and ideas to be generated on possible options. Once the options have been establish their suitability can be assessed.
4 *Decision making* – the options are evaluated and the decision is taken on the best course of action.
5 *Implementation* – this requires planning what needs to be done and implementing the action plan.
6 *Reviewing success* – this is a critical stage which can often be missed out and involves assessing what went well, what went less well and implications for the future.

Each of the steps is important, but, as Francis (1990) describes, it is sometimes possible to use the structure flexibly.

3 Techniques used in problem solving

There are a number of techniques that can be used to solve problems more effectively. Problem identification techniques include situational appraisal and significance analysis. Situational appraisal is used by Francis

(1990) and has two stages: first, structured fact-finding, where all the questions which need asking about the situation are written down on individual 'post-it notes' and then grouped together with other similar questions; second, situation analysis, which involves all information related to the situation being written down on 'post-it notes' and attempts being made to answer the questions generated in the structured fact-finding stage. Significance analysis provides a way of analysing the importance of various issues. Four key questions are asked.

1 Why is this issue a concern?
2 How important is the issue relative to other things requiring attention?
3 Who should be concerned with resolving the issue?
4 What are the real constraints or limitations faced?

Brainstorming, the fishbone technique, Pareto charts, and histograms are all techniques used for information gathering or analysis. Brainstorming was developed by Alex Osborn in the 1950s to encourage groups to be more creative when generating ideas. It is a group problem-solving technique and is described in detail by Robson (1988). Ideas are generated freely and recorded on a flip chart. People must be willing to free-wheel and disclose any ideas. Judgement is suspended until later when the ideas are then evaluated.

The fishbone technique was developed by Ishikawa and is widely used for problem solving in total quality processes (see ISHIKAWA, K.). It helps in the understanding of cause and effect and is shown diagrammatically in Figure 1. Pareto charts and histograms are used to display numerical information on the possible causes of the problem and are described by Wilson (1993). These vertical bar charts are named after the Italian economist who

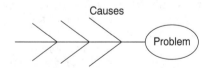

Figure 1 The fishbone technique
Source: Majaro (1988)

established the 80/20 principle. They show diagrammatically the relative importance of different issues.

The decision matrix, described by Kepner and Tregoe (1981), is a decision-making technique in which the different options for decisions are listed (see DECISION MAKING). Each option is then assessed against selected criteria set out in a matrix. On the basis of this comparison various alternatives can be assessed.

Force-field analysis is a useful technique to evaluate factors which will help implementation and change, and identify and overcome factors which could inhibit change. It is shown diagrammatically in Figure 2. A number of steps need to be undertaken: (1) the desired outcome is clearly stated; (2) helping and hindering forces are identified; (3) ways of reducing the strength of hindering forces, or eliminating them, and increasing helping forces are identified; and (4) actions to achieve the desired change can then be undertaken.

The techniques outlined above can be used individually, but they can equally well be used by teams, especially those which require creative thinking.

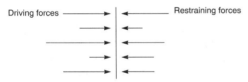

Figure 2 Force-field analysis

Helping others solve problems

In recent years managers have been expected to use different styles which are appropriate to the particular situation they are managing (see LEADERSHIP). This will often require them to adopt a less directive style and instead act as a facilitator and enabler. Egan (1986) specified a number of key skills needed for operating this enabling style. When helping others solve problems the skills of attending, listening, empathy, probing and challenge are necessary to help others develop a clear view of their situation. People can then be helped to develop future scenarios and commit to a specific action plan for problem resolution.

4 Problem solving in teams

Team-based problem solving has increased in importance for a number of reasons (see GROUPS AND TEAMS). Mainly, as organizational problems become more complex more than one person is often involved in a particular problem, making a team approach more suitable. Teams are more able to develop creative solutions using the appropriate tools available to them.

While the models and techniques for problem solving remain the same, the process of teamworking does need to be managed to play to the strengths of the team members. Teams can experience certain difficulties which block effective problem solving if left unresolved. Some team members will contribute ideas, others will ensure that the ideas can be developed into workable solutions.

Belbin (1981) conducted research at Henley Management College to identify characteristics of successful teams. He identified nine roles and their associated behaviours which all contribute to team success. Each of the roles also have their part to play in effective problem solving. There are those who generate the ideas, those who evaluate the usefulness of the ideas and those who turn the ideas into solutions which can be applied in the working environment. Others are needed to help the team work together effectively and to ensure that the task gets completed.

Robson (1988) identified three key problems external to the problem solving group which have to be addressed. Sometimes the problem the group has been tasked to solve just disappears. Alternatively, people may be reluctant to join a problem-solving group for fear of the unknown, or the groups may also be viewed with suspicion by other employees.

Robson also highlighted internal problems. These range from the use of time, to interpersonal difficulties, lack of appropriate skills and motivation, and problems with the process of the team problem solving. Francis (1990) makes reference to the research of Irving Janus into the concept of group think. According to Janus, as teams become cohesive, people with dissonant views are expelled by the majority who share common views. Team members gain reassurance from one another when taking decisions which results in groups sometimes taking much riskier decisions than individuals would take.

5 Problem solving at work

There are many ways of dealing with problems which arise at work, but much can be learnt from the Japanese when striving to solve the problems faced by organizations today of achieving and maintaining competitive edge. Reference will be made to the *kaizen* approach, use of cross-functional teams and quality circles.

The *kaizen* philosophy, as described by Walker (1993), originated in Japan and is considered to be fundamental to the country's competitive success in the world market. The technique is now used extensively in manufacturing, even in companies with no Japanese connections. *Kaizen* is an approach to achieving continuous improvement by a system of making many small changes to improve the workplace. The system is customer-focused, both internal and external customers, and views people as the organization's most important asset. It requires involvement, commitment and openness.

The PDCA cycle is a powerful technique used in the approach. It is an endless improvement cycle which involves:

- Plan – survey/understand/identify
- Do – adequate actions
- Check – verify effect/ evaluate
- Act – feedback to upstream sources

It is often said Japanese managers spend 80 per cent of their time planning while Western managers spend 80 per cent of their time acting. What Japanese managers tend to do is move through the PDCA cycle quite quickly, particularly the first two steps. They are then meticulous at standardization and examining each stage to develop a system.

The Japanese have also led the field in the use of quality circles as an approach for achieving total quality. In years to come this is likely to assume as great an importance as the Industrial Revolution and impacts significantly on the level within the organization at which problem solving takes place.

Hutchins (1990) gives a clear definition of quality circles and emphasizes that they engage in solving problems which are identified by the circle in their own work area and which they in turn are able to solve. The circles are led by the team supervisor and quality improvement issues within the control of the work team are the focus of the circle.

6 Problem-solving culture and climate

Stephens (1988) emphasizes the importance of the climate within an organization as a stimulant or a barrier to effective problem solving (see OCCUPATIONAL PSYCHOLOGY). Many organizations have failed in the past to have problems solved creatively because the prevailing management style prevents people from taking risks. Successful organizations have encouraged commitment, acknowledged failure as a development opportunity and rewarded innovative ideas. An authoritarian, critical management style encourages people to adopt a low risk strategy. Managers who delegate problem solving to their staff enable the process to take place at the level where people have the information to solve the problems and the problem solvers are committed to the solutions they recommend.

In the next ten years problem solving will not only cross functional boundaries but also company and cultural boundaries. As more businesses become global people will have to develop their skills of problem solving cross-culturally. The extent to which the process is successful will depend on the use of a range of problem-solving techniques and the recognition of the differing strengths which people can offer depending on their cultural background.

JANE CRANWELL-WARD
HENLEY MANAGEMENT COLLEGE

Further reading

(References cited in the text marked *)

* Belbin, R.M. (1981) *Management Teams: Why They Succeed or Fail*, Oxford: Heinemann. (Provides a useful understanding of roles played by successful team members and includes those associated with problem solving.)

Bird, M. (1992) *Problem Solving Techniques That Really Work*, London: Piatkus. (Helpful book on the management of information for problem solving and how to make the solution work.)

* Egan, G. (1986) *The Skilled Helper*, Belmont, CA: Brooks/Cole. (Focuses on the way to help others solve problems.)

* Francis, D. (1990) *Effective Problem Solving*, London: Routledge. (An excellent workbook approach for solving problems systematically.)

* Hutchins, D. (1990) *In Pursuit of Quality*, London: Pitman. (Understanding problem solving in the context of quality and continuous improvement.)

* Kepner, C. and Tregoe, B. (1981) *The New Rational Manager*, London: John Martin. (A classic book on problem solving which is particularly useful for decision analysis.)

* Majaro, S. (1988) *Managing Ideas for Profit–The Creative Gap*, Maidenhead: McGraw-Hill.

* Robson, M. (1988) *Problem Solving in Groups*, Aldershot: Gower. (Includes thorough coverage of problem-solving techniques that are useful for groups.)

* Stephens, M. (1988) *Practical Problem Solving for Managers*, London: Kogan Page. (Covers a wide range of aspects on problem solving, including creating a climate for problem solving.)

* Walker, V. (1993) 'Kaizen: the art of continuous improvement', *Personnel Management* August. (Describes the use of the *kaizen* approach to continuous improvement.)

* Wilson, G. (1993) *Problem Solving and Decision Making*, London: Kogan Page. (Offers a good range of tools and techniques and provides an excellent overview of the various approaches to problem solving.)

See also: DECISION MAKING; ISHIKAWA, K.; MANAGERIAL BEHAVIOUR; TOTAL QUALITY MANAGEMENT

Related topics in the IEBM: COGNITION; DEMING, W.E.; INDUSTRIAL REVOLUTION; JURAN, J.M.; LEWIN, K.; MANAGEMENT EDUCATION IN JAPAN; MANAGEMENT IN JAPAN; ORGANIZATION STRUCTURE

Productivity

Overview

Webster's *Dictionary* defines productivity as: 'A state of yielding or furnishing results, benefits or profits'. This definition may be intuitively appealing, but it is of little use to managers of economic activities since it overlooks the resources used to yield the results. Economists overcome this shortcoming by defining productivity as the ratio of output to input, or the results achieved per unit of resource; a measure of how effectively the resources are utilized.

This entry emphasizes the role of management in increasing the productivity of the firm. There is an extensive body of literature covering techniques for measuring and improving productivity, and a representative selection of these references is listed at the end of the article. The details of the techniques contained in the references will not be covered. The aim of this entry is to provide an overview, or conceptual framework, to enable a manager to define a productivity improvement programme that is appropriate for the firm and select the techniques to be used for its implementation.

1 Macroeconomic significance

Economic activities can be viewed as processes for converting input factors, or resources, into outputs that are of economic value. This value-adding conversion is depicted in Figure 1.

For example, manufacturing processes convert inputs of labour, material, capital and energy into products such as automobiles or appliances. In microeconomic theory, the

Figure 1 Economic activity model

production function defines the output quantity per time period for given input quantities. The elasticity coefficients for the inputs – the percentage increase in output for a given percentage input increase – determine the productivity level. These coefficients are normally assumed to be a function of the state of technology in the firm's industry. Research, however, has shown that major productivity differences often exist among firms within a given industry. The differences are explained by variations in management, hence the productivity of a firm can be a measure of managerial performance.

At the national level, productivity increases are necessary for a country to achieve long-term economic growth, improved living standards and price stability. In today's global economy, productivity levels also influence the international competitiveness of a country's products. The need to increase productivity is particularly crucial in developing nations, as emphasized by the International Labour Organization: 'It is clear ... that the vicious cycle of poverty and unemployment can be broken only by increasing productivity' (Prokopenko 1987: 6).

If national productivity is significantly to increase, there must be an aggregation of widespread improvement in individual enterprises. Effective monetary, fiscal and regulatory policies by government can certainly help to create an economic climate favourable to high productivity. However, a favourable climate by itself is not sufficient. The major responsibility for productivity improvement must be met by the managers of individual enterprises.

2 An operational model of productivity

The equation that defines productivity as the ratio of output to input must be expanded to define more clearly the input resources and to identify the opportunities available to managers for increasing productivity. There are two types of resource: fixed and variable. By definition, the quantity of fixed resources utilized does not vary with output during the time period considered. Fixed inputs could include indirect labour and energy for office heating. In contrast, the quantities of variable inputs, such as direct material and direct labour, vary with output.

To derive a more useful form of the productivity equation, the following variables are defined:

Let:

P = productivity
t = time period
q = output rate
Q = total output = qt
F = fixed resource input per period (t)
v = variable resource input per output unit

We begin with the basic equation:

$$P = \frac{\text{Ouput}}{\text{Input}}$$

The output during the period t will be Q and the input will be the sum of the fixed and variable inputs, or $F + vQ$. Therefore:

$$P = \frac{Q}{F + vQ}$$

Dividing through by Q, we get:

$$P = \frac{1}{F/Q + v}$$

This equation identifies the opportunities for increasing productivity, P. To increase the value of P, the magnitude of the denominator, $F/Q + v$, must decrease. There are two ways of achieving this in the short run:

1 decrease the value of v, the amount of variable resources required per unit of output;

2 decrease the value of F/Q, the portion of fixed input allocated to each output unit. Since F cannot be reduced in the short run, the total output Q must be increased by increasing the output rate q.

Beyond the short run the fixed inputs can also be varied. Because successful productivity improvement requires long-range programmes, there is a third opportunity:

3 decrease the value of F by reducing the amount of fixed resources required per time period.

This conceptual approach to productivity improvement can help managers to focus on productivity programme results instead of on programme activities. If, as a result of the programme, the values of the fixed and variable inputs are decreased, and output is increased, the firm's productivity must increase. Conversely, if the improvement programme fails to achieve any of these results it will be a failure regardless of the amount of enthusiasm and activity it generates within the firm. The approach also emphasizes the need for developing adequate measures for evaluating the performance of improvement programmes, measures that track reductions in variable and fixed inputs and increases in output to ensure actual productivity improvements.

3 Where to begin

A comprehensive programme to improve the productivity of the firm requires a substantial commitment of resources. Therefore, a logical starting point is the productivity of the programme, a concern for maximizing the ratio of the improvements to the resources used. This requires a strategic approach similar to that proposed by Garvin:

> There is no one, best route to superior productivity. A wide range of approaches have proved to be successful. The task for managers is to recognize the alternatives that are available and then choose the approaches that best match their company's culture, capabilities, and competitive needs.

(Garvin 1992: 209)

A strategic assessment of the competitive position of the firm's products and services, its culture, and the availability and quality of its resources is a critical first step to improving productivity. If a programme is to 'make a difference' in the performance of the firm, the resources employed must be directed at products, services and processes that are 'highly leveraged', where there are opportunities for productivity improvements to impact significantly on cost, quality and customer service.

The strategic assessment must be appropriate to the size and resources of the firm. In large firms it can be a formal strategic planning process, using techniques such as benchmarking and quality function deployment (see TOTAL QUALITY MANAGEMENT). In smaller firms the process will, by necessity, be less formal, less quantitative and depend more heavily on executive judgement and experience. It is, however, no less critical than in larger companies. Embarking on a productivity programme without a clear sense of direction is a serious error. It creates the situation described by Billy Crystal, portraying a cowboy in the film *City Slickers*: on a cattle drive where no one knows where the herd is heading, he comments 'We're lost but we're making good time.'

4 Characteristics of successful programmes

The definition and design of a productivity programme should be 'custom tailored' to the needs and capabilities of the firm. 'Off the peg' programmes offered by consultants or management books should be avoided. There are, however, some generic characteristics of successful programmes that should be pursued.

Strategic integrated programmes

The traditional approach to productivity improvement focuses on direct labour productivity in manufacturing. The emphasis is on short-term cost reductions and no attempt is made to integrate the manufacturing programme with the strategic plan or the other functions within the firm. This approach is clearly sub-optimal. For example, manufacturing can expend resources to improve the production of a component that could be eliminated by an engineering design change.

In contrast, an integrated strategic approach links the productivity programme to the firm's business needs. The major departments within the firm, as well as key outside suppliers participate and contribute in a coordinated manner. There is a trend in manufacturing towards reduced vertical integration and increased reliance on outside suppliers to provide specialized technology and expertise. As a result, key suppliers are important 'partners' in productivity improvement programmes. Integrated programmes are particularly important in those firms whose strategy is based on using their manufacturing competence as a competitive weapon.

Top management support

No comprehensive productivity improvement programme can be successful without the strong support and involvement of the chief executive. A successful programme requires strategic input, a high priority, a commitment of resources and an integrated effort throughout the firm. Only the chief executive can deliver all of these and also provide the leadership needed to initiate and sustain a programme. Top management support is also needed to help 'keep the faith' in the early stages of a programme. There can be an initial decrease in productivity as resources are diverted from productive short-term activities to the learning phase of the new programme. Maintaining the commitment to the programme during these negative returns is obviously aided by strong support at the top.

Emphasis on breakthrough opportunities

Strategic productivity programmes emphasize 'breakthrough' improvements, as compared to the incremental improvements sought by activities such as employee quality circles. The two are not mutually exclusive. Continuous improvement programmes with employee involvement help to promote a productivity improvement culture. They also provide continuity of improvement since breakthroughs can be achieved only intermittently. The design of the goods and services offered by the firm and the design of the processes used by the firm are two activities that offer high potential for achieving productivity breakthroughs.

Product designs can be improved by using design for assembly (DFA) and design for manufacturability (DFM) techniques. These are computer programs that systematically subject a design to a series of decision rules to identify opportunities for reducing the number of parts. IBM used DFA/DFM to achieve a breakthrough in the design of their personal computer, Proprinter. They reduced the number of parts by 67 per cent and assembly time by 50 per cent – decreasing variable inputs and increasing production output.

Breakthroughs in services can be achieved through business process re-engineering (BPR), a technique that combines the use of industrial engineering process flow analysis with the power of information technology. A US supplier of industrial goods re-engineered its order entry system that hitherto required 600 employees at 25 regional offices and corporate headquarters and which took two weeks to process an order. The re-engineered system is run by 150 employees, organized into multi-functional teams at headquarters and linked to customers by fax and e-mail. The order processing time has been reduced to under two hours.

Process analysis of the flow of products can enable managers to identify bottlenecks in the production process – namely, points of low capacity and minimum flow that control the total output rate. Eliminating these bottlenecks, through new technology or the reorganization of work, can often achieve output breakthroughs. A UK heavy machinery manufacturer used bent tubular assemblies in all of its machines. The wide variety of tubular configurations and long set-up times on the tube bender created a bottleneck. A computer-controlled bender was installed, thereby eliminating lengthy set-ups, removing the bottleneck and helping to double output.

Managed use of technology

Technology is a key resource and an important factor in increasing productivity. Its importance is confirmed by the research of Hayes and Clark (1995). They studied the factors that account for differences in productivity among factories and reported that: 'Our data show unequivocally that capital investment in new equipment is essential to sustaining growth in Total Factory Productivity (TFP) over a long time.' But they also point out that: 'Simply investing money in new technology or systems guarantees nothing' (Hayes and Clark 1995: 475). A firm cannot simplistically automate its way to increased productivity. The effect of capital investment on performance is determined by the way in which the introduction of the technology is managed. Hayes and Clark conclude that: 'Managed right, new investment supports cumulative, long term productivity improvement and process understanding – what we refer to as "learning" '.

Installing new technology without properly training the workforce and without making required changes in the design of products, processes and systems can have a negative effect on productivity. It can disrupt existing methods, create confusion and frustration among the workers and seriously damage the credibility of management.

Hammer (1990) reaches the same conclusion regarding information technology. The failure of US companies to manage properly the massive investment in information technology during the 1980s resulted in an absence of significant increases in productivity. The major fault was in computerizing existing systems and processes instead of improving or eliminating them – an approach Hammer calls 'paving the cowpaths'.

Long-term view

A long-term view is essential if productivity improvement is to have a real impact on the firm's performance and profitability. Successful programmes imbue a concern for productivity into the culture of the firm. Cultures change slowly, and the change process tends to face resistance (see ORGANIZATION CULTURE). Programmes must exhibit continuity and success to overcome these barriers.

Long-term continuity builds credibility as employees become convinced that top management is serious about improving performance. Continuity also promotes organizational learning and competence in improvement techniques. Productivity successes add to the credibility of the programme and also generate confidence and enthusiasm among employees. It is important to celebrate these successes through effective communications and recognition programmes. Japanese firms make it a practice to list the names of employees contributing successful ideas and post sketches of the ideas on bulletin boards to recognize the contributors and stimulate additional applications.

5 Barriers to success

Most attempts to implement comprehensive productivity enhancement programmes face a variety of obstacles. Improving productivity can be viewed as an exercise in constrained optimization, where the objective is to achieve the maximum improvement consistent with the constraints or barriers that are faced. If the constraints can be relaxed, the 'solution space' – the range of feasible alternatives – can be increased.

In practical terms, attempting to overcome the barriers should be part of any productivity programme. Most of the major difficulties encountered are highlighted in the references. These include resistance to change by employees and managers, the use of invalid or confusing productivity measures, short-term performance measures and reward systems that conflict with long-term improvement, and fear of job losses due to increased productivity.

One barrier that tends to be overlooked in the productivity literature results from the limitations on management actions caused by restrictive work rules or 'custom and practice' in union shops. Restrictive practices can increase v, the amount of variable resources required; they can increase F, the necessary fixed resources; and they tend to reduce the total output Q. The result can be a sharp decrease in productivity. Table 1 shows the negative effects of a few restrictive practices. These are typical of a broad range encountered in union shops – prompting efforts by management to change them in order to improve performance more effectively.

In the UK, during the 1960s, productivity bargaining was often used. Payments over and above regular compensation were made to workers in return for changes in work practice. In many cases the restrictive practices were gradually restored through union guile and management neglect, resulting in a cycle of periodic buyouts of the same practices. During the 1980s the nature of these agreements changed, resulting in actual manning reductions through redundancies to prevent the deterioration of the new levels of flexibility.

In the USA managers have pursued changes in restrictive labour contract clauses primarily through 'concession bargaining'. Work practice concessions on the part of the unions usually result from either the 'carrot' of improved worker job security or the 'stick' of plant closure threats.

Table 1 Effects of restrictive work practices

Increase in v	Increases in F	Decreases in Q
Excess manning in direct labour	Excess manning in indirect labour due to narrow craft demarcations and restrictions on operators doing simple crfat tasks	Delays waiting for craft support for set-ups, minor adjustments and inspections – even if operators are capable
Demarcation limits – 'not my job' – preventing idle workers from helping busy ones		Overtime bans

6 Productivity and quality

High quality is a competitive necessity in virtually all markets, placing an added constraint on productivity programmes. Productivity improvements cannot be made at the expense of quality. Fortunately the trade-off is not a zero-sum situation. IBM, for example, simultaneously improved productivity and quality by reducing the number of parts in their printer.

This potential for a symbiotic relationship between quality and productivity improvement was first demonstrated on a large scale by manufacturers in post-war Japan, particularly in the motor industry and in consumer electronics. To achieve this potential, the objectives of a productivity programme should include the enhancement of both productivity and quality.

7 Conclusion

During the 1990s, several factors have combined to create a heightened awareness of the importance of productivity. Global competition is an increasing reality. The countries of eastern Europe and developing nations face the daunting challenge of this competitive arena, creating the spectre of cheap labour competition for the industrialized countries. Many of the economies of western Europe are experiencing zero growth and historically high levels of unemployment. Any solutions to these challenges must include substantial productivity improvement.

The key players in this scenario are the managers. Productivity must be measured and managed in order to be improved. Today's managers have at their disposal an unprecedented array of technological and innovative means for organizing the production of goods and services. The effectiveness with which they utilize these resources will be a major influence on the survival and success of their firms.

ROBERT CONTI
BRYANT COLLEGE

Further reading

(References cited in the text marked *)

Blackburn, J. (1991) *Time-Based Competition: The Next Battleground in American Manufacturing*, Homewood, IL: Business One Irwin. (An approach to increasing productivity by reducing throughput time in manufacturing and product development.)

Costin, H. (ed.) (1994) *Readings in Total Quality Management*, Fort Worth, TX: Harcourt Brace. (Excellent collection of readings covering all aspects of total quality management, including details of productivity improvement techniques.)

* Garvin, D. (1992) *Operations Strategy: Text and Cases*, Englewood Cliffs, NJ: Prentice Hall. (Insightful coverage of manufacturing as a competitive weapon, with an excellent module on 'competing on productivity'.)

* Hammer, M. (1990) 'Re-engineering work: don't automate, obliterate', *Harvard Business Review* July–August: 104–9. (Describes the rationale for BPR and outlines the steps required for its implementation.)

* Hayes, R. and Clark, K. (1995) 'Why some factories are more productive than others', in V. Sower, J. Motwani and M. Savoie (eds), *Classic Readings in Operations Management*, Fort Worth, TX: Dryden. (Chapters on operations strategy, quality and productivity. The last contains ten worthwhile articles.)

Hronic, S. (1993) *Vital Signs*, New York: AMACOM. (Well-organized coverage of the development and use of performance measures that emphasize operating results instead of process activities.)

Lawlor, A. (1985) *Productivity Improvement Manual*, Westport, CT: Quorum. (Well-written, detailed manual for implementing a total productivity improvement programme.)

* Prokopenko, J. (1987) *Productivity Management: A Practical Handbook*, Geneva: International Labour Office. (Excellent overview of productivity and broad coverage of specific steps for an improvement programme; recommended for a productivity bookshelf.)

Steudel, H. and Desruelle, P. (1992) *Manufacturing in the Nineties*, New York: Van Nostrand Reinhold. (Lucid introduction to all aspects of the newest forms of high-performance production, including just-in-time and cellular manufacturing.)

Wilson, S., Ballance, R. and Pogany, J. (1995) *Beyond Quality, An Agenda for Improving Manu-*

facturing Capabilities in Developing Countries, Aldershot: Edward Elgar. (Detailed coverage of a programme for improving labour productivity in developing nations through continuous improvement techniques.)

See also: HUMAN RESOURCE MANAGEMENT; TOTAL QUALITY MANAGEMENT

Related topics in the IEBM: BENCHMARKING; BUSINESS ECONOMICS; GLOBALIZATION; INFORMATION TECHNOLOGY; LOGISTICS IN MANUFACTURING MANAGEMENT AND OPERATIONS; ORGANIZATION PERFORMANCE; ORGANIZATIONAL LEARNING; RE-ENGINEERING; SHORT-TERMISM; STRATEGIC MARKETING PLANNING; STRATEGY, CONCEPT OF

Stress

Overview

Early work on stress focused on explaining the nature of stress. It was originally perceived as an external force. More recently stress has been viewed as the reaction to pressure. The nature of stress will be explained and the physiological and psychological reactions will be described which can be used to identify increased levels of stress. Stress is becoming a global phenomenon affecting all countries, professions and all categories of worker. Stressors will be identified, both those created by individuals and organizational causes of stress. Studies have focused on particular categories of people including executives and their experiences of stress. Strategies for stress management originally focused on individual approaches, concentrating on lifestyle and addressing work-related problems. With the threat of litigation, organizational initiatives are assuming growing importance.

1 Understanding stress

The term 'stress' is used in a variety of ways, often synonymously with pressure. Understanding of stress has developed from both medical and psychological research. Originally it was viewed from an engineering perspective and seen as an external force on the person giving rise to strain and finally permanent damage. It is now widely viewed today as the physiological and psychological reaction which occurs when individuals meet a threat or challenge and the individuals' perception, whether consciously or subconsciously, that it is beyond their immediate capacity (see OCCUPATIONAL PSYCHOLOGY).

A recent report published by the Institute of Employment Studies (Rick *et al.* 1997) highlights the extent to which stress has become an umbrella term comprising a number of elements, stressors, strain – the symptom and stress outcomes.

The physiological reaction is what is referred to as the fight/flight response. It equips the individual to face life-threatening situations by increasing their arousal level. This is a natural response and can be described as acute stress. When it occurs occasionally and the body quickly returns to a normal level of arousal this does not have detrimental effects. However, in the modern world individuals are experiencing long-term, unacceptably high levels of arousal which give rise to chronic stress. This initially gives rise to tiredness, then exhaustion and ultimately illness and long-term side effects. This chronic stress gives organizations most cause for concern and is the type most likely to lead to litigation for employers. Cases have been heard in a range of countries including the USA, Australia and Canada.

Most writers on the topic of stress usually make use of an extension of the Yerkes Dodson Law that demonstrates the relationship between performance/quality of working life and levels of pressure. Andrew Melhuish (1978) identifies a medical component as shown in Figure 1.

Figure 1 shows that low levels of pressure can be as unhealthy and stress inducing as high levels of pressure. The relationship between pressure and stress levels is not linear. It also dispels the myth that the higher up one progresses in the organization the more likely one is to experience excessive stress levels. People undertaking very routine work describe the stress experienced which results from boredom.

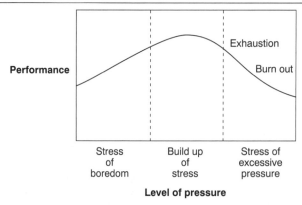

Figure 1 The relationship between stress and performance
Source: Adapted from Melhuish (1978)

At optimum levels of pressure the stress experienced is positive. People at this point on the performance curve describe feeling challenged, in control of the situation, achieving high levels of job performance and job satisfaction (see MOTIVATION AND SATISFACTION). Sports people concentrate on performing at these pressure levels to enable them to maximize their performance.

There is a fine line between optimum pressure and excessive pressure causing people to change their perceptions of the situation. At excessive levels of pressure people describe feeling out of control, unable to cope and overloaded. The point at which positive stress turns to distress is personal. It depends on the perceptions of people, personality characteristics and their perceived capacity to cope with the pressures of the situation. If people operate at excessive levels of pressure for lengthy periods, the excessive stress experienced can be extremely harmful to them.

Excessive stress is now viewed as a killer. A report in *Personnel Journal* (Solomon 1993) described an illness suffered in Japan, a nation known for its employees working very long hours. The fatal illness is known as *karoshi*. People die from high stress levels and the pressure of overtime work. In 1990 the Labour Ministry received 777 applications for compensation because of *karoshi*. Not all symptoms of excessive stress are as serious, but it certainly impacts on quality of life and job performance as the next section will demonstrate.

2 Symptoms of stress

Care must be taken not to exaggerate the effects of excessive stress. While it is a killer, some illnesses known to be stress-related may develop for other reasons and excessive stress levels just exacerbate the problem. For example, the relationship between stress and heart disease remains controversial.

The symptoms of stress are best understood having first explained the physiological reactions which take place when a person's stress level becomes raised either by a sense of danger, pressure at work or an irritation in daily life. The stressor sets off a complex chain of physiological and psychological reactions. This was described by Walter Cannon of Harvard as the 'fight or flight reaction'. The reaction was part of the survival mechanism of prehistoric man, needed to give extra energy to flee from life-threatening situations.

At the first sign of a threat, signals from the brain alert the body of the need for action. The adrenal glands produce adrenaline and noradrenaline and corticoids. These chemicals trigger activity in the short term but if produced over long periods of time can have negative effects.

The blood is diverted from the skin to the brain, increasing alertness, and to the muscles, fuelling them for action. In the short term digestion stops, the pulse becomes more rapid, blood pressure rises as a result of adrenaline and noradrenaline increasing the force and speed of contraction of the heart. The hormones also enlarge the airways so that more oxygen reaches the lungs. Glucose is released from the liver for energy and the cooling system is activated resulting in the person sweating.

This chain of reactions happens very quickly and if triggered to deal with a single emergency is not harmful. In today's climate this reaction is repeatedly triggered which gives rise to long-term harmful effects. These include high blood pressure, the breakdown of the immune system, muscle tension resulting in headaches and backache and constant perspiration resulting in skin allergies and eczema.

A range of symptoms are listed in Table 1. People tend to develop their own response patterns and when monitoring stress any changes in behaviour may be indicative of increased stress levels. Ashton (1993) identified a number of signs that can be used as stress indicators: reduced performance; increased absenteeism; excessive consumption of alcohol; irritability; rapid and inappropriate mood changes; indecisiveness; and an appearance of fatigue, nervousness and/or depression.

Table 1 Spotting the signs of stress

Physical reactions	Emotional reactions	Mental reactions	Behavioural reactions
Not all physical changes are caused by increased pressure but many are:	A change in feelings often accompanies a change in pressure level:	A change in thought processes often accompanies a change in pressure:	There are many ways behaviour can be affected:
Indigestion/heartburn	Irritability	Inability to concentrate	Excessive drinking
Constipation/ diarrhoea	Anxiety/panic	Difficulty establishing priorities	Excessive eating/loss of appetite
Tiredness	Anger	Indecisiveness	Craving for sweet food
Insomnia	Depression	Tunnel vision	Withdrawl from people/ absence from work
Muscle tension/cramp and spasms	Guilt	Confused/illogical thinking	Clumsiness/accident prone. Changed driving behaviour
Palpitations	Feeling unable to cope	Procrastination	Irritability/hostile behaviour
Persistent headaches/ migraine		Forgetfulness	More speech/faster speech
Nervous twitches		Difficulty recalling information	Mood swings
Reduced resistance to illness			Loss of sense of humour

3 Causes of stress

The triggers of the stress reaction are many and varied depending on the person. Some writers, including Cooper *et al.* (1988), concentrate on identifying external sources of stress, others, including Arroba and James (1992) focus on self-imposed stressors. Another approach is to focus on life event changes, first developed by Holmes and Rahe (1967) in the 1960s and extended further by Cooper *et al.* (1988). This approach explores events in life which can be stress-inducing and draws attention to the cumulative effects of several stressors which can result in chronic stress.

The Cooper model identifies six sources of work stress.

1 *The job itself.* This includes the working environment, hours worked including shift work, travel, workload and keeping up with new technology. This last factor was particularly experienced by Japanese executives.
2 *Role in the organization.* This covers role conflict, ambiguity of role, particularly lack of clarity, and responsibility for other people as part of the job role.
3 *Relationships at work.* One of the most stressful aspects of work is building and sustaining positive and supportive relationships with colleagues, bosses and subordinates (see ORGANIZATION BEHAVIOUR).
4 *Career development.* This includes job insecurity, redundancy, skill obsolescence, reaching one's career ceiling or being over-promoted (see CAREERS).
5 *Organization structure and climate.* This impacts on the extent to which individuals feel able to participate in decisions affecting them.
6 *Home–work interface.* Increasingly stresses at work escalate stress at home as partners experience difficulty providing the necessary support. There is also the challenge of dual career families. In the USA only 7 per cent of wives followed the conventional child rearing role and family unit while in the UK 65 per cent of wives

work. Studies have also suggested that husbands have greater difficulty than wives separating home and work when experiencing difficult relations with their children (see EQUAL EMPLOYMENT OPPORTUNITIES).

In the 1990s Cartwright and Cooper (1994) focus on three fundamental causes of stress: first, change (resulting in uncertainty, job insecurity and changes in corporate culture which lead to significant changes in managerial style); second, increased workload (as organizations strive to become leaner and increase their competitive position in Europe and internationally, fewer staff have more work to do); and third, loss of control (as European and international networks become established, rules and regulations take away autonomy and control from organizations and individuals) (see HUMAN RESOURCE MANAGEMENT; HUMAN RESOURCE MANAGEMENT, INTERNATIONAL).

4 Studies on stress

The relationship between gender, work and stress

According to the *International Labour Organization Conditions of Work Digest* (1992) the relationship between gender, work and stress is complex and varied. A survey conducted in the USA reported women being more affected by stress than men. Two reasons were cited: first, women are often earning less than men; and second, many companies lack policies covering family issues. Research conducted in Sweden concluded that women work longer hours than men. In Sweden 86 per cent of women work but spouses share duties equally at home (see EQUAL EMPLOYMENT OPPORTUNITIES).

Executive stress

Cooper conducted a study of 1,100 senior to top-level executives in ten countries and discovered work pressure variations cross-culturally, particularly between developed and developing countries. US managers reported the stress of lack of power, incompetent bosses and a conflict of beliefs with the organization. Japanese managers cited the pressure of keeping up with changes in technology and German managers complained of work pressures and working with inadequately trained subordinates. In Brazil executives appeared under extreme pressure with very high mental ill health and low job satisfaction. The stresses were work pressure, keeping up with new technology and inadequately trained personnel (see MANAGERIAL BEHAVIOUR).

5 Managing personal stress

In today's world many are likely to need to manage personal stress. There is no one right way to manage it but different ways which will suit different people. Ashton (1993) describes stress management as one step in his twelve-week Executive Health Plan. Cranwell-Ward (1990) emphasizes the need for the right balance in life and the importance of physical, emotional and spiritual well-being. Cartwright and Cooper (1994) focus on how to respond to the fundamental causes of stress, particularly overload, relationship difficulties, the home–work interface and responding to unexpected events and changes in the organization (see DOWNSIZING). David Fontana (1989) and Arroba and James (1992) address personally-induced stress. From the various approaches a number of core elements emerge.

1 Maintaining a healthy and balanced lifestyle – this acts for stress prevention as well as a cure. A balanced diet, adequate sleep, time for relaxation and taking regular physical exercise helps maintain stress at an acceptable level.
2 Participating in a programme of exercise – 3–4 sessions of 30 minutes per week. Exercise helps to reduce the sudden hormonal surges of the stress response and increases endorphins which reduce anxiety. It also helps to restore a normal sleep pattern.
3 Ensuring an adequate balance between home and work – avoidance of excessive overwork, taking work home and becoming involved in excessive business travel.
4 Keeping a positive outlook – the importance of turning negative stress into positive stress.
5 Self-management – the importance of prioritizing, being assertive and making the best use of time.
6 Effective problem solving – particularly when problems are causing stress.
7 Adopting realistic expectations for self and others – much stress is self-imposed resulting from excessive personal demands.
8 Ensuring adequate emotional support – both at home and networks at work to allow for release of emotions.
9 Managing the job effectively – ensuring pressure is kept at appropriate levels and if necessary seeking help from others.
10 Managing change appropriately – creating stability zones at times of change and facing up to change positively.
11 Stress monitoring – in terms of stress levels, signs of stress and triggers of stress.
12 Seeking outside help when this is necessary.

6 Organizational perspective

In recent years organizations have become much more aware of the need to help employees manage stress (see ORGANIZATIONAL BEHAVIOUR). Help has taken a number of different forms, ranging from counselling help to cope with post traumatic stress to stress prevention by creating a healthy environment, staff development and organizational development.

Arroba and James (1992) suggest interventions at three levels to make organizations fitter to cope and perform well. At employee level they emphasize the need to clarify expectations placed on staff, the importance of giving feedback on performance and developing the appropriate skill base to fulfil roles (see PERFORMANCE APPRAISAL). Teams can be developed to ensure effective teamwork and, at the organizational level, values, organization design and job design must be examined to ensure each is appropriate to achieve organizational objectives (see GROUPS AND TEAMS).

Rick *et al.* (1997) emphasized the need for much more focused interventions by organizations to deal with stress. Five key elements of good practice were identified in research:

1 assessement and diagnosis
2 solution generation
3 implementation
4 evaluation
5 ongoing monitoring and feedback

Melanie Williams in an article entitled 'Facing up to frontline stress' in *Managing Service Quality* (1993) explored the extent to which stress can be minimized in organizations. The Automobile Association, which deals with 4.8 million breakdowns a year, was given as an example of an organization which sometimes has to work under intense pressure and deal with very stressful situations and stressed customers. A number of measures are taken to ensure stress is kept to a minimum. Care is taken to recruit the right staff, train them adequately and empower them to make their own decisions. A good team spirit is created and good use made of positive feedback.

As litigation by employees against employers increases in the USA for compensation for work-related stress illnesses there is likely to be a similar trend in the UK. Earnshaw and Cooper (1996) cite the first successful personal injury action brought by a social worker, John Walker, against Northumberland County Council, in the UK. This is likely to focus attention more sharply on creating healthy organizations for employees. Williams (1994) outlines four elements of organizational health. He suggests a holistic approach to managing health of employees as the four elements – environment factors, physical, mental and social health – all interact with one another and all have a bearing on stress.

Stress is likely to remain a critical issue from an individual, team and organizational perspective (see OCCUPATIONAL PSYCHOLOGY). The focus for the next few years is likely to be the healthy organization.

JANE CRANWELL-WARD
HENLEY MANAGEMENT COLLEGE

Further reading

(References cited in the text marked *)

* Arroba, T. and James, K. (1992) *Pressure at Work: A Survival Guide*, 2nd edn.Maidenhead: McGraw-Hill. (An excellent practical guide to help managers understand and keep pressure at a constructive level.)
* Ashton, D. (1993) *The 12 Week Executive Health Plan*, London: Kogan Page. (An excellent informative health plan to manage stress more effectively.)
* Cartwright, S. and Cooper, C. (1994) *No Hassle! Taking the Stress Out of Work*, London: Century. (A new approach to problems which generate stress at work and how to manage them.)
* Cooper, C., Cooper, R. and Eaker, L. (1988) *Living with Stress*, London: Penguin. (An excellent comprehensive summary of stress and how to manage it; particularly good at comparing different occupational and cultural groups.)
* Cranwell-Ward, J. (1990) *Thriving on Stress*, London: Routledge. (A workbook designed to help managers recognize and manage stress effectively.)
* Earnshaw, J. and Cooper, C. (1996) *Stress and Employer Liability*, London: IPD. (A good overview for managers of employer liability related to stress and stress related issues.)
* Fontana, D. (1989) *Managing Stress*, London: Routledge & Kegan Paul. (A good overview on stress, the causes and how to manage them.)
* Holmes T.H. and Rahe (1967) 'The social readjustment rating scale', *Journal of Psychosomatic Research* 11: 213–8. (One of the first studies focusing on life event changes as a factor in stress.)
* International Labour Office (1992) *Preventing Stress at Work*, vol. 2, *International Labour Office Conditions of Work Digest*, Geneva, Switzerland: International Labour Office. (An excellent reference book summarizing current international research. Good reading list.)
* Melhuish, A. (1978) *Executive Health*, London: Business Books. (A good view of stress written by a medical practitioner.)
* Rick, J., Hillage, J. Honey, S. and Perryman, S. (1997) *Stress: Studies of the Big Issue, but what are the problems?*, Brighton: Institute of Employment. (An informative report which gives an overview of stress, workplace stress interventions and well-documented case studies of stress interventions.)
* Solomon, C.M. (1993) 'Working smarter: how H.R. can help', *Personnel Journal* June: 54–64.

(Useful article on the human cost of overwork and how human resource professionals can help employees prioritize, make better decisions and lead balanced lives.)

Williams, M. (1993) 'Facing up to frontline stress', *Managing Service Quality* July: 11–14. (A useful article examining stress in organizations, exploring quality of management as a source of stress and describing a case study on an organization attempting to minimize stress in the workplace.)

Williams, S. (1994) 'Ways of creating healthy organisations', in C. Cooper and S. Williams (eds), *Creating Healthy Work Organizations*, Chichester and New York: Wiley. (A useful collection of contributions focused on creating healthy organizations, with international examples. The chapter gives a useful overview of health from a holistic perspective, addressing the impact of the environment on physical, mental and social health.)

See also: JOB DESIGN; OCCUPATIONAL PSYCHOLOGY; ORGANIZATION BEHAVIOUR; ORGANIZATION CULTURE; PRODUCTIVITY; TOTAL QUALITY MANAGEMENT; WORK ETHIC; WORK AND ORGANIZATION SYSTEMS

Related topics in the IEBM: CONTEXTS AND ENVIRONMENTS; MANAGEMENT IN BRAZIL; MANAGEMENT IN GERMANY; MANAGEMENT IN JAPAN; ORGANIZATION DEVELOPMENT; ORGANIZATION STRUCTURE; ORGANIZATIONAL PERFORMANCE; WORK AND LEISURE

Total quality management

Overview

What is the secret of the apparently 'magic' expression 'total quality management' (TQM)? An operations management person may associate it with a modern management approach as adapted to cope with the recent and acute worldwide quality economics problem; a quality-orientated person may emphasize the quality origin of TQM and describe it as a climax of the stepwise evolution of quality-orientated schemes and techniques; and a production person may see it as yet another manifestation of improved productivity. As often in such cases, the answer lies somewhere in between.

Whatever its source, dissemination of the term TQM was very quick, reaching people in industry, research, education and health. Many wrote about it, describing it as a miraculous and universal cure for all organizational maladies. Perhaps the very fact that so many organizations (manufacturing and service alike) were, and some still are, in desperate need of being cured explains the quick climb of TQM. On the verge of disaster when everything else failed, managers were prepared to try new remedies. As TQM seemed a reasonable and tangible way out of the disastrous situation, many managers eagerly adopted it. For some it was indeed an economic success, but for others it was a failure. Why? Was it too late? Were the expectations too high or the preparations too hasty?

This entry introduces the notion of TQM (starting from its quality core concept and historical development), emphasizing its underlying principles and philosophy (the principle of continuous improvement and the customer/supplier quality chain) and its system-orientated approach with the required infrastructure for supporting the improvement process. It also attempts to explain the spread and successes of the TQM strategy, while offering an international perspective and providing some guidance on how to avoid the pitfalls. The entry concludes with a short exploration of future collaboration prospects between management theories and total quality strategies.

1 Introduction

This entry is about quality and management not as separate entities or organizational functions but as a united concept within which they complement each other. It is this melding that has generated so many success stories, such as Xerox and Motorola, Ford and General Motors, to name but a few. As a first step the concept is examined at a strategic level, both from a management perspective as well as from a quality-orientated perspective.

The fierce international competition, the ever-growing power of the customers, their discrimination between companies and between their respective products and services on the basis of quality, the Japanese market conquests, all brought about what may be called the quality management 'revolution'. It consists of the recognition of quality by top management as a 'strategic competitive edge'. Indisputably, this is the main ingredient on which the partnership relies, marking a turning point in the management attitude towards the economic importance of quality. The road had been paved with many disappointing experiences of quality leaders (bred in the Western world), who for several decades failed to find listeners and followers among managers in their part of the world.

Nonetheless, within the quality function itself, a stage-by-stage evolution of methods and techniques (from product inspection to statistical quality control and beyond) could be observed. By the 1960s this organic development reached (in the Western world) a stage that became known among quality practitioners and analysts as 'total quality control'. This stage was distinguished by breadth and functional integration, as expressed in the word 'total', but was still relatively limited in scope, as imposed by the name 'quality control'. By the 1970s the Japanese developed and practised their own special version of total quality control called 'company-wide quality control', which enriched total quality control and can be regarded as the first materialization of what is now internationally designated as total quality management (TQM). By the mid-1980s, in the Western world, the separate goals of the two disciplines – quality and management – got closer. While quality people were striving towards quality system implementation, top managers began to understand the tremendous economic importance of quality. These developments showed that any further progress for each could only be achieved through a fruitful partnership.

For a partnership to last, there is a need for both partners to benefit continuously from it. Apart from there being strategic reasons for the union, the partnership also needs to be supported by a collaboration based on common tactical concepts and operational activities, to be generated by one partner and enriched by the other. The operational means which provided the binding ties between quality and management, making the partnership durable, were the quality tools and techniques, used as 'universal tools for management improvement', and management's perception of the importance of time, as transformed into a 'universal product quality characteristic'. The great potential of the quality tools (such as statistical process control and cause-and-effect diagrams) to support company-wide improvement programmes became immediately apparent, reaching areas that on the surface had no relation to quality, such as sales, purchasing, invoicing, finance, training, and service generally.

The truth of the saying 'time is money' applies as much to management activities as to process activities, and is best emphasized by the just-in-time philosophy, originally intended to reduce inventories. Time is an important characteristic of the processes involved in designing, producing and marketing products. Reducing performance time (of any kind) had always been given high priority by management, simply because less time meant more quantity, a favourite managerial goal. By using a broad interpretation of product quality characteristics so that they include 'timeliness', any conflicts arising in assigning priorities between improvement of quality and improvement of productivity (reducing performance time) are solved. Through an enhanced TQM perspective, reducing cycle time or improving productivity is considered as yet another aspect of quality improvement to be carried out under the auspices of TQM: this is known as 'time-based management'. There are no more weaknesses, no more contradictions between quality and management. When managers do not improve quality *per se* but are busy encouraging cycle time reduction (as in the past), everybody is happy; after all, the organization is performing a quality activity. These ideas are illustrated in Figure 1.

2 Quality

In order to understand the various meanings of quality and appreciate its economic importance, some basic quality concepts set within an historical context are presented. (A more detailed presentation can be found in, for example, Garvin 1988.)

Quality definitions

Quality is looked at by quality gurus (such as Juran, Deming, Feigenbaum, Crosby and Taguchi) from three viewpoints: customer, producer and society. Product quality is described as 'fitness for use' (Juran 1991) or 'conformance to requirements' (Crosby 1979); it has 'to satisfy the needs of customer present and future' (Deming 1986). It can be

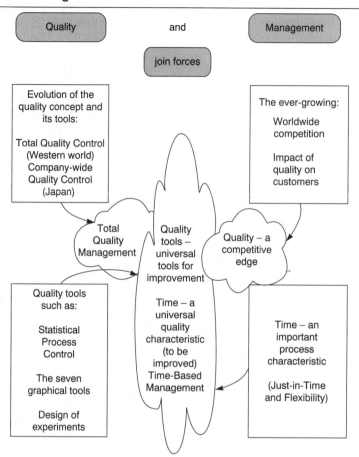

Figure 1 Quality and management join forces

seen that Deming is also concerned with the time-orientated ability of a product to perform satisfactorily, in other words with its reliability. Feigenbaum's definition is more elaborate: 'the composite product and service characteristics of marketing, engineering, manufacture and maintenance, through which the product and service in use will meet the expectation by the customer' (Feigenbaum 1991: 7). This definition is an expression of the total quality control concept, stressing an integrative view of quality as reflected on other functions; also, the notion of a product quality is extended to the quality of service.

A different way of defining quality, providing a new way of thinking, is Taguchi's approach: 'quality is the loss imparted to the society from the time a product is shipped' (Taguchi 1986: 1). This approach considers costs and benefits of quality improvement projects from an overall and interactive economic view representing the 'society' (integrating the economics of producers and customers). According to Taguchi's philosophy, not investing in a prevention project likely to avoid future customer costs higher than the project investment cost will later incur a much higher loss on the producer in terms of lost market share.

The quality definitions above reflect the organizational development of quality over the years in different parts of the world. This development is now briefly reviewed, focusing on two countries: the USA and Japan. The review first considers quality developments in the USA before the management recognition of quality as a strategic competitive edge (roughly from the beginning of the century to the mid-1980s); it then moves to Japan, viewing it first (from the end of the Second World War roughly until the mid-1960s) as a receiver of the quality techniques and principles preached by famous Western quality gurus, and afterwards as a source of new quality philosophies, well supported by its own gurus who enhanced important practical aspects of (Western) quality theories.

Development of quality organization in the USA (until the mid-1980s)

Three main evolutionary stages can be distinguished: inspection, statistical quality control, and quality assurance.

Inspection
Inspection of final manufactured products is connected with the development of mass production, and as such it started before the end of the nineteenth century. A formalization of this activity was supported by Taylor in his book *Scientific Management*, published in 1911 (see TAYLOR, F.W.). The goal of inspection was to separate 'good' and 'defective' units through sieving. Organizationally, an inspection department (or section) was responsible for carrying out inspection. Typically, this section was under the jurisdiction of the production department.

Statistical quality control
The beginning of statistical quality control is identified with the publication in 1931 of Shewhart's book *Economic Control of Quality Manufactured Products*. This book introduced 'quality control' charts as a basic graphical tool for implementing statistical process control. On these charts the quality characteristics to be monitored are plotted at constant time intervals, for example, an hourly plot of a detergent package weight). Typically, such a control chart consists of a central line (which occasionally represents the process target value) and two control lines drawn at (+/−) (standard deviation) of the quality characteristic to be monitored. Later on, additional types of control charts were

developed, among which 'cumulative sum' charts are the best known and most practised. The goal of statistical process control is to control the quality of products during their manufacture (online) and thus (by the eventual stopping of the process and its readjustment as necessary) prevent manufacturing of defective units. Commonly, process control activities were carried out under a shared responsibility of the production and the engineering departments.

Judging by the title of his book, Shewhart intended to stress that the use of control charts should be guided by economic principles and practised 'selectively'. It seems that the wisdom of this was not well understood, because following the book's publication control charts appeared all over the USA, only to be soon removed as not useful. Statistical sampling procedures, which were intended to reduce inspection costs, constituted another aspect of the statistical quality control methodology.

Quality assurance
As products became more complex and product quality requirements more demanding, the quality methods gradually grew into a body of knowledge comprising wider topics, such as 'quality costs', total quality control, reliability engineering and 'zero defects', known together as 'quality assurance' methods.

'Quality costs' represented the first formalization of the economic aspects of quality tasks. The topic was introduced by Juran in the first edition of his *Quality Control Handbook*, first published in 1951. The approach trades off 'unavoidable' costs (stemming from 'appraisal' of product quality and from investments intended to 'prevent' the manufacturing of defective units) against 'failure' costs that are considered 'avoidable'. The latter are the costs incurred by the defective units produced, some of which are discovered prior to shipment to customers, causing internal failures, and others of which reach the customers, thus incurring external failures that may also result in loss of reputation. The model prescribes a cost-minimizing 'optimal' quality level, as appropriate to a specific company, with lower than 100 per cent non-defective (conforming) units, implying an 'optimal higher than zero' percentage of defective units. This 'optimal' percentage of defective units is expected to vary with the type of company, its size and the type of industry, and in principle it can get so low as to be expressed in terms of parts per million. This classical model used to be generally accepted, but as it was in direct opposition to the theories advocating 'zero defects' as an optimal conformance level, it became controversial and was banned, although its logic was undeniable. However, within TQM there is renewed use of this important quality economics tool.

The phrase 'total quality control' is derived from Feigenbaum's book, which appeared in 1961. It presented a first version of quality integration within a company, and its goal was to achieve quality through cross-functional coordination and collaboration. Quality was viewed as a 'system', within which the traditional (online) quality control activities on the shop floor were expanded to include (offline) preparation activities such as quality design of new products and control of raw materials. Feigenbaum's pioneering principle was that quality responsibility had to be shared by all departments.

Reliability engineering developments concerned modelling and estimation of time-orientated product performances. Though dealing with quality characteristics, such topics were typically within the jurisdiction of research and development (R&D) departments.

'Zero defects' expressed an entirely different aspect of quality development, ultimately intended to achieve workers' participation to reducing the alarming level of defective items among US products during the 1960s and 1970s. The zero defects 'movement' started with Crosby's book *Quality is Free*, published in 1979, which was a great commercial success. In Crosby's view quality is free because the cost of prevention will always be lower than the costs of appraisal (detection) and failure (correction, scrap, warranty, reputation).

Quality organization in Japan

One of the most successful US export areas after the Second World War was quality control methods, which were particularly well received in Japan. Until the mid-1960s the Japanese absorbed the methods introduced by the well-known quality control ambassadors such as Deming, Juran and Feigenbaum. The quality theme became nationwide in Japan. The Japanese managers who eagerly attended the seminars and lectures of the famous Western quality gurus were taught not only statistical wisdom for controlling quality but sound principles of quality management and quality economics as well.

Deming presented to managers a series of seminars focusing on statistical process control. In his well-known fourteen points, besides stressing the importance of process quality 'improvement' and the advantages of the statistical methods over mass inspection, he also stressed the need to preserve workers' pride and the importance of 'training' for stimulating workers' motivation to improve quality. He considered management commitment and leadership as crucial to achieving quality improvement. Deming's cycle of improvement – plan, do, check, act – is a methodology intended to support his fundamental concept of 'continuous improvement'. It consists of defining the problem objectives and planning the necessary data collection (plan), gathering the data (do) and analysing the results (check). If these are all right, the next step is implementing them (act); if not, the next step is starting anew.

Juran emphasized the necessity of a 'quality system' approach and the importance of 'managing' quality. He viewed the management role as defining quality goals, providing recognition and communicating results. He encouraged analysis of quality costs, which could offer good opportunities for improving quality. Feigenbaum brought to Japan his total quality control principles, the tools for system 'integration'.

All these gurus had some themes in common. They believed that 'management' and the 'system' are the cause of poor quality, that 'commitment and leadership' by top management are essential ingredients for successful quality programmes, that quality programmes need organization-wide 'long-term efforts' and that 'quality precedes timeliness' (see LEADERSHIP).

The total quality control methods described in Feigenbaum's book were applied in Japan by the 1970s under the name of 'company-wide quality control'. This enhanced Japanese version of total quality control viewed the quality system through the different but 'interacting' perspectives of its main elements: employees, customers and managers. An integrative approach, it attempted to satisfy the separate concerns of each element, that is work motivation for the employees, products with on-target and consistent (low-variance) characteristics for the customers, and increased market share and reduced costs for management. This approach is shown in Figure 2.

Among the Japanese quality gurus who extensively contributed to this integration are Kaoro Ishikawa (see ISHIKAWA, K.) and Genichi Taguchi. Ishikawa's main contribution is related to providing simple graphical tools for employees participating in improvement programmes that were used within 'quality control circles'. Taguchi's main contribution is identified with developing methods promoting the use of 'design of experiments' to improve product and process quality. It was important that these methods be applied during the development stage of products and processes, the ultimate result being products exhibiting on-target and low-variance quality characteristics (features that according to Taguchi's philosophy made products attractive to customers) and reduced costs.

The quality tools and techniques imported from the West were assimilated by top management and disseminated downwards. This movement did not produce satisfactory participation at the lower levels and resistance to applying the new methods thus occurred. The Japanese answer to the lack of work motivation at the bottom was the creation of the

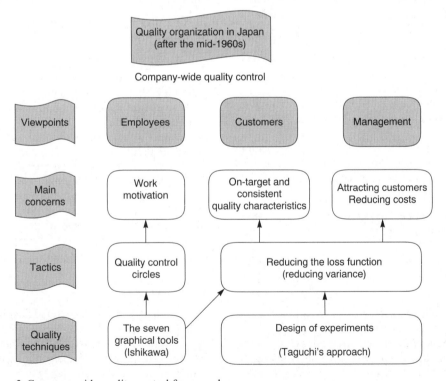

Figure 2 Company-wide quality control framework

quality control circle. (A thorough presentation of this topic can be found in Lillrank and Kano (1989).) These were voluntary, homogeneous, small groups intended to open implementation channels for quality improvement. The Japanese quality leaders developed simple tools for improvement to be used by members of the quality circles.

Ishikawa calls these graphical tools 'the seven basic tools':

1 Pareto diagrams are meant to distinguish quantitatively between the 'vital' few and the 'trivial' many, so as to find out what are the main problems necessitating improvement.
2 Flow charts are intended to define the problem boundaries through a graphical illustration of what is being done and where.
3 Cause-and-effect diagrams, also called 'fishbone' or Ishikawa diagrams, present logical connections between causes and symptoms of problems.
4 Histograms give a visual presentation of the data: their central location (median or mean) as well as their dispersion (variance).
5 Check sheets are helpful to organize data in terms of problem factors with their respective frequencies.
6 Scatter diagrams illustrate quantitative relationships between two variables, X and Y.
7 Quality control charts help in deciding what processes have to be controlled and what process variances have to be reduced.

Deming's cycle of improvement provided the logical connections between these tools, some of which pertain to 'plan' and others to 'do', 'check' or 'act'.

Two essential components make up Taguchi's strategy, aimed at 'selling' design of experiments:

1 providing 'economic' motivation for management to use experimental design, in terms of a loss function expressing customers' discontent with products whose quality characteristics are not on target and/or exhibit high variation;

2 providing 'easy-to-use' instructions for implementing the experimental design methodology, originally an elitist statistical method known to statisticians and few engineers.

Taguchi's loss function is directly related to the deviations of a quality characteristic from its target value. It can be expressed in terms of its variance, thus showing that the higher the variance, the higher the loss. Hence, reducing performance variance means reducing loss. As the design of experiments is an effective tool for reducing performance variance, it is also, according to Taguchi's logic, a tool for reducing losses and attracting customers.

Both types of technique – the simple graphical techniques used by Japanese workers participating in quality control circles and the 'sophisticated' design of experiments used by Japanese engineers – brought about the great quality improvement of Japanese products and the improved efficiency of their manufacturing processes.

3 Total quality strategies: a global view

A corporate strategy is the pattern of decisions in a company that determines its goals, produces the policies, plans to achieve the goals and defines the kind of economic and human organization it intends to be. While quality *per se*, and even quality techniques, are old concepts, quality as a 'strategy' is a new idea. Traditionally, strategic 'quantity' goals always preceded 'quality' goals. Since companies seldom change unless forced to do so by the environment, the recognition of quality as a strategic competitive edge by managers in the West came only as a result of the extensive market-sharing losses in the 1960s and 1970s.

Basic principles

At the core of TQM philosophy is Deming's pioneering concept of 'continuous improvement' (initially adopted in Japan, where it became well known as *kaizen*), implying a culture change. 'Create constancy of purpose towards improvement of product and service.

Adopt the new philosophy' (Deming 1986: 23). It is worth mentioning that the Deming Prize, established in Japan in 1951, defined the first and very demanding self-auditing process of quality improvement. The name TQM can be traced to another quality prize, the famous Malcolm Baldrige National Quality Award, instituted in the USA in 1987 to encourage the implementation of the same concept.

The major rationale for the creation of the Malcolm Baldrige Award was foreign competition. As it was realized that customers wanted quality (not advertising), the original aim of the award was to support national efforts to improve quality and thus satisfy customer 'desires'. Soon it became clear that the principle of meeting customer requirements and desires could be applied not only to

separate companies, but within the same company as well. A manufacturing department is the customer of the engineering department that produces the design, whose quality has to meet the manufacturing requirements, for example tolerances that are true requirements of the product and can be achieved using the designed process. In each section and department there are various series of customers and suppliers and all are part of a quality chain. The 'customer/supplier quality chain' thus became another fundamental concept of TQM.

The tremendous impact of the award on US and Western industry in general and later on global industry can be attributed to its excellent 'structural quality framework', enabling companies to assess themselves against it. Here this framework, as described by the

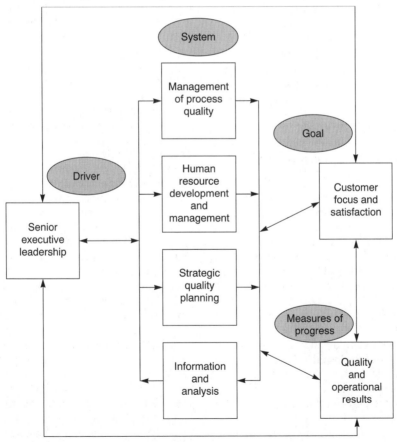

Figure 3 Baldrige Award criteria framework
Source: NIST (1993: 33)

National Institute of Standards and Technology (1993), is used as a TQM general reference frame (see Figure 3). It consists of:

1 a 'driver' (top management leadership);
2 a 'system', whose elements are management of process quality, development and management of human resources, strategic quality planning and information and analysis;
3 a 'goal', focusing on customer satisfaction (and implicitly on market share gain);
4 'measures of progress' in terms of quality and operational results (product quality, productivity, supplier, waste reduction).

Based on the Baldrige Award framework, TQM consists in essence of:

1 the provision of high-quality products (services) to satisfy customer wishes (a dynamic goal to be achieved through a continuous improvement process);
2 the achievement of high total quality in products and processes at low cost (managing process quality so as to increase productivity, get suppliers' collaboration and reduce waste);
3 the management of total quality through involvement of all employees, measurement of progress and communication of results.

To create a model of excellence for business across Europe, the European Foundation for Quality Management instituted in 1991 a European Quality Award for business. The model distinguishes between two major types of criteria, 'results' and 'enablers' (the means to achieve results). The results concern 'customer satisfaction', 'people (employee) satisfaction' and 'impact on society' (or community, including meeting the demands of shareholders), ultimately leading to excellence in 'business results'. The enablers are expressed by five criteria: 'leadership' that drives 'people management', 'policy and strategy', 'resources' and 'processes'. The results are assessed by internal (self) assessment (representing prerequisites for improvement), as well as by external assessments, that is comparisons with competitors and best-in-

class organizations. Self-assessment is the systematic measurement and review of all key activities and results of the organization, allowing it to discover its areas for improvement.

Challenging problems for managers are how to create a 'best path' to improvement in terms of organizational structures, how to measure and communicate progress and how to achieve and sustain active participation (collaboration) of employees at all levels. These topics are considered below.

Generic quality strategies

Since quality strategies (and their fundamental principle of continuous improvement) revolve around the 'competitive advantages' of quality, the different approaches to carrying out the quality improvement process are now examined in some detail and from a competitive perspective. A competitive strategy is a 'broad formula for how a business is going to compete' (Porter 1980: xvi); competitive 'edges' focus on the distinctive competitive 'advantages' of the competing companies, each emphasizing its specific strength. There are two basic types of competitive advantage that may be emphasized by a company (or a nation): 'differentiation' (unique and superior value to the buyer in terms of product quality and/or after-sales service, for example German machine tools) and 'lower cost' (for example Korean semiconductors).

Porter's notion of 'generic strategies' is drawn upon here to define generic 'quality strategies' as combinations of types of competitive 'quality advantage' and different competitive 'quality means' for achieving them. A product-driven quality strategy will express a differentiation competitive advantage, building on high-valued products with unique quality and service characteristics, whereas a process-driven strategy will focus on lowering costs through improved process quality and efficiency. As quality and fast response to customers' requirements are both important from a competitive perspective, both types of competitive advantage can be achieved either through a quality *per se* improvement orientation and/or through a time reduction and just-in-time orientation. This is the rationale of the two competitive quality means, making some large worldwide organizations (for example, Asea Brown Boveri (ABB)) distinguish specifically between a TQM and a time-based management approach. Both TQM and time-based management can be applied to each of the two types of competitive advantage, thus leading ultimately to the four generic quality strategies appearing in Figure 4.

TQM applied to the differentiation advantage (the product-driven strategy) means an improved quality of design. This may be supported by appropriate methodologies such as 'quality function deployment' (a systematic approach for designing a product or a service based on customer requirements with the participation of members of all functions) and design of experiments. TQM applied to the lower-cost advantage (the process-driven quality strategy) essentially means reducing the non-conformance level of the process.

Viewing the product-driven quality strategy from a time-based perspective means reducing the time to market of a new product (from its design to successful delivery), thus emphasizing that it is important not only to develop highly innovative quality products but also to be able to market them ahead of competitors. To achieve that, the system configuration should quickly adapt to the changes required to introduce new products, that is it should possess 'marketing' flexibility. The process-driven strategy as perceived from a time orientation emphasizes reducing cycle time and inventories, results that could eventually be realized with the support of the just-in-time methodology and the existing 'production' flexibilities of the organization.

In contrast to the quality gurus who all believed that 'quality' precedes 'timeliness', the TQM philosophy (as expressed by the Baldrige framework) does not impose any 'hierarchical' discrimination between these two notions. Both are identified with quality in the broad sense of the word. It is seen that measures of progress appear in terms of quality and operational results, being associated with improved product quality and service as well as with increased productivity and waste elimination. Perhaps this is the real secret of TQM – the universality and flexibility of the quality concept whose flag it carries. In a customer-driven and well-managed system the 'dynamics' of improvement (representing the relative importance attributed to TQM versus time-based management and to product quality versus process quality over time) will be determined by the 'priority' of the

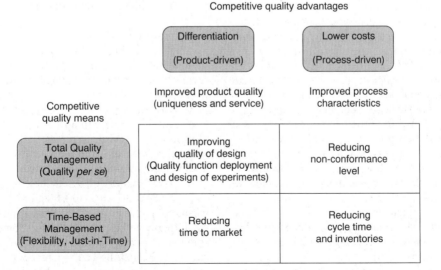

Figure 4 Generic quality strategies

improvement needs of the company at any given point in time, as seen from a customer and a business perspective.

The role of the quality system in the improvement process

The continuous improvement process has to be planned and supported by an appropriate system with distinctive organizational and structural features. For the purpose of describing and analysing them, the major system dimensions are here considered as: 'quality management', 'human resources' and 'quality information'.

Quality management
Within quality management the following are to be distinguished: planning for improvement, infrastructure for improvement and process management.

Planning for improvement concerns setting improvement objectives and priorities to improvement projects. To do this, up-to-date information on product and process performances and analysis, meant to assign relative importance to the various performance indicators and accordingly establish their improvement priorities, are absolutely necessary.

Infrastructure for improvement consists of the organizational efforts devoted to building and upgrading improvement support systems, such as 'improvement teams' and 'communication channels', to carry out improvement projects. The development and organization of improvement teams, encouraging wide and active collaboration of all human resources, has proved to be a crucial factor to the success of TQM. A wide participation of employees in improvement projects will achieve two different aims: successful improvement solutions will be obtained as a result of gathering the 'wisdom' of the company; resistance to changes (an inherent human feature), in this case to implement project results, is likely to be reduced on account of collaboration between workers and managers within improvement teams.

The establishment of clear-cut communication channels enables the smooth exchange of valuable information and understanding within the company as well as outside it (between the company and its customers and suppliers) (Oakland 1993: 285). Well-developed communication channels between employees and management regarding TQM programmes are relevant at the beginning of the programme to inform the employees (downward informal communication) and then get feedback on their reactions. During projects, improvement team members may initiate communication to keep management informed about the problems encountered and get advice. At the end of improvement projects, horizontal communication links are useful to communicate results so as eventually to extend their applications to the benefit of additional departments or sections.

Process management, in an improvement environment, means perpetually exercising and upgrading quality process organization and control, by using quality control tools as universal process control tools to reduce variation, as well as just-in-time methods to reduce set-up time and inventory, thus improving productivity. Applying the concept of the customer/supplier quality chain to all processes is another effective angle from which to approach improvement. A pitfall of process control is strict adherence to rigid methods and procedures, where a human approach may be more appropriate.

Human resources
Some of the attributes of the management and development of human resources briefly reviewed here include participation, training, job structure, and incentives and rewards (see HUMAN RESOURCE MANAGEMENT).

A central idea regarding human resource utilization in TQM is active participation in the improvement efforts through motivational involvement. Participation in process improvement is typically carried out in teams or cells (see GROUPS AND TEAMS). Involvement means commitment and personal responsibility. Experience has shown that empowering employees to make decisions and solve problems is typically followed by a higher drive to achieve. This is in contrast to old procedures, encouraging imposition, a posture likely to initiate a reaction chain of negative attitudes, such as lack of acceptance, lack of personal responsibility, ultimately leading to a lower drive to achieve (Ross 1995: 119).

Knowledge acquisition in terms of training is a crucial factor in sustaining workers' participation. Training challenges are concerned with two areas: avoiding failure patterns in training and planning for training. Training sometimes fails because it is practised without insight and understanding (see TRAINING). In some organizations the workers receive training but are not given the opportunity to use the tools and techniques they acquire. In other organizations top managers do not expose themselves to training. Management training in total quality represents evidence of the managers' personal involvement in TQM and is bound to have a significant effect on the improvement process. It is likely that managers will make good use of their own training, either by being active within improvement teams or as knowledgeable (and thereby more energetic) promoters of the improvement process.

Planning for training means answering questions about who should be trained, in what order, how much and how fast. There is only one answer to the first question, which is that within a TQM programme everybody should ultimately receive at least a minimal amount of training. A sequential training scheme for introducing and upgrading TQM tools and techniques in a company will recommend an appropriate amount of training time for different types of personnel (such as top management, middle management, technical staff, team facilitators and the regular workforce) according to the level of sophistication of the technique (for example basic total quality concepts such as continuous improvement, customer/supplier quality chains and simple graphical improvement tools; team facilitation that may include problem solving, group leadership and communication skills; then statistical process control and just-in-time, followed by more advanced methods including failure mode analysis and design of experiments). Other relevant questions are about where to train (on site or off site) and how to evaluate training. In this context it would be useful to know whether or not the trainees used what they had learned and, if they did, how.

The practice of 'job enrichment' is encouraged by TQM principles, which also recommend the alignment of incentives and rewards with principles of shared responsibility. However, deciding on which is best, individual or team compensations, may still pose some problems.

Quality information

Quality information is made up of 'measures and performance indicators' (such as defects and defective items by contingencies, central values and dispersion measures of product quality characteristics, throughput time of parts, work in process, equipment downtime, customer complaints and preferences, supplier performances), 'analysis of performance indicators' for evaluating and establishing performance goals (such as quality costs or time to market of new products) and 'flow of information' for decision making. Relevant questions are about what information is needed and by whom, whether the data are reliable, how they should be presented from the perspective of the recipient, and in what way this information is important to people in other departments.

Since external information is typically poorer than internal information, more exposure to the outside is required, to be achieved through the 'benchmarking' technique. The measure of the management will be its ability to define and exploit information. A small-scale study was carried out in Australia to investigate interactions of organizational structures as input indicators to create a 'best path' to improvement (Barad and Kayis 1995). The input indicators of 'organizational improvement' were the 'measured' system dimensions, that is quality management, human resources and quality information. The output indicator of improvement was the flow of successfully completed improvement projects per year. The study provided evidence that the measured input indicators had a positive causal effect on the output indicator. A relatively high and 'balanced' distribution of input efforts of a company over all the defined dimensions, and attributes within dimensions, was found to be a 'best path' towards improvement.

The quality improvement measurement system

Quality improvement measures are used to evaluate how well processes and people are doing and eventually to motivate them to do better. It is often said that what gets measured, gets done. A measurement system concerns the quality of products and services as well as of processes, functions or organizational infrastructures. Measurement is needed to identify improvement opportunities for each of these (by discovering unmet customer desires, highlighting vital process quality problems, locating costs of poor quality or tracing organizational deficiencies), to compare performances (within the company as it relates to its suppliers and customers and also to other companies) and to evaluate progress (including improvement of business performance and personal performances).

To achieve its purposes, the design and planning of the measurement system should be organized as customer/supplier quality chains, relating measures of 'input' (supplied) quality performances (and improvement) to measures of 'output' quality improvement, as perceived by their respective customers. This is illustrated in Figure 5. For instance, as both employees and processes are 'customers' of the organizational infrastructure of a company, the quality improvement of the organizational structure (measured as input) is likely to affect the employees' behaviour (measured as output in terms of absenteeism) as well as the functioning of the improvement team process (measured as output in terms of the rate of successfully completed improvement projects). Manufactured products are customers of manufacturing processes, and the quality of the former should meet the requirements of the 'external customer', whose satisfaction will depend on its perception of the company quality improvement as related to service, products and eventually to the functional organization of the company as well. The business performance as a whole

may be measured in terms of growth (increased market share), increased profit (through improved process efficiency and productivity) and employees' well-being (reflected in their commitment to the company).

In a quality measurement system two other factors have to be considered: the 'measurability' and the 'complexity' of the quality features or performances to be measured. 'Measures' of product and process quality features may be directly expressed as attributes or numbers (defects, defective items, work in process), ratios (defective levels), cost (failure, appraisal), time (cycle, delivery, life) or some other measuring unit as appropriate to specific product characteristics such as strength, resistance or dimensions. In contrast, the intangible nature of some service characteristics, such as the behaviour of the service providers, makes their measurement difficult. Hence, indirect measures or 'quality indicators', intended to quantify quality features (such as human behaviour or human satisfaction) that by their nature are not measurable, are used instead.

Measuring the breaking strength of a material or the dimension of a part are examples of measurements whose results serve welldefined and simple purposes. Sometimes the purpose of measurement is more complex, for example to assess the quality organizational structure of a company or its business performance. In cases such as these, the measuring process becomes more intricate. It is then necessary to define the quality organizational structure of the company (or the business performance) in terms of measurable components to be separately evaluated and eventually integrated into overall 'performance measures'. Other examples of integrated performance measures associated with quality are 'efficiency' (which measures actual versus planned input efforts) or 'productivity' (which measures process outputs relative to its inputs). Customer satisfaction is a time-orientated complex concept, difficult to define and to measure.

'Quality costs' can be looked upon as another integrative way of assessing a company's economic quality performance. Quality costs analysis aims at an efficient use of prevention costs and appraisal costs to reduce failure costs. Through this model a corporate assessment of the quality costs is provided by the relative contribution of its three component costs. An alternative model is the process cost model, which rationalizes quality costs into the costs of conformance and the costs of non-conformance of each process.

'Benchmarking' is the process of comparing a company's strategy and achievements

with those of the best in the same class in an attempt to match and overtake them. The best-known example of benchmarking was provided by Xerox during the 1980s where sensational results were obtained. These included reducing the number of suppliers and the time to market of new products, instituting improvement teams and practising concurrent engineering. Other examples of companies that successfully applied benchmarking are

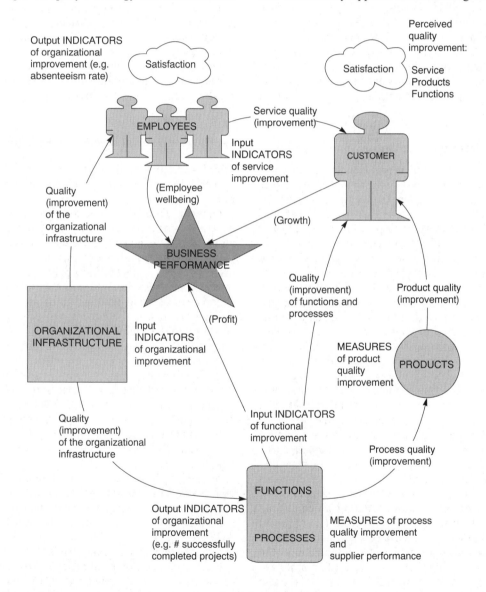

Figure 5 The quality improvement measurement system

Ford and Motorola. Benchmarking may be classified as strategic or operational. Strategic benchmarking is related to key success factors in terms of functional performances (sales, distribution, suppliers, R&D) and product differentiation criteria (such as reliability). Operational benchmarking focuses on particular processes or activities.

The benefits of benchmarking are associated with providing a model for setting new and realistic targets with respect to product, service and process and closing the gaps through improved performances. The pitfalls of benchmarking are disruption of operations, stemming from trying to imitate the best-in-class without possessing the necessary fundamental TQM structural and organizational features.

Infrastructure of improvement teams

Organizational efforts devoted to building quality team systems contributed strongly to successful implementation of the change in culture towards a realization of continuous improvement processes (Juran 1991). Typically, there are two types of team: first, breakthrough and selective teams (also called cross-functional because of their structure, as needed to approach the relatively complex improvement projects they deal with); and second, continuous improvement teams, which are intended to boost employees' participation (through solving simpler, local improvement problems) and are accordingly non-selective and homogeneous. The challenge to management is to determine the extent to which monitoring and control should be applied to improvement teams.

It was suggested that the infrastructure of improvement teams should be modelled as a three-stage sequential process representing the infrastructure elements. The three stages are: (1) a preliminary stage necessary to set the process in motion, during which companies must establish a steering committee to guide the approach, and basic training and initiatory improvement teams, typically of the breakthrough/selective type; (2) a more developed stage intended to improve process operation through monitoring and control of the teams; and (3) an advanced stage aimed at ensuring process continuity and progress. During the latter stage there is a danger of process stagnation. To avoid this, it is recommended that the active participation of employees should be extended by upgrading training and establishing additional improvement teams of the continuous improvement type. These teams resemble the quality control circles in Japan, except that they are not voluntary. The establishment of such teams (also called 'cells') is related to changes in the organizational structure of the companies, which become 'cellular organizations'. The validity of the above three-stage model was tested on a small sample of Australian companies, yielding positive results.

ISO 9000: universal standards of quality

The aim of a good quality system is to provide the conditions that ensure operational 'uniformity' in terms of methods, materials and equipment. To achieve this, the procedures have to be written in a standard format, so that all the people involved can use them consistently. Intense worldwide competition has driven the development and application of international standards. In contrast to the Baldrige or Deming criteria, which are for judging excellence, the standards of quality, such as BS5750 published in the UK in 1979 or the US ANSI/ASQC Q-90 series, are for establishing minimum requirements for a system of quality management aimed at assuring the quality of the processes that make the product or deliver the service. ISO 9000 is a set of worldwide standards (published in 1987) which are used in the European Union, and were also adopted by the Japanese, to provide a universal framework for quality systems that will enable companies to meet quality standards. The ISO 9000 standards are compatible with the second issue of the British standard BS5750 as well as with the US ANSI/ASQC Q-90 series. An interesting element in the application of the standard is that companies are assessed and registered by an approved body that is independent of both supplier and customer organizations.

A quality manual describing the quality system and explaining how the organization carries out the quality policy is established; it summarizes the procedures through which the quality objectives are carried out by the organization. A management respresentative having adequate authority is normally appointed. Responsibilities are defined and delegated throughout the system. Documentation for preparing a company's quality plan has to consider the level of the required quality system. Level 1 relates to design production and installation and is appropriate when the customers' requirements are expressed in terms of performances. It addresses topics such as: design control, document control, purchased items, calibration, inspection status of items, non-conformance and corrective action, records, training and techniques. Level 2 relates to organizations that produce goods and services. Level 3 is limited to final products and service inspection or test procedures. The problem with certification is that sometimes the required documentation may give rise to bureaucracy and unproductive activity.

4 Cultural/geographical styles in quality strategies and practices (West versus East)

A cultural style is a universal human feature expected to be reflected in a company's approach to its human resources. As there is no guarantee that theories developed in one country can, with good effect, be applied in another, continuous improvement is bound to take different forms in different countries (see ORGANIZATION CULTURE). The development of quality techniques in the USA and Japan has been reviewed above. The similarities and differences between these two quality management pillars are now examined, as reflected in the criteria of their respective national quality awards, Baldrige and Deming.

The criteria of the two awards are consistent with respect to 'continual improvement', 'a customer-orientated quality policy', 'participation of all employees' and 'deployment of these principles' in all the company's functions. The differences are mainly in the emphasis placed on the principles by the two approaches. In the US approach there is emphasis on 'leadership', which fits well within a US cultural pattern that consistently considers it as a crucial factor for organizational success. There is less emphasis on 'education and training' in general and on quality control methods in particular. Traditions of education and learning seem to be more deeply rooted in Japan than in the USA. Other relevant criteria of the Baldrige award are 'management by fact', supported by credible data and 'measurement'. These principles do not imply use of 'statistical methods', to which particular importance is attributed by the Deming criteria. According to Ishikawa, the Japanese quality control movement has benefited from the high level of Japanese basic education in mathematics. Senior managers in Japanese companies are currently much better trained in TQM and statistical thinking than their colleagues in Western companies. 'Collectivism' or 'groupism' is considered a basic principle of Japanese management, being strongly mirrored in the quality control circles, whose importance is stressed by the Deming award criteria. Activity theories on hierarchy of needs have been used to explain the congruence between people's psychological needs, accepted authority and peer pressure (Lillrank and Kano 1989).

The comparison between Western and Eastern styles of quality management has further implications (Barad 1995). Application of quality control circles was not commonly accepted in Western countries. In a large-scale study comparing quality control circles as applied in Japan, Korea and Denmark, significant differences between Denmark and the two Asian countries were brought to light. In Japan as well as in Korea, only a small percentage of the companies studied did not practise quality control circles, whereas the reverse situation existed in Denmark. Similar results were provided by a small-scale comparison between China and Australia. However, evidence contrary to the above is supplied by the findings of an international large-scale study (Ernst & Young and the American Quality Foundation 1992).

Another way to apply 'groupism' is through 'cellular organizations' (as created in the West), intended to meet two different organizational needs: first, a simplification of material handling and material flow through process redesign or re-engineering (providing favourable conditions to apply just-in-time and become an 'agile' enterprise); and second, reorganization and the boosting of 'participation' in continuous improvement teams on the shop floor. The marked difference between the quality control circles and the cells in a cellular organization is that the former are practised on a voluntary basis, whereas the latter are not, being part of the system's formal organization. The cellular organization model has been successfully adopted by many companies all over the world such as Ingersoll-Rand, IBM and Caterpillar.

5 Management theories and total quality

Thus far TQM has been examined from a 'total quality' point of view. In contrast, this section views it from a management theory perspective as reflected in some of the papers published in a special issue devoted to TQM by The Academy of Management Review in July 1994. The publication of this special issue provides evidence that TQM is here to stay (to be kept 'in fashion', its name may eventually change somewhat). The purpose of the issue was to stimulate the development of management theories on total quality by exploring the relationship between the principles of total quality and those of management theory, using the Malcolm Baldrige Award criteria as a bridge between them. As total quality and management theory cover similar topics, both disciplines may benefit from theory development. Total quality practitioners may benefit by an improved understanding of the factors leading to success and failure; for management theory researchers the total quality perspective will open up new research questions, such as ways to improve strategy formulation processes and the relative contributions of person and system factors to individual performance. The papers contributed to the special issue by Dean and Bowen, Waldman and Spencer are referred to here.

Dean and Bowen list three categories of topic: (1) areas in which total quality is consistent with management theory (leadership and practices of human resources); (2) subjects about which total quality should be informed by management theory (for example, to beware of overreliance on formal analysis of information, to place more importance on the human selection process and to apply a contingency approach to customer–supplier relationships and employees' involvement); and (3) new directions for management theory (for example, whether and in what ways strategy can be improved). Waldman considers the contribution of TQM to a theory of work performance. To model the determinants of individual performance, personal features such as knowledge, skills and motivation must be considered simultaneously with system factors such as person enhancers as well as system constraints and demands.

Spencer examines the similarities and differences between TQM and three models of organization: 'organismic', 'mechanistic' and 'cultural'. TQM shows signs of strong organismic concepts, similar to those exhibited by system thinkers. These are the concepts of 'open systems', which view an organization as a 'flow of interdependent processes' (analogous to the customer/supplier quality chains), and 'cross-level' relationships (cross-functional improvement teams), which are fundamental to TQM. Examples of mechanistic concepts can be found in some of Deming's ideas, namely the emphasis placed on 'reducing variation' (a mechanistic idea) and the general idea of viewing management in terms of (mechanical) principles. The cultural model calls attention to the 'value' judgements. It forces organizational researchers to make implicit values explicit and to recognize that individuals have purposes that warrant consideration. Spencer also provides meaningful explanations of management research that considers TQM ideas as 'old hat' (a fad of the organismic model, built on mechanistic principles). However, future fruitful research collaborations between the two disciplines can be envisaged, studying for example the interactions of organic components with cultural concepts, expressing the fact that human beings are not like other organisms.

6 Conclusion

In the TQM play there is a cast of three major characters: the promoters of total quality; the researchers of management theories; and the managers, who are the real and active players. In times of economic crisis, managers look for new and practical guidance to perform their roles. Pragmatic and successful guidance is provided by total quality, a 'management practice' that has evolved from a narrow focus on process quality control to embrace system structure and behavioural methods intended to achieve an 'overall improvement' of the organizational performances.

'Management theory is a multidisciplinary academic area whose links to practice are controversial' (Dean and Bowen 1994: 396). However, managers do need some theoretical grounding in addition to practical guidance, in order to gain a better understanding of the reasons for success and to beware of failure. When taken separately, the 'pure' managerial theories (such as the mechanistic, organismic and cultural models) cannot accurately describe 'real' systems like organizational systems, whose behaviour is much more complex. When taken together, theories such as the above may become a powerful tool for 'analysing' the more practical TQM models, 'enhancing' and 'improving' them through a deeper understanding of the interactions involved in their implementation, so as not to use them in a universal (simplistic) way, but through contingencies as appropriate to individual companies.

Seen in perspective, the quality concept and its organization has travelled a long way. First, it developed as a discipline, then it acquired strategic management credibility, and lately it has attracted the attention of management researchers as well. A promising future for TQM is chiefly related to its cultural philosophy of continuous improvement, driving its human orientation within organizations towards 'creativity' (a goal that is superior to mere 'organistic adaptability' to environment), enabling the highest level of individual need to be materialized, that is the 'self-actualization' need expressed by personal development and accomplishment.

MIRYAM BARAD
TEL AVIV UNIVERSITY

Note

The author wishes to acknowledge the kind help of Professor Barry Popplewell in suggesting and providing additional material.

Further reading

(References cited in the text marked *)

Akao, Y. (1990) *Quality Function Deployment*, Cambridge, MA: Productivity Press. (A detailed presentation of the house of quality concept and its many stages.)

* Barad, M. (1995) 'Some cultural geographical styles in quality strategies and quality costs revisited (P.R. China versus Australia)', *International Journal of Production Economics*. (Discusses some principles and practices of quality management across cultures, based on comparison of state-owned enterprises in China and small sample of Australian enterprises.)

* Barad, M. and Kayis, B. (1995) 'Total quality management experiences in some New South Wales manufacturing companies', *Total Quality Management* 6 (2): 107–22. (A quantitative approach to analyse input and output performance indicators of organizational structures.)

Buchanan, D. and McCalman, J. (1989) *High Performance Work Systems: The Digital Experience*, London: Routledge. (Provides an insightful, detailed account of Digital's experience with work teams.)

* Crosby, P.B. (1979) *Quality is Free*, New York: McGraw-Hill. (Provided the starting point for the 'zero defects' movement.)

Dale, B.G. and Plunkett, J.J. (1995) *Quality Costing*, 2nd edn, London: Chapman and Hall. (Useful advice on designing a quality cost collection and reporting system.)

* Dean, J.W., Jr and Bowen, D.E. (eds) (1994) *Total Quality*, special issue of *Academy of Management Review* 19 (3): 387–584. (A stimulating discussion of total quality as a new management practice versus some older management theories.)

* Deming, W.E. (1986) *Out of the Crisis*, Cambridge, MA: MIT Press. (Transformation of the US management style in the direction of continuous improvement, as viewed by the famous visionary quality management pioneer.)

* Ernst & Young and the American Quality Foundation (1992) *International Quality Study (IQS) Computer Industry Report*, Cleveland, OH: Ernst & Young. (Reveals dynamic international trends of the quality movement around the world.)

* Feigenbaum, A.V. (1991) *Total Quality Control*, 3rd edn, New York: McGraw-Hill. (Advocates quality integration within companies through cross-functional collaboration.)

* Garvin, D.A. (1988) *Managing Quality: The Strategic Competitive Edge*, New York: The Free Press. (An interesting presentation of the quality concept and its historic development in the USA and Japan.)

Ishikawa, K. (1989) 'How to apply company-wide quality control in foreign countries', *Quality Progress* September: 70–4. (Emphasizes the differences between Japanese and Western approaches to quality management.)

* Juran, J.M. (1991) 'Strategies for world-class quality', *Quality Progress* March: 81–5. (An analysis and explanation of the quality improvement team movement.)

Juran, J.M. and Gryna, D.S. (1993) *Quality Planning and Analysis*, 2nd edn, New York: McGraw-Hill. (A classic book that illustrates a well-structured view of quality management and practices.)

* Lillrank, P. and Kano, N. (1989) *Continuous Improvement*, Ann Arbor, MI: University of Michigan Centre for Japanese Studies. (A deep and critical review of quality control circles based on thorough and methodical research.)

Melcher, W.A., Dumont, P. and Khouja, M. (1990) 'Standard maintaining and continuous improvement systems: experiences and comparisons', *Interfaces* 20 (May–June): 24–40. (A discussion of the elements involved in moving from a standard maintaining culture to a continuous improvement culture, supported by numerous examples.)

Montgomery, D.E. (1991) *Introduction to Statistical Quality Control*, 2nd edn, New York: Wiley. (A very good textbook on quantitative quality control techniques with emphasis on process control; also includes an introduction to the design of experiments methodology.)

* National Institute of Standards and Technology (1993) *Malcolm Baldrige National Award Criteria*, Gaithersburg, MD: Department of Commerce.(Sets out the criteria framework for the well-known US quality award.)

* Oakland, J.S. (1993) *Total Quality Management: The Route to Improving Performance*, 2nd edn, East Brunswick, NJ: Nichols Publishing. (A core book on TQM with a well-structured presentation of the many intricacies of quality management.)

* Porter, M.E. (1980) *Competitive Strategies: Technique for Analyzing Industries and Competitors*, New York: McGraw-Hill.

Porter, M.E. (1985) *Competitive Advantage*, New York: The Free Press. (An exciting book about how a firm actually puts the generic strategies into practice.)

* Ross, J.E. (1995) *Total Quality Management: Text, Cases and Readings*, 2nd edn, Delray Beach, FL: St Lucie Press. (A core book on TQM built around the main criteria of the Baldrige award, supplemented by test cases.)

* Taguchi, G. (1986) *Introduction to Quality Engineering*, Tokyo: Asian Productivity Organization. (A methodology for designing products and processes whose quality characteristics are robust with respect to noise factors; many practical examples.)

See also: ISHIKAWA, K.; ORGANIZATION BEHAVIOUR; ORGANIZATION CULTURE;

Related topics in the IEBM: BENCHMARKING; COMMITMENT IN JAPAN; DEMING, W.E.; GLOBALIZATION; GURU CONCEPT; JAPANIZATION; JURAN, J.M.; JUST-IN-TIME PHILOSOPHIES; MANAGEMENT IN JAPAN; STRATEGY, CONCEPT OF

Women managers in organizations

1 **Theoretical perspectives on women's roles in management**
2 **Progress made**
3 **Barriers and opportunities**
4 **Actions to be taken by organizations**

Overview

International Women's Day is held in March of each year, providing an annual opportunity to review opportunities available to the world's women. Each year's findings are similar: while the world's women are making progress, much more progress is possible. According to a 1997 United Nations report, women remain an under-utilized human resource worldwide.

In many countries, differential treatment for women includes poor access to basic safety, security, nutrition or healthcare resources; in other countries, differential treatment frequently is related to educational opportunities; and in other parts of the world – particularly industrialized nations – differential treatment often is reflected in unequal pay for women and men. For example, the International Labour Organization (ILO) reports that Japanese women earn about 57 per cent of men's earnings for comparable work, while in Norway women typically earn 85–93 per cent of what men are paid. In addition, the Human Development Report, 1997, reports that in developing countries women earn only three-fourths of what men earn, plus they have less access to land, credit and employment opportunities. Available data also show that women in business worldwide frequently have limited access to professional and managerial jobs. The Human Development Report, 1997, compared 94 countries in terms of the amounts of professional, economic and political opportunities available to women. Norway, Sweden, Denmark and Finland were the recipients of the highest rankings, 1–4 respectively.

Just as women in different countries face a range of challenges, women in the same country also might experience distinctive obstacles in becoming part of the paid workforce. Women are by no means a monolithic group either within or across nations. For example, according to the US Department of Labor 1996 data, while white women executive administrators earn 68 per cent of what white male managers are paid, African-American women earn only 60 per cent and Hispanic women earn only 61 per cent.

Furthermore, national cultures differ in how they view women's actual or potential contribution to the paid workforce and, as a result, different theories have emerged to explain women's contributions to this area. Cultural differences also may account for the barriers that women face in becoming managers, and cultural stereotypes about women can play a large role in shaping the educational, legal and organizational opportunities offered to women. Just as women in different nations are not likely to face the same challenges to paid workforce participation, neither are they likely to share the same aspirations, hopes or dreams. Accordingly, this entry focuses primarily on women who share the experience of working for pay, or who are in managerial positions. Unfortunately, information about these experiences often is not readily available. One result is that the following information comes from those countries where data are available, principally from the USA and other industrialized nations.

While the available evidence demonstrates that the status of women remains lower than that of men, it is also evident that women increasingly are part of the paid workforce and continue to make progress in achieving managerial positions. For example, according to the ILO, between 1985 and 1991 the percentage of women managers increased in thirty-nine of the forty-one countries that report comparative labour statistics. This progress was made in a variety of ways and may be explained by a range of reasons. One of those reasons is culture's perspective on the role women can or should play in the paid workforce. Theoretical perspectives vary from country to country, so we begin this review with an examination of perspectives that can serve as a baseline for assessing and explaining progress made and progress which still needs to be made on behalf of working women worldwide.

The review of theoretical perspectives on women and paid work is followed by specific evidence of women's employment progress organized according to the major and enduring ways in which such progress has been achieved. Despite the evidence provided, there is considerable proof to show that women are absent from many organizations, and are particularly scarce in middle and top management positions. For example, a 1994 *Wall Street Journal* study of data collected by the Equal Employment Opportunity Commission for over 38,000 US-based firms showed that strides made by women are numerous but men remain firmly in control of top management and decision-making jobs. The Human Development Report, 1997, showed that, globally, women still hold only 13 per cent of parliamentary seats and 6 per cent of cabinet posts. This evidence suggests that while barriers to occupational equity have been reduced, many remain. Accordingly, this review provides additional information of two types: barriers that women frequently face in becoming part of the paid workforce; and ways these barriers could be or have been lowered. Finally, this entry concludes with an examination of some worldwide conditions that continue to draw women into the paid workforce and into managerial positions.

1 Theoretical perspectives on women's roles in management

The world is not one with respect for the opportunities accorded to women, nor is there universal agreement as to the role women can or should play in the business world. These differences are evident in several major theories of women's roles in business and

management. While explanations for perceived or actual differences between men and women vary widely, three primary perspectives have been proposed. These theoretical perspectives are useful not only as research frameworks, but also because they describe the perspectives organizational leaders implicitly or explicitly adopt when addressing gender equity issues (see EQUAL EMPLOYMENT OPPORTUNITIES).

Person-centred or gender-centred perspectives

One approach to understanding gender differences is known as the 'person-centred' or 'gender-centred' approach (Fagenson 1993). The basic argument here is that gender is a powerful determinant of many, if not most, of one's preferences, abilities, skills and behaviours. Accordingly, one might expect men to think and act in certain prescribed ways and women to act in other prescribed ways. Organizational practices prior to the mid-1960s in the USA favoured men almost exclusively as managers, operating on the gender-centred belief that men alone possessed qualities suitable for managerial positions; the theory also holds that women are unlikely to possess the skills, abilities and attributes needed for management. Research evidence shows that this perspective remains alive and well in workplaces in the USA and in other countries (Adler and Israeli 1994; Fagenson 1993). This perspective is likely to find adherents primarily in those countries where gender roles are clearly prescribed.

Another variation on the gender-centred approach to management is that women have different, perhaps even better, skills than men for managing the demands of an increasingly global workplace. The list of managerial skills important to what has been called the 'global century' continues to grow, but some theorists argue that caring for and nurturing others is an important skill for empowering others, and that this is a skill that women frequently possess (Helgesen 1990). That is, women have a greater concern for relationships, disdain complex rules and structures and emphasize process over product or task.

Yet a third gender-centred approach is represented in what has been called the complementary contributions approach; its argument is that men and women are different but that as managers each has an equally valuable organizational contribution to make (Adler and Izraeli 1994). As compared to other gender-based perspectives, the complementary contributions approach does not suggest that either gender is inherently better than the other. This approach to gender differences is often voiced in western Europe, but it is also found in many US firms and among individuals who believe that while men and women as managers are different, these differences are not hierarchical.

Organizational structure perspective

A second theoretical perspective on women as managers argues that observed or observable differences in managerial behaviour for men and women are due to situational differences in the workplace (Kanter 1977). This perspective has been called the situation or organizational structure approach, and it argues that differences in how women and men manage at work are a function of the different organizational structures they experience. As compared to men, women managers are delegated little organizational power, are situated in positions with little job mobility or opportunity and, as a group, are few in number in the ranks of management. Research supportive of this approach has shown that women managers will change their behaviour as a function of their organizational situations. In organizational environments where men dominate and determine who receives promotions, women often downplay their femininity and take on the traits of the individuals who promote them, traits that are traditionally considered more masculine (Fagenson 1993) (see CAREERS).

Gender–organization–system perspective

A third, more recent approach used to describe gender diversity in management is called the gender–organization–system (GOS) approach (Fagenson 1993). It supports both the gender-centred and situational perspectives presented above by arguing that men and women in organizations are likely to act differently because of differences in their gender, and their organizational situations (a concept broader than organizational structure which includes an organization's history, culture, strategy, etc.). Moreover, the GOS approach proposes that individuals and organizations cannot be understood separate from their societies or cultures, and that changes in either the individual, the organization or the system are likely to occasion changes in the other factors. In viewing the status of men and women in organizations simultaneously with the organizational and societal contexts from which those status differentials or equalities emerged, this theory is more complex than either the gender-centred or situational perspectives on gender.

As compared to the gender-centred and situational theories, the systems-orientated aspect of the GOS theory approach does not so much assign blame for past inequities as suggest directions for future equity. An organization following a GOS approach would view managerial equity for women as part of a systemic change requiring some amount of adaptation on the part of society, organizational members, organizational design and organizational strategy and vision. Ideally, this vision would define equity as a strategic imperative for would-be world-class competitors.

The theory can be used to argue that opportunities for women in the business world result not from a single stand-alone event, but rather from complex interactions and convergence among multiple forces, including political and legal activity, societal beliefs, values, practices, and organizational and individual action. The complex nature of these interactions means that change often occurs in a discontinuous fashion rather than according to a predictable pattern. This being the case, progress is not likely to be identical from country to country, or even within the same country over time.

2 Progress made

Winning a place for women in the paid workforce has not come without a struggle, although the nature of the struggle has varied considerably from country to country. Nonetheless, as the following review suggests, enduring progress has come about as a result of profound changes occurring in the global environment. The following review looks at changes in cultural values and norms relating to work, legal changes not only allowing women to work but also to prepare educationally for work, and changes in the economic priorities of individuals, families and nations.

Changes in cultures

Culture has been defined in many ways but a recurring theme is that culture represents a highly integrated and intensely interrelated set of learned symbols and values. Interrelationships among sets of cultural symbols and norms are important because they serve to reinforce the values, beliefs and behaviours expected from individuals. Although culture does not change quickly, it begins to change when prior solutions to social problems no longer work. A quick review of world events should be enough to suggest that globalization has posed many challenges that countries are unable to resolve using traditional norms and beliefs. Answers to questions of national importance like economic development, comparative advantage, workforce deployment and resource development are subject to continual review in most, if not all, countries. One result of the search for new answers to societal questions is that many people experiment with new, culturally diverse options in an effort to find new solutions to the problems societies face.

Included among the problems culture typically resolves are two issues especially pertinent to this review of women in business and management; how to divide labour among people and how to provide girls and boys with instruction in socially accepted and useful behaviour. Some cultures have coped with these issues through prescribed sex roles for females and males, but as this review indicates, there is considerable cultural variation in resolving these problems.

For example, in the aftermath of the Second World War when work was relatively scarce, both the USA and Japan coped with the overabundance of labour by consigning women almost exclusively to a place in the home rather than in the paid workforce and consigning men to paid jobs outside the home. Sex roles were clearly defined and similarly assigned in both countries; women assumed nurturing and caretaking jobs within the family while men toiled outside the home to earn resources for the family. These prescribed roles were reinforced with a variety of available cultural tools, including appropriate stereotypes of what was expected of men and women.

Communist countries took a different approach to labour division by expecting both women and men to join the paid workforce. In the former Soviet Union and in many of the countries controlled by the USSR, both women and men were expected to work outside the home (Adler and Izraeli 1994). China charted a similar path, and Chinese women, who had historically faced discrimination, were rewarded with important constitutional rights for having fought alongside men to establish the People's Republic of China (PRC). China's first constitution in 1954 guaranteed women the right to work and vote, and during the 1960s and 1970s additional measures were introduced to guarantee women's participation in employment and state affairs. By the early 1990s, 89 per cent of China's urban women were employed in the industrial sector.

Thus, in the PRC as in the former Soviet Union and its satellites, central guidelines against sex discrimination led to relative job equality for women and men. This is not to say that sex roles were eliminated altogether, because evidence from communist and previously communist countries shows that women in those countries still assumed the majority of household and child-rearing functions. Similarly – and this is also true in many other countries – many jobs performed primarily by women in Russia continue to be viewed as lower in status than male-dominated work, and often the wage rates are lower for jobs in female-dominated fields (Adler and Izraeli 1994). In both the USSR and the PRC opportunities for women in the paid workforce were enhanced by universal childcare but are under pressure as market-led reforms are implemented. This policy was largely intended by these countries' governments to be a response to the cultural challenge to train children with appropriate values, norms and behaviours, and not necessarily to benefit women and their families.

As outlined above, the link between economic priorities, political/legal systems, childcare systems and women's labour outside the home shows that cultural factors well outside individual control affect individual opportunity. Changes in the ways societies need to resolve problems associated with allocating labour in society have led many countries to not only *under-utilize* women's vast resources, but to also make changes to *facilitate* female employment. Progress has been achieved mainly through the political process and through laws and regulations which make it difficult to exclude women from organizational life. Progress has been uneven but for many women measurable change has followed political/legal change and has been facilitated by the work of grass roots movements on behalf of occupational equity for women.

Equal opportunity legislation

One catalyst for increased occupational equity for women is legal action. As the example of the PRC indicates, legal action can result from central government decree or constitutional change, but in other countries legal change has resulted from political and grass roots activities on the part of women and other minority groups. For example, the US political environment for civil rights in the early 1960s led to a series of executive orders and legislative acts mandating equity. Although these new laws were passed principally to eradicate racism, women also were able to benefit from this legislation (see EQUAL EMPLOYMENT OPPORTUNITIES).

More specifically, until passage of the US Equal Pay Act of 1963, US women had few employment opportunities and almost no legal expectation of pay or treatment equal to what men received at work. At best female workers were viewed as a reserve workforce to be invited into or phased out of paid jobs according to the current state of the economy. Since women's opportunities to remain in the paid workforce depended on employer needs, few women remained in the workforce long enough to achieve managerial positions. Those few who did remain found advancement very difficult and pay low; executive, professional and administrative jobs were not covered by the Equal Pay Act until June 1972. The Civil Rights Act of 1964 (Title VII) provided basic guarantees for equal opportunity in jobs and pay but none of these laws as yet have achieved full equity for women in paid jobs.

Many countries facing similar labour shortages have introduced laws intended to provide social or occupational equity for women, but many leaders in these countries recognize that it is easier to pass an equal opportunity law than to implement one. This is in part due to the fact that men fear the competition women pose if they are guaranteed equal rights in the workplace, and it is due to the reality that cultural habits and stereotypes change slowly. Ironically, it is also due to the fact that other laws exist that make equity laws difficult to implement. For example, while Swiss voters guaranteed equal rights for men and women in the early 1980s, a provision in an earlier law allowed the half-canton of Appenzell Inner-Rhoden to withhold some voting rights from women until a Federal Tribunal overruled the practice a decade later. Similarly, while Japan passed an Equal Employment Opportunity Law in 1985, a national law prohibiting women from working between 10 p.m. and 5 a.m. has made it difficult for some employers to comply with this law. Norway's 1978 Equal Status Act similarly provides legal protection, but the fact that limited childcare exists for infants and children not yet of school age effectively prevents many women from taking full-time paid positions.

In summary, in most countries that have equal opportunity laws, full equity has yet to be achieved. In the PRC, for example, an anti-discrimination law created to protect women from discrimination in employment, housing, politics and education in 1992 is difficult to enforce since there are few mechanisms to enforce the law. Thus, in the PRC and other countries the law proves most useful in informing women of their rights and in helping women become aware of opportunities. At the same time, because they are sometimes difficult to enforce, laws mandating equal employment opportunity for women are not a singular solution to improving equity at work.

Educational opportunities

The reason that equal opportunities under the law may not result in equal opportunities at work is that past practices may have made it impossible or unfeasible for women to prepare educationally for business or managerial work. In addition, the same laws that permitted occupational inequities frequently contributed to educational inequities. For example, Title IX of the Education Amendments changed educational opportunities for US women in 1972 by requiring all institutions receiving federal monies of any kind to eradicate discrimination against students and employees on the basis of gender; virtually all educational institutions are covered by Title IX. The effect of this type of legislation in the USA was to provide opportunities for women to consider fields previously considered closed to them, particularly business, science and engineering fields, and to participate fully in the academic and co-curricular activities of educational institutions.

Education is a critical barometer of women's progress since it offers one of the few ways to circumvent other restrictions women might face such as cultural norms or stereotypes. Yet, obtaining higher education is likely to be difficult for the world's girls and women who are not permitted access to basic learning such as reading and writing, as documented in the United Nations 1993 report on the status of women. Progress made to improve women's educational opportunities varies from country to country but the net effect is the same: women with little or no education are not perceived as likely candidates for jobs. This problem is especially evident in developing countries, where literacy rates may be especially low for women. For example, according to the 1997 Human Development Report, in developing countries illiterate women outnumber men by 60 per cent.

Recognition of the tight link between economic development and education has led many countries to improve women's literacy rates (Adler and Izraeli 1994). For example, while colonial segregation in Kenya provided education only for Kenyan males, independence led to changes in national priorities including compulsory education up until the age of 12 for all children. One result of this policy has been an increased literacy rate nationwide, but also an increase in the number of girls and women who continue their education.

Many developing countries are similarly working to raise literacy rates, and where once girls and women were not recipients of education, now they are viewed as an untapped resource to be cultivated with education in order to increase production and enhance social progress. Although as many as 90 per cent of rural women and 60 per cent of urban women in Egypt are illiterate, female enrolment in primary and secondary schools tripled in Egypt between 1960 and 1976. Social status and education also are dual roads to job access for Egyptian women and for women in much of the developing world, suggesting that women from advantaged families will be the first movers in job markets.

This link between education, social class and employment is found in many developing countries. That is, highly educated women often are part of the upper classes and also are likely to have paid employment in civil service or private sector jobs. In some cases families educate their women so that they can play an active role in family businesses, some of which are powerful economic entities. Thus, while education is seen as a critical variable for economic development, in the short term education is not yet available to the poor in great numbers, and is particularly inaccessible for impoverished girls and women.

Singapore is an exemplar of a progressive, newly-developed nation. Singapore's economic priorities include an educational emphasis, and its success at reaching this goal is measured by the fact that its women are generally better educated than its men. If the trends towards higher education for women continue in Singapore there are likely to be more women than men with completed degrees. In addition, increasingly women are enrolling in professional studies in Singapore and are the majority of those seeking medical or law degrees.

When women have access to education and to higher education they frequently are directed towards those degrees that are most consistent with traditional female roles which, in turn, provide most of the job opportunities for women. These include teaching, nursing and community services. However, when educational opportunity under the law changes, one result often is a change in enrolment patterns for women in higher education. Presently the majority of US college students are women and the increased enrolment of women is credited by the American Accreditation Association of Collegiate Schools of Business as the single most important factor contributing to enrolment growth in US business education from the 1970s to the 1990s. However, women have been ghettoized, with far more female than male business majors concentrating their studies on accounting and far fewer concentrating on finance. According to the US Department of Education, where once there were few women holding PhDs in business, by the mid-1990s approximately 27 per cent of such degrees were earned by women, suggesting that opportunities that attract more women to undergraduate programmes also will encourage some women to seek advanced degrees.

The US Department of Education reports that the progress for US women continues to lag in the fields of engineering and physics. Women account for only 4 per cent of America's engineers and continue to seek a greater proportion of degrees in fields other than science or engineering. Women hold fewer than 10 per cent of all electrical and aeronautical engineering degrees. This gender gap in science may be increasing rather than decreasing in the USA, but it is not found to the same extent in western Europe or Asia, where both girls and boys are encouraged to acquire higher level maths skills according to the American Association of University Women. Overall, research has consistently shown that US females make better students than males. For example, girl's and women's grades are consistently higher than the grades attained by boys and men. Yet, women's superior academic achievements are not rewarded in the workplace. Women at all educational levels experience greater unemployment than men and US women have achieved equity with men in only seven of thirty-three major occupations. Moreover, women with college degrees earn less than men who have not finished high school according to the American Association of University Women.

Under-utilization of educated women also occurs in other countries (Adler and Izraeli 1994). For example, while Kuwaiti women are well educated and have earned college degrees at home and abroad, they are not encouraged to work outside the home. Despite comprising 45 per cent of the population, Kuwaiti women represent only 2 per cent of the workforce; those few who are employed are generally concentrated in teaching and clerical positions and few find it possible to advance to high-level organizational positions. While few developing or developed countries can afford to educate women to work only at home, many continue to track women toward degrees more consistent with traditional gender roles than with individual skills and abilities.

Overall, this review of educational opportunities shows that while barriers to women in some academic fields have all but disappeared, other fields remain unattractive to women. In some countries the problem of educational equity is access to education, while in others the problem is access to particular fields of study. In addition, it has been shown that even as women earn degrees in fields traditionally reserved for women their opportunities for obtaining and advancing in employment have been limited. Moreover, when women pursue fields traditionally reserved for and currently dominated by men, according to the American Association of University Women, they are often discouraged and harassed by teachers and peers, especially those of the male gender.

Changes in economic priorities

Entrepreneurship
In addition to changes in cultural values and legal opportunities, a third enduring factor contributing to enhanced occupational equity for women has been economic need and the changes in social priorities which economic need has fuelled. Evidence from around the world shows that women increasingly contribute to economic development both in the industrialized and developing worlds. In many cases the role women play in economic development is not via existing organizations but rather through entrepreneurial activities. As much as one-third to one-half of small entrepreneurs in Latin America are believed to be women, and in urban areas that number may be as high as 80 per cent (Adler and Izraeli 1994). Development projects in many countries involve development of traditional cottage industries that include women's labour. Projects emphasizing pottery, textiles and similar handicrafts often benefit families and development by providing cash income for the work carried out by women. Not surprisingly, contributing to the economic status of the family has had a positive effect on the status of the woman who provides that income. Many developing countries recognize that this income-producing ability develops the country's economic base, and this could lead nations to invest more resources in women and to recognize the valuable role women can play in economic development.

Estimates vary but according to the US Small Business Administration women own about 30 per cent of all US sole proprietorships and partnerships. In contrast to many women entrepreneurs in developing countries who initiate businesses because they have no other options, US women entrepreneurs often establish small businesses because of frustrations with current work options (Fagenson 1993). Leaders in corporations often underestimate and under-utilize women's skills and abilities and this leads many women employees to strike out on their own to create jobs that can utilize their abilities. According to many women who have established their own companies, entrepreneurship offers a number of opportunities: being one's own boss, flexible work hours and responsive work policies, for example. At the same time, working for oneself is said to be demanding, sometimes requiring more hours of work than is expected from an employee, and it is not without financial risk (Fagenson 1993).

In-home work
Another way to earn a cash income is to work for an employer either inside or outside the home. Many women work at home assembling garments or similar products for an employer; this occurs particularly in developing countries, but also is practised among immigrants and other groups in developed countries (Adler and Izraeli 1994). In addition, the technological capacity of some countries makes it possible for some women to work via telecommunication. In entrepreneurial jobs and in jobs that permit in-home labour, women retain some amount of control over their workload and schedule. This allows them to balance work with other life demands, and in particular to provide daycare for young children or elderly parents. However, for most women paid labour involves working outside the home, and for many this work is available only at some distance from their homes. This has resulted in disruptions of traditional cultural habits and norms.

Work outside the home: migration to work
In most countries, the greatest number of jobs are found in and around cities. One consequence of this trend for industrialized countries is that most people live near larger cities. However, the situation is quite different in developing countries where agricultural life has been the norm. Increasingly these norms are being abandoned by both men and women who journey to cities in search of paid work.

As the male heads of families migrate to the cities in search of paid work, women may take on new roles in managing the home or farm, and this has changed some social practices. In Kenya, for example, male migration has left women with farm roles, but these roles have been altered as women band together with others in similar situations to develop self-help groups to improve their community (Adler and Izraeli 1994). The government of Kenya has also played a role assisting women by organizing a Women's Bureau to provided financial and educational assistance to self-help community groups. While the long-term effect of this type of reorganization cannot be known, it is clear that women's roles in the family and the community will be changed as they make more family and economic decisions.

In addition, where once women stayed at home and men worked outside the home, women are increasingly found among the world's migrants, similarly searching for jobs but in some cases pursuing safety and other opportunities not found at home. According to the United Nations, among the 100 million people who typically are migrants, over half are women and children in search of better opportunities for themselves. This too has had a disruptive effect upon traditional beliefs about women's roles at work and in the family. Where once young Mexican women lived at home until they married, jobs at maquiladora plants located along the US-Mexico border have attracted many young women from southern Mexico to work in these northern Mexican factories. According to some estimates over 80 per cent of labourers in maquiladors are young women, many of whom are on their own for the first time in their lives. This experience not only provides young women with a variety of new opportunities but also has changed some social roles and institutions. For example, many new support industries for young women have sprung up along the US-Mexico border. Moreover, the father's traditional authority within the Mexican family is interrupted when children leave the home for work elsewhere. These disruptions are occurring in many developing countries as young people leave their homes to seek paid work in cities and even in other countries. Part of the latter practice occurs when women cannot find suitable employment in their own countries. For example, many young women from Sri Lanka and the Philippines migrate to Asia and to the Middle East to seek jobs not available to them at home (Adler and Izraeli 1994). While most continue to send money and goods to their families, others remain abroad and never return to their country of origin.

Work outside the home: working for an employer

Job creation in some countries has been high and this has permitted women to seek and find work in their own countries. Development patterns vary widely according to national economics, even within regions. For example, according to the International Labour Organization (ILO), the workforce participation rates for women in the European Union (EU) range from a low of 37.5 per cent in Portugal to a high of 75 per cent in Denmark. The average workforce participation rate for EU women is 50.5 per cent.

In developing countries, women's occupational opportunities tend to follow similar patterns, with women working first in agricultural jobs and then in light assembly (Adler and Izraeli 1994). With increased education women begin to move to clerical work, then to commerce and finally to managerial positions. Only 21 per cent of women in Kenya are formally employed and most are found in lower level jobs. On the other hand, Singapore's rapid economic growth has provided numerous opportunities for women, many of whom are well educated. Over one-half of recent college graduates in Singapore are female, and females increasingly seek higher degrees, particularly in professional fields such as law and medicine. Furthermore, opportunities for women in Singapore have shifted from a concentration in agricultural, manufacturing and community services to greater representation in finance and commerce.

Progress towards achieving equal access and representation of women in management positions to date has been lacking in developing countries, where women as a group hold few managerial positions and generally have poor access to educational opportunities to prepare them for management. According to the 1997 Human Development Report, in industrialized countries the unemployment rate among women is higher than among men. In many cases the height and breadth of barriers for women in management varies according to race and ethnicity, employing industry or level of the managerial position (Fagenson 1993). Overall, women have made their greatest gains in attaining lower level managerial positions worldwide, but most have some difficulty obtaining midlevel positions and much greater difficulty reaching top-level positions (Powell 1993).

According to the US Census Bureau only 33.9 per cent of US women were employed outside the home in 1950, but 57.5 per cent were similarly employed by 1990. The US Department of Labor reports that during the 1980s the number of women in executive, administrative and managerial fields nearly doubled in the USA to about 6.2 million. Women constituted about 42 per cent of the number of people employed in such positions. Of the 6.2 million women employed in executive, administrative and managerial fields, about 83 per cent were white women, 8 per cent were black women and about 4.5 per cent were women of Hispanic origin. As these data would indicate, women face barriers to their participation in managerial ranks, but women of colour are less well represented in managerial ranks than white women.

In general, women are not equally represented in all segments of the workforce. Employed women, according to the US Department of Labor, are most frequently found in those professions that have traditionally been considered appropriate for women, particularly in the helping professions such as nursing, teaching and clerical work. Women also tend to be concentrated in sales, particularly at the retail level. More specifically, in 1991 women held 80 per cent of administrative support jobs, 99 per cent of secretarial positions and 66.7 per cent of all retail and sales jobs while 94.8 per cent of registered nurses were women (Fagenson 1993). Unfortunately,

most of these occupations pay women relatively meagre wages for their efforts as compared to the occupations dominated by men. This is not due to the fact that traditional women's occupations are any less important than traditionally male occupations. Rather, research shows that the status of an occupation declines the more women there are in that occupation, a finding reported by the American Psychological Association, whose membership is increasingly female.

3 Barriers and opportunities

The glass ceiling to advancement

According to a recent ILO report, men all over the world hold the highest management positions, with greater inequalities occurring between men and women the closer they get to the top of organizational hierarchies. According to the US Department of Labor, only 3 per cent of senior management jobs were held by US women by 1991, and many argue that this occurs because a 'glass ceiling' exists preventing women from advancing up the corporate ladder. What is responsible for this impenetrable barrier? According to several high-level managers there are six major organizational barriers that constitute the glass ceiling (Morrison 1992). These include a lonely and non-supportive working environment, the treatment of gender differences as weaknesses, exclusion from group activities because of these differences, the failure to help individuals prepare for management, the inability of people to balance work/personal life issues and the failure to develop organizational awareness and shrewdness.

The glass ceiling, as well as 'glass walls' for lateral movement into line positions, are both key features of the dim organizational landscape encountered by women in many nations. In the USA the barriers to top-level jobs are perceived to be numerous although many are subtle and well embedded in organizational culture and life. According to an estimate provided by the Women's Research and Education Institute, at the current rate of change attaining full economic integration for women at every organizational level would take seventy-five to one hundred years.

In addition to encountering barriers to advancing toward senior-level positions, women also face barriers associated with particular industrial sectors. For example, according to the US Department of Labor, US women are more likely to hold senior management positions in human resources and communications, and are far less likely to hold senior management positions in production or plant facilities functions. Opportunities for women in management may be greater in industries like computers and telecommunications that are experiencing a rapid pace of change. This may be because emergent industries simply have not been in existence long enough to have established rules about who is or should be a manager, relying more on managerial ability than on gender to make employment decisions.

Earnings

It was shown earlier that gains for women in management have been greatest at lower managerial levels; earning gains show a similar profile. That is, in the USA female cashiers earned about 95 cents to every male dollar in 1992 as compared to female securities brokers who earned only 52 cents for every dollar men earned from the same profession. The biggest gender gaps occur for sales employees where women earn 57 per cent of male earnings, and in executive and managerial positions where women earn approximately 63 per cent of what men earn.

Despite overall increases in earnings in some sectors, gains in comparative earnings for women overall have been slow, particularly at senior management levels. In 1990 *Fortune* magazine conducted a compensation study of the 1,000 largest industrial and service businesses in the USA and discovered that only nineteen women (0.005 per cent) were counted among the highest paid officers and directors. Similarly, a recent Korn/Ferry International Study showed that while individual women made wage progress, on average there had been no group progress in wage increases among executive women when their

earnings were compared with those of executive men (see PAYMENT SYSTEMS).

As compared to the rest of the world, working women in the USA are paid proportionately less than working women in most industrialized nations. According to the ILO, the female–male weekly wage ratio ranged from 80–90 per cent in Australia, Denmark, France, New Zealand, Norway and Sweden, while other countries in western Europe had ratios of roughly 65–75 per cent. However, as noted earlier, Japanese women earn about 57 per cent of what a Japanese man would earn in a similar job. The overall pattern that emerges across nations is that women are paid less than men for comparable work.

Work/personal life balance

Managerial work has traditionally made high demands on the individual, but perhaps no demand is higher than the belief that work should have higher priority than family or personal concerns. This order of priorities may have been viable when men worked outside the home and women toiled inside, but it is not feasible and may be fatal for families when women work outside the home as well.

While many women try to balance their careers and family life others make a choice between the two. Some women choose a personal life, perhaps a family, and never become organizational employees or breadwinners, a role that enhances self-esteem. Other women choose paid work and may postpone or bypass some aspect of personal or family life which can offer them personal fulfilment. In the USA Hennig and Jardim's study of managerial women in the 1970s showed that few were married or had children. Nearly twenty years later the average corporate woman officer in the *Fortune* 1,000 largest industrial and service companies was found to be married but childless, and spent less than ten hours per week on homemaking tasks.

The same pattern emerges in many other countries. Working women in Japan frequently face the choice of having a business career or a family, but they have great difficulty combining both. The practice of late evening social functions in Japan is but one example of why a personal and a business life are not usual for the individual woman. In Indonesia the conflict between wife/mother and career has also led most women to choose between the two. The same situation occurs in many other nations including Israel, Switzerland and Singapore.

Where once US women had to make a choice between career and family, economic pressures for dual-job or dual-career families have rendered it difficult for US women to choose not to work outside the home. One result has been an increase in the number of dual-career families in the USA and a relatively higher level of US women managers who are married with families. Korn/Ferry International compared 1982 survey data of women executives to 1992 data to find that while about 49 per cent of the women executives were married and 61 per cent had no children in 1982, nearly 70 per cent of the women executives were married in 1992 and of them, most had children.

Dual careers

Women who choose to both work outside the home and have families find that this can be a very stressful personal strategy without help from their families, organizations or both. According to research on the topic, women pursuing the 'have it all' strategy experience a great deal of stress at home and on the job, although these stressors are not immutable and can be relieved (Fagenson 1993). For example, two key sources of stress are house-care and childcare responsibilities. Much research shows that women are expected to – and do – perform the majority of such work. Personal solutions for these sources of stress include selecting a partner who will take major responsibility for house-care and child-care responsibilities, or, in the case of executives who are compensated at the high end of the salary scale, selecting others who can be paid to perform these tasks. According to reports on a US Census Bureau study released in 1993, social and economic changes in the USA have resulted in increases in the number of fathers providing in-home daycare. That is, fathers provided primary care for one in seven

children under the age of five in 1988 as compared to one in five by 1991 (see CAREERS).

Childcare

Organizations have been successful in reducing some amount of work/personal life conflict by providing on-site programmes for childcare and household tasks and supporting flexible work schedules and job sharing for women and men alike. Unfortunately, despite evidence to show that on-site childcare results in lower employee absenteeism, lower job turnover and greater job satisfaction and commitment, fewer than 2 per cent of companies provide such programmes (Fagenson 1993). Thus, this is an area where organizations have been lax in finding ways to reduce barriers faced by families but particularly by women in management. In 1989 Felice Schwartz of Catalyst suggested that organizations could help women balance work and family lives by providing separate career tracks for women with children. The career track for women choosing to have children was later dubbed the 'mommy track'. The article and the concept of the mommy track generated a great deal of debate, with some feeling it categorized women unfairly and others believing it provided a viable option for women and men alike in organizations. In addition, the mommy track debate carved out a new perspective on having it all, which was to suggest that women and men could have it all, although not necessarily at the same time.

The Family and Medical Leave Act was enacted in the USA in February 1993 in response to concerns from men and women that they could not exercise the choice to nurture children or care for sick or ageing family members without sacrificing their jobs. Prior to enactment the USA had no family leave laws at all, as compared to almost all other industrialized countries where opportunities to balance work and family life were well institutionalized. For example, Finland provides thirty-five weeks of fully paid family leave; Austria provides twenty fully paid weeks; Canada provides for fifteen weeks of family leave time at 60 per cent pay. Although the US Family and Medical Leave Act represents an improvement over the void preceding it, the Act provides no guarantees for paid leave. It allows for many exemptions on the basis of organizational size and for employees viewed as key to the organization. What this is likely to mean is that women who are in higher managerial positions may not be permitted family leave if their positions are perceived as critical to the organization. This example also suggests that society and its social institutions are by no means universal in their support for families or a personal life for workers. The work/personal life conflict remains a significant challenge for individuals, and particularly for women who aspire to managerial positions.

Sexual harassment

According to the ILO report 'Combating Sexual Harassment at Work', 15–30 per cent of women surveyed said they had experienced conduct on the part of supervisors or co-workers that they consider to be sexual harassment. The survey also reports that 82 per cent of Japanese working women had been subjected to sexual harassment. Increased attention to sexual harassment worldwide has led to a new awareness of work problems associated with sexual harassment and to actions that can address the problem.

So new is the concept of sexual harassment that the legal system in several countries – for example, The Netherlands – had not provided a legal definition by 1992; but lack of a definition does not prevent individuals from understanding the concept and its affect upon their work. For example, while there was no phrase for sexual harassment in Russia when the study was conducted, women quickly recognized the concept when it was described.

At the time of the ILO's international study in 1992 only eight nations had laws specifically prohibiting sexual harassment, but many other countries now are considering or have passed such rules. The subtle nature of sexual harassment has made it very difficult to define, but many definitions focus less on direct sexual advances and more on the fact that sexual harassment can create a work environment hostile to full productivity. In Japan the Labour Ministry defined sexual harassment as unpleasant speech and conduct with sexual references or connotations that create a difficult working environment. In the USA the courts have recognized six instances where sexual harassment can occur. These are:

1 when unwelcome sexual advances are made inside or outside of work and the harassed individual generally has to tell the harasser that such behaviour is unwelcome;
2 stated or implicit coercion, when an individual feels that sexual favours are associated with promotions or other rewards;
3 a hostile work environment, generally understood as one where women individually or as representatives of their gender are subject to intimidation;
4 indirect harassment, namely when someone else is subject to harassment and another individual is not able to avoid being around such situations;
5 physical conduct, the courts ruling that unseemly gestures can constitute harassment;
6 graffiti, comments written about a female employee or pervasive displays of nude or pornographic pictures.

Sexual harassment lawsuits have led US courts to broaden the legal guideline of the 'reasonable man', who was assumed to be the prototype of how the average man would judge a situation, to the 'reasonable woman'. Thus, women's claims of sexual harassment on the job are now judged by whether the alleged acts would offend the reasonable woman. This ruling suggests that men and women have different views about what is offensive or acceptable behaviour at work.

Mentorship/networking

This review shows that women have not been readily admitted to organizations, and many studies report that once women are hired into managerial positions they find it difficult to become part of the existing power coalition. In the USA this coalition is sometimes called the 'old boy network', a reflection of the fact that power coalitions are built not only upon work relationships but also upon other social and relational networks. Research shows that women and men who are part of these networks generally earn more promotions and advance faster in their jobs than people who are not sponsored. One way that women have begun to break into these networks is by locating sponsors or developing mentor relationships with men or women in higher level organizational positions. These relationships are expected to help the new employee acquire the knowledge and skills one needs to become a valued member of the management cadre. According to somoe research, women frequently perceive that they do not have as many opportunities for developing these relationships as men.

In the absence of joining existing networks, and perhaps in addition to being part of these networks, another way that women have responded to exclusion from networks is to develop their own networks. Networks made up of managerial women from the same or different organizations meet in informal and formal settings to share information and provide one another with help in advancing in organizations. Alliances of both these types are generally viewed as helpful for people who wish to enhance their careers.

Stereotypes and assumptions

According to traditional gender roles, women are believed to be more caring and nurturing, while men are believed to be more competitive and less concerned about feelings. These gender roles have led to assumptions about how women and men should behave, and to stereotypes that make it difficult to view the individual except in relation to traditional gender-typed behaviour. In the business world, a stereotypical assumption is that women are not interested in jobs that are demanding or that require a competitive attitude, and that women who display these attitudes are not acting appropriate to the female role. Price Waterhouse's experience with accountant Ann Hopkins illustrates how an organization might create a situation that favours gender-typed behaviour. In a lawsuit Hopkins initiated, she was able to

demonstrate that the men evaluating her for partnership had used unfavourable gender stereotypes to decide against her. Furthermore, she was able to provide testimony 'that she had been told to walk and talk more femininely, to wear makeup, and to have her hair styled if she wanted to be named a partner in the firm' (example cited in Fagenson 1993). Thus, this example shows that stereotypes such as these are not easily put to rest.

Despite the fact that 47 per cent of the US workforce is female, the images of women in advertisements, newspapers, books, television programmes and other forms of popular culture tend to depict women as less competent than men, if women are visible at all, according to feminist writer Susan Faludi. An analysis of pictures in a sample of *Fortune* 500 annual reports found that females were underrepresented in annual reports by about 27 per cent, whereas males were overrepresented by approximately 39 per cent. Additionally, according to a survey by UCLA (University of California, Los Angeles), 81 per cent of 200 female Chief Executive Officers identified stereotyping and preconceptions of women managers as a primary factor impeding progress for women in managerial positions. Negative images of women can be damaging to self-esteem, but when women and girls are not considered appropriate organizational members the result is a sense of exclusion for women and perhaps a feeling among men that women do not belong or act appropriately in the workplace. For example, many people assume that women are not as committed to their organizations as men, but a statistical review of over twenty-five studies reveals that there are no differences in the organizational commitment of men and women.

Stereotypes and assumptions constraining opportunities for equal opportunity have been overcome in a number of ways. One of the more important ones has been to challenge traditional assumptions about women's place in research, in organizations and in society. Much of the research on women in organizations has focused attention primarily on how work has traditionally been organized and how women can fit into existing structures. Many argue that this type of approach forces researchers to think of males as the norm and females as those who do not fit into existing organizations. Accordingly, research practices have reinforced the maleness of current organizations, where women are expected to do most of the adapting that occurs.

4 Actions to be taken by organizations

Challenging the status quo produces resistance to change and this factor alone impedes progress to managerial equity. In addition, results are difficult to achieve because while it is challenging to imagine organizations that are equitable, it is even more challenging to structure these organizations. Nevertheless, change may occur by adapting current models and developing new ones.

As was indicated earlier, a variety of tactics have been successfully pursued to lower barriers to women in management. In a study of corporations with $100 million or more in annual sales, among the 400 women executives polled, 64 per cent believe large companies have improved in the last five years in hiring and promoting women managers, but most assert that many barriers remain. According to this group, these barriers will be overcome by various actions including women taking a strong public stand on hiring and promoting women executives, women taking legal action when they see evidence of discrimination and women building networks with other women to help one another. Thus, some amount of progress will be made by individuals acting on their own.

Organizational efforts to recruit qualified women have had positive results, and recent evidence shows that organizational initiatives for gender equity in management have been broadened to include development and retention of women hired: organizational action that has retained more women in management includes developing workplaces that are more congenial for women. According to a *Business Week* report on 'woman-friendly' companies, criteria that make a company friendly include the numbers of women in key executive positions and on the board of directors,

efforts to help women advance and sensitivity to work/family issues. Organizational leaders increasingly acknowledge that their ability to compete worldwide depends on hiring and retaining the best employees they can find, and further acknowledge that many of the best employees will be those who represent some aspect of diversity, including gender. Indeed, Covenant Investment Management's 1993 study found that Standard & Poor's 500 firms that had hired and advanced women (and minorities) and complied with Equal Employment Opportunity Commission and regulatory requirements outperformed firms that had poorer equal employment track records. In fact, five-year annualized returns for the 100 firms with the best equal employment track records were 18.3 per cent as compared to 7.9 per cent for the 100 firms with the worst equality track records: overall, Standard & Poor's returns for the period were 15.9 per cent. These data suggest that diversity initiatives can be successful and can have a positive impact on organizational profits. Thus, the opportunities for families, for organizations and for nations are inextricably tied to equitable opportunities for the world's women.

BARBARA PARKER
SEATTLE UNIVERSITY

ELLEN A. FAGENSON-ELAND
GEORGE MASON UNIVERSITY

Further reading

(References cited in the text marked *)

* Adler, N.J. and Izraeli, D. (1994) *Competitive Frontiers: Women Managers in a Global Economy*, Cambridge, MA: Blackwell. (Describes the status of women managers from an international perspective focusing on twenty-one regions.)

Cox, T., Jr (1993) *Cultural Diversity in Organizations*, San Francisco, CA: Berrett-Koehler. (Successfully dealing with gender, racial, cultural and other aspects of workplace diversity.)

Davidson, M. and Burke, R. (1994) *Women in Management: Current Research Issues*, London: Paul Chapman Publishing. (Reviews selected research topics on women in management.)

* Fagenson, E. (ed.) (1993) *Women in Management: Trends, Issues and Challenges in Managerial Diversity*, Newbury Park, CA: Sage Publications. (A multidimensional analysis of and commentaries on the personal and work lives of women managers.)

* Faludi, S. (1991) *The Undeclared War Against American Women*, New York: Crown Publishers. (Looks at how women are undermined and manipulated by the political, legal and media communities.)

* Helgesen, S. (1990) *The Female Advantage: Women's Ways of Leadership*, New York: Doubleday/Currency. (Helgesen looks at the unique leadership styles of women managers.)

* Hennig, M. and Jardim, A. (1977) *The Managerial Woman*, Garden City, NY: Anchor/Doubleday. (One of the first books to look at managerial women in the USA; finds that access to the top is difficult, often including a trade-off between career advancement and any type of peronal life.)

* Kanter, R.M. (1977) *Men and Women of the Corporation*, New York: Basic Books. (The factors that help and hinder the careers of women workers are presented.)

* Morrison, A.M. (1992) *The New Leaders: Guidelines on Leadership Diversity in America*, San Francisco, CA: Jossey Bass. (The factors that help to promote leadership diversity are discussed.)

* Powell, G.N. (1993) *Women and Men in Management*, 2nd edn, Newbury Park, CA: Sage Publications. (A review of sex differences for men and women in many facets of their personal and professional lives is presented.)

* Schwartz, F. (1989) 'Management women and the new facts of life', *Harvard Business Review* 67 (1): 647–64. (In suggesting that corporations need to accomodate their employees by allowing managerial women to step off the promotional track for a time to rear children, Schwartz triggered off a furore in the USA over what came to be called the 'mommy track'.)

United Nations (1991) *Women: Challenges to the Year 2000*, New York: United Nations. (Covers current and projected needs for female education, health and security, and reviews the worldwide impact of female labour and political activity.)

United Nations (1994) *Human Development Report*, New York: United Nations. (Contains indicator tables on the female workforce and political participation; includes wage gaps due to gender.)

* WuDunn, S. (1992) 'Women face increasing bias as China focuses on profits', *New York Times* 28 July: A1–A5. (One of several reports by the author, this piece outlines ways in which women have lost equal rights gained during Maoist years.)

See also: CAREERS; EMPLOYEE RELATIONS, MANAGEMENT OF; EQUAL EMPLOYMENT OPPORTUNITIES; HUMAN RESOURCE MANAGEMENT; INDUSTRIAL AND LABOUR RELATIONS; PAYMENT SYSTEMS

Related topics in the IEBM: ENTREPRENEURSHIP; GENDER AND ACCOUNTING; MANAGEMENT IN NORTH AMERICA; MANAGEMENT IN THE UNITED KINGDOM; WOMEN IN MANAGEMENT IN JAPAN

Work ethic

Overview

The work ethic is an important concept, since working is an essential activity in every economy. A considerable amount of cross-national research evidence is available and some findings have practical policy relevance. The original historically derived concept of a 'Protestant work ethic' is no longer appropriate, since particularly high work ethic (centrality of work) scores exist in Japan, Israel and Slovenia. However, almost everywhere one or more of four values are thought to characterize working; it can be seen as a burden, a constraint, a responsibility, or a social contribution. Another useful distinction shows that people distinguish between work as an obligation or an entitlement. The USA, for instance, has very low entitlement expectations while several European countries have high scores on entitlement and Japan is in a middle position.

It should also be noticed that the term 'work' in the work ethic concept should include many important but usually unpaid activities, like rearing children, looking after a household, and doing voluntary jobs for local as well as international societies and charities.

The most policy-relevant practical findings from the available literature suggests that work ethic values everywhere are high with people who have interesting, varied jobs which enjoy a fair amount of autonomy or self-regulation. This would suggest that investment in education and job design are appropriate policies for strengthening the work ethic.

1 Some introductory thoughts

> Those of us who study work are unsurprisingly convinced of its importance while. . . (for) those who merely do it, it may have less cosmic significance.
>
> (Albert Cherns)

In everyday usage the term 'work ethic' is almost indistinguishable from work satisfaction or simply attitudes to work. Do people value work or not, or are they in various degrees indifferent to it? Since most adults are expected to work and most do so in order to make a living, the work ethic in this popular use of the term is, on average, positive for most people. Nevertheless, there are bound to be variations in this average and in the distribution around the average for different groups of people.

Social scientists tend to define the term with greater precision and want to compare and contrast the emphasis people tend to give to working with their valuation or preference for other activities in their lives, most obviously leisure, but also religion, community, the family, hobbies and so on. In such an approach, human activities are seen to offer choices. Working may still be very central, but at the margin, people will have other preferences and the margin may be different for a variety of reasons that are interesting to explore. Another approach is to differentiate attitudes that regard work as an obligation – something we owe society – or an entitlement – something society owes us.

Probably the most influential writing on the work ethic comes from the sociologist Max Weber (1930). In trying to explain why people pursue wealth and material gain for its own sake, not because of necessity, Weber found the answer partly in Puritan asceticism and the concept of 'calling'. Puritans sought to achieve salvation through economic activity. Weber believed the introduction of capitalism as a mass phenomenon was facilitated

327

by factors like urbanization, the development of cooperatives and guilds, the development of a legal system, bureaucratic nation-state, and the development of a moral system, which he called 'the Protestant Work Ethic', the core notion of the Protestant work ethic being the idea of calling and Puritan asceticism. The notion of calling requires individuals to fulfil their duty in this world and interpret occupational success as a sign of being elected, and the notion of Puritan asceticism adds the positive evaluation of hard, continuous, bodily or mental labour, and a negative view of idleness, luxury, and time wasting. The term Protestant work ethic is still used to describe a positive attitude to hard work, possibly unconsciously as a way of indicating an expectation of social approval. As we shall see, modern research casts doubt on the Protestant connection in the twentieth century, though it appears to have had such an influence in the past.

Another related concept that has become very popular among managers and organization psychologists is work commitment or attachment to work (see OCCUPATIONAL PSYCHOLOGY; ORGANIZATION BEHAVIOUR). The assumption here, as well as with the work ethic is that people who demonstrate high values on these characteristics are somehow more effective or productive and consequently more valuable as employees and managers. Such a causal relationship is more often assumed than tested. Causality, as we shall see, is more likely to run in the other direction. People having high levels of education and skill and occupying jobs with a fair measure of autonomy are likely to hold high work ethic values. People with lower skills, education and control over their work tend to espouse low work ethic values (MOW 1987: 261–3).

2 Research evidence

Research has discovered a relationship between the work ethic and social policy values, such as lack of sympathy for the unemployed, who are regarded as lazy and therefore responsible for their own predicament (Furnham 1987). People who hold these values believe that economic, social and other outside environmental conditions should not be considered to be causal agents or excuses for social deprivation, poverty and related misfortunes. There is clearly an association between these private beliefs and political values, but the rapid and substantial rise in unemployment in the last decades of the twentieth century in parallel with unprecedented changes in technology and several severe economic depressions has made these views less plausible.

Extensive tests to measure the work ethic have been developed and have shown association with achievement, motivation, ambition, and other personality factors and attitudes like economic, political, and social conservatism, and self-control and self-reliance. (Technically known as 'internal locus of control', self-control is a measure which shows that a person perceives him/herself as having control over one's own behaviour rather than being influenced by external environmental factors.)

For all those who are not unemployed or retired, work takes up a major slice of the week; this is true even when work is unpaid, as for large numbers of women. Work is, therefore, closely associated with self-identity and feelings of self-worth. This is why involuntary retirement and unemployment create many individual problems, tensions and stress. Stress can also be a consequence of excessive work. Stress-related illness seems to have increased in the run up to the twenty-first century and has received a lot of attention from social scientists. It is sometimes attributed to inappropriate forms of leadership (Fiedler *et al.* 1992) (see LEADERSHIP; STRESS). Work stress can also be self-induced and, among managers in some organizations, long hours and homework have become a cultural prescriptive that cannot easily be rejected. The workaholic's singular dedication tends to exclude the variety of human experience we associate with civilization; it narrows or excludes social intercourse, including family relations, and has been likened by some to a form of psychopathology.

In the last decade of the twentieth century, as a result of combination of technological development and economic conditions, part-time work has grown rapidly, particularly in Europe, and women have taken up a larger share of the labour market (see LABOUR MARKETS). These labour market developments, if sustained, will have an effect on the work ethic.

While intellectual enquiries into the work ethic are usually considered to be within the field of the behavioural social sciences, economics has recently claimed a stake. Buckley and Casson (1994) have argued that the main threat to the position of economics as an explanation of economic behaviour 'comes from accumulating evidence that cultural factors are key determinants of economic performance'. They argue that culture (see CULTURE) can be considered to be a major component of human capital. The argument is that people in two different countries may have identical skills, but one country's workers may be more productive 'because the moral content of the local culture makes them better motivated' (Buckley and Casson 1994: 1040). The 'moral content of the local culture' seems very similar to our description of the work ethic but the validity of the argument that local cultural differences or the work ethic can be considered as 'key determinants of economic performance' has not been established.

A fair amount of cross-national research on the work ethic has been carried out.

3 International perspectives

In the past decade the Meaning Of Working Study and its offspring (MOW 1987; Ruiz-Quintanilla 1991) have collected evidence on how cultural, societal and individual factors shape the work ethic. Intensive personal interviews were conducted with respondents representing all segments (occupational, educational, age-groups) of societies in Europe, the USA and Asia. In some countries additional data were collected for societal groups of special interest, like socialization agents (teachers). In other countries the study was replicated eight years later to estimate changes on the group level. Three-year longitudinal studies were undertaken with

youngsters entering the labour market and additional evidence was collected in complementary case studies. All in all, more than 30,000 respondents from Belgium, Bulgaria, the Czech Republic, China, England, France, Germany (both former Federal Republic as well as Democratic Republic), Hungary, Israel, Italy, Japan, the Netherlands, Poland, Portugal, Slovenia, the Slovak Republic, Spain and the USA were involved in one or other study. To summarize such a large amount of data we will confine ourselves to major cross-cultural similarities and differences, and their sources.

Employment and working is characterized by one of four values: work can be seen as a burden, a constraint, a responsibility (give and take) or a social contribution (see EMPLOYMENT AND UNEMPLOYMENT, ECONOMICS OF). This is true whether we talk to a professional athlete or an unskilled factory worker, in Beijing or Antwerp, or to a person starting their working career or entering retirement. For about 95 per cent of the respondents in any given society, one of these work values clearly dominates their understanding and, thus, their evaluation of work. Comparing the dominant view across countries we learn that the work as responsibility view dominates in Japan, two-thirds of the respondents endorsing it, while the same portion of the Slovak and Czech Republics sees work as a social contribution. Seeing work as a burden or constraint became more prominent in the USA between 1982 and 1989 (Ruiz-Quintanilla and England 1993).

We have seen that work can be perceived as an obligation (something one owes society) or as an entitlement (something society owes to a person). Differences between countries on these values are important considerations to help us understand contractual relations between employees and the organization (Rousseau 1995). While there is high agreement between Western and Asian societies in what contributes to entitlement (for example, responsibility to receive retraining or participation in decision making) and what belongs to the obligation side of the equation (for example, to give value and quality, etc.), this black-and-white picture becomes blurred in the former communist states and Israel. In the latter, respondents have a hard time distinguishing between rights and duties of work. This can be understood as a consequence of a mixture between an individualistic and more collectivistic approach in the dominant ideology. Being able to distinguish between rights and duties assumes that people tend to distinguish between themselves as 'private' person and citizen, and their role in the world of work, between employees and employers, or between the partners of a contract. Comparing the entitlement/obligation results for Belgium, Germany, the USA, and Japan (Ruiz-Quintanilla and England 1993) we can summarize that the two European labour forces have the highest entitlement expectations; the Japanese follow and the US American have the lowest entitlement expectation. The reverse is true for the obligation scores. In addition, these results proved to be fairly stable over a period of six to nine years. Obviously, the respective labour forces start from different expectation points about what society or organization owes individuals in terms of interesting and meaningful work, work as a right versus a duty, and whether the organization or the employees themselves should plan or provide for their own future. We can assume that this result derives from a different understanding of 'what is fair and what isn't' in these countries. Finally, in all countries the obligation orientation becomes more dominant and the entitlement expectations weaker with age and with higher educational and occupational level.

In the seven-country MOW study the measure of work centrality was highest in Japan and lowest for the UK. The US sample came somewhere in the middle. Israel and Slovenia had high work centrality, and Germany and the Netherlands had low scores. In the same countries the research took samples of different occupational groups. The findings show that jobs requiring high skills and relatively low centralized control (that is to say a higher measure of independence) had high work centrality (chemical engineers, self-employed and teachers).

Adding other research data, it seems that people who have high work ethic values have

skilled and moderately autonomous jobs, are older rather than younger and come from countries like Japan, China, the Slovak Republic, Slovenia and Israel that have only recently moved away from agriculture and towards industrialization. The work ethic is lower but emphasis on hobbies, sport, recreation and social activity is higher in countries like the UK, Germany and The Netherlands, which had their industrial revolutions some two and a half centuries ago.

The Strathclyde Centre for the Study of Public Policy (1994) has carried out survey work in ten central and eastern European countries and included a question on what people would do if by luck they unexpectedly came into a lot of money. One theoretical alternative was: 'To try to get a better job'. The answers varied from 4 per cent in Slovenia to 16 per cent in Croatia. An alternative that attracted many was: 'Start business, buy farm'. In every country the answer was 20 per cent or above, 57 per cent in Romania, 41 per cent in Croatia and 40 per cent in Bulgaria. There were also substantial variations in those who wanted to take the money and stop working: 4 per cent in Slovakia and Romania, but 19 per cent in Bulgaria and 21 per cent in Belorussia.

To be really useful this type of data would have to be followed up with analysis of the degree of realism or fantasy these answers imply. For instance, the question about a realistic opportunity of starting a business or buying a farm; are the 57 per cent of Romanians who answered that question indulging in a daydream or are they genuinely motivated to become entrepreneurs? This type of survey work needs to be followed up. In general, country differences are interesting but are difficult to explain and have little policy relevance.

4 Work ethic and policy

There can be little doubt that at the moment and for the vast majority of people, work occupies an important place in life and takes up a considerable amount of the available time between the end of education and retirement. There is now a trend in western as well as eastern countries for education to take up more time and for retirement to come earlier, while at the same time life expectancy is increasing. The consequence of these developments suggests that in future over the life span from birth to death, work as traditionally conceived will become less important or at least will take up less of the available time (Heller 1991).

Nevertheless, the work ethic usefully underpins the economic system. The goods and services, including food production, which we need for survival as well as for higher standards of living, require human activity. That part of activity for which people receive pay is called work. In this sense the term 'work' in the phrase work ethic is slightly misleading because men and women undertake many different activities that are important for our standard of living that require considerable effort – the equivalent of hard work – and are capable of being characterized as being rational, frugal, achievement-orientated and deserving. Child rearing and housewifery are probably the best modern examples, but one can also include studying, amateur sports and unpaid work for voluntary organizations like the Red Cross and Amnesty International.

We will stay with the term 'work ethic' but mentally include the important range of unpaid activities that sustain the social fabric of our society. The importance of the work ethic is its provision of a motivational dynamism that gets things done. It is this characteristic that Max Weber identified when he attributed the rise of modern capitalism in part to the Protestant ethic. Today, as we have seen, this ethic thrives in several parts of the world which espouse different religions. In the older western industrialized countries the centrality of working retains an important position but is complemented by other salient life interests, like the family and recreational activity.

What implications do these findings have for policy at organizational and national levels? Accepting that, other things being equal, a high work ethic has practical utility, what can be done to increase it in companies or countries where it is considered to be exceptionally low? It is not sensible to increase the age level in an organization because we know that older people have a higher work ethic, nor

can one advance or retard industrialization by a century or so. We know from other social science research that exhortation alone is not very effective in changing attitudes or behaviour, though parental and school influences can be important. It seems that findings which relate the work ethic to the nature and designs of jobs offer useful policy recommendations but need to be tested further. Several studies have shown that high work ethic values are related to educational achievement, senior level jobs and work which allows self-expression, a measure of autonomy and self-regulation (Penn *et al.* 1994; Lundberg and Peterson 1994; MOW 1987).

These factors are interconnected but an underlying dimension is the nature of skill. Rose (1991), using the results of a large-scale survey on social change and economic life in the UK, comes to the conclusion that the nature of a person's job and the level of skill largely determine the strength of the work ethic. From the data Rose concludes that work involvement and the work ethic can be strengthened by improving education and skill training (see CAREERS; TRAINING, ECONOMICS OF). Similar improved work ethic effects would result from redesigning jobs to have higher and more varied skill content.

Here, then, are several practical and feasible policy options at the level of a country (educational improvement) and at the level of organization (work design changes) which seem capable of having a positive effect on the work ethic.

FRANK HELLER
TAVISTOCK INSTITUTE, LONDON

S. ANTONIO RUIZ-QUINTANILLA
CORNELL UNIVERSITY

Further reading

(References cited in the text marked *)

* Buckley, P. and Casson, M. (1994) 'Economics as an imperialist social science', *Human Relations* 45 (9): 1035–52. (Argues that economics has a methodology capable of also analysing the social and political environment and economists should pay more attention to people's values.)

* Fiedler, F., Potter, E., III and McGuire, M. (1992) 'Stress and effective leadership decisions', in F. Heller (ed.), *Decision-making and Leadership*, Cambridge: Cambridge University Press. (Gives empirical evidence in support of a theoretical model which analyses the effect of stress on the under-utilization of human competence.)

* Furnham, A. (1987) 'Work related beliefs and human values', *Personality and Individual Differences* 8: 627–37. (The study examines the relationship between work beliefs and general human values).

* Heller, F.A. (1991) 'Reassessing the work ethic: a new look at work and other activities', *European Work and Organization Psychologist* 1: 147–60. (Argues that while nearly everybody has to work in order to sustain life, in future non-work activities will become more important over a total life span as work will start later in life and end earlier.)

* Lundberg, C.D. and Peterson, M.F. (1994) 'The meaning of working in US and Japanese local governments at three hierarchical levels', *Human Relations* 47 (12): 1459–87. (Presents the results of a research project on the work ethic based on community organizations in the USA and Japan.)

* MOW (1987) *The Meaning Of Working: An Eight Country Comparative Study*, London: Academic Press. (An empirical study comparing work related values and attitudes across eight nations and a diversity of occupational groups.)

* Penn, R., Rose, M. and Rubery, J. (1994) *Skill and Occupational Change*, Oxford: Oxford University Press. (A chapter on the changing British work ethic based on a large-scale survey comes to the important conclusion that the strength of the work ethic reflects skill levels.)

* Rose, M. (1991) 'The work ethic: women, skill and the ancient curse', presidential paper to section N (sociology), British Association for the Advancement of Science. (Based on a large-scale survey, it argues that women's commitment to work differs little from men's but their employment opportunities are inferior.)

* Rousseau, D.M. (1995) *Promise in Action: Contracts in Organizations*, Newbury Park, CA: Sage Publications. (A behavioural theory of contracts and the fundamental role they play in organizations with special emphasis on how changing contracts impact on the employer–employee relationship.)

* Ruiz-Quintanilla, S.A. (ed.) (1991) *Work Centrality and Related Work Meanings*, Hove: Lawrence Erlbaum. (A collection of articles discussing work ethic assessments across nations and time.)

* Ruiz-Quintanilla, S.A. and England, G.W. (1993) *Balanced and Imbalanced Societal Norms about Working*, CAHRS working paper no. 93–120, Ithaca, NY: Cornell University Press. (The empirical work compares two normative orientations: work as an obligation and work as an entitlement among representative samples from the US, German, Belgium and Japanese labour forces.)

Ruiz-Quintanilla, S.A. and England, G.W. (1996, forthcoming) 'How working is defined: structure and stability', *Journal of Organizational Behavior*. (A cross-national study supporting the belief that one dominant dimension ranging from individual cost to social contribution underlies the way in which people define working.)

* Strathclyde Centre for the Study of Public Policy (1994) 'Between State and Market' Glasgow: University of Strathclyde. (Professor Richard Rose has carried out a series of attitude surveys in central and eastern Europe; attitudes to work are included.)

* Weber, M. (1930) *The Protestant Ethic and the Spirit of Capitalism*, London: Allen & Unwin. (Classic study of the apparent relationship of Protestantism with the rise and development of capitalism.)

See also: HUMAN RESOURCE MANAGEMENT; HUMAN RESOURCE MANAGEMENT, INTERNATIONAL; MOTIVATION AND SATISFACTION; ORGANIZATION BEHAVIOUR; WORK AND LEISURE

Related topics in the IEBM: ORGANIZATION BEHAVIOUR, HISTORY OF; WEBER, M.

Work and leisure

1 **Definitions**
2 **Division and re-integration of labour**
3 **Sectors of work and employment**
4 **Towards self-service**
5 **New work and leisure**

Overview

Human work and leisure are being radically redefined. The key words are empowerment, self-reliance, autonomy and self-service, replacing the more traditional notions of division of labour, specialization, manual work and the physically remote workplace of the mass production, mass assembly and mass consumption era. Most human activities – work, labour, jobs, leisure, recreation and the overall ways and quality of life – have changed and are going to change even more before this millennium is over.

1 Definitions

Human action can be loosely differentiated into work (creation) and leisure (recreation) activities (see MOTIVATION AND SATISFACTION). This is not an exhaustive distinction – there could also be non-voluntary human activities that are neither work nor leisure (breathing, eating, sleeping), or either work or leisure depending on the person (sex, escort or companionship for money), or even mixtures of work and leisure (hobbies such as gardening and do-it-yourself).

The key to any useful differentiation of this kind must be the *purpose*, the why, the motivation of the activities being carried out. If the purpose is a direct or indirect economic exchange – for money, goods, time or any other reciprocity of economic value – then humans engage in work. If the purpose of such activities is not directly economic or exchange motivated, then we can speak of leisure. That is why somebody doing 'absolutely nothing' in exchange for money would be working, while

somebody sweating in the garden for their own pleasure and satisfaction would be at leisure – and even having a 'good time'. Professional sports are work, amateur sports are a mixture of leisure and work, and recreational sports activities are leisure.

Also domestic, household and at home work or chores, as well as all forms of do-it-yourself and self-service, represent bona fide work because their purpose is substituting for an exchange or economic alternative, like having such in-house work performed by paid (external, for exchange) help or professionals. The purpose of a given activity provides the key. Yet, some governments still consider taking care of one's own children as leisure and taking care of someone else's children as highly taxable work – with the obvious societal impacts. The sheer exertion of neuromuscular energy does not necessarily amount to work if it is not economically motivated and cannot or would not be exchanged. An individual going out to plant some tulips, for relaxation and enjoyment, is at leisure. An individual going out to plant the same tulips in order to avoid the high costs of landscaping services, is working.

Leisure activities must be voluntary, noncontractual and unforced, seeking recreation rather than economic gain or exchange of value. Forced unemployment or serving a jail term are not leisure as they have no alternative. Forced labour is work only if remunerated, at least partially. Work and leisure are not mutually exclusive and exhaustive categories.

'Work' can be defined as economically purposeful activity requiring substantial human coordination of task and action. 'Job' designates the kind of work that is performed contractually, that is, explicitly for remuneration and in the employ of others. 'Labour' (often used as a synonym for hard work or toil) can more properly be related to performing simplified work-components or tasks without engaging in their substantial coordination towards given purposes. Work often involves labour but not vice versa. Work involves coordination of tasks while labour relates only to their performance. Building a fish pond is work, digging a hole is labour (see HERZBERG, F.). 'Leisure' and activities of leisure are motivated by non-economic and non-exchange purposes, like relaxation, pleasure, joy, recreation, satisfaction and so on.

2 Division and re-integration of labour

If we divide the work into its components we break it into labour. Historically, since the time of Adam Smith, we refer to such a division as the 'division of labour' (although division of work would be more appropriate). Any work-task can be broken down into a large number of sub-tasks and operations. Such task disaggregation allows parallel processing and may translate directly into increased productivity. This kind of 'division of task' is directly related to the number of parts constituting the product. Some products consist of thousands of parts, including all sorts of accessible or less accessible screws, nuts, washers, bolts, caps and pins.

In order to realize the parallel processing of thousands of specialized tasks, different tasks have to be performed or controlled by different workers: labour itself has to be appropriately divided. Only in this sense can we talk about the division of labour. Division of task may or may not be accompanied by the division of labour. Together with the division of labour, we are also disaggregating, dividing and dispersing the knowledge necessary for the coordination of work. When one person makes a chair, from cutting the proper wood to selling the product at the market, such a person commands a full contingent of the chair-making knowledge. As the task and labour become divided, each person can claim only a part of the overall knowledge. The knowledge itself has become divided and the phenomenon of the 'division of knowledge' must be considered.

Modern concepts of 're-engineering' are helping to redefine work through reunifying the previously broken down tasks into coherent work processes. The traditional industrial paradigm – the division of labour, economies of scale, hierarchical control and so on – represented the old ways of doing business.'The division of labour around which companies have been organized since Adam Smith first articulated that principle – simply don't work anymore', insist Hammer and Champy (1994: 17). Modern re-engineering of work processes is based on the following efforts:

1 Re-integrating the task: combining smaller process sub-tasks and sub-activities into larger, integrated units and packages; reducing the number of parts, components, segments and constituents in products and processes.
2 Re-integrating the labour: allowing workers to perform and coordinate larger rather than smaller portions of the process; encouraging multi-functionality, job rotation, despecialization and integrated process design; letting people work in autonomous teams and coordinate an integrated process rather than labour individually on narrowly defined and linearly conceived tasks of assembly lines.
3 Re-integrating the knowledge: workers must know (that is, be able to coordinate successfully) larger and larger portions of the process and product, not smaller and smaller portions. Knowledge is the ability to coordinate one's actions purposefully. If one is specialized, atomized, reduced to a machine appendage – one cannot coordinate action (work), but only perform single and simple commands (labour).

As Hammer and Champy explain:

Today's airlines, steel mills, accounting firms, and computer chip makers have all been built around Smith's central idea – the division or specialization of labor and the consequent fragmentation of work. The larger the organization, the more specialized is the worker and the more separate steps into which the work is fragmented. This rule applies not only to

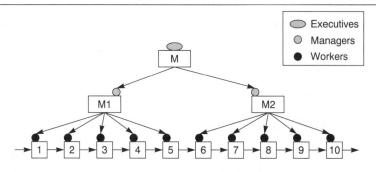

Figure 1 Division of labour

manufacturing jobs. Insurance companies, for instance, typically assign separate clerks to process each line of a standardized form. Then they pass the form to another clerk, who processes the next line. These workers never complete a job; they just perform piecemeal tasks.

(Hammer and Champy 1994: 12)

It appears that Smith and Marx's concepts of the 'division of labour' have been overcome in the 1990s.

In Figure 1, observe how the division of labour leads to the emergence of coordinating agents (M1, M2 and M), organized properly in a coordinative hierarchy, because of the individually limited span of control. Although the productivity increases, the complexity and the cost of coordination are increasing even faster. Division of labour is limited by its own requisite transaction cost and complexity of coordination, not simply by the extent of the market.

Every subsequent doubling of the number of specialized sub-tasks (and labourers), as in Figure 1, leads – under the conditions of a finite span of control (how many people can a manager effectively manage) – to more than a doubling of the requisite number of coordinators (managers). Coordinative hierarchy is therefore bound to grow in size, complexity and costs (see ORGANIZATION BEHAVIOUR).

Through the re-integration of task, labour, and knowledge, labour is again becoming work, meaning is replacing alienation, professionalism and skill are replacing expertism and specialization. Basic coordinative mechanisms of the traditional administrative management of labour-performing operators are being replaced by the self-coordinative systems of mutual adjustment and consensual reciprocity of teams of empowered skilled workers.

In Figure 2 we present these three re-integrations schematically. Compared to Figure 1: if each worker now performs two instead of just one task (with the aid of the requisite high technology), task productivity would be maintained, the number of workers cut in half, the number of managers cut by two-thirds and the whole process made simpler, more streamlined, cheaper, leaner, more flexible and of higher quality.

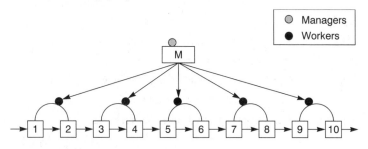

Figure 2 Re-integration of labour

3 Sectors of work and employment

Re-integration of work is accompanied by very strong co-trends towards self-service and do-it-yourself modes of work activities. Mature economies, especially in the USA, are characterized by a large percentage of people working in the service sector. In the 1980s, services in the USA added 21 million jobs and employed almost four out of five workers. Some 70 per cent of the total US workforce is in the services. However, the service sector is no different from any other economic sector, for example agriculture or manufacturing, that went into irreversible loss of employment decades ago. The accelerating productivity growth rates in those sectors have caused a steady decline in their job-generating capacity. The service sector is simply following the pattern: increasing automation, increasing productivity, global competitive pressures, high relative costs and overgrown hierarchies are annihilating its own employment opportunities.

In Figure 3 we display the general sectoral dynamics that all economies, slowly or rapidly, sooner or later, are bound to follow. Due to its productivity growth rate, each sector has to emerge, grow, persist, stagnate, decline and dissipate in terms of its employment-generating capacity.

The high-productivity growth sectors are emerging and dissipating first, the low-productivity growth sectors (like services) are completing their cycle only now. Different productivity growth rates in different sectors are accompanied by essentially uniform growth rates in wages and salaries across all sectors. This simple empirical fact implies that the costs and prices grow relatively faster in low-productivity sectors and relatively slower in high-productivity sectors (see PRODUCTIVITY).

In other words, in mature economies, the prices of food and manufactured goods are getting relatively cheaper and the prices of services are getting relatively more expensive. In slow-developing or laggard economies of the Third World this may still be the

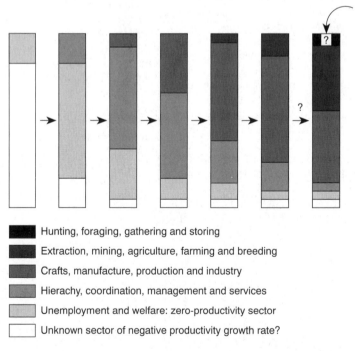

Hunting, foraging, gathering and storing

Extraction, mining, agriculture, farming and breeding

Crafts, manufacture, production and industry

Hierachy, coordination, management and services

Unemployment and welfare: zero-productivity sector

Unknown sector of negative productivity growth rate?

Figure 3 Sectoral evolution and differentiation (in a rapdily maturing economy)

other way around: food and manufactured goods are most expensive while services remain relatively cheap. That is, in developed countries, chicken, bread, computers and cars are getting cheaper, while insurance, healthcare and education costs are skyrocketing without adequate quality, productivity or availability improvements. In Figure 4 we represent this phenomenon.

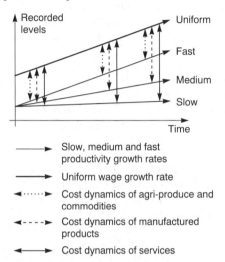

Figure 4 Price gap: differential sectoral productivity growth rates, combined with the uniform wage growth in the whole economy, cause the prices to grow faster in the 'lagging' sectors

4 Towards self-service

The fundamental systemic disharmony of Figure 4, that is, between differential productivity growth rates and the uniform wage/salary growth rates across sectors, points to a self-organizing, spontaneous mode of resolving the tension.

Rational economic agents will exhibit and support the tendency towards substituting relatively cheap capital-intensive manufactured goods for relatively dear labour-intensive services. Consumers will tend to use goods instead of services wherever economical and possible, while the producers will tend to respond by supplying them with goods instead of services wherever economical and possible. As a collective result of this

individually rational decision making, one shall observe the emergence of automated teller machines instead of bank tellers, self-service petrol stations instead of full-serve stations (except where prohibited by law), self-driving instead of chauffeurs, do-it-yourself pregnancy kits rather than hospital test services, self-handled optical scanners rather than cashier-handled services and personal computers instead of centralized mainframes. In other words, self-service and do-it-yourself activities are replacing the traditional, other-person-delivered services at an increasingly accelerating rate. Mature economies are entering the era of self-service and do-it-yourself societies.

Self-service activities are characterized by high efficiency: they can be delivered when, where and at whatever quality the user desires, at lower costs and in a shorter time period. They require user-friendly requisite products with easy-to-use, reliable instructions and support, sufficient time and the high costs of alternative services. All these conditions are present in mature economies. The self-service society is characterized here by increasing autonomy of workers and consumers, growth of work-at-home, telecommuting, self-employment, community self-help, home office, part-time and seasonal work, early retirement, barter and exchanges, networking, flexible work hours, self-management, decline in supervisory and administrative 'services', decentralized self-reliance and so on.

5 New work and leisure

There is no conspicuous increase in leisure and leisure-related activities perceived in the modern economy: the traditional leisure activities are themselves becoming overpriced services and thus being substituted by self-service. There is a tendency for jobholders to work even longer hours, although the overall amount of time worked per person is declining. The time spent for self-service and do-it-yourself activity is one of the few expanding categories of economic activities, and it is sketched in Figure 5.

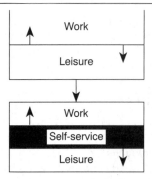

Figure 5 Transition from the sharp separation of work and leisure to a self-service 'grey' region of working

Households are again becoming primary investment/production units, producers and consumers are merging into 'prosumers'. One of the fastest growing sectors in developed industrial economies, especially in the USA, is 'work at home'. Work at home relates to self-employment, part-time self-employment, work after regular office hours, work instead of regular office hours, self-service and do-it-yourself, typically relying on a home office, telecommuting, neighbourhood networks, virtual office, personal computers, modem, fax, multiple and cellular telephone lines and similar technologies. Work at home is the most potent job-generating sector, moving the self-reliant population towards more productive and efficient self-service activities, reducing the pressures on energy, ecology, human stress, traffic congestion and the cost-intensive physical commuting inherited from factories from the turn of the century. Clearly, individual or corporate telecommuting presents a powerful alternative to the traditional emphasis on 'railroads, highways and bridges'.

Modern production is primarily based on the processing of information, not on the hauling of goods, humans and machinery over large distances. One can more effectively 'haul the information', to produce goods and provide services locally. Information and knowledge travel effortlessly through electronic superhighways, through telecommunications networks and the World Wide Web. Citizens and employees working at home are now in control of their time, can take care of their own children, can invest in home technologies; they do not have to pay excessively for petrol, insurance, childcare and waste most of their precious off-work hours on commuting to work. Temporary, freelance, contingent and interim workers are increasingly forced into or voluntarily choose new modes of economic action. They support and accompany empowerment, autonomy, self-reliance and professionalization – main attributes of the future work and jobs. Knowledge, enhanced by education and training, is taking over as the main form of capital. Self-employed people (in the USA) earn about 40 per cent more hourly than those employed by others. Hired operators, labourers and farmhands are rapidly declining in number.

The most qualified workforce – in terms of education, computer literacy and worker motivation – is found in Singapore, Denmark, Germany, Japan and the USA. However, over 96 per cent of Japanese students attend high school, Hong Kong's per capita spending is $810, and Korea moved from $33 in 1975 to $450 per student by 1989. Such numbers underline that educational spending is rapidly becoming the main arena of global competition: in search of the knowledge capital, human and social.

In spite of the continued governmental obstacles and barriers, there were already about 40 million Americans working at home in 1992. This is to be compared with only some 25 million in 1988. From these 40 million home workers, there are 12.1 million self-employed, 11.7 million part-time self-employed, 8.6 million working at home after regular office hours, and 6.6 million working at home instead of regular office hours. High technologies, e-mail, computer teleconferencing, real-time teleconferencing, and video teleconferencing – are all helping to create the electronic networks necessary for self-help and work-at-home business styles. However, the distributed and asynchronous communication systems are the key: they allow global interaction to take place at different places and at different times – creating time/space collaborative systems of unprecedented productivity. The physically 'going-to-work-with-a-lunch-box' type of interaction is becoming rapidly outmoded: unless there is an actual physical transformation taking place *in situ*, all the necessary information processing is becoming location-independent.

The US economy appears to serve as an experimental laboratory for many new forms of work and leisure, from work-at-home and telecommuting to self-employment and virtual offices. Spending on home improvement products by individuals was about $25 billion in 1980, but has reached about $95 billion in 1995, and the trend is accelerating rather rapidly.

MILAN ZELENY
FORDHAM UNIVERSITY AT LINCOLN CENTER

Further reading

(References cited in the text marked *)

Champy, J. (1995) *Re-engineering Management*, New York: HarperCollins. (The follow-up book to *Re-engineering the Corporation*, calling for the re-engineering of management.)

* Hammer, M. and Champy, J. (1994) *Re-engineering the Corporation*, New York: HarperCollins. (One of the first and simplest introductions to re-engineering of a business process.)

Kochen, M. and Zeleny, M. (1981) 'Self-service aspects of health maintenance: assessment of current trends', *Human Systems Management* 2 (4): 259–67. (Self-service aspects of modern medical care and prevention.)

Schor, J.B. (1992) *The Overworked American*, Cambridge, MA: Harvard University Press. (Extensive study of the dilemma of less work and less leisure for modern Americans.)

Zeleny, M. (1980) 'Towards a self-service society', *Human Systems Management* 1 (1): 77. (Simple exposition of basic principles of self-service.)

Zeleny, M. (1979) 'The self-service society: a new scenario of the future', *Planning Review*, 7 (3): 3–7, 37–8. (One of the earliest arguments predicting the rise of self-service, do-it-yourself and work-at-home.)

Zeleny, M. (1989) 'Knowledge as a new form of capital, part 1: division and reintegration of knowledge; part 2: knowledge-based management systems', *Human Systems Management* 8 (1–2): 45–58, 129–43. (Extensive discussion of the demise of the division of labour and the rise of integrated knowledge.)

Zeleny, M., Cornet, R. and Stoner, J.A.F. (1990) 'Moving from the age of specialization to the era of integration', *Human Systems Management* 9 (3): 153–71. (Management and business viewpoint of the decline in the division of labour and the rise in re-integration of labour.)

See also: BRAVERMAN, H.; LABOUR PROCESS; PRODUCTIVITY; TAYLOR, F.W.; WORK ETHIC

Related topics in the IEBM: INFORMATION REVOLUTION; INFORMATION TECHNOLOGY; INFORMATION TECHNOLOGY AND SOCIETY; INTERNET AND BUSINESS; MANAGEMENT IN PACIFIC ASIA; MARX, K.H.; ORGANIZATION STRUCTURE; RE-ENGINEERING; SMITH, A.

Work and organization systems

Overview

Around the world, the issues associated with changing work organization and work systems are important for practitioners and scholars in several fields, including human resources, industrial relations and organization design, and for those concerned with the broader issues of management, public policy and political economy. How has work organization developed since the nineteenth century? After outlining the historical context and offering a definition, the entry discusses a series of approaches to work organization: craft, bureaucracy, Taylorism/Fordism, sociotechnical, neo-human relations, labour process, neo-human relations, lean management, empowerment, service areas and the influence of unions.

The development of work organization is influenced by many factors including: technology; national, industry and enterprise culture; product and labour markets; and government and union regulation. However, there also appears to be scope for 'strategic choice'. This entry examines competing views of determinism versus choice and argues that some choice was exercised even in the most mechanistic work organizations. Nevertheless, the role of choice should not be exaggerated.

1 Historical context

As early as 2000 bc in ancient Mesopotamia there were records of the organization and management of work. Work plays a central role in the lives of most of us. People derive several meanings from work. Through work, we seek to justify our own existence, to develop a feeling of participation in a design which is grander than our personal lives. Through work, we join a community of individuals with common experiences, skills or goals. Through work, we may be induced to have a sense of alientation, or we may derive feelings of competence and achievement, making contributions which enable us to believe in our own worth.

People's understanding of and relationship to work has changed throughout history and varies across cultures. For example, in the days of ancient Greece, work was deemed the plight of those to whom Plato referred as 'the meaner sort of people'. The role that such privileged philosophers occupied was seen as separate from and above work. More recent conceptions of work placed a divine importance on the need for and importance of work. The Protestant work ethic, puritanism and Calvinism extol the virtues of work as a means to greater divine salvation. Others argue that work is in essence a social process, and culture is the ultimate determinant of what meaning and value people assign to work (see WORK ETHIC).

2 What is work organization?

People combine their skills and knowledge in an effort to produce and distribute goods and services. It becomes necessary to combine the various inputs in the work process: labour and capital (including raw materials and energy) in the context of the available technologies, such as equipment and buildings, then produce an output of goods or services. Work organization is the manner in which these variables are arranged.

Work organization determines the way that employees undertake their specific tasks. This usually involves the formation of a hierarchy which shapes the relationships between members of an enterprise, an arrangement for the division of labour and a set of explicit or implied work rules. Through these arrangements, certain individuals may be subordinate to, and controlled by, others.

3 Different ideal types of work organization

Different models of work organization can be compared by examining in each such factors as hierarchy, authority structure, units of responsibility (individual versus group), formalization of work rules, structure of job design and flexibility or division of labour. Although an 'ideal type' in the Weberian sense is an exaggerated abstraction, simplifying types of organization, the various elements are 'more or less present and occasionally absent' in particular cases. Actual policies and practices can be better understood by comparing them with the 'ideal type'. This does not imply a moral value of an 'ideal prescription' for the management and organization of work. In practice, no exact replica will be found of the ideal type, but examples will usually display variations of these characteristics.

There are at least three reasons why work organization changes over time and across cultures. First, work organizations are influenced by their context, such as product and labour market demand, geography, demographics and culture. In view of the economic and social distinctiveness of Japan, managers there have developed different forms of work organization from those in Western countries.

Second, work organization is influenced by technology For example, in the first half of the twentieth century, industrial engineers used assembly lines to change work organization fundamentally. More recently, others have used microelectronics to revolutionize processes and products. Such technological change may precipitate significant alterations to work organization. The notion of technological determinism is that technology tends to determine a particular pattern of management and work organization. However, although technology may be an important

influence, it is by no means the sole determinant (Bamber and Lansbury 1988).

Third, there is scope for key decision makers to exercise a strategic choice about work organization, although they are constrained and possibly partially determined by the above-mentioned variables, including national and corporate cultures as well as technology, labour markets and payment systems. Work organization is also constrained by employers' and unions' policies, styles and organizational structures (including centralization or decentralization), the extent to which decision making is participative and about how innovations are introduced and maintained.

Craft production

Images of craftwork before industrialization have often been idealized. Craftworkers' jobs were broadly defined. Such work was seen as satisfying; it provided workers with feelings of identity and control over their labour processes. Before the Industrial Revolution work organization could be characterized by a relative lack of a division of labour and little formalization of job design. Craft production or cottage industry often involved an extended family. There would be only a few individuals involved in production, but they might work in a team. These self-employed people might have owned some means of production and sold what they made at a market. Production was set at the pace dictated by the head of the family business and was strongly influenced by demand and by the supply of materials. Loyalty was to a family or an individual rather than to a larger enterprise. While workers would have access to intensive collective knowledge of their craft or occupation, most of this knowledge was not systematically organized or recorded. One example of such work organization was the family farm. Although there were general methods for core activities such as ploughing a field or fitting parts of machinery, there was a degree of variation in these activities. Family members, owners and employees decided the specifics of how and by whom these tasks would be carried out.

Workshops had a decentralized control system: most owners had only a nominal control of a semi-autonomous workforce. Work was loosely organized around the traditional apprentice–master system. This gave a degree of structure to the relationships of those involved. In some cases such arrangements were regulated by guilds or incipient unions. Different products might be designed and built in the same workshop and, depending upon their complexity, by the same people. These companies predominantly employed skilled craftworkers that combined their skills to build products, mainly by hand. There was a limited division of labour which was based upon different crafts including plumber, joiners and painters. For example, in the early production of cars, parts would be hand cut and produced by skilled contractors. These parts would probably be assembled into a car elsewhere, by other craftworkers. There was little standardization and parts would vary. Those assembling the product would have to manipulate the parts further, filing and cutting them as necessary. Many products were built to the specific needs of customers. There was, therefore, considerable scope for choice in, for example, the design of work, the development of authority structures and the relationship between people and technology.

After industrialization, work organization was fragmented, as illustrated by Adam Smith's famous analysis of pin making in *The Wealth of Nations*. He argued that increasing the division of labour (by process) led to higher labour productivity. As the nineteenth century drew to a close, managers began to use more complex arrangements for the division and control of labour to supplement craft-based approaches. Craft production was not completely eliminated, but survived to varying extents, especially in agriculture and to service niche markets. However, a bureaucratic approach based on mass production became more typical.

Bureaucratic work organization

In the twentieth century there were increasing calls for more systematic forms of work organization to facilitate increases in efficiency, standardization and quality. Weber made an important contribution to the understanding of such work organization. He diagnosed a fundamental process of rationalization that characterized the modernization of industry. This process was considered inevitable due to the increasing role that technology and structured enterprises were having in the lives of working people. The former decentralized and loosely structured craftwork organization was being replaced with more centralized organizations characterized by formal rules, regulations, hierarchy and formal structures. Weber saw such a progression in organization as the office equivalent to the change from non-mechanized to mechanized forms of factory production.

Weber's conception of a bureaucratic enterprise builds on the work of Adam Smith, Babbage and others who analysed the division of labour and the importance of a systematic system of management. Weber provided several characteristics of the 'ideal type' bureaucratic form of work organization:

1 fixed, clearly understood and demarcated, division of tasks;
2 hierarchical means of authority based on impersonality and governed by clear rules and regulations;
3 focus on the position and not the person (that is, power and authority which emanates from the position and maintains control over other positions);
4 separation of management and ownership of the enterprise;
5 clear method of hiring and promotion based on merit.

Weber argued that bureaucratic work organization was more efficient than the relatively haphazard work organization found in most family enterprises or small firms. Weber was writing against a background of class consciousness and work organization in Europe. His notion of *impersonality* and *rationality* in the management of the enterprise was conceived in opposition to the overemphasis on *personal interests* in small family-run businesses and many state-operated enterprises (for example, the military), at the expense of the needs of clients and employees.

Taylorism and Fordism

Several others attempted to develop more prescriptive methods by which bureaucratic organization could be implemented most effectively. Both Frederick Winslow Taylor and Henry Ford had a profound impact (see FORD, H.; TAYLOR, F.W.). They were concerned with raising labour productivity. Taylor argued that tradition be replaced by management based on scientific study, hence his term 'scientific management'. The need for a systematic approach to management had already been identified by others, however Taylor was possibly the most influential in conceptualizing these approaches.

Taylor was working against a background of rapid industrialization. The USA, for example, was changing from craft production to a factory system. There was no existing blueprint for the scale of labour organization that was then occurring. Scientific management partially filled this gap. While working as a steel-company engineer, Taylor attempted to find the solution to the problem of employee 'soldiering' (employees not working to their potential). He developed four principles designed to deal with the problem of soldiering and, in general, of organizing labour effectively (Taylor 1911):

1 scientific study should be used to develop the best way for doing a task;
2 workers should be scientifically selected and trained;
3 management should cooperate with employees to make sure workers use the scientific principles;
4 work and responsibility should be divided, with management responsible for planning and deciding upon work issues and workers executing the work.

Taylor recommended that time-and-motion studies be used to gauge and plan the amount of work that an employee should do. The employee was then given strict instructions on this method, as well as a monetary incentive to undertake these tasks. The method was exemplified with his dealings with a pig-iron handler, Schmidt. Taylor wanted to increase the amount of pig iron loaded from 12.5 tonnes per day to 47.5. He gave strict instructions to Schmidt to obey a manager (presumably one versed in the science of loading heavy objects). In return, Schmidt was paid as a 'high-priced man' (he received US$1.85 instead of US$1.15 a day). The following is an excerpt from their discussion:

> Well, if you [Schmidt] are a high-priced man, you will do exactly as this man tells you tomorrow, from morning till night. When he tells you to pick up pig and walk, you pick it up and you walk, and when he tells you to sit down and rest, you sit down. You do that right straight through the day. And what's more, no back talk.
>
> (Taylor 1911: 39)

Such work was analysed and the best procedure for doing each task was determined. These tasks would then be assigned to those who were specially trained in doing them. A high degree of control was needed to make this work successfully. The methods by which jobs are designed have subsequently changed, but job design as a method of productivity improvement has become a central strategy in the management of work organization (see JOB DESIGN).

Scientific management also emphasized areas other than job design: the formalization of authority and responsibility, standardization of means for control, development of task specialization and separation of responsibility and authority. These strategies are still used to varying degrees in contemporary work organization.

Henry Ford refined and built upon the work of Taylor. The opening of his mechanized assembly line in the USA in 1913 revolutionized manufacturing and heralded the age of mass production. Mass production is typified by long production runs of a standard product and the use of a moving assembly line. However, it is important not simply to equate Ford's techniques strictly with the assembly-line form of mass production which prevailed in some industries for much of the twentieth century. Ford also developed innovative techniques in factory layout, stock handling and labour usage before the adoption of the assembly line. His innovations exemplify the potential for choice in even the most mechanistic work organization: according to Williams *et al.* (1992: 525) 63 per cent of the 1910–16 labour hours reduction and 70 per cent of the material cost reduction was achieved without benefit of assembly lines. Ford adopted innovative techniques which were subsequently forgotten, and it was not until later the term 'Fordism' became synonymous with mass production.

Taylorism and Fordism provoked a great deal of controversy among managers, workers and others. Critics argued that such mechanistic approaches de-skilled and de-humanized working people. This was manifested in increased rates of labour turnover, for example, which on Ford's first assembly line was approximately 380 per cent per year. Ford also had to double wages to US$5 per day before he could maintain a relatively stable workforce. However, these methods appeared to induce tremendous productivity gains. These gains, coupled with the large amount of power that employers wielded in their own establishments, meant that Taylorism and Fordism had a major impact upon work organization, especially in larger manufacturing enterprises in the USA, Europe, the former USSR and elsewhere. Fragmented forms of work organization were institutionalized by job regulation (custom and practice, collective bargaining, arbitration or professional codes). Industrial engineers, job evaluation specialists and labour negotiators further defined jobs and demarcations.

The advent of bureaucratization, Taylorism and Fordism was partially induced by industrialization. However, different countries and enterprises adopted varying bureaucratic methods. Bureaucracy was a means by which management could extend a greater degree of control over the means of production. While it took a degree of control of the individual elements of work organization away from skilled workers, perhaps managers and owners could then exercise a greater degree of choice in the direction and control of the enterprise and the pattern of work organization. Clawson (1980: 57) argues that moves to such fragmented forms of work organization came before a technological revolution and were not determined by it. According to Thompson and McHugh, the 'minute division of work was not necessarily more efficient; rather, it provided a role for the capitalist to play in organizing production and to take a greater portion of the rewards' (1990: 49).

Taylorism, while providing standards for individual work tasks, was applied in varying ways and influenced by different reactions from managers, employees and unions. Taylorism was not a precondition of industrialization, but was a chosen method of control. 'Human relations' was a rather different approach.

Human relations

In partial reaction to the drawbacks of Taylorism and Fordism, the human relations school advocated that management should focus on the role of employees and work groups (see HUMAN RELATIONS). People could not or would not always follow instructions exactly and there were other problems with regard to working conditions and the importance of job satisfaction which Taylorism and Fordism neglected. Led by Elton Mayo (see MAYO, G.E.), the human relations school was inspired by reports of experiments at Western Electric's Hawthorne Plant which began in 1924. These experiments found that employee motivation increased with attention from higher-status people (see HAWTHORNE EXPERIMENTS).

The human relations school argued that informal social processes could have a large impact on issues such as productivity, morale and the effectiveness of work organization. Therefore, when constructing a work organization, social issues are as important as technical requirements. While the Hawthorne experiments drew attention to the importance of the social system, perhaps the increased attention to social issues replaced technology as a key determinant of work organization, while not necessarily increasing the potential for choice.

The methodology and conclusions of the Hawthorne experiments have been widely criticized. However, human relations ideas had a major effect on subsequent approaches to work organization. Managers paid more attention to interacting with employees. Under Taylorism, work organization was seen as primarily a technical (engineering) problem and hence it advocated a 'one best way' approach, as determined largely by technology. The human relations school contradicted this argument. Two advocates, Roethlisberger and Dickson (1939), when describing their experiments, invoked the notion of a social system. Given the dominance of 'structural functionalism' in sociology in the subsequent period, it is unsurprising that other studies of work used a similar paradigm.

Sociotechnical systems

Another approach to work organization is derived from research and consulting by the Tavistock Institute of Human Relations, which ranged from British coal mines to Indian textile mills. Its adherents saw a sociotechnical system as consisting of two elements: (1) *technical factors* such as mechanical equipment, technical processes and the physical environment; (2) *social factors* such as the relationships amongst workpeople and their individual and collective attitudes to it and to each other. The idea of a work organization as a system includes a series of assumptions:

> that it comprises a set of interdependent 'parts' such that a change in one part will affect some or all of the others, but that the whole system is more than just an aggregation of these parts; that there is some relatively clear continuity about this set of interdependent parts so that it can be considered the same enterprise despite the changes which may take place; and that it has a relatively clear *boundary* which separates it from a wider 'environment'. In addition, most conceptions of enterprises as systems assume that there is an overarching set of values and/or goals which secures the *integration* of the system; and, in open system models, that the maintenance of the system (and the achievement of its goals) are secured by exchanges between the system and its environment.
>
> (Brown 1992: 42–3; emphasis added)

The Tavistock analysts' insight included the notion of work being arranged around people. Compared with scientific management (which underlined the technical aspect of work) and human relations (which emphasized the social aspects), a sociotechnical understanding recognizes the importance of both of these vital aspects of work organization.

Tavistock researchers criticized the formal methods used to introduce new technology and to organize tasks. They argued that employees could not be treated as separate individuals isolated from their work groups. The sociotechnical school emphasized the need to find a proper fit between the social and technical systems. They argued that when this did not occur, low productivity, poor morale and high turnover of staff often resulted (Trist *et al.* 1963).

The organization of work by sociotechnical precepts includes two main characteristics. First, are semi-autonomous work groups; work groups should have a degree of freedom in regulating the manner of their work. Although details of this approach were published in the 1950s, relatively few managers in the English-speaking world seem to take its message fully into account when embarking on technological and organizational change. The message has had more impact in Scandinavia. For instance, at Volvo's Uddevalla plant, production employees were given control over the pace of work and the division of tasks (Berggren 1992: 146–83). However, the concept of employee self-regulation may apply beyond the work-group level. The use of joint labour–management consultative committees is also recommended. Such forums are seen as appropriate for making decisions about the organization of work.

Second, is the adoption of ergonomically sound methods of production and the de-emphasis of assembly lines in favour of 'cellular production'. Semi-autonomous teams of workers are given responsibility for the production of a whole task or a whole unit of production.

How can 'social' objectives be incorporated into the design of a technical system of work organization? Such questions apply in general to the design of work organizations and the use of new technologies. Graversen (1989), for instance, draws on the sociotechnical approach in a Danish study of the phases of the design of work organization in a new brewery. He identifies four different patterns:

1 technical systems are designed without regard to social systems;
2 objectives for, and the design of, social systems are separated from the design of technical systems;
3 objectives for, and the design of, social systems are introduced after the design of technical systems;
4 technical and social objectives and solutions are integrated in the design process.

Heller (1989) draws on French and British examples to argue that engineering solutions ('the technological fix') are often designed to maximize technological effectiveness, on the assumption that people, being adaptable, will make all the necessary adjustments to work with any technologies. He shows that such one-sided solutions can fail completely and advocates the sociotechnical approach as appropriate for analysing the range of choices available when designing technologies.

The notion of choice, as conceptualized by the Tavistock school has been criticized. The Tavistock researchers argued that the social, technical and economic variables must be mediated. However this may indicate a decrease in choice. According to Rose, if the consideration of social requirements is a 'necessary precondition of more productive arrangements... [then] the socio-technical concept may be seen as a device for helping production engineers to discover better "best ways" ' (1975: 216). This is a concept shared with Taylorism.

The 'technological imperative' tends to ignore the requirements of people and thereby usually fails to realize its full potential. The sociotechnical approach implies an integrated solution rather than a compromise. Both the technical–economic system and the social system may operate at sub-optimum levels, but overall efficiency may be maximized by allowing the social as well as the technical factors to operate in coordinated harmony.

A labour process perspective

Braverman (1974) inspired a revival of interest in the Marxist notion of the labour process. This is the management function which converts people's potential for work into productive work effort under conditions which permit capital accumulation (see LABOUR PROCESS). This perspective can highlight the influence of technology on work organization. Braverman's major criticism of the earlier scientific management approach is not of the technological imperative as such, but the underlying drive for capital accumulation and control.

Since the mid-1970s there has been much debate about work organization and management from a labour process perspective. Such research has made an important contribution by directing attention to managerial strategies and the importance of skills. Braverman and some of his followers, however, tend to regard new technology as inevitably causing de-skilling and the degradation of work. They appear to assume that most managers invariably follow a technological imperative, use scientific management principles and give the utmost priority to maximizing the control of labour.

In spite of the de-skilling argument, technological change can be associated with re-skilling and a demand for new skills. Depending on the choice of work organization, flexible automation may provide operators with opportunities to use a wider range of skills than traditional machine tools (Child 1984). New technologies may provide possibilities for technicians to use mechanical and electronic engineering skills, and for operators to programme and maintain their machines and to supervise themselves.

It may be true that the principal reason for introducing new technology during the early stages of assembly-line manufacturing was to reduce direct labour costs through economies of scale and standardization of production. In the more advanced stages, however, the main objective for introducing technological change in manufacturing is to achieve greater quality and flexibility in the production process, through the use of innovations such as computer-aided design/computer-aided manufacturing (CAD/CAM) and robotics. Although most managements aim to achieve consistent profitability and thereby retain the goal of minimizing labour costs, increasing emphasis is being given to customizing products and achieving fast responses in terms of changes in specification, delivery times and so on.

When deciding about new technologies, most employers are primarily concerned with achieving greater control over production processes, improved product quality and cost reduction. Labour processes and work organization are invariably of secondary importance and are often considered only in the implementation stage, rather than initially when making high-level corporate decisions about technological innovation.

Braverman has been criticized for underestimating the potential for worker resistance, union action and even of worker control of aspects of labour regulation, and his followers for concentrating too narrowly on the point of production and exaggerating the pervasiveness, coherence and conspiratorial nature of management. In reality, business strategy specialists tend to focus on finance, marketing, research, production and corporate structures, while neglecting work organization and the labour process.

Automating versus informating

Zuboff (1988) highlights two stark options in the introduction of information technology (IT). IT may be used to *automate* work, robbing people of whatever skill and gratification they may retain and increasing management's impersonality. Alternatively, IT can be used to *informate*, empowering people with knowledge about production and distribution processes, which in turn may provide new opportunities for individual workers and their employing enterprises.

Zuboff asked people 'to draw pictures that represented their "felt sense" of their job experience before and after conversion to the new computer system' (1988: 141ff.). One set of pictures and captions drawn by clerks and their supervisors shows 'both the sense of the

isolation of the individual office worker and a new sense of distance between the clerical function and those who supervise it' (1988: 151). IT had been used to automate rather than to informate the clerks' jobs; that is, to push them away from acting with other people to acting on office machines. Paradoxically, this may allow some informating of supervisors' jobs so that they can become more closely integrated into management.

Taylorist styles of work organization appear to be inimical to the adoption of an informating approach. Hierarchical control is not suitable for the new informating regime. Zuboff's analysis shows how an 'informating process can provide the impetus for new models of organization and management' (1988: 223).

A neo-human relations approach

Several of Peters and Waterman's (1982) prescriptions are consistent with elements of the earlier human relations school. Peters and Waterman do not formulate a new behavioural model, but include a series of common-sense prescriptions, based on their observation of the USA's most successful companies. They recommend, for example, that 'employees should be trusted':

> Treat people as adults. Treat them as partners; treat them with dignity; treat them with respect. Treat *them* – not capital spending and automation – as the primary source of productivity gains. These are the fundamental lessons from the excellent companies' research. In other words, if you want productivity and the financial success that goes with it, you must treat your workers as your most important asset
> (Peters and Waterman 1982: 238; original emphasis)

Although their book has also been a bestseller internationally and has inspired similar studies elsewhere, outside the USA many scholars regard the remedies of Peters and Waterman as inapplicable, on the grounds that they are too prescriptive and too ethnocentrically American. Even in the USA work organization issues for such renowned 'excellent' companies as McDonald's and Walt Disney Productions in the private service sector are very different from many of those confronting most practitioners in the public sector, mining or manufacturing. Within manufacturing, work organization issues differ greatly, for example, depending on the technologies, methods of production and type of business strategy. Even in the private service sector, work organization strategies may vary depending, for example, on whether the business policy is to concentrate on specialist market niches with emphasis on high quality (and high pay) as the basis for a competitive advantage, or to concentrate on mass markets with an emphasis on the quantity of low-cost output (and low pay), which gives a fundamentally different competitive advantage.

Lean management

Particularly since the 1973 oil shock, the ability of Japanese enterprises simultaneously to produce high-quality and relatively low-cost goods gave these firms a competitive advantage over most of their Western counterparts. The work organization of these Japanese enterprises are an aspect of their success.

In breaking the assumed nexus between high quality and low productivity, Japanese enterprises overthrew much of the accepted 'wisdom' about the modern organization of work. They altered the prevailing way in which work systems are judged. Traditional mass producers emphasized output *quantity* as a key measure of success. Other criteria, such as *quality*, were considered subordinate and even incompatible with this focus. A certain proportion of defective output was seen as acceptable; it could either be rectified later or scrapped.

To survive in the face of Japanese and international competition, many non-Japanese enterprises saw a need to increase the efficiency of their work systems and the quality of their outputs. In North America, Europe and elsewhere many managers and academics sought to apply the 'secrets' of Japanese success. Furthermore, many of their enterprises tried to emulate Japanese work systems or to develop forms of work organization which could build a similar competitive advantage.

Deming, Juran and others who fostered the approach to quality found in large Japanese manufacturing enterprises found Western business leaders were an enthusiastic audience. They developed strategies for improving quality and productivity, the adoption of which changed work organization.

Deming stresses the importance of training, especially in statistical tools of process control. Operational employees are the main target of this training. They are given a greater control over production processes; employees are expected to supervise the quality and efficiency of their own work. This decreases the need for direct supervision. In return for such *empowerment* the enterprise can expect an increase in quality and productivity.

The concept of the 'internal customer' is crucial. All employees in the enterprise are seen as customers of those who supply them with parts, information, services and so on. Ideally this concept extends to all levels of an enterprise and can change the relationships that develop in work organizations. For example, a finance officer would provide budgetary advice to other departments of an enterprise. This advice is expected to equal or surpass the service that an external finance consultant could provide, and is judged on this basis.

In the early 1980s, in response to Japanese competition, the Ford Motor Company embarked on an 'After Japan' (AJ) strategy. This was an attempt to change from Fordist mass production to Japanese-style management practices. Ford aimed to change its workforce from being relatively unskilled and untrained to more highly skilled and trained. Ford's leaders saw these changes as a way of building higher quality cars more productively. This was a means to an end: winning a more satisfactory return on its investment.

In the 1980s the Massachusetts Institute of Technology's (MIT) International Motor Vehicle Program (IMVP) undertook a major study into the sources of the competitive success of Japanese car manufacturers. The IMVP researchers argued that most of this success could be traced to the type of work system; they contended that just as mass production (Taylorism and Fordism) replaced craft production, lean production 'will become the standard global production system' (Womack *et al.* 1990: 278).

The IMVP coined the idea of 'lean' because lean production uses 'less of everything compared with mass production – half the human effort in the factory, half the manufacturing space, half the investment in tools, . . . [and] far less than half the needed inventory on site' (Womack *et al.* 1990: 13).

Lean production is primarily concerned with achieving a competitive advantage by operating at the highest levels of efficiency possible. This is accomplished by the continuous reduction of everything used in the production process and specifically every process not involved in adding value to the product. The notion of *kaizen* (continuous or incremental improvement) is a key to lean production. This drive for continuous improvement has de-emphasized the role of technical experts as the sole source of innovation in work systems. Operational employees are closest to the point of production, and hence much of the *kaizen* effort is focused upon their efforts. MIT's Commission on Industrial Productivity argued that a focus on *kaizen* can be more effective than the older notion of aiming to achieve large technological breakthroughs (Dertouzos *et al.* 1989: 74). *Kaizen* is promoted in training and suggestion schemes. Frequent rewards are given for suggestions. These rewards tend to encourage all suggestions, no matter how small (Shadur and Bamber 1994).

The *andon* system is an aspect of lean production whereby operators are given responsibility for stopping the production line to remedy problems at their source. The *andon* system played an integral part in improving the quality and efficiency of Japanese car manufacturers. However, it is not easy to adopt such methods in older Western assembly plants with entrenched customs and practices.

Another important aspect of lean production is just-in-time (JIT). Units of production are delivered by suppliers (internal and external) 'just in time' to meet the demands of the next stage of production. Such a process helps to cut costs by removing inventory, the resulting storage space and the workers required to handle inventory. There is a growing interest in these approaches in most industries including the service sector. For this reason we prefer the term lean *management*, rather than lean *production*.

Lean management is also supported by an array of human resource management strategies such as teamworking, multi-skilling and cross-functional training. With regard to teamworking, teams normally consist of five to fifteen members. In large Japanese enterprises teams tend to be compulsory, whereas in non-Japanese enterprises they are frequently voluntary. In either case, teams are expected to work towards the solution of specific problems and make general quality improvements (see GROUPS AND TEAMS).

Non-Japanese enterprises that also arrange their employees into teams do so as a means of improving performance (Federal Express, General Electric, Hewlett Packard, Honeywell and Rank Xerox). There are several advantages of operating in teams rather than individually. When dealing with tasks, the combination of individuals' knowledge and experience found in a team should produce quicker and higher quality results than individuals. Teams may also foster creativity and innovation.

To operate successfully, teams may depend upon an increase in the inputs to the work system, such as cross-functional training. Team members can be trained in the functions of all members of the team. Members can therefore cover the jobs of absent colleagues. However, where the team concept is implemented, there tends to be less absenteeism, for there is considerable peer pressure to minimize absenteeism. Also, cross-trained team members can be readily shifted to respond to changing production requirements. Teams are often given a greater degree of autonomy than individual employees. Consistent with the notion of built-in quality, teams are responsible for their own quality.

Japanese firms pioneered the use of cross-functional teams in the design and manufacture of cars. Japanese cars are designed more quickly and are often more manufacturable than comparable US ones (Womack *et al.* 1990: 97). Lean-managed enterprises can respond more quickly and effectively to changing consumer preferences. Similarly, multi-function teams are being used effectively in many leading-edge companies to deal quickly with current or potential problems.

The sociotechnical school of thought was one inspiration for the later advocates of teams and self-managing work groups. However most sociotechnical analysts are critical of such later developments of the team concept. For it would appear that, in Japan and other countries, teams are being adopted in a subordinate role to the technological infrastructure. Sociotechnical researchers tend to be critical of Japanese-style work organization. Instead, Berggren (1992) recommends the sociotechnical forms of work organization pioneered by Swedish enterprises.

Supporters of the sociotechnical style of work organization claim that the changes to work systems associated with lean management enhance the quality of employees' working lives. However, detractors hold that, from an employees' point of view, these methods may lead to a degradation of human dignity. After a study of several US and Japanese firms, Klein (1989) is also critical of JIT, arguing that a reduction in inventory often leads to an increased work pace and worker dissatisfaction. Such critics suggest that these systems do not augment the skills of employees – instead, for most workers, they imply de-skilling.

Lean management aims to eliminate as many 'buffers' as possible. Hence the work system is operating as close to its failure point as possible. Some critics argue that this system places undue stress on employees and represents a return to Taylorism. Other critics cite the pace of work as a key drawback. For example, at Toyota in Japan, supervisors reportedly run to the workstations to assist employees to keep up with the line or alleviate problems. Attempts at continuous improvement create increasing demands on employees and managers.

At the enterprise level two more strategies are influencing work organization: empowerment and the decentralization of authority. These strategies can be encapsulated within the broader models of quality improvement and lean production mentioned above. However, they also merit further discussion.

Empowerment

Empowerment is defined by Vogt and Murrel as a process by which employees achieve individual and cooperative goals by working in teams (1990: 8–10). While this emphasizes the *team* focus of empowerment programmes, empowerment is also reported as an *individual* process whereby employees can become increasingly involved in the maintenance and improvement of their enterprise. By working in self-managing teams, employees can take more direct control over their own jobs. Empowerment, then, resembles tenets of the sociotechnical school.

Empowerment may increase the effectiveness of a work system, for an empowered workforce should be able to initiate and make changes and adjustments in a work system more quickly than if each process were controlled strictly by management. Thus, an enterprise with such a workforce could be more responsive to their various customers' needs. Operational employees are the closest to the point of production and often have most knowledge about it, and many of these employees are excellent 'troubleshooters'.

To assist the strategy of empowerment, enterprises are trying to decentralize and devolve authority. There are several other reasons for this: first, a holistic approach to quality improvement requires a large degree of communication up, down and across organizational structures. This is easier in enterprises with 'flatter' hierarchies. Second, there have been attempts to remove as many non-value-adding costs and employees as possible. Middle managerial and levels are being eliminated. These employees are either removed or given greater autonomy. Third, tall hierarchical organizations tend to be less responsive to market conditions than flat organizations. Many levels of authority may actually create work and can lead to an insular focus. Feedback from employees who deal with customers tends to be slower to reach upper management. Moreover, it is more difficult to change an enterprise with a long chain of command. MIT's Commission on Industrial Productivity found '[in] virtually all successful firms. . . [investigated]. . . the trend is toward greater functional integration and fewer layers of hierarchy, both of which promote greater speed in product development and greater responsiveness to changing markets' (Dertouzos *et al.* 1989: 122).

Work organization in service areas

Services generate approximately 70 per cent of gross domestic product in highly developed countries. The importance of this sector is increasing since the distinction between manufacturing and service enterprises is blurring, and many manufacturing enterprises attempt to increase the level and quality of, for example, their customer service, distribution and finance operations. White-collar support staff, comprising approximately one-third of the employment in the US service sector, also are a large component of the total workforce of manufacturing enterprises. Despite the increasing importance of services, the general productivity of services appears to lag behind manufacturing.

The increasing importance of services and the need to improve the efficiency of this sector has implications for contemporary work organization. Work organization that was designed for the manufacturing sector may be inappropriate for the service sector. Traditionally, commentators recommended a Tayloristic production-line approach to services. McDonald's is the archetype of this strategy. McDonald's has a set procedure for greeting customers, taking and assembling orders, and this procedure results in a standardized, highly efficient operation in which the customers know exactly what they will receive. Customers' expectations for a more customized service may not be compatible with the production-line approach to services which has subsequently come under increasing criticism.

In parallel, many employers are seeking to change the work organization among their managerial *cadres* too. The production-line approach may not be applicable to knowledge-based services that encompass a range of managers, executives and professionals such as doctors and lawyers. Nor may it be applicable to white-collar support functions that are highly complex and difficult to standardize. For example, while there have been attempts at extending the features of lean management to staff areas, lean management has so far had less influence on white-collar staff than on operational employees. Many Japanese enterprises that have pioneered lean production on the shop floor are overstaffed and less well organized in the white-collar areas. The adoption of quality-management strategies in US service enterprises has also had only sporadic success. The adoption of these strategies, which were initially developed in a manufacturing setting, relied on standardization. It is difficult to transpose such strategies to the management of services despite the rapid introduction of advanced telecommunications and information technologies. These technologies have increased the mechanization of services, especially in the white-collar support areas, but there has not been a correlated increase in the efficiency of services.

There have been calls for the adoption of a work system for services which shares many of the underlying philosophies of lean production yet is more flexible and stresses empowerment over the standardization of tasks. However, such strategies as flatter management hierarchies are probably more suitable in enterprises with highly skilled and polyvalent operational workers who may seek greater autonomy than their less skilled and univalent counterparts. Perhaps such 'unskilled' workers can effectively be managed by Theory X approaches of 'direct control', but typically the highly skilled are more appropriately managed by a Theory Y-type strategy (see HUMAN RELATIONS). Transformations have been taking place in the management hierarchies of enterprises. Some are aiming to be less bureaucratic and to share information horizontally as well as vertically.

As Burns and Stalker (1961) found, such flexible (organic) organizational structures are more appropriate than bureaucratic (mechanistic) ones in enterprises which face turbulent environments.

The influence of unions

As unionism grew in the nineteenth and early twentieth centuries, it reflected the contemporary forms of work organization. Consequently a pattern of occupationally structured unionism is evident to varying extents in many countries including the UK, Ireland, Canada, the USA, Australia and New Zealand. (Independent forms of occupationally based unionism were largely destroyed in Germany and Japan in the 1930s.) As unions tend to be defensive, they may appear to be suspicious about attempts to change work organization. Many employers are opposed to unions participating in decisions about work organization. When employees and their unions are not consulted in advance but are merely confronted with a *fait accompli* about new work systems, it is not surprising if their initial response is negative.

There is some evidence that conflict about work organization changes is less likely if the changes are also associated with technological change. None the less, where there have been industrial disputes about technological change, the conflicts have often involved the introduction of new technology that may impinge on the work organization of traditional occupations which are threatened with extinction, or at least a transformation, such as railway firemen, miners, dockers and printers. For example, working with hot metal was the basis of the newspaper printers' old craft. The craftworkers and their unions feared the prospect of extinction by the introduction of computerized typesetting, with direct keying by journalists. Several newer occupations have also been involved in disputes about technological change, including computer staff, TV and telecommunications technicians, air traffic controllers and chemical workers.

Despite the media's focus on such industrial conflicts, complete resistance by unions to changing work organization associated with new technology is relatively rare. In recent years there have been many such changes, most of which have been introduced peacefully. Most innovations are not accompanied by industrial disputes (and are, therefore, less newsworthy). Only 7 per cent of a large British sample of managers of manufacturing establishments using new technologies reported opposition from the shop floor or unions as a major difficulty (Northcott *et al.* 1985: 37).

Unions have long sought to exert some control over work organization through various means, including collective bargaining and government action (see TRADE UNIONS; COLLECTIVE BARGAINING). Increasingly, some unions have been seeking to shape the introduction of organizational and technological change, which they realize can have a significant impact over the quality of their members' working lives. Why have certain national union movements had much more influence than others? As an influential observer puts it:

> The unions which have been most effective in securing positive outcomes for their members seem to have been those which have adopted a strategic response involving generally positive attitudes towards technological and organizational change and a willingness and ability to engage in consultation and collaboration with management at the workplace level.
> (OECD 1992: 252)

Union responses are not the only variable, however, especially since union power and density has declined in many contexts. The role of the State is invariably important. The role of governments tends not to be that of direct intervention, rather of helping to establishing a climate, while perhaps providing minimum standards. Governments can also play a powerful leadership role by fostering appropriate education and training, disseminating information about 'best practice' exemplars and providing advice and assistance to managers, employees and unions.

4 Conclusions

As the above discussion of different approaches to work organization was approximately in a chronological order, one might infer that, within a century, conventional wisdom about work organization has almost turned full circle, from autonomous craftwork with flat hierarchies, through bureaucracy, Taylorism/Fordism and tall hierarchical bureaucracies, to semi-autonomous work groups and flatter hierarchies again. Decision makers' views of 'best practice' work organization vary according to their particular circumstances, but dominant coalitions in many enterprises are aiming to reorientate work, away from individuals to teams, with more emphasis on decentralization. They are seeking more input from more employees, for instance, by their participating in making and implementing decisions.

There is, however, a fundamental difference between nineteenth-century autonomous craftwork and late twentieth-century semi-autonomous work groups. Typically, the latter are allowed to have only a degree of 'relative autonomy' about some details of how they work and are still, in many cases, employees (or sub-contractors) of a large enterprise that has sophisticated control mechanisms. The late twentieth-century emphasis on total quality management (and, as the Japanese put it more bluntly, total quality *control*) has often induced a rigorous and systematic approach to management that resembles Taylorism.

Is there an international convergence of 'best practice' work organization? There are parallel moves in most industrialized market economies in an attempt to introduce forms of lean management. None the less, there are also differences of approach between countries. To begin to characterize these differences, Anglo-Saxon approaches tend to be seen all too often as trying a one-off 'quick fix' that is not integrated with enough appropriate training and other elements of corporate strategy. By contrast, Japanese approaches are integrated with complementary elements in the political economy, and foster a mind-set that sees training as an investment rather than a cost. Scandinavian approaches build on a legacy of industrial democracy, with pervasive union and employee influences, so that Volvo's form of teamworking is quite different from Toyota's approach.

Anglo-Saxon countries can be characterized as having an adversarial industrial relations context. By contrast, Japan and another group of countries can be characterized as currently having a more consensual approach, for instance, Scandinavia, Germany and Austria (where there was little pre-capitalist industry, as they were primarily agrarian societies and the industrial workforce was recruited rapidly from peasants). Other things being equal, more employers in these latter countries have tended to be more innovative in terms of work systems and have introduced more integrated approaches than most of those in the Anglo-Saxon countries.

Although there are many exceptions – some enterprises in Anglo-Saxon countries have been innovative in terms of work organization and have a consensual rather than an adversarial approach – there are many similarities between different countries. Hence such generalizations can be sustained more easily for particular industries, occupations, or organizations.

In most of the countries characterized as consensual, there have been substantial public policy initiatives emphasizing novel forms of work organization. Such initiatives have been complemented by a high priority devoted to education and training. There is less likelihood of fully flexible work organization being successfully implemented and maintained in situations with an adversarial context than in some of the continental European countries, where there have been more constructive moves away from Taylorism, with a backcloth of public policies that aim to improve the working environment. The broader context is crucial. Reformers, unions and their members are better able to exert a constructive influence in countries, industries and enterprises that have a relatively harmonious tradition and a long-term approach to training, career development and investment, rather than a tradition of conflictual industrial relations and short-termism.

There are numerous examples of convergence in work organization. Management styles in Japan are changing to incorporate Western ideas and a greater degree of variation in management practice. In the USA, Canada, the UK, Australia and New Zealand, Japanese enterprises are having remarkable success at transplanting lean management systems which are almost as successful in terms of productivity and quality as those in Japan. Similarly, US enterprises such as Ford, Motorola and Hewlett Packard are adopting forms of work organization which resemble those in Japan, but also incorporate insights from the sociotechnical and other schools. Scandinavian enterprises are having difficulty maintaining their distinctive approach to work organization. The closing of Volvo's Uddevella plant, as well as General Motors' takeover of Saab may signal the end of the Swedish car industry's divergence from others. However, these examples draw upon the experience of large enterprises. There may be less convergence among small to medium-size enterprises, especially those which service niche markets.

International and comparative research reinforces the view that there are no universally applicable prescriptions for 'best practice' work organization. A contingency approach is likely to yield more useful insights into work organization. Accordingly, the most effective managers draw selectively on research and experience, analyse their own national and corporate cultures and constraints, diagnose the opportunities and problems which they face, then devise the policies and practices which are most appropriate in their precise circumstances. This is a contingency approach to designing work organization, which is more demanding than buying 'off-the-shelf' prescriptions. For most managers, however, a contingency approach is more likely to be successful in the longer term. An important aspect is that those who are involved in conducting their own investigations and devising their own solutions tend to feel a sense of ownership and are then committed to their success.

While most contemporary enterprises use more advanced technology than their predecessors, they also have more informed choices about its introduction, management and change. Arguably, technologies can provide a competitive advantage, but only if they are well integrated with work organization, drawing insights from several of the above-mentioned schools of thought as appropriate. These findings are consistent with our analysis of different approaches to work organization. Each approach is constrained and influenced by technological and environmental factors, however, these are not the sole determinants of work organization. While proponents of various approaches to work organizations, such as Taylorism and lean production, argue that these represent 'one best way', there is considerable diversity in the practical application of these forms of work organization, and the associated choices of key decision makers. Several different styles of work organization can exist at any one time in any given industry. For example, aspects of each 'ideal-type' work organization discussed above can be found in the car industry.

Innovation in work systems has been influenced by technological change, as well as by such factors as: changing notions of work and its organization; a more demanding and highly-educated workforce; greater expectations on the part of consumers for high-quality and low-cost products; shortening of product life cycles; overcapacity in some markets (for example, cars); privatization; growing international trade; de-regulation, and the growth of regional trade blocs (for example, the European Union and North American Free Trade Agreement); increasing competition and the growth of small and medium-sized enterprises. Policy-makers may have a degree of choice in the way in which work organization is designed. Nevertheless, as shown by this discussion of the development of work organization, choice does not occur in a vacuum, but is strongly influenced by contextual factors.

GREG J. BAMBER
GRIFFITH UNIVERSITY

DAVID E. SIMMONS
QUEENSLAND UNIVERSITY OF TECHNOLOGY

Further reading

(References cited in the text marked *)

* Bamber, G.J. and Lansbury, R.D. (1988) 'Management strategy and new technology', *Journal of Management Studies* 25 (3): 197–216. (Interesting case study illustrating ways in which technology can affect the organization of work.)

* Berggren, C. (1992) *Alternatives to Lean Production: Work Organization in the Swedish Auto Industry*, Ithaca, NY: ILR Press. (Reviews the drawbacks of lean production (and related systems) and offers alternatives.)

* Braverman, H. (1974) *Labor and Monopoly Capital: The Degradation of Work in the Twentieth Century*, New York: Monthly Review Press. (Marked a revival of the Marxist notion and popularized the labour process perspective.)

* Brown, R.B. (1992) *Understanding Industrial Organizations, Theoretical Perspectives in Industrial Sociology*, London: Routledge. (Discusses organization design from a sociological perspective.)

* Burns, T. and Stalker, G.M. (1961) *The Management of Innovation*, London: Tavistock Publications. (Explores how organizations react to change. Many subsequent organization theory and related texts build upon this work.)

* Child, J. (1984) *Organization: A Guide to Problems and Practice* , 2nd edn, London, Harper & Row. (Discusses the major issues relating to organization design and organization theory.)

* Clawson, D. (1980) *Bureaucracy and the Labour Process: The Transformation of US Industry, 1860–1920*, New York: Monthly Review Press. (Reviews the major changes to US organizations from 1860–1920.)

* Dertouzos, M.L., Lester, R.K. and Solow, R.M. (1989) *Made in America, Regaining the Productive Edge*, New York: MIT Press. (Discusses the findings of a major US study of the sources of competitive success.)

* Graversen, G. (1989) 'Social factors in the introduction of new technology: a Scandanavian case study', in G.J. Bamber and R.D. Lansbury (eds), *New Technology: International Perspectives on Human Resources and Industrial Relations*, London: Routledge. (Discusses perspectives to the introduction of new technology from a sociotechnial viewpoint.)

* Heller, F. (1989) 'Human resource management and the socio-technical approach', in G.J. Bamber and R.D. Lansbury (eds), *New Technology: International Perspectives on Human Resources and Industrial Relations*, London: Routledge. (Discusses perspectives on the introduction of new technology from a sociotechnical viewpoint.)

* Klein, J.A. (1989) 'The human costs of manufacturing reform', *Harvard Business Review* 60 (6). (Discusses the problems relating to the introduction of innovative work systems and related technology.)

* Northcott, J., with Rogers, P., Knetsch, W. and de Lestapis, B. (1985) *Microelectronics in Industry, An International Comparison: Britain, Germany, France*, London: Policy Studies Institute. (An international comparison of the different implications relating to the introduction of new technology.)

* OECD (1992) *New Directions in Work Organisation: The Industrial Relations Response*, Paris: Organization for Economic Cooperation and Development. (An international perspective on the industrial relations issues associated with the introduction of innovative approaches to work organization.)

* Peters, T.J. and Waterman, R.H. (1982) *In Search of Excellence: Lessons from America's Best-Run Companies*, New York: Harper & Row. (Popular management book that ushered in a flood of related texts.)

* Roethlisberger, F.J. and Dickson, W.J. (1939) *Management and the Worker*, Cambridge, MA: Harvard University Press. (Text written by human relations advocates that discusses the experiments of the period.)

* Rose, M. (1975) *Industrial Behaviour: Theoretical Development Since Taylor*, London: Penguin. (A comprehensive overview of the different approaches to industrial organization since Taylor.)

* Shadur, M.A. and Bamber, G.J. (1994) 'Towards lean production? The transferability of Japanese management strategies to Australia', *International Executive* 36 (4): 343–64. (Analysis of the effectiveness of *Kaizen* in a non-Japanese setting.)

* Taylor, F.W. (1911) *The Principles of Scientific Management*, New York: Harper & Row. (Classic work by the father of scientific management; introduced the concepts of scientific management to the world.)

* Thompson, P. and McHugh, D. (1990) *Work Organisations: A Critical Introduction*, London: Macmillan. (Reviews the different issues relating to work organization theory.)

* Trist, E.L., Higgin, G.W., Murray, H. and Pollock, A.B. (1963) *Organisational Choice*, London:

Tavistock Publications. (Seminal work on the sociotechnical perspective.)

* Vogt, J.F. and Murrel, K.L. (1990) *Empowerment in Organisations*, San Diego, CA: University Associates. (Extols the benefits of the popular concept of empowerment.)

* Williams, K., Haslam, C. and Williams, J. (1992) 'Ford versus "Fordism": The beginning of mass production', *Work Employment and Society* 6 (4): 517–55. (Provides historical data on Henry Ford's manufacturing operations and the beginning of mass production.)

* Womack, J.P., Jones, D.T. and Roos, D. (1990) *The Machine That Changed the World*, New York: Macmillan. (Popularized the lean production notion.)

* Zuboff, S. (1988) *In the Age of the Smart Machine: The Future of Work and Power*, New York: Basic Books. (A critical review of the influence of new technology, especially information technology, on work organization and workers.)

See also: HUMAN RELATIONS; HUMAN RESOURCE MANAGEMENT; INDUSTRIAL CONFLICT; JAPANIZATION; MAYO, G.E.; TAYLOR, F.W.

Related topics in the IEBM: DEMING, W.E.; JURAN, J.M.; JUST-IN-TIME PHILOSOPHIES; MANAGEMENT IN JAPAN; ORGANIZATION STRUCTURE; ORGAHNIZATION TYPES; PETERS, T.J.; SMITH, A; STRATEGIC CHOICE; TEAMS IN MANUFACTURING; TECHNOLOGY AND ORGANIZATIONS; TOYODA FAMILY; WEBER, M.

Global dimensions

Bata's system

Overview

The Bata system of management originated from Henry Ford's ideas – before 1926 – as summarized in his seminal book *Today and Tomorrow* (Ford 1926). Ford's early view of management was based on worker autonomy, knowledge, just-in-time, waste minimization, quality and customer's involvement (customization): it was all but abandoned by Ford's turnaround embrace of mass production, Taylorism and hierarchical management in the 1930s.

In Moravia, Tomas Bata remained true to Ford's original ideas and brought them to practical fruition in the late 1920s and early 1930s. Young Tomas, who repeatedly visited, trained and worked in the USA, brought home the lessons of self-reliance, total quality management, strategic flexibility, high technology, worker participation and use of knowledge as capital. In the 1920s and early 1930s, in Moravia (in Zlin of former Czechoslovakia), Bata practised a remarkable management system which was some fifty years before its time.

1 What is the Bata system?

The Bata system is a management system of extraordinary productivity and effectiveness. Its main characteristics include: integration instead of division of labour, whole-system orientation, continuous innovation and quality improvement, team and workshop self-management, profit-sharing and autonomy, workers' participation and co-determination, clearly-defined responsibilities, organizational flexibility, vigorous automation and most importantly – an uncompromisingly human-orientated capitalistic enterprise. Every employee was a partner, co-worker or associate and all workers were to become owners and capitalists.

To the contrary, mass production was based on employee disempowerment and political dependency, collective bargaining, command hierarchy of control, low quality, simplicity, extreme division of labour and disregard for the customer (see FORD, H.; TAYLOR, F.W.). This system had reigned supreme essentially from the 1930s until the 1970s. By then the Japanese-style management – with mass customization, lean production, total quality management, integrated-process management and trade-off free management – started replacing the dysfunctional hierarchies of mass production.

2 Basic principles

There are clearly identifiable principles which Tomas Bata evolved, adhered to and ultimately made to work.

His first slogan 'Thinking to the people, labor to the machines!' he proclaimed at the factory gate. He eliminated the intermediaries: a large network of Bata-run stores and outlets complemented and extended his production operations by integrating customers into the production process. He also made the consumer and the public not only the purpose, but the very foundation of his enterprise. 'Our customer – our master' and 'Service to the public' were not just slogans, but sound principles of business. Production and profits were not the ends, but the means towards improving the individual lives of all Bata employees (Bata-people liked to call themselves 'associates'). Employment was stable and long term: part of each worker's earnings was reinvested in the company (the initial endowment put up by the company) – each worker became a capitalist and partial co-owner. Bata claimed that the quality of employee life was a primary concern of the employer (not of the state). He offered economic incentives to employees to stop drinking and smoking, or to lose weight. He provided family housing (with gardens) and a minimum social infrastructure: hospitals, museums, churches, swimming pools, leisure facilities, sport stadiums, roads – all part of the self-imposed responsibilities of Bata Enterprises. He also established and ran his own school of management: an institution considered too important to be left to the external and traditional providers of business education. He was seeking enhanced self-reliance, independence and vertical integration: railroads, waterways, airports, land, forests, even local government – all became connected to his enterprise. He strove to operate with no debt and with no credit: all state taxes were paid according to almost fanatical principles of integrity.

Thanks to these and similar principles, Bata's business grew and flourished even during the worldwide depression of 1929–32. He was fully aware of the qualities of his system: he knew it was a whole which could not be copied in parts – there were no 'company secrets'. Often he assured his associates that no fair competition could ever pose a threat to their performance. However, the Bata system was gravely damaged by the 'unfair competition' of politics and ideology in 1939 by the Nazis, then it was vilified and later proscribed by Marxists and communists of the post-1948 era. Bata's own family, managers and workers were forced into exile. This story is recounted in Tomas' son's book (Bata 1990), which also describes the current scope of Bata international operations. Surprisingly, after 1989 and the subsequent dissolution of Czechoslovakia, the Bata system continued to be vilified, its promoters and practitioners still ignored or ridiculed by the ex-communist regime.

3 Operational practices

Bata's symbiosis of workers' autonomy and empowerment through technology was unique and even by today's standards still remains somewhat 'futuristic'. Modern US and Japanese companies have only recently started to experiment with similar concepts.

Let us consider a short sample of Bata practices:

1 the process of continuous innovation and improvement; the total system of preventive maintenance: machine shop working as 'clockwork';

2 in-house adaptation and rebuilding of all purchased machinery; 10 per cent of the engineering employees involved directly in the R&D function;

3 the assurance of continuously high-quality output with processes streamlined to eliminate breakdowns and stoppages and individual workers given quality responsibility;

4 total manufacturing flexibility achieved:
   (i) by breaking the traditional large factory plant into smaller, semi-autonomous and specialized workshops; and
   (ii) by making all machines self-contained, independently powered and motorized by electric motors (referred to as 'electric robots' by Bata);

5 changes in product styles and types were achieved quickly (in a few hours) by rearranging machine sequences and layouts, by pulling out machines temporarily ('decoupling the line') and by designing all adjustments and customization into the final stages of the production process;

6 a close personal 'ownership' relationship between workers and 'their' machine: not only was there no suspicion of the machinery but there was also no neglect, only pride of ownership, emotional involvement and total care;

7 all operators were able to stop production line conveyors at will; all waste in production was minimized (everything had to be just in time for the next step); all machines were designed to serve 'the process', not just perform individual operations;

8 dedication to automation: one of the Bata machines 'did everything but talk and sing' (the note-scribbling overseas visitors were never able to copy it; a machine called 'Union press' produced a pair of shoes in a single movement);

9 a perfect, semi-automated, rotational system of preventive maintenance of all ma-

chinery (including full overhauls and updates), carried out without ever stopping the production.

4 Human capital at Bata Enterprises

Another set of Bata's concepts is related directly to people. The need for total involvement of top management was never questioned. In order to be promoted to a top managerial position, one had to personally make a pair of shoes. All executives remained close to their product and actually had to learn how to make it themselves (compare this with top executives who have never even observed how their company's products are made or used).

Quality circles (see TOTAL QUALITY MANAGEMENT) also emerged spontaneously because they had to – the very system design of Bata management required it. More interesting is that top executives (and Bata himself) were part of the continuous quality improvement process: their suggestions ranged from company-store door design to teaching all workers statistics and profit calculations.

Many decades before the collapse of management hierarchies, Bata and his entire directorship ate in the company cafeteria (to assure proper quality of food and operations). It was insisted that each executive must be replaceable and that competent leaders must be continually trained and educated: the company-run school, the Tomas Bata School of Work and Management, was the answer. Bata was no fool: 'High wages can only be attained through human intelligence', he insisted.

Bata was also an optimist ('A day has 86,400 seconds'): he simply knew it was possible to succeed. And management by walking around? He put his office in an elevator – in order to be close to his workers. He laughed at the notion that any acquired wealth must be taken from somebody else (the 'zero-sum' fallacy): his workers were paid eight times more than the prevailing average. He projected that each worker should be able to retire at 40 and live from their accumulated capital.

The best savings strategy, he taught, was the repayment of debts. He warned that producers asking for state customs and quota protections ultimately harm the public and minimize employees' gains. To beg for subsidies or bailouts was not only unworthy of a professional manager, but to Bata, any such managed competition was unacceptable.

He also dreamt, almost longingly, about the 'new machines' which would ease human mental work, computations and accounting. He had big plans for such computing machines. Bata's response to the ravages of the Depression was masterful and yet not tried anywhere else: he achieved workers' approval to reduce wages by 40 per cent; at the same time he took steps to reduce their cost of living expenditures by 50 per cent; finally, he reduced the prices of all Bata products by 50 per cent. It worked: Bata Enterprises and employees flourished even during the Depression. Bata was fond of saying: 'And how do they do things in England?' He liked to answer, rather proudly: 'Just the other way around. In England there is no understanding between managers and workers. They do not trust each other. They even have powerful adversary organizations, separately for employers and employees. Employers are not allowed to raise wages without approval . . .workers cannot accept work on their own terms . . . .' Tomas Bata was never short of courage: 'We are the pioneers. The cowards did not even start on the journey, the weak were lost on the way. Forward!'

MILAN ZELENY
FORDHAM UNIVERSITY AT LINCOLN CENTER

Further reading

(References cited in the text marked *)

Bata, T. (1992) *Knowledge in Action: Bata-System of Management*, Amsterdam: IOS Press. (First English translation of Bata's own thoughts and speeches.)

* Bata, T.J. (1990) *Bata: Shoemaker to the World*, Toronto, ONT: Stoddart Publishing. (Describes the current scope of Bata international operations.)

* Ford, H. (1926) *Today and Tomorrow*, Garden City, NY: Doubleday, reprinted 1988, Cam-

bridge, MA: Productivity Press. (Seminal work describing Ford's early view of management.)

Vlcek, J. (1971) 'Das Bata-Führungssystem', *Industrielle Organisation* 40 (11): 615–19. (One of the first resurrective discussions of the Bata system.)

Zeleny, M. (1987) 'The roots of modern management: Bat'a-system', *Human Systems Management* 6 (1): 4–7. Also (in Japanese) in *Standardization and Quality Control* 40 (1): 50–3. (English and Japanese discussion of the Bata system.)

Zeleny, M. (1988) 'Bat'a-system of management: managerial excellence found', *Human Systems Management* 7 (3): 213–19. (Detailed essay including statistics, quotes and excerpts for a serious student.)

Zeleny, M. 'Three men talk on Bat'a-system' (in Japanese), *Standardization and Quality Control* 41 (1): 15–24. (Discussion in Japanese of the Bata system.)

Zeleny, M. (1988) 'Practical roots of IPM', appendix to 'Integrated process management: a management technology for the new competitive era', in M.K. Starr (ed.), *Global Competitiveness: Keeping the United States on Track*, New York: W.W. Norton & Co., Inc. (The Bata system related as a case relevant to the US efforts for improved productivity.)

See also: HUMAN RESOURCE MANAGEMENT; LABOUR PROCESS; ORGANIZATION BEHAVIOUR

Related topics in the IEBM: MANAGEMENT IN JAPAN; ORGANIZATION BEHAVIOUR, HISTORY OF

Fordism

Overview

At its very simplest level, Fordism refers to the production methods utilized by Henry Ford in his car assembly plants at River Rouge and Highland Park in Detroit in the first two decades of the twentieth century. In these plants, Ford further developed both the American System of Manufacturing – consisting of the use of single purpose machinery; manufacture of standardized products; and the interchangeability of parts – and Taylorist scientific management. However, the most innovatory aspects of the Ford plants were the introduction of the moving, mechanized assembly line, the use of the firm's *sociology department* to control worker behaviour and the introduction of the 'Five-Dollar' day. The application of Fordist techniques is not a universal phenomena but can only occur under certain social and economic conditions such as the presence of mass consumption, Keynesian economic regulation and widespread state economic intervention.

1 Introduction

It is difficult to over estimate the importance to the process of manufacturing the innovations and changes introduced at Ford's Detroit factories between 1910 and 1915 and their later incorporation into the business practice of organizations throughout the Western world. By producing the Model T and 'diffusing of the techniques' of mass production, 'Fordism', a concept which encompasses both the Ford production system and its parallel system of labour relations, (see INDUSTRIAL AND LABOUR RELATIONS) may be said to have 'changed the world' (Hounsell 1984: 218). Whilst it may be the case that the introduction of Japanese production techniques is restructuring the labour process in major industrial sectors such as that of automotives (Womack *et al.* 1990), it is Fordism and not Lean Production that is *The Machine That Changed the World.* The importance of Fordism as a mass production system, defined as 'long runs of standardised products made on dedicated special purpose equipment by semi-skilled workers' (Williams *et al.* 1987: 1) can be overstated, as mass production itself is often 'used interchangeably with the concept of "Ford" as a kind of historical shorthand for the manufacturing system discovered by Ford and then, supposedly, widely imitated' (1987: 1). Williams *et al.* (1987) dispute whether the traditional definition of mass production describes what Ford actually did and describe methods such as lack of vertical integration, miraculous reductions in labour hours per car, running with low stock levels as proto Japanese. However, the analysis of Japanization and Fordism are here linked to labour process issues (see LABOUR PROCESS). Fordism, however, refers to much more than the methods of Henry Ford, as it describes practices in the political and economic realms as well as in the realm of production.

However 'Fordism' from its first usage by Gramsci (1978) up to its re-invention by Aglietta (1979) has had a wider purchase and latterly refers to the dominance of wider social and economic processes such as Keynesian economics and the politics of the welfare state in post-war western Europe and the USA. It is only at this level that we can properly relate Fordism to mass production and its corollary in mass consumption. In the analysis of the effects of Fordism in the post-war period there are two distinct theoretical positions. On one hand, 'regulationists' such as Aglietta see Fordism as a determinant stage in the development of capitalism in which at the level of the factory, the technical division of labour and the use of semi-skilled labour constitutes a particular form *or regime of accumulation* supported by *a mode of regulation* consisting of a mixed economy, the re-distribution of wealth through welfare provision and the post-war compromise between capital and labour. A second, 'institutionalist' framework, particularly the work of Piore and Sabel (1984), sees Fordism as a particular set of social choices, arising out of the 'first industrial divide' at the turn of the twentieth century. Although there are significant methodological, political and theoretical differences between the 'regulationists' and the 'institutionalists' they both agree that sometime between 1965 and 1975 Fordism entered a period of crisis in which both mass production and mass consumption could no longer be sustained because of the development of microprocessor technology, the information society and the increasing disaggregation and fragmentation of customer demand. Out of this crisis arose a third aspect of Fordism, in which new forms of labour processes such as flexible specialization and new flatter organizational forms replaced Taylorism and the bureaucratic organization under the general aegis of the *enterprise culture* (see TAYLOR, F.W.; LABOUR PROCESS)

2 Fordism as a labour process

Standardization, single purpose machinery and flow line mass production

The main elements in the technical definition of Fordism are; standardized production and interchangeable parts; the use of dedicated single purpose machine tools; and mechanized flow-line mass production. The Model T was the mainstay of Fordist commodity production through the decision in 1909 that the Ford company would 'only make Model Ts and the runabout, touring car, town car and delivery car would all consist of the same chassis' (Hounsell 1984: 227). It was made possible through processes of standardization and interchangeability of parts inherited from

the American armament, sewing machine, watchmaking and bicycle industries. Indeed in its marketing literature the Ford company stated: 'We are making 40,000 cylinders, 10,000 engines, 40,000 wheels, 20,000 axles, 10,000 bodies, 10,000 of every part that goes into a car ... all exactly alike (1984: 221). By 1913 with a car coming off the line every 40 seconds, the company had increased, within 5 years, production from about 6,000 Model Ts to roughly 200,000 (1984: 228).

Although in the nineteenth century, 'most machine tools were still general purpose' (Littler 1985: 15) with the automation of vehicle production new machine tools dedicated to high volume, large batch production designed 'to run continuously at high speeds' began to appear (1985: 15). With the decision to concentrate on Model T production, superintendents in the plants began to 'initiate the design, construction or procurement of large numbers of special or single purpose machine tools'. (Hounsell 1984: 227), out of which Ford's 'tool experts designed almost all of the fixtures and gauges so that they could be used by unskilled machine tenders' (1984: 230).

The distinguishing feature of flow line production as opposed to craft-based forms of production was that instead of craft workers moving round the work-in-progress the flow of parts was achieved by a mechanization process with assembly workers being tied to their work position (Littler 1985: 15). The assembly line brought not only a regularity to production but extended its 'dynamism to all phases of the factory operations' (Hounsell 1984: 237). Consequently, mass production is more than mechanized high quantity production, it is 'the focusing upon a manufacturing project of the principles of power, accuracy, economy, system, continuity and speed' (*Encyclopaedia Britannica*, quoted in Hounsell 1984: 217).

Labour Aspects of Fordism – Taylorism

In Braverman's (1974) classic analysis of the capitalist labour process, he identifies deskilling of labour as the key element in the application of Taylorism (see TAYLOR, F.W.) in blue and white collar employment. In breaking down production into its smallest possible elements, task fragmentation takes place and in so doing reduces the labourer to the boring and mundane repetitiveness of short cycle times. Decision making over task allocation or planning of production rests only in the hands of management. On the shop floor, the foreman took over the control function of the craft worker and the machine the skill element, leaving semi-skilled operators the task of feeding the machinery and removing the finished pieces. The Fordist system of mass production in turn intensified the Taylorist division of labour and fragmentation of skills by which 'the pace of work was mechanically controlled' (Meegan 1988: 141).

With the mechanization of the flowline systems, the effects were that the pace of the line was increased and the intensity of the labour effort required was controlled by the machine and not by the operator. Increasing mechanization also meant that the required skill levels of the labourer were not particularly high. Indeed, Ford himself reported that of the lightest jobs in his factory '670 could be filled by legless men, 2637 by one legged men, two by armless men, 715 by one-armed men, and ten by blind men' (quoted in Littler 1985: 15).

The increased technical division of labour meant that any skills required were firm-, product- or even station-specific and unlikely to be transferable either within the firm or from firm to firm. In 1916 for example, a Swiss car factory superintendent reported to the US Federal Trade Commission that:

There applied for work at this factory one day a man who represented himself to be a skilled erector of automobiles. The plant needed such a man, hired the applicant, and assigned him to the assembly of an automobile. It soon became apparent that this employee did not even know where or how to commence the assembly. The superintendent said to him
'We thought you were a skilled erector of automobiles'
'I thought I was' replied the new employee.

'Where did you work'
'At the plant of the Ford Motor Company'
'What did you do'
'I screwed nut No. 58.
(Gartman 1979: 203, quoted in Meegan 1988)

Sociological and cultural aspects of Fordism

Littler (1986: 56–7) describes how Ford incorporated aspects of Taylorism such as the disaggregation of planning from the execution of work, task fragmentation and the timing of specific operations and enhanced them through the introduction of the flow-line principle in the form of the moving assembly line and new forms of labour control. However, in the early days the Ford factories experienced high levels of labour turnover and in order to combat this Ford introduced the Five Dollar Day. It was not a universal benefit, however, and there were strict qualifying criteria such as six months' continuous employment, aged over 21, satisfactory personal habits at home and work ... and no consumption of alcohol or tobacco (Littler 1986: 57), all of which were controlled by the factory's Sociological Department. Ford sought to control not just the behaviour of his employees at work but also outside of the factory in an attempt to produce a new form of collective labourer. Ford believed that the proper exercise of corporate power could build a new kind of society with the five-dollar day being 'only in part to secure worker compliance' to the new discipline required for assembly line work.' It was also designed to provide workers with sufficient income and leisure time to consume the mass produced commodities the corporations were about to turn out in ever vaster quantities (Harvey 1989: 126). Ultimately what separates Taylorism from Fordism was Henry Ford's belief that mass production was intrinsically linked to mass consumption, a belief underscored by the presence of a 'new politics' of labour control and resistance leading to a 'new aesthetics ... and a new kind of rationalised modernist and populist democratic society' (Harvey 1989: 126).

3 Fordism as a social model

Thus far, we have concentrated the analysis on Fordism as a means of organizing production, but the real distinctiveness of the Fordist system is the 'way in which consumption is brought into the balance with the goods produced' (Meegan 1988: 139). The 'Five Dollar' day was seen by some of Ford's contemporaries as creeping socialism and doomed to failure, but in practice the rationale behind the innovation was to move the consumption of consumer goods away from the hegemony of the upper classes of society. Increased productivity and lower factory gate prices, reductions in man hours per car, the increased prosperity of blue collar workers brought more and more consumer goods into the homes of the ordinary working class family.

Ford was a proponent of the idea that 'corporate power' could be used as a positive economic and social regulator. Although the experiments in his factories had little effect on economic policy during the inter-war years, it is in the post-war settlement in Europe and America that we can begin to detect the wider dissemination of Fordism. Harvey (1989) identifies two stumbling blocks which stood in the way of the full development of the Fordist model in the inter-war years. First, the continuance of hostile class relations on the shop floor with the organizations of labour able to successfully resist the implementation of the Taylorist/Fordist model. Second, state intervention in the economy was spasmodic and uneven and therefore lacked the regulatory power to ensure the development of a Fordist model of production.

The post-1945 settlement

The growth in national level collective bargaining (see COLLECTIVE BARGAINING) signalled on the one hand the acceptance by trade unions of the managerial prerogative – the rights of management to manage in the factory 'in exchange for increases in line with productivity growth and inflation' across industrialized countries (Brenner and Glick 1991). Enterprises were therefore able to secure investment and innovation with less worker opposition. On the other hand the new economic enterprises began to recognize the rights of trade unions to represent the interests of their employees in negotiations over the setting of terms and conditions of employment. Outside of the factory, national level collective bargaining was incorporated into 'the States adoption of Keynesian fiscal and monetary policies, which made up for the shortfalls of demand and so smoothed out the business cycle and prevented high levels of unemployment' (Brenner and Glick 1991). The welfare state provided a 'safety net for the structurally or temporarily unemployed' and 'redistributed income towards the working class' whilst at the same 'functioned in counter cyclical fashion to keep the economy turning over' (Brenner and Glick 1991). With the facilitation of long-term consumer credit, the outcome was the 'regular matching of production with consumption, thus transcending the tendency towards underconsumption and providing the basis for the great post-war boom' (Brenner and Glick 1991).

In the USA the widespread adoption of Keynesian economics increased 'federal control' over tax levels and interest rates , enhancing Roosevelt's 'new deal' revolution of the late 1930s. The state intervened more and more into such areas as restructuring 'economic institutions in accordance with technological imperatives' (Piore and Sabel 1984: 95–7); social welfare provision for the unemployed, aged and disabled; expenditure in public works and into the wage–effort bargain between employers and employees. In the UK, the election of the Attlee government and the introduction of the mixed economy signalled more than just the introduction of welfare provision which saw a shift away from a process of redistribution through 'common ownership of the means of production' to redistribution through programmes of progressive taxation and free social provision for all citizens irrespective of the means to pay. In France the economy was sheltered from the vagaries of the market place by the erection of trade barriers and the concentration of productive effort into satisfying the demands of the domestic consumer. This was matched by an increase in the minimum wage as a means of absorbing the increased output and lowering worker resistance to technological change (Piore and Sabel 1984: 140), as well as increasing state intervention into the collective bargaining arena. Germany, perhaps as a consequence of the 'attachment' of neo-corporatist, Keynesian ideologies to the policies of the National Socialists in the 1930s, remained an outsider and, developed its own, non-Fordist, model of economic management. Reliant, in the immediate aftermath of the war, on low wage, liberal policies in which the market over-ruled state management of the economy, it was only in the early 1960s that 'economic success' led more and more to the development of mass production techniques and 'Keynesian macroregulation' (Piore and Sabel 1984: 148).

The post-war period 'brought Fordism to maturity' in which 'living standards rose, crisis tendencies were contained, mass democracy was preserved and the threat of inter-capitalist wars kept remote' (Brenner and Glick 1991). The economic underpinning of this stability was the widespread implementation of Keynesian economics and the redistribution of corporate taxation into infrastructural investment and rebuilding in such industries as transport, extraction, energy and construction and growths in employment in white collar and service class occupations, and public sector organizations.

The key to the contingent rise of Fordism in the post-1945 period across the OECD member countries was stability and growth – growth in product markets and in the real surplus in consumer incomes and stability in labour markets, the bureaucratic organizational form, the tripartite neo-corporatist welfare state, in the labour–capital relationship and in employment patterns. The role of large corporate power was to assure steady growth investments to enhance 'productivity, guaranteed growth, and raised living standards while ensuring a stable basis for gaining profits' (Harvey 1989: 134). The tripartite partnership between labour, capital and the state worked towards 'defining the paths of mass consumption growth ... keeping effective demand at levels sufficient to absorb the steady growth of capitalist output' (1989: 134).

These general patterns should not be mistaken either for a lack of trade union resistance, inter-class conflict or the end of poverty: so called the 'end of ideology' thesis and favoured by many conservative political theorists of the period it in fact reflected governmental intervention in the economic and social issues attempting to stifle or marginalize voices of discontent. The pattern was widespread throughout the West and with nation-states being able to engineer 'stable economic growth and rising material living standards' by the use of 'welfare statism', Keynesian economic management, and control over wage relations' (Harvey 1989: 138).

Internationalization

The increase in consumption and production necessary for the stability of the Fordist model was not confined to the developed capitalist economies but depended upon an expansion in world trade which resulted in 'the formation of global mass markets and the absorption of the mass of the worlds into the global dynamics of a new kind of capitalism' (Harvey 1989: 137). None the less, the spread of Fordism, although uneven, with countries developing their own, distinct, modes of industrial relations, welfare policies and fiscal regimes, was largely under the sway of American hegemony. It was uneven because not everyone enjoyed the fruits of Fordist growth as 'wage bargaining was confined to certain sectors of the economy and certain nation states' and 'other sectors of high risk production still depended on low wages and weak job security. And even Fordist sectors could rest upon a non-Fordist base of subcontracting (Harvey 1989: 138). This resulted in the continuance of inequalities producing social tensions and new sources of resistance based upon race, gender and ethnicity struggles.

None the less, Fordism held sway till the oil crisis of the mid-1970s and held together the fragile tri-partite neo-corporatism which spread the 'benefits' of mass production and mass consumption to an ever-widening citizenry. 'Material living standards rose for the mass of the population in the advanced capitalist countries and, a relatively stable environment for corporate profits prevailed' (Harvey 1989: 140). However, with the onset of crisis, productivity growth declined as labour systematically began to challenge work intensification, deskilling of blue collar tasks, and the increased perceptions of labour as an alienating process leading to an inertia in the innovatory focus of labour. Consequently, it was the internal 'socio-technical' contradictions embedded within the Fordist labour process which led to the crisis in this particular mode of capitalist development (Harvey 1989: 141). A fall in corporate profitability on a global scale was exacerbated by the oil crises of the early to mid 1970s and led to a series of political, economic and cultural changes in the late 1970s and early 1980s which, although unsatisfactory, have been subsumed under the rubric of post-Fordism (see Table 1).

4 Post-Fordism

As we saw in the last section the 1970s witnessed a crisis of profitability in the Fordist production mode which the neo-corporatist state found more and more difficult to regulate. At an economic level this signalled the beginnings of what has become known as the enterprise culture described in the following terms:

Economic characteristics
1 continual process of privatization;
2 the deregulation of industry;
3 the structural re-organization of public funded bodies;
4 a reduction in reliance upon the culture of dependence throughout all organizations and business sectors – this includes reliance on each other as well as upon government agencies for support.

Socio-cultural characteristics
1 The view of the competitive market organization becomes the dominant role model for all others including public statutory agencies and voluntary sector.

2 The vocabulary of management theory becomes predominantly that of commercial practice (market niche, product differentiation, sustainable competitive advantage).
3 A noticeable trend towards the homogenization of organization models. All organizations are normatively encouraged to adopt commercial modes of operation, especially where they are expected to lead directly to increased organizational performance and success.
4 The idea of running even one's own personal life as if it were a business becomes highlighted. Individuals should organize their lives around economic concepts of opportunity cost and operate under norms of overt market competition (Keat and Abercrombie 1990 quoted in Wilson 1992: 39).

Within the realm of organizational and work-based issues we can identify four different visions of a post-Fordist future: 1) *flexible specialization* which relates to issues such as technological development, and inter-firm relationships; 2) the *flexible firm model* which related to labour market issues and 3 and 4), *lean production* and the *enriching production* models which more properly limit themselves to organizational issues of production.

Flexible specialization

Piore and Sabel (1984) argue for the development of a second industrial divide or new production system which they call *flexible specialization* – a system which recognizes the possibility for strategic choice over production techniques, working practices and organizational forms. Flexible specialization relies upon a decentralized organizational form, the replacement of mechanized flow-line technology by new, more innovative production techniques utilizing multi-skilled and flexible workers supported by a teamwork environment better equipped to satisfy the demands of developing niche markets for high quality and customized products and services (Grint 1991: 296).

Micro-chip technology allowed for the critical distinguishing factor in the new

Table 1 From Fordism to Post Fordism

Fordism	Post-Fordism
Economy competition, technology and production process	
Protected national markets	*Global competition*
Mass production of standardized products, economies through fixed capital and labour productivity within the production process. Stock control on a just-in-case basis	Flexible production systems/small batch/multiple products in niche markets, economies through capital productivity between production and distribution. Stock control on a just-in-time basis
Bureaucratic, hierarchical and vertically integrated organizations, split into dispersed and remote site plants or branches	Flatter and flexible organizational structures alongside organizational decentralization, organizations moved to greenfield sites
Technology focused upon single purpose machinery	CNC, multi-purpose and adaptable machine tools
Compete by full capacity utilization and cost cutting	Compete by innovation, diversification, sub-contracting
Domination of manufacturers over retailers, producers over users	Domination of retailing
Labour and management	
Fragmented and standardized work tasks, strict division between mental and manual labour	Flexible specialization/multi-skilled workers, open ended tasks with closer integration of mental and manual labour.
Semi-skilled workforce represented by large general trade unions	Multi-skilled workers with no-strike agreements or by derecognition. Management strategies aimed at achieving high individual performance and people identified as a key organizational resource. Management theories lean towards human relations management supported by numerically flexible peripheral workers
Wages collectively bargained at national level	Individualized payment – PRP
Low trust/low discretion, majority employed in manufacturing sector and blue collar jobs	High trust/high discretion. Majority employed in service sector/white collar jobs
Little 'on the job training', little formal education required for most jobs	Regular 'on the job' training. Greater demand for 'knowledgeable workers
Small managerial and professional elite utilizing scientific management	Growing managerial and professional class/service class
Industrial/economic change seen as natural process of facilitating mass production and consumption	Need for change viewed as a natural result of facing up to economic crises and depressions.
Fairly predictable labour market histories	Unpredictable labour market histories due to technological change and increased economic uncertainty
Politics, culture and ideology	
Trade union solidarity and class based political affiliation	Decline in trade union membership and class based political affiliation
Importance of locality/class/gender based lifestyles	Fragmentation and pluralism, 'global' village
Cultural icons are the television set, the cinema, the theatre, other forms of collective entertainment. and the package holiday	Culture becomes individualized and fragmented through the Walkman, the computer game and travel becomes individualized through the packaging of the independent holiday
Mass consumption of consumer durable 'You can have any colour as long as it is black' (Ford)	Individualized consumption/consumer choice 'You can have any colour or size or shape you want' (Bennetton)

Table based on data gathered from numerous sources in bibliography.

system, that is its flexibility; flexibility in labour utilization, product range and design, CNC multi-purpose machine tools, batch sizes in which the scale of production can be switched to suit the flexibility and range of demand 'without any significant impact on overall operating costs' (Meegan 1988: 167). It is thus that *economies of scope* – the ability to produce a range of commodities to suit a wide range of consumer tastes, supports *economies of scale* – reductions in cost per unit – the byword of standardized mass production. Williams *et al.* (1987) question whether there is such a conceptual distance between flexible specialization and mass production and there is evidence that team working in the Nissan plants outside of Japan retain elements of Taylorist working practice and joint ventures between Japanese and American automotive firms, elements of Bureaucratic Scientific Management (Warner 1994).

The flexible firm

The demands of the new system of production require new types of labour contract and new skills profiles. Simply put, *functional flexibility* refers to the distinction between core and peripheral workers in which skilled, core workers – in return for relatively stable wages, access to an internal labour market and security of contract – allow themselves to become multi-skilled in firm or sector specific tasks. However, this was achieved at a price. Peripheral workers such as part time, temporary or subcontract workers who – more easily replaceable – became *numerically flexible* and retained their position in the work force only as and when required. The evidence suggests that there has been a large increase in this form of employment (Harvey 1989: 150). Half of all large firms in the UK have increased their utilization of subcontracted labour, with two-thirds of respondents to an ACAS survey reporting use of temporary workers across a range of industries and tasks. Part timers working 16 hours a week or less have increased significantly in the 1980s and 1990s and increased access to information technology has increased the numbers of home and teleworkers (Thompson and McHugh 1995: 176–7). Pollert (1988) however, questions whether the flexible firm is indeed new and points out that women workers and workers from ethnic background, have long historical experience of the peripheral labour market.

Lean production

Associated with the Toyota production system in Japan (see OHNO, T.; JAPANIZATION) and popularized through the work of Womack *et al.* (1990) who state that the 'principles of lean production can be applied equally in every industry across the globe' and 'the conversion to lean production will have a profound effect on human society – it will truly change the world' (1990: 8). Thus, although lean production is usually associated with the automotive sector, as it spreads beyond, the utilization of the model 'will change everything in almost every industry – choice for consumers, the nature of work, the fortune of companies, and ultimately, the fate of nations (Womack *et al.* 1990: 12). In contrast to mass production, lean production utilizes multi-skilled teams of workers, flexible multiple purpose machinery able to produce a variety of products. and is called *lean* because it uses half the human effort, manufacturing space, stock levels, investment in tools and product development time compared to mass production resulting in 'many fewer defects, and produces an ever growing variety of products' (Womack *et al.* 1990: 13). In terms of work organization it changes blue collar working methods by empowering workers, making work more challenging and stressful which in the process increases productivity by making them more responsible and anxious about making 'costly mistakes' (Womack *et al.* 1990: 14). Williams *et al.* (1992) dispute the veracity of the lean enterprise model outlined by Womack *et al.* on three main grounds: the empirical unsustainability of the difference between mass and lean production; the exaggerated claim of lean production's utilization of half the human effort and their failure to account for the peculiarity of the Japanese system of employee relations.

Enriched production

Based upon the Volvo production system the enriching production model is said to be more human centred, underpinned by a 'reflective production' system in which organizational development is seen in terms of active and co-creative people with the ability and will to create, gather and use knowledge (Volvo internal documents). Volvo's experiment in organizational design is unique in that they are based around individual learning processes, developed through co-operation with engineering, architectural, sociological and psychological practitioners actively involved in plant layout, new production technologies and the organization of work teams. In the first phase of implementation new working practices were aimed at reducing absenteeism and labour turnover. However, in an increasingly globalized environment they are now entering a more advanced phase in which performance criteria are now placed firmly alongside those of work organization. In Volvo's global empire there is no one dominant system of production outside of a recognition that global players have to take cognisance of local product, market and labour conditions. Thus for instance, we can find evidence of the presence of traditional mass production flow line technology alongside small batch, dock based technologies which have reverted to craft-based ideologies of the worker moving round the work in progress. In terms of payment, there are examples of traditional piece rates payments based around MTM (a system in which work is analysed before it is actually performed (Berggren 1992: 112)) and payment for knowledge systems based around the development of competence based training. What does distinguish the enriched production model from all the others is the widespread adoption of autonomous team-based forms of work organization which is moving rapidly towards such things as devolved decision making down to the lowest level in the team, the elimination of middle and supervisory levels of management, the use of rotating team leaders, and the widespread involvement of trade unions (see TRADE UNIONS) at all levels in the organization. As of yet, most of these developments have been limited to the organization's plants in Sweden with only spasmodic application elsewhere in Europe and the Americas.

5 Conclusion

During the 150 years after the first wave of industrialization, two factors coalesced to limit a generalized and strategic mode of labour regulation in the factory. First, there was a lack of systematic and nationally co-ordinated trade union resistance in the form of strikes and lockouts while it was only round the beginning of the twentieth century that national structures of collective industrial agreements began to be put in place. Equally, with inter-firm competition being largely based in local and regional market places it was difficult, if not impossible, for employers' organizations to have more than an ephemeral existence and only in times of local disputes between capital and labour. In the UK the beginnings of the Engineering Employers Federation signalled both the demise in the importance of local disputes and the institutionalization of bureaucratic, national level bargaining. Second, most business organizations in the nineteenth century were small scale, encompassing a range of labour contracts ranging from direct labour to the 'putting out' system, and it was only in the early years of the twentieth century that the 'chaotic and ad-hoc factories' were transformed into 'rationalized, well-ordered manufacturing settings' (quoted in Thompson and McHugh 1995: 24). However, economic growth in Germany, France and the USA challenged Britain's hegemony in global market places which alongside the increasing links between nationally based institutions of finance capital tended to move competition onto a global stage which required a more disciplined organizational structure better able to control the increasing size of the business organization. These developments required not only new forms of functional management – such as the personnel function – but also the isolation of the managerial function as worthy of intellectual analysis. Writers such as Fayol and Urwick began to publish across a range of managerial and organizational issues in Europe and North America. However it was Taylor's theory of Scientific Management and its concentration on the control of the labour process which has had the most profound impact upon the managerial process outside purely academic circles. In terms of the labour process scientific management was based upon three main principles:

1 The separation between the design and planning of works tasks and their execution.
2 The disaggregation of work tasks into their smallest possible component part and the allocation of the appropriate individual workers to carry out these 'deskilled' tasks.
3 Scientific methods should be utilized to find out the best, most efficient and quickest way to carry out these tasks.

Between 1913 and 1915, these principles were applied and developed in the Detroit factories of Henry Ford, primarily through the introduction of the mechanized assembly line and the Five Dollar day. Just how far these processes were innovatory is open to question and much like the current interest in Japanese forms of production the importance of Fordist production techniques has been the subject of heated debate and has created much controversy within academic circles. Indeed questions as to the precise relationship between mass production, mass consumption and mechanization have been rekindled by the current interest in the transfer of Japanese production methods to Europe and the Americas (Williams *et al.* 1987). However, just as Fordism and Taylorism are distinct, albeit related concepts, Fordism itself relates to more than just an analysis of the production methods initiated in the US automotive industry in the early decades of the twentieth century. The concept of Fordism has entered the lexicon of such diverse disciplines as human geography; education and training; social policy; political science and economics and has concerned itself with such issues as fiscal policy, welfare provision, consumer demand, democracy and popular culture. It is at this level that the concept takes a wider, more inclusive and contemporary importance, for it could be argued that Fordism stands for all our experience of the modern world. At a general level, it parallels the development of the bureaucratic organization, the welfare state, the neo-corporatist post-war compromise between capital and labour and Keynesian economic restructuring.

However, there are two distinct schools of thought which have to explain the nature of the Fordist compromise and the relationship between economic and social policy, manufacturing output and performance; and the rapid rate of economic growth between 1945 and 1973. Although there are real differences between the 'regulationists' such as Aglietta (1979) and the 'Institutionalists' (Piore and Sabel 1984). They both agree that our understanding of the interaction between 'boom' and 'stagnation' in western economies lies in the rise and decline of Fordism and mass production (Meegan 1988: 138). What distinguishes the two positions is that the regulationists see Fordism, or state Monopoly Capitalism, teleologically, as a distinct, but necessary, stage in capitalist development resulting from the crisis in the previous, competitive, mode of capitalism. This stage is itself ridden with crisis tendencies such as the oil and debt crises of the mid 1970s, which necessarily leads to the next and current stage defined as neo-Fordism. The form and structure of neo-Fordism are determined by the nature of Fordism and the form that the crisis of Fordism took and not by the strategic choices of key social actors. The Institutionalists reject 'the acceptance by the Marxist regulationists of a 'natural law' or 'narrow path' of capitalist technological and industrial development and emphasize 'instead the role of "social struggle" and the accidents of history' (Meegan 1988: 145).

Consequently, the institutionalists offer a series of alternative visions of the future open to capital. At the cross-roads of the 'first industrial divide', mass production was *the* chosen alternative as opposed to a model based on the development of craft skills. So although political, economic and social factors coincided in favour of the chosen path the *choice* could have been different (Meegan 1988: 146). For the 'institutionalists' then the crisis of Fordism is indeterminate and open. They suggest two alternative possibilities. A series of external shocks such as the oil crisis set an 'inflationary spiral' prompting 'recessionary policy responses and break up of mass markets' (Meegan 1988: 151). An alternative theory revolves around a set of internal, structural problems within mass production such as the disjuncture between 'productive capacity' and levels of consumer demand leading to 'market saturation' and a reduction in consumer spending and a crisis in profitability. Piore and Sabel remain neutral as to the validity of these two positions (Meegan 1988: 151). The regulationists have no such problems and see the crisis very much in terms of Piore and Sabel's second proposition and they see 'post--Fordism as generating a new cohesion, a neo-Fordism' (Aglietta 1979: 385).

In terms of post-Fordism – a term which itself covers both *flexible specialization* and *neo-Fordism* the visions of the 'institutionalists' and the 'regulationists' are closer together. For Piore and Sabel the 'Second Industrial Divide' implies a choice between patching up Fordism into what they call 'Multi-national Keynesianism' or the development of *flexible specialization* (Piore and Sabel 1988: 164). The presence of micro-chip technology and such external forces as the discursive politics of the '*new times*' replace class-based turmoil, with struggles around ethnicity, gender, sexuality and ecology. This phase presents a new 'futurology, in which the workplace becomes more democratic and work itself regains some of the intrinsic value associated with craft-based forms of production. However:

> While ambition, satisfaction, fulfilment and co-operation are commonly present in the office and on the shopfloor, they continue to co-exist alongside (and in many cases remain secondary to) feelings of frustration, boredom, resistance and the pursuit of strategies designed to make it easier to get through the working day
>
> (Noon and Blyton 1997: 2).

TERRY WALLACE
CARDIFF BUSINESS SCHOOL
UNIVERSITY OF CARDIFF

Further reading

(References cited in the text marked *)

* Aglietta, M. (1979) *A Theory of Capitalist Regulation* London: New Left Books. (Marxist analysis of the Fordist Mode of Production and outline of Regulation Theory.)
* Berggren, C. (1992) *The Volvo Experience: Alternatives to Lean production in the Swedish Auto Industry.* London: Macmillan (Description of working practices and technological structures in Volvo's and Saab's truck and bus plants.)
Braverman, H. (1974) 'Labour and Monopoly Capital: the Deregulation of Work in the Twentieth Century'. New York: *Monthly Review*. (A marxist critique of Taylorism and its application across a range of different environments.)
* Brenner, R. and Glick, M. (1991) 'The Regulation Approach: Theory and History' *New Left Review 188, July/August 1991.* (Theoretical critique of regulation theory, particularly the work of Aglietta.)
* Gramsci, A. (1978) 'Americanism and Fordism' in Hoare, Q. and Nowell Smith, G. (eds) *Selection from Prison Notebooks* London: Lawrence and Wishart. (Analysis of the effects of the spread of Fordism on European trade unionism and working class political activity.)
* Grint, K. (1991) *The Sociology of Work: An Introduction* London: Polity (Overview of Regulation theory and the work of the Institutionalists.)
* Harvey, D. (1989) *The Condition of Postmodernity* Oxford: Blackwell (Traces the development of Fordism and Post-Fordism in cultural, political, social and economic environments.)
* Hounsell, D. (1984) *From the American System to Mass Production, 1800–1932* Baltimore: Johns Hopkins University Press (Technical description of pre-Fordist and Fordist methods of production.)
* Keat, R. and Abercrombie, N. (eds) (1990) *Enterprise Culture* London: Routledge. (Sociological account of the rise of Thatcherism and the enterprise culture in the UK.)
* Littler, C. (1985) 'Taylorism, Fordism and job design' in D. Knights, H. Willmott and D. Collin-

son (eds) *Job Redesign* Aldershot: Gower (Historical account of scientific management in the US and Europe.)

* Meegan, R. (1988) 'A Crisis of Mass Production' in Allen, J. and Massey, D. (eds) *The Economy in Question* London: Sage (Traces the genesis of Regulation Theory and the work of Piore and Sabel from the perspective of Human Geography.)

* Noon, M. and Blyton, P. (1997) *The Realities of Work* London: Macmillan (Analyses of skill, gender, practices of 'making out' and emotional labour in the contemporary workplace.)

Phillimore, A.J. (1989) 'Flexible specialization, work organization and skills: approaching the "second industrial divide" ', New Technology, Work and Employment 4, 79–91 (Outline of the introduction of flexible specialization in the textile industry.)

* Piore, M.J. and Sabel, C.F. (1984) *The Second Industrial Divide* New York: Basic (Seminal text in which flexible specialization is opposed to mass production for the first time.)

* Pollert, A (1988) 'The Flexible Firm: Fixation or Fact?', *Work, Employment and Society*, 2 (3): 281–316 (Seen as *the* critique of the flexible firm model from a feminist and socialist perspective.)

* Thompson, P. and McHugh, D. (1995) *Work Organizations: A Critical Introduction* London: Macmillan (Standard textbook on the development of different forms of working practices.)

* Warner, M. (1994) 'Japanese Culture, Western Management: Taylorism and Human Resources in Japan', *Organization Studies* 15 (4) (Highlights the impact of Taylorism on Japanese management practice.)

* Williams, K., Cutler, T., Williams, J. and Haslam, C. (1987) 'The end of mass production?', *Economy and Society* 16 (3): 405–439.

Wilson, D. (1992) *A Strategy of Change* London: Routledge.

* Womack, J., Jones, D. and Roos, D. (1990) *The Machine That Changed the World* New York: Macmillan. (Prescriptive and atheoretical account of the Toyota production system and its application across all sectors of industry.)

See also: BEDAUX, C.E.; COLLECTIVE BARGAINING; GILBRETH, F.B. AND GILBRETH, L.E.M.; INDUSTRIAL RELATIONS IN EUROPE; INDUSTRIAL RELATIONS IN JAPAN; INDUSTRIAL RELATIONS IN THE USA; JAPANIZATION; LABOUR PROCESS; OHNO, Y.; TAYLOR, F.W.; TRADE UNIONS

Human resource management, international

Overview

The successful operation of a multinational firm is contingent upon the availability of technology, technological know-how, capital and human resources. Without a highly developed pool of human resources (including managerial and technical talent), technology, technological know-how and capital cannot be effectively and efficiently allocated or transferred from corporate headquarters to the scattered subsidiaries. Developing and managing this managerial and technical talent is the function of international human resource management.

International human resource management has five main dimensions: first, the selection and recruitment of qualified individuals capable of furthering organizational goals; second, the training and development of personnel at all levels to maximize organizational performance; third, the assessment of employee performance to ensure that organizational goals are met; fourth, the retention of competent corporate personnel who can continue to facilitate the attainment of organizational goals; and fifth, the management of the interface between labour and management to ensure smooth organizational functioning.

This entry examines the international dimension of these five aspects of human resource management. Where relevant, the international human resource management policies and practices of a sample of US,

European, Japanese and Australian multinationals will be discussed and compared.

1 Selection and recruitment

An assumption is often made that an effective manager at home will also be an effective manager abroad. Moreover, many companies continue to focus primarily on the technical competence criterion for expatriate assignments. There are two reasons for this: (1) task requirements are usually more easily identifiable; and (2) since technical competence almost always prevents immediate failure on the job, particularly in high pressure situations, the selectors play safe by placing a heavy emphasis on technical qualifications and little on the individual's ability to adapt to a foreign environment. Both these assumptions are suspect, however, when one examines the rate of expatriate failure and the reasons for such failure.

Some US multinationals experienced expatriate failure rates as high as 30–40 per cent; in contrast, European, Japanese, and Australian multinationals experienced significantly lower rates of expatriate failure (Tung 1990). Nevertheless, these casualties of selection not only represent substantial lost investment, they also constitute a human resource waste since most of those who fail seem to have a noteworthy home track record (see HUMAN RESOURCE MANAGEMENT). Failures often constitute a heavy personal blow to the expatriates' self-esteem. Hence, even if they are accepted back by corporate headquarters, it may take some time before they regain confidence in their own abilities. The unsettling experience for the person's family, both emotionally and physically, represents yet another consequence.

What are the causes of expatriate failure? In the US sample the most important reasons for expatriate failure, in descending order of importance, were:

1 inability of the manager's spouse to adjust to a different physical or cultural environment;
2 the manager's inability to adapt to a different physical or cultural environment;
3 other family-related problems;
4 the manager's personality or emotional immaturity;
5 the manager's inability to cope with the responsibilities posed by overseas work;
6 the manager's lack of technical competence;
7 the manager's lack of motivation to work overseas.

These findings are consistent with other studies which show that the family situation and an inability to relate are factors usually responsible for failure or poor performance abroad. The family situation is also the principal cause of failure among European and Australian multinationals. For Japanese multinationals the most important reasons for failure were significantly different. In this sample the reasons for failure, given in descending order of importance, were:

1 the manager's inability to cope with the larger responsibilities posed by the overseas work;
2 the manager's inability to adapt to a different physical or cultural environment;
3 the manager's personality or emotional immaturity;
4 the manager's lack of technical competence;
5 inability of the manager's spouse to adjust to a different physical or cultural environment;
6 lack of motivation to work overseas;
7 other family-related problems.

In Japan status shock, not culture shock, is a primary cause of failure. The Japanese, who are more used to working as a team, suddenly take on the burden of overseeing a diverse range of responsibilities and functions, in isolation, in a foreign subsidiary.

The principal causes of failure among US, European and Australian multinationals are the family situation and lack of human relation skills of the manager, rather than technical incompetence. This brings us to the question of what should be the selection criteria for overseas assignments.

Selection criteria

Overseas managerial assignments can be classified into four major categories: (1) the chief executive officer (CEO), whose responsibility is to oversee and direct the entire foreign operation; (2) the functional head, whose job is to establish functional departments in a foreign subsidiary; (3) the troubleshooter, whose function is to analyse and solve specific operational problems; and (4) the operative, or rank and file.

Jobs in each of these categories involve varying degrees of contact with the host culture and varying assignment lengths. For example, one would expect a CEO to have more extensive contact with members of the local community than a troubleshooter, and the troubleshooter's job in a certain country to be of shorter duration than the CEO's.

It is possible to create an eighteen-point criteria list for expatriate assignments across these four job types:

- experience within the company
- technical knowledge of the business
- knowledge of the language of the host country
- overall experience and education
- managerial talent
- interest in overseas work
- initiative and creativity
- independence
- previous overseas experience
- respect for the culture of the host country
- sex/gender of candidate
- age
- stability of marital relationship
- spouse's and family's adaptability
- adaptability and flexibility in a new environmental setting
- maturity and emotional stability
- communicative ability
- same criteria as for other comparable jobs at home

For US multinationals, for each job category certain criteria were considered more important than others. Attributes like 'adaptability and flexibility in a new environmental setting' and 'communicative ability' were more frequently identified as very important for jobs requiring more extensive contact with the local community (CEO and functional head) than for jobs that were more technically orientated (troubleshooter). Despite this recognition of the need to select candidates who are adaptable and flexible in new environmental settings, only 5 per cent of the US companies surveyed administered any test to assess these attributes. However, nearly half of the companies did interview both the candidate and spouse to gauge their interest in living and working overseas. This latter practice may reflect the growing awareness that the spouse's attitude towards an overseas posting can be pivotal to success. A potential problem is where the candidate and spouse feign enthusiasm for fear that a negative attitude towards an overseas posting may adversely affect the candidate's career within the company.

For the west European sample the most important criterion for selecting candidates in the CEO category was 'managerial talent'. The most important criterion for selecting candidates in the functional head, trouble-shooter and operative categories was 'technical knowledge of business'. 'Adaptability and flexibility in a new environmental setting' was also considered very important for all job categories except operatives. 'Interest in overseas work' was cited as a very important criterion for each of the four job categories by a majority of the firms, although this was not cited as frequently as the other aforementioned criteria. While 'adaptability and flexibility' was not mentioned as the most important criterion, 21 per cent of the European firms used tests to assess the candidate's relational abilities. In common with the US multinationals, many of the European firms conducted interviews with both the candidate and spouse to determine their interest in working abroad.

In the Japanese sample, like their European counterparts, the most important criterion for selecting candidates in the CEO category was 'managerial talent', and the most important criterion for selecting candidates in the functional head, troubleshooter and operative categories was 'technical knowledge of business'. Most of the Japanese companies considered 'experience within the company' a very important criterion for jobs in three of the four job categories (CEO, functional head and troubleshooter). This perhaps reflects the system of employment in Japanese society which emphasizes length of service in the company and experience acquired over that time. 'Adaptability and flexibility in a new environmental setting' was also cited as a very important criterion for each of the four categories by a majority of the firms, although this was not cited as frequently as the other criteria. None of the Japanese firms used any psychological test to determine the candidate's relational abilities. While the majority of companies interviewed the candidate about the overseas position, none of them included the spouse in such meetings. This was very different from the practice in US and European multinationals and could be attributed to the fact that Japanese culture has a different view of the spouse's (in this case, the wife's) role and status in the family.

While Japanese multinationals may not administer a specific test or include the spouse in the interview, the characteristics of the Japanese employment system are such that it permits ample opportunity for the supervisor to determine a candidate's suitability for an overseas assignment. Given the intense socialization during the after-hours sessions in drinking bars (*karaoke*) and restaurants, a supervisor often has detailed knowledge of an employee's background and family situation. Most Japanese companies also keep very detailed personnel inventories on their career staff. These are compiled from the annual or semi-annual performance evaluations completed by the individual, his or her immediate supervisor and the chief of the division. In addition, candidates who are considered for an overseas assignment (excluding those who have been selected to study abroad) typically have been with the company for ten years. Hence, the company has ample time to assess capabilities and qualifications, including adaptability to a new environmental setting.

In Australian multinationals, while the criteria used for selecting candidates for international assignments varied, two dimensions stood out. One pertained to the willingness of the individual to undertake the overseas assignment. In fact, several of the multinationals relied exclusively on volunteers. Given the present emphasis on international experience in most Australian corporations and the desire of many Australians to travel to foreign lands, there appears to be no shortage of highly qualified individuals who would volunteer for an overseas assignment. A second major criterion was the potential of the candidate for senior management positions. In other words, an overseas assignment is used as part of the overall career development strategy of high flyers in the company. Some of the Australian multinationals surveyed tried to select those who had demonstrated a certain resilience in their character and who were tolerant of things foreign. Several of the Australian executives indicated that they look for a 'Paul Hogan' mentality: in the Australian hit movie, Crocodile Dundee, the hero (played by actor Paul Hogan) typified the Australian spirit and mentality – adventurous, friendly and adaptable. A number of Australian executives perceived this trait as critical to success in living and working abroad. Even those Australian companies which did not use the adaptability criterion in their selection decision believed that it would be important to incorporate this dimension in the future.

A question can be raised as to whether the gender of the candidate should be taken into consideration in identifying appropriateness for an international assignment. Over one-half of the west European and Japanese multinationals used 'sex/gender of a candidate' as a criterion in all four job categories. Gender was not mentioned as a criterion by any of the US multinationals. This is probably due to differences in equal employment legislation. Despite the assertion by US multinationals that the gender of the candidate is not a consideration in the selection decision, the low percentage of women who are sent on expatriate assignments may suggest that there is a

discrepancy between officially stated policy and actual practice. In the late 1990s about 17 per cent of US expatriates were female, an increase from 5 per cent a decade ago (Tung and Arthur Andersen 1997) (see WOMEN MANAGERS IN ORGANIZATIONS).

What are the reasons for such limited use of women expatriates? Sixty-nine per cent of the nearly 5,000 respondents in US multinationals surveyed by the firm of Moran, Stahl & Boyer (1988) did not perceive any advantage in expatriating a woman over a man, citing the following barriers to the use of women in overseas postings:

1 cultural prejudices and limitations;
2 male-dominated management group in the company;
3 employment of the accompanying male spouse;
4 inflexibility and resentment of male peers, subordinates and superiors;
5 lack of support groups for working expatriate females;
6 lack of access to local male networks;
7 pregnancy;
8 acceptance of working women in the expatriate community;
9 militant feminism of some US female employees;
10 unwillingness of women to accept foreign assignments.

Despite their limited use in overseas assignments, how have women expatriates fared? The same study showed that 93 per cent of the respondents who had expatriated women abroad were extremely satisfied with their performance overseas. Similarly, in another study of women expatriates in Pacific Asia it was found that women were accepted by Asian businesses (Adler 1987).

A barrier to the use of women as expatriates was employment of the accompanying male spouse. According to another survey of twenty chief executives of US multinationals, the majority of respondents believed that the issue of dual-career families will become a major problem confronting their companies in the next decade (Tung 1988). Because most Japanese wives do not work outside their home, the issue of dual-career couples is not a concern among Japanese multinationals. In both European and Australian multinationals this problem was less prominent because of the lower percentage of women who were employed as professionals in these countries.

Selection of parent-, host- and third-country nationals

Multinationals have three sources of human power supply available to them: (1) parent-country nationals (PCNs), or those who are citizens of the home country of the multinational corporation; (2) host-country nationals (HCNs), or citizens of the country of foreign operation; and (3) third-country nationals (TCNs), or nationals who are neither citizens of the home country of the multinational nor of the country in which the foreign operation is located.

Analysis thus far has focused on the use of PCNs. The reasons for using PCNs, HCNs

and TCNs are multiple and varied, and the selection criteria may be summarized as in Figure 1.

It is noteworthy that west European multinationals seem to use expatriate assignments as a mechanism for developing an international orientation among their management personnel. In the 1990s, US multinationals are also following this trend (Tung and Arthur Andersen 1997). In order to compete effectively in a world characterized by the globalization of industries, European multinationals recognize the need to develop this orientation among its management personnel.

The extent to which PCNs, HCNs and TCNs are used at various levels of management in different geographic regions of the world varies. For the US and west European samples, HCNs are used to a much greater extent at all levels of management in developed regions of the world compared to less-developed countries. This is logical as one would expect the more developed nations to

	US			EUROPE			JAPAN		
	PCN	HCN	TCN	PCN	HCN	TCN	PCN	HCN	TCN
Start-up foreign enterprise	X			X					
Technical expertise	X		X	X					
Familiarity with culture		X			X				
Knowledge of language		X			X				
Reduced costs		X							
Good public relations		X							
TCN best person for the job			X			X			
Development of an international orientation for headquarters' management				X					
PCN best person for the job							X		
HCN best person for the job								X	

(Not applicable. None of Jap. MNCs used TCNs, except for Africa)

Figure 1 Reasons for using parent-country nationals (PCNs), host-country nationals (HCNs) and third-country nationals (TCNs)
Source: Tung (1982)

have a larger pool of personnel that would possess the necessary human power and technical skills to staff management-level positions. Unfortunately, the countries staffed by a smaller percentage of HCNs at management levels of US and European subsidiaries tend to be ones whose culture, values and business practices differ substantially from those at home. Consequently, the issue of selecting a candidate who would be able to live and work in a very dissimilar cultural environment still constitutes a pressing problem.

Japanese multinationals, on the other hand, employ considerably more PCNs in their overseas operations at the senior and middle-management levels. This phenomenon may be attributed, in part at least, to the significant differences that exist between Japanese and non-Japanese styles of management which can create problems of integration, particularly at the senior management level. One problem pertains to language differences. Virtually all communication between corporate headquarters in Japan and the foreign subsidiary is in Japanese. There are very few non-Japanese who are thoroughly proficient in the Japanese language. The more extensive use of PCNs at the senior and middle management levels in Japanese multinationals may also be a function of the stage of internationalization of Japanese firms. Compared with their US and European counterparts, Japanese companies are more recent entrants into the multinational scene. Aside from the large general trading companies, the majority of Japanese firms only began overseas expansion in the 1960s. In start-up phases there is a greater tendency for multinationals to use PCNs.

Another characteristic of international human resource management practices in Japanese multinationals is the limited use of TCNs. Except for Africa, the Japanese multinationals studied did not use TCNs at all. When asked why, the Japanese multinationals indicated that since they already experience difficulties in trying to integrate a local workforce with their expatriate staff, they do not wish to confound the situation by adding a third dimension, namely TCNs.

The trend towards the increased use of HCNs at various levels of management in overseas operations has continued for US multinationals. While acknowledging the obvious advantages associated with the use of HCNs, such as reduced costs and greater familiarity with the local environment, there can be limitations associated with relying exclusively on HCNs. Because of geographic distance and cultural differences, corporate control becomes more tenuous.

Duration of overseas assignment

Most overseas assignments of US multinationals are for two or three years. Such short stints are not conducive to high performance because the expatriate barely has time to adjust before transfer home or to another overseas location. Research has shown that when expatriates are exempted from active managerial responsibilities in the first several months of foreign assignment, particularly to countries where the cultural distance is great, it can facilitate acculturation. However, extending the overseas assignment can lead to concern by the employee about repatriation.

Japanese multinationals tend to have a longer duration of overseas assignment, with an average of five years, except for assignments to the Middle East, which are generally of two years' duration. This latter policy stems from the perceived harsh living conditions in that geographic region. The longer duration of overseas assignments means that the Japanese expatriate has more time to adjust. Many Japanese multinationals do not expect the expatriate to perform to full capacity until the third year of assignment, as the first two years abroad are viewed as part of the basic period of adjustment.

Except for overseas assignments that are strictly for career development purposes, expatriate assignments in European multinationals average five years or more. Some of the European multinationals allow an adjustment period of up to one year. Besides allowing more time to adjust, the longer duration of overseas assignment also provides a greater incentive for the expatriate to learn more about the host country, including its language.

2 Training for cross-cultural encounters

The focus here is on training programmes that are designed to improve the relational skills crucial to effective performance in expatriate job assignments. Training programmes or procedures employed typically fall into the five categories below, presented in ascending order of rigour. They constitute a continuum ranging from low rigour (area studies) to highly rigorous training programmes (field experiences). Depending upon the type of job and the country of foreign assignment the individual should be exposed to one or several of these programmes (see CULTURE, CROSS-NATIONAL; ORGANIZATION CULTURE).

Area studies programmes. These include environmental briefing and cultural orientation programmes designed to provide the trainee with information about a particular country's sociopolitical history, geography, stage of economic development and cultural institutions. The content is factual in nature.

The basic assumption behind this approach is that knowledge will lead to increased empathy, thus modifying behavioural patterns and facilitating intercultural relationships. Although there is some indication that increased knowledge will remove some of the fear and aggression that tend to be aroused by the unknown, evidence that knowledge will invariably result in increased empathy is sparse and usually not the result of rigorous experimental control. When used alone area studies programmes are inadequate for preparing trainees for assignments which require extensive contact with the local community overseas. Furthermore, since cultural differences between any two countries could be innumerable, training programmes of an area studies nature could not possibly pass on to the trainee all the knowledge that would be required over the duration of the overseas assignment.

Culture assimilator. This consists of a series of seventy-five to one hundred short episodes briefly describing an intercultural encounter. Encounters which are judged (by a panel of experts, including returned expatriates) to be critical to the interaction situations between members of two different cultures are included.

Studies have shown that this training device can be effective preparation for cross-cultural encounters. Culture assimilators, however, are designed specifically for people who have to be assigned overseas on short notice. Consequently, where time is not a critical factor, and in assignments which require extensive contact with members of the local community, this technique should be supplemented by the more rigorous training programmes.

Language training. The candidate is taught the language, usually verbal only, of the host country. While knowledge of the host country's language can facilitate cross-cultural interaction, it often involves months, or sometimes years, before a candidate can master the foreign language.

Sensitivity training. These programmes focus upon learning at the affective level and are designed to develop an attitudinal flexibility within the trainees so that they can become aware of and acclimatize to unfamiliar modes of behaviour and value systems. Although the effectiveness of sensitivity training sessions has been questioned, there is some indication that sensitivity training can reduce racial/ethnic prejudice.

Field experiences. These involve sending the candidate to the country of assignment or microcultures in the home country (for example, Indian reservations, urban black ghettos) where the trainees may undergo some of the emotional stress that can be expected while living and working with people from a different culture or subculture. Research indicates that even though differences in cultural content exist between these microcultures and the country to which the trainee is ultimately assigned, trainees seem to benefit from an encounter with people whose way of life is different from their own, since the process of adaptation can be similar. The US Peace Corps has used this technique successfully with their volunteers.

These programmes vary in their focus upon cognitive and affective learning and in the medium of instruction, information content, time and resources required. They are by no means mutually exclusive and should be complementary. Japanese multinationals by far provide the most rigorous training to prepare their expatriates for cross-cultural encounters. While the type and nature of programmes provided by the Japanese multinationals vary, a typical programme would include the following components.

(1) *Language training*. Most Japanese companies sponsor intensive language training programmes, ranging from three months to one year in duration. To promote fluency in a foreign language, many Japanese companies invite Caucasians to share the same dormitories in order to provide their trainees with ample opportunity to practice their language skills and to gain a better understanding of the foreign country.

(2) *Field experience*. Many Japanese multinationals select members of their staff to serve as trainees in their overseas offices for one year. As trainees their primary mission is to observe closely and, hence, learn about the company's foreign operations. The trainees also try to acquire as much information as possible about the foreign country, including non-economic variables. This kind of training prepares them for an eventual offshore assignment, which is viewed as part of one's career development.

(3) *Graduate programmes abroad*. Every year many Japanese multinationals send between ten and twenty career staff members to attend graduate business, law and engineering programmes abroad. The company pays tuition and all expenses in addition to the employee's regular salary. While attending graduate school the Japanese employee is exposed to foreign principles of management which would prepare him for an eventual overseas assignment. Furthermore, the two years abroad would allow the Japanese employee to experience first hand the problems of living in and adapting to a foreign society.

(4) *In-house training programmes*. Besides language training the expatriates take courses in international finance and international economics and are exposed to environmental briefings about the country of assignment.

(5) *Outside agencies*. Besides in-house training programmes there are several institutes in Japan that prepare expatriates for overseas assignments. The Institute for International Studies and Training, for example, was established under the auspices of the Japanese Ministry of International Trade and Industry in 1967. It offers three-month and one-year residential programmes.

3 A contingency framework for selection and training

In light of the different categories of overseas job assignments and the contributions of various factors to success on the job, any comprehensive selection and training paradigm has to incorporate a complex set of variables and allow for their interaction. The selection criteria and training programmes that should be used for different categories of overseas assignments can be summarized in a contingency framework of selection and training shown in Figure 2.

Due to the variability of each situation in terms of the country of foreign assignment and the task to be performed, constant weights applicable to all instances could not be assigned to each of these factors. A more feasible strategy is to adopt a contingency approach to the selection and training of personnel for overseas assignment (see ORGANIZATION BEHAVIOUR).

This approach requires a clear identification of task, environment and the psychological characteristics of the individual under consideration. Before headquarters launches a search (at home) for an appropriate individual to fill an overseas job, it should consider if the job in question can be filled by a HCN. If the answer is yes, this alternative source should certainly be considered. If the position cannot be filled by a HCN then a search must be conducted among those who are already with domestic operations or within competing industries (either PCNs or TCNs).

An indication should always be obtained as to whether a candidate is willing to serve abroad. If the individual is averse to serving abroad then no training programme is capable of changing this basic attitude. If the individual is willing to live and work in a foreign

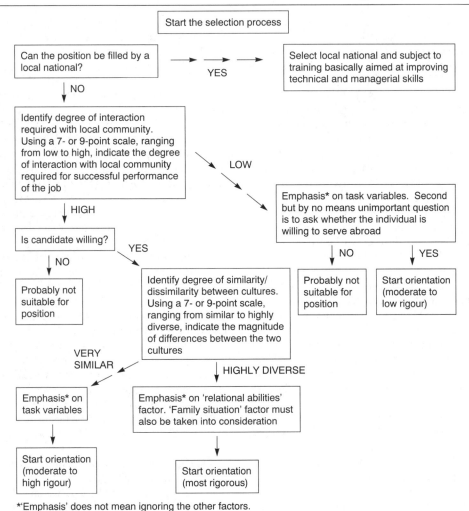

Figure 2 Flow chart of the selection–decision process
Source: Tung (1981)

environment an indication of the extent to which he/she is tolerant of cultural differences and his/her ability to work towards intercultural cooperation should be obtained. Several psychometric instruments are available for assessing a candidate's suitability for an overseas assignment.

Another step in the decision process is the identification of the degree of interaction with the local community that is required by the job. In positions involving extensive contact

with the culture and an understanding of the local value system (such as CEOs and functional heads), 'relational abilities' and 'environmental variables' become more critical and should become dominant factors in the selection decision. The selector should then proceed to examine the degree to which the foreign environment differs from the home situation. This is referred to as the cultural distance. If the cultural distance is low, that is, differences are insignificant (such as those between the USA and Canada), the selection should focus primarily on task variables. Where cultural distance is great, the selection decision should focus on the 'relational abilities' and 'family situation' factors.

The subsequent step involves the provision of training programmes to prepare candidates for cross-cultural encounters. In jobs requiring a great deal of interaction with the local community and where the differences between the two cultures are great, the candidate should be subjected to all five types of training, with particular emphasis on sensitivity training and field experiences. In jobs requiring minimal contact with the local community and where the differences between cultures are small, the area studies programme would probably be sufficient. Between these extremes is a continuum of situations requiring varying degrees of contact with the local culture and involving varying magnitudes of difference between the cultures. Human resource administrators should locate the job under consideration along this continuum and determine the type of training programme that would be suitable for the expatriate in question.

Research has shown that firms which used more appropriate selection criteria and training programmes for each of the four job categories experienced significantly lower rates of expatriate failure (Tung 1981; Arthur and Bennett 1995).

4 Assessment of performance

The international aspect of performance assessment raises three basic questions: (1) what standards should be used in assessing performance abroad?; (2) who should perform the evaluation?; and (3) what time horizon should be used in assessing performance?

Standards in assessing performance

There are four basic approaches to assessing performance in the multinational context: (1) ethnocentric (home country standards); (2) polycentric (host country standards); (3) regiocentric (standards within a given geographic region); and (4) geocentric (global standards) (Heenan and Perlmutter 1979).

While the appraisal of an expatriate's performance should, in theory, be separate from the overall assessment of a foreign subsidiary's performance, in reality, the two often run in parallel. Thus, executives who operate in a subsidiary which is profitable tend to be evaluated positively, regardless of their actual performance. Conversely, in a subsidiary which is not profitable, even though the factors responsible for the loss are beyond the executives' control, corporate headquarters' assessment of their performance would generally be negative.

Where ethnocentric standards are used to evaluate expatriate performance, the latter may be liable for factors or situations which are beyond their control. In countries where there is rapid depreciation of the local currency, and/or hyperinflation accompanied by government price controls, the subsidiary may operate at a loss, particularly where the local currency has to be converted or translated back into the currency of the home country. For this, expatriates may be penalized even though they may be performing as efficiently as possible under the circumstances.

On the other hand, where poly- and regiocentric standards are used to evaluate an expatriate's performance, there is little incentive for the person to adopt strategies which can maximize the firm's global position. Where the firm chooses to adopt geocentric standards, which may entail, for example, the rationalization of production activities around the world, leading to plant closures or worker layoffs in some locations, host governments may not view such policies favourably. This dilemma epitomizes the classic tension between a national/local responsiveness strategy and a global rationalization strategy.

To overcome some of the problems associated with the use of ethnocentric standards, it has been suggested that a 'difficulty level' index should be incorporated into the assessment of an expatriate's performance (Oddou and Mendenhall 1991). This index would take into consideration three factors: (1) the operational language used in the subsidiary (operational language refers to the language used in the day-to-day operations of the subsidiary); (2) cultural distance; and (3) the stability of factors which affect the expatriate's performance.

If expatriates are not proficient in the operational language it may take them longer to communicate with others both within and outside the context of the work situation. The higher the cultural distance, the higher the index. Similarly, the more unstable the factors, such as volatile exchange rates, the higher the index. Thus, for a 'somewhat more difficult' country, performance appraisal would be multiplied by an index factor of 1.2, whereas for a country which is 'much more difficult' the index factor would be 1.6.

Who should perform the evaluation?

A related issue is who has the necessary perspective to assess the expatriate's performance. If, for example, corporate headquarters were to perform the assessment, they may not have a full and accurate understanding of the circumstances and situations affecting the employee's performance. On the other hand, if the assessment were to be performed by the local management, the latter may not have the perspective necessary to evaluate performance within the broader context of the firm's global strategy. To obtain a more accurate picture of the expatriate's performance, both corporate headquarters and local management should be involved.

Time horizon to be used in assessing performance

US multinationals generally possess a short-term orientation with regard to planning and assessment of performance. This overemphasis on short-term results may be detrimental to the attainment of the long-term goals of the company. In contrast, European, Japanese and Australian multinationals espouse a longer term orientation in their human resource management practices. In these areas employers are generally more tolerant of circumstances that may temporarily

affect a person's performance. Consequently, they tend to make allowances for performance that is below average in the initial period of assignment abroad (see HUMAN RESOURCE MANAGEMENT).

5 Retention of personnel

Two factors which can affect a firm's ability to retain competent corporate personnel to meet their international human resource management needs are: (1) compensation – is there adequate compensation for service abroad? and (2) repatriation – does the overseas assignment have a positive impact upon the expatriate's subsequent career advancement within the organization on repatriation?

Compensation

The typical cost of expatriating a family abroad is three to four times base salary. A compensation package is comprised of base salary and one or more of the following allowances/premiums.

(1) *Cost-of-living differential*. This takes into consideration the differences in costs in various parts of the world so that expatriates can enjoy the same, if not better, standard of living they were accustomed to at home.

(2) *Foreign service premium*. Besides cost-of-living differentials, some multinationals pay a foreign service premium to induce an employee to accept a foreign assignment.

(3) *Relocation allowance*. Some multinationals pay a lump sum outright to offset non-recurring incidental costs necessitated by relocation.

(4) *Hardship and danger premiums*. Danger pay applies to specific emergency situations such as war, revolution or political unrest, and is discontinued once the emergency situation ceases. Hardship premiums, on the other hand, represent an ongoing allowance for assignments to countries with harsh living conditions, such as climate or inadequate amenities.

Besides monetary incentives many multinationals adopt other measures to make assignments to hardship locations more bearable, such as shorter durations of overseas assignments and more frequent vacations to seaside resorts or home leave.

Repatriation

Although companies make an effort to facilitate adaptation to the foreign environment – such as providing pre-departure training and other types of relocation assistance, including finding accommodation – most do little for the individual upon repatriation because they assume that the problems of re-entry to the home country and home operation are minimal. Unfortunately, this is not always true: the process of re-entry after several years of absence – including settling into a new position, a new home and the spouse's searching for a job – may be traumatic. Research has shown that repatriates and their families often experience a reverse culture shock upon re-entry (Harvey 1989).

The re-entry process can be particularly painful when expectations of upward career advancement are not realized. Frustration sets in when repatriates find they are not able to use immediately the skills and experience acquired abroad. This phenomenon is relatively common among US multinationals where international experience is not considered a very important criterion for promotion to senior management positions (Tung and Miller 1990). This practice stands in sharp contrast to the policies and practices in many leading European, Japanese and Australian multinationals. Worse yet, according to Tung and Arthur Andersen (1997), almost 60 per cent of US expatriates were not guaranteed a position at home upon successful completion of an international assignment. Another one third were guaranteed a position at the same level at which they were expatriated.

Two factors account for this difference in attitude towards an international assignment among US, European, Japanese and Australian multinationals. First, the majority of European, Japanese and Australian companies derive a significantly larger proportion of their corporate revenues from abroad. Thus, overseas positions are often viewed as exciting and challenging. Second, because of the heavier emphasis on domestic operations in US multinationals, many fear that if they are removed from corporate headquarters for an extended period of time, they will be out of the mainstream and, hence, bypassed for promotion. The ease or difficulty of reabsorption is influenced by three factors: (1) the duration of the overseas assignment; (2) the overall qualification of the expatriate; and (3) the attitude of top management towards international experience.

In general, the longer the duration of an offshore assignment, the more difficult reabsorption is. The problem is generally magnified when the repatriate has only mediocre skills and talents. Now that most European firms have phased out career expatriation, expatriate assignments are primarily used for career development purposes. An international assignment is viewed as an expedient means to acquire broad management experience and so only those individuals with high potential for senior management positions are sent abroad. An overwhelming majority of the companies in Japan and Australia, and now Europe, will refuse to send people on international assignments unless they are identified as having senior management potential.

To minimize the downside risks associated with repatriation, multinational firms should provide a better support system to allay expatriate concerns about career issues while serving abroad. A comprehensive support system should entail one or more of the components listed below.

A mentor–mentee programme should be instituted, where there is a one-on-one pairing of an expatriate with a member of senior management in the home organization. The latter has responsibility for monitoring the career path of the expatriate while abroad. This allays expatriates' concern about career opportunities back home and lets them devote full attention to the duties and responsibilities of the overseas assignment.

Where one-on-one pairing is not possible, a separate organizational unit should be established with primary responsibility for the specific needs of expatriates, such as career planning with the individual prior to departure, continuing guidance and/or counselling to help expatriates keep their career path on track while abroad, and career planning about their next assignment at the home office or another foreign location six to eight months prior to their return.

Constant contact between the home office and expatriates should be maintained to make them feel that they are still an important part of the home organization. In many Japanese multinationals there are special courier services for delivering newspapers, mail and gifts from the home office. According to a Japanese bank executive, his company provides both moral and financial support to its expatriates. An executive of an Australian natural resources company suggests the use of teleconferencing to provide that 'personal touch' to mitigate the isolation expatriates often experience overseas.

6 Managing the labour and management interface

There are two major issues in this area: (1) the extent to which industrial relations and practices around the world can constrain the activities of multinational firms; and (2) the labour unions' perspective of multinational corporations.

Labour's constraints upon multinationals

There is a diversity of industrial relations practices across countries in terms of the strength of unions, difference in wages and other compensation packages. The extent of worker participation in management also differs (see INDUSTRIAL AND LABOUR RELATIONS; TRADE UNIONS).

Strength of the unions. Some multinationals are concerned about locating manufacturing plants in places which are heavily unionized because they associate strong unionization with frequent work disruptions. Japanese automobile makers avoid 'union territory' in locating sites for their manufacturing plants in the USA. For example, Nissan chose to locate in Smyrna, Tennessee and Toyota in Georgetown, Kentucky.

Difference in wages. Other aspects of industrial/labour relations policies which can affect the operations of the international firm, particularly from the cost standpoint, are minimum wage rates, average number of hours worked per week and per year, and number of days of annual vacation plus other holidays.

Worker participation in management. Another salient way in which labour unions can affect and/or constrain the activities of international firms is the extent to which they are involved in management. This is referred to as industrial democracy (see INDUSTRIAL DEMOCRACY). Another variation is co-determination, where labour participates in the economic management of the firm.

The heterogeneity of labour policies and practices poses problems of adjustment for the international firm. In particular it frustrates attempts at central coordination from headquarters and the rationalization of manufacturing facilities worldwide.

The organic solution to this dilemma would be multinational unionization. At present multinational unions do not exist even though the term 'international' is used by some national unions. National unions can be affiliated with International Trade Secretariats; these are autonomous entities which are organized on the basis of trade or industry and which have working relations with the International Confederation of Free Trade Unions (ICFTU). Some national unions have also entered into international confederations across industry lines. The ICFTU, for example, which has its headquarters in Brussels, Belgium, has a membership including most European national unions. It is a less powerful force in developing countries, however.

There are two major impediments to the formation of multinational unions. First, in some countries unions are heavily involved in the political process of their country and may constitute the backbone of a political party. Hence these unions have a strong national identity which is not conducive to multinationalization. Second, the ideological differences across unions can be significant. Some have a strong political or religious orientation, while others may subscribe to the principles of co-determination or corporate ownership. Even in the EC pan-EC worker rights have yet to be realized. The diluted version of the Social Charter, adopted by the EC heads of states (with Margaret Thatcher dissenting) in December 1989, is a non-binding agreement which provides rather vague and incomplete guidelines on social and labour policies.

Multinational unionization which can harmonize standards for multinational corporations and which can also increase the bargaining power of unions does not seem attainable in the 1990s. Labour unions have attempted, however, to establish a set of labour relations standards which could guide the activities of multinational corporations around the world. One such standard has been adopted by the International Labour Organization (ILO) and by the Organization of Economic Cooperation and Development (OECD). This set of standards is generally referred to as the OECD Guidelines and is non-mandatory. The Guidelines, first adopted in 1976 and subsequently revised, established standards on disclosure of information, competition, financing, taxation, employment and industrial relations, and science and technology. They call on international companies to: 'within the framework of law, regulations, and prevailing labour relations and employment practices . . . respect the right of organizations of employees, and engage in constructive negotiations'.

Unions' perspective of multinational corporations

Unions also view multinationals as a threat. They perceive the growing might of the geographically dispersed empire of multinationals as reducing their bargaining position with management, which resides in corporate head office somewhere offshore.

From the unions' perspective, multinationals can constrain the bargaining power of labour unions in four significant ways (Gladwyn and Walter 1980).

(1) *Employment displacement/transfer of production*. In attempts to reduce costs and to rationalize their production activities around the world, multinationals can relocate their manufacturing facilities from one region of the world to another, thus leading to plant closures and downsizing of some existing operations. These result in displacement of workers in some countries.

(2) *Reduced strike vulnerability*. In the event of a strike, a multinational firm can source from plants abroad to continue servicing the needs of the local market. This diffuses the effectiveness of local strike actions.

(3) *Reduced negotiating authority*. Many unions believe that local subsidiaries of foreign-based multinationals are not vested with genuine authority to make decisions on collective bargaining. Thus, they feel that their concerns may not be adequately represented to and/or understood by decision makers in corporate headquarters, who may be less attuned to local social, economic and cultural conditions.

(4) *Lack of information on ability to pay*. Many unions allege that they have limited access to financial data on the multinational corporation. They argue, for example, that profit and loss figures on the subsidiary may be distorted through intra-firm transfer pricing. Furthermore, many multinationals, in pursuing a global strategy, may deliberately sacrifice the profits of a local subsidiary to maximize worldwide performance. Thus, relying upon financial data on the local operation alone, instead of utilizing financial data for the multinational as a whole, may distort pay criterion often used in collective bargaining.

7 Conclusion

Each of the five salient aspects of international human resource management (selection, training, evaluation of performance, retention and labour–management relations) can affect organizational functioning. In the future international human resource management will take on even greater significance in the overall strategic management and planning of multinational firms for several reasons: (1) the globalization of the world economy; (2) the globalization of the workforce; and (3) regional economic integration.

The globalization of the world economy has resulted in an unprecedented demand for managers who can adopt an international perspective in decision making, strategic planning and management. Such international orientation, among other things, can be developed over one or two stints of overseas assignments. Thus the primary objective of expatriation will increasingly shift from one of filling a job opening overseas to serving as a mechanism for the overall career development of employees with high potentials for senior management positions.

Johnston (1991) coined the term 'Global workforce 2000' to refer to the increasing mobility of the workforce across international boundaries. There is a growing trend towards the emigration of younger workers from developing countries to industrialized nations. Several factors have contributed to this development. First, many governments have been lowering barriers to immigration and emigration. Second, low birth-rates and an ageing workforce in many developed economies have resulted in labour shortages. Younger, mobile workers from developing nations can fill such a void. The emergence of regional trading blocs (such as the EC and the North American Free Trade Agreement) has contributed to the growing mobility of workers and harmonization of labour policies and practices among countries within a trading bloc.

These developments necessitate that international human resource management, in addition to the five main dimensions discussed in this piece, devote more attention to the issues of dual-career couples, managing diversity and the development of an international orientation. As more women enter into professional and managerial positions, multinational corporations have to deal with the relocation of dual-career couples. So far, US multinationals have not addressed this issue adequately. The problem of dual-career couples will also pose an increasing challenge to European multinationals in the future.

Thus far, the focus of managing diversity has been primarily on cross-national differences, such as selection criteria for effective performance abroad and training for cross-cultural encounters. With the increasing participation of women and ethnic minorities in the labour force at various levels, including managerial and professional positions, corporations have to devote greater attention to managing and valuing intra-national diversity. There are many similarities, as well as differences, in the dynamics and processes of managing cross-national versus intra-national diversity (Tung 1993). Research findings and experiences acquired in the field of managing cross-national diversity can be fruitfully applied and/or adapted to managing intra-national diversity.

With respect to developing an international orientation, three issues are noteworthy. First, the development of a global mentality requires a fundamental reorientation in all dimensions of human resource management policies and practices, in particular, the design of a reward structure to encourage employees to think and act globally. Second, in some countries with large domestic markets, and thus a more ethnocentric orientation (such as the USA), the successful development of a global mentality also necessitates fundamental changes to the education system in elementary and secondary schools. For example, requiring proficiency in a second language and the study of world geography and history can help raise young people's awareness and consciousness of other cultures and their *modus operandi*. Third, while stressing the need to develop a global mentality, a delicate balance must be struck between a local/national responsiveness strategy and a global rationalization strategy. In general, host governments are suspicious of global rationalization strategies which may result in plant closures and/or worker layoffs in their respective countries.

The challenges which lie ahead in the international human resource management arena can be daunting. However, if organizations seek to gain and/or maintain their global competitiveness in the decades ahead, these issues must be addressed.

ROSALIE L. TUNG
FACULTY OF BUSINESS
SIMON FRASER UNIVERSITY
CANADA

Further reading

(References cited in the text marked *)

* Adler, N.J. (1987) 'Pacific basin managers: a *gai-jin*, not a woman', *Human Resource Management* 26 (2): 169–91. (Interviews with North American female expatriates on their experiences of living and working in the Asia Pacific region.)

* Arthur, W. and Bennett, L. (1995) 'The international assignee: the relative importance of factors perceived to contribute to success', *Personnel Psychology* 48: 99–114. (An empirical investigation of factors important for expatriate success, along with their relative importance.)

Dowling, P.J., Schuler, R.S. and Welch, D.E. (1994) *International Dimensions of Human Resource Management*, Boston, MA: PWS-KENT Publishing Company. (A text in international human resource development, including selection, training, development and compensation.)

* Gladwyn, T. and Walter, I. (1980) *Multinationals under Fire*, New York: Wiley. (A survey and analysis of the dangers and challenges confronting multinationals in their worldwide operations.)

* Harvey, M.C. (1989) 'Repatriation of corporate executives: an empirical study', *Journal of International Business Studies* 20 (1): 131–44. (A survey of the problems and issues faced by repatriates upon returning home.)

* Heenan, D.A. and Perlmutter, H.V. (1979) *Multinational Organization Development*, Reading, MA: Addison-Wesley. (An analysis of how companies can develop an international perspective to take advantage of global opportunities.)

* Johnston, W.B. (1991) 'Global work force 2000: the new world labor market', *Harvard Business Review* 69 (1): 115–27. (A discussion of changes in the international labour market and their implications for management.)

* Moran, Stahl & Boyer (1988) *Status of American Female Expatriate Employees: Survey Results*, Boulder, CO: Moran, Stahl & Boyer. (A survey of the deployment of women in expatriate assignments and reasons for their underutilization.)

* Oddou, G. and Mendenhall, M. (1991) 'Expatriate performance appraisal: problems and solutions', in M. Mendenhall and G. Oddou (eds), *Readings and Cases in International Human Resource Management*, Boston, MA: PWS-KENT Publishing Company. (A discussion of the problems associated with the performance appraisal of expatriates, and their solutions.)

* Tung, R.L. (1981) 'Selection and training of personnel for overseas assignments', *Columbia Journal of World Business* 16 (1): 68–78. (A theoretical framework for the selection and training of personnel for international assignments.)

Tung, R.L. (1982) 'Selection and training of U.S., European and Japanese multinationals', *California Management Review* 25 (1): 57–71. (A survey of the policies and practices on expatriate assignments among US, Japanese and western European multinationals.)

* Tung, R.L. (1988) 'Career issues in international assignments', *Academy of Management Executive* 2 (3): 241–4. (A discussion of two key issues associated with international assignments, dual-career couples and repatriation.)

* Tung, R.L. (1990) 'International human resource management policies and practices: a comparative analysis', in G.R. Ferris and K.M. Rowland (eds), *Research in Personnel and Human Resources Management*, suppl. 2, Greenwich, CT: JAI Press Inc. (A comparative analysis of international human resource management practices among US, western European, Japanese and Australian multinationals.)

* Tung, R.L. (1993) 'Managing cross-national and intra-national diversity', *Human Resource Management Journal* 23 (4): 461–77. (An analysis of the similarities and differences in dynamics of managing cross-cultural versus intranational diversity.)

* Tung, R.L. and Arthur Andersen (1997) *Exploring International Assignees' Viewpoints: A Study of the Expatriation/Repatriation Process*, Chicago, IL: Arthur Andersen Inc. (A study of 409 international assignees' attitudes to and experience with expatriation and repatriation.)

* Tung, R.L. and Miller, E.L. (1990) 'Managing in the twenty-first century: the need for global orientation', *Management International Review* 30 (1): 5–18. (A survey of career development of senior management personnel in US companies.)

Related topics in the IEBM: APPRAISAL METHODS; ECONOMIC INTEGRATION, INTERNATIONAL; GLOBALIZATION; GLOBALIZATION AND CORPORATE NATIONALITY; GLOBALIZATION AND SOCIETY; INTERNATIONAL BUSINESS ELITES; MANAGEMENT EDUCATION AND DEVELOPMENT,

INTERNATIONAL; MANAGEMENT IN AUS-
TRALIA; MANAGEMENT IN EUROPE; MAN-
AGEMENT IN JAPAN; MANAGEMENT IN
NORTH AMERICA; MIGRANT MANAGERS;
MULTINATIONAL CORPORATIONS, ORGANI-
ZATION STRUCTURE IN; ORGANIZATIONAL
PERFORMANCE

Human resource management in Europe

1 **Managerial autonomy**
2 **The human resource management–economic success equation**
3 **Alternative approaches to human resource management**
4 **A 'European' model?**
5 **Comparing European and United States human resource management**

Overview

Human resource management as a concept developed and was popularized in the USA. It has been extensively criticized in Europe. A key question is whether the concept in its US guise is applicable to this other continent. The discussion here draws on existing analyses and data, and presents more recent data, to argue that the essentially unlimited managerial autonomy that is an underlying assumption in most US texts is not found in Europe. Consequently, there is a need to develop a new perspective; a 'European' model of human resource management. This entry examines the basis of the human resource management concept as it has come to Europe from the USA, emphasizing the notion of managerial autonomy and the inability of that vision to link human resource management to economic success, and examining some of the ways in which autonomy in Europe is limited. It then discusses alternative approaches to the problem and proposes a 'European' model of human resource management which takes account of external and internal limitations on managerial autonomy. Finally, some implications for practitioners are drawn from the model.

Emphasis will be placed on a contrast between the situation in the USA and that in Europe which, it will be argued, has led to different approaches to the notion of human resource management. There is, as a result, the need for a theory which encompasses these

variations. By its very nature, the argument will involve a considerable degree of generalization: conflating differences within the USA and, more tendentiously, within Europe. The analysis is built on the assumption that despite the differences in the conditions and circumstances within western Europe, taken as a whole Europe stands out as being distinct from other economic areas like the USA or Japan. The argument is weakened also by a lack of hard data available on representative practices in the USA. Indeed, in this area there is a real danger of comparing empirical evidence from Europe with normative statements of what should be from the USA. Much of the US literature can be read as a prescriptive indictment of what is not happening rather than a description of what exists. A final point is that the core elements abstracted from the 'US' texts are precisely that; abstractions. No conception of human resource management in the USA or among its adherents in Europe mirrors this version exactly and many have other perspectives. Nevertheless, it is clear that the fundamental basis of the human resource management concept noted here, that of managerial autonomy, underpins nearly all of the leading texts.

1 Managerial autonomy

The notion of organizational independence and autonomy is central to the concept of human resource management as currently propounded. Defining and prescribing human resource management strategies only makes sense if the organizations concerned are free to develop their own strategies. The fact that US views of human resource management may be culture-bound, particularly in this stress on organizational autonomy, has been recognized by North American authors. Meanwhile in the UK, Guest (1990) has argued that this view of freedom and autonomy is peculiar to the US; that it is related to the US view of their country as the land of opportunity in which any individual, through hard work or self-improvement, can be a success; where the ideal model is that of the 'rugged individualist' or self-reliant small businessman, and where a vision of the 'frontier mentality' exists. We can see these ideals reflected in the comparatively low levels of support, subsidy and control provided, or at least commonly understood to be acceptable, by the State. We can see them in the 'private enterprise' culture of the US, in the concept of 'the right to manage' and in the antagonism of management towards trade unions (see INDUSTRIAL AND LABOUR RELATIONS; TRADE UNIONS).

These factors are not typical of most European countries (for a more detailed review see Brewster *et al.* 1992). Certainly they have some limited acceptability in the UK but even in this country each point remains the focus of considerable controversy, while in countries such as Germany and Sweden these assumptions would be held by only a minority of the population.

In the European system organizations are less autonomous. Their autonomy is constrained at a national level by culture and legislation; at the organizational level by patterns of ownership; and at the human resource management level by trade union involvement and consultative arrangements. This different view of autonomy affects, among other things, the debate about the contribution of human resource management to economic success.

2 The human resource management–economic success equation

It is frequently argued that there is a direct correlation between strategic human resource management and economic success (see HUMAN RESOURCE MANAGEMENT). Porter (1985) believes that human resource management could help a firm obtain competitive advantage. Other authors make the point explicitly that 'firms that engage in a strategy formulation process that systematically and

reciprocally considers human resources and competitive strategy will perform better . . . over the long term' (Lengnick-Hall and Lengnick-Hall 1988: 468). Human resource management has even been propounded as the only truly important determinant of success. Pieper extended this logic and argued that 'since HRM is seen as a strategic factor strongly influencing the economic success of a single company one can argue that it is also a strategic factor for the success of an entire nation' (1990: 4): Porter (1991) has supported this point.

There have been attempts to apply the argument at the organizational level too, some of them based on careful analysis of performance data. In the USA, which has led the field in this area, there are a number of studies which claim to prove a positive relationship between the two (see Huselid 1995 for a review). Indeed, Huselid goes beyond establishing a correlation to arguing for a causal link: that good HRM has an

> economically and statistically significant impact on both immediate employ outcomes (turnover and productivity) and short and long term measures of corporate financial performance
>
> (Huselid 1995: xx)

The debate in Europe, by contrast, has been much more sceptical. Metcalfe and Fernie (1994) used WIRS (the UK's workplace industrial relations survey) to resurrect the attack on HRM instituted by the famous 'big hat – no cattle' taunt (Skinner 19xx). They argued that the work of the HR department was linked, in practice, to poorer industrial relations and lower financial performance. The differences between these two outcomes can be attributed in part to methodological differences, in part to the measures used (Guest 1994), and in part to the range of organizations studied. A significant element, however, lies in the definitional differences. It is significant, for example, that the UK study, and its challengers, draw the data from and include in the subject area, relationships with the trade unions. These are notably absent from the US texts.

The problem with the argument about the HRM performance in the UK is that there is a marked dearth of evidence to support it. Indeed, at the most visible level, the national level, data from evidence based on the most generalized assumptions points in the opposite direction: countries with less evidence of human resource management, namely those nations who allow least autonomy to their managements and possess the most legal regulation and trade union influence, tend to have been the most successful in recent years. National differences in human resource management and in practices linked frequently with US views of good human resource management practices have no correlation with national differences in economic performance.

Part of the answer to this problem is undoubtedly methodological, based around the impossibility of finding nations (or organizations) which are equal in all substantial areas except human resource management strategies. It seems unlikely, however, that better methodology would resolve the issue. This raises two possibilities: (1) the link with economic success, despite its apparent logic, is a fallacy; (2) more promising, current conceptions of human resource management are inadequate. This would go some way towards explaining the lack of correlation of a narrowly conceived view of organizational human resource management strategies with economic success – by failing to include external constraints, the 'autonomous' human resource management models miss important factors. A number of the factors which are omitted by these theories are explored below: culture and legislation; patterns of ownership; trade union representation; and employee involvement. Clearly this is not a comprehensive list and nor can each item be explored in other than an indicative fashion. However, these examples will be enough to enable us to develop a model of European human resource management which fits much better with the circumstances on this continent.

Culture and legislation

At the most general level the evidence available on national, cultural differences although limited, points clearly to the uniqueness of the USA. The USA is, according to one of the leading researchers in this field, quite untypical of the world as a whole (Trompenaars 1985): US culture is more individualistic and more achievement-orientated than most other countries.

National, cultural differences are inevitably reflected in legislation. One German authority, Pieper, pointed out that 'the major difference between HRM in the US and in Western Europe is the degree to which [HRM] is influenced and determined by state regulations. Companies have a narrower scope of choice in regard to personnel management than in the US' (Pieper 1990: 8).[1] Pieper included here the greater regulation of recruitment and dismissal, the formalization of educational certification and the quasi-legal characteristics of the industrial relations framework in comparison to the USA. Going beyond the concerns of the German system to include other European countries, it is possible to add legislative requirements on pay, health and safety, the working environment and hours of work, and to supplement these with legislation on forms of employment contract, rights to trade union representation, requirements to establish and operate consultation or co-determination arrangements, as well as a plethora of other legal requirements (see CORPORATISM).

Furthermore, Europe is unique in the world in having fifteen of its countries committed to a supranational level of legislation on a considerable range of aspects of the employer–employee relationship. The European Union, particularly through the steps associated with its Social Action Programme, is having an increasing legislative influence on human resource management.

State involvement is not restricted to legislation. In Europe an organization's external labour market will often include highly skilled individuals whose vocational training has been paid for by the State; Organization for Economic Development (OECD) figures show public expenditure on labour market programmes to be substantially higher in Europe than in the USA.

The State is also a major player in human resource management in Europe through a variety of other mechanisms. In broad terms, in Europe as compared to the USA, the State has a higher involvement in underlying social security provision, a more directly interventionist role in the economy, provides far more personnel and industrial relations services and is a more extensive employer in its own right by virtue of a more extensive government-owned sector.

Patterns of ownership

Patterns of ownership in the private sector also vary between North America and Europe. Although public ownership has decreased to some extent in many European countries in recent years it is still far more widespread than in the USA. In Sweden, for example, more than half of all employment is in the public sector; and even in the UK, which has done most to privatize services, around one-quarter of all employees still work in that sector. Nor should it be assumed that ownership in the private sector implies the same thing. In Germany, for example, most major companies are owned by a tight network of a small number of substantial banks. Their interlocking shareholdings and close involvement in the management of these corporations mean less pressure to produce short-term profits and a positive disincentive to drive competitors out of the marketplace. In some of the southern European countries family ownership of most businesses, even some household names, remains the common pattern.

Trade union representation

There are not only external constraints on organizational autonomy. These are reinforced by a variety of internal constraints; particularly in the form of employee representation. Studies of human resource management in the USA have tended to take place in the non-union sector and a constant thread in research programmes has been the link between human resource management practices and non-unionism.

Although it is the case that union membership figures have different implications in different countries it is quite clear that, in general, the European countries are more heavily unionized than the USA. Some, such as Germany, France and the Benelux countries, have legislation requiring employers over a certain size to recognize unions for consultative purposes. In France, Greece and Portugal employers have to negotiate with a union if it can show that it has any members in the workplace.

Europe is a highly unionized continent. Trade union membership and influence varies by country, but is always significant. The Nordic countries have union membership of over 85 per cent of the working population, the UK around 40 per cent and, even in the less unionized countries such as France, the unions negotiate terms and conditions of employment for a substantial majority of employees. In many European countries union recognition for collective bargaining purposes is required by law wherever there are trade unions, and even in the UK, where there is no legal mechanism for enforcing recognition, seven out of every ten organizations with more than 200 employees recognize the trade unions (Gunnigle *et al.* 1993) as do 53 per cent of all establishments with over twenty-five employees (Millward *et al.* 1992).

Trade unionism remains widespread and important in Europe; an importance that current European Union (EU) approaches will certainly not diminish, and may well enhance. Furthermore, in most European countries many of the union functions in areas such as pay bargaining, for example, are exercised at industrial or national level, outside the direct involvement of organizational managers (see INDUSTRIAL AND LABOUR RELATIONS; INDUSTRIAL RELATIONS IN EUROPE; TRADE UNIONS).

Employee involvement

In itself, a measure of trade union membership underestimates the constraining nature of employee action on managerial behaviour. This is emphasized by the European practice

Country	Statutory works councils	Statutory Board-level employee representation
Belgium	■	■
Denmark		■
Fed. Rep. Of Germany	■	■
France	■	■*
Greece	■	■*
Ireland		
Italy		
Luxembourg	■	■
The Netherlands	■	■
Portugal	■	■*
Spain	■	
United Kingdom		

Table 1 Incidence of statutory works councils/supervisory/board-level employee representation in the twelve member states of the European Union
Source: European Foundation for the Improvement of Living and Working Conditions (1990: 5)
*Note:** Statutory requirements confined to state-owned enterprises

of employee involvement: in many countries the establishment of workers' councils is required by law (see INDUSTRIAL DEMOCRACY).

In Germany, and Portugal employers have to deal with workplace (and often wider) works councils wherever employees request it. In Greece the unions can insist on the establishment of a works council where the organization is larger than twenty employees; there have to be thirty-five or more employees in the Netherlands; fifty or more in Spain and France; and one hundred in Belgium. These various forms of works councils have differing degrees of power, most of which would shock US managers brought up on theories of 'management's right to manage'. In Germany and the Netherlands, for example, employee representatives can resort to the courts to prevent or delay managerial decisions in areas (recruitment, termination, changing working practices) which in the USA would be sites of almost unfettered managerial prerogative.

Beyond the workplace, legislation in Denmark, the Netherlands and Germany requires organizations to have two-tier management boards, with employees having the right to be represented on the more senior Supervisory

Board. Employee representation, depending on country, size and sector, can be up to 50 per cent of the Board and employee involvement is recognized by law in most European states (see Table 1).

These arrangements give considerable (legally backed) power to employee representatives. Some of the proponents of US-style human resource management argue that consultative and involvement systems can be used to supplant the trade union. In the differing European context these systems tend to supplement the union position. In relatively highly unionized countries it is unsurprising that many representatives of the workforce are, in practice, trade union officials. In Germany, for example, the majority of works council and Supervisory Board employee representatives are drawn from union representatives.

At the supranational level it is clear that the EU is committed to maintaining the role of what it calls, instructively, the 'social partners': namely, employers and trade unions. In particular the latest European Directive on European Works Councils, whilst it offers several alternative structures which have no formal role for the trade unions, is clearly designed to increase the involvement of representative employee organizations in the overall direction of the companies. It is likely that the next step in Europe will be the resurrection of the works councils in each country debate.

3 Alternative approaches to human resource management

The argument here is that the concept (or perhaps bundle of concepts) of human resource management that has come to Europeans from the USA has as a key component the notion of organizational autonomy. It also argues that such autonomy looks very different from this side of the Atlantic.

This implies either abandoning the human resource management concept, an approach which, even if possible, would imply throwing out a considerable body of work and insight along with the proverbial bath water or, more positively, developing a model of human resource management which fits European circumstances more closely. The groundwork for such an approach has already been laid. Europeans are increasingly critical of the US model. Looking at the UK, Guest sees 'signs that . . . the US model is losing its appeal as attention focuses to a greater extent on developments in Europe' (1990: 377), and the same author elsewhere is sceptical of the feasibility of transferring the US model to the UK.

The inapplicability of US models in Europe has also been noted in Germany. 'An international comparison of human resource practices clearly indicates that the basic functions of HR management are given different weights in different countries and that they are carried out differently' (Gaugler 1988: 26). Another German, Pieper, surveying European personnel management similarly concluded that 'a single universal model of HRM does not exist' (1990: 11). Critiques of any simplistic attempts to 'universalize' the US models have also come from France.

There is a general trend in theorizing on the eastern side of the North Atlantic towards arguing that an over-ready acceptance of US models has gone beyond its provable value:

that the time is now ripe for distinguishing specifically European approaches. It is surely no coincidence that this coincides with the revitalization of the EU and Europe's economic success compared to the USA.

Thurley and Wirdenius, for example, were concerned with the development of a functional model of management, particularly in the context of international business activities, rather than with human resource management in particular or the comparative analysis of different national models of human resource management. However, they are relevant here because they tried to distil what is particular to 'Europe' rather than to the US or Japan. They argued that despite the predominance of US and Japanese conceptions of management, the need was 'now to distinguish "European Management" as a possible alternative approach'. Such an approach argues that European management:

- is emerging, and cannot be said to exist except in limited circumstances
- is broadly linked to the idea of European integration, which is continuously expanding further into different countries (i.e. the [EuropeanUnion])
- reflects key values such as pluralism, tolerance, etc., but is not consciously developed from these values
- is associated with a balanced stakeholder philosophy and the concept of Social Partners

(Thurley and Wirdenius 1991: 128)

There has been criticism of the importation of US theory elsewhere too. In the context of human resource management specifically, European authors have argued that we should not copy solutions which result from other cultural traditions.

It has been argued elsewhere (Brewster 1995) that this search for a more European concept of human resource management has to include a key role for the influence of factors and institutions beyond the immediate management of the organization. Furthermore, to see these as merely 'external' may lead to their influence being either overvalued or undervalued. In the first case it is easy for commentators to be driven towards a form of determinism in which the only rational choice for the management of an organization is to find the appropriate style of human resource management. These attempts to establish some sort of contingent determinism have linked human resource management strategies to life cycles, markets or other aspects of the organization's situation. Although some European authors have adopted this approach, contingency theories have come under attack in Europe on three grounds. First there are those who, adopting a European perspective, are sharply critical of the idea that human resource management must necessarily derive from corporate strategy rather than contribute to it (Conrad and Pieper in Pieper 1990; Staehle 1988). Second, there are those who argue that the notion of strategic choice is incompatible with situational determinism (Poole 1990). And third, there are the pragmatists who see retail outlets or airlines in similar contingent situations adopting different and equally successful human resource strategies.

Undervaluing the influence of the external factors, by contrast, leads academics to adopt 'autonomous' models of human resource management, consultants to propound 'one best way' and organizations operating internationally to make some fundamental errors in their human resource policies and practices. Seeing these factors as part of human resource management changes the nature of the analysis.

4 A 'European' model?

Evidence (Brewster *et al.* 1992; Brewster and Hegewisch 1994) suggests that there are clear country differences in human resource management within Europe which can only be understood and explained in the context of each national culture and its manifestations in history, law, institutions, and trade union and employing organization structures. However, at a higher level of abstraction it is possible to identify regional clusters within Europe. And

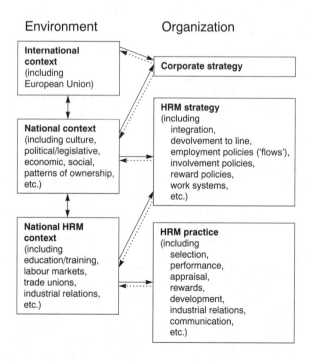

Figure 1 'European' (contextual) model of human resource management

at a higher level of abstraction still there is an identifiable difference between the way in which human resource management is conducted in Europe and the situation in the USA; a difference which allows us to speak of a European form of human resource management and to question the universality of the US concept. A number of attempts have been made to create a model of human resource management that re-emphasizes the influence of factors such as culture, ownership structures, the role of the State and trade union organization (Brewster and Bournois 1991; Brewster 1993a; Sparrow and Hiltrop 1994).

What is needed is a concept of human resource management in which the State and its agencies, employers and their associations and employees and their representative bodies form the constituent elements. Older readers will recognize a similarity between this and Dunlop's 'industrial relations systems' (1958). Kochan *et al.* (1986) rejuvenated the old theory and their argument that governmental, market and labour management are interwoven looks even more powerful in the European context. The new concept would therefore include all of these elements within a model of human resource management, not as external influences to it (Figure 1).

The advantages of such an approach include a better fit of the model to the European scene and experience. This changes the focus of debate in Europe in two ways.

On the normative side, where commentators and consultants have criticized employing organizations for not adopting the 'US' model, this approach allows a change. Rather than searching for human resource management, discovering that, according to the model usually applied, it does not exist and then criticizing employing organizations and their personnel specialists for not adopting these 'modern' approaches, the model enables consultants to be more modest and employers to be less defensive. What the analysts may be observing is, certainly, an absence of US-style human resource management, but they may be missing alternative, and perhaps more effective, 'European' human resource management.

On the analytical side, where academics have found little evidence of human resource management in practice and significant shortcomings in the concept as it has come across to us from the USA, the model enables analysts to move beyond discussions of whether human resource management should be 'accepted' or 'rejected' to a more positive debate about the forms and styles of human resource management. By including the environment in which the organization is located, this approach takes us beyond the 'autonomous' models. Furthermore, because a wide variety of external factors are indicated, the model also avoids the 'determinism' associated with previous attempts to take account of environmental factors: organizations here clearly have options in the decisions about how much weight to give to which elements. Thus, this approach possesses the capability to account for the fact that organizations in similar circumstances can choose different human resource management strategies and still succeed. Perhaps in part because of this reasoning, the model provides a closer fit between human resource management and national success. Also, the fact that personnel aspects are brought into corporate strategy by culture, legislation and union involvement can be encompassed here. As a result the model goes a considerable way towards explaining why some countries, even those with limited natural resources, that do not meet the traditional criteria of human resource management none the less take people management issues very seriously, and hence (Porter 1991) are among the most successful in the world. Thus, the link between positive human resource management and economic success is restored.

5 Comparing European and United States human resource management

This chapter has focused upon outlining the challenge that the European perspective provides to many 'US' notions of human resource management. Without some adaptation to take into account the European (and perhaps other?) non-US situations, the human resource management concept will continue to attract fundamental critiques, even in its most sophisticated form; for its failure to accept different degrees of managerial independence, different approaches to working with employee representatives and governmental involvement and, most damagingly, for its inability to link human resource management to economic performance. By attempting to clarify some of these fundamental bases of the concept, a way forward can be proposed.

The argument here has been developed from European data and hence the analysis is restricted to Europe. It is believed that the 'European' approach projected here accords much better with the reality of current and developing practice than many of the more straightforward personnel management or human resource management approaches elsewhere. Moreover, it may be that it is closer to reality in other continents and countries too. One test of this will be the challenge of extending these concepts to the ex-Communist countries of central Europe: clearly there human resource management has been, and is, different to that in western Europe. Research currently being undertaken in the new Länder of Germany and in the Czech Republic already shows initial indications that the European model of human resource management has explanatory value under those particular circumstances.

An oversimplification in the model, and one which clearly needs work, is in its relation to multinational enterprises. Clearly it shows the need for international organizations, and particularly international managers, to be aware of, and to adapt to, local environments – as in practice they do (Brewster 1991; 1993b). However, a more complicated, perhaps three-dimensional, model would be required to provide a full picture of the world environment within which many international organizations operate. Fruitful ways forward have been indicated by Dowling and colleagues (1993).

The implications of this 'European' approach to human resource management for

	Personnel management	Prescribed human resource management	European human resource management
Environment	Established legal framework	Deregulation	Established legal framework
Objectives	Social concern	Organizational objectives	Organizational objectives AND social concern People as key resource
	People as the organization	People as resource (internal or external)	Focus on cost/benefits management AND environment
Focus	Focus on systems formalization	Focus on cost/benefits autonomy	Union AND non-union
Relationship with employees	Trade unions	Non-union	Specialist/line liaison
Relationship with line managers	Specialist responsibility for systems	Specialists as support to line	Specialist managers – Ambiguity Tolerance Flexibility

Table 2 Personnel/human resource/European human resource management: a comparison
Source: Brewster (1993a)

the personnel practitioner can be indicated by a simple table first published in the *International Journal of Human Resources Management* (Table 2; Brewster 1993a). Column 1 indicates the traditional 'personnel management' approach still widespread within Europe (and possibly within the USA). Column 2 is an attempt to abstract the key features of the normative concept of human resource management as it has reached Europe from the USA. Column 3 identifies what a 'European' view of human resource management would look like. It can be seen that key features of the latter are a combination of the practices listed in the two previous columns and a potential flexibility and tolerance of dual concerns.

The first row in each column identifies the preferred environment; the second row the objectives of people management; the third row the focus of the personnel or human resource department activities. In the first column the rows indicate an established framework and the resultant drive towards formalization and systematization by personnel specialists, based on a view of the organization as consisting of the people within it – people who will be most effective if treated fairly. In contrast the second column indicates the normative view of human resource management apparent in much of the literature: governments should leave organizations and the labour market as free as possible and within that the human resource department's job is to view people inside or outside the organization as resources which can be used to achieve corporate objectives. Echoes of the difference in approach between mainland Europe and the UK throughout the period of the 1980s–1990s Conservative government may be detected here. The fourth row addresses relationships with employees (union for personnel management; 'non-union', or even anti-union, for human resource management). Row five shows the different relationships with line managers; with personnel management having responsibility for employee systems in the classic personnel model and human resource management serving the line in the prescribed human resource model.

The final row examines the role, or potential role, of the specialists.

The human resource challenge to personnel management has arisen partly as a way of expounding, or propounding, a new role for the personnel/human resource management department given that the previous one is seen as inappropriate to changing times. However, evidence from this paper and from other data collected across Europe (Brewster and Hegewisch 1994) is that human resource management is not developing as a straightforward opposite, or negative, of personnel management. What is happening in Europe at least is that, as the third column of Table 2 indicates, there is a move towards the human resource management concept but one which, within a clearly established external environment, accepts the duality of people management. Thus, objectives include both organizational requirements and a concern for people: the focus on both costs and benefits means fitting organizational policies to external cultures and constraints; union and non-union channels are utilized; and the relationship with line managers at all levels is interactive rather than driven by either specialists or the line.

In this context the specialist department requires the ability to manage ambiguity and flexibility – issues which the management strategy gurus tell us are going to become ever more important. They are also perhaps issues where Europe has a lead.

CHRIS BREWSTER
CRANFIELD SCHOOL OF MANAGEMENT

Note
1 The closest German equivalent to the linguistic distinction between personnel management and human resource management is between *'Personalwesen'* or *'Personalverwaltung'* (administration) and *'Personalmanagement'*; this differentiation is much weaker and concentrates more on the shift from administration to management, rather than emphasizing a different valuation of employees.

Further reading

(References cited in the text marked *)

* Brewster, C. (1991) *The Management of Expatriates*, London: Kogan Page. (A short book summarizing the research position in Europe up until the beginning of the 1990s.)
* Brewster, C. (1993a) 'Developing a "European" model of human resource management', *International Journal of Human Resources Management* 4 (4): 765–84. (Article attempting to distinguish 'European' from 'US' models of human resource management.)
* Brewster, C. (1993b) 'The paradox of adjustment: UK and Swedish expatriates in Sweden and the UK', *Human Resource Management Journal* 4 (1): 1–14. (Reports on an empirical investigation of expatriates transferring within Europe.)
* Brewster, C. and Bournois, F. (1991) 'Human resource management: a European perspective', *Personnel Review* 20 (6): 4–13. (First attempt to clarify what is specifically European, rather than US or universal, in human resource management.)
* Brewster, C. and Hegewisch, A. (eds) (1994) *Policy and Practice in European Human Resource Management: Evidence and Analysis from the Price Waterhouse Cranfield Survey*, London: Routledge. (Substantial book containing data and a full analysis of a major survey of human resource management in Europe.)
* Brewster, C., Hegewisch, A., Holden, L. and Lockhart, T. (eds) (1992) *The European Human Resource Management Guide*, London: Academic Press. (Detailed summaries of the different human resource management environments in thirteen countries.)
* Conrad, P. and Pieper, R. (1990) 'Human resource management in the Federal Republic of Germany', in R. Pieper (ed.), *Human Resource Management: An International Comparison*, Berlin: Walter de Gruyter. (Excellent summary of human resource management in West Germany prior to reunification.)
* Dowling, P.J., Schuler, R. and De Cieri, H. (1993) 'An integrated framework of strategic international human resource management', *International Journal of Human Resources Management* 4 (4): 717–64. (A thoughtful early attempt to theorize international human resource management.)
* Dunlop, J.T. (1958) *Industrial Relations Systems*, New York: Henry Holt & Co. Inc. (Seminal text on Anglo-Saxon industrial relations.)

Ferner, A. and Hymen, R. *Industrial Relations in the New Europe*, Oxford: Blackwell. (Seventeen chapters, each summarizing industrial relations in a European country.)
* Gaugler, E. (1988) 'HR management: an international comparison', *Personnel* 65 (8): 24–30. (A brief paper outlining the importance of national systems in human resource management.)
Gold, M. and Hall, M. (1990) 'Legal regulation and the practice of employee participation in the European Community', working paper EF/WP/90/41/EN, in *European Foundation for the Improvement of Living and Working Conditions*, Dublin: EFILWC. (Careful, detailed summary of employee involvement in twelve European countries.)
* Guest, D. (1990) 'Human resource management and the American Dream', *Journal of Management Studies* 27 (4): 377–97. (A well-written, entertaining and thought-provoking analysis of why human resource management in the USA is different from that elsewhere.)
* Gunnigle, P., Brewster, C. and Morley, M. (1993) 'Evaluating change in industrial relations: evidence from the Price Waterhouse Cranfield Project', *Journal of the European Foundation for the Improvement of Working and Living Conditions* 7: 29–35. (Summary of organizational level change and continuity in European industrial relations.)
Hall, M., Carley, M., Gold, M., Margison, P. and Sisson K. (1995) *European Works Councils: Planning for the Directive*, London: Industrial Relations Research Unit, University of Warwick, and Industrial Relations Services, Eclipse Group Ltd. (Clear, informative guide to a key issue in European human resource management.)
* Kochan, T.A., Katz, H.C., McKersie, R.B. (1986) *The Transformation of American Industrial Relations*, New York: Basic Books. (After Dunlop (1958), the key text on industrial relations in the USA.)
* Lengnick-Hall, C.A. and Lengnick-Hall, M.L. (1988) 'Strategic human resources management: a review of the literature and a proposed typology', *Academy of Management Review* 13 (3): 454–70. (Careful and influential analysis of the writing on strategic human resource management up to 1988.)
* Millward, N., Stevens, M., Smart, D. and Hawes, W.R. (1992) *Workplace Industrial Relations in Transition*, Aldershot: Dartmouth. (Detailed but well-written analysis of workplace industrial relations survey data for the USA.)

* Pieper, R. (ed.) (1990) *Human Resource Management: An International Comparison*, Berlin: Walter de Gruyter. (One of the first European texts on international human resource management; still valuable.)
* Poole, M. (1990) 'Human resource management in an international perspective', *International Journal of Human Resources Management* 1 (1): 1–15. (Introductory article outlining the field of international human resource management for a new journal on the topic.)
* Porter, M. (1985) *Competitive Advantage*, New York: The Free Press. (Classic text emphasizing the importance of human resources to organizational and national success.)
* Porter, M. (1991) *The Competitive Advantage of Nations*, New York: The Free Press. (Classic text analysing why, in international competition, some nations succeed while some fail.)
Schuler, R. and Macmillan, S. (1984) 'Gaining competitive advantage through human resource management practices', *Human Resource Management* 23 (3): 241–55. (An early article by leading US academics arguing the competitive value of human resources.)
* Sparrow, P. and Hiltrop, J.-M. (1994) *European Human Resource Management in Transition*, Hemel Hempstead: Prentice Hall. (An excellent student text summarizing the knowledge on human resource management in Europe.)
* Staehle, W.H. (1988) 'Human resource management', *Zeitschrift für Betriebswirtschaft* 5/6: 26–37. (One of the first German analyses of the subject.)
Storey, J. (ed.) (1995) *Human Resource Management: A Critical Text*, London: Routledge. (Variety of authors critically evaluate different aspects of the topic, mainly from a British perspective.)
* Thurley, K. and Wirdenius, H. (1991) 'Will management become "European"? Strategic choices for organisations', *European Management Journal* 9 (2): 127–34. (A seminal 'think piece' on what is distinctive and coherent in European management.)
* Trompenaars, A. (1985) 'Organisation of meaning and the meaning of organisation: a comparative study on the conception of organisational structure in different cultures', unpublished PhD thesis, Philadelphia, PA: University of Pennsylvania (DA 8515460). (Trompenaars' original research on national cultures. Also available in a more accessible form in the 1993 publication *Riding the Waves of Culture*, London: Economist Books.)

See also: CORPORATISM; CULTURE, CROSS-NATIONAL; HUMAN RESOURCE MANAGEMENT; INDUSTRIAL AND LABOUR RELATIONS; INDUSTRIAL RELATIONS IN EUROPE; TRADE UNIONS

Related topics in the IEBM: ECONOMIC INTEGRATION, INTERNATIONAL

Human resource management in Japan

1 Introduction
2 Origins of Japanese human resource management
3 The strategy of Japanese human resource management
4 Policies and practices of Japanese human resource management
5 Behavioural outcomes of human resource management
6 Ultimate outcomes of human resource management
7 Changes in human resource policies and practices

Overview

Japanese corporations place great importance on the management of human resources. Their human resource management is generally characterized by lifetime employment and seniority-based compensation systems.

Corporate strategy derives from basic corporate philosophy and its goals are blended by the nature of and the changes in the business environment. Corporate strategy for HRM is represented as an 'internalization of human resources' which means hiring, training and promoting from within the workforce. The philosophy of HRM in Japanese corporations is summarized as human resource emphasis, paternalism, egalitarianism, groupism and non-class consciousness.

The policies and practices of HRM in Japanese corporations are expressed in the following way: hiring new school graduates; operating gender distinction; undertaking systematic training, exercising job rotation; systems of promotion, holistic evaluation, and seniority- and age-based compensation systems; and ensuring employment security. Information sharing, employees' participation in managerial decision making, and enterprise-based unionism are also popular.

Policies and practices are formulated to achieve such behavioural outcomes as the improvement of employees' skills and motivation, better teamwork, more organizational commitment, flexible working patterns, a lower attrition rate, the observation of corporate discipline, and a reduction in the number of labour disputes.

Behavioural outcomes need to be achieved in order to improve labour productivity and product/service quality, and then to improve profit growth and corporate development, or other such goals as defined by individual corporations.

The problem is whether or not traditional HRM policies and practices will continue to be useful and meaningful in the future. Japanese corporations face potential changes in the business environment such as severe global competition, an ageing workforce, new technology, etc.

The conclusion is that those Japanese practices which are derived from non-corporate social practices – such as compensation systems based on age and length of service – will be slow to change. On the other hand, other areas of Japanese HRM practices will be adjusted more quickly, such as the flexible transfer of employees. It should also be noted that current Western practices such as team working, outsourcing, contingent wokers, cross training and empowerment were originally developed within Japanese corporations.

1 Introduction

A particular style of human resource management comes from a particular style of management overall (see HUMAN RESOURCE MANAGEMENT). Japanese style management stresses the importance of human resources which is frequently expressed by Japanese managers by the phrase 'the people are a castle'.

Ouchi and Johnson (1978) presented two ideal types of organizational controls. Type A represents a typical US corporation and Type

Z represents a typical Japanese corporation. If their styles of corporate governance were to be compared, Type A would be seen to prioritize the common interests of shareholders and management, while Type Z would be seen to have the common interests of management and employees as their priority. Their ways of organizational control would also be different. Type A is more individualistic than Type Z in that it encourages individual decision making and responsibilty. Type Z is more collective than Type A as it encourages collective decision making and collective responsibility. Type A is further characterized by short-term employment, explicit/formalized evaluation, and a segmented concern for employees, while Type Z is exhibits long-term employment, implicit/informal evaluation and an holistic concern for employees.

Whether or not Type A control is more efficient when compared to Type Z, there are differences between Japanese-style and non-Japanese-style management. Companies and other organizations are likely to be interdependent in Japanese markets, whereas their counterparts abroad are more likely to be independent. Japanese companies (see JAPANIZATION) tend not to compete but to collaborate with each other, although this may result in *dango* (bid rigging) and *keiretsu* (a vast pyramid structure of affiliated companies).

2 Origins of Japanese human resource management

Japanese-style HRM is said to have been formed in the decades after World War II with its roots in the industrial development which took place after the Mejii Restoration (see INDUSTRIAL RELATIONS IN JAPAN). Kim (1992) has shown that industrialized Confucian philosophy had a significant impact. The origins of HRM will be discussed as follows: (1) philosophy; (2) strategy; (3) policies and practices; (4) behavioural outcomes; and (5) ultimate outcomes (see UENO, Y.). Figure 1 shows the structure of these relationships as a series of concentric circles.

The philosophy of Japanese corporations

Above all else, Japanese organizational philosophy emphasizes the importance of human resources, and group and organizational commitment are strongly encouraged based on an egalitarian approach. Retaining staff in long-term employment is a well-known policy of Japanese firms, while class consciousness is weak among Japanese workers.

On the subject of corporate governance, it has often been pointed out that Japanese corporations were apt to neglect shareholders' interests. Their concern was internal, and management and employees were regarded as the main stakeholders. However, as companies began to face global competition, thay started to look outside and to follow the global standard. At this time, however, the division of shareholders and executives is still not clear, and outside auditors are not popular.

3 The strategy of Japanese human resource management

The basic strategy of human resource management in Japan has been the 'internalization of labour markets', which means enclosing the workforce within the firm. In large corporations, in particular, the workforce was hired and fostered by the firm, for the firm. Their internal rules of human resource management eatablished a unique labour market within an organization. Organizations thus tended to be independent from each other and rejected interference from external labour markets.

The reason why Japanese corporations originally chose an internalization policy was because the labour market had not been fully developed to allow for a fluid exchange of the workforce. Secondly, Japanese corporations, facing successive changes in technology, were not provided with a sufficient quantity or quality of workers by the external labour market. Thirdly, after in-house training, corporations had to retain their workforce within the firm to protect their investment. Fourthly, workers were encouraged to move from rural areas to industrial areas, by the provision of housing and living facilities, which in turn

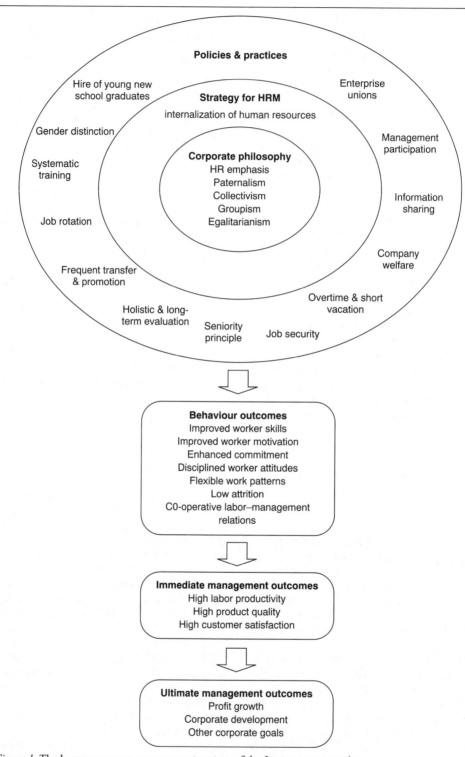

Figure 1 The human resource management system of the Japanese corporation

encouraged the workforce to make a long-term commitment to the corporation.

4 Policies and practices of Japanese human resource management

Recruitment

Japanese corporations tended to hire new school graduates and young people, because a young person with a low level of experience, but of potentially high competence is the most appropriate for educating and training inside an organization. It costs less, as young workers are paid lower rates under the *nenko* (age and seniority) wage rule.

Training

Japanese corporations established their own system of human resource development. The key concepts were off-the-job training, on-the-job training, job rotation, internal transfer and promotion. The system was intended to develop employees' general skills and adaptability, more so than in Western countries.

Evaluation

Japanese corporations can be seen to have put a greater emphasis on comprehensive and holistic views when compared to the segmented evaluation demonstrated in Western countries. It meant a slow, infrequent and long-term evaluation for pay raises and promotion with the stress placed on age, length of service, schooling and gender. The performance evaluation of individual employees has not been developed, nor even considered.

Employment security

Japanese corporations were most concerned with employment security, even if it were something that was not fully protected by legislation. Instead of making middle-aged and senior employees redundant, Japanese companies would transfer them to the subsidiary and affiliated organizations under their umbrella. Compared to the workforce as a whole, male senior management were found to experience better employment security.

Working hours

Japanese corporations established practices of working systematic overtime and taking short vacations. In order to secure their employment, employees were found to prefer lower discretionary time/vacation allowances to being laid-off, and this was especially true for the senior male staff.

Corporate welfare programmes

Japanese corporations established housing programmes in order to facilitate transfers to remote regions. Recreational facilities were built to encourage good human relations and to reinforce the organizational commitment.

Information sharing

Japanese corporate policy has proved successful with rank-and-file employees. From time to time, management circulate general corporate information through newsletters, company notice boards, letters from the President, morning gatherings, in-house broadcasts, dinner parties, socials and, sometimes, via the mass media.

Participation in management

Japanese corporations generally encourage rank-and-file employees to speak out and make their opinions heard. Examples of the mechanisms to allow for this to happen are: workplace roundtable conferences, small group activities, proposal systems, grievance procedures, consultatuion sessions, self-report systems and opinion surveys.

Trade unions

Japanese corporations have allowed union shop agreements whereby employees are required to be members of enterprise unions. This is especially popular among large companies. Such internal enterprise unions are said to co-operate with management and to play the role of a secondary personnel department.

5 Behavioural outcomes of human resource management

Improvement of employees' skills

New employees are trained on the job by seniors. At the same time, for those companies at the frontiers of technology, new skills are constantly required. It is less costly for employers to provide training to selected groups of employees. Skill formation is an important outcome of human resource managment.

Improvement of employees' motivation

Motivation is usually a major concern for employers and the maintenance of high motivation for repetitive, unexciting jobs should be properly controlled. This is an area which can indicate how successfully a company's human resource management programme is being implemented.

Enhancement of teamwork

Japanese management is most concerned with teamwork – part or most of the training programmes in large organizations aim to build on teamwork instead of training on an individual basis. Japanese corporations screen applicants for their suitability for teamwork, and educate employees to ensure the sustainability of that ability.

Organizational unity

Employees are fostered to become 'company people'. Japanese corporations sometimes secure employees with the privileges of their company names. When employees are satisfied with their status, they will be proud of their companies, thus leading to an increased feeling of organizational unity.

Flexible patterns of work

An example of a flexible pattern is working hours. Employees should accept management's need to extend working hours when necessary in order to improve customer satisfaction, and thereby to increase company profitability. Another example is job demarcation. Loose job categories are common in Japanese organizations, where employees are trained to cover their colleagues' jobs.

Low turnover of the workforce

Japanese corporations are extremely concerned with the attrition behaviour of employees. It is the managers' responsibilty to maintain long employment. From the employees' point of view, a change of employer is actively discouraged with the only reasonable excuse for females being marriage and, for males, going into one's father's business.

Disciplinary behaviour

It is considered extremely important in Japanese organizations that work rules are observed. Punctuality is highly appreciated, as it is in schools. Employees are praised for extremely low levels of absenteeism. Workers in Japan are sometimes dismissed from employment following traffic accidents. The philosophy behind this is that employees are seen to represent the company at all times and should therefore act accordingly.

Co-operative labour management relations

Industrial disputes can cause an enormous amount of damage to profitable companies. It is considered plausible in Japan to regard the presence of militant unionism as a failure of human resource management.

6 Ultimate outcomes of human resource management

The immediate management targets of human resource management were to raise labour productivity and product quality. Ultimately the targets were to continue the growth of sales and to increase the profit of companies. Japanese corporations have been successful in setting these common goals with both employees and enterprise unions.

7 Changes in human resource policies and practices

Human resource management in Japan faced new challenges after the oil crisis in 1973, when rapid economic growth reached its peak and forced management to make changes. After organized labour had received pay rises as high as 30 per cent in 1974 Japanese leaders – politicians, businessmen, government bureaucrats and union leaders – became aware of an impending crisis. Of necessity they collaborated to overcome the difficulties facing the Japanese economy.

It should be pointed out that union leaders at every level – national, industrial and enterprise – changed their strategies at this time and strove to lower employee benefits. They tried to persuade union members to slow down their payclaims in order to secure employment.

Successful results were thus achieved through peaceful industrial relations in the post-1975 period. Japanese economic growth continued to excel, although less so than in the previous period, with moderate growth, stable prices, low umployment, and an international trade surplus. Japanese corporations enjoyed a successful period until 1990 and Japanese-style management attracted attention from abroad for its achievements in growth and in employees' well-being.

At the beginning of the 1990s Japanese corporations began to experience problems. A trigger was the so-called bubble explosion, but in fact the fundamental surrounding business environment had changed in various ways. Global competition, international friction, yen appreciation, the inefficiency of regulated industries, a lack of domestic consumer demand, structural changes in industries, continuous innnovation and an aging population were all likely to force change on Japanese management.

What form are these changes expected to take in human resource management in Japan? Lifetime employment and a compensation system based on age, length of service, schooling and gender cannot be maintained due to rising costs, an aging population and internationally competitive prices.

Whether or not the philosophy, strategy and policies of HRM undertaken in the past will continue to be applicable in the future is questionable. Will these polices and practices achieve the same level of success in term of their behavioural outcomes as they have in the past?

There are differing views. One view maintains that a Japanese style of human resource management should be derived from the global standard. Another holds that Japanese practices should follow the established Japanese framework. The former view is mostly held by commentators and researchers in academia and the latter view mostly by practitioners in the traditional area. Discussions about corporate governance are starting and will continue to be developed further.

Evaluation and conclusion

The corporate environment changes rapidly, while corporate institutions and practices are stagnant. Global competition has become severe; the aging of the population is increasing more quickly; industrial structures are changing towards a post-industrial and service-oriented perspective and there is international and economic pressure to deregulate industries. The changing values of the younger generation have made employers reconsider some work patterns. The role of women has also changed: women have become more powerful both as consumers and as life planners.

On the other hand, laws, institutions and practices appear to have been supported by a considerable part of the population. More importantly, direction is created by leaders known as a power elite. In terms of human resource practices, Japanese corporate management, in fact, reveals a realistic attitude, contradicting many of their commentators. That is, practices which are derived from non-corporate, social concepts are now recognized as obstacles to industrial and managerial change.

Traditional compensation systems based on such personal characteristics as age, length of service, gender and schooling are known as *nenko* systems. *Nenko* means age and length of service in a narrow sense. 'Seniority' means only length of service, and seniority-based compensation is not the same as *nenko*-based compensation. This is commonly accepted across a wide range of organizations. It is felt that the effect of *nenko* should be reduced and some industrial unions have agreed to change to a more performance-based compensation policy. However, the evidence suggests that this change is taking place very slowly.

Conversely, adjustments to the size of the workforce are taking place quickly. Internal transfers are becoming more frequent; external transfers to subsidiary and related companies are proving to be more popular among middle-aged and senior employees. Schemes for early retirement, extending the retirement age and re-employment after retirement are gaining popularity and becoming more flexible, although the scale of the flexibility depends on the individual orgainization. Obviously, some organizations take on more workers while other organizations reduce the number of employees. The different situations facing different organizations dictate the ease with which the size of the workforce can be adjusted.

A final question is whether Japanese-style HRM will disappear or whether it will still be useful. An article in *Business Week* (17 October 1994) discussed a new wave of work patterns emerging in the USA. The following work patterns were considered to be highly up-to-date and innovative: mobility, empowerment, cross-training, restructuring, virtual offices, telecommuting, re-engineering, outsourcing, contingent workers, and team working. It is surprising to find that five of the above eleven originated in traditional Japanese practices of management. Empowerment, cross-training, outsourcing, contingent

workers and team working have been popular practices in Japanese corporations.

Quality circle activities and just-in-time production (see ISHIKAWA, K.) are also well-known as Japanese management practices. Further analysis of Japansese HRM practices may be beneficial for management studies on a world wide scale.

YOKO SANO
TOKYO INTERNATIONAL UNIVERSITY

Further reading

(References cited in the text marked *)

Abegglen, J.C. (1958) *The Japanese Factory: Aspects of its Social Organization*, Glencoe,IL: Free Press. (A milestone of Japanese-style management: focuses on lifetime commitment, collective responsibility and paternalistic human resource management.)

Kikuno, K. (1995) *Humanization of Work and Japanese Personnel Management*, Tokyo, Raku. (Discusses personnel management systems from the viewpoint of humanization of work.)

* Kim, B.W. (1992) *Seniority Wage Systems in the Far East*, Aldershot: Avebury. (A quantitative analysis of Korean and Japanese wage systems with a comprehensive review of possible theories and stressing socio-cultural Confucian hypotheses.)

Koike, K. (1997) *Human Resource Development*, Tokyo: The Japan Institute of Labour. (Careful and enlightening observation of Japanese-style human resource management.)

Kakbadse, A., Okazaki-Ward, L. and Myers, A. (1996) Japanese Business Leaders, London: International Thomson Business Press. (A result of interview studies of high-level business leaders which partly consists of global comparative studies undertaken at Cranfield School of Management.)

Miyamoto, M. (1994) Straitjacket Society, Tokyo: Kodansha International. (A result of participant observation at a ministry of Japanese central government, showing an internal system of informal bureaucratic practices which in turn represent a condensed model of Japanese management style.)

Okazaki-Ward, L. (1993) Management Education and Training in Japan, London: Graham & Trontman. (An intensive and comprehensive study of Japanese management education including a number of case studies collected by the author.)

Sako, M. and Sato, H. (eds.) (1997) *Japanese Labour and Management in Transition: Diversity, Flexibility and Participation*, London: Routledge. (A frontier edition of fifteen researchers in industrial relations, labour economics and human resource management indicating current stages of each topic.)

Sano, Y. (1995) *Human Resource Management in Japan*, Tokyo: Keio University Press. (A textbook to present human resource management systems in Japanese organizations.)

Shimizu, R. (1992) Company Vitalization by Top Management in Japan, Tokyo: Keio Tsushin. (A unique study of interviews with CEOs emphasizing traditional Japanese systems.)

Takezawa, S. (1995) *Japan Work Ways 1960–1976–1990*, Tokyo: The Japan Institute of Labour. (A panel study of emloyees' attitudes at two large manufacturing plants during 1960–1976–1990 showing changes in a rapid economic growth period.)

Whitehill, A.M. (1991) *Japanese Management Tradition and Transition*, London: Routledge. (A wide-ranging study of Japanese management including a description of the role of informal organizations.)

See also: HUMAN RESOURCE MANAGEMENT INDUSTRIAL RELATIONS IN JAPAN; ISHIKAWA, K.; JAPANIZATION; UENO, Y.

Related topics in the IEBM: LABOUR MARKETS

Industrial relations in developing countries

Overview

Industrial relations in developing countries have been products of both endogenous and exogenous factors. In several cases, being predominantly former colonial dependencies, the sudden creation of the original and formal cradle of industrial relations – wage-employment – had been externally induced. Subsequently, these initial structures gradually grew in the designated countries and remained intact for varying periods beyond political independence and through the 1970s. But, for reasons also internally and externally accounted, the industrial relations institutions in these countries have undergone further regimes of transformation and regeneration – sometimes chaotic and disruptive of macro-level development – through the 1980s and 1990s.

The major elements of industrial relations in developing countries have been: the colonial impact; nationalism, post-colonial states and crises of development; an overbearing role of government, coupled with political problems and instability; the impact of structural adjustment programmes; the democratic challenge; the emergent demands of social partnership; and the glacial effects of the contemporary trends in globalization.

The patterns of industrial relations in developing countries are still largely disparate, but with a few coherent features gradually emerging. The continuity of these in the very long term, and the probable additional benefits of social well-being and political peace in these nations, should strengthen the overall framework of relationships.

1 Introduction

The developing countries are comparatively new nations in the geo-political sense of nationhood. Therefore, industrial relations or patterns of the employment relationship that are associated with them are also relatively new and still evolving. Furthermore, it should be borne in mind that much larger proportions of the total and economically active population in virtually all of these countries still lie outside the formal wage-employment sector – where, technically, industrial relations exist (see ILO 1990a, 1990b; Diejomaoh 1979: 169–70).

The term 'developing countries' is a generic conceptual label for that large and diverse group of nations, mostly located in Africa, Asia, Latin America (central and south America), and the Caribbean. Perhaps the amorphous composition of this group is best depicted by its varying characterization in the subject matter literature. For example, Yesufu (1966: 90–91) included the following in his index of 'under-development': low average *per capita* national income, low standard of living and social welfare, an unbalanced – often monocultural – economic structure, and general poverty of the population. Similarly, Bean (1994: 208) has defined 'developing or third world societies' broadly in terms of *per capita* gross domestic product (GDP) levels, increasing social and political modernization, and predominant spatial or geographical location. Thus, the generality of developing countries exhibit various development needs and gaps in all ramifications of socio-economic life, particularly when standard international parameters are applied.

However, in spite of the perceived general social, political and economic similarities, these countries are far from monolithic when viewed, either generally in terms of their present levels of development or mainly on account of their industrial relations. The contiguous sub-Saharan African countries, as a case, even with their identical configuration, are still very different in levels of infrastructural acquisition for expanding the wage-employment and industrial sectors. The overall scale of comparison further widens when these countries are compared with regionally faster-growing and relatively more rapidly industrializing South Africa, or with the industrial 'models' of Latin America such as Mexico, Venezuela and Brazil. The same is true of the north African and the Asian countries, with differential social background, population density and natural endowment, and therefore different economic structures and orientations (Yesufu 1966: 91; Poole 1986: 11–37Bean 1994: 208–9; ILO 1994a: 11–26; World Bank 1995: 249).

In particular, one vivid manifestation of the sometimes superlative variability among developing countries is the Human Poverty Index (HPI) ranking for a panorama of these countiies, computed by the United Nations Development Porgramme (UNDP) in New York. The HPI was computed for some 78 different countries from the developing world and, naturally, the index ranged from 4.1 per cent for Trinidad and Tobago in the Caribbean to 66.0 per cent for Niger in west Africa. Consequently, the overall distribution of national estimates gives quite a statistical spread, both in terms of the quantum and global location of these countries, with United Arab Emirates scoring 14.9 per cent, Peru 22.8 per cent, Congo 29.1 per cent, Zambia 35.1 per cent, India 36.7 per cent, Nigeria 41.6 per cent and Ethiopia 56.2 per cent. Significantly, the gross HPI values in percentages directly depict the extent of poverty in a given country, that is, whether less than 5 per cent of the national population is affected by extreme human poverty or deprivation, as in Trinidad and Tobago, or more than 60 per cent as in Niger (see UNDP, 1997: 19–23).

2 Colonial impact

The origin of industrial relations in developing countries is generally traceable to the creation and popularization of wage work during the period of colonial rule (see INDUSTRIAL AND LABOUR RELATIONS). Given the backdrop of the mainly agrarian and rural economies that sustained the traditional societies in Africa, Asia, Latin America and the Caribbean, the introduction of wage labour and gradually, later, the modern work method, by the colonial powers – for example, in sub-Saharan Africa from about the late nineteenth century onwards – was new and different from the indigenous values and traditional mechanisms of compensation for individual or communal labour through non-pecuniary forms. One immediate salutary effect was the sudden activation of individual-level motivation to work for monetary or material utility.

Thereafter, and through several decades of elaboration before eventual political independence from British, French, German, Spanish or Portuguese hegemonies as the case might have been, the various colonial powers had gradually expanded the wage-employment sectors (largely public but also private or business) in these countries and, through these initial basic structures, also created the early necessary legislative framework that legitimized trade unionism as well as provided the instrumentality for the concession of a semblance of labour rights that lasted until national independence at different periods by the countries.

However, as noted earlier in the Introduction, the scope of the wage–employment sector in these countries (which is still largely urban-skewed) and the associated labour force relative to the total population (that is, the economically active proportion) has remained small (Southall 1988: 111; ILO 1990a, 1990b). This reflects the status and structure of their economies, and the fact that even when they are rapidly pursuing industrialization, they are mostly (with the exception of pockets, particularly in east and southeast Asia, as well as in Latin America) at considerably low levels of economic growth and subject to serious crises, often with serious consequences for employment generation and human resource utilization potentials as well as for the larger framework of socio-economic development (see ILO 1994a: 25–6). In another sense, that situation also portrays the overall scope of industrial relations.

3 Nationalism, post-colonial states and crises of development

In developing countries, there was affinity between the early labour movement and nationalistic opposition to colonial hegemonies. Yesufu has noted of these countries that:

> The most significant trade union development started after the Second World War, and thus coincided with the period of intense nationalist agitation. Although the size of the labour force organised in trade unions was (often) small ... their value to the nationalist movement and the struggle for political advance and independence was immense ... . Accordingly, the recruitment of the trade unions into the nationalist movement was vital to its success.
>
> (Yesufu 1966: 104–5)

The colonial administrators did not initially tolerate this, as this was reflected in series of anti-labour and anti-political legislation in the strongholds of colonial power before the dawn of independence. However, the benefits to nationalists and trade unions were mutual in the short term, as the pro-independence struggles also promoted labour unionism. But, the post-colonial experience of trade unions in developing countries did not necessarily reflect the rapport of the previous nationalism era. The hitherto robust relations with the new indigenous governments were soon deflated, especially when the astute unions became critical of the blunders of the latter. The impatient post-colonial governments often became fascist and repressive (Kraus 1994). Against

all odds, the labour movement in many of these countries – through the benefit of labour education over the years and the larger assistance of international organizations such as the ILO – has produced formidable leaderships with cross-national recognition. These leaders have been able to influence policy and participate in the tortuous development process – even under hostile regimes in some of these countries and the often harrowing environments of unilateral legislation by dictatorial states, alongside the contextual albatross of autocratic labour policies – apart from the pursuit of business unionism.

4 Role of government, political problems and instability

A recurring theme in industrial relations in developing countries has been the conspicuous presence of government. The logic of state intervention, particularly in a developing country, has often been defended. The major thrust of the apologists is that government can probably best protect public good (for example, quality of life, greater employment generation, human resource development, and accountability for development finance, and a desirable, probable commitment to transparency in public governance) (Yesufu 1966: 90–92). More specifically, the provision of an enabling framework for positive industrial relations, in the form of legislation to moderate the employment relationship and protect vulnerable workers is also an appealing rationale (see INDUSTRIAL AND LABOUR RELATIONS).

However, when the government role in industrial relations becomes all-pervading and overbearing, as in the developing countries – where for reasons of malfeasance or outright ineptitude labour policies are sometimes inconsistent or not enforced at all (see Fashoyin, 1992), – such a government presence is futile. Bronstein (1995: 163–4) has found that ' ... two most distinctive characteristics of Latin American industrial relations systems are the legal (heteronomous) regulation of employment and working conditions and the very high degree of state intervention in collective labour relations'. The implication is that free collective bargaining, in particular, is often stifled. Although some social gains in these countries have been reported on the front of 'human rights – freedom of association and autonomous collective bargaining' (Bronstein 1995: 185), he cautions that only future trends will confirm the stability of these changes.

The situation in Africa also conforms to the foregoing profile of government. For example, in Nigeria, the degree of robustness of labour rights has been very much a function of the relative dispositions of successive national governments from colonialism to this era of protracted military dictatorship. The general pattern has been government's penchant for taking complex industrial and labour relations actions by fiat (for example, wage determination in the public sector, with often serious inflationary consequences). This has accounted for the poor record of collective bargaining in the public sector, which commands the largest proportion of wage-earning population, and from where the first three trade unions – of civil servants, railway workers and teachers, respectively – had emerged in the country during the colonial period. On the contrary, the culture of collective relations has endured in the private sector (see Matanmi 1997).

In general, the larger environment of industrial relations in developing countries has been a burden. In almost all cases, the new sovereign states were highly pluralistic right from their creation or independence and, in addition, lacked democratic culture as well as the maturity and tolerance of political leadership to carry along the wider populace. Hence the pursuit of often parochial interests in the face of widespread poverty and scarcity soon fanned the embers of inter-ethnic confrontation. The human vices of official corruption, greed and conspicuous consumption have not aided the conservation of pockets of affluence and natural endowment, such as the crude oil, gold and diamonds in the African and Latin American continents, which could prudently have been harnessed for the public good (see Gabre-Michael 1994: 211). Thus, the characteristics of structural instability that persisted in the new nations also tended to boomerang into serious political and economic development problems that have remained. This, too, has been an issue of grave concern, both to the international community because of the potential conflagration effect, and also to the creditor nations. Nevertheless, there are real pressures for comprehensive change through democratization and good government in these societies.

5 Collective relations

The practice and benefits of collective bargaining – an ideal democratic and self-regulating system for governing employer–employee relations, and therefore the heart of industrial relations (see Kochan and Katz 1988: 1) – naturally gradually accompanied the evolution and development of trade unionism and employers' associations in developing countries (see COLLECTIVE BARGAINING). However, from the beginning, the entire course and pattern of collective relations in these nations have always been determined by the demands of their individual systems, and particularly by the framework of labour laws.

Mostly within the first four decades of the twentieth century, the early trade union movement – initially generally organized along house or craft/enterprise unionism – emerged in the regions. With the additional aid of the early scanty legislative provisions that were made by the colonial governments, these developments immediately facilitated collective relations, although on a lesser scale. The legal frameworks had conceded critical labour (or collective) – embodied in labour codes or Acts, particularly the right to organize and to bargain collectively, including the stipulation of grievance procedures for trade dispute processing.

For example, in Africa, countries like Egypt and Somalia have, for example, 'ful--fledged labour codes' containing various provisions. Similarly, Ghana, Nigeria, Kenya, Zambia and Mauritius – to mention just a few – have adopted specific industrial relations Acts that also recognize various rights (ILO 1983: 28–9). Moreover, in Latin

America, Chile in 1924, Guatemala in 1926 and Ecuador in 1928, respectively, had adopted acts on labour contracts, followed by Mexico in 1931, Brazil from 1934 and Venezuela in 1936 (Bronstein 1995: 164).

As indicated earlier under this sub-theme, the scope of both labour policy or legislation and collective relations was rather limited until the 1970s or 1980s, depending on the various countries. For example, in Africa, even up until now, with the exception of Egypt, Ethiopia, Libya and Tanzania, the existing legislation has yet to include the rural (traditional) and the urban informal sectors (ILO 1983: 31; The World Bank 1995: 5) – partly a fall-out of the highly urban-skewed wage-employment sector which was also mentioned in the previous discussion of colonial impact.

In other developing areas of Africa, Asia and Latin America, the main reasons for the restriction of collective relations have included the unequal bargaining power relations between workers and the capitalist owners, especially in the context of development and largely unfavourable economic trends in the 1980s and 1990s (Fashoyin 1992); in addition to governments' predilection to 'keep unions in check' and therefore create practical obstacles in the way of development of collective bargaining (Bronstein 1995); as well as the relatively new experience of workers and unions with collective bargaining, in terms of tool skills and strategy. In the long term, sustained stewardship training and general labour education will serve the workers and their unions well on tool orientation.

Be that as it may, another common and comparatively new pattern in developing countries is industrial unionism, whereby workers in the same industry, irrespective of occupational or skill differentiation, belong to the same union. Thus the earlier existing unions were often later, through state policy, reorganized along predominantly industrial lines. The various national unions normally operate from designated labour centres (central labour organizations).

It cannot be overemphasized that the primary function of a trade union as an organization is the continuous representation and protection of workers' interests. A complementary perspective is that trade unions also have social responsibility in contributing to the development of society (Kochan and Katz 1988). This overlapping continuum and periodic sliding between 'bread and butter' and the wider social unionism have been reflected in the pursuits of labour movements in developing countries from colonialism to the present.

The emergence of seemingly powerful industrial unions in the critical sectors of many of these countries – for example, in Ghana, Nigeria, Zimbabwe, India, Argentina and Brazil (because of the implication of centralized and multi-employer bargaining) – has also influenced the proliferation of employers' associations and federations. It is significant that tripartite organizations have increasingly included members of unions, employers' associations, and government. A further development has been the deregulation or decentralization of machineries of collective bargaining, mainly as a result of the recession and continuing predicament of these developing countries.

The original centralized structures of bargaining have been strained and rendered unviable. The implication is that aspects of national labour contracts, even under multi-employer bargaining, are increasingly being subjected to individual employer conditions. Although this is one dimension of the new flexibility in the labour markets, it is an important instrument of the ascendancy of concession bargaining, and the new economy-imposed challenge of employer–employee cooperation, in these countries.

6 Structural adjustment programmes (SAPs)

Most of the developing countries, whether in Africa, Latin America or Asia, had been under one form of structural adjustment programme (SAP) or another by the mid-1980s. These are economic recovery strategies comprising a battery of policy measures aimed at finding effective solutions to macroeconomic problems. The problems generally include monoculture, lack of self-reliant growth and development, low productivity and stagflation, serious imbalance of payments, huge external debts, and government budget deficit. Moreover, the SAPs have often been prescribed by the Bretton Woods institutions (the International Monetary Fund and the World Bank), on whom the crisis-laden economies of these nations are dependent for development credit and finance (Simpson 1994: 191–200).

Unfortunately for these countries, a lot appears to be wrong with the instrumentation of the SAPs. The policy demands are overwhelming. The prescriptions are usually comprised of the following: devaluation, removal of subsidies on basic commodities, reduction of government expenditure, labour market reforms, reduction of trade protection, and increased incentives for the traditional sector (agriculture and mining) (Simpson 1994: 193). And, because the doses have so far not jolted the countries into early signs of possible recovery, the industrial relations actors – and in many societies, as a result of the human toll, the larger populace – have been unanimous in protesting against the pangs of structural adjustment.

In the main, the effects of SAPs on industrial relations have been unfavourable to the developing countries. These are: gross union membership decline with the contraction of the formal employment sectors; growing informalization of the economy; the toughening of collective bargaining as a result of unfavourable pressures on job security and employee welfare, for example, through deregulation and other institutional realignments; the ascendancy of concession bargaining; and the continuing precarious predicament of the national labour forces (Fashoyin, *et al.* 1994: 1–38; Bronstein 1995: 167–9).

SAPs have generally adversely impacted labour-market policies and approaches as well as industrial relations in these countries (Simpson 1994: 191–200), and it is probably a vicious circle. But since most of the adjustment programmes began around 1985, the long-term effects should crystallize by the start of the next millennium.

7 The democratic challenge

One of the structural elements differentiating modern industrial relations in the West from practices in the developing countries has been the political framework of relations. Although it took the advanced countries of the West, for example, several generations of experimentation with the tenets of liberal democracy to attain their present status, democratic values and institutions in particular have survived. In essence, the principles of democratic society (see Adams 1995) have also influenced the tradition of industrial relations in Western countries, one of which is the mechanism of collective bargaining in the wider context of industrial democracy.

In the developing countries, the principles of democratic society are hardly embraced, to the effect that government not only sits tight but is omnipresent even in the sphere of industrial relations, while autocratic labour policies have been the norm. One illustration of the spill-over effect is the fact that not only the unions and employers but the entire citizenry are expected by government to 'subordinate' individual and collective trade interests to that of the nation (Barbash 1984: 122; ILO 1995: 70). In a way, such a development burden could be a positive impetus to widespread nationalistic consciousness and patriotic feeling. Nevertheless, the exigencies of the times have been causing gradual social and political transformation in these countries, especially since the 1990s. Thus, in Africa, for instance, industrial relations have had to subsist under changing political institutions. Just as most economies therein are being rapidly deregulated and governments are suddenly opening up channels of participation with other actors (employers and unions), the larger political context is also increasingly being pressured for democratic changes (Gabre-Michael 1994). The same processes are occurring in Latin America, for example, Argentina, Chile, Uruguay, Brazil and El Salvador (see Bronstein 1995), as well as in Asia, for example, India, where major institutional changes have also either taken place, or new developments are rapidly unfolding, in favour of ultimate democratization of workplace management and the necessary synergy between the major actors, such as through increasing social unionism and concertation (Mankidy 1995: 41; see also Verma *et al.* 1995).

By and large, it is noted that there is uneasy political calm, especially in Africa and Latin America – mostly enforced with military hardware – while the practice of protracted political transition is widespread. But events of the future years will portray the extent of democratization of the political machinery of governance in these countries, and the degree of flexibility of industrial relations.

8 Demands of social partnership

The logical conclusion from the account so far is that industrial relations in developing countries henceforth will particularly benefit from new alliances, positive orientations and approaches. The other side to the challenge of ongoing changes is that these have opened new possibilities for concertation and accommodation by the triparties. Therefore, employers, labour and government – being the principal stakeholders – should embrace the culture of tolerance, consultation, compromise and cooperation. The horrendous problems of these nations demand collective effort, trust and goodwill to be tractable, perhaps in the very long term.

9 Trends in globalization

From about 1985 onwards, the international trend has been towards a greater integration of the global economic and political system. In particular, a new world order has emerged in which countries that historically belonged to the Western and Eastern blocs are now increasingly more ideologically united and their economies more integrated, just as a new pattern of international division of labour, among various other parameters, is fast coagulating (see Fajana 1996). Undoubtedly, globalization has continued to have a glacial effect on international affairs, including the particular realms of economics and industry, where the 'gospel' of market orientation has continued to spread. Thus, when we consider

that the old world order had manifested a wide development gulf, and heavy dependency relationships, between the north and the south, it is clear why the trend of globalization portends greater implications and challenges, in terms of vast opportunities, especially for the latter (that is the developing) nations.

Among some positive developments that have been associated with the trend of greater integration of national economies into the global markets has been the ascendancy of certain developing countries in the east Asian region, to the extent that such countries as Korea, Malaysia and Thailand have become capital exporters (Fajana 1996). These achievements have prompted the conclusion that the generality of developing countries can, among other things, also improve their economic standing through the deployment of mechanisms of strategic policies for sound economic, political and social management. In this way, the benefits of globalization can be harnessed through greater participation in international commerce and industry, and the demonstration effects of national investments in human capital for the sake of favourable terms for the international mobility of labour.

10 Conclusion and prospects

Empirical evidence obviates further explanation of the perceived direct relationship between good industrial relations policies and practices, and the probable achievement of social and economic development. Human resources and solid employment relationships in collective output are critical for this development. The various cross-national accounts have also shown how employment policies and general industrial relations practices, such as wage determination, trade union status and collective relations are products of given systems and contexts of industrial relations.

The trends in industrial relations in the developing countries are major elements in the calculus of functions that block the necessary development process. Hence national planners and change agents in these countries cannot downplay the role of the industrial relations climate, particularly as a barometer of the degree of labour market well-being and the guarantee of human resources rights – an embodiment of the benchmarks of quality of the contemporary world of work.

In the years ahead, industrial relations in developing countries will continue to attract international attention and interest because the environment of work and contextual factors in these countries, which often contrast with those in the advanced countries of the world, have been changing rapidly. The direction of this change and a proper comprehension of the various internal and external agencies will further determine the trajectory of future relations and the extent to which enduring models of the employment relationship will emerge.

It cannot be overemphasized that, beyond industrial relations, the general economic and political problems of the developing countries have global overtones and indirect ramifications for the developed nations, because of the potential threats of social poverty and instability to international order.

There is a continuing need for general institution building in these countries to strengthen the existing machineries for collective labour relations. In particular, strategic human resource management, including training and other development processes, will improve their capacities for promoting favourable overall climates of stable employment relationships, and social development itself.

SEGUN MATANMI
LAGOS STATE UNIVERSITY

Further reading

(References cited in the text marked *)

* Adams, R.J. (1995) *Industrial Relations Under Liberal Democracy: North America in Comparative Perspective*, Columbia, SC: University of South Carolina Press. (A treatise on North American industrial relations and the structure and processes of differences as compared with the European and Asiatic models.)

Barbash, J. (1984) *The Elements of Industrial Relations*, Madison: University of Wisconsin Press. (An account of the elements of industrial relations from a comparative perspective.)

* Bean, R. (1994) *Comparative Industrial Relations: An Introduction to Cross-National Perspectives*, London: Routledge. (A synthesis of comparative evidence on cross-national practices of industrial relations.)

* Bronstein, A.S. (1995) 'Societal change and industrial relations in Latin America: trends and prospects', *International Labour Review*, 134 (2): 163–86. (This journal contribution portrays the complexity, change and diversity that characterize Latin American industrial relations.)

* Diejomoah, V.P. (1979) 'Industrial relations in a development context: the case of Nigeria', in U.G. Damachi, H.D. Seibel and L. Trachtman (eds.) *Industrial Relations in Africa*, London: Macmillan Press. (Demonstrates the critical importance of industrial relations for social and economic development.)

* Fajana, O. (1996) 'Global economic environment and the new world economic order', Text of a keynote address at the national seminar of the Nigerian Industrial Relations Association, held at the University of Lagos.

* Fashoyin, T. (1992) *Industrial Relations in Nigeria*, Lagos: Longman Nigeria. (This is an appraisal of past and present policies and practices in industrial relations, and views collective bargaining as realistic for determining wages and other conditions of employment.)

Fashoyin, T. and Matanmi, S. (1996) 'Democracy, labour and development: transforming industrial relations in Africa', *Industrial Relations Journal*, 27 (1). (An assessment of labour development in Africa and the constraints on existing systems of industrial relations.)

* Fashoyin, T., Matanmi, S. and Tawose, A. (1994) 'Reform measures, employment and labour market processes in the Nigerian economy: empirical findings', in T. Fashoyin (ed.), *Economic Reform Policies and the Labour Market in Nigeria*, Lagos: Friedrich Ebert Foundation/Nigerian Industrial Relations Association. (The product of a formative research on the impact of structural adjustment programmes on the Nigerian labour market.)

* Gabre-Michael, M. (1994) 'Second sub theme: changes in the roles of public authorities, employers' organizations and trade unions: an overview', in International Labour Office, *Political Transformation, Structural Adjustment and Industrial Relations in Africa: English-speaking Countries*, Geneva: ILO. (A comprehensive review of tripartite roles in African industrial relations.)

* ILO (International Labour Office) (1983) *Labour Relations in Africa: English-speaking Countries*, Geneva: ILO. (One of the critical and usually comprehensive ILO accounts of labour–management relations in Africa.)

* ILO (International Labour Office) (1990a) *Yearbook of Labour Statistics*, retrospective edition on population censuses, 1945–89, Geneva: ILO. (A rare data bank, particularly on the developing countries – where empirical data are a problem – but also on the developed ones.)

* ILO (International Labour Office) (1990b) *Yearbook of Labour Statistics, 1989–90*, Geneva: ILO. (An update on previous longitudinal data.)

* ILO (International Labour Office) (1994a) *World Labour Report*, Geneva: ILO. (A yearly overview of the employment situation and regional patterns throughout the world.)

* ILO (International Labour Office) (1994b) *Political Transformation, Structural Adjustment and Industrial Relations in Africa: English-speaking Countries*, Geneva: ILO. (This volume of a labour-management series is devoted to an anlysis of the impact of structural adjustment programmes and other aspects of continuing transformation on African industrial relations.)

* ILO (International Labour Office) (1995) *World Labour Report*, vol. 8. Geneva: ILO. (An account of significant events, trends and indicators in connection with international and comparative industrial relations.)

* Kochan, T.A. and Katz, H.C. (1988) *Collective Bargaining and Industrial Relations*, 2nd edn, Homewood, IL: Irwin. (A foundation text on the role of collective bargaining in the employment relationship.)

* Kraus, J. (1994) 'Trade Unions and Democratization in Africa', in M. Doro (ed.), *Africa Contemporary Record 1989–90*, New York: Africana Publishing. (This chapter discusses the predicament of African unions within the overall political framework.)

* Mankidy, J. (1995) 'Changing perspectives of worker participation in India with particular reference to the banking industry', *British Journal of Industrial Relations*, 33 (3): 443–58. (A situation account of industrial democracy in a critical south Asian industry.)

* Matanmi, S. (1997) 'Trade unions and labour rights in Nigeria', in K. Wohlmuth *et al.* (eds.) *Regional Perspectives on Labour and Employment, African Development Perspectives Yearbook 5, 1995/6*, Hamburg: Lit Verlag. (A contribution on the status of labour unions and semblance of labour rights in a pre-eminent African country.)

* Poole, M. (1986) *Industrial Relations: Origins and Patterns of National Diversity*, London: Routledge & Kegan Paul. (The book employs comparative analysis to explain the phenomenon of national diversity in industrial relations.)

Rothman, M., Briscoe, D.R. and Nacamulli, R.C.D. (eds.) (1993) *Industrial Relations Around the World: Labour Relations for Multinational Companies*, Berlin: Walter de Gruyter. (A reader on various national systems of industrial relations in both developing and developed countries.)

* Simpson, W.R. (1994) 'First sub theme: structural adjustment and its impact on labour relations', in International Labour Office, *Political Transformation, Structural Adjustment and Industrial Relations in Africa: English-speaking Countries*, Geneva: ILO. (A position paper on ILO views on structural adjustment programmes and their effects on African industrial relations.)

* Southall, R. (1988) *Labour and Unions in Asia and Africa: Contemporary Issues*, London: Macmillan Press. (The author compares the labour movements in Asia and Africa, and reflects on particular organizational and development issues.)

* UNDP (United Nations Development Programme) (1997) *Human Development Report 1997*, New York: Oxford University Press. (The latest output in the series of annual accounts of the global configuration of human development, since the maiden issue in 1990.)

* Verma, A., Kochan, T.A. and Lansbury, R.D. (1995) *Employment Relations in the Growing Asian Economies*, London: Routledge. (A most recent reader on industrial relations and human resource management in the relatively faster-growing and more rapidly industrializing developing countries of the Asia region.)

Wohlmuth, K. and Messner, F. (eds.) (1996) *Active Labour and Employment Policies in Africa, African Development Perspectives Yearbook 4, 1995/5*, Hamburg: Lit Verlag. (The product of multi-disciplinary synergy aimed at projecting the employment problem and associated social policies in the African continent.)

* World Bank (1995) *World Development Report*, New York: Oxford University Press. (An updated multilateral account of development trends around the world with copious use of international and comparative social statistics.)

* Yesufu, T.M. (1966) 'The state and industrial relations in developing countries', in A.M. Ross

(ed.), *Industrial Relations and Economic Development*, London: Macmillan. (A formative work on the state's role in industrial relations in developing countries.)

See also: COLLECTIVE BARGAINING; HUMAN RESOURCE MANAGEMENT; INDUSTRIAL AND LABOUR RELATIONS; TRADE UNIONS

Related topics in the IEBM: ECONOMICS OF DEVELOPING COUNTRIES; GOVERNMENT, INDUSTRY AND THE PUBLIC SECTOR; MANAGEMENT IN AFRICA

Industrial relations in Europe

Overview

Since the 1970s industrial relations in Europe have undergone much change, the majority of which has come from beyond the boundaries of Europe. The emergence of a global economy dominated by large multinational companies, structural transformations in the economies of western Europe from manufacturing to services, developments in new technology, an increase in white-collar employment at the expense of manual jobs and a continuing rise in unemployment have all had a major effect on industrial relations in all European countries.

The major impact on European industrial relations has been: increased decentralization in collective bargaining; a decline in trade union membership and influence; the emergence of new forms of management, including human resource management; new forms of participation and work organization; and the growing importance of European Union employment initiatives. Because of the wide diversity in industrial relations systems across different European countries, the changes have affected countries in Europe in different ways and there is little evidence to suggest that a European-wide industrial relations model is developing.

1 Context

From the 1970s onwards all western European economies have faced a number of common developments which have fundamentally shaped the evolution of employment relations. First, they have been continuously undergoing a structural transformation in the transition from manufacturing to services. By 1989 services accounted for nearly 70 per cent of employment in several countries, and in only two countries (Portugal and Greece) did services account for less than half the labour force (OECD 1991). As services expanded there was a significant shift from manual to white-collar employment.

At the same time, developments in international trade meant that the European economies became increasingly integrated into a global economy dominated by large multinational companies. The emergence of the Single Market in the European Union (EU) can be seen as an element in these developments as European businesses seek to enhance their competitiveness in world markets. As new technological innovations based on microelectronics and telecommunications have developed, European firms have sought to compete by moving away from mass standardized production to customized, quality 'high-tech' products which are aimed at niche markets.

Superimposed upon all these developments has been the inexorable rise in unemployment which has affected all Western industrialized countries, with two recessions in the early 1980s and the early 1990s. For example, unemployment in the twelve EU countries rose from 2.3 per cent in 1970 to 9.5 per cent by 1992, a rise which was significantly higher than in the EFTA (European Free Trade Association) countries, the USA and Japan (Commission of the European Community 1993b). This has been one of the main factors responsible for a shift in the balance of power against labour over the past decade or so, both at the political level and within labour markets, although as we will see later the effects of this shift have been uneven across different European countries.

Coupled with these economic changes, major political changes have affected western European countries. The post-war consensus between management and labour, the reliance on Keynesian demand management economic policies being pursued by governments and the growth of the welfare state all began to erode after the oil shock of 1973–4. Since then the growth rates of western European countries have been at more modest levels. European nation states have had to face growing budget constraints and an endemic fiscal crisis of the welfare state has severely limited their ability to offer concessions to trade unions in exchange for restraint in wage claims. Governments began to concentrate on monetarist policies as they were forced to adapt to a tighter international monetary regime. The economies of western Europe became increasingly interdependent and this severely restricted the ability of national governments to pursue economic policies to maintain full employment independently of other countries. As the Commission of the European Community puts it in its Green Paper on Social Policy: 'All the evidence points to deep underlying structural problems in Europe which makes a return to full employment unlikely in the foreseeable future unless significant changes of policy are introduced' (1993a: 17).

The consequences of change

The economic and political changes taking place in Europe over the past decade have been the cause of many changes in the field of employment relations. Trade unions in Europe have had to adapt to a much more diverse constituency of groups and interests as a result of these economic and political changes (see TRADE UNIONS). Apart from the shift of employment to the services sector and the increasing importance of 'knowledge' – with its attendant demand for white-collar workers – they have had to become accommodated to increasing female participation within the workforce; a transformation of the traditional family structure; the growing individualization of lifestyles; and the expansion of 'atypical' work (part-time, temporary, agency, seasonal work). This has meant that European trade unions are no longer able to appeal to a heterogenous population but must cater for a range of diverse interests.

The new technology has offered management a new range of strategic choices which were not available in the pre-microelectronics era. European manufacturing enterprises now rely less and less on cost-efficient, price-competitive, high-technology mass production and increasingly on high-skill, high-wage, customized, quality-competitive production. Service industries also have undergone a major transformation as a result of the introduction of new technology.

Associated with the introduction of this new technology is the trend towards 'flexibility'; flexibility in hours, flexibility in pay, flexibility in tasks and a move towards company-specific rather than industry-specific training (see FLEXIBILITY). Meanwhile, the recession in Europe in the early 1990s has encouraged management to embark on 'numerical' flexibility (Atkinson and Meager 1986) in order to contain labour costs.

Linked with this trend towards increased flexibility has been an increasing tendency towards a devolution of industrial relations issues to lower levels (see INDUSTRIAL AND LABOUR RELATIONS), often as a result of management using their enhanced bargaining power and exercising their prerogative to shift bargaining down from national or industry-wide levels to the level of the enterprise (Ferner and Hyman 1992). While management have frequently taken the initiative in this trend towards decentralization, major political and economic forces have also been at work, international competition increasing while international markets have grown increasingly volatile.

The tendency towards decentralization of industrial relations has been accompanied by organizational changes in companies such as the growth of company 'business units' with their own profit centres and autonomy in conducting the management of employee relations. All this means that European unions find it difficult to bring their organizational strength to bear within the political arena. Decentralization and deregulation have been most pronounced in the UK, although they have occurred to a lesser extent in countries such as Italy, Spain, Portugal and France.

It would be a mistake, however, to assume that the nature and extent of decentralization has been uniform across Europe; for example, there has been little evidence of changes in collective bargaining structures or the introduction of human resource management initiatives in Austria or Switzerland (Ferner and Hyman 1992). Similarly, although there is some evidence that there has been increased devolvement of industrial relations issues to workplace level in countries such as Germany (Lane 1989) and Denmark (both of which are renowned for their relatively high degree of centralization of collective bargaining and extensive regulation of their labour markets), such changes have generally been accommodated within existing procedures. In France and Italy, two countries which in the 1960s and 1970s were traditionally characterized by antagonistic power relations between management and labour, significant changes have taken place in industrial relations since the early 1980s at enterprise level, in the former as a result of the Auroux institutional reforms (Segrestin 1990) and in the latter as a result of informal collaboration between rival union bodies and a greater degree of accommodation with management in Italian firms.

As stated above, the level of commitment towards decentralization and flexibility has varied throughout Europe. And, although some changes could well be reversed if there were to be significant political changes such as the election of governments sympathetic to trade unions, all the indications are that the shift towards decentralization and increased flexibility is part of a continuing long-term trend which would not be possible were it not for a shift in bargaining power against labour at the political level during the 1980s. Throughout Europe social democratic policies have been in retreat. In Spain a nominally socialist government presided over avowedly conservative economic strategies and in 1994 embarked on a radical policy of deregulation of the Spanish labour market. Similarly, although there was a socialist government in office in France throughout most of the 1980s, it

pursued de-regulatory labour market policies and trade union membership density in France sank to its lowest post-war level. In Sweden a new conservative government was elected in 1991 and the country's powerful employers' association, the SAF (*Svenska Arbetsgivareföreningen*), finally withdrew all its nominees from public bodies and used the shift in bargaining power to weaken the 'Swedish model' of centralized negotiations which had characterized Swedish industrial relations ever since 1938.

However, it should not be assumed that the political shift to the Right in Europe in the 1980s and early 1990s necessarily means that all centre–right administrations not only made significant inroads into welfare state assumptions, but also carried their policies of liberalization and deregulation into the labour market. On the contrary, countries in northern Europe such as Denmark, Holland and Germany pulled back from implementing radical labour market reforms.

2 Trade unions

With the notable exceptions of the Scandinavian countries of Finland, Norway and Sweden (OECD 1991), there was a substantial decline in union density throughout western Europe during the 1980s (see TRADE UNIONS).

All estimates of union density are notoriously difficult to measure and it is difficult to obtain accurate comparisons between one country and another. Europe is no exception. Nevertheless, such estimates do provide a crude measure of the degree to which trade union membership declined throughout Europe during the 1980s. While the 1970s were a decade favourable to growth in membership levels in nearly every European country, with levels reaching a peak at the turn of the decade, during the 1980s levels decreased by so much that one has to go back to the 1920s and 1930s to find a comparison. This drop was particularly pronounced in the private sector. The expansion of the public sector, however, assisted union growth in three of the five countries which evaded this overall trend – Sweden, Norway and Finland – while participation in the administration of unemployment insurance in Belgium and Denmark accounts in part for their relative stable membership levels. Of the other countries, the UK, France, Ireland, The Netherlands, Spain and Portugal all witnessed severe union decline although Irish and Dutch trade unions managed to stem their decline in the late 1980s.

This decline was the result of economic and structural changes in the 1980s, which had a marked impact on trade union membership within Europe. Unions were slow to adjust both to the changing circumstances, to the contraction of employment in their traditional strongholds and to the expansion in sectors and segments where union penetration has generally been low. They also failed to recruit and retain members in the burgeoning services sector and to attract women, young workers and part-time employees.

There have been a number of studies (Visser 1988; Blanchflower and Freeman 1990) which have sought to identify reasons for changes in union membership levels across countries. Common factors are as follows:

1 structural and economic characteristics such as the size of the agricultural or manufacturing sectors, unemployment, employment concentration and size of enterprise, foreign ownership of domestic firms and international competition;
2 institutional and political factors such as the government's antagonism towards or support for unions, development of the public sector, social and labour legislation, deregulation policies and union access to parties and governments;
3 employer organization and policies;
4 the collectivist nature of the workforce;
5 union organization skills.

Nearly all these explanatory factors were favourable across Europe during the 1970s but, as we have already seen, they were very unfavourable during the 1980s. However, it would be misleading to assume that trade unions in Europe during the 1970s were as strong, purposeful and solidaristic as the union density figures imply. It would be equally inadequate to simply extrapolate current unionization trends into the future.

The future of trade unions

The question remains: How can European trade unions stem the decline in membership given the adverse trends that face them as they move towards the millennium?

One possibility, given the gradual decline of collective bargaining in Europe, is to seek to become providers of services to individuals, just as the early unions formed 'friendly societies' to help individual members. The problem with this approach is that it strays away from the whole *raison d'être* of trade unions being recognizable as a collective entity. Moreover, there is no guarantee that the provision of such friendly services could compete with financial institutions in a fiercely competitive market.

Another alternative is to adapt to the enhancement of employer bargaining power and seek to work with management on a collaborative basis to ensure company competitiveness and survival. There are already elements of this in approaches by trade unions in Germany and in Italy. The difficulties with it is that in adverse economic conditions there is a likelihood of competitive underbidding of pay, job protection or conditions of employment, with the associated problems of conflicts of interest between different groups of employees in the firm.

One might argue that unions must seek influence at the level of government and industry decision making: the European Trade Union Confederation (ETUC) would seem to have been particularly successful at the supranational level in ensuring its legitimacy in its representative role in its dealings with the institutions of the EU. Presence at this level might assist recruitment and enable unions to achieve results for their members. The risk in this approach is that it could divert union attention away from the workplace. Unions may seem too remote to members who may then become increasingly disenchanted. Unions also need to strengthen their international links, particularly now that the European Works Council Directive has been agreed (see below).

A final possibility for ensuring the survival of trade unions in Europe has been pursued by

Nordic unions with some success, particularly in Sweden. Here, unions have focused their efforts not only on offering discounted financial benefits to members but also in widening their workplace efforts to concentrate not just on pay and job security but on the quality of working life and on skill development and training (see INDUSTRIAL AND LABOUR RELATIONS; TRAINING).

3 Collective bargaining

Collective bargaining has long been the dominant form of determining pay and working conditions in Europe (see COLLECTIVE BARGAINING). From the end of the Second World War up to the end of the 1970s elements of the employment relationship which had traditionally been regarded as the prerogative of management were gradually drawn into the bargaining process. Such collective bargaining, generally over pay, took place at national or sectoral level and was seen as providing a stable framework for the institutionalized management of conflict in the European developed industrial societies, although there were wide variations in practice.

Both employers and trade unions supported centralized forms of collective bargaining for a number of reasons. The unions saw it as a means of controlling and sometimes reducing wage differentials – between firms, sectors and regions as well as between occupational and skill groups. This enabled them to cater to the great diversity of their membership. Since centralized bargaining favoured large over small firms, it also had the support of the large corporations because they realized that it was less prone than workplace bargaining to interfere with managerial prerogative at the point of production.

Governments also supported the centralization of both collective bargaining and union organization. As far as they were concerned, it enabled them to monitor wage agreements so that settlements were 'reasonable', were not excessively inflationary and could be reconciled with democratic capitalism's core commitment to maintain full employment. However, from the 1980s onwards there were growing pressures from employers and some

governments to decentralize elements of the bargaining process in order to promote more flexibility. The initiative for such change came largely from employers and increased in intensity throughout the 1980s. This trend, however, has not been uniform across the western European countries. For example, the level of bargaining in Germany remains at industry-wide level and at regional levels while collective bargaining in Austria and Finland is still relatively centralized.

One remarkable example of a radical change in bargaining levels occurred in Sweden, where the famous 'Swedish Model', which since 1938 had been based on centralized bargaining between the two central bodies for trade unions and employers, the LO and the SAF, was severely weakened as a result of the decision by the SAF in 1990 that they would no longer be involved in wage negotiations with the LO. In 1991 SAF decided to withdraw all its representatives from the governing boards of all public authorities, triggering the emergence of the widespread decentralization of collective bargaining which is now commonplace in many large Swedish companies. The SAF are keen to continue to use their enhanced bargaining power to press for further decentralizations and even to replace collective bargaining altogether, replacing it with negotiations between management and 'co-workers', with the local union's role limited to a periodical review of the outcomes of such individualized discussions. However, the election of a Social Democratic government in 1994 which is more sympathetic to the union's position makes it difficult to predict how much decentralization there will be in Sweden in the future and on whose terms.

Overall, while there has been a general trend towards a greater emphasis on enterprise-level industrial relations, decentralization has taken a different form in each country. It has been particularly far-reaching in the UK and The Netherlands but much less so in Germany and Denmark. None the less, the general trend towards decentralization has also involved critical decisions as to how work is to be organized and labour to be deployed on a more flexible basis, as well as how management is to be devolved within the enterprise.

4 The emergence of human resource management

Some commentators have argued that collective bargaining itself is threatened not only by the decline of trade unions and the trend towards decentralization but also by the rise of human resource management in a European context (see HUMAN RESOURCE MANAGEMENT; HUMAN RESOURCE MANAGEMENT IN EUROPE). Human resource management emphasizes individualism rather than collectivism by seeking to foster the commitment of individual employees to the aims of the business in which they work. Opinion is sharply divided on the implications of human resource management for the future of collective bargaining. Legge has argued that the emergence of human resource management is a reflection of the rise of the 'new right': 'our new enterprise culture [in Britain] demands a different language, one that asserts management's right to manipulate, and ability to generate and develop resources' (Legge 1991: 40). The proponents of human resource management present it as being concerned with 'a coherent positive and optimistic philosophy about management. . . built around the possibility of achieving personal growth in an integrated, human organisation' (Guest 1990: 17).

Human resource management in Europe has taken a different form from that in the USA, where it has been more closely associated with either anti-union activities or alternatives to collective bargaining. In Europe, as Storey (1991) and Regini (1994) observe, unions and collective bargaining are retained in part as a result of the legal framework, in part owing to higher levels of unionization and in part as a feature of the 'social democratic' version of human resource management at the macro level, as represented by the approach taken in the EU's Social Charter (see below).

A major survey carried out by the Cranfield School of Management and financed by Price Waterhouse (Brewster 1992) sought to ascertain what forms of employee involvement existed and whether the emergence of human resource management in Europe had given a fillip to collective participation practices or if instead there had been a move towards greater individualization and the concomitant isolation of trade union representation. The survey covered ten European countries and concentrated on gathering data on a range of human resource management departments and human resource policies.

The findings painted a 'conflicting picture'. Everywhere the respondents mentioned increases in employee communication, yet at the same time the form, level and strategic importance of that communication was highly variable. For example, staff bodies were used least for communication purposes in Portugal, Spain, Ireland and the UK where verbal communication channels were preferred. With regard to other methods of employee involvement, the researchers found that quality circles had not spread dramatically, with less than 20 per cent of employers favouring them. On the other hand, there was some indication of the increased use of employee attitude surveys. Overall there seemed to be little difference in the transmission of strategic and financial information between countries regardless of whether or not they had legislative frameworks for worker participation.

The results also showed variations across European countries in the levels of trade union membership, trade union recognition, trade union influence and the locus of policy determination in industrial relations. In general, they tended not to support the thesis that human resource management weakens trade union influence: while union membership was falling in several countries, union recognition and influence had remained resilient. Industrial relations strategy in companies remained relatively centralized, although the survey reported that there was a shift in industrial relations decision making down to line management. In sum, the findings confirmed that the way human resource management is practised in Europe is very different from the US model; the Europeans tend, in their human resource management systems to take account of more factors than the Americans, such as cultural factors, the role of the state, differences in company shareholding and legislation.

5 The changing nature of participation

There has been considerable debate throughout Europe for some time about the most appropriate forms of employee participation in decision making within the enterprise (see INDUSTRIAL DEMOCRACY). Until the 1980s the main emphasis was on indirect forms of participation through works councils, co-determination and collective bargaining. In this context, trade unions were generally the main channel of representation for employees. During the 1980s there was a switch in focus to direct forms of participation, which have been defined as:

> Opportunities which management provide, or initiatives to which they lend their support, at workplace level for consultation with and/or delegation of responsibilities and authority for decision-making to their subordinates either as individuals or as groups of employees relating to their immediate work task, work organisation and/or working conditions.
>
> (Sisson 1994)

Indirect participation

Indirect forms of participation have a long history in many European countries. In Germany the Co-determination Act (1951) and Works Constitution Act (1952) extended a range of rights to employees to participate in decision making. These were considerably extended and consolidated during the 1970s. The main instrument for participation is the works council, elected by all employees in a firm regardless of their union affiliation and operating on a defined legal status. Works councils of various kinds now play an important role in many European countries; eleven of the fifteen member states of the EU had some form of works council in 1995.

During the 1970s and early 1980s a number of countries adopted legislation on

employee participation, although few were as extensive as the German model. In Sweden, which traditionally favoured national collective agreements, new rules for indirect participation were established in the 1976 Co-determination Act, which permitted the inclusion of employee directors on company boards. Legislation also was enacted in The Netherlands, France and Belgium which provided for some form of indirect participative practices, while in Denmark the role of cooperation committees was strengthened in 1982, but through collective agreements rather than through legislation.

The introduction of new technology into enterprises is central to the concerns of employees. A study was carried out by Gill *et al.* (1993) on the diffusion of participation in new technology in the then twelve member states of the EU. It reported a wide diversity of levels of participation throughout the EU (see Figure 1). The authors of this study, under the auspices of the European Foundation for the Improvement of Living and Working Conditions, concluded that five variables play a crucial role in shaping the opportunities for participation in new technology: (1) management's reliance on the workforce to achieve its objectives for introducing new technology; (2) management style and culture; (3) the bargaining power of organized labour; (4) regulatory provisions, including legislation providing for participation; and (5) the degree of centralization of the industrial relations system in the particular country. Although the authors warn that these variables are no more than generalizations, their study provides an important reminder of the complex array of factors that influence the types and levels of participation found in Europe.

Direct participation

Compared to indirect participation, little is known about the extent and significance of direct participation in Europe. The European Foundation for the Improvement of Living and Working Conditions launched a major investigation into its extent and nature in 1993 focusing on all the twelve member states of the European Union as well as the three

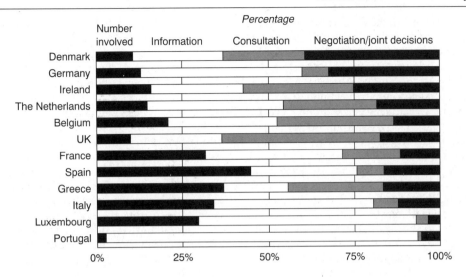

Figure 1 Management participation levels in 1992 for the implementation of new technology

countries who subsequently joined the Union in 1995 – Austria, Finland and Sweden. Preliminary results (Sisson 1994) indicate that direct participation is probably confined to approximately 20 per cent of establishments in Europe and is particularly likely to be found in organizations which compete in international markets and are in close competition with Japanese firms. More advanced forms of direct participation are also more likely in firms which produce high value-added, high-quality, customized goods rather than in establishments concerned with high-volume, low value-added, labour-intensive products.

Recent direct participation initiatives tend to be far more coherent and strategic in nature than older experiments. They concentrate on enhancing competitiveness and tend to go hand in hand with the introduction of a set of human resource management techniques. It would appear from the preliminary results of the investigation by the European Foundation for the Improvement of Living and Working Conditions that organizations adapt particular strands of human resource management techniques to suit their own circumstances.

Some of the examples of direct participation identified by the European Foundation highlight the fact that direct and indirect forms of participation may be complementary. Indeed, it appears that a strong institutional

basis for indirect participation stimulates the emergence of direct forms. The lesson that might be drawn from this is that, on their own, the individualistic approach of direct participation and the collectivist approach inherent in indirect participation are unlikely to succeed. There is a need for a mixture of both; examples from the European Foundation suggest that successful organizations tend to have integrated both forms of participation in their employment policies.

6 The European Union: the social dimension

No discussion of employment relations in Europe would be complete without considering the growing influence of the EU on industrial relations in Europe. The Maastricht summit of heads of government in December 1991 represented a landmark in EU affairs. One of the most controversial issues at Maastricht was the social dimension of the internal market programme; in other words, issues about to what degree the European community (EC) should adopt positive policies and legislation on such matters as employment and working conditions (health and safety issues, information and consultation rights, working time arrangements, training, job placement schemes, etc.) so that the citizens and employees of the Union would have some form of 'safety net' to protect them from the substantial economic changes accompanying the establishment of open markets in Europe.

Prior to the Single European Act, European social and employment policy was limited, and given the absence of any clear EC competence deriving from the Treaty of Rome in this area apart from equal pay, initiatives were few and far between until the mid-1980s. Such initiatives were restricted to the areas of equal pay and treatment, collective redundancies, acquired rights for employees in the event of transfer of ownership of a business and insolvency. During the early 1980s EC employment initiatives were consistently vetoed by the British government. None the less, the Single European Act extended qualified majority voting in the Council of Ministers on measures that 'pay particular attention to encouraging improvements, especially in the working environment, as regards the health and safety of workers' (Article 118A), but Article 100A limits its applicability by deliberately excluding from majority voting those provisions 'relating to the rights and interests of employed persons'. Whether or not a particular proposal is subject to qualified majority voting or unanimity can have considerable implications for its prospects of adoption.

Fresh attempts were made in the late 1980s by the Belgian government, which proposed a range of social and employment rights which later became enshrined in the 'Social Charter' (or more accurately termed, The Community Charter of Fundamental Social Rights for Workers) subsequently adopted at the Council of Ministers in December 1989 (although the UK refused to sign). The European Commission was charged with the responsibility for drawing up an 'Action Programme' of measures to put the Social Charter into effect. Although the Commission interpreted the scope of Article 118A very broadly, the results of the Social Charter have been disappointing to those who saw them as an opportunity for creating a minimum 'floor of rights' for employees in Europe. Measures have been implemented including health and safety, proof of an employment contract, equal pay, working hours, maternity rights and provisions relating to young workers. However, all these measures have been considerably watered down on their passage through the Council of Ministers.

One measure which will influence participation in European multinational companies is the European Works Council Directive which came into effect on January 1 1995. It was the first measure introduced under the Maastricht Social Protocol which enables member states (apart from the UK which has an 'opt out' from the Social Chapter) to proceed with European-level legislation by qualified majority voting. The European Works Council Directive requires transnational corporations employing at least 1,000 employees in one member state and at least 150 employees in two other member states to set up European-wide works councils or transnational information and consultation procedures. It applies to all EU member states (except the UK), plus the two other countries in the European Economic Area, Iceland and Norway and, according to estimates, it will affect around 860 companies in total (Hall *et al.* 1995).

7 Conclusions

Despite the initiatives which have emanated from the EU to facilitate the integration of social and economic policies among member countries, many of the influences on industrial relations within Europe come from outside this arena. As outlined above, markets have become globalized and segmented so that production and the provision of services are often being organized on an international, if not global, level. Accordingly, the global trend towards more customized products and services has accentuated the search for improved labour and capital flexibility.

Linked with this trend are perhaps the two key issues facing Europe during the 1990s and beyond, the twin problems of rising unemployment and European competitiveness in world markets. The Union of Industrial and Employers' Confederations of Europe (UNICE) argues that the relatively high labour standards in Europe when compared with, for example, the USA, is a contributory factor to the problems facing European companies in competing in world markets and has led to a rise in unemployment. ETUC, however, maintains that European companies can best compete in the newly emerging high technology markets with a highly skilled, well-paid and highly trained labour force, and claim that the problem of unemployment cannot be solved by lowering labour standards.

Although the search for improved labour and capital productivity is common throughout Europe, the wide diversity in the industrial relations systems from one country to another will mean that the manner in which changes are introduced, mediated and handled in European workplaces may lead to different outcomes.

COLIN GILL
JUDGE INSTITUTE OF MANAGEMENT STUDIES,
UNIVERSITY OF CAMBRIDGE

Further reading

(References cited in the text marked *)

* Atkinson, J. and Meager, N. (1986) *Changing Patterns of Work*, London: NEDO. (This book outlines the changing patterns of employment and argues that a new 'flexible firm' model will emerge.)
* Blanchflower, D.G. and Freeman, R. (1990) *Going Different Ways: Unionism in the US and Other Advanced OECD Countries*, discussion paper no.5, London: London School of Economics and Political Science, Centre for Economic Performance. (A comparative paper on trade union membership.)
* Brewster, C. (1992) *The European Human Resource Management Guide*, London: Academic Press. (An international survey by Cranfield School of Management and Price Waterhouse on the role of personnel management in Europe.)
* Commission of the European Community (1993a) *European Social Policy: Options for the Union*, Luxembourg: Office for Official Publications of the European Community. (An influential European Commission document setting the scene for future EU initiatives.)
* Commission of the European Community (1993b) 'January 1992 to June 1993: 18 months of community social policy', *Social Europe* 2: 14.

* Ferner, A. and Hyman, R. (1992) *Industrial Relations in the New Europe*, Oxford: Blackwell. (This book provides a detailed expert account of industrial relations in seventeen western European countries, including all the countries of the EU.)
* Ferner, A. and Hyman, R. (1994) *New Frontiers in European Industrial Relations*, Oxford: Blackwell. (This book examines some of the key comparative themes of European industrial relations in the 1990s.)
* Gill, C., Krieger, H. and Fröhlich, D. (1993) *Roads to Participation in the European Community: Increasing Prospects of Employee Representative Involvement in Technological Change*, vol. 1, 2nd report on the attitudinal survey on technological change, Luxembourg: European Foundation for the Improvement of Living and Working Conditions, Office for Official Publications of the European Community. (A survey covering 3,400 enterprises in the EC on levels of participation in various aspects of technological change.)
* Guest, D. (1990) 'Human resource management and the American dream', *Journal of Management Studies*, 27 (4): 377–87. (A critical perspective on human resource management.)
* Hall, M., Carley, M., Gold, M., Marginson, P. and Sisson, K. (1995) *European Works Councils: Planning for the Directive*, London: Industrial Relations Research Unit, University of Warwick, and Industrial Relations Services, Eclipse Group Ltd. (A detailed guide to the European Works Council Directive.)
* IDE (1993) *Industrial Democracy in Europe Revisited*, Oxford: Oxford University Press. (A comprehensive survey of industrial democracy and participation in Europe.)
* Jacobi, O. and Müller-Jentsch, W. (1990) 'West Germany: continuity and structural change', in G. Baglioni and C. Crouch (eds), *European Industrial Relations*, London: Sage Publications. (A good account of the industrial relations changes in West Germany during the 1980s.)
* Lane, C. (1989) *Management and Labour in Europe*, Aldershot: Edward Elgar. (A detailed comparison of management and labour in the UK, France and Germany.)
* Legge, K. (1991) 'Human resource management: a critical analysis', in J. Storey (ed.), *New Perspectives on Human Resource Management*, London: Routledge. (One of a number of critical perspectives on human resource management.)

* OECD (1991) *OECD Economic Outlook. Historic Statistics 1960–69*, Paris: OECD. (General economic statistics provided by the OECD.)

* Regini, M. (1994) 'Human resource management and industrial relations in European countries', in J.R. Niland, R.D. Lansbury and C. Verevis (eds), *The Future of Industrial Relations: Global Change and Challenges*, London: Sage Publications,. (An outline of likely developments in industrial relations in the 1990s based on the Proceedings of the 1992 World Conference of the International Industrial Relations Association.)

* Segrestin, D. (1990) 'Recent changes in France', in G. Baglioni and C. Crouch (eds), *European Industrial Relations: The Challenge of Flexibility*, London: Sage Publications. (An outline of industrial relations changes in France during the 1980s.)

* Sisson, K. (1994) *Workplace Europe: Direct Participation in Organisational Change*, Fourth IIRA European Congress, Helsinki. (An overview of direct participation in Europe.)

Sisson, K., Waddington, J. and Whiston, C. (1992) *The Structure of Capital in the European Community: The Size of Companies and the Implications for Industrial Relations*, Warwick Papers in Industrial Relations 38, University of Warwick: IRRU. (An outline of future developments in industrial relations in Europe.)

* Storey, J. (1991) *New Perspectives on Human Resource Management*, London: Routledge. (Outlines the major changes in personnel management during the 1990s in the UK, particularly the emergence of human resource management.)

* Visser, J. (1988) 'Trade unionism in western Europe: present situation and prospects', *Labour and Society* 13 (2): 18–38. (An excellent account of past and future trends in trade union membership in western Europe.)

See also: COLLECTIVE BARGAINING; FLEXIBILITY; HUMAN RESOURCE MANAGEMENT; HUMAN RESOURCE MANAGEMENT IN EUROPE; INDUSTRIAL DEMOCRACY; TRADE UNIONS; WORK AND ORGANIZATION SYSTEMS

Related topics in the IEBM: ECONOMIC INTEGRATION, INTERNATIONAL; NEW TECHNOLOGY, INVESTMENT IN

Industrial relations in Japan

Overview

Industrial relations in Japan is one example of cooperative employer–employee relations in an industrialized country. These relations are based on the following mechanisms: enterprise union, works council, and spring labour offensive. The essential elements of the enterprise union and works council also apply to some Japanese companies operating abroad under different styles of industrial relations.

Good employer–employee relations are beneficial for several reasons. They have contributed to the competitiveness of Japanese companies in the 1980s and to the high nominal wage level of Japanese workers when compared with other developed countries. Enterprise unions can stimulate joint efforts between employers and employees to increase productivity and thus maintain employment levels. Works councils can promote the exchange of opinions concerning management policies as well as discussion of the working condition of the company. These two mechanisms provide conditions for information sharing between employees and their employer which further develops the feeling of joint commitment. Meanwhile, the establishment of the Japan Trade Union Congress in 1989 indicates a new direction taken by Japanese enterprise unionism.

One drawback of such a system, however, is that it may promote the overcommitment of Japanese employees to their company. In addition, ideological differences among workers supporting different political parties disturbs uniform political action to improve the social system for the working class as a whole.

1 Historical development of trade unions

Peaceful industrial relations was not one of the original characteristics of the Japanese system of management but was shaped after the severe struggle between workers and employers during industrialization (see INDUSTRIAL CONFLICT).

The first labour union in Japan was organized in 1897 during the early stages of industrialization. However, the Law for the Maintenance of Public Peace of 1900 prohibited the development of labour unions in order to forcefully pursue quick industrialization. It was thus not until after the First World War, with the creation of *Yuai Kai* (Fraternity Association, led by Bunji Suzuki), that such an organization established itself as a real labour union, with a corresponding standing in society. This association followed the philosophy of the US-based American Federation of Labour (AFL). Other parts of the labour movement in the 1920s and 1930s followed socialist or communist ideologies, but these unions suffered oppression as the government tried to maintain industrial peace and a policy of militarization. Despite this, by 1931 the estimated unionization rate was 7.9 per cent of the workforce, with a total union membership of 368,975 workers (see TRADE UNIONS).

During the Second World War labour unions were absorbed into the *Sangyo-Hokokukai* (an association serving the State through industry) to promote the military policy of the resident government. However, in the wake of the war, unions developed rapidly as separate entities. This was facilitated by the Labour Union Act of 1945, which first approved the basic right to organize workers, to

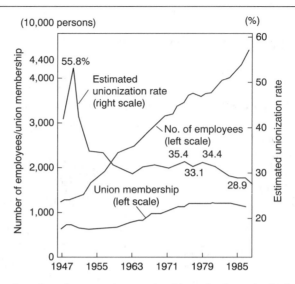

Figure 1 Trends in number of employees, union membership and estimated unionization rate
Source: Utuda (1986: 1)

bargain collectively and to strike. Such legal recognition, coupled with the democratization policy established by Allied Occupation Forces, resulted in union growth in all forms of industry. By 1949 the Ministry of Labour estimated a unionization rate of 55.8 per cent (see Figure 1).

During this growth period national federations of labour unions such as *Sodomei* (Japanese Federation of Trade Unions; socialist-orientated; 850,000 members in 1946) and *Sanbetsu-kaigi* (Congress of Industrial Unions of Japan; communist-orientated; 1,630,000 members in 1946) led the labour movement. In the early stages of development these federations were closely linked to political movements, which meant the Japanese labour movement experienced many conflicts between left- and right-wing unions connected with corresponding political parties. Such political affiliations also raised opposition among the Allied Occupation Forces; the 'General strike' scheduled to commence 1 February 1947 was prohibited the occupying forces. As a result, some union leaders promoted a union democratization movement, in opposition to the communist domination of *Sanbetsu-kaigi*. Then, in 1949 *Sohyo* (General Council of Trade Unions of Japan)

split from the *Sanbetsu-kaigi*. *Sohyo's* aim was to follow the basic line of trade unionism, not that of political parties, and brought together mainly private-sector trade unions and non-communist public-sector unions.

The basic framework of the Japanese industrial relations system was established around 1956 after the economic boom of the Korean War. The Economic White Paper published in that year by the government concluded: 'post-war economic reconstruction has been completed'. *Shuntohoshiki* (spring labour offensive) was also established at this time, its aim to coordinate the collective bargaining of enterprise unions and thus strengthen union bargaining power with each company. Meanwhile, in 1955 the Japan Productivity Centre had been founded to promote peaceful industrial relations.

Beginning in 1959, Japan underwent another period of rapid economic growth. *Sohyo*, which led the labour movement during this period, included a lot of labour unions from the public sector. These unions were essentially hostile towards the conservative government, and as the unionization rate for this sector was estimated as high as 76.4 per cent by 1985, thus *Sohyo* constituted a major anti-government force. *Domei* (Japanese

(1,000 persons)

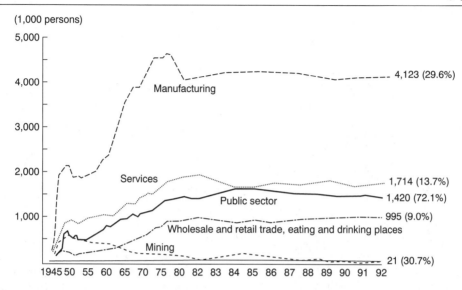

Figure 2 Trends in union membership and estimated unionization rate among major industries
Source: Ministry of Labour

Confederation of Labour), the second biggest national federation of labour unions, had its constituent labour unions mainly in the private sector. Within this sector union members tended to be concentrated in the larger companies (usually around 1,000 employees or more (Ministry of Labour 1985)). This meant that employees of large companies in the private sector more often enjoyed the benefits of trade unions than employees of small and medium-sized companies. Differences in union density between the public and private sector and between the larger and smaller companies in the private sector help to reveal some characteristics of the Japanese industrial relations system.

As is the case in all industrialized countries, Japan's overall unionization rate has been declining since 1980, with the impact of the second oil crisis on the country. Total union membership increased from 12,369,262 in 1980 to 12,540,691 in 1992, but the estimated unionization rate dropped from 30.8 per cent in 1980 to 24.4 per cent in 1992 (Ministry of Labour). Trends in union membership and the estimated unionization rate among major industries are shown in Figure 2.

One of the main reasons for this decline was the low unionization rate in areas such as

wholesale and retail trade, and eating and drinking trade (9 per cent) and services (13.7 per cent) (see Figure 2). Low numbers in these areas impacted particularly on unionization rates because they absorbed many non-union workers made redundant from manufacturing industries. Other reasons for the decline were an increasing number of non-regular employees (part-time, temporal, contracted and dispatch workers) ineligible for union membership and the growing number of young workers uninterested in the role of trade unions.

This feeling of crisis provided a positive atmosphere for the unification of several national federation of enterprise unions previously divided by political ideology. This move culminated in the creation of *Rengo* (Japanese Trade Union Confederation), which quickly established itself as the national centre of trade unions. The relationships between *Rengo* and the various associations preceding it are outlined in Figure 3.

Essentially the changes are as follows. *Domei*, which supported the Democratic Socialist Party, and *Churitsuroren* (Federation of Independent Unions of Japan), whose aim was to be independent of the political struggle among trade unions, and *Shinsanbetsu*

435

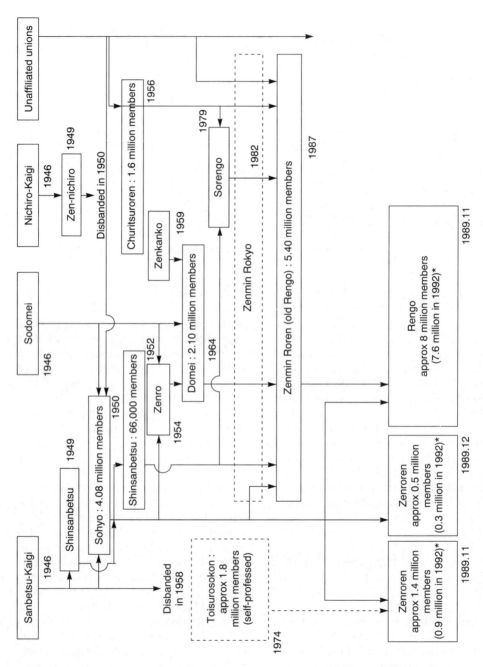

Figure 3 History of post-war labour organizations
Source: Japan Institute of Labour (1993: 50–1)

(National Federation of Industrial Organizations) merged in 1987 into *Zenmin-roren* (Japanese Private Sector Trade Union Confederation), which was set up to revitalize the trade union movement. The organization focused primarily on the private sector.

Sohyo, essentially a public sector association and one of the national leaders of Japanese trade unions supporting the Socialist Party, also decided to dissolve itself in 1989 so that main body of its member unions could join *Rengo*. This association included both private and public sector trade unions and had as its aim political influence for the purpose of improving social institutions for the working classes. Growth was rapid: by 1992 it constituted approximately eight million members. The establishment of such a new form of union is expected to change the direction of the Japanese labour movement.

2 Forms of trade union

Enterprise unions

The dominant type of union within the private sector is the *kigyobetsu-kumiai* (enterprise union): 91.1 per cent of private sector union members in 1975 belonged to an enterprise union in contrast to 1.4 per cent for craft unions and 5.5 per cent for industrial unions. Unlike in the public sector, where unions are usually organized on the basis of individual ministries, offices, public bodies and individual public corporations, an enterprise union is a labour union whose membership is confined to regular employees of a certain company regardless of whether they are blue-collar or white-collar workers. Non-regular workers who are temporarily employed by a company or workers who are employed long-term as employees of a sub-contractor working at shops of its parent company are not included in the membership. Foremen of blue-collar workers or sub-section heads of white-collar workers can be union members but this depends on the collective agreement between their company and the trade union (see COLLECTIVE BARGAINING). Top executives or middle managers are often ex-members because they are usually rank and file employees or were union leaders under the union shop clause in collective agreement.

Union leaders of enterprise unions are elected from union members, and are thus necessarily regular employees of the company. Therefore, according to work rules or collective agreement, union officers are put on the list of unpaid employees on leave from duty. They can only return to their original jobs when they leave union office. This too is the case for union officers working in the federations of enterprise unions or national centres, who are also classed as officers of enterprise unions.

Foremen and sub-section heads can be included in union membership under the organization principle of enterprise unions. They sometimes play an important role in forming the union organization or in choosing the basic policies of the labour union because they come from rank-and-file workers and are at the same time influential opinion leaders on the shop floor. As the first line of management against employees on the shop floor, their role is one of mediator between employees and employer during conflict.

There are many theories concerning why the culture of enterprise unions is so strong in Japan. *Shushin-koyo* (lifetime employment) may be one of the primary reasons given that enterprise unions are based on the deep commitment of workers to their company.

Other elements can be pinpointed which greatly influenced the formation of enterprise unions. The Trade Union Law of 1946 demanded the rapid establishment of labour unions under conditions at a time when workers were unaccustomed to the idea of self-organization among workers or collective bargaining. The quickest and most effective way to organize workers is to unify employees of an establishment or a company who can communicate easily with each other. *Sangyo-hokokukai* was an employees' organization including both blue- and white-collar workers and managers to promote production for military purposes during the World War II. This may have provided the stimulus for unions based on a single company.

Another possibility is that the new idea of democracy emphasized by the Allied Occupation Forces stimulated the demand of blue-collar workers for the destruction of the strong differences of status and wage between white-collar and blue-collar employees existing before the Second World War. This may have promoted the formation of an enterprise union which included in its membership both blue- and white-collar workers within the same company.

Employers' associations

These are four main employers' associations in Japan: *Keidanren* (Japan Federations of Economic Organization); *Nikkeiren* (Japan Federations of Employers' Associations); *Keizaidoyukaiu* (Japan Committee for Economic Development; and *Nippon Shokokaigi-syo* (Japan Chamber of Commerce and Industry). These employers' associations do not have rights or the power to negotiate collective agreements with the national centres or industrial federations of trade unions. Instead, they represent the interests of employers as a whole, coordinating opinions on labour problems and presenting opinions and proposals concerning economic policies and industrial relations problems to the public and the government. Although separate bodies, no deep political or ideological conflict exists between them (see EMPLOYERS' ASSOCIATIONS).

Of these employers' associations, the *Nikkeiren* plays a particularly influential role, especially in the field of industrial relations and labour problems. It includes fifty-four trade associations and all of the prefectural employers' associations. Its economic policies have a strong influence on its member employers. In addition, the association has input into the economic and labour policies of the national government and the selection of employers' representatives for various governmental organizations and international organizations such as the International Labour Organization.

Documents or guidelines concerning wage negotiation and other working conditions are released by the *Nikkeiren* to the general public as well as its member trade associations. This creates the atmosphere of *Shuntohoshiki* (spring labour offensive), at which time many employers and employees annually negotiate wages and other working conditions. Opinion-leaders of the *Nikkeiren* thus often release an official or unofficial comment on wage levels or wage increases. Leaders of the opposing *Rengo* also make attempts to try and gain the initiative during collective bargaining on behalf of its member unions.

3 Collective bargaining

In Japan collective bargaining is based on negotiations between an enterprise union and its employer. Of the labour unions surveyed by the Labour Policy Bureau of the Ministry of Labour in 1977, 81 per cent concluded a collective agreement with their employers. However, while 60 per cent of the unions negotiated the collective agreement themselves, 35 per cent applied the agreement negotiated by upper organizations such as industrial confederations or industrial unions to their workshops. The proportion of each type of negotiation has continued despite the creation of *Rengo*.

The content of the collective agreement consists of clauses such as wages, annual wage increases, fringe benefits, working hours and criteria for dismissal (see COLLECTIVE BARGAINING). Also included are obligatory clauses such as union shop, clocking-off and union activators during working hours. Finally, the agreement includes institutional clauses such as joint consultation machinery and grievance procedures. However, the main issues at the bargaining table surveyed in 1977 were economic in form. These were basic salaries and wages (an issue raised by 57 per cent of the unions surveyed), bonuses or lump-sum payments in summer and winter (by 50 per cent), monthly allowance (by 30 per cent), retirement allowance (by 30 per cent), days off and vacation (by 29 per cent) and hours of work and rest periods (by 25 per cent). Later, in the 1980s an increase in the number of aged workers and slow increase of wages under stable economic growth meant that postponement of the mandatory retirement age and welfare plans became an important part of the agenda at negotiation.

The bargaining power of enterprise unions is not strong due to the lack of solidarity at an industrial and national level. *Shuntohoshiki* was established in 1956 to overcome this weakness and now around 80 per cent of labour unions schedule their negotiations for the beginning of spring (particularly March, April and May). This time was chosen because April is the beginning of the financial year and the month when new school graduates join companies. *Shuntohoshiki* is particularly important to unions because employers feel forced to accept the coordinated wage settlement in order to avoid severe competition among themselves.

Four industrial confederations of trade unions – iron and steel, motor, electrical machinery, and shipbuilding and engineering – are the main unions making up the International Metal Federation – Japan Council (IMF–JC). The four federations play a lead role during wage negotiations and offer a blueprint for bargaining to other non-member industries like private railways, electricity power supply and the public sector.

Higher profits mean it is easier for labour unions in these industries to obtain higher wages. The high standards of wage increase set by the IMF–JC are usually followed by other industries, including public-sector and small and medium-sized companies. Thus, *Shuntohoshiki* has been effective in increasing the general wage level and living standard of many workers. However, whether it works well even in the stable economic growth after 1978 is an open question. One alternative to this method may be found in the development of the *Rengo*.

4 Joint consultation system

Alongside collective bargaining, *roshikyogisei* (joint consultation system) plays an important role in promoting cooperative Japanese industrial relations. Of those companies with over 5,000 employees, by 1988, 73.3 per cent had adopted the system according to the survey carried out by the Ministry of Labour. Under this system, representatives of employees from each level of a company – for example the shop floor, factory and company as a whole – meet regularly with their counterparts in management to exchange information about company policies, production schedule, changes of shop-floor practices and so on (see INDUSTRIAL DEMOCRACY).

Employee representatives are usually, in practice, union officials and shop stewards. Owing to this, rigid differentiation between collective bargaining and a joint consultation system is very difficult in the sense that both work effectively to promote communication between management and employees. Surveys of labour unions have revealed that around one-third of unions consider that the two systems cannot be separated when reaching consensus between management and the employees. Around one-third believe that the joint consultation system is a kind of pre-stage of bargaining mechanism which can easily turn into collective bargaining when an agreement cannot be reached. Another third of labour unions insist that a joint consultation system, which usually deals with issues of mutual interest between management and employees, can be distinguished from collective bargaining, which usually deals with issues of conflicting economic interests for both parties.

Some basic differences between the two systems can be outlined. Table 1 shows areas which are covered both by the joint consultation system (works council) and by collective bargaining. Issues such as wages, bonus, retirement allowance and working hours, which seem to be economic conflicts between management and employees, are dealt with primarily through collective bargaining. This supports the above distinction. A joint consultation system, meanwhile, often deals with overtime and holiday work, vacations, job assignment and transfer, welfare and the introduction of new technology and related matters, areas which are thought to be of common interest to management and employees. In this way a joint consultation system prohibiting the use of a strike or lockout as a solution can easily co-exist with collective bargaining, which presumes the use of such methods as a means to an end.

Table 1 Percentage of unions according to subjects to be covered by works councils (WC) or collective bargaining (CB)

Subjects	CB (%)	WC (%)
Wages	89.0	14.4
Bonus	88.8	15.1
Retirement allowance	52.4	23.9
Working hours	50.8	29.2
Overtime, holiday work	45.0	37.2
Holidays	47.9	28.5
Vacation	40.8	30.8
Retirement	46.0	23.7
Job assignment, transfer	19.0	36.0
Voluntary retirement, dismissal	16.4	15.1
Welfare	39.0	44.4
Introduction of new technology and related matters	15.6	31.7
Foreign investment and related matters	6.0	12.3
Conclusion and amendment of collective agreement	45.2	27.1
Interpretation of collective agreement	24.3	22.2
Others	4.0	3.7

Source: Ministry of Labour

A joint consultation system based on intensive discussion in order to achieve consensus complements collective bargaining in the sense that both systems function as an effective mechanism to communicate between management and employees. Management can consult jointly with union representatives over issues which are sometimes confidential even to lower management. In this way employees, especially trade union members, can easily share information about the future of their company. Thus, both systems contribute towards enhancing the common interests between management and employees, one of the basic requirements for good industrial relations (see INDUSTRIAL AND LABOUR RELATIONS).

Agenda which are discussed at shop-floor level of joint consultation (*shokuba kondankai*) are shown in Table 2. Of the enterprises surveyed, 36 per cent explained management strategy to the representatives of the employees at shop-floor level (that is, they outlined management policy, production plans and sales plans). At the same time, 76.9 per cent discussed matters related to daily business, such as production schedule, temporary transfer of workers to other shop floors and changes in some production methods. Owing to their acquaintance with the situation, employees refrained from insisting on their own economic interests regardless of the overall effect on the company. They more easily accepted occurrences such as transfer to another shop proposed by management when the company had to reduce production volume or change products themselves.

Collective bargaining permits trade unions to strike when they cannot agree with a proposal made by management. However, under the joint consultation system employee representatives cannot oppose a management proposal. In these cases management either modifies the proposal according to the opinions of the employee representatives or suspends execution of the proposal, if only for a cooling-off period. In general, management follows the unofficial consensus in order to avoid severe conflict between management and employees.

Issues discussed at *shokuba kondankai* are graded in terms of employee participation. Table 3 identifies the degree of participation for management policy. In the case of basic policies on management, production and sales plans and the introduction or

Table 2 Subjects discussed in shokuba kondankai (round table at a workshop)

Subjects discussed	Percentage of enterprises
Management policy, production and sales plans	36.0
Matters related to daily business	76.9
Safety and hygiene	42.4
Matters related to welfare	20.8
Education and training	8.1
Others	1.7
No answer	0.2

Source: Ministry of Labour (1990: 20)

restructuring of company organization, management usually explains the situation and does not wait for agreement by employees. Where rationalization is concerned, however, management usually has to wait for consensus from the employees because such an issue has a major impact on employee security and working conditions.

As far as the area of working conditions (change of work schedule, working hours and wages) is concerned, management has to reach consensus with employee representatives. Table 4 shows that many such issues are graded as 'consultation' or 'co-determination', meaning that management is highly unlikely to execute its proposal without consensus. Thus management tries to persuade employees through the joint consultation system, promoting communication without resort to industrial action (see WORK AND ORGANIZATION SYSTEMS).

5 Future developments

The main characteristics of Japanese industrial relations were shaped in the short period of rapid economic growth following the Second World War. The enterprise union has established its social position as the representative organization of the working class, while *Rengo* has unified the main body of workers, including those in the public sector, so that it can improve their economic and political situation. As a complement, *Shuntohoshiki* was devised to supplement the bargaining power of each enterprise union by coordinating their bargaining schedule and demands at a national level. Enterprise unions may also obtain information about their company and express opinions through the joint consultation system. These mechanisms have contributed to the peaceful industrial relations experienced in Japan since the 1960s.

Table 3 Degree of participation according to subject (management decisions)

	Degree of participation (%)			
	Asking for			
Subject	Information	Opinions	Consultation	Co-determination
Basic management policy	77.6	8.5	11.7	2.2
Basic production and sales plan	66.3	12.5	18.6	2.5
Introduction or abandonment of company organization	61.3	13.0	19.4	6.3
Rationalization (introduction of new technology)	39.3	18.5	37.5	4.6

Source: Ministry of Labour (1990: 16)

Table 4 Degree of participation according to subject (working conditions)

| | Degree of participation (%) | | | |
| | Asking for | | | |
	Information	*Opinions*	*Consultation*	*Co-determination*
Change of work schedule	11.1	11.7	57.9	19.4
Working hours, holiday	9.1	9.6	56.3	25.1
Safety and hygiene in the workplace	11.5	17.8	61.9	8.8
Retirement	13.1	6.9	48.4	31.6
Wages, allowances	16.2	4.4	52.7	26.6
Retirement allowance, pension	16.6	5.5	49.7	28.3

Source: Ministry of Labour (1990: 16)

In spite of such a stable background, there exist many concerns about future developments in Japan. First, a declining trade unionization rate is considered a problem both by researchers and practitioners. The Japanese unionization rate of 24.4 per cent in 1992 is low compared with 43.9 per cent in 1990 in the UK and 42.0 per cent in 1991 in Germany. The establishment of *Rengo* may not halt the decline in unionization.

Another concern is the social role of trade unions. As collective bargaining becomes institutionalized and concentrated at a national level, at the enterprise level individual unions can no longer express any great influence. Workers of an enterprise union no longer expect outstanding increases in wages through bargaining because joint consultation has familiarized them with the economic performance of the company and they can anticipate the trends of general wage increases due to the detailed information available about national economic activity. Trade unions are thus being forced to discover new areas in which they can offer aid. Some such new fields are based social activities like environment protection, volunteer activities and international cooperation for refugees.

Finally, the role of national government will alter due to the changing activities of trade unions. The government has played an important role in establishing a framework for employer–trade union relations since the enactment of Industrial Relations Law in 1947. Since then it has refrained from directly interfering in industrial relations' problems. However, in the wake of the second oil crisis and the declining ability of trade unions to act effectively, the Ministry of Labour played an active role in improving employment conditions for all workers. Some laws such as the Equal Employment Opportunity Act (1986) and the Mandatory Retirement Age of Sixty Act passed the Diet under the strong support of the Ministry of Labour, while the Labour Standard Law of 1945 was also amended by that ministry to promote shorter working hours and increasing employment of female workers (see CORPORATISM).

These new laws and amendments of traditional labour laws reflect the fundamental change in the traditional framework of Japanese industrial relations. The future direction of these changes is still uncertain, given the turbulent political situation under the coalition between the Liberal Democratic Party and the Socialist Party. However, that things will change into the twenty-first century is beyond doubt.

KOJI OKUBAYASHI
KOBE UNIVERSITY

Further reading

(References cited in the text marked *)

Cole, R.E. (1979) *Work, Mobility and Participation: A Comparative Study of American and Japanese Industry*, Berkeley, CA: University of California Press. (Compares employment and participative management systems in Japan and the USA to clarify Japanese characteristics.)

Dore, R.P. (1973) *British Factory and Japanese Factory: The Origin of National Diversity in Industrial Relations*, Berkeley, CA: University of California Press. (Defines Japanese characteristics of industrial relations compared with those of the UK.)

Fujita, Y. (1981) *Employee Benefits and Industrial Relations*, Tokyo: Japan Institute of Labour. (Explains the practices of employee welfare plans based on empirical data.)

Hanami, T. (1991) *Managing Japanese Workers: Personnel Management Law and Practice in Japan*, Tokyo: Japan Institute of Labour. (Outlines labour laws concerning employees, including the Labour Standard Act and the Industrial Relations Act.)

Inagami, T. (1988) *Japanese Workplace Industrial Relations*, Tokyo: Japan Institute of Labour. (Focuses on labour management consultation systems at shop-floor level, as well as collective bargaining system at enterprise level.)

* Japan Institute of Labour (1993) *Japanese Working Life Profile 1993–1994*, Tokyo: Japan Institute of Labour. (Contains statistical data regarding Japanese workers, trade unions, forms of collective bargaining, etc.)

Kuwabara, Y. (1989) *Industrial Relations System in Japan: A New Interpretation*, Tokyo: Japan Institute of Labour. (Explains basic characteristics of Japanese industrial relations from the viewpoint of their history.

* Ministry of Labour (1985) *Basic Survey on Trade Unions*, Tokyo: Ministry of Labour. (Explains statistical data based on questionnaire survey concerning number of trade unions, union membership, etc. Good data source for researchers.)

* Ministry of Labour (1989) *Saisin Rohdoh Kyoyaku toh no Jittai* (Newest Data of Collective Agreements etc.), Tokyo: Ministry of Labour. (Statistical survey on labour union forms, contents and industrial disputes.)

* Ministry of Labour (1990) *Nihon no Rohsi Komyunikeision no Genzyoh* (Present Reality of Communication Between Labour and Management in Japan), Tokyo: Ministry of Labour. (Explains communication channels between labour and management including suggestion system, labour–management consultation, group production method.)

Okubayashi, K. (1989) 'The Japanese industrial relations system', *Journal of General Management* 14 (3): 67–88. (Explains the development of Japanese industrial relations since 1945.)

Shirai, T. (ed.) (1983) *Contemporary Industrial Relations In Japan*, Madison, WI: University of Wisconsin Press. (Provides a wide-ranging introduction to Japanese industrial relations in the 1970s.)

Takanashi, A. *et al.* (1989) *Shunto Wage Offensive: Historical Overview and Prospects*, Tokyo: Japan Institute of Labour. (Focuses on the new practices of collective bargaining known as *Shunto*.)

* Utada, T. (1986) *Labour Unions and Labour–Management Relations*, Tokyo: Japan Institute of Labour. (Gives elementary information on Japanese trade unions, collective bargaining and labour–management consultation.)

Whitehill, A.M. (1991) *Japanese Management: Tradition and Transition*, London: Routledge (Gives an overview of Japanese management from the viewpoint of its history and the culture of Japanese society.)

See also: COLLECTIVE BARGAINING; EMPLOYERS' ASSOCIATIONS; INDUSTRIAL AND LABOUR RELATIONS; TRADE UNIONS

Related topics in the IEBM: COMMITMENT IN JAPAN; MANAGEMENT IN JAPAN

Industrial relations in the United States of America

1 **The historical, economic and political context**
2 **The major participants in industrial relations**
3 **The main processes of industrial relations**
4 **Issues of current importance**
5 **Conclusions**

Overview

Both the relative power of the US economy and the global influence of its managerial and industrial relations models justify the effort necessary to understand it, despite the difficulties posed by its exceptionalism and complexity. The magnitude of the US economy is illustrated by its gross domestic product of $726 billion and population of over 263 million. The US influence on the global economy derives from the early development of professional management techniques in the USA, its guidance and financing of the post-Second World War recovery, and the size and world-wide scope of US multinational corporations.

1 The historical, economic and political context

Prior to industrialization, beginning in the 1790s, US skilled craftsmen formed unions (see TRADE UNIONS). According to the widely accepted view, this was in response to downward pressures on pay that were produced by growing and increasingly competitive markets. According to this view, being pre-factory, unionization was not, as might be expected in Marxist theory, stimulated by changes in the mode of production (Commons 1913). It is also generally believed that the skilled trades' nature, practical goals, and economic strategy of these early, pre-factory unions had a permanent influence on US

unions (Sturmthal 1973). It should be noted, however, that as is often the case in matters of US labour history, 'Versions of the past [serve] aims of the present' (Cooper and Terrill 1991: 46). Marxist scholars, not surprisingly, (see, for example, Foner 1947) disagree with the above analysis, seeing the market as only 'hastening' the inevitable development of working-class organizations among the wage-earning class.

The industrialization of the USA, which was later than that of Britain, began in the period 1810–40. From the mid-1820s to 1860, manufacturing developed in a broad range of industries, with textiles being among the most significant. Prior to the 1850s, however, production was mainly in small shops and in workers' homes. This extensive use of part-time home-working ameliorated the labour shortage that existed throughout this period. The establishment of the factory system in the 1850s and 1860s brought into the industrial system large numbers of native rural women and children, and eventually many immigrants from Ireland, Britain, Germany and other countries. These early factory workers did not unionize. This may have been partly because their pay was generally comparable to US farm earnings and higher than those of factory workers in Europe. In addition, vigorous repression of unionization by employers, both directly and through government action, inhibited unionization. It may also be that the high rate of worker mobility to other jobs, and considerable social mobility, hindered the development of the solidarity among workers that would have facilitated widespread organization of unions.

In spite of the difficulties, skilled craftsmen did form national unions in the 1860s. Also, the social reform-orientated Knights of Labor rose to prominence in the 1880s. By 1886, they organized 700,000 mainly unskilled workers. Unlike the craft unions, which focused on wages and the working conditions of their members, the Knights aimed at reforming society as a whole, turning back the clock to an earlier and better time before the rise of capitalism. Their strategy was 'cooperation', which meant forming worker cooperatives. The Knights had only a brief history. In the same year that they reached their peak of membership – 1886 – the craft unions organized on a national basis into the American Federation of Labor (AFL). These pragmatic 'business' unions drove the Knights from the field. By the turn of the century, the Knights had ceased to be an important force. This experience of idealistic unionism rising for a time – only to fall before pragmatic economic unionism – has occurred several times in the history of US labour.

Around 1900, building on a large home market made accessible by an improved transportation system, large corporations achieved dominance in US industrial life. These complex, impersonal organizations required systematic strategies for managing their workers. Responding to this need, Frederick Taylor, the father of 'scientific management', and his industrial engineer disciples gained a powerful influence on the ideology and practice of management in the USA (see TAYLOR, F.W.). These ideas became widely accepted in the USA some time before they were accepted in Europe and other parts of the world. By declaring 'scientific' principles for the design of work and pay, the Taylorists undermined the rationale for determining these matters through power-based bargaining by unions. Added to this difficulty for the unions was the continuing vigorous opposition of the capitalists, who had both enormous power and high prestige.

Nevertheless, the craft unions were able to survive and prosper in the first two decades of the century, partly because of the cooperative mechanisms put into place during the First World War, and their patriotic support of the war. During this same period the craft unions were challenged by the rise of the first powerful US union of the Left, the Industrial Workers of the World (IWW). The IWW, or 'Wobblies' (a title allegedly derived from

their drinking habits), combined philosophies of anarchism and syndicalism with tactics that included songs and martyrs, to rise to prominence during the pre-war years. Like the reformist Knights, they had only a brief moment of glory, and during the First World War (which they opposed) and the post-war reaction to the Russian revolution, they were crushed by the forces of capitalism and patriotic fervour.

By the 1920s, a combination of the influence of Taylorism, employer use of company-dominated unions as a union-substitution device, tough employer action in collective bargaining, widespread use of anti-union propaganda by employer groups, and a hostile legal environment had reduced even the proud and once-powerful craft unions to a very weak position.

It was during the Great Depression of the 1930s that US unions rose from the ashes and, for the first time, penetrated mass-production industry, organizing large numbers of factory workers. Working conditions and pay had deteriorated. There was a changed political environment with the election of President Franklin D. Roosevelt in 1932. A great wave of strikes, most of which were successful, broke out in 1934. The Wagner Act was passed in 1935, giving workers for the first time a federally guaranteed right to organize and strike. The unions, organized by industry rather than by craft (United Automobile Workers, United Mine Workers, United Steel Workers), adopted the strategy of mass organizing campaigns. This strategy and the fact that the unions were united in a new labour movement – the Congress of Industrial Organizations (CIO) – led to unionization of the car, steel, rubber, coal and other industries.

In the 1940s and 1950s the unions continued to grow and to develop the collective bargaining system (see COLLECTIVE BARGAINING). Since the 1950s, they have organized large numbers of government employees, but have declined in strength overall. In the early 1990s, US unions covered less than 16 per cent of the workforce. Up until this point they had been comparatively militant, although the number of working days lost due to industrial stoppages decreased in the 1980s (but at least part of the apparent reduction reflects the change in the basis of collecting stoppage data).

Employment patterns in the USA are probably prototypical. The services sector employs over two-thirds of civilian employees (along with Canada this is a higher percentage than any other OECD (Organization for Economic Cooperation and Development) country); less than one-quarter are employed in industry, and only a few are employed in agriculture. The level of unemployment in the USA has historically tended to be higher than that in Australia, Japan and most of western Europe, but this relationship reversed in relation to Europe in the 1980s (see EMPLOYMENT AND UNEMPLOYMENT, ECONOMICS OF).

Although the USA is heavily engaged in international trade, exports of goods constitute less than 11 per cent of its gross domestic product – smaller than any other OECD country. The relative unimportance of exports to the economy reflects the USA's large home market which creates a greater potential for self-sufficiency than exists in most other countries. However, large international trade deficits have been a major problem for the economy since at least the 1980s.

The politics of the USA are largely politics of the centre. The two major parties that dominate national politics, the Republicans and Democrats, have generally absorbed and moderated the ideas of more extreme groups. However, during the Great Depression of the 1930s, Franklin Roosevelt's Democrats moved some distance to the left, and in the early 1980s, Ronald Reagan's Republicans moved to the right. Even in these instances, substantial segments of the other major party moved in the direction set out by the party in power, thereby shifting the centre. Distinctions between them are further blurred by the fact that, unlike most political parties in other English-speaking countries, party discipline is weak.

Nevertheless, the two political parties do differ with respect to the part of the centre that they occupy. The Democrats, while not a labour party, are clearly more left-inclined than the Republicans. In general, they have more 'liberal' political goals, and are more supportive of government action to achieve social and economic justice. As a party, the Democrats enjoy the support of the unions.

Under Ronald Reagan and his successor George Bush, the Republicans moved further to the right, drawing upon traditional US notions of individualism and distrust of 'big government', a 'backlash' reaction to demands of blacks for opportunity and equality, and what was for a time at least a rising tide of religious fundamentalism. They also used appeals to patriotism to salve the wounds to national pride inflicted by the loss of the Vietnam War, George Bush as a presidential candidate 'wrapping himself in the flag' during his successful 1988 presidential campaign. This was combined with a new move toward market-orientated economic policies, increases in military expenditure (at least until the end of the Cold War), and record high government budget deficits, associated with strong, but uneven, economic prosperity until the recession of the early 1990s. The election of the Democratic president Bill Clinton – and in particular, Clinton's appointment of Robert Reich as US Secretary of Labour – may mark the beginning of a trend back towards a more centrist position, but at time of writing the political and economic situation in the USA remains uncertain (see REICH, R.M.)

Since the 1950s policy issues relating to unions and collective bargaining have not often been high on the national agenda, but there has been a great deal of legislative activity in the broad area of employment relations. Legislative initiatives in the areas of minimum wages, termination of employment, race and sex discrimination in employment, pensions, health and safety, plant closing, drug testing, discrimination against workers with disabilities and polygraphs (lie detector machines) all drew a great deal of attention and produced a plethora of new laws in the 1980s and early 1990s.

The nature of industrial relations

The industrial relations system in the USA consists of two rather distinct sectors: a unionized sector and a non-union sector. These two sectors interconnect in many ways and share common legal and social underpinnings, but do differ significantly.

The unionized sector has historically been characterized by openly adversarial relations between labour and management (Barbash 1981). The traditional US view sees unions and management as performing the functions of serving discrete, and fundamentally opposed, interests. The conflict between unions and management is circumscribed, however, by the limited goals of US unions. As the unions are still mainly concerned with the 'pure and simple' goals of the founders of the US labour movement, that is, better wages, hours and conditions of work, and do not wish to be broadly involved in management, their challenge to management has been rather constrained. They have been willing to enter into what the old radical trade unionists called a 'treaty with the boss' – a collective bargaining agreement covering those matters that concern them, even giving up the right to strike for the duration of this 'treaty'. Conflict in the unionized sector is further bounded by the recognition by managers and unions that there are some broad areas of mutual interest.

The end result in the unionized sector is a fairly stable situation where conflict is legitimate but bounded as to grounds, timing, and emotional intensity. The main threat to its stability is endemic managerial resistance to unions, which from time to time results in efforts to move establishments from the unionized sector to the non-union sector – either by disestablishing a union in an existing location or moving the work to a southern or western location where unions are weak. In the late 1980s and early 1990s, managers and unionists who are proponents of labour–management cooperation (one of the issues discussed at length below) have challenged the basic adversarial nature of the US system. It remains to be seen whether this is a fundamental change or merely a tactical expansion of the area of accepted common interest.

The non-union sector is characterized by broad management discretion and control over the terms and conditions of employment. This is limited only by labour–market constraints, protective labour legislation, the

desire of managers to avoid unionization, and the strong influence of a 'positive' managerial philosophy that holds that firms 'ought to' offer favourable conditions of employment to employees. This sector includes private white-collar employment, electronics, small firms, most of the textile industry, most of the service sector, and manufacturing employees in a variety of industries. The main threat to the stability of this sector is the sporadic efforts of unions to organize it.

The environment of industrial relations

The economic environment has always had a powerful influence upon the US industrial relations system. The predominant employers are large private-sector enterprises. Unions in the USA were created to deal with, and have adapted to, operating in a capitalist economy dominated by such firms. Government's role in the economic system, although it has fluctuated over the years, has largely remained more limited than in other countries. Economic growth has helped to produce relatively favourable terms and conditions of employment for the majority of workers in the USA since the Second World War.

A reduction in demand for US goods was part of the general decrease in demand during the post-1974 recession, and was exacerbated by the competition from high quality goods produced in other countries. In the home market, competition from higher quality or lower cost foreign goods has particularly affected major industries such as cars, textiles and steel. In these and other industries, improvements in technology, encouraged by this competition, have caused workers to be replaced by machines. To further complicate matters, the type of labour demanded has been changed both by new technology and the shift of the US economy from manufacturing to services. All of this has weakened the bargaining power of labour. In periods of relative economic growth, collective bargaining demands and results are generally more favourable to labour. However, with a return to general prosperity in the late 1980s, unions remained weak and wage improvements were only moderate. The early 1990s' recession did not change this situation.

The political environment in the USA, with its representative democratic institutions, has historically provided a structure for the development of both free trade unions and free management. The political strength of capital and its representatives has always been sufficient to preserve broad areas of managerial discretion from government regulation. The balance of political forces has also permitted the development of reasonably strong trade unions and the imposition of some governmental constraints upon managerial freedom in the industrial relations arena. The government endorsed the formation of private-sector unions during the period 1935–47. The federal government established bargaining with its own employees, and many state and local governments followed suit in the 1960s and 1970s. However, in some areas of the USA, particularly in the south, state and local governments do not permit collective bargaining by their employees.

During the 1980s and early 1990s the political environment accentuated the trend towards ever-increasing management power in industrial relations. Conservative national administrations 'deregulated' the transport industry, increasing competition and placing downward pressure on wages. They have lessened the influence of government upon employers generally by moderating the enforcement of laws protecting workers from health and safety hazards and discrimination.

2 The major participants in industrial relations

In the USA, of all the participants in the industrial relations system, it is the employers who have generally been the most powerful of the actors.

Employers and their organizations

As Kochan has written, 'Management is the driving force, in any advanced industrial relations system' (Kochan 1980: 179). In the USA and in other industrialized countries this derives, at least in part, from the crucial role of management in ensuring the efficiency and survival of work organizations. It may further stem from the high general social status of managers and their relatively high position in the organizational hierarchy.

By the mid-1990s, the non-union sector of the US workforce included more than 85 per cent of the workers. Throughout most of this sector, redundant workers can be laid off in whatever order the employer desires, and terminated for any or no reason. Furthermore, the conditions under which employment takes place are essentially employer-determined, limited only by labour-market forces and the protective labour legislation (discussed below).

In some non-unionized firms, the conditions of employment are relatively favourable. 'Personnel welfarism' has been a strong movement in the USA since the early years of the twentieth century. Modern personnel practice is oriented towards human resource management (HRM) – the notion that the labour factor of production is valuable, worth investing in, and worth preserving (Heneman *et al.* 1980: 6). In this 'enlightened' view, it is in the interests of the corporation as a whole to attract, retain and improve workers. It is a unitary perspective that sees no necessary conflict between the interests of managers and other workers.

Employers' organizations are relatively unimportant in the USA (see EMPLOYERS' ASSOCIATIONS). In contrast to many other countries, there have never been national employers' confederations engaging in a full range of industrial relations activities. In the non-union sector, however, there have long been employers' organizations with a mission to avoid the unionization of their members' employees. The National Association of Manufacturers was formed for this purpose in the nineteenth century. At both the regional and national levels, the Chamber of Commerce includes union avoidance in its activities. These employer groups and others engage in anti-union litigation, lobbying and publicity campaigns. They, along with management consultants, engage in the lucrative business of educating employers in techniques of union avoidance.

There has been a considerable increase in employer anti-union activities since the mid-1970s. These actions have ranged from locating plants in non-union areas in the south and west (the so-called 'Sun Belt'), to openly violating the labour laws, to providing higher pay than the union range. The reasons for this increase are not entirely clear. It may be, at least in part, the result of a movement arising from the lower levels of management in protest against the strictures which unions impose on the performance of work (Piore 1982: 8). This is especially ironic as many union rules were developed in the context of management application of the Taylorist notions of scientific management described earlier. Another cause of increased employer resistance may be managers seizing the opportunity to defeat their historic adversary when it is weak. The acceptance of unions by US managers has always been somewhat grudging, and based more upon necessity than choice.

The unions

The fundamental characteristics of the US labour movement are as follows:

1 goals which are largely those of 'bread and butter' unionism;
2 a strategy that is mainly economic;
3 collective bargaining as a central well-developed activity;
4 relatively low total union density;
5 strength *vis-à-vis* the employer on the shop floor;
6 an organizational structure in which the national union holds the reins of power within the union;
7 financial strength;
8 leadership drawn largely from the rank-and-file.

Selig Perlman long ago argued that the US labour movement exhibited a 'Tom, Dick and Harry' idealism – an idealism derived from the ordinary worker (1970: 274–5). Perlman believed that unions, because they reflected the aspirations of their members, adopted those goals which seemed most important to the workers. These goals, said Perlman, had nothing to do with the imagined utopia of the Marxist 'intellectuals', but rather with the 'pure and simple' goals espoused by such labour leaders as Samuel Gompers, the 'father' of the US labour movement. Perlman's argument still affords a basic understanding of the US labour movement. Although US unions have also pursued wider goals, and are now newly interested in cooperation with management to increase worker feelings of self-worth, what has endured has been their emphasis upon practical improvements in wages, hours and conditions of work. Of course, unions in other countries have also sought 'bread and butter', but US unions have focused more closely upon this outcome than have most others.

The ideology of US unions is still much as it was expressed in 1911 by Samuel Gompers:

> The ground-work principle of America's labour movement has been to recognize that first things must come first. The primary essential in our mission has been the protection of the wage workers, now; to increase his wages; to cut hours off the long workday, which was killing him; to improve the safety and the sanitary conditions of the workshop; to free him from the tyrannies, petty or otherwise, which served to make his existence a slavery.
>
> (Gompers 1919: 20)

Unions in the USA have relied upon collective bargaining, accompanied by the strike threat, as their main weapon (see INDUSTRIAL CONFLICT). This strategy has influenced the other characteristics of the US labour movement. It has provided the basis for an effective role on the shop floor, as the day-to-day work of administering the agreement requires this; it has required unions to be solvent financially in order to have a credible strike threat, and it has resulted in an organizational structure in which the power within the union is placed where it can best be used for collective bargaining – with the national union. Centralization of power over strike funds in the national union has been a crucial source of union ability to develop common rules and to strike effectively. It has facilitated, and perhaps even required, an independence from political parties that might be tempted to subordinate the economic to the political. It is one reason why there is a relatively low total union density, as collective bargaining organizations have a concern about density only as it pertains to their individual economic territories. It has also contributed to one of the concomitants of low density – weak political power.

Although US unions have emphasized collective bargaining, they have also engaged in politics. Their political action has for the most part taken the form of rewarding friends and punishing enemies among politicians and lobbying for legislation. They have avoided being involved in the formation of a labour party. The American Federation of Labor–Congress of Industrial Organizations (AFL–CIO) Committee on Political Education (COPE) and similar union political agencies are major financial contributors to political campaigns. The goals of such political activity have often been closely related to unions' economic goals, being aimed at making collective bargaining more effective. However, the US labour movement has also been a major proponent of progressive political causes such as laws on civil rights, minimum wages, plant closing notice, and other subjects of benefit to citizens generally.

Why does the USA have no labour party? First, it would be difficult to operate as an independent national political force when representing only a small proportion of the workforce. Second, US workers have traditionally been highly independent politically, often voting in ways other than those desired by their union leaders. Third, the limited US experience with separate labour parties has not been favourable. Formed in 1828, the Working Men's Party was arguably the first labour party in the world. Its collapse, and the severe problems that it engendered, caused unions to steer clear of a repeat of that experience. Some later attempts were made, but were not much more successful. These were probably hindered by the historic difficulty of forming any third party in the USA. Fourth, the idea of a labour party is one which has often been urged by left-wing unionists who were the losers in struggles for control of unions in the 1930s and 1940s, and were purged during the 'Red-scare' years of the 1950s. The

failure to form a labour party may be accounted for in part by the narrow economic orientations of US unions, making the unions themselves and their federations seem logically to be the exclusive organizations for labour. Although others are puzzled by the American failure to have a labour party, US trade unionists are unable to see why they should do such a peculiar thing.

Yet, in the 1980s, the AFL–CIO did move towards greater identification with a party (the Democratic Party) than has been the case in the past. This move was accompanied by many statements by labour leaders which provide evidence of a new awareness of the importance of politics.

The structure of the US labour movement is rather loose compared to that of other western union movements. The AFL–CIO is a federation of national unions that includes approximately 85 to 90 per cent of US union members. It has been strengthened in the 1980s by the re-affiliation of such major unions as the International Brotherhood of Teamsters (IBT), United Auto Workers (UAW), United Mine Workers (UMW) and several others. This has given the US labour movement the greatest degree of cohesiveness that it has seen in thirty years. The AFL–CIO serves as the chief political and public relations voice for the US labour movement, resolves jurisdictional disputes among its members, enforces codes of ethical practices and policies against racial and sex discrimination, and is the US labour's main link to the international labour movement.

The national unions have been described as occupying the 'kingpin' position in the American labour movement (Barbash 1967). They maintain ultimate power over the important function of collective bargaining, in large part through their control of strike funds. The national unions can establish and disestablish local unions and can withdraw from the AFL–CIO if they wish. The national presidents of unions are generally considered to be the most powerful figures in the US labour movement.

The local unions perform the day-to-day work of the labour movement. They usually conduct the bargaining over the terms of new agreements and conduct strikes. They administer the agreement, performing the important function of enforcing the complex set of rights that the US collective bargaining agreement creates. Social activities among union members take place at the local level, where there exists what there is of a union culture in the USA (Barbash 1967).

The composition of the US labour movement has gradually come to include more white-collar and female workers. As one would expect from the national shift of employment to non-manufacturing, the majority of union members now work in non-manufacturing occupations.

The US labour movement is generally considered an exceptional case because of its apolitical 'business unionism' ideology, focusing rather narrowly on benefits to existing membership. The most convincing explanations for this are historical (Kassalow 1974). First, there is no feudal tradition in the USA, which has made the distinctions among classes less obvious than in much of Europe and, unlike Australia, the USA lacks any other special historical circumstances giving rise to strong class feelings. Second, US capitalism developed in a form that allowed fairly widespread prosperity. Third, the great diversity of the population has always hampered the organization of a broad-based working-class movement. Fourth, the early establishment of voting rights and free universal public education eliminated those potential working-class issues in the nineteenth century. Fifth, social mobility from the working class to the entrepreneurial category blurred class lines, creating a basis for the widely-held belief in the 'log cabin to White House' myth. In consequence, the US labour movement has seldom defined itself in class terms. Additionally, the historical experience of US unionists was that class-conscious unions, that is, those that assumed the 'burden of socialism', tended to be repressed by the strong forces of US capitalism. A related but somewhat different explanation (Sturmthal 1973) is that US labour formed an economic strike-based strategy in its early years because this was appropriate to the conditions of labour shortage under which

it began, and it has continued to pursue this course, even when it might be inappropriate.

Government

Government has three main roles in industrial relations: the direct regulation of terms and conditions of employment; regulation of the manner in which organized labour and management relate to each other; and as an employer.

Historically, the direct regulation of terms and conditions of employment was limited to the areas of employment discrimination, worker safety, unemployment compensation, minimum wages and maximum hours, and retirement. In 1964, the government acted to prohibit discrimination in employment on the grounds of race, colour, sex, religion, national origin or age. It has also proscribed discrimination against disabled persons and Vietnam War veterans. Most recently, it acted to broadly prohibit discrimination against disabled workers.

The government has addressed problems of worker safety; mainly through the Federal Occupational Safety and Health Act 1970 (OSHA), state health safety laws, and state workers' compensation laws. OSHA mandates a safe workplace, both by imposing a general duty of safety upon employers and by providing a detailed set of regulations for each industry. Employers flouting safety and health standards are subject to fines and remedial orders. Workers' compensation laws provide for medical care and income protection for workers injured on the job. Also, they encourage safety indirectly by increasing the costs of insurance for employers experiencing a large number of on-the-job injuries. Unemployment compensation is provided for on a state-by-state basis, but with some federal control and funding. It involves payments to people who become involuntarily unemployed and are seeking work.

Retirement benefits are regulated in two main ways. First, through the Social Security system employers and employees are required to pay a proportion of wages (7.65 per cent each in 1992) into a government fund. It is out of this fund that pensions are paid by the government to eligible retired employees (Social Security Act). The second way in which government controls pensions is by regulation of the private pension funds that are set up voluntarily by employers. The Employee Retirement Income Security Act of 1974 requires retirement plans to be financially secure, and insures these plans. It also mandates that employees become permanently vested in their retirement rights after a certain period.

There are a number of long-standing issues in the area of government regulation of conditions of employment. A major public policy debate has long taken place over the minimum wage laws. As in the UK, many economists believe that such laws tend to create unemployment, particularly among the young. This belief has led to proposals for a sub-minimum wage for this group of workers, for whom unemployment has been particularly high. Opponents of this idea see it as creating unemployment for adults and greater employer exploitation of low-wage workers. The debate leading up to the 1989 changes in the law was curiously muted; the only disagreement between a mainly Democratic Congress and a Republican President was over the amount of increase and the adoption of a youth training wage.

In the field of sex discrimination laws, the concept of 'comparable worth' was much debated in the 1980s. This is the notion that different jobs should carry equal rates of pay if they are worth the same to the employee. That is, the job of secretary, which is mostly held by women, should pay as well as that of a truck driver, which is mostly held by men, if its worth is comparable. The chief argument against this theory is its difficulty of application. In the early 1990s, sexual harassment gained visibility as an issue because of charges of this conduct raised against a nominee for the Supreme Court, Clarence Thomas, who had headed the government agency charged with enforcing anti-discrimination laws. Also in 1991, Congress enacted amendments in the employment discrimination laws. They reversed restrictions which had made it more difficult for employees to assert claims under the law. These restrictions had been read into them originally by a conservative

Supreme Court. Over the years occupational safety and health laws and pension regulations have been challenged by employers and conservative politicians because of their cost to employers and their alleged ineffectiveness.

Government regulation of the labour-management relationship consists largely of a set of ground rules through which these actors establish, and work out the terms of, their relationship. Through the National Labor Relations Act (NLRA) of 1935, as amended in 1947 and 1959, government provides a structure of rules that establishes certain employee rights with respect to collective action. The right to organize and bargain, as well as the right to refrain from organizing and bargaining, is set out in the law. These rights are made effective through the establishment of an election process for workers to choose whether they want union representation, and the prohibition of certain 'unfair labour practices' on the part of employers and unions.

Since the late 1970s, there has been a continuing debate over the adequacy of laws protecting workers' rights to form and join unions. Management spokespersons have argued that unions are too powerful and should not be encouraged by more benevolent organizing rules. The unions have maintained to the contrary, citing numerous violations of employee rights by many employers. The unions argue for reforms to facilitate the enforcement of laws prohibiting discrimination against workers for union activity, and to expedite the process of choosing union representation. Union leaders have gone to the extreme of suggesting repeal of the NLRA as useless. The reality is that employers can violate the labour laws with impunity, knowing the enforcement mechanisms are too weak to do them much damage. The unions tried to correct these problems in their support of the proposed Labor Law Reform Act of 1977. The failure of this legislative initiative in 1978 was a crushing blow to the political credibility of organized labour. This was one of the main spurs to increased union political activity in the 1984 presidential election and since. The main effort by labour to change these laws at present is the proposed Workplace Fairness

Act which would prohibit employers from permanently replacing striking workers (as discussed above in relation to the Caterpillar strike).

Since 1959, the government has regulated the internal affairs of unions. Federal law creates a 'Bill of Rights' for union members, requiring that unions accord them rights of free speech and political action. It also punishes union officials who mishandle union funds and outlaws certain anti-democratic practices by unions. In 1991, an election held under government supervision resulted in a state of 'reform' candidates taking power in the historically corrupt Teamsters union (IBT).

An explosion of federal employment legislation took place in 1988. In that year the Employee Polygraph Protection Act placed limitations on the use of lie detectors by employers. These machines, notorious for their unreliability and degrading uses, were being widely used by employers for both pre-employment testing and investigations of employee wrongdoing. This increased protection of employees was balanced, however, by the Drug-Free Workplace Act of 1988. This applies to employers that do business with the federal government and strongly encourages drug testing and punishment of employees for both on- and off-duty drug use. Employer actions in this area have received further encouragement from regulations of the US Department of Transportation and Department of Defense requiring broad drug testing of employees in those industries. Drug testing of federal and railroad employees, at least under some circumstances, was approved by the US Supreme Court in two 1989 decisions (*National Treasury Employees Union* v. *Von Raab; Skinner* v. *Railway Labor Executives Association*). The issue of employee drug testing is a battleground on which the traditional protections of individual human dignity are under siege by public panic over a crisis in drug use.

An additional piece of legislation adopted in 1988 is the Worker Adjustment and Retraining Notification Act (WARN), or 'plant closing' law. This federal statute requires employers, with some exceptions, to give 60 days' advance notice of a plant closing or a mass layoff.

This trend in government action continued into the 1990s. The changes in the employment discrimination laws mentioned above make it easier for workers to prevail in their claims. The adoption of these changes was an important attempt by Congress to reverse the weakening of these laws by conservative judges. Perhaps of more practical importance is the Americans With Disabilities Act which, since 1992, has imposed on most employers the obligation to make reasonable accommodation to the needs of disabled employees. This may even include protection for employees with infectious diseases such as AIDS.

The rapid increase in public sector unionization in the 1960s and 1970s was probably the most important development in the US labour movement since the 1930s. Teachers initiated this, as they successfully protested about declines in their salaries and benefits relative to those of other workers. Unionization spread rapidly through most areas of government employment. As a result of this wave of unionizing, there has been an important change in the composition of the US labour movement, with public-employee unions now representing slightly over one-third of union members. It remains to be seen to what degree this will affect the basic goals and activities of the movement.

3 The main processes of industrial relations

In the non-union sector, employers have devised a set of HRM practices to systematically determine pay and conditions of work. With respect to compensation, a combination of job evaluation and individual performance evaluation systems is common. The range of possible wage rates to be paid to workers in a job of, say, clerk are determined by an assessment of the worth of the job to the firm, that is, job evaluation. A particular employee is assigned a wage rate within this range depending upon seniority, performance, or other factors. In addition to pay, fringe benefits such as health insurance, pensions and holidays are determined by company policy. All of this is done with an eye to the external labour market, with total compensation having to be adequate to attract and keep needed workers.

With respect to conditions of work, non-union employers establish job design and conditions in two principal ways. First, there is what has been called the 'conventional management theory' approach, in which jobs are standardized and specialized, in the spirit of Frederick Taylor. Jobs are designed in such a way as to maximize efficiency. Second, the 'behavioural science' approach, originally founded in human relations theory, looks to the internal motivation of workers to provide efficient and high quality production. It attempts to design jobs in such a way that workers can fulfil their goals and the employer's at the same time. The enrichment of jobs, or at least their enlargement to provide more variety, is a major thrust of this notion. Quality circles and other schemes for worker participation in the design of jobs are consistent with this approach.

Collective bargaining, which chiefly determines the outcomes in the unionized sector, has reached an advanced stage of development in the USA. Since the 1940s, collective bargaining has produced a high standard of living for most unionized workers, protection for the worker interest in fair treatment and a complex and detailed set of rules governing the employment relationship, while generally preserving the managerial ability to ensure efficiency.

The collective bargaining structure is highly fragmented, and this fragmentation is increasing. Single company or single plant agreements are the norm in manufacturing. Most collective bargaining takes place at such levels. Even where national agreements exist, as in the car industry, substantial scope is left for local variation. Yet, in this large and diverse country, there is diversity as to this also, and much bargaining still occurs at higher levels.

Third party intervention is widespread. In the private sector, government mediators are active in the negotiation of new agreements, and their work is generally admired in negotiations involving government employees, many state laws provide for binding arbitration of unresolved disputes over the terms of a new agreement. This is especially common where the government employees involved, such as fire fighters or police officers, are considered to be 'essential'. Interest arbitration of the terms of the new agreement is very rare in the private sector. However, in both the private and public sectors, rights arbitration of disputes over the application and interpretation of an existing agreement is nearly always provided for in collective bargaining agreements. Decisions of arbitrators have historically been treated by the courts as final, binding and unappealable, although their finality has been weakened somewhat since the 1970s.

Although there is considerable variety in collective bargaining agreements (contracts), they share certain nearly universal aspects. Most are very detailed, although the craft-union contracts are less so. Agreements generally cover wages, hours of work, holidays, pensions, health insurance, life insurance, union recognition, management rights, and the handling and arbitration of grievances. Most agreements have a limited duration, usually of one, two or three years.

At least for unionized workers, the relative lack of government welfare programmes in the USA is somewhat compensated for by the extensive protection included in these agreements. However, the very substantial declines in holidays, and automatic wage adjustments, although balanced by gains in other areas, reflect the decreased strength of US unions in what has traditionally been their bailiwick. Furthermore, although union wages and benefits continue to be substantially higher than those of non-union workers, their increases have been slightly smaller than those of non-union workers in several recent years.

During the 1980s substantial pressures were brought to bear upon unions to reduce wages. In the early 1980s the chief response to this was union agreements to general wage cuts in what was known as 'concession bargaining'. Although the unions often obtained a *quid pro quo* for these concessions, such as membership on a corporate board of directors, it was an extraordinary event for established unions to agree to a reversal of the historic upward trend of wages in collective bargaining. This wave of concession bargaining was followed by a series of 'two-tier' wage agreements in which certain workers, usually new employees, received a lower rate of pay for doing the same work as other employees, violating the traditional union rule of equal pay for equal work. The two-tier system provides a means for employers to reduce labour costs without offending (and perhaps losing) their experienced workers, while at the same time permitting the experienced majority of workers at the firm to project their wages at the expense of the minority of newer workers. However, as was obvious from the outset, there is tremendous potential for dissatisfaction of newer workers, conflict among groups of workers, and difficulty in attracting new hires.

Collective bargaining dealt with a variety of challenging issues in the late 1980s and early 1990s. The rapid rise of health care costs, most of which had been borne by employers, has prompted them to shift some of this burden to employees, and unions and employers to work together to contain these costs. Profit-sharing plans have been proposed and accepted at such firms as Weyerhauser, Chrysler and Uniroyal-Goodrich. Childcare has become a major item on the union bargaining agenda for the 1990s, although employer interest in providing these benefits appears to be limited. Corporate mergers and acquisitions have given rise to union insistence on 'successorship clauses' in contracts with such diverse employers as Bloomingdale's Department Stores, and Firestone. In such a clause the company agrees to require a buyer of the business to retain the union relationship. Technological changes have sparked agreements on early retirement, preferential hiring, pay continuance guarantees and retraining.

Although the US collective bargaining system is currently being widely criticized for its adversarial nature and obsolescence, a review of its accomplishments in the 1980s and early 1990s provides clear testimony to its strength and flexibility. It may bear some share of blame for the problems of US competitiveness, at least for its invention of automatic wage adjustment based upon increases in the consumer price index (COLA clauses), which raised wages unexpectedly during the high inflation of the 1970s. However, in reviewing the adjustments that it has made to the enormous economic disturbances of the 1980s and 1990s, one is struck with its ability in times of change to meet the efficiency requirements of management while providing workers with as much protection as possible.

4 Issues of current importance

Of the many issues concerning US industrial relations, let us discuss three, in particular: industrial justice, labour–management cooperation and union decline.

Industrial justice

Industrial justice has become one of the most widely discussed issues, chiefly because of increasing public dissatisfaction with the common law doctrine of employment at will. Under this legal doctrine an employee can be dismissed at any time, for any (or no) reason. Historically, the only exceptions to this rule have been statutory prohibitions against dismissals that discourage union membership or discriminate on other forbidden grounds, and contractual obligations that the employer voluntarily assumes.

In the unionized sector, employers agree to refrain from dismissing or disciplining employees except for 'just cause'. To enforce this, US collective bargaining agreements provide for a multi-step grievance procedure, with the ultimate step being arbitration by an outside neutral, employed jointly by the union and management. The concept of 'just cause' is one that has been reasonably well defined in the decisions of arbitrators. A distinction is made between 'major' offences, such as theft and insubordination, and 'minor' offences. For a major offence a worker can be discharged immediately upon first office. For a minor offence, 'progressive' discipline must be used. Progressive discipline means the imposition of progressively more severe discipline, ordinarily beginning with an oral warning, and moving to a written warning, suspension, and eventually discharge for repeated offences. An employer is also required to impose discipline evenly across employees.

The contrast between the protections available to unionized workers and minority employers on the one hand, and other workers on the other hand, has led to proposals for a general system of legislative protection of all workers. One state, Montana, has adopted such legislation. Also, numerous court decisions have weakened the employment-at-will doctrine. Courts have held that employees cannot be terminated for refusing to violate a law or for 'whistle blowing' when an employer violates a law or endangers public safety. They have found employers liable for money damages for terminating employees in violation of the implied obligation of good faith and fair dealing, and for acting contrary to provisions in employee handbooks. Terminating an employee in an abusive manner can also give rise to a claim of unjust termination.

Labour–management cooperation

Labour–management cooperation's prominence as an issue is perhaps the most unusual feature of the current discussions about industrial relations in the USA. This is somewhat odd in a system that is still characterized by adversarial relations between management and unions. But the pressures of international competition and the Japanese example, among other things, have caused a re-examination of the foundation principle of the necessity of labour–management conflict. Recognition that there are broad areas of common interest amenable to a problem-solving approach, known as win/win or integrative bargaining, is not new. However, the emphasis upon this has reached new highs in recent years. This trend has been encouraged by scholarly writing, such as the influential *The Transformation of American Industrial Relations* (Kochan *et al.* 1986), the establishment and activities of a Bureau of Labor–Management Relations and Cooperative Programs in the US Department of Labor, the 1978 Labor–Management Cooperation Act adopted by the Federal Congress, and the 1988 report of the President's Advisory Committee on Mediation and Conciliation.

Cooperation takes many forms. Scanlon and Rucker plans, which share productivity gains with workers, have been around for many years, as have joint health and safety committees. More recent innovations are quality circles, quality of working life (QWL) programs, and even scattered instances of union representation on corporate boards of directors. Some of these have been initiated by strategic management decisions aimed at improving productivity or quality. In some instances, innovations such as membership on corporate boards have come in exchange for union wage concessions. A number of union leaders, such as Douglas Fraser, former president of the United Auto Workers, and Morton Bahr, president of the Communication Workers of America (CWA), have become vigorous advocates of increased direct worker participation in the decisions that affect their working lives. The shop floor version of this amounts to adding direct industrial democracy to the more traditional representative industrial democracy.

There are numerous well-publicized instances of successful ventures in labour–management cooperation. These include the experience at New United Motor Manufacturing Inc. (NUMMI); a joint venture between General Motors and Toyota; General Motors' Saturn contract with the UAW; non-adversarial negotiations between Xerox and the Amalgamated Textile Workers Union (ATWU), and the relationship worked out between National Steel Co. and the United Steelworkers of America (USWA). The claimed benefits are improved satisfaction of workers, higher productivity and better quality. There have, however, been numerous, less well-publicized examples of failures of attempts at cooperative programs. There has also developed in some unions something of a rank-and-file anti-cooperative movement. The 'New Directions' movement in the UAW is the prime example of this. Another problem in the credibility of managements in proposing cooperation while working avidly to destroy or avoid unions, thereby removing the grounds for the trust that is necessary for co-operative programs. In spite of the difficulties, however, there does seem to be a generally shared opinion among managers and many union leaders that cooperation is a necessary condition for economic survival in a competitive world.

Union decline

The decline of the union movement is an issue receiving increasing attention in the USA. Union density has slipped substantially since 1980. A number of reasons are probably associated with its decline, including:

1 the shift in the economy from manufacturing to services;
2 the challenges of technological change and foreign competition;
3 employer anti-union activities, both positive and negative;
4 changing employee preferences and values away from 'bread and butter' (Allen and Keaveny 1988).

Furthermore, the recession of the early 1980s hit hardest at unionized basic industries, causing massive losses of union members. These industries recovered somewhat in the late 1980s but did not return to former levels of employment, and are unlikely ever to do so. It may also be that equally important causes of union decline are the failure of unions to exert sufficient efforts to organize new members and a rising tide of employer opposition.

The opposition of employers to unions has been especially intense since the mid-1970s. Attempts to disestablish existing unions reached new heights in the 1980s, as did convictions of employers for fighting against unions in violation of labour laws. In the 1990s, the unremitting opposition to unions of most employers has become a fact of industrial life. Given the well-known inability of the labour laws to protect workers from employer retribution, it is hardly surprising that unions have experienced difficulty in organizing new members.

It perhaps bears repeating that employer power is very great in the USA in both the political and economic spheres. To the extent that changes in the law are needed for unions to regain and preserve power, change is blocked by the superior political power of employers. This, in turn, makes it more difficult to operate in the sphere of economic action, as the example of the Caterpillar strike shows. Friends of labour in the USA have been known to look across the northern border and cry 'Oh, Canada!' in wistful admiration of the Canadian legal system which is more friendly to unions (Geoghegan 1991). Added to this is a high unemployment rate in the early 1990s, which also makes economic action difficult. It is also easy to understand why US unions are having trouble regaining the ground they lost when employment has declined in sectors which traditionally have been organized.

The crucial question is whether the US labour movement can survive the current difficulties and re-emerge as a powerful, lively movement. The alternative is for it to slip into a moribund condition, as it did in the 1920s – a period not unlike the 1980s and early 1990s in political and social climate. Another possibility is a dramatic slide to the left, changing from an economic orientation to a more political one. However, neither of these outcomes seems likely. Although the unions appear to have a new awareness of the importance of politics, it is still politics directed at achieving their survival for collective bargaining. It seems most unlikely that US unions will become as political as those in western Europe and Australia. It is also unlikely that they will wither away under the various pressures described above. Unions in the USA still have millions of members. As those who have worked with labour's 'grassroots' can testify, its ranks are filled with energetic, dedicated and intelligent unionists who appear to be capable of weathering the storm.

On the negative side, the continuing competitiveness of the international economy gives support to those in management who oppose unions as fetters to efficiency and profitability. Furthermore, until there is once again a shortage of labour, which is the condition under which a strike-based strategy is most effective, the ability of unions to achieve large gains in collective bargaining is probably going to remain limited. Demographic forecasts do furnish some hope in this regard. Loss of major strikes, such as at Eastern Airlines and Caterpillar, and endemic problems with democracy and honesty, continue to hurt the unions' public image. Perhaps most importantly, the continuing aversion of the legal system to unions remains a severe problem.

5 Conclusions

The pressures of international competition have, for the US industrial relations system as for others, opened a Pandora's box of troubles. Kochan *et al.* (1986) argued that these pressures and others had already, in the early 1980s, fundamentally changed the nature of the US system. Yet, in the 1990s, the extent and depth of these changes still are not clear.

Certainly, the move from oligopolistic markets to competitive ones has created the need for many industries in the USA to create new ways to organize work and cut costs. It may be that the necessary level of quality of some goods, such as automobiles and electronic equipment, cannot be attained without developing cooperative mechanisms that are inconsistent with the adversarial US model. However, it is unclear whether more cooperative work methods can endure under US capitalism, where the 'fast buck' is held in reverence, the pressures of predatory takeover artists keep management constantly squeezing for more profits, managers hold opposition to employee collective action to be a holy cause, and hierarchical habits are deeply ingrained. The trust that is the foundation stone of labour–management cooperation is difficult to build in such an environment. Management choosing to share power with union and non-union workers in the highest councils of corporate decision making is also something about which this writer is highly sceptical. It seems that the best chance for cooperation lies on the shop floor where the workers have expertise, power and the desire to exercise both of these.

Meanwhile, the traditional collective bargaining structure in the USA has fared rather well. It has devised means to cut labour costs.

Unions have generally not opposed the adoption of new technology, and have bargained for innovations in cooperation, profit sharing, healthcare costs, and holidays. Childcare may be the next frontier. Similarly, in the unionized sector, the grievance and arbitration procedures continue to guarantee worker protection from, as put earlier, the 'tyrannies, petty or otherwise, which served to make [the worker's] existence a slavery'.

In the non-union sector, many employers are adopting progressive and positive employment policies, making workers' jobs both better and better paid. The network of laws has increased, providing new protections for workers, although the enforcement of both old and new laws may not be sufficiently energetic. Also, rights of human dignity of employees are being challenged by new employer anti-drug policies.

An enduring concern is the continued strength of the US labour movement which, like those in many other countries, has declined in recent years. However, as noted earlier in this chapter, in labour's Pandora's box of troubles there is, as there was in Pandora's, one important remaining item – hope. There is also a fundamental logic to collective action by workers that is not repealed by international competition. Indeed, the historical roots of US unions lie in a time when markets expanded in this young country, forcing workers to gather together in a protective response.

In summary, the parties in the US industrial relations system continue to muddle through. As the only certainty appears to be change, a history of muddling through reasonably well is rather reassuring.

HOYT N. WHEELER
UNIVERSITY OF SOUTH CAROLINA

Further reading

(References cited in the text marked *)

Adams, R.J. (1980) *Industrial Relations Systems in Europe and North America*, Hamilton, Ont.: McMaster University. (Useful text on international industrial relations.)

* Allen, R.E. and Keaveny, T.J. (1988) *Contemporary Labor Relations*, 2nd edn, Reading, MA: Addison-Wesley. (Basic textbook on labour relations.)

* Barbash, J. (1967) *American Unions: Structure, Government and Politics*, New York: Random House. (The classic work on the US trade union movement.)

* Barbash, J. (1981) 'Values in industrial relations: The case of the adversary principle', *Proceedings of the Thirty-third Annual Meeting, Industrial Relations Research Association*, Madison, WI: IRRA, 1–7. (Specialist article, focusing on the adversarial nature of industrial relations.)

Bean, R. (1994) *Comparative Industrial Relations*, London: Routledge. (Good introductory study of different forms of industrial relations.)

Beaumont, P.B. (1995) *The Future of Employment Relations* London: Sage. (Chapter 4 deals specifically with industrial relations in the USA.)

BNA (1992) *Collective Bargaining Negotiations and Contracts*, Washington, DC: Bureau of National Affairs. (General guide to collective bargaining.)

* Commons, J.R. (1913) 'American shoemakers, 1648–1895', in *Labor and Administration*, New York: Macmillan. (Specialist labour history, which gives some useful historical examples.)

* Cooper, W.J. and Terrill, T.E. (1991) *The American South: A History*, New York: Knopf. (Regional history, which includes material on the development of the labour movement in this historically less-industrialized part of the USA.)

Donn, C.V. and Lipsky, D.G. (eds) (1987) *Collective Bargaining in American Industry*, Lexington, MA: Lexington Books. (Edited collection of useful articles on collective bargaining.)

* Foner, P.A. (1947) *History of the Labor Movement in the United States*, vol. 1, New York: International Publishers. (Large and comprehensive history of the US labour movement.)

* Geoghegan, T. (1991) *Which Side Are You On: Trying to be for Labor When It's Flat on Its Back*, New York: Farrar, Strauss & Giroux. (Polemical publication on the labour movement.)

* Gompers, S. (1919) *Labor and the Common Welfare*, New York: Dutton. (Classic text on labour in the USA, very valuable for a historical perspective.)

Hecksher, C. (1988) *The New Unionism: Employee Involvement in the Changing Corporation*, New York: Basic Books. (A look at how employee involvement is affecting industrial relations.)

* Heneman, H.G. III, Schwab, D.P., Fossum, J.A. and Dyer, L.D. (1980) *Personnel/Human Resource Management*, Homewood, IL: Irwin. (Good textbook on human resource management.)

* Kassalow, E.M. (1974) 'The development of Western labor movements: some comparative considerations', in L.G. Reynolds, S.A. Masters and C. Moser (eds), *Readings in Labor Economics and Labor Relations*, Englewood Cliffs, NJ: Prentice Hall. (Short article which considers differences in the developments of labour movements in the West.)

* Kochan, T.A. (1980) *Collective Bargaining and Industrial Relations*, Homewood, IL: Irwin. (Key text on collective bargaining, with a focus on the USA.)

* Kochan, T.A., and Katz, H.C. and McKersie, R.B. (1986) *The Transformation of American Industrial Relations*, New York: Basic Books. (Established text on industrial relations.)

Ledvinka, J. (1982) *Federal Regulation of Personnel and Human Resource Management*, Belmont, CA: Kent. (Good general summary of US industrial relations regulation.)

* Perlman, S. (1970) *The Theory of the Labor Movement*, New York: Augustus M. Kelly. (Classic text on labour theory; reprinted several times since first edition published in 1928.)

* Piore, M.J. (1982) 'American labor and the industrial crisis', *Challenge* (March–April): 5–11. (Useful summary of the decline of US industry and its effect on labour relations.)

* Sturmthal, A. (1973) 'Industrial relations strategies', in A. Sturmthal and J. Scoville (eds), *The International Labor Movement in Transition*, Urbana, IL: University of Illinois Press. (Useful if dated source on industrial relations strategies.)

Taft, P. (1964) *Organised Labor in American History* New York: Harper & Row. (Classic work on the history of labour organization and trade unions.)

Wever, K.S. (1994) 'On the future of trade unionism in the US', in J. Niland, R.D. Lansbury and C. Verens (eds), *The Future of Industrial Relations*, London: Sage Publications. (Poses some interesting views on how trade unions will fare in the future in the USA.)

Wheeler, H.N. (1985) *Industrial Conflict: An Integrative Theory*, Columbia: University of South Carolina Press. (Good text on industrial conflict.)

See also: BRAVERMAN, H.; COLLECTIVE BAR-
GAINING; EMPLOYMENT AND UNEMPLOY-
MENT, ECONOMICS OF; HUMAN CAPITAL;
HUMAN RESOURCE MANAGEMENT, INTER-
NATIONAL; INDUSTRIAL CONFLICT; INDUS-
TRIAL DEMOCRACY; INDUSTRIAL AND
LABOUR RELATIONS; INDUSTRIAL RELA-
TIONS IN EUROPE; INDUSTRIAL RELATIONS
IN JAPAN; LABOUR MARKETS; MOTIVATION
AND SATISFACTION; TAYLOR, F.W.

Related topics in the IEBM: CONTEXTS
AND ENVIRONMENTS; GOVERNMENT, IN-
DUSTRY AND THE PUBLIC SECTOR; MAN-
AGEMENT IN NORTH AMERICA

Japanization

Overview

'Japanization' is the process by which Japanese industry is influencing the policies and practices of Western industry. There are two aspects to this: Japanese direct investment in Western economies and the emulation of Japanese practice by Western companies.

This entry discusses Japanese industrial conditions in four main areas: manufacturing practice; human resource policy; buyer-supplier relations; and economic context. The extent of Japanese investment across the world is assessed, along with the attempts by Western companies to emulate Japanese practice. Finally, the key positions and debates in the area are mapped out.

1 Western interest in Japan

For much of the twentieth century the USA was the country to which people looked for best practice in manufacturing. Towards the end of the 1970s, this changed as Japan emerged as a leading manufacturing nation. From the economic ruin of the Second World War, Japan rapidly attained industrial pre-eminence in several industrial sectors, principally vehicles and consumer electronics. From a 1950s position of world domination, by the 1970s and 1980s the three big US car manufacturers were asking the US government for protection from the Japanese car industry, an industry which scarcely existed thirty years previously. The dent to Western manufacturing pride was enormous. By the mid-1980s Japan held 84 per cent of the world market for 35mm cameras, 55 per cent for motorcycles and 53 per cent for colour televisions.

At this time evidence of the superior manufacturing performance of Japanese producers was accumulating. Western economies, particularly those who were experiencing decline (such as the USA and the UK) eagerly looked to Japan in order to extract lessons to improve their own economic fortunes.

In 1982, Schonberger's *Japanese Manufacturing Techniques* was published, which rendered many Japanese ideas accessible to a Western audience. More influential still was *The Machine that Changed the World* (Womack *et al.* 1990). This book reported a 2 to 1 difference in productivity and quality between Japanese car assembly plants in Japan and car assembly plants in the West. The authors ascribed these differences to a distinct package of management practices, for which they coined the term 'lean production'. Japanese 'transplant' car factories in the USA, although not performing at the same levels as their sister plants in Japan, were well ahead of indigenous US plants. Womack *et al.* argued that this proved that lean production principles, found in their purest form in Japan, were transferable anywhere in the world.

The impact of *The Machine that Changed the World* was twofold. First, it sent an alarming message to the West about the performance of the Japanese car industry. Second, it contained a ray of hope. The idea that Japanese principles were universally applicable suggested that there *was* an answer to Western manufacturing woes and, moreover, an answer that was within the grasp of individual companies, plants and managers.

Thus, the concept of Japanization developed in the context of a decline in confidence in Western manufacturing methods, the rapid rise of Japan as a manufacturing nation and a desire on the part of many Western companies to emulate Japanese practice. There is one further element in the picture, and that is the

461

movement of Japanese manufacturers overseas. Faced with the appreciation of the yen and increasing trade friction with the West, many Japanese manufacturers established overseas manufacturing facilities in the 1970s and 1980s. These facilities provide test cases of the transferability of Japanese methods and of the impact of these practices in the host economy.

2 Approaches and agendas

Japanization may be defined as the process by which Japanese industry influences Western industry through Japanese direct investment in Western economies and the attempts at emulation of Japanese practice by Western companies. The term was first used by Turnbull (1986) to describe changes at Lucas Industries (UK). Turnbull observed that Japanese-inspired changes which Lucas was making to its manufacturing systems affected social relations around the production process and argued that the success of Japanese production methods was:

> Dependent on a social organization for the production process intended to make workers feel obliged to contribute to the economic performance of the enterprise
> (Turnbull 1986: 203)

The idea that change in one arena – manufacturing systems – creates pressure for changes in the social relations of production lies at the heart of the concept of Japanization. Does the adoption of Japanese production methods mean other aspects of Japanese management, such as their human resource policies, must inevitably follow if the methods are to work? Is the Japanese management system a culturally-bound configuration, an accident of history, or does it represent a set of universal principles of business organization, which properly applied can yield success anywhere in the world? What happens to workers, managers and suppliers when a Japanese company sets up an operation in the West? Or when a Western company emulates these methods? These questions lie at the heart of the Japanization debate.

The phrase 'Japanese manufacturing methods' is one of a number of terms that describe a particular type of production system, other terms being Womack *et al.*'s (1990) 'lean production' (which is really a description of the Toyota production system), 'Toyotaism' (Wood 1992), 'Fujitsuism' (Kenney and Florida 1993) and the Toyota Production System (Monden 1983). The appropriateness of the term Japanization is a source of considerable debate, but before considering the points of contention, let us examine the elements of Japanese practice and the transfer of such practice to the West.

3 Japanese industrial practice

There is an enormous volume of published work on industrial conditions in Japan (see Oliver and Wilkinson 1992 for a review). This section provides an overview of these in four main areas: (1) manufacturing methods; (2) human resource policy; (3) supplier relations; and (4) wider context.

Schonberger (1982) was one of the first Western writers to provide a popular account of Japanese manufacturing methods. Central to the Japanese model are just-in-time factory operations, which run with minimum inventory and total quality principles.

Total quality (see TOTAL QUALITY MANAGEMENT) is an umbrella term covering several practices. The key idea is that responsibility for quality lies at the point of production, rather than in the hands of a specialist quality department. Effort is focused on the prevention of errors rather than on their detection and subsequent correction. There is also an ethos of continuous improvement in the system, frequently backed up by bottom-up problem-solving structures such as quality circles, improvement teams and so on.

Just-in-time methods clearly help in this by reducing levels of inventory in a factory to reveal problems and thereby generate pressure for improvement. In Japan, these methods are used in the context of flexible and multi-skilled workforces, with production organized into teams. On the human resource side, many Japanese firms offer long-term employment security, at least for core workers, company-based welfare and social activities and seniority-based payment systems. The net effect of these is to create a long-term orientation towards the company on the part of the employee, which greatly facilitates labour flexibility, and to identify the fortunes of the employee with those of the firm. Indirectly, this encourages employees to suggest improvements, an important part of the Japanese practice of *kaizen*, or continuous improvement. Such a social system is an important support to a highly fragile manufacturing system which requires willing cooperation rather than mere compliance on the part of those who operate it.

Similar dynamics exist in relations between firms. Sako (1992) characterizes buyer-supplier relations in Japan as obligational and long-term in nature, contrasted with traditional Western relations, which have traditionally tended to be short-term and contractual. The norm is for suppliers to make just-in-time deliveries of quality-assured supplies.

Although a continuing point of debate, several commentators have argued that the net effect of Japanese production arrangements, both internal to the factory and between buyers and suppliers, is to create a highly interdependent system between the company and its workers, suppliers and so on. Long-term, obligational relations may be both a cause and a consequence of this. Yet the story goes further than this, extending to relations between the Japanese financial and manufacturing worlds. The relationships between banks and companies are much closer than in the West, with the former offering the latter long-term low interest finance. 'Safe shareholding' is commonplace, a practice which developed after the Second World War, when many Japanese firms were concerned about foreign takeovers. It is virtually unthinkable in Japan for a shareholder to divest of shares without consulting those in the company itself. The net effect of this is to create a financial stability which is unusual in publicly-quoted Western companies. According to Dore (1986) this allows Japanese managers to focus on a strategy of increasing market share rather than the short-term defence of profit margins to appease external stakeholders.

4 Direct investment and emulation

Japanese overseas investment increased exponentially in the 1980s. The three main reasons for this were: (1) the rapid appreciation of the yen, which began to erode Japanese cost advantages; (2) an increase in trade friction leading to a Japanese fear of being locked out of major markets; and (3) the spectre of 'global localization', with the consequent need to have presence in the three major trading blocs of Europe, the Pacific Rim and the USA. The destinations and share of Japanese overseas investment are shown in Table 1. Of the total amount, 26.3 per cent represents manufacturing investment.

North America has seen the largest share of Japanese investment, followed by Europe. Within Europe the UK has been the favoured destination. In the early 1990s Japanese manufacturing investment into Western economies greatly reduced, a function of recession in both the Japanese domestic economy and host economies, and an indication that many of the major investments were already in place. East Asia, in particular the People's Republic of China, became the main target for Japanese manufacturing investment in the 1990s, an indication of the increasing significance of the Pacific Rim as a trading bloc.

To use the UK as an example, incoming Japanese manufacturers typically use

Table 1 Cumulative Japanese investment by region 1951–90

Region	Value ($m)	%
North America	136,185	43.8
Europe	59,265	19.1
Asia	47,519	15.3
Latin America	40,483	13.0
Oceania	18,098	5.8
Africa	5,826	1.9
Near and Middle East	3,431	1.1
World total	310,808	100

Source: Elger and Smith (1994)

greenfield sites, although there has been some joint venture activity. Japanese plants use many of the manufacturing practices found in Japan itself. In terms of human resource policy (see HUMAN RESOURCE MANAGEMENT; HUMAN RESOURCE MANAGEMENT IN JAPAN), Japanese-style work teams, performance appraisal for production workers, common uniforms and single status facilities are the norm. About 50 per cent of Japanese companies in the UK are unionized, nearly all of them recognizing only one union. One of the pressure points for Japanese companies operating overseas is the buyer-supplier interface. The three most commonly reported problems with suppliers are quality, price and delivery.

Towards the latter part of the 1980s and into the 1990s several surveys have been conducted into the adoption of Japanese practices (see for example Voss and Robinson 1987; Oliver and Wilkinson 1992). The picture of these is clear: many Western companies are adopting – or claiming to adopt – aspects of the Japanese manufacturing practice. To use the UK as an example again, over two-thirds of companies surveyed in 1991 claimed to be using just-in-time methods; over 90 per cent claimed total quality programmes.

There is plentiful case material on the experiences of Western companies with these methods (see Elger and Smith 1994; Oliver and Wilkinson 1992). Practitioner-produced cases tend to be success stories. Cases produced by academics tend to spend more time exploring the issues and difficulties in implementation. The picture to date may be summarized thus:

1 There are widespread claims that Western companies are introducing Japanese methods.
2 Success is mixed: great claims for these methods are made by some companies, but these claims are rarely backed up by hard evidence of tangible results.
3 Organizational-political issues in implementation are commonplace, particularly in larger organizations.
4 There are signs that the 'Japanese threat' is used to make legitimate changes which mangers wished to implement anyway (Graham 1988).

5 Perspectives on Japanization

The purpose of this section is to map out the main points of debate within this field. Essentially, there are four objections to the use of the phrase 'Japanization' to describe changes which are currently occurring in Western industry:

(1) 'There is no such thing as *Japanese* management.' The basis of this objection is that the term 'Japanization' implies a homogeneity of management practices in Japan and skirts over the diversity of practice found there. Cusumano's (1985) discussion of Toyota and Nissan illustrates this point.

(2) 'Describing the process of change as Japanization obscures the *real* process.' This position is typically held by those writing from a Marxist perspective, who argue that the term 'Japanization' implies a battle between capital of different *nationalities* rather than a battle between *capital* and *labour*. They argue that Japanese management methods are just another set of management practices and should be recognised and treated as such by labour.

(3) Japanization represents an oversimplification.' The main argument here accepts that change is taking place in Western economies and that some of the changes may resemble aspects of the Japanese model. However, 'Japanization' implies a strategic intent and a coherence which does not actually exist. Industrial change is piecemeal and complex, and a response to a variety of local contingencies.

(4) 'Nothing has changed.' This argument is frequently found among the orthodox industrial relations community. Their argument is that Western industrial structures are characterized more by continuity than change, and that where change is occurring it has more to do with structural change in the economy than with anything which is driven by management strategy, Japanese-inspired or otherwise.

In addition to these four objections to the term Japanization, advocates and critics of the Japanization process are fiercely divided on several issues. Their positions are

Table 2 Perspectives on Japanization

Level of analysis	Subject	Critics' perspective	Advocates' perspective
The economy	Japanese direct investment	Economic domination by multi-national capital	Japanese companies regenerate host economies via direct job creation and diffusion of management methods
	Quality of investment	Japanese plants are 'screwdriver' assembly plants; the high value-adding operations are retained in Japan	All globalizing compnaies send their simpler operations overseas first; the Japanese are still at an early stage in the process and core operations will follow
The firm	Performance levels	The performance gap between Japanese and Western firms has been exaggerated	Real (and substantial) gaps in performance between Japan and the West have been systematically measured and proved
	Explanations of performance	Economic structures and conditions within which firms are embedded largely explain any performance differential	Management practices and managerial competence largely explain performance
	Methods	Japanese methods are a reponse to a unique set of historical, cultural and economic circumstances	Japanese methods embody a universal set of principles which properly implemented can yield good results anywhere
Individuals	Work experience	'Working harder' and a more pressured, stressful work experience	'Working smarter.' Opportunities for involvement due to problem solving and improvement activities. Wasteful activities are eliminated so people work more effectively

summarized in Table 2 and, where appropriate, examples of each position are provided.

It is beyond the scope of this entry to assess the evidence for and against each position given in Table 2. Suffice to say, the polarity of opinions makes for a rich research agenda. That these issues have implications for emotive issues such as the experience of work and, potentially, for economically important questions of national competitiveness implies that the Japanization debate – or whatever phrase one uses to describe it – is likely to endure for several years.

NICK OLIVER
JUDGE INSTITUTE OF MANAGEMENT STUDIES,
UNIVERSITY OF CAMBRIDGE

Further reading

(References cited in the text marked *)

Crowther, S. and Garrahan, P. (1988) 'Invitation to Sunderland: corporate power and the local economy', *Industrial Relations Journal* 19 (1): 51–9. (Describes the investment of Nissan in the northeast of England – Orwellian.)

* Cusumano, M. (1985) *The Japanese Automobile Industry: Technology and Management at Nissan and Toyota*, Cambridge, MA: Harvard University Press. (Detailed history of the development of the Japanese motor industry, with particular reference to Nissan and Toyota.)

Delbridge, R. (1988) *Life on the Line in Contemporary Manufacturing*, Oxford: Oxford University Press. (An insider's account of life on the production lines of a Japanese transplant factory in the UK and of an 'emulating' firm.)

* Dore, R. (1986) *Flexible Rigidities*, London: Athlone. (Economic analysis of selected Japanese industries.)

* Elger, T. and Smith, C. (1994) *Global Japanization?*, London: Routledge. (A labour-process-orientated collection of readings on the process of Japanization in several countries.)

Fucini, J.J. and Fucini, S. (1990) *Working for the Japanese*, New York: The Free Press. (A critical account of the start-up and operation of Mazda's US assembly plant.)

* Graham, I. (1988) 'Japanization as mythology', *Industrial Relations Journal* 19 (1): 69–75. (Describes the political 'shaping' of messages about Japan.)

James, B. (1989) *Trojan Horse: The Ultimate Japanese Challenge*, London: Mercury. (Argues that the quality of much Japanese investment overseas is suspect, as high value-adding activities are retained in Japan.)

Kamata, S. (1982) *Japan in the Passing Lane*, London: Allen & Unwin. (A journalistic account of life on a Toyota assembly line.)

* Kenney, M. and Florida, R. (1993) *Beyond Mass Production: The Japanese System and its Transfer to the US*, Oxford: Oxford University Press. (Qualified and sophisticated analysis, sympathetic to the 'universal applicability' argument.)

Lillrank, P. (1995) 'The transfer of management innovations from Japan', *Organization Studies* 16 (6): 971–89. (Description of how knowledge is coded and transferred from one context to another.)

* Monden, Y. (1983) *Toyota Production System*, Atlanta, GA: Industrial Engineering and Management Press. (Rather dry, but a comprehensive account of the Toyota production system.)

* Oliver, N. and Wilkinson, B. (1992) *The Japanization of British Industry: Developments in the 1990s*, Oxford: Blackwell. (Overview of the whole field.)

* Sako, M. (1992) *Prices, Quality and Trust* Cambridge: Cambridge University Press. (Discusses different models of buyer-supplier relations.)

* Schonberger, R. (1982) *Japanese Manufacturing Techniques*, New York: The Free Press. (Clear and lucid; an early example of Western dissemination of Japanese principles.)

* Turnbull, P. (1986) 'The 'Japanization' of production and industrial relations at Lucas Electrical', *Industrial Relations Journal* 17 (3): 193–206. (One of the first uses of the term Japanization.)

* Voss, C. and Robinson, S. (1987) 'The application of just-in-time techniques', *International Journal of Operations and Production Management* 7 (4): 46–52. (Early survey of the use of Japanese methods.)

Wickens, P. (1987) *The Road to Nissan*, London: Macmillan. (Written by the personnel director of Nissan UK; an example of the 'good news' about Japanese management methods.)

Williams, K., Haslam, C., Johal, S. and Williams, J. (1994) *Cars: Analysis, History, Cases*, Providence: Berghahn Books. (A critique of the managerial nature of the writings on the Japanese car industry.)

Williams, K., Haslam, C., Williams, J., Cutler, T., Adcroft, A. and Johal, S. (1992) 'Against lean production', *Economy and Society* 21 (3): 321–54. (Lively critique of lean production.)

* Womack, J.P., Jones, D.T. and Roos, D. (1990) *The Machine that Changed the World: The Triumph of Lean Production*, New York: Rawson Macmillan. (Colourful and readable account of performance and management practices in the international car industry.)

* Wood, S.J. (1992) 'Japanization and/or Toyotaism?', *Work, Employment and Society* 5 (4): 567–600. (Dry but solid discussion of the concept of Japanization.)

See also: COMMITMENT; HUMAN RESOURCE MANAGEMENT; HUMAN RESOURCE MANAGEMENT IN JAPAN; OHNO, T; TOTAL QUALITY MANAGEMENT

Related topics in the IEBM: BUSINESS STRATEGY, JAPANESE; COMMITMENT IN JAPAN; FINANCIAL MARKETS, JAPANESE; JUST-IN-TIME PHILOSOPHIES; MANAGEMENT IN JAPAN; MANAGEMENT IN PACIFIC ASIA; TOYODA FAMILY

Focal policy-areas of HRM

Careers

Overview

The historical view of a career has been of a progression up an organization and an occupation which we chose near the beginning of our working lives. Events have overtaken this model. Increased competition, cost competitiveness, information technology and customer focus have all resulted in de-manning and de-layering of organization structures. Organizations have removed the rungs of the career ladder and instead are concentrating on the optimal use of their 'human resources'.

The study of careers and of the interventions designed to develop them has changed accordingly. The move is away from the determinants of success, where success is defined as position achieved in the corporate hierarchy, towards understanding how individuals construe their careers, how they might better manage them and what is the appropriate relationship between organization and employee. Above all, current research and theory seeks to place careers in the context of individual, organizational and environmental change.

I The changing face of careers

The historical view

The concept of career is changing its meaning rapidly. Historically, careers have been seen as progression within an occupation and an organization. People got around to settling on an occupation, sometimes after some 'immature' job changes in their youth. Having made their final occupational selection, they then arrived at an organizational choice. They found an organization which would employ them and enable them to further their occupational career. Both occupational and organizational choices were seen as likely to be for the rest of one's working life. Careers were referred to as ladders or paths. The former metaphor implies a steady sequence of promotional steps; the latter the possibility of planning to tread the same career steps as those who have been there before. Typically, having chosen each other the organization and the individual entered into a psychological contract in which the organization offered secure employment and career development in return for the individual's loyal commitment.

This view of career was appropriate to the context in which it was developed. This context was one of stable markets and static organizations. Organizations were so structured as to allow a steady progression up many hierarchical levels. Managers and professionals sometimes reached a plateau but this was more often regarded as a level of comfort than as a barrier to further promotion. This type of career structure could be characterized as based upon an internal labour market. Organizations recruited young people and developed them up through a series of levels, each level being closely related to an age range. Thus, at least at the lower levels of the hierarchy, groups of employees were promoted when they reached the appropriate age. This internal group-focused career strategy is associated with the business strategy of 'Defender'. That is, if an organization wishes to retain or enhance its share of a stable market, it will foster this club-like working environment (Sonnenfeld and Peiperl 1988).

People who have been brought up to understand the organization, its products or services and its market are required by

Defenders. Given the environment of stable markets and steady market shares it is hardly surprising that many organizations were clubs.

The changing context of careers

The business context has changed radically, however. A summary of the changes is given in Table 1.

Increased competition has led to an increasing emphasis on cost competitiveness. Consequently many layers of middle management have been taken out and many middle managers made redundant. The same is true for many professional employees, whose skills have been either automated or else their work given to contract professionals. A second consequence of increased competition is the emphasis on product and service quality. This has led to authority being delegated to those employees who directly produce the goods or provide the services; they are given the discretion to adapt to the customer's requirements. The traditional managerial functions of control and coordination are therefore less in demand. Another managerial function that has also been eroded is that of information channel. The increased use of information technology means that information up, down and across the organizational hierarchy does not require a middle manager to transmit it.

The consequences of these developments for organizational careers and career structures have been profound. The organizational pyramid is typically far flatter, with many fewer levels. Consequently the difference between one level and the next is greater; there is a qualitative leap rather than a quantitative step involved. Moves sideways rather than moves upwards are therefore more frequent, for two reasons: (1) there are now fewer moves upwards available; and (2) wider experience is necessary to prepare an individual for the next level up. In particular, a wide experience is necessary to operate internationally.

As Kanter (1989) has observed, these changes have thrown the traditional ideas of career as a series of promotions into the melting pot. Instead of predictable progress today's employees suffer career uncertainty. They cannot be sure of remaining within the functional specialization or occupation in which they were originally trained; nor, indeed, can they be confident of security of employment, let alone of promotion. A variety of alternative employment contracts is now on offer, none of them offering permanent full-time employment. Most of these are offered primarily because they cut costs. Employees' major asset is their employability, both within and outside their organization. For as long as they maintain or enhance their employability

Table 1 The old and new career realities

Old	New
Full-time permanent contracts	Part-time temporary contracts
Assured employment	Employment insecurity
One-off career choice	Repeated changes in career
Occupation for life	Several occupations
Organization for life	Several or no organizations
Regular promotions	Maintenance of employability
Multi-level hierarchy	De-layered pyramid
Predictable job moves	Unpredictable job moves
Internal labour market	External labour market
Organizations manage careers	Individuals manage careers
Organizations develop people	People develop themselves
Career national	Career international

in the internal or external labour market they enhance their careers. Now middle-class employees have the same insecurity as the working class has always had; they too are subject to the vagaries of the labour market.

Is the concept of career still useful?

Given this changed scenario, we may ask whether the concept of career still has any explanatory use. Is the idea of career now merely an attempt at *post hoc* rationalization of the accidents of the labour market by the individual? There are several reasons for retaining the concept of career and for broadening its meaning beyond the idea of progress within an occupation or organization. The first is that the concept of career is dynamic in time (Arthur *et al.* 1989). It enables *individuals* to give meaning to their experience. In particular, individuals can make sense of their working lives as they reinterpret their past in the light of present realities; and as they adjust their aspirations for the future in the light of those same realities. The concept of career may also still be of use to *organizations*. In their need to achieve business advantage they will seek to use the potential of their employees to the full. The idea of managing their organizational careers so as to develop this potential will be extremely attractive to them. It will form a major plank of their human resource strategy.

Finally, the concept of career is likely to be of use to *both organizations and individuals* in order to express the relationship between them. As Schein (1978) pointed out in his classic treatment of this relationship, the idea of the psychological contract has a lot to offer. It is important to pay attention to what the employee believes the employment agreement to be. Instead of the old once-for-all, security-for-loyalty bargain, the psychological contract has to be renegotiated as both parties' circumstances change. Perhaps all that can be offered in some organizations is the promise of at least three months' notice of redundancy and outplacement counselling in exchange for staying to help in its bid for survival.

Like organizations, people too want different psychological contracts at different stages of their lives. Thus careers may be helpfully reconstrued as a sequence of renegotiations of the psychological contract (Herriot 1996).

2 Organizations' management of careers

Research and theorizing about careers reflects these changes. We first examine research and practice on organizations' management of careers before considering both objective and subjective aspects of individuals' careers.

Career management is embedded in the ideology of human resource management (see HUMAN RESOURCE MANAGEMENT). Human Resource Management is an ideology because it is 'an action related system of ideas… involving value choices' (Horwitz 1990: 10). These value choices are that: unitarism is preferable to pluralism; the interests of management and employees should be congruent; and conflict is external in origin and a challenge to managerial authority. The essential features of human resource management are that it involves:

1 the use of planning to meet business needs;
2 the integration of personnel systems within an overall strategy;
3 the matching of this human resources strategy to the business strategy; and
4 treating people as a strategic resource for achieving competitive advantage (Hendry and Pettigrew 1990).

Just as traditionally a business strategy of Defender implied a human resource strategy of internal group-based career development, so other business strategies imply different human resource approaches. Typically, for example, Reactors who are fighting for survival go outside for a new top team to rescue the business and cheaper labour *en masse* to cut costs. Or a Prospector organization seeking to colonize new markets will recruit individual stars from outside to manage new acquisitions or to develop new lines (Sonnenfeld and Peiperl 1988). Thus career management by the organization is an element of a human resource strategy designed to support the business aims of the organization.

Research evidence suggests, however, that the current level of practice of these precepts is patchy to say the least. This doubtless partly because few organizations can now boast a consistent long-term business strategy. Organizations tend to introduce new systems (for example, performance-related pay) piecemeal rather than strategically (see FINANCIAL INCENTIVES; PAYMENT SYSTEMS). Many of those systems which were of strategic intent have been overtaken by events. For example, many large organizations with a well developed human resource function developed fast track 'high flier' schemes whereby a cohort of young employees identified as having potential to reach the top were singled out for special treatment. They were moved across functions, across businesses and increasingly across countries in order to give them the breadth of experience assumed necessary for executive responsibility. Not only were there unwanted consequences – the 'lower fliers' were demotivated – but also such schemes became impracticable. So changed are organizational structures that a planned sequence of jobs is no longer possible. And so subject is the cohort to losses to other organizations that a steady supply to the top cannot be guaranteed. Instead organizations are offloading the responsibility for career development. Individuals are urged to develop themselves. Career development is not through a series of positions to an ultimate seat on the Board. It is rather through the individual's acquisition of competencies which enable him or her to manage change at the next level of responsibility. And organizations are becoming more segmented internally in terms of the differing degrees of support they are prepared to offer to different categories of staff (Hirsch and Jackson 1996).

Competencies

The move towards competencies as a basis for organizational and individual development is widespread. The term 'competencies' is used at three levels of analysis (Sparrow 1994). *Behavioural competencies* are 'behavioural repertoires which people input to a job, role or organisation context'. *Management competencies* are 'knowledge, skills and attitudes', while *organization competencies* are the 'resources and capabilities of the organisation linked with business performance'. The link with human resource strategy is clear: the organizational level of analysis focuses on the core capabilities associated with business success (Prahalad and Hamel 1990). The managerial level competencies follow from these and the behavioural level ones in their turn from the managerial level. The language and assessment methods of competencies are used to tie together and integrate human resource systems and to relate them to business needs.

As Sparrow (1994) observes, however, the use of competencies analysis runs the risk of improving organizations' and individuals' performance in the jobs and tasks of the past. This is because traditionally competencies have been defined on the basis of an analysis of the jobs people do at present. The need is for competencies for the future and for a methodology for discovering them. As Sparrow notes, this will require anticipating likely strategic changes and the future competencies they imply. From the point of view of the organization, then, career management means building up the knowledge and skills capital of the business to meet future requirements. Individual development is geared to this end, and the individual is regarded as a unit of human capital resource (see HUMAN RESOURCE DEVELOPMENT). Indeed, the use of the term human resource implies acquisition, ownership, conservation, investment and expenditure.

3 The careers of individuals

Objective careers

As Ornstein and Isabella (1993) note, the field of careers is moving towards an increasing emphasis on the individual as opposed to the organization and on the individual's subjective perception of their career rather than its objective reality. We now turn to individuals, moving from the consideration of their objective job sequences in organizations through to more developmental and subjective perspectives.

Considerable evidence is available about how managers and professionals have progressed through organizations and what predicts such progress (Rosenbaum 1989). One line of research suggests that objective careers in organizations are like tournaments. The earlier rounds of the tournament are crucial, in that failure to achieve promotion at one of these hurdles may have lasting effects. Indeed, the length of time spent in the very first job in an organization predicts the level an individual ultimately reaches. Intra-organizational mobility, then, can help career progress (defined as promotion) but it is not so clear why this should be so. Multiple jobs are likely to increase the knowledge and skills of individuals and therefore make them more promotable (the human capital explanation). On the other hand, they are also able to build up networks, acquire patrons and gain visibility; organizations are social and political systems. What is also clear is that while mobility within and between organizations is high in periods of economic prosperity (Nicholson and West 1988), it decreases markedly in recession. Objective careers, too, change with the times.

An interesting set of employees with respect to organizational careers are technical professionals such as research and development scientists and engineers. As Van Maanen and Barley (1984) explain, such employees always have a dual career loyalty – to their profession and to their organization. Although these are not necessarily mutually exclusive, research clearly demonstrates that only those who place their professional work firmly in the context of the needs of the business achieve high status positions (Dalton and Thompson 1986). There are a few organizations (for example, Unilever) which have successfully developed separate career ladders to a senior level for professional experts. In general, however, the trend is towards the participation of professional experts in project teams, where their skills and knowledge have to be directed towards achieving task success. For those who do not wish or are not suited to take managerial responsibility for projects or teams, career can consist of participation in a sequence of projects. Technical professionals would then hope to enhance their employability internally and externally as a consequence of the new skills and knowledge they acquire from each project.

A second interesting research area concerns not the sequence of positions occupied *per se* but the nature of the transitions between them. Four stages in the transition process are proposed (Nicholson and West 1989: 182–3):

1 Preparation (the processes of expectation and anticipation before change).
2 Encounter (affect and sense-making during the first days or weeks of job tenure).
3 Adjustment (subsequent personal and role development to reduce person–job misfit).
4 Stabilization (settled connection between person and role).

Such was the rapidity of job change in Nicholson and West's sample of British managers, however, that the stabilization stage was often omitted before the next transition cycle began.

Individual differences as predictors

Moving on from career as a sequence of jobs and the transitions between them, we turn now to differences between individuals as predictors of career. Much of this research was based historically on notions of career choice as a one-off event, the choice therefore being the degree of match between the person's characteristics and the chosen occupation.

Perhaps the best researched theory in this tradition is that of Holland (1985). He isolated six interest areas, which are more properly construed as relatively enduring attributes of personality. They are:

• realistic
• investigative
• artistic
• social
• enterprising
• conventional

They may be arranged hexagonally in the above order to indicate their degree of similarity to each other. Underlying dimensions are people-orientated versus non-people-orientated (namely social, enterprising versus realistic, investigative) and intellectually-orientated versus practically-orientated (namely investigative, artistic versus conventional, realistic). Recent research suggests that people are more likely to change their interests and aspirations in the light of their experience of the labour market than to consciously change occupations.

Another individual difference theory is that of Schein (1978). He defined five career anchors, anchors being the talents, motives and values which people believe underlie their careers. These are labelled:

- technical/functional competence
- managerial competence
- security and stability
- creativity (subsequently labelled entrepreneurship)
- autonomy and independence

Schein later added three more anchors:

- service/dedication
- pure challenge
- lifestyle integration

Schein supposed that individuals formed and then maintained throughout their lives one dominant anchor which they express more and more clearly as they gain work experience. In Schein's highly educated sample (of MBA graduates) different anchors led to different sorts of relationship with organizations. Those for whom managerial competence was their dominant anchor were more likely to favour hierarchical progression in a large organization whereas those favouring autonomy and independence tried to disengage entirely from such a context.

A promising theoretical approach from this era of research was that of Super. He insisted on the developmental nature of careers and argued that it was the individual's self-concept, namely their view of themselves and their abilities, which was the prime determinant of their occupational behaviour.

Unfortunately the processes whereby the self-concept was related to the individual's career were not clearly elucidated, nor were the effects of the social, economic and organizational contexts spelled out. Nevertheless, Super (1981) went on to develop the notion of the life career, the series of roles which the individual typically plays during the course of their life. For example, for many in western industrialized society the twenties is a decade of one's life when the roles of worker, partner and parent commence. Despite the normative nature of this model it has proved valuable in directing attention towards the ever changing relationship of individuals' work career with their life career.

A particular offshoot of this awareness has been a recent concentration upon the careers of women (Gutek and Larwood 1987). Rather than concentrating upon the various forms of discrimination suffered by women in traditional promotional terms, this research discusses whether women's careers can be theorized in the same terms as men's careers. There is clearly room for debate about the extent to which the observed differences between women's and men's careers are attributable to inherent differences between men and women. Alternatively, there is a case for concentrating attention upon the economic, social and organizational context. Either way, it is clear that any account of careers which fails to incorporate a specifically female perspective is inadequate (see EQUAL EMPLOYMENT OPPORTUNITIES; WOMEN MANAGERS IN ORGANIZATIONS).

Considering first the usually cited differences between men and women, the masculine competitive motive is less appropriate now that individual promotion is less possible, while the feminine collaborative preference is more suited to the teamworking project mode increasingly prevalent in organizations. However, of course not all men are masculine nor women feminine in terms of this collaborative versus competitive dimension. Moving on to contextual developments, there is agreement that women will constitute an ever increasing proportion of the workforce. Developments such as dual-career couples for whom neither's career is more important than the other's and the increasing frequency of women returners are forcing organizations to rethink career policies. How, for example, can there be a strong relationship between age and stage when people enter, exit and re-enter the labour market at different ages?

Individuals' perceptions of their career

Consideration of women's careers leads to our next topic: individuals' perceptions of their career. Historically, the trend of research and theory has been to look at objective career progress as the outcome, or dependent variable, and individual characteristics, interests, aspirations and attitudes as the predictors, or independent variables. There is, however, a strong case for reversing this emphasis. It is important to understand how individuals' past and present experiences affect their career attitudes and intentions. This is not only important from the individual's point of view; their career satisfaction, for example, is a valuable outcome in its own right. It is also useful to help organizations understand what career aspirations and options they should consider providing for.

One obvious candidate for investigation is *career satisfaction*. There are a variety of predictors of career satisfaction which have been evidenced. For example:

1 the degree to which the individual's skills and knowledge are utilized;
2 the degree of fit between the individual's and the organization's plans for their career;
3 the extent to which the individual is certain of their career future;
4 perceived equity of pay relative to the pay of others in your organization who do the same sort of work; and
5 perceived equity of assessment and promotion procedures.

As one might expect, satisfaction with career is related, in its turn, to job satisfaction and to career commitment.

The emphasis on equity is interesting, particularly in the light of the idea of career as psychological contract. Theorists distinguish

between procedural and distributive justice (Rousseau and Parks 1993), and there is some evidence that procedural justice is more important for career satisfaction. In other words, employees are more dissatisfied about unfairness in the way in which, for example, promotion decisions are taken than in the actual outcome. Particular feelings of injustice and consequent dissatisfaction may result from the perceived breaking of a psychological contract by the organization. For example, an individual may believe that he or she will get a promotion in return for taking on an unpopular role. When this expectation is disappointed they will feel strongly that they have been unfairly treated. The implications of these findings for organizations are obvious: to avoid making promises which they cannot fulfil; and to ensure that all promotion procedures are fair and seen to be so.

4 Developmental stages in careers

There are other subjective aspects of careers which are only now beginning to receive attention; for example, how salient is their work career for individuals relative to other aspects of their lives and how does this change as they grow older? There is some evidence that careers have different meanings for different people at different stages of their lives. Indeed, they interpret particular organizational events, such as the appointment of a new chief executive or the introduction of a quality improvement programme, in different ways, depending upon their stage of career development. While a variety of theories exists about life careers and work careers, there is some agreement on three broad stages: early career, middle career and career maturity (Arthur and Kram 1989). At the first stage the individual's prime need is to explore: what their abilities are, what organizations are like, what the future might hold. Reciprocally, organizations expect and tend to receive high energy and optimism driving work at the technical/occupational level. The meaning of career at this stage is often discovering what one's expertise is and becoming more expert in it.

In middle career individuals start looking for autonomy and the opportunity to become visible and recognized in their organization. They are often concerned with organizational success and will contribute to the extent that they believe their efforts will achieve these outcomes.

In career maturity the concern is with maintaining and securing their outcomes and with passing on their experience to others. They are interested in being generative and productive and therefore anxious that what they have to offer is still relevant and useful. Arthur and Kram (1989) use the word 'stewardship' to describe this period.

There is an obvious danger in being normative, and in particular of assuming that women's development follows this pattern which is derived from research on, primarily, men. Nevertheless, the first stage is usually ended in the early thirties, the second in the mid-forties and the third in the early sixties. Often, however, women are just arriving at career maturity when men are opting out for good. Such is the rapidly changing pattern of employment, indeed, that even these broad generalizations are hazardous. Recently, for example, we have seen managers and professionals leaving or being forced out of organizations at around 50. They frequently use their experience in the role of consultant thereafter.

Clearly, if such different stages, each building upon the previous one(s), do exist then the views of career held by employees will differ markedly as a function of age. Equally obviously, if they are wanting to offer different benefits to the organization and derive different outcomes in return then the organization should renegotiate the psychological contract. One impetus, then, for such renegotiation is the individual's stage and anchor. Another impetus is, of course, the organization's own business development and human resource strategy. In the final section, therefore, consideration is given to how careers can be integrated; how, in other words, the career expectations of employees can be matched with the business needs of organizations.

5 Career management interventions

Few career interventions which have been described in the literature have attempted to address these two expectations simultaneously. There is a considerable literature on how to manage careers from the organization's perspective. For example, Mayo (1991) describes a set of systems based upon practice at ICL (Europe). For Mayo the career management process is 'the design and implementation of organisational processes which enable the careers of individuals to be planned and managed in a way that optimizes both the needs of the organisation and the preferences and capabilities of individuals'. This enlightened definition goes a long way towards recognizing the contractual nature of the career relationship. However, inherent in the definition is a crucial ambiguity; who is doing the planning and managing?

Mayo lists a variety of systems under three headings: *individual career planning processes*; *joint career planning processes*; and *organizational processes*. Included among the individual processes are:

- occupational counselling
- career planning workshops
- self-development plans
- career resource centres

The organizational processes include:

- appointment processes
- career/grade structures
- succession planning
- development postings
- manpower planning
- high flier schemes

The joint processes contain the following:

- appraisal and development reviews
- assessment centres for potential
- development centres
- joint career planning

All of these processes or systems might in principle serve both organizational and individual needs. However, whether they actually succeed in so doing probably depends upon the culture of the organization. Specifically, only if certain basic assumptions and value priorities are held by line managers and others in power in the organization will real negotiation take place. Among such assumptions and values might be:

1 Organizations exist for the benefit of individuals as much as, if not more than, the converse.
2 If the individual's employability is enhanced, this adds to the organization's knowledge assets and therefore to its competitive advantage.
3 People's career aspirations differ, both between individuals and within the same individual over time.
4 Unless these differences are discovered, recognized and negotiated about, career satisfaction and commitment will not ensue.
5 Valued employees will consequently leave the organization or contribute less than they could.
6 A change in the state of the labour market (for example, a buyer's labour market in recession) may result in a different balance of power (in this case, with the employer). However, these variations in power should not in principle affect career negotiations.
7 On the other hand, organizations too have needs. Survival is the most basic need of all, and the need to survive may justify very demanding expectations of the employee.
8 Career negotiation can only work if the individual and the representative of the organization are open about their expectations and prepared to compromise.

Unfortunately, both the systems listed and the culture necessary for them to work effectively are rarely found together. Indeed, it is possible that many of them are not relevant to the current needs of small and medium-sized organizations, or even some large ones. A variety of current trends render them inappropriate. First, if more and more projects or functions are outsourced then there will only remain a core of full-time employees for whom such processes are needed. The nature of the psychological contract with staff on temporary employment contracts will be entirely different. It will be far less of a relational, far more of a transactional, contract (Rousseau and Parks 1993); or, in other words, less a matter of mutual understandings, more an explicit exchange of payment for services rendered. Second, increased inter-organizational mobility will result in much more caution in organizations regarding investment in long-term development; remaining high flier schemes, for example, will be jettisoned. Third, the uncertainty of the business environment and the consequent constant adaptive organizational change mean that career futures are hard to foresee. As a result, organizations will expect individuals to develop themselves so as to be generally prepared for change.

Perhaps the only psychological contract left available is to learn to cope with change in exchange for an enhancement of one's employability. Learning to cope with change may itself be a way of enhancing employability so the bargain may be a mutually convenient one for some. On the other hand, there are many for whom coping with change does not accord with their career motivations. What of those, for example, whose career anchor is safety and security?

6 Approaches to career counselling

Perhaps it is appropriate to conclude, therefore, with those forms of career help which are available to the individual outside their employing organization. Careers counselling has passed through a series of historical stages which reflect our changed view of careers (Kidd and Killeen 1992). To match a model of one-off career choice, the earliest view of counselling was as an expert process. The counsellor made recommendations regarding the client's occupational choice on the basis of an assessment of their aptitudes and interests. Placement in an occupation which required those aptitudes and interests was the desired result.

A later model of counselling took account of developmental views of careers. It was

Table 2 Some key products and outcomes

Predictor	Author(s)	Outcome
Interests	Holland (1985)	Occupational choice
Self-concept	Super (1957)	Career development
Anchors	Schein (1985)	Career direction
Gender	Gutek and Larwood (1987)	Women's careers
Equity	Rousseau and Parks (1993)	Career satisfaction
Age/stage	Arthur and Kram (1989)	Career motivation
Counselling model	Kidd and Killeen (1992)	Career management

concerned with helping clients with self-awareness, opportunity awareness, decision making and transition learning. This model is not necessarily associated with younger people, although most of the research based upon it investigates school leavers and students.

The final and current model of career guidance is aimed at helping individuals to manage their own careers. Such management implies the ability to place one's career in the context of changing labour market, social, political and organizational realities. It requires individuals to develop themselves in such a way as to maintain and enhance their employability.

One form of counselling where this latter model is sometimes employed to good effect is that of outplacement counselling. Individuals, usually managers or professionals, who have been made redundant, are helped to feel more in charge of their own careers. It must be said, however, that probably for the majority of outplacement clients the outcome of greatest concern is the attainment of a new job which they feel continues their traditional sense of career progression. We may sum up the different research directions we have reviewed in Table 2.

There are two possible scenarios for the future. One suggests that organizational and individual career management will diverge. That is, organizations will increasingly treat employees as human resources to be utilized for business purposes; individuals will be concerned solely with their own interests; and contracts with employers will be strictly transactional, with terms and conditions spelled out on either side. The other alternative suggests that there will be a renewal of the idea of the relational contract. Careers will be developed as a sequence of renegotiations of the psychological contract, necessitated by changes in the lives of both organizations and individuals. This second alternative is more probable for individuals with labour market power – in particular for knowledge-based professionals.

PETER HERRIOT
INSTITUTE FOR EMPLOYMENT STUDIES

Further reading

(References cited in the text marked *)

* Arthur, M.B., Hall, D.T. and Lawrence, B.S. (1989) 'Generating new directions in career theory: the case for a transdisciplinary approach', in M.B. Arthur, D.T. Hall and B.S. Lawrence (eds), *Handbook of Career Theory*, Cambridge: Cambridge University Press. (A persuasive case for broadening the scope of research and theory on careers.)

* Arthur, M.B. and Kram, K.E. (1989) 'Reciprocity at work: the separate yet inseparable possibilities for individual and organizational development', in M.B. Arthur, D.T. Hall and B.S. Lawrence (eds), *Handbook of Career Theory*, Cambridge: Cambridge University Press. (An attempt to relate individual and organizational stages of development.)

* Dalton, G.W. and Thompson, P.H. (1986) *Novations: Strategies for Career Management*, Glenview, IL: Scott Foresman. (Traces stages in the career development of professionals based on a long-term research project into four different professions.)

* Gutek, B.A. and Larwood, L. (1987) *Women and Career Development*, Beverly Hills, CA: Sage Publications. (Argues powerfully that current approaches to career are male-centred, and suggests alternative career models for women.)

* Hendry, C. and Pettigrew, A. (1990) 'Human resource management: an agenda for the 1990s', *International Journal of Human Resource Management* 1 (1): 17–44. (A thorough account of the principles and practice of human resource management.)

* Herriot, P. (1996) 'Contracting careers', *Human Relations* 49, 757–90. (Argues for a model of career as a psychological contract between individual and organization.)

Herriot, P. and Pemberton, C. (1995) *New Deals: The Revolution in Managerial Careers*, Chichester: Wiley. (Examination of the attitudes of individual managers towards career change and management. Argues in favour of the need for innovation in creating new jobs.)

* Hirsch, W. and Jackson, C. (1996) *Strategies for Career Development: Promise, Practice and Pretence*. Brighton: Institute for Employment Studies, Report 305. (Reviews current career development practice in a sample of large UK organizations.)

* Holland, J.L. (1985) *Making Vocational Choices*, 2nd edn, Englewood Cliffs, NJ: Prentice Hall. (The theory and evidence for the most thoroughly researched model of occupational choice.)

* Horwitz, F.M. (1990) 'HRM: an ideological perspective', *Personnel Review* 19 (2): 10–15. (Analyses the human resource approach as an ideology designed to buttress managerial control.)

* Kanter, R.M. (1989) 'Careers and the wealth of nations: a macroperspective on the structure and implications of career forms', in M.B. Arthur, D.T. Hall and B.S. Lawrence (eds), *Handbook of Career Theory*, Cambridge: Cambridge University Press. (The new economic and organizational realities and the consequent individualizing of careers.)

* Kidd, J. and Killeen, J. (1992) 'Are the effects of career guidance worth having? Changes in practice and outcomes', *Journal of Occupational and Organisational Psychology* 65: 219–34. (Includes a valuable historical account of the development of careers guidance theory.)

* Mayo, A. (1991) *Managing Careers: Strategies for Organizations*, London: IPM Press. (A full account of the career management processes potentially available in a large organization.)

* Nicholson, N. and West, M.A. (1988) *Managerial Job Change: Men and Women in Transition*, Cambridge: Cambridge University Press. (Evidence regarding the mobility of a large sample of British managers.)

* Nicholson, N. and West, M.A. (1989) 'Transitions, work histories and careers', in M.B. Arthur, D.T. Hall and B.S. Lawrence (eds), *Handbook of Career Theory*, Cambridge: Cambridge University Press. (A theory of transitions between jobs.)

* Ornstein, S. and Isabella, L.A. (1993) 'Making sense of career: a review 1989–1992', *Journal of Management* 19: 243–67. (Points to new directions for career theory and research, especially towards subjective responses to career events.)

* Prahalad, C.K. and Hamel, G. (1990) 'The core competence of the corporation', *Harvard Business Review* 90 (3): 79–91. (Prescribes the knowledge base for an organization's competitive advantage, with obvious human resource implications.)

* Rosenbaum, J.E. (1989) 'Organization career systems and employee misperceptions', in M.B. Arthur, D.T. Hall and B.S. Lawrence (eds), *Handbook of Career Theory*, Cambridge: Cambridge University Press. (The objective career progress of individuals in internal labour markets and how they judge their progress.)

* Rousseau, D.M. and Parks, J.M. (1993) 'The contracts of individuals and organisations', in L.L. Cummings and B.M. Staw (eds), *Research in Organizational Behavior* 15: 1–43, Greenwich, CT: JAI Press Inc. (Outstanding review of the idea of the psychological contract and the limited evidence currently available to support it.)

* Schein, E.H. (1978) *Career Dynamics: Matching Individual and Organisational Needs*, Reading, MA: Addison-Wesley. (The original classic on careers in organizations; the origin of much subsequent theorizing and research.)

* Schein, E.H. (1985) *Career Anchors: Discovering Your Real Values*, San Diego, CA: University Associates. (The questionnaire used by Schein in his research on the careers of MBA graduates, here packaged as a self-administered instrument.)

* Sonnenfeld, J.A. and Peiperl, M.A. (1988) 'Staffing policy as a strategic response: a typology of career systems', *Academy of Management Review* 13: 588–600. (A clear integration of human resource strategies with business strategies regarding markets.)

* Sparrow, P.R. (1994) 'Organisational competencies: creating a strategic behavioural frame-

work for selection and assessment', in N. Anderson and P. Herriot (eds), *Handbook of Assessment and Appraisal*, London: Wiley. (Competency analysis as a way of anticipating the strategic human resource needs of the future.)

* Super, D.E. (1957) *The Psychology of Careers*, New York: Harper & Row. (The original statement of Super's developmental theory based on the self-concept.)

* Super, D.E. (1981) 'A life span, life space approach to career development', *Journal of Vocational Behavior* 16: 282–98. (Super's influential 'life career rainbow', an account of the roles which have traditionally been played at different points in our lives.)

* Van Maanen, J. and Barley, S.R. (1984) 'Occupational communities: culture and control in organisations', in B.M. Staw and L.L. Cummings (eds), *Research in Organizational Behavior* 6: 287–365, Greenwich, CT: JAI Press Inc. (A most insightful account of the potential conflict between occupational and organizational values.)

See also: EQUAL EMPLOYMENT OPPORTUNITIES; HUMAN RESOURCE DEVELOPMENT; HUMAN RESOURCE FLOWS; HUMAN RESOURCE MANAGEMENT; FINANCIAL INCENTIVES; OCCUPATIONAL PSYCHOLOGY; ORGANIZATION BEHAVIOUR; ORGANIZATION CULTURE; PAYMENT SYSTEMS; WOMEN MANAGERS IN ORGANIZATIONS

Related topics in the IEBM: ORGANIZATION DEVELOPMENT; ORGANIZATION STRUCTURE

Commitment

Overview

Commitment in the workplace, commitment to work and committed employees are all aspects of work commitment. Definitions of work commitment vary depending on the focus. In time-series development 'organizational commitment' is the most popular definition, meaning commitment to an organization, company or any other employer. Other work-related aspects of commitment are commitment to a job, occupation, profession or trade union. 'Commitment to a job' is more often known by the established term 'job involvement'. 'Professional commitment' is another term which appeared a little later and which attracts some interest in the field of human resource management as 'career commitment'.

The concept of organizational commitment has been developed during the 1970s and 1980s because it is regarded as a strategic variable in the promotion and achievement of business goals. One recently developed human resource device is the concept and encouragement of 'teams'. Efficient teamwork is based on a commitment to the team, workplace, division and/or corporation.

Originally, the concept of organizational commitment was to be utilized to manage employees within hierarchical and mass-producing organizations. Since the 1980s, industrial structure has been changed into a softer, more service-oriented economy in advanced countries. At the same time firms facing new information technology and global competition tried to introduce new organizational systems which were more flexible, more local and more innovation-led.

Organizational commitment should also contribute to flexible, local and innovative systems.

The definition of organizational commitment used in this entry is 'identification with an organization and acceptance of its goals and values as one's own' following the now commonly used definition of March and Simon (1958).

1 Introduction

From the viewpoint of human resource management the ultimate aim of firms or organizations is to achieve a certain goal with the least amount of cost, time, human input, etc. The selection, assignment and compensation of employees, employee relations and employees' career development are all important. Given the human resources existing in any company, the internal management is a key factor influencing employees' productivity,

Managers are most concerned to maintain their employees' job satisfaction, salary levels, degree of organization, etc. both at the present time and into the foreseeable future. Common problems, routinely faced by managers, are, for example, low levels of morale, high absenteeism, a high turnover of staff, human relations difficulties, militant unionism and even legal action by employees.

Workers who are more committed to their companies, are more likely to have a high level of morale, maintain a good attendance record, be less likely to leave, have good human relations with co-workers and management, reasonable union interaction and few legal problems.

In terms of quality of working life it is highly desirable that workers feel satisfied with organizations and the conditions there. Industrial stress, human relations stress, alienation and other disputes should be avoided. Organizationally committed workers are

481

more likely to accept organizational goals and values as their own, and to be less affected by industrial stress.

Historical context

Organizational commitment constitutes several elements: workers' attitudes, orientation towards an organization, identification with an organization, individual–organizational transactions, and investments.

Until the early 1950s the term 'loyalty' was generally used instead of 'organizational commitment'. J.C. Abegglen (1958) introduced the term 'lifetime commitment' to express Japanese workers' low turnover. Abegglen attributed this tendency to the traditional pattern of Japanese management and to a certain extent to the cultural background (see HUMAN RESOURCE MANAGEMENT IN JAPAN; INDUSTRIAL RELATIONS IN JAPAN). This concept was clearly based on the notion of 'attitudinal commitment' in much the same way as in the work of March and Simon (1958)

H.S. Becker (1960) first investigated the ability of 'job satisfaction' to raise labour productivity, improve attendance and promote retention of workforce in the early 1950s. But he found no significant correlation between job satisfaction and job performance. Becker's interest then moved to organizational commitment, as he argued that individuals commit to their organization in order to benefit from the return of past investment (time, money and effort). This idea was also called the 'side-bets theory' and later named 'calculative commitment' to contrast it with 'attitudinal commitment'. These terms were used as a dichotomic classification.

In the 1980s the term 'value commitment' was introduced by O'Reilly and Chatman (1986) drawing a distinction between organizational value and individual value. Matching of the two values should result in a high level of commitment.

In the 1990s a trichotomic classification was suggested by Allen and Meyer (1990; Meyer and Allen 1997). The three components are 'affective commitment', 'continuance commitment' and 'normative

commitment'. Affective commitment relates to emotional attachment. Continuance commitment emphasizes cost-consciousness (close to calculative commitment). Normative commitment reflects obligation-consciousness (see WORK ETHIC).

Measurement of organizational commitment

Mowday *et al.* (1979) constructed the Organizational Commitment Questionnaire suggesting that there are three components of organizational commitment: (1) a strong belief in and acceptance of an organization's goals and values; (2) a willingness to exert considerable effort on behalf of an organization; and (3) a strong desire to maintain membership in an organization (Mowday *et al.* 1979: 226). The Porter Organizational Commitment Scale was also developed. The scale has been widely used since then, but it has been criticized for its vagueness and oversimplification.

O'Reilly and Chatman (1986) proposed another three components of organizational commitment as psychological attachment: (1) compliance; (2) identification as involvement desire; and (3) internalization as vague congruence. In their studies they found identification and internalization were significant when explaining prosocial behaviour and turnover.

Allen and Meyer (1990) originally constructed twenty-three scale items for the three components. A sample of the organizational Commitment Questionnaire was as follows: (1) affective commitment (8 items, for example 'I would be very happy to spend the rest of my career in this organization'); (2) continuance commitment (9 items, for example 'I am not afraid of what might happen if I quit my job without having another one lined up'); (3) normative commitment (6 items, for example 'I do not feel any obligation to remain with my current employer') Responses were on a 7-point agree–disagree scale for each item. (Meyer and Allen, 1997: 118–119).

2 Research and empirical findings

Organizational type and commitment

Ouchi and Johnson (1978) introduced two ideal types of organizational control: Type A characterized by large firms and bureaucracy and Type Z characterized by such features as life-time employment, consensus decision making, collective responsibility, slow evaluation and promotion, implicit informal control, non-specialized career path and holistic concern. In summary Type A is a dry organization and Type Z is a wet organization.

Ouchi and Johnson examined employees' affiliative behaviour and attachment to the company as dependent variables after they chose two companies representing Type A and Type Z. They found that attachment to the company revealed the greatest difference between the two types of company. This variable consisted of loyalty; perceived support at work; satisfaction with the company; and congruent values in a work group. All of the elements scored higher for the wet company than for the dry company. The greatest difference was for the item 'reject a job offer with a 20 per cent rise'.

Among company practices the greatest differences for the wet company were the firm's attempts to avoid layoffs, to have an informal organizational structure, and to have more months employed by the company. The least significant differences were visiting a supervisor's home, the tendency towards group decision making and shared concerns.

Findings of meta-analysis

There have been a great number of empirical studies of organizational commitment. Mathieu and Zajac (1990: 174) published results of their meta-analysis grouping factors relating to organizational commitment into eight categories as follows:

1 *Personal characteristics*. Age, gender, education, marital status, tenure of position and in the organization, perceived personal competence, ability, salary, Protestant work ethic and job level.
2 *Role states*. Role ambiguity, role conflict and role overload.
3 *Job characteristics*. Skill variety, task autonomy, challenge and job scope.
4 *Group/leader relations*. Group cohesiveness, task interdependence, leader initiating structure, leader consideration, leader communication and participative leadership.
5 *Organizational characteristics*. Organizational size and organizational centralization.
6 *Motivation*. Overall motivation, internal motivation, job involvement, stress, occupational commitment and union commitment.
7 *Job satisfaction*. Overall job satisfaction, intrinsic job satisfaction, extrinsic job satisfaction, supervision, co-workers, promotion, pay and work itself.
8 *Job performance*. Others ratings of performance, output measures, perceived job alternatives, intention to search for job alternatives, intention to leave, attendance, lateness and turnover.

The above factors were considered likely to create organizational commitment except for motivation and job satisfaction. In the past studies of job satisfaction and organizational commitment showed close correlation. Some researchers assumed job satisfaction was the cause and others assumed organizational commitment was the cause. Motivation has also been in this situation.

In fact, contrary to the factors which showed sufficient explanatory power, the factors related to job performance gave poor results. Adjusted correlation coefficients between organizational commitment and its consequences were estimated as follows (Mathieu and Zajac 1990: 184):

intention to search for job alternatives –0.599
intention to leave –0.464
turnover –0.277
lateness –0.116
attendance 0.102
perception of job –0.085

483

The factors considered in the studies were mostly the perceived reaction of respondents. Mathieu and Zajac's analysis showed that organizational commitment (attitudinal and calculative) was explained by a great number of the factors listed above. On the other hand consequence factors seemed to be fewer in number and arbitrary.

3 Human resource management and organizational commitment

Organizational commitment is a consequence of human resource management (see HUMAN RESOURCE DEVELOPMENT; HUMAN RESOURCE MANAGEMENT) as well as demographic and organizational characteristics and it is a cause of organizational performance. Figure 1 shows all the relationships around organizational commitment in a human resource management context.

Organizational commitment and job satisfaction are located in the centre. They are most closely related although they are conceptually independent. Background factors are organizational policy on HRM, labour market conditions, organizational context, and employees' propensity to commit.

Beneficial consequences of organizational commitment are as follows: good attendance, less lateness, low turnover, less industrial stress, less alienation, good discipline, flexible job behaviour, high motivation, good teamwork, good human relations, few industrial disputes, stable industrial relations and fewer legal disputes as shown in Figure 1. Detrimental consequences of organizational commitment are as follows: high levels of stress, overwork, death, family strains, less self-development, less creativity and eventually an unhappy retirement.

Organizational performance means high productivity, innovative work, customer-driven services and globalization. Organizational performance should contribute to the ultimate organizational goals of profit and growth.

Changes in organizational commitment over thirty years.

Employees at two manufacturing plants in the Tokyo metropolitan area were surveyed three times in thirty years: 1960, 1976 and 1990. One was a steel mill at NKK which was one of the five largest steel companies in Japan. The second was a glass manufacturing plant at Asahi Glass which was one of the oligopolistic glass companies in Japan.

Takezawa (1995) conducted workers' attitude surveys including organizational commitment and finally finished his analysis following Takezawa and Whitehill's Japan and America studies (Takezawa 1995). The year of 1976 was picked out by Takezawa as a particularly difficult time for heavy industry, following the oil crisis. The sample consisted of male, regular employees. The sample size was 230 in 1960, 370 in 1978 and 500 in 1990 at each plant.

The only commitment question in the survey was one relating to withdrawal behaviour as follows: 'If you expect that your company will experience a prolonged decline in business, and if you can get a job with a more prosperous company, would you:

1 stay with the company and share whatever the future may bring because you have confidence in the management;
2 stay with the company provided management pledges to try to keep you employed though perhaps at reduced pay;
3 stay with the company provided management pledges to try and keep you employed and not reduce your pay;
4 leave the company and take the job with the more prosperous company?'

The overall picture shows a similar pattern for the two plants over the thirty years. At NKK the first answer, suggesting the strongest level of commitment, was chosen by 43.8 per cent in 1960, 39.9 in 1978 and 22.8 in 1990. At AGC the results for the same chioce were 48.3 per cent in 1960, 36.3 in 1978 and 14.4 in 1990. The majority in 1990 chose to stay but without a of reduction pay (no. 3). Also the percentage opting to move (no. 4) increased from 4.3 to 17.2 at NKK and from 1.7 to 18.8 at AGC over the thirty years.

Takezawa also analysed a young workers sample and a cohort sample. His findings during the period were that young workers' commitment especially was reduced. The cohort analysis showed that commitment rose in 1976 for those aged 35–44 and then reduced in 1990 at the age of 50 and over.

It is striking to know that choosing to leave (no. 4) was selected by only 17–18 per cent, even in 1990, and that for young leaving workers in the same year the figure was 32 per cent. It is not easy to compare one questionnaire with another, differently designed, questionnaire. A survey of American workers conducted by Lincoln and Kalleberg (1990), however, showed a higher level of commitment there than among Japanese workers.

4 Evaluation and conclusion

Excellent studies of organizational commitment have been accumulated. There seems to have been considerable advancement in the past decades. The common features of most of

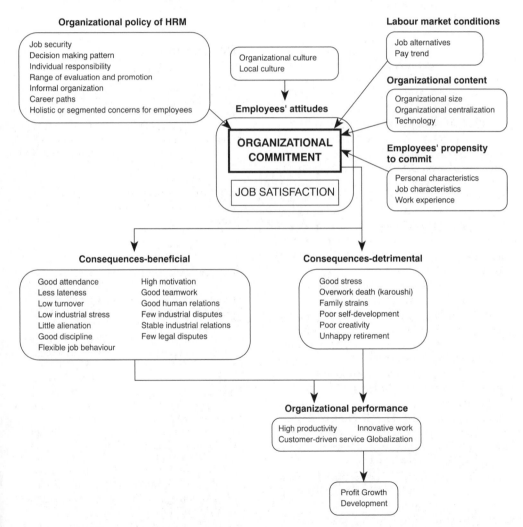

Figure 1 Causes and consequences of organizational commitment in human resource management context

the studies are a psychological approach, employees' questionnaire survey, multivariate analysis and use of meta-analysis. Some problems, however, still remain.

Organizational commitment was originally divided into two: attitudinal and calculative commitment. Subsequently it was divided into three or even four. The terms used proliferated. Researchers introduced a concept of dimensionality which was difficult to follow. Other terms employed to divide the commitment concept are dimensions, facets, components, constructs, definitions, foci and nature. Extraordinary, sophisticated terms become obstacles for outsiders wishing to enter the territory.

Secondly, the psychological approach has limitations. Organizational commitment is measured by the OCQ (organizational commitment questionnaire). A high correlation between organizational commitment and job satisfaction should be explained within a highly theoretical framework, but too much reliance on questionnaires may be problematical. Statistical data are available in organizations including employees' withdrawal behaviours and job performance. Furthermore, financial data would also be useful. Some psychologists have stated that 'perception is more important than reality' (Meyer and Allen 1997: 88) which has an unrealistic sound.

A third limitation of the psychological approach is its micro approach. Researchers from the psychological school tend to be concerned with employees' attitudes and behaviours and not so much with organizational factors and market factors. If they do not consider such environmental conditions, they will surely fail to tell the whole story.

Fourthly, more multi-cultural studies should be developed. The OCQ surveys of the past were mostly conducted in USA. This is one reason why the research became overly micro in its analysis – the variances of the variables was too small. If researchers include the wider world, they will inevitably need to introduce more variables.

Multi-commitment is another problem which will need to be explored further in the future. It is a fully accepted view that commitment to unions is not compatible with commitment to companies (Colon and Gallagher 1987). Commitment to the job is called job involvement which has some relationship with organizational commitment (Blau and Boal 1989). Professional commitment is another growth area in the study of work commitment (Wallace 1993). Organizational commitment is the most advanced research area at the present time and it is encouraging the development of multi-commitment studies.

YOKO SANO
TOKYO INTERNATIONAL UNIVERSITY

Further reading

(References cited in the text marked *)

* Abegglen, J.C. (1958) *The Japanese Factory: Aspects of its Social Organization*, Glencoe, IL: The Free Press. (A milestone of Japanese-style human resource management: focuses on lifetime commitment and collective responsibility.)
* Allen, N.J. and Meyer, J.P. (1990) 'The measurement and antecedents of affective, continuance and normative commitment to the organization', *Journal of Occupational Psychology* 63(1): 1–18. (A study emphasizing three sub-dimensions of the concept of commitment.)
* Becker, H.S. (1960) 'Notes on the concept of commitment', *American Journal of Sociology* 66(1): 32–42. (A milestone of the successful studies. The concept of organizational commitment; introduced for the first time into the field of industrial sociology.)
* Blau, G. and Boal, K. (1989) 'Using job involvement and organizational commitment interactively to predict turnover', *Journal of Management* 15: 115–27. (Significant correlations and distinctive differences were found between job involvement and organizational commitment.)
* Conlon, E. and Gallagher, D.G. (1987) 'Commitment to Employer and Union: The effect of membership status', *Academy of Management Journal*, 30(1): 151–62. (A pioneering work of multi-commitment showing strong commitment to employers with strong commitment unions.)
* Lincoln, J.R. and Kalleberg, A.L. (1990) *Culture, Control and Commitment: A study of work organization and work attitudes in the United*

States and Japan, Cambridge: Cambridge University Press. (A most comprehensive and advanced study examining workers' attitudes and commitment towards work and organizations. US workers showed stronger commitment to their jobs and firms compared to Japanese workers.)

Luthans, F., McCaul, H.S. and Dodd, N.G. (1985) 'Organizational commitment: a comparison of American, Japanese and Korean Employees', *Academy of Management Journal* 28(1): 213–19. (A close examination of three countries indicating higher commitment level for Americans.)

March, J.G. and Simon, H.A. (1958) *Organizations*, New York: Wiley. (Defines organizational commitment as identification with an organization and acceptance of its goals and values as one's own.)

Mathieu, J.E. and Zajac, D.M. (1990) 'A review and meta-analysis of the antecedents, correlates and consequences of organizational commitment', *Psychological Bulletin* 108 (2): 171–94. (A useful meta-analysis reviewing a trend of studies of organizational commitment on the basis of quantitative approach.)

* Meyer, J.P. and Allen, N.J. (1997) *Commitment in the workplace: Theory, Research and Application*, Thousand Oaks: Sage Publications. (The latest and best book to show theories, current state of researches and their applications of organizational commitment.)

Morrow, P.C. and Wirth, R.E. (1989) 'Work commitment among salaried professionals', *Journal of Vocational Behavior*, 34: 139–45. (Professional commitment which is a kind of work commitment needs to solve a measurement problem.)

* Mowday, R.T., Steers, R. and Porter, L. (1979) 'The measurement of organizational commitment', *Journal of Vocational Behavior*, 14: 224–47. (The authors constructed the concept of organizational commitment and developed the well-known Porter Organizational Commitment Scale.)

Mowday, R.T., Steers, R. and Porter, L. (1982) *Organizational Linkages: The Psychology of Commitment, Absenteeism and Turnover*, San Diego: Academic Press. (One of the most comprehensive and the most influential works on organizational commitment.)

* O'Reilly, C. and Chatman, J. (1986) 'Organizational commitment and psychological attachment: the effects of compliance, identification and internalization', *Journal of Applied Psychology* 71 (1): 492–99. (After a careful examination of the Porter approach, gives some comment on the three sub-dimensions of the commitment concept.)

* Ouchi, W.G. and Johnson, B. (1978) 'Types of organizational control and their relationship to emotional well being', *Administrative Science Quarterly* 23(2): 293–317. (A comparison of a prototypical US work organization and a US version of the prototypical Japanese organization based on an intensive questionnaire study.)

Randall, D.M. (1993) ' Cross-cultural research on organizational commitment: a review and application of Hofstede's value survey module', *Journal of Business Research* 26(1): 91–110. (Reviewing twenty-seven organizational commitment studies of ten countries; does not include USA.)

Shoire, L.M. and Wayne, S.J. (1993) 'Commitment and employee behavior: a comparison of affective and continuance commitment with perceived organizational support', *Journal of Applied Psychology* 78: 774–80.

* Takezawa, S. (1995) *Japan Works Ways: 1960–1976–1990*, Tokyo: The Japan Institute of Labour. (Panel data of three manufacturing plants over thirty years shows a great change in workers' commitment in a period of rapid economic growth.)

* Wallace, J.E. (1993) 'Professional and organizational commitment: Compatible or incompatible?' *Journal of Vocational Behavior* 42: 333–49. (A meta-analysis of 15 researches on professional commitment indicating differences were related to measurement.)

See also: HUMAN RESOURCE DEVELOPMENT; HUMAN RESOURCE MANAGEMENT; HUMAN RESOURCE MANAGEMENT IN JAPAN; INDUSTRIAL AND LABOUR RELATIONS; INDUSTRIAL RELATIONS IN JAPAN; WORK ETHIC

Related topics in the IEBM: COMMITMENT IN JAPAN; MANAGEMENT IN JAPAN; ORGANIZATION STRUCTURE

Communication

Overview

Effective communication is essential for the management of organizations. Individuals within the organization may be involved in oral, written and visual communication, with those above or below them in an organizational hierarchy, laterally with colleagues in other departments and externally. The emphasis in this entry is on interpersonal skills and how they may be developed. Other aspects that are covered are evaluation, cultural barriers, organizational structure and electronic communication.

1 The importance of communication

Studies have shown that managers spend most of their time in oral communication (Stewart 1988). Much of the rest of the time may be spent preparing or studying messages or reports. The volume of information a manager has to digest and impart and the need for accuracy means that one cannot manage effectively unless communication skills are adequate (see MANAGERIAL BEHAVIOUR). Unfortunately this crucial aspect of managerial work is often taken for granted and people may be appointed to managerial and other jobs who do not have the necessary communication skills. To compound matters, little may be done in terms of monitoring, evaluation, training and remedial action to develop appropriate communication skills. Consequently, dangerously optimistic assumptions may be made about the efficiency of the communication process (Rees 1996). The basic concepts covered here will help in developing an increased awareness of the fallibility of communication processes and the skills that need to be developed.

2 Barriers to effective oral communication

The barriers to effective oral communication are many, and include failure to recognize that such barriers even exist. People tend to view communication skills as the ability to communicate with others, although it may be even more important to ensure that others are able to communicate with you. Most oral communication needs to be in the listening role. This is because, even with only two people, on average the time spent talking and listening will need to be evenly distributed. When people meet in groups the share of the time that each person will have for talking will fall according to the size of the group. People often do not listen actively, for a variety of reasons, but the whole communication process will break down if the people for whom messages are intended do not receive those messages accurately.

3 Enabling others to communicate with you

For managers to take decisions they need accurate information. Although listening may appear to be a low status activity, accurate decision making necessitates good listening skills (see INTERPERSONAL SKILLS). Managers need to judge when to respond in such a way that communication is encouraged and when pro-actively to seek people out so that they can be properly briefed by them. As all this takes time, and judgement has to be used about when it is necessary to listen and when it is not, listening may need to include searching for attitudes and feelings behind words and looking for non-verbal clues such as body language to see what else needs to be communicated. If the manager is in an authority relationship with the potential giver of information it is necessary to recognize barriers that may discourage the free flow of information. It is easy enough to impart good news, the problem arises when bad news or potential criticism needs to be imparted. If the manager rebukes a person for offering unwelcome news or views, further adverse messages may be withheld. The manager may then in future receive carefully edited information without realizing that they are not being told the full story. The more authoritarian the style in an organization, or in an individual manager, the more likely this is to happen. The art is to be able to receive unfavourable news without retaliating, thus developing a reputation for being approachable.

Potential barriers to communication include recognizing when people are shy, or intimidated by their surroundings, for example physically or because of the presence of other people, as in the case of meetings. Often when managers have said something they fail to concentrate on the response. The need to develop communication skills has been neglected historically, yet it is difficult to think of an area where there is a greater need and greater return on the effort invested for those who are prepared to try and make the appropriate adjustments in their behaviour.

4 Effective communication by you

Having stressed the importance of effective listening, it is necessary to look at the skills involved in imparting information effectively. Many assume that information distributed, by whatever means, is understood and acted upon. Information that is imparted, but which is not understood and where necessary acted upon, is of no value. What managers often lack is timely feedback about comprehension of and commitment to information

they have imparted. In the case of oral instructions, it may be appropriate to look for positive proof that people have really understood. Lack of questions at the end of an instruction may not mean that people have understood. There may be many reasons – such as boredom, reluctance to cause trouble or offence, fear or failure to appreciate the consequences of error – for people giving the impression that they have understood and accepted something when they have not. This demonstrates also that talking and listening may need to be carefully sequenced to enable effective (two-way) communication to occur. Sometimes this will need to be combined with 'assertiveness' so that parties involved say what they need to say and recognize the need for others to do likewise (Back and Back 1990).

As with listening, so with presentation, managers are likely to reap handsome dividends if they recognize this as a core skill and devote adequate time and thought to it. Timing and location can be important. Another key issue is terminology. Many people simply seek to communicate using those words which are most convenient to them. If, however, the language is inappropriate this may defeat the purpose of the exercise. If communication is with a group of people it may be necessary to use a variety of languages or try and express oneself in a language that is as simple as possible, consistent with accuracy. Tone and variety of voice and use of bodily gestures may also need thought. Particularly in group situations, consideration of aids to effective communication such as visual aids, practical examples, exercises, demonstrations, humour, and an understanding of the audience's time span of concentration may also be needed. With emotional issues, or matters affecting the vital interests of an individual or group of people, particular care must be taken to ensure communication is accurately received. Factors such as ambiguity, preconceptions and selective perception can all too easily cause distortion. Such factors may lead people to hear just that which it is convenient to hear, with inconvenient or unpleasant aspects being 'blocked out'. People may also overreact to 'trigger' words so that the context in which they are used is misunderstood. All this underlines the need for positive checks to ensure that communication really has been effective.

5 Written communication

Much of what has been said about oral communication also applies to written communication. The use of clear and unambiguous language is important because, unlike in face to face communication, the author cannot immediately be questioned. Again, careful preparation may be necessary to ensure that, as well as appropriate language being used, the structuring of any message is logical and unambiguous, and irrelevant information is excluded. A welcome innovation from some manufacturers is the provision of a telephone helpline so that customers can get rapid assistance if they cannot follow written instructions on how to use a product.

6 Cultural barriers

Different countries have different cultures and subcultures. Some of the differences are obvious – such as language. Others may be more of a trap because they are less visible. Factors such as climate, history, politics and religion may have a deep impact on the customs and values in a culture. This may affect the openness of expression that is considered acceptable. If there is a strong tradition of politeness and avoidance of open criticism or conflict it may require considerable patience to get accurate responses. Some cultures may encourage exaggeration of statements, and others understatement. Attitudes to authority, to one's elders and outsiders may be important. The list of potential variations is endless but the key issue is the need to try and comprehend the difference between your own culture and another and to make appropriate adjustments. Even if mistakes are made, much credit may be given for the sheer politeness in trying to make appropriate adjustments in behaviour (see COMMUNICATION, CROSS-CULTURAL).

7 Organizational structure

The 'fit' between the objectives of an organization and its structure may have an important impact on the quality of communications. Often the fit is wrong because of such factors as ignorance about organizational structures and the options available, changed circumstances, power politics and failure to understand that different parts of an organization need to be structured in different ways. Common weaknesses are barriers to the upward flow of information and to the lateral flow of information across departmental boundaries (Rees 1996; Peters 1992).

8 Electronic communication

Mention must be made of the electronic communications dimension. There has been a dramatic increase in the variety and use of rapid, high volume electronic communication. This includes fax machines, electronic mail, electronic data processing, interlocking computers, electronic markets, satellite transmission of data, broadcasts and television pictures and electronic conferencing. These developments have had a powerful effect on economic and organizational structures, and on society, and have contributed greatly towards the process of globalization. Organizations are able to respond much more quickly and often more cheaply; they have a greater chance to succeed or fail, and in any event their structures are likely to keep changing – often quite dramatically. Clearly managers need to try and master these processes. Data needs careful evaluation and interpretation. The bias towards quantification may obscure the need to consider important intangible issues and the need for subjective decisions. The scale of potential errors may be much greater. The dangers of manipulation by data or visual presentations needs to be recognized and also the need for security and confidentiality.

W. DAVID REES
LONDON

Further reading

(References cited in the text marked *)

Argyle, M. (1990) *The Psychology of Interpersonal Behaviour*, Harmondsworth: Penguin. (Covers theory and application, and also includes a section on culture.)

* Back, Ken and Back, Kate (1990) *Assertiveness at Work: A Practical Guide to Handling Awkward Situations*, London: McGraw-Hill. (A useful explanation of the concept of assertiveness and how to apply it.)

Davenport, J. and Lipton, G. (eds) (1993) *Communication for Managers*, London: Industrial Society. (A basic practical guide based on a text by British Telecommunications Employee Communications.)

Fontana, D. (1990) *Social Skills and Work*, London: British Psychological Society and Routledge. (Advice on how to handle different professional situations including case studies and exercises.)

Gowers, Sir E. (1986) *Complete Plain Words*, rev. by S. Greenbaum and J. Whinart, London: HMSO. (The seminal work on clarity of expression in written English.)

* Peters, T. (1992) *Liberation Management*, London: Macmillan. (A comprehensive account of the impact of information technology and globalization on organizations.)

* Rees, W.D. (1996) *The Skills of Management*, 4th edn, London: International Thomson Business Press. (See chapter 8 for an expanded account of this entry on Communication, chapter 3 for an explanation of the options in organization structure and chapter 4 for managerial style and culture.)

Scott Morton, M.S. (ed.) (1991) *The Corporation of the 1990s*, Oxford: Oxford University Press. (A set of papers explaining the impact of information technology on organizations and their structure.)

* Stewart, R. (1988) *Managers and their Jobs*, London: Macmillan. (A research-based account of what managers do, emphasizing the importance of communication.)

Trompenaars, F. (1993) *Riding the Waves of Culture*, London: Nicholas Brealey Publishing. (A practical look at different cultural approaches to business.)

See also: COMMUNICATION, CROSS-CULTURAL; INTERPERSONAL SKILLS; MANAGERIAL BEHAVIOUR; NEGOTIATION SKILLS; ORGANIZATION CULTURE

Related topics in the IEBM: CYBERNETICS; INFORMATION AND KNOWLEDGE INDUSTRY; INFORMATION REVOLUTION; INFORMATION TECHNOLOGY; INTERNATIONAL BUSINESS NEGOTIATIONS; INTERNET AND BUSINESS; ORGANIZATION STRUCTURE; ORGANIZATIONAL INFORMATION AND KNOWLEDGE; ORGANIZATIONAL LEARNING; TELECOMMUNICATIONS

Communication, cross-cultural

1 Culturally sensitive communication
2 Some cultural contrasts
3 Managing cultural differences in communication
4 Communicating across national cultures
5 Meeting the challenges ahead

Overview

In the literature on cross-cultural communication, the terms 'cross-cultural communication', 'intercultural communication' and 'international communication' are frequently used interchangeably. Although 'cross-cultural communication' and 'intercultural communication' can be treated synonymously, an important distinction needs to be made between 'cross-cultural communication' and 'international communication'. 'International communication' takes place across political or national borders while 'cross-cultural communication' takes place across cultures. Both terms have their usefulness. If one is talking about communications between a multinational organization and its subsidiaries located in other countries, either 'international communication' or 'cross-cultural communication' can be used. However, if one is speaking of communications between colleagues working in a multicultural organization but in the same country, the term 'cross-cultural communication' is obviously more appropriate. In this study, the term 'cross-cultural communication' is used.

Two words need to be defined: 'culture' and 'communication'. As both have various meanings, depending on one's intention and persuasion, for present purposes their definitions are as follows.

Culture can be defined as a community's shared values, attitudes, behaviour and acts of communicating which are passed from one generation to the next. Communication means a goal-directed and context-bound exchange of meaning between two or more parties. In other words, communication takes place between people for a specific reason in a particular medium and environment. An American meets a Japanese to negotiate a business deal. The context in which the purpose of communication takes place can be either within the same culture or across different cultures. In the example given, the business negotiation takes place across different cultures. Communication is therefore a culture-bound activity. To communicate means expressing the uniqueness of one's cultural heritage, and this includes not only the verbal and non-verbal peculiarities but also the preferred medium and context of communication.

The scope for cross-cultural communication is extremely wide. It is a multidisciplinary field of study with roots in anthropology, sociology, psychology, cognition and linguistics, among other disciplines. For the purposes of this study, the focus will be on cross-cultural communication in business and management.

1 Culturally sensitive communication

As a field of study, cross-cultural communication can be characterized as the unceasing quest for a culturally sensitive model of communication (see COMMUNICATION). Underlying this quest is the dissatisfaction with the early linear-based and culturally impoverished models of communication such as those in Shannon and Weaver (1949). Such communication models fail to account for the role and impact of culture in communication. The growing realization of the importance of culture in communication has led more scholars to modify the earlier models as well as to construct new models that are able to capture the complexity and dynamics of cross-cultural communication.

In the 1990s, a rapidly changing world propelled by technological advances in communications compels its people to communicate across many cultural and geographical boundaries. In Britain, Europe, America, Asia and other parts of the world, the workplace is seeing greater interaction and communication among peoples of different cultures and experiences. The multicultural communication environment of business organizations is an indisputable thriving reality.

With more businesspeople needing to communicate with others from different cultures, more businesses are concerned about the importance and impact of cross-cultural communication. This is because the way in which businesses manage cross-cultural communication will determine their economic survival and competitiveness in the global marketplace.

Multinational and multicultural managers increasingly realize how vital it is to have a better understanding of the social system, the organizational as well as technological environment in which their businesses function. Insights from cross-cultural communication are increasingly important to management who wish to improve their understanding of organizational behaviour as well as the multicultural nature of business communication. Managers who have a systematic understanding of the cultural and organizational dynamics of cross-cultural communication will enhance organizational effectiveness and business performance.

2 Some cultural contrasts

Eastern and Western cultures

Many scholars have written about the cultural differences between the West and the East (see ORGANIZATION CULTURE). Among them, three are highlighted here: cognition, relationship with nature, and the concept of truth. Western culture is said to incline to think in a linear fashion. A cause leads to an effect. In Eastern culture, a cause can be an effect as well as that which leads to an effect. The past, present and future are interconnected and therefore they can affect one another. Western culture tends to be oriented towards mastery over nature while Eastern culture seeks harmony with nature. Regarding the concept of truth, the view of Western culture of ultimate truth or reality is based more on scientific and empirical explanation while that of Eastern culture is based more on revealed truth. Cultural differences between East and West have a significant impact on the communication behaviour and pattern.

Perceptions of cultural differences between East and West are insufficient to help business people get by when communicating across cultures. These perceptions have to be backed up by a clear understanding of the context of communication. According to Hall and Hall (1990), context refers to the information that circumscribes communication. One needs to understand that the informational context, that is, the kind of information (whether verbal or non-verbal) and the degree of background data (whether required or assumed) that has to be transmitted, varies from culture to culture.

High-context and low-context cultures

One fundamental area that concerns cross-cultural communication scholars is the communication differences between high-context cultures and low-context cultures. According to Hall (1976), any cultural transaction can basically be divided into two communication systems: high-context and low-context. In high-context cultures, the transactions feature preprogrammed information which is in the receiver and in the setting, with only minimal information in the transmitted message (implicit code). By contrast, in low-context cultures, transactions are the reverse, with most of the information in the transmitted message (explicit code).

Although no one culture exists exclusively at either extreme, in general, low-context cultures refer to groups of cultures that value individual orientation and overt communication codes and maintain a heterogeneous normative structure with low cultural demand characteristics. Conversely, high-context cultures refer to groups of cultures that value group-identity orientation and covert communication codes and maintain a homogeneous normative structure with high cultural demand characteristics. For

Hall, Germany, Scandinavia and the USA are situated at the low-context end of the continuum; Chinese, Japanese and Korean cultures are located at the high-context end. It is obvious that philosophy can influence communication – Confucianism, for example, has permeated the culture of all three east Asian countries.

In high-context cultures, that of Japan, for example, a larger portion of the message is left unspecified and accessed through the context, non-verbal cues and between-the-lines interpretation of what is actually said or written. The Japanese also prefer oral communication to written communication. In contrast, in North America, which is labelled as a low-context culture, messages are expected to be explicit and specific. More is spelt out than left for the receiver to deduce from the context. Thus it can be concluded that relative emphasis either on written or oral communication is a function of whether the country has a high- or low-context culture.

Polychronic and monochronic cultures

Another area of concern in cross-cultural communication is how temporal conception contributes to cultural differences in communication. Hall (1983) distinguished two patterns of time that govern the individualistic and collectivistic cultures: monochronic time schedule (M-time) and polychronic time schedule (P-time). According to Hall, P-time stresses the involvement of people and completion of transactions rather than adherence to preset schedules. Appointments are not taken as seriously and, as a consequence, are frequently broken. P-time is treated as less tangible than M-time. For Hall, Latin American, Middle Eastern, African, Asian, French and Greek cultures are representatives of P-time patterns, while North American and German cultures are representatives of M-time patterns.

M-time patterns appear to predominate in individualistic, low-context cultures while P-time patterns appear to predominate in group-based, high-context cultures. M-time cultures tend to have a linear and compartmentalized view of time while P-time cultures

generally have a more flexible one. In P-time cultures, time is seen as more contextually based and relationally orientated. Differences in time conception affect the management and resolution of conflicts in cross-cultural communication.

People in monochronic cultures tend to be direct when communicating good news or neutral news. Very little 'contexting', that is, the process of filling in background information, is needed, as people usually come to the point very quickly. Also, people in monochronic cultures tend to value quick responses in discussions with little introductory phrasing or politeness. Owing to the linear conception of time, communication tasks are segmented into predetermined units of time which can circumscribe the time span of business communication.

By contrast, oral and written communication in polychronic cultures can be more indirect or circular. A business talk can go off at tangents as business people view all information as having its proper place and function in the whole context of communication. Conflicts may arise when a business person from a monochronic culture interacts with another from a polychronic culture as the latter may consider the direct approach preferred by the other party as being rude.

3 Managing cultural differences in communication

An understanding of cultural differences will not only assist business people to bridge the communication gap between cultures but also multinational or multicultural managers to manage cultural differences more effectively. Studies on managing cultural differences in communication have grown both in number and popularity. They now form the basis of multicultural training and cultural diversity training of multinational companies operating in various cultural environments.

Courses and seminars offering participants 'new skills for global success' inevitably focus on the development and sharpening of cultural competence for cross-cultural business communication, including written communication, negotiations and conducting meetings. For instance, businesspeople from Britain are taught how to deal with the negotiating styles of the Japanese and Koreans. French salespeople learn how to make an effective sales presentation to a Japanese, Indonesian or Chinese prospect. Banking employees in mainland China are taught how to communicate with American and European clients.

One practical application of the insights obtained from studies on the East–West cultural divide is cross-cultural conflict management, an important area in cross-cultural communication studies. An example of such a study is Ting-Toomey's attempt at formulating a theory of culture and conflict (1994). In her analysis of factors that may lead to cross-cultural conflict, she explains how communication clashes can arise from such cultural differences as that between high-context cultures and low-context cultures, collectivistic cultures and individualistic cultures, and polychronic cultures and monochronic cultures. For instance, the maintenance of 'face' or self-respect in a conflict situation differs between a high-context culture and a low-context culture. Ting-Toomey also offers specific suggestions on how to deal with such conflicts. In resolving conflicts in cross-cultural communication, all parties involved must not only know about their own cultures but also demonstrate a willingness to accept differences in other cultures.

4 Communicating across national cultures

If communication is culture-bound and culture-specific, then the communication policies, patterns and preferences vary according to national cultures. Communication is therefore as individual as every culture because every culture has its own set of values. And these values have an impact on management and organizational behaviour. In his landmark study on the consequences of culture on management, Hofstede (1980) contended that each culture provides 'value sets' or 'mental programmes' which are culture-

specific. These programmes affect the way people in each culture perceive and interpret the world, influencing their expectations, goals, beliefs and ultimately behaviour in everyday life, including their work experiences and communication (see ORGANIZATION CULTURE).

Hofstede identified four major attitudes or value dimensions which differentiate national cultures: power distance, uncertainty avoidance, individualism–collectivism and masculinity–femininity. Power distance refers to the extent to which members of a culture accept the distribution of power in institutions and organizations. Uncertainty avoidance refers to the degree to which members of a culture feel uncomfortable with uncertainty and ambiguity, which leads them to support beliefs promising certainty and to maintain institutions protecting conformity. Individualism refers to a preference for a loosely knit social framework to take care of themselves and their immediate families only, as opposed to collectivism, which stands for preference for a tightly knit social framework in which individuals can expect their relatives, clan or other in-group members to look after them in exchange for unquestioning loyalty. Masculinity refers to a preference for achievement, heroism, assertiveness and material success, as opposed to femininity, which stands for a preference for relationships, modesty, caring for the weak, and the quality of life.

Hofstede's major conclusion is that different cultures have different value systems. Consequently, management and organizational theories and practices appropriate to some countries may be wholly inappropriate to other countries with different value systems. Ethnocentric US solutions do not always solve the management dilemmas of other nations. For instance, Peter Drucker's management by objectives works well in the USA and other individualistic cultures but not in collectivistic cultures which regard the performance of individuals as part of the relationship with the boss.

Cross-cultural communication, like organizational behaviour and management practices, is affected by the manifestation of national values or beliefs in corporate

495

communication, including the four identified by Hofstede: power distance, uncertainty avoidance, individualism (or collectivism), and masculinity (or femininity). The implication is that business people and managers have to be sensitive to the peculiar cultural mindset of nations, especially when they have to deal with people from other countries.

5 Meeting the challenges ahead

In looking ahead, researchers and scholars in cross-cultural communication will have to contend with two kinds of challenge. The first is in improving the theory and model of cross-cultural communication. Distinguishing communication along cultural parameters such as individualism versus collectivism, high-context versus low-context, and polychronic versus monochronic, or even along value dimensions as identified by Hofstede, may have useful but limited applications in cross-cultural communication: useful because they serve as reference points of comparison; limited because as soon as they are identified, they tend to highlight only those that are distinguishable by those parameters. Culture is difficult to pin down. Anyone who is seriously interested in studying cross-cultural communication must guard against the temptation to oversimplify cultural differences and differences between national cultures. Scholars of cross-cultural communication should be alert to the dangers of stereotyping cultural or national characteristics. Further research on the differences between national cultures, for instance between macroculture and microculture, dominant culture and subcultures, is required.

In their review of existing work on cross-cultural business communication, Limaye and Victor (1995) identified major weaknesses in the existing corpus. One of their main criticisms is that most of the studies conducted so far have been too culture-specific or have examined only narrow slices of those cultures, and therefore its findings may not apply across cultures. Future research has to focus on developing a culturally sensitive theory and model of cross-cultural communication as well as establishing a stronger empirical foundation.

The building of that foundation can be brought about by fostering greater collaboration among scholars from various cultures. An immediate benefit of such cooperation is the chance of overcoming potential cultural biases among researchers. Another is the possibility of obtaining greater insights into the multidimensional, multilayered, and multifaceted nature of cross-cultural communication. Given that cross-cultural communication is a multidisciplinary field of study, scholars and researchers from various related disciplines also need to come together to bring to bear their various forms of expertise and training.

The second challenge is to cope with changes in communications technology. The world today is experiencing rapid advancements in communications technology with the advent of the fax, e-mail, teleconferencing, video-conferencing and multimedia communication. Truly, cross-cultural communication has become borderless communication with people surfing on the global information superhighway anywhere and anytime. Virtual communication is the next frontier in cross-cultural communication. Business people have to learn to cope with the demands and changes wrought by the information revolution and face new problems of communication brought about by the swift pace of communication and information explosion.

The growing interdependence of nations in the global economy has resulted in the formation of regional trading zones and groups which promote economic cooperation among many nations, for instance the European Union (EU), the North America Free Trade Agreement (NAFTA), the Asia Pacific Economic Cooperation (APEC), and the ASEAN Free Trade Area (AFTA – 'ASEAN' is the Association of Southeast Asian Nations). When nations come together, their cultures will also come into contact. Cultural differences exist among member countries of multicultural APEC (which consists of the USA, Japan, Korea, China and the dynamic economies of southeast Asia) as well as within member countries of the EU. Inevitably, cross-cultural communication will be pivotal in the arena of international business collaboration and multinational management.

JOO-SENG TAN
NANYANG TECHNOLOGICAL UNIVERSITY,
SINGAPORE

Further reading

(References cited in the text marked *)

* Hall, E.T. (1976) *Beyond Culture*, New York: Doubleday/Currency. (A classic text on the contexts of culture, high context versus low context.)
* Hall, E.T. (1983) *The Dance of Life*, New York: Doubleday/Currency. (Another classic text on how time conception, monochronic versus polychronic, leads to cultural differences.)
* Hall, E.T. and Hall, M.R. (1990) *Understanding Cultural Differences*, Yarmouth, ME: Intercultural Press. (Illuminating cross-cultural comparisons of the Germans, French and Americans.)
Harris, P.R. and Moran, R.T. (1991) *Managing Cultural Differences*, 3rd edn, Houston, TX: Gulf Publishing. (Discussions and practical pointers on how to manage for cross-cultural effectiveness.)
* Hofstede, G. (1980) *Culture's Consequences: International Differences in Work-Related Values*, London: Sage Publications. (A classic text on how national cultures can affect organizational behaviour and management policies.)
Jackson, T. (ed.) (1995) *Cross-cultural Management*, Oxford: Butterworth Heinemann. (A helpful anthology of articles on various aspects of cross-cultural management, including managing cultural differences.)
* Limaye, M.R. and Victor, D.A. (1995) 'Cross-cultural business communication research: state of the art and hypotheses for the 1990s', in T. Jackson (ed.), *Cross-cultural Management*, Oxford: Butterworth Heinemann. (Presents ten useful and illuminating hypotheses on cross-cultural business communication.)
Samovar, L.A. and Porter, R.E. (eds) (1994) *Intercultural Communication: A Reader*, 7th edn, Belmont, CA: Wadsworth Inc. (A useful introduction to the theories and practice of intercultural communication.)
* Shannon, C.E. and Weaver, W. (1949) *The Mathematical Theory of Communication*, Urbana, IL: University of Illinois Press. (A classic text on the linear model of communication.)
Terpstra, V. (1985) *The Cultural Environment of International Business*, Cincinnati, OH: South-Western Publishing Co. (Analyses how multinational corporations adapt to the multicultural environment.)
* Ting-Toomey, S. (1994) 'Managing intercultural conflicts effectively', in L.A. Samovar and R.E. Porter (eds), *Intercultural Communication: A Reader*, 7th edn, Belmont, CA: Wadsworth Inc. (Examines the issue of cross-cultural conflict management.)
Trompenaars, F. (1994) *Riding the Waves of Culture: Understanding Cultural Diversity in Business*, London: Nicholas Brealey Publishing. (Explores four types of corporate culture and the cultural differences between them.)
Victor, D.A. (1992) *International Business Communication*, New York: HarperCollins. (Textbook for students of cross-cultural business communication with detailed review of literature and direct business applications.)

See also: COMMUNICATION; CULTURE; CULTURE, CROSS-NATIONAL; ORGANIZATION BEHAVIOUR; ORGANIZATION CULTURE

Related topics in the IEBM: GLOBALIZATION; HOFSTEDE, G.; INFORMATION TECHNOLOGY; INTERNATIONAL BUSINESS NEGOTIATIONS

Discipline and dismissals

Overview

Discipline at work is the regulation of human activity to produce a controlled and effective performance. It ranges from the guard's control of a rabble to the accomplishment of lone individuals producing spectacular performance through self-discipline in the control of their own talents and resources; from the threat or implementation of dismissal to the subtle persuasions of mentoring. Maintaining discipline is one of the central activities that managers have to exercise. Here we consider the sources of managerial authority and what makes it effective. Each organization has a framework of organizational justice within which managers administer rules and procedures and carry out disciplinary interviewing. In extreme cases employees are dismissed, although there are a series of legal rights to protect them against dismissal that is unfair.

Of all management activities, discipline is one of the most culturally constrained, making any international perspective difficult to discern. The burgeoning literature on international human resource management is silent on this topic because of the varied ways in which authority – the basis of discipline – is construed in different countries. The leading study on management and cultural variation is by the Dutchman Geert Hofstede, who takes the concept of power distance as one of the central ways in which culture causes management practice to vary.

1 The sources of managerial authority

If the different forms of discipline require a person of authority for them to be effective, from where do managers derive their authority? In part from the law and in part from human predilection and conditioning.

The law

The authority of the law is conferred on managers as agents of the employer, exercising the authority that employers enjoy as parties to a contract of employment (see INDUSTRIAL AND LABOUR RELATIONS). The employer has a range of duties. The main duty is to pay the employee according to the terms of the contract. The employer is also required to take reasonable care of the employee, as in matters of health and safety, and to be reasonably cooperative with the employee. Employers are not normally obliged to provide work, but they can be so obliged if their failure to provide work jeopardizes the employee's income, currently or in the future.

The employee's part of the bargain is generally to obey reasonable lawful orders and not to impede the employer's business. An accountant would not be obliged by the contract of employment knowingly to produce a set of false accounts. An employee is not obliged to discharge duties falling outside the terms of the contract, so the accountant would not be obliged to act as a chauffeur unless there was some wording of the contract which explicitly allowed for that. Employees also have a legal duty not to allow their own interests to compete with their duty to their employer.

The law therefore confirms a working relationship in which the employer has a legal right, working through the agency of managers, to exercise power and authority in relation to employees, including the right to terminate the contract of employment if dissatisfied.

The gradual development of employment law has been to curb that authority, especially in regard to contract termination, but employees have a fundamental duty to obey lawful orders.

Legal processes vary widely between different countries. Germany, for instance, requires employers to notify the Works Council of any proposed dismissal. In Sweden a termination cannot be completed by an employer until after legal proceedings have been exhausted, if the employee wishes to contest the dismissal decision by going to law. In Malaysia and Singapore due enquiry must be held before an errant employee can be dismissed for misconduct.

Human predilection and conditioning

The exercise of authority in an organization is partly impersonalized by the use of role in order to make it more effective. Quality-assurance staff in factories are likely to wear white coats and send unfavourable reports in writing so as to deploy the authority of their role rather than test the authority of their own selves. Dependence on role is not always welcome to those in managerial positions, who like to claim part of their effectiveness to lie with their own leadership, persuasive skill or similar qualities. Some managers are undoubtedly better than others in getting things done through other people, but the importance of role within the organization cannot be under-estimated.

The Milgram experiments

Stanley Milgram was a US psychologist who conducted a series of highly original and controversial experiments to investigate obedience to authority. Through advertisements in his local press, he recruited a number of volunteers who were led to believe that a study of memory and learning was being carried out which involved the volunteers giving progressively more severe electric shocks to learners who gave incorrect answers to a series of simple questions. If a volunteer questioned the procedure a standard response was received from the authority figure conducting the experiment, such as: (1) 'Please continue' or 'Please go on'; (2) 'The experiment requires that you continue'; (3) 'It is absolutely essential that you continue'; and (4) 'You have no other choice: you must go on'. These responses were given sequentially: (2) only after (1) had failed, (3) after (2) and so on.

The 'learner' was not actually receiving shocks but was a member of the experimental team simulating progressively greater distress as the shocks were made stronger. Eighteen different experiments were conducted with over 1,000 subjects, with the circumstances varying between each experiment. No matter how the variables were altered the subjects showed an astonishing compliance with authority even when giving 'shocks' of 450 volts. Up to 65 per cent of subjects continued to obey throughout the experiment in the presence of a clear authority figure and as many as 20 per cent continued to obey when the authority figure was absent and there was no reinforcement of the original instruction. Milgram was extensively criticized for this study, largely because of questions about the ethics of requiring subjects to behave in such a distressing way, but we cannot evade the fact that he induced a high level of obedience from a large number of people who would otherwise have considered their actions to be wrong.

Milgram's work is mentioned here simply to demonstrate that individuals have a predilection to obey instructions from authority figures, even if they do not want to. Milgram explains the phenomenon of obedience for us by an argument which he summarized thus:

(1) organized social life provides survival benefits to the individuals who are part of it, and to the group; (2) whatever behavioural and psychological features have been necessary to produce the capacity for *organized* social life have been shaped by evolutionary forces; (3) from the standpoint of cybernetics, the most general need in bringing self-regulating automata into a co-ordinated hierarchy is to suppress individual direction and control in favour of control from higher level components; (4) more generally, hierarchies can function only when internal modification occurs in

the elements of which they are composed; (5) functional hierarchies in social life are characterised by each of these features, and (6) the individuals who enter into such hierarchies are, of necessity, modified in their functioning.

(Milgram 1974: 132; emphasis added)

He then points out that the act of entering a hierarchical system causes individuals to see themselves acting as agents for carrying out the wishes of another person, and this results in these people being in a different state, described as the *agentic state*. This is the opposite to the state of *autonomy*, when individuals see themselves as acting on their own. Milgram then sets out six factors which lay the groundwork for obedience to authority.

(1) *Family*. Parental regulation inculcates a respect for adult authority. Parental expectation becomes the basis for moral imperatives, as telling children what to do has a dual function. 'Don't tell lies' is a moral injunction carrying a further implicit instruction, 'And obey me!' It is the implicit demand for obedience that remains the only consistent element across a range of explicit instructions.

(2) *Institutional setting*. Children emerge from the family into an institutional system of authority: the school. Here they learn how to function in an organization. Their activities are regulated by teachers but they can see that the teachers in turn have their activities regulated by head teacher, board of governors and central government. Throughout this period they are in a subordinate position. When, as adults, they go to work it may be found that a certain level of dissent is allowable but the overall situation is one in which they are to do a job prescribed by someone else.

(3) *Rewards*. Compliance with authority is generally rewarded while disobedience is frequently punished. Most significantly, promotion within the hierarchy not only rewards the individual but ensures the continuity of the hierarchy.

(4) *Perception of authority*. Authority is normatively supported: there is a shared expectation among people that certain institutions do, ordinarily, have a socially controlling figure. Also the authority of the controlling figure is limited to the situation. The usher in a cinema wields authority which vanishes on leaving the premises. As authority is expected it does not have to be asserted, merely presented.

(5) *Entry into the authority system*. Having perceived an authority figure, this figure must then be defined as relevant to the subject. The individual does not only take the voluntary step of deciding which authority system to join (at least in most of employment), but also defines which authority is relevant to which event. The fireman may expect instant obedience when calling for everybody to evacuate a blazing building, but not if asking employees to use a different accounting system.

(6) *The over-arching ideology*. The legitimacy of the social situation relates to a justifying ideology. Science and education formed the background to the experiments Milgram conducted and therefore provided a justification for actions carried out in their name. Most employment is in realms of activity regarded as legitimate, justified by the values and needs of society. This is vital if individuals are to provide willing obedience as it enables them to see their behaviour as serving a desirable end.

Making authority legitimate

The authority of a person in authority is greatly increased if the person is also an authority, with some element of expertise or even personality which makes their instructions both welcome and convincing. French and Raven (1959) suggest that there are five main bases of power that help us to influence others. We can examine this using management examples.

1 There is the situation where the manager is able to control the rewards of the employee. Direct, line managers are an important source of praise: they influence promotions and often decide on pay rises. Other managers decide on features of fringe benefit, such as the type of company car one may be able to use.

2 The second basis is where the manager is able to coerce the employee as a result of having punishments available. They can

withhold praise, block promotion, produce unenthusiastic (but rarely damning) performance appraisals, assign boring duties, rebuke and perhaps eventually dismiss.

3 The managerial role may provide legitimate influence in relation to the employee. Just as police officers have a right to constrain ordinary citizens in ways that are not available to other people, so most managers have duties that give them legitimate power in relation to their colleagues, like the auditor who can look at the books or the quality assurance official who can examine work done by other people.

4 Where the employee wishes to identify with the manager, the manager then has referent power. Managers with attractive personalities and an air of self-confidence often have a degree of referent power.

5 A manager has power when in possession of expertise that the employee recognizes and wants to use. The value of this particular power base is that it does not depend on the relative hierarchical position of 'the manager'.

The general willingness of people to do as they are told is something of which managers need frequent reassurance, but that alone is not sufficient for the manager to produce a performance from 'the managed'. Milgram's volunteers mainly complied with the instructions they received, but a substantial minority disobeyed. In most working situations the manager has to build something on top of the general predilection of subordinates to comply. The need in some way to be *an* as well as *in* authority is paramount.

2 Organizational justice

A framework of justice surrounds the everyday employment relationship so that managers and supervisors, as well as other employees, know where they stand when dissatisfaction develops. A system of organizational justice will have various features (see HUMAN RESOURCE MANAGEMENT; THIRD PARTY INTERVENTION).

Procedures

The formality of procedure provides a framework which avoids the risk of inconsistent *ad hoc* decisions and the employee knows at the outset how the matter will be handled. The key features of procedure are *fairness, facilities for representation, procedural steps* and *management rules.*

Fairness is best supported by the obvious even-handedness of the ways in which disciplinary matters are handled, but it will be greatly enhanced if there is an appeal stage either to a joint body or to independent arbitration as the management is then relinquishing the chance to be judge of its own cause.

Representation can help the individual employee who lacks the confidence or experience to take on the management single-handedly. There is always the risk that the presence of the representative produces a defensive management attitude, so the managers involved have to cast the representative in the correct role for the occasion.

Procedural steps should be limited, so that there are sufficient for justice to be done but not so many that matters become hamstrung by long drawn-out waiting. The steps are typically associated with actions that can only be taken by managers of specified authority, together with the series of warnings that have to be issued as a preliminary to dismissal except in the most serious of instances.

Management rules place limitations on how managers behave and about how decisions are to be reached. 'Last in – first out' is a decision rule often applied in situations of redundancy. If agreed by employer and employee before any redundancy arises, the decision about which employees should be dismissed when redundancy does arise is already taken. The pre-determined and agreed decision rule ties the hands of individual managers and legitimates the decision, which is accepted as just – even though unwelcome.

Another aspect of management rules is the need to deal with matters promptly in order to avoid the frustration that can come from delay and the risk of managers being seen to dither and lack the confidence to make a decision. The typical safeguards of ensuring, for instance, that first-line managers do not take major disciplinary decisions alone are necessary to achieve reasonable justice in the system, but prevarication can undermine the justice it is intended to ensure. Furthermore, the manager whose decision is being questioned will have a difficult time until the matter is resolved.

Rules of behaviour

Every workplace has rules. Some come from statutes, like the tachograph requirement for HGV drivers, but most are tailored to meet the particular requirements of the organization in which they apply. Rules about personal cleanliness, for example, are essential in a food factory but less stringent in a garage. Rules should be clear, readily understood and no more than are sufficient to cover all obvious and usual disciplinary matters. This will help people to remember them and to comply with them. Employees should have ready access to the rules, through the employee handbook and notice board.

Rules fall into six categories, relating to different types of employee behaviour.

1 Negligence is failure to do the job properly even though one could. Incompetence is different because the incompetent employee is not able to do the job properly and should not be subject to discipline.
2 Unreliability is failure to attend work as required, such as being late or absent.
3 Insubordination is refusing to obey an instruction or deliberate disrespect to someone in a position of authority.
4 Interfering with the rights of others covers a range of behaviours that are deemed socially unacceptable. Fighting is clearly identifiable, but intimidation or sexual harassment may be more difficult to establish.
5 Theft is unacceptable when it is from another employee. Theft from the organization can be difficult unless supported by very explicit rules, as 'stealing' company property is regarded by many offenders as one of the perks of the job. Private telephone calls, unauthorized private mileage,

stationery, material 'on its way to the tip' are all examples.
6 Safety rules are often extremely strict and are intended to avoid hazard.

The greatest value of rules is not to justify penalties but to provide guidelines on what people should do; the majority will comply, providing that they understand what they should do and providing that managers are consistent and prompt in making sure that the rules are kept.

Implementing the rules

Rules are only effective if employees conform to them, so managers have to make sure that the rules are observed.

Information about the rules needs to be thoroughly and imaginatively conveyed to those affected. Written particulars may be adequate to satisfy an industrial tribunal, but informal methods of communication are just as important as formal statements, as most people follow the advice and behaviour of their colleagues in determining how they will behave.

Training is a means of making the rules coherent and reinforcing their understanding. The background can be described and the reason for the rule explained, perhaps with examples, so that employees not only know the rules but also understand why they should be obeyed.

Placement and relocation can both avoid the risk of rules being broken by placing a new recruit with a working team that has high standards of compliance. If there are the signs of disciplinary problems in the making then a quick relocation can put the problem employee in a new situation where offences are less likely.

Rules periodically require review to ensure that they are up-to-date and to ensure that their observance is a live issue. This is an excellent feature of employee involvement in decision making. If, for instance, there is a monthly meeting between management and employee representatives, it could be appropriate to have a rules review every twelve months. The simple fact that the rules are being discussed will sustain the general level of awareness of what they are.

Penalties

The framework of organizational justice is completed by an understanding of what penalties can be imposed, by whom and for what. The following is a typical system of penalties.

(1) *The rebuke*. The simple 'Don't do that' or 'If you're late again, you'll be in trouble' is all that is needed in most situations, when someone has forgotten one of the rules, or has not realized it was to be taken seriously or was perhaps testing the resolution of the management. Too many managers are afraid that they will be defied or faced down, so they prefer to wait until they have good evidence for more serious action rather than deploying their own, there-and-then authority. Such managers should remember the evidence from Stanley Milgram's experiments: we all have a predilection to obey rather than defy authority.

(2) *Warnings*. Great care is required when issuing warnings: first because the manager is making some sort of commitment to action if the behaviour is repeated; and second because the legislation on dismissal has made the system of warnings an integral part of disciplinary practice which has to be followed if the employer is to succeed in defending a possible claim of unfair dismissal at tribunal. For the employer to show procedural fairness there should normally be a formal oral warning, or a written warning, specifying the nature of the offence and the likely outcome of the offence being repeated. It should also be made clear that this is the first, formal stage in the procedure. Further misconduct could then warrant a final written warning containing a statement that further repetition would lead to a penalty such as suspension or dismissal. All written warnings should be dated, signed and kept on record for a period agreed by rules known by both sides. Details must be given to the employee and to his or her representative, if desired. The means of appeal against the disciplinary action should also be pointed out.

(3) *Disciplinary transfer or demotion*. A penalty which is substantial but which falls short of dismissal is moving the employee to less attractive work, possibly carrying a lower salary. The seriousness of this is that it is public, as the employee's colleagues know the reason, as well as the tangible loss of earnings or potential earnings that may be involved. Demotion is rare. Those demoted usually either leave or continue (probably because they cannot leave) with considerable resentment and having lost so much confidence that their performance remains inadequate.

(4) *Suspension*. A tactic that has the benefit of being serious and avoids the disadvantage of being long-lasting is to suspend the employee for a short period. The employer has a contractual obligation to provide pay, but not usually to provide work, so it is easy to suspend someone from duty – with pay – either as a punishment or while an alleged offence is being investigated. If the contract of employment permits, it may also be possible to suspend the employee for a short period without pay.

Penalties should be appropriate in the circumstances. Where someone is persistently late or absent, for instance, suspension would be inappropriate as the penalty seems to reinforce the offence.

3 Dismissal

If all else fails the contract will be terminated by the management, and there is a mass of legal statute and precedent intended to safeguard the individual employee against unreasonable management action in dismissal, although most employees do not acquire legal protection against dismissal until they have been employed by their employer for a minimum period. In the UK in 1997 this minimum period was two years. The point of legal intervention varies from one country to another. In some the dismissal cannot be completed until its legality has been tested. In the UK the dismissal takes place and can then be tested by a dismissed employee making a claim to an Industrial Tribunal that the dismissal was unfair.

Potentially fair grounds for dismissal

A dismissal is potentially fair if there are fair grounds for it. Such grounds may exist in the following circumstances.

1 *Lack of capability or qualification.* If an employee lacks the skill, aptitude or physical health to do a job satisfactorily then the employer has a fair ground for dismissal. Someone who cannot do what is required now, even if they were highly skilled for work that is no longer needed, can be fairly dismissed. Ill health is a misfortune rather than a privilege in employment and no protection against dismissal, although employers are frequently reluctant to terminate the employment of someone who is incapacitated.
2 *Misconduct.* Disobedience, absence, insubordination, criminal activity and taking industrial action all provide grounds for dismissal.
3 *Redundancy.* If a job ceases to exist there is no protection against dismissal, although there may be an argument about which job has ceased to exist.
4 *Statutory bar.* The 'driving licence' clause. Employees who can no longer discharge their duties without breaking the law can be fairly dismissed. This most commonly applies to disqualified drivers.
5 *Some other substantial reason.* In addition to the above list there is this catch-all category for other behaviours that clearly justify dismissal but which are too diverse to be listed.

Actual fairness

As well as being potentially fair, dismissals also need to be actually fair. This mainly relates to following agreed procedures and going about dismissals in a way that does not offend against natural justice. Was the dismissal reasonable in the circumstances? Examples would be whether or not the application of rules was consistent, whether warnings were issued and recorded, whether an employee dismissed on grounds of ill health was dismissed after the condition had been investigated and a prognosis obtained, and whether employees dismissed as incompetent were given appropriate training and supervision.

Remedies

If a tribunal finds that an employee has been unfairly dismissed it will determine a remedy for the individual. This will be either *reinstatement*, *re-engagement* or *financial compensation*.

Reinstatement was intended by the legislators to be the primary remedy, but is rarely found in practice because the employment relationship has broken down beyond repair. An employee who is reinstated resumes the contract as if it had never been terminated, with length of service, seniority and pension rights restored.

Re-engagement is also rare and provides for the dismissed employee to be employed on a new contract comparable to that from which the dismissal was made. There is no continuity of service.

Financial compensation is the actual remedy in most circumstances. Employers are not likely to be keen on either reinstatement or re-engagement if they have resisted the claim at tribunal, and dismissed employees usually prefer a fresh opportunity. Neither reinstatement nor re-engagement can be imposed if either party is unwilling. The level of compensation is first a *basic award* which is computed by a formula according to the employee's length of service and actual pay at the time of dismissal. A *compensatory award* is to compensate for financial loss at the time of dismissal. In the rare circumstances where the tribunal awards reinstatement or re-engagement and the employer fails to comply, there is then an *additional award*.

4 Equity in discipline and dismissal

For these processes to work they must command support, and they will only command support if they are seen as equitable. At first it would seem that it is concern for the individual employee that is paramount, but the individual cannot be isolated from the rest of the workforce. Fairness is linked to the interests that all employees have in common in the organization and to the managers who must also perceive the system as equitable if they are to abide by its outcomes (see EQUAL EMPLOYMENT OPPORTUNITIES).

Procedures have a potential to be fair in that they are certain. The conduct of industrial relations becomes less haphazard and irrational; people 'know where they stand'. The existence of a rule cannot be denied and opportunities for one party to manipulate and change a rule are reduced. Procedures also have the advantage that they can be communicated. The process of formalising a procedure that previously existed only in custom and practice clarifies the ambiguities and inconsistencies within it and compels each party to recognize the role and responsibility of the other. By providing pre-established avenues for responses to various contingencies there is the chance that the response will be less random and so more fair. The impersonal nature of procedures offers the possibility of removing hostility from the workplace since an artificial social situation is created in which the ritual displays of aggression towards management are not seen as personal attacks on managers.

The achievement of equity may not match the potential. Procedures cannot for instance impart equity into situations that are basically unfair. It is impossible to overcome accepted norms of inequity in a plant, such as greater punctuality being required of manual employees than of white-collar employees.

A further feature of equity is the degree of similarity to the judicial process. All adopt certain legalistic mechanisms, like the right of individuals to be represented and to hear the case against them, but some aspects of legalism, such as burdens of proof and strict adherence to precedent, may cause the application of standard remedies rather than the consideration of individual circumstances.

5 Conclusion

Discipline and dismissal are key features of managerial authority in the workplace. Practice varies between national legal systems and between cultures that have contrasted views of power distance and compliance. To be effective managerial exercise of authority through discipline and the sanction of dismissal needs to be seen as equitable by those who are subject to it. In most Western countries discipline requires rationality and transparency, with the clear option of managerial decision being challenged. In some other countries the management/worker relationship may be complicated by the assumption that the manager will act in a quasi-parental capacity towards subordinates.

In Western societies we are seeing the crumbling of large organizational hierarchies and the fragmentation of corporate empires. Perhaps this will lead to further impersonalization of the employment contract that gradually becomes not a contract for employment, but a contract for performance, with a relationship that is not master and servant but purchaser and provider. Elsewhere attitudes and practices will be different. Geert Hofstede makes a telling cultural comparison (see ORGANIZATION CULTURE). First an extract from an official United States Office of Education publication on teaching Vietnamese children in US schools:

> Student participation was discouraged in Vietnamese schools by liberal doses of corporal punishment, and students were conditioned to sit rigidly and to speak only when spoken to. This background makes speaking freely in class hard for a Vietnamese. Therefore, don't mistake shyness for apathy.
>
> (Hofstede 1991: 233)

He then provides a hypothetical statement that might have been written if US students were attending Vietnamese schools:

> Students' proper respect for teachers was discouraged by a loose order and students were conditioned to behave disorderly and to chat all the time. This background makes proper and respectful behavior in class hard

for an American student. Therefore don't mistake rudeness for lack of reverence.

(Hofstede 1991: 234)

DEREK TORRINGTON
UNIVERSITY OF MANCHESTER INSTITUTE OF
SCIENCE AND TECHNOLOGY

Further reading

(References cited in the text marked *)

Edwards, P.K. (1989) 'The three faces of discipline', in K. Sisson (ed.), *Personnel Management in Britain*, Oxford: Blackwell. (A comprehensive analysis of how discipline is practised in factories and the purposes it serves.)

* French, W.L. and Raven, S. (1959) 'The bases of social power', in D. Cartwright (ed.), *Studies in Social Power*, Ann Arbor, MI: University of Michigan. (A classic study of power which focuses on the organization of personal aspects.)

Hofstede, G. (1980) *Culture's Consequences: International Differences in Work-related Values*, Beverly Hills, CA: Sage Publications. (An explanation of cultural variations in organizations.)

* Hofstede, G. (1991) *Cultures and Organizations*, Maidenhead: McGraw-Hill. (A work that expands the arguments set out in the author's 1980 publication to include further interpretation of the data with special relevance to oriental cultures.)

Huberman, J. (1964) 'Discipline without punishment', *Harvard Business Review*, 42 (4): 62–8. (A simple proposal about a positive approach to discipline that discounts any punishment at all,

except in the most extreme circumstances, although contract termination is a clear possibility.)

Macchiavelli, N. (1981) *The Prince*, Harmondsworth: Penguin. (A classic study of power and influence, written nearly 500 years ago. Relevant and incisive in its advice, it remains unnerving because of its distinction between ethical behaviour and political behaviour.)

* Milgram, S. (1974) *Obedience to Authority*, London: Tavistock Publications. (This famous study of human willingness to obey authority figures within a hierarchical system provides clear evidence that those in positions of authority can expect compliance from subordinates much more readily than defiance.)

Pfeffer, J. (1981) *Power in Organizations*, Marshfield, MA: Pitman. (Although Jeffrey Pfeffer has expanded his original thesis since, this early work remains his most lucid account of how power works in organizations.)

Wrong, D.H. (1979) *Power: its Forms, Bases and Uses*, Oxford: Blackwell. (This book, by an American philosopher, probes the issue of power, including an illuminating analysis of how it is described in literature from diverse cultures.)

See also: CAREERS; EQUAL EMPLOYMENT OPPORTUNITIES; HUMAN RESOURCE MANAGEMENT; INDUSTRIAL CONFLICT; INDUSTRIAL AND LABOUR RELATIONS; ORGANIZATION BEHAVIOUR; ORGANIZATION CULTURE; THIRD PARTY INTERVENTION

Related topics in the IEBM: POWER

Empowerment

Overview

The term 'empowerment' generally refers to a form of employee involvement initiative which was widespread from the 1980s and focused on task-based involvement and attitudinal change. Unlike industrial democracy there is no notion of workers having a right to a say: it is employers who decide whether and how to empower employees. While there are a wide range of programmes and initiatives which are entitled 'empowerment' and which vary as to the extent of power which employees actually exercise, most are purposefully designed not to give workers a very significant role in decision making but rather to secure an enhanced employee contribution to the organization with 'empowerment' taking place within the context of a strict management agenda. Empowerment schemes tend to be direct and based on individuals or small groups (usually the work group), a clear contrast with industrial democracy and participative schemes such as consultative committees which are collectivist and representative in nature.

Empowerment can be seen as a child of the mid-late 1980s when the term became common currency and it was also associated with influential movements of the 1980s, particularly Human Resource Management (HRM) and Total Quality Management (TQM) (see HUMAN RESOURCE MANAGEMENT; TOTAL QUALITY MANAGEMENT). However, there are significant problems with much of the prescriptive literature on empowerment, in that there is little detailed discussion of the problems employers may experience implementing empowerment or the conditions which are necessary for such an approach to be successful. It is assumed that employees will simply welcome the new way of working. Moreover, it is also assumed that empowerment is a universal solution appropriate to all organizations in all circumstances. Empowerment itself is not seen in a contingent way. Such literature has also been criticized as superficial and furthermore trivializes the conflict that exists within organizations.

This entry contains a description of the theoretical foundations of empowerment, descriptions of the major forms, an account of historical developments, and an evaluation of the practice.

I Theoretical foundations

In one sense it can be seen as a new phenomenon – standard texts on involvement and participation make scant reference to the term. However in a more meaningful sense, the roots go much deeper and it can be seen to be based on a number of key assumptions about methods of work. Empowerment can be seen in many respects as a rejection of the traditional classical model of management associated with F.W. Taylor and Ford (see FORDISM; TAYLOR. F.W.) where standardized products were made through economies of scale and the division of labour, and workers carried out fragmented and repetitive jobs. Economic man was seen as accepting a trade-off of high wages (extrinsic motivation) for a poor quality of working life. A number of theoretical arguments have been used to justify the utilization of empowerment.

(1) *Democratic humanism* which was a response to the excesses of scientific management and the problems of alienation and was associated with enlightened managers. This view of human nature can be seen in the work of McGregor and his Theory X and Theory Y

constructs. While Theory X assumes employees to dislike work and responsibility and to be motivated purely by financial considerations, Theory Y assumes employees would prefer to exercise self control and contribute to the organization so as to meet their needs for self-actualization. These sets of assumptions were also reflected in the work of humanist psychologists such as Maslow with his model of the hierarchy of needs, and also Herzberg's motivation–hygiene theory (Watson 1995) (see HERZBERG, F.). Participation would satisfy human growth needs of self-actualization and fulfilment and through this mechanism increase motivation and performance (seE MOTIVATION AND SATISFACTION; ORGANIZATIONAL PERFORMANCE). The socio-technical systems school stressed the need to design technical and social components alongside each other to optimize the two and their influential study of coalmining in Britain showed how work could be redesigned within the existing technical basis so as to retain traditional features such as skill variety and a degree of autonomy (Trist *et al.* 1963) (see TRIST, E.L.). In the 1970s the Quality of Working Life (QWL) movement consolidated and developed these ideas and put them into practice, most famously in the Swedish car plants such as Volvo at Kalmar. Furthermore developments in the broader political and social environment, including better-educated workers, has led to a higher level of expectation concerning quality of working life (Cotton 1993).

(2) The *economic argument* is essentially a pragmatic one. It is assumed first that workers have the opportunity to contribute to organizational success and as they are closer to the work situation they may be able to suggest improvements which management would not suggest by virtue of their position in the hierarchy. Secondly, empowerment would also increase job satisfaction and reduce turnover as workers feel more committed to organizational goals. Thirdly, as workers are empowered this reduces the need for complex and indeed dysfunctional systems of control, and thus increasing efficiency.

(3) *Flexible organization theory* brought together the above ideas and openly advocated empowerment within a wider business context. The move to customized products with flexible specialization (Piore and Sabel 1983) and flatter and leaner structures is seen as the new route to competitive advantage and this means increasing the focus on labour as a resource and not just as a cost. Furthermore, jobs are seen as far more complex than in the days of scientific management and change much quicker. It is seen as vital to achieve greater flexibility through the use of people. Rather than trying to control employees, they should be given discretion to provide a better service and achieve a higher standard of work. The argument emphasizes the need for faster decisions in a changing marketplace with employees closest to the customer/product being best placed to make decisions concerning related issues.

All these theories share a common assumption that workers are an untapped resource with knowledge and experience and an interest in becoming involved which can be released by employers providing opportunities and structures for their involvement. It is also assumed that participative decision making is likely to lead to job satisfaction and better quality decisions.

2 Types of empowerment

Empowerment has been used very loosely by managers and indeed academics. At its simplest, empowerment would common sensically be associated with the redistribution of power, but in practice empowerment is usually seen as a form of employee involvement. Employee involvement refers to schemes designed by management and intended to generate commitment and enhance employee contributions to the organization. While some forms of employee involvement may provide employees new channels through which their influence is enhanced, employee involvement does not involve any *de jure* sharing of authority or power. With employee involvement, the onus is on employers to involve employees or give employees the opportunity to be involved. Empowerment in the context of its usage in recent years can be seen as reflecting this approach. It is individualist rather than collectivist in its orientation, i.e. empowerment is based on individual workers or work groups but not on larger groups such as trade unions. It encompasses direct involvement in work practices rather than indirect. Financial participation and representative participation were not part of the agenda rendering it distinct from some parts of employee involvement, employee participation and industrial democracy. Thus a distinction could be made between empowerment initiatives as defined above and initiatives which may empower (the latter including industrial democracy).

The new terminology is important. The term is associated with an upbeat view of management and the vague but positive associations make the appeal immediate and extensive. But one needs to question who is empowering whom and why, as well as examining to whom do the benefits (if any) belong? No doubt the empowerment movement appropriates language and concepts from wider political movements – feminism, and the ecology movement where empowerment is seen as a positive force, but a key difference is that these movements are rooted in the oppressed whereas the empowerment movement is driven by those in power, i.e. management not workers.

Empowerment can be seen as a flexible and even elastic term (Lashley 1997). It clearly fits within the 'voluntarist' tradition which left managers and workers (in practice reflecting power structures, usually the former) to decide on a suitable approach for the organization. Empowerment is different to the 1970s QWL Movement which emphasized labour issues such as job satisfaction, absenteeism and labour turnover. In contrast empowerment emphasizes more direct business considerations, such as quality, flexibility and productivity (see FLEXIBILITY; PRODUCTIVITY). It is management who empowers employees and the initiatives have tended to cover direct workforce involvement over a relatively small number of issues usually connected with the production process or service delivery, with the rationale that highly committed and empowered staff were more likely to engage in a 'beyond contract' effort,

i.e. beyond the normal call of duty. There has tended to be little union negotiation concerning the principle of the initiative (an empowerment paradox) with design and planning excluding union involvement (see TRADE UNIONS). In practice, issues arising out of the implementation of empowerment often become industrial relations matters. For example job enlargement can threaten traditional demarcation lines.

What the quantitative growth of empowerment initiatives means for empowerment in practice is another issue. There is tendency in the existing literature to lump together all the various forms of empowerment. No categorization scheme for empowerment is entirely satisfactory as the boundaries between different types are not clear and much depends on the definition adopted. As there are no legal imperatives behind empowerment schemes, unlike co-determination for example in much of Western Europe, it is difficult to generalize about patterns of empowerment in different countries as decisions tend to be made at a decentralized level. With empowerment not existing as a single unified entity, it can cover a very wide range of schemes which in turn may involve a variety of diverse management motivations. However they are united by sharing a common assumption that employees and employers' interests are inextricably connected. They can range from the mechanistic (i.e. structural change) to the more organic (concerned with attitudes/culture). However, taking account of these notes of caution we can identify five main types, namely (1) information sharing; (2) upward problem solving; (3) task autonomy; (4) attitudinal shaping; (5) self-management.

Information sharing

This takes a number of forms. There has been a great deal of interest in recent years in management increasing *downward communication* to employees typically via newsletters, the management chain or team briefing, which communicates organizational goals and the business position of the organization to 'win hearts and minds' (see COMMUNICATION). The logic here is that employees will be more understanding of the reasons for business decisions and as a result more committed to the organization's action. Moreover, communication is made directly to the workforce rather than being mediated by employee representation or trade unions. Thus critics have argued that such schemes 'incorporate' workers and/or by-pass trade unions. It is also seen as important that employees should have the opportunity to express their views and grievances openly and independently through a form of *upward communication*, rather than being able to raise only task-related problems. Of course 'voice' could be achieved through trade union organization and collective bargaining (see TRADE UNIONS), through formally established grievance and disputes procedures but empowerment tends to favour individual action through speak-up schemes which offer employees protection if their complaints are not heard sympathetically. Employees may also be asked to collect information outside their immediate work group, perhaps through cross functional teams, as issues here may impact upon their work. This introduces a *horizontal communication* dimension. It is usually accompanied by a problem solving aspect as well (see below).

Upward problem solving

At its simplest this may involve informing management of problems and letting them deal with it (see PROBLEM SOLVING). A typical example in manufacturing would be workers having the ability to halt the line because of production problems. In services employees may be able to make customer related decisions (often unanticipated) without seeking higher approval (e.g. replacing defective products) while in manufacturing, employees may reject defective material. In the middle of the continuum would be a form of suggestion involvement (Bowen and Lawler 1992), where workers make suggestions but management decides whether or not to act upon them. Another form of this type of empowerment can involve workers having autonomy outside their basic work process such as addressing problems through quality circles/teams and implementing improvements themselves.

Alternatively there may be greater autonomy and responsibility at the point of production or service delivery.

Task autonomy

At its most basic level this may mean removing inspectors from the production line as workers take on wider responsibility, or it may involve the more significant restructuring of work units into cells (often around product flows), teams or the creation of semi-autonomous work groups now commonly referred to as teamworking or self-managing teams. This differs from job rotation, enlargement and enrichment in that the work group itself decides details of production and work group norms to a much larger extent than the former job restructuring schemes. Such teams can have autonomy, concerning task allocation and scheduling, monitoring of attendance, health and safety issues, the flow and pace of production and can also be responsible for setting improvement targets (Wall and Martin 1987). Teams can also have responsibility for the recruitment and training of temporary staff as well as controlling overtime levels. Developing a cell-based team structure is seen as helping communication, acceptance of change, and through peer pressure reduces the need for tight supervision and other forms of external control. This then facilitates delayering. Such groups can have what psychologists term skill discretion (solving problems with the knowledge of the group) and means discretion (choice in organizing the means and tools of work) (Cooper 1973).

Attitudinal shaping

This sees empowerment as a psychological process and is often seen in the service industry. There may be no change in work or organizational structure but employees are trained/educated to 'feel' empowered (a state of mind) and play a more confident role in their interaction with the customer. Internalization of the new values is seen as the key to new behaviour. Such initiatives have been criticized as 'smile campaigns' with critics arguing that the end result is a better apology rather than improved service.

Indeed there is some research that suggests changing attitudes through education and programmatic change is to misunderstand the process of change. It is changed behaviour that leads to changed attitudes rather than the reverse. What matters is how management organizes work so as to ensure new responsibilities, relationships and roles which in turn force changed behaviour (Beer *et al.* 1990).

Self-management

This tends to be fairly rare in any real sense. Clearly self-managing work groups are a limited form of this approach, but are constrained by working within certain limits set by senior management (e.g. self-managing in relation to a set of work tasks). Ideally self-management should involve divisions between managers and workers being eroded and decisions, rules and executive authority no longer set by the few for the many (Semler 1989). Others have referred to high involvement (Bowen and Lawler 1992) where business information is shared and employees participate in wider business decisions.

Clearly these types may overlap as many initiatives incorporate several of these dimensions. For example, information is important to empowerment in general and not just as a separate form. Similarly, a change in attitude and self-efficacy is seen by some writers as being at the core of empowerment (Conger and Kanungo 1988).

3 Historical background

Innovations at work group level have a long history. Prior to the industrial revolution, goods were made by craftsmen who had responsibility for the entire job – deciding how to make the product and also having control over the process itself. In the 1920s the ideas of F.W. Taylor (see TAYLOR, F.W.), the father of scientific management, were influential in breaking down jobs into small tasks and deciding the best method of carrying out each task. Workers had little discretion – conception was separate from execution and was centred on management. The system was based on worker compliance. While scientific management was very successful in boosting productivity there was concern over the alienation of workers reflected in high labour turnover, absenteeism and conflict. The work of Elton Mayo (see MAYO. G.E.) and the Human Relations School (see HUMAN RELATIONS) criticized Taylorism and suggested that involving workers had strong business as well as moral benefits. Workers could be self-motivated and carry out good work without close supervision.

While many problems were apparent with traditional forms of organizing work from this time it was not until the 1960s that an alternative work paradigm, job enrichment was established, the aim being to provide meaningful work for employees with some degree of control and feedback on performance. In short intrinsic motivation was seen as critical to job satisfaction and jobs were to be enriched by reintegrating maintenance tasks and providing some decision making opportunities. Walton (1985) lists firms such as General Motors, Procter & Gamble and Mars as leaders in work innovation in the USA during this time. In the 1970s there was great interest in industrial democracy which emphasized workers' rights to participate, and legislative backing for worker directives in much of Western Europe (excluding the UK) provided impetus for such structures. By the 1980s there was continuing interest in getting workers to participate but less concern with the concept of joint negotiation and much greater emphasis on employee involvement such as quality circles, team briefing and profit sharing as part of a wider set of reforms in working practices. The key point about the these schemes is that they did not challenge management prerogative.

It was the late 1980s which saw empowerment emerge in its modern form. While earlier involvement initiatives may have been empowering, empowerment needs to be seen in a particular business and political context. The rhetoric of enterprise which reflected the shift to the political right in Western Europe and the USA underpinned the new management approach. The discourse of empowerment fitted with notions of enter-prise culture with individuals seen as entre-preneurs taking their destiny into their own hands. Such ideas were advocated by the in-fluential popular management writers of this period, such as Peters and Schonberger whose ideas filtered back into the more academic writing on TQM and HRM. Peters ('involve everyone in everything; leading by empower-ing people') and Schonberger both became more explicit in their ideas for empowerment in the late 1980s and 1990s, as mass produc-tion in a predictable environment was no longer the norm. A flood of books on empow-erment began to appear (Foy 1994). However, the voluntarist approach to involvement was altered in the 1990s as the Clinton Democratic Administration launched a number of initia-tives designed to minimize bureaucracy and empower employees which then impacted on the private sector.

In retrospect it could be argued that Peters and Waterman's much derided best selling book *In Search of Excellence* published in 1982 was influential in helping lay the foun-dations for the modern empowerment move-ment. While many may not have read the book, their perceived wisdom and buzzwords became fully dispersed within management circles. A central message was the need to move away from the hard rationalist models driven by accountants and engineers to a more simple intuitive style of management. 'Produ-ctivity Through People', 'Autonomy and En-trepreneurship' summed up the new philosophy which, when combined with the 'Customer is King', provided the context for current empowerment ideas. The message was that successful organizations focused on managing culture. Implicit in this analysis was the view that managers could unleash the talents of individuals by dismantling organ-izational bureaucracy. Managers were ex-horted to trust and involve employees. Different forms of control were demanded. 'Simultaneous loose–tight properties' re-ferred to control through shared values (cus-tomer service, etc.) with employees having greater discretion with regard to how they car-ried out their jobs to meet these core corporate values.

By the late 1980s business thinking had also become attracted by the notion of new modes of managing. It was argued that markets were now more competitive (in-deed turbulent and chaotic) partly due to the globalization of competition and liber-alization by governments and customers were becoming more demanding in terms of choice, quality, design and service. Nor was the public sector immune from such pressures as privatization and commer-cialization increased the pressure on them to meet various performance criteria. In the private sector, organizations were now tar-geting their products at niche markets and attempting to respond swiftly to customer demands rather than selling mass produced goods in stable markets. As a result the em-phasis changed from utilizing economies of scale to more flexible, innovative and re-sponsive organizations. This shift was variously referred to as post-Fordism (see FORDISM), flexible specialization (see FLEXIBILITY) and lean production. The new management paradigm emphasized by writers such as Drucker and Kanter include de-bureaucratization (end of hierarchy and prescriptive rules), downsizing and delay-ering, decentralization and the utilization of project based teams as part of a move-ment towards a new knowledge based organization.

The new approach carried implications for people management and employers were urged to move away from an approach based on compliance, hierarchical authority and limited employee discretion to one where there was greater emphasis on high trust rela-tions, team-working and empowerment, with calls for employee commitment and the utili-zation of workforce expertise (Walton 1985). Furthermore, sectoral and labour market changes shifted the balance of power to em-ployers so as to facilitate the introduction of empowerment and other employee involve-ment mechanisms, which changed work rela-tionships on employers' terms. Whereas the Scandinavian experiments were born of a po-litical and economic context with a strong la-bour movement and supportive government, the context of empowerment was quite different.

The quality movement was also influential during this period. While its principles had been developed by Japanese companies in the late 1950s and 1960s, interest in the West peaked in the 1980s, and it appeared to carry a message of empowerment. Under Total Quality Management (TQM), continuous improvement is undertaken by those involved in a process and this introduces elements of 'bottom up' issue identification and problem solving. As a result TQM may empower employees by delegating functions that were previously the preserve of more senior organizational members. Thus supervisory roles are taken over by workers particularly in relation to quality control. Operators could use their tacit knowledge of work processes to achieve substantially higher levels of quality, with the task of management to create the conditions which would facilitate such efforts. However, operators activity would be confined to diagnosing improvements in their own work not necessarily being able to implement these themselves unless the organization had also moved towards semi-autonomous working that combined authority with the responsibility for work. Middle managers become facilitators, encouraging participation, teamwork and the delegation of responsibility and accountability and this helps foster pride, job satisfaction, and better work. The practice of continuous improvement is seen as increasing employee involvement in decision making although there is little discussion as to whether it is relatively low grade task-centred involvement or a more significant form of participation and shared decision making. In practice there is a basic ambiguity in TQM in that, while employers seek the commitment and empowerment of their employees, increased control over the work process is a cornerstone of TQM (Hill and Wilkinson 1995).

There is also a profoundly negative force which has driven the empowerment initiatives. In the 1980s and 1990s rationalization and downsizing were very much the order of the day. In this context empowerment became a business necessity as the destaffed and delayered organization could no longer function as before. In this set of circumstances, empowerment was inevitable as tasks had to be allocated to the survivors in the new organization. Thus talk of enrichment and job satisfaction were very much secondary to simply getting the job done. The Business Process Re-engineering movement reflected these types of considerations.

4 Evaluation of empowerment practices/issues

There has been considerable criticism of the transformation thesis implying a shift from Fordism to post-Fordism (see FORDISM). It has been pointed out that the pursuit of flexibility has not led to widespread multiskilling and indeed reflects sectoral change and opportunism rather than strategic choice. Lean production as implemented has strong elements of continuity with Taylorism. Nor have high trust relations appeared to be any more widespread than in previous times, with commitment largely calculative.

Effectiveness can be examined from a number of perspectives, and much depends on how one sees management motivation for the introduction of such initiatives. While there has been much discussion of empowerment from a humanist perspective there is no doubt that in the 1980s and 1990s management have regarded business considerations as the primary force behind empowerment. Thus the empowerment agenda of the 1980s and 1990s is much more pragmatic and business oriented than the QWL movement of the 1970s. Furthermore, management have defined the redistribution of power in very narrow terms. The degree of participation offered by empowerment is strictly within an agenda set by management and it tends not to extend to significant power sharing or participation in higher level strategic decisions such as product and investment plans. It tends to be within systems rather than over systems. It is also true to say that radical forms of empowerment are not on the current empowerment agenda. While there have been business benefits arising from empowerment it is often difficult to disentangle the contribution of empowerment given that it is typically part of a wider organizational change process (TQM, BPR, etc.) with other changes such as new payment systems and new technology often part of the package (see INFORMATION TECHNOLOGY; PAYMENT SYSTEMS). In terms of whether it leads to greater worker influence over decisions the answer appears to be yes but within heavily constrained terms.

The rhetoric of senior management, and the names given to their empowerment initiatives, sound superficially similar when comparing organizations. Research suggests the need to move away from any simplistic or unilinear conceptions of empowerment. Not only is it the case that varying types of empowerment carry different meanings, but also techniques with the same name, structure and processes may be experienced in very different fashions by different workforces. As a result empowerment initiatives cannot be analysed in isolation from the other organization policies that impact on the employment relationship. In particular, attention must be directed towards the work organization, the nature of the workforce, existing technology and business strategy, and whether initiatives are designed to create the climate in which changes in these areas can be introduced or whether they are merely bolted-on in a context where wider changes are already underway. While the catalyst for the introduction of empowerment initiatives may have been the same at the most general level, i.e. intensifying competitive pressure, the extent of these pressures may differ. In one organization empowerment may be part of a wider move to a more progressive and open style of management while in another, management may be forced towards changes in work organization and empowerment as part of an immediate and desperate struggle to survive, with increased intensification the outcome, and workers putting up with the new regime because of a fear of dismissal (see DISCIPLINE AND DISMISSALS).

However the credibility and acceptance of any initiative is partly governed by the management's treatment of the workforce. Studies point to the importance of supporting changes in human resource policy such as moves towards single status in producing a conception among the workforce of an 'open management style' and helping to produce a more positive evaluation of management. Research on high performance work teams which encompass empowerment identifies the context within which the teams operated as critical to their success. Management had a clear vision of how the teams fitted in with the broader business strategy and this was shared with all employees. Moreover, the teams were supported by a whole raft of other initiatives such as an open management style, open plan layout, flexitime and the removal of clocking and a payment system based on skills acquisition (see SKILLS). Thus empowerment needs to be nurtured by the whole work environment within which it operates. Teamworking is unlikely for example to be very successful with an individualized payment system which cuts across the group ideal. While there is little evidence that traditional distrust is eliminated by empowerment there may be greater loyalty within the reconstructed workgroups which may equally serve management goals. Similarly, best practice theory implies that interrelated elements produced benefits, not a piecemeal approach. Key human resource practices included empowerment but also identified training, rigorous selection, employee ownership and performance related reward as critical success factors (Pfeffer 1994).

Research is often polarized into those who report greater work effort and more demanding jobs and those who report more job satisfaction, but there is evidence of both occurring simultaneously. Thus work could be more satisfying with increased discretion over the work process but demands may also be more explicit and rigorous. While traditional external controls such as supervisory attention may have been eradicated, sophisticated measurement systems (technical control) monitor the performance of individuals and teams and peer pressure (social control) also serves management's objectives. From this perspective empowerment is more significant as ideology rather than as practice.

It is important to see empowerment in a wider context and reiterate that empowerment as defined by employers is largely task-based and aimed at operational issues. It is taken for granted in much of the prescriptive literature that employees will welcome and indeed be committed to the new approach (see COMMIT-MENT). Indeed there is evidence that workers welcome the removal of irritants (e.g. close supervision) and welcome the opportunity to address problems at source as well as the ability to decide work allocation. However, there is also evidence that employees are not sufficiently trained for empowerment in the West especially where empowerment is as a result of downsizing. Empowerment becomes abandonment (Adler 1993). In contrast in Japan the success of job enrichment has been attributed to newly hired workers being trained to do all the jobs on the line (a process taking six to twelve months), so they understand the entire process and are better able to identify problems. Another common problem is that the decision making process is neither clear nor developed, so that workers suggest ideas but management are unable to respond adequately to these. These problems are partly the result of the need to adapt to new production techniques and downsizing rather than enhancing empowerment *per se*. In other words empowerment is not without costs both in terms of establishing a new approach to management (involving training costs, costs of new reward and information systems) and in its operation (involving issues of integration, consistency and unintended consequences) (Lawler 1996). Thus the new paradigm of work organization remains an ideal, with elements adopted but in an *ad hoc* piecemeal manner. Some commentators have suggested that employees' 'empowerment' is more akin to taking responsibility previously held by others without a commensurate improvement in their own terms and conditions.

However, the evidence indicates that employees do not simply buy into rhetoric in an unconditional way and their support is dependent upon trust in management and the perceived benefits to themselves. Employees interpret, evaluate and (re)act towards managerial initiatives, and in its way serve to 'audit' in their own way the viability of managerial initiatives. Thus while workers' representatives may be becoming enmeshed in a management discourse which makes it difficult for them to challenge any management strategy which is grounded in business logic, in reality they may oppose the initiative implemented and indeed may subvert management goals (Roberts and Wilkinson 1991). Thus it could be argued that although management try to limit 'empowerment', employees themselves may question the extent to which they are treated and rewarded in the organization as a whole, and the extent to which they participate in key business decisions and hence construct their own independent agenda.

Because a passive view of the workforce is often taken, the potential variability of understanding of individual initiatives consequent upon diversity of industrial sectors is often overlooked. Thus for example in the services sector, moves towards empowerment may be seen by individual workforces as routine in the context of other firms already providing such schemes; in manufacturing the situations may be very different. Indeed the differences between the sectors suggest that the views expressed by the workforce towards empowerment initiatives is not just a matter of degree; rather, the specific nature of employment relationships in the different sectors serves to indicate whether or not such initiatives will involve immediate questions about the frontier of control. The importance of such initiatives lies in the context of the translation of their supposed formal properties within the real terrain of the organization and workplace. This is also important in helping us understand whether empowerment erodes other forms of involvement or participation. By restructuring work responsibilities and making the team central to the workplace, as well as encouraging employees to identify with managerial objectives, it can marginalize unions and in some cases is clearly intended to do so. From a business perspective a concern in recent years is the implication in terms of a loss of management control. An individual acting alone brought down a British Bank, Barings, and in other organizations such as Sears Roebuck, embarrassing headlines resulted from employees using their initiative and subverting control mechanisms (Simons 1995).

Empowerment suggests that it changes the role of middle managers and supervisors from holders of expert power to facilitators (or coaches). Removal of expert power is perceived as a significant threat and participative management is seen as a burden to many middle managers and it is not surprising that they do not universally welcome it. Their sense of anxiety is exacerbated by fears of job loss as levels in the hierarchy may be reduced as part of wider changes. Indeed some resist its introduction or alternatively go along with it but emphasize the 'hard', controlling aspects as a way of maintaining the existing power relationship. Moreover many see moves towards employee empowerment as 'soft' management removing their authority over subordinates. However, research suggests that opposition may owe more to the fact that they were not provided with the resources required, were not sufficiently trained or were not evaluated on this in terms of performance appraisal and therefore did not see it as of much importance. In other cases middle managers may feel that they themselves gain influence over decisions taken elsewhere in the organization that affect their work. Some may also feel that it gives them a chance to show their initiative and so increase their career prospects despite losing a degree of functional expert power.

In practice empowerment can be seen as depending contingently on other factors. For lower level employees, empowerment in organizations with more flexibly specialized processes, which rely on employee skill, discretion and organizational capabilities, is associated with more influence over decisions than empowerment in organizations where there are routinized and standardized processes that are capable of being tightly controlled from above and where there is a tradition of such control. Empowerment in terms of identifying and solving problems can be found in the latter environment, as was evident at the New United Motor Manufacturing Inc (NUMMI) – GM–Toyota joint venture in California, a Taylorised auto plant, but the scope for radical empowerment appears to be limited (Adler 1993). There is clearly a paradox in the empowerment process in that while workers may be empowered to improve a process once that change has been made it is standardized and hence constraining.

5 Conclusion

Empowerment has arisen from the employee involvement initiatives of the 1980s and has been conceived in an era where notions of industrial democracy were seen as old fashioned. Empowerment has largely been aimed at shopfloor workers with the twin goals of increasing productivity and commitment to employer's goals. While there has developed a variety of forms of empowerment they share a common basis in being managerially driven and hence within a management agenda which allows for largely task-based empowerment. Empowerment may not in practice dilute overall management control: rather it can reconstitute the nature of such control. Paradoxically empowerment as currently practised has been less empowering than employee participation of earlier times.

ADRIAN WILKINSON
MANCHESTER SCHOOL OF MANAGEMENT

References

(References cited in the text marked *)

* Adler, P. (1993) 'Time and motion regained', *Harvard Business Review*, Jan–Feb: 97–108. (A study of NUMMI car plant where Taylorism facilitates learning and continuous improvement.)
* Beer, M., Eisenstat, R. and Spector, B. (1990) 'Why change programmes don't produce change', *Harvard Business Review*, Nov–Dec. (A study of organizational change which criticized the programmatic route to revitalization.)
* Bowen, D. and Lawler, E.E. (1992) 'The empowerment of service workers: why, how and when?' *Sloan Management Review*, Spring, 33: 31–39 (A discussion of empowerment contingent on organizational strategy and circumstances.)
* Conger, J. and Kanungo, R. (1988) 'The empowerment process: integrating theory and practice', *Academy of Management Review* 13 (3):

471–82. (Provides an analytical treatment of the term looking at management and psychology literature.)

* Cooper, R. (1973) 'Task characteristics and intrinsic motivation', *Human Relations*, 26, August 387–408. (Analysis of task characteristics and job dimensions.)

* Cotton, J. (1993) *Employee Involvement*, Newbury Park, CA: Sage. (A wide ranging study of various forms of employee involvement.)

* Foy, N. (1994) *Empowering People at Work*, London: Gower (A practical text including case studies.)

* Hill, S. and Wilkinson, A. (1995) 'In search of TQM', *Employee Relations* 17 (3): pp 8–23. (An analysis of the quality movement and empowerment.)

* Lashley, C. (1997) *Empowering Service Excellence: Beyond the Quick Fix*, London: Cassell. (Examines empowerment in service sector organizations.)

* Lawler, E.E. (1996) *From the Ground Up*, San Francisco: Jossey-Bass. (A discussion of new approaches to organizing firms.)

* Peters, T. and Waterman, R. (1982) *In Search of Excellence*, New York: Harper Row (The best-selling guru book which identifies corporate culture as a key factor in achieving competitive advantage.)

* Piore, M. and Sabel, C. (1983) *The Second Industrial Divide*, New York: Basic Books. (Argues mass production has been replaced by flexible specialization as a result of product market changes and new technology.)

* Pfeffer, J. (1994) *Competitive Advantage Through People*, Boston, MA: Harvard Business School Press. (Argues that Best Practice People Management provides long term competitive advantage.)

* Roberts, I. and Wilkinson, A. (1991) 'Participation and purpose: boilermakers to bankers', *Critical Perspectives on Accounting* 2, 385–413. (A study of the nature of participation and its impact.)

* Semler, R. (1989) 'Managing without managers', *Harvard Business Review* September–October, 76–84. (An account of a Brazilian firm which has empowered its workforce.)

* Simons, R. (1995) 'Control in an age of empowerment', *Harvard Business Review*, March–April, 80–88. (Argues the need to balance control and empowerment.)

* Trist, E., Higgin, G., Murray H. and Pollock, A. (1963) *Organisational Choice: Capabilities of groups at the coalface under changing technologies*, London: Tavistock. (A classic study on socio-technical systems.)

* Wall, T. and Martin, R. (1987) Job and work design in Cooper, C. L. and Robertson, I.T. (eds.), *International Review of Industrial and Organisational Psychology*, pp. 61–91, Chichester, UK: John Wiley. (An overview and evaluation of the job design experiments.)

* Walton, R. (1985) 'From control to commitment in the workplace', *Harvard Business Review* March–April: 77–84. (A classic article arguing a shift for the control to commitment paradigm of work.)

* Watson, T. (1995) *Sociology, Work and Industry* (3rd edition) London: Routledge. (Standard textbook on industrial sociology.)

See also: DISCIPLINE AND DISMISSALS; FLEXIBILITY; FORDISM; HERZBERG, F.; HUMAN RESOURCE MANAGEMENT; MOTIVATION AND SATISFACTION; PRODUCTIVITY; TOTAL QUALITY MANAGEMENT; TRADE UNIONS

Related topics in the IEBM: COMMUNICATION; COMPETITIVE STRATEGIES, DEVELOPMENT; GLOBALIZATION; MASLOW, A. H.; ORGANIZATION PERFORMANCE; TRIST, E. L.

Financial incentives

Overview

Incentives have grown in popularity across a wide spectrum of employing organizations worldwide, particularly during the past ten years or so. The motivating effect of 'extra income' has enjoyed growing interest even in times of recession. Incentive payment schemes represent an attempt to influence the behaviour, and therefore work performance, of employees through the provision of a cash or cash equivalent reward which is extra to basic remuneration. This reward is assumed to bring forward a level of contribution to the company which is greater than that normally forthcoming in return for basic pay. Such payments can be made for extra effort on the shop floor, shouldering extra responsibility in the office, selling more than quota in the sales division or achieving increased profits in the boardroom. In one form or another, therefore, incentives can be applied to all categories of work.

Incentive schemes have traditionally been more popular in the United Kingdom than in many other industrial nations. In the USA remuneration practices have tended to concentrate on the total package of cash and non-cash payments with any innovations concentrated on the whole remuneration rather than some individual element such as cash incentives.

The most notable recent development in remuneration for American companies therefore has been 'cafeteria' or flexible systems which have grown in popularity since the early 1980s. The motivating effect of such flexibility has been largely ignored in the UK, where the cash incentive is still regarded as the prime motivator of human resource performance. There is also evidence that US companies view pay as an integral element of a strategic approach to human resource management thus linking payroll costs to business performance (Schuler 1995). In Europe incentives tend to be less available to company workforces than in the UK: certainly this is so in the Netherlands, France, Italy and Denmark, although ex-Eastern bloc countries use incentives to a greater degree than is the case in the UK (Logger *et al.* 1995). In Asia and Australasia incentives are as popular as they are in the UK. Interestingly, the Third World economies in the East parallel British industry conditions of the early twentieth century when shop-floor incentives grew apace (Tung 1991).

In some industries incentives represent a considerable proportion of the task of managing remuneration. For the individual on incentive the payment can represent a significant element of earnings. For the trade union incentives are a subject for negotiation. For management the incentive scheme is deemed to offer some hope of a reduction in unit costs of production or in more general terms an improvement in corporate well-being. Unfortunately, translating an incentive effect into some measure of improvement in corporate performance has proved difficult and it is a paradox that reward for employee performance is very rarely linked to the strategic approach to company objective achievement. What follows examines the origins of financial incentives, the various schemes, their strengths and weaknesses and their application to all categories of work.

I The rise of incentives

The dissolution of the craft guild system in the UK in the sixteenth century saw the rise of a system of merchant capitalism in which workers were hired to work at home for an income based on piecework. Such a system can be deemed to be the first application for an incentive scheme in the world, and it survived to the end of the eighteenth century when the industrial revolution brought the age of the factory to the UK. The factory system did not see the introduction of incentives on any significant scale until the end of the nineteenth century, when schemes which are now popularly associated with the Scientific Management theories in general and F.W. Taylor (see TAYLOR, F.W.) in particular were introduced in the form of 'merit differential piece rates' for cyclical or repetitive work in 1884. By the beginning of the twentieth century the names of Halsey, Emerson, Gantt and Bedaux (see BEDAUX, C.E.) could be attached to a list of schemes aimed at improving manual worker performance, improvements which were rewarded by some form of financial bonus. It is from such origins in the UK and the USA that today's work measurement-based incentive schemes have grown (Niebel 1972).

The age of the factory and urbanization also saw the rise of the department store with hired sales staff. Apparently not documented, the idea of commission on sales surfaced during the latter half of the nineteenth century, with employees paid a flat rate or percentage of the value of the goods sold. To this day commission survives as a financial incentive for sales personnel at all levels, from shop assistant to sales executive.

It is also worth noting that the nineteenth century also saw the introduction of the non-monetary incentive. In the UK several industrialists, including Robert Owen and Seebohm Rowntree, saw the importance of worker welfare as a contribution to employee motivation and performance. Rowntree can be credited with introducing a pension scheme, participative procedures for drawing up and monitoring work rules and worker performance, and the employee representative role. These qualitative means of improving worker contributions helped the performance of a confectionery company which certainly prospered.

Incentive schemes, therefore, have a long history which began on the shop floor of industry and financial incentives for the shop floor have been subjected to considerable development over the course of the past eighty years. In the USA developments were limited to the application of measures of labour productivity to underpin the efficiency of mass production technology. In the UK the use of these measures was extended to justify the payment of incentives within schemes such as the Halsey–Weir, Atkinson, Allingham, Bedaux, Rowan, Differential and Accelerating incentive methods. These are a few of the more than seventy types of incentive schemes developed in the UK between 1900 and 1950. The impact on British manufacturing efficiency in the inter-war years was notable particularly in the automobile, defence and general engineering industries.

In Europe incentives have been scarce until recently, while post-war experience has underlined the importance of generous wages and salaries as reward in themselves and of bringing forth required levels of employee contribution without the need for measures of labour productivity to determine extra incentive payments (Adler 1986). In Japan individual employee pay is frequently based on seniority, although a trend in the 1980s was towards bonuses based on company performance (Lawler 1987).

In Africa, Asia and Australasia the growth of incentives has been noticeable in the past forty years. Pockets of application are Nigeria, Tanzania, Israel, India, Indonesia, Malaysia, Hong Kong and Australia. This list is not exclusive but reveals some nations where the use of incentives for manual work has been part of a more general push to increase national wealth.

The Western world has seen a significant emphasis on incentives for white-collar, technical, professional and managerial employee groups, particularly since the middle of this century. This development has been in pursuit of white-collar efficiencies as blue-collar workforces have declined.

2 Performance and behaviour

The incentive is an addition to basic pay provided for additional effort and/or performance. Basic pay is remuneration for the time the employee spends at the employer's disposal. Thus, incentives are offered to improve the level of worker performance to levels which management considers necessary to maintain a required level of performance and which are higher than those which would be forthcoming in response to basic pay. Worker performances may be defined in terms of: (1) quantitative effort (measured in terms of time or physical output); (2) some target to be achieved; or (3) a broader grouping of elements including skill, responsibility and general behaviour. The first type of measure is normally used in schemes for blue-collar employees (such as piecework), the second type in management schemes (such as profit sharing and sales bonuses) and the latter in white-collar schemes (such as merit rating) (see PAYMENT SYSTEMS; PROFIT SHARING AND EMPLOYEE SHAREHOLDING SCHEMES). The incentive scheme should normally cause management to ask themselves what they want of their employees in terms of a performance-based contribution and to determine how much they are prepared to pay for it.

Incentive schemes are an intervention in the process of behaviour at work. They are sometimes based on the simplistic assumption that employees are indifferent to corporate needs and require some 'carrot' to bring forward positive and contributing behaviour. It is often not considered necessary to create conditions which will help and allow the employee to change attitudes but rather to concentrate the incentive effect on behaviour. Any negative attitudes held by the employee towards the company tend to be 'smothered' by the reward in the hope that they will cease to be an obstacle in the relationship between employee contribution and corporate requirement. In these terms incentive schemes are concerned with the structural elements of the working environment and aim to modify employee behaviour. Incorporating behavioural elements to more positively influence behaviour within a job design has proved difficult in

practice (Lawler 1987). The objectives of technical excellence in work measurement, production control and scheduling, and pay system design are all too often not balanced by behavioural excellence, in the form of a socio-psychologically motivating environment where high levels of performance are permanently maintained. Lacking such an environment, the majority of schemes have tended to provide only a temporary improvement in employee performance (Bowey et al. 1982; Gregg et al. 1993).

It should be noted, however, that the debate in US literature on the subject of incentives reveals a lack of confidence in the ability of financial rewards in any form to influence employee performance (Redling 1981). Much of this argument has concluded that organizations achieve success because of cooperation among the labour force rather than any direct relationship between pay and performance (Pearce 1987).

3 Rewards, measures and objectives

The reward may be given to the individual in recognition of his/her personal effort or results. Such a direct and individual approach has traditionally been preferred in shop-floor and management schemes. Alternatively the reward may be distributed among a group of employees on a pre-determined basis. This approach has increasingly been used with shop-floor schemes in recent years, but has been more popular with white-collar schemes. The provision of group rewards with the addition of an extra payment to reflect individual performance is also currently growing in popularity. Because the payment is normally based on performance, measures of employee contribution are required. These measures have been found among the techniques of work measurement for shop-floor operations and in the form of measures possessing less precision for white-collar and managerial work. Profits and sales values have been used for executive schemes. Value added rewards have enjoyed a 'patchy' history as a measure to underpin blue-collar and white-collar incentives.

The payment of the reward is normally made close in time to the achieved performance. For manual schemes the payment has usually been in the same weekly or monthly pay packet and salary, and for white-collar employees in the next salary payment. Some recent schemes, particularly of the value added type, have not met such a requirement, delaying payment by months, and the results have been decidedly mixed, with goodwill sometimes generated but not necessarily an improved level performance.

The objectives for incentive schemes are normally built around the expected gains in company performance which management expect. Motivating after-tax rewards are the usual objectives for employees. The reward is therefore deemed to be a real incentive, bringing forward demanding levels of effort and/or performance and providing for earnings which exceed basic pay by a substantial margin. Determining the size of that margin requires some effective judgement on management's part if the incentive effect is to be achieved. Shop-floor schemes were originally designed to provide a bonus of some 33.3 per cent of basic pay; anything less than 25 per cent of basic pay has traditionally been regarded as unlikely to improve employee effort (Currie 1969). This may indicate a potential problem with white-collar methods which often add little more than three or five per cent of basic pay. Although employee performance may improve with such schemes, it may be due to reasons very different from any incentive effect deriving from the reward, and may also be limited to a 'goodwill' effect (Murliss 1992).

Incentive schemes of any type should be self-financing but this can prove difficult in practice. The costs of measurement and preparatory work, coupled with the cost of any bonuses, can be considerable. Savings from efficiency and the better utilization of staff should at least balance, and preferably exceed, such costs.

Within the processes of design, implementation and maintenance of incentive schemes a key requirement is for the scheme to be readily understood by managements and employees. The financial reward is designed to improve employee effectiveness at work, an improvement which can be assured and enhanced by better utilization of equipment and services and more effective work methodologies and company organization structures. Thus, incentive schemes may have more to offer than just concentration on the quantitative aspects of work. The qualitative elements of performance measurement and the decisions based on that information can be improved simultaneously on the basis of financial and physical data needed for the incentive scheme. This improvement in the database for management represents an opportunity for improved effectiveness at the level of the corporate entity.

4 Some considerations for white-collar schemes

The majority of schemes for white-collar employees provide an additional payment linked to performance, as is the case with manual schemes. The issue of achievable levels of performance is therefore as important to white-collar schemes as to manual schemes. It is inescapable, however, that the means of determining white-collar performance is problematic except in cases where sales and profits can be used. Clerical work measurement schemes have been developed to deal with the problem, but they remain limited in terms of application and effectiveness. Length of service has been one popular determinant of white-collar incentives (used in salary progression schemes) but it is doubtful whether this provides any real incentive effect in terms of raising performance. The main consideration in such schemes appears to be the provision of an inducement to the worker not to change his job, rather than some stimulus to greater contribution. The majority of white-collar schemes are based on subjective measures and can provide a weaker incentive effect than shop-floor methods (Fowler 1988). They may require a greater degree of management control of performance than has been traditionally the case with manual schemes, although managerial intervention has often proved necessary even with the most generous shop-floor rewards (Smith 1976).

5 Non-cash incentives

Schemes such as profit sharing and employee shareholding are indirect incentives in that they are designed to improve the employee's commitment to the organization, while recognizing a higher order of need than immediate cash (Knight 1986). Such a recognition can create a positive climate for employee attitudes towards the company, which can in turn facilitate the application of direct monetary incentives and their positive influence on employee and corporate performance (Incomes Data Services 1987).

The provision of long service awards, suggestion awards, expenses, subscriptions to private health schemes and company cars also represent indirect incentives, although they are also classified as employee benefits and perquisites. The incentive effect of such benefits is not as clear as direct monetary rewards and their influence on behaviour is usually lost soon after they have been awarded. As an immediate and short-lived incentive they need careful timing in their application. Other non-monetary incentives can include working conditions, education and training. This kind of provision has so far been minimal but reported success with education and training linked to performance has been notable (Pickard 1990).

6 Incentive, earnings and performance

There are three basic questions to be asked by management and employees in their approach to the subject of direct financial incentives:

1 What level of payment should employees earn?
2 How hard should they work for that payment?
3 How hard can they work?

The answer to the first question depends on a mix of issues including manpower supply, the relative bargaining power of employee representatives and management, the economic health of the industry and the expectations of the workforce. The second question is equally difficult to answer: management may be clear about how hard they want their human resources to work, but the employees may determine a pace of work which may be acceptable to them but at variance with management's aim. Faced with difficulties in the control and determination of pay levels and the effort exerted by manpower, management have found some confidence by adopting various measurement methods as an answer to the third question. This confidence has derived from the (disputed) claim that measurement reveals how hard people can work (or the value of their contribution), and these findings are then normally used to determine the level of reward for such effort. Thus, within an incentive scheme management believe they are paying for measured effort or contribution on the basis of three assumptions:

1 measured effort equates to the maximum level of effort forthcoming from the organizations' human resources;
2 employees are willing to contribute to the achievement of corporate objectives through a financial inducement; and
3 contribution varies in relation to earnings.

All three assumptions are open to question. The maximum level of effort or contribution is tied up with the issue of how hard people should work and, as mentioned above, this is not always or fully under the control of management. In the case of the second and third assumptions, it is well to remember that money is not the only motivating factor and socio-psychological factors should also be taken into account (Humner 1973; Pearce 1987) (see HUMAN RESOURCE MANAGEMENT).

In the last analysis financial incentive schemes represent no more than a bargain and that bargain may be 'official' or 'unofficial'. They represent a compromise of management and employee beliefs about performance and pay. Incentive payments reflect conceptions of pay, performance and measurement, in whatever form. The question of whose objectives are met by incentive schemes cannot therefore be answered easily. Both parties are looking for gain, and the responsibility placed on management includes an obligation to ensure that the employees achieve their own objectives of higher levels of earnings and standard of living while simultaneously contributing to the achievement of corporate objectives. Therefore it is management's task to ensure the permanent balance of effort and reward. Given that such a balance is determined by compromise rather than precision, doubts arise about whether such balance can be achieved. The overwhelming evidence shows that at best it has proved difficult (Smith 1993). Against the background of this knowledge, many commentators inside and outside British industry have claimed that incentive schemes should be put aside and replaced by consolidated pay rates (Humner 1973; Pearce 1987). Unfortunately such a move would replace a compromise based on the complex exercise of designing an incentive which at least involves measurement with a compromise mainly based on little understood pressures influencing general earnings levels. Incentives may be difficult to manage, but so are the alternatives (Smith 1989).

7 Payment by results for manual work

Traditional schemes are normally time-based and piecework derivatives. (Piece-time bonus systems, which are based on the principle of management and employee sharing any financial gain from any improved production are popular mainly in the USA and have enjoyed minimum application in the UK). They are based on job fragmentation, repetition, piece rate pay and individual worker reward for effort. They rely for success on the usual assumption that a financial reward can cause an increase in worker effort and, consequently, an increase in the level of productivity of the enterprise. Thus the worker must be able to vary their output in some kind of relationship to the effort exerted. Linked to this is

the assumption that worker effort varies in proportion to the level of earnings. Some precision is brought into the process of defining the effort–reward relationship, and it is here that the techniques of work measurement have perhaps played their greatest role in British industry (Currie 1969).

In theory bonus is designed to raise the effort by one-third from seventy-five to one hundred on an effort-rating scale. The assumption is that this one-third improvement will be forthcoming for a bonus which represents one-third of basic pay. The industrial engineer is trained to use rating as a means of determining just how hard people are working, although to what kind of tolerance is often difficult to determine. A 5 to 10 per cent tolerance is normally expected depending on the type of work being studied.

The incentive scheme may be based purely on time saved or may have times converted into units or pieces produced. In cases where time, and indeed work measurement, are not involved in the determination of effort workers are paid a fixed sum for each unit produced irrespective of time taken to produce the unit. Such a scheme is called straight or fixed piece rate.

Standard time-based schemes have proved most popular because the requirement for work measurement involves comprehensive analysis of the work situation and the provision of production control and standard cost data based on achieved standard times. In addition, these schemes allow different rates to be set for different workers. This last point is a key feature of traditional payment by results (PBR), namely the emphasis on the individual employee.

Modern payment by results

More recent alternatives to traditional PBR have been the types of day-work scheme which grew in popularity during the 1960s and 1970s. Unfortunately these schemes have not matched the longevity of piecework, and a move away from them was clearly discernible in the early 1980s. On introduction they were considered to be the ultimate alternative to traditional PBR and a sound basis for revitalizing wage systems, collective bargaining and industrial performance (North and Buckingham 1969). An important feature of day-work schemes is the emphasis on group or plant-wide payments as opposed to the payments for individuals in traditional schemes. Thus it was hoped that these newer schemes would provide for a greater degree of rationality in incentive payment structures and would drastically reduce opportunities for disputes on the issue of comparability which marked the history of traditional PBR. The motor industry in particular saw some considerable applications of day-work schemes, as did the light and medium engineering sector of industry. British Leyland's scheme at the Cowley Oxford plant regularly featured in the media in the early 1970s, although more often than not for the wrong reasons (including strikes about the incentive payments and their application).

There are three categories of day-work scheme worthy of note, and they have normally been applied to manual work only:

(1) *Controlled* or *measured day work* involves a fixed standard bonus for a fixed level of worker performance applied to groups of employees, or sections, or departments, or indeed the whole plant. It is possible for these arrangements to be applied to direct and indirect employees. This type of day-work scheme proved the most popular in terms of reported applications.

(2) *Graduated* or *stepped day work* provides a whole range of pay and performance levels and is usually applied factory-wide. The most developed form is the premium pay plan which required the development of a pay and performance matrix with job grades determined by job evaluation and performance determined by work measurement (Smith 1989). Workers are able to increase earnings by improving their performance as well as by moving up to jobs of greater degrees of complexity and responsibility. These schemes are able to provide a greater degree of flexibility in earnings and performance and have proved to be the most successful and durable of the day-work schemes.

(3) *High day* or *time-rate schemes* offer a consolidated and high level of pay linked to the employees' commitment to work at a performance level determined unilaterally by management decision. In many respects this follows the pattern employed in many North American companies, but it has not proved popular in the UK.

When introduced, many consultants and managers claimed that day-work schemes offered an opportunity to develop rationalized incentive payment structures, thus giving management more control over labour costs than was the case with traditional PBR. Employees normally benefited in the short run from an across-the-board increase in earnings. In the long run they benefited (one hopes) from stability of earnings brought about by the fixed incentive payment; from fewer interruptions to workflow through improved production planning and management; and from the knowledge that workers expending the same effort in similar work were receiving the same level of bonus. Unfortunately evidence proving the realization of such hopes is extremely rare.

8 Schemes for managerial and white-collar staff

It has traditionally been the case that the encouragement of white-collar commitment to the success of the organization has been founded on schemes peculiar to these employee groupings and somewhat distant from manual schemes. Such schemes have included bonuses, salary progression, merit rating, profit sharing, shareholding and cash allowances. Significantly, recent developments have seen such arrangements replacing PBR schemes for manual workers (Sheard 1992).

Bonuses for management

Supervisory staff may be paid an incentive on the basis of the output of the department or the achievement of departmental standard hours. Such arrangements are possible with traditional PBR schemes. While on day-work schemes the foremen normally receive a payment which is equivalent to the incentive element paid to the people they supervise. This arrangement can extend to inspection and test personnel. In addition bonuses can be paid to foremen on the achievement of delivery targets, for reducing departmental costs, improving quality and reducing waste. This use of performance indicators for supervisors in cost centres is an arrangement which has appeared in recent years (Smith 1991).

Bonus schemes for executives are very popular and can vary widely in nature and scope. The majority, however, are based on company profitability and are either distributed on a group basis or to the individual. It is becoming popular for such bonuses to be pensionable, and the reductions in marginal rates of income tax during the 1980s enhanced the attractiveness of bonuses as methods of increasing the real amount of disposable income (Armstrong and Murliss 1988). Some examples are described below.

Bonus fund schemes provide a bonus from profits or cost savings which exceed a predetermined target. Bonuses are normally distributed as a proportion of salary on a group basis. Although normally limited to directors and senior managers, the schemes may be applied to middle management if deemed appropriate.

Bonus schemes for individual executives are normally based on the standard of performance achieved by the division, department or function for which the executive has responsibility. A performance target must be determined and some means of measuring performance, such as return on capital employed or value of output, is required to determine individual effectiveness.

Bonuses for sales staff are often overvalued by organizations and evidence certainly suggests that they are not the pre-requisite to sales performance as traditionally thought (Langley 1987). They are of two types: commission based on sales volume; and commission based on contribution to the costs and profits associated with the sales of products or product groups. Commission can be distributed on a group basis or related to individual

results. Since commission is added to basic salary it is important to ensure that this salary on its own is sufficient to provide for financial security.

Christmas bonuses have traditionally been popular in the finance and retailing sectors and can equate to one month's salary although there is no standard rate.

Bonuses in kind are the provision of goods, travel and luxury items in the attempt to provide a short-term improvement in sales and for senior executive performance. A veritable industry has now developed to meet company needs for such services and its growth suggests that incentives in kind are popular.

Schemes for clerical workers

The design of salary ranges to provide some form of progression in earnings has sometimes been used to provide the incentive effect of achieving the next higher grade job. Alternatively, group incentives have been used in offices, based on the measurement of work volume over a particular time-period. Individual incentives have been based on work which can be measured such as typing, processing of documentation and computer operations.

Salary progression is a phenomenon of the public sector and takes place within a salary range for the job, on the basis of experience or merit: it is declining in terms of application. Progression on the basis of experience is normally through fixed increments awarded at regular intervals in line with the individual's service. For example, in the British university system lecturers move through a salary range of sixteen steps, with each increment worth some 6.66 per cent of the minimum salary in the range.

One traditional major advantage of fixed increments has derived from government policy because the increments can be paid in times of a pay 'freeze'. This decision was based on the grounds that incremental systems are held to be self-financing. The assumption is that people are leaving the organization (and therefore the salary range) with salaries which are greater than those joining the scale. Whether this happens in

Table 1 Appraisal scheme with points score

Factors	Grades					Score	Final grade
	Excellent	Very good	Satisfactory	Acceptable	Unsatisfactory		
Judgement	50	40	30	20	10	40	
Cooperation	30	25	20	15	10	25	
Initiative	30	25	20	15	10	20	
Supervisory ability	30	25	20	15	10	25	
Written expression	50	40	30	20	10	50	
					Total score	160	Excellent

practice is doubtful. None the less, unions have traditionally preferred these systems, considering them to meet the requirements for equity and an annual pay award, while management have found them easy to control.

It is doubtful however that fixed increments provide any incentive effect since the poor performer receives the same size pay increase as the 'high flyer'. Some flexibility has been introduced in the form of 'performance bars' which cannot be passed if employees are below par; by doubling the increments paid to the more effective staff; and by introducing a special 'add on' bonus for such people. The main improvement, however, has more and more been seen as the scrapping of salary progression and replacement by performance appraisal-based incentives (Brindle 1987; Wilson and Cole 1990).

Performance appraisal-based incentives

To provide the incentive effect missing in the fixed increment methodology in salary progression schemes has required the adoption of an approach which provides progression on the basis of employee merit. This involves the use of performance appraisal (or merit rating) which, although carried out on an annual basis, should preferably be carried out continuously (see HUMAN RESOURCE MANAGEMENT). These methods were not originally intended as part of the management of remuneration (they have historically been used for promotion purposes, training and development and drawing up redundancy lists). While accepting that there are strong reasons for keeping money and appraisal separate, many

organizations have concluded that the salary review can usefully benefit from appraisal information and growth in popularity for this method has been a major feature of incentives since the early 1980s. With performance-related schemes definitions of performance assessment are required and are usually along the following lines:

1 excellent, outstanding or ready for promotion;
2 very good, very effective or exceeds job requirements;
3 satisfactory or adequate;
4 barely satisfactory or struggling to meet job requirements;
5 unsatisfactory or totally unsuited to the job.

Five grades (as above) are often used to provide the most effective spread for assessment purposes although there is always a danger that an indecisive or less brave manager will opt out and choose the middle grade. The use of four or six grades therefore may be preferable where doubts exist about managerial competence in handling the assessments. Factors which are considered to be elements of the performance required by the organization must then be determined. These often include the following: judgement; knowledge; organizational ability; relationships with others; attitudes; initiative; supervisory ability; and written expression. Points are normally awarded as shown in Table 1 above.

The total score ranges are defined as follows:

Grade	Grade
Excellent	156–190 points
Very good	121–155 points
Satisfactory	86–120 points
Acceptable	51–85 points
Unsatisfactory	50 points

The factors may be apportioned equal points values or they may be weighted. Non-point systems may be used, in which the assessor provides a written assessment of the individual against the factors. Appraisal can also be carried out by the rank-order or forced distribution method, where each employee is ranked by class; these classes are normally defined in percentage terms as follows:

top	10 per cent;
next	20 per cent;
next	40 per cent;
next	20 per cent;
bottom	10 per cent.

Whichever method of assessment for white-collar performance is used, it is necessary to define percentage increases in salary for the total scores of assessments. These scores will fall into the performance categories of excellent, very effective, satisfactory, acceptable and unsatisfactory. This will then provide for incentives to be paid in one of the two ways discussed below.

Merit-rating schemes

Merit-rating schemes provide an additional personal payment above the basic salary for the job. Against each of the performance categories an appropriate merit rate of pay will be established. Scores in each category may directly relate to percentages of pay: for example, 0–25 points (unsatisfactory) no increase; 26–50 points (acceptable) 2–5 per cent of basic pay; 51–75 points (satisfactory) 7.5 per cent; 76–100 points (very good) 10 per cent; and 100–125 points (excellent) 12.5 per cent. Otherwise, a straight points to money conversion may be used, with 0–25 points receiving no bonus, 26–50 points receiving £2.50 per week, 51–75 points receiving £5.00 and so on. In both methods of determining bonus the levels can be stepped to reflect differentials in performance.

Performance-related salary progression schemes

Performance-related salary progression schemes do not provide a bonus as such but take the performance category scores to determine the increments to be paid to the individual employee and therefore his/her rate of progression through the salary range for the job. To facilitate this the performance categories may be allocated an increase which is a percentage of the salary, as follows:

Assessment	per cent salary increase
Excellent	10.0
Very effective	7.5
Satisfactory	5.0
Unacceptable	2.5
Unsatisfactory	No increase in salary

Alternatively, the increase may be a percentage of the minimum salary of the range. It is usual to apply limits to salary progression which allow a maximum time limit to reach a maximum salary level within the range.

9 Competency-based pay

The linking of remuneration to competencies is currently growing in the UK with 45 per cent of employing organizations reportedly considering its introduction (Sparrow 1996). This approach to determining incentive payments is only a step away from performance appraisal and is consistent with the British pre-occupation with pay for the individual. What is different about the competency approach is that in addition to assessing achievement (the what) the behaviour of the employee in meeting targets is taken into account (the how). Thus pay is linked to the 'process' aspects of the job. The competencies involved with the process normally include skills in communication, leadership, teamwork, innovation, quality and customer service.

These competencies are of course measures of capability and like many other measures are being used to drive remuneration. Many organizations have merely taken their existing pay systems and 'force-linked' them to the competencies deemed appropriate; usually this has seen the replacement of methods of assessment used in performance appraisal, by the competencies.

A major claimed advantage for competency-based pay systems is that concentration on the individual rather than the job allows the incentive payments to 'track' changes in the tasks completed by people at work (Lassler 1991). Since such changes have now become endemic in the Western world competencies are seen as an adaptable basis for determining financial incentives. But they are not a panacea: instead they represent another choice among the incentive methodologies available. Introducing competency-based pay requires the organization to define appropriate competencies; set 'prices' for those competencies; initiate the means for people to acquire competencies; introduce measures for competencies; and allow for competencies to change over time. In summary, the organization should be placing as much, if not more, emphasis on encouraging the existence of the competencies (through incentive payments) as is placed on ensuring the outputs.

10 Allowances

Monetary allowances are often provided to cover unsocial hours and expenses incurred by employees in connection with their work. Non-monetary allowances are also provided, particularly time off in lieu for overtime working, although cash may be preferable to the employee. Although not technically an incentive, where these payments more than compensate for expenses and inconvenience then an element of profit for the employee enters into the situation and they may represent some incentive to do the work. Living in large conurbations, particularly London, has often been considered justification for a special allowance to cover the higher costs of travel and living associated with these areas. Any incentive effect deriving from these allowances is very difficult to determine and is probably secondary at best to the influence of cash earnings.

11 Profit-related pay

Profit related pay (PRP) was introduced in the 1987 Finance Act (No. 2), and is designed to relate the pay of employees to the fluctuations in the fortunes of companies (Greenhill 1988; Self 1991). The main features of PRP are detailed below:

1   In a PRP scheme a part of earnings moves with profit.
2   PRP is calculated on the basis of the profits on the ordinary activities of the company after taxation (Companies Act 1985).
3   PRP can be calculated by two alternative methods:
    (a) as a PRP pool calculated as a fixed percentage of profits;
    (b) as a PRP pool based on profits versus previous year profits.
4   A PRP scheme must be registered with and approved by the Inland Revenue before the start of the first profit period it is to cover. It must operate for at least a year. Written rules must be drawn up before an application for registration is made.
5   Tax relief is given by the employer on the profit-related pay through the PAYE system.
6   The operation of the scheme and the profits generated by the selected unit must be independently audited.

Sadly, the Conservative government began to phase out PRP in its last budget of November 1996. This devlopment should not overshadow the benefits and innovation of the method, which could yet re-appear in modified form.

Advantages of PRP

PRP is unique in that it offers tax relief on cash payments which would be fully taxed under any other cash performance reward scheme. PRP has initially proved more interesting to employers than other performance-linked reward plans promoted by British governments. The government suggested that PRP can be an alternative to future annual pay increases, but whether employees would have accepted this is difficult to determine. In application, however, PRP schemes have experienced problems.

PRP may only use profit as the measure of performance. Therefore, in cases where the performance objectives of the business are significantly dependent on measures other than profit, for example return on assets, quality or market share, it may be detrimental and impossible to provide employee incentives based on profit. The calculation methods for PRP do not allow for failure to reach targets caused by conditions outside the control of the company. Where, for example, markets are volatile and unpredictable, PRP is best left alone.

Should the PRP scheme run into trouble, for example by being inappropriate to the company conditions, it cannot be modified or removed unless the PRP office is satisfied with the reasons, such as reorganization or takeover. PRP requires companies to generate documentation for audits and the Inland Revenue, which will be considerably more than is required for other types of scheme. Finally PRP calculations can sometimes provide lower payments in a high profit year than a low profit year, thus depressing employee motivation.

Despite these problems with PRP, further development would have been welcome. In the long term the objective for a majority of organizations is profit or surplus. There is, therefore, a very real purpose for resolution of the matter if incentives are used as part of a managerial strategy which relates those incentives to the needs of employees and the profit requirements of the company (see PROFIT SHARING AND EMPLOYEE SHAREHOLDING SCHEMES).

12 Conclusion

Incentives have become complex and significant elements of wage and salary administration and nowhere has that been more noticeable than in the UK. Since the mid-1980s the use of incentives has become entrenched within the concept and practice of what has been called 'reward management'. This term is used to represent the attempt to 'juggle' the wage and salary administration

exercise into a strategic approach linking human resource performance and remuneration (Smith 1993). The use of the concept underlines the vital role of pay linked to performance within employing organizations – public and private sector – in the UK. Thus, the majority of methodologies for incentive schemes, wherever they are applied, have their origins in the UK.

In Africa, Asia and Australasia the significant use of incentives is based on ideas developed in a British context, particularly applications for manual work. The successfulness of these applications is difficult to determine as cultural issues and preferences and attitudes to incentive systems may well generate a different set of results from those experienced in the UK (Adler 1986). None the less, increasing industrialization and the need to improve the productivity of the human resource is likely to spur on the application of incentives particularly in southeast Asia (Tung 1991). Should developments in this part of the world follow those in the UK, the next major step forward may be the wider application of incentives to professional, technical, administrative and managerial groups. Squeezing manual worker productivity can reach a limit and further gains will have to come from these other employee categories.

Incentive schemes have stood the test of time at least in so far as they have endured for most of this century. But questions continue to be asked of their motivational effect, and whether non-pecuniary elements of motivation should be mobilized in addition to cash incentives. It is also worth considering how changes in employment arrangements will affect incentives in the future. Increasing use of part-time and temporary employees may well mean a reduced need for incentives. Against this however, the sub-contracted employee (who may work at home for example) may be paid solely for work done and may never appear on any organization's payroll. The system of payment by commission only already exists in the finance and leisure sectors of the British economy. The growth of such methods in the future seems likely, and may presage a return to some modernized form of the commission piecework system of the Middle Ages – which is where we began.

IAN SMITH
CARDIFF BUSINESS SCHOOL

Further reading

(References cited in the text marked *)

* Adler, N.J. (1986) *International Dimensions of Organisational Behaviour*, Boston, MA: PWS–Kent Publishing Company. (This work contains a study of cross-cultural motivation issues and their effect on attitudes to work and rewards.)

* Armstrong, M. and Murliss, H. (1988) *Reward Management: A Handbook of Salary Administration*, 1st edn, London: Kogan Page. (Chapter one presents a very optimistic look at developments in white-collar remuneration in the UK during the 1980s. Chapter two of the second edition provides a more restrained view of the same subject matter.)

* Bowey, A.M. *et al.* (1982) 'Effects of incentive payment systems, United Kingdom 1977–80 ', research paper 36, London Department of Employment. (An in-depth analysis of the design of incentive schemes and their applications and outcomes. Attitudes to incentives are also covered usefully.)

* Brindle, D. (1987) 'Will performance pay work in Whitehall?', *Personnel Management* (August): 36–9. (An overview of experience with incentive schemes in the British Civil Service.)

* Currie, R.M. (1969) *The Measurement of Work*, London: British Institute of Management. (An extensive and intensive text on work measurement and its application.)

* Fowler, D. (1988) 'New directions in performance pay', *Personnel Management* (November): 30–4. (A retrospective assessment of managerial incentives and their requirements.)

* Greenhill, R.J. (1988) *Performance Related Pay*, Cambridge: Simon & Schuster. (A full explanation of recent developments in performance-related pay with particular emphasis on profit-related pay.)

* Gregg P., Machin, S. and Szymanski, S. (1993) 'The disappearing relationship between directors' pay, and corporate performance', *British Journal of Industrial Relations* 31 (1): 1–9. (This article presents evidence to prove that incentives have not improved corporate performance.)

* Humner, W.L. (1973) 'How to ruin motivation with pay', *Compensation Review* 7 (3): 17–27. (This article provides an interesting counter-argument to the use of incentives for purposes of improving motivation.)

* Incomes Data Services (1987) *Executive Share Options*, special study, London: Incomes Data Services. (An overview of the various management share-option schemes in the UK and their characteristics.)

* Knight, V. (1986) 'Does profit sharing improve employee performance?', *Personnel Management* November: 46–50. (A balanced examination of profit-sharing schemes which reveals that their impact may be marginal at best.)

* Langley, M. (1987) 'Selling the pass on sales pay', *Personnel Management* March: 22–5. (This article assesses the performance of sales managers and the impact of incentives on that performance. The use of incentives is put into context for sales work.)

* Lassler, E. (1991) 'Paying the person : a better approach to management', *Human Resource Management Review* 2, 145–154. (A thorough presentation of competency-based pay.)

* Lawler, E.E. (1987) 'The design of effective reward systems', in J.W. Lorsch (ed.), *Handbook of Organizational Behavior*, Englewood Cliffs, NJ: Prentice Hall. (This work provides an extensive analysis of the decisions that management needs to take in designing incentive schemes.)

* Logger, E., Vinke R. and Kuytmans, F. (1995) 'Compensation and appraisal in an international perspective', in Harzing, A.W. and Ruyseveldt, J.V. (eds.), *International Human Resource Management*, London: Sage. (A useful international perspective on pay policies and methods.)

* Murliss, H. (1992) 'The search for performance improvement', *Public Finance and Accountancy* February: 14–16. (An assessment of the causes of failure in public sector incentives and identification of the means to improve.)

* Niebel, B.W. (1972) *Motion and Time Study*, 5th edn, Homewood, IL: Irwin. (A complete text on work measurement by a US writer. Chapter one provides an interesting explanation of the development of work measurement in the USA.)

* North, D.R.B. and Buckingham, G.L. (1969) *Productivity and Wage Systems*, Aldershot: Gower. (A comprehensive discussion of the demise of piecework and the swing to day work group incentives in the British manufacturing industry during the 1960s.)

* Pearce, J.L. (1987) 'Why merit pay doesn't work: implications from organisation theory', in A.B. Balkin and L.R. Comez-Meiza (eds), *New Perspectives on Compensation*, Englewood Cliffs, NJ: Prentice Hall. (This work presents an argument for aligning elements of remuneration with organizational contexts.)

* Pickard, J. (1990) 'Awards for employees who go through the mill', *Personnel Management* (February): 6–41. (This article reports on the experiences of one company using incentives coupled to training and career development. The importance of training and the relative unimportance of incentives is revealed.)

* Redling, E.T. (1981) 'Myth vs reality. The relationship between top executive pay and corporate performance', *Compensation Review* 13 (4): 16–24. (Another article which reveals the inability of executive incentives to improve company performance.)

* Schuler, R.S. (1995) *Managing Human Resources*, 5th edn., St. Paul, MN: West Publishing. (See chapter 5 for the examples of links between pay and business performance.)

* Self, R. (1991) *Developments in Profit-Related Pay, Pay and Benefits*, special report no. 2 (April) Kingston upon Thames: Croner Publications. (An analysis of the characteristics and requirements of profit-related pay coupled to reported experiences in several British companies.)

* Sheard, A. (1992) 'Learning to improve performance', *Personnel Management* (November): 40–5. (An article which assesses the importance of non-financial motivators alongside financial motivators.)

* Smith, I.G. (1976) 'Why wage systems fail', *Management Today* (July): 44–106. (An analysis of the experiences of two companies using group-based day-work incentive schemes.)

* Smith, I.G. (1989) *Incentive Schemes: People and Profits*, 1st edn, Kingston upon Thames: Croner Publications. (This book discusses the design and applications of, and experiences with, all types of incentive scheme for all types of employee category.)

* Smith, I.G. (1991) *Incentive Schemes: People and Profits*, 2nd edn, Kingston upon Thames: Croner Publications. (As for the first edition but with the addition of cost-centre-based performance indicator schemes to measure manager and employee performance linked to company performance.)

Smith, I.G. (1992) 'Reward management and HRM', in P. Blyton and P. Turnbull (eds), *Reassessing Human Resource Management*, London: Sage Publications. (An assessment of the effectiveness of reward management as a strategic element of human resource management.)

* Smith, I.G. (1993) 'Reward management: a retrospective assessment', *Employee Relations* 15 (3): 45–59. (This article reports on the use of reward management to revolutionize pay administration in British companies.)

* Sparrow, P. (1996) 'Too good to be true?' *People Management*, December, 22–27. (A critical review of competencies linked to pay.)

* Tung, R.L. (1991) 'Motivation in Chinese industrial enterprises', in R.M. Steers and L.W. Porter (eds), *Motivation and Work Behaviour*, 5th edn, New York: McGraw-Hill. (A useful assessment of the attitudes and expectations of Chinese workers to incentive schemes. Cultural issues and their implications for motivational strategies are discussed.)

* Wilson, J. and Cole, G. (1990) 'A healthy approach to performance appraisal', *Personnel Management* (June): 46–9. (Addresses the development of performance appraisal schemes in the private sector of the British economy. Also usefully assesses their effectiveness.)

See also: BEDAUX, C.E.; HUMAN RESOURCE MANAGEMENT; INDUSTRIAL AND LABOUR RELATIONS; OCCUPATIONAL PSYCHOLOGY; ORGANIZATION BEHAVIOUR; PAYMENT SYSTEMS; PRODUCTIVITY; PROFIT SHARING AND EMPLOYEE SHAREHOLDING SCHEMES; TAYLOR, F.W.; TRADE UNIONS

Related topics in the IEBM: BENCHMARKING; MANAGEMENT IN JAPAN; MANAGEMENT IN NORTH AMERICA; MANAGEMENT IN THE UNITED KINGDOM; ORGANIZATIONAL PERFORMANCE

Job design

1 Introduction and definitions
2 Designing jobs for individuals
3 Conclusion

Overview

For most of this century job design has been one of the most frequently researched topics in the fields of management and organizational behaviour. The purpose of this entry is to summarize the most significant historical and contemporary developments in this area. We begin by defining job design and discussing its importance to the management of organizations. Several of the major approaches to the design of jobs for individuals are then discussed. These include industrial engineering, motivation–hygiene theory, job characteristics theory and an interdisciplinary framework. The design of jobs for groups of employees, or teams, is discussed next. We describe Hackman's model of work group design and briefly review research regarding self-directed work teams. We conclude by suggesting several future directions for both individual and group approaches to job design.

1 Introduction and definitions

At its most basic level job design refers to changing the actual structure of jobs that people perform. Unlike other change strategies that focus on training employees or altering the context of the work (for example, the pay system or managerial practices), job design focuses squarely on the work itself – that is, on the tasks or activities that individuals complete in their organizations on a daily basis (see JOB EVALUATION; PAYMENT SYSTEMS; TRAINING).

It is this focus on the work itself that is undoubtedly most responsible for the popularity of job design as a research topic and managerial strategy. Individuals may be able to avoid contact with many aspects of the work context

but they cannot avoid contact with their jobs. When people are at work they spend most of their time performing their jobs. Jobs, then, represent the most fundamental point of contact between the employee and the organization. Therefore the way jobs are structured and designed should play a major part in determining how people respond in their employing organization.

Many different approaches can be taken in designing jobs and a variety of criteria can be used in deciding what is a well designed job. Some of the approaches reviewed here focus on the minute motions and procedures that compose a job, whereas others involve a broader view of the entire job for which the employee is responsible. Some approaches emphasize criteria of engineering efficiency in evaluating how well jobs are designed; others emphasize the motivation and satisfaction of the employees who perform the job. And some approaches deal mainly with jobs performed by individual employees, while others address larger jobs that are performed by teams of employees.

For the purposes of this entry we have grouped the various approaches to job design into two general categories: (1) individual approaches, which focus on the design of work for employees working independently of one another; and (2) team approaches, which focus on the design of work for groups of employees working interdependently with one another. After reviewing and critiquing these various approaches we suggest some future directions for attention and research regarding the design of jobs.

2 Designing jobs for individuals

Industrial engineering

The overall objective of the industrial engineering approach is to maximize the productive efficiency of individual employees. In general, this approach argues that this can be accomplished by structuring jobs so that any unnecessary work is eliminated and so that the quickest and most practical work methods are standardized for all employees who perform that job.

The individual most responsible for developing the ideas that underlie the industrial engineering approach to the design of jobs is Frederick W. Taylor (1911) (see TAYLOR, F.W.). His principles of 'scientific management' can be summarized as follows (Hackman and Oldham 1980: 49–50):

1 The work to be done should be studied scientifically to determine how the work should be partitioned among various employees and how each segment of the work should be done most efficiently. These analyses should indicate the exact equipment that should be used and the exact spacing of rest breaks for maximum efficiency.
2 Employees should be well matched to the demands of the job. That is, individuals should be mentally and physically capable of performing the work but should not be overqualified for the job.
3 Employees should be trained so that they perform their jobs exactly as specified by the scientific analysis of the work. In addition, employees should be regularly monitored to make certain that they are performing their jobs as required.
4 Finally, to provide motivation for employees to follow the detailed practices described above, a substantial monetary bonus should be paid upon the successful completion of each day's work.

Advocates of the industrial engineering approach argue that organizations obtain a number of benefits by adopting this approach to job design. First, because job specialization and simplification reduce the prerequisite qualifications for a job, the pool of potential applicants is larger and organizations can hire more selectively. Given the larger applicant pool, organizations can offer lower wages to selected workers. Second, since jobs are highly specialized and simplified in a scientific management approach, worker training

expenses are reduced considerably and supervisors have greater flexibility when assigning workers to particular tasks. Third, worker efficiency is maximized because all resources needed to accomplish a particular task can be centrally located and, therefore, time and motion spent gathering materials or changing tools is minimized.

The industrial engineering approach gained tremendous popularity in many organizations during the first six decades of this century. Indeed, by the 1950s most manufacturing jobs were designed on the basis of Taylor's principles. Yet, despite its popularity there is substantial evidence that the industrial engineering approach induced a variety of unintended negative consequences. For example, many early studies showed that employees were quite adamant in their disaffection with standardized, routinized work. Employees often failed to show up for work on time or restricted their productivity on such routinized jobs, or they sabotaged their work or their equipment, resulting in productivity losses. In sum, the gains in productive efficiency that were achieved by the industrial engineering approach were more than offset by the losses incurred when this approach was implemented (Walker and Guest 1952).

The problems associated with the industrial engineering approach led to the emergence of several more behavioural approaches to job design which focused on designing work to achieve high productivity without incurring the human costs that are associated with standardized, routinized work. Several of these approaches are reviewed below.

Motivation–hygiene theory

The first attempts to redress the problems associated with industrial engineering approaches to job design involved expanding the scope of the job by adding tasks to an employee's job assignments. This approach, called *job enlargement*, often involved adding tasks that were similar in complexity and challenge to those already completed by the employee. Job enlargement, however, met with little success in early investigations, probably because adding more routinized tasks did not address the negative consequences of the standardized nature of the work. Later efforts involved expanding both the content and scope of the job by providing employees with increased opportunities for personal responsibility and control over their work activities. This approach, called *job enrichment*, met with substantial success in numerous studies. These studies demonstrated that job enrichment often resulted in both enhanced productivity and employee satisfaction (Davis and Taylor 1972). However, early approaches to job enrichment lacked a clear theoretical direction. This changed in the late 1960s, when Frederick Herzberg and his colleagues (1966) developed a specific approach to job enrichment, entitled motivation–hygiene theory.

In its most general form motivation–hygiene theory proposes that the primary determinants of employee motivation and satisfaction are factors intrinsic to the work itself – recognition, achievement, responsibility, advancement and personal growth in competence. These factors are called *motivators* because employees are motivated to obtain more of them through good job performance. Dissatisfaction, on the other hand, is caused by *hygiene factors* that are extrinsic to the work. These include company policies, salary, co-worker relations and supervisory practices. Herzberg's theory argues that job enrichment changes will enhance motivation and productivity only to the degree that motivators are designed into the work. Changes that deal only with hygiene factors are expected to reduce dissatisfaction but not to generate motivational gains.

Much to the credit of Herzberg's theory, it prompted a great deal of research and inspired a large number of successful change projects (Herzberg 1976). Results of these projects appear to demonstrate, for diverse jobs and organizations, that increasing a job's standing on motivators such as recognition, responsibility and achievement can lead to numerous beneficial outcomes for the job holders and for the employing organization. Moreover, Herzberg developed a set of step-by-step procedures for implementing job enrichment, and these procedures continue to guide many change projects.

However, despite its considerable merit there are several difficulties with Herzberg's theory that compromise its usefulness. First, a number of researchers have been unable to provide support for the core of the theory – the motivator–hygiene dichotomy (House and Wigdor 1967). It appears that some aspects of the workplace can serve at times as motivators and at other times as hygiene factors. For example, a pay raise would be classified as a hygiene factor, yet it may serve as a motivator if it is provided as a form of recognition for achievement. The ambiguity in the distinction between motivators and hygiene factors is problematic because it creates considerable uncertainty when decisions are made about the specific changes that should be introduced to enrich a job. Second, Herzberg does not provide an instrument for measuring the presence or absence of motivating factors in existing jobs. Thus it is difficult to systematically diagnose the status of jobs on the motivators prior to introducing job changes or to measure the effects of job design activities on the jobs after the changes have been carried out. Finally, the theory does not provide for differences in how responsive people will be to enriched jobs that are high on the motivators. Herzberg's theory suggests that all individuals will respond similarly and positively to the presence of motivators in jobs. Yet, numerous research studies have demonstrated that some people respond more positively to responsible, challenging positions than other people.

Job characteristics theory

In an attempt to overcome some of the major shortcomings of Herzberg's approach to job enrichment, job characteristics theory (Hackman and Oldham 1976 and 1980) was developed. This theory, which has its roots in early work by Turner and Lawrence (1965) and Hackman and Lawler (1971), focuses on several measurable characteristics of jobs and recognizes that people may respond differently to these job characteristics.

The basic job characteristics model, taken from Hackman and Oldham (1980: 90), is

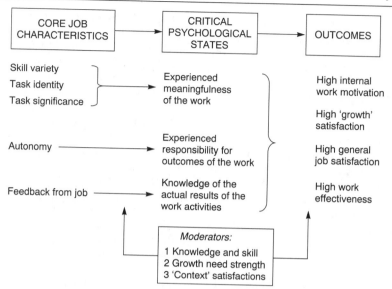

Figure 1 The job characteristics model
Source: Adapted from Hackman and Odlham (1980: 90)

shown in Figure 1. At its most general level, five core job characteristics are seen as prompting three psychological states which, in turn, affect a number of beneficial personal and work outcomes. The links between the job characteristics, the psychological states and the outcomes are shown as 'moderated' by three individual difference variables.

The theory posits that all three of the psychological states must be experienced by the employee if desirable outcomes are to emerge. First, the employee must experience the work as meaningful and worthwhile by some system of values that he or she accepts. Second, the employee must experience personal responsibility for the results of the work, believing that he or she is personally accountable for the work outcomes. Finally, the individual must have knowledge of the results of his or her work efforts.

When all three of these states are present simultaneously, several outcomes are predicted to result. First, the employee should be internally motivated at work – that is, to feel good when performing well and feel bad when performing poorly. Second, the employee should be satisfied with the opportunities for personal and professional growth at work and

with the job in general. Finally, the employee should perform effectively at work. However, if one or more of the psychological states is missing or absent fewer desirable outcomes should result.

The three psychological states are, by definition, internal to individuals and therefore not directly manipulable in designing jobs. Thus, the theory suggests five measurable, changeable characteristics of jobs that prompt these psychological states and, through them, enhance work outcomes.

The three characteristics that are believed to be especially powerful in influencing the experienced meaningfulness of the work are: (1) *skill variety*; (2) *task identity*; and (3) *task significance.*

Skill variety is the degree to which a job requires a variety of different activities in carrying out the work, involving the use of a number of different skills and talents of the person.

Task identity is the degree to which the job requires completion of a whole, identifiable piece of work – that is, doing a job from beginning to end with a visible outcome.

Task significance is the degree to which the job has a substantial impact on the lives of other people, whether those people are in the immediate organization or the world at large.

The characteristic that is expected to lead to feelings of responsibility for work outcomes is *autonomy*, the degree to which the job provides substantial freedom, independence and discretion to the individual in scheduling the work and in determining the procedures to be used in carrying it out.

Finally, knowledge of results of one's work is proposed to be directly affected by the amount of *job feedback*, the degree to which carrying out the work activities required by the job provides the individual with direct and clear information about the effectiveness of his or her performance.

Hackman and Oldham (1980) also propose a single index, the Motivating Potential Score (MPS), that reflects the overall potential of the job to foster work motivation in job holders. Following Figure 1, a job high in motivating potential must be high on a least one of the three characteristics that prompt meaningfulness, and high on both autonomy and feedback as well, to create conditions that foster all three of the psychological states. When numerical scores are available, they are combined as shown in Figure 2.

Jobs with high MPS scores are considered enriched, challenging pieces of work. Yet job characteristics theory recognizes that not all employees will respond positively to these enriched, high MPS jobs. As shown in Figure 1, the theory identifies three individual difference characteristics that influence the way employees react to jobs that are high on the five characteristics. First, the theory posits that employees must have sufficient *knowledge and skill* to perform the enriched work effectively. Second, employees must have strong needs for personal growth at work. Only individuals with high *growth need strength* are likely to appreciate and respond positively to the opportunities for personal accomplishment provided by enriched, high

MPS jobs. Individuals with low growth need strength may experience a high MPS job as threatening and baulk at being 'stretched' too far by the work. Finally, the theory argues that if employees are to respond positively to enriched jobs they should be satisfied with several aspects of the *work context* (such as pay, job security, co-workers and managers). Active dissatisfaction with such contextual factors may distract employees' attention from the work itself and orient their energy instead toward coping with the experienced problems.

In addition to developing the model shown in Figure 1, Hackman and Oldham (1980) developed an instrument, the Job Diagnostic Survey (JDS), that can be used in tests of the theory and to diagnose jobs prior to and after initiating a job enrichment programme. The JDS assesses job holders' perceptions of the five job characteristics, the psychological states, their growth needs, their internal work motivation, and their satisfaction in several domains. The JDS does not assess employee knowledge and skill and work effectiveness.

More than 200 studies have used the JDS in testing job characteristics theory, and the results provide general support for the major tenets of the theory (Fried and Ferris 1987; Oldham 1996). In particular, results indicate that the higher the job on each of the five characteristics, the higher the employees' satisfaction, internal motivation and work effectiveness. Moreover, evidence from numerous change projects shows that when jobs are boosted on the five characteristics, substantial increases in employee productivity and satisfaction typically result (Kopelman 1985). Research evidence also suggests that the job characteristics positively affect the outcomes by influencing the three psychological states specified in the model. Finally, research shows that employees with high growth need strength often respond most positively to enriched, high MPS jobs.

$$MPS = \frac{Skill\ variety + Task\ identity\ +\ Task\ significance}{3} \times Autonomy \times Job\ feedback$$

Figure 2 The motivating potential score

In summary, job characteristics theory overcomes several of the shortcomings associated with motivation–hygiene theory. The theory suggests five characteristics that might be boosted to enhance motivation and work effectiveness, all of which are more specific than the 'motivators' included in Herzberg's theory. Second, the theory identifies important individual difference characteristics – knowledge and skill, growth need strength and context satisfactions – that clarify the conditions under which enriched, well-designed jobs should have their strongest effects. Finally, the instrument that accompanies job characteristics theory, the JDS, can be useful in: (1) diagnosing jobs prior to enrichment to determine which characteristics (if any) may require change; (2) determining whether the job holders are ready for enrichment and are likely to respond positively to it (that is, whether they have sufficient growth need strength and context satisfactions), and; (3) evaluating the effects of a job enrichment programme on employees' perceptions of the core job characteristics.

Despite all of these positive features, job characteristics theory is not without its own shortcomings. One of these involves the focus of the theory on a relatively narrow set of five characteristics. This narrow focus does not include social or interpersonal aspects of the job or attention to the broader organizational context, which may have a substantial impact on the way people respond at work. Second, the theory views job characteristics and individual difference characteristics (such as knowledge and skill and growth need strength) as independent constructs that do not influence one another. But research suggests that, over time, the characteristics of jobs might influence individuals' needs and talents. For example, after continued exposure to enriched, challenging jobs individuals may begin to desire more opportunities for personal growth at work. Finally, job characteristics theory is not explicit about the process that should be used to introduce changes at work. That is, it is not clear from the theory if employees should be involved in generating ideas for changing their jobs or if managers should unilaterally introduce job enrichment changes.

An interdisciplinary framework

One of the more recent developments in job design is the interdisciplinary viewpoint espoused by Campion and his associates (Campion and McClelland 1993; Campion and Thayer 1987). This approach attempts to integrate various job design approaches into a single framework. Specifically, the interdisciplinary approach classifies previous job design approaches into four types and argues that changes associated with each will lead to different outcomes.

The *motivational approach* (such as motivation–hygiene theory and job characteristics theory) focuses on how to enhance the motivational nature of jobs in order to increase employees' motivation, satisfaction and effectiveness.

The *mechanistic approach* (such as the industrial engineering approach), on the other hand, emphasizes human resource efficiency, which is associated with efficiency and flexibility outcomes such as ease of staffing and low training costs.

The *biological approach* focuses on issues related to strength and endurance requirements as well as noise and climate limits. The objective of this approach is to design jobs to minimize physical efforts, fatigue, aches and pains, and health complaints. Job changes congruent with this approach will produce more physically comfortable workers.

Finally, the *perceptual/motor approach* attempts to assure that people's cognitive capabilities such as attention and concentration are not exceeded by the nature of the job or the physical characteristics of the workplace or equipment. Changes in line with this approach are associated with reduced mental overload, fatigue, stress and boredom; more positive employee attitudes towards work stations and equipment; and reduced error rates and accidents.

The interdisciplinary perspective contends that no one approach to job design can serve as the basis for a full and comprehensive understanding of how job design affects employees' responses. Campion argues that advocates of each job design approach identify and promote intended benefits but give little recognition to potential, perhaps unanticipated, costs. The interdisciplinary perspective, in contrast, is advantageous because it increases awareness of potential costs and benefits of each job design approach. For example, the mechanistic and perceptual/motor approaches advocate incorporating into the design of jobs features that minimize information processing demands. In contrast, motivational approaches argue for increasing the complexity of jobs, thereby increasing the information and processing demands. Whereas motivational approaches would argue that implementing mechanistic or perceptual/motor recommendations may decrease employee motivation and satisfaction and increase absenteeism, mechanistic or perceptual/motor approaches would argue that implementing motivational approach recommendations may result in jobs that are more difficult to staff, require more training, have higher error rates, and generate greater employee stress and mental overload. Advocates of the interdisciplinary approach argue that both costs and benefits of minimized information processing should be considered in design efforts. A summary of all expected costs and benefits of the four job design approaches, adapted from Campion and Thayer (1987: 76), is provided in Table 1.

Like job characteristics theory, the interdisciplinary framework is accompanied by a

Table 1 Summary of expected costs and benefits from the four job design approaches

Job design approach	Benefits	Costs
Mechanistic	Decreased training time	Lower job satisfaction
	Higher utilization levels	Lower motivation
	Lower likelihood of error	Higher absenteeism
	Less chance of mental overload and stress	
Motivational	Higher job satisfaction	Increased training time
	Higher motivation	Lower utilization levels
	Greater job involvement	Greater likelihood of error
	Higher job performance	Greater likelihood of mental
	Lower absenteeism	overload and stress
Biological	Less physical effort	Higher financial costs because
	Less physical fatigue	of changes in equipment or job
	Fewer health complaints	environment
	Fewer medical incidents	
	Lower absenteeism	
	Higher job satisfaction	
Perceptual/motor	Lower likelihood of error	Lower job satisfaction
	Lower likelihood of accidents	Lower motivation
	Lower likelihood of mental overload and stress	
	Lower training time	
	Higher utilization levels	

Source: Adapted from Campion and Thayer (1987: 76)

survey, the Multimethod Job Design Questionnaire (MJDQ), which assesses employee perceptions of the job elements associated with each of the four job design approaches. Studies using the MJDQ provide some support for the interdisciplinary approach by demonstrating that the job elements associated with each of the approaches are related to the outcomes associated with that approach (Campion and McClelland 1993).

The advantage of the interdisciplinary framework is that it is more comprehensive and integrative in nature than previous models. Yet, more research is clearly needed to assess its contribution. Future work is also needed to better integrate the various approaches to job design into a single, clear theoretical framework. Finally, the framework needs to be expanded to account for differences in how individuals will react to each of the four design approaches.

Designing jobs for teams

Each of the approaches we have discussed thus far has focused on the design of jobs for employees who work relatively independently of one another. But sometimes work is designed to be performed by a team of employees rather than by individuals. There are several reasons why practitioners often choose to design work for teams rather than for individuals. First, if the work is extremely complex and demands multiple special skills, it may require more expertise than a single individual can effectively learn and manage. Second, jobs designed for teams provide employees with more opportunities to develop satisfying social relationships with one another. And sometimes jobs are designed for teams simply because the technology that is in place in the organization requires employees to work interdependently.

Most of the research on the design of jobs for teams has been integrated into the more general area of the design of effective teams, and has focused on 'autonomous', 'self-managing', or 'self-directed teams. Because these teams typically have substantial amounts of responsibility for managing their own work activities and processes, understanding how their work is designed requires also examining how the teams are structured and motivated in general.

Many of the basic ideas and concepts involving self-directed teams were originally developed by researchers interested in socio-technical systems theory, an approach that attempts to optimize the relation between the social and technical aspects of the organization (Trist *et al.* 1963; Trist *et al.* 1977). A more recent and comprehensive model of

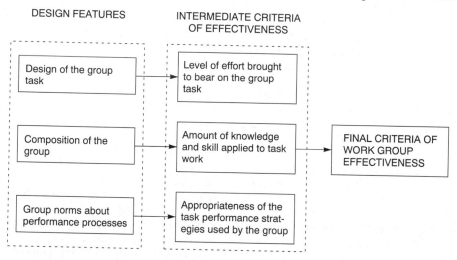

Figure 3 Hackman's model of self-directed work teams
Source: Adapted from Hackman and Oldham (1980: 187)

self-directed teams was developed by Hackman and his colleagues (Hackman 1987; Hackman and Oldham 1980). This model, adapted from Hackman and Oldham (1980: 187), is shown in Figure 3. The Hackman model argues that the overall effectiveness of work teams in organizations is a joint function of three intermediate 'process criteria': (1) having a sufficient level of effort applied to the group task; (2) assuring that sufficient knowledge and skill of group members is applied to the task; and (3) having members devise and use performance strategies or ways of working together that are appropriate for the group task.

Hackman proposes three primary design features of groups as critical in achieving these process results. First, group members' efforts are expected to be a function of the *group task* structure. Building on the previously discussed job characteristics theory, Hackman proposes that the group task should be high in motivating potential. Thus, the task should require team members to use a variety of skills; it should be a whole and identifiable piece of work; it should provide team members with regular and trustworthy feedback about how the team is performing; it should provide autonomy for members to decide together how they will carry out the work; and the outcomes of the task should have significant consequences for others.

Second, Hackman expects *group composition* to directly affect the amount of knowledge and skill that is applied to the task. He proposes four aspects of composition that are particularly relevant: (1) members should have high task-relevant expertise; (2) the group should be just large enough to do the work; (3) members should have a moderate level of interpersonal skill; and (4) members should be moderately diverse in terms of their backgrounds and talents.

Finally, Hackman argues that *group norms* affect the performance strategies members use in carrying out the task. Norms influence how teams scan the environment and regulate member behaviour, thereby influencing what strategies are chosen and how effectively they are implemented. According to Hackman the challenge in designing a work group is to help

members collectively develop and maintain norms that reinforce scanning and member behaviour regulation in a way appropriate for the team's tasks.

Although no study has systematically tested Hackman's entire framework, a number of studies of self-directed work teams are directly related to some of its criteria. For example, some self-managing teams are responsible for decisions that directly affect the groups' composition. That is, they are given substantial input into hiring and firing decisions involving group members. Individual members also often have responsibility for evaluating the performance effectiveness of their fellow team members. Thus, some of these teams may well incorporate the group design feature of ensuring that each member of the group willl have an appropriate mix of both task-relevant and interpersonal skills.

In addition, in several of these studies the team is assigned to complete a large product or work process. The teams typically schedule their own work, make decisions about which employees will complete particular tasks during the workday, decide when rest breaks will be taken, decide on an equipment maintenance schedule and decide how often product quality will be checked. Moreover, the team receives regular feedback about its performance effectiveness. Thus, many of the self-managing teams incorporate the task design features of autonomy and feedback, to ensure a high level of monitoring potential in the work, and a high degree of team effort as a result. Finally, several of the more descriptive studies of self-managing organizational teams emphasize the existence and variety of group norms, that may play a role in shaping and reshaping how the team designs its work (Hackman 1990).

In general the results of studies examining the effects of these design elements on team productivity, group member attendance and group member satisfaction have been very positive. For example, Cotton (1993) reviewed several of these studies and concluded that introducing self-directed work teams resulted in increased productivity in 83 per cent of the studies, decreased absenteeism in 79 per cent of the investigations and increased job satisfaction in 93 per cent of the studies. Moreover, only a trivial percentage of the studies showed that these work outcomes actually decreased after the introduction of teams.

Despite these very promising results, work team approaches, like the other approaches to job design discussed here, are not without their limitations. One of these is the failure of work team advocates to recognize that there may be individual differences in how members respond to the dynamics of a team. With few exceptions, advocates simply assume that all individuals will respond similarly and positively to the experience of working in a group. Yet, as we have noted previously, abundant evidence suggests that there are substantial individual differences in how people respond to various work arrangements. Second, like motivation–hygiene theory, an instrument for measuring the various components of work teams currently does not exist. Thus, it is difficult to determine whether the effects of teams are a function of their impact on features related to group composition, the group task, group norms or some other element of the team design. Finally, if teams are to have positive effects on productivity and member attitudes, changes in a variety of other organizational programmes and practices may be required. For example, the behaviour of managers external to the team may have to be more facilitative than under traditional work arrangements. And new training and pay practices that support team-based performance may be needed. Introducing self-directed teams without these support elements may result in fewer and shorter term positive effects on personal and organizational outcomes.

3 Conclusion

This chapter reviewed five approaches to the design of jobs – four focusing on the jobs of individual employees and the fifth on jobs for teams. Each of the approaches reviewed has received a good deal of research attention and, as we have noted, each has its own strengths and weaknesses. Research is now needed that compares and contrasts the long-term effects of each of these approaches. In addition, studies are needed that examine the effects of these approaches across several cultures and nations. Given preliminary evidence that people in different countries tend to define work differently (see England and Harpaz 1990), research is essential to determine whether individuals respond differently to job arrangements based upon their national or cultural definitions of work and the activity of working. Third, research is warranted that identifies organizational practices and policies (for example, training practices, pay plans, managerial behaviours) that support and reinforce each of the job design approaches described in this chapter. Finally, studies are needed that examine the procedures that are necessary to implement the various design approaches. Should managers alone implement these job design changes or should employees be consulted before jobs are changed? If the latter, exactly how much input should employees have in the design of their own jobs? Research on questions such as these is critical if we are to continue to develop effective strategies for designing jobs in organizations.

YITZHAK FRIED
WAYNE STATE UNIVERSITY

ANNE CUMMINGS
UNIVERSITY OF PENNSYLVANIA

GREG R. OLDHAM
UNIVERSITY OF ILLINOIS AT
URBANA-CHAMPAIGN

Further reading

(References cited in the text marked *)

* Campion, M.A. and McClelland, C.L. (1993) 'Follow-up and extension of the interdisciplinary costs and benefits of enlarged jobs', *Journal of Applied Psychology* 78 (3): 339–51. (This is an analysis of task and knowledge enlargement effects in financial services industry using MJDQ; two-year follow-up of quasi-experiment shows changed costs and benefits.)
* Campion, M.A. and Thayer, P.W. (1987) 'Job design: approaches, outcomes, and trade-offs', *Organizational Dynamics* 15 (3): 66–79. (This readable evolution of the interdisciplinary approach includes a comparison of the four ap-

proaches and sample questions for assessment or redesign.)

* Cotton, J.L. (1993) *Employee Involvement: Methods for Improving Performance and Work Attitudes*, Newbury Park, CA: Sage Publications. (This book comprehensively reviews various employee involvement strategies, including quality circles, gainsharing plans, and self-directed work teams.)

* Davis, L.E. and Taylor, J.C. (1972) *Design of Jobs*, Baltimore, MD: Penguin. (This volume includes articles on both the mechanistic and motivational approaches and provides a historical perspective on job design.)

* England, G.W. and Harpaz, I. (1990) 'How working is defined: national contexts and demographic and organizational roles influences', *Journal of Organizational Behaviour* 11: 253–66. (This project summary examines work rationales, outcomes and constraints and identifies six definitions of work across western Europe, Israel, Japan, and the USA.)

* Fried, Y.C. and Ferris, G.R. (1987) 'The validity of the job characteristics model: a review and meta-analysis', *Personnel Psychology* 40: 287–322. (This article presents a narrative review of 200 studies and meta-analysis of seventy-six studies using the JDS.)

* Hackman, J.R. (1987) 'The design of work teams', in J.W. Lorsch (ed.), *Handbook of Organizational Behavior*, Englewood Cliffs, NJ: Prentice Hall. (This extension of the 1980 model presents a normative design model for work team effectiveness, including supporting contextual features.)

* Hackman, J.R. (1990) *Groups that Work (and Those that Don't): Creating Conditions for Effective Teamwork*, San Francisco, CA: Jossey-Bass. (This edited volume describes 27 work teams in a variety of organizations. The author presents a framework for examining the teams and their effectiveness, as well as a concluding chapter that identifies comon themes and issues.)

* Hackman, J.R. and Lawler, E.E., III (1971) 'Employee reactions to job characteristics', *Journal of Applied Psychology* 55: 259–86. (This monograph presents a conceptual framework for motivating jobs and a study of telephone company jobs using self-report, supervisor report and observational methods.)

* Hackman, J.R. and Oldham, G.R. (1976) 'Motivation through the design of work: test of a theory', *Organizational Behavior and Human Performance* 16: 250–79. (This article presents job characteristics theory and an empirical test of its validity.)

* Hackman, J.R. and Oldham, G.R. (1980) *Work Redesign*, Reading, MA: Addison-Wesley. (This book presents job characteristics theory in the context of enriching individual jobs and group work. It includes the complete Job Diagnostic Survey with norms.)

* Herzberg, F. (1966) *Work and the Nature of Man*, Cleveland, OH: World. (This book presents a description of motivation–hygiene theory and several tests of its validity.)

* Herzberg, F. (1976) *The Managerial Choice*, Homewood, IL: Dow Jones–Irwin. (This readable statement of motivation–hygiene theory is accompanied by a question-and-answer defence of this approach to work and examples of its application.)

* House, R.J. and Wigdor, L. (1967) 'Herzberg's dual-factor theory of job satisfaction and motivation: a review of the evidence and a criticism', *Personnel Psychology* 20: 369–89. (This paper critiques motivation–hygiene theory on conceptual and methodological grounds.)

* Kopelman, R.E. (1985) 'Job redesign and productivity: a review of the evidence', *National Productivity Review* Summer: 237–55. (This readable summary of the productivity, work quality and absenteeism impact of thirty-two job redesign efforts includes implementation suggestions.)

* Oldham, G.R. (1996) 'Job design', in Cooper, C.L. and Robertson, I.T. (eds.), *International Review of Industrial and Organizational Psychology*, Vol. 11, New York: John Wiley & Sons. (This article presents a comprehensive narrative review of research focusing on job characteristics theory.)

* Pearce, J.A. and Ravlin, E.C. (1987) 'The design and activation of self-regulating work groups', *Human Relations* 40: 751–82. (This paper reviews ten US field experiments on self-regulating work groups and integrates other studies of relevant group issues.)

* Taylor, F. (1911) *The Principles of Scientific Management*, New York: Norton. (This is the original presentation of 'scientific management' practices, which promoted time and motion studies to specialize duties and simplify work.)

* Trist, E.L., Higgin, G.W., Murray, H. and Pollock, A.B. (1963) *Organizational Choice*, London: Tavistock Publications. (This book includes a thorough description of sociotechnical systems theory and follows self-directed work teams over time in British coal mines.)

* Trist, E.L., Susman, G.I. and Brown, G.R. (1977) 'An experiment in autonomous working in an American underground coal mine', *Human Relations* 30: 201–36. (This is an informative consultants' report on the formation of self-managing work teams in a coal mine.)
* Turner, A.N. and Lawrence, P.R. (1965) *Individual Jobs and the Worker*, Cambridge, MA: Harvard University Press. (This is a seminal study of the relationship between 'requisite task attributes' and employee responses to work.)
* Walker, C.R. and Guest, R.H. (1952) *The Man on the Assembly Line*, Cambridge, MA: Harvard University Press. (This book summarizes home interviews of assembly-line workers about their jobs and working conditions.)

See also: HERZBERG, F.; HUMAN RESOURCE MANAGEMENT; JOB EVALUATION; MAYO, G.E.; OCCUPATIONAL PSYCHOLOGY; ORGANIZATION BEHAVIOUR; PAYMENT SYSTEMS; TAYLOR, F.W.; TRAINING; WORK AND ORGANIZATION SYSTEMS

Related topics in the IEBM: HUMAN-CENTRED MANUFACTURING SYSTEMS, DESIGN OF; MANUFACTURING STRATEGY; TRIST, E.L.

Job evaluation

Overview

Job evaluation is a technique that systematically compares jobs with each other to produce a rank order on which pay differentials can be based. A job evaluation scheme can be used to compare jobs across a whole country or an entire industry in that country, but normally it is confined to a single organization. In that organization it would be unusual for all jobs to be covered by job evaluation. Typically only some occupational groups are covered and there will generally be different schemes for categories such as manual, non-manual, professional and managerial staff.

Employers normally will have some of the following objectives in seeking to introduce job evaluation: to establish a rational pay structure; to create pay relationships between jobs which are perceived as fair by employees; to reduce the number of pay grievances and disputes; to provide a basis for settling the payment rate of new or changed jobs; to provide pay information in a form which enables meaningful comparisons with other organizations

Job evaluation is often introduced to bring some order into a pay structure. Payment for different jobs may appear to be arbitrary or to have little logical justification. It may have evolved as a result of *ad hoc* decisions sometimes made under pressure and without consideration for the wider consequences. As a result management will face grievances and possibly disputes.

Most of the reasons given for introducing job evaluation are concerned with raising the efficiency of the organization or improving relations with employees. However, the decision may, at least in part, be taken in response to external pressures or constraints. In both the USA and the UK some organizations introduced job evaluation following the imposition of national pay controls. Pay increases could be justified only where a change in the work could be demonstrated clearly. The systematic nature of job evaluation allowed such changes to be legitimized and it was therefore in the interests of both management and unions to agree upon a scheme.

Job evaluation has also been introduced in response to equal pay policies and legislation. Where an analytical scheme is operated without any gender bias it will normally be accepted that men and women are being paid equally for work of equal value.

1   A brief history of job evaluation

Formal job evaluation was first introduced by the US Civil Service Commission in 1871, which used a method of job ranking to try to eliminate wage anomalies between different government departments. By 1909 similar methods were being used by the Civil Service Commission of Chicago and by the Commonwealth Edison Company. In 1923 the US Government passed the Classification Act which introduced job evaluation in order to harmonize the federal wage structure.

The emergence of the ideas of Scientific Management (see TAYLOR, F.W.) encouraged the development of work study and job analysis techniques. The Bureau of Personnel Research at the Carnegie Institute of Technology was influential in developing non-analytical classification methods of job evaluation. In

1920 Charles E. Bedaux published details of the first known analytical job evaluation method on behalf of the American Management Association (see BEDAUX, C.E.).

A major extension of job evaluation came in the 1930s when the growth of union power in the USA meant that employers needed to justify wage differentials in ways that would make them acceptable to employees. Two of the best known schemes, applied to hourly paid factory jobs in the late 1930s, were those developed by A.L. Kress for the Electrical Manufacturers' Association and the National Metal Trades Association. The success of these schemes, which influenced other sectors of the economy, has been attributed to the fact that they were relatively simple and therefore more easily understood and implemented. Instead of a wide range of disparate factors Kress accommodated all the job demands within the four generic factors of skill, responsibility, effort and job conditions.

Further development was stimulated by the 1942 Act on Economic Stabilisation. The aim of this law was to prevent the sudden increases in wages caused by severe shortages of labour during the war. Wages were frozen but the National War Labor Board could approve increases where there were manifest anomalies and inequities. Systematic job evaluation could be used to demonstrate anomalies and therefore there were strong incentives for both employers and unions to develop schemes. Some of these were still in existence years later.

Outside the USA there was little interest in job evaluation before the Second World War, although there were a few isolated examples in the UK, Germany and Switzerland, notably its introduction into the British factories of Imperial Chemical Industries in 1935. In the post-war period many western European countries sought wage stability as they worked to restore their damaged economies and job evaluation was often seen as a means of identifying anomalies which justified pay increases despite general wage restraint or control. The most pervasive scheme was introduced by the Dutch government and was intended to apply to all manual jobs in the country.

In the UK job evaluation slowly gained acceptance after the Second World War. In 1968 a survey by the National Board for Prices and Incomes found that one in four employees was covered by a scheme. However, these schemes were concentrated in only 10 per cent of establishments, with large employers much more likely to have job evaluation, particularly in the coal mining, tobacco, oil refining, chemicals and air transport industries. In the following decades further growth occurred and a survey in 1990 discovered that 26 per cent of workplaces had job evaluation schemes. These were spread equally across private manufacturing, private services and the public sector, but were concentrated particularly in large establishments and in workplaces that were unionized.

2 Job evaluation methods

Numerous methods of job evaluation have been devised. Normally these are divided into 'analytical' and 'non-analytical' types, with non-analytical methods being the simplest. They are relatively cheap to implement and operate and compare whole jobs with other whole jobs. The most popular types are 'job ranking' and 'grading' or 'classification'.

Job ranking

With this method jobs are considered as a whole, using job titles or simple job descriptions to compare one with another. It is easily understood and simple to implement. It is most likely to be suitable for small organizations with a limited range of jobs. However, there are several potential disadvantages with this approach: jobs may be ranked using incomplete information; since there is no detailed analysis of jobs it may be difficult to explain why jobs have been ranked in a particular order; it does not give any indication of the degree of difference between job rankings; the ranking is more likely to be influenced by the person doing the work rather than the job itself; new jobs are not easily slotted into the structure; and those carrying out the evaluations may be heavily influenced in their judgements by the prevailing pay rates.

Grading or classification

With the classification method the grading structure is determined first. The number of grades is decided and a broad definition of the work appropriate to each grade is established. Using the description of the job the evaluators assign it to the most suitable grade. The method is relatively simple, inexpensive and easy to understand. It has been used successfully to evaluate clerical jobs and a wide range of Civil Service posts. It is easy to fit new jobs into the structure. The classification method is less subjective than the ranking method since the jobs are compared with pre-existing definitions. It is most likely to be used successfully where groups of jobs can be clearly defined. Where there is a wide variety of jobs it will be difficult to fit them into the limited grade descriptions, although this can be made easier by using imprecise definitions that allow the evaluators greater flexibility.

The important difference between non-analytical and analytical methods is that in the latter each job is compared with others using a variety of factors such as skill, knowledge, responsibility or working conditions. Each factor is allotted points or a value. The rank order of the jobs is derived by adding together the factor scores for each of them. Two well-known approaches are the 'factor comparison' and the 'points rating' methods. There are also schemes developed by consultancy companies. Of these the 'guide chart profile' method introduced by Hay and Associates in the early 1950s is used extensively in the UK and the USA.

Factor comparison

With the factor comparison method key jobs (often known as benchmark jobs) are chosen. Each factor of every key job is allocated a proportional amount of current wage or salary value. A job can then be evaluated by comparing it factor by factor against the scale for each job factor. This method, originally devised by Benge in 1926, is now little used despite modifications being introduced to try to make it more acceptable. Although it is an analytical approach it is more complex and expensive to

introduce and maintain than most other schemes. It also links payment rates directly to evaluation results which introduces an unnecessary rigidity, particularly during times of change.

Guide chart profile

The Hay guide chart profile method is used in many countries and is the most popular proprietary method in the USA and the UK. It is used primarily for managerial and professional employees but also increasingly for other categories. It uses three main factors: know-how; problem-solving and accountability. Each basic factor is shown in a 'guide chart' in which eight sub-factors are broken down into different degree levels, which may vary according to the size and complexity of the organization. This method enables a company to make pay comparisons between itself and others using the same scheme. However, it is complex and not always easily understood by those to whom it applies.

Points rating

The points rating method is easily the most common approach used today. There are many variations on the basic approach. Typically each job is examined using what appears to be relevant factors and sub-factors. These factors and sub-factors must be given definitions and they may be given differential weightings. It is an adaptable method and when jobs change they can be quickly reassessed if necessary.

3 Introducing a job evaluation scheme

Consultants

Organizations considering introducing a job evaluation scheme must decide whether to manage the process entirely in-house or to employ the services of a consultant. Only a minority actually use consultants since most believe they have sufficient expertise within the organization; usually because a senior member of the personnel staff has prior experience of introducing or operating job evaluation. Consultants are used partly for their expertise and partly because they are seen as impartial, thereby conferring a greater legitimacy to the process.

Typically consultants will gather information on the organization and then advise on the design of an appropriate scheme; the range of jobs to be evaluated; the selection of representative benchmark jobs; and the evaluation of these jobs. Also they will normally train the job analysts and participate in the evaluation committee.

Coverage

Organizations must decide whether job evaluation should cover all or only some of their employees. Typically, where different groups such as manual, clerical or managerial staff are covered, they are in different schemes. It is argued that the factors appropriate for evaluating one type of work are not suitable for very different kinds of task and that separate schemes are necessary. Recently some organizations have been introducing a single scheme to cover the whole workforce. One influence has been the growing popularity of the 'Single Status' employment philosophy, where differences between groups are kept to a minimum and an integrated pay structure applied to all staff. Another reason is that under equal pay policies and legislation women are able to claim pay equal to that of men carrying out very different work. For example, a female clerical worker may compare herself with a male electrician. If they are in two different job evaluation schemes or one is in a scheme but the other is not, there is no way the relative values of the jobs can be assessed. However, if they are in the same scheme and it contains no obvious gender bias in its construction or application, a court will accept that any higher pay for the man is not the result of sex discrimination.

Organizations must also decide whether one scheme should cover all establishments or whether local circumstances are such that different schemes are appropriate. Different schemes or differential coverage of job evaluation is most likely in those organizations which operate in more than one product market, since they will have to adapt to different labour market pressures. Normally one scheme will cover managerial and professional employees because in most cases they are part of a national labour market.

Choice of scheme

After deciding who should be covered by a job evaluation scheme it is necessary to choose an appropriate method. Where a consultant is being used the decision will be influenced by his or her prior experience, while taking into account the circumstances of the organization. Often the consultant will be associated with a proprietary brand of job evaluation and that will be chosen, albeit with small modifications to suit the particular organization.

If it is decided to develop a scheme especially for the organization a series of choices must be made. First, should the scheme be analytical or non-analytical? Most organizations choose analytical schemes because the methods are more detailed and more transparent: all job evaluation requires human judgement, but an analytical approach displays the reasoning and values underlying this judgement. Courts have accepted that evaluations carried out using such schemes are less vulnerable to gender bias. However, the greater complexity of analytical schemes means that they are less easily understood and are more expensive to implement and maintain. Where job evaluation is not expected to alter significantly the existing pay relationships between employees, and therefore is unlikely to experience sustained challenges which require the employer to explain the changes in detail, a non-analytical scheme might be adequate.

After deciding between analytical or non-analytical methods the employer must choose one of the existing schemes, possibly with some modifications. Sometimes they will devise one themselves, taking into account the advantages and disadvantages of the various types outlined above. Crucially they must choose a method which is acceptable to the employees concerned and thus discussions with employee representatives may be carried out before a final decision is made. Cost is another factor which will influence the decision.

Since the points method is by far the most popular method, the remainder of this discussion about the introduction and operation of job evaluation will assume that this is the method in use.

Employee involvement

The involvement of staff is important if the results of job evaluation are to command the support of employees. Research has suggested that participation in the introduction of a payment system brings greater commitment from employees and that they are more likely to perceive the resulting pay structure as equitable (Jenkins and Lawler 1981). Many organizations include employee representatives in their initial deliberations. Others seek greater control by conducting preliminary investigations and trials before opening the issues with representatives. However, not all employers believe that the extra time and costs associated with involving employees outweigh any benefits which may be gained. Equally, trade unions may not want full involvement in the process, preferring to distance themselves sufficiently to be able to dispute the results if necessary (see INDUSTRIAL DEMOCRACY; TRADE UNIONS).

Steering groups

A project management team or steering group will oversee the process of introducing a scheme. Typically it will make decisions on the type of scheme, the use of consultants, communications with those affected by the scheme, the setting up of an evaluation committee and a timetable for each stage of the process. It will monitor progress and ensure the quality of the job analyses, job descriptions and evaluation of benchmark jobs. Near the end of the evaluations it will spot problems and politically sensitive results and seek ways of making these more acceptable to the parties involved before they are confirmed and published.

Job analysis

Job analysis is an essential component of any analytical approach to job evaluation and it can also be used to provide information for other purposes, including training, appraisal and selection. Typically it involves the collection of information about the context of the job, the tasks carried out, the skills and knowledge required to do the work and the conditions under which the job is performed.

There are many ways by which information can be gathered. A common approach is to interview the job holder using a structured questionnaire. A similar interview will be conducted with the supervisor. Where time or money is more limited the job holder or supervisor can be given a questionnaire or simply asked to check off from a list those tasks which are undertaken. This information may be supplemented by observation of the work process and by asking the job holder to keep a diary of their activities. A further source of information may be work-related documents, supplied by the job-holder or supervisor, which can clarify the depth of involvement in the tasks carried out and provide insights into the cognitive skills and the knowledge needed for the work.

In recent years some organizations have introduced quantitative methods of job analysis which allow the information to be analysed statistically using computer software. Whilst this is an efficient way of processing a mass of information and may appear to be more objective, it has the disadvantage of involving managers and employees less and is likely to be more difficult for them to understand.

Who should carry out the job analyses? The task can be entrusted to an experienced consultant, although more often a group of staff are trained in the technique. Where this is not feasible or not thought desirable the supervisor or the job holder will be responsible for the analysis and production of the job description. However, this approach will result in job descriptions of widely varying quality, which puts less analytical and articulate staff at a disadvantage.

4 Implementing a job evaluation scheme

Once the scheme has been designed it must be tested before it is fully implemented. If necessary it can then be modified. Normally up to 25 per cent of the jobs to be evaluated are chosen as representative benchmark jobs and some of these are used for the initial testing. Benchmark jobs should cover a range of posts across the organization from different departments and varying levels. They should be well known, relatively stable jobs with established rates of pay in the external labour market.

Who should carry this out? In a few organizations it may be handled by the payment specialists within the personnel department, but there are advantages in setting up a job evaluation committee drawn from a range of people in the organization. This brings wider experience to bear and generates more commitment to the outcome. However, a great deal of time is involved and managers may not be keen to give their own or their staff's time to an activity which falls outside their normal responsibilities and rarely brings much prestige. However, it does provide a good opportunity for staff to get to know other parts of the organization and can be a valuable learning opportunity.

Once the members of the job evaluation panel have been trained they will carry out the test evaluations, unless this has already been done by the internal or external payment specialists during the initial design of the scheme. Following this the other benchmark jobs are evaluated and the main structure is established. The remaining jobs can be fitted into this structure through further evaluations.

Increasingly the evaluation process is being assisted by computer software. At the very least this can help in sorting and storing the information, but more sophisticated packages may aid consistent judgements by defining rules of evaluation and asking questions of the evaluators (Murlis and Fitt 1991).

Communication to managers and staff

Communication of information about a new job evaluation scheme and the reasons for its introduction should be carefully planned. Some staff will feel threatened by the process and must be reassured where possible. In addition to meetings and written explanations for staff, a full brief, preferably in question and answer format, should be given to managers to help them discuss the changes with their staff. Union representatives should be given information as soon as possible and consulted about potential problems, particularly when the early results are available. However, it is wise for senior management to discuss what appear to be contentious results before they are disclosed.

Appeals

Inevitably there will be losers as well as winners with a job evaluation exercise. In order to avoid unnecessary problems all assessments should be checked for technical inaccuracies and for their political impact. If sufficient money is made available there may be little need for significant numbers of staff to face a pay cut. The position of such staff can be ameliorated by allowing them to retain a personal salary equal to their previous one and giving them subsequent general salary increases. A less favourable treatment is to let them retain their salary, but with no further salary rises until their salary has fallen to the level appropriate to their new grade.

None of these measures will avert the need to deal with aggrieved staff whose pay or status is threatened. An appeal or review mechanism must be put in place before the announcement of new grades. Mass appeals could overwhelm an appeal process and therefore the grounds on which they will be allowed may need to be restricted. Where a strong occupational group feels that it has been wrongly evaluated and obtains union support the scheme may come under extreme pressure. Management will be anxious to avoid being seen to manipulate the scheme thereby undermining its legitimacy, but it has to balance that against the possibility of damaging industrial action.

5 Operating a job evaluation scheme

The introduction of a new job evaluation scheme is normally a time-consuming and frequently exhausting process. It is all too easy to breathe a sigh of relief when it is successfully implemented and to concentrate on other issues. However, it is a costly investment which needs maintenance if it is to have a reasonable lifespan.

A senior manager should be responsible for the operation and development of the scheme. The person chosen should not see their role simply as one of ensuring that the rules are adhered to and that the administrative arrangements are operating smoothly. They must also have the experience and authority to recognize when changes need to be made. Where resources are available the scheme should be audited regularly. Administration of a job evaluation scheme includes the maintenance of accurate job descriptions, responding to requests for re-evaluations, the keeping of accurate records and the implementation of new job grades.

Changes and pressures within the organization may challenge the scheme, although there will be fewer difficulties where the initial introduction of the scheme was well planned and fully supported by management and employees. Maintaining the commitment and involvement of management can be difficult, particularly where there are changes in key personnel.

Pressures can come from various sources. First, labour market shortages in particular occupations may mean that the evaluated rate becomes less than the market rate and that staff leave and cannot be replaced. Where this is a temporary phenomenon it is advisable to pay a 'market supplement'. However, in the longer term the solution will have to lie in modifications to the scheme. Second, the scheme may need to respond to the changing bargaining power or priorities of unions or attempts to re-establish traditional pay relationships. Third, changing technology and work organization will normally mean that some jobs become more demanding and others less so. Where technology has reduced the skills needed in a job, as for example in printing, management must decide whether to carry out an immediate re-evaluation or to disregard the situation and wait until the next major overhaul of the evaluation system occurs. This poses a particular dilemma because the new technology will have made the individual worker more productive and a consequent downgrading will be seen as unfair. Fourth, fundamental changes in business strategy or in the market for the organization's products or services will change the value it places on certain skills. For example, British clearing banks facing competitive and cost pressures have placed more emphasis on extending their financial services and marketing new products. Their job evaluation schemes therefore have needed to give greater weight to skills which support these new priorities. Finally, increased pressures or legislation seeking to eliminate sex discrimination in the design and operation of job evaluation schemes has required changes in schemes or the introduction of new ones (Arthurs 1992).

In responding to pressures the key issue is how much to defend the integrity of the job evaluation scheme in the pursuit of consistency and control and when to make changes. This requires difficult judgements and the ability to make uneasy compromises.

6 Limitations and criticisms of job evaluation

Despite the increase in the use of job evaluation over the past fifty years it is still regarded with scepticism and sometimes hostility by many employers. They argue that it is expensive to install and operate; that there is little evidence to show that it reduces pay grievances; that it introduces a rigidity which makes it difficult to respond quickly to market conditions; and that it encourages an inflexible attitude amongst employees, which in extreme cases results in them 'working to the job description'.

Unions and their members show no consistent attitude towards job evaluation. Some, particularly at the workplace, accept it as a useful technique that prevents the arbitrary fixing of payment rates by management and reduces grievances. Criticisms often relate to particular local circumstances: suspicion of management's motives for introducing a scheme; lack of consultation or involvement; or the complexity and jargon associated with the scheme which makes it difficult to understand. Objections in principle include the belief that it limits collective bargaining; that it undermines the role of the union in securing pay increases; that it may lead to union representatives having to take responsibility for some of their members taking pay cuts; and that its outcome is unpredictable and may result in some of their members being paid less than they could get in the local labour market.

7 Perspectives on job evaluation

Much recent research on job evaluation has concentrated on efforts to refine the technique in order to eliminate bias. The passing of legislation and the pursuit of public policies designed to ensure that women are paid equally where their work is of equal value to that of a man has meant that job evaluation has been subjected to unprecedented scrutiny and legal challenge.

Although it is commonly asserted that discrimination can take place at all stages of the process, experimental research has not unambiguously demonstrated that it does. Research has found that the results of evaluation are dependent on the method used and that significant variations in job hierarchy can occur when different schemes are applied. Results also vary from one evaluator to another, although reliability is much improved where a team of evaluators is used. It has also been shown that many methods use more factors than necessary in order to evaluate jobs since there is a high correlation between many of the factors. Surprisingly there is little evidence that the gender of the evaluator influences the results of an evaluation or that it is affected by knowing the gender of the job holder (Schwab 1985).

From a different perspective the search for the perfect job evaluation scheme is a chimera. Job content is not the sole criterion of the value of a job. The purpose of job evaluation is not to find some 'correct' value for a job but to produce a pay structure which is acceptable to all the parties involved. It must take account not only of the demands of the job but also its value in the market, tradition and the bargaining power of the parties involved. Indeed some writers have insisted that the design of a scheme is of less practical importance than the context into which it is introduced and the way in which it is administered (Kerr and Fisher 1977).

8 Equal pay

The pressure for equal pay for women has meant that job evaluation has been subjected to increased analysis and criticism. The criticism has been directed at all stages of the process. First, it is claimed that the design of even the more transparent analytical methods can contain unconscious or even deliberate gender bias. This occurs because the factors chosen for the evaluation may reflect the priorities and the values of the times in which many of the methods were first formulated; namely, when lower pay for women carrying out the same work as men was explicitly sanctioned. Efforts to produce methods free of bias have concentrated on ensuring that the factors used, and the weight given to them, take full account of the skills, experience and responsibilities associated with those jobs typically carried out by women. For example, interpersonal skills, dexterity and caring responsibilities are given substantial weight, whereas factors often associated with male-dominated jobs, such as physical strength and responsibility for money, are given less prominence (see PAYMENT SYSTEMS). Gender bias can also be reduced by ensuring that women are knowledgeable about job evaluation and are fully involved in the design or choice of the scheme, the job analyses and the evaluations (see EQUAL EMPLOYMENT OPPORTUNITIES).

9 The future of job evaluation

For a hundred years, and particularly in the last fifty years, job evaluation has grown in popularity as a management technique. Will it continue to grow? How might it develop as a technique?

In the UK job evaluation is found mostly in medium-sized and large organizations and in unionized environments. However, despite the precipitate decline in union membership in the 1980s and 1990s and the trend towards workplaces with smaller numbers of employees, job evaluation is used more widely than ever. While many employers modify their schemes or introduce new ones, evidence suggests that very few abandon job evaluation entirely. Two explanations may be given. First, that job evaluation is simply part of a wider development of rational management techniques promoted by business schools, consultants and the management literature. Second, that job evaluation, despite the management time it takes and its expense, continues to provide the best legitimation of pay differences. In the process it usually can be expected to minimize discontent about pay. In a unionized environment this means less time spent dealing with grievances and less disruption. In a non-unionized organization it means that there are fewer perceived injustices and therefore less likelihood that employees will feel a need to join a union. Third, the use of a proprietary scheme such as the one developed by Hay enables employers to compare jobs, and their appropriate payment rates, across a wide range of organizations. However, one recent development which may inhibit the growth in popularity of job evaluation is the trend towards the individualizing of pay, with emphasis on the employee's competencies and contribution rather than on the demands of the job (Lawler 1994) (see PAYMENT SYSTEMS).

ALAN ARTHURS
UNIVERSITY OF BATH

Further reading

(References cited in the text marked *)

* Arthurs, A. (1992) 'Equal value in British banking: the Midland Bank Case', in E. Meehan and P. Kahn (eds), *Equal Value/Comparable Worth in Britain and the United States*, London: Macmillan. (Study of the strategy behind a new job evaluation scheme introduced in response to equal pay legislation.)

IRS Employment Trends (1994) 'Developments in job evaluation: shifting the emphasis' 551: 10–16. (Argues that job evaluation is being used increasingly to underpin pay structures rather than to determine individual payment rates.)

* Jenkins, G.J., Jr and Lawler, E.E., III (1981) 'Impact of employee participation in pay plan development', *Organizational Behavior and Human Performance* 28: 111–28. (A study of the introduction of a new pay system designed by a commitee of employees and managers.)

* Kerr, C. and Fisher, L.H. (1977) 'Effects of environment and administration on job evaluation', in C. Kerr (ed.), *Labor Markets and Wage Determination*, Berkeley, CA: University of California Press. (An outstanding analysis by two eminent US labour economists with practical experience of job evaluation.)

* Lawler, E.E., III (1994) 'From job-based to competency-based organizations', *Journal of Organizational Behaviour* 15: 3–15. (Challenges the assumption that organizations should be built around 'jobs'.)

* Murlis, H. and Fitt, D. (1991) 'Job evaluation in a changing world', *Personnel Management* May: 39–43. (Describes and advocates the use of computers in job evaluation for processing information and aiding judgements.)

Pritchard, D. and Murlis, H. (1992) *Jobs, Roles and People: The New World of Job Evaluation*, London: Nicholas Brealey Publishing. (A thorough, well-presented account by two very experienced consultants and writers.)

* Schwab, D.P. (1985) 'Job evaluation research and research needs', in H.H. Hartmann (ed.), *Comparable Worth: New Directions for Research*, Washington, DC: National Academy Press. (Incisive review of research, with suggestions for future directions.)

See also: EQUAL EMPLOYMENT OPPORTUNITIES; HUMAN RESOURCE MANAGEMENT; INDUSTRIAL DEMOCRACY; INTERPERSONAL SKILLS; JOB DESIGN; PAYMENT SYSTEMS; TRADE UNIONS; TRAINING, ECONOMICS OF; WORK AND ORGANIZATION SYSTEMS

Management development

Overview

Management development covers a wide
spectrum of activities ranging from self-
development through improving communication and presentation skills or specific skills
such as managing information in the office,
performance appraisals, financial management, managing other people, managing in
different cultures and aligning the capabilities
of managers with changes in the strategies and
structures of the organization. This field is
characterized by a rich diversity of
approaches, methods, philosophies, techniques and ideas about human and organizational development. However: 'This very
richness has its downside. Many of us fall into
bee-like behaviour, sipping momentarily
from every flower . . . a balance needs to be
sought between the need to explore . . . and the
need to work deeply from a well-considered
position' (Megginson and Pedlar 1992).

Global flows of currency and information
impact directly on management development,
which was originally defined during earlier
periods of relative stability when it was possible to screen out uncertainty rather than engage with it. Management is in transition from
the command and control structures appropriate to relative stability to the distributed
decision-making structures necessary in rapidly changing conditions. Managers now require new approaches to decision making in
uncertainty, and they must also do much more
to create an atmosphere where people can
cope with uncertainty not only in making

decisions but also in the patterns of their
working lives. Best practice in management
development integrates the development of
individuals within the design of the
organization.

1 Background

The 1990s are an important and testing time
both for managers and for management development. Global flows of capital and information impact on each and every organization,
whatever its scale or location. Managed or
planned economies are breaking down all
over the world, assumptions of continuous
growth and relative stability no longer hold,
and large organizations can no longer control
economic development. Instead these organizations now have a 'humbler perception of
their powers' (Benton 1990), and 'share a
common fate' in the face of the dynamic complexity that characterizes the global
environment.

The impact of this complexity on the structures of organizations, on what is expected of
the people who work in them and on the understanding of power and authority, is sharply
focused on individual managers as they sit at
their desks reflecting on how to organize priorities (see ORGANIZATION BEHAVIOUR). In
this situation, managers and those responsible
for supporting them in their development face
both confusion and opportunities.

Confusion can easily arise when managers
feel that they are being exhorted to behave in
one way and then being treated in another. Although theorists perceive 'a rapidly growing
shift in management style away from one
based on control and aggression. . . toward
one based on "caring and connection" '
(Parikh 1991), there is evidence that some
companies have a long way to go: the finance
director of a large media organization commented on his own firm, 'This company depends directly on the creativity of its people

who make the programmes and it treats them like tiddlywinks!'

Where is management development coming from?

In the past, in relatively stable times with assumptions of growth, employment security, regular promotion and unquestioned authority, management development provided systematic training based on detailed job descriptions and followed standard syllabi (see TRAINING). Management development was about learning new skills and abilities, and the answer to every problem was to send the manager on a course. This kind of approach faced a 'transfer of training problem', and the focus then shifted to the individual learner and the learning process.

However, the socio-economic and organizational context in which development took place remained relatively unchanged. Providing returns to shareholders remained the primary goal of most companies; command and control hierarchies prevailed, jobs were highly specialized, the planning of work was separated from its actual execution and management reserved the choice of methods by which a particular task was carried out. Analytical skills dominated; the managerial task was to select rationally from among growth options and then to construct new rationales for behaviour based on analyses of the problems of control currently faced. The influential approach of Taylorism saw 'initiative and incentive' as barriers to efficient mass production, and advocated: 'the substitute of a science for the individual judgement of the workman' (Freedman 1992) (see TAYLOR, F.W.). Most decisions were taken in situations where all the facts were knowable, allowing managers to analyse, predict and use their knowledge and experience to guide data collection, make deductions, draw conclusions and manage deviations from stability. In this environment people were, quite appropriately, instructed, controlled and discouraged from communicating with each other.

Economies entering the field later faced the necessity of establishing themselves in the face of competition and amassing large amounts of capital quickly. This need created a more dispersed pattern of relationships with providers of capital, customers, employees, suppliers, and communities. Entering at a point when technologies were already sophisticated, they faced higher fixed capital per employee. Many thus chose to multi-skill rather than specialize, to encourage people to use their judgement in the light of economically useful on-the-spot information, and to trade specialized production time for participatory time in which information could be shared (see FLEXIBILITY).

2 The current state of management development

Management – particularly in mature economies – is in a phase of transition from command and control to a new balance between the authority of hierarchy, the price controls of the market, and the trust that is essential if people are to use their initiative. In supporting this transition, management development is faced with the same dilemmas as is management itself, and by the sharpness with which these dilemmas impinge on individual managers, who may well fear that their development will be followed by redundancy but who can also be helped to strengthen their own self-understanding in preparation for a change of career.

In a managed economy, authority is the primary mechanism for control inside the organization. But, to remain viable in a turbulent environment where no one group controls the destiny of the business, organizations must be much more responsive to price and thus to cost. To remain viable in a global economy, where the emphasis is on recruiting information, handling uncertainty, know-how and teamwork, organizations have to be more aware of their human assets and the mechanisms of trust for their commitment. However, the mechanisms of authority embodied in the command and control hierarchy remain very strong, and market considerations are felt to dictate tight financial control; substantial redundancies are often a consequence.

Management development in the mid-1990s is in a transition stage from command and control to cost-cutting and culture (see ORGANIZATION CULTURE). But while command and control are not mutually contradictory and can produce security, loyalty and dependable workforces in stable conditions, cost-cutting and culture rest less easily together. This conflict can have a severe impact on managers and their development.

Expectations of the managerial role

Companies have very high expectations of their managers (see MANAGERIAL BEHAVIOUR). According to one chief executive officer (CEO), the manager must be an impresario: 'skilled in generating the enthusiasm and focusing the aspirations of many individuals with distinct talents. He listens, he shapes vision and structure, he inspires'. According to another the manager must be a sculptor: 'forming managers who can judge well, rather than the highly polished cogs of yesterday' (Benton 1990). Other views of the managerial role postulate that managers should 'let go and allow things to happen', or be the conductor of an orchestra, a gardener, a guide, a listener, a coach or a counsellor. In the words of Parikh (1991): 'The role of management is to create within the organization a climate, a culture and a context in which corporate enrichment and individual fulfilment collaborate and resonate progressively in the development of a creative and integrative global community'.

Managers are expected to run effective profit centres, control costs tightly, compete with other departments, be audited and audit, be rewarded and reward with performance-related pay, all at one and the same time. Most structures and systems support the market mechanism within the authority of the command and control hierarchy, and this is a powerful combination. At the same time, awareness of the potential for people to innovate, be alert to market opportunities and use their judgement in dealing with uncertainty, and of trust as the 'lubricant' of social networks, enters the managerial role through the considerable emphasis in current management development on culture, people, communication, and interpersonal and team-building skills. By and large, however, the structures and systems remain authority-driven despite reduced numbers of hierarchical levels and the growing economic significance and power of networks and alliances. The contradictions inherent in these expectations of the managerial role – that it will be both authoritarian and egalitarian at one and the same time – lead to considerable problems. These are summed up succinctly by Peters (1989):

> Approximately 97 per cent of your people are creative, vigorous, loyal, committed, caring and energetic – except for the eight hours they work for you. And the serious question we've got to ask ourselves is – What kind of a hell hole have we created as managers that has taken this talent and turned it into turned-off people?

Beyond analysis

Effective managerial performance involves learning to handle complexity, diversity and ambiguity. Success depends on trust: managers must be in a position to trust their own inner resources and intuition and take responsibility for creating a climate in which their subordinates can do the same.

> For more than thirty years, a management world whose prime task should be the creation of business has treated intuition as a dirty word ... but now as companies search for ways of creating more business, and with excessive rationality in retreat after more than a decade of strategic planning disasters, intuition is making a comeback. The problem is how to integrate it with the rigour and deep understanding of markets, technologies, strategy and competitive behaviour which managers need at a time of global competition, complexity, uncertainty and rapid change.
>
> (Lorenz 1994).

When the facts of a situation are knowable – as they are more likely to be in stable economic and market conditions – managers can use their knowledge and experience to analyse the situation and take the right decision. However, when an important part of work is to engage with uncertainty, managers are forced beyond fully-informed decision making. The managerial task becomes extralogical; managers must rely on their judgement and make choices for which they, rather than data, must bear responsibility (Spender 1989).

As a result, a new value has been placed on insight, intuition and tacit knowledge, and it is becoming more and more widely accepted that people make decisions as a consequence of an interplay between that which is articulated and that which is not, and that the thought process that led to the decision cannot always be clearly set out. This can lead to problems for managers who have been trained to analyse and be rational, and to oversee and control those who work for them for that they do the same.

Managers are faced on the one hand with a new need for the use of intuition, and on the other hand by anxiety that important decisions – their own, and also those of their managers and subordinates – rely on anything so intangible and 'unscientific'. Intuition that leads to sound judgement is highly prized, but it is also elusive in that it depends on a very fine balance between what people feel they can grasp and do and the challenges with which they are faced. Managers who are either overwhelmed or insufficiently challenged by their jobs will be much more reluctant to trust their intuition: they are likely to feel that their support structure is flimsy to the point of disintegration, and as their anxiety increases their competence correspondingly decreases.

A management development programme in the South African company Anglo American was specifically designed to minimize overstretch and insufficient challenge. The programme includes development centres where a procedure known as Career Path Appreciation is used to evaluate the current capacity of individuals to make decisions in the face of irreducible uncertainty. The evaluations provide the bases for individually-tailored programmes that match increase in responsibilities with the predicted growth of that capacity in the future. One of the primary purposes of this programme has been to identify the capacities of Black managers and give them proper opportunities for advancement. Until very recently, Black managers have been significantly underused, and the purpose of this programme is to make sure as far as possible that they are neither overwhelmed nor underused in the future. In order to achieve this, it has been necessary to use a procedure that is completely free of cultural bias.

Beyond supervision

It is because this balance is so delicate that asking people to use their intuition may be to ask more than they may be willing to give. Willingness or lack thereof depends directly on the conditions in which they are asked to work. Physical working conditions may be significant, but cultural aspects – how expectation is framed, how meaning is given to actions and events, how learning is arranged and valued, how behaviours are encouraged or discouraged – are likely to be most important.

In a command and control hierarchy, the responsibility of managers is simply to supervise. In the transition to new patterns of organization, however, managers are expected both to maintain tight financial control – which can make them feel completely inhuman – and to create a climate where those who work to them are 'nurtured', 'encouraged' and 'mentored'.

3 Best practice

In a climate in which managers are expected to use their judgement and trust their intuition, and encourage others to do the same, management development must include concepts such as learning to learn, listening, being a team member, influencing others, communication and individual understanding of growth capability. As managers meet new and wider challenges, development must proceed at a pace that neither pushes managers too fast, leading to anxiety and loss of confidence, nor holds them back, to similar deleterious effect.

In best practice, these concepts are integrated not only into the development of the organization as it reshapes itself to meet the challenges of its environment, but also with an understanding of why these changes in culture and behaviour are necessary. When these links are clear, the uneasy relationship between tight financial control, redundancies and the nurturing of people can be better understood. Organizations need people to be creative and act on their own initiative, whether in serving customers or in making products, because the survival of an organization depends on its ability to be flexible and adaptive in a highly competitive environment, and individual behaviour is the source of that flexibility. Organizations need people to work together in teams because effectiveness in rapidly changing conditions depends on people sharing, rather than hoarding, information and insights. In command and control hierarchies, where functions have considerable power, information is not readily shared and so the value it could generate is lost. And, with the high levels of fixed capital represented by each person employed, organizations need to make the most of their investment.

Beyond the long-term employment contract

The era of jobs for life is over, and the consequent job insecurity rests heavily on managers, producing both anxiety for themselves and for those who work for them (see CAREERS; FLEXIBILITY). Some writers have suggested that there has been a return to – or no move away from – the master–servant relationship of early industrialization where workers had minimal rights. For many workers this is indeed the case. In countries where welfare provision is deemed to be too costly to both the state and organizations, employers may design contracts in such a way that they do not have to contribute to national insurance; women and young people in particular may be employed on a part-time basis with no rights. In nations struggling to build an economy, there may be different degrees of legislative protection ranging from employment conditions at the behest of the employer to recognized trade unions.

Managing a plethora of different kinds of contract is an entirely new experience for managers and one in which they need development. There are technical and legal issues to be dealt with; there is also the expectation that the relationships represented in the contracts will be handled in a 'culture of care and connection' (Parikh 1991). This kind of expectation can pose a real moral dilemma for managers who are being encouraged to treat people not as units of production, but as individuals with potential. There is much talk of 'managing paradox', the kind of paradox that asks managers to plan a culture of nurture and encouragement in an environment in which dismissal may be called for at any time. Managers need to be helped to understand the nature of contracts from both a technical and a cultural, partnership point of view; there is also a need for transparency in the direction of the organization.

To support self-understanding, best practice may also include the use of a variety of psychological instruments to help people to reflect on themselves and on how they are perceived by others. These may include the Myers Briggs Type Indicator, the 16 PF (Personality Factor), personality assessments, tests of critical thinking, and feedback from peers and subordinates (see OCCUPATIONAL PSYCHOLOGY). To use these instruments in assessment without feedback to the individual is not best practice, although there are organizations that do not distinguish between assessment and development.

Best practice places management development at the heart of the business, contributing to strategic development and the definition of long-term direction. A 1990 survey of CEOs around the world revealed their priorities for developing managers to be as follows: strategic awareness (mentioned by 71 per cent of those surveyed), adaptability in new situations (67 per cent), sensitivity in different cultures (60 per cent), ability to work in international teams (58 per cent), relationship skills (40 per cent) and high task orientation (19 per cent).

The widely used competency approach integrates management and organizational development by combining careful analysis of role with thorough evaluation of the competencies of the individual. As with psychological instruments, this approach can strengthen the individual's self-understanding; this is increasingly important as people move in and out of different organizations at different stages of their working lives and perhaps also look for different balances between work and other aspects of their lives.

Beyond the given

One CEO described the role of experience in decision making as follows: 'good judgement depends on experience and experience depends on bad judgement'. It is not what people have done or how long they have worked in a particular area, but what they have made of the experience that counts.

An understanding of how the interaction between knowledge, experience and judgement changes in the move from stability to turbulence (see Figure 1) can release managers from the sense that if they do not know something, it is because they are not educated, experienced or careful enough: 'While knowledge is one of the essential tools of work, it is not the work itself. . . knowledge alone will not see you through. . . in work you are confronted by problems that have no absolutely correct answer. You have to use knowledge and judgement in interaction' (Jaques 1990). Seeing knowledge as a tool eases people away from the feeling that it is their fault they do not know enough, and helps them to accept not just the unknown but a growing degree of unknowability in many of the situations where decisions must be made.

Knowledge is no longer a static model carried from one situation to another, but a capacity to adapt and re-coordinate familiar ways of seeing, talking, and acting in new situations (Linde 1993). In complex work settings, the ability to monitor the state of the world, generate both tacit and articulable knowledge and weave these together ('the helical process' in the words of Nonaka, quoted in Hampden-

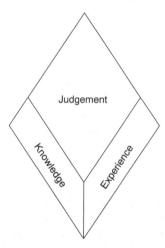

Figure 1 Knowledge, experience and judgement

Turner and Trompenaars (1993)) confers crucial corporate advantage.

Again, this means a substantial shift in understanding for managers accustomed to applying and supervising the application of the given knowledge assumed in command and control hierarchies and stable conditions. Not only have they to come to terms with the fact that knowledge and qualifications previously obtained – sometimes through many years of evening or part-time study – may no longer be relevant, but they must also create a climate for the sharing of information and generating new knowledge. This can pose another dilemma as to whether the time for sharing information should be deducted from time devoted to production. The trade-off must be made in an informed way, and this in turn requires full understanding of the issues involved. Best practice for management development will support managers in making these decisions by helping them to a greater understanding of how their own intuition works, of how they as individuals contribute to a team, and of the context which must inform their decisions. Through this understanding of context, managers will be able not only to reconcile costs and culture but combine them in ways that make sense for them, for the people who work for them, and for the company that employs them. Managers are too often left without this contextual understanding, while still being expected to be part of a 'learning organization'.

The twenty-first century company has to promote and nurture the capacity to improve and to innovate. That idea has radical implications. It means learning becomes the axial principle of organization. It replaces control as the fundamental job of management.

(Zuboff 1992)

In the words of Argyris (1991): 'success in the market place increasingly depends on learning, yet most people don't know how to learn' (see ARGYRIS, C.). Best practice in management development focuses on the learner and the learning process, freeing people from assumptions that it is what they learn that is most important, and that if they have not 'learned it properly' then they have failed. Again this is a matter of culture and atmosphere, of whether people are encouraged to 'honour their errors' and be open about what has worked and what has not, so that learning can take place. The command and control hierarchy encourages the covering up of mistakes, 'passing the buck' and avoiding blame. The shift to a culture of honouring errors can only be brought about by example; the culture of blame avoidance goes too deep to be changed by words alone. Managers may do their best to create a learning environment, but if their mistakes are held against them and this affects their performance-related pay, then protection of their own position will become paramount despite all exhortations.

There is yet another point at which managers – and especially middle managers – can be torn between exhortation and reality. All organizations are now more outwards-directed, watching for signals or indications in the environment that could suggest either opportunities or threats. Information is needed from every possible source, but the command and control attitude that it is only knowledge at the centre that counts – and that only the centre is in a position to transform information into knowledge – inhibits middle managers and slows response times. However, middle managers who are expected to control costs and provide cultural change have an excellent opportunity to do both, and to benefit the company by generating information, from impressions collected at the periphery of the organization by people working directly with customers or production. These middle managers know they could be powerful agents for change; they are in a key position to combine strategic macro (context-free) information and hands-on micro (context-specific) information, and to serve as a starting point for action to be taken by both upper and lower levels. Management development can support middle managers in this position, strengthening their understanding of the commercial value of information gained at the periphery, their capacity to communicate that information to senior management, and their skills in encouraging people who work for them to share and not hoard, to talk together about new ways of doing things and improvements in practice.

External focus

Two groups of words come up frequently in writing about management development. The first group is concerned with being alert and includes 'listen', 'observe' and 'watchfulness', reflecting the need for awareness of all the nuances of the ever-changing,

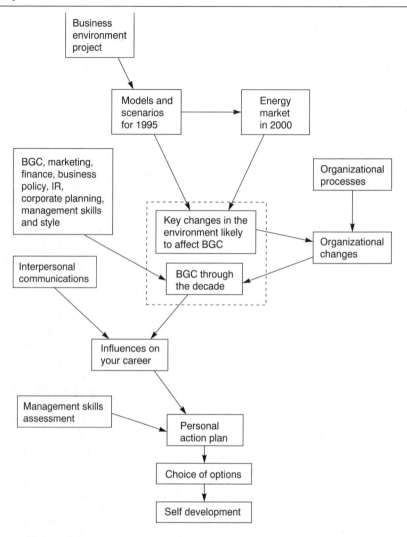

Figure 2 How middle management integrates its various inputs
Source: Saunders (1984)

opportunity-rich but contradictory environment. For example, 'awareness' is the first word of the name of the AVIRA (awareness, vision, imagination, responsibility and action) programme for top executives established at INSEAD in France. AVIRA, which was set up as a result of a worldwide study carried out to identify the needs of senior managers in large international corporations in Europe, the USA and the Asia Pacific region, focuses on the interconnections between the executive, the organization and the environment.

This external focus, on customers, competitors, joint venture partners and suppliers, adds greatest value when it is made the responsibility of everyone and when each person knows that his or her insights will be received with respect. Managers at all levels can make sure this is the case, but to do so requires a substantial change in attitude from the view that only the knowledge of and from the centre counts.

4 Integrating organizational and management development

The need for organizations to be flexible, adaptable and information-rich can best be met by integrating the development of people with the design of the organization so that the relationships between the two are coherent at every point. They can be linked through the level of complexity in the work to be done and the individual capacity to cope with that complexity (Jaques 1976; Stamp 1989).

While many issues are experienced in similar ways by all managers, the impact of these issues may be very different depending on the manager's level of responsibility. Best practice in management development is therefore to fine-tune programmes to the needs of particular levels of responsibility, and to help prepare people for the transition from one level to the next. An example of best practice can be found in the work of the British Gas Management Centre in the 1980s and 1990s (Saunders 1984, 1992). When British Gas was privatized in 1986, the board of directors came to the conclusion that their core business would become fully mature around the turn of the century; after exploring alternatives, they decided on a strategy of international expansion in the gas and oil sector.

During the early 1980s the British Gas Management Centre had evolved a middle-management programme centred around scenario thinking (de Geus 1988), likely organizational changes and helping managers to see what skills they would need in future years. The content and scope of this programme are shown in Figure 2.

A second series of programmes, called business issues programmes, was developed for more senior managers. These also used a scenario approach to management development, action learning and syndicate work. These programmes were an important broadening experience which helped counterbalance the strong functional organization that had been in place before privatization. In

the late 1980s the experience of middle-management programmes, the business issues programmes and emerging cross-cultural understandings were applied in the design of a Strategic Management Development Programme to give an understanding of the strategic direction of the business to senior managers from Canada, America, Africa, Russia, Germany and the UK.

All these programmes were designed on the basis of an executive development framework developed over the last thirty years at Brunel University in the UK (Jaques 1989; Isaac and O'Connor 1975; Stamp and Isaac 1990) and shown in Figure 3.

The British Gas Management Centre drew on this framework when events focused attention on eastern Europe, and the centre hosted three senior executives from the Russian company Gasprom for three weeks. In discussion it was learned that Gasprom heads of enterprise often operate in remote areas where their first job is to create a town where the employees can live before they can get gas out of the ground or transmit it. This means that managers are responsible not only for an executive organization, but also for farms, schools and hospitals; in many cases they are among the most senior people in the local authority structure. The executive development framework made it easier to establish the complexity of the role and to tailor inputs accordingly.

These visits led in turn to contacts with the Leningrad Management Institute (LIMI) and SDA Bocconi in Milan and to a proposal by LIMI for a joint programme for British Gas directors and potential heads of enterprise in Gasprom. Two courses were held in St Petersburg. The first two weeks of each course was provided by LIMI, which gave a basic understanding of western management and economics, while the third week was a joint programme with directors from all British Gas business units. The starting point for the programme design was again the executive development framework, which made it possible to identify the heads of enterprise in Gasprom as operating on the same level as managing directors and with experience strongly focused on production in a stable and

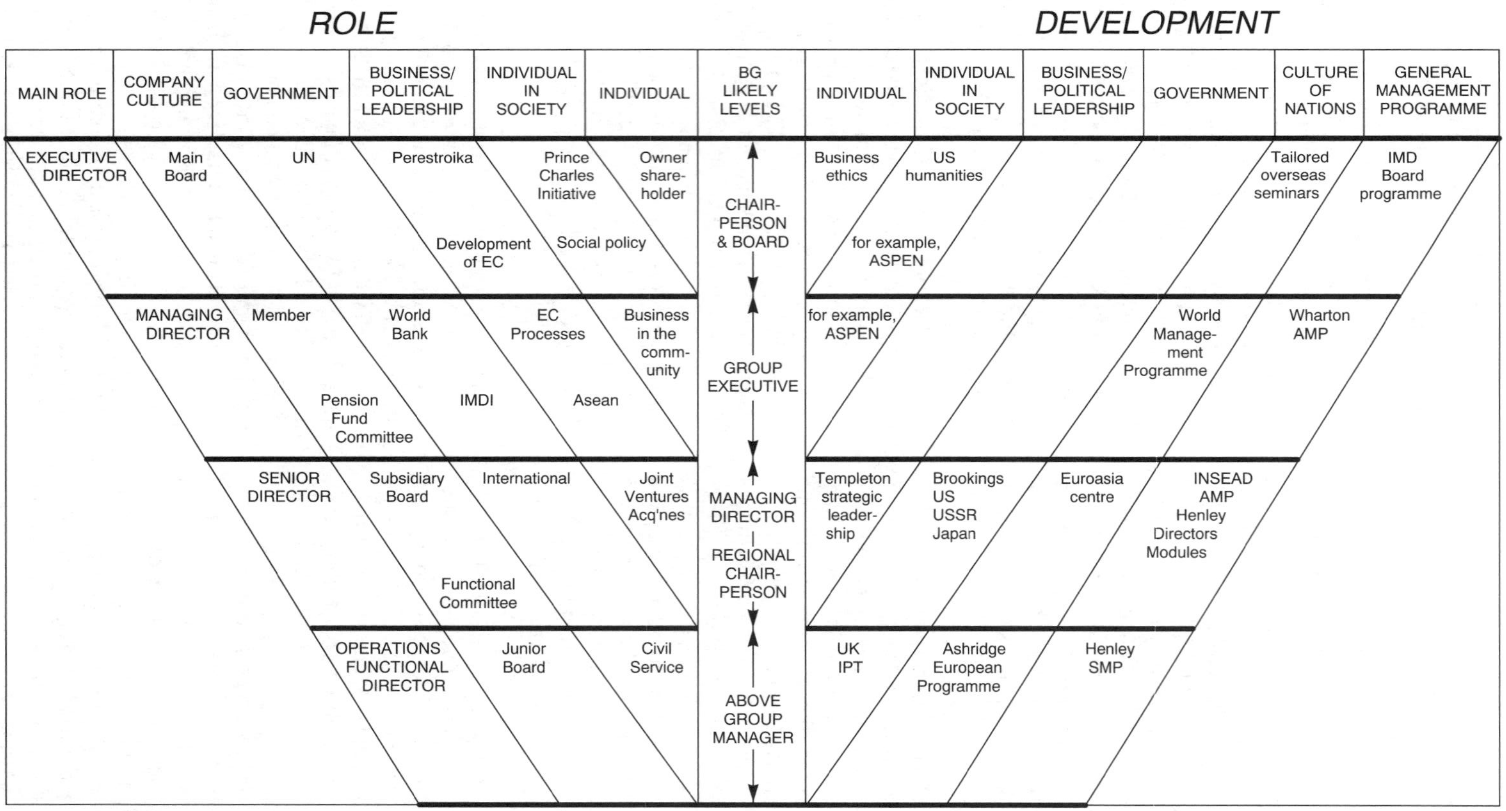

ROLE

DEVELOPMENT

Figure 3 Executive development framework
Source: Saunders (1992)

unchanging political and economic environment. This made it possible to fine-tune the input of the programme and provide both support for people already at that level in Gasprom and proper preparation for those likely to be promoted within the next couple of years. The framework has also been used in development courses for managers from Kazakhstan, the Czech Republic, Australia, South Africa, India, Indonesia, Sweden and Germany.

5 Management development in the future

As complexity and change in the environment continue to increase, external focus – hunger for information about what is going on in the environment – and internal focus – nurturing the capacity to generate shared knowledge from that information – will become even more powerful drivers of management development and organization design. Command and control structures will continue to shift towards distributed control and decision making in direct response to the pull of the environment. The counter-pull of the primacy of shareholders in Anglo-Saxon economies is likely to remain strong but, as other systems of raising capital such as leveraged buyouts become more common, changes in relationships with the providers of capital are likely to support distributed control and responsiveness to a greater number of stakeholders.

The single most powerful driver of management development will be global and personal information technology. The Internet is already tapped by organizations all over the world for information which can be used for competitive leverage. The spread of information has also had a profound effect on individual development because it can provide personally tailored learning at any time, any place and any pace. This learning is also available outside the control of the manager's superiors: 'There is no central keeper of knowledge in a network, only curators of particular views' (Kelly 1994). In the words of Golzen (1994): 'When George Orwell came up with the notion of Big Brother watching

you in his novel *1984*, he did not envisage the possibility that the same technology might enable Little Brother to stare right back'.

External focus and the need to make the most of the information gathered is likely to strengthen the need for people to use their individual judgement to discern what information may be of significance to them, and then to give meaning to that information and leverage it for maximum advantage. It will also strengthen the need for people to share information and thus generate added value (Aoki *et al.* 1990; Crémer 1990; Koike 1987). However, people will use their judgement and collaborate only if there is mutual trust between them and the organization; this trust will be developed not because it is 'nice to have' or because people like to be 'nurtured', but for hard reasons of viability. 'The fast-moving organization will rise or fall on the trust the remaining cadre of managers places on those in the front line' (Peters 1994).

This need is likely to resolve some of the dilemmas in current practice, not by shifting from command and control to care and connection but by redesigning employment contracts in such a way that they take account of the need for 'studied trust' (Sabel 1993). This trust is not a global feeling of warmth or affection but rather the conscious regulation of one person's dependence on another, which cannot be taken for granted but must be produced and sustained on the basis of credible commitments made between people who are working together whether they are in the same division, the same organization and the same culture, or are independent long-term or short-term contractors. Managing credible commitment contracts is likely to be a primary responsibility for managers, and best practice is already preparing them for this through courses on partnership behaviour and understanding interdependence.

GILLIAN STAMP
BRUNEL UNIVERSITY

Further reading

(References cited in the text marked *)

* Aoki. M., Gustafsson. B. and Williamson, O. (eds) (1994) *The Firm as a Nexus of Treaties*, London: Sage Publications. (Examination of how firms operate as a series of relationships.)
* Argyris, C. (1991) 'Teaching smart people how to learn', *Harvard Business Review* May–June. (Article on learning processes by a leading thinker on organization behaviour.)
  Barham, K. and Devine, M. (1990) *The Quest for the International Manager: A Survey of Global Human Resource Strategies*, London: Economist Intelligence Unit. (Report on a survey of human resources practices, with strong implications for management development.)
* Benton, P. (1990) *Riding the Whirlwind*, Oxford: Blackwell. (Benton's book examines the challenges facing managers in the modern business environment, and how they need to adapt their attitudes and skills.)
  Briggs Myers, L. (1983) *Consulting Psychologists*, Palo Alto, CA: Press Inc. (Work on psychological development for managers.)
  Capra, F. (1983) *The Turning Point: Science, Society and the Rising Culture*, New York: Bantam Books. (A good, readable work on changes in society, with implications for business and managers.)
  Cox, T. (1993) *Cultural Diversity in Organizations*, San Francisco, CA: Berrett-Koehler. (Good recent study of diversity within organizations and companies.)
* Crémer, J. (1990) 'Common knowledge and the coordination of economic activities', in M. Aoki, B. Gustafsson and O. Williamson (eds), *The Firm as a Nexus of Treaties*, London: Sage Publications. (A look at how knowledge can be used as a form of linkage within organizations.)
* Freedman, D.H. (1992) 'Is management still a science?', *Harvard Business Review* November–December. (A critique of current attitudes to management and management training.)
  Garratt, B. (1987) *The Learning Organisation*, London: Fontana Collins. (In-depth definition and study of learning organizations.)
* Geus, A. de (1988) 'Planning and learning', *Harvard Business Review* March–April. (Excellent article which explains the concept of the learning organization, by a former director of planning with Royal Dutch Shell.)
* Golzen, G. (1994) 'Communicating with a super-highway code', *Observer* July. (Article on how the spread of technology is also spreading personal control over it.)
* Hampden-Turner, C. and Trompenaars, F. (1993) *The Seven Cultures of Capitalism*, London: Piatkus. (Already becoming a classic, this book looks at different global cultures of management and argues for a more holistic view.)
  Handy, C. (1992) 'Balancing corporate power: a new federalist paper', *Harvard Business Review* November–December. (Article from a European perspective looking at new models of corporate control.)
  Handy, C. (1994) *The Empty Raincoat*, London: Hutchinson. (One of Handy's best-known works, looking at paradigms of managerial work.)
* Isaac, D.J. and O'Connor, B. (1975) 'Discontinuity theory of psychological development', *Human Relations* 29 (1): 41–61. (Examines theories of psychological development for managers.)
* Jaques, E. (1976) *A General Theory of Bureaucracy*, London: Heinemann. (Study of hierarchies and controls.)
* Jaques, E. (1989) *Requisite Organisation*, Cason Hall & Co. (Proposes new ways of ordering organizations and management tasks.)
* Jaques, E. (1990) *Creativity and Work*, Madison, CT: International Universities Press Inc. (Book which emphasizes the creative nature of management.)
  Jaques, E. and Clement, S. (1991) *Executive Leadership*, Oxford: Blackwell. (Another study of management and the managerial task.)
* Kelly, K. (1994) *Out of Control: The New Biology of Machines*, London: Fourth Estate. (The author postulates that technology systems in corporations may be hampering managerial control.)
* Koike, K. (1987) 'Skill formation systems, a Thai–Japan comparison', *Journal of the Japanese and International Economies* 1: 408–40. (An article which looks at differences in development in learning between Japan and Thailand.)
* Linde, C. (1993) *Reflections on Workplace Learning*, Palo Alto, CA: Palo Alto Research Center. (A look at the nature of knowledge in a managerial context.)
* Lorenz, C. (1994) *Financial Times* July. (Article by a leading management journalist on the changing nature of the management task.)
  Mant, A. (1993) *Leaders We Deserve*, Canberra: Australian Commission for the Future. (Report from Australia highlighting changes in management development.)

* Megginson, D. and Pedlar, M. (1992) *Self Develop-ment: A Facilitators Guide*, London: McGraw-Hill. (Leading work on self-development for managers.)

* Parikh, J. (1991) *Managing Your Self*, Oxford: Blackwell. (Parikh contrasts Eastern and Western paradigms of management and calls for a more holistic view.)

Parikh, J., Neubauer, F. and Lank, A. (1994) *Intuition – The New Frontier of Management*, Oxford: Blackwell. (An insightful look into the role of intuition in management.)

* Peters, T. (1989) *The Tom Peters Experience – The Customer Revolution*, London: BBC Enterprises. (Training video by one of the leading management gurus from the USA.)

* Peters, T. (1994) 'Trust in the front line', Palo Alto, CA: TPG Communications (syndicated in newspapers including the *Independent on Sunday*). (Peters argues for greater decentralization and more intuitive, hands-on management.)

Reich, R. (1991) *The Work of Nations*, New York: Simon & Schuster. (Widely-cited work on management and business cultures by the current US Secretary of Labor.)

* Sabel, C.F. (1993) 'Studied trust: building new forms of cooperation in a volatile economy', *Human Relations* 46 (9): 1133–70. (An examination of theories of relationship building.)

* Saunders, A. (1984) 'The use of model building and scenario construction in management development programmes', paper presented at the Fourth International Symposium on Forecasting at London Business School. (Paper stemming from the author's experiences with British Gas.)

* Saunders, A. (1992) 'Executive development in CIS countries – the experience of British Gas', paper presented at AMED Conference at London Business School. (A look at British Gas management programmes in the former Soviet Union.)

Senge, P. M. (1990) *The Fifth Discipline: The Art and Practice of the Learning Organization*, New York: Doubleday. (Now famous work on organization management.)

* Spender, J.C. (1989) *Industry Recipes: The Nature and Sources of Managerial Judgement*, Oxford: Blackwell. (A look at the critical faculty of managerial judgement.)

* Stamp, G. (1989) 'The individual, the organization and the path to mutual appreciation', *Personnel Management* July. (The author writes on the relationship between individuals and organizations.)

* Stamp, G. and Isaac, D.J. (1990) *A Matrix of Working Relationships*, Uxbridge: Brunel University. (A detailed look at relationship matrixes within organizations.)

* Zuboff, S. (1992) 'The search for the organization of tomorrow', *Fortune* April. (Somewhat speculative article which looks at business organization in the future.)

See also: CAREERS; HUMAN RESOURCE MANAGEMENT; ORGANIZATION BEHAVIOUR

Related topics in the IEBM: EXECUTIVE TRAINING; GLOBALIZATION; MANAGEMENT EDUCATION, FUTURE OF; MANAGEMENT EDUCATION AND DEVELOPMENT, INTERNATIONAL; MANAGEMENT IN SOUTH AFRICA; MBA CONCEPT; ORGANIZATION DEVELOPMENT; ORGANIZATIONAL LEARNING; ORGANIZATIONAL PERFORMANCE

Motivation and satisfaction

Overview

Work motivation and work satisfaction continue to be major topics in organizational behaviour because it is assumed that they exert important influence on action and behaviour in organizations. However, as opposed to so called *hard factors* like hardware, costs and benefits etc. motivation and satisfaction are often called *soft factors*. These soft factors constitute hidden realities in organizations which can hardly be measured in a direct, objective way, nor do research results concerning these soft factors provide much evidence for a relationship between motivation/satisfaction and action responsive behaviour. Despite these not very encouraging results work motivation and satisfaction are regarded as very important human resources in organizations, resources one should not only take seriously with respect to organizational culture and identity but should also take into account for managing effectiveness and quality. The article gives a short description of well-known work motivation theories which can roughly be divided into process and content-orientated types. Theories of both types show considerable limitations, especially with respect to the prediction of action from motivation. Therefore, several modern theories of motivation, volition and action are introduced. Some of them are distant ('distal') others are close ('proximal') to action, and some of them allow for a link between the content, process and action perpectives of motivation. It appears that these integrative approaches to motivation and volition of goal-directed action may substantially contribute to a better prediction of work satisfaction, employee withdrawal or job performance. Work satisfaction is the most prominent result of work motivation. Its research continues to produce a large number of results relevant to organizational behaviour. However, while work satisfaction is one of the most frequently studied concepts in industrial and organizational psychology it is also suffering from critical shortcomings, especially from its mostly theory-free concepts and from the very large proportions of satisfied workers and employees in almost all studies since the early 1970s up to the point that more and more researchers speak of an artificial character of these results. To overcome these problems a new dynamic view of work satisfaction is presented by introducing a model of different forms of work satisfaction. This model distinguishes forms ('qualities') and not quantities of work satisfaction and allows researchers to explain the processes behind these forms. By differentiating forms of satisfaction (e.g. resigned, stabilized, progressive) this model permits an understanding of the high percentages of satisfied employees in earlier studies. Finally, the entry points to future directions and discusses the implications of work motivation and work satisfaction with regard to work design and organizational development.

1 Introduction

Motivation continues to be a major topic of industrial and organizational psychology as well as of organizational behaviour. Motivational concepts, such as expectancy, valence, goal setting, self-efficacy and self-regulation are often used to analyse and to predict a wide range of individual expressions relevant to organizations like attitudes, perceptions, emotions and behaviour, for example work satisfaction, stress and burn-out, withdrawal, turnover, absenteeism, performance, etc. Progress in work motivation research has led to a wide scope of results about both the factors and the processes of behaviour and performance in the workplace. This growth of new ideas and concepts from allied fields of psychology is accompanied by a growing concern that influential theories and concepts of work motivation are not sufficient for addressing relevant problems in organizations. For example, to date, prevailing theories of work motivation are not able to predict why knowledge is not transformed into action in many areas of organizations, they have not substantially contributed to distinctions between the effects of motivational processes in simple and complex jobs, the effects of motivation in the interrelationship between work and non-work, or how motivation operates in work groups and teams etc. Therefore, the aim of this chapter is not only to summarize past research. Rather, new developments will briefly be presented that show promising advances in work motivation theory.

2 Work motivation: past research and further developments

Work motivation theories were commonly categorized into two groups: content and process oriented types of theories (Campbell and Pritchard 1976) (see ORGANIZATION BEHAVIOUR). The first group of theories (see Figure 1) asks for central human needs and motives such as basic or higher order needs, human needs for existence, relatedness and growth, motivational and hygiene factors, intrinsic or extrinsic motivation responsible for particular aspects of work like feedback or autonomy that are supposed to relate to motivation, while the second group of theories (see Figure 1) deals with process variables that are posited to determine cognitive choices for action. Theories of the process type (e.g. the Value-Instrumentality-Expectancy [VIE] model or achievement motivation theories) concentrate on the process of choice for behaviour and emphasize two determinants of

choice: the individuals expectation and the individual's subjective valuation of expected consequences associated with alternative actions at the workplace (For more detailed overviews on work motivation theories see Campbell and Pritchard 1976; Kanfer 1990, 1992; Kleinbeck, Quast, Thierry and Häcker 1990; Locke and Henne 1986).

Both content and process oriented theories of work motivation show considerable limitations. With respect to content theories it seems impossible to identify needs and motives that are universal, i.e. most important for everybody and effective independent of time and space. Moreover, the impact of constructs from content theories on behaviour and performance is frequently spurious and indirect. What is lacking is a specification of mechanisms for how specific needs and motives lead to specific behaviour. However, while one should assume that these mechanisms are subject to process theories, these theories actually focus almost exclusively on the cognitive processes underlying choice, instead of any other part of the motivational process. For example, by calculating the expectancy (subjective probability) of various possible outcomes (e.g. good or bad quality from a certain work behaviour, the instrumentality (subjective correlation) of these outcomes for subsequent outcomes (e.g. reduction of income because of slower high quality work or positive feedback from supervisors for fewer inaccuracies and errors), and finally the valence (subjective value) of these second order outcomes in terms of Vroom's VIE-model, one cannot expect to predict actual behaviour because the VIE model is solely able to determine motivational states for certain behaviour, or the most probable choice for a certain effort. Hence, the process theories that dominated the published industrial/organizational literature during the 1960s and 1970s posit almost entirely cognitive choice or cognitive evaluation models based on the expectancy or the equity-inequity theory.

Since it is common to evaluate and compare theories of work motivation by the extent to which they are able to correctly predict job behaviour and job performance one should be concerned by the fact that content as well as

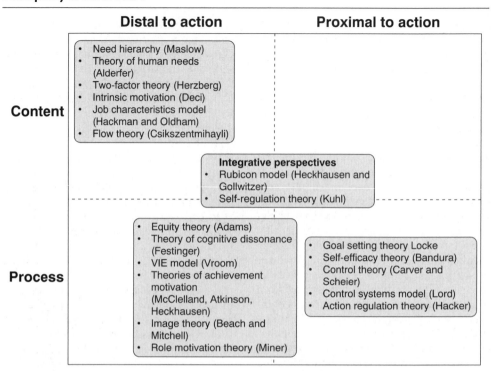

Figure 1 Taxonomy of (work) motivation theories

most of the process theories of work motivation are more or less 'distal', i.e. distant from action. Therefore, we clustered (work) motivation theories and their associated constructs by their 'proximity' (i.e. closeness) to action according to Kanfer (1992) and by the traditional distinction into content responsive process theories. The taxonomy in Figure 1 reveals that modern (work) motivation theories are proximal to action as well as typically process oriented. They comprise goals and self-regulation as dominant constructs.

Among these theories the goal-setting paradigm, established by Locke and his colleagues (e.g. Locke and Latham 1991), dominated work motivation research during the past two decades. According to this theory, goals influence task behaviour through four mechanisms: directing attention, mobilizing on-task effort, encouraging task persistence, and facilitating strategy development. The theory states two important goal attributes: intensity and content. While goal intensity refers to the strength of goals in terms of

importance and commitment, goal content is directed towards aspects like difficulty, specifity, and complexity. Most research has focused on the effects of goal content in the sense of difficulty and specifity by comparing a non-specific goal assignment condition like 'do your best' with a specific and difficult assigned goal condition such as 'process x orders this week without any mistakes'. Because numerous studies show support for the positive impact of difficult and specific goal assignment on work performance, goal setting techniques enjoy widespread use in industry. However, studies examining an assignment of goals and feedback cycles indicate that the combination of moderately difficult and specific goals along with performance feedback and, therefore, an enhancement of self-regulation, resulted in higher levels of performance than either goal assignment or feedback alone.

Self-regulation and control theories relevant to work motivation have been posited by Bandura (1986), Carver and Scheier (1990),

Hacker (1985) and Lord (e.g. Lord and Levy 1994). Even though these theories are rooted in different traditions of psychology they have some basic theoretical and methodological positions in common e.g. goal orientation or (cybernetic) self-regulation modelling. Altogether, these different theories provide complementary, rather than contradictory, perspectives. Empirical research testing predictions of work behaviour and work performance derived from these models have generally been supportive. Nevertheless, none of these theories take an integrative perspective in linking distal constructs like needs, motives, dispositions, flow, affect, etc. and proximal constructs of work motivation like goal setting and self-regulation.

Recent developments in (work) motivation theory try this link. Important attempts are the theory of self-regulation by Kuhl (e.g. 1992) and the Rubicon-model by Heckhausen and Gollwitzer (e.g. Gollwitzer, 1990). The latter considers the motivational/volitional phases of (work) behaviour, while the models mentioned before (see Figure 1) are restricted to one or two specific phases. The Rubicon-model connects motivation with volition and distinguishes between four phases of motivation/volition with respect to action: weighing (first motivational or choice phase), planning (volitional phase), acting (volitional phase), and evaluating (second motivational phase). Crossing the Rubicon means bridging the gap between weighing and willing, between motivation and intention (see Figure 2). The model combines distal aspects of motivation as well as proximal constructs of goal setting and self-regulation. Therefore, despite the fact that little is known so far about the validity of the Rubicon-model for predicting job behaviour and performance, it appears that this integrative approach, or 'frame' approach, to motivation and volition of goal-directed action may substantially contribute to a better prediction of work satisfaction, employee withdrawal or job performance (see Kanfer 1990, 1992).

3 Work satisfaction: its level, causes and consequences

Over 20 years ago Locke (1976) identified over 3,000 studies dealing with different aspects of work satisfaction. There are several reasons for this strong interest in work satisfaction. These reasons include the presumed ease of measurement with paper-and-pencil devices and the common-sense linkages between satisfaction and other main-stream concepts like leadership, performance, reward systems, group processes (see LEADERSHIP; PERFORMANCE APPRAISAL) and so forth. Even though in recent years there has been a cutback in the total amount of papers, research activities dealing with work satisfaction are still quite alive today. Work satisfaction continues to be a major area of interest in the study of industrial and organizational psychology. Indeed, a large proportion of the empirically oriented articles published in this

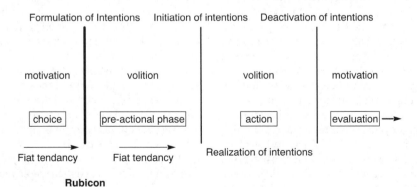

Figure 2 Rubicon model of action releasing by Heckhausen and Gollwitzer
Source: Adapted from Gollwitzer (1990)

field include work satisfaction as an independent, dependent and/or moderating variable.

Although a large body of research has been accumulated there are still major shortcomings in work satisfaction research. One of these is the loose coupling between its few theories and its measurement. It is a paradoxical situation that while work satisfaction is one of the most frequently studied concepts in industrial and organizational psychology, it is also one of the most theory-free concepts in the field. That is, a 'pleasurable or positive emotional state resulting from the appraisal of one's job or job experience' (Locke, 1976: 1300) or 'the achievement of one's job values in the work situation results in the pleasurable emotional state known as *job satisfaction*' (Locke and Henne 1986: 21) is understood as being work satisfaction. Most of the definitions of work satisfaction are quite similar, although they may differ in the conceptualization of what they conceive as 'achievement of ones job values'.

Work satisfaction research can be grouped into three major categories: causes and moderators of (dis)satisfaction, consequences of (dis)satisfaction, and surveys of (dis)satisfaction levels. Some of the *causes and moderators* related to work satisfaction have included conditions like job quality, union membership, autonomy, job tension, flexible working hours as well as personal variables like realistic expectations, self-esteem, value importance, or sex differences (see Locke and Henne 1986). With respect to the *consequences* of work satisfaction research has focused on some commonly presumed forms of job behaviour like turnover and absenteeism and on job performance. Meta-analytic studies on turnover and absenteeism clarify that one cannot expect a strong relationship between work satisfaction and turnover as well as absenteeism because correlations with work satisfaction do not reach beyond -0.40 for absenteeism (e.g. Hackett and Guion 1985) and for turnover (e.g. Williams and Hazer 1986). Apart from this overall result the relationship between satisfaction and absenteeism is generally much less consistent than that reported between satisfaction and turnover, and both

turnover and absenteeism research with respect to work satisfaction are affected by some severe methodological problems related to the conceptualization and measurement of absenteeism and turnover (e.g. Hackett and Guion 1985). Moreover, various meta-analyses confirm a rather weak relationship between attitude-based measurement of work satisfaction and different kinds of job performance. Correlations from these studies range between 0.20 and 0.40 (e.g. Iaffaldano and Muchinsky 1985; Petty, McGee and Cavendar 1984). Therefore, these results from work satisfaction research can give only small support to the solution of practical problems like work redesign or other kinds of intervention in organizations (see GROUPS AND TEAMS).

Most studies apparently continue to use relatively atheoretical attitude-based measurement questionnaires to estimate work satisfaction. The wide acceptance of this method of work satisfaction measurement and its abundant use in research – almost to the extent that some researchers see moments of a 'throw-away' variable (Staw 1984: 630) – is one side of the problem. The other side is the high rate of survey studies on satisfaction levels which find a large proportion of satisfied employees, including blue collar workers. These results seem to be widespread, that means they seem to be especially independent of population and culture. For example, Weaver (1980) found 88 per cent satisfied among 4,709 persons between 1972 and 1978. Szilagyi and Wallace (1983) could refer to results of 81 per cent (minimal) up to 92 per cent (maximal) satisfied in a period between 1958 and 1980. These examples are not typical for the US. Similar results can be stated independent of country and the specific type of attitude measurement. In Germany for example several studies found more than 80 per cent or even 90 per cent satisfied among fulltime employed blue and white collar workers. Our inspection of a large amount of work satisfaction research since 1980 offers no interpretation for a decreasing tendency of these large proportions of satisfied employees in recent studies.

What are the reasons for this impressive proportion of satisfied persons? Since the early 1990s quite a few researchers have become more and more critical and speak about the artificial character of traditional work satisfaction results. Taking into account diverse negative conditions stated in many studies, as for example accidents, insufficient work conditions and unsatisfactory work environment, high division of labour, absenteeism or turnover, positive work satisfaction results in these studies seem superficial. This is not only true for industry, trade or administration. Similar high percentages of satisfied personnel were also calculated in health care settings like hospitals (see Büssing 1992).

4 A dynamic view of work satisfaction

Work satisfaction research traditionally uses attitude based measurement, as mentioned before. This method of conceptualization and measurement is criticized for several reasons. Three of these reasons will be outlined. First, despite the large amount of studies, we do not find many reliable results for determinants and consequences of work satisfaction (see above). Second, attitude-based measurement of work satisfaction is prone to distortion by several well-known factors, i.e. social desirability or cognitive dissonance. Third, attitude-based measurement of work satisfaction does not consider situational factors like, for example, controllability of work conditions. However, it is hard to tell much about the amount of variance explained by the person or by the situation at work by evaluating work satisfaction results gained by attitude measurement. Therefore, critics point to the important validity problems of traditional attitude measurement of work satisfaction which supposedly supports artificially high work satisfaction rating patterns mentioned above (see Büssing 1992). With respect to these critics, it seems to be insufficient to measure work satisfaction in quantitative terms, e.g. the *amount* of satisfaction. Instead, work satisfaction should be looked at in terms of quality, which seems to be a much more important perspective.

One basic point in this debate is, among others, that traditional concepts of work satisfaction and related methods of measurement are not dynamic. Another point touches the person–environment problem. Work satisfaction has to be interpreted as a product of an interaction process between a person and his/her work situation. Variables like control or power to regulate this interaction and, therefore, possibilities to influence the work situation play an important role. Therefore, we should see work satisfaction in a different, qualitative perspective. In this light, work satisfaction is not merely a product but rather a result of a complex process. Thus, we have to consider changes of the work situation by a person depending on his or her situational control and motives/aspirations on the one hand, as well as changes of the person and his or her motives/aspirations etc. on the other.

In recent studies by Büssing and his work group (Büssing 1992; Büssing, Bissels, Fuchs and Perrar 1997) a dynamic concept of work satisfaction was analysed that was first suggested by Bruggemann in 1974 (see Bruggemann, Groskurth and Ulich 1975). This concept depends on an interactional view of work satisfaction as shown in Figure 3 and distinguishes between different forms of work satisfaction. The model consists of three basic variables: (1) differences between actual value of the work situation and nominal value of the person, (2) changes in level of aspiration, (3) problem-solving behaviour (coping). According to this model, work satisfaction is developed in a three-step process. Depending on the match between expectations, needs, and motives on the one hand, and the work situation on the other, a person builds up a certain degree of satisfaction or dissatisfaction with her/his job. Moreover, depending on subsequent changes in levels of aspirations of satisfaction or dissatisfaction and subsequent problem-solving behaviour (coping), six forms of work satisfaction or dissatisfaction can be developed.

In case of diffuse dissatisfaction at the first step – i.e. in case of differences between actual values of the work situation and nominal values of the person – the model suggests two different outcomes for the level of aspiration

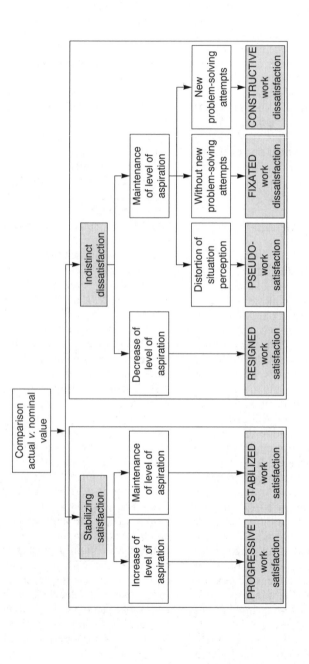

Figure 3 Different forms of work satisfaction
Source: Bruggemann *et al.* (1975: 135)

according to the second step: decrease or maintenance. A decrease in the level of aspiration should lead to what is called resigned work satisfaction. This form of work satisfaction is supported by results from qualitative interviews which find quite a lot of people adjusting themselves to work situations either by decreasing or by shifting their motivation and aspirations to non-work activities. The high percentage of satisfied workers often found in this kind of study can be claimed to be caused by a more or less large proportion of workers who have passively shifted their aspirations away from their work situation. Therefore, according to this model, resigned satisfaction is only one out of three forms of work satisfaction and must be distinguished from these other forms.

Maintaining one's level of aspiration in case of diffuse work dissatisfaction can result in three forms, of which the pseudo-work satisfaction is the most critical one. For further research, this form was disregarded as the authors doubted the possibility of finding valid systems. The model suggests that the two other forms, fixated and constructive work dissatisfaction, are closely connected to coping options, coping resources and problem-solving behaviour a person can mobilize. These coping options, coping resources and problem-solving behavioural patterns are relevant variables at the third step to developing different forms of work satisfaction. Both fixated and constructive work dissatisfaction seem to depend largely upon the well-known coping options in organizations like control or social support at work in one respect, and what in short form is called coping resources – abilities to use these options – in another respect. Constructive dissatisfaction is obviously a counterpart to resigned work satisfaction.

Table 1: Different forms of work satisfaction

Progressive work satisfaction: A person feels satisfied with the work. By increasing the level of aspiration a person tries to achieve an even higher level of satisfaction. Therefore, a 'creative dissatisfaction' with respect to some aspects of the work situation can be an integral part of this form.

Stabilized work satisfaction: A person feels satisfied with the job, but is motivated to maintain the level of aspiration and the pleasurable state of satisfaction. An increase of the level of aspiration is concentrated on other areas of life because of little work incentives.

Resigned work satisfaction: A person feels indistinct work dissatisfaction and decreases the level of aspiration in order to adapt to negative aspects of the work situation on a lower level. By decreasing the level of aspiration a person is able to achieve a positive state of satisfaction again.

Constructive work dissatisfaction: A person feels dissatisfied with the job. While maintaining the level of aspiration a person tries to master the situation by problem solving attempts on the basis of sufficient frustration tolerance. Moreover, available action concepts supply goal orientation and motivation for altering the work situation.

Fixated work dissatisfaction: A person feels dissatisfied with the job. Maintaining the level of aspiration, a person does not try to master the situation by problem-solving attempts. Frustration tolerance makes defence mechanisms necessary for efforts at problem solving seem beyond any possibility. Therefore, the individual gets stuck with its problems and pathological developments cannot be excluded.

Pseudo-work satisfaction: A person feels dissatisfied with the job. Facing unsolvable problems or frustrating conditions at work and maintaining one's level of aspiration, for example because of a specific achievement motivation or because of strong social norms, a distorted perception or a denial of the negative work situation may result in pseudo-work satisfaction.

The model of different forms of work satisfaction points to the insufficiency of a merely quantitative view, even if this view is complex and comprises several facets, like colleagues, work conditions, work content, promotion, and so on. Therefore, the work satisfaction we usually think of and traditionally measure has to be differentiated. Being represented by the forms of stabilized, progressive and resigned work satisfaction on the one hand, and fixated as well as constructive dissatisfaction on the other, work (dis)satisfaction can no longer be merely regarded and used as a product; rather it has to be seen as a process-oriented outcome of a person-work-interaction largely dependent upon mechanisms of control to regulate this interaction.

So far, studies employing the model of different forms of work satisfaction have led to three important results. First, forms of work satisfaction can be validly differentiated according to the model; while the proportions of forms in various samples may vary, several forms (e.g. resigned satisfied, constructive dissatisfied) emerge consistently across studies (Büssing 1992; Büssing et al. 1997). Second, forms of work satisfaction depend on situational factors, such as controllability at the workplace by the workers, rather than on dispositional factors. Third, forms of work satisfaction do not function like psychological types, i.e. they are not stable over a longer period of time. Even though this model is a most important advance in work satisfaction research, little is known about antecedents and consequences connected with the different forms of work satisfaction. Moreover, so far there has been a lack of substantial research comparing this model with other prevailing concepts of work satisfaction.

5 Future directions in work motivation and work satisfaction

Work motivation research is rapidly giving way to new, more complex theories that are proximal to action and that incorporate elements of older theories, especially distal approaches to motivation. The sharp distinction between various theories is therefore reduced, and although models of human need, intrinsic motivation or motivators and dissatisfiers may provide relatively poor predictions of job behaviour and job performance, few researchers would argue that dispositions play no role in sophisticated models of motivation and volition. Many of the recent advances in work motivation research have been more theoretical. Though they clearly aid our understanding of behaviour and performance at the workplace, we lack unique and specific applications of modern motivation and volition theory to the workplace. These applications are needed and they will be instrumental in developing better understanding and predictions of work attitudes (e.g. satisfaction), job and organizational behaviour (e.g. turnover, absenteeism, commitment, stress reactions, burn-out) and job performance constructs.

It seems, since expectancy and equity theory had their important impact on work satisfaction in the 1960s and 1970s, that we find only a limited influence of new developments in work motivation theory on work satisfaction. However, progress in the area of work satisfaction is dependent on advances in work motivation research. This is especially true for the dynamic model of different forms of work satisfaction presented in this chapter. It is a person-environment model which assumes a close interdependency between motivational and dispositional variables on the one hand, and situational determinants at the workplace on the other. Especially if one takes into account a distribution of explained variance of work satisfaction according to Arvey, Carter and Buerkley (1991) where 40 to 60 per cent of work satisfaction variance is associated with situational factors, 10 to 30 per cent account for person factors and about 10 to 20 per cent of the variance is explained by interactive elements.

The dynamic view provided by the model of different forms of work satisfaction is of special importance to work in complex organizations which offer many opportunities for rapid socio-technical changes, and therefore demand a high level of adaptability and dynamic behaviour from the structural and technical system as well as from the personnel. That is, differentiation of forms of work satisfaction could have a considerable impact on organizational studies and their consequences.Workers and employees could not just be divided into a large group of satisfied and a small group of dissatisfied as is the custom; therefore, comfortable work satisfaction figures could not easily underline and justify organizational structures, internal selection and promotion procedures, production processes, and so on. Taking the idea of different forms of work satisfaction seriously, new perspectives for processes in organizational behaviour and conflict should be questioned. First of all, the large group of resigned satisfied in all studies so far should be regarded as strong evidence for a failed person-work-interaction, and, therefore, they should be considered necessary reasons to doubt and not to justify, among other things, aspects of organizational structures, internal selection and promotion procedures as well as production processes. According to the results of various studies, and especially the ones of our longitudinal study, we must take into account that resigned work satisfaction is related to reduced well-being, performance and effort as well as resistance to change on the person side and – at least – less adaptability and performance on the organization side (see PERFORMANCE APPRAISAL). Moreover, another remarkable aspect on the persons side of resigned satisfaction seem to be reduced goal-setting activities and, closely connected, a restricted professional development and job socialization.

Resigned work satisfaction is one variable of influence noteworthy with respect to studies in organizations; constructive work dissatisfaction is another. Turnover and absenteeism appear to be only one side of this form of work dissatisfaction, and probably not even the most important one. Another side seems to be activities and engagement in organizational change as well as a higher potential for differential goal setting of the constructive dissatisfied. Therefore, this group should not be – in a one-sided perspective – considered a dangerous potential factor for organizational conflict; instead the critical potential of this group should be emphasized with regard to organizational change, adaptability, and improvement. A transformation of this potential into organizational change on one side and personal development on the other requires new strategies of conflict management in organizations and a willingness to broaden control at work, as well as participation in decision making for the personnel.

More than the other forms of work satisfaction or dissatisfaction, resigned work satisfaction and constructive work dissatisfaction might have remarkable influence on performance and intervention efficiency in organizations. We know by now that resigned satisfaction is closely connected with reduced effort and willingness to adapt to new and complex demands; however, such demands are typical of the daily situation in complex organizations. Resigned work satisfaction seems to be an obstacle to changes inside an organization and to the adaptability of an organization to external challenges. Hence, resigned work satisfaction is supposed to be connected to growing rates of absenteeism, notification of illness and a reduced quality of work. Therefore, management and other responsible groups in organizations should take a close look at the group of resigned satisfied personnel to prevent negative effects on performance and quality. Managing resigned work satisfaction seems to be a difficult task, as resignation is not a matter of short periods of time. It seems to be more a consequence of a longer lasting conflict between individual aspirations on the one hand and organizational structures as well as specific working conditions on the other. Therefore, the cost-effectiveness of strategies regarding resigned work satisfaction are not to be questioned: prevention seems to be a far more cost-effective strategy than subsequent changes or correction for dealing with it.

In cases of constructive dissatisfaction of their personnel, organizations are faced with a quite different problem. As mentioned before, constructive work dissatisfaction might become a background for growth in organizations as constructive dissatisfied personnel tend to show sufficient frustration tolerance and action concepts for new problem-solving attempts. Because of this, their goal orientation and motivation for altering the negative work situation has to become an integral part of an organizational change planned, or at least supported, by the management. Offering this group of personnel an opportunity to discuss critical issues in quality circles or autonomous teams might give them a higher feeling of control over the situation and might encourage their motivation for job control and their willingness to change. Aside from intrinsic task-related aspects like job control, organizations are also faced with corresponding and growing aspirations with respect to extrinsic features of the job like, for example, pay, promotion or flexible as well as reduced working time. Dealing with constructive work dissatisfaction is generally costly; there are structural, task related and extrinsic monetary expenses. But by meeting and regulating these problems an organization prepares itself for better outcomes and higher quality. As a result, organizations should look at constructive work dissatisfaction in a positive manner. This form of dissatisfaction demands new and intelligent problem solving attempts by the personnel as well as by the organization. Organizations need highly motivated and qualified personnel to work with growing standards of work processes and technology. Organizations which fail to meet these growing challenges are prone to fail in meeting other challenges of their sociotechnical system as well.

Both work motivation and work satisfaction cannot be restricted to the workplace. On leaving an office or a plant, employees and workers do not leave their work experiences, their thoughts, motivation and feelings behind. Indeed, we find a strong interrelationsship between life at work and life outside work with respect to work motivation and work satisfaction. This interrelationship includes constructs that are central to motivation and satisfaction, like changes in levels of aspiration or goal-setting (Büssing 1995). Not only for intervention and organizational design, but also for purposes of analysis, the work–nonwork interdependency has to be integrated into work motivation and work satisfaction research.

ANDRÉ BÜSSING
TECHNICAL UNIVERSITY OF MUNICH

Further reading

(References cited in the text marked *)

* Arvey, R.D., Carter, G.W. and Buerkley, D.K. (1991). 'Job satisfaction: Dispositional and situational influences', in C.L. Cooper & I.T. Robertson (eds.), *International Review of Industrial and Organizational Psychology* (Vol. 6: 359–84). Chichester: Wiley. (This review article provides competing explanations for antecedent conditions of job satisfaction by dispositions or situations.)

* Bandura, A. (1986). *Social Foundations of Thought and Action: A Social Cognitive Theory.* Englewood Cliffs, NJ: Prentice Hall. (This book gives an impressive presentation of Banduras work on social cognitive theory which is most important for work motivation theorizing and experimentation.)

* Bruggemann, A., Groskurth, P. and Ulich, E. (1975) *Arbeitszufriedenheit [Job satisfaction].* Bern: Huber. (This book is a classic on work satisfaction in the German language.)

* Büssing, A. (1992) 'A dynamic view of job satisfaction', *Work & Stress*, 6 (3): 239–59. (This article introduces the model of different forms of work satisfaction and presents evidence from questionnaire data.)

* Büssing, A. (1995) 'Work and leisure. A study of subjective concepts in health care', in M. Hagberg, F. Hofmann, U. Stößel and G. Westlander (eds.), *Occupational Health for Health Care Workers*, Landsberg: Ecomed. (This article is dealing with subjective concepts of the relationship between work and leisure with respect to well-being and work satisfaction.)

Büssing, A. and Bissels, T. (1997) 'Different forms of work satisfaction: concept and preliminary evidence from qualitative research', *Journal of Organizational Behaviour* (in press). (Deals with the model of different forms of work satisfaction in conceptual detail and offers illustrative cases.)

* Büssing, A., Bissels, T., Fuchs, V. and Perrar, K.-M. (1997) 'A dynamic model of work satisfaction: Qualitative approaches', in *Human Relations* (in press). (Presents evidence for the model of different forms of work satisfaction from various qualitative methods.)

* Campbell, J.P. and Pritchard, R.D. (1976) 'Motivation theory in industrial and organizational psychology', in M.D. Dunnette (ed.), *Handbook of Industrial and Organizational Psychology.* New York: Wiley. (This handbook article

is a classic of work motivation theory in industrial and organizational psychology.)

* Carver, C.S. and Scheier, M.F. (1990) 'Principles of self-regulation: Action and emotion' in E.T. Higgins and R.M. Sorrentino (eds.), *Handbook of motivation and cognition*, (Vol. 2: 2–52). New York: Guilford Press. (This handbook article gives a comprehensive overview over the principles of self-regulation with regard to emotion, motivation and action.)

* Gollwitzer, P.M. (1990) 'Action phases and mindsets' in E.T. Higgins and R.M. Sorrentino (eds.), *Handbook of Motivation and Cognition*, (Vol. 2: 53–92). New York: Guilford Press. (This handbook article gives a comprehensive overview over the rubicon model of motivation, volition and action.)

* Hacker, W. (1985) 'Activity: A fruitful concept in industrial psychology', in M. Frese and J. Sabini (eds.), *Goal Directed Behavior: The Concept of Action in Psychology*, Hillsdale, NJ: Erlbaum. (This article gives a good overview of the influential work on action theory by the German work psychologist Hacker.)

* Hackett, R.D. and Guion, R.M. (1985) 'A reevaluation of the absenteism–job satisfaction relationship', in *Organizational Behavior and Human Decision Processes*, 35 (3): 340–81. (This article presents a meta-analytic sight of the absenteeism job satisfaction relationship.)

* Iaffaldano, M.T. and Muchinsky, P.M. (1985) 'Job satisfaction and job performance: A meta analysis', *Psychological Bulletin*, 97 (2): 251–73. (This article gives a meta-analytic view of the job satisfaction and job performance relationship.)

* Kanfer, R. (1990) 'Motivation theory and industrial and organizational psychology', in M.D. Dunnette and L.M. Hough (eds.), *Handbook of Industrial and Organizational Psychology* (2nd edition, vol. 1: 75–170), Palo Alto, Cal.: Consulting Psychologists Press. (This handbook article provides an extensive summary of work motivation theory and its application in industrial and organizational psychology.)

* Kanfer, R. (1992) 'Work motivation: New directions in theory and research', in C.L. Cooper and I.T. Robertson (eds.), *International Review of Industrial and Organizational Psychology* (Vol. 7: 1–53) Chichester: Wiley. (This review article provides a sophisticated and integral view of work motivation theory and its application in industrial and organizational psychology.)

* Kleinbeck, U., Quast, H.-H., Thierry, H. and Haecker, H. (1990) *Work Motivation*, Hillsdale,

NJ: Erlbaum. (This reader contains articles that provide for an advanced treatment of central concepts in work motivation and satisfaction.)

* Kuhl, J. (1992) 'A theory of self-regulation: Action versus state orientation, self-discrimination, and some applications', *Applied Psychology* 41 (2): 97–129. (This lead article gives a comprehensive overview over Kuhl's action and state orientation theory of motivation, volition and action including examples for application.)

* Locke, E.A. (1976) 'The nature and causes of job satisfaction', in M.D. Dunnette (ed.), *Handbook of Industrial and Organizational Psychology*. New York: Wiley. (This article is a classic on job satisfaction theory and method.)

* Locke, E.A. and Henne, D. (1986) 'Work motivation theories', in C.L. Cooper and I.T. Robertson (eds.), *International Review of Industrial and Organizational Psychology* (Vol. 1: 1–35), Chichester: Wiley. (This review article provides a thorough overview on work motivation theories including information on job satisfaction.)

* Locke, E.A. and Latham. G.P. (1991) *A Theory of Goal Setting and Task Performance*, New York: Prentice-Hall. (This book provides for a comprehensive presentation of goal-setting theory and research. It is central to work motivation and satisfaction.)

* Lord, R.G. and Levy, P.E.. (1994) 'Moving from cognition to action: A control theory perspective', *Applied Psychology* 43 (4): 335–98. (This lead article gives a sophisticated overview of theoretical issues regarding the relationship between cognition and action; it is of particular interest to work motivation and satisfaction.)

* Petty, M.M., McGee, G.W. and Cavender, J.W. (1984) 'A meta analysis of the relationships between individual job satisfaction and individual performance', *Academy of Management Review* 9 (4): 712–21. (This article gives a meta-analytic view of the job satisfaction and job performance relationship.)

* Staw, B.W. (1984) 'Organizational behavior: A review and reformulation of the field's outcome variables', *Annual Review of Psychology* 35: 627–66. (This review article is a concise summary of organizational behaviour research with strong relations to work motivation and work satisfaction research)

* Weaver, C.V. (1980) 'Job satisfaction in the United States in the 1970', *Journal of Applied Psychology* 65 (3): 364–67. (This article gives an overview of the state of job satisfaction in the US; it can be regarded as representative up to the present day.)

* Williams, L.J. and Hazer, J.T. (1986) 'Antecedents and consequences of satisfaction and commitment in turnover models: A reanalysis using latent variable structural equation methods', *Journal of Applied Psychology* 71 (2): 219–31. (This article gives a meta-analytic view of the function of job satisfaction in turnover models.)

See also: FLEXIBILITY; GROUPS AND TEAMS; HUMAN RESOURCE MANAGEMENT; HUMAN RESOURCE MANAGEMENT, INTERNATIONAL; INDUSTRIAL AND LABOUR RELATIONS; LEADERSHIP; OCCUPATIONAL PSYCHOLOGY; ORGANIZATION BEHAVIOUR; PERFORMANCE APPRAISAL; PRODUCTIVITY; TAYLOR, F.W.; WORK AND LEISURE

Related topics in the IEBM: COGNITION; CONFLICT AND POLITICS; INNOVATION AND CHANGE; ORGANIZATION DEVELOPMENT; ORGANIZATION STRUCTURE

Payment systems

Overview

A payment system can be defined as a method or means for determining employee wages or salary. As such, it represents a central mechanism for the regulation of the employment relationship. For management the importance of payment systems is reflected in what often appears to be an ongoing preoccupation with finding new and better ways of paying employees.

Given that pay is one of the defining characteristics of the employment relationship and consequently a powerful means for the exercise of managerial control, the pursuit of ever more 'efficient and effective' techniques for its allocation is hardly surprising. However, as a technique for the pursuit of managerial control, payment systems have been subject to countervailing workplace pressures exercised by employees, work groups and their representatives. Indeed, a well-established academic literature has developed which has sought to analyse the degeneration or decay of the payment systems in terms of competing managerial and employee interests as they relate to the operation of such systems.

It is clear, therefore, that payment systems cannot simply be perceived as structural artefacts captured through passive categorization or by simple typologies. Rather, a payment system is a process which raises questions about the exercise of choice, implementation, operation and impact. The discussion here seeks to focus on payment systems in this broader sense, reviewing the forms taken by the different methods of pay allocation but also addressing issues related to their functioning.

The discussion is divided into three main parts. The first identifies the principles underlying different payment systems and then distinguishes the range of payment systems available. The second reviews trends in the use of payment systems over the years, concentrating on the variable use of different systems in the post-war period and concluding with an evaluation of current usage. The third looks at payment systems in practice, assessing the relationship between payment systems, managerial goals and organizational context as well as evaluating their operation and impact upon employees, managers and organizations.

First, however, it is important to distinguish between payment systems and other terms, such as pay structure and pay level. These terms are often closely associated with payment systems but are analytically distinct. A pay or grading structure is a rational ordering of jobs, often devised through the application of job evaluation and usually reflecting the different roles and the contributions they make to the organization. A pay level is the amount or rate received by an employee and is usually generated through the combined operation of payment systems and structures. While closely related to the development and operation of payment systems, the techniques associated with the establishment of pay structures or setting of pay levels are analytically separate and not dealt with here.

1 Types of payment system

Payment systems can be distinguished broadly on the basis of two founding principles: time and performance. Payment by time can be dealt with relatively briefly as in structural and administrative terms it can be characterized in relatively simple terms. Employees are paid for being at work for a stipulated period of time. Their pay is expressed on the basis of these time-periods as an hourly rate, a weekly wage or an annual salary. Payment by time is sometimes

Unit of performance		
	Individual	*Collective*
Type of performance		
Output	Payment by results	Measured daywork
	Commission	Team bonus
	Individual bonus	Profit sharing
	Performance-related pay	Gainsharing
Input	Skill/knowledge-based pay	Employee share ownership
	Merit pay	

Figure 1 Types of performance-based payment systems

supplemented by performance-based pay while the time-rate may also be used as the fall-back provision for an employee failing to meet a minimum standard of performance.

The notion of pay for performance, in contrast, embraces a wide range of different payment systems. These systems might be seen to vary according to the unit of performance (the individual or the collective) and the nature of the performance (whether in the form of input or output) (Purcell 1992). These two dimensions provide the basis for Figure 1, which sets out the main performance-based payment systems.

Individual output systems

Payment-by-results

In the context of this discussion, payment-by-results is used to refer to the traditional forms of individual shop-floor incentive. At their simplest they emerge as piecework schemes. Under 'straight' piecework a fixed price per unit is paid while under 'differential' piecework a standard price is paid up to a certain level of output and a higher price for any production thereafter. Alternatively, payment-by-results is sometimes based on time. Thus, under standard time systems earnings are dependent on the difference between the time taken to complete a job and an allowed time. The fixing of prices and times is based upon work study which in turn comprises method study (a critical evaluation of the 'best' way to perform a job) and work measurement (the time taken to perform the task in relation to the rate of effort expended in so doing).

Commission

This is a payment system operating primarily among sales staff, which pays a proportion of sales value. Commission may be the only source of income or may operate in combination with a basic salary and/or individual bonuses.

Individual bonuses

Individual bonuses are non-consolidated payments given in addition to base pay which are related to the achievement of particular targets. These targets may be linked to financial indicators, the completion of a project or other features of individual performance. Individual bonuses are particularly significant at the executive level where pay is linked to financial indicators such as earnings per share, return on capital, cash flow and profit. These schemes are often self-regulating to a certain extent in that the achievement of certain targets will often lead automatically to a given bonus payment.

Performance-related pay

The term performance-related pay is used in this discussion specifically to refer to a type of payment system which links pay to quantitative individual objectives or targets. However, it differs from a individual bonus scheme in a number of respects. First, performance-related pay is based on a wide range of potential objectives. These may include those of a financial or budgetary kind but may also cover a range of more focused, personalized targets – completing a particular report, improving the individual's attendance record and so on. Second, the link between performance and pay is not mechanistic: an appraisal will take place and some overall evaluation made which then gives rise to a pay increase. Finally, payment made under this system takes a number of different forms. A given level of performance, for example, may result in a number of increments on a fixed scale; a percentage increase within a salary range (that is, a grade without fixed increments); or a number of 'range' points available once the maximum of a service-based scale has been reached.

Collective output systems

Measured daywork

This type of scheme pays a particular time-rate or bonus to a group of workers, usually manual, within or across a plant for a fixed and predetermined level of performance. Under a variation of this system, stepped measured daywork, employees can choose to maintain one of a series of performance levels, each attracting a different rate of pay.

Team bonuses

Team bonus schemes operate in a similar way to those based on the individual in that a lump sum payment is generated for the achievement of specified, quantitative targets. Clearly the difference lies in the fact that the targets are based upon a team performance, with the bonus paid to all members. A range of targets can be used: under an existing scheme at a brewing company production workers are given a bonus for every barrel of beer produced above a threshold of 10,750 per week, while Parcel Force staff in the sorting office are given a team bonus related to the number of parcels sorted against target.

Profit sharing

Generally, profit-sharing schemes can be divided into those which provide a cash bonus from profits and those which distribute the profit bonus in the form of shares. In the UK a further distinction can be made between approved and non-approved: under the former, tax concessions are granted to those schemes meeting particular structural and administrative requirements (see PROFIT SHARING AND EMPLOYEE SHAREHOLDING SCHEMES).

Gainsharing

These schemes generate a collective bonus based on the workforce performance of a plant or enterprise. The bonus might be linked to volume of output, as under the Scanlon Plan, or to sales value, as under the Rucker Plan. Such schemes involve establishing a baseline ratio between volume or sales value and wage bill costs, with any subsequent improvement in that ratio giving rise to a bonus.

Individual input systems

Skill-based pay

Skill- or competency-based pay is a payment system in which pay progression depends upon the acquisition by individual employees of new skills. It is very unusual for pay progression to depend solely on skill acquisition and these schemes are usually underpinned by general pay increases. The form taken by the pay progression may be a lump payment related to the completion of specific skill modules or may take place within a particular pay structure which allows movement through a grade as skills are acquired.

Merit pay

Merit pay schemes share many of the characteristics of the performance-related pay schemes described above. They also rely on an appraisal of the individual's performance, leading to some general evaluation and linked, in turn, to different forms of pay progression. The major difference lies in the nature of the performance criteria used. Under merit schemes employees are evaluated according to what they bring to the job, in particular what specified behavioural traits or characteristics. These 'softer', more qualitative criteria may include factors such as leadership and planning skills, personal motivation, dependability, initiative or flexibility.

Although a distinction has been made between appraisal-related schemes based on quantitative output factors and those based on qualitative input factors, some organizations do use a combination of both. In other words, an employee's pay increase will be dependent on performance as rated against a series of qualitative and quantitative criteria. Moreover, recent usage of the term 'individual performance-related pay' has tended to cover those payment systems which involve an appraisal of the employee on the basis of input, output or a combination of both.

Collective input systems

Employee stock ownership plans
Although employee stock ownership plans (ESOPs) relate more to the issue of ownership and control, they still deserve a mention within this section. They represent a collective input payment system in that capital is brought into the organization, usually in the form of a bank loan, to be used to buy shares in the company for the employees. The employees receive their reward in the form of the distributed shares and the resultant dividends.

The schemes outlined above should not be seen as mutually exclusive. Organizations sometimes employ a number of systems, using individual, group or company performance pay underpinned by time-based rates to achieve a variety of managerial goals. It is equally apparent, however, that there are variations in practice across both time and space in the use of different systems.

2 Trends in payment systems

In evaluating trends in the use of payment systems within an international context it is important to avoid generalization. The use of different payment systems is strongly linked to the national, cultural context. In part this can be related to different patterns of industrialization within countries. The emergence of specific types of payment system can be linked with the pace and process of industrial development as well as with particular industries and product markets. Clearly there are marked variations between countries in these respects.

In addition, the value and viability of a payment system can be linked to the fundamental values, attitudes and beliefs underpinning a national culture. As Trompenaars points out:

> The internationalisation of business life requires more knowledge of cultural patterns. Pay for performance, for example, can work out well in the culture where the author has had most training: the USA, the Netherlands and the UK. In more collectivist cultures like France, Germany and large parts of Asia it may not be so successful, at least not in the Anglo-Saxon versions of pay for performance.
> (Trompenaars 1993: 4–5)

This section draws extensively upon more accessible material related to trends in British and US payment systems. However, wherever possible attention is drawn to the available evidence on variable developments in continental Europe and Japan which highlight national and cultural differences in payment system practices.

Early developments

The centrality of the 'cash nexus' to employment and the work relationship enables the operation of payment systems to be traced back over many years. There are, as noted, relatively few cardinal principles for payment systems and, although there is considerable scope for variation in technical detail, only a limited number of major schemes available for use at any given time. As a result it is possible to find evidence, albeit patchy, of many of the systems identified appearing at different points over the years.

Early forms of pay incentive can be traced back to the most ancient of civilizations. A number of writers have drawn attention to the use of crude output-based incentives by the Babylonians. In 604 bc weavers of cloth were paid in food, the quantity granted depending on the spinner or weaver's output (Peach and Wren 1992). In succeeding centuries, however, prevailing doctrines and philosophies mitigated against the development of incentives and placed much more emphasis on payment systems based on input. The Roman concept of *verum pretium* or 'true cost' attempted to pay at the approximate cost of the labour input. This approach was succeeded by the Church's notion of a *justum pretium* or 'just price' based on the cost of production. This in turn led to a disapproval of excess profiteering and similarly proved an unfavourable climate for incentives (Peach and Wren 1992).

The early Middle Ages and feudalism provided some examples of piecework systems for agricultural workers (Marriot 1961). Yet it was not until the later Middle Ages that such schemes were more in evidence. Lipson (Marriot 1961), for example, highlights the importance of the shift in the ownership of work materials for changing pay practice. In the 'household' and 'guild' stages of the Middle Ages work material was owned by the householder or artisan and the product was used in the producers' own households. During the 'domestic' stages, spanning the sixteenth to the eighteenth centuries, work was still carried out in the home but the material was supplied by an employer. This transformed the artisan into a wage earner 'paid by piece'. It was the next stage, industrialization and the emergence of factory work, however, which proved to be the turning point in the development of payment systems.

Early industrialization and into the twentieth century

The emergence of industrial society marked a fundamental shift in the organization of production and necessitated the development of new types of payment systems. The nature of the payment systems which developed was also intimately related to the changing economic philosophies which underpinned the process of industrialization.

Industrialization removed producers from the home and placed them directly under the discipline of the factory and the authority of the employer. In general terms, stable means of payment became essential as a way of facilitating managerial control. However, the character of the system of payment used at the time was also related to prevailing assumptions about what motivated employees and stimulated productivity. Peach and Wren point to the shift in economic thinking that paved the way for the broader use of incentives. Thus the view of the mercantilist economists, that 'it is a well known fact . . . that scarcity, to a certain degree, promotes industry . . . (with a reduction of wages in the woolen manufacture [being] a blessing and advantage, and no real injury to the poor . . .)' (1992: 10), gave way to Adam Smith's views, which were much more in line with the assumptions underlying incentives that higher performance reward levels are linked to higher performance. As Smith noted: 'The liberal reward of labour . . . increases the industry of the common people. The wages of labour are the encouragement of industry . . . [and] where wages are high, accordingly we shall always find the workmen more active, diligent and expeditious than where they are low' (1969: 214).

There is evidence of piecework schemes in the early stages of industrialization and the end of the eighteenth century and the early nineteenth century among cotton mill workers, engineers, coal miners and other craftworkers. In the late nineteenth century there was some extension of proportional piecework, particularly in outworking employment, in clothing, footwear and in the light metal trades. Yet, as Gospel notes: 'most nineteenth century workers were paid by time-rates with levels fixed according to customary rates' (1992: 23).

It was not until almost century later, however, with the work of F.W. Taylor in the USA, that the next major development in payment systems took place (see TAYLOR, F.W.). The distinctive contribution made by Taylor at the turn of the century, reflected in the term scientific management, lay in the systematic evaluation of work for pay purposes. Rather than relying on intuitive assessment, Taylor devised work measurement techniques – method and time study – which laid the foundation for the many individual and group payment-by-results discussed earlier.

The spread of Taylorist principles from the USA to the UK and Continental Europe was slow and uneven. However, after the First World War and into the 1920s, the use of Taylorite payment schemes in the UK began to increase, especially in the engineering industry. In the 1930s the spread of piecework schemes was given a further boost by the Bedaux system, which was seen to further reinforce the 'scientific' character of work measurement by dealing 'more effectively' than Taylor with employee rest and relaxation in the workplace.

By early 1917, some one-third of engineering firms had piecework schemes. By 1926 the proportion of fitters on such schemes was 51 per cent and by 1938 this had risen to 62 per cent, with over 80 per cent of turners and machinists receiving payment-by-results in some form (Gospel 1992).

Although the spread of piecework systems remained the dominant trend throughout the nineteenth and into the twentieth centuries, two qualifications must be made. First, at least in the UK, the majority of workers remained on time-based payment systems (Gospel 1992). Second, payment systems other than those based on time or piecework were in evidence although to a far lesser degree.

Merit and other appraisal-based schemes were not unknown. Performance appraisal was used by Robert Owen in his New Lanark textile mills in the early 1800s as means of recognizing the worthy and encouraging the less able to improve. Performance pay was apparent among teachers in the early 1860s. Meanwhile Schloss highlights the use of qualitative and as opposed to quantitative performance indicators as the basis for pay in the later 1890s. He notes:

In some instances, in which a fixed or minimum is supplemented by a premium, the amount of this premium is made dependent upon the qualitative, rather than the quantitative, character of the work done, as exhibited in the avoidance of waste, in the perfection of results obtained and so on. Examples of this method will be found in the workings of the railways. Engine drivers in many cases are paid a premium based upon the economy effected in the use of coal and oil, also rewards based upon the punctuality with which their trains are run and receive special additions to their regular pay in respect of special zeal and discretion by which accidents are avoided.

(Schloss 1898: 106)

Although precise information as to the extent and coverage of such merit pay schemes is not available, the development of another payment system emerging during this period, that of profit sharing, has been more precisely charted (see PROFIT SHARING AND EMPLOYEE SHAREHOLDING SCHEMES). Early evidence of profit-sharing schemes can be found in 1775 espoused by the French economist A.R.J. Turgot and introduced by the Parisian housemaking firm *Maison Leclaire*. Such a system was held to encourage workers to produce more at less cost because they would share in the profits (Peach and Wren 1992). However, it was at the end of the nineteenth century that the practice of profit sharing became more widespread: in the USA over thirty firms had schemes by 1887 while in the UK also there was growing interest in the 1880s and 1890s, followed by renewed interest just before and after the First World War.

The immediate post-war decades

In the immediate post-war years the spread of piecework continued. For example, the proportion of workers in British manufacturing covered by such a system increased from one-third in 1938 to some 40 per cent in 1951 (Behrend 1959). This rise was related to a combination of labour and product market pressures. Behrend (1959), for example, when noting that around one-third of the firms she studied in the mid-1950s were changing their payment systems, stated that there were various reasons for taking action, including: the need to meet increasing foreign competition; the need to meet an increasing number of orders; the desire to lower labour costs; and the necessity of meeting trade union pressure for a shorter working week.

The continued and growing significance of piecework stimulated a preoccupation among policy makers and researchers with the operation of this type of payment system. In general terms there was not only a progressive disillusionment with such an approach to pay but a growing realization by some observers that it was at the root of many of the difficulties being experienced by the British economy during the 1960s and 1970s. A number of pay developments occurring during this period can be seen as a backlash against piecework.

A range of studies began to highlight some of the difficulties linked to the use of piecework which served to distort its operation (Lupton 1963). They highlight the importance of work group behaviour and, in particular, the development of workplace norms in providing some informal regulation of the way schemes worked and in undermining their incentive effect. It was apparent in some cases, for example, that workers were deliberately controlling output to below attainable levels using quotas and social sanctions in order to stabilize earnings. In other instances the 'tightness' or 'looseness' of times influenced whether employees were prepared to put in the effort to earn the bonus.

Other studies concentrated more on the impact piecework was having on wage levels and structures. The 1968 report by the British National Board for Prices and Incomes (NBPI), *Payment by Results Systems*, concluded that piecework caused 'excessive' wage drift, as times were loosened or prices negotiated upwards, and a proliferation of wage anomalies. It reported an average rate of drift of 4 per cent per year and noted that: 'Earnings gains from drift are necessarily so unequally distributed between different groups of workers that they induce anomalies in pay which, to be remedied, require selective increases in minimum wages or earnings' (NBPI 1968: 69).

The NBPI findings were echoed in the Donovan Commission's analysis of British industrial relations, where piecework was not only perceived to have generated wage drift but also to be linked to high-level unofficial industrial action, to extensive restrictive practices and to the general 'informality, fragmentation and autonomy' of workplace industrial relations.

The concerns highlighted by this work were reflected in a number of developments in the academic, policy-making and practitioner spheres. On the academic front the assumptions underlying scientific management, in particular the belief that workers are driven primarily by economic considerations, began to be challenged. The pioneering work carried out at the Hawthorne plant in the USA highlighted the importance of social considerations in workplace relations which in turn spawned the more sophisticated 'human relations' analysis of the behavioural scientists. Based on the view that employees had a number of 'needs' to be met in the workplace they placed a far greater emphasis on non-monetary rather than monetary reward (see HUMAN RESOURCE MANAGEMENT).

For policy makers in the UK efforts to deal with wage drift and the difficulties associated with piecework were reflected in attempts at reform through a third party agency, the Commission on Industrial Relations (CIR) between 1969 and 1975 and the Advisory Conciliation and Arbitration Service (ACAS). Although these bodies functioned in very different ways their general remit to 'improve industrial relations' inevitably led to a shared concern with the state of payment systems. As a matter of course CIR procedural cases involved an analysis of the organization's payment system (CIR 1974) while ACAS has continued to provide in-depth advice on the design and implementation of payment systems. In addition, however, successive governments used incomes policies with a concomitant encouragement of productivity agreements as a means of providing a 'sound' basis for payment increases. These agreements were in part designed to address some of the rigidities of workplace employment practices by providing pay increases in return for greater worker flexibility.

Finally, there were also a number of developments in payment systems at the level of practice. First, there was some evidence to suggest that interest in merit pay schemes was increasing. Marriot (1961: 79), writing in the late 1950s, draws upon a British Institute of Management observation: 'In both the United

States and the United Kingdom there appears to be a growing body of thought in favour of a bonus scheme known as ''merit rating'' or the ''individual assessment bonus scheme'' '.

Marriot also refers to a US survey of 231 firms which found that over half (52 per cent) were using merit rating and a smaller survey carried out five years later which showed a lower but still significant proportion of companies (40 per cent) using such a system. However, what was most striking about this type of scheme was the manner in which the focus of attention was upon its application to private sector manual, supervisory and clerical workers. This can be accounted for by the fact that these schemes were seen at the time as an effective means of addressing some of the weaknesses in the piecework system. Thus merit was seen as means of rewarding workers who could not be covered by piecework and as a way of encouraging greater flexibility and more attention to quality by including them as assessed factors.

Second, measured daywork schemes achieved a degree of popularity at this time. These schemes were generally seen as providing a much greater degree of managerial control of paybill costs than traditional piecework schemes (NBPI 1968).

Third, the disillusionment with manual incentives led some organizations to move away from such systems altogether (Smith 1989). This gradual disillusionment does not mark the end of managerial interest in innovatory payment systems but a decisive shift in the focus of attention as organizations moved into the 1980s.

Current patterns

Research suggests that there have been recent changes in British payment systems. For example, an ACAS survey (1988) found that almost 40 per cent of the companies covered had altered their payment systems within the past three years. Further consideration of these changes suggests a number of trends and issues which are distinct and distinguishable from those in the past. First, there has been increased debate surrounding the use of individual performance-related and merit-based

payment systems rather than traditional payment-by-results schemes. Moreover, this debate has led to a significant extension of the coverage of these systems. Second, and partly related, the focus of interest among policy makers and practitioners in the development of 'improved' payment systems appears to have shifted from manual to non-manual staff. As Smith (1989: 61) succinctly puts it: 'the only group not experiencing the changes brought about by the reward culture are shopfloor employees'. Third, there has been some growth of interest in collective bonuses, especially share ownership schemes. However, the proportion of the workforce covered by these schemes is still relatively limited. These three trends are each considered in turn.

A review of the prescriptive and much of the analytical literature highlights the extent to which individual performance-related and merit-based payment schemes have dominated recent debates. The literature has by no means been united on the viability and value of these individual schemes. It is noteworthy, for example, that some of the higher profile 'management gurus' have been critical. Deming refers to merit pay as a 'deadly disease' and includes as one of his fourteen points the 'elimination of such schemes'. Moss Kanter is critical of the assumption that individuals alone are responsible for their performance and suggests that the establishment of a 'fair' link between pay and performance is difficult for many professional groups. Peters, meanwhile, places greater store on group-based schemes as opposed to individual incentives as a means of improving organizational performance.

This scepticism has been balanced, however, by alternative opinion leaders strongly supportive of individual performance pay. The Confederation of British Industry (CBI: 1988), for instance, has called for payment systems which 'focus on the performance and needs of individuals'. Equally significant, Conservative governments of the 1980s have encouraged this type of performance system both generally and especially in relation to the public service sector. As the Citizen's Charter (1991: 35) states: 'Pay systems in the public sector need to make a regular and direct link between a person's contribution to the standards of the service provided and his or her reward'.

Setting aside the rhetoric, it is clear that individual performance-related or merit-based schemes have increased in popularity. A recent Policy Studies Institute survey (Casey *et al.* 1991) highlighted the spread of such schemes in two regional labour markets and concluded that 'an individualization of pay has indeed taken place'.

With regard to the shift in focus, evidence indicates that performance pay schemes are spreading down through the organization and across different sectors of the economy. While the British Workplace Industrial Relations Survey (WIRS) in 1990 (Millward *et al.* 1992), found that merit pay was prevalent at the higher reaches of organizations, operating in 40 per cent of establishments for middle and senior managers, it was still found in around one-third (31 per cent) of establishments for clerical and administrative staff and even in just under one-quarter (21 per cent) of establishments for skilled manual workers. The emergence of merit pay across sectors can be seen in its growing significance within the public service sector. An Institute of Personnel Management/National Economic Development Office survey indicated that although less prevalent than in the private sector, merit pay was still found in 37 per cent of public sector organizations. Certainly for around 500,000 non-industrial civil servants, for whom the government has a direct influence over pay determination, assessed performance is now integral to salary progression for most grades. In local government approximately one-half of local authorities have such schemes, at present primarily for the more senior managerial levels.

The spread of individual performance pay needs to be qualified in a number of respects however. First, time-based payment systems or time-rates remain the single most important basis of payment in the UK. The ACAS survey (1988), for instance, indicates that in two-thirds of their organizations time was the basis for pay for at least some of their employees. Moreover, while all merit increases are spreading, in many organizations merit increases are still underpinned by general across-the-board increases; in other words, merit pay remains 'the icing on the cake'.

Second, and as stressed above, it is important to point out that there are significant cross-cultural variations in the popularity of individual performance-related pay. This is reflected in the variable incidence of performance-related pay. In the USA, for example, such schemes are widely used. A survey conducted by the American Association in 1986 found that practically all the firms in their sample relied on annual performance appraisals by supervisors for input when making pay decisions. This was confirmed by a major survey of salary practices in large companies which showed that 80 per cent of the companies had merit plans, with over 50 per cent saying that at least 95 per cent of their employees received merit increases. Drawing upon a survey of employers across Continental Europe, it has also stressed the popularity of performance-related pay in France, Italy and Switzerland while noting that it remains marginal in Scandanavian countries.

There is evidence to suggest that individual performance-related pay is increasing in popularity in Japan: such schemes have been introduced for Japanese employees at Nissan, Fujitsu and Honda. However, team or group bonuses have traditionally been more in evidence. As Alston (1982) notes: 'The American rule is: make the individual happy and the group will become more productive. The group exists for the good of the individual. In Japan, the individual exists for the group. The whole is more important than its parts'.

Third, and confirming earlier observations, it is apparent that new approaches to performance pay have not reached the shop-floor to any greater degree. The WIRS (Millward *et al.* 1992) indicates that merit pay is far less likely to be found among manual than non-manual staff. Such schemes were found in well under one-quarter of establishments for skilled, semi-skilled and unskilled manual workers. This figure is put into perspective by developments in other countries and particularly in France where a recent Ministry of Labour survey found that over 50 per cent of employees in around 1,300 companies had a merit element in their pay packets (IDS Focus 1991).

The one innovative development in payment systems for manual workers which can be classified as an appraisal-based payment scheme is that relating to skills acquisition. These skill-based schemes appear prevalent particularly on 'greenfield sites', where their introduction is linked to the drive for flexibility in the context of technological change. Recently they appear to have increased in popularity, with around 100 British companies now operating them. Pay is also closely related to skill in Germany.

Yet the more general the withering away of incentives, particularly of an individual or work group kind, highlighted by Smith is reflected in a number of general and more specific trends. The proportion of manual workers on incentive bonuses has fallen significantly over the last decade. The New Earnings Survey indicates that the proportion of male manual workers on bonuses fell from 46.5 per cent in 1984 to 33.6 per cent in 1992 while for female manual workers the fall was from 35.3 per cent to 25.5 per cent. Those surveys which allow for a disaggregation of individual bonuses suggest that while a core of companies retain some form of piecework these schemes are now relatively limited in their coverage. The ACAS survey (1988), for example, found that only 12 per cent of establishments had piecework schemes in place.

The incidence of collective bonuses or more specifically those covering the plant or company also remains relatively low. It is certainly apparent that interest in profit sharing and employee share ownership has grown in the 1980s. The Inland Revenue, for example, estimated that nearly 1.3 million employees received shares or share offers in 1991/92. Since statutory support was provided for such schemes some 2.9 million employees in total have received shares or options worth at the outset some £10.3 billion. Yet ACAS found only 13 per cent of establishments with collective bonus schemes while the Policy Studies Institute (Casey *et al.* 1991) finds very little evidence of their more general growth.

This review of trends has highlighted how the interest shown by policy makers and practitioners in different types of payment system has shifted across space and, more particularly, time. Given this changing picture, the question which inevitably arises is why have there been such shifts of interest over the years. This question is considered below.

3 Payment systems in practice

The selection of payment systems

There have been three broad schools of thought on the selection of payment systems, crudely reflecting more general theories on the nature of decision making within organizations. The first has seen selection as part of a rational and considered decision-making process; the second has viewed choice as being driven by *ad hoc*, immediate and reactive managerial concerns; the third has suggested that approaches have been governed less by a direct and tangible means–end relationship and more by the pursuit of ideological goals and the manipulation of social reality and meanings.

The view that payment systems are selected on the basis of a rational and considered decision-making process has attracted the most attention in recent years. It has informed much of the prescriptive literature and is underpinned by the theoretical proposition that payment system effectiveness is likely to be enhanced if this route is taken. In its most sophisticated form, this approach has merged within contingency theory. Lupton and Gowler (1969) have suggested that the selection of payment systems should involve: identification of pay goals; an awareness of the type of payment systems likely to further such goals; and an appreciation of the appropriateness of such payment systems given the organization's circumstances. Success in the choice of payment systems is therefore viewed as crucially dependent upon a degree of congruence between organizational circumstances and needs.

This approach has been developed over the years. Many standard lists are available distinguishing the range of managerial goals which might be furthered through the use of different payment systems. Bowey and Thorpe (1986), for example, note that these goals include: recognizing what jobs deserve; retaining good employees; responding to demands for more pay; motivating high performance; encouraging interest in promotion; encouraging loyalty to the company; rewarding merit generally; and compensating for adverse conditions.

More recently this range of goals has been extended to include the use of payment systems to change organizational culture. Individual merit pay, for example, is often presented as a way of developing a performance-driven culture given the manner in which it is associated with procedures which encourage changes in employee and management attitudes, values and beliefs. For example, performance pay played an important part in the restructuring of the Italian firm Fiat in the late 1980s. There are, however, differences of view on the role payment systems can play in the process of organizational change. It is interesting that two of the leading human resource management texts take views which are diametrically opposed in this respect: Fombrun *et al.* (1984) see pay as a lead technique promoting change: '[rewards are] the most underutilized tool for driving organizational performance', while Beer *et al.* (1984) suggest that: 'The design of a compensation system should rarely be the place to start in solving business and human resource problems'.

Attention has also been drawn to the range of internal and external contingent circumstances influencing the appropriateness of any given payment system for a particular company. Thus technology, product and labour markets have all been highlighted as significant in this respect. Again the range of influential circumstances has been extended by commentators to include, as noted above, national culture.

More significant has been the manner in which general contingency has re-emerged within the context of human resource management literature and, in particular, in that strain which has placed emphasis on 'fit'. Payment systems have figured prominently

here. It has been suggested that different compensations and benefits are appropriate for different business life cycle stages: Fombrun *et al.* (1984) relate the character of payment systems to product market strategy and organizational structure, while others highlight the difference in approaches to reward according to whether the business strategy is one of innovation, quality enhancement or cost reduction.

The extent to which these relationships are reflected in actual practice remains open to some debate. Certainly the Milkovich (1991) inquiry suggested that US organizations were concentrating on seeking to relate pay more directly to their specific context. None the less, the second school of thought on the selection of payment systems is founded on the suggestion that choice in many organizations is based more on *ad hoc* reactions to immediate pressures than on systematic and rational considerations.

Recent developments again on the introduction of individual performance-related pay, particularly in the UK, have been seen to lend some support to such a view. Contrasting reactive British practice with the more considered US approach to the selection of pay systems, it has been suggested that the move to merit pay in the mid- to late 1980s was primarily driven by short-term cost considerations. The financial difficulties faced by companies at this time simply encouraged a desperate search for greater control over the paybill, achieved through a more selective targeting of pay increases on the basis of perceived merit as a replacement for indiscriminate across-the-board general pay increases.

In addition, there is evidence to suggest that a number of organizations were 'bounced into' the use of merit pay to deal with short-term labour market pressures at this time. It is noteworthy, for example, that in a survey of local authorities the most common reason for introducing such a system was to address recruitment and retention needs. Despite textbook strictures that such needs are best dealt with through pay levels rather than merit pay, which is after all designed to reward individual performance not labour market position, some companies were left with a sophisticated pay bureaucracy to deal with what emerged as a cyclical problem.

The general fickleness of organizations in relation to their payment systems may also be indicative of a tendency to 'sway in the wind'. This is not a new development. A survey of US firms in the late 1950s found that almost 80 per cent would like to change or modify their payment system, even though in the same survey 96 per cent indicated that they considered their systems 'successful' (Crandall 1962). More recently an observer commenting on moves towards performance pay in the UK noted: 'Many organizations were vague and uncertain about what they were doing; some were swept away by the mood of the times' (IDS Focus 1991: 6).

While the basis for the selection of a payment system using these contrasting approaches is clearly very different, they are nonetheless both founded upon the assumption of relatively uncontested and straightforward managerial decision making. The final school of thought challenges such an assumption. Given differences of interest and power within organizations, not only between management and employee but within these respective and far from unified groups, the selection of a payment system becomes a complex, ongoing process. Behrend (1959), for instance, has argued that management support for manual worker incentives, based on a set of unverified and arguably unverifiable beliefs, served to support covertly the ideology of managerial authority. More recently, emphasis was placed on the importance of symbolism as a means of explaining the continuation of productivity-based payment systems which according to any objective criteria had failed to meet managerial goals.

The view that the selection of payment systems can be seen as rooted in a contested decision-making process perhaps accounts for the finding that the way in which payment systems are introduced is a more likely predictor of success than their substantive character. The importance attached to widespread managerial and employee involvement in the design and implementation of payment systems has been reflected in a number of prescriptive texts. The ACAS advisory booklet on appraisal-related schemes, for example, states that:

> Adequate resources and suitable training should be provided; Employers should consult with managers, employees and their representatives before appraisal related pay is introduced; All employees involved must receive full and clear information about how the scheme will operate'
>
> (ACAS 1990: 7)

If the selection of a payment system is perceived as a contested, political process the articulation of competing interests is unlikely to cease when a choice is made. This school of thought can therefore be extended to provide useful insights into the way payment systems operate and the impact they are likely to have on employees and managers.

Operation

The managerial difficulties associated with the implementation and operation of payment systems are well recognized. As Beer *et al.* note:

> The design and management of reward systems constitute one of the most difficult HRM tasks for the general manager. Of the . . . major policy areas in HRM, this is where we find the greatest contradiction between the promise of theory and the reality of implementation.
>
> (Beer *et al.* 1984: 113)

As already noted, these difficulties have been highlighted by a long-standing research interest in the decay of payment systems. Some of the pioneering workplace studies carried out by Whyte, Lupton and Brown focused on the degeneration of such payment systems in the context of ongoing social, political and economic pressures. The notion of control was central to these and other studies. Pay as a managerial control system has to be continuously administered. This administration provides the focus for the ongoing articulation and pursuit of distinctive managerial and employee interests which can distort the original goals held for pay.

Yet it has not been essential to adopt such an analytical framework to appreciate the operational difficulties associated with payment systems. Prescriptive texts routinely suggest the need to review the operation of a payment every three to five years to ensure that original managerial intentions continue to be met. This advice is based on a recognition that there is inevitably a degree of managerial discretion in the operation of payment systems which over time may undermine initial purpose. The extent to which such monitoring and review actually takes place is more questionable, not least because organizations are often unsure of what their intentions are.

An appreciation of operational difficulties has also been reflected in the observation that there is 'no such thing as a perfect payment system' and in the standard presentation of the advantages and disadvantages associated with different payment systems. Table 1 provides an overview of the kind of managerial pros and cons associated with three of the main payment systems discussed.

This kind of 'advantages' and 'disadvantages' table indicates the structural strengths and weakness of different types of payment systems, usually from a managerial perspective. Academic research has added to this kind of listing exercise by examining how, when and where such operational difficulties and benefits might arise in practice. In recent years, for example, the popularity of individual performance-related pay has encouraged concentration on its associated problems.

Attention has been drawn to the difficulties of setting performance criteria. Thus over one-third of the respondents in a survey of almost 600 British organizations conducted by Wyatt (1990) suggested that 'targets were hard to establish', while just under one-third indicated that there was 'no objective measure'. The difficulty of establishing meaningful and consistent criteria has been particularly apparent for certain occupational groups in, for instance, caring professions where performance is not easily measured in quantifiable terms. Problems have similarly been identified in the assessment of employee performance for pay purposes. Inconsistent

Table 1 Pay systems: advantages and disadvantages

Pay system	Pros	Cons
Time-rates	Simple and cheap to administer efficiency/productivity	Limited incentive effect to improve
	Easy for employees to understand	
	Predictable/stable pattern of earnings for employees	
	Few industrial disputes	
Piecework	High incentive effort	Tendency to wage drift
	Lower manufacturing costs per unit, spreading overheads	Problem of rewarding indirect staff
	Higher earnings for operatives	Problems of rate fixing
	Less supervision needed	Quality suffers
		Resistance to improved work methods
Merit pay	Way of rewarding qualities not rewarded by other pay systems	Difficulties in setting performance criteria for some staff
	Methods of bonus for employeess' work not easily measured	Subject in assessment
		Undermines team work

and subjective assessments have been seen to undermine the credibility of schemes while tensions have arisen between appraisal for pay and staff development purposes. Finally, the process of actually linking appraisal to pay has been plagued by difficulties associated with limited financial resources available to reward good performers and by a tendency for line managers to use their pay budget to deal with perceived grading anomalies and labour market pressures rather than to support the 'high fliers'. More recently the equal opportunities implications of individual performance-related pay schemes have also emerged. The European Court of Justice decision in the Danfoss case has placed the burden on employers to prove that any differential payouts are not discriminatory against women, but recent work by Bevan and Thompson (1992) has suggested that such discrimination may exist in reality.

Given the difficulties associated with individual performance-related pay schemes a violent backlash against their use might be expected. While there are examples of organizations withdrawing from the use of such schemes, these remain isolated. Such a reaction highlights the need for care in seeking to assess managerial judgements on the effectiveness or impact of payment systems.

Effectiveness

Discussion on the effectiveness of payment systems needs to be founded on a number of observations. First, assessment of effectiveness must be sensitive to what management is trying to achieve. In this respect it may be possible to distinguish between the goals underpinning some of the more traditional manual piecework and bonus schemes and the more recent individual performance-related pay schemes introduced for white-collar workers.

Smith (1989), for example, has highlighted a number of studies which suggest that bonus schemes for manual workers can achieve certain managerial goals, particularly if enough money is attached to these schemes. He cites a US survey of 514 incentive schemes used in the late 1940s which suggested increases in output of 39 per cent, labour costs lowered by

11.5 per cent and earnings increased by 17.5 per cent. These findings were supported by research in the UK in the mid-1950s which indicated that the use of incentives increased output by 60 per cent and earnings by 20 per cent. Further work can be marshalled to argue that payment systems can help to retain staff. In 1960 a study by Scott and colleagues found that labour turnover fell by 370 per cent to 16 per cent with the introduction of a bonus scheme (Smith 1989).

More recent work on the impact of white collar performance-related payment schemes, however, has been sceptical about their positive impact. This research has tended to rely more on the attitudes of staff and concentrate on whether such schemes motivate. Thompson (1993), reviewing attitudes in a wider a range of organizations, has concluded that performance pay does not have a positive impact on motivation. This research has tended to use the basic tenets of expectancy theory and argues that performance pay does not appear to motivate because the tenets are not met. Thus, this survey suggests that performance goals are not clear and unambiguous; that the link between such goals is weak; and that the importance attached by employees to the amounts of money at stake is limited. The implication in much of Smith's work (1989) is that these tenets are far more likely to be met for manual workers given the nature of the work and the incentive schemes used.

Such work has not, however, sought to explore in the same depth the extent to which some of the more ambitious goals held for performance pay and associated with organizational change have been achieved. This gives rise to a second observation on the evaluation of the effectiveness of payment systems.

Measuring the impact of pay on the performance of the individual employee or the organization is an extremely difficult process. Given that performance in both senses is dependent on such a wide range of variables the viability of isolating the impact of a particular payment system remains highly problematic. It is perhaps for this reason that the Milkovich Committee in its thorough review of US academic work on performance pay concluded that: 'we found virtually no research on merit pay that directly examined its effect' (Milkovich 1991: 77). It may also explain why the choice of any given payment system is often viewed as an 'act of faith' by management.

The difficulty of measuring the effectiveness of payment systems is further exacerbated by the fact that the use of a payment system is often inextricably linked to the use of other techniques. This makes it extremely difficult to untangle the respective influences of these different techniques upon the employee and the organization. Such intertwining, particularly in pursuit of an extended project such as organizational change, sometimes encourages management to take a longer term view of the impact of a payment system. Indeed, if symbolic importance is attached to such a system it may be a misconception to suggest that managers evaluate effectiveness in systematic and rational terms.

In the absence of the 'perfect payment system' and the exercise of choice as an act of faith in the absence of viable measures of effectiveness, the processes by which payment systems are selected, operated and evaluated are perhaps best seen as a responses to a series of dilemmas and judgements. There are no 'right' or 'wrong', 'good' or 'bad' decisions but rather different approaches adopted in response to competing pressures and the assessment of circumstances and needs carried out in a more or less systematic and rational fashion.

IAN KESSLER
TEMPLETON COLLEGE
UNIVERSITY OF OXFORD

Further reading

(References cited in the text marked *)

* ACAS (1988) *Developments in Payment Systems*, occasional paper 45, London: ACAS. (Survey of pay developments in some 600 organizations. Provides good empirical data on extent and nature of changes.)
* ACAS (1990) *Appraisal Related Pay*, advisory booklet 14, London: ACAS. (Prescriptive test on how to introduce appraisal-related pay.)
* Alston, A. (1982) 'Awarding bonuses the Japanese way', *Business Horizons* 25 (5): 46–50. (Analysis of Japanese style merit pay based on group or team bonuses. Contrasts this with the US approach based on individual merit.)

Armstrong, M. and Murlis, H. (1991) *Reward Management*, 2nd edn, London: Kogan Page. (A comprehensive prescriptive text which outlines the mechanics of the main pay systems, how to design and implement them and their respective advantages and disadvantages.)

Balkin, D. and Gomez-Mejia, L. (eds) (1987) *New Perspectives on Compensation*, London: Prentice Hall. (Collection of essays by leading US academics in the field of reward. Critically evaluates merit pay, other incentive schemes and executive compensation.)

* Beer, M., Spector, B., Lawrence, P., Mills, D. and Walton, R. (1984) *Managing Human Assets*, New York: The Free Press. (Comprehensive review of human resource management using the 'stakeholder' approach. Has a chapter on rewards.)

* Behrend, H. (1959) 'Financial incentives as the expression of a system of beliefs', *British Journal of Sociology* 10 (2): 137–47. (Looks at the use of payment systems as a way of manipulating and structuring employee perceptions. Useful counter to rational approaches to the design of pay systems.)

* Bevan, S. and Thompson, M. (1992) *Merit Pay Performance Appraisal Attitudes to Women's Work*, Brighton: Institute of Manpower Studies, University of Sussex. (Research carried out for the British Equal Opportunities Commission providing a number of case studies investigating whether merit pay discriminates against women.)

* Bowey, A. and Thorpe, R. (1986) *Payment Systems and Productivity*, Macmillan: Basingstoke. (Assessment of the effectiveness of productivity schemes introduced in the UK in the 1980s. Also includes a thorough review of literature and research on pay.)

* Casey, B., Lakey, J., Cooper, H. and Eliot, J. (1991) 'Payment systems: a look at current practice', *Employment Gazette* (August): 53–8. (Survey of organizations in different parts of the UK looking at the contrasting developments in the use of pay systems.)

* CBI (1988) *People at the Cutting Edge*, London: CBI. (Policy document highlighting different personnel techniques to improve employee performance in the workplace.)

* CIR (1974) *Final Report*, no. 90, London: HMSO. (Highlights the role of payment systems in controlling wage drift and piecework.)

* *Citizens' Charter* (1991), Cmnd 1599, London: HMSO. (Statement of intent by the British government on ways to improve the quality of public services.)

Crandall, R. (1962) 'De-emphasised wage incentives', *Harvard Business Review* 4 (2): 110–13. (Report on a survey of 100 US companies on their approach to the introduction of new pay systems.)

* Fombrun, C., Tichy, N. and Devanna, M. (1984) *Human Resource Management*, New York: Wiley. (Leading US text on human resource management which follows the 'matching' school. Has a chapter on pay.)

* Gospel, H. (1992) *Markets, Firms and the Management of Labour in Modern Britain*, Cambridge: Cambridge University Press. (Thorough historical review of the use of internal and external labour by British companies. Good historical material on the use of different pay systems.)

* IDS Focus (1991) *Merit Pay*, no. 49, December, London: IDS. (Overview of merit pay trends in the UK. Critical evaluation of merit pay and some case study material.)

Lawler, E. (1990) *Strategic Pay*, San Francisco, CA: Jossey Bass. (Leading monograph on the development of new payment systems within the context of new company structures and organizational change. Balances critical evaluation of different approaches to pay with practical recommendations.)

* Lupton, T. (1963) *On the Shopfloor*, Oxford: Pergamon Press. (Ethnographic study of employee shop-floor behaviour. Stresses the importance of group norms in regulating the operation of pay systems.)

* Lupton, T. and Gowler, D. (1969) *Selecting a Wage Payment System*, research paper III, London: Engineering Employers' Federation. (Work carried out for the British Engineering Employers Federation on how to select a pay system. Definitive attempt to apply the contingency approach to this process.)

* Marriot, R. (ed.) (1961) *Incentive Payment Systems*, London: Staples Press. (Comprehensive review of incentive schemes in the 1950s and 1960s. Mixes research material and recommendations on 'good practice'.)

* Milkovich, G. (1991) *Pay for Performance*, Washington, DC: National Academic Press. (Report by the Committee on Performance Appraisal for Merit Pay for the US government to inform the debate on performance pay for federal employees. A comprehensive and systematic review of practice and evidence on performance pay in the USA.)

* Millward, N., Stevens, M., Smart, D. and Hawes, W. (1992) *Workplace Industrial Relations in Transition*, Aldershot: Dartmouth Press. (Survey of the distribution of merit pay systems within organizations. Highlights the lack of such schemes at lower levels.)

* NBPI (1968) *Payment by Results Systems*, report no. 65, Cmnd 3627, London: HMSO. (Critical evaluation of payment by results systems in the UK. Combines survey and case study material.)

* Peach, E. and Wren, D. (1992) 'Pay performance from antiquity to the 1950s', in T.C. Mawhinney (ed.), *Pay for Performance: History, Controversy and Evidence*, New York: Haworth Press. (Sweeping overview of developments in pay systems across the centuries. Highly generalized but some useful source material included.)

* Purcell, J. (1992) *Payment Systems*, unpublished lecture notes, Oxford: University of Oxford. (Outlines the various types of payment system available.)

* Schloss, D. (1898) *Methods of Industrial Remuneration*, London: Williams & Norgate. (Fascinating discussion of remuneration systems at the turn of the century. Shows that nothing much has changed in terms of approaches and issues.)

* Smith, A. (1969) 'The wealth of nations', in A. Briggs (ed.), *How They Lived*, vol. 3, Oxford: Blackwell. (A classic text originally published in 1776.)

* Smith, I. (1989) *Incentive Schemes: People and Profit*, London: Croner Publications. (Analysis of the effectiveness of payment schemes in terms of management aims.)

* Thompson, M. (1993) *Pay for Performance: The Employee Experience*, Brighton: Institute of Manpower Studies, University of Sussex. (Attempt to evaluate the impact of merit pay using employee attitude surveys in four organizations.)

* Trompenaars, F. (1993) *Riding The Waves*, London: Economist Books. (Discussion of cross-cultural management issues which touches briefly on pay. Not particularly scholarly but very readable.)

* Wyatt (1990) 'Do you play the ratings game?', *Personnel Today* (October): 27–9. (Small survey of organizations asking for their views on the advantages of merit rating, especially for pay purposes.)

See also: HUMAN RESOURCE MANAGEMENT; INDUSTRIAL AND LABOUR RELATIONS; PERSONNEL MANAGEMENT; PRODUCTIVITY; PROFIT SHARING AND EMPLOYEE SHAREHOLDING SCHEMES; TAYLOR, F.W.

Related topics in the IEBM: DEMING, W.E.; ORGANIZATIONAL PERFORMANCE

Performance appraisal

Overview

Organizational productivity hinges upon controlling the interplay of at least three variables, namely capital, technology and human resources. Effective control systems require information on what is occurring and a means of correcting or adjusting inputs when sensors indicate that change is needed. Productivity gains due to capital are typically measured by sophisticated accounting systems (for example, profits and costs, pro-forma balance sheets and budgets). Gains due to technology are assessed through the control systems of similar operations (for example, comparisons of inputs and outputs, process time, equipment efficiency and effectiveness). The contribution of an organization's human resources to productivity is more difficult to measure but it can be assessed in terms of work outputs produced or work behaviours exhibited over a specified time period. Performance appraisal involves assigning a value to employee behaviours or work outputs in terms of a criterion of productivity effectiveness (quantity, quality, timeliness).

1 Introduction

Appraisal systems have several objectives. They provide employees and the organization with data about current performance and serve as a medium through which organizations communicate future expectations. The objective is to ensure that the goals of employees match those of the organization. Data from performance appraisal also help to pinpoint employees who might be good candidates for development and to specify the type of development opportunity that is best for them. Performance appraisal is also a precursor of employee motivation. By making the distribution of organizational-sanctioned rewards (compensation, promotion, transfer and termination and job assignments) contingent upon the results of performance appraisal, employees are signalled that good performance is a route to desired rewards.

Traditionally, performance appraisal has focused only on individual assessment and reward allocation processes. More recent conceptualizations of the appraisal process, however, examine how the work system affects an individual or work group's performance. This broadens the scope of performance appraisal to include an analysis of system-level factors (such as organizational policies, politics, corporate objectives, spans of control, reward systems) that impact on human performance. The identification and correction of system obstacles increases the likelihood that employee performance will lead to organizational productivity. Finally, the data collected through performance appraisal provide documentation for decisions on basic human resources. Information thus generated is useful during strategic transformations which require new or different skill mixes. This information allows organizations to administer training and development programmes and to validate selection processes. How well the performance appraisal achieves these objectives depends on how it is integrated into the organization's control system (see HUMAN RESOURCE MANAGEMENT; TRAINING).

Unfortunately, performance appraisal systems have traditionally been so mismanaged that they have come under attack from managers, employees, psychologists and even the courts. One reason why organizations feel that their appraisal systems are not working effectively is that managers are seldom proficient in the basics of performance planning. Most managers spend far more time acquiring technical competencies (accounting, marketing, operations management) than they do learning to manage human resources (determine performance objectives, provide feedback and administer performance-contingent rewards). Second, an often-cited reason why performance appraisals fall short of achieving strategic objectives is that organizations are not clear as to who is responsible for managing human resources. At the heart of the debate is whether performance management falls into the domain of human resources or line departments. Third, performance appraisal is time-consuming. An enormous amount of time is required to develop performance standards, identify behaviours leading to peak performance, and prepare and conduct appraisal interviews. Organizations and their managers are frequently unwilling to commit to performance appraisal unless there is an immediate measurable payoff. Often there is not.

Given that performance appraisal processes touch on one of the most emotionally charged activities in business life – the assessment of a person's contribution to an organization – these processes often lead to conflict between managers and employees. The organization needs thorough and valid information about the competencies of its employees to achieve its objectives, but it is often not in the best interests of employees to provide such data. The signals an employee receives about his or her performance have a strong impact on self-esteem and on subsequent performance. A low rating may produce negative consequences (firing, demotion) for the employee; the supervisor may not want to be personally responsible for the consequences. Managers may rate their subordinates higher than deserved to appear successful themselves, to enlist subordinate cooperation for future work, to enhance their popularity, or to compare favourably with other supervisors. Conversely, managers may mete out strict ratings in order create an image as a task master, to signal a change in leadership, to motivate employees to work even harder or to control human resources costs. Research has focused on minimizing these conflicts through the design of purported better rating formats, better rater training and restructured control systems.

2 Historical context

Although the measurement of work performance has been a concern of organizational psychologists for only the past seventy years, the practice of assessing performance has existed for centuries. A third-century AD Chinese philosopher, Sin Yu, charged that raters employed by the Wei dynasty seldom rated men according to merits but always according to personal likes and dislikes. In Western cultures, the philosophy of pay for performance dates back to the Protestant Reformation of the sixteenth and seventeenth centuries (see FINANCIAL INCENTIVES; PAYMENT SYSTEMS). During this period, hard work was assessed by the economic success it brought and was viewed as self-sacrifice in the service of God. Hence, economic success was seen as a willingness to serve God (Heneman 1992). Concern over performance criteria and rating bias emerged as early as 1640. The *Dublin Evening Post* ran an editorial in that year that criticized the process of rating legislators on personal qualities rather than performance.

The first industrial application of performance appraisal in Europe is believed to have been during the early 1800s. At his cotton mills in New Lanark, Scotland, Robert Owens used wooden cubes of different colours to indicate different degrees of merit. As an employee's performance changed, so did the cubes hanging over the work station. In the USA, formal performance appraisal probably began in 1813. Army General Lewis Cass submitted to the US War Department an evaluation of each of his men using such terms as 'good natured' or 'despised by all'. Merit or efficiency ratings in the US Civil Service have been in place since at least 1890.

The translation of pay-for-performance philosophy into formal organizational policy and systematic appraisal system is a more recent phenomenon. One impetus to the development of the performance measurement process was the Industrial Revolution. Frederick W. Taylor in the USA theorized that the most important objective of both workforce and management should be the training and development of each individual in the establishment so that he or she could achieve (at the fastest pace and with the maximum efficiency) the highest level of work that his or her natural abilities allowed (Taylor 1911) (see TAYLOR, F.W.). Writing at about the same time in France (although no English translation was widely available until 1949), Henri Fayol delineated the duties of a manager as organizing work, commanding employees and coordinating performance. Both of these industrial scientists advocated the use of time and motion studies to determine optimum work design and rewards based on direct output.

The scientific study of the performance ratings process can be traced to work of organizational psychologists at Carnegie-Mellon University in the USA. These researchers developed 'man-to-man' rating forms based on trait psychology for use in the selection of a salesperson (see OCCUPATIONAL PSYCHOLOGY). The 'man-to-man' appraisal format was used in the US Army during the First World War to rank officers. With this approach, each individual is compared with every other individual in the work group to derive a numerical rating of ability. One drawback of this approach is that an overall 'subjective' criterion was utilized to rank employees. For one rater, the criterion may be leadership ability and for another it may be sales. Although it is not used frequently today, the 'man-to-man' ranking process was the impetus for normative appraisal processes such as ranking, paired comparison and forced choice.

Designed to overcome the limitations of man-to-man ratings, the graphic rating scale became popular in the early 1930s. Rather than rely on relative comparisons of individuals, this format requires absolute judgement of personality traits which are purported to be linked to performance-related traits.

Judgements are recorded on numerical rating scales. The 1940s produced a major breakthrough in performance assessment, namely the development of the critical incident technique of job analysis. As a first step to develop an appraisal instrument, subject matter experts (SMEs) generated critical incidents of effective and ineffective job performance (Flanagan 1949). These descriptions were then clustered into performance dimensions and scored in terms of the performance level represented by the incident. By-products of the critical incident technique include the behaviourally anchored rating scale (BARS), the mixed standard scale (MSS) and the behavioural observation scale (BOS).

Following the Second World War, the emphasis in performance appraisal shifted to organizational productivity and employee effectiveness. Management by objectives (MBO) emerged as a complete systematic process to align the goals of employees with those of the organization. Performance is assessed in terms of output and results rather than behaviour. The first attempt to model the entire performance appraisal process (not just the rating decision) also came at this time. Taking as his basis a series of projects for the US Army, Robert Wherry (1957) used a theory of reliability to develop a mathematical model of the rating process. A number of unique, but testable, theorems about rating bias, the rating process and rater motivation were generated. Corollaries of Wherry's theory of rating focused on physical features of the rating scale, reliability of ratings, the time span of the evaluation period, and the number and type of raters and methods to control rater bias. Unfortunately, Wherry's work lay buried in unpublished technical reports and did not come to the attention of researchers until the 1980s. Still, it provided the impetus that researchers needed to look beyond appraisal instrumentation for solutions to the rating accuracy dilemma. By the 1980s, research attention had shifted towards the cognitive processes associated with appraisal decision making and the political/social context in which performance appraisal occurs. A decade later, 80–90 per cent of organizations in the USA and the UK were utilizing some form of performance appraisal.

3 Psychometric research

Researchers initially viewed performance appraisal as a measurement problem. The emphasis was upon criterion measurement and rating accuracy (ratings that are conceptually near the true score level of performance). Error variance was assumed to be due to the rating format. Working under this psychometric umbrella, psychologists have spent years attempting to develop an ideal appraisal instrument. Their efforts have generated a variety of rating formats. One particular viable approach to classifying different performance measurement formats is Smith's (1976) three-dimensional taxonomy. His multi-dimensional model classifies performance appraisal instruments according to the time span covered, the specificity of the rating scale and the closeness of the measure to organizational goals.

4 Graphic/trait rating formats

Introduced in the late 1920s, the graphic/trait rating scale remains the most widely used scale format. Essentially, the rater is asked to rate employees on a number of job characteristics (quality and quantity of work, care and use of equipment) or traits (work quantity, quality, dependability, leadership) thought to be related to successful job performance. Ratings are made using an interval scale that ranges from one extreme to another, for instance, from well below standard to well above standard or from poor to excellent. Numerical values are associated with each interval of the scale. Since judgements are absolute, it is possible for multiple ratees to receive the same ratings for any or all dimensions of performance.

The graphic rating format is often preferred to behavioural- and output-based formats by managers because they are easy to use, require no job analysis, and one set of scales can be used for a variety of jobs. But the benefits of trait rating scales are overshadowed by their drawbacks. What is important in one job is not necessarily critical in another. For example, creativity may be a critical attribute for a research scientist but a negative attribute for a data entry operator who must enter data accurately, not originally. Second, raters do not interpret trait categories (dependability, communication skill) or scale anchors ('fully competent', 'outstanding') consistently. Consequently, trait scales are notoriously unreliable and invalid (Bernardin and Beatty 1984: 65). At best, traits ratings indirectly relate to predictors of performance rather than to performance itself.

5 Behaviour-focused formats

Disillusioned with trait-based formats, psychologists launched a search for a better, more accurate, rating format. Researchers assumed that more accurate ratings could be obtained by replacing 'fuzzy' trait criteria with explicit behaviourally based criteria. An interactive process is utilized to develop all behaviourally focused appraisal scales. As a first step, critical incidents are collected from raters and ratees. Incidents are then clustered according to independent dimensions of behaviour. Next, a numerical value or weight is assigned to each incident in proportion to its contribution to the behavioural criterion. The product of this process is a set of behavioural criteria.

Behaviourally anchored rating scales

Various scaling formats are associated with behavioural appraisals. A behaviourally anchored rating scale (BARS) clusters the behavioural examples associated with a single dimension of performance along a single rating scale. To evaluate performance, the rater chooses the behavioural item that best represents the ratee's performance. Developers of BARS maintain that the scales are less ambiguous and more reliable than error-prone graphic rating scales. Because they participate in the delineation of the appraisal criterion, acceptance of BARS is assumed to be high among raters and ratees. A major drawback of BARS relates to the potential non-monotonicity of scale anchors; a ratee simultaneously may display behaviour associated with high and low performance. Raters also may have difficulty in matching a ratee's performance to the highly specific behavioural descriptors that anchor the scale. Consequently, raters may be based on perceived or stereotypical performance rather than actual performance.

Mixed standard rating scales

A mixed standard rating scale (MSS) is designed to minimize rating leniency. Like BARS, the critical incident method of job analysis underscores the development of this format. Rather than multiple behaviours anchoring a single numerical scale, an MSS consists of sets of three statements that describe high, average and low levels of performance for each dimension of performance. To minimize leniency, the behavioural examples are randomly ordered on the rating form. A score on each performance dimension is calculated on the basis of the pattern of responses. For each item, the rater determines whether the employee's performance is 'worse than', 'better than' or the 'same as' the behaviour described by the scale item. The purported advantage of an MSS is that the rater is not dealing with anything numerical. Consequently, the rater is more likely to focus on comparing job performance with the behaviour exemplars.

Behavioural observation scales

A third derivative of the critical incident technique is called the behavioural observation scale (BOS). It differs from BARS in one important respect. With a BARS format, a set of behaviours anchors a single rating scale. Judges numerically rate each behavioural incident in terms of the extent to which each behaviour represents effective job performance. Endorsement of an incident implies endorsement of all lower-rated behaviours on a specific performance dimension. Since it is possible for an employee over time to display various behaviours, this endorsement may be unwarranted. BOS formats eliminate this problem. Rather than choosing the one behaviour that best represents the employee's

performance, each behavioural item is evaluated independently with BOS. The rater observes employee performance over a time and rates the frequency of each behaviour (Latham and Wexley 1994) on a numerical scale. This increases reliability by reducing sampling error. The limitations of BOS are connected with this format's advantages. Without the time and opportunity to observe and record the frequency of performance, raters may revert to evaluations based on their overall impression of the employee's performance.

Comparative studies indicate that behavioural scales produce slightly higher reliability and rater confidence than trait scales. Research is inconclusive regarding the relative accuracy of trait and behavioural scales. However, the accuracy of each format – BARS, BOS, MSS and graphic scales – is affected by the rating context, rater motivation and the temporal, spatial and sensory proximity of the appraiser to the employee's behaviour. A second definitive conclusion is that the minimization of rating errors (leniency, central tendency) and user acceptance is proportional to the degree of involvement users have in scale development.

6 Output-based formats

Rather than the behaviours that lead to performance, output-based formats focus on the performance outcomes (see HUMAN RESOURCE MANAGEMENT). Output-based formats can be categorized in several ways. First, they can be broken down into whether they are non-judgemental or judgemental. Direct indices of productivity, namely criteria that can be counted and/or seen (for example, scrap rates, production rates, task completion time and cost reductions) are non-judgemental measures. Judgemental measures require the rater to collect information about performance outcomes and compare these data with organizationally sanctioned standards of performance. Output-based formats can also be classified according to whether performance is measured in absolute or relative terms. The former suggests an optimization standard of performance, the latter suggests a comparative standard of performance. In terms of sales performance, an optimization criterion would focus on total sales per month. A comparative criterion would emphasize the deviation in sales from the standard established for that job. Landy and Farr (1983) argue convincingly that comparative judgements are easier to make and more reliable than absolute or optimization criteria. The quality improvement movement also favours comparative indexes. Deming and his associates stress that the key to continuous improvement lies in reducing variability. Applied to performance assessment, individual, group or organizational output should be examined in terms of its variability or deviation from the standard rather than in terms of maximum output.

Direct index approach

The direct index approach utilizes objective, impersonal, criteria, such as productivity, absenteeism and turnover, to assess performance. Direct measures of productivity can focus on quality measures such as scrape rates, customer complaints and the number of defective units produced, or quantity measures, including units of output per hour, new customer orders and sales volume. Direct indices of performance are generally assumed to be objective, reliable and valid. The implication is that they are not open to interpretation or rater bias. Unfortunately, there are problems with this format. First, performance may not be totally controllable by the employee (for instance, unit turnover may be due to a labour supply and demand imbalance or non-competitive pay (a market lag compensation policy). A second concern is that performance maximization is emphasized over performance optimization. The goal is to produce the most or the fastest rather than to produce the highest quality or the right amount (just enough with nothing left over). Thus, performance maximization may result in short-term gains but may not be the best tactic to sustain long-term productivity. Employees may also not be able to sustain high levels of performance indefinitely. Finally, the process by which

these outcomes are achieved may be neglected. This is problematic if the behaviours or the way one achieves results matter (for example, the employee uses proper safety equipment, or does not threaten debtors over the telephone).

Performance standards

With performance standards, the rater compares actual output to organizationally sanctioned performance norms. After assessing the degree of congruence between the standard and the actual performance, the rater assigns a numerical rating the performance. Useful standards are specific, time-bound and weighted and therefore enable the user (manager and job-incumbent) to differentiate between acceptable and unacceptable results. A specific standard limits the number of acceptable outcome matches. The outcome of behaviour also must be reported in precise terms so that it can be confidently compared against performance standards and subsequently mapped on a global rating scale. The specificity of the global rating scale upon which the rating inputs are mapped also affects the accuracy of the appraisal judgements. Scale anchors act as categorization cues which help the rater to translate rating inputs into a overall judgement of performance (Kahneman and Tversky 1973). The more explicit and differentiated the anchors, the easier it is to map the rating inputs onto the global rating scale. For example, a graphic rating scale with vague anchors (such as 1 = below average, 5 = excellent) provides more judgement latitude than a rating scale with anchors that relate explicitly to performance standards (such as 1 = 'fails to meet all standards'; 5 = 'exceeds all standards').

The use of standards to motivate performance builds from three related lines of research: goal setting, participative decision making and objective feedback (see MOTIVATION AND SATISFACTION). Findings in the goal-setting literature indicate that performance is higher when individuals work towards the attainment of specific, difficult goals rather than vague, easy ones or none at all. Although the goal-setting literature is pivotal in explaining how performance is motivated, performance standards are distinct from goals. Locke and Latham (1990) describe goals as the aim or end of an action and standards as a rule to measure or evaluate things. Goals tend to be individualized, focusing on individual ability and performance. Standards, on the other hand, are constant across individuals and determined by organizational criteria (Bobko and Colella 1994). To influence performance positively, externally imposed standards must be accepted by employees. This is accomplished through participation in the setting of standards and reward linkages. Research further indicates that feedback is necessary. Specific, descriptive feedback about performance relative to the standards will increase motivation more than vague, delayed and general feedback (Bobko and Colella 1994). Huber (1989) examined the usefulness of specific performance standards in controlling appraisal rating bias. Huber found that true performance was the most important determinant of rated performance. However, several other factors (the order of evaluation, gender of rater, prior performance rating) biased judgements in the vague but not the specific standards condition (see EQUAL EMPLOYMENT OPPORTUNITIES).

Management by objectives

The use of standards as an appraisal process is generally operationalized through management by objectives (MBO). Central to this approach to performance management is the issue of goal congruence. An individual's goals must be in harmony with those of his work team; these in turn must be linked to department or division goals; goals for the division must support the objectives and overall mission of the organization. Objectives (goals) can refer to desired outcomes to be achieved, to means for achieving the outcomes, or both. Goals may be related to routine activities that comprise day-to-day duties or to the identification and solution of problems that hamper individual and organizational effectiveness; they may also be innovative or have special purposes (Odiorne 1979). A recent study of MBO systems

showed that productivity increased in 68 out of 70 cases with an average gain in productivity of 46 per cent when management was committed (Rodgers *et al.* 1993). Performance gains, however, are not immediate. It takes an average of two years for MBO systems to work effectively and efficiently.

The major advantage of judgemental formats – when done correctly – is that they provide clear unambiguous direction to employees regarding desired job outcomes. When exceptional performance also is specified, these scales can motivate the average as well as the exceptional employee. One disadvantage is that they require time, money and cooperation to develop. Second, concern centres on controllability. As implemented in many organizations, objectives may hold employees accountable for outcomes over which they have little or no control. Third, the essence of job performance may not be captured completely by output-based criteria. Consequently, important job behaviours may be ignored in the evaluation process. When linked to scarce organizational reward, the production of desired products or output may also induce unintended competition among employees.

7 Social/cognitive research on performance appraisal

Despite years of study devoted to developing an 'ideal' (accurate) appraisal format, only one result is clear – rating errors are made whatever the rating format. Rather than continue the search for an appraisal elixir, research since the 1970s has concentrated on the way in which raters mentally process information about performance and subsequently recall information to make a performance judgement. The first widely cited model to treat performance appraisal as a social/cognitive process was proposed by DeCotis and Petit (1978). In stark contrast to the earlier psychometric models, they recognized the importance of organizational and situational factors in shaping rating outcome. They proposed that rating accuracy was determined by rater motivation, rater ability and the avail-ability of rating norms.

Subsequent cognitive models of the ap-praisal process (for example, Landy and Farr 1983; Ilgen and Feldman 1983; DeNisi *et al.* 1984) suggest that the quality of performance judgements is dependent upon the information-processing capabilities and strategies of the rater. The decision maker must first attend to and recognize relevant per-formance information. This information must then be aggregated and stored in the rater's short-term memory. The evaluator may use formal or informal cognitive categories to store information about another's perform-ance. When informal or self-generated cate-gories are utilized, categorization of performance may be inaccurate. Because of long appraisal periods, information often must be condensed further and stored in long-term memory. With time, information decay occurs. When a performance judgement is re-quired, relevant performance information must be retrieved from memory and com-pared with behavioural descriptors or output standards. Unfortunately, raters' memories are often fallible. Consequently, they fall prey to a variety of cognitive errors.

Cooper (1981) generated a sequential model of the rating process which identifies potential sources of cognitive distortion or bias in appraisal, including, but not exclu-sively, under-sampling, engulfing and dis-counting. Cognitive distortion refers to the tendency of raters to lose and add information about performance. This distortion is due to such cognitive factors as inadequate observa-tion of behaviour, short-term and long-term memory decay, and inaccurate aggregation of performance data. Behaviourally anchored rating scales and performance standards were introduced to minimize this bias. With under-sampling the rater bases his or her judgement on an insufficient sample of the ratee's behav-iour or output. Engulfing relates to the ten-dency for ratings to be inappropriately anchored by an overall impression of the per-son or by a single salient aspect of the person's performance. Discounting refers to the ten-dency to undervalue or discount inconsistent information. For example, a new employee may perform well for the first few weeks on the job. As a result, his or her supervisor may classify the employee as a good performer. Once categorization is made, inconsistent data (for instance, did not complete the proj-ect on time) is discarded and confirming data (for instance, secured a new account) is over-weighted during the appraisal process.

Research on cognitive obstacles to rating accuracy indicate that reliable judgements are more likely if the rater: (1) understands the relevant behaviour set; (2) is provided with organizationally sanctioned rating categories; and (3) is provided with a global rating scale that facilitates the match of the two and the combination of information across behav-ioural categories (Ilgen and Feldman 1983). The use of specific rating formats assists the rater to classify the employee's behaviour ap-propriately, recall the behaviour in terms of job relevant categories and accurately make a performance judgement. Research indicates that rating accuracy may be enhanced through training focused on improving the observa-tion skills of raters. The reliability of ratings can be enhanced through frame of reference training. This type of training focuses on pro-viding raters with a common nomenclature for defining the importance of each compo-nent of behaviour observed or output evaluated.

8 Interactive approach to performance appraisal

Although cognitive models of performance appraisal have stimulated study, they are often criticized as being 'nice in theory but ineffectual in practice'. The interactionist's perspectives contend that rating accuracy hinges on the rater, instrumentation and con-text (that is, organizational control structures, politics, values) in which evaluations occur. Pivotal to this view is the belief that appraisal is a communication and social process (Mur-phy and Cleveland 1991). The interactionist line of research differs significantly from early psychometric and cognitive perspec-tives in three respects. First, it recognizes the interdependence of behaviour in organizations. The behaviour of a rater is influenced by the behaviour of the ratee and other factors in the environment and vice versa. Second, it assumes that the rater is not passive but an active agent pursuing specific goals which may or may not include accurate ratings. Third, there is an explicit distinction between a rater's ability and motivation to rate accurately. Given appropriate training, and specific criteria, a rater may be able to make accurate performance judgements but may still be motivated to inflate or deflate perform-ance ratings.

Consider the problem of lenient or inflated ratings. The psychometric perspective as-sumes that leniency can be reduced by im-proving the specificity and job relatedness of the rating formats. The cognitive approach fo-cuses on a decision-making process and a sec-ond key variable, namely the rater. If raters are trained to be better observers, are given appro-priate decision aids (specific performance cri-teria), and are cued to recall performance data, ratings will not be inflated. The interaction-ist's perspective of rating leniency is more ho-listic. Rating leniency is as much a product of the situation as of the rater (that is, organiza-tional control structures, politics and power, the rater and ratee).

Little is known about the contextual factors that raters perceive or consider in determining a course of action to pursue through appraisal (Murphy and Cleveland 1991), although one factor found to affect rater motivation is the purpose of the rating (Landy and Farr 1983). Performance appraisals conducted for the purposes of administrative decision making result in significantly higher ratings than ap-praisals conducted for other purposes such as employee development or selection criterion validation. Research clearly indicates that ra-ters consciously distort (inflate) their ratings when they perceive that the distribution of im-portant organizational rewards are contingent upon the appraisal.

9 Conclusion

Initial research focused on minimizing rating errors such as leniency, halo and horn, first impression, primacy and recency through the redesign of appraisal formats. Numerous studies also compared the accuracy of rating formats. Despite years of study devoted to developing an 'ideal' (accurate) appraisals format, only one result is clear – rating errors are made regardless of the rating format. More recent investigations have focused on cognitive bias inherent in the judgement process. Prescriptive training in which raters are merely instructed not to rate too high or too low to improve rating accuracy is less effective than experiential training in which raters actively participate and learn observa-tional skills (Latham and Wexley 1994). The interactionist's viewpoint distinguishes between judgement and rating.

Despite the knowledge that has been gleaned from these investigations, additional research is still needed under each umbrella (see Murphy and Cleveland 1991 for a par-ticularly comprehensive list of questions). One particularly important emerging issue re-lates to the effects of technology. For exam-ple, what is the effect on appraisals of employees telecommuting as opposed to working in-house? How does computer moni-toring affect ratee performance and rater judgements of that performance? Does the conveyance of performance feedback or ap-praisal ratings via electronic media (via e-mail, for example) differ significantly from more traditional practices? With regard to performance in general, it is unknown how variable (that is, deviating from standard) per-formance must be before it affects a rater's judgement. Finally, research is needed to un-derstand the interplay between the rater, ratee and the rating context.

VANDRA L. HUBER
SALLY RIGGS FULLER
UNIVERSITY OF WASHINGTON SCHOOL OF
BUSINESS ADMINISTRATION

Further reading

(References cited in the text marked *)

* Bernardin, H.J. and Beatty, R.W. (1984) *Perform-ance Appraisal: Assessing Human Behavior at Work*, Boston, MA: Kent Publishing Co. (Com-prehensive review of the literature, with an

overview of criteria by which the effectiveness of appraisal systems can be assessed.)

* Bobko, P. and Colella, A. (1994) 'Employee reactions to performance standards: a review and research propositions', *Personnel Psychology* 47: 1–29. (Comprehensive review of research relating to standards for performance. Covers aspects of the performance standard process that influence incumbent performance, satisfaction and motivation.)

* Cooper, W. (1981) 'Ubiquitous halo', *Psychological Bulletin* 90: 218–44. (Influential early work in which a sequential model of the rating process illustrates the potential sources of bias in appraisal.)

* DeCotis, T. and Petit, A. (1978) 'The performance appraisal process: a model and some testable propositions', *Academy of Management Review* 3: 635–46. (An early paper which viewed the appraisal process as a social as well as judgemental process.)

* DeNisi, A.S., Cafferty, T.P. and Meglino, B.M. (1984) 'A cognitive view of the performace appraisal process: a model and research proposition', *Organizational Behavior and Human Performance* 33: 457–67. (Presents a cognitive model of the performance appraisal process which identifies the various sorts of bias associated with collecting, storing and recalling performance information to make a rating.)

Farr, J.L., Dobbins, G.H. and Cheng, B.S. (1991) 'Cultural relativity in action: a comparison of self ratings made by Chinese and American workers', *Personnel Psychology* 44: 129–47. (Interesting comparative study which examines performance ratings of 900 pairs of supervisors and their subordinates in the USA and the Republic of China.)

Fayol, H. (1949) *General and Industrial Management*, London: Pitman. (Includes a complete translation of his classic theory of administration.)

* Flanagan, R. (1949) 'The critical incident technique', *Psychological Bulletin* 2: 419–25. (Classic article describing the critical incident process of job analysis. Delineates strengths and weaknesses of the technique.)

Harris, M.M. and Schsaubroeck, J. (1988) 'A meta analysis of self–supervisor, self–peer and peer–supervisor rating', *Personnel Psychology* 41: 43–62. (Comprehensive review of the research on various rater groups. While self and supervisory ratings are only moderately linked, peer and supervisory ratings are strongly related.)

* Heneman, R.L. (1992) *Merit Pay: Linking Pay Increases to Performance Ratings*, Reading, MA: Addison-Wesley. (Reviews the literature on incentive pay allocated on the basis of a subjective evaluation of an employee's past or current performance rather than future performance.)

* Huber, V.L. (1989) 'Comparison of the effects of specific and general performance standards on performance appraisal decision', *Decision Sciences* 20: 545–57. (One of the few empirical investigations of performance standards. Examines the utility of specific standard in reducing rating bias.)

* Ilgen, D.R. and Feldman, J.M. (1983) 'Performance appraisal: a process focus', in B. Staw and L. Cummings (eds), *Research in Organizational Behavior*, vol. 5, Greenwich, CT: JAI Press. (Identifies the components of the appraisal rating process.)

* Kahneman, D. and Tverksy, A. (1973) 'On the psychology of prediction', *Psychological Review* 93: 429–45. (Classic article which examines decision-making bias.)

* Landy, F.J. and Farr, J.L. (1983) *The Measurement of Work Performance: Methods, Theory and Application*, New York: Academic Press. (Presents a comprehensive judgemental model of the rating process, reviews the literature and provides a summary of R.J. Wherry's theory of rating.)

* Latham, G.P. and Wexley, K.N. (1994) *Increasing Productivity Through Performance Appraisal*, Reading, MA: Addison-Wesley. (Assessment of various issues in performance management; examines behavioural criteria and discusses strategies to improve productivity or discharge people.)

* Locke, E. and Latham, G.P (1990) *A Theory of Goal Setting and Task Performance*, Englewood Cliffs, NJ: Prentice Hall. (The definitive work on goal setting and its relationship to motivation and performance.)

Mager, R.F. and Pipe, P. (1970) *Analyzing Performance Problems, or You Really Oughta Wanna*, Belmont, CA: Fearon Pitman. (Practitioner-orientated classic which delineates the systems problems that may limit employee motivation. Includes a decision tree to determine whether training or system redesign is needed.)

Meyer, H.H., Kay, E. and French, J.R.P., Jr (1965) 'Split roles in performance appraisal', *Harvard Business Review* 43: 123–9. (Classic article which explores the conflict between using appraisal instruments for developmental and evaluative purposes.)

* Murphy, K.R. and Cleveland, J.N. (1991) *Performance Appraisal: An Organizational Perspective*, Boston, MA: Allyn & Bacon. (One of the most comprehensive reviews of current thinking on performance management. Traces the organizational–political influences that affect appraisal judgements.)

Northcraft, G.B., Neale, M. and Huber, V.L. (1988) 'The effects of cognitive bias and social influence on human resources management process', in G. Ferris and K. Rowland (eds), *Research in Personnel and Human Resources Management*, vol. 6, Greenwich, CT: JAI Press Inc. (Examines the sources of social influence and cognitive biases that affect human resource decisions. Utilizes behavioural decision theory as an explanatory tool.)

* Odiorne, G. (1979) *MBO II: A System of Managerial Leadership for the 80s*, Belmont, CA: Lake Management and Training. (Classic which delineates the philosophy of management by objectives systems. Views MBO as a systems approach to management.)

* Rodgers, R., Hunter, J.E. and Rogers, D.L. (1993) 'Influence of top management commitment on management program success', *Journal of Applied Psychology* 78: 151–60. (Demonstrates the importance of management commitment in MBO systems.)

Schwab, D.D., Heneman, H.G. and DeCotis, T.A. (1975) 'Behaviorally anchored rating scales: a review of the literature', *Personnel Psychology* 28: 549–62. (Reviews the research on behaviourally anchored rating scales. Traces conditions under which these scales work well. Examines reliability and validity.)

* Smith, P.C. (1976) 'Behaviors, results and organizational effectiveness', in M. Dunnette (ed.), *Handbook of Industrial and Organizational Psychology*, Chicago: Rand-McNally. (A systematic classification of aspects of performance appraisal instrumentation.)

* Taylor, F. (1911) *The Principles of Scientific Management*, New York: Norton & Co. (Describes Taylor's classic experiment in which a pig-iron handler improved his performance fourfold and delineates Taylor's principles of scientific management.)

* Wherry, R.J. (1957) 'The past and future of criterion evaluation', *Personnel Psychology* 10: 1–5. (A foundation work for examining rating criterion and accuracy. Presents a theoretical perspective that has withstood the test of time.)

See also: EQUAL EMPLOYMENT OPPORTUNITIES; HUMAN RESOURCE DEVELOPMENT; HUMAN RESOURCE MANAGEMENT; FINANCIAL INCENTIVES; INDUSTRIAL AND LABOUR RELATIONS; JOB EVALUATION; ORGANIZATION BEHAVIOUR; PAYMENT SYSTEMS; PRODUCTIVITY; TRAINING; WORK AND ORGANIZATION SYSTEMS

Related topics in the IEBM: APPRAISAL METHODS; DEMING, W.E.; FAYOL, H.

Profit sharing and employee shareholding schemes

Overview

During the past fifteen to twenty years, profit sharing and employee share ownership schemes have experienced a dramatic increase in popularity in Western industrialized countries, and numerous countries have introduced supportive legislation.

The prime motives for profit-sharing plans are to improve employee and company performance, to serve as a pension plan and to provide a more attractive benefits package, as well as for philosophical reasons. The importance of each motive varies across countries, largely depending on the legislative context. Research indicates that profit sharing is generally associated with improved company performance, but this varies with the nature of the plan and numerous other factors.

The prime motives for employee share ownership are improvement of employee and company performance, the provision of a tax supported employee benefit plan, the transferral of ownership from retiring owners of private corporations and the development of cooperative employee–management relations. As with profit sharing, these motives vary across countries depending on the legislative context. Evidence indicates that, when combined with employee participation in decision making, employee ownership is usually associated with a substantial improvement in company performance.

This entry begins by defining profit sharing and employee shareholding schemes and providing a background of their evolution. It is followed by a discussion of the arguments for and against their use, the extent to which they actually are in use at present and the consequences and reasons for this. Finally there is a summary of what the future holds for organizations implementing profit sharing and employee shareholding schemes.

1 Profit sharing

At its most basic, profit sharing can be defined as any system that distributes a bonus to employees based on the profitability of the entire company or a major division. However, 'true' profit sharing contains two additional elements. First, there should be a pre-established formula to determine the amount of the profit-sharing bonus in a given year. Second, profit sharing should apply to a broad spectrum of employees, not just management.

There are three main types of profit-sharing plans – *current distribution, deferred,* and *combination.* Current distribution plans (often known as cash plans) disburse the payout to employees as soon as it is declared (typically annually), usually in the form of cash but sometimes in the form of company shares. Deferred profit-sharing plans defer the payout, usually until retirement or termination of employment, in order to reap tax advantages. Combination plans provide some immediate disbursement and defer the remainder.

Profit-sharing plans can differ on a number of important dimensions, including employee eligibility, the formula that determines the size of the profit-sharing bonus, the basis for distributing the bonus across employees and the nature of the payout. For example, should all employees be included, both full-time and part-time? Should the profit-sharing bonus be based on a straight percentage of company profits or should there be some threshold level that must be reached before profit sharing is initiated? Should the bonus be distributed across employees according to salary, seniority or simply equally? These differences can affect the nature of the consequences that arise (see FINANCIAL INCENTIVES; PAYMENT SYSTEMS).

Although profit-sharing schemes have been around for a long time, they have experienced a very uneven growth rate. The first known profit-sharing plan was introduced in the USA in 1794 at the New Geneva (Pennsylvania) glass works of Albert Gallatin, one of the founders of the USA (Coates 1991). However, very few plans were introduced until the 1860s and 1870s, after the Civil War. There was a fairly steady growth in plans until the depression, when most were eliminated due to lack of profit. In the late 1930s the US Senate conducted hearings on the desirability of profit sharing, and concluded that it 'unified the interests of workers and employers, promoted greater cooperation between the parties, and created the most effective means of promoting capitalism as an economic system' (Florkowski 1991: 96).

In 1939 legislation was passed that permitted employers to deduct their contributions to deferred profit-sharing plans, on the same basis as wage costs, up to 15 per cent of total compensation. Employees were allowed to treat these earnings as capital gains rather than ordinary income, which reduced the taxes payable. These plans were regarded by many employers as a convenient substitute for pension plans, and enjoyed steadily increasing popularity, with about 261,000 plans in place by 1979, and nearly 443,000 by 1989.

The first recorded plan in the UK was implemented by Lord Wallscourt on his farms in Galway in 1829 (Bell and Hanson 1987), but few, if any, others were established until 1865. Between 1865 and 1873 at least twenty-five schemes were established, often for philanthropic reasons (Poole 1989). Between 1889 and 1892 there was another wave of development, often to forestall unionization. Other surges occurred in 1908–9, 1912–14 and during the 1920s, brought on by economic buoyancy and labour unrest. A decline in implementations in the 1930s was followed by a gradual expansion after the Second World War.

The major surge in British implementation occurred after passage of legislation in 1978 that provided tax incentives for certain types of profit sharing. Plans that qualify for tax incentives combine deferred profit sharing with employee share ownership, as companies are required to use the profit-sharing bonus to purchase company shares for their employees. Employees are not taxed on this income until the shares are sold and are taxed at a reduced rate if the shares are held at least five years. Supplemental legislation was passed in 1987 to encourage current distribution profit-sharing plans and employees can exclude 25 per cent of profit-sharing earnings from income taxation, up to a limit of 5 per cent of total pay. Other European countries that provide some legislative support for profit sharing include Denmark, Germany and Greece.

Only one other Western industrialized country has encouraged profit sharing through tax incentives. Until 1983 Canada had tax incentives for deferred profit-sharing plans similar to those in the USA, with the underlying intention that they serve as pension plans. However, new legislation which defers taxation on all employee investments for pension purposes has in effect removed the special tax advantages previously provided by deferred profit-sharing plans.

In western Europe, France is the leader in use of profit-sharing plans, since deferred profit-sharing plans were made mandatory in 1967 for firms employing at least 100 employees (extended in 1990 to include firms employing 50 or more employees) (see INDUSTRIAL RELATIONS IN EUROPE). Besides France, a number of countries impose mandatory profit sharing, including Bolivia, Brazil, Chile, Colombia, Ecuador, India, Mexico,

Nigeria, Pakistan, Panama, Peru and Venezuela (Florkowski 1991).

2 Employee ownership

Firms with employee ownership can vary greatly, but three main categories can be distinguished, depending on the degree of employee ownership. First, there are firms that are completely owned by their employees. These firms may use a cooperative or private corporation structure. Under a cooperative form, each worker is required to purchase one (and only one) voting share, which they must relinquish if they leave the cooperative. Under the corporate form, voting for the board of directors is based on the number of shares held (which can vary greatly across employee owners), and employees are not usually required to purchase shares as a condition of employment.

Second, there are firms that are majority-owned by their employees but which also have other shareholders. These can be either public or private corporations, and are often firms in transition to full employee ownership. Third, and by far the most common, is partial employee ownership, where there is no intention for employees to become majority owners. Many large public corporations have such schemes.

There are three main types of partial ownership plans: stock bonus plans, stock option plans and stock-purchase plans. Stock bonus plans put shares in the hands of employees at no cost to them. Profit-sharing plans that pay out in shares would be one example, as well as employee stock-ownership plans (ESOPs) in the USA. Stock options provide an opportunity to buy shares at some point in the future at a pre-determined price. If the actual value of the shares is higher than the option price when the options mature, then it will be in the best interests of the employee to purchase company shares (although they may turn them over immediately in order to realize their gain). Stock-purchase plans provide the opportunity for employees to purchase shares in their employer, usually with some incentive to do so, such as a discounted share price.

Although examples of completely employee-owned firms can be found in the USA as early as the 1840s (four foundry cooperatives), the most significant early cluster occurred in the 1880s, when 200 cooperatives were formed under the auspices of the Knights of Labor. However, formation dropped off sharply in the following decades, and did not revive again until the 1930s, when at least 250 self-help cooperatives were formed. Interest died again, and did not revive until the 1970s and 1980s (Jones 1984).

Employee share purchase plans in the USA enjoyed increasing popularity during the first part of the century, culminating in the 1920s when employee ownership became a fully fledged movement called 'The New Capitalism'. However, most plans were discontinued with the stock market crash of 1929. Subsequently, they regained popularity slowly, with many public corporations introducing them during the 1950s and 1960s, mainly as an employee benefit.

A turning point came in 1974, with the passage by the US Congress of the Employee Retirement Income Security Act, which provided strong tax incentives for employee ownership. This legislation resulted from the efforts of two men. During the 1950s a lawyer named Louis Kelso became concerned that wealth, in the form of stock ownership, was overly concentrated in the USA, and that this inequity could eventually serve to undermine the political legitimacy of the capitalist system. He argued that all employees should have income not only from their labour, but also from capital. His ideas gained no political acceptance until 1973, when he met with Senator Russell Long, Chair of the Senate Finance Committee. Long immediately liked Kelso's idea and pushed through supportive legislation.

This legislation established the 'Employee Stock Ownership Trust' as a vehicle for companies to provide shares to employees at no cost to the employee. There are two main kinds of ESOP. Under the *leveraged* ESOP, the trust borrows money from a financial institution to purchase company shares, which are held by the trust as collateral for the loan. The company then contributes money to the trust over a period of years, which the trust uses to repay the loan. The primary advantage of this to the employer is that it can deduct the principal as well as the interest for tax purposes. For employees income taxes are deferred until they sell their shares, which might not be until retirement. Even then, if employees 'roll over' these funds into other investments, no taxes are payable until these other investments are liquidated.

A *non-leveraged* ESOP does not borrow money but simply contributes company shares to the trust. Employers are permitted to expense the full value of the shares for tax purposes, which provides an immediate source of cash for the firm. Under the Tax Reduction Act of 1978 this option was made even more attractive to corporations since they then received one dollar of tax credit for every dollar of shares contributed to the trust. However, this legislation was repealed in 1986 after its enormous costs had become evident.

Many amendments have been made over the years to fine tune the ESOP legislation and make ESOPs more attractive. Under one of these amendments financial institutions were allowed to exclude from their revenues half of their interest income on ESOP loans, which provided an incentive for granting these loans and also lowered the cost of these loans to the borrower. Dividends paid directly to ESOP members were also made tax deductible. Another amendment provided an additional 1 per cent investment tax credit for contributions to an ESOP (later changed to 0.5 per cent tax credit on payroll), but this was repealed in 1988 because of its high cost to the treasury (Blasi and Kruse 1991).

To encourage owners of private firms who want to sell their firm to consider allowing their employees to purchase it, employers who sell at least 30 per cent of company stock to employees are allowed to defer capital gains if the proceeds are rolled over into purchase of US stocks or bonds. The idea here is to make it as attractive to sell to employees as it is to sell to a large corporation which is able to use its shares to provide the same tax advantage to the seller.

Finally, another type of incentive for stock ownership is available outside of the ESOP

vehicle. Known as 401(k) plans (named after the section describing them in the US tax code), employees can defer current income to purchase shares and employers are allowed to fully match these contributions, also on a tax-deferred basis. Many firms prefer 401(k) plans to ESOP plans since they are much less complicated (Rosen and Young 1991).

Although no other country in the world has as much legislation as the USA to support employee ownership, the UK would rank second. As seen earlier, the tax incentives for profit sharing promulgated in 1978 automatically result in employee share ownership schemes. In addition, legislation was passed in 1980 that provides tax support for employee stock-purchase plans. Recent legislative changes in the UK have also made it possible for a structure resembling the ESOP trust to be developed, although the tax advantages are much more limited than in the USA.

Besides Britain, numerous countries in the European Union have legislation to support employee ownership (Belgium, Denmark, France, Germany, Greece and Ireland), but these provisions generally provide only modest support. In Canada there is no special support for employee ownership at the federal level, but the three largest Canadian provinces (Ontario, Quebec and British Columbia) have passed supportive legislation (Long 1992). Other countries that have changed their tax laws to favour employee ownership include Australia, Argentina, Egypt, Poland and the Philippines.

3 Motives for profit sharing

The motives for a company to introduce profit sharing tend to fall into four major groups: (1) use as a pension plan or employee savings investment plan; (2) simply as one element in developing an attractive compensation system that will both retain current employees and enable the firm to attract new employees; (3) as a means to enhance company performance by increasing employee motivation, commitment, cooperation and interest in the company; and (4) philosophical, as some business owners believe that it is only fair that the company shares its profits with those who helped to earn them.

The relative importance of these motives varies across countries, partly in response to the legislative inducements surrounding them. For example, in the USA the first motive seems to predominate (Coates 1991), in the UK the second is most important (Poole 1989) and in Canada the third is the prime motivator (Long 1991).

At a macro, or public policy, level profit sharing has been advocated for several reasons, including productivity improvement, encouragement of labour–management cooperation and reinforcement of the capitalist system. Weitzman (1984) has argued for the widespread implementation of profit sharing as a means of facilitating non-inflationary full employment. His argument is that an economy populated by profit-sharing firms should experience a higher demand for labour since firms will attempt to hire workers to the point where the value of the marginal product of labour equals the base wage. If profit sharing substitutes for a portion of base wages then base wages will be lower, which will cause higher employment.

A related argument is that by replacing a portion of fixed wages with a component that depends on firm performance, firms will be more likely to add labour in boom times and less likely to shed labour in poor economic times. Both of these forces should work to permanently increase the level of employment in a society (see FLEXIBILITY).

4 Objections to profit sharing

Given the potential advantages of profit sharing, why is it that only a minority of firms have it? Employers may object to profit sharing for several reasons. First, some see little gain in it for them. Why should they simply 'give away' their hard-earned profits? Second, there are philosophical objections: if employees are not sharing in the risks (that is, through investment of their own capital), why should they be entitled to share in the profits? Third, many firms, especially private corporations, do not wish to divulge any financial

information, which profit sharing necessitates. Fourth, many firms believe that either their profits or their workforce are too unstable for profit sharing to work. Finally, many firms might be receptive to the idea but do not have the expertise necessary to design and implement a plan.

Unions have traditionally opposed profit sharing, for several reasons. First, as noted by Karl Marx, profit sharing was to be regarded 'as a special way of cheating the workers and of *deducting a part of their wages* in the more precarious form of a profit depending on the state of the business' (Poole 1989: 9; emphasis added). In general, labour unions prefer fixed wages and benefits which can be negotiated. Employees themselves may object to profit sharing if they believe it will substitute for fixed wages and benefits. Although most profit-sharing plans do not detract from other wages and benefits (Mitchell *et al.* 1990), occasionally they do so. Finally, some unions see profit sharing as a ploy to lessen solidarity of the workers by causing them to identify more closely with the employer.

Some economists have criticized profit sharing, based on their belief that it will reduce company productivity. Under profit sharing, they argue, the direct increase in remuneration to an individual resulting from additional individual effort on the job will be insignificant. Thus, the incentive is for each worker to 'shirk' their efforts while hoping to share in the gains produced by the additional exertion of others, thus getting a 'free ride'. If everyone does this there will be no productivity gain at all. However, supporters of profit sharing counter that it will put in place a set of social dynamics and group norms that will prevent free riding.

5 Current incidence of profit sharing

To what extent is profit sharing actually used, and by what kinds of companies? Given its long history of tax incentives, it is no surprise that the USA has a very significant amount of profit sharing. In 1989 about 16 per cent of employees in medium and large firms were covered by profit-sharing plans (Coates 1991). About 41 per cent of these plans were introduced during the period 1979 to 1989. Given the nature of the tax incentives, it is not surprising that the majority of plans – about 82 per cent – were deferred profit-sharing plans. Of the others, about 6 per cent were current distribution plans and 12 per cent were combination plans.

In the UK, Poole (1989) found that 14 per cent of firms had broad-based profit sharing in 1985, covering just under one million workers. Over 90 per cent of these plans had been introduced since 1978 when the first supportive British legislation was implemented. About 62 per cent of the plans were deferred plans and 38 per cent were current distribution. In Canada, Long (1992) found that about 17 per cent of Canadian firms (that employed at least twenty persons) had profit-sharing plans in 1990. The majority of these plans (60 per cent) had been introduced during the 1980s. The great majority (75 per cent) were current distribution plans, while about 15 per cent were deferred profit-sharing plans and 10 per cent were combination plans. This pattern is almost certainly due to the lack of incentives for deferred profit-sharing plans in Canada.

The pattern of utilization also depends on whether the company is a public or private corporation. Public corporations are much more likely to have profit sharing than private corporations, and are much more likely to have deferred plans, while those private corporations that do have profit sharing are more likely to have current distribution plans.

6 Motives for employee ownership

There can be an enormous variety of motives for introducing employee ownership, but there are six main categories: (1) in hopes of improving company performance by improving employee motivation and commitment and labour–management relations; (2) to serve as an employee benefit, as part of the compensation package; (3) to serve as a source of capital, especially for smaller firms;

(4) to preserve employment (through buyouts of failing firms), or to create employment (through new starts); (5) to transfer ownership if the current owner is interested in selling out; and (6) for philosophical or ideological reasons.

As far as philosophical/ideological reasons are concerned, some see employee ownership as a way of expanding and strengthening capitalism since only a small minority of the population in most countries directly owns shares in companies. Others see employee ownership as a way of creating economic democracy, while some owners simply feel that it is 'only fair' for employees to share in the success of the firm. It may also be part of a change in managerial philosophy to increase employee involvement in the firm, a process that has been advocated by numerous prominent commentators.

There are also a number of less common reasons for employee ownership. Some governments have used employee ownership to privatize government-owned businesses, as in the case of National Freight in Britain. Occasionally shares have been demanded by unions as a *quid pro quo* for accepting wage concessions, as at the Chrysler Corporation. Some US firms (such as Polaroid) have used employee ownership to thwart hostile takeovers.

The motives for employee ownership vary from country to country. In the USA providing an employee benefit and tax advantages are the most important reasons, followed by improving productivity and then transfer of ownership (usually from a retiring owner). In the UK the motives focus more on fostering employee commitment and involvement, although tax advantages are important. In Canada improving worker commitment and motivation are the most important motives.

7 Objections to employee ownership

Despite all these possible motives, only a minority of firms have employee ownership. Why? First, owners may not wish to dilute their shareholdings. Second, employers often believe that the benefits of these plans do not justify the costs, particularly where the tax advantages are not significant. Aside from the cost of any incentives involved, developing and administering the plan may be expensive and complicated, particularly for private corporations which have no publicly traded stock. Third, and especially in private corporations, owners may be reluctant to share the power that goes with ownership, or the financial information. Moreover, many private corporations are family-owned and want to stay that way. Fourth, managers may oppose employee ownership because they feel that it will make the management task more difficult if employees expect to have a say in the operation of the firm. Employee owners may also become more critical of poor managerial performance once they have money at risk. Finally, many owners believe that employees do not want ownership since they would risk losing both their jobs and their savings in the event of company failure.

In many cases unions have opposed employee ownership. McElrath and Rowan (1992) identify five main concerns: (1) that ESOPs will be used to substitute for pension and benefit plans, increasing employee risk through lack of portfolio diversification; (2) that workers will identify more closely with the company and undermine union solidarity; (3) that employee ownership could compromise the collective bargaining process if employee owners are willing to take lower wages than they would otherwise; (4) that employees may be burdened with owning financially distressed firms; and (5) that being an owner and a union negotiator could contravene legislation regarding fair representation.

While these are potentially valid fears, McElrath and Rowan (1992) note that in fact they seldom materialize. Indeed, they argue that as organized labour has gained greater experience with employee ownership, the concept has enjoyed greater acceptance, to the point where some unions see employee ownership as a useful tool in the protection of their members' interests. Some unions, such as the United Steel Workers 'have perceived the leverage secured from employee ownership as part of a strategy for gaining control of relatively prosperous companies, restraining capital mobility, organizing workers, and defending their interests in cases of mergers and takeovers' (McElrath and Rowan 1992: 101).

8 Current incidence of employee ownership

Because of the legislative inducements the world leader in the use of employee stock-ownership plans is the USA, where at least 11,000 companies, employing more than 12 million persons, have introduced ESOPs since 1974 (Rosen and Young 1991), and this does not include the numerous employee ownership plans not falling under the ESOP umbrella. The number of wholly employee-owned firms is much lower, probably in the hundreds. Although most are quite small, some are large, such as Publix Supermarkets with 95,000 employees, and United Airlines with 78,000 employees. There are also a significant number of majority-owned firms, most of which are private corporations in the process of conversion to complete employee ownership.

In Europe the UK has experienced the most rapid growth in employee ownership, almost certainly due to its legislative support. As of 1985, Poole (1989) reported that 10 per cent of British firms had broad-based share option or other share ownership schemes, covering about 700,000 employees. (This does not include the profit-sharing plans that pay out in stock, which covered another 8 per cent of companies and 689,000 employees.)

Although not supported by federal legislation, Canada has experienced rapid growth in employee ownership, with about 7.5 per cent of firms having some type of broad-based ESOP as of 1990 (Long 1992). There is also very significant use of employee stock-purchase plans in several Asian countries, most notably in Japan, where some analysts believe that as many as 60 per cent of Japanese corporations have such plans despite lack of supportive legislation.

Most employee ownership in North America and the UK uses the corporate model, and there are relatively few wholly employee-owned firms. For worker cooperatives the leader is Italy, where there are thousands of such firms, although they are also common in France. However, the most well known and successful set of workers cooperatives is located in and around Mondragón, Spain (Whyte and Whyte 1988). The Mondragón Cooperatives now consist of over 100 affiliated cooperatives, employing about 20,000 workers. Since the establishment of the first cooperative in 1956 additional cooperatives have been established at a rapid pace, in industries ranging from machine tools to consumer electronics. A key feature of this group of cooperatives is the bank owned by the group, the Caja Laboral Popular, which provides financing and business advice to new cooperatives and serves as a type of head office for the group.

9 Consequences of profit sharing

Where profit sharing has been used, most managers believe that it has been beneficial to the company. They report that profit sharing has caused greater employee interest in the company, increased employee motivation and effort and increased employee satisfaction and loyalty (Long 1991; Poole and Jenkins 1990). Poole and Jenkins also found that employees believed that profit sharing increased employee commitment to the firm, made employees more interested in the success of the firm, served as an incentive to greater productivity and led to greater employee–management cooperation.

Most studies that have attempted to relate profit sharing to hard measures of company performance have found positive results, while virtually none have found negative results. Based on all available evidence, Weitzman and Kruse (1990) concluded that profit sharing raises company productivity between 2.5 and 11 per cent on average. However, it is not clear whether this productivity increase completely offsets the costs of the profit

sharing. There is also insufficient evidence to draw firm conclusions about whether use of profit sharing results in higher employment levels on an economy-wide basis, although there are some indications that it does so.

Most observers believe that there are a number of factors that will increase the success of profit sharing. These include employee participation in the development of the plan, extensive communication about the plan and company financial results and a participative approach to management. Specific plan characteristics may also bring about different results. For example, it is commonly believed that the wider the degree of employee eligibility and participation in the plan, the more successful the plan will be.

If profit sharing indeed raises company productivity, how does it do so? Two theoretical frameworks have attempted to explain this, based on either psychological or economic theory. Using psychological theory Florkowski (1987) argues that profit sharing can lead to increased integration of employee and company goals and increased psychological commitment to the company. This increased organizational commitment will lead to a variety of favourable outcomes, including lower absenteeism, lower turnover and improved employee motivation (see MOTIVATION AND SATISFACTION; PRODUCTIVITY).

The economic model is based on agency theory. This theory argues that owners must incur costs ('agency costs') in order to ensure that their 'agents' (managers and workers) are acting in their best interests. These costs are primarily the costs of monitoring managers and workers to ensure that all resources are directed towards organizational goals. By aligning the goals of employees more closely with those of the owners (shareholders) it is possible that the costs of monitoring and supervising employees can be reduced.

10 Consequences of employee ownership

Most studies of employee ownership have found positive effects on employee job attitudes, such as commitment, motivation, satisfaction and interest in the company, although some studies have found neutral effects and a few have found some negative effects. In terms of company performance, most studies have shown either neutral or mildly positive effects, with one major exception. Where implementation of employee ownership has been accompanied by a process for employee participation in decision making, dramatic positive effects have been found (Conte and Svejnar 1990). Other factors thought to relate to greater success include a greater proportion of the company owned by employees, a greater proportion of employees within the firm holding shares and effective communication of information about the plan, financial results and key management issues facing the company.

Some evidence is available from examining the experience with employee buy-outs. For example, it appears that about half of the firms involved in 'distress buy-outs' during the 1980s have survived, which is impressive when considering that virtually none of these firms would have survived otherwise (Rosen and Young 1991). Another study found that firms in the USA that had undergone leveraged employee buy-outs (not necessarily in distress situations) performed at least as well as firms that had not.

Most of the foregoing results apply to firms using the corporate model. Worker cooperatives have been found to be highly successful in some western European countries, most notably Italy, where they appear to be more productive than conventional enterprises, and France, where they have a high survival rate. They have been less successful in the UK and the USA, although exceptions can be found in both countries.

Like profit sharing, there are two main theoretical models to explain the impact of employee ownership; one based on economic theory and the other on psychological theory. The economic argument is based on agency theory and is very similar to the argument for profit sharing.

Using the psychological perspective Long (1978) developed a model for employee ownership leading to beneficial consequences through increasing organizational integration, involvement and commitment. Integration of individual and organizational goals through employee ownership is thought to lead to improved group work norms and higher motivation. Psychological involvement is believed to lead to cooperative behaviours and satisfaction, and commitment is thought to lead to lower turnover, absenteeism and grievances.

Pierce *et al.* (1991) extended this model by focusing on variables that may intervene between formal employee ownership and the attitudinal and behavioural variables posited in Long's model. They contend that the key intervening variable is psychologically experienced ownership, which is determined by the extent to which three core ownership rights (rights to equity, influence and information) are brought about by employee ownership. As discussed earlier, rights to influence (worker participation in decision making) appears to be the single most important variable.

11 Future prospects

It is likely that both profit sharing and employee ownership will continue to increase in popularity for several reasons. The first stems from the legislative support that these concepts, especially employee ownership, have been receiving in recent years. Given the difficult economic circumstances facing most countries, governments in all probability will continue to support these concepts, particularly as the benefits from doing so become more apparent. It is also likely that governments will continue to see these concepts as a way of building more competitive business organizations, with improved labour–management relations. Indeed, the European Union has issued a directive urging its member countries to legislate incentives for employee financial participation schemes (see INDUSTRIAL AND LABOUR RELATIONS; INDUSTRIAL RELATIONS IN EUROPE).

From a management point of view these concepts fit well with a new philosophy of management which is currently emerging. Termed the 'industrial humanistic' or 'human resources' or 'high involvement' approach to management, this philosophy argues that companies will be most productive when they regard employees as partners in the enterprise. These firms entrust decision making and other responsibilities to front-line workers, giving them considerable latitude in how they perform their work activities. Proponents argue that this type of firm will be best suited to deal with the economic and social conditions that have emerged toward the end of the twentieth century – such as a turbulent business environment, complex and quickly changing technologies, a highly educated and quite prosperous work force and social values that emphasize democratic involvement.

To put this in historical context, Poole (1989) notes that there has been a general advance in economic and organizational democracy during the twentieth century in most Western industrialized countries. Although organizational democracy tends to advance in waves that peak and ebb, even after the ebb the level of organizational democracy remains higher than what it was at the beginning of the wave.

Although not every firm will be willing and able to implement employee profit sharing or share ownership, those that do so effectively will no doubt enjoy a significant competitive advantage. As knowledge about these concepts spreads an increasing number of firms will likely attempt to harness this competitive advantage.

RICHARD LONG
UNIVERSITY OF SASKATCHEWAN

Further reading

(References cited in the text marked *)

* Bell, D.W. and Hanson, C.G. (1987) *Profit Sharing and Profitability: How Profit Sharing Promotes Business Success*, London: Kogan Page. (Presents the findings of a major study of the impact of profit sharing plans in the UK.)

Blasi, J.R. (1988) *Employee Ownership: Revolution or Ripoff?*, New York: Harper Business. (Provides a comprehensive evaluation and critique of ESOP legislation in the USA along with prescriptions for change.)

* Blasi, J.R. and Kruse, D.L. (1991) *The New Owners: The Mass Emergence of Employee Owner-* *ship in Public Companies and What it Means to American Business*, New York: HarperCollins. (Describes the rapid increase by public companies in the USA in the use of ESOPs and the potential consequences.)

* Coates, E.M. (1991) 'Profit sharing today: plans and provisions', *Monthly Labor Review* 114 (4): 19–25. (Presents data on the extent and nature of profit-sharing plans in the USA.)

* Conte, M. and Svejnar, J. (1990) 'The performance effects of employee share ownership plans', in A.S. Blinder (ed.), *Paying for Productivity: A Look at the Evidence*, Washington, DC: The Brookings Institution. (Comprehensive review of the evidence on employee ownership and company performance.)

* Florkowski, G.W. (1987) 'The organizational impact of profit sharing', *Academy of Management Review* 12 (4): 622–36. (Based on theory and empirical evidence, proposes a conceptual framework to explain the effects of profit sharing.)

* Florkowski, G.W. (1991) 'Profit sharing and public policy: insights for the United States', *Industrial Relations* 30 (1): 96–115. (After reviewing the extent of profit-sharing legislation around the world, discusses whether the USA should increase its support for profit sharing.)

Jenkins, G. and Poole, M. (eds) (1990) *New Forms of Ownership*, London: Routledge. (Useful set of nineteen theoretical and empirical readings on employee ownership and profit sharing.)

* Jones, D.C. (1984) 'American producer cooperatives and employee owned firms: a historical perspective', in R. Jackall and H.M. Levin (eds), *Worker Cooperatives in America*, Berkeley, CA: University of California Press. (Traces the evolution of worker cooperatives in the USA.)

Kruse, D.L. (1993) *Profit Sharing: Does it Make a Difference?*, Kalamazoo, MI: W.E. Upjohn Institute. (Provides the most up to date and thorough review of the evidence on the productivity and employment effects of profit sharing.)

Kruse, D.L. (1996) 'Why do firms adopt profit sharing and employee ownership plans?' British Journal of Industrial Relations 34 (4) 515–538. (Presents the results of a major US study of factors affecing the adoption of profit sharing and share ownership plans.)

Kruse, D. and Blasi, J. (1995) 'Employee ownership, employee attitudes and firm performance: a review of the evidence', in D. Lewin, D. Mitchell and M. Zaidi (eds), *Handbook of Human Resources*, Greenwich, CT: JAI Press Inc.

(Presents a review of the empirical evidence relating employee ownership to employee attitude and company performance.)

Long, R.J. (1978) 'The effects of employee ownership on organizational identification, job attitudes, and organizational performance: a tentative framework and empirical findings', *Human Relations* 31 (1): 29–48. (Provides a theoretical framework attempting to explain the consequences of employee share ownership.)

Long, R.J. (1991) *Employee Profit Sharing and Share Ownership in Canada: Results of a Survey of Chief Executive Officers*, Toronto: Profit Sharing Council of Canada. (Provides the results of a major survey of the extent and nature of profit sharing and employee ownership in Canada, including objectives for implementation and perceived success.)

Long, R.J. (1992) 'The incidence and nature of employee profit sharing and stock ownership in Canada', *Relations Industrielles* 47 (3): 463–88. (Presents data on the incidence and nature of profit sharing and employee ownership in Canada.)

Long, R.J. (1997) 'Motives for profit sharing: A study of Canadian chief executive officers', *Relations Industrielles* 52 (4): in press. (Provides an anlysis of the motives of Canadian chief executive officers for adopting or not adopting employee profit sharing.)

McElrath, R.G. and Rowan, R.L. (1992) 'The American labor movement and employee ownership: objections to and uses of employee stock ownership plans', *Journal of Labor Research* 8 (1): 99–119. (Analyses the reaction of US unions to employee ownership and suggests how it could be used to their advantage.)

Mitchell, D.J.B., Lewin, D. and Lawler, E.E. (1990) 'Alternative pay systems, firm performance, and productivity', in A.S. Blinder (ed.), *Paying for Productivity: A Look at the Evidence*, Washington, DC: The Brookings Institution. (Provides an analysis of the evidence on the performance effects of alternative pay systems, particularly profit sharing.)

Pierce, J.L., Rubenfeld, S.A. and Morgan, S. (1991) 'Employee ownership: a conceptual model of process and effects', *Academy of Management Review* 16 (1): 121–44. (Provides a comprehensive theoretical model of the effects of employee ownership.)

Poole, M. (1989) *The Origins of Economic Democracy: Profit-sharing and Employee-shareholding schemes*, London: Routledge. (Provides a detailed description of the current extent of profit sharing and employee owner-ship plans in the UK and the forces underlying their expansion.)

* Poole, M. and Jenkins, G. (1990) *The Impact of Economic Democracy: Profit-sharing and Employee-shareholding Schemes*, London: Routledge. (Provides the results of a comprehensive study of the consequences of profit sharing and employee ownership in British firms.)

Rosen C., Klein, K. and Young, K. (1986) *Employee Ownership in America: The Equity Solution*, Lexington, MA: Lexington Books. (Major study and description of employee ownership in the USA, including many case examples.)

* Rosen, C. and Young, K.M. (eds) (1991) *Understanding Employee Ownership*, Ithaca, NY: ILR Press. (Comprehensive set of readings on employee ownership in the USA, with an excellent chapter on share ownership plans in other countries.)

Tyson, D.E. (1996) *Profit Sharing in Canada: The Complete Guide to Designing and Implementing Plans that Really Work*, Toronto: John Wiley. (Provides an exellent outline of the specific issues involved in designing a profit sharing plan.)

* Weitzman, M.L. (1984) *The Share Economy*, Cambridge, MA: Harvard University Press. (Expounds Weitzman's theory that widespread use of profit sharing as a substitute for a portion of fixed pay will stimulate a full employment society.)

* Weitzman, M.L. and Kruse, D.L. (1990) 'Profit sharing and productivity', in A.S. Blinder (ed.), *Paying for Productivity: A Look at the Evidence*, Washington, DC: The Brookings Institution. (Provides a careful review of the empirical evidence linking profit sharing to company productivity.)

* Whyte, W.F. and Whyte, K.K. (1988) *Making Mondragón: The Growth and Dynamics of the Worker Cooperative Complex*, Ithaca, NY: ILR Press. (Comprehensive study of the evolution of the worker cooperative complex at Mondragón, Spain.)

Young, K.M. (ed.) (1990) *The Expanding Role of ESOPs in Public Companies*, New York: Quorum Books. (Set of readings on the financial, technical and performance aspects of ESOPs in US public companies.)

See also: DECISION MAKING; EMPLOYEE RELATIONS, MANAGEMENT OF; FLEXIBILITY; FINANCIAL INCENTIVES; HUMAN RESOURCE DEVELOPMENT; INDUSTRIAL

DEMOCRACY; INDUSTRIAL AND LABOUR RELATIONS; INDUSTRIAL RELATIONS IN EUROPE; PAYMENT SYSTEMS

Related topics in the IEBM: AGENCY, MARKETS AND HIERARCHIES; LABOUR MARKETS; ORGANIZATIONAL PERFORMANCE

Recruitment and selection

Overview

Recruitment and selection make up the staffing function in organizations. The primary goal of staffing is to assure that companies get the qualified people they need in order for the company to operate as efficiently and effectively as possible. Prior to recruitment and selection, two steps must be taken. First, a company must scan and analyse the external environment and examine the company's internal situation to develop human resource plans and forecasts; these actions anchor the staffing effort. More broadly, these human resource plans form an integral part of an organization's strategic business plan. Ultimately, to be effective, the staffing function should be thoroughly integrated with the company's overall business strategies. The second precursor to beginning the recruitment and selection effort is job analysis. Although the human resource plans and forecasts identify general personnel needs, job analysis is used specifically to determine the types of individuals the company wishes to recruit and select. Each type of job is described in terms of its purpose, its major duties and activities, the conditions under which it is performed, and the necessary knowledge, skills, abilities and other requirements. This information guides recruitment and selection activities.

1 Introduction

Getting the right individuals interested in applying for a job at a company is the essence of recruitment. Effective recruitment depends on knowing how individuals view recruitment as well as how an organization views it. Thus, it is important for human resource management (HRM) to know the needs of the applicant and the needs of the business (see HUMAN RESOURCE MANAGEMENT; JOB EVALUATION). Which of these needs gets priority depends on the situation. When there are many more applicants than jobs, it is a buyer's market, and the business needs could get priority. Conversely, in times with many more jobs than applicants, there is a seller's market, and the needs of the applicant might win out. Given labour market fluctuations, supply and demand are likely to flip/flop over time. For example, until quite recently, the market for nurses in the USA was clearly a seller's market. However, with the changing emphasis on cost-cutting in health care institutions, a substantial number of nursing positions were eliminated and nurses were laid off; these factors dramatically changed the market through increased supply relative to demand.

Given the possibility of these varying conditions, an organization's best tactic is to develop a specific set of recruiting procedures and use them consistently rather than attempting constantly to adjust to a changing market. Although this may at times result in giving more to individuals than is necessary or than some firms might wish, it also can result in the firm being attractive to candidates regardless of employment and economic conditions.

After job applicants have been recruited, the process of selection begins, that is, the organization deciding whether to extend an offer and the individual deciding whether to accept it. The organization must develop and utilize procedures for selecting the people who are most likely to perform well once hired. In addition, the entire recruitment and selection process must be conducted in a manner consistent with relevant civil rights laws, that is, in a non-discriminatory fashion.

A commonly held myth concerning staffing is that the organizational cost of establishing and using a rigorous, valid selection procedure does not pay off (Podsakoff *et al.* 1988). However, assuming that the person hired does in fact perform well, the organization's level of productivity should increase. Research has shown that the ratio of the performance of highly productive workers to those with low productivity is as high as three to one (Schmidt and Hunter 1983). Therefore, the cost of utilizing a staffing procedure that will increase the likelihood of hiring good performers should actually save the company money in the long run. This positive impact will be greatest when the company is able not only to hire the best but also to effectively retain high-performing individuals.

As Dunnette (1976) pointed out, two types of errors in staffing decisions can occur. In a 'false positive' error, a person is placed in a job but fails to be successful. A 'false negative' error is when a candidate is not hired or placed in a job in which he or she could have been successful. Although it is clear that both of these wrong decisions would be costly to an organization, a 'false positive' mistake can have major financial consequences because of training costs, lost productivity and replacement costs.

2 Recruitment

The general purpose of recruitment is to provide an organization with a pool of potentially qualified job candidates (see HUMAN RESOURCE MANAGEMENT; HUMAN RESOURCE MANAGEMENT, INTERNATIONAL). The underlying objectives embedded in this process are: acquiring this pool at the lowest possible cost; reducing the number of obviously overqualified or underqualified candidates; reducing the likelihood that an applicant, once hired, would leave the organization after a short time; and meeting the organization's legal and social obligations. There is also a more subtle consideration in recruitment. Research indicates that in developing recruitment strategies, organizations should be cognizant of the types of inferences applicants may make based on a company's recruitment practices. Candidates view factors such as recruiter competence, sex composition of interview

panels, recruitment delays and even rejection letters as indicative of broader organizational characteristics (Rynes *et al.* 1991). The various aspects of recruitment are further described below (see PERSONNEL MANAGEMENT).

Sources and methods for obtaining job applicants

An organization must consider a number of issues when developing a strategy for recruitment. One of the most important decisions is whether to recruit internally, externally, or both. Potential advantages of internal recruitment over external include: (1) performance information on current employees is available; (2) selection is generally less costly since initial information has been analysed; (3) positions may be filled faster (no time spent contacting employees or getting recommendations); (4) candidates are already familiar with organizational norms, etc., which helps to reduce training (see TRAINING) and socialization; and (5) promotion from within can be a motivator signalling to other employees that peak performance will be rewarded (Breaugh 1992).

An external recruitment orientation also often realizes some advantages: (1) outside individuals can import new ideas and/or trade secrets; (2) external candidates may reduce the need for employee training and development, particularly if they have been trained elsewhere; (3) hiring outsiders can indicate a changing business; and (4) there may not be a viable internal person.

The internal versus external recruitment decision is especially important to managerial hiring. Top decision makers often believe that there is need for continuity in managers, and therefore, promote high-level managers from within the company (see MANAGERIAL BEHAVIOUR). However, caution in this area is advised. The risk is that managers all have the same organizational experience, have become familiar with the status quo, and therefore may approach strategic issues similarly. This can result in the organization being unable to adapt to changing environmental and business demands (Falvey 1987; Schuler and

Jackson 1987) (see HUMAN RESOURCE MAN-
AGEMENT).

In general, research indicates that a combination of internal and external recruitment
produces the best results. The exact mix depends on the organization's strategic plan.
Factors such as the amount of money that can
be expended, how quickly the position is to be
filled, as well as careful consideration of the
organizational business environment, all feed
into decisions regarding the internal/external
recruitment mix (Olian and Rynes 1984). Unfortunately, there has been little research comparing internally recruited and externally
recruited employees with respect to their motivation, productivity and/or job satisfaction
(see MOTIVATION AND SATISFACTION).

Internal sources and methods

There are four recruitment sources for candidates inside the organization, namely promotions from within, lateral transfers of
employees, job rotation, and rehiring or
recalling former employees. Two frequently
used methods to recruit internal employees
are job posting and skills inventories. Job
posting involves prominently displaying current job openings in order to invite all employees of the organization to apply. In the past,
this method has been most often used for clerical and blue-collar jobs. However, it is
increasingly being used for all types of jobs at
all levels of organizations. This strategy is
consistent with the trend towards high
involvement and open communication in
organizations. Job posting has the advantages
of making all types of employees (for example, minorities and women) aware of openings, uncovering hidden talent that may have
been overlooked, and encouraging employees
to be responsible for their own career development (see CAREERS). It also helps to ensure
that anyone with the requisite skills who
wishes to apply will be considered, thus helping to eliminate the similar-to-me bias that
often leads to discrimination (Gist and Fuller
1995) (see EQUAL EMPLOYMENT OPPORTUNI-
TIES).

The skills inventory method uses a human
resource information system to compile skills

information on all employees. Information
could include name, employee number, job
classification, previous jobs and experience,
salary levels, skills assessment results, work
sample results, employee interests and career
goals. In addition to these two internal recruitment methods, employees often become candidates for open jobs through informal
systems in the organization such as simple
word of mouth.

External sources and methods

Several reasons for organizations wishing to
recruit externally were discussed earlier.
External sources of recruits include employee
referral programmes, walk-ins, employment
agencies, other companies, temporary help
agencies, trade associations and unions, contract agencies, schools and colleges. The most
common methods used to locate external
applicants are radio, television, newspaper
and trade journal advertisements. Techniques
that are gaining in popularity include electronic postings via electronic mail and telephone job listings. When companies create
the recruiting advertisements, they should
consider what they want to accomplish with
the advertisement, specifically, the required
qualifications, the number of candidates
desired, the timeframe to fill the position, the
available advertising budget, and the target
candidate population.

The job search from the applicant's perspective

For organizations to attract potentially qualified applicants, they need to understand how
candidates are attracted, and to what they are
attracted. An important part of this understanding of job search strategies is knowing
the sources applicants use to learn about jobs.
Surveys indicate that across all jobs, informal
methods – referrals from friends and relatives,
direct applications – are used most often by
recruits. More formal sources, such as advertisements and employment agencies, are used
often by managerial and clerical employees.
Interestingly, employees using the informal

methods are more likely to still be in the job one year after hiring.

Another major factor concerning applicant job searches is the intensity with which people conduct their search. This intensity can be influenced by financial need, that is, individuals who are currently employed spend less time searching for other jobs than do unemployed workers. In addition, applicants with high self-esteem and a high need for achievement tend to conduct more intensive job searches than individuals with lower expectations.

A final important factor is for organizations to be familiar with how applicants evaluate job offers. Applicants focus on both occupational choice and organizational choice. Occupational choice occurs throughout an individual's life and results in narrowing the job offers perceived as of interest. Organizational choice is normally a sequential process except in the case of new college graduates who, because of more than one offer, may consider jobs simultaneously. In evaluating job offers, individuals consider such job attributes as wages, co-workers, benefits, hours and job security.

Ensuring organizational fit

As emphasized earlier, it is costly for an organization to hire the wrong individuals. Therefore, through the recruiting process, it is in an organization's best interest to increase the likelihood that high-quality applicants will be successfully recruited, hired and retained as employees. Five organizational strategies can help to achieve this recruitment goal. The first is to convey to the applicant thorough, accurate and realistic information concerning both the job and the overall organization. This is facilitated by devoting careful attention to the job interview, having a job-matching programme, carefully timing recruiting efforts, providing realistic job information, and developing appropriate policies regarding job offer acceptances. Research has shown that because providing recruits with accurate information (positive and negative) shapes their expectations, they are less likely to leave once they have accepted the job, and they are more likely to

have higher levels of eventual job satisfaction and organizational commitment (Wanous *et al.* 1992).

The second strategy is to expand career opportunities within the organization (see CAREERS). This can include career management programmes and work–family interface programmes. In a third strategy, organizations can offer alternative work arrangements such as flexible work schedules, compressed work weeks, part-time employment, job sharing, and work-at-home arrangements. The fourth strategy is to provide employment security.

The fifth strategy is effective socialization, that is the process of exposing new employees to the company's culture and way of doing things. Managing socialization successfully increases the likelihood of employees being loyal to and staying with the company, thus avoiding potential future problems with labour shortages. Initial socialization is frequently accomplished through formal orientation programmes in which new employees are advised of benefits, work rules and regulations, organizational history and structure and expected behaviour. In addition, job assignments of new employees serve a similar function. The characteristics of the first job, the first supervisor and experiences in that job all serve a socialization function by sending signals about the organization. Informal socialization occurs through all of the new employee's early experiences as he or she discovers the informal norms and organizational politics.

3 Selection

Through the recruitment process, companies acquire a pool of potentially qualified applicants (see HUMAN RESOURCE MANAGEMENT). Next, selection is used to gather legally defensible and performance-relevant information about these applicants in order to determine who to hire. The following sections describe types of job applicant information, techniques for obtaining the information (including information on the validity of various selection techniques) and methods of using the information.

Types of applicant information

Selection techniques, or devices, are used to assess candidates' qualifications concerning such factors as knowledge, skills, abilities, preferences, interests and personality. The purpose of gathering this information is to allow the company to predict which applicants will be successful if hired. These types of information, therefore, are called 'predictors'. Elements of job performance such as work quality and absenteeism are referred to as 'criteria'. Jobs must be thoroughly analysed before selection begins in order to identify the important predictors and criteria for a job. The goal is to find reliable and valid predictors that will increase the likelihood that the candidates who are selected will subsequently perform well on the important criteria. Identifying appropriate and readily measurable criteria is a challenge in validating selection devices.

The reliability and validity of predictors refer to the degree to which the devices measure the information in dependable and accurate ways. A reliable measure is one that consistently produces the same results time after time. For example, if a mechanical ability test were administered several times to the same applicant, the scores should be equivalent. This type of reliability is 'test-retest reliability'. A second important type of reliability is termed 'inter-rater reliability'. If, for instance, several people used a device to score an applicant in an interview, and they all gave the candidate equivalent scores, the device would have a high degree of inter-rater reliability.

In addition to the reliability, or consistency, of a measurement device, it must also be valid, or accurate. Three types of validity are important. First, the device should in fact measure the concept it is intended to measure. For example, if an interview-scoring device purports to measure the communication skill of the applicant, then a high score should mean that the applicant has strong communication skills. This is referred to as 'construct validity'.

The second type of validity is 'criterion-related validity', referring to whether the selection device accurately predicts performance on the important criteria. An example of high criterion-related validity is a cognitive ability test designed such that scores on the test correlate mathematically with people's performance on the job. The validity correlation coefficient can range from -1.00 to $+1.00$. The closer the correlation is to 1.00, the more valid the selection device. One example of a valid selection device is a paper and pencil test that assesses perceptual capability to discern differences in stimuli; this test has been shown to be a valid predictor for such jobs as quality control inspectors, electronic repair jobs and copy editors.

'Content validity' is the third type of validity. Although similar to criterion-related validity, content validity is based on a judgement that the predictor is related to the job-performance factors rather than an actual measurement and calculation of the relationship. The types of information discussed below must be measured with reliable and valid selection devices. The techniques used to assess the information are presented in the next section.

An important decision facing companies is whether to hire individuals who possess the specific knowledge, skills and abilities the job demands or whether to train people after they are hired. This decision hinges primarily on the difficulty of finding someone with the requisite knowledge, skills and abilities to perform the job, as well as the extent of training that would be required, and whether there are other predictors that may be more important.

The next sub-set of applicant information includes personality, interests and preferences. Personality is a set of relatively stable traits that characterize individuals and identify their disposition to function in certain ways. Research examining the validity of personality traits as predictors of job performance has been mixed. The most encouraging results indicate the predictive value of five major personality categories – extroversion, emotional stability, agreeableness, conscientiousness, and openness to experience – for a variety of occupations (Barrick and Mount 1991). Studies showed that conscientiousness was related to performance across five occupational groups, and the other four personality characteristics predicted performance in some situations. In spite of some promising research, however, personality tests remain controversial. In some countries (Australia, for example) they have yet to meet with widespread acceptance (Dowling *et al.* 1994).

In addition to personality, matching a candidate's interests and preferences with those required for the job can lead to employees who are more satisfied and have less absenteeism and turnover (Dawis 1991). For example, a person who is investigative and likes activities requiring order, analysis, attention to detail and little social interaction would be better suited to such jobs as computer programmer or accountant than to an office receptionist.

A final type of information being used in selection is biographical data, or biodata. These data go beyond general background information to things such as academic achievement, work attitudes, physical orientation, self-perception, and beliefs and feelings about past experiences. Through this information, organizations attempt to better predict how individuals will behave in the future. However, like other selection tools, biodata should be used only if it has been shown to be reliable and valid. One interesting example of valid biodata is the information used to predict success of pilots in flight training during the

Second World War. Those who, before the age of twelve, had constructed a paper aeroplane that flew were more likely to become successful pilots.

Techniques for gathering applicant information

Job applicant information can be collected via many different types of device. In choosing which device(s) to use, organizations must consider cost, type and amount of information collected, and the validity of the predictor. Also, recent research has shown the important effect of selection procedures on the impressions applicants form concerning both the job and the organization. For example, applicants who perceived selection techniques such as cognitive tests and assessment centres more favourably were more satisfied with the selection process, the job and the organization, which in turn made them more likely to accept a job offer (Macan *et al.* 1994). Several commonly used devices are shown in Table 1 and described below.

Application blanks
The application blank is used to gather a variety of information about the applicant's background and present position. This information

Table 1 Usage and validity of common selection devices

Selection device	Firms using device (%)	Criterion-related validity
Situational interview	5–20	0.54
Cognitive ability test	42	0.53
Work sample test	6	0.44
Assessment centre	6	0.44
Biodata	11	0.37
Personality	5	0.10–0.25
Interest inventory	5	0.10
Education rating	(no data)	0.10
Standard interview	70	0.07
Drug screening	25	(varied)
Alcohol screening	13	(varied)
Genetic screening	1	(varied)

includes: past and present work experience; education level, degrees and content of education; training; and references. The application blank is often used as an initial screening device to assess whether the applicant meets minimum job requirements. Unfortunately, the accuracy of application blanks is a concern. It has been reported that nearly 30 per cent of applications contain false information.

In designing application blanks, organizations must be particularly careful to avoid questions that are illegal or inadvisable. For example, in the USA, questions concerning race, age, sex, religion and national origin, while not strictly illegal, may signal to applicants that the organization will use these data for selection. Therefore, a safer strategy would be to avoid asking these types of questions. Organizations may ask about criminal convictions but not about arrests. Questions relating to such issues as marital status and dependants should be avoided but, if they are asked, men and women must be treated equally. Physical requirements should only be considered if they are truly necessary for job performance.

Finally, education and prior work experience are commonly used worldwide to select employees for entry level positions. However, these factors predict performance for the first job in an organization only. To select employees for promotion, unionized firms and companies in Pacific Rim often use experience (seniority); however, its validity in predicting performance is questionable.

Written tests

Another important method by which to gather applicant information is through written tests. Common types are those that assess ability, personality and interests. Cognitive ability tests can measure such things as verbal comprehension, numerical aptitude, inductive reasoning, perceptual speed and memory. Other types of ability tests are those that measure mechanical ability and psychomotor ability (the correlation of thought with body movement). As discussed previously, personality, preference and interests can lead to several generally favourable organizational outcomes. A difficult task associated with using

personality as a predictor has been that of defining relevant personality variables and validly measuring those variables. The validity issue with personality tests primarily involves criterion-related validity; it is difficult to identify personality predictors for specific types of job.

Other types of written tests include interest inventories, preferences for different types of work and work situations (Hogan 1988), and the applicant's knowledge and acquired skills. As with personality tests, the challenge is to ensure that any written test is work-related and will, in fact, predict job performance. Finally, to reduce the likelihood of such possibilities as employee theft, written honesty tests have been developed and are being used for selection.

Work simulations

In work simulations, an applicant completes verbal or physical activities that replicate actual work. These techniques have a high degree of validity, in part due to the fact that they are difficult to fake. To be effective, work simulations must be specific to the job; therefore, they can be costly to develop. Examples include asking candidates to write a memo, process mathematical data, deal with customers on the telephone, use specific word-processing equipment and repair machinery.

Assessment centres

Assessment centres build from the more simple work simulations and use situational tests or exercises so that specific behaviours of the candidates can be observed and scored by trained evaluators. Assessment centres, which are especially appropriate for complex attributes and abilities, are unique in that they combine several different types of selection tools into one device. They have been used for some time as managerial development tools, but their popularity as a selection device has grown in recent years. An important consideration in assessment centres as selection devices is that, to be effective, an assessment centre should specifically fit the job human resource decision for which it is intended

(Thornton 1992); therefore it can be costly to develop.

Research into the use of assessment centres at the US telecommunications giant AT&T revealed that the scores for the assessment centre evaluations were valid predictors of future performance on the job. In addition, simply being a participant in the assessment centres predicted future promotions.

Interviews

The job interview is the device most often used to determine who to hire. Although past research has questioned its reliability and validity as a selection device (Arvey and Campion 1982), recent meta-analyses (analysing results from a large number of studies) have reported a more encouraging picture (McDaniel *et al.* 1994; Wright *et al.* 1989). Overall, the research reveals that the value of the selection interview appears to vary dramatically according to several factors (Dipboye 1992; Schuler and Huber 1993).

The first consideration is the relevance of the interview questions to the specific job. General questions give an overall impression, but may not predict job success. Therefore, the predictive interview will contain specific questions about the duties and skills that were identified in the job analysis.

The second factor is the degree of structure in the interview, that is, the degree to which the questions and order of questions are defined in advance. Too little structure results in inconsistent information across interviews and wandering into often non-productive and non-relevant conversations. Research supports a more structured interview approach. The same questions are asked of all applicants and responses are recorded and compared against established criteria. There are two types of valid structured questions: the experience-based and the situational-based. The former asks applicants to relate their behaviour in past job or life situations which is relevant to the job requirements. In contrast, the situational questions are future orientated, asking candidates to indicate how they would behave in a hypothetical, job-related situation. Consistent with the philosophy that past behaviour is the best predictor of future

behaviour, the experience-based questions have been shown to be slightly more valid than the situational ones (Pulakos and Schmitt 1995).

The third important factor is the method used to score the interviews. A systematic method with specific criteria, behaviourally anchored rating scales and a defined scoring key increases reliability by ensuring consistent ratings and also increases validity, especially construct validity. The fourth consideration is the number of interviewers. A panel of interviewers, all assessing the candidate at same time, rather than the applicant being interviewed sequentially by several interviewers, generally increases the consistency of the information. The fifth factor affecting the quality of interviews is interviewers' training. This training involves definition of criteria, and interpreting and scoring interviews.

Physical tests

Several additional devices can be used to obtain applicant information. Because drug and alcohol abuse exist and can have significant impacts on both individuals and society (Schuler and Huber 1993), organizations often implement drug and alcohol testing programmes. In the USA, the Employee Polygraph Protection Act of 1988 severely restricts the use of polygraphs as a selection device (Labato 1988). Physical examinations can also be used to gather applicant information. In doing so, organizations must ensure that a physical exam is necessary to predict job performance, and that it does not systematically screen out disabled applicants in countries in which they are legally protected.

A recent addition to physical selection tests stems from advances in technology. Genetic screening is now available to organizations. It provides the capability to test applicants and identify those who may be hypersensitive to pollutants in the workplace, thus allowing the placement of hired staff out of harm's way. Another potential use of genetic screening is to identify job candidates who may be susceptible to various diseases and physical or mental conditions.

Use of information for selection decisions

All of the above selection devices can be used to choose a potential employee. The decision over which selection devices to use involves assessment of time constraints, job related-ness of the information and the costs associated with gathering the information. Sometimes, for relatively unskilled or simple jobs, organizations can use a single device as a predictor. For example, to fill a job in a typing pool, the candidate's score on a typing test may be enough information on which to base a hiring decision. More often, however, organizations use multiple devices, or predictors, to select from a pool of applicants. This can be accomplished in several different ways. One is to use a multiple hurdle approach such that an applicant must exceed certain levels of proficiency on all of the predictors in order to qualify. A second approach is the compensatory model in which excellent scores on one predictor can compensate for poorer scores on another. The final selection is then based on a composite index of scores on all predictors. An example is selection to an MBA programme in which an applicant's grade point average is multiplied by 200 and added to his or her General Management Aptitude Test score to create the index. A third common approach is a combination model. In this case, organizations have one or more hurdles that must be cleared; applicants who clear those hurdles are scored on other predictors and a composite index is then used to make a final selection. For instance, selecting nurses might involve meeting licensing requirements (a hurdle) then assessments of competence in technical and interpersonal skills (compensatory).

4 Issues in recruitment and selection

Within the recruitment and selection processes, several important organizational issues emerge. The first of these is the management of workforce diversity. Current radical transformations of the demographic make-up of the workforce, including internationalization, mean that staffing efforts must be concerned with maintaining the appropriate balance among job applicants and hired employees. The 'appropriate' balance will depend on a number of factors including type of job, organization and industry, and national customs, norms and laws.

A second staffing concern is whether companies' efforts are indeed effective. As mentioned earlier, incorrect staffing decisions can be quite costly to organizations; therefore, the quality of staffing decisions should be examined. To assess the recruitment process, organizations examine, in general, whether they have attracted the right people at the right time within legal constraints. Specifically, a utility analysis can be conducted. The analysis includes criteria at all stages of the recruitment process such as number and type of applicant, cost per applicant, offers extended, number and type of hires, and initial expectations of newcomers. In order to identify reasons for recruiting success or failure, evaluations should cost out (in terms of long- and short-term benefits) the different recruiting methods, types of recruiters, applicant sources and advertising approaches (Breaugh 1992).

To carry the assessment through to the selection process, the organization must evaluate the predictive validity of the procedures and devices that were used. That is, did the selection process result in high-performing employees exhibiting positive organizational attitudes and behaviours?

A third issue in staffing is the potentially negative effect of cognitive biases. The recruitment and selection processes are complex and involve human decision making; unfortunately, however, human information-processing capabilities are limited. Therefore, managers and other decision makers rely on inferences and shortcuts in judgement, and biases become a critical issue (Huber *et al.* 1980). Two general human tendencies are the over-utilization of certain intuitively appealing but biased inferential strategies, and the under-utilization of logical, formal and statistical strategies (Nisbitt and Ross 1980). The distortions adversely affect staffing by producing decisions that are often far from optimal.

Although it is impossible to rid people of biases, steps can be taken to minimize their adverse effect on staffing (Huber *et al.* 1980). The first is to train decision makers to understand biases in general, to be aware of their own biases and to institute methods to correct them. One such method is to provide the decision maker with decision aids that force him or her to make concrete and to quantify the sometimes hidden assumptions and intuitions that often guide decisions. This can be accomplished by assigning to the decision maker the role of devil's advocate, or by the decision maker's use of a formal decision analysis procedure. In contrast to the above methods, decision programmes actually take the decision making out of human hands and place the function in a computerized mathematical model. With this approach, human resource personnel identify important factors and assign weights to them, but do not make the final selection decision, thus reducing judgemental bias. However, managers are not readily accepting of this approach, contending that the finer subtleties of decision making cannot be captured in a computer program.

A final issue relevant to selection stems from additional information that organizations may currently have available to them. Examples include the results of genetic screening and HIV testing. Armed with this type of information, organizations could screen out those applicants who it determined might, in the future, be costly to insure. This, of course, raises both ethical and legal questions about the use of genetic screening and other methods to obtain sensitive information.

5 Conclusion

The staffing processes of recruitment and selection are critical to organizational effectiveness. Just as organizations carefully weigh decisions to expend financial capital, so too should they carefully weigh human resource decisions. Recruitment and selection are an integral component of other human resource activities including employee training and development, compensation and employee relations (see EMPLOYEE RELATIONS, MANAGEMENT OF; FINANCIAL INCENTIVES;

HUMAN RESOURCE DEVELOPMENT; PAYMENT SYSTEMS; TRAINING). Even more broadly, these human resource functions affect and are affected by overall organizational strategies. Ultimately, to be successful, organizations must ensure that they are effectively recruiting and selecting the best possible individuals.

SALLY RIGGS FULLER
VANDRA L. HUBER
UNIVERSITY OF WASHINGTON SCHOOL OF
BUSINESS

Further reading

(References cited in the text marked *)

* Arvey, R.D. and Campion, J.E. (1982) 'The employment interview: a summary and review of recent research', *Personnel Psychology* 35: 281–322. (A conceptual review covering the employment interview research.)
* Barrick, M.R. and Mount, M.K. (1991) 'The big five personality dimensions and job performance: a meta-analysis', *Personnel Psychology* 44: 1–26. (Analyses 117 criterion-related validity studies of personality as a predictor of performance and other relevant organizational variables.)
* Breaugh, J.A. (1992) *Recruitment: Science and Practice*, Boston, MA: PWS–KENT Publishing Company. (A comprehensive book covering all aspects of recruitment, appropriate for practitioners, researchers and students.)
* Dawis, R.V. (1991) 'Vocational interests, values, and preferences', in M.D. Dunnette and L.M. Hough (eds), *Handbook of Industrial and Organizational Psychology*, vol. 2 (2nd edn), Palo Alto, CA: Consulting Psychologists Press. (Reviews the literature on interests, values and preferences and provides good comparative knowledge of techniques.)
* Dipboye, R.L. (1992) *Selection Interviews: Process Perspectives*, Cincinnati, OH: South-Western Publishing Co. (An integration of theory, research and applications in the use of interviews for making selection decisions.)
* Dowling, P.J., Schuler, R.S. and Welch, D.E. (1994) *International Dimensions of Human Resource Management*, 2nd edn, Belmont, CA: Wadsworth Inc. (Focuses on international human resource management practice issues that confront multinational enterprises.)
* Dunnette, M.D. (1976) *Personnel Selection and Placement*, Monterey, CA: Brooks/Cole.

(Classic volume that describes basic issues in recruitment and selection with particular emphasis on validity and placement strategies.)

* Falvey, J. (1987) 'Best corporate culture is a melting pot', *Wall Street Journal*, 16 April: 18. (Addresses the need for outside hiring in order for businesses to be successful.)

* Gist, M.E. and Fuller, S.R. (1995) *Discrimination and Workforce Diversity: A Multilevel Model of Action Versus Intent*, University of Washington working paper. (Theoretical model of the psychological and environmental antecedents of a company's climate relating to workforce diversity issues.)

* Hogan, J. (1988) 'Interests and competencies: a strategy for personnel selection', in R.S. Schuler, S.A. Youngblood and V.L. Huber (eds), *Readings in Personnel and Human Resource Management*, 3rd edn, St Paul, MN: West Publishing Co. (Article asserts that to match individuals to work organizations must assess vocational suitability and competencies.)

* Huber, V.L., Northcraft, G.B. and Neale, M.A. (1980) 'Foibles and fallacies in organizational staffing decisions', in R.S. Schuler, S.A. Youngblood and V.L. Huber (eds), *Readings in Personnel and Human Resource Management*, 3rd edn, St Paul, MN: West Publishing Co. (Article presents a framework for examining the human judgement shortcomings associated with staffing decisions.)

* Labato, S. (1988) 'Business and the law: new rules limit lie detectors' use', *The New York Times*, 28 November: 22. (Reviews the guidelines for companies as a result of the Employee Polygraph Protection Act of 1988.)

* McDaniel, M.A., Whetzel, D.L., Schmidt, F.L. and Mauer, S. (1994) 'The validity of employment interviews: a comprehensive review and meta-analysis', *Journal of Applied Psychology* 79: 599–616. (Review and analysis of empirical studies that examine the validity of interviews as selection devices.)

* Macan, T.H., Avedon, M.J., Paese, M. and Smith, D.E. (1994) 'The effects of applicants' reactions to cognitive ability tests and an assessment center', *Personnel Psychology* 47: 715–38. (Empirical study examining applicants' reactions to selection techniques and the effect of those reactions on perceptions of the selection process, the job, the organization, and intent to accept a job offer.)

* Nisbitt, R. and Ross, L. (1980) *Human Inference: Strategies and Shortcomings of Social Judgment*, Englewood Cliffs, NJ: Prentice Hall.

(Classic book that discusses cognitive biases and distortions in human judgement.)

* Olian, J. and Rynes, S.L. (1984) 'Organizational staffing: integrating practice with strategy', *Industrial Relations* 23: 170–83. (Overview that applies different strategic conceptualizations to the staffing process.)

* Podsakoff, P.M., Williams, M.L. and Scott, W.E. (1988) 'Myths of employee selection systems', in R.S. Schuler, S.A. Youngblood and V.L. Huber (eds), *Readings in Personnel and Human Resource Management*, 3rd edn, St Paul, MN: West Publishing Co. (Explains and debunks four common misconceptions regarding selection and cognitive ability tests.)

* Pulakos, E.D. and Schmitt, N. (1995) 'Experienced-based and situational interview questions: studies of validity', *Personnel Psychology* 48: 289–308. (Article reporting the results of an empirical study that tested the predictive value of experience-based and situational-based interviews.)

* Rynes, S.L. and Barber, A.E. (1990) 'Applicant attraction strategies: an organizational perspective', *Academy of Management Review* 15: 286–310. (Comprehensive review of the factors that influence applicant decisions to join an organization.)

* Rynes, S.L., Bretz, R.D. and Gerhart, B. (1991) 'The importance of recruitment in job choice: a different way of looking', *Personnel Psychology* 44: 487–521. (Empirical study that used longitudinal structured interviews to examine the role recruitment played in job-seeker decisions.)

* Schmidt, F.L. and Hunter, J.E. (1983) 'Individual differences in productivity: an empirical test of estimates derived from studies of selection procedure utility', *Journal of Applied Psychology* 68: 407–14. (Classic investigation in which utility analysis is used to compare the cost and benefits of selection processes.)

* Schuler, R.S. and Huber, V.L. (1993) *Personnel and Human Resource Management*, 5th edn, St Paul, MN: West Publishing Co. (Comprehensive college-level text that includes an extensive review of the recruitment and selection literature.)

* Schuler, R.S. and Jackson, S.E. (1987) 'Linking competitive strategies with human resource management practice', *Academy of Management Executive* 1: 207–20. (Places recruitment and selection processes within a strategic management perspective.)

* Thornton, G.C. (1992) *Assessment Centers in Human Resource Management*, Reading, MA:

Addison-Wesley. (Provides a review of assessment centre research and practice using description, analysis and prescription.)

* Wanous, J., Poland, T.D., Premack, S.L. and Davis, K.S. (1992) 'The effects of met expectations on newcomer attitudes and behaviors: a review and meta-analysis', *Journal of Applied Psychology* 7: 281–96. (Reviews and analyses empirical studies that address new recruits' expectations and their effects on attitudes and behaviours.)

* Wright, P.M., Lichtenfels, P.A. and Pursell, E.D. (1989) 'The structured interview: additional studies and a meta-analysis', *Journal of Occupational Psychology* 62: 191–9. (Comprehensive investigation of variables affecting interview validity.)

See also: EMPLOYEE RELATIONS, MANAGEMENT OF; EQUAL EMPLOYMENT OPPORTUNITIES; FINANCIAL INCENTIVES; HUMAN RESOURCE DEVELOPMENT; HUMAN RESOURCE MANAGEMENT; HUMAN RESOURCE MANAGEMENT, INTERNATIONAL; JOB EVALUATION; ORGANIZATION BEHAVIOUR; PAYMENT SYSTEMS; PERSONNEL MANAGEMENT; TRAINING

Related topics in the IEBM: SKILLS

Relocation

Overview

Relocation, with both an operational and strategic role in international organizations, represents a major component in international human resource management (IHRM) research and practice. There are three phases in the relocation process. Each phase – pre-departure, expatriation and repatriation – has specific implications for the employees involved, human resource practitioners, and organizational strategy. Effective IHRM policies and practices throughout these phases in the relocation process will maximize the opportunities for successful outcomes for individuals and organizations.

1 The context of international human resource management

Growth in international trade, worldwide diffusion of technology and the globalization of the world economy have all contributed to the development of new strategic imperatives for multinational enterprises (MNEs). Realization of these strategic imperatives typically requires a transnational structure, a network of multiple MNE units that recognize and respond to the often conflicting pressures for integration and local responsiveness (Bartlett and Ghoshal 1992). Inter-unit coordination in the transnational may be achieved through a variety of mechanisms, including bureaucratic control (reflected in the systematic rules and procedures utilized in decision making), centralization (the extent to which the locus of

decision making lies in the higher levels of the organizational hierarchy), normative integration (the building of common perspectives, purposes and values among managers across different units) and critical flows of capital, technology and people (Edström and Galbraith 1977; Martinez and Jarillo 1991). The flow of people, through staff transfers within and between MNE units, impacts on the MNE corporate culture and disseminates knowledge, skills and ideas (see HUMAN RESOURCE FLOWS). Effectively managed international staff transfers therefore form an important strategic dimension of international human resource management (IHRM) (Schuler et al. 1993; Taylor et al. 1996) (see HUMAN RESOURCE MANAGEMENT, INTERNATIONAL). These staff transfers are alternatively referred to as relocation.

2 Defining relocation

Relocation involves the transfer of employees – and often families – for work purposes, between two locations and for a period of time that is deemed to require a change of address and some degree of semi-permanent adjustment to local conditions. The relocation process involves a pre-departure phase, the duration of the assignment in the host location and a repatriation phase. Although relocation may be either domestic or international, the focus of this review is on international relocation, or expatriation.

Reflecting its common usage in the literature, 'expatriate' is used here as a generic term to refer to an employee being relocated internationally. However, the alternatives of 'inpatriate' – a host country national relocated to the parent country headquarters – and 'transpatriate' – suggested by Adler and Bartholomew (1992) to represent international assignments in transnational firms – are also recognized in the IHRM literature. This literature predominately focuses on relocation as applied to employees transferring between international units of an MNE, or intra-organizational relocation. However, individuals who relocate with a change of company (inter-organizational relocation) experience the same relocation phases as those transferring within a single MNE. The contrast between these two types of relocation is that for those who relocate between firms, more than one organization is involved over the phases of relocation. Similarly, where an organization recruits externally as opposed to using solely intra-MNE transfers, the organization may not handle all phases of the relocation process for every individual. Although inter-organizational relocation has, to date, received minimal attention, the increasing pool of skilled labour and expatriate talent internationally can be expected to increase the viability of organizations fully utilizing the global labour market (see HUMAN RESOURCE MANAGEMENT).

3 Staffing approaches and relocation

Relocation may include the transfer of parent country nationals (PCNs), host country nationals (HCNs) and third country nationals (TCNs). The MNE's orientation towards relocation is determined, to a large extent, by the organization's approach to staffing. The approach of MNE headquarters towards local unit staffing may be categorized as ethnocentric, polycentric, regiocentric and geocentric (Heenan and Perlmutter 1979). An ethnocentric approach to staffing results in all key management positions being held by PCNs. A polycentric staffing approach decentralizes human resource management to each national location, resulting in HCNs occupying management positions in the local units, while PCNs occupy positions at corporate headquarters. Regiocentric staffing develops regional staff for key positions anywhere in that region, while a geocentric approach is one where the 'best' people are sought for key positions throughout the organization, regardless of nationality.

The MNE may use any 'mix' of these approaches, whether deliberate or *ad hoc* (Dowling *et al.* 1994). The extent to which each approach is adopted within the MNE is influenced by several factors. These include the socio-economic and political environment in which the MNE units operate, the strategic predisposition of the MNE (Welch 1994), the specific tasks involved and the corporate and national cultures of the MNE units (Dowling *et al.* 1994; Newman and Nollen 1996).

Relocation may be utilized for a variety of organizational purposes. These include filling positions or solving staffing shortages, exerting parent-firm control and coordination in local units and developing global capabilities in HCNs, PCNs and TCNs (Edström and Galbraith 1977; Feldman and Thomas 1992). For example, relocation of PCNs provides an opportunity for PCNs to gain international experience, as well as exchange expertise and knowledge with HCNs and TCNs. Kobrin (1988) asserts that relocation is essential in the MNE to maximize identification with, and knowledge of, the global organization by staff in all locations. When PCNs are placed in senior positions at local units, relocation constitutes pseudo-centralization. The use of relocation as a subtle mechanism for coordination typically expands as the integration of the MNE's activities increases (Martinez and Jarillo 1991).

Despite these advantages of relocation, Kobrin (1988) has observed a US trend of expatriate reduction. Perceived benefits to MNEs of expatriate reduction may include: lowering costs associated with managing expatriates and operating in uncertain environments; meeting host country employment requirements; and contributing to host country managerial and technical development. The growing resistance of employees to international mobility is attributable to several factors, including career uncertainty arising from home company restructuring during the employee's absence and an unwillingness to disrupt the career of one's partner or children's education (Gomez-Mejia and Balkin 1987; Harvey 1996a). Kobrin (1988) argues, however, that the benefits of expatriate relocation outweigh the perceived costs, and suggests that the trend of expatriate reduction may, in part, be due to the high 'failure' rate of international relocations.

4 Success and failure in international relocation

Successful relocation involves adjustment to the new culture, environment and tasks (Feldman and Thomas 1992). It often requires an ability to develop constructive relationships with HCNs, and the enhancement of the expatriate's work-related skills. In addition to specific performance appraisal criteria, 'success' is frequently measured by length of stay relative to the originally agreed term, and whether positive attitudes to the relocation – which lead to increased job and organizational commitment – are developed. The absence of stress levels which inhibit performance, health or general well-being is also often used as an indicator of success (Feldman and Thomas 1992).

Expatriate turnover or 'failure' is typically defined as including all individuals who end the assignment or return to their home base prior to the expected completion of the expatriate assignment (Dowling *et al.* 1994). It has also been suggested to include separation from the organization up to a year after repatriation (Harvey 1989). Expatriate turnover rates have been suggested to be at least twice domestic rates, with between 20 and 50 per cent of US MNE expatriates returning home early or being dismissed. Harzig (1995) has, however, raised doubts about these estimates, and in a UK study Forster (1997) found that an average of around 8 percent of expatriate employees return home before the agreed end of the assignment. When the definition of expatriate failure was broadened to include the negative effects, stresses and strains of an international assignment on expatriates and their families, the level of 'failure' rose to up to 28 per cent of expatriates and their partners (Forster 1997). This failure can be very expensive in terms of lost investment. The direct costs of maintaining an expatriate overseas may exceed US$250,000 per year. Indirect costs include reduced productivity and

efficiencies, lost sales, market share and competitive position, an unstable corporate image and damage to international networks (Naumann 1992; Welch and Welch 1993).

Common reasons for expatriate turnover include premature return due to the employee's or family's inability to adapt, parent–local unit alienation and poor relationships between MNE and host country agents. It is also possible that companies contribute to turnover rates through poor management development and misuse of talented people. Expatriate management researchers and practitioners have therefore recognized the need for attention to both individual and organizational requirements throughout all phases of relocation, in order to reduce the high costs of turnover (Naumann 1992). Each of these phases has specific HRM requirements across the functional areas of organizational staffing, and maintaining and retaining employees (see HUMAN RESOURCE MANAGEMENT).

5 The process of relocation

The pre-departure phase

Major issues in the pre-departure phase of relocation include determination of the assignment objectives, development of selection and performance appraisal based on these objectives, consensus on the remuneration package of the expatriate and the design and implementation of preparatory training and development initiatives. Each of these issues requires consideration of both organizational and individual needs.

The international staffing function should be integrated with the organization's strategy. Many efforts have been made to describe and prescribe expatriate selection factors that meet organizational objectives, with the assumption that certain factors are likely to be predictive of success in expatriation. The factors may be grouped as: (1) strategic characteristics (characteristics or skills which fit the organization's strategic objectives directly); (2) professional expertise, including technical qualifications (which may be necessary but not sufficient for the success of the expatriation assignment); (3) general managerial skills, including leadership style; (4) communication skills, such as host-country language proficiency (see COMMUNICATION, CROSS-CULTURAL); and (5) individual characteristics such as cultural tolerance (Black *et al.* 1992). Many criteria used for expatriate selection may be adapted from an employee's domestic work performance appraisal, and utilized in the management of expatriate performance. The emphasis placed on the selection and appraisal criteria used may vary according to the context, which includes cultural and country norms, organizational characteristics and task requirements (Harvey, 1996b; Tung 1982).

In the selection process, many organizations also consider partner and family factors, such as the partner's career, personal attributes, and the educational needs of children (De Cieri *et al.* 1991). These factors also affect employee decisions to accept relocation offers. Despite growing awareness of the importance of the family in expatriate selection, there remain some complex issues related to incorporating the family into the selection process, including issues of privacy and informal knowledge. Overall, the establishment of expatriate selection criteria remains problematic. While several predictors of success have been suggested, the measurement of these is yet to be refined (Dowling *et al.* 1994). These complications are exacerbated when selection of HCNs and TCNs is involved.

According to Scullion (1995), a number of factors make recruitment of HCNs more difficult than recruitment and selection of PCNs (see RECRUITMENT AND SELECTION). These factors include lack of local labour market knowledge, lack of knowledge of local education systems and qualifications, language and cultural differences and inappropriate attempts to transfer parent country staffing practices to different host countries and cultures. However, it may be important to overcome these problems. As Dowling *et al.* (1994) have suggested, there are both advantages and disadvantages in selecting parent, host and third country nationals. These relate to varying levels of control and coordination desired or possible, host government

responses, overcoming language and cultural barriers, observing equal opportunity requirements and impact on the career paths of other groups. Career path management is an important consideration in maintaining and retaining international employees, which also involves the establishment of performance management and remuneration systems, and pre-departure training and development (Harrison 1994) (see CAREERS; FINANCIAL INCENTIVES; PAYMENT SYSTEMS).

Expatriate performance management and performance appraisals may be used by the MNE for individual and organizational purposes. They will be influenced by the MNE's approach to staffing. In an ethnocentric approach, for example, standards are typically set and administered by PCNs, whereas in a polycentric approach the standards are usually set and administered by HCNs (Dowling *et al.* 1994). Whichever approach is used, the first step in developing performance appraisal criteria for expatriate employees is to identify the goals of the assignment, the expectations of the raters relating to the expatriate, and the specific purpose of the performance appraisal. Clarification of and consensus regarding these objectives and expectations facilitates the expatriate's decision, first, to accept or decline the assignment, and second, to approach the assignment in a manner conducive to organizational objectives.

Possible performance appraisal criteria include performance-based or outcome-based criteria including sales, profit, or market share, criteria based on relationships (for instance, with subordinates) and traits such as negotiating skills or adjustment (Gregersen *et al.* 1996) (see PERFORMANCE APPRAISAL). Appraisal may also take into account contextual elements, currency fluctuations for example, which may affect the apparent financial performance of the local unit. The combination of performance criteria used will depend upon the objectives of the organization's units – parent and local – and the ability to measure the indicators with reliability. Each type of criterion provides challenges to accurate measurement. Performance appraisal based on multiple criteria should reduce bias and recognize the multi-dimensionality of the expatriate role.

International relocations also present a number of complexities related to the remuneration of expatriates. Considerations include financial, legal, and customary standards and practices in each of the locations in which the MNE operates. International remuneration policies are required to meet several organizational objectives, including fairness and equity for all categories of employees, the ability to attract, motivate and retain desired personnel, the facilitation of transfer of international employees in the most cost-effective manner and consistency with organizational strategy, structure and needs (Dowling *et al.* 1994). The perspective of parent and host country units, host governments, and expatriates and their families need to be taken into account. Expatriate remuneration packages may include base salary, expatriate premium, cost-of-living allowances and additional fringe benefits. Taxation advice is also of prime consideration in relocation. With such complexities in mind, there appear to be some trends towards flexibility in remuneration packages and cost containment (Harvey 1993) (see FLEXIBILITY; PAYMENT SYSTEMS).

Home-based remuneration policies are the most common, with the emphasis on 'keeping the expatriate whole'. This involves maintaining relativity to home colleagues, with supplements for cost-of-living adjustments, housing, education and other premiums (Reynolds 1986, cited in Dowling *et al.* 1994). Establishment of this policy prior to expatriation facilitates repatriation and may be the simplest method for shorter expatriation assignments. However, inequities may be perceived as expatriates from different countries in the one host location will be paid different amounts. An alternative method is to adopt host- or region-based remuneration policies. An important issue for global organizations is the extent to which remuneration systems are customized to achieve effectiveness across cultures and countries, while maintaining some degree of inter-unit integration. It has been argued that MNEs that consider local culture when designing reward systems will achieve greater success in managing workforce diversity. Thus, the remuneration system may act as an integrative mechanism for the alignment of individual and organizational goals, thereby contributing to the performance of the firm.

An additional consideration in the pre-departure phase is that of expatriate training and development, and several authors have proposed models. A common recommendation is that the extent of training to be provided should be contingent upon factors such as the task, environment, individual, length of stay, level of integration into local culture, and cultural distance between home and host cultures (see Mendenhall *et al.* 1995). In addition, when management development is integrated with business strategy and staffing approaches, it can become a tool for organizational development (Evans 1992). As such, training and development are not limited to PCNs. One of the key objectives for some MNEs with regard to HCNs and TCNs is to develop a global cadre of expatriate managers (Welch 1994). Expatriate training and development programmes should be adapted to be sensitive to the cultural differences of participants across local units (Adler and Bartholomew 1992).

Both formal and informal training and development opportunities may be offered for expatriate and family orientation (see HUMAN RESOURCE DEVELOPMENT; TRAINING). These may include cross-cultural training, language training, discussions with returned expatriates (repatriates), provision of reading materials, informal briefings, preliminary site visits and career planning. With regard to employee development, Feldman and Thomas (1992: 289–90) suggest that 'the longer term issues of integrating the expatriate assignment into logical career paths can be as important as the shorter run issues of language training and pre-departure training in facilitating expatriate success'.

The duration of pre-departure training may vary from one day to several years, depending on organizational factors, assignment type, and individual requirements (Mendenhall *et al.* 1995). In particular, cross-cultural training (CCT) has been advocated as important in developing effective interactions with HCNs. Black and Mendenhall (1990) reviewed twenty-nine US empirical studies of CCT and found a positive relationship between it and the development of appropriate perceptions relative to members of another culture. CCT was also positively correlated with expatriate adjustment and performance. There has, however, been some lag between recognition of the usefulness of CCT and the uptake of such practices by MNEs. Failure to use CCT effectively and, indeed, the effectiveness of pre-departure preparations in all areas of staffing and maintenance, have implications for the success of the assignment throughout the expatriation phase.

The expatriation phase

There are several important aspects to consider in the expatriation phase of relocation, including the enhancement of the expatriate's adjustment to the new environment and conditions. International relocation often requires individual adjustments to a local unit with a different organizational culture from that of the parent organization, and to a societal culture different to that of the individual's home. Relocation to a new environment may result in 'culture shock', which refers to the experience of psychological disorientation by people living and working in cultural environments radically different from that of their home. This may hinder the expatriate's ability to adjust to the new conditions (De Cieri *et al.* 1991).

Berry *et al.* (1988: 63) define adjustment as a 'process by which individuals change their psychological characteristics, change the surrounding context, or change the amount of contact in order to achieve a better fit (outcome) with other features of the system in which they carry out their life'. Several researchers have investigated the psychological adjustment process of relocation, often represented as a curve applicable to expatriation and repatriation (Black and Gregersen 1991a). Prior to departure, individuals typically increase their focus on the relocation, not least due to the many arrangements required. For many, expatriation initially

involves a 'honeymoon' stage during which expatriates report a sense of novelty in their new location. This typically gives way to a feeling that 'the party is over', an experience characterized by unrealistically negative appraisals of the environment. This stage leads to a 'turning point' at which, ideally, expatriates become accustomed to the environment and make more realistic appraisals; the alternative here may lead to a crisis of inability to adjust. The fourth stage documented in psychological adjustment to relocation is 'healthy recovery' as expatriates accept and adjust to their new lifestyle and circumstances.

The relocation adjustment process is multifaceted and affects employees and their families (Aycan 1997; De Cieri *et al.* 1991). Further, several empirical studies have found a positive and significant relationship between the reported adjustment of the expatriate spouse and that of the employee (Black and Gregersen 1991b), thereby influencing success or failure. It is therefore important for the MNE to consider the adjustment of the employee and family, and to provide support mechanisms to assist in adjustment to the new situation. Several practices may be used by companies to support their expatriates. These include regular contact with home nationals for information exchange and continued efforts to organize social gatherings (usually led by the most senior expatriate in the local unit). Expatriates themselves have also suggested mentors at both the local and home sites, and ongoing language training. The latter may be vital in building host country networks.

Schein's (1971) work on career movement (cited by Feldman and Thomas 1992), suggests that expatriates may face difficulty crossing the inclusionary boundary (that is, an expatriate's position in the informal information and influence networks). As the expatriate is on the periphery in terms of culture and organization, the informal networks and information most required by the expatriate – and the expatriate family – may in fact be the least accessible. Cross-cultural training (CCT) in the pre-departure phase may assist in the adjustment process during the expatriation phase. It may also facilitate crossing of the inclusionary boundary, particularly where the expatriate community is small (see TRAINING).

Despite effective CCT, difficulties in crossing the inclusionary boundary may arise when the expatriate employee faces competing demands for commitment from the parent firm and the local unit. Black and Gregersen (1992) have identified four types of employee response to this dilemma and suggest that the best one is dual citizenship, where the employee develops strong dual commitment to parent company and local unit. Although such dual citizenship may be highly desirable, the ability of MNEs to engender such commitment through IHRM policies remains in doubt. Expatriate performance management provides one illustration of the difficulties.

Even when performance criteria have been developed prior to expatriation, problems in performance management may still arise. For example, if the expatriate's career is dependent upon performance appraisals at headquarters, the expatriate may find difficulty in pursuing strategies which, although critical for subsidiary operations, are opposed by headquarters (Black and Gregersen 1992; Feldman and Thomas 1992). Thus, performance appraisal can be an interesting control mechanism in MNEs. The problem of rater bias, which also exists in domestic appraisals, is amplified in expatriate performance appraisals where the distance separating the parent company and local unit may result in inadequate information gathering. Effective performance appraisal of expatriates thus requires reconciliation of parent and host country raters' perceptions of 'performance'. Further, long-term goals and appraisal criteria need to be flexible enough to cater for volatility in the international environment and changes in the strategic direction of the MNE units (Dowling *et al.* 1994). Appraisals throughout the expatriation phase are not only important in maintaining the individual while on an international assignment, but also in retaining the employee when repatriated (see PERFORMANCE APPRAISAL).

The repatriation phase

The MNE's goal in repatriation – the process of returning from a foreign assignment to the home country – is to return and retain an expatriate employee who will be a valuable addition to the organization in contributing knowledge, experience and networks gained overseas. Repatriation issues should be considered in the pre-departure and expatriation phases. Although many firms emphasize the selection, training and initial relocation to the foreign environment, often insufficient attention is given to returning the expatriate to the domestic environment (Forster 1994; Gomez-Mejia and Balkin 1987).

The difficulties in repatriation adjustment may, in fact, be greater than the culture shock experienced during expatriation. Black and Gregersen (1991b) have identified three interrelated facets of adjustment required in repatriation: adjustment to work, adjustment to interacting with home nationals and adjustment to the general environment and culture.

Repatriation requires adjustments on the part of both the returned expatriate and parent company, with career issues being of prime consideration. It can be particularly difficult if career aspirations are not realized upon return (Dowling *et al.* 1994). Because of the geographical and cultural distance separating the parent firm and foreign unit, the expatriate is often literally 'out of sight, out of mind' of the parent company for the duration of the international assignment (Harvey 1989; Tung 1982). The propensity of the organization to find a position for the repatriated employee may be affected by this distance, as well as the performance appraisal of the expatriate while abroad and the availability of a position in MNE home-base operations.

One of the most devastating circumstances for the repatriated employee is being placed in a 'holding pattern' without a clear assignment or set of responsibilities (Harvey 1989). For example, in a US study of 126 repatriates and 76 spouses, role clarity was found to have a significant positive relationship with work adjustment (Black and Gregersen 1991b). An inability to use new skills and experience gained through an international assignment –

in which the expatriate had substantial responsibility – can lead to frustration upon repatriation. The loss of autonomy, a restricted career path upon return, lower prestige and status of the new assignment, and removal from the mainstream of corporate advancement while abroad (resulting in less experienced domestic counterparts climbing the corporate ladder in the expatriate's absence) are all potential problems for the repatriate (Gomez-Mejia and Balkin 1987). These problems are amplified where the parent firm does not highly value international experience. US firms in particular have been criticized for not valuing international experience as a criterion for promotion to senior management. In a study of 123 US companies, Tung and Miller (1990) found that 93 per cent of respondents did not consider 'international experience or perspective' a criterion for promotion or recruitment. In contrast, countries with a smaller domestic market tend to place a greater premium on international experience (Hendry 1994).

A common recommendation of the prescriptive literature has been for the organization to give an assurance of the position to be held upon return, prior to expatriation. This may reduce expatriate anxiety over career development and enhance productivity, particularly in the latter stages of the international assignment as well as upon return (Naumann 1993). However, such 'job guarantees' must be flexible enough to cater for changes over time in the MNE's internal and external environments (see CAREERS; EQUAL EMPLOYMENT OPPORTUNITIES).

Career issues are also important for the repatriate spouse. The repatriation shock experienced by the spouse, whose career may have been interrupted by the relocation, may be severe. A high proportion of repatriate spouses do not return to work, at least for some time after their return (Black and Gregersen 1991b; De Cieri et al. 1991). If spouse and expatriate adjustment is significantly related as suggested, it is in the MNE's interest to assist with family adjustment.

In addition to work-related adjustment, the repatriated employee and family must become reaccustomed to the home environment, including developing networks of friends, absorbing changes in the political and economic environment, and often accepting a reduction in lifestyle as expatriate allowances are removed. The returning family may view their home country with a different perspective, and therefore need to adjust not only to changes in the environment, but also to changes within themselves. The ease with which repatriates are able to re-integrate into society may vary not only between individuals and corporations, but also between societies. For example, Japanese repatriates may face greater difficulties in crossing the inclusionary boundaries in the Japanese society than, for example, British or US repatriates (Enloe and Lewin 1987).

Lowered performance levels upon repatriation may also be a major concern. It may take between twelve and eighteen months for the repatriate to adjust fully to the new environment (Adler 1986). Without adequate attention to the repatriation issues described here, expatriate commitment to the parent firm may be eroded substantially during the latter stages of the overseas assignment and upon return (Gregersen 1992). The average repatriation turnover rate – that is, individuals who return from overseas assignments but then leave the organization within one year – has been estimated at 25 per cent in the USA (Black and Gregersen 1991b).

Poor repatriation management has strategic implications for international human resource management (see HUMAN RESOURCE MANAGEMENT, INTERNATIONAL). Potential expatriates within the organization may observe repatriate turnover, and therefore conclude that an international assignment is detrimental to one's career and decline expatriate assignments (Black and Gregersen 1991a). In turn, the MNE will experience difficulty finding suitably qualified candidates for expatriation. As less suitable candidates are sent on expatriate assignments, a 'downward spiralling vicious cycle' results (Black and Gregersen 1992) with long-term consequences for international operations. Effective repatriate programmes are therefore an imperative for MNEs.

The programmes that have received most attention in repatriation have been: career path counselling; assistance with relocation problems such as housing and transportation; and interim financial assistance. Many MNE repatriation programmes have focused on only tangible aspects of relocation, and are lacking in attention to the social and psychological problems confronted by many repatriates and their families. Some approaches that may be used to address repatriation adjustment include pre-departure training and development which includes repatriation planning, written job guarantees, sponsors or mentors for expatriates, pre- and post-return counselling, and financial counselling and short-term assistance.

6 Emerging issues in relocation

Throughout the three phases of relocation – pre-departure, expatriation and repatriation – greater attention could be given by MNEs to several areas of international human resource management (IHRM). These include offering pre-departure training such as language instruction, providing clear performance criteria and appraisal information, establishing congruent expectations between home and local units, integrating relocations into career development and providing support systems during the expatriation and repatriation phases. Organizations may also seek to develop job characteristics, such as work role clarity, and realistic expectations of the relocation destination and objectives.

To promote expatriate commitment to the organization and maximize the opportunities for successful relocations, MNEs need to recognize the strategic importance of IHRM. Top management support is necessary to ensure adequate planning and preparation for relocation assignments, and accurate forecasts of staffing needs throughout the MNE network. Indeed, an issue of growing importance in IHRM is the role relocation will play as the MNE's international operations and staffing approaches evolve. The promotion of a global, integrative perspective among all organizational stakeholders, and the creation of an environment in which relocation is valued by every member of the MNE network, will broaden the pool of potential expatriates and maximize the opportunities for successful relocations.

HELEN DE CIERI
CORNELL UNIVERSITY

SARA L. MCGAUGHEY
PETER J. DOWLING
UNIVERSITY OF TASMANIA

Further reading

(References cited in the text marked *)

* Adler, N.J. (1986) *International Dimensions of Organizational Behaviour*, Belmont, CA: PWS-Kent. (Provides an overview of crosscultural management issues for individuals and organizations.)
* Adler, N.J. and Bartholomew, S. (1992) 'Managing globally competent people', *Academy of Management Executive* 6 (3): 52–65. (Provides results of a survey of fifty North American firms, a set of required managerial skills and a framework for assessing competences in transnational firms.)
* Aycan, Z. (1997) 'Expatriate adjustment as a multifaceted phenomenon: individual and organizational level predictors', *The International Journal of Human Resource Management* 8 (4): 434–456. (A conceptual model that identifies critical antecedents of expatriate adjustment is proposed.)
* Bartlett, C. and Ghoshal, S. (1992) *Transnational Management: Text, Cases, and Readings in Cross Border Management*, Boston, MA: Irwin. (General textbook covering strategic, organizational and management issues for MNEs. Each chapter comprises text, several useful cases and readings.)
* Berry, J.W., Kim, U. and Boski, P. (1988) 'Psychological acculturation of immigrants', in Y.Y. Kim and W.B. Gudykunst (eds), *Cross-cultural Adaptation: Current Approaches*, Beverly Hills, CA: Sage Publications. (Conceptual model of the process of psychological acculturation is presented, identifying five types of acculturating groups.)
* Black, J.S. and Gregersen, H.B. (1991a) 'Antecedents to cross-cultural adjustment for expatriates in Pacific Rim assignments', *Human Relations* 44 (5): 497–515. (Examines the impact of job, personal and general factors on cross-cultural adjustment for 220 American ex-

patriates in Japan, Hong Kong, Korea and Taiwan.)

* Black, J.S. and Gregersen, H.B. (1991b) 'When Yankee comes home: factors related to expatriate and spouse repatriation adjustment', *Journal of International Business Studies* 22 (4): 671–94. (Examines anticipatory and in-country individual, job, organizational and non-work variables and their association with repatriation adjustment.)

* Black, J.S. and Gregersen, H.B. (1992) 'Serving two masters: managing the dual allegiance of expatriate employees', *Sloan Management Review* 33 (4): 61–71. (Four patterns of expatriate employees' allegiance to parent company and to host country unit are described.)

* Black, J.S., Gregersen, H.B. and Mendenhall, M.E. (1992) *Global Assignments*, San Francisco, CA: Jossey Bass. (This book focuses on the phases of relocation and provides brief case studies. It is based on the authors' own research but targeted primarily towards practitioners.)

* Black, J.S. and Mendenhall, M.E. (1990) 'Cross-cultural training effectiveness: a review and a theoretical framework for future research', *Academy of Management Review* 15 (1): 113–36. (Following a review of the cross-cultural training literature, a theoretical framework based on social learning theory is presented.)

* De Cieri, H., Dowling, P.J. and Taylor, K.F. (1991) 'The psychological impact of expatriate relocation on partners', *The International Journal of Human Resource Management* 2 (3): 377–414. (Examines relationships between personal and company factors, and cross-cultural adjustment for fifty-eight expatriate and repatriate partners from several countries.)

Deresky, H. (1994) *International Management: Managing Across Borders and Cultures*, New York: HarperCollins. (Covers the behavioural aspects of international management, with comparative applications highlighted. Both brief and long case studies are provided.)

* Dowling, P.J., Schuler, R.S. and Welch, D.E. (1994) *International Dimensions of Human Resource Management*, 2nd edn, Belmont, CA: Wadsworth. (Concise overview of international HRM covering functional areas and developments, with examples from many countries. Includes a glossary of international HRM terms.)

* Edström, A. and Galbraith, J.R. (1977) 'Transfer of managers as a coordination and control strategy in multinational organisations', *Administrative Science Quarterly* 22: 248–63. (Explores the multiple purposes of relocations, focusing on the use of relocations by organizations as a tool to develop control based on socialization.)

* Enloe, W. and Lewin, P. (1987) 'Issues of integration abroad and readjustment to Japan of Japanese returnees', *International Journal of Intercultural Relations* 11: 223–48. (Explores issues of integration for Japanese expatriate families through an empirical study of twenty-one repatriate families.)

* Evans, P.A.L. (1992) 'Management development as glue technology', *Human Resource Planning* 15 (1): 85–106. (Outlines the mechanisms used to integrate units within and between MNE subsidiaries in order to escape the centralization–decentralization dilemma.)

* Feldman, D.C. and Thomas, D.C. (1992) 'Career management issues facing expatriates', *Journal of International Business Studies* 23 (2): 271–93. (Expatriation and career development are examined through organization-level programmes and individual-level strategies, using data from 118 expatriates in Saudi Arabia, Europe, South America and Japan.)

* Forster, N. (1994) 'The forgotten employees? The experiences of expatriate staff returning to the UK', *The International Journal of Human Resource Management* 5 (2): 405–25. (Reports survey responses from 124 UK repatriates, identifying difficulties faced, psychological well-being and general adaptation to repatriation.)

* Forster, N. (1997) 'The persistent myth of high expatriate failure rates: a reappraisal', *The International Journal of Human Resource Management* 8 (4): 414–33. (This article argues that traditional measures of expatriate failure have limitations and do not reflect the true extent of the problems. A broader definition of 'failure' is stressed.)

* Gomez-Mejia, L.R. and Balkin, D.B. (1987) 'The determinants of managerial satisfaction with the expatriation and repatriation process', *Journal of Management Development* 6 (1): 7–17. (Surveys eighty-nine US repatriates and their spouses, with reference to satisfaction with company assistance, career development and expatriation/repatriation overall.)

* Gregersen, H.B. (1992) 'Commitments to a parent company and a local work unit during repatriation', *Personnel Psychology* 45: 29–54. (This study of 174 American repatriate managers examines the extent to which individual, job, organizational and non-job factors influence commitment.)

* Gregersen, H.B., Hite, J.M. and Black, J.S. (1996) 'Expatriate performance appraisal in U.S. mul-

tinational firms', *Journal of International Business Studies* 27 (4): 711–38. (This article reports on a survey of expatriate performance appraisal practices in 58 US multinational firms.)

* Harrison, J.K. (1994) 'Developing successful expatriate managers: A framework for the structural design and strategic alignment of cross-cultural training programs', *Human Resource Planning* 17 (3): 17–35. (This article presents a practical, prescriptive framework for the structure, sequence, and content of cross-cultural training programs.)

* Harvey, M.G. (1989) 'Repatriation of corporate executives: an empirical study', *Journal of International Business Studies* 20: 131–44. (Survey of seventy-nine personnel administrators examined repatriation issues and associated programmes.)

* Harvey, M. (1993) 'Empirical evidence of recurring international compensation problems', *Journal of International Business Studies* 24 (4): 785–99. (A survey of managers responsible for IHRM reports five common problems in international compensation strategies and practices.)

* Harvey, M.G. (1996a) 'Addressing the dual-career expatriation dilemma', *Human Resource Planning*, 19 (4): 18–39. (This article presents a model of stressors for dual-career expatriates and discusses coping strategies and organizational programs to address the needs of these people.)

* Harvey, M. (1996b) 'The selection of managers for foreign assignments', *Columbia Journal of World Business* 31 (4): 102–18. (This article discusses issues and criteria to be considered in expatriate selection.)

* Harzig, A.K. (1995) 'The persistent myth of high expatriate failure rates', *The International Journal of Human Resource Management* 6 (2): 457–74. (This article provides a critical analysis of past research on expatriate failure, casting doubt on some of the reported high failure rates.)

* Heenan, D.A. and Perlmutter, H. (1979) *Multinational Organization Development: A Social Architectural Perspective*, Reading, MA: Addison-Wesley. (Focuses on organization development in public and private sector multinational enterprises, identifying central problems and possible action strategies.)

* Hendry, C. (1994) *Human Resource Strategies for International Growth*, New York: Routledge. (Focuses on internationalization of the firm and

the human resource management implications, with emphasis on European issues.)

* Martinez, J.I. and Jarillo, J.C. (1991) 'Coordination demands of international strategies', *Journal of International Business Studies* 22 (3): 429–44. (This study of fifty MNE subsidiaries shows a connection between their strategy and use of different mechanisms of coordination.)

* Mendenhall, M.E., Punnett, B.J. and Ricks, D. (1995) *Global Management*, Oxford: Blackwell. (Balances global approaches with management of diversity, covering issues related to the global environment, organization strategy and structure, and general and human resource management.)

* Naumann, E. (1992) 'A conceptual model of expatriate turnover', *Journal of International Business Studies* 23 (3): 499–531. (A conceptual model of the expatriate turnover process shows the contributing factors, intermediate linkages and relationships. Related propositions are offered.)

* Naumann, E. (1993) 'Antecedents and consequences of satisfaction and commitment among expatriate managers', *Group and Organisation Management* 18 (2): 153–87. (Survey of 184 US expatriates tests the applicability of concepts from domestic employee turnover models to expatriates.)

* Newman, K.L. and Nollen, S.D. (1996) 'Culture and congruence: The fit between management practices and national culture', *Journal of International Business Studies* 27 (4): 753–79. (Financial performance outcomes for work units in eighteen countries are analysed, and support found for the thesis that business performance is better when management practices are congruent with national culture.)

Pucik, V., Tichy, N.M., and Barnett, C.K. (1992) *Globalizing Management: Creating and Leading the Competitive Organization*, New York: Wiley. (Collection of major readings dealing with a range of issues in MNE management and the implications for IHRM.)

* Schuler, R.S., Dowling, P.J. and De Cieri, H.L. (1993) 'An integrative framework of strategic international human resource management', *Journal of Management* 19 (2): 419–59. (A framework is presented, with numerous propositions reflecting the relationships between exogenous and endogenous factors, MNE components and strategic IHRM.)

* Scullion, H. (1995) 'International human resource management', in J. Storey (ed.), *Human Resource Management: A Critical Text*, London:

Routledge. (Provides an overview of international human resource management issues.)

* Taylor, S., Beechler, S. and Napier, N. (1996) 'Towards an integrative model of strategic international human resource management', *Academy of Management Review* 21: 959–85. (This article develops a theoretical model of determinants of international human resource management strategy.)

* Tung, R.L. (1982) 'Selection and training procedures of U.S., European and Japanese multinationals', *California Management Review* 25 (1): 57–71. (Expatriate selection and training policies and practices are discussed, presenting questionnaire data from 80 US, 29 western European and 35 Japanese MNEs.)

* Tung, R.L. and Miller, E.L. (1990) 'Managing in the twenty-first century: the need for global orientation', *Management International Review* 30 (1): 5–18. (The results of a questionnaire completed by 123 US executives, with reference to management succession policies and practices.)

* Welch, D.E. (1994) 'HRM implications of globalization', *Journal of General Management* 19 (4): 52–68. (Discusses a range of HRM and expatriate management issues in global enterprises.)

* Welch, D.E. and Welch, L.S. (1993) 'Using personnel to develop networks: an approach to subsidiary management', *International Business Review* 2 (2): 157–68. (The interaction model is applied to the role of networking in MNE management, identifying the nature of subsidiary networks and the contribution of staffing decisions.)

See also: CAREERS; FINANCIAL INCENTIVES; HUMAN RESOURCE DEVELOPMENT; HUMAN RESOURCE FLOWS; HUMAN RESOURCE MANAGEMENT, INTERNATIONAL; PAYMENT SYSTEMS; PERFORMANCE APPRAISAL; RECRUITMENT AND SELECTION; TRAINING

Related topics in the IEBM: MANAGEMENT IN JAPAN; MIGRANT MANAGERS; MULITNATIONAL CORPORATIONS; ORGANIZATIONAL DEVELOPMENT; ORGANIZATIONAL PERFORMANCE; ORGANIZATION STRUCTURE

Training

Overview

Training is any systematic process used by organizations to develop employees' knowledge, skills, behaviours, or attitudes in order to contribute to the achievement of organizational goals. It is also referred to as human resource development. Training is used to improve the performance of employees in their present positions; to prepare workers for positions to which they are likely to be promoted in the future; and to respond to changes in the workplace, such as new technology and systems, internationalization, global competitiveness and the need for greater service orientation. In addition, training is provided by governments and organizations to improve the future employability of the hard-core unemployed, under-employed minority groups and workers whose present skills are becoming obsolete. Training is directed toward employees at all levels of the organization, from workers on the shop floor through to executives, and covers applications from specific technical skills to complex social and cognitive skills.

Most organizations dedicate substantial resources to training and see it as an integral function of achieving their goals. In the USA alone training expenditures have been estimated to be as high as $100 billion per year and training professionals have estimated that organizations' commitment to training is likely to grow.

Despite its pervasiveness in industry, however, training must be viewed as only one of several human resource interventions used to improve the match between the knowledge, skills, behaviours or attitudes possessed by employees and those required in particular jobs. Alternatives to training include changing the way in which personnel are selected; changing job requirements through job redesign or technological change; and changing the way in which performance is managed (for example, introducing goal setting, feedback or reward systems). All of these alternatives can be used in place of, or in conjunction with, training initiatives.

The development of training programmes involves three phases: (1) training needs analysis; (2) training design and delivery; and (3) training evaluation. In the first phase, specific training needs which address organizational objectives are identified. Within the training design and delivery phase, training objectives are set, specific training content is identified and principles that will maximize learning and transfer of skills are applied. In training evaluation, criteria are established and a method of evaluation is developed: (1) to ensure that training has met its objectives; and (2) to make necessary changes to improve the programme's effectiveness.

1 Training needs analysis

In order for training to contribute to the achievement of an organization's goals, training needs must be identified through an analysis which links training to relevant organizational outcomes – a process referred to as training needs analysis. In the first major book written on organizational training, McGehee and Thayer (1961) presented a three-part system for training needs analysis which, despite slight changes in terminology, is still the most prevalent model presented in textbooks today. Their approach involves three analyses: (1) organization analysis; (2) task analysis (sometimes referred to as operations analysis or job analysis); and (3) person analysis (originally referred to as man analysis, sometimes called individual analysis). The purposes and commonly used procedures

Table 1 The McGehee and Thayer approach to identifying training needs

Analysis	Purpose	Examples of specific needs analysis techniques
Organization analysis	To determine where in the organization training is needed	Identify knowledge and skill requirements from organizational goals, objectives, business plans
		Compare efficiency and quality indices against expectations
		Conduct personnel and succession plans, including personnel audits which identify knowledge/skill-base of present employyes
		Assess organizational climate for training
Task analysis	To determine what training content should be	For individual jobs, identify performance outcomes/standards, tasks required to achieve them and knowledge, skills, behaviours and attitudes necessary for successful task completion
Person analysis	To determine who should receive training and what training they need	Using performance appraisals, identify knowledge/skill, causes of performance discrepencies
		Collect and analyse critical incidents
		Conduct training needs analysis surveys

Source: Adapted from McGehee and Thayer (1961)

for each of these three analyses are summarized in Table 1.

Organization analysis

An organization analysis (see ORGANIZATION BEHAVIOUR) is conducted to determine exactly where in the organization training is needed. Organizational goals, objectives and business plans are reviewed to identify knowledge and skill requirements of the organization. For example, an Australian beef export firm which wishes to increase sales in Asia may determine that its product quality and uniformity must first be improved and that training in quality improvement processes will be necessary to achieve its goal.

In addition to reviewing goals, efficiency indices (for example, production figures, scrap rates and quality data) are compared with targets to identify performance discrepancies which might be addressed by training. Personnel (manpower) and succession plans are conducted to determine future staffing requirements and the replacement of people who vacate positions due to promotion, retirement or leaving the organization. These plans typically include a *personnel audit*, in which the knowledge and skills of employees are compared with future requirements to identify training needs.

Goldstein (1993) has suggested that, as part of an organization analysis, the climate for training should also be assessed. Conflict between the goals of a training programme and those of a particular group in the organization (for example, management, union), or between behaviours taught in training and those supported by trainees' supervisors, indicates that trainees are unlikely to apply newly learned skills to the job, and thus that the organization is not ready for the training.

Task analysis

While organization analysis is conducted at the level of the entire organization or within divisions, task analysis is conducted at the level of a specific job. Through task analysis the specific content of the training is identified. Similar to job analysis used for personnel selection (see JOB EVALUATION), task analysis involves the identification of performance outcomes and standards for a job, the tasks which must be completed for an individual to achieve those outcomes, and finally the knowledge, skills, behaviours and attitudes required for successful task completion.

Person analysis

A person analysis is used to determine who in the organization needs training and what training each person needs. Performance appraisals can be used for person analysis by identifying areas of discrepancy between individuals' expected and actual performance and by determining whether such discrepancies are due to a lack of knowledge or skills, thus indicating training needs. Based on what the employee and supervisor determine to be the employee's training needs, through performance appraisals and a discussion of the employee's career goals, a *learning contract* (also known as a learning agenda) can be developed between employee and supervisor.

A person analysis can also be conducted using critical incidents, in which supervisors record actual occurrences of particularly effective or ineffective job behaviour. Unlike performance appraisals, in which training needs are identified on an individual basis, critical incidents are grouped across all individuals in a particular job to identify training needs at a group level.

Alternatively, surveys can be used for person analysis. Employees or their supervisors are asked to indicate training needs, usually by checking or rating each of a list of knowledge and skill areas. Such surveys have been expanded in two ways for the identification of managers' training needs: (1) subordinate and peer ratings are often used to supplement self- and supervisor ratings; and (2) two rating scales for each knowledge/skill area are frequently used, one indicating the optimal level of proficiency for the job and one the actual proficiency of the individual. Training needs are indicated where a significant gap exists

between these two actual and optimal performance levels.

Training needs analysis surveys are popular because they are relatively easy to administer and analyse and because they provide quantitative information, but they suffer from a fundamental weakness: they do not necessarily link training to organizational goals. Responses to needs analysis surveys may reflect respondents' own (unstated) personal objectives more than those of their organization. Evidence of this limitation is found in studies which have compared, and found significant differences between, self-rated and supervisor-rated training needs. Further research is needed to determine whether these differences reflect different objectives for identifying training needs or simply different views of what training is needed to meet the same objectives.

Demographic analysis

Some writers have extended the three analyses (organization, task and person) to include a fourth, demographic analysis, because studies comparing self-reported training needs of various levels of management, of different ethnic groups and of male and female employees have often indicated statistically significant (albeit small) differences. They suggest that training practitioners should look for differences in training needs identified by various groups of employees (see WOMEN MANAGERS IN ORGANIZATIONS).

Equal employment opportunities and training

Related to the concern for differences in the training needs of various demographic groups of employees, training personnel should ensure that women and minority groups have equal access to training and equal probabilities of successfully completing training (see EQUAL EMPLOYMENT OPPORTUNITIES). For example, if a minority group does not receive the same access to training necessary for promotion as its majority group counterpart, the training can be viewed as failing to provide equal employment opportunities. Similarly, if minority group members have a lesser chance of succeeding in training required for promotion, the training can be considered to have an adverse impact on that group.

Performance analysis

While McGehee and Thayer's (1961) organization–task–person analysis model is the most widely recognized approach to training needs analysis in textbooks, an alternative approach referred to as performance analysis has become popular among practitioners. The basic process of performance analysis is presented in Figure 1. Gaps between expected and actual job performance are identified, as in performance appraisals for person analysis. Unlike performance appraisals, however, performance analysis looks for factors in the work environment (for example, rewards or punishments) which sustain poor performance, instead of assuming that the gap is caused by a deficiency in employee skills, knowledge or attitudes.

Performance analysts have criticized the traditional training needs analysis approach for failing to link training to organizational outcomes by relying too heavily on needs analysis surveys and for overlooking the role of (often subtle) rewards and punishments in the work environment when assessing the causes of performance discrepancies (Gilbert 1978; Mager and Pipe 1984). This latter criticism is much the same as some writers' suggestion for greater cooperation between training and organization development, which focuses more broadly on long-range planned organizational change.

The extent to which organizations actually use these training needs analysis techniques is surprisingly low. In one study, organizations in four out of five European countries reported that they identified training needs most frequently through employee and line manager requests (Holden 1990) (see HUMAN RESOURCE MANAGEMENT IN EUROPE). Similarly, only 27 per cent of 611 companies surveyed in a study of organizations in the USA indicated that they had practices or procedures for determining training needs (Saari et al. 1988). In a sample of large organizations in New Zealand, most reported using no formal training needs analysis procedures (O'Driscoll and Taylor 1992). Some training practitioners may be unfamiliar with these procedures or see little value in applying them. McGehee and Thayer (1961) suggested that practitioners rarely apply a systematic needs analysis procedure because of the pressure to get training started quickly. Further research is needed to understand and resolve the practice–theory gap in training needs analysis.

2 Training design and delivery

In order to design an appropriate training programme to meet identified needs, training objectives must be established, for they guide the development of training content, training method and evaluation criteria. Training objectives can state what trainees will know after training; what they will do on the job, referred to as *behavioural objectives*; or what end results will be achieved for the organization through training. For example, a safety training programme may have the knowledge-related objective that 'each trainee will be able to accurately describe the correct procedure for lifting heavy items off the floor'; a behavioural objective that 'observed violations of safety procedures should occur no more than one time per year per employee'; and a results objective that 'lost-time accidents at the plant are reduced by 30 per cent'. Knowledge, behavioural and results objectives each can be stated in terms of either desired performance levels (as in the first two examples above) or performance changes (as in the last example).

Of the three types of training objectives, behavioural objectives have received the most attention because virtually all organizational training efforts are expected to affect outcomes relevant to the organization through changed employee behaviour. Guidelines for the development of behavioural objectives can be found in Mager and Pipe (1984) and Goldstein (1993).

Once training objectives have been developed, specific training content is established. General tasks to be learned are broken down into smaller, component tasks, which are sequenced so that each component builds upon those that have been presented earlier. Principles of learning are applied to the development of the training process in order to maximize skill retention and transfer of training to the workplace. These principles have been developed largely from behavioural, social learning, educational and cognitive psychologies. Learning principles most commonly employed in training include:

1 operant conditioning (in which desired behaviours are intentionally reinforced during and after training);

2 modelling (in which desired behaviours are modelled through videos, as well as by trainers and trainees' supervisors);

3 knowledge of results (in which trainees are given frequent and accurate performance feedback);

4 distributed practice (in which sessions are spaced rather than massed together);

5 identical elements (in which the similarity between what learners face in training and job situations is maximized).

Goldstein (1993) has provided a comprehensive review of these and other learning principles which have been applied to training.

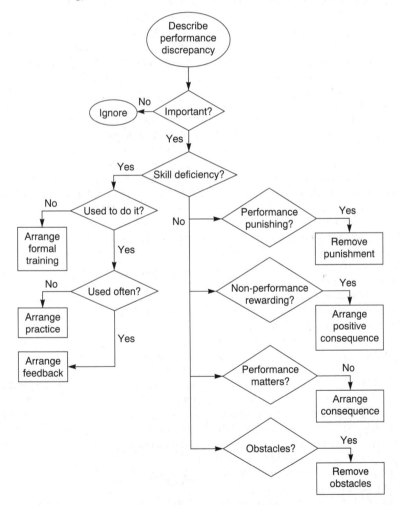

Figure 1 The performance analysis approach to identifying training needs
Source: Mager and Pipe (1984)

Various training methods have been developed which combine principles of learning and available technology for particular applications. Training is usually thought of in terms of programmes conducted in classroom settings, but also includes on-the-job learning activities such as job rotation, apprenticeships and vestibule training. Many training programmes in organizations employ multiple methods. For example, while most training programmes have a lecture component, few would use lecture alone. Further details on training methods can be found in Craig (1987) and Nadler and Nadler (1990). Commonly used training methods are described below.

Job rotation

Employees at virtually all levels of an organization may be rotated through a series of jobs to expand their knowledge and skills. Job rotation allows the organization greater flexibility because employees' responsibilities can be shifted easily with changing human resource needs. In the interest of flexibility some organizations have adopted pay-for-knowledge schemes (sometimes referred to as competency-based pay), in which a portion of workers' pay is influenced by the knowledge and skills they have acquired through voluntary job rotation and formal training experiences. Job rotation can also be used to prepare workers for promotion and to provide a more enriching work experience for employees. Job rotation may not be appropriate when workers are paid on a piece-rate system and would be less productive in jobs other than their primary one (see WORK AND ORGANIZATION SYSTEMS).

Apprenticeships

In the trade field apprenticeships are a common means of providing training to new employees. The apprentice serves as an assistant to a more senior worker, often for a fixed period of time, receiving one-to-one, on-the-job modelling, instruction and feedback. This method is usually cost-effective because the organization receives the benefit of the apprentice's work, usually at a relatively low rate of pay. Apprenticeships are only appropriate when there are enough skilled individuals to work on a one-to-one basis with new employees. A further limitation is that, because apprenticeship periods are usually fixed, they do not take into account individual differences in pre-apprenticeship skill levels and learning rates.

Vestibule training

New employees who are to work on production lines that require a particular speed or skill level may be trained on a simulated production line which often operates at a slower rate. Using this technique organizations avoid having to slow down regular production lines or risk product damage or poor quality due to the introduction of unskilled workers.

Lecture

The lecture method consists of a trainer presenting information to trainees, and is one of the least expensive forms of training because it incurs little development costs and can be used with large training classes. Despite criticism that it lacks the opportunity for practice and feedback, evaluations of training using the lecture method have shown that it can have at least a moderate level of effectiveness.

Conference

The conference method uses structured discussion between trainer and trainees in relatively small groups. While the lecture method involves one-way communication, the conference approach provides for two-way discussion and so can be used to test participants' understanding and to invite reactions to what is presented. Because it entails a high degree of participant involvement, the conference method is particularly effective for enhancing trainee commitment or attitude change.

Video

Video can be used in training to stimulate interest in the training topic, to present information, to model the use of skills and to provide trainees with accurate feedback about their use of newly learned skills. Videos can be used to present course information to employees at remote sites, which can be a cost-effective alternative to bringing trainer and trainees physically together. In behaviour modelling training video is used to present trainees with a positive role model of the skills they are learning, shown in realistic settings to enhance credibility. Trainees are often videotaped as they practice complex interpersonal skills, such as in simulated selling situations, and immediate playback provides them with feedback.

Video use in training evolved from the use of slides and films, and is growing increasingly sophisticated and powerful through computer and laser disk technologies. These developments allow trainees to interact with video material, which can stimulate interest and provide very controlled feedback. For example, management trainees may be shown a simulated discussion concerning a job performance problem and asked how they would respond. Based on their response, realistic replies by the video-simulated employee would be shown.

The primary disadvantage of using video to present training material is cost, of both the initial development and of making later modifications. Videotaping of trainees for the purpose of feedback is not as costly but requires considerably more training time. Despite these disadvantages the use of video in training is likely to continue to grow.

Computer-assisted instruction

Computerized training permits the presentation of information in a logical sequence, testing trainees' understanding, providing feedback and tailoring lessons to the knowledge/skill level of individual trainees through an assessment of their responses (called *branching*). Computer-assisted instruction (CAI) developed from programmed instruction, which followed the same basic approach of presenting information and testing understanding in a logical sequence, but using either workbooks or teaching machines. Programmes designed to teach a wide variety of knowledge and skills have been developed using CAI, from tutorial programmes that accompany PC software to complex interpersonal and problem-solving skills.

Despite initial enthusiasm about CAI as an innovative training method, research comparing its effectiveness to more traditional training approaches has found little difference. Furthermore, rapidly changing computer hardware has made it difficult to develop CAI programmes that will not be soon outdated. For example, large investments were made in PLATO, a mainframe-based CAI environment, during the early 1970s, but the unexpectedly high processing power and memory of PCs that followed have rendered PLATO obsolete. As PC hardware grows increasingly standardized, the development of CAI training programmes becomes more cost-effective.

Simulation

Simulations are carefully developed exercises, modelled on realistic situations, in which trainees participate and receive feedback. Simulations are particularly useful for jobs in which the risk and costs of mistakes are high (for example, pilot training) or in which direct observation and feedback are typically absent (for example, managerial decision making). With the aid of computer technology, machine simulators (such as flight simulators) can be created to be amazingly realistic. Simulations are frequently used in management training and include assessment centre exercises such as in-tray (or in-basket) exercises, business games and case studies. Management training simulations allow participants to collect information and make decisions as if they were in a real situation and to receive feedback on their behaviour based on careful observation by other participants and training staff.

A particularly popular simulation for managers has been outdoor training, which includes a series of exercises in a wilderness setting that, according to its proponents, simulate job-related group and individual problem-solving situations. For example, a group of trainees might be instructed to scale a high wall without the use of any equipment. After each exercise the trainer links behaviour on the task with trainees' work environment, facilitating feedback to individuals under the assumption that their behaviour on the exercise is similar to how they address challenges at work. The fidelity of outdoor training exercises is not as high as more job-related simulations mentioned earlier, and so the effectiveness of such training may depend on the trainer's ability to show links between the outdoor exercise and job behaviour.

Role play

Role playing is used in teaching interpersonal skills such as managerial and sales interactions. Trainees adopt relevant roles (for example, manager and staff member; salesperson and customer) and play out a particular kind of discussion (for example, taking disciplinary action; making a sale). Background information on the nature of the roles is provided for the role players but the interaction is generally unscripted.

A particularly effective role playing approach is behaviour modelling training, developed from social learning theory. Participants are first shown a model of someone using a set of clearly defined skills appropriately (typically with actor on video) and then asked to role play; they then receive feedback on a similar interaction using those same skills.

Burke and Day (1986) have conducted a major review of training research which compared the effectiveness of various training approaches. They found that all methods which they included in their review yielded at least moderately positive effects. Which particular training technique is used seems of less importance than the determination of training content, despite the fact that much of the past training research has focused on comparing new training methods with traditional approaches. Future research could focus less on the effectiveness of alternative training methods and more on developing generalized training content for common jobs and tasks.

While earlier training design research focused on the application of learning principles

and comparing training methods, later research has focused on techniques which can be added to training to increase transfer of skills to the job. For example, having trainees set goals concerning how they will apply newly learned skills to their jobs, identify potential causes of reverting to pre-training behaviours and to brainstorm solutions have all been shown to increase training transfer if added at the end of training sessions.

Transfer of training is not only a function of how training is designed but is also related to characteristics of trainees and their work environment. For example, researchers have demonstrated that trainees' self-efficacy (their beliefs about their skills and likelihood of success) influences training transfer. In the work environment factors which affect training transfer include the opportunity to apply newly learned skills and the degree to which trainees' supervisors support the use of trained skills.

While organizations can do little to change trainees' individual characteristics to increase training transfer, their work environments can be positively influenced, such as through the provision of supervisory support workshops to accompany training. Given the concern that a substantial proportion of training does not get transferred to the workplace (Baldwin and Ford 1988), research into ways that training transfer can be maximized is likely to continue to be important.

3 Training evaluation

In addition to ensuring that training has met its objectives, training evaluation provides critical information for several organizational decisions. Training programmes are often piloted and evaluated to determine whether they should be continued throughout the organization and, if so, to identify changes that could be made to improve them. Favourable training evaluations within an organization can document that training dollars have been well spent, which enhances the future credibility of training initiatives. An evaluation of training effectiveness in one organization can be useful to other organizations in deciding whether to implement a particular programme.

Like all other human resource interventions in organizations, training can only be evaluated in relation to criteria, which should be based on training objectives established at the beginning of the training design and delivery phase. Kirkpatrick (1983) developed a set of four criteria for training evaluation, including trainees' *reactions, learning, behaviour* and *results*. (Note the parallel between the last three training evaluation criteria and the three types of learning objectives discussed earlier.) These four criteria are often referred to as levels of training evaluation. Trainee reactions represent Level I evaluation, while results reflect Level IV.

Reactions are trainees' impressions, usually sought at the conclusion of training sessions through a brief questionnaire. Most reaction questionnaires include both open-ended questions such as 'What could be done to improve the training?' and questions with anchored response scales such as 'Overall, how effective did you find the training? 1 – quite ineffective, 3 – somewhat effective, 5 – very effective'.

Learning is typically measured with paper-and-pencil tests which are administered both before and after training. For example, managers of a multinational firm who attend training to prepare them for working in another country could be tested for their knowledge of facts concerning that country. Such tests must contain a representative sample of the training content.

Behaviour refers to change in employees' on-the-job behaviour after training and is usually rated by trainees themselves and those working closest to trainees, such as managers, co-workers or subordinates. Ratings are often made on behavioural observation scales (BOS). For example, subordinates of supervisors attending training might be asked to complete a BOS concerning the extent to which their supervisors engage in each of a list of effective managerial behaviours, such as asking for their help in solving problems. When ratings are made by trainees' supervisors either BOS or existing performance appraisal rating forms may be used.

Results refers to changes in organizationally relevant outcomes of trainee behaviour such as increased production rates of supervisors' work groups after supervisors have attended training. Ultimately the purpose of training is to contribute to the achievement of organizational goals, and the most meaningful level of training evaluation is results. Unfortunately changes in organizational results due to training are difficult to isolate from those caused by factors outside trainees' control. For example, salespeople who attend training may improve their sales strategies, which should increase their organization's volume of sales, but increased cost-cutting by competitors may reduce the organization's sales over the period surrounding training.

There are also special difficulties in measuring behavioural change due to training. Those rating trainees' behaviours usually know whether training has been attended and their expectations of the effect of training can bias ratings. In addition, it is difficult to determine if differences in self-rated behaviour before and after training are due to genuine changes in behaviour rather than trainees interpreting the rating scale differently after attending training.

These difficulties in evaluating training at the behavioural and results levels may account in part for why practitioners continue to rely most heavily on reaction-level training evaluations (Holden 1990; Saari *et al.* 1988). Another explanation for the infrequent use of behavioural and results evaluations is that much of training in organizations is provided as an end in itself, rather than to change specific on-the-job behaviours and results, and so evaluation at more than the level of trainees' reactions is considered unnecessary.

Training validity

In order to establish the validity of a training programme, namely, whether a training programme has achieved its stated objectives, evaluation criteria must be measured through an *evaluation design* which permits unambiguous interpretation of results. Consider, for example, an evaluation of technical training provided to new employees, using a comparison of pre- and post-training ratings of on-the-job behaviour for a single group of trainees. Higher post-training ratings could be a result either of the training or of increased job experience, leaving interpretation ambiguous. Controls in the evaluation design are required to eliminate potential threats to the validity of the conclusions.

A common control used in training evaluations is the use of a control group, which does not receive the training and serves as a comparison. If individuals are assigned to training and control groups randomly, which is called an *experimental design*, group differences in post-training performance can be attributed to training with some degree of certainty. Unfortunately, random assignment of individuals to training and control groups is not often practical in work situations because existing work groups frequently must be trained together. Designs that use intact work groups as training and control groups are referred to as *quasi-experimental designs*. Results of the quasi-experimental design can not be interpreted as clearly as those from true experiments, mainly because we are uncertain about pre-existing differences between the groups, but they are still considered superior to evaluations with no control group at all.

In cases where control groups are difficult to establish, a *time series design* may be an effective alternative. Criterion measures are taken repeatedly for a period of time before training and again after training. The repeated measures before training act as a control, and so a single individual, group or even organization can be studied without a control group. Time series designs are most appropriate when the criterion can easily be measured repeatedly over time, such as when existing records, called archival data, can be used.

Training evaluation studies are subject to many potential threats. A study of these potential threats and suggested evaluation designs to address them have been developed and are reviewed in Goldstein (1993). One of the most ubiquitous threats in training evaluation is referred to as the Hawthorne Effect, named after an assembly plant in which individuals' productivity increased for short periods after virtually all of a series of experimental changes to working conditions, some of which would logically be expected to have either no or even detrimental effects. In the Hawthorne study these increases were attributed to employees' knowing that they were part of an experiment. In training evaluations the Hawthorne Effect could account for positive reactions immediately after training; favourable self-reports of learning, behaviour change and results; or even temporary increases in actual job performance.

Even a true experimental design does not control for the Hawthorne Effect because those trained may respond favourably to the fact that they are part of a training group being studied while the control group does not. One suggested way of addressing the Hawthorne Effect is to provide the control group with bogus training, often called *placebo training*. For example, the control group might only view a video, read a book or have a discussion on the training topic. Because both the training and control groups are expected to be influenced by the Hawthorne Effect in this design, differences in post-training performance between groups can be unambiguously attributed to the effect of training. Placebo training is often not practical. Another solution is to take post-training measures some time after training has been completed, when a potential Hawthorne Effect might be expected to have worn off.

Training validity has been extended beyond the traditional four criteria since Kirkpatrick first introduced them in the 1960s. Training *content validity* has been presented as a means of reflecting the match between training content and job content, much as the content validity of a test reflects the match between test and job content. People familiar with the job (frequently supervisors) specify all elements of the job and of the training programme and a comparison of the two reflects the degree of the training programme's content validity. However, content validity can not serve as a replacement for criterion-related validity because the extent to which training criteria are achieved is influenced by multiple factors, including the training methods used and characteristics of trainees and their work environments.

Goldstein (1993) has also extended the way in which training validity is viewed by proposing four levels of validity relevant to training programmes:

1 training validity (whether trainees achieve performance criteria established within the training programme);
2 transfer validity (whether trainees apply newly learned skills to the job);
3 intra-organizational validity (whether the training is also effective with subsequent training groups within the organization);
4 inter-organizational validity (whether the training is also effective when conducted within other organizations);

Few published studies of training effectiveness have extended beyond the first two of these four levels (Burke and Day 1986).

The traditional approach to experimental training evaluation compares trained individuals' performance on a criterion with either their pre-training performance or the performance of an untrained control group. Inferential statistics are used to determine whether differences between trained group and control group scores (or between post-training and pre-training scores) are greater than would be expected by chance alone at a particular significance level (for example, 0.05). Three criticisms of this traditional approach have been raised.

The first criticism is that the typical training evaluation lacks sufficient statistical power to detect statistically significant differences when, indeed, the training has had a true effect. Statistical power is a function of many variables, but in training evaluation the primary cause is small sample sizes. The second criticism, also related to the inferential statistics used in the traditional training evaluation design, is that statistical tests of significance tell us only whether training has had an effect, but not the size of that effect. We know from the cumulation of training evaluation studies that training is generally effective across a variety of methods and applications, and so the question of whether training has had an effect is less informative than what the size of the effect has been.

Determining the size of the effect indicates training's practical significance and can help organizations estimate the utility of training, which is its value to the organization in monetary terms. Training utility estimates can be used to compare the anticipated value of a training programme to other training programmes; non-training human resource interventions (for example, improving employment selection procedures); and investments in other areas of the organization (for example, marketing programmes, equipment upgrades, research and development).

The third criticism of the traditional approach to training evaluation concerns a frequent mismatch between how training objectives are stated and training is evaluated. Objectives of training are often stated in terms of trainees attaining a particular level of performance (for example, 'observed violations of safety procedures should occur no more than one time per year per employee'), but training is usually evaluated using a *change model* (for example, 'Significantly fewer violations of safety procedures were observed among employees who attended safety training than among those of a comparable control group'). When training objectives refer to obtaining a particular performance level after training, the method of evaluation must focus on whether that level has been achieved. Together, these three criticisms suggest that training evaluation practices and future research should focus on the practical, rather than just statistical, significance of training effects and should link more closely training evaluation with training objectives.

In conclusion, training has become an increasingly important function within business and industry, due largely to technological advances, workers' need for greater involvement in decision making and organizations' interest in developing workforces which reflect their particular values and cultures. Systematic approaches to determining training needs, developing programs to meet those needs and evaluating training effectiveness are required to ensure that training meets its objectives.

PAUL TAYLOR
UNIVERSITY OF WAIKATO

Further reading

(References cited in the text marked *)

* Baldwin, T.T. and Ford, J.K. (1988) 'Transfer of training: a review and directions for future research', *Personnel Psychology* 41 (1): 63–105. (An extensive review and integration of theory and research on transfer of training, including an exhaustive bibliography.)
* Burke, M.J. and Day, R.R. (1986) 'A cumulative study of the effectiveness of managerial training', *Journal of Applied Psychology* 71 (2): 232–45. (A quantitative review of various managerial training content and methods.)
* Craig, R.L. (ed.) (1987) *Training and Development Handbook*, 3rd edn, New York: McGraw-Hill. (A comprehensive training text for practitioners.)
* Gilbert, T.F. (1978) *Human Competence: Engineering Worthy Performance*, New York: McGraw-Hill. (Provides a detailed description of the performance analysis approach to training needs analysis.)
* Goldstein, I.L. (1993) *Training in Organizations*, 3rd edn, Monterey, CA: Brooks/Cole. (A comprehensive overview of training useful to both academics and practitioners, including an extensive bibliography.)
* Holden, L. (1990) 'European trends in training and development', *International Journal of Human Resource Management* 2 (2): 113–31. (Reports on a major survey of training practices in five European countries.)
* Kirkpatrick, D.L. (1983) 'Four steps to measuring training effectiveness', *Personnel Administrator* 28 (11): 19–25. (Presents the commonly referred to four levels/types of training criteria.)
* Mager, R.F. and Pipe, P. (1984) *Analyzing Performance Problems*, 2nd edn, Belmont, CA: Lake. (Provides an easy-to-read guide for writing behavioural training objectives and for using performance analysis to identify training needs, primarily for practitioners.)
* McGehee, W. and Thayer, P.W. (1961) *Training in Business and Industry*, New York: Wiley. (The first major text on training, which provided seminal ideas about training needs analysis.)
* Nadler, L. and Nadler, Z. (eds) (1990) *The Handbook of Human Resource Development*, 2nd edn, New York: Wiley. (A compilation of training topics for the practitioner which includes chapters on some specialized and practical topics not found elsewhere.)
* O'Driscoll, M.P. and Taylor, P.J. (1992) 'Congruence between theory and practice in management training needs analysis', *International Journal of Human Resource Management*, 3 (3): 593–603. (Reports on a survey of training executives concerning how training decisions have actually been made.)
Phillips, J. (1994) *In Action: Measuring Return on Investment*, Alexandria, VA: American Society for Training and Development. (Useful resource for developing results-based training evaluation strategies.)
Prior, J. (ed.) (1994) *Gower Handbook of Training and Development*, Aldershot: Gower. (Practitioner-orientated handbook covering a wide field of training topics.)
* Saari, L.M., Johnson, T.R., McLaughlin, S.D. and Zimmerle, D.M. (1988) 'A survey of management training and education practices in U.S. companies', *Personnel Psychology* 41 (4): 731–43. (Presents findings from a large survey of training practices in US companies.)

See also: EQUAL EMPLOYMENT OPPORTUNITIES; HUMAN RESOURCE DEVELOPMENT; HUMAN RESOURCE MANAGEMENT; HUMAN RESOURCE MANAGEMENT, INTERNATIONAL; HUMAN RESOURCE MANAGEMENT IN EUROPE; INDUSTRIAL RELATIONS IN JAPAN; JOB DESIGN; OCCUPATIONAL PSYCHOLOGY; ORGANIZATION BEHAVIOUR; PRODUCTIVITY; TRAINING, ECONOMICS OF; WOMEN MANAGERS IN ORGANIZATIONS; WORK AND ORGANIZATION SYSTEMS

Related topics in the IEBM: ORGANIZATIONAL PERFORMANCE

Training, economics of

Overview

The economics of work-based training comprises two overlapping theories: human capital and institutionalism. Human capital theory, assuming rational individualism and competitive markets, analyses the incentives to employers and trainees to develop skills. Its view of the training outputs of an unregulated market system is broadly optimistic. Its extension to include recruitment costs, informational attributes and wage rigidities results in a more institutionally-orientated and less optimistic account. Further institutional influences evident in national training patterns include industrial relations, labour market structure, collective organization, system-wide interdependences and historical path dependence.

1 Definition and importance

The term 'training' denotes the learning of work-related skills and knowledge (see TRAINING). The scope of the definition is, however, variable. Economists include all forms of work-related learning, ranging from vocational education to learning by doing. Managers include only planned learning under instruction (Oatey 1970). This survey focuses on *on-the-job training*, that is, work-based learning, the most complex part of the wider whole. Apprenticeship and learning by doing are included, full-time vocational education is excluded.

Economic interest in training is generated by several attributes. Vocational learning, of which it is part, contributes strongly to the economic performance of companies, regions and countries (Prais 1989). Increased knowledge and skill are associated with higher pay. Unequal skill is an important cause of economic inequality. Public unemployment policies nowadays emphasize training rather than job creation and income maintenance. Training is central to theories of internal labour markets, efficiency, wages and labour market segmentation. Finally, market failure is endemic to training, creating a potential case for public intervention.

2 Evidence

Empirical work on training is beset by measurement problems. In addition to definitional variability, the jointness of training with production impedes the measurement of its prevalence and effects. Surveys of employer training outlays produce unreliable estimates (see PERFORMANCE APPRAISAL). Case studies offer better estimates but they are costly and rare. Age-earnings profiles involve too many restrictive assumptions to give valid estimates of worker investments (Jones 1986; Ryan 1991; Mincer 1995).

The empirical literature on training is accordingly dominated by qualitative, partial indicators – for workers, trainee status; for employers, share of employees with trainee status. Such measures are associated for workers with subsequently higher pay, upward occupational mobility and reduced unemployment – although public training is often associated with lower pay (Greenhalgh and Stewart 1987). Company-based measures are positively associated with productivity, but appropriate human resource and product strategies are often required as well (Prais 1989; Brown *et al.* 1993).

3 Human capital theory

The economics of training has, since the 1960s, been dominated by human capital theory, which treats training as an investment, involving a short-term sacrifice of income in return for subsequently higher income (see HUMAN CAPITAL; HUMAN RESOURCE MANAGEMENT). Agents are rational egotists, undertaking all investments for which discounted net benefits are positive. Markets are assumed competitive: pay adjusts to equate supply and demand in markets for trained, trainee and untrained labour (Becker 1975).

The pattern of training provision and finance in the absence of public intervention can be considered in a two period model, in which the first period comprises work-based training, the second, work without additional training. In Figure 1, Q represents individual output (net marginal value product) for trained, unskilled and trainee workers (subscripted s, u and t, respectively). Assuming identical abilities, zero unemployment, full information on present and future, and no learning in unskilled work, total costs and benefits of training are then areas *abcd* and *cefg*, representing respectively the initial loss and the subsequent gain in output when an

employee is trained instead of doing unskilled work. If discounted net benefits are positive, the training is economically viable.

The division of costs and benefits between employer and trainee is mediated by the payroll costs (W, henceforth 'pay') of the three employee categories. When skills are *general*, that is as valuable to many other employers as to the employer which provided the training, the pay profile tracks the output one and trainees bear all of the costs – in Figure 1, forgone earnings amounting to *abcd*. Any employer which subsidizes general training (for example, by paying W_1 to trainees, incurring costs of abih) has to pay its trained workers less than they produce (for example, W_2) in order to earn a return on its investment. Competitors who do not pay for training will be able to lure its trained workers away by paying them their full value (Q_s). Employers cannot therefore invest in general training. However, that need not be a problem: trainees are willing to bear the entire cost themselves, as the external market ensures high pay and a

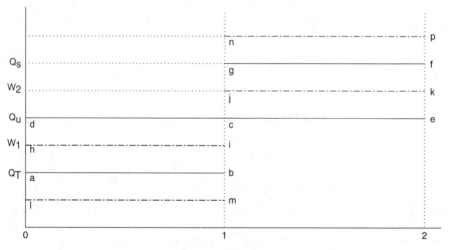

Skill	Pay	Outlay		Return	
		trainee	employer	trainee	employer
general	abgf	abcd	0	cefg	0
specific	hijk	hicd	abih	cejk	jkfg

Figure 1 Pay, outputs and investments in training
Note: Outlays and returns have not been discounted to present values

return on the investment. Training for costly general skills involves prolonged low pay – if not explicit training fees – for trainees but employers meet trainee demand as it costs them nothing.

The problem is that trainees may not be able to finance the investment. As human capital is embodied in people, legal and motivational factors prevent its use as collateral against a training loan. Trainees who lack other assets cannot finance training, which reduces training volumes and raises skilled pay relative to the economic optimum.

Apprenticeship contracts can solve the problem. The trainee is bound to receive low pay, the employer to teach a skill, and each party to avoid separation, for a fixed duration, longer than required to learn the skill. When the trainee's net product rises over the contract from less than to more than his or her pay, the employer consequently invests in training during the first phase and reaps a return during the second one. By relieving the financial strain on the trainee without laying the employer open to poaching before its investment has been recouped, apprenticeship can make both parties better off than under short-term contracts.

Two anomalies are visible for general skills. Employers sometimes invest significantly in the general training which they provide. Examples include manual and technical skills, both certified and uncertified, traded in external labour markets (Ryan 1984; Jones 1986). At the other extreme, employers may exploit trainees by offering them little training as well as low pay, benefiting from their output during training. 'Contracts of apprenticeship, in which the main advantage accrues to the employer, leaving very little to the apprentice who has been "trained" are only too familiar' (Hicks 1969: 140; Ryan 1994). The two situations may be represented by pay profiles *dcgf* and *lmgf*, respectively.

As neither anomaly could survive in highly competitive labour markets, alternative assumptions are needed. Three ways of explaining employer finance of general training have been proposed. The first involves monopsony power, present whenever an employer's labour supply would not disappear totally were its pay lower. The employer may then retain enough ex-trainees to provide a return on the investment (Becker 1975). Employers will rationally provide and finance costly general training when the alternatives – increased recruitment of trained workers or deskilling jobs – are more expensive (Oatey 1970). Hiring costs for skilled labour have been a major influence on apprentice numbers in the UK (Stevens 1994).

The second approach assumes costly and asymmetric information. When training is costly for outside employers to observe, the trained worker cannot effectively signal skill to the external market. An employer can then finance general training without losing trained workers, to an extent which increases with the informational asymmetry. When effective external certification is available the asymmetry disappears and employers refuse to finance training (Katz and Ziderman 1990).

Wage rigidity is the third potential explanation. Pay profiles are set not by labour market clearing but rather by the rules stipulated by law, collective agreement and job evaluation. When such rules specify a trainee wage greater than trainee productivity, employers must finance whatever training they provide – and are correspondingly discouraged from providing it. Evidence of such effects has been found for statutory minimum wages and collective agreements (Hashimoto 1982; Ryan 1984).

Theories which invoke wage rigidity should explain it. One factor is trade union pursuit of high trainee pay, an objective which may reflect several motives. Unions may respond to the interests of trainee members, who may make short-term job rewards their priority. Unions may want to curb exploitation, the second anomaly noted above, by raising the price of trainee labour. Better training would have the same effect, but under asymmetric information the enforceability of collective agreements is greater for trainee pay than for training quality (Ryan 1994).

At the other extreme, skills are *specific*, that is, of value only to the employer which provided the training. As a mutually beneficial asset is then destroyed if employer and trained worker separate, each party requires protection against separations induced by the other. A suitable contract allocates to each party a significant share of both costs and benefits, reassuring each that the other will lose something from ending the relationship – as under *hijk* and similar pay profiles (Becker 1975). The drawback is that both parties may seek opportunistically after training to bargain up their shares of the joint benefit. As such bargaining is costly, an efficient contract debars it by covering both periods and specifying trained worker pay in advance.

An efficient contract must also induce an optimal separation rate for trained workers – which will usually not be zero, as specific training may not work out for both parties. Various contractual provisions, in terms of duration, wage growth and restriction on separation rights, prove optimal according to what is known in advance about the productivity and job satisfaction of trained workers. For example, employers must bear most of the costs when: (1) higher pay for trained workers raises layoffs by more than it reduces quits; and (2) when less is known *ex ante* about the productivity and job satisfaction of trained workers in the training firm than elsewhere (Hashimoto and Yu 1980).

The theory of specific training provides insights into the variable importance of long-term employment and seniority pay. The unmeasurability of specific skills makes it hard to test but empirical difficulties have surfaced nevertheless (see EMPLOYMENT AND UNEMPLOYMENT, ECONOMICS OF). Its prediction that senior employees are paid less than their productivity is contradicted by evidence from the USA and from Japan, where employers pay 'window watching' senior employees more than their value (*np* and *gf* respectively). Mandatory retirement intensifies the problem: why would employers require senior employees to leave if their productivity exceeded their pay?

Seniority effects in pay and productivity may reflect motivational factors rather than training finance but they can be reconciled with human capital theory. The turnover-optimizing long-term wage contract for specific training involves low trainee pay initially and a seniority-based pay increase, taking pay above product value, during the post-training period. It optimizes labour turnover by requiring each party to incur the entire *joint* loss if it induces a separation after training – the trained worker by having borne all the costs of training, the firm by losing a trained worker without saving on pay, having to promote a junior trained worker if a senior one is laid off (Hutchens 1989).

The explanation is perhaps too ingenious. Its prediction that the trainee will bear all the costs (*abcd*) of specific training conflicts with evidence that employers bear most or all of the costs of any training which they provide. A contract which responded to the problems of trainee finance and risk aversion might account for that, but given endemic uncertainty and bounded rationality, training contracts cannot be expected simultaneously to prevent opportunistic behaviour, induce efficient risk bearing and solve trainee financing problems (Granovetter 1985). Instead, contracts go only part of the way, leaving to personnel policy the extra-contractual task of restricting turnover and protecting the employer's investment in skills.

The human capital research programme sheds less light on international differences in training. In Sweden and France vocational learning occurs largely in formal schooling; in the UK, USA, and Germany, largely in association with work. Only the latter category lies within scope here, but differences are marked there too. German training relies primarily on two to four year apprenticeships undertaken early in the working life; training often begins in the USA only after several years of work experience and increases in frequency over the first half of the work-life. German apprentices receive allowances well below earnings in the occupation for which they are training; US trainees are normally paid at the rate for the job to which their training is orientated. More generally, the relative pay of young trainees varies considerably from country to country (Marsden and Ryan 1991b).

Such differences can hardly be understood primarily in terms of the worker preferences and technology to which human capital theory looks. British youth may indeed be less willing to invest in its future than German youth, and German production methods may require more general skills than British ones, but such differences are at most second order influences – and, rather than being intrinsic attributes, may themselves be fostered by national training systems. An explicitly institutional approach is needed in order to address the heterogeneity of national training systems.

4 Institutional theories

The above discussion has considerable institutional content: the 'new institutional economics' interprets such institutions as long-term employment, seniority rights and apprenticeship as the result of rational choices under imperfect information and skill specificity. The contribution of the new institutionalism is however limited by its methodological individualism and efficiency-orientated interpretations. A richer institutional account must also consider industrial relations, labour market structure, cooperation, systemic interdependences and path dependence.

Training is often intertwined with industrial relations. An extreme case is craft union regulation of the content and availability of training in the post-war British newspaper industry (Child 1967). More generally, pay structures reflect the goals of the unions and employers which negotiate them, although their implications for training are often neglected. British, Swedish and Italian bargainers gave little thought to the implications for training of egalitarian pay policies; their German counterparts have however kept in mind the implications of trainee pay for training provision (Marsden and Ryan 1991b; Crouch 1993).

Labour market structure also affects training. Occupational markets encourage skilled workers to move between employers to build careers and gain security, in association with certified skills, rather than relying on any particular employer. Occupational structures often rely on low trainee pay under traditional apprenticeship to encourage employers to offer training. Internal labour markets are organized around particular workplaces and employers. Job vacancies are filled by internal mobility; skills are learned along career promotion ladders. The dichotomy between occupational and internal markets corresponds in part to that between general and specific skills but, as similar products and technologies are associated with different labour market structures in different countries, structure is important in its own right. Internal structures predominate in US, Japanese, French and Italian labour markets; occupational ones in German, Swiss and, historically, UK ones. The decay of occupational markets and apprenticeship has posed problems for the post-war UK (Doeringer and Piore 1971; Marsden and Ryan 1991a, 1991b).

Finally, successful training, particularly apprenticeship geared to occupational markets, may require a degree of cooperation between agents which purely contractual relations cannot provide. The simpler aspect is employer–employer cooperation. The employer who considers financing general training acts as a player in a Prisoners' Dilemma game, in which all employers will be best off when all train (the cooperative solution), all will be worst off if none train, but any one employer will be better off if it alone avoids training and 'poaches' trained workers (Chapman 1993). Cooperative solutions may be attainable in repeated games when discount rates are low and non-cooperative players can be punished effectively. The latter option usually requires an employers' association possessing the authority to deter free riding. The weakness of employers' associations in the UK and the USA accounts partly for those countries' poor training performance (Soskice 1990).

Tripartite cooperation between employers, unions and government is also needed for training to transcend job-specific skills and attain wider occupational and educational goals, for example under apprenticeship. The willingness and ability of political agents to build and run neo-corporatist, tripartite structures with training responsibilities vary greatly across countries, with Germany at one pole and the USA at the other (Streeck *et al.* 1987; Crouch 1993).

A fourth issue is the interdependence of the panoply of national institutions relevant to training. The UK and USA have been depicted as stuck in 'low skill equilibria', the result of mutually reinforcing influences which include, in addition to weak employer associations: Fordist managerial strategies (standardized product markets supplied by mass production methods using deskilled production techniques); managerial short-termism, encouraged by external takeover threats and penalising investment in intangibles like training; arms-length, insecure relationships between suppliers and producers; low social respect for skill; and political short-termism, driven by partisan advantage rather than agreed institutional development. The high skill equilibria enjoyed by Japan and Germany reflect interlocking favourable attributes in the same dimensions (Finegold and Soskice 1988).

Such arrangements constitute an equilibrium in that: (1) agents act rationally within their wider institutional context; and (2) changes in only one component, for example, public training subsidies, often fail, given systemic inertia. The efficiency claims of competitive equilibria are absent. Such holistic interpretations have difficulty however explaining intranational variation, for example, how some UK employers have succeeded with high skill strategies despite an unfavourable context.

Finally there is path dependence: national training systems result from unique, cumulative historical paths, in which random effects and positive local feedback produce enduring international differences – in contrast to the universalism of human capital theory (David 1986). Path dependence helps to account for the persistent heterogeneity of national training systems within an increasingly integrated global economy. A low skill equilibrium represents only one of several historical possibilities. Opportunities to change radically a national training system may arise episodically and its redirection can be informed by economic theory and comparative practice, but economic theory *alone* can neither explain

how a national training system came to be what it is nor specify what can be done to improve it.

PAUL RYAN
UNIVERSITY OF CALIFORNIA AT BERKELEY
KING'S COLLEGE, UNIVERSITY OF
CAMBRIDGE

Further reading

(References cited in the text marked *)

* Becker, G.S. (1975) *Human Capital*, 2nd edn, Chicago, IL: University of Chicago Press. (The original, lucid account of human capital theory, using job training as the exemplar.)
* Brown, C., Reich, M. and Stern, D. (1993) 'Becoming a high-performance work organization: the role of security, employee involvement and training', *International Journal of Human Resource Management*, 4 (2): 247–75. (Discusses factors determining success in high-tech product markets, with training as a leading component.)
* Chapman, P. (1993) *The Economics of Training*, Hemel Hempstead: Harvester Wheatsheaf. (A textbook survey of economic and institutional approaches to training.)
* Child, J. (1967) *Industrial Relations in the British Printing Industry*, London: Allen & Unwin. (A classic case study of craft union regulation of training.)
* Crouch, C. (1993) *Industrial Relations and European State Traditions*, Oxford: Oxford University Press. (An analysis of the industrial relations systems and links to national political structures in a large group of advanced economies.)
* David, P.A. (1986) 'Understanding the economics of QWERTY: the necessity of history', in W.N. Parker (ed.), *Economic History and the Modern Economist*, Oxford: Blackwell. (Path-dependent economic outcomes illustrated from the history of the standard keyboard layout.)
* Doeringer, P.B. and Piore, M.J. (1971) *Internal Labour Markets and Manpower Analysis*, Lexington, MA: D.C. Heath & Co. (A classic eclectic account of internal and occupational labour markets.)
* Finegold, D. and Soskice, D. (1988) 'The failure of training in Britain: analysis and prescription', *Oxford Review of Economic Policy* 4 (3): 21–53. (The case for seeing British training in terms of a multi-dimensional low skill equilibrium.)

* Greenhalgh, C. and Stewart, M.B. (1987) 'The effects and determinants of training', *Oxford Bulletin of Economics and Statistics* 49 (2): 171–89. (Discusses patterns of training receipt and training outcomes in the UK labour force.)
* Granovetter, M. (1985) 'Economic action and social structure: the problem of embeddedness', *American Journal of Sociology* 91 (3): 481–510. (A critique of the new institutional economics.)
* Hashimoto, M. (1982) 'Minimum wage effects on training on the job', *American Economic Review* 72 (5): 1070–87. (Presents theories and evidence that higher minimum wages reduce youth training.)
* Hashimoto, M. and Yu, B. (1980) 'Specific capital, employment contracts and wage rigidity', *Bell Journal of Economics* 11 (2): 536–49. (Contractual options for specific training.)
* Hicks, J.R. (1969) *A Theory of Economic History*, Oxford: Oxford University Press. (Comprehensive study of economic history.)
* Hutchens, R.M. (1989) 'Seniority, wages and productivity: a turbulent decade', *Journal of Economic Perspectives* 3 (4): 49–64. (An accessible account of debates over the role of training in seniority-pay relationships.)
* Jones, I.S. (1986) 'Apprentice training costs in British manufacturing establishments: some new evidence', *British Journal of Industrial Relations* 24 (3): 333–62. (Case study estimates of employers' costs for craft and technician training.)
* Katz, E. and Ziderman, A. (1990) 'Investment in general training: the role of information and labour mobility', *Economic Journal* 100: 1147–58. (How informational failures permit employers to finance general training.)
* Marsden, D.W. and Ryan, P. (1991a) 'Initial training, labour market structure and public policy: intermediate skills in British and German industry', in P. Ryan (ed.), *International Comparisons of Vocational Education and Training for Intermediate Skills*, Brighton: Falmer. (An account of divergent post-war training paths in the UK and Germany drawing on human capital, institutional and path dependence themes.)
* Marsden, D.W. and Ryan, P. (1991b) 'The structuring of youth pay and employment in six European economies', in P. Ryan, P. Garonna and R.C. Edwards (eds), *The Problem of Youth: The Regulation of Youth Employment and Training in Advanced Economies*, London: Macmillan. (Evidence on the institutional background to trainee pay in the European Union.)
* Mincer, J. (1995) 'Investments in education and training in the USA', in C.F. Buechtemann and D. Soloff (eds), *Investment in Human Capital and Economic Performance*, New York: Russell Sage Foundation. (A review of methods and evidence from an orthodox human capital standpoint.)
* Oatey, M. (1970) 'The economics of training within the firm', *British Journal of Industrial Relations* 8 (1): 1–21. (An explanation of employer investment in training, couched primarily in terms of recruitment costs.)
* Prais, S.J. (ed.) (1989) *Productivity, Education and Training: Britain and Other Countries Compared*, London: National Institute for Economic and Social Research. (Sector-level investigations of links between vocational skill and productivity in matched sectors in the UK and other European Union countries.)
* Ryan, P. (1984) 'Job training, employment practices and the large enterprise: the case of costly transferable skills', in P. Osterman (ed.), *Internal Labour Markets*, Cambridge, MA: Massachusetts Institute of Technology. (Wider implications of a case study of shipyard welder training.)
* Ryan, P. (1991) 'How much do employers spend on training? An evaluation of the "Training in Britain" estimates', *Human Resource Management Journal* 1 (4): 55–76. (Examines the difficulties of costing on-the-job training, with reference to a major UK survey.)
* Ryan, P. (1994) 'Training quality and trainee exploitation', in R. Layard, K. Mayhew and G. Owen (eds), *Britain's Training Deficit*, Aldershot: Avebury. (Looks at the determinants of trainee exploitation and trade union responses.)
* Soskice, D. (1990) 'Reinterpreting corporatism and explaining unemployment', in R. Brunetta and C. dell'Arringa (eds), *Labour Relations and Economic Performance*, London: Macmillan. (Employer associations and public policy options.)
* Stevens, M. (1994) 'An investment model for the supply of training by employers', *Economic Journal* 104: 556–71. (Recruitment and borrowing costs as influences on apprentice intakes.)
* Streeck, W., Hilbert, J., Kevalaer, K.-H. van, Maier, F. and Weber, H. (1987) *The Role of the Social Partners in Vocational Training and Further Training in the FRG*, Berlin: European Centre for Vocational Education and Training (CEDEFOP). (An account of the multilayered tripartite regulatory context of German apprenticeship.)

See also: HUMAN RESOURCE DEVELOPMENT; HUMAN RESOURCE FLOWS; HUMAN RESOURCE MANAGEMENT, INTERNATIONAL; HUMAN RESOURCE MANAGEMENT IN EUROPE; INDUSTRIAL AND LABOUR RELATIONS; MANAGEMENT DEVELOPMENT

Related topics in the IEBM: INSTITUTIONAL ECONOMICS

Industrial and labour relations

Collective bargaining

Overview

Collective bargaining can be defined as the institutionalized process by which workers (usually combined into unions) negotiate with employers with the aim of jointly determining terms and conditions of employment. Collective bargaining is institutionalized because the process in each country and industry is circumscribed by laws, customs and rituals which make the parties' relationships predictable.

As an introduction to collective bargaining, this entry is divided into four parts. The first focuses on collective bargaining as an institution, its history and its relationship with other methods of determining employment relationships. The second part examines institutional components such as bargaining structure and the status of collective bargaining contracts. The third section looks at the process of negotiations themselves. The conclusion looks to the future.

1 Collective bargaining as an institution

Collective bargaining can be justified on the assumption that bargaining between management and individual employees gives management an unfair advantage, given its position as a monopsonist. To counterbalance this advantage employees band together collectively.

While a certain amount of bargaining occurs in every employment relationship, collective bargaining has developed as a stable and pervasive institution only recently (see discussion below). In many countries it still exists only in a rather rudimentary form and there are important differences in its extent and nature in those countries where it is prevalent.

Stable collective bargaining requires a rejection of both the *unitary* and *radical* models of industrial relations (see INDUSTRIAL AND LABOUR RELATIONS). The unitary model assumes that the interests of workers and management are basically identical and that therefore unions and collective bargaining are unnecessary and illegitimate. The radical model, in contrast, assumes that these interests are fundamentally irreconcilable and that wholesale changes in power relationships are required.

Stable collective bargaining is a *pluralist* approach. It is based on a variety of assumptions.

1 While employers and employees have different interests, these differences are not irreconcilable. Instead they are somewhat the same as the differences between buyers and sellers in general. Therefore, through bargaining, a deal can be cut which sets the price and regulates the conditions under which employees sell their labour.

2 Each side accepts the legitimacy of the other and its right to survive.

3 The sides are roughly equal in strength; otherwise one side will dominate rather than bargain with the other.

4 The union legitimately represents the interests of all of those it claims to represent (a claim sometimes questioned by women and members of minority groups) (see EQUAL EMPLOYMENT OPPORTUNITIES).

5 Both parties are willing to negotiate seriously with the aim of reaching agreement.

6 If agreement cannot be reached it is legitimate for either side to exert economic pressures (such as strikes or lockouts) in order to induce the other to make concessions.

The types of pressures which may be used are usually regulated by law or generally accepted rules of fair play, which differ among countries (see INDUSTRIAL CONFLICT).

7 The government plays only a limited direct role in bargaining (see discussion below) (see CORPORATISM).

As we shall note later, however, collective bargaining is considerably more complex than buying a used car. Indeed, collective bargaining is somewhat akin to a marriage contract. As in a stable marriage the parties develop the skills and mind-set for compromises and adjustments; they accept the likelihood of continued differences of interest but have worked out a variety of mechanisms to resolve these. Also as in a stable marriage, these mechanisms work better when there is underlying trust.

Collective bargaining is not the only system for determining employment conditions. There are at least three others: governmental action, unilateral employer decisions, and participation. These systems are somewhat mutually exclusive. To the extent that these other systems are strong, collective bargaining is restricted. But note: all four alternatives are subject to economic constraints. Regardless of how wages are determined, a company cannot pay wages so high that it suffers consistent losses. Neither can it pay wages so low that it cannot recruit employees.

The role of government

The government may influence collective bargaining and employment conditions in ways which differ greatly among countries.

1 It may determine employment conditions by law, for example, through setting minimum wages, legislating the length of holidays or preventing ethnic discrimination.

2 It may provide some benefits directly, for example, pensions.

3 It may set the ground rules which govern the parties' conduct, for example through giving unions the right to bargain, restricting the conditions under which strikes may occur or determining the scope of bargaining.

4 It may settle disputes which the parties are unable to settle themselves, often through mediation or arbitration. In Australia conciliation and arbitration play a major role in determining the conditions of employment.

5 Through its macro-economic and social policies it affects the terms of bargaining agreements.

6 The government is a major employer itself and often bargains with unions representing its employees, frequently setting a pattern for the entire economy. In fact, union density is higher in the public than in the private sector in most countries today.

Furthermore, as the presumed representative of the public interest the government is interested in industrial peace, price stability, increased productivity and non-discriminatory employment patterns. To achieve these objectives it can pressure the parties (often through legislation). On the other hand, the parties can pressure the government (often through political action). Thus the government is a third party in collective bargaining, combining the often conflicting roles of neutral and bargainer.

Three examples illustrate the range of governmental roles: in the USA the government is primarily (and perhaps ineffectively) a referee in collective bargaining; in 'corporatist' systems (now less common) it is often one of three direct participants; in Latin American countries, where collective bargaining is poorly developed, the parties pressure the state to obtain conditions which in other countries might be obtained through bargaining.

Almost regardless of the form government intervention takes, the greater the extent of government participation the less scope there is for voluntary collective bargaining.

The impact on management

The purpose of collective bargaining is to subject to joint control issues over which management previously had unilateral control. But even without formal bargaining management never has complete discretion. It is subject to government regulation and market pressures. Furthermore, it is often forced to engage in informal, implicit bargaining with its employees: for example, unless it provides acceptable working conditions (including wages), employees may leave, sabotage or shirk.

Collective bargaining strengthens workers' hands in negotiations. Moreover, it formalizes the process of bargaining. When it encompasses workplace issues, as it does formally in the USA and informally in the UK, collective bargaining can bring dissatisfaction into the open. It provides workers with an opportunity to release tension and gives them a voice. It eliminates abuse and often engenders a sense of participation and commitment.

According to empirical research (mostly American), workers who have the benefits of collective bargaining generally enjoy higher wages, better benefits, fewer injuries, narrower wage dispersions and greater equality between genders and ethnic groups. Through raising labour costs, collective bargaining reduces turnover and better qualified employees are hired. On balance it may increase efficiency (Freeman and Medoff 1984), although this is debatable.

Employers complain that it also has other effects. It exaggerates and dramatizes differences: hostilities developed during negotiations may be carried over to day-to-day relations. Collective bargaining reduces management flexibility and makes it more difficult to adapt to technological and market changes. In Europe it restricts management's ability to set working hours and to lay off employees; in the USA and the UK it restricts management's ability to assign workers to tasks. Finally, collective bargaining increases costs. Not only are wages increased, but time is lost through strikes and negotiations. The net impact is considerably greater when there is comprehensive bargaining regarding shop-floor issues, as in the USA, than where bargaining involves wages only (see INDUSTRIAL AND LABOUR RELATIONS).

Relationship to participation

The distinction between collective bargaining and participation is somewhat blurred (see INDUSTRIAL DEMOCRACY). In some countries an effort is made to distinguish between topics handled through collective bargaining and an additional range of topics, such as productivity, quality and amenities, which are to be handled participatively through works councils and the like. Hopefully these later discussions will take place in a non-adversarial atmosphere (Heller *et al*. 1998).

Handling collective bargaining and participation as separate processes with separate actors may lead to jealousy and tension, particularly if the union seeks to control both. Furthermore, adversarial bargaining can easily poison the participative part of the relationship. If handled as a single process, however, participation may verge into integrative bargaining (discussed later). Unfortunately, few situations have been fully successful in separating the adversarial from the non-adversarial.

A brief history

Collective bargaining normally requires the presence of unions, and stable collective bargaining requires the acceptance of pluralism. Consequently collective bargaining's development lagged behind that of unions. Early unions in the USA and the UK sought to impose employment conditions unilaterally. When bargaining began it was generally quite informal, with unwritten agreements and no formal provisions for ongoing relationships. In time procedures for resolving differences became formalized, albeit with significant differences between the two nations. By the 1890s business unionism and collective bargaining were the predominant modes of dispute settlement in English-speaking countries generally, although these were often confined to a few sectors.

Revolutionary and reform unions persisted much longer on the Continent (see INDUSTRIAL AND LABOUR RELATIONS; TRADE UNIONS), stable collective bargaining systems not developing until much later. But by the

1950s some variant of collective bargaining had become well established generally throughout most developed non-Communist countries, although in many it was still overshadowed by government regulations. As unions grew stronger a trend toward corporatism developed in some European countries.

Collective bargaining developed more fully in the UK, the USA, Japan, Germany, Sweden and much of northern Europe than it did in France or Italy. Indeed, French unions never viewed collective bargaining as the main method of determining employment conditions. The largest union, the Confédération Générale du Travail, traditionally saw its role as political action and fomenting strikes.

The 1980s and early 1990s saw a reversal of these trends in most advanced countries. Union density and power declined almost everywhere, leading to a reduction in the number of workers covered by collective bargaining and in collective bargaining's ability to determine employment conditions independently of market pressures. On the other hand, deregulation and privatization meant that the government played a diminished role in industrial relations, in principle leaving more scope for collective bargaining (or, in the case of New Zealand, individual bargaining). The de-Communization of eastern Europe also created the potential for bargaining relations to develop. In practice, however, in neither East nor West have these trends led to more widespread bargaining.

Little stable collective bargaining has developed in Latin American and other underdeveloped countries where the unions' main concern is with their relationship with the state (Collier and Collier 1991; Frenkel 1993). In some of these countries (for example, Korea until recently) strikes and collective bargaining are heavily restricted by law, with employment conditions determined unilaterally either by management or the government. In others (for example, Singapore and Mexico) unions have been co-opted by the government or the dominant political party. Weak independent unions exist in some countries (Taiwan), but strikes tend to be directed against the government rather than the employer. Even where strong unions develop (as

in present-day Korea) they may lack the traditions or skills to negotiate a stable relationship with management. Indeed, in most underdeveloped countries unions lack the strength to be accepted by management as equal bargaining partners.

2 The elements of the bargaining relationship

There are substantial differences in the forms which collective bargaining takes among various countries. Furthermore, within any one country there may be substantial variations in collective bargaining practices among industries. In this regard dockworkers in one country may be closer to dockworkers in another than they are to university staff in their own country.

Some of the main elements of bargaining are discussed below.

The nature of representation

Collective bargaining typically involves an employer or group of employers, often bound together in an employers association, and a group of employees, bound together in a union. (The fact that employees join together to bargain through a union or a union-like institution distinguishes collective from individual bargaining.)

There are wide differences among countries in how unions obtain the right to represent a group of employees. In the USA representation rights are gained through a government-run election. In many other countries they are based on tradition or past practice; originally they may have been wrested from unwilling employers through industrial action. Similarly, there are differences whether only one union has the right to represent a given set of employees (that is, it is their 'exclusive bargaining agent') or whether there may be several. Exclusive bargaining agents are the general rule in English-speaking countries and much of northern Europe. In France, Italy and Spain several rival unions (typically differing in political or religious orientation) may claim to represent the same group of employees, although the practice in most situations is for one union to take the lead in negotiations. Many European countries have a 'dual system', with the union representing workers at higher levels and works councils representing their workplace interests. However, since unions often dominate works councils, this difference may be of only minor importance.

Bargaining structure

The term 'bargaining structure' is applied to the arrangement of who bargains with whom and whom the parties represent. There are three main issues here.

1 Does each firm negotiate separately or do firms join together to negotiate in employers' associations? The role of employers' associations varies considerably across countries: they are weak in the USA and strong in Germany (see EMPLOYERS' ASSOCIATIONS).

2 Is bargaining on an industry or occupational basis? In other words, does the resulting agreement apply to all the workers in a given industry, regardless of occupation – or to all the workers in a given occupation, regardless of industry? The answer is partly determined by (and partly determines) union structure. Both are highly influenced by the nature of the labour and product markets. Occupational bargaining (and occupational unions) are common, but not universal, in Australia, the UK and in some US industries (construction, health and transportation). Elsewhere bargaining by industry is the rule.

3 At what level does bargaining occur? How centralized is bargaining? As discussed below, five main types of bargaining structure can be distinguished: economy-wide; industry-wide; area-wide; plant or enterprise; and workplace. (A sixth type, European Union-wide, is still more dream than reality.) Note, however, that the bargaining structure in no country conforms perfectly to one type and there has been much change recently. Furthermore, these forms are not mutually exclusive. Agreements

negotiated at a higher level are often supplemented at lower levels.

Austria (and until recently Sweden and The Netherlands) provides the clearest examples of *economy-wide bargaining*. Here the key negotiations have been highly centralized, being between the peak national union federation and its management counterpart. Agreements reached are binding nationally (with exceptions). Another form of economy-wide negotiation involves corporatist arrangements (see CORPORATISM). Here the peak union and management organizations join with the government during inflationary periods to establish incomes policies which set limits on wage and price increases (with the government often subsidizing the policy through improved social benefits). A more limited form of economy-wide bargaining used to occur in France where peak employer and union organizations bargained on specific issues, such as vocational training, but left wages and other issues to be determined at lower levels.

Industry-wide bargaining is typically conducted at a national level between a national union and a national industrial association. It is common in many Continental countries and was once so in the UK. Typically industry-wide agreements include specific provisions regarding wages and perhaps hours and benefits (such as superannuation). Other topics, such as training or shop-floor representation, may be totally ignored; alternatively the industry-wide agreement may provide a 'framework', a broad set of principles which are applied and supplemented by further company- or plant-level negotiations. For example, German industry-wide agreements typically cover wages and hours; on other topics they often provide only general policies, with the details to be bargained out by works councils and their managements. In some countries industry-wide agreements provide merely minimum wages, with actual levels set at lower levels.

Even where negotiations are not formally industry-wide, a key agreement set in one company may set a pattern which is followed elsewhere, establishing a form of *de facto* industry-wide bargaining. Thus in the USA an agreement between the United Automobile Workers and one auto company is followed with little change by the other companies. Similarly in Japan the annual 'spring offensive' helps spread wage increases. In some countries the terms of a presumed industry-wide agreement may be extended by law to cover non-union firms.

Not all agreements between employers' associations and unions are negotiated at the national level. In the USA, the UK and (formally) in Germany important agreements are negotiated at regional or local levels. This *area-wide bargaining* is especially common where individual employers are small.

To the extent to which bargaining exists, *company or enterprise bargaining* is the rule in Japan, in many US and Canadian industries and increasingly in the UK, Australia, and New Zealand. During times of prosperity unions sometimes prefer company to industry-wide bargaining because they can play off (whipsaw) one company against another; in recession it may be the companies which prefer decentralization. Often company-level negotiations are monitored by the employers' association and the national union; not so in Japan where national union federations are weak. In the USA company-wide contracts in multi-plant companies are themselves often supplemented by plant-level agreements covering such topics as promotional sequences and training rights.

There are widespread differences both between and within countries as to the extent and form of *workplace bargaining*. Most workplace bargaining involves work rules – topics such as the scope of an employee's duties, work pace and the length of rest breaks. These have been a major source of contention in some countries where management seeks to set work rules unilaterally while the union insists they should be jointly determined. Battles over what are variously called 'management prerogatives' or 'the frontier of union control' are almost continuous in many organizations.

In the USA, where contracts are detailed and of set duration, workplace bargaining typically involves the application of written agreements to specific situations. Union demands take the form of written grievances which, if not settled locally, are resolved at higher union–management levels or through arbitration. (Despite legalities the union's position is often reinforced by 'go-slows', work-to-rule and, increasingly rarely, wildcat strikes.) In the past, at least, British contracts were less detailed and workplace rules were embedded in unwritten 'custom and practice'. No-strike agreements are still rather rare in the UK.

Both the USA and the UK have well developed steward systems. Workplace organization is weaker in many other countries. In Japan the formal grievance procedure is largely ignored. Indeed, one of the reasons why national and regional bargaining became so common in some European countries was that management was adamant to keep the union 'outside the plant gate'. In these countries works councils often negotiate work rules and handle cases of workplace discontent. Elsewhere there are few rules restricting management's workplace discretion or providing for the orderly resolution of workplace grievances. Disorderly ways remain, such as sabotage or go-slows.

Historically the level of centralization depended on a number of factors, especially on the geographical scope of the labour and product markets existing at the time unions were formed and the role of government in determining employment conditions. Centralization is also moderately correlated with union density: industry-wide bargaining is difficult if only a portion of industry is unionized. The trend in many countries until roughly the 1970s was toward greater centralization, especially in those countries which experimented with incomes policies or, as in the case of Sweden, solidaristic policies of minimizing wage inequalities (see PAYMENT SYSTEMS; TRADE UNIONS). Particularly since 1980 there has been a movement in the opposite direction. Bargaining in many countries has become considerably decentralized, for example, in the USA, the UK (especially in the public sector), France, Sweden, Australia, New Zealand and even (slightly) in Germany. Among the reasons for this trend is that unions have lost members as well as political and economic power throughout most of the world: corporatism has been losing popularity. Meanwhile, new laws, especially in the UK, Australia and New Zealand, have accelerated the change. Furthermore, industry-wide bargaining sought to establish a 'common rule' or 'level playing field' which eliminated labour costs as a factor in competition. But growing international trade makes this objective difficult to attain on a national basis. Job involvement and union-management cooperation schemes in the USA often give work teams and joint committees the right to vary conditions previously determined contractually on a plant- or company-wide basis.

The scope of bargaining

Wages are a principal topic of bargaining almost everywhere. Beyond this there are considerable differences. US contracts cover a broad range of other topics: individual pay scales, holidays, grievance and arbitration procedures, no-strike provisions, training, grounds for discipline, layoffs and recalls, workloads, pensions (superannuation), profit sharing and health benefits, among others. Consequently US contracts are quite long and are often supplemented by appendices.

By contrast, in other countries many of these topics have been pre-empted by the government. Health and superannuation (pensions) may be provided directly by the state, while other topics, such as length of holidays, are regulated by law and workplace issues remain under unilateral management control. Furthermore, as previously noted, some topics may be negotiated at one level and others at another. Still another difference is that in the USA all issues are negotiated simultaneously, thus promoting trade-offs; by contrast, in France various issues may be negotiated separately.

The nature of the agreement

In Germany, Austria, Scandinavia, the USA and Canada contracts are of fixed duration and are legally binding. Moreover, 'peace agreements' or 'no-strike clauses' prohibit industrial action while the contract is in effect. In most of these countries a fairly sharp distinction is drawn between disputes over rights and those over interests. Rights disputes relate to the application and interpretation of an existing contract while interest disputes concern the provisions of a new contract. Rights disputes often take the form of grievances alleging contract violations. These are handled with various degrees of bureaucratic legalism, depending on the country.

Labour courts exist in many European countries. They adjudicate rights disputes which the parties are unable to settle themselves. In the USA and Canada the function of labour courts is played by private arbitrators, selected and compensated by the parties (see THIRD PARTY INTERVENTION). The rights/interest distinction is weaker in the UK; here contracts are not generally viewed as legally binding and are open-ended as to length. If disagreements as to these persist the parties may resort to industrial action. In Italy and France contracts have never been seen as binding as they are in the USA.

The use of pressure

Collective bargaining involves more than persuasion. Any resulting agreement depends heavily on the parties' abilities to exert economic and political pressures to achieve their goals.

Usually the union is the party seeking change, and its primary weapon is the strike. For management it is often enough to indicate its willingness to take on a strike. But strikes are not the union's only weapon (see INDUSTRIAL CONFLICT). Depending on the country the union may organize a go-slow or a work-to-rule campaign, or apply pressure tactics (including unfavourable publicity) against the employer's suppliers, customers or financiers.

Management has weapons of its own. It may lock out its employees; it may enforce rules strictly; it may dare the union to strike through unilaterally cutting wages or changing work rules; and it can bolster the credibility of its threat to withstand a strike through such tactics as recruiting strike breakers, training clerical employees to handle production jobs or accumulating a large inventory of products. Either side may appeal to the government or to public opinion. In stable bargaining relationships there are understood limits, set by laws or the parties' expectations, as to types of techniques which may legitimately be used.

In Australia strikes tend to be short and are intended chiefly to warn management or influence arbitration tribunals. In contrast the average US strike is long: it occurs only after extensive bargaining sessions have broken down. In countries where collective bargaining is weakly developed (such as in Latin America) strikes are directed not so much against management as against the government.

Since public sector employers seek to maximize votes rather than profits, unions are likely to use strikes to embarrass the public employer politically rather than to force it to take a financial loss.

3 The bargaining process

Recent years have seen the development of the academic field of 'negotiations', with its roots in psychology (Neale and Bazerman 1992), economics, especially game theory (Raiffa 1982; Schilling 1960) and international relations as well as industrial relations (Walton and McKersie 1965; Kennedy *et al.* 1982). The field has a considerable literature and a specialized jargon. The analysis below makes use of this jargon and is based chiefly on American experience in collective bargaining as practised by experienced negotiators. There has been considerable research as to cross-national differences in bargaining styles, but little on differences in specific collective bargaining processes among countries.

Collective bargaining versus buying a used car

To demonstrate what is distinctive about collective bargaining, it may be useful to compare this complex process with a simpler one: buying a used car.

(1) Negotiations over a used car involve only two parties; the buyer and seller. In contrast, collective bargaining is conducted usually by professional negotiators who act as agents for their respective constituents (the principals), the union membership and top management. Professional negotiators may spend as much energy managing their constituents as dealing with each other.

(2) Complicating matters, neither constituency is homogeneous. Older union members, for example, may give top priority to better superannuation allowances, while younger people may prefer more take-home pay. Similarly, on management's side, Finance may insist on keeping wages low while Manufacturing is more interested in winning working rules concessions and Sales seeks to avoid a strike at all costs. Resolving these differences requires considerable *intra-party bargaining*.

(3) Buying a used car is a one-time transaction. Once it is over the parties may not see each other again. Union–management relations are continuous. Hostilities developed during formal negotiations may transfer to the contract's day-to-day administration.

(4) In selling a used car the terms of trade are quite specific: a car is exchanged for a set sum of money. But a collective bargaining agreement is more like a marriage contract. Not only are there numerous areas for possible future disagreement, but predicting these in advance is difficult. New problems are constantly arising. Settling these may require almost daily negotiations.

(5) In used car negotiations, if no agreement is reached either party can 'walk away'. But unions and managements are bilaterally dependent. Management can avoid eventually reaching an agreement only by going out of business, by moving to another location or by breaking the union – all costly alternatives. Similarly the union can avoid an eventual agreement only by giving up its membership – something unions

are quite reluctant to do. The parties have no cheap alternative to settling eventually. But this fact may not make settlement easier: knowing that its opponent cannot withdraw may make a party more intransigent.

Some basic principles

Two elements which collective bargaining has in common with most simpler forms of bargaining are resistance points and the use of trade-offs to reach agreement.

First, each side has a *resistance point*. For instance, the union may be willing to settle for a £2 an hour increase, but not for less. Thus its resistance point is £2. Management is willing to pay £3 to avoid a strike, so its resistance point is £3.

Each side's resistance point is largely determined by its BATNA (Best Alternative to a Negotiated Agreement). For example, based on their own (perhaps inaccurate) evaluation of the company's competitive position and their members' own militancy, the union's negotiators may conclude that they could win £5 through a long strike. But such a strike would expensive. Furthermore there is a good chance it might lose. Therefore it arrives at its £2 figure by discounting the £5 by highly subjective factors representing the costs and uncertainty of a strike. Going through a similar process, management sets its resistance point at £3.

In this case there is a positive *contract zone* (the difference between the two resistance points) of £1, and the main task of bargaining is to divide the £1 between the parties. But, if the union's bottom line is £4 while management refuses to make any concessions at all, the contract zone is negative and a strike is likely unless the parties change their reservation prices.

But even with a positive contract zone settlement is difficult, since neither side reveals its reservation price. To take the previous example, if the union were to say it would settle for £2 management might accept this offer immediately. By not revealing its resistance point the union may win up to £1 more. So the union bluffs and claims it needs £4.

Second, agreement is facilitated by the possibility of making trade-offs. Trade-offs require the existence of at least two issues, with the parties differing as to the priority they give these: one side may think issue A (perhaps wages) most important; for the other party it is issue B (working rules). Thus the first side makes a concession on issue A in return for the other side's concession on issue B. In such trade-offs neither side gets everything it wants, but both sides are better off than they were previously (technically they are closer to the Pareto frontier). Thus trade-offs can create *value*. But value-creating trade-offs do not come easily because each side has an incentive not to reveal its priorities. Were the union, for instance, to announce publicly that its top priority was winning a closed shop, management might hold this item 'hostage' and concede it only for major union concessions.

Bargaining stages

With this introduction let us describe the stages through which collective bargaining normally passes. Prior to bargaining each side gathers arguments and formulates its position. Union members and individual managers may be polled as to their preferences. The union must choose, for example, whether to give top priority to higher wages or to some other demand. There are widespread internal discussions which serve two purposes: they discover constituents' preferences and they mobilize support for each side's demands, including, if necessary, industrial action.

Each side begins negotiations by making exaggerated demands which its sophisticated opponent rarely take seriously. So why not be 'honest'? First, unrealistic demands leave room for a party to make concessions which it might trade off for concessions by its opposite. Second, a negotiator who opens negotiations with an 'honest' moderate position may inadvertently give away 'value' which the other side might have been prepared to concede. Finally, tough opening demands are designed to convince less sophisticated constituents that their interests have not been forgotten.

During the early stages of negotiations the parties demonstrate their determination and their willingness to engage in a long strike. As mentioned earlier, management may recruit possible replacements for those who might go on strike and the union may accumulate a strike fund. Although most negotiations take place in private, away from the press and out-siders, at this stage each side's team tends to be rather large and each side engages in con-siderable oratory (sometimes called *attitudi-nal structuring*).

Despite the rhetoric, skilled negotiators spend the early period seeking to discover the other's priorities. Eventually they begin to ex-plore possible concessions and value-creating trades. Often they do this indirectly through signalling. Example: the union asks for three new holidays. Management replies, '*Three* holidays is too much', emphasizing the three. Translation: we might consider one new holi-day. The advantage of signalling is that a sig-nal can be disavowed, while an explicit concession is more difficult to disclaim.

In time the parties begin a 'concession dance'. Each side makes a small concession with the expectation that the other side will make a concession in return. Often conces-sions start with trivial items first. Gradually the parties come closer to agreement. The ne-gotiating team size is reduced. The parties spend considerable time floating possible trade-offs. At this stage there may be more 'intra-party bargaining' within each team than actually bargaining between teams. Often concessions are combined with trade-offs. One side says: 'I'll give you X if you give me Y'. Then negotiations take place over the size of Y. Occasionally one of the parties may come up with a genuine 'breakthrough', a so-lution not previously considered which meets both parties' needs and which both sides can claim as a victory.

The pace starts accelerating as the parties approach a strike or contract-expiration dead-line. (Without a deadline negotiations might go on indefinitely as each party waits for the other to make another concession.) Inter-changes are shorter and more rapid; caucuses are more frequent. Final settlement is often reached just before or shortly after the deadline arrives. Once the goal is achieved, tensions are reduced and often there is a small celebration.

The final step in many negotiations is for the union membership and the company board of directors to ratify the contract. If intra-party bargaining has been successful ratification may be simple. Otherwise the key negotiators must fight hard to sell their agree-ment or otherwise suffer loss of face and pos-sibly job.

If unassisted bargaining does not lead to a settlement the parties may utilize concilia-tion, mediation and arbitration. In some cases parties become so dependent on arbitration that there is little real bargaining (see THIRD PARTY INTERVENTION).

The key role of negotiators

As middlemen, professional negotiators have complex relations with each other and their constituents. This both complicates and facilitates negotiations. Since negotiators are hired by their constituents they must con-stantly demonstrate their devotion to their interests. At some points this may require the-atrics such as screaming or pounding the table. But negotiators must also manage their constituents' expectations and behaviours. At first they must mobilize them to support their demands, but they must also educate them to keep their expectations realistic and eventu-ally persuade them to accept the concessions necessary for agreement.

Skilful negotiators often work in tandem with their opposites, translating opponents' demands into terms which constituents find acceptable. They pass signals to each other as to when concessions will be most successful. They recognize the political realities facing their opponents and may make it easier for them to retreat without lost face. In 'mature bargaining' each negotiator knows fairly well where the other stands. The longer they work together the more likely they are to exchange favours which prolong each other's political survival.

Integrative bargaining

In theory skilled negotiators who have exchanged appropriate information, especially as to their preferences and BATNAs, should be able to reach a settlement without a strike or lockout – either that or they should agree that no mutually beneficial solution is possible and they should dissolve their relationship voluntarily. In practice this rarely happens.

Negotiations fail for many reasons. The parties do not trust each other. Differences are dramatized and exaggerated. Hostilities multiply as the parties personalize their opponents' opposition. Insufficient information is exchanged or, if exchanged, not believed. In an effort to demonstrate their determination, the parties commit themselves to no-further-concession positions which they cannot abandon without loss of face. Negotiators make inaccurate estimates of their opponents BATNAs or are blind to possible value-creating trade-offs which would leave both sides ahead. All these problems are multiplied if the parties have a past history of poor relations.

There has been growing interest in new forms of negotiations which have been variously called 'integrative', 'win–win' or 'mutual gains' bargaining (Fisher and Ury 1981). The hope is to make bargaining less adversarial and to develop more harmonious relations. Parties engaged in integrative bargaining seek to understand the other side's needs, to focus on interests (underlying problems) rather than positions (demands), to evaluate a range of alternative solutions rather than advocating a single one and, above all, to concentrate on generating solutions (acceptable propositions) that simultaneously meet both parties' needs.

US experience suggests that parties which have been trained in the use of integrative techniques are frequently able to negotiate contracts amicably and without resort to industrial action. But this is not always the case. Past history and suspicions are often too strong to be overcome. Furthermore, the 'prisoners' dilemma' is at work: integrative bargaining succeeds only as long as both sides play according to its rules; either side can gain by 'defecting' (playing by traditional adversarial rules), leaving the other side only the 'suckers' payoff'.

Furthermore, integrative bargaining will not automatically leave both sides better off than they were before. Neither does it completely eliminate the need for 'distributive' or 'win–lose' bargaining. Through facilitating value-creating trade-offs, integrative bargaining may increase the size of the contract zone to be distributed. However, once it is understood that such a zone exists – that settlement is better than non-settlement – the distributive question of how to divide this zone remains.

4 The future of bargaining

Bargaining is dependent on union strength and a favourable political environment. Unions are in retreat throughout much of the world. They have lost both political and economic strength. Among the reasons for this are high overall levels of unemployment, the shift from well-unionized mass production to service work and the internationalization of product markets. (Industry-wide bargaining functions best when national markets can be effectively insulated from external pressures (see INDUSTRIAL AND LABOUR RELATIONS).) Managers are pushing everywhere for greater flexibility in the management of their workforce (see FLEXIBILITY). Although unions remain an important force in many countries (especially Germany), bargaining is being decentralized. Furthermore, there is a trend in many organizations towards forms of workplace participation in which unions play little direct role. It is hard to predict whether or when these trends will be reversed. At least until some form of successful multinational unionism develops, it seems questionable whether collective bargaining will regain its significance.

GEORGE STRAUSS
UNIVERSITY OF CALIFORNIA AT BERKELEY

Further reading

(References cited in the text marked *)

Bean, R. (1985) *Comparative Industrial Relations: An Introduction to Cross-National Perspectives*, London: Croom Helm. (This basic text has a strong section on collective bargaining.)

* Collier, R. and Collier, D. (1991) *Shaping the Political Arena: Critical Junctures, the Labor Movement, and Regime Dynamics in Latin America*, Princeton, NJ: Princeton University Press. (This comparative analysis of the history of government–union relations in eight Latin American countries argues that stable collective bargaining has rarely developed in these countries.)

Clegg, H.A. (1976) *Trade Unionism Under Collective Bargaining*, Oxford: Blackwell. (A comparative work explaining differences in unions and bargaining in six countries.)

* Fisher, R. and Ury, W. (1981) *Getting to Yes: Negotiating Agreements Without Giving In*, Boston, MA: Houghton Mifflin. (A best-selling handbook for bargaining for mutual gains by stressing interests rather than positions.)

* Freeman, R. and Medoff, J. (1984) *What Do Unions Do?*, New York: Basic Books. (A study of union impact which argues that unions may increase managerial efficiency.)

* Frenkel, S. (ed.) (1993) *Organized Labor in the Asia-Pacific Region*, Ithaca, NY: Cornell University Press. (Compares nine countries and illustrates how collective bargaining plays a minor role in the underdeveloped seven.)

* Heller, F., Pucik, E., Strauss, G. and Wilpert, B. (1998) *Organization Participation: Myth or Reality*. Oxford: Oxford University Press. (Chapter 4 deals with the relationship between participation and collective bargaining.)

* Kennedy, G., Benson, J. and McMillan J. (1982) *Managing Negotiations*, London: Macmillan. (A practical guide to how to bargain.)

* Neale, M. and Bazerman, M. (1992) *Negotiating Rationally*, New York: The Free Press. (Based on extensive psychological research, this study demonstrates how biases and social pressures can lead to negotiators behaving less rationally.)

Poole, M. (1986) *Industrial Relations: Origins and Patterns of National Diversity*, London: Routledge & Kegan Paul. (A sociological approach to comparative industrial relations.)

* Raiffa, H. (1982) *The Art & Science of Negotiations*, Cambridge, MA: Belnap/Harvard. (The application of game theory in a form directly relevant to collective bargaining; deals with issues such as trade-offs and the concession dance.)

* Schilling, T.C. (1960) *The Strategy of Conflict*, Cambridge, MA: Harvard University Press. (A major contribution by a game theorist, of relevance especially to international relations, but also applicable to industrial relations.)

* Walton, R. and McKersie, R. (1965) *A Behavioral Theory of Labor Negotiations*, New York: McGraw-Hill. (A pioneering study which suggests how psychological and economic game theory can he helpful in understanding collective bargaining, giving us the concepts of distributive and integrative bargaining, attitudinal structuring and intra-party bargaining.)

See also: CORPORATISM; EMPLOYERS' ASSOCIATIONS; EMPLOYMENT AND UNEMPLOYMENT, ECONOMICS OF; EQUAL EMPLOYMENT OPPORTUNITIES; FLEXIBILITY; HUMAN RESOURCE MANAGEMENT; INDUSTRIAL CONFLICT; INDUSTRIAL DEMOCRACY; INDUSTRIAL AND LABOUR RELATIONS; INDUSTRIAL RELATIONS IN EUROPE; INDUSTRIAL RELATIONS IN JAPAN; INDUSTRIAL RELATIONS IN THE USA; PAYMENT SYSTEMS; THIRD PARTY INTERVENTION; TRADE UNIONS

Corporatism

Overview

Corporatism describes a form of organizational behaviour in which associations, while representing the particular interests of their members, also discipline them in the interests of some wider collectivity. It has mainly been used to describe systems of industrial relations, although it can be more widely applied to the role of certain kinds of trade association and other industry bodies outside the sphere of labour.

Its significance is that it might enable firms, unions of employees and other participants in a market economy to achieve a high level of cooperation and shared pursuit of collective goods that also serve a wider public interest, despite the fact that they are also in competition with one another. Associations will act in this way only under certain specific and rather precisely balanced situations of organizational design. Within modern social science the concept of corporatism should therefore be used with care and precision. This can be difficult given that it has had a long and strange history. It has mainly been associated with northern Europe, but also with Japan. Some economic branches, in particular agriculture, tend to be corporatist in a wider range of countries. Corporatism enjoyed a peak period of both actual performance and theoretical recognition during the 1970s, since when it has undergone important challenges and changed its form in interesting ways.

There is much confusion over the relationship between corporatist arrangements and the State; in the UK in particular there is a tendency to use the term to describe situations in which government, usually in a crises, tries to cajole organized interests to behave themselves. This is far too loose and general. Indeed, within an existing corporatist structure a need for government intervention is evidence of *failure of the system*.

1 Introduction

Corporatism describes a form of organizational behaviour in which associations, while representing the particular interests of their members, also discipline them in the interests of some wider collectivity. It has mainly been used to describe systems of industrial relations, with the organizations concerned being trade unions and employers' associations (see TRADE UNIONS; EMPLOYERS' ASSOCIATIONS), usually though not solely referring to long-term arrangements for keeping collectively negotiated wage development in line with price competitiveness (Dell'Aringa 1990; Crouch 1993), but is usually associated with voluntary incomes policies. It can however be extended outside the labour context to refer to the work of trade associations, in relations with governments or with each other (Streeck and Schmitter 1985). Examples would be German *Kammer* (chambers) ensuring that their member firms play their part in the training of young workers, or an association of Japanese motor manufacturers allocating production quotas to firms under a voluntary export restriction agreement.

The significance of corporatism is that it might enable firms, unions, associations of employees and other participants in a market economy to achieve a high level of cooperation and shared pursuit of collective goods that also serve a wider public interest, despite the fact that they are in competition with each other. Since associations of economic actors might normally be expected to pursue their collective interests at the expense of the wider public – for example, by forming special-interest lobbies and protectionist cartels –

associations will act in a corporatist way only under certain specific and rather precisely balanced situations of organizational design.

The term 'corporatism' has a long and strange history, and for that reason has been the subject of major misunderstandings. In contemporary practice, although by no means as a historical idea, it is associated primarily with northern Europe (with a contrast between a 'social democratic' form in Scandinavia and a more employer-dominated system in Germany, The Netherlands, Belgium, Austria and Switzerland). However, in some cases it is also associated with Japan (Dore 1990), while some economic branches, in particular agriculture, tend to be corporatist in a wider range of countries. After a peak period of both actual performance and theoretical recognition during the 1970s, it has since undergone important challenges and changed its form in interesting ways.

There is much confusion over the relationship between corporatist arrangements and the State (see Cawson (1986) for the clearest discussion of the issue). In the UK in particular there is a tendency in public debate and journalism to use the term to describe situations in which government, usually in a crisis, tries to cajole organized interests to behave themselves. But government intervention of that kind may be found in crises for virtually all types of organized interests, not just corporatist ones. The aim of governments in such situations may well be to try and encourage the formation of corporatist structures among pluralist interest groups that are becoming oligopolistic, but the intervention itself does not constitute corporatism. Indeed, within an existing corporatist structure a need for government intervention is evidence of the failure of the system.

The view that corporatism is somehow associated with a high profile for the State also stems from a past association of certain forms of corporatism with fascism. This aspect will be discussed in detail below. Confusion caused by this has led many authors to distinguish sharply between two forms of corporatism, using such contrasting adjectives as 'state and societal' (Schmitter 1974), or 'authoritarian and liberal' (Lehmbruch 1982).

More generally, societal or liberal corporatism, which is the form encountered in certain contemporary democratic societies, is called 'neo-corporatism', to distinguish it from both fascist and other historical meanings of the term. In this entry this usage will be followed where appropriate.

2 Theory

From the perspective of economic theory, when interests organize themselves they are likely to conspire against the public interest. They pursue their shared collective interest by dumping or externalizing the costs of what they do onto those outside their circle – the general public. For example, they might exercise political pressure to receive special treatment for their activities or they might fix artificially high prices for their products. There are, however, three kinds of situation in which they might not act in this way:

(1) The first is when the organized group is so large that: (a) its actions have a clear, perceptible effect and cannot just disappear into the general 'noise' of everybody's special pleading; and (b) its membership overlaps with at least a significant minority of the general public. In such instances the distinction between insiders who gain, at the expense of outsiders who lose, breaks down as the two groups become partly co-terminous. Olson (1982) describes such cases as 'encompassing organizations'. Examples would be large, centralized, national trade union organizations bargaining on behalf of, say, thirty per cent of the employees in a country. Whereas the leaders of a small union might argue that any inflationary consequences of their actions will be (a) infinitesimally small, and (b) in any case borne in general by outsiders, the leaders of a centralized national federation know that the outcomes of their bargaining will (a) have a macro-economic effect, (b) that will be directly borne by their members as part of the general public.

(2) The second instance is where the group is sufficiently large and sufficiently responsive to its leaders for the latter to have a strategic capacity enabling them to identify and respond to negative consequences that would

eventually be felt by the group were it to maximize its immediate interests. Examples would be centralized employers' associations and unions bargaining: (a) in a context where they know that any inflationary outcome of their bargaining will lead to deflationary action by a central bank likely to create unemployment in the sector (Lange and Garrett 1985; Crouch 1994; Streeck 1994); or (b) in an industry heavily dependent on price-sensitive export trade (Crouch 1990).

(3) Third is where the group is small, decentralized and operating in a context of many rival groups analogous to a pure market: that is, no one group can affect the overall outcome or have more than a small impact.

The first and second instances are both examples of where organizations are likely to behave in a corporatist way as they have strong incentives to restrain their pursuit of self-interest, if necessary disciplining their members in order to do so. The third instance is an example of organizations compatible with the public interest due to pluralism, not corporatism. The optimal conditions of corporatism and pluralism are the opposite of each other, and pluralism serves as a useful antithesis to corporatism in the study of different systems of organized interests. Corporatism will be more stable the more oligopolistic, the more centralized and the more capable of strategic action are the organizations; pluralism will be more stable the more there is a highly competitive free market (see INDUSTRIAL AND LABOUR RELATIONS).

Both corporatist and pluralist systems begin to acquire rent-seeking attributes, associated in economic theory with interest organizations, as they start to converge; that is, if they slip towards the middle ground between them. This middle position would exist if there were a number of competing interest organizations, each too small to have strategic capacity but too large and too uneven and partial in their coverage to produce a true market. It is an interesting case of a middle-ground position being less stable than the two extremes on either side of it: a bipolar or U-curve model of stability. Research has supported this theory of interest group behaviour and the public

interest (Calmfors and Driffill 1988; Crouch 1993, 1995).

Corporatist theory and research have gone further in establishing the conditions for optimal functioning. The more that central leaders retain strategic capacity while being linked to lower levels of the organization through various interdependencies. The more they will avoid the dangers of remoteness endemic to centralization; the more that potentially hostile interests interact with each other, the more they are likely to develop trust relations and suspend short-term maximization of their interests (Marin 1990).

3 History

The historical development of corporatism, whether as an idea or as practice, bears little relationship to the above theories that have retrospectively sought to understand it. In the late nineteenth century a number of social thinkers became alarmed at the growing confrontation between capitalism and socialism. They identified the former with an atomization of social solidarities, the latter with excessive collectivism and statism; and both were associated with social conflict and materialism. These writers often looked back with a rather romantic nostalgia to what they saw as the more orderly world of medieval cities, where guilds and other corporations sustained a balance between the individual and the collectivity through organized occupational identities. They explored the scope for modern versions of such organizations within industrial society as an alternative to individualistic capitalism and statist socialism, focusing in particular on industrial relations conflicts. Since both capitalism and socialism were associated with secularism and materialism, it is not surprising that most of these corporatists were Christians, the Roman Catholic Church in particular associating itself with corporatist social policies. There were important exceptions, however: Hegel (a very secularized Lutheran) and Durkheim (a secularized Jew).

From this unpromisingly romantic and idealistic base some practical proposals developed; the idea of works councils originates here (see INDUSTRIAL DEMOCRACY). They made little headway in the everyday world, however, although outside the area of industrial relations trade associations in the German-speaking world did routinely behave in a corporatist way (Streeck 1983).

During and immediately after the First World War governments became alarmed at the dangers of widespread industrial conflict – first during a major war and second in the wake of the Russian revolution (see INDUSTRIAL CONFLICT). They sought to bring unions and employers together in consultative fora. This led to some policy initiatives resembling corporatist ideas, although not necessarily directly influenced by the movement. Some edifices from this period still exist: the International Labour Office at Geneva was established in this spirit as part of the Treaty of Versailles, while in the UK the Whitley Councils in the public services were part of the same movement. However, the appearance of widespread unemployment in the early 1920s weakened the threat of organized labour in many countries, and there was far less concern over its power among the established forces of conservative and liberal politicians and businessmen. Nor did labour interests, apart from those associated with Catholicism, appear interested in corporatism, being too committed to the overthrow of capitalism.

Corporatism was instead taken up by a new and surprising source. The emerging fascist movements in southern Europe were also staking a claim as alternatives to capitalism and socialism, and included a good deal of romanticism in their rhetoric. A corporatist model of industrial relations fitted this perfectly and was incorporated into fascist ideology (Williamson 1985). When fascist movements took control of governments they established a pattern of what they called corporatist industrial relations: autonomous trade unions were abolished, and in their place were established, industry by industry, cooperative syndicates of both worker and employer representatives. This happened in Italy, Portugal, Spain, Austria and in Vichy France. The Nazi movement in Germany included a similar rhetoric, but it was far weaker; the idea of consultation contradicted the more important leadership principle, or *Führerprinzip*, which was extended to management as well as to politics. Thus, when Nazi Germany annexed Austria, the institutions of the existing Austrian fascist regime were abolished.

In reality none of the fascist regimes really developed corporatism in the way that had been envisaged by nineteenth century writers. Since existing labour leaders were all executed, imprisoned or exiled, and no open debate was permitted, the organizations established became little more than dummies for the fascist parties, empty shells with few real functions.

By the time the Second World War was over ideas of corporatism had become thoroughly discredited through these associations. The only exception in a democratic country was The Netherlands, where the strength of the Christian corporatist tradition had been exceptionally strongly embedded in a compromise between Christian democracy and social democracy; there people spoke quite openly of a corporatist system. Elsewhere, the Spanish and Portuguese regimes continued to use the term, albeit in an increasingly ritualistic way, and it became important to some Latin American regimes, especially Peronism in Argentina.

Industrial relations in newly democratic Germany and Austria embodied many corporatist ideas and practices, in particular in works councils and the general concept of *Mitbestimmung*, or co-determination, within economies that already featured highly corporatist trade associations (see INDUSTRIAL RELATIONS IN EUROPE). The term corporatism was not used in these countries, however, as no one wanted to sustain concepts that carried reminders of the fascist past. In general the concept disappeared from view, other than as a term of abuse.

Meanwhile, industrial relations practices resembling important elements of the nineteenth century corporatist model were developing in Scandinavia – ironically the region of democratic Europe most remote from social Catholicism. Here, very powerful trade unions and social democratic parties had given up the old socialist dream of overthrowing capitalism and instead sought to manage economies alongside capitalist entrepreneurs and their associations. Despite occasional conflicts the groups worked in close cooperation, and were not restricted to collective bargaining (see COLLECTIVE BARGAINING). Logically, this entailed behaviour similar to the corporatist model. Neither unions nor employers' associations could risk a strategy of pressing their own interests to the full; the need for self-discipline, restraint and constructive compromise was paramount if these small, open economies were to thrive. In part because the economies were small, in part because the model was driven by social democratic political strategy, the main focus of activity was the whole national economy rather than individual sectors or companies, as had been embodied in the corporatist theories. In spite of these similarities the model did depart substantially from the nineteenth-century model. The term corporatist was of course never used as a self-definition of the Scandinavian systems.

The term itself was rehabilitated in the 1970s, by both North American and western European scholars. In the face of the inflationary crises surrounding the two oil price shocks of 1973 and 1978, governments in nearly all western countries, including the USA, sought to persuade peak organizations of business and labour to cooperate in self-discipline over prices and incomes. Observers noted that governments were encouraging the interest organizations to set up structures resembling those in the German-speaking countries and in Scandinavia; they also noted that these countries tended to be performing relatively well in conquering the inflationary crisis. They searched for ways of describing such a pattern of cooperative, self-restraining organizational behaviour. The word 'corporatism' was rediscovered quite separately by different scholars, and then applied in a range of researches (Schmitter 1974; Crouch 1977; Schmitter and Lehmbruch 1979; Lehmbruch and Schmitter 1982; Streeck and Schmitter 1985; Scholten 1987; Crouch and Dore 1990).

Although during the 1970s it appeared that elites in most capitalist democracies (including for a time the USA) wanted to experiment with neo-corporatist schemes, they remained strongly implanted only in northern Europe and (in a rather different form) Japan. In the Anglo-Saxon world pluralist systems were far more in evidence, even though Australian industrial relations achieved considerable success in turning itself into a corporatist pattern during the early 1980s (Singleton 1990). In France, Italy and southern Europe different terms of analysis are needed, despite neo-corporatist attempts continuing throughout the 1980s and beyond, particularly in Spain.

4 Neo-corporatism today

Since the 1980s the concept of corporatism, and in particular *neo*-corporatism, has been developed theoretically as a form of collective action, as shown above. Meanwhile empirical research has extended beyond industrial relations to embrace many other areas of business behaviour. Studies have been made of the relative economic performances of corporatist, pluralist and other structures (Goldthorpe 1984; Bruno and Sachs 1985; Lange and Garrett 1985; Dell'Aringa 1990). These tend to show that neo-corporatist systems have a record of minimizing inflation and unemployment superior to pluralist systems, although they have been less successful in sustaining economic growth.

The context in which corporatism is viewed has undergone considerable change. Recurrent economic recession has weakened the power of organized labour, and hence reduced the need for business or government to take account of trade unions (see TRADE UNIONS). The restructuring crises which have affected all economies have had two important results. They both reduced the size of the workforces in export-orientated manufacturing industries which had borne the burden of wage restraint, and shifted the locus of problem solving to the company, away from the sectoral or national level where previously neo-corporatist arrangements have been most prominent. Within general economic policy there has been a return to popularity of free-market solutions, which tend to exclude any constructive role for organized interests. Finally, for the transnational corporations the globalization of the world economy has reduced the importance of individual national association networks.

All these changes have undermined the importance and effectiveness of neo-corporatism. The German and Japanese models have retained much of their stability, but the Scandinavian systems have undergone considerable crises. There have been counter-trends, however. Although nation and sector have loomed large in the literature, there has always been an important company-level component to some neo-corporatist arrangements, in particular in Germany, Austria and Switzerland, while in Japan it is only at this level that labour has been important. Recent reforms to some Scandinavian systems have also paid more attention to the scope for company autonomy (Due *et al.* 1995; Pestoff 1995). European firms trying to imitate the Japanese model of company cultures, or Japanese-owned plants overseas, may similarly develop new forms of neo-corporatism.

It must also be remembered that by no means all modern firms are transnational; a particularly important part is being played by small companies drawing on the resources of their particular region or district to give themselves competitive advantages and distinctive niches. In so doing they build on informal, or sometimes even formal, cooperative networks with other firms and local deals with local governments and trade unions. Central Italy in particular has been identified as home to such arrangements (Amin and Thrift 1994; Mitchie and Grieve Smith 1995; Kogut 1993; Regini 1996) (see INDUSTRIAL AND LABOUR RELATIONS).

Interesting developments relevant to neo-corporatism are therefore taking place within the company and within the geographical region. This parallels the first of the two divergent trends in contemporary economies towards both the local and the global, away from the national. The global shift, in contrast, leaves neo-corporatism very much at a disadvantage. Corporatist structures exist only where there are strong, disciplined organizations which become involved in a dense web of interactions. This cannot take place at the world level. It happens to some extent at the level of the European Union, where interest organizations play a part in the formulation of policy. However, European associations of business and labour have a very weak capacity for self-discipline over national affiliates, and are rarely part of substantial neo-corporatist relationships. Euro-corporatism remains a very weak, diluted phenomenon.

Nevertheless, the European Commission tends to attract interest organizations into a relationship as it extends its own influence. Here a type of exchange, resembling corporatism in form but concerning primarily symbolic business, takes place. The Commission and the associations exchange legitimacy: the Commission can grant an association a voice at an important level of decision making, which is particularly important to trade unions at a time when they are weak; the associations can help the Commission acquire some of the attributes of a national state.

Something similar to this continues to take place in relations between associations and national governments, where the latter fear threats to social order: examples include Spain, Italy and, occasionally, France and the new united Germany. Weak associations are grateful to be taken into the circle of those consulted by the State, while states want to demonstrate their centrality and stability to groups who might challenge them. This takes us away from the main interest that business management might have in neo-corporatism, but these essentially political criteria may well be important in shaping the context within which business operates. Tendencies of this kind counteract the otherwise dominant trend in industrial relations, whether corporatist or not, to move down to company level and to become technical and non-political. Furthermore, it is also at this point that one sees a slight convergence between western and eastern Europe. Governments and employers in the latter countries have little to offer trade unions, and in any case are largely pursuing neo-liberal policies. Most of them do however want a relationship with organized interests to bolster their own legitimacy within troubled societies, even more strongly than in, for example, Spain. And trade unions in these countries desperately want a badge of respectability. A similar equation is therefore at work: a mutual exchange of legitimacy. Away from the trade union connection there are, within several nations, paradoxical developments. The general trend towards de-regulation and marketization is normally seen as hostile to the role of associations, since these often thrive on mediating between regulatory regimes and individual businesses (Streeck 1993). On the other hand, a move away from government regulation might lead to re-regulation at an association level; this may also be true of privatized state services, which usually remain monopolistic, or at least oligopolistic, and require some form of regulation.

An interesting example of corporatist re-regulation is the City of London, home of the British financial sector. In many respects this is as far removed from corporatism as possible: it is global in focus, labour relations play virtually no part, and the work of the institutions is to perform within the most perfect markets imaginable. However, for a number of reasons there has to be a regulatory regime (see CAPITAL MARKETS, REGULATION OF). When this was reformed in the 1980s it took the form of self-discipline by membership associations operating under state licence. As such it constitutes about as pure an instance of the corporatist form as one could find. Furthermore, although the City's business is global and operates across non-spatial electronic networks, it continues to be very important to its operations that it is geographically highly concentrated: a real example of an industrial district. And it has been such since the Middle Ages, when it was governed by the city guilds and corporations – prime examples of the institutions from which nineteenth century corporatist theorists took their inspiration.

The most recent writing on neo-corporatism has extended its focus and located the phenomenon within the larger field of the political and social institutions within which economies are located. It has therefore become part of the literature on the diversity of forms of modern capitalism (Hollingsworth *et al.* 1993; Boyer and Hollingsworth 1996; Crouch and Streeck 1996). Research has identified both formal associations and informal networks as instances of such institutions; and in the contrast between 'Rhenish' and 'Anglo-Saxon' capitalism popularized by Michel Albert (1993) neo-corporatism can clearly be seen to constitute part of the definition of the former model.

Within many European states organizational structures have an embedded strength which leads them to adapt to change rather than be overwhelmed by it, refuting predictions of their imminent demise (Traxler 1996). A recent survey of the state of neo-corporatist institutions in Western Europe uses the appropriate imagery of the labour of Sisyphus: they never fully succeed in their goals and frequently collapse, but immediately thereafter the work of reconstruction begins, because they can tackle certain problems in a manner unrivalled by other mechanisms in these social contexts (Schmitter and Grote 1997). Also, as recent developments in the Netherlands have shown, corporatist structures can be successfully used to introduce major innovatory labour market reforms without sacrificing social consensus (Visser and Hemerijck 1997).

COLIN CROUCH
EUROPEAN UNIVERSITY INSTITUTE,
FLORENCE
AND TRINITY COLLEGE, OXFORD

Further reading

(References cited in the text marked *)

* Albert, M. (1993) *Capitalism Against Capitalism*, London: Whurr. (Focuses on the contrast 'between 'institutional' and free-market forms of capitalism.)
* Amin, A. and Thrift, N. (eds) (1994) *Globalization, Institutions and Regional Development in Europe*, Oxford: Oxford University Press. (Outlines the economic prospects of various European countries in light of increasing globalization.)
* Boyer, R. and Hollingsworth, J.R. (eds) (1996) *Contemporary Capitalism: The Embeddedness of Institutions*, New York: Oxford University Press. (Studies of institutional forms of economic organization.)

* Bruno, M. and Sachs, J. (1985) *The Economics of World-wide Stagflation*, Oxford: Blackwell. (Study of 1970s economies, using corporatism as a variable.)

* Calmfors, L. and Driffill, D.G. (1988) 'Bargaining structure, corporatism and macro-economic performance', *Economic Policy* 6 (April): 13–62. (Article developing the theory of the U-curve of corporatist success and failure.)

* Cawson, A. (1986) *Corporatism and Political Theory*, Oxford: Blackwell. (Thorough textbook introduction to the political theory of corporatism.)

* Crouch, C. (1977) *Class Conflict and the Industrial Relations Crisis*, London: Heinemann. (Study of corporatism and pluralism in British industrial relations, from the 1950s to the 1970s.)

* Crouch, C. (1990) 'Trade unions in the exposed sector: their influence on neo-corporatist behaviour', in R. Brunetta and C. Dell'Aringa (eds), *Labour Relations and Economic Performance*, London: Macmillan and the International Economic Association. (Empirical study of the relevance of export exposure to trade union behaviour.)

* Crouch, C. (1993) *Industrial Relations and European State Traditions*, Oxford: Oxford University Press. (Account of neo-corporatist theory and its long-term development in certain European countries.)

* Crouch, C. (1994) 'Incomes policies, institutions and markets: an overview of recent developments', in R. Dore, R. Boyer and Z. Mars (eds), *The Return to Incomes Policy*, London: Pinter. (Account of the interaction between markets and institutions in contemporary economies.)

* Crouch C. (1995) 'Reconstructing corporatism? Organized decentralization and other paradoxes', in C. Crouch and F. Traxler (eds), *Organized Industrial Relations in Europe: What Future?*, Aldershot: Avebury. (Theoretical analysis of the effect of decentralization on neo-corporatist institutions.)

* Crouch, C. and Dore, R. (eds) (1990) *Corporatism and Accountability. Organized Interests in British Public Life*, Oxford: Oxford University Press. (Studies of the extent of neo-corporatist arrangements in the UK in the 1980s.)

* Crouch, C. and Streeck, W. (eds) (1996) *The Future of Capitalist Diversity*, London: Pinter. (Series of primarily national studies of the viability of different institutional forms of capitalism.)

* Dell'Aringa, C. (1990) 'Industrial relations and the role of the state in EEC countries', in Commission des Communautés Européennes, DG V, *Salaire et intégration européene*, Brussels: European Commission. (Analysis of economic performance and indices of neo-corporatism.)

* Dore, R.P. (1990) 'Japan: a nation made for corporatism?', in C. Crouch and R. Dore (eds), *Corporatism and Accountability: Organized Interests in British Public Life*, Oxford: Oxford University Press. (Account of how Japanese corporatist institutions operate.)

* Due, J., Madsen, J.S., Petersen, L.K. and Jensen, C.S. (1995) 'Adjusting the Danish model: towards centralized decentralization', in C. Crouch and F. Traxler (eds), *Organized Industrial Relations in Europe: What Future?*, Aldershot: Avebury. (Study of the trend among Danish institutions towards greater autonomy.)

* Goldthorpe, J.H. (ed.) (1984) *Order and Conflict in Contemporary Capitalism: Studies in the Political Economy of Western European Nations*, Oxford: Oxford University Press. (Major collection of case studies of corporatist performance.)

* Hollingsworth, J.R., Schmitter, P.C. and Streeck, W. (eds) (1993) *Governing Capitalist Economies*, New York: Oxford University Press. (Series of cross-national comparisons of the institutions governing several key economic sectors.)

* Kogut, B. (ed.) (1993) *Country Competitiveness*, Oxford: Oxford University Press. (Studies of various institutional forms underlying economic behaviour in a number of countries.)

* Lange, P. and Garrett, G. (1985) 'The politics of growth: strategic interaction and economic performance in the advanced industrial democracies', *Journal of Politics* 47 (3): 792–828. (Empirical study of the relationship between corporatism, political variables and certain indicators of economic performance.)

* Lehmbruch, G. (1982) 'Neo-Corporatism in comparative perspective', in G. Lehmbruch and P.C. Schmitter (eds), *Patterns of Corporatist Policy-Making*, Beverly Hills, CA: Sage Publications. (Major forerunner of neo-corporatist analysis.)

* Lehmbruch, G. and Schmitter, P.C. (1982) *Patterns of Corporatist Policy-Making*, Beverly Hills, CA: Sage Publications. (Seminal collection of essays in neo-corporatist analysis.)

* Marin, B. (1990) 'Generalized political exchange: preliminary considerations', in B. Marin (ed.), *Generalized Political Exchange*, Frankfurt am Main: Campus. (Theoretical account of the behaviour of actors in neo-corporatist contexts.)

* Mitchie, J. and Smith, J.G. (eds) (1995) *Managing the Global Economy*, Oxford: Oxford Univer-

sity Press. (Outlines key trends and indicates the possible direction institutions may take in the future.)

* Olson, M. (1982) *The Rise and Decline of Nations: Economic Growth, Stagflation and Social Rigidities*, New Haven, CT: Yale University Press. (Path-breaking analysis of collective action in large organizations.)

* Pestoff, V.A. (1995) 'Towards a new Swedish model of collective bargaining and politics', in C. Crouch and F. Traxler (eds), *Organized Industrial Relations in Europe: What Future?*, Aldershot: Avebury. (Discusses recent trends among Swedish institutions.)

* Regini, M. (1996) 'The future of the Italian model', in C. Crouch and W. Streeck (eds), *The Future of Capitalist Diversity*, London: Pinter. (Discussion of Italian small business communities and their future.)

* Schmitter, P.C. (1974) 'Still the century of corporatism?', *Review of Politics* January. (Seminal source for 1970s debate on corporatism.)

* Schmitter, P.C. and Grote, J.R. (1997) *The Corporatist Sisyphus: Past. Present and Future*. EUI Working Paper SPS No. 97/4, Florence: European University Institute.

* Schmitter, P.C. and Lehmbruch, G. (eds) (1979) *Trends Towards Corporatist Intermediation*, Beverly Hills, CA: Sage Publications. (First major collection of neo-corporatist studies.)

* Scholten, I. (ed.) (1987) *Political Stability and Neo-Corporatism, Beverly Hills*, CA: Sage Publications. (Studies, primarily of national cases, of the operation of neo-corporatist institutions.)

* Singleton, G. (1990) *The Accord and the Australian Labour Movement*, Melbourne: Melbourne University Press. (Study of the development of neo-corporatist imitations in Australia.)

* Streeck, W. (1983) 'Between pluralism and corporatism: German business associations and the state', *Journal of Public Policy* 3 (3): 265–84. (Account of neo-corporatist behaviour, primarily outside the industrial relations context.)

* Streeck, W. (1993) 'The social dimension of the European Economy', in D. Mayes, W. Hager, A. Knight and W. Streeck (eds), *Public Interests and Market Pressures*, London: Macmillan. (View of the likely impact of the European single market on neo-corporatist business organizations.)

* Streeck, W. (1994) 'Pay restraint without incomes policy: institutionalized monetarism and industrial unionism in Germany', in R. Dore, R. Boyer and Z. Mars (eds), *The Return to Incomes Policy*, London: Pinter. (Account of how German neo-corporatist institutions operate in industrial relations.)

* Streeck, W. and Schmitter, P.C. (eds) (1985) *Private Interest Government: Beyond Market and State*, Beverly Hills, CA: Sage Publications. (Collection of research studies on neo-corporatism applied to business associations outside the labour context.)

* Traxler, F. (1996) 'Collective bargaining and industrial change: A case of disorganization? A comparative analysis of eighteen OECD countries', *European Sociological Review* 12 (3): 271–87.

* Visser, J. and Hemerijck, A. (1997) *A Dutch Miracle, Job Growth, Welfare Reform and Corporatism in the Netherlands*. Amsterdam: Amsterdam University Press.

* Williamson, P.J. (1985) *Varieties of Corporatism*, Cambridge: Cambridge University Press. (Discusses the development of corporatist ideas and institutions under fascism.)

See also: COLLECTIVE BARGAINING; EMPLOYERS' ASSOCIATIONS; INDUSTRIAL AND LABOUR RELATIONS; INDUSTRIAL RELATIONS IN EUROPE; TRADE UNIONS

Related topics in the IEBM: BUSINESS CULTURES, EUROPEAN; DURKHEIM, É.; ECONOMIC INTEGRATION, INTERNATIONAL; MANAGEMENT IN EUROPE; MANAGEMENT IN SCANDINAVIA

Employee deviance

Overview

Deviance, as a term, comes from criminology, but in practice covers a wider range of behaviours than crime, which only refers to actions that break the law. When used in management, it normally covers illicit workplace behaviours, not all of which are illegal. Employee deviance focuses on pilferage and cheating by employees at all levels, with benefits taken from employers, customers and clients, or both. It is frequently extended to thefts of time, tax evasion/avoidance, payroll and expenses padding, restrictive 'customs and practice' and sabotage; in short, all behaviours formally disapproved of by managements that involve illicit movement of resources to employees and to managers. Called 'fiddling' in the UK, 'skimming' and 'scamming' in the USA, self-report studies have consistently shown its widespread extent, while recorded examples of employee deviance have a long history from Pharaoic Egypt through Classical Greece to the present.

Psychological explanations for deviance attempt to identify propensities associated with particular personality types. This 'rotten apple in the barrel' approach, whereby one deviant personality allegedly contaminates others, has led to extensive commercial screening programmes, especially in the USA. Situational explanations that examine how the social context of the workplace contributes to deviance and often creates it have, however, been more fruitful both for understanding and control.

Various attempts have been made to classify employee deviance, although some commentators have argued that since deviance is a feature of all occupations it is therefore not worth classifying. Most attempts, however, have been based on type of victim or type of occupation. These approaches are useful to criminologists, but do not address the wider issues of deviance of concern to managers. Other works have identified archetypes based on how jobs are designed and structured. In addition, a number of factors have been shown to facilitate deviance irrespective of how jobs are organized. Some factors derive from an imbalance of power between deviant and victim, others from the nature of goods involved and the structures mediating between them and those handling them.

Many attempts to check deviance have been, and will continue to be, problematic since deviance satisfies undeclared and covert interests, often including those of management, and because new variants and opportunities are continually offered by changing markets, forms of organization and technology. Endeavours to change work systems that ignore deviance or aim to eradicate it without understanding its social context and functions are likely to involve serious and often unanticipated effects.

1 Deviancy-prone factors

However jobs are classified, deviants need opportunities to exploit the differential powers they possess relative to those they exploit. Deviancy-prone factors include opportunities to make collaborative links, to operate in receptive markets and to be able to exploit various kinds of ambiguity. Several factors often operate together.

Passing trade is found where two sides to a transaction typically meet only once, thus precluding the build up of goodwill. Large cities are a typical milieu. Trades that deal with tourists, especially foreign tourists, offer good examples; others can be found in the hotel and restaurant trades.

Exploiting expertise is found where real or suggested expertise is involved in a transaction. Mechanical servicing and repairs, particularly garage servicing, are archetypal. O'Brien (1977) specifically discusses garage 'scams', but his observations also apply more widely. As he observes, since garage customers typically demonstrate ignorance, cannot judge the service they receive and are frequently unable to move from a specific manufacturer's agent, they are particularly vulnerable. Garages can perform incomplete services but charge for complete ones, install used or cheap pirated parts but charge for premium ones and replace parts unnecessarily. Accordingly, cars break down more frequently than they otherwise would, involving further costs. Specialists exploiting expertise in these ways benefit from 'perverse incentives'. This explains why garages that perform poorly are likely to be more successful than ones that perform well. Thus, bad garages drive out good and faulty service becomes the norm. These techniques and implications extend to most repair and service trades, such as plumbing and computer repairs and to professional and quasi-professional groups; that is, whenever there is a marked imbalance in expertise and power and where normal market assessments cannot be made by customers. Incidence increases where customer needs are urgent.

Gatekeepers exist where imbalance exists between supply and demand and where institutional constraints inhibit competition whether it be of goods or information. Gatekeepers typically process applications for scarce permits ahead of queues, allow access to important decision makers and leak commercially sensitive information. Gatekeepers thus specialize in clearing bottlenecks for a consideration. They are particularly rife in command economies and the Third World, as discussed by Sampson (1987) in the wider context of 'informal economies' and by Altman (1989) with reference to the USSR.

Triadic occupations are a feature of the personal service industries, where there are customers or clients as well as employers and employees. These triadic occupations offer opportunity for collusion between any two of the triad at the expense of the third. They are very common among driver deliverers, waiters, cashiers and throughout the retail trades, all of which feature in Mars (1994).

Control systems are responsible for occupational crime by their absence; that is, when they are too expensive or complicated to install relative to possible savings, or where costs of installation fall to the employer but cost of losses is borne by customers. For example, it is not considered financially viable to control the issue of trading stamps or free gifts in stores or garage forecourts. Cheap electronic controls are eroding this area.

Ambiguity exists where ambiguity over the quantity of a good, its quality or its exact category is inherent in its nature. This may cloak theft and be specially developed to do so. It is not easy, for example, to compute the quantity of drink consumed at a wedding; or, in the building trade, the number of bricks delivered to a site, the thickness of concrete on a path, the exact amount of copper in a building, or the gauge of zinc on a roof. Gilding (1971) gives an excellent example of constructed ambiguity in the theft of alcohol from distilleries which use traditional wooden barrels, a practice which lasted for hundreds of years until the introduction of metal barrels. Whenever market conditions move against buyers, especially at busy times, ambiguity is often deliberately increased. Price lists go missing and cash register windows become covered over or obscured when ice cream is sold on hot days, when customers surge about at New Year sales or when drinks are ordered at theatre bars during crowded intervals.

The conversion and smuggling of goods is relatively common. In Royal Air Forces stores watches and micrometers are categorized as 'V & A' ('valuable and attractive items'), well known as more prone to 'consumer conversion' than, say, the side of a fuselage. Storemen who guard such convertible items often operate with little supervision. They can, therefore, juggle records over time to match them to physical stocks during checks (but these rarely match between checks). Such goods, if stored in warehouses and storerooms, need to be smuggled out. Thus, V & A items which are small or can easily pass as the property of the pilferer, and items in or awaiting transit, are particularly at risk.

Anonymity and scale. The most common deviancy-prone factor is scale, involving the impersonality of large organizations. Henry (1988) discusses the range of justifications used by deviants and discusses how theft from a corporation is often not regarded as immoral, unlike theft from a known individual.

2 Ways of classifying crime and deviance at work

In some jobs deviance involves the collusion of management; in others, deviants are ruthlessly and swiftly punished. In others, deviance is organized and carried out by individuals in isolation; others require group cooperation. While deviance is seen by some employers as an incentive, almost a part of wages, and is therefore tacitly welcomed and even encouraged, some deviance undoubtedly occurs because of resentment, as a way of hitting out at the boss, the company, the system or the State.

In attempting to classify different types, the difficulty lies in imposing some form of order on such wide variations, which is probably why few attempts have been made to offer them. Green (1990) is a laudable exception, and he divides occupational crime into four categories: (1) crimes for the benefit of an employing organization; (2) crimes by officials through exercise of their state-based authority; (3) crimes by professionals in their capacity as professionals; and (4) crimes by individuals. However, this classification is restricted to crime rather than also covering the illicit but non-criminal deviant behaviours which are of interest to managers, and its categories are insufficiently exclusive; in particular, there is overlap between the third and fourth categories. A further difficulty is that classifications based on what is illegal are essentially limited: what is illegal in one country might not be so in another, and what is illegal at one time is not necessarily so at another. An approach that makes the classification of

deviance follow from the classification of jobs avoids these problems.

The most effective classification, based on the exclusivity of its categories and clustering of distinct characteristics, involves a division of jobs into sub-types and follows a model derived from social anthropology called 'cultural theory'. Cultural theory, as demonstrated by Thompson *et al.* (1990), shows that the values and attitudes of people and their behaviours are directly related to the way that their social relationships are organized. Applied to the workplace, it is dependent upon analysing the organization of work. This division of work into types based on its organization involves studying work from two standpoints. The first is whether work is group-based or carried out by individuals in isolation; the second, whether it allows a degree of autonomy or imposes strong rules and classifications on its incumbents (see GROUPS AND TEAMS).

These two dimensions of group strength and rules, when graded as strong or weak, can be placed on a 2 × 2 matrix to give four rough and ready cultural archetypes, as shown in Figure 1. This is the approach taken by Mars (1994, 1998), who divides occupations into four categories: 'hawks', 'donkeys', 'wolfpacks' and 'vultures'. Jobs in each category not only possess structural characteristics in common but also distinct arrangements to rob, cheat, short-change and pilfer customers, employers, subordinates and the State. These categories also reflect clusterings of different kinds of illicit training and career as well as distinct and different values, attitudes and justifications. Each elicits a different

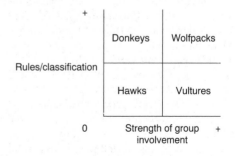

Figure 1 The four archetypal work cultures

managerial response. A do-it-yourself guide on how to allocate occupations to these categories, with a discussion of policy implications for each category, is contained in Mars (1998).

Hawks (weak rules/classification; weak group involvement)

Hawks, like their feathered counterparts, are competitive individualists. They perch unhappily in organizations and tend to make the rules or bend them to suit themselves. These are autonomous entrepreneurs and fixers, innovative professionals and small businesspersons. Their aim is to 'make it'. To do so they work to preserve and enhance their autonomy.

The hawks' greatest capital is knowledge and flair followed by extra-organizational networks of contacts. Their method involves insulating one set of activities from others. One senior medical hawk had buying rights to a million dollars' worth of specialized equipment. Three US companies competed for his orders so he travelled from London and visited all three:

> You can buy an 'all over' ticket that gives you unlimited travel in the States for two weeks. . . but you've got to buy it in Europe. So one company pays for me to go and see them in New York. Then I go to another company in Los Angeles and the third in Las Vegas, and I use my 'all over' ticket. But I charge the regular charge from New York to Los Angeles. . . and from New York to Las Vegas. . . . They don't mind paying at all, it's peanuts to them for a big order, but it means quite a bit to me. If I was really unscrupulous, mind, I could charge all three from London return!

The point is not that this hawk carries out unremarkable cheating but that he exploits several groups who neither know nor care that he claims similar expenses from all. They are prepared, indeed keen, to pay expenses, and each transaction is insulated. Hawk justifications are that benefits reward merit and position, no one is cheated and a scarce resource is maximally used. Attempts to control hawk deviance without building in alternative reward systems can lead to the loss of key staff. Their talents tend to be highly marketable, and because their networks are well developed, they are prone to move to rivals and take resources with them, including company clients. Hawks are not noted for loyalty or long-term strategic planning. Controls and limits to deviance are independently set, and are based on perceived market values. Managerial collusion is frequently implicit and even on exposure, sanctions are often minimal.

Donkeys (strong rules/classification; weak group involvement)

Donkey jobs are dominated by rules, lack autonomy, are often of low status and are relatively isolated from each other. Many transport jobs are donkeys. They tend to be constrained by timetables and rules governing safety and often involve isolation. Supermarket cashiers and machine-minders are similarly constrained. Responses involve increasing their autonomy and interest by breaking rules, resentfully sabotaging systems, products and, especially in personal service occupations, relationships, or cheating. Such effects can be highly disruptive and sometimes dangerous in these jobs, especially since isolation from group influence necessarily results in an absence of group restraints. Unlike classic wolfpacks, such as traditional dockworkers, who typically work in teams, their excesses are not regulated by group controls. As a result the press periodically reports cases of donkey-job shop assistants whose houses, when raided, are often described as an 'Aladdin's cave'.

One shop cashier, each day for six months, abstracted five times her daily salary by ringing up less than the proper charge on the till and taking the difference. This was in addition to letting friends and relatives pass the checkout at minimal charge. She was never caught. Her response derived from frustration at the constraints of the job, its low status and resentment of managerial controls. As she said:

> Of course, it's a lousy firm, a really lousy firm; girls are always leaving and so are

managers. A friend of mine was once ten pounds down on her till. She never fiddled a penny but the manager said she must have taken it. She was so upset she said she couldn't work there if they thought she'd taken the ten pounds, so she left. Afterwards when they'd checked it all they discovered the error but they never wrote to her, just asked me if I saw her to tell her that it was OK. That's typical, they treat you like dirt, as if you have no intelligence at all. It's the little things like that, things you can't often remember, that makes them a horrible firm. It's horrible too because the pay is so low, even compared to similar jobs in other shops.

A lack of social solidarity is always a strong factor in donkey jobs:

> It's also a lousy firm in other ways. The girls are always backbiting and bitchy; there's a lot of gossip all the time. Nobody ever accuses anyone of stealing from the tills, though. That's never ever mentioned by anyone. Nothing is ever said, even by management, even when you first start. It's just not done to mention it. New girls just have to find out for themselves.

The more managements control donkey jobs by their typical tactic of tightening constraints and strengthening rules, the more likely they are to be counterproductive. Schemes to increase autonomy and interest through job enlargement, job enrichment and job rotation are better alternatives, especially if linked to development of promotion prospects and measures to increase job security.

Wolfpacks (strong rules/classification; strong group involvement)

Wolfpacks practise team theft; they work and steal in well-defined and stratified packs. Traditional dockwork gangs are archetypal examples, with hierarchy, order and internal controls based upon group work involving different but coordinated tasks. Many maintenance and construction crews are wolfpacks. When they pilfer or indulge in other deviance they act according to agreed rules, within

agreed limits and through well-defined divisions of labour. Unlike the isolated donkeys, they therefore have to be taught the techniques and practice of deviance. Like real-life wolves, they know who is their leader and who are the led. They use their internal organization to penalize and reward their own deviants, particularly those who exceed group set limits. They often command strong group loyalties.

Wolfpacks invariably invoke sanctions over members from jesting, through ridicule, to expulsion, the latter being effected by making it difficult to work with them. They also frequently aim to control recruitment. This is particularly effective when workers live and work in the same vicinity, as is often the case in mining, shipbuilding and dock work. Here, they merge leisure and work lives by, for instance, drinking together after work and recruiting relatives. They are able to adopt a vigorous and united role in negotiations with management and often sustain a body of what management define as 'restrictive practices', including tolerated access to activities considered deviant. Whereas hawks are impressive innovators and donkeys tend towards fatalism, wolfpacks are inherently conservative and work to long-term strategies in deviance and other concerns. They are the most stable of the work groupings. When linked to industrial strength, this frequently allows them to exchange industrial peace for managerially tolerated levels of deviance. They often resist change and innovation.

Vultures (weak rules/classification; strong group involvement)

Vultures are also team-based but their teams, unlike wolfpacks, are minimally differentiated by rank or function. Travelling salesmen are vultures, as are waiters when linked and supported from a common base such as working for a common supervisor. Cab drivers, particularly those working from a single depot, are vultures, as are train and ship stewards. They depend upon information and support from colleagues and need the support of a group but are competitive in their own interests. The lack of established leadership roles that derives from weak classification and their paradoxical combination of competition and need for cooperation cause vultures difficulty in resolving their disputes and makes them particularly subject to rumour and to scapegoat selection. Vulture groupings tend to be unstable, both in their constituent parts and in industrial relations behaviour, which is inclined to be turbulent. The introduction of functional ranking as, for instance, is applied to waiters in top level restaurants, however, causes them to operate more as wolfpacks.

In vulture jobs, behaviour is not reactive (as in donkey jobs) or creative (like individualist hawks) but responsive to the changing opportunities presented by management. Acceleration of pace, increases in scale, alterations in price or incentives tend not to be opposed, as they would be by wolfpacks. Instead, changes offer employees their chances. They 'ride' an unstable system which constantly bucks and threatens to throw them off.

A group of waiters at a north of England seaside resort, was convicted of overcharging for drinks. The hotel manager was cast as group ringleader. His defence was that he had 'to make a profit and ensure that stocks were right'. He said he allowed overcharging and maintained:

> The directors' attitude was the same as mine, and on occasions directors have said, in a jocular manner, 'Are these visitors' prices or ours?' I told them they should be satisfied as we were getting our share, meaning that the company was benefiting, through good stocks.

Explicit collusion of this sort between workers and first-line management is common among vultures, particularly when the victims are outside the firm. Collusive toleration to deviance by higher managements is often implicit until subject to visibility, which further enhances the inherent instability of vultures.

3 Conclusion

Managers face five difficulties when assessing deviance, aside from the fact that being covert it is very difficult to identify. One is a difficulty in suspending their own morality so as to make calm, rational assessments. A second is accepting that deviance is rarely 'wild' or normless but operates within culturally set moral codes, rules and limits. Although managers may not share such standards, they do need to understand them. A third difficulty lies in personalizing employee deviance ('rotten apple' theories) instead of concentrating on understanding the contexts that facilitate it. This can of course create difficulties when the context is one for which they may be formally responsible. A fourth is to accept that deviance often produces benefits, not only to deviants but also to their employers. It can bond members of teams, offer informal incentives for merit or effort when formal systems are too rigid; make boring jobs more interesting, buy off labour dissatisfaction and permit differential favouritism.

The fifth factor, linked to all of these, is that attempts to change work systems are much more likely to succeed if the jobs' culture is first identified, as the cases in Mars (1998) demonstrate. Otherwise, particularly where deviance is integral to the rewards of workers, attempts at controlling it are likely to produce unanticipated consequences, especially resistance to innovation that might seem 'mindless'. The current widespread introduction of electronic controls that attempt to limit deviancy-prone factors must be considered in this context.

GERALD MARS
UNIVERSITY OF BRADFORD

Further reading

(References cited in the text marked *)

* Altman, Y. (1989) 'Second economy activity in the USSR', in P. Ward (ed.), *Corruption, Development and Inequality*, London: Routledge. (This article looks at behaviour in the USSR, and describes the role and activity of 'gatekeepers'.)

Dalton, M. (1959) *Men Who Manage*, New York: Wiley. (The classic forerunner of much subsequent work which concentrates on the inevitable deviance involved in managing managerial careers.)

Ditton, J. (1977) *Part-time Crime: An Ethnography of Fiddling and Pilferage*, London: Macmillan. (Superb account of the deviant training of baker's roundsmen as they learn and incorporate illegal 'vulture-type' work practices.)

Gabor, T. (1994) *Everybody Does It: Crime by the Public*, Toronto, Ont.: University of Toronto Press. (Sets occupation crime, but not deviance, in the context of crimes by 'ordinary' citizens. Interesting case studies.)

* Gilding, B. (1971) *The Journeymen Coopers of East London*, History Workshop pamphlet no. 4, Oxford: Ruskin College. (This historical trade study contains details of the example of theft mentioned in the text.)

* Green, G. S. (1990) *Occupational Crime*, Chicago, IL: Nelson-Hall. (Presents an overview and attempts a classification of occupational crime. Limited to activities against the law rather than incorporating deviance. Good account of self-report studies and references to computer crime.)

* Henry, S. (1988) *The Hidden Economy: The Context and Control of Borderline Crime*, Port Townsend, WA: Loompanics Unlimited. (A highly readable classic, originally published in 1978. Concentrates on the context in which occupational crimes occur and particularly on the nature of social relationships between the people who take part and the sub-economy they form.)

Hollinger, R. and Clark, J. (1983) *Theft by Employees*, Lexington, MA: Lexington Books. (An account of a survey of 9,000 employees and their deviance at work.)

* Mars, G. (1994) *Cheats At Work: An Anthropology of Workplace Crime*, 2nd edn, Aldershot: Dartmouth Press. (A comprehensive situational analysis which classifies occupations as cultures and assesses resulting deviance, values, motivations, moralities and techniques. Covers history, categories, proneness factors plus implications of deviance and its control for practical industrial relations.)

* Mars, G. (1998) *Occupational Scams: How to Identify and Understand Them*, Aldershot: Dartmouth Press. (Part I contains twenty-eight personal accounts; Part II offers a guide to dealing with occupational deviance.)

* O'Brien, D.P. (1977) 'Why you may be dissatisfied with garage servicing', *Motor*, 10 September. (Neatly outlines the economic bases of perverse incentives.)

* Sampson, S.L. (1987) 'The second economy of the Soviet Union and eastern Europe', *The Annals of the American Academy of Political and Social Science*, special issue on the informal economy (L.S. Ferman, S. Henry and M. Hoyman (eds)): 120–36. (A seminal collection of articles that examines the wider economic implications of all non-formalized economic activity, including occupational deviance.)

Stevenson, C.H. (1990) *Auto Repair Shams and Scams: How to Avoid Getting Ripped Off*, Los Angeles, CA: Price, Stern, Sloan Inc. (Written very effectively for the consumer by a former mechanic; useful in conjuction with O'Brien (1977).)

* Thompson, M., Ellis, R. and Wildavsky, A. (1990) *Cultural Theory*, Boulder, CO: Westview Press. (A comprehensive development of cultural theory which expands on the work of Mary Douglas, its originator.)

Zeitlin, L.R. (1971) 'Stimulus/response: a little larceny can do a lot for employee morale', *Psychology Today* 14 (June): 22, 24–6, 64. (Demonstrates how managements can avoid reorganizing jobs and raising wages by permitting a controlled amount of theft.)

See also: GROUPS AND TEAMS; MOTIVATION AND SATISFACTION; ORGANIZATION BEHAVIOUR; WORK ETHIC

Related topics in the IEBM: BUSINESS ETHICS

Employee relations, management of

Overview

The term 'employee relations' has been used for many years as an alternative to other, better-established descriptive terms such as 'personnel management', 'industrial relations' and now 'human resource management'. Each of these is used to describe a particular feature of the world of work and employment, but each overlaps with the others across ill-defined margins. The result is both confusing and misleading, especially when, as in recent years, the meanings of the terms begin to change. 'Employee relations', used as a descriptive label, has the potential to unify this confusing picture, and may well become widely adopted as 'human resource management' falls out of favour.

To explore this, it is necessary first to look more closely at the everyday usage of these terms associated with the management of people at work to see how each has become limited or specialized. This will allow employee relations to be defined in terms of a combination of approaches to individual employees and to collective employee organizations. This mix of individualism and collectivism will be used to identify differing styles of management and link them to business strategies and external environmental conditions. In this way it is hoped that 'employment relations' and 'employee relations management' can come to be recognized as the most useful terms in the field of work.

1 Definitions and fashions in the world of work

In the last two decades there appears to have been a substantial shift in the terms used in companies to describe the specialist functional managers responsible for people issues, and the functions they perform or the departments they work in. 'Personnel' departments and 'personnel' managers, as they were called, have increasingly been relabelled 'human resource' or shortened to 'HR' as in 'the HR Department' (see PERSONNEL MANAGEMENT; HUMAN RESOURCE MANAGEMENT). In higher education the term 'human resource management' is widely used to describe specialist courses previously labelled 'personnel management'. (See Purcell 1994 for an assessment of the growth of human resource management.)

Subtle differences are implied by these changes. Human resource management is widely seen as strategic, or at least linked to business and corporate strategies, while personnel has a more routine, operational image. Personnel was also associated with stand-alone departments generally concerned with administration. In contrast, the claims of HRM are that responsibility is returned to line management and integrated into the practice of management in the firm. Thus, while human resource management was increasingly seen as progressive, strategic and integrated, personnel management seemed to gain a reputation as routine, bureaucratic and unable to contribute to bottom-line business performance. Such descriptions stereotype, if not stigmatize, the past and idealize the future. Although the spread of 'human resource' in job titles was slower than expected, with only around 9 per cent of specialist staff in large firms using it in 1992, compared with 63 per cent calling themselves 'personnel' director or manager (Marginson *et al.* 1993), in everyday language it is much more common now to find 'human resource' in use.

While 'personnel management' as a term was becoming unfashionable, the meaning of 'industrial relations' was rapidly being narrowed and hollowed out, in Anglo-Saxon countries at least (see INDUSTRIAL AND LABOUR RELATIONS). Declines in union membership, rapid and marked falls in the number of days lost in industrial action, and a shift towards individualism all combined to reduce the importance of industrial relations in the public mind. Originally the term 'industrial relations' was intended to cover the whole of the world of work and employment, both within organizations and, more importantly, in the economy and society as a whole. In academic terms it was the applied or practical crossroads for labour history, labour law, labour economics, industrial sociology and industrial psychology (see OCCUPATIONAL PSYCHOLOGY; ORGANIZATION BEHAVIOUR). In this very broad sense, personnel management (or, now, human resource management) was defined as a branch of industrial relations, while trade union studies was another. The leading research institute in the UK, the Industrial Relations Research Unit at the University of Warwick, still uses the term in this way. They are, however, very much in a minority. In everyday usage 'industrial relations' has now become associated exclusively with collective labour relations: trade unions, collective bargaining, joint consultation, arbitration, strikes and other forms of industrial conflict (see TRADE UNIONS; COLLECTIVE BARGAINING; INDUSTRIAL CONFLICT). Behind this is the view that industrial relations is primarily concerned with the development of institutions at the level of the state, industry and company to deal with labour conflict and provide a collective voice for employees.

In the 1990s, this concentration on the institutions of collectivism was very much out of fashion. Interestingly, this has led to calls for 'industrial relations' to be replaced by the term used here, 'employee relations' (Kaufman 1993; Purcell 1983). This would have the advantage of dropping the word 'industrial' at a time when less than one-fifth of employees work in manufacturing or production

industries and an even smaller proportion are blue-collar manual workers. More importantly, 'employee relations' allows for a combined analysis of the policies and practices of the firm towards the individual employee, from recruitment to retirement or resignation, and of all aspects of the collective determination of the terms and conditions of employment.

Initially there were grounds to expect that 'human resource management' would have a definition wide enough to incorporate these aspects of individual and collective relations from a management perspective. Gospel (1983: 12–17) provided one of the earliest comprehensive attempts to do this by defining human resource management as management's policies and plans which integrate work relations (the design of jobs and social relations such as authority patterns), employment relations (job tenures and contracts, types of remuneration system and other rules of employment) and industrial relations (collective relationships and rule-making between management and representatives of the workforce.) Used in this way, 'human resource management' becomes a descriptive and holistic term indistinguishable from 'employee relations'. This allows us to study (and practise) a wide variety of approaches to the management of the workforce, including managers themselves (see HUMAN RESOURCE MANAGEMENT).

It would follow that types of human resource management could come to be identified and classified and these then used to assess which type best suited different economic and market circumstances. What type of human resource management is best applied to a high-tech greenfield organization? Is this different from the needs of a large, mature public-sector agency? There is no reason to suppose that the same type or style of human resource management would fit both. This type of approach, known as the matching model, is associated with the work of Schuler and Jackson (1987) and Dyer (1985) in the USA. More recently, it has been tested by Arthur (1994) in a detailed examination of US steel mini-mills to see how far given product and manufacturing strategies are associated with different types of human resource management. Crudely put, he found some association between firms focusing on achieving lowest-cost market advantage and 'control'-type human resource policies based on cost reduction and low levels of investment in employees. By contrast, other firms were seeking a product differentiation strategy based on product variety and a flexible response to customer needs, including the development of longer-term supply contracts with them. This differentiation strategy was associated with the more extensive use of 'commitment'-type policies involving greater expenditure on training, higher pay, more skilled workers, greater decentralization of problem solving and empowerment of employees. The fit between product strategy and human resource management was by no means perfect but good enough to provide some empirical support for the theoretical matching model.

If the matching model of human resource management provided the agreed base for the definition of the term, there would be little difference with those who use 'employee relations' instead. However, increasingly the normative model of human resource management – or what some call the Harvard model, after the work of Michael Beer and his colleagues at Harvard Business School (Beer *et al.* 1985) – has begun to dominate the field and is reflected in numerous recent textbooks. Here the search is for a bundle of good or progressive employment practices which are applied in organizations to maximize the human contribution to profitability while simultaneously increasing satisfaction and motivation. Understood in this way, it is possible to refer to human resource management in the singular: 'it'. For example, one of the leading authorities in the UK classifies firms as those with and those without human resource management (Guest 1995). This body of good practice, sometimes called high-commitment management (Wood 1995), is linked to teamworking, empowerment policies, high levels of training and wider notions of performance management.

This is not the place to debate at length the problems with this definition of human resource management, but it is necessary to note two major limitations to its use, and thus show why the term 'employee relations' is preferable. First, all claims for human resource management suggest that it is the link with business strategy that makes it different from personnel management. This is not plausible in the normative model based on a set of good practices, since it implies that these are universally applicable and can fit every firm in every circumstance. Strategy is based on differentiation, the achievement of sustained competitive advantage, as in the resource view of strategy (see Purcell 1995: 80–4). If all firms managed their employees in the same way, there would no competitive advantage to be gained from human resource management and it would not therefore be strategic. Second, empirically it has proved very hard to find the widespread adoption of these bundles of good HR practices, as they are called. Indeed, so unusual is it to find the full-blown adoption of these good-practice policies across the whole of the enterprise that the problem is not to explain why so few firms seems willing or able to adopt human resource management but rather why these few 'HRM firms' exist in the first place. It is also highly instructive to note that some of the original exemplars of human resource management, such as IBM, abandoned some of these policies after a collapse of profitability (see HUMAN RESOURCE MANAGEMENT).

There is a third objection of a different sort. The normative model of human resource management does not allow for, or virtually ignores, collective labour regulation. In part this is because of its US origins, but in part also because the rapid adoption of the language of 'soft' human resource management in the UK occurred at a time of labour market deregulation and trade union weakness. It is possible in these circumstances to adopt what Storey (1994) has called a 'dualist' approach, where the management of trade unions and collective labour institutions is divorced from human resource policy development. In many continental European countries, however, with traditions of legislative support for the institutions of collective bargaining and collective consultation, such as Germany and The Netherlands (see INDUSTRIAL RELATIONS

IN EUROPE), it is neither sensible nor feasible to develop normative human resource policies which do not take account of the requirements for collective representation. This is of course equally true of the many firms in the UK where trade union membership remains relatively high, for example in the public sector and privatized corporations.

In summary, the argument here is that all the terms most commonly used to describe the quality and nature of the relationship between the firm and its employees and workers are inadequate. 'Personnel management' is either dated or limited to the profession; 'industrial relations' has been narrowed down to mean just collective bargaining, trade unions and conflict resolution; while 'human resource management' is seen to be something based on high-commitment policies that some firms (in fact only a few) have. 'Employee relations' thus becomes the preferred term since it covers all firms and allows for a combined approach to both the individual worker and the collective system of employee representation, whether this is via collective bargaining or joint consultation, and whether it involves an independent trade union or some kind of works council arrangement. Employee relations management thus relates to the type of policies and practices that firms pursue to maximize their competitive advantage. Different employee relations styles can be identified according to the interconnection of the firm's policies towards the individual employee and those directed towards the trade union or collective labour body. These styles, once identified, can be related to company strategy.

2 Management styles in employee relations

It is often observed that firms can vary quite considerably in the way they manage employees and, more broadly, how the culture of organizations differs so that each has a well-established way of 'doing things' that has evolved over many years. Many have sought to explain such differences by reference to the technology employed, the size of the unit and the firm as a whole, the degree of organizational maturity or pace of innovation, and the market position of the firm in terms of its basic strategy. These all deeply influence choices relating to the type and number of people working in the establishment and the degree of organizational commitment expected of them.

In recent decades an extra dimension has been added as the framework for industrial relations and labour law has been dismantled and firms have been required to determine a wider range of policies, indeed to think more seriously about the whole nature and rules of the employment relationship. Originally industrial relations was considered something external to the firm, with organizations relying on decisions taken by employers' associations in negotiation with trade unions, all in the context of labour law. There were always a few, generally large, employers which developed their own internal systems of employee relations, but these were exceptional. As external regulatory mechanisms have disappeared and as firms have decentralized their operations down to the operating or strategic business-unit level, a wider range of choices have been made in linking employee relations to business strategies. This has either been negatively defined, in the sense of removing inhibitors to the 'proper' utilization of labour through a process of internal deregulation, or more positively designed to link employee relations with the needs of the firm. Strategic choice has often been forced on a reluctant management by the collapse of external institutions, rather than being deliberately chosen. In these circumstances it is not surprising that many organizations are unable to make strategic choices in employee relations, instead 'muddling through' as Edwards *et al.* (1992) call it.

This process of 'internalization', where the managers of the organization must decide for themselves how they want to structure and manage employee relations, has essentially two dimensions. They must decide how to manage employees as individual workers – how much training to provide, what sort of jobs to design, what sort of contracts to offer, and much more besides. They need also to

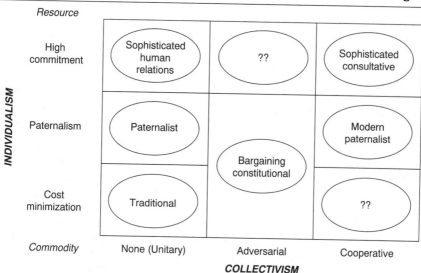

Figure 1 The management style matrix
Source: Purcell and Ahlstrand (1994)

consider their policy towards trade unions and other types of employee representational systems. Should these be opposed, kept very much at arm's length or considered as partners in the workplace? Decisions in the first area (loosely described as 'individualism') will influence the type of decisions that can be taken about trade unions and other employee bodies (termed 'collectivism' here), and vice versa. This is shown in Figure 1.

The individualism scale

The vertical axis in Figure 1, individualism, is designed to help identify different approaches to the management of individual employees. It is deliberately bounded by two polar extremes which, in their pure forms, are unlikely to exist in more than a handful of firms. Most firms can be placed somewhere along the continuum at less extreme positions. At the top end of the scale, high commitment, an emphasis is placed on employees as the firm's 'most important resource'. Here it is assumed that there will be extensive investment in employees to help them become effective and willing to take on new work as technology and procedures change. High performance and high productivity are required, providing the justification for the relatively

high level of investment. This demands highly motivated staff. It is likely here that the firm will try to keep a high proportion of its staff in order to recoup the training and selection costs; and therefore a form of internal labour market, linked to careful selection at the point of entry, will be preferred.

At the other end of the scale, at the bottom of the vertical axis, a quite different type of employment policy is pursued. This type is based on the achievement of cost minimization and the pursuit of the lowest-cost option. In firms adopting such a policy, the level of investment in training and development will be low, the cost of hiring and recruiting kept to the minimum, and all other employment costs such as fringe benefits avoided as far as possible. Job security is likely to be low, matched only by the low pay. These employers are very unlikely to develop promotional ladders and other features of an internal labour market, relying instead on the external labour market as long as there is an excess of supply of the type of people they wish to employ. Workers, often referred to in the generic sense as labour, are treated as a commodity.

In the centre of the vertical axis is the firm which has developed a paternalist approach to employee relations. Paternalism is defined in the *Oxford Concise Dictionary* as restriction of the freedom of the subject through well-meant regulations. In employment it refers to the type of firm which is not overtly exploitative and often uses terms like 'welfare' and 'caring' to describe its fundamental approach to subordinate employees. At the same time there are few promotion opportunities, and what training is provided is at the minimum level to enable a person to do the job assigned. Such firms are likely to be rather bureaucratic, hierarchical and 'old-fashioned' in their management.

The collectivism scale

The horizontal axis on the matrix in Figure 1 seeks to classify a firm's approach to trade unions and other types of institutions where employees' interests are articulated by elected representatives. In addition to trade unions, therefore, we include here works councils, as commonly established by statute in most countries of the European Union, and other such consultative mechanisms whatever their title, be they joint consultative committees, company councils, staff associations or members' advisory committees. This is not to imply that these bodies created to represent employees are all the same, since they will vary according to the type of *de jure* and *de facto* power they can exert and this will influence the employer's response in terms of management style (see INDUSTRIAL RELATIONS IN EUROPE; TRADE UNIONS).

From an employer's point of view the choice as implied on the horizontal axis is twofold. First, does the firm wish to, or feel compelled to, recognize a trade union for collective bargaining and consultative purposes, or does it intend to avoid all forms of collectivism? The latter option is shown on the left of the collectivism axis as 'none' or 'unitary'. 'Unitary' means that management believe there to be a single management focus and channel of communication and commitment, and a single unified organizational goal to which all subscribe. This is in contrast to so-called 'pluralist' organizations, where a plurality of interests is expected and management recognize the legitimacy of trade unions or works councils to represent these employee

interests (Fox 1966). The second choice is concerned with the nature or quality of the relationship between management and union or works council. Is it adversarial or cooperative? Under adversarial relationships, emphasis is placed on negotiating skills which often involve exaggeration of claim and counter-offer, stylized behaviour, a restriction of shared information (as in the poker player keeping cards close to the chest) and a polarization of views and beliefs as seen in the language of 'us and them'. Relations may also be marked by the use or the threat of sanctions by either 'party'. Adversarial relations are not unique to the world of work, and indeed are influenced by wider societal expectations such as those reflected in parliamentary behaviour or in the conduct of legal cases, where adversarialism is assumed to be both normal and necessary. In contrast, the 'cooperative' pattern shown on the right-hand side of the scale refers to a situation where management seeks to share information and to engage in open discussion and longer-term relationship building with the union or works council to achieve 'mutual gain' (Kochan and Osterman 1994). Here we would expect to find the language of 'partnership' in play and a widespread use of joint working parties and other forms of shared activity that integrate the two sides (see INDUSTRIAL DEMOCRACY).

Patterns of employee relations

Management style in employee relations is described as the *preferred* way of managing employees. The choice, which may have been made, or just happened, years earlier, sets the parameters for employee relations. The choice on one axis will have a strong impact on the other, such that the emerging patterns of employee relations are a combination of the firm's approach to collectivism and to individualism. A management team thinking strategically about employee relations and the links with business policy is required to consider the two dimensions together. These are explored in depth by Purcell and Ahlstrand (1994), but a summary of the different styles is given in the following list. This describes, in note form, the type of management style found in each of the matrix segments and indicates the type of firm where it is most likely to be found.

(1) *Sophisticated human relations* (high-commitment management/no collectivism). Employees (excluding short-term contract or sub-contract labour) are viewed as the company's most valuable resource. Great care taken with selection. Above average pay. Internal labour market structures with promotion ladders are common, with periodic attitude surveys used to harness employees' views. Emphasis is placed on flexible reward structures, employee appraisal systems, employee development and training, teamwork competences, internal grievance, disciplinary and consultative procedures, and extensive networks and methods of communication. The aim is to inculcate employee loyalty, commitment and dependency and thereby to maximize productivity and responsiveness to change. As a by-product these companies seek to make it unnecessary or unattractive for staff to unionize. Most often found in US electronic/information firms and high-tech/professional service firms. Typical of the aims of greenfield sites opting for no trade unions or works councils. Many firms seek to develop managers through this style (see HUMAN RELATIONS).

(2) *Paternalist* (paternalism/no collectivism). Welfare/caring image projected which emphasizes the employee's place in the firm. Emphasis on loyalty and downward communication. Fixed grade structures through job evaluation. Often a high proportion of lower-grade women employees. Little internal mobility or promotion across grades. Job training provided. Stability, order and hierarchy, with everyone knowing his/her place. Conflict seen as a failure of communication. Unions avoided. Most often found in service/financial/distribution firms.

(3) *Traditional* (cost minimization/no collectivism). Labour is viewed as a cost or factor of production and employee subordination is assumed to be part of the 'natural order' of the employment relationship. Fear of outside union interference. Unionization opposed or unions kept at arm's length. Often low pay and low job security. The prime driving force

in employment policies is cost minimization. Little or no training provided. Most often found in labour-intensive contract/franchise firms, hotels and catering.

(4) *Sophisticated consultative* (high-commitment management/cooperative). Similar to the sophisticated human-relations companies except that unions or company councils are recognized. The attempt is made to build 'constructive' relationships with the trade unions and incorporate them into the organizational fabric. Broad-ranging discussions are held, with extensive information provided to the unions, on a whole range of decisions and plans including aspects of strategic management, but the 'right of last say' rests with management. Emphasis is also placed on techniques for enhancing individual employee commitment to the firm and the need to manage change (share option schemes, profit sharing, briefing or cascade information systems, joint working parties, quality or productivity circles/councils, training and development). Most often found in greenfield-site companies recognizing single unions with no-strike deals or where traditional manufacturing firms have sought a radical change in work organization and industrial relations. Similar to Japanese corporations.

(5) *Modern paternalist* (paternalist/cooperative). Emphasis placed on 'constructive' relationships with trade unions, with extensive information provided and a network of collective consultative committees established to communicate to employee representatives the needs of the business and to aid the management of change within the context of a caring/welfare image. Fixed grade structures based on job evaluation with union–management review teams and appeal bodies. Average pay. Little internal mobility. Overall emphasis on stability, order and hierarchy, with employees knowing their place. Most often found in large, relatively stable process industries such as foods or oil.

(6) *Bargaining constitutional* (paternalist or cost minimization/adversarial). Somewhat similar to the traditionalists (or paternalists) in basic value structures (an emphasis on cost minimization or welfare provision), but

unions have been recognized for some time and accepted as inevitable. Employee relations policies centre on the need for stability, control and the institutionalization of conflict. Management prerogatives are defended through highly specific collective agreements, and careful attention is paid to the administration of agreements at the point of production. The importance of management control is emphasized, with the aim of minimizing or neutralizing union constraints on both operational (line) and strategic (corporate) management. Relations with trade unions range from conflict-prone (collective bargaining restricted to terms and conditions of employment) to stable, more formalized relationships where the rules of employment are determined. Most often found in public service sector, mass-production or large-batch manufacturing firms, or in firms with large workforces and a high proportion of manual workers such as the postal service.

Two pattern boxes in the matrix are marked '??'. These are styles which are likely to be highly unstable. The combination of cost minimization with a cooperative style of union–management relations (bottom right) implies that the union is cooperating in the exploitation of its members. How long can this last before the members resign or seek to throw out the union leadership and revert to a more traditional and appropriate adversarial style? It may be, in certain circumstances, that the union prefers to adopt this cooperative stance in order to avoid, or fend off, de-recognition. This has occurred in recent years in parts of the public service sector. It is, however, still appropriate to ask how stable a condition it is.

The other '??' box is where adversarialism in industrial relations is combined with high-commitment management, with its emphasis on investment in training and development, empowerment policies and flexible reward structures. In one large organization this style was described as 'human resource bungee jumping'. Lots of initiatives were planned and implemented in areas such as total quality management, employee involvement and performance-related pay, but they did not take

root. Neither side could escape from the pattern of adversarial industrial relations, of defending long-established practices. Management's failure to address the issue of relationships with the trade union, and the continuance of traditional, low-trust bargaining behaviour, made it impossible to gain acceptance of moves towards high-commitment management. In the case of Rover, however, the unions were initially reluctant to see the introduction of high-commitment management in part because it was linked, as it often is, with substantial job cuts and the company was not prepared to negotiate on them. Eventually the unions accepted the changes and worked cooperatively with management as high-commitment policies were introduced, with a favourable response from the employees. In a third case, union membership began to fall as the employees' positive response to high-commitment work practices meant they were no longer prepared to support the adversarial stance of the union leadership outside the company. Recognition was eventually withdrawn and the prevailing pattern became sophisticated human relations.

Changes to patterns of employee relations and the link to business strategy

The importance of this high-commitment–adversarial '??' box is that it illustrates how an organization has to choose simultaneously to develop new approaches to both the individual and the collective aspects of employment. Historically many organizations in the UK have combined cost minimization, or sometimes paternalism, towards employees with adversarialism towards trade unions; that is, the prevailing pattern has been bargaining constitutional. There is strong evidence, discussed by Purcell and Ahlstrand (1994: chapter 6), that growing competition and expenditure restrictions are driving out paternalism, for example in insurance companies. Changes in attitudes towards strike action and the growing need for companies to be much more flexible in their labour policies are reducing the attractiveness of adversarialism. This suggests a growing bifurcation in patterns of employee relations in both dimensions of the matrix. There is clear evidence of a growth in non-union cost minimization, the traditional pattern (Millward *et al.* 1992). The growth of interest in total quality management, teamworking and empowerment is indicative of the top line of the matrix, high commitment, whether non-union (top left) or unionized (top right). Recent US research suggests that the type of companies embarking on this type of 'workplace transformation', as it is called, are likely to have a high proportion of skilled or knowledge-based workers, to trade in competitive international markets, and to pursue product differentiation strategies in niche markets rather than opt for lowest-cost leadership (Osterman 1994). This very much confirms the research in the US steel mini-mills, referred to earlier, in support of the matching model of human resource management (see HUMAN RESOURCE MANAGEMENT).

This allows us to suggest that the conditions under which high-commitment employee relations styles are likely to be adopted are very different from those impacting on traditional cost-minimization firms. To put it simply, a firm in a competitive, low-cost volume market with little requirement for technical sophistication, such as a fast-food retail outlet, is unlikely to adopt the high-commitment work practices of sophisticated human relations. If it did, it would be highly unlikely to make a profit, especially if the competitors were driving down labour costs through lower wages following the abolition of minimum pay. The converse of this illustration is the firm in a quality market requiring knowledge-based workers but managing them in a typical cost-minimization control-and-command fashion. Could this organization achieve the levels of quality required for sustained competitive advantage, or make almost continuous changes to products and processes to keep ahead of the competition? It seems unlikely, especially if competitors were managing their labour costs by investment in both capital and people in order to achieve higher levels of productivity, and lower unit labour costs. Such a firm, if it were unionized, as would be likely, would be caught in the

bargaining constitutional pattern and would find it difficult to manage change without a deliberate effort to reform the relationship with trade unions. The prediction here, then, is that this organization would resist change until it was forced by crisis to do something.

Choices about the response to collectivism are less likely to be a product of business policy. They come from the personal beliefs and experiences of the senior management and from the external environment of labour laws and patterns of unionization. This explains why the same multinational firm will have different approaches to collectivism in different countries. For example, Nissan is non-union in the USA but recognizes the engineering union in the UK. In each it pursues high-commitment practices in its dealings with individual employees. Many non-union British companies operate works councils in the Netherlands and Germany, and in many cases seek to develop high levels of cooperation.

3 Conclusion

Employee relations management styles can be related to a variety of internal and external conditions in the business, economic and legislative environment. Choices about the way individuals are managed can be related to business strategies and underlying requirements for the type of employees recruited, defined in terms of skills, qualifications and experience. In general terms, the greater the pursuit of added-value, product differentiation strategies, the more likely it is that high-commitment work practices will be required. This also applies where there is a need to employ a high ratio of knowledge-based or skilled and experienced workers. In contrast, cost-minimization policies are more likely where product strategy is based on lowest-cost price leadership and where work processes are simple and it is easy to recruit cheap labour.

This best-fit approach, with the associated choices about relations with collective labour organizations, has become much more important as the process of internalization has spread into the public service sector and external mechanisms of labour regulation have been abolished or weakened, as in health and local authorities. The renaissance of interest in employee relations comes from the requirement of organizations to make choices, and a growing realization that the best-practice model of human resource management is inappropriate or irrelevant to many firms.

JOHN PURCELL
UNIVERSITY OF BATH

Further reading

(References cited in the text marked *)

* Arthur, J. (1994) 'Effects of human resource systems on manufacturing performance and turnover', *Academy of Management Journal* 37 (3): 670–87. (Excellent research on the link between human resource management and business policy in US steel mini-mills.)

* Beer, M., Spector, B., Lawrence, P., Quinn Mills, D. and Walton, R. (1985) *Human Resource Management: A General Manager's Perspective*, Glencoe, IL: The Free Press. (The first definitive text in human resource management produced for Harvard Business School.)

* Dyer, L. (1985) 'Strategic human resource management and planning', in K.M. Rowland and G.R. Ferris (eds), *Human Resource Planning: Evolving Roles and Responsibilities*, Greenwich, CT: JAI Press Inc. (Explores how human resource management can be matched to business policy.)

* Edwards, P. *et al.* (1992) 'Great Britain: still muddling through', in A. Ferner and R. Hyman (eds), *Industrial Relations in the New Europe*, Oxford: Blackwell. (The best analysis of British industrial relations in one chapter.)

* Fox, A. (1966) *Industrial Sociology and Industrial Relations*, Research Paper 3, Royal Commission on Trade Unions and Employers' Associations, London: HMSO. (Path-breaking analysis of management approaches to trade unions that influenced a generation of researchers and practitioners – still well worth reading.)

* Gospel, H.F. (1983) 'Management structures and strategies: an introduction', in H.F. Gospel and C.R. Littler (eds), *Management Strategies and Industrial Relations*, London: Heinemann. (One of the earliest authoritative analyses of human resource management in the UK, taking a business history perspective.)

* Guest D.E. (1995) 'Human resource management, trade unions and industrial relations', in J. Storey (ed.), *Human Resource Management: A Critical Text*, London: Routledge. (A good example of the normative, or 'soft', model of human resource management.)

* Kaufman, B.E. (1993) *The Origins and Evolution of the Field of Industrial Relations in the United States*, Ithaca, NY: ILR Press. (Riveting account of the rise and fall of industrial relations as an academic subject in the USA.)

* Kochan T.A. and Osterman, P. (1994) *The Mutual Gains Enterprise: Forging a Winning Partnership among Labor, Management and Government*, Boston, MA: Harvard Business School Press. (Explores how cooperative industrial relations can be combined with high-commitment management for the benefit of all.)

* Marginson, P., Armstrong, P., Edwards, P., Purcell, J. and Hubbard, N. (1993) *The Control of Industrial Relations in the Multi-Establishment Company*, Warwick Papers in Industrial Relations 45, Coventry: University of Warwick Industrial Relations Research Unit. (Research on how the UK's top companies manage and control personnel and industrial relations.)

* Millward, N., Stevens, M., Smart, D. and Hawes, W. (1992) *Workplace Industrial Relations in Transition 1980–84*, Aldershot: Dartmouth Press. (Reports on the third massive national survey of industrial relations in the UK.)

* Osterman, P. (1994) 'How common is workforce transformation and who adopts it?', *Industrial and Labor Relations Review* 47 (2): 173–88. (US research on the type of firm adopting high-commitment work practices.)

* Purcell, J. (1983) 'The management of industrial relations in the modern corporations: agenda for research', *British Journal of Industrial Relations* 21 (2): 1–16. (One of the earliest papers to establish the research agenda for studying the management of industrial relations.)

* Purcell, J. (1994) 'Human resource management: implications for teaching, theory, research, and practice in industrial relations', in J.N. Niland, R.D. Lansbury and C. Verevis (eds), *The Future of Industrial Relations: Global Change and Challenges*, Thousand Oaks, CA: Sage Publications. (Explores the origin of human resource management and the problems with the diffusion of best practice.)

* Purcell, J. (1995) 'Corporate strategy and its link with human resource management strategy', in J. Storey (ed.), *Human Resource Management: A Critical Text*, London: Routledge. (Explores how the new thinking in business strategy on resource strengths can be applied to human resource management.)

* Purcell, J. and Ahlstrand, B. (1994) *Human Resource Management in the Multi-divisional Company*, Oxford: Oxford University Press. (Explains the management-style model in detail in the context of large company strategy and structure.)
* Schuler, R. and Jackson, S. (1987) 'Linking competitive strategies with human resource management practices', *Academy of Management Executive* 1 (3): 207–19. (Explores the logical connection between business policy and human resource management. Good example of the matching model.)
* Storey, J. (1994) 'The take up of human resource management by mainstream companies: key lessons from research', in J. Niland, R. Lansbury and C. Verevis (eds), *The Future of Industrial Relations: Global Change and Challenges*, Thousand Oaks, CA: Sage Publications. (Summary of major research into the response of sixteen major companies to human resource management.)
* Wood, S. (1995) 'Can we speak of a high commitment management on the shop floor?', *Journal of Management Studies* 32 (2): 215–47. (Tests whether 'soft' human resource management, better described as high-commitment management, is applied in UK manufacturing companies.)

See also: COLLECTIVE BARGAINING; HUMAN RESOURCE MANAGEMENT; HUMAN RESOURCE MANAGEMENT, INTERNATIONAL; HUMAN RESOURCE MANAGEMENT IN EUROPE; INDUSTRIAL AND LABOUR RELATIONS; INDUSTRIAL RELATIONS IN EUROPE; PERSONNEL MANAGEMENT; TRADE UNIONS

Related topics in the IEBM: MANAGEMENT IN JAPAN; MANAGEMENT IN THE UNITED KINGDOM; STRATEGY, CONCEPT OF

Employers' associations

Overview

Employers' associations represent the interests of business to government and engage in collective bargaining with trade unions. Associations in some countries, such as Germany, undertake a much wider range of functions than associations in other countries, for example the UK. In countries with associations that display a high level of organizational development, tasks are undertaken that would otherwise be the responsibility of public agencies and a more comprehensive range of services is provided to members.

Associations are influenced by the political systems in which they operate and three broad patterns of government–business relations can be identified: company state; associative state; and party state.

There has been an increasing emphasis in recent years on the need for employers' associations to organize at the European Union level. This is achieved both through European federations of national federations and direct membership associations.

Even in countries where it has been relatively centralized, collective bargaining is increasingly undertaken by individual firms. Large firms have also developed their own government relations divisions to represent their interests to government. Although these developments undermine the role of employers' associations they remain the main mechanism for defining and representing business interests.

1 Definitions

Employers' associations are organized in a number of different ways. Some associations are concerned just with collective bargaining and other industrial relations issues and are referred to as *employers' organizations*. Those associations that confine themselves to commercial issues such as taxation, trade policy and government regulation are known as *trade associations*. *Peak associations* organize associations representing individual sectors and endeavour to represent general business interests. In some countries, such as the UK, individual firm membership is combined with association membership. Many countries, such as Germany and Sweden, have separate peak associations for the systems of employers' organizations and trade associations. Some organizations represent all business interests in a particular city or region. Chambers of commerce are particularly important in those countries such as Austria, Germany and The Netherlands where businesses are required to be members. Regional business associations are, however, also important in Italy where powerful regional organizations such as that for Lombardy are represented in the national business association, Confindustria, alongside sectoral associations. There are many organizations which confine their membership to smaller scale businesses. The Handwerk organizations in Germany are public law institutions with compulsory membership which artisan firms have to join if they wish to practice a particular trade. Where membership is not compulsory, smaller firms are less likely to join employers' associations than their larger counterparts for whom the subscription is a much smaller proportion of turnover (see INDUSTRIAL RELATIONS IN EUROPE).

2 The importance of employers' associations

Employers' associations act as the principal intermediaries between business and government. Despite the move in the 1980s throughout advanced industrial countries towards less interventionist government policies, privatization and deregulation there are many government policies that have a direct and often considerable impact on the day-to-day activities of businesses. These range from exchange rate policies, through taxation policies, to education and training policies. Indeed, the increasing emphasis on environmental and health and safety regulations and equal opportunities legislation has opened up a whole new area of government activity which affects the operation of business.

Governments are generally willing to consult businesses about proposed new legislation because they want to ensure that the economy will continue to prosper, in part because their own chances of re-election depend on continued economic success. They therefore need to know if a proposed new regulation will have a harmful effect on business activity which offsets the other benefits that it seeks to achieve. In many areas government does not have specialist expertise to match that found in firms and it therefore needs to draw on that expertise in framing legislation.

Government can and does consult with individual firms and direct contacts between government firms and large departments are increasing. However, when government wants a collective view from a particular industry, or from business as a whole, the only way it can obtain this is by turning to an employers' association. The associations therefore have to collect the views of their member firms and assemble them into a coherent set of policy proposals which take account of current government policy. Uncompromising opposition to existing policy is unlikely to achieve anything. Successful associations learn to work with the grain of government policy, modifying it to benefit their members and helping to steer it in new directions.

Employers' associations act as intermediaries between business and government. They have to explain to government what is likely to be acceptable to their members and they have to explain to their members what is likely to be acceptable to government. They have to retain credibility with both audiences. The success of this difficult political balancing act depends to a large extent on the skill of the 'industrial politicians', often the heads of leading firms, who serve terms as the organization's president or as the chair of a key committee and on the permanent staffs of the organization. These staffs have become increasingly professional through the 1980s and 1990s, with work for an employers' association increasingly being seen as a long-term career.

Many associations also act as intermediaries between their members and the trade unions. For some associations collective bargaining and associated industrial relations issues constitute their sole purpose. The rhythm of business in an employers' association operating in a centralized system of collective bargaining is rather different from that whose main focus of attention is on government and whose working calendar is likely to be geared to the legislative year. In an employers' organization all activity focuses on a short, intensive and crucially important period of negotiation with the trade unions.

Employers' associations may also represent the interests of their members in relation to their suppliers and customers. For example, an association of energy producers will usually have continuing discussions with a counterpart organization of industrial energy consumers. Supplier–customer interactions have been particularly important in the food chain between farmers, food manufacturers and retailers. As the market power of supermarket chains has grown relative to that of food manufacturers in a number of countries, associations of manufacturers and retailers have sought to address some of the consequent tensions through discussions.

3 Historical development of employers' associations

The development of employers' associations is closely associated with the emergence of a modern industrial economy. The specific stimulus for association formation varies from case to case. The need to establish a countervailing force to newly formed trade unions was an important motive in many countries in the latter part of the nineteenth century and the early years of the twentieth century. Some associations were formed with state encouragement in order to stimulate exports, undertake training or raise quality standards. Other associations emerged as cartels, operating price fixing or market-sharing agreements. In the UK the chambers of commerce in many towns were formed in response to what was seen to be the high rates and poor service of the railway companies.

In Sweden trade unions in the form of local industry organizations began to appear in the 1860s and became increasingly common in the 1870s. The national umbrella organization for trade unions, the Landes Organisationen, was founded in 1898. A general strike over the universal suffrage issue in 1902 accelerated existing plans for a general employers' federation in Sweden, leading to the formation of the Swedish Employers' Confederation (SAF).

The emergence of trade unions was also an important factor in the development of employers' associations in Germany, with rapid growth in the decade after 1890. A national confederation of employers' associations, the Vereinigung der Deutschen Arbeitgeberverbände, was formed in 1913. An agreement with the unions in 1918 not only recognized them as bargaining counterparts but also gave employers' associations the task of representing business interests in collective bargaining.

The formation of key sectoral associations in the UK was also stimulated by trade union activity. One of the earliest sectoral associations, that in the building industry, was formed in response to the development of labour organization, while the key Engineering Employers' Federation was formed in 1896 and organized a lockout against the unions in 1897. The Federation of British Industries (FBI) was formed in 1916 with encouragement from the government which thought it would help to expand British trade during and after the war. The first two chief staff members of the new body were seconded from the Commercial Section of the Foreign Office.

The modernization of the Japanese economy after the Meiji Restoration in 1868 led to the formation of business associations, one of the first being the Japan Paper Manufacturing Federation established in 1880. Chambers of commerce were officially recognized in 1890. These early bodies were primarily trade associations, concerning themselves with such functions as sharing technical information to enable their members to compete with Western imports. They became increasingly concerned with industrial relations issues, particularly as labour costs began to rise.

As in other countries, in the USA there was a substantial increase in the formation of employers' associations in the 1890s in response to increased union activity. The National Association of Manufacturers (NAM) was formed by Ohio firms concerned about protectionist trends in the 1890s. In its early years the NAM largely represented the minority of US firms, usually larger ones, with significant export markets. The Department of Commerce and Labor took an active part in attempting to form a US Chamber of Commerce in the first decade of the twentieth century, finally succeeding in 1912. During the 1920s Herbert Hoover as Secretary of Commerce made a considerable effort to encourage the formation of trade associations.

The years of the inter-war depression were difficult ones for some employers' associations. In the UK the FBI found it difficult to take a position on the tariff policy issue which would not upset one group of its members. In Sweden, however, the SAF concluded the landmark Saltsjöbaden Accord with the employers, culminating in a General Agreement in 1938 which was based on the principle that the two sides would make national agreements and try to avoid open conflict. In Germany the Nazis brought the system of business associations under their control, integrating 1,500 trade associations into thirty-one sector groups.

The Second World War revitalized many employers' associations. They were often the best mechanism for collecting the information needed to run the war economy, while they themselves were often given such tasks as operating price controls or allocation arrangements for scarce raw materials. In many ways, however, the war served to reinforce existing patterns of employer organization. In the UK, for example, a chaotic and confused system of employers' associations was complicated by the development of new 'wartime associations' with government encouragement. Their persistence after the war had the effect of further intensifying fragmentation and competition among British employers' associations.

In the defeated countries the war did not lead to dramatic structural transformations in employer organization. In Japan organizations such as the Keidanren (Federation of Economic Organizations) and many sectoral associations were largely extensions of organizations that existed before the war. In Germany the Nazi rationalization effort meant that organizations that had previously had a separate existence were reconstituted as specialist sections of larger organizations, something that was rarely achieved in the UK. For example, the Verband deutscher Maschinen- und Anlagenbau serving the machine-building industry replaced a pre-war association, which had coordinated a considerable number of autonomous organizations, with a much more effective association in which the former sectoral associations became internal groups.

The post-war policy framework

Increased government intervention in the economy during the war period was maintained in most countries in the post-war period, in part because of the widespread adoption of Keynesian techniques of aggregate demand management. The post-war period was less amenable to the exercise of cartel functions by associations, with the 1956 Restrictive Trade Practices Act in the UK transforming the roles of some associations and leading to the disappearance of others. Protectionist tariffs were also gradually dismantled under the influence of the General Agreement on Tariffs and Trade. The

increased exposure of domestic economies to intensified competition, not just through trade liberalization but because of a general trend towards greater international economic integration, led many countries to resort to industrial policies to attempt to revive declining industries and to assist the growth of new, high-technology sectors. This created a new interface between government and employers' associations, but in countries where trade associations were perceived to be relatively ineffective, such as the UK, alternative structures were created for the development of industrial policy, for example, the tripartite Economic Development Committees.

One consequence of increased government intervention in the post-war period was the nationalization of significant areas of economic activity. In some countries where public enterprises accounted for a significant proportion of the national economy, as in Italy, this led to the formation of separate employers' associations to represent public enterprises. In other countries, such as the UK, nationalized industries had their own representative organizations but also were admitted, initially as associate members, to the new Confederation of British Industry (CBI) formed in 1965.

Another trend in the post-war period was the development of corporatist arrangements in a number of countries, particularly smaller European democracies such as Austria, Sweden and The Netherlands (see CORPORATISM). Corporatist arrangements involved employers and unions not just in the formation of economic and industrial policies but also in their implementation. It was hoped that their active consent would ease the implementation of policies which might otherwise encounter union and employer resistance. The adoption of prices and incomes policies from the 1960s onwards reinforced this trend towards corporatist arrangements, giving an enhanced importance to the CBI in the UK in the 1970s. Elsewhere, in countries such as Austria, with its long-established compulsory membership structures for chambers of commerce and labour, and Sweden, with its long-established tradition of social partnership, such arrangements did not work well. Effective elite accommodation was easier in the smaller countries, while the openness of their economies to international competition acted as a check against any tendency to create privileged categories of economic activity. Even in those countries it is uncertain whether social partnership was a cause of economic prosperity or its effect. In any case, these corporatist arrangements tended to disintegrate under the impact of recession and increased economic liberalization in the 1980s. One consequence was that peak associations became less important relative to sectoral associations of employers.

Changes in collective bargaining

In many countries, collective bargaining at a national or sectoral level has become less important, diminishing the significance of employers' associations in a key area of their activities (see COLLECTIVE BARGAINING). The general trend in many British industries, evident since the 1950s, has been away from multi-employer bargaining towards increasingly decentralized bargaining by individual employers. The general decline of collective bargaining as an institution has had a profound impact on the role of employers' organizations in the UK. Between 1980 and 1990 the number of workplaces in the UK which were members of employers' organizations declined by 50 per cent so that by 1990 only one in eight were members. Throughout the 1980s there was a significant increase in the number of large firms withdrawing from multi-employer agreements, leading in some cases to the collapse of the national agreements.

These trends are not so surprising in the UK, where collective bargaining has always been less centralized than in most other countries, and where there has been a determined effort by the Conservative government to deregulate the labour market. Similar trends are, however, also apparent in countries which have had more centralized collective bargaining arrangements. In Germany the system has been put under strain by unification and by differentials in pay between the former western and eastern parts of the country.

In Sweden, which has operated a highly centralized system of collective bargaining, increasing strains and tensions have appeared. From the late 1970s the engineering employers, the largest group within the SAF, pressed for more decentralized negotiations. In October 1986 the engineering employers informed SAF of their intention to engage in direct negotiations with the metalworkers' union on all questions. The bakery employers also broke away and signed their own agreement. In 1990 SAF decided that it would no longer negotiate on wages or general working conditions in the manual workers' sector. In the white-collar sector there would be a period of transition. SAF would continue to negotiate on some issues such as job security. No further money would be transferred into its strike insurance fund which would no longer be able to cope with large-scale disputes.

As their collective bargaining role has declined, employers' associations have sought to retain members by providing them with a wide range of services. These selective incentives for membership are particularly important to smaller firms, who are less likely to have specialized services 'in-house'. The types and levels of service offered vary from country to country and association to association, with German associations, for example, generally offering a wider and more sophisticated range of services than many of their British counterparts. Examples of services provided are legal advice, including handling cases before labour courts; advice on technical developments; and a variety of training courses and seminars.

Many of these services can be purchased from commercial suppliers, but employers' associations do have an advantage in providing some types of service to their members. For example, confidential comparative performance statistics can be more readily processed and collected by an association than by a commercial firm. Inspection and certification of the quality of the processes and products of member firms, sometimes using legal powers delegated by the state, is a task particularly suited to employers' associations.

National variations in relationships with the political system

The roles performed by employers' associations are significantly influenced by the characteristics of the political systems in which they operate. Three broad patterns of relationship between employers' associations and government exist in advanced industrial countries, depending on the predominant form of the interrelationship between business and government. These three broad patterns are:

- the company state (the UK and the USA)
- the associative state (Germany and Sweden)
- the party state (Italy and Japan)

In the company state direct contacts between large firms and government are encouraged and are of considerable importance. Large firms have their own specialist government relations divisions which coordinate their relationships with government. Direct company–government relationships undermine the significance of employers' associations. They are often confined to more technical or product-specific issues. The delegation of public policy functions to employers' associations is limited.

In the associative state employers' associations are the principal intermediary between business and government. It is in such political systems that employers' associations have their greatest importance. Government relations divisions are either absent or very weakly developed in such countries and prevalent political norms encourage the channelling of business representation through employers' associations. There is extensive delegation of public policy functions to employers' associations.

In the party state political power is concentrated in a dominant political party which has remained in power over a long period of time. Patronage in the form of contracts is dispensed through the political party. Because of the ineffectiveness of the official opposition parties the ruling party becomes factionalized and employers' associations seek to identify themselves with particular factions in the dominant party.

These are general characterizations of the form taken by business–government relationships. All forms of contact are going to exist to some extent in any country. For example, although British governments have placed increasing emphasis on direct contact with companies, they have not neglected the reform of the system of employers' associations which they have seen as being particularly important in ensuring that the views of smaller companies are represented. In an effort to stimulate reform of the trade association system in the UK, the President of the Board of Trade, Michael Heseltine, announced in 1993 that in future his department would not talk to all associations but to only one leading association in each sector.

Countries can shift between the categories outlined above over time. The attachment to a company state model was at its strongest in the UK in the late 1980s in the latter part of the Thatcher government. With successive Conservative victories at general elections the UK shifted more in the direction of a party state model, with the Conservative Party displaying greater factionalization. The Labour government elected in 1997 seemed likely to move in an associative state direction, while maintaining direct contacts with companies. In Italy and Japan, on the other hand, the position of the dominant party has been eroded, and they have started to move away from the party state model, which is seen as increasingly inconsistent with the effective operation of a modern economy.

The emergence of employers' associations in Russia and eastern Europe

Moves towards less centrally controlled economies and liberal democratic systems of government in eastern Europe and Russia have created opportunities for the development of employers' associations which have been seized by some entrepreneur organizers (see INDUSTRIAL AND LABOUR RELATIONS). It has to be emphasized, however, that the circumstances in which employers' associations operate in these countries, particularly in Russia, are very different from those faced by their counterparts in countries with long experience of operating a market economy and a liberal democracy. Substantial portions of the economy remain in state hands, and this creates a division in most countries between employers' associations representing state enterprises and those representing the new entrepreneurial sector. The organizations representing state enterprises are often themselves split between conservative managers preferring the retention of something as close to the old system as possible and those more liberal managers who would like to see privatization, or at least extensive reform.

Particularly in Russia, there has been a proliferation of associations claiming to represent the interests of employers. Often these are very small organizations, based around a single charismatic individual and linked with a political party. In some eastern European countries employers' associations have initially been based on a refurbished version of the chambers of commerce which existed in some communist regimes. There has been a debate in Hungary about the appropriateness of the Austrian compulsory chambers model to Hungarian needs. Some of the most successful associations have been those which represent the new small-scale enterprises emerging in eastern European countries. In Hungary the National Association of Entrepreneurs organizes companies with an average size of seventy employees. Although it includes both large and very small firms as part of its membership its main constituency is made up of medium-sized firms.

Employers' associations in former communist countries have a broader political task than their counterparts in long-established democracies. As well as representing the interests of their members and providing them with services, an important role in countries which often lack an adequate business infrastructure and reliable independent advice, the associations contribute to the construction of a civil society in countries where political life was formerly controlled by the state. This broader political role is reflected in their often close links with political parties.

The development of employers' associations in these countries depends in large part on how successful they are in privatizing their state sectors and maintaining liberal democratic institutions. One trend in Russia is that the most effective organizations appear to be forming at the regional or city level. Territorially based employers' associations seem likely to be of more significance in these societies than they have been in most Western countries.

Employers' associations at the European Union level

As decisions taken by the European Union (EU) have grown in scope and importance, particularly since the Single European Act, it has become increasingly important for employers' associations to organize at the EU level (see INDUSTRIAL RELATIONS IN EUROPE). This is particularly necessary given the attachment of the Commission to the continental European belief in social partnership, which attaches value to tripartite discussions between state agencies, employers' associations and trade unions. In 1984 the so-called 'Val Duchesse' discussion was set up between the Commission, the Union of Industrial and Employers' Confederations of Europe (UNICE), the trade unions and public enterprises.

Much of the influence exerted by employers' associations in relation to the EU is still exercised at the national level. Employers' associations persuade their governments to adopt their position on a particular issue in the Council of Ministers. However, this is a risky strategy if it is not combined with action at the Union level. The national government may be defeated through the use of qualified majority voting or, more likely, their position on a particular issue will be sacrificed as part of a more general political bargain.

In some sectors, such as petrochemicals and motor vehicles, employers are already organized in direct membership associations at the EU level. The European Round Table, organized on the lines of the US Business Round Table, has a membership of around forty-five chief executives from major

European companies with membership by invitation only. The Round Table focuses on particular issues such as transport infrastructure or taxation. Some of the leading US multinationals are organized through the EU Committee of the US Chamber of Commerce.

Most employer association activity at the EU level takes place through federations of national associations. At the peak level there is UNICE, which was reorganized to enhance its effectiveness in the late 1980s. Each industrial sector, and many product groups, have their own European federations which vary considerably in their effectiveness. Even the more effective, however, suffer from the problem of attempting to reconcile twelve national positions, a process which often results in 'lowest common denominator' policy positions which have little practical impact.

4 Future developments

There has been a trend throughout the 1980s and 1990s for large companies to develop their own government relations divisions to coordinate their relationships with political actors. Centralized systems of collective bargaining operated through employers' associations have tended to weaken further in countries in which they were already weak and to start to disintegrate in countries where they have been well established. This move towards more individualistic action by companies, reflecting the more general move away from corporatist arrangements and towards greater deregulation and liberalization in the 1980s, does not mean that employers' associations face a future of decline.

In the EU, the increasing impact of EU decisions on business has opened up a new arena of activity for employers' associations. Throughout advanced industrialized countries, environmental and health and safety regulations increasingly require collective action by employers to influence their development and implementation. For their part governments continue to show an interest in the effectiveness of employers' associations as organizations which can contribute to enhanced competitiveness. Three trends are likely in the future. There will be an increased emphasis on the provision of high-quality services to members. Organizations made up of leading firms concentrating on a few crucial issues like the EU Round Table will become more common. Various forms of public/private partnership in areas such as training, research and development, and quality control will increase. The roles performed by employers' associations will continue to develop and change, but their future is assured.

WYN GRANT
UNIVERSITY OF WARWICK

Further reading

Coleman, W. and Grant, W. (1988) 'The organizational cohesion and political access of business: a study of comprehensive associations', *European Journal of Political Research* 16: 467–87. (Uses internationally comparative data set to examine roles of 'peak level' employers' associations.)

Coleman, W. and Jacek, H. (1989) (eds) *Regionalism, Business Interests and Public Policy*, London: Sage Publications. (Comparative examination of territorially organized employers' associations.)

De Geer, H. (1992) *The Rise and Fall of the Swedish Model: the Swedish Employers' Confederation and Industrial Relations over Ten Decades*, Chichester: Carden Publications. (Succinct history of the SAF, particularly useful on recent deterioration of the Swedish model.)

Grant, W. (1993a) *Business and Politics in Britain*, 2nd edn, London: Macmillan. (Provides analysis of employers' associations in the UK set in a comparative context.)

Grant, W. (1993b) 'Business associations in eastern Europe and Russia', *Journal of Communist Studies* 9 (2): 86–100. (Summarizes the findings of a conference on the emergence of employers' associations in former communist countries.)

Grant, W., Nekkers, J. and van Waarden, F. (1991) (eds) *Organizing Business for War*, Oxford: Berg. (Nine-country comparison of the impact of the Second World War on employers' associations.)

Greenwood, J. (1997) *Representing Interests in the European Union*. London: Macmillan. (Comprehensive assessment of interest representation in the EU.)

Greenwood, J., Grote, R. and Ronit, K. (1992) *Organized Interests and the European Community*, London: Sage Publications. (Examines the impact of the single market on employer association activity, emphasizing diversity of response.)

Lynn, L. and McKeown, H. (1988) *Organizing Business: Trade Associations in America and Japan*, Washington, DC: American Enterprise Institute. (Systematic and well-informed comparative analysis of the different roles of trade associations in Japan and the USA.)

McLaughlin, A., Jordan, J. and Maloney, W.A. (1993) 'Corporate lobbying in the European Community', *Journal of Common Market Studies* 31 (2): 191–212. (Analysis of the development of employers' association activity at the EU level in the motor industry.)

Martinelli, A. (ed.) (1991) *International Markets and Global Firms*, London: Sage Publications. (Comparative study of employers' associations in the chemical industry.)

Richardson, J. and Mazey, S. (eds) (1992) *Lobbying in the European Community*, Oxford: Oxford University Press. (Includes contributions by employers' association staff members and Commission officials as well as academics.)

Windmuller, J.P. and Gladstone, A. (eds) (1984) *Employers Associations and Industrial Relations*, Oxford: Clarendon Press. (Well-edited accounts of employers' associations in collective bargaining in major industrial countries.)

See also: COLLECTIVE BARGAINING; HUMAN RESOURCE MANAGEMENT; INDUSTRIAL AND LABOUR RELATIONS; INDUSTRIAL RELATIONS IN EUROPE; INDUSTRIAL RELATIONS IN JAPAN; INDUSTRIAL RELATIONS IN THE USA; TRADE UNIONS

Related topics in the IEBM: CONFLICT AND POLITICS ; EMPLOYEE RELATIONS, MANAGEMENT OF; GENERAL AGREEMENT ON TARIFFS AND TRADE (GATT)

Employment and unemployment, economics of

Overview

The historical evolution of employment follows the evolution of spending patterns that accompanies economic growth. At early stages of growth employment is concentrated in agriculture and raw materials. Later, employment grows in the production sector and finally in the public and private services. At any particular time, a country's employment structure tends to reflect its stage of growth and its particular comparative advantages n international trade. Short-run changes in employment and unemployment are influenced by the fact that in modern industrial economies there are both fixed and variable costs associated with hiring labour. When fixed labour costs are important, employers are more likely to adjust hours of work before they change the number of employees in response to changes in output. Changes in employment and unemployment thus lag behind changes in output. Fixed labour costs associated with turnover and training tend to rise with the skill of a worker. As a result, employers are more reluctant to lay off skilled than unskilled workers, and the unemployment of unskilled workers is more responsive to cyclical changes than the unemployment of skilled workers.

Economic analysts identify four general types of unemployment. Deficient demand unemployment can be reduced by fiscal and monetary policies that increase the demand for labour. Frictional, structural and seasonal unemployment, which exist even when business conditions are good, depend more on relative wage adjustments, labour mobility and other aspects of the functioning of labour markets. There are significant international differences in unemployment, and since the 1970s unemployment in Europe has increased relative to unemployment in North America and Japan. Much of this change appears to reflect an increase in the structural and frictional components of unemployment in European labour markets.

Frictional and structural unemployment can be reduced by avoiding policies that raise the incidence and duration of unemployment and by pursuing policies that reduce them. The structure of unemployment insurance provides an example of the former. Unemployment durations will generally be lower when unemployment benefits are low relative to prior earnings and when benefit eligibility periods are relatively short. Policies that may reduce unemployment include retraining programmes, wage subsidies, and subsidies for worker relocation. Most industrialized countries have pursued such policies in the postwar period, but the results have been mixed.

1 Introduction

Employment and unemployment are among the most frequently watched indicators of economic performance at both the aggregate and market level of economic activity. Figures 1–3 describe some key features of employment and unemployment in industrialized countries during the period following the Second World War. Figure 1 indicates that movements in employment tend to follow movements in output. Employment increases with the general growth in the economy but also has a pronounced cyclical component that tends to lag behind cyclical developments

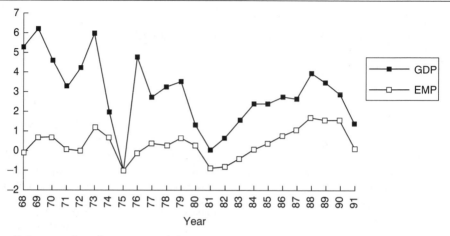

Figure 1 Output and employment growth in European Community countries (annual per cent change)

in product markets. The unemployment rate also moves cyclically but lags behind output, taking low values during economic booms and high values during recessions. (If comparable data were available for the entire twentieth century, they would show the highest unemployment rates during the great depression of the 1930s and the lowest during the Second World War.)

Figure 2 illustrates two key features of the structure of employment. First, over long periods of time the structure of employment evolves similarly in most industrialized countries. As economic growth proceeds, the share of employment in agriculture and eventually industry declines and the share of employment in the services expands. At any particular time, the distribution of employment by

industry is by no means identical for countries at the same stage of economic development, however. Second, the effects of short-run fluctuations in demand are not evenly distributed in the labour market. Employment in some occupations and industries responds much more rapidly to product market developments than in others.

Similarly, unemployment is not the same in all markets. Figure 3 shows distinct international differences in unemployment rates, for example, and indicates that these differences can change over time. Relative to the USA, Europe had low unemployment rates in the early post-war period and high unemployment rates more recently. Unemployment in Japan has been still lower during the post-war period, rarely exceeding 2.5 per cent of the

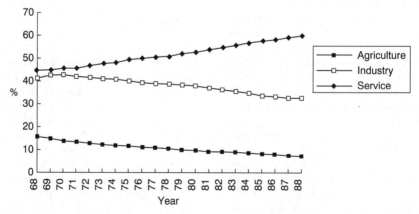

Figure 2 Evolution of employment shares in European Community countries

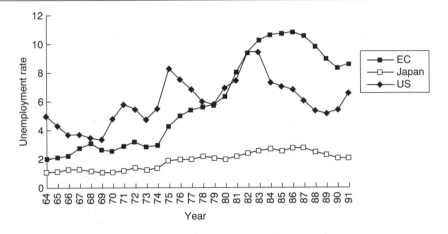

Figure 3 International unemployment differences

workforce. Unemployment rates also typically vary by occupation, industry, age, race, and other personal characteristics, and unemployment in some sectors is more sensitive to cyclical developments than in others. Figure 3 also indicates that the unemployment rate remains well above zero even in the best of times in peacetime market economies.

Economic analysis, therefore, needs to explain the fact that: (1) the structure of employment varies across countries and changes over time; (2) employment and unemployment lag behind output changes; (3) not all dimensions of employment and unemployment are equally responsive to changes in output; (4) market economies may experience significant unemployment even when business conditions are good; and (5) the structure of unemployment varies across markets and countries. Before addressing these features of the data, we will briefly discuss the measurement of employment and unemployment.

2 Measuring employment and unemployment

In modern workforce accounting, members of the population are either in or out of the workforce (see HUMAN RESOURCE MANAGEMENT). It consists of individuals who are employed or who desire employment but have not found a job and hence are considered unemployed. All

other individuals are considered out of the workforce. In most industrialized countries, estimates of the number employed, unemployed, or out of the workforce are developed from periodic household surveys that apply conventions developed over the years by government statisticians and codified by the International Labour Office. An alternative approach, estimating the number of unemployed from the number of unemployment benefit recipients, generally yields biased estimates because not all unemployed may be eligible for benefits. Like most statistical conventions, the definitions of employment, unemployment, and out of the workforce may deviate in some respects from common understandings of the terms.

To be employed, a person must have worked for pay or profit for some period of time – usually as little as an hour – in a particular reference week preceding the survey date. Those who did not work during the reference week must then be allocated to either the unemployed or not in the workforce categories. In modern workforce accounting, the touchstone is whether the non-employed individual is available for work and has engaged in job search activity in the recent past. Individuals who were not at work but who made specific efforts to obtain a job, such as registering with an employment exchange or answering employment advertisements, are counted as unemployed. Individuals who were not at work and did not engage in job-seeking activities are counted as not in the workforce. The unemployment rate is the per cent of the workforce that is unemployed.

Like other statistical conventions, these definitions are not free of ambiguity. The employed include some people who are not fully employed – either because they are working fewer hours than they prefer or because their productivity would be higher in a different job, if it were available. The count of unemployment will be sensitive to the length of the reference period for determining job search activity. Longer reference periods will produce higher estimates of unemployment. Moreover, individuals who cease job-seeking activities because they come to believe that no jobs are available will not be included in the official count of the unemployed, although many countries make a separate enumeration of these 'discouraged workers'.

The conventions adopted by workforce statisticians generally reflect judgements informed by extensive pre-testing of alternative definitions. For example, some observers have argued that 'discouraged workers' should be included in official estimates of unemployment. This view reflects a judgement that such individuals would quickly re-enter the workforce and seek work as economic conditions improved. Yet the evidence does not support this assumption, and statistical authorities continue to require evidence of recent job search before including non-workers in the count of the unemployed. The US Bureau of Labor Statistics and other statistical organizations often publish alternative indicators of joblessness along with the official unemployment rate. As the discouraged worker example indicates, alternative definitions generally influence the levels of employment and unemployment more than their movements over time, and it is the latter that are generally most important for interpreting economic developments. Moreover, the ranking of countries by level of unemployment is not very sensitive to different definitions of unemployment (Sorrentino 1995).

3 Historical evolution of employment

Employment is derived from the demand for the products and services produced by labour. Since employment is a derived demand, one important determinant of a country's structure of employment is the spending patterns of its population. Broad changes in employment structure over time reflect changes in spending patterns that occur with the increases in income that accompany economic growth, which in turn are driven by income elasticities of demand. At the early stages of economic development, most spending is in the primary sectors, such as agriculture, forestry and fishing. As output and incomes increase, spending on manufactured goods increases. In still later stages of economic development much increased spending occurs for services. Thus, at early stages of development, a country's employment tends to be mainly in agriculture. Later, employment growth occurs in the goods-producing industries. At higher income levels, the share of employment in private and public service industries grows at the expense of employment in agriculture and manufacturing.

Historically, these effects of changing spending patterns have been enhanced by rapid productivity growth in agriculture and manufacturing relative to the services. The decline of agricultural employment and rapid expansion of employment in services has been a key feature of employment trends in advanced industrial countries over the past twenty years (Figure 2). Indeed, the service sector has been the major source of new job creation in industrialized countries in modern times.

In economies that engage in international trade, the connection between domestic spending patterns and the structure of employment is somewhat weakened. In the absence of barriers to free trade, countries can specialize in production (and hence employment) according to their comparative advantages and then trade to obtain their desired consumption mix. With free trade, countries at the same stage of development are therefore likely to have rather different employment structures reflecting their different comparative advantages.

The role of international trade raises an important public policy influence on the structure of employment. To the extent that a country adopts tariffs, quotas or other trade protection policies that inhibit specialization according to comparative advantage, the employment structure of that country will be altered. Developments since the Second World War have been more in the opposite direction. Successive rounds of the General Agreement on Tariffs and Trade (GATT) and the development of free trade areas, such as the European Community (EC), have altered domestic employment structures to reflect more closely patterns of comparative advantage. Trade policy can be an important influence on the structure of employment.

4 The employment decision

Moving from the historical evolution of employment to specific employment issues requires a closer examination of the hiring decisions that produce employment. Economic analysis assumes that firms seek to maximize their profits and therefore will hire additional workers so long as they raise profits. The key decision rule implied by profit maximization is that additional workers will be hired as long as they add more to revenues than to costs, and that hiring will cease when the marginal revenue from a new hire just equals the marginal costs of the new employee. Virtually all economic analyses of employment are based in some way on this proposition, so that a key aspect of employment analysis is to identify the relevant revenues and costs and to trace the implications for employment of changes in these factors.

The additional revenue to a firm from hiring another worker consists of the additional physical output resulting from the hire (that is, the marginal productivity of the worker) times the revenue that can be obtained by selling the output. A key technological feature of most organizations in the short run is that beyond some employment level, the marginal productivity of additional workers declines, thus diminishing the additional revenue generated by successive new hires. For any hiring cost, this factor will limit the number of employees that it is profitable to hire.

The additional cost to a firm from hiring another worker can depend very much on legal requirements and details of personnel practice. In the most basic economic models of hiring, the hourly or weekly wage is presumed to be the marginal cost of a new worker. When this is the case, employment increases until the value of the additional output per hour or week produced by the last hire just equals the hourly or weekly wage. At lower wages, employers can afford workers with lower marginal productivity, and employment will expand. At higher wages, employment will contract until the marginal productivity of labour equals the increased marginal cost.

Even this limited view of the marginal cost of labour provides certain useful policy implications. Most notably, efforts to raise the wage in competitive labour markets by institutional means are likely to reduce employment and efforts to reduce the wage are likely to expand employment. This explains the opposition of most professional economists to statutory minimum wages as an anti-poverty policy. While such legislation will raise wages for low-productivity workers who remain employed, it is likely to reduce the number of low-productivity workers who are employed. Only in monopsonistic labour markets will a carefully set minimum wage raise employment. Efforts to raise wages above market levels through collective bargaining should have similar effects (see COLLECTIVE BARGAINING). Conversely, wage subsidy policies, in which the government effectively pays some fraction of a worker's wage, should expand employment. Some of the empirical regularities of employment noted earlier are not easily explained by this model, however. For example, the model does not explain why employment changes lag behind output changes and does not explain why employment in some occupations adjusts to output changes much more slowly than in others.

5 The role of fixed labour costs

The economic analysis of employment is strengthened by recognizing the importance of non-wage labour costs in modern industrial economies. These include hiring and training costs, legally required and voluntarily provided fringe benefits and severance pay or other termination costs. A key feature of many of these employment costs is that they constitute a cost per employee hired rather than a cost per hour worked. That is, there is a fixed cost associated with each new hire – a cost that does not vary with the amount of work performed. The effects of fixed labour costs on employer hiring decisions are important, for non-wage labour costs have increased relative to wages in virtually all industrialized countries during the post-war period.

Recognition that new hires involve an element of fixed costs alters the behaviour of profit-maximizing firms in important ways. When costs per employee increase relative to costs per hour worked, employers have an incentive to achieve a given labour input with fewer workers and more hours per worker. Increased fixed non-wage labour costs effectively lead firms to favour existing employees (insiders) at the expense of job applicants (outsiders).

This helps explain the tendency (noted earlier in the discussion of Figure 1) of employment changes to lag behind output changes over the business cycle, a phenomenon that results in distinctive pro-cyclical movements in labour productivity (output per employee) (see PRODUCTIVITY). When faced with significant fixed labour costs, firms are unlikely to respond to an increase in demand by hiring new workers initially. Instead they will first increase labour input by increasing the number of hours worked per employee. (Without fixed labour costs, firms would be indifferent between these two methods of adjusting labour input.) When fixed costs are sufficiently high, it may even be cheaper to pay overtime premia to the existing workforce than to incur the costs of hiring new workers. Employers will postpone new hiring until they consider the increased demand to be permanent. Conversely, employers will initially respond to a downturn in economic activity by reducing weekly hours and only later turn to layoffs if the downturn persists. Thus, changes in unemployment as well as changes in employment lag behind changes in output.

The role of employment versus hours adjustments may also be influenced by specific public policies. For example, there is evidence that in countries that permit workers to collect unemployment benefits for short-time work (such as Germany), hours are adjusted more than employment relative to countries, such as the USA, in which only workers who have lost their jobs can collect unemployment benefits (in most states) (Abraham and Houseman 1993) (see FLEXIBILITY).

Increased non-wage labour costs also raise the average cost of labour, thereby providing an incentive to reduce total labour input. This may contribute to the persistence of unemployment observed in many European countries in recent decades. Finally, fixed hiring costs raise the cost of low-wage relative to high-wage labour, creating an incentive for employers to substitute skilled for unskilled labour. The growth in fixed non-wage labour costs therefore lowers the employment probability of unskilled and inexperienced workers relative to skilled workers.

Some fixed labour costs, notably those associated with turnover and training, tend to rise with the skill of a worker (see TRAINING, ECONOMICS OF). As a result, employers are more reluctant to lay off skilled than unskilled workers. This helps to account for occupational variations in the sensitivity of employment and unemployment to changes in output. Employers are reluctant to lose their investments in skilled workers, and hence adjust the hours of skilled workers more than their employment in response to changing output. Layoffs of unskilled workers involve little or no loss of investment, and so the unemployment of unskilled workers is much more sensitive cyclically.

Fixed labour costs have also had an influence on another post-war employment trend – the modest growth in the proportion of the workforce in part-time and temporary employment in most industrialized countries. These developments appear tied in part to the growth of employment in the service industries, which offer more part-time opportunities. In addition, part-time and temporary workers are often cheaper to employ than full-time workers, because many countries exempt such employment from certain non-wage labour costs, such as paid holidays, maternity pay and leave, and redundancy payments. In addition, some countries exempt such workers from labour market regulations governing dismissals and payment of unemployment compensation.

6 Unemployment

The pronounced cyclical movements in unemployment noted in Figure 1 encourage the idea that joblessness predominantly results from the layoff and hiring decisions of firms and represents a waste of labour resources. In fact, inflows to unemployment are from four sources: layoffs by firms (see DOWNSIZING), employed people quitting to search for new jobs, the entry of new workers into the workforce, and the re-entry of workers with prior work experience who withdrew from the workforce for a period of time (for example, to continue their education or to raise children). While cyclical movements in the unemployment rate are indeed driven by changes in joblessness resulting from layoffs, spells of unemployment initiated by supply-side decisions to quit, enter or re-enter the workforce constitute over half of the unemployment observed in full employment years in North America and as much as 80 to 90 per cent of unemployment in Europe (Sorrentino 1995). In fact, during economic expansions, employment and unemployment may both increase for brief periods when the number of new jobs is insufficient to absorb workforce growth.

Types of unemployment

Economic analysts identify four types or components of measured unemployment – deficient-demand unemployment, seasonal unemployment, frictional unemployment and structural unemployment. All four may contribute to total unemployment at any particular time.

Deficient-demand unemployment occurs when the aggregate demand for labour declines and real wages do not decline rapidly enough to maintain employment. This is the cyclical component of unemployment observed in Figure 1. Sufficiently flexible real wages could prevent many of the layoffs that produce this type of unemployment, but modern wage-setting institutions and policies do not produce such flexibility. Where the terms and conditions of employment are set by collective bargaining, contracts often establish fixed wage levels for two or three years at a time (see COLLECTIVE BARGAINING). In some union agreements, part of the wage may be indexed to a price or cost-of-living index, but contractual wages rarely vary with profitability or labour market conditions. The influence of collective bargaining may be particularly important in most countries of Europe, where union representation is more widespread than in the USA and Japan (see TRADE UNIONS).

The specific features of a country's wage-setting institutions can influence the degree of wage flexibility and hence the extent of deficient-demand unemployment that results from a general decline in spending. There is some evidence that unionized countries with relatively centralized collective bargaining arrangements, such as Austria and the Scandinavian countries, experience less unemployment, for example (Bruno and Sachs 1985; Layard *et al.* 1991; Calmfors and Driffil 1988). Unions that bargain on a nationwide basis are likely to recognize that wage increases in excess of productivity gains will lead to higher prices that erode the real wage gains of workers. In less centralized bargaining structures, each union may feel that its negotiations are too small a part of the total picture to generate much inflation, but when all unions reason similarly, wage restraint is unlikely. The most decentralized bargaining systems – such as the plant-level bargaining that is common in the USA and Japan – may also permit wage flexibility, because unions have less bargaining power in these settings.

Non-union wage determination, as is now most common in the USA, provides the most decentralized pay determination system. Non-union wages are more responsive than union wages to changing demand, and layoffs are less frequent in non-union than in union firms. None the less, even non-union wages are not sufficiently flexible to prevent all deficient-demand unemployment. Employers who have invested substantially in the training do not wish to provide incentives for trained workers to quit (see TRAINING). Others may be trying to limit the risk of income variation faced by more senior workers. Such a policy also provides incentives for less senior workers to work harder in order to attain the benefits of greater seniority later in their career.

In the absence of sufficient wage flexibility to prevent the emergence of deficient-demand unemployment, cyclical fluctuations in unemployment are addressed by economic policies. In principle, deficient-demand unemployment can be eliminated by fiscal and monetary policies that increase the demand for labour by increasing public and private spending.

Seasonal unemployment results from fluctuations in the demand for and supply of labour that occur regularly year in and year out. Examples include school-age youth who become part of the labour supply in the summer or other vacation periods, construction workers who may be out of work when the weather is bad, and agricultural workers who are jobless after a harvest. The key distinction from deficient-demand unemployment is that seasonal variations do not signal a permanent improvement or deterioration in labour market conditions. Monthly and quarterly unemployment data are invariably adjusted for seasonal variations before publication in order to provide a more reliable guide to general economic conditions.

Frictional unemployment arises from the normal turnover that occurs among firms and workers in the labour market even when there is no deficient-demand or seasonal unemployment. Turnover occurs when workers enter or re-enter the workforce and when workers quit jobs to seek other employment. (Recall that on average most unemployment begins from such labour supply decisions by individuals.)

Turnover also occurs as some firms downsize or go out of business, while others expand.

Such turnover generates frictional unemployment because labour market information is imperfect and it takes time for unemployed workers and employers with job vacancies to find each other. While unemployed search has its costs, it may also benefit a worker to the extent that search identifies more desirable jobs. Some unemployment is therefore productive rather than a waste of labour resources. This provides at least a partial explanation for the observation that unemployment rates in market economies never reach zero. Some frictional unemployment is an unavoidable and even rational consequence of the process of allocating labour to higher productivity jobs. None the less, institutions such as computerized employment exchange services that improve labour market information can reduce this component of joblessness.

Structural unemployment arises from imbalances in the skill structure or geographic distribution of unemployed workers and of job vacancies. In principle, such imbalances need not result in extensive unemployment. To the extent that wages rise in response to labour shortages and fall or rise relatively slowly in response to labour surpluses, the imbalances may be eliminated if workers respond by investing in higher-paying skills or relocation to high-wage areas. There are many practical barriers to such labour market adjustments, however. Institutional influences on pay setting may prevent relative wages from changing in response to the imbalances, or workers may not be well informed about some relative wage changes. Moreover, the costs of skill acquisition or relocation may be too great for the necessary occupational or geographic mobility to occur. This is particularly true for older workers, who have a shorter time horizon over which to collect returns on such investments. When such practical barriers are important, structural unemployment will result. On the other hand, labour market policies that reduce such barriers can reduce structural unemployment. These include subsidized training programmes for skill development, subsidies to defray relocation costs, and information about distant job opportunities. Institutional arrangements facilitating relative wage flexibility will also mitigate structural unemployment. All of these are discussed at greater length in the concluding section.

Frictional and structural unemployment may also be attributed to the wage policies of employers. Employers may voluntarily pay wages above the market-clearing rate in order to improve productivity by reducing turnover costs and providing incentives for greater effort. The payment of such 'efficiency wages' could discourage turnover and poor performance that could result in dismissal, since workers would likely receive lower wages at other employers. High wages would substitute to some degree for supervision costs. While workers at other firms might be willing to work for less than the efficiency wage, employers adopting the policy would be reluctant to lower their wages because they would lose the incentive effects. Unemployment therefore results as workers quit lower-wage jobs to search and wait for vacancies to occur at high-wage firms.

The boundary between structural and frictional unemployment is necessarily imprecise. Both result from efforts by labour market participants to adjust to economic change. The key distinction appears to be that sufficient information about job alternatives will end a spell of frictional unemployment, while information plus a change in skill or location will also be necessary to end a spell of structural unemployment. This is not a distinction that is tractable with existing data, and statistical agencies do not produce tabulations of frictional and structural unemployment. None the less, the difficulties in eliminating either of these types of unemployment account for the fact that even when economies are strong, measured unemployment is still significant.

How then do economists determine the level of unemployment consistent with 'full' employment – that is the point of zero deficient-demand unemployment? The key point is that when an economy experiences deficient demand, there should be downward pressure on wages and prices, but when aggregate demand exceeds resource supplies, wage

and price inflation will appear. A target for macroeconomic policy is therefore the unemployment rate that produces neither upward nor downward pressures on wages and prices. In policy discussions, this rate is sometimes referred to as the non-accelerating inflation rate of unemployment (NAIRU). In academic discussions, it is sometimes called the 'equilibrium' or 'natural' rate of unemployment. It can also be thought of as the sum of frictional, structural and seasonal unemployment.

Post-war growth of unemployment

As Figure 3 illustrates, unemployment has increased in both Europe and North America since the 1960s, and the increased European joblessness has been particularly persistent. In contrast to the early post-war period, Europe now routinely experiences higher unemployment rates than North America. If increased unemployment primarily reflected deficient demand, stimulating demand through monetary and fiscal policies could reduce joblessness, but deficient demand has been only part of the explanation, particularly with regard to Europe.

The growth in total unemployment was accompanied by an increase in the NAIRU, so that efforts to expand the economy with government fiscal and monetary policies would produce inflationary pressures at higher unemployment rates than previously. During the late 1970s and 1980s, many countries experienced outward shifts in their Beveridge curve, the relationship between the aggregate unemployment and job vacancy rates. For a given labour market structure, this curve describes the negative cyclical relationship between the two rates; as demand declines, vacancies decrease and unemployment increases, and conversely. Changes in frictional and structural unemployment are reflected in shifts in the Beveridge curve, since changes that impede the adjustment of labour supply to labour demand increase the amount of unemployment associated with a given vacancy rate.

Thus, monetary and fiscal policies would eliminate only some of the increased unemployment before generating inflationary pressures. Further reductions require policies that are tailored to the nature of increased labour market maladjustment. Shifts in the NAIRU and the Beveridge curve could reflect increasing structural unemployment – a growing mismatch between the skill or regional structure of demand for and supply of labour. As noted earlier, a permanent rise in the amount of structural unemployment in an economy requires both an increase in the ongoing pace of structural changes in employment and a failure of traditional labour market adjustment mechanisms to work sufficiently well to cope with the pace of structural change. The many studies that have measured the mismatch between the structure of unemployment and of job vacancies across sectors in major European countries conclude that structural imbalances in the labour market did not increase during the period of increasing unemployment. This raises the question of why a given job vacancy rate was associated with so much more unemployment in virtually all sectors in most European countries by the early 1980s.

Analyses of the relation between unemployment inflows and unemployment duration help one to understand the growth of European unemployment and the increasing unemployment differential between Europe and the North America. The amount of unemployment in an economy depends on the weekly flow of new unemployment and the average duration of a spell of unemployment. If 100 people per week become unemployed and remain unemployed an average of 10 weeks, on any given day 1,000 people will be unemployed. In another economy, if 10 people become unemployed and each is unemployed 100 weeks, unemployment will also be 1,000. In the first economy, a comparatively large percentage of the workforce experiences relatively brief durations of unemployment. In the second, very long spells of unemployment are concentrated on a comparatively small fraction of the workforce. The first economy is more descriptive of North America; the second is more descriptive of Europe.

Changes in the stock of unemployment observed at any job vacancy rate equal the difference between the inflows to unemployment (discussed above) and the outflows from unemployment. Outflows from unemployment occur when firms offer jobs to unemployed workers and those offers are accepted, or when unemployed workers end their job search and leave the workforce. Outflows control the duration of unemployment. Secular increases in European unemployment since the 1970s largely resulted from a decline in the outflows from unemployment. Once unemployed, the probability that a worker will leave unemployment declined substantially. A major consequence of this pattern is that European unemployment durations tend to be quite long, and European unemployment tends to be concentrated in a comparatively small fraction of the workforce. The persistence of unemployment in Europe has become a major policy problem.

In contrast, secular increases in North American unemployment largely reflect increases in the inflows to unemployment. (The pattern in Australia and Japan is closer to North America than to Europe.) There has been little change in the likelihood of leaving unemployment. As a result, spells of unemployment are comparatively short and distributed across a comparatively broad spectrum of the workforce. The differences in the resulting unemployment experience are dramatic. In 1990, about 5.6 per cent of the unemployed in North America had been without a job for over a year. Among major European countries, the proportion unemployed for over a year ranged from 36.1 per cent in the UK to 71.1 per cent in Italy (Organization for Economic Cooperation and Development 1993). (Experience in the Scandinavian countries is closer to North America.) Expressed differently, in a full-employment year, about 0.3 per cent of the workforce has been unemployed for over a year in the USA and Japan, while the comparable proportion ranges from ten to eighteen times greater in EC countries (Sorrentino 1995). Long duration unemployment tends to feed on itself, in the sense that long periods of joblessness produce depreciation of skills, discouragement and demoralization. Employers may also interpret long unemployment durations as signals of low ability, so that long unemployment spells effectively stigmatize workers.

The differences in the flow patterns guide the search for an explanation of higher European unemployment. Since the key difference is the increasing difficulty of leaving unemployment, explanations focus on the willingness of employers to hire the unemployed and the willingness of the unemployed to accept job offers. Declines in the willingness of employers to make job offers would be tied to increases in the costs of hiring labour, *ceteris paribus*. Some of these were noted above in the discussion of the economic effects of non-wage labour costs. Dismissal regulations may also produce a reluctance to hire. When employers know that it has become more difficult (costly) to dismiss workers, they will avoid hiring additional workers until they are sure that there will be a long-term demand for their services. Dismissal regulations thus feed back into hiring behaviour. The willingness of the unemployed to accept job offers will be influenced by the nature of the unemployed insurance system. Systems that provide benefits equal to a large fraction of a worker's normal wage or provide benefits for a long duration will discourage the acceptance of job offers.

Structure of unemployment

The structure of unemployment displays certain broad similarities across countries. Unemployment tends to be higher among younger workers, women, less-skilled workers, and racial minorities. In addition, virtually all countries have important regional differences in unemployment.

Many of these unemployment rate differentials reflect differences in the amount of labour turnover experienced by different demographic groups. Young workers move in and out of the workforce frequently and often seasonally because of school schedules. Each return to the workforce generally requires a new period of job search, so that unemployment among youth is higher than for workers with a full-time attachment to the workforce. Turnover is also high for young workers who have completed their schooling, as they change jobs until they find a suitable job environment. With low seniority, young workers are also subject to more frequent layoffs.

None the less, the relationship between youth and adult unemployment rates varies substantially across industrialized countries. The exception to the general rule is Germany, where the rates are essentially equal. Elsewhere the ratio of youth to adult unemployment rates varies from about 1:6 in the UK to 5:9 in Italy (Sorrentino 1995). This ratio can be reduced by labour-market institutions that facilitate the transition from school to work by providing school-leavers with vocational training (as in Germany) and information about labour market opportunities. Higher unemployment rates for women also reflect greater movement in and out of the workforce.

High turnover is often a symptom of low investment in human capital (see HUMAN CAPITAL). The earlier discussion of the economic effects of fixed costs of employment concluded that turnover and unemployment should be inversely related to the degree of investment in an employee. Young workers are often employed in unskilled jobs that have little specific training. Under historical child-rearing arrangements that resulted in intermittent workforce participation for many women, men may have received more specific training and been relatively insulated from unemployment. The role of fixed investments in workers also fits the occupational pattern of unemployment. Unemployment rates are lowest in occupations requiring substantial skill and education.

Regional differences in unemployment tend to be a consequence of regional patterns of industrial specialization. Changing spending patterns, technological change, and more open international markets can stimulate major changes in the structure of production. To the extent that declining and expanding industries are regionally concentrated, regional unemployment differentials emerge. These are a component of structural unemployment. Whether regional unemployment differentials persist depends crucially on the flexibility of the labour market. If wages fall in declining regional markets and rise in expanding markets, two adjustments will tend to eliminate regional unemployment differentials. First, workers may respond to both wage and unemployment differentials and move from declining to expanding regions. Second, industry may be attracted from the areas where labour is expensive and hard to recruit to areas where wages are lower and labour is plentiful. On the other hand, if relative wages remain rigid in the face of growing unemployment and/or the costs of mobility are high, regional unemployment differences may persist for long periods.

Unemployment policies

Broadly speaking, the problem of unemployment can be attacked by both macroeconomic and microeconomic policies. The former policies address deficient-demand unemployment; the latter address seasonal, frictional and structural unemployment. They are discussed below in turn.

The classic approach to reducing deficient-demand unemployment is to increase aggregate demand by fiscal policies or monetary policies. Increased government expenditure raises public spending, tax reductions raise private consumption spending, and policies to increase the money supply tend to lower interest rates and increase investment spending. The political process often delays formulation and implementation of macroeconomic policies, and there may be further lags in their economic effectiveness since consumers and firms usually do not respond immediately to a change in spending power or incentives. While policy makers may intend to eliminate deficient-demand unemployment by using monetary and fiscal policy to maintain unemployment at the NAIRU, in practice achieving this goal over long periods of time is difficult.

Deficient-demand unemployment might also be mitigated by greater wage flexibility. As discussed above, differences in the degree of wage flexibility associated with different collective bargaining structures are believed to influence the amount of unemployment experienced in response to a reduction in aggregate spending. The policy implications to be drawn from such findings are by no means clear, however. Bargaining arrangements tend to develop out of rather special historical circumstances, and often appear to reflect deeply rooted social commitments that are not easily transferred to other countries by policy action. Moreover, experience in Nordic countries indicates that centralized bargaining structures, which may produce greater wage flexibility and lower unemployment, can be difficult to maintain as the interests of different groups covered by a central bargain come into conflict.

Microeconomic policies to attack unemployment can seek to reduce either the inflow to or duration of seasonal, frictional and structural unemployment. If unemployment insurance were financed by employer contributions that depended on the extent to which employees from each firm received unemployment payments, for example, inflows to unemployment would be reduced. With experience-rated contributions, employers have an incentive to minimize their contributions by reducing layoffs – for example, by reducing the seasonality of their operations.

The amount of frictional unemployment in a country will also reflect the rules governing the collection of unemployment insurance benefits. The existence of such benefits reduces the costs of being unemployed and may prolong job search by the unemployed. This is most likely to occur when benefits replace a large fraction of a worker's normal earnings and when workers can collect benefits for a relatively long period of time. At the same time, longer spells of unemployment might result in higher post-unemployment wages and better job matches, which would reduce subsequent job turnover. Empirical studies of the effects of unemployment insurance systems find that more generous payments (relative to a worker's normal wage) are associated with longer durations of unemployment but not necessarily with higher wages. Thus, with lower unemployment insurance benefits and shorter periods of benefit availability, unemployment durations would be lower. But unemployment insurance policies also have distributional objectives; benefits are desired to support people who would have no hope of finding a job. There is a classic conflict between efficiency and equity objectives.

Structural unemployment may be reduced by the availability of public retraining programmes designed to provide the unemployed with skills for which job vacancies exist. Historically, Sweden has had the most extensive investments in training and retraining programmes, but there has been little evaluation of whether these investments have paid off. Many industrialized countries have emulated Swedish labour market policies, albeit at a much smaller scale. Evaluations in the USA and other countries indicate that the returns from such programmes are quite mixed. While there are some examples of successful programmes, this has by no means been the general case. Trained workers do not always experience better labour market outcomes than similar untrained workers.

Subsidies to encourage labour mobility are an approach to reducing structural unemployment associated with regional imbalances. (Industrial relocation policies, which are much less frequently tried, address the same issue from the demand side of the labour market.) These programmes are most likely to be successful with younger workers. Programmes to assist the relocation of older workers have generally failed to overcome resistance to leaving familiar communities and social relationships. These programmes now play a small role in labour market policies in most countries.

Wage subsidies reduce the cost of employing low-productivity workers and should reduce unemployment. Experience in the USA with wage subsidies that were targeted on specific disadvantaged groups has been disappointing, however. Employer participation in the programmes was very low even though the programmes appeared economically advantageous. In some cases it appeared that employers preferred to hire workers who would not qualify for a subsidy. One explanation for this behaviour is that employers assume that participation in public labour market programmes is a signal of low productivity and that the lower productivity exceeds the subsidies available through the programmes. Such stigmatization can be a serious barrier to the ability of such programmes to reduce unemployment.

Overall, post-war experience in industrialized countries suggests that labour market policies such as those discussed above have yet to achieve major reductions in unemployment.

ROBERT J. FLANAGAN
STANFORD UNIVERSITY

Further reading

(References cited in the text marked *)

* Abraham, K. and Houseman, S. (1993) *Job Security in America*, Washington, DC: The Brookings Institution. (A comparison of differences in the adjustment of employment and working hours to economic changes in Germany and the USA.)

* Bruno, M. and Sachs, J. (1985) *Economics of Worldwide Stagflation*, Cambridge, MA: Harvard University Press. (An influential study of the simultaneous development of unemployment and inflation in industrialized economies during the 1970s and early 1980s.)

* Calmfors, L. and Driffil, J. (1988) 'Bargaining structure, corporatism, and macroeconomic performance', *Economic Policy* 6: 14–61. (A pioneering effort to link collective bargaining structures with macroeconomic outcomes.)

Flanagan, R. (1987) 'Labor market behavior and European economic growth', in R.Z. Lawrence and C.L. Schultze (eds), *Barriers to European Growth: A Transatlantic View*, Washington, DC: The Brookings Institution. (A comparative analysis of unemployment experience in Europe and the USA.)

* Layard, R., Jackman, R. and Nickell, S. (1991) *Unemployment: Macroeconomic Performance and the Labour Market*, Oxford: Oxford University Press. (A major study of the determinants of the level and fluctuations in unemployment, including analyses of international unemployment differentials.)

Lindbeck, A. and Snower, D. (1988) *The Insider–Outsider Theory of Employment and Unemployment*, Cambridge, MA: MIT Press. (A theoretical study of how experienced employees gain market power and use it in ways that increase the unemployment of less experienced or jobless workers.)

* Organization for Economic Cooperation and Development (1993) *Employment Outlook*, Paris: OECD. (Presents employment and unemployment statistics for European countries.)

* Sorrentino, C. (1995) 'International unemployment indicators', *Monthly Labor Review* 56: 31–50. (An international comparison and dis-

cussion of seven different indicators of unemployment.)

See also: HUMAN RESOURCE MANAGEMENT; HUMAN RESOURCE MANAGEMENT, INTERNATIONAL

Related topics in the IEBM: BUSINESS CYCLES; ECONOMIC INTEGRATION, INTERNATIONAL; GENERAL AGREEMENT ON TARIFFS AND TRADE (GATT); INDUSTRIAL STRATEGY; INFLATION; INTERNATIONAL TRADE AND FOREIGN DIRECT INVESTMENT; NEO-CLASSICAL ECONOMICS; SUPPLY-SIDE ECONOMICS

Employment law

Overview

The law has become an increasingly important influence on employment practices. While employment has always had a legal basis in the contract between the individual worker and his or her employer, there is little legal regulation of what could and could not be part of this 'agreement' in many countries. By 1960, for example, a clear majority of the British labour force had their conditions of employment settled by collective bargaining between trade unions on the one hand and individual employers or employers' associations on the other. In Britain, this process has never been the subject of detailed legal regulation. But it does take place within an enabling legal framework which became increasingly restrictive in the 1980s and 1990s. At the same time the coverage of collective bargaining declined from over two thirds of the labour force to just under one third (see COLLECTIVE BARGAINING). By the late 1990s, however, legal regulation of employment at the level of the individual employer–worker relationship had become extensive as a result of legislation at both British and, after the UK joined the European Economic Community in 1973, European levels. Employment law remains an intricate patchwork of individual rights and obligations as between employer and worker surrounded by a complex and little understood framework for relations at the collective level, which in Britain is still largely confined to employer–trade union relations (for wider comparisons see CORPORATISM; INDUSTRIAL AND LABOUR RELATIONS; TRADE UNIONS).

1 Introduction

Employment or 'labour' law can be divided into two parts. 'Individual employment law' is concerned with the individual worker–employer relationship. In legal terms this is a 'contract', that is a legally binding agreement the terms of which are, in theory, determined by bargaining between the parties. In practice the superior economic bargaining power of employers would generally allow them to dictate these terms, but it is constrained by two factors. The first is the collective power of workers expressed largely through trade unions. 'Collective labour law' concerns the relationship of workers acting collectively – through trade unions or otherwise – employers and the State.

The second constraint is provided by the law. While the courts have always implied certain terms into the 'contract of employment', since the 1970s this has been overshadowed by the provision of rights for workers by legislation, at least in the UK. Part of the impetus for this development has come from the social policy of the European Community (EC). Some indication of the importance of the law is provided by the number of disputed claims processed by Industrial Tribunals (ITs) which adjudicate on most disputes over individual employment rights. In 1995–96 this was 73,472 and 1,358 cases were taken on appeal from ITs to the Employment Appeal Tribunal (EAT). Most litigation arising out of collective labour law issues takes place in the High Court with appeals from either the EAT or High Court decided by either the Court of Appeal or the highest appellate court, the House of Lords (see Pitt 1997) (see INDUSTRIAL AND LABOUR RELATIONS; TRADE UNIONS).

2 Collective labour law

Freedom of association

Convention No 87 of the International Labour Organisation, the United Nations' specialist agency for labour issues, provides that workers shall have the right to form and join trade unions and Convention No 98 extends this to give workers the right to protection against acts of anti-union discrimination by employers. The UK ratified both these Conventions by 1950, but there were no laws on this issue before the 1970s.

In outline, the legal protection for this, the 'positive' aspect of freedom of association, is currently as follows. It is unlawful for an employer to refuse to employ someone because of their union membership. It is also unlawful for an employer to take *action short of dismissal* against employees for the purpose of *preventing* or *deterring* them from being members of an independent trade union or taking part in union activities or *penalizing* them for doing so. Dismissal for any of these reasons is automatically unfair for the purpose of the law on unfair dismissal (see below) and gives rise to special compensation rights (see DISCIPLINE AND DISMISSALS). An independent trade union is one with a certificate of independence from the Certification Officer, a government official, which certifies that it is not under the domination or control of an employer or liable to interference tending towards such control.

Where employees are members of an independent union which is recognized by their employer for collective bargaining, they have the additional right to a reasonable amount of paid time off to take part in union activities. Lay officials of recognized independent unions – often called shop stewards – have the right to paid time off to carry out duties concerned with collective bargaining or other agreed functions.

Over the 1980s parallel rights were enacted for non-union members. They provide remedies for job seekers who are refused employment because they are not, or refuse to become, union members, employees who are subject to action short of dismissal to *compel* them to join a union and those who are dismissed because they are not union members when the special compensation provisions referred to above again apply (see COLLECTIVE BARGAINING; TRADE UNIONS).

Trade union government

The law provides a framework for the way trade unions are run centred on the contractual right of members to ensure that a union abides by its rules. Eligibility for membership has always depended on a union's rules and unions were able to discipline and expel members according to their rules. Since 1993, however, individuals in Britain have had a statutory right not to be excluded or expelled from a trade union except in specified circumstances which permit unions to confine their membership to particular types of worker, geographical areas, or those employed by particular employers, but otherwise severely limit their freedom to regulate their own membership. Moreover, in 1988 members were given highly controversial rights not to be 'unjustifiably disciplined', defined to include the disciplining of members for refusing to take part in industrial action even where that had been, as the law requires (see below) approved by a majority vote in a ballot.

Members' rights to ensure that unions act in accordance with their rules were supplemented in the 1980s by a mandatory requirement for all unions to hold elections for their principal executive committee, President and General Secretary by postal ballot of all the members at least once every five years. While unions have generally changed their practices to come into line with this legislation, the new laws have had little impact on the exercise of authority within trade unions (Undy *et al.* 1996) (see COLLECTIVE BARGAINING; INDUSTRIAL AND LABOUR RELATIONS; TRADE UNIONS).

Collective bargaining, consultation and information

In Britain, collective labour relations have traditionally focused on 'collective bargaining' – negotiations between employers and trade unions over terms and conditions of employment – which in Britain has never been a legally regulated process. The 'collective agreements' reached by unions and employers are not legally binding contracts unless the parties expressly so provide, which in practice almost never happens. The provisions of collective agreements may however become implied terms in the employment contracts of those workers for whom the unions are negotiating.

Where independent trade unions are recognized they have the right to seek disclosure of information for collective bargaining purposes in accordance with good industrial relations practice on which guidance is provided by a code of practice (ACAS 1978). Recognized independent unions also have the right to appoint safety representatives who have rights to be consulted over, and access to certain information relevant to, safety issues. In workplaces where there are no recognized unions, a parallel obligation to inform and consult either the workforce directly or elected 'representatives of employee safety' was introduced in 1996. Information and consultation rights are also provided where employers are proposing either redundancies or to transfer their undertaking to another person. Since 1995 they must inform and consult either 'employee representatives', who may be elected by employees specifically for the purpose, or, where there are recognized independent unions, union representatives.

The shift towards information and consultation rights independent of collective bargaining will be underlined once the UK becomes a signatory to the social protocol to the 1991 Maastricht Treaty, the so called 'social chapter' which extended the competence of the EC to legislate on social issues. The European Works Councils' Directive of 1994 will then have to be given effect as part of British law. It requires transnational undertakings with a workforce of over 1000 and at least 150 in each of two EC member states to establish European Works Councils, or other procedures for informing and consulting their workforce about matters relating to the undertaking. In practice almost all the arrangements made by transnational organizations up to 1996 included their British workforces within them even though the UK's 'opt out' from the social chapter was then in force (see Bercusson 1996). In 1996, the EC Commission proposed that all undertakings above an unspecified size should be required to establish Works Councils whether or not they operate on a transnational basis. By the end of the century the legal obligations on British employers to inform and consult workforce representatives may well be extensive (for further comaprisons see COLLECTIVE BARGAINING; INDUSTRIAL AND LABOUR RELATIONS; TRADE UNIONS).

Industrial disputes

Workers who take industrial action may lay themselves open to legal sanctions in a number of ways. If they join a picket line they may be at risk of prosecution for criminal offences such as obstruction of the highway. They may also be committing civil wrongs known as torts. The statutory right to picket peacefully might provide a defence against some of these liabilities, but since 1980 it has been confined to picketing by workers at their own place of work and it has always been very narrowly interpreted by the courts (see Lewis 1986).

Workers who take part in industrial action are breaking their employment contracts. This means that they are liable to dismissal without any notice and only in limited circumstances can the fairness of this be challenged under the law of unfair dismissal. In the 1980s the courts upheld employers' rights to make deductions from the pay of workers taking limited industrial action – for example by refusing to perform particular tasks – or even not to pay them at all so long as the employer made it clear that nothing short of normal working would be acceptable.

Where the law is invoked in industrial disputes it is normally directed at union(s) or individuals who called for or organized industrial action, rather than the workers taking part. From 1906 to 1980 as long as they acted 'in furtherance of a trade dispute' they were generally protected against liability in the law of tort. Legislation from 1980 to 1993 put limits on this immunity in a range of circumstances. Calling on the workforce of employers other than those party to disputes to take action was excluded. So too was organizing industrial action over union membership issues.

The most important of the changes to the law was the introduction of an obligation on trade unions to hold a ballot of those members to be called on to take action and secure majority support among those voting, in order to be able to claim the protection of the remaining immunities. While this does not apply to unofficial action, the circumstances when unions are legally responsible for action taken by their officials and members were extended in 1990 to include a lot of what would popularly be regarded as unofficial action. Unions can only escape liability for this through a complex repudiation process which leaves those members who continue to take part in the action exposed to dismissal with no possibility of any legal redress.

The legal requirements for a valid ballot are highly complex and expensive for unions. Since 1993 all ballots have had to be postal and the balloting process has to be integrated with various notices to the employer concerning the ballot and industrial action consequent on a majority 'yes' vote. While unions may be tripped up over the details, there is evidence that they can successfully negotiate these technicalities and thereby retain the ability to make a credible threat of industrial action, which is crucial to their bargaining power (see Elgar and Simpson 1996; Undy *et al.* 1996) (see INDUSTRIAL CONFLICT; TRADE UNIONS).

3 Individual employment law

The nature of the individual employment relationship

Most of the labour force work as 'employees' under a 'contract of employment'. An increasing minority, however, work under different arrangements which usually means that they are 'self-employed'. When they enter into an agreement to work for someone, this will normally be a 'contract for services'. Where there is a dispute over the status of a particular individual it has to be resolved ultimately by the courts applying criteria developed over time. The oldest of these focuses on the extent of 'control' exercised by the employer; the greater this is, the more likely it is that the relationship is a contract of employment. While control is still relevant, the courts now consider other factors as well. In the 1980s considerable prominence was given to the need for 'mutuality for obligation' – continuing obligations on the employer to provide work and the employee to be available to do it – before a relationship could be classified as a contract of employment.

The importance of this issue has increased with the growth of 'atypical' employment which does not conform to the pattern of regular full-time working under indefinite contracts. Homeworking may become more common as employers make increasing use of 'teleworkers' whose tasks can be performed at home through the use of information technology. Although homeworkers have not generally been treated as employees, case law has established that they may be able to claim employee status at least after continuously working for one employer over a reasonable period.

While there is no reason why temporary workers on fixed term contracts should not be regarded as employees, the legal status of temporary workers supplied through employment agencies remains unclear. A 1991 EC Directive seeks to ensure that all temporary workers have the same health and safety protection as the rest of the workforce. Casual workers will fail to qualify as employees if the 'mutuality of obligations' test is strictly applied. On the other hand the employee status of part-time workers and job sharers is not usually in doubt. In 1997 agreement was reached on a proposal for another EC Directive requiring part-time workers to have the same rights, *pro-rata*, as their full time equivalents.

Terms of employment

Except in so far as legislation otherwise requires, an employment contract can contain any terms which are expressly agreed by the parties. The courts have, however, developed a number of duties which are automatically implied into all contracts of employment. The employer is under an implied duty to pay the employee the agreed wage or salary and to take reasonable care for the employee's health and safety. The employee owes the employer implied duties not to commit misconduct and to obey lawful orders. The duty of fidelity prevents the employee from misusing confidential information which belongs to the employer. An important development in this area of the law recognized a duty on employees to adapt to new ways of working so that a refusal to change the way tasks were performed to one which involved working with computers was found to be a breach of contract by the employees concerned (*Cresswell* versus *Board of Inland Revenue* 1984). The courts have also recognized a mutual duty owed by both parties, variously described as a duty of trust and confidence or duty of cooperation. Since 1964 employers have been required to provide their employees with a written statement which provides particulars of certain basic terms of their employment – including pay, hours, holidays and sickness – as well as information about disciplinary rules, and disciplinary and grievance procedures.

The most important terms are those concerned with pay. All employees have the right to an itemized pay statement which sets out gross pay, deductions and net pay. Deductions from pay are unlawful unless authorized by statute – income tax and national insurance contributions for example – or provided for by a written term of the employment contract or a separate written agreement between the employer and worker made before the matter in respect of which the deduction occurred.

Since 1983, employers have been required to pay Statutory Sick Pay (SSP) to employees who are off work due to sickness or injury. In practice, most employers have their own sick pay schemes which provide more generous sick pay entitlement than SSP and cover most of the regular workforce. Since 1994, it has only been possible for employers to recoup the amounts paid – in 1997 £55.70 per week – from the State, to a limited extent in certain exceptional circumstances. Employers are also required to bear the full cost of making guarantee payments to employees who are laid off because there is no work for them to do. In industries where this is a common occurrence, guaranteed week agreements negotiated with trade unions which specify fall-back payments are the norm. The statutory obligation applies to all employees who have been employed for at least a month and is limited to a maximum five days' guarantee pay in any 13 week period with the daily payment subject to a maximum – in 1997 £14.50 – where this is greater than a normal day's pay. One of the most important statutory rights for employees in relation to pay is the right to recover certain arrears of pay, up to specified maximum amounts, from the State where their employer has become insolvent.

In Britain, there has been a tradition of only limited regulation of working time and in the 1980s much of this was repealed. It will however be necessary for a degree of re-regulation to be introduced into the law to comply with the 1994 EC Directive on working time. This provides for a maximum working week of 48 hours, a daily rest period of at least 11 hours plus a weekly rest period of at least an additional 24 hours and minimum annual holiday provision of four weeks. It should, however, be noted that the details of the Directive are complex and admit to a mixture of derogations through both individual and collective agreement (see Bercusson 1996).

While working time has traditionally been recognized as an appropriate issue for regulation by employers and workers themselves, in 1991 in a case concerning the hours of junior hospital doctors, the Court of Appeal recognized that if a contract of employment requires the employee to be available for work for a number of hours such that their health is put at risk, the employee may have a legal remedy (*Johnstone* versus *Bloomsbury Health Authority*) (see WORK AND LEISURE).

Parental rights, equal pay and discrimination

The maternity rights of working women are extensive but undesirably complex. All pregnant employees have the right to a reasonable amount of paid time off for ante-natal care. Those who satisfy the qualifying conditions – basically 26 weeks' employment and weekly pay above the 'lower earnings limit' (£61 in 1996–97) – are entitled to Statutory Maternity Pay (SMP). This is nine-tenths of a week's pay for the first six weeks absence from work followed by the prescribed lower SMP rate (£55.70 in 1997) for the following 12 weeks. Following implementation of the EC's Pregnant Workers Directive in 1994, all women workers are entitled to 14 weeks maternity leave, which must include the two weeks immediately after childbirth. Women with at least two years' employment are entitled to longer leave starting at any time from the eleventh week before the expected week of childbirth and continuing for up to 29 weeks after birth. Dismissal for any reason connected with pregnancy or childbirth is automatically unfair (see generally Palmer 1997).

An important extension of the law from maternity rights to parental rights will occur when measures are put in place to give effect to the Parental Leave Directive adopted by the EC under the so-called 'social chapter' (see above). This entitles both parents to up to three months' unpaid parental leave during the first eight years of a child's life.

As explained by the Equal Pay Directive of 1975 the EC equal pay principle requires men and women to receive equal pay not only where they do the same work but also where their work is of equal value. As amended in 1983, the British Equal Pay Act 1970 (EqPA) seeks to give effect to this principle by modifying the terms of employment of a woman to substitute any more favourable terms from the contract of a man in the same employment who is employed on 'like work' – work that is the same or broadly similar – 'work rated as equivalent' – in a valid job evaluation study – or 'work of equal value' – determined by an IT usually after receiving the report of an

independent expert. Exceptions are allowed only in respect of variations due to a 'genuine material factor other than sex'. In 1987, the House of Lords decided that this could cover any factor which was significant and relevant and that this extended to both economic and other objectively justified grounds such as administrative efficiency (*Rainey* versus *Greater Glasgow Health Board*). To avoid infringing EC law, however, the means chosen to achieve the stated goal must correspond to a real need on the employer's part and be appropriate and necessary to achieving it. Since a majority of part-time workers are women, less favourable conditions for part-time workers may have to meet these criteria to avoid infringing the law.

The EC Equal Treatment Directive of 1976 requires equal treatment of men and women in all aspects of employment (with appropriate exceptions for the special treatment of women in relation to maternity) outside those covered by the equal pay principle. In the *Marshall* case in 1986, the European Court of Justice (ECJ) held that this included retirement age. The British Sex Discrimination Act 1975 (SDA) makes it unlawful for an employer to discriminate in recruitment and by denying workers access to benefits or subjecting them to any detriment (including dismissal) on the grounds of sex or marital status. The definition of discrimination is in two parts. 'Direct' discrimination covers less favourable treatment on the ground of sex. 'Indirect' discrimination occurs where ostensibly neutral 'conditions' or 'requirements' have an adverse impact on women (or men) in that a smaller proportion of women than men (or vice versa) can meet them. Where this is to a particular worker's detriment, it is unlawful unless the employer can 'justify' it. To be consistent with EC law, justification must relate to sex-neutral objectives and the conditions or requirements imposed must be appropriate and necessary to fulfilling them.

The Race Relations Act 1976 (RRA) is identical in scope to the SDA save that it extends to contractual as well as non-contractual employment issues. It covers direct discrimination on racial grounds – colour, race, nationality, or ethnic or national origins – and indirect discrimination against racial groups defined by reference to one of these characteristics. The Disability Discrimination Act 1995 (DDA) has a more restricted scope. Subject to an exception for 'small' employers of less than 20 workers, it makes it unlawful for employers to discriminate against disabled persons in recruitment, terms of employment and access to benefits, or by subjecting them to detriments. The definition of discrimination is, however, much narrower being limited to less favourable treatment which the employer cannot justify. But it is accompanied by a duty on employers to make adjustments to working arrangements which place disabled people at a substantial disadvantage. The compensation awarded under the SDA, RRA or DDA is not subject to any upper limit (see EQUAL EMPLOYMENT OPPORTUNITIES).

Termination of employment

Employees' legal rights are of particular importance when their employment has come to an end. Pursuing legal entitlements against an employer does not then run the risk of adversely affecting a subsisting employment relationship. Dismissed employees who have been employed for at least two years have the right to ask for a written statement of the reasons for their dismissal; the penalty for an unreasonable refusal to provide this is an automatic award of two weeks' pay. The oldest right in relation to termination of employment is the right to be given due notice – or pay in lieu. Legislation has laid down minimum notice periods. After one month's employment, at least one week's notice must be given by either party. Thereafter the minimum notice which the employer must give is one week for each year of employment up to a maximum of twelve. Summary dismissal without notice is only justified if the employee has committed a serious breach of contract.

The main remedy for wrongful dismissal is monetary compensation called 'damages'. In the majority of cases this is limited to the net pay that the employee would have earned during the period of notice which should have been given. In all cases it is subject to the employee's 'duty to mitigate' their loss, basically by looking for other comparable employment. The courts will not normally make any order which requires the continued employment of someone against the employer's wishes. There have nevertheless been a small number of cases where injunctions have been issued which prevent an employer from giving effect to a wrongful dismissal at least until certain procedures which were part of the employee's contractual rights, were exhausted (see Ewing 1993).

The limited nature of the remedies for wrongful dismissal was one reason for the introduction in 1971 of a separate right for dismissed employees to make a complaint of 'unfair dismissal' to an IT. This right is confined to those employees who have been employed for at least two years save in specified exceptional cases where dismissal is stated to be always unfair, these include dismissals for the reasons related to union membership and pregnancy referred to above, when there is no qualifying period of employment before a complaint can be made. 'Dismissal' includes circumstances where an employee leaves the job without being formally dismissed, but is legally entitled to do so because the employer has committed a serious breach of the contract of employment, for example of the implied duty of trust and confidence (see above); termination of employment in these circumstances is known as 'constructive dismissal'.

Except in the specified cases where dismissal is always unfair, the fairness of a dismissal is determined by reference to whether the employer acted reasonably in all the circumstances in treating the given reason as sufficient to justify dismissal. What the law of unfair dismissal requires of employers which the common law on wrongful dismissal does not, is that they follow a fair procedure in reaching a decision to dismiss. Some guidance on procedural fairness is provided by an ACAS code of practice (ACAS 1977). In an important decision the House of Lords in the UK ruled that it will not normally be open to ITs to find that a dismissal was fair on the grounds that although the employer failed to follow a fair procedure, it would not have made any difference had this been done (*Polkey* versus *Dayton Services* 1987).

Although the primary remedy for unfair dismissal is stated to be an order for reinstatement or re-engagement, in practice only 1 or 2 per cent of successful claims result in such an order. The main remedy is therefore compensation which in most cases is a two part award. The 'basic award' is calculated in the same way as a redundancy payment (see below). The compensatory award is for proved financial losses, of which past and future loss of earnings and loss of valuable rights such as pension rights are the main components. It is subject to an upper limit which in 1997 was £11,300.

Where the reason for dismissal is redundancy, which is defined in terms of a reduction in demand for work of a particular kind, employees with over two years' continuous employment have the right to a 'redundancy payment'. This sum is calculated by reference to a fixed formula: one and a half week's pay for each year of service over the age of 41, a week's pay for years between 22 and 41 and half a week's pay for years between the ages of 18 and 21. A week's pay is subject to a maximum which in 1997 was £210. The right is lost where a redundant employee unreasonably refuses the employer's offer of suitable alternative employment.

An important addition to the rights of employees was made by the Transfer of Undertakings (Protection of Employment) Regulations 1981 which were intended to give effect to the EC's Acquired Rights Directive of 1977. This Act provides that on the transfer of an undertaking from one employer to another, the contracts of employment of the workforce are automatically transferred as well. As amended in 1993, the right of an employee to refuse to transfer is recognized, but in this event the termination of employment is deemed not to be a dismissal. To reinforce the policy of protecting the employment rights of the workforce where the ownership of an undertaking is transferred, the dismissal of an employee for any reason connected with the transfer is made automatically unfair unless the reason is an economic, technical or organizational reason affecting the size of the workforce. In this event, the fairness of any dismissal has to be determined by ITs in

accordance with the normal criteria applied under the law on unfair dismissal (see McMullen 1997) (see DISCIPLINE AND DISMISSALS).

4 Conclusions

The last four decades of the twentieth century have seen a progressive increase in the importance of the law as an influence on employment relations. As the coverage of collective bargaining has declined since 1980 the potential value of employment rights for individual workers has increased. The need for social or employment rights to accompany moves towards greater integration of the economies of member states has been a notable feature of EC developments in the 1980s and 1990s. While this may underwrite the existence of some collective institutions for the process of social dialogue at EC, national, enterprise and maybe establishment levels, its main impact is likely to continue to be by way of underpinning individual employment relations with a floor of legal rights. For individual employers of whatever size, however, the extent to which they have direct experience of the enforcement mechanisms of the law in respect of either individual or collective issues will continue to depend mainly on the acceptability and effectiveness of their own autonomous structures for employment relations. While the law may be an influence on these, their successful operation necessarily depends on a wide range of other, non-legal issues.

BOB SIMPSON
LONDON SCHOOL OF ECONOMICS AND
POLITICAL SCIENCE

Further reading

(References cited in the text marked *)

* Advisory Conciliation and Arbitration Service (ACAS) (1977) *Disciplinary Practice and Procedures in Employment*. Code of practice 1, London: ACAS. (Provides guidance relevant to the law on unfair dismissal.)
* Advisory Conciliation and Arbitration Service (ACAS) (1978) *Disclosure of Information to Trade Unions for Collective Bargaining Purposes*. Code of practice 2, London: ACAS.

(Provides guidance on compliance with the law.)

* Bercusson, B. (1996) *European Labour Law*. London: Butterworths. (A text on EC labour law which explains its implications for the UK.)

Deakin, S. and Morris, G.S. (1995) *Labour Law*. London: Butterworths. (Comprehensive, authoritative text on employment law.)

* Elgar, J. and Simpson, R. (1996) *Industrial Action Ballots and the Law*. London: Institute of Employment Rights. (Reports on research into trade unions' experience of the law on industrial action ballots.)

* Ewing, K.D. (1993) 'Remedies for breach of the contract of employment', *Cambridge Law Journal* 52 (3): 405–36. (Analysis of the development of the law on this issue.)

* Lewis, R. (ed.) (1986) *Labour Law in Britain*. Oxford: Blackwell. (A collection of contributions on most aspects of labour law, valuable for their critical perspective.)

* McMullen, J. (1997) *Business Transfers and Employment Rights*, 3rd edn, London: Butterworths. (A full analysis of the developing law in this area.)

* Palmer, C. (1997) *Maternity Rights*. London: Legal Action Group. (A comprehensive, accessible account of the law.)

* Pitt, G. (1977) *Employment Law* 3rd edn. Andover: Sweet & Maxwell. (A readable introductory text.)

* Undy, R., Fosh, P., Morris, H., Smith, P. and Martin, R. (1996) *Managing the Unions: The Impact of Legislation on Trade Unions' Behaviour*. Oxford: Clarendon. (An analysis of evidence from research into the effect of legislation in the 1980s and 1990s on trade unions.)

See also: COLLECTIVE BARGAINING; CORPORATISM; DISCIPLINE AND DISMISSALS; EQUAL EMPLOYMENT OPPORTUNITIES; INDUSTRIAL AND LABOUR RELATIONS; INDUSTRIAL CONFLICT; TRADE UNIONS; WORK AND LEISURE

Related topics in the IEBM: TELEWORKING

Equal employment opportunities

Overview

The provision of equal employment opportunities is regarded in many countries as a desirable situation in the labour market and in work organizations. International conventions and recommendations establish standards for equal employment opportunities and have encouraged the enactment of legislation and the implementation of policies which seek to remove discrimination in employment. Affirmative action is one of the means used to create equal employment opportunities. It has consequences for the formulation and implementation of all human resource management policies.

1   Concept of equal employment opportunities

Equal employment opportunities refers to a desirable situation in the labour market and work organizations. It refers to a situation in which access to employment opportunities and rewards is based on individual merit and ability rather than a personal characteristic which is not job-related. Equal employment opportunities is an international standard established by International Labour Organization (ILO) Conventions and countries which ratify the Conventions are obliged to take action to apply the principles embodied in the conventions.

The concept of equal employment opportunities can be interpreted in a number of ways. First, it can refer to a situation when employment decisions are made on the basis of individuals' performance and qualifications. This interpretation ignores the processes involved in the acquisitions of these qualifications and performance skills. It fails to acknowledge that some individuals are unable to develop their skills because of social disadvantage and as a result are disadvantaged at the start, and during the 'employment race'.

A second interpretation of equal employment opportunity is that it involves the implementation of policies which attempt to redress the effect of past disadvantage. This facilitates the development of an individual's skills and qualifications which had previously been unable to develop.

The third way of looking at equal employment opportunities is even broader. It refers to a situation in which policies seek to redress not only the effects of social disadvantage, but also of an individual's natural disabilities. The distinction between these two forms of equal employment opportunity is not clear cut as natural disabilities can really be disguised forms of social disadvantage. For example, physical disability is more common in some occupations than others and access to these occupations is closely related to class position.

The concept of equal employment opportunity is one which requires an understanding of the distinction between the notions of *equality of outcome* and *equality of opportunity*. The issue of equality of outcome is based on the desire to have proportional representation of individuals from different groups in employment or educational categories identified as desirable by the dominant social group. Equality of outcome in the labour market would result in the breaking down of sexual segregation in the labour market. Consequently, men and women would be more widely dispersed across occupations and industries and have greater conformity of working hours and rewards. However, such an approach does not acknowledge that existing practices embodied in work and occupational structures need to be re-evaluated. For example, one of the reasons for the persistent differences in male and female wage rates is that work in occupations in which women are concentrated is valued less highly than the work in occupations traditionally carried out by men (see PAYMENT SYSTEMS).

Equality of opportunity, that is equal access to employment benefits through individual ability and capacity has been argued for on two grounds. First, on the grounds of social justice and the rights of individuals; second, on utilitarian grounds associated with claims that it fosters the efficient operation of organizations and the labour market (Poiner and Wills 1991: 4). Social justice is not an absolute concept; because of its association with social values and social structures it changes with developments in society. The rights associated with social justice are sometimes enshrined in ILO Conventions, laws and moral codes.

Equal employment opportunity is claimed to improve the operation of organizations and the labour market through the promotion of greater efficiency. It is argued that efficiency is enhanced by removing discrimination from employment decisions. As a result of equal employment opportunity policies which are non-discriminatory, the 'best' person for a job is selected or promoted, and organizational productivity improved.

Equality of opportunity and equality of outcome are not mutually exclusive. It is possible that policies designed to create equality of employment opportunity will result in equality of labour market outcomes such as the redistribution of men and women between occupations and positions of power in organizations.

2 Economic dimensions

Labour market outcomes, particularly the structure of employment and the relative earnings of men and women, indicate that there is a need to create equal employment opportunities. In most countries, men and women have different employment experiences, with women being concentrated in a narrower range of occupations and industries than men. In addition, women work fewer hours than men and they tend to earn less than men. Most part-time employees are women and, in part a reflection of this, women earn only about two-thirds of male earnings. Similarly, in the UK women represent 87 per cent of the part-time workforce (*European Industrial Relations Review* 1995). The position of women in the labour market and their access to employment opportunities was the subject of concern of the United Nations' Fourth World Conference on Women in Beijing in 1995 (Ledwith and Colgan 1996: 4).

A variety of explanations for these differences in labour market outcomes for men and women have been given. Economists provide a number of reasons. These include the fact that men and women possess different amounts of human capital, such as different educational qualifications, years of employment and differing amounts of training. Another explanation proposed by institutional labour market economists is that employees are concentrated in different sectors of the labour market as a result of employer perceptions of the relative employment stability of men and women. The concentration of women in part-time, 'female' occupations is explained in terms of employer policies which discriminate against women. This discrimination occurs because women are believed to display unstable employment behaviour and to therefore be unsuitable for jobs associated with career paths, promotion opportunities and investment in training. A third explanation involves the influence of social relationships and institutions on the choices women and employers make about employment.

Policies have been developed to deal with these causes of the different labour market experience of men and women. Labour market and education policies which seek to increase the educational qualifications of women and the selection of technical and scientific courses by women attempt to remove labour market disadvantage resulting from differential human capital. Policies and legislation which prohibit discriminatory employment practices attempt to deal with employer policies and behaviour which limit women's access to training, employment vacancies and employment rewards. Finally, policies which support the funding of childcare arrangements and flexibility in working hours can attempt to deal with the social and institutional arrangements influencing the employment of women.

3 International Labour Organization Conventions

The ILO and the United Nations have developed a series of Conventions and Recommendations which cover a broad range of matters in the area of labour. A number of these deal with issues associated with the removal of discrimination from employment and the creation of equal employment opportunities.

The most significant Conventions and Recommendations include Convention (no. 111) and Recommendation (no. 111) on Discrimination (Employment and Occupation), Convention (no. 100) and Recommendation (no. 90) on Equal Remuneration, Convention (no. 156) and Recommendation (no. 165) on Workers with Family Responsibilities and Convention (no. 142) and Recommendation (no. 150) on Human Resources Development. The Convention on Discrimination (Employment and Occupation) provides comprehensive standards for the removal of discrimination on the grounds of race, gender, religion, colour, political opinion, and national extraction or social origin, and since its adoption in 1958 has had a significant influence on the promotion of equal employment opportunities. Many member countries have implemented a variety of practical measures and enacted legislation designed to eliminate discrimination (see HUMAN RESOURCE

DEVELOPMENT; HUMAN RESOURCE MANAGEMENT).

In 1981 Convention (no. 156) and Recommendation (no. 165) on Workers with Family Responsibilities was adopted by the ILO as a recognition that the creation of full equality between men and women required changes in the traditional roles of men and women. These instruments recognize that workers with family responsibilities can be disadvantaged by existing employment arrangements. They provide that men and women workers must be able to exercise their right to obtain or engage in employment without being subject to discrimination because of family responsibilities. The Convention is broad, requiring ratifying nations to take account of the particular needs of these workers in a number of areas such as by promoting childcare and family-care services and acknowledging their needs in employment, social security arrangements, vocational guidance and training. It also requires ratifying members to foster public understanding of the principle of equal opportunity for men and women and the problems of workers with family responsibilities (ILO 1987: 28–30).

4 Discrimination

Discrimination takes a variety of forms. It can be the result of intentional or unintentional behaviour or policies. Three forms of discrimination which disadvantage individuals have been identified: direct; indirect or structural; and systemic.

Direct discrimination refers to decisions which exclude an individual from an employment benefit because they are treated differently as the result of a personal characteristic which is not job-related. The decision not to appoint a woman to a job usually carried out by a man, such as a carpenter's job, is an example of direct discrimination.

Indirect or structural discrimination is more complex and not as easy to understand. It refers to employment decisions which appear neutral because individuals are treated the same but which are discriminatory because the treatment has an unjustified, adverse effect on individuals from certain groups. An example of indirect discrimination is the requirement of a minimum height for certain jobs when height is not an essential prerequisite for the performance of the job. This policy indirectly discriminates against women and some nationalities because a substantially higher proportion of men than women, and certain nationalities, will satisfy the requirement.

The doctrine of indirect discrimination was introduced into North American law by the US Supreme Court in *Griggs* v. *Duke Power Co.* In the USA indirect discrimination is known as disparate or adverse impact. The *Griggs* v. *Duke Power Co.* case involved the use of aptitude tests and educational achievements as qualifications for jobs in situations where Black individuals performed much less well than White individuals. Although the employer was not responsible for the individuals' under-performance, the employer's liability arose because the educational requirement operated in fact to exclude large numbers of Black individuals when the requirement was not necessary for job performance.

The Sex Discrimination Act 1975 and 1986 and the Race Relations Act 1976 move the concept of indirect discrimination into English law. These prohibit both direct and indirect discrimination on the grounds of gender, marriage and race in a number of areas, including employment. The Equal Opportunities Commission (EOC) has among its powers the ability to enforce legislation through investigations of claims of discrimination and to issue non-discrimination notices which are enforceable through the courts. Similarly, proposed amendments to the Equal Opportunities Act 1986 in Finland prohibit direct and indirect discrimination on the grounds of gender.

Systemic discrimination is a very subtle but pervasive form of discrimination. It is embodied in the values underlying human resource management practices, organizational culture and the value systems of the coalitions in organizations with power. Systemic discrimination reflects the structural arrangements in society which inhibit or encourage particular employment behaviours of individuals with different personal characteristics.

The grounds for discrimination are wide ranging. These include gender, marriage, family responsibilities, pregnancy, race, colour, religion, national origin, sexual preference, age, and physical and mental handicap. Different countries have adopted different grounds for discrimination and even within countries the grounds for discrimination vary between states and federal laws. In the European Union the Council, Commission and Parliament have issued a joint declaration condemning discrimination on a number of grounds including racial.

A further form of discrimination is *positive discrimination* or *reverse discrimination*. This refers to action which improves the employment prospects of members of groups which have been identified as facing discrimination and are regarded as disadvantaged. Positive action can take a number of forms including the adoption of criteria which a higher proportion of the members of the disadvantaged group than the general population satisfy; the implementation of measures to enable members of the disadvantaged group to compete more favourably in the labour market; and the preferential treatment of some members of the disadvantaged group.

5 Affirmative action

Affirmative action refers to policies and other measures, such as legislation, taken to achieve equal employment opportunities. There are a range of approaches to affirmative action. Jewson and Mason (1986) identify two extremes of a continuum along which these affirmative action measures can be considered. At one extreme there are measures which can be regarded as constituting a liberal approach, while at the other extreme are measures which can be regarded as radical. The liberal approach is primarily concerned with establishing formal procedures enhancing individuals' access to jobs and rewards, while the radical approach promotes the use of policies which discriminate in favour of individuals from disadvantaged groups in order to overcome the effect of past discrimination.

The earliest attempts to promote affirmative action measures were undertaken in the USA during the 1960s and 1970s. Policy was mandated through federal and state measures. Federal measures involved Executive Orders 11246, 11141, 11625 and 12138 and legislation such as Title VII of the Civil Rights Act of 1964 which outlaws employment discrimination on the basis of gender, race, colour, religion or national origin in any employment policy including hiring, firing, promotion, transfer, provision of training and compensation. Title VII extends to all employees of government and educational institutions as well as private employers with more than fifteen employees. It also bans discrimination because of pregnancy, childbirth, or related conditions and sexual harassment. Additional legislation providing affirmative action in the USA includes the Equal Pay Act 1963, the Age Discrimination in Employment Act of 1967, the Equal Employment Opportunity Act of 1972 and the Rehabilitation Act of 1973 and the Vietnam Era Veterans Rehabilitation Act of 1974. In addition, there is a variety of legislation which covers state and local government.

A number of organizations are involved in the administration and enforcement of affirmative action laws. In the USA The Civil Rights Act 1964 established the Equal Employment Opportunity Commission (EEOC) which oversees Title VII enforcement. Since 1972 the EEOC has had the power of litigation which it can pass on to individual plaintiffs. It has the authority to investigate and reconcile charges of discrimination against employers, employment agencies and unions. However, in cases involving state or local government agencies or political subdivisions the Department of Justice enforces Title VII. Part of the Department of Labor, the Federal Contract Compliance Programs, is responsible for administration of Executive Order 11246.

Executive Order 11246 requires all organizations with fifty or more employees and/or parties to federal contracts exceeding $50,000 per year to develop written affirmative action plans and to take steps to eliminate discrimination from employment policies, including hiring, firing, layoff, recall, promotion and compensation. Affirmative action plans are required to include an analysis of the employment of women, establishment of goals and timetables, the development of policies and a display of good faith to achieve these goals.

A variety of sanctions for not implementing affirmative action exist in the USA. These include withdrawal of federal funds and/or federal contracts, long and costly fights in the courts and the possibility that a case could result in the payment of large settlements. Two well-known examples of these settlements are the American Telephone and Telegraph (AT&T) case in which $US 15 million was paid in back pay to 13,000 female employees as compensation for past discrimination and the long drawn out Harris Trust and Savings Bank case in which $US 14 million was paid to about 5,000 women and minorities who were employed but not promoted between 1974 and 1986.

In Australia the US affirmative action model has been adopted. Federal and state laws seek to promote equal employment opportunities by preventing discriminatory behaviour and by requiring private sector organizations and trade unions with 100 or more employees and public sector and tertiary education organizations to develop affirmative action programmes. Although the details of the programmes can be determined by the employer, the federal legislation provides a framework of eight steps for the development of the programmes. The Affirmative Action (Equal Employment for Women) Act 1986 requires employers to undertake these eight steps in their affirmative action programme and to report to a government body, the Affirmative Action Agency on their progress in developing them. These steps are:

1 the issuing of a statement by senior management that the development and implementation of affirmative action programmes has commenced;
2 conferring responsibility for the development and implementation of the programme on a senior manager or managers;

3 consulting each trade union with members affected by the programme;

4 consulting employees, particularly women;

5 collecting and recording information and statistics on the employment of men and women within the organization, including the number of employees of either sex and types of jobs undertaken by, or job classifications of, employees of either sex;

6 reviewing all employment policies to identify any policies that discriminate against women and patterns which indicate lack of equal employment opportunity;

7 setting objectives and forward estimates in the programme;

8 monitoring and evaluating the implementation of the progress.

Almost all organizations covered by the legislation comply with the law, with formal compliance amounting to almost 99 per cent of organizations covered by the Affirmative Action (Equal Employment Opportunity for Women) Act. The sanctions for not complying with the affirmative action legislation are limited, including being named in Parliament and not securing government contracts.

In Japan legislation has been enacted in an attempt to remove discrimination from employment practices. The enactment of the Japanese Equal Employment Opportunity Law of 1985, effective in April 1986, represents a liberal approach to affirmative action. This law prohibits discrimination on the grounds of gender with respect to recruitment, hiring, promotion, training, fringe benefits, retirement and job assignment. It provides guidance to employers about how to develop policies which do not discriminate. Its enforcement is however moot. Meanwhile, in Finland proposed amendments to legislation will require employers with thirty or more employees to provide measures to hasten equality in the workplace. These measures will be reflected in annual personnel and training plans or in annual occupational health and safety plans.

6 Equal employment opportunities and human resource management policies

The requirement to create equal employment opportunities and remove discrimination has implications for the development of human resource management policies (see HUMAN RESOURCE MANAGEMENT). These implications are clearly illustrated in the requirements for non-discriminatory selection policies. In order to be non-discriminatory, selection policies for hiring, promotion and training need to satisfy at least four criteria:

1 they must be unbiased regarding personal characteristics such as gender and race;

2 employment policy and practice must ensure individuals satisfy criteria which are job-related;

3 the selection process must be clearly understood and documented; and

4 selectors must be able to implement effectively the selection policies.

There are a number of ways non-discriminatory selection can be enhanced. These include changing stereotypical attitudes of selectors towards women, men and minority groups so that each individual is assessed in terms of the extent to which they satisfy stated job requirements; ensuring there is a pool of suitably qualified candidates with different personal characteristics available for selection; ensuring managers perceive it as their line responsibility to make non-discriminatory selection decisions; and ensuring thorough documentation of the stages of the selection procedures by providing written job descriptions, person specifications and reports of the selection process which include reasons for the particular selection decision.

The requirement for non-discriminatory selection has implications for a variety of human resource management policies. For example, non-discriminatory recruitment which seeks to ensure a pool of well-qualified candidates with a variety of personal characteristics could entail advertising vacancies in magazines which target particular markets such as women or particular minority groups. Similarly, there are major implications for training policies, including the provision of training for women and minority groups so that they can compete for other positions and the training of selectors so they are aware of the way they construct stereotypes of members of different groups. There are even implications for the job structures and job descriptions. Assumptions about the working hours associated with a particular job, for instance whether it is part-time or full-time, should be reviewed to enable individuals from a variety of different groups to apply for the job (see JOB EVALUATION).

A variety of factors have been identified as encouraging the implementation of programmes which seek to create equal employment opportunities. Schaeffer and Lynton (1979) found in a survey of senior personnel executives in large US corporations that the three most important factors contributing to the overall success of efforts to create equal employment opportunities in the USA were the awareness of federal laws and regulations; commitment on the part of the chief executive officer; and the establishment of goals and timetables for action. The finding of the importance of awareness of federal laws and regulations seems justified given that most employers in the United States only started to remove discrimination from employment policies after they were aware of the federal laws. This awareness followed the Supreme Court's endorsement of disparate impact discrimination in 1971, the requirement for government contractors to file written affirmative action plans in 1971 and the consent agreement signed by AT&T in 1973.

Similar findings were made in a study by Johns and Moser (1989) which found equal employment opportunities legislation in the USA was a major stimulus for the formulation of human resource management policies seeking to promote equal employment opportunities. Policies generally developed or changed included the provision of training in equal employment opportunity to supervisors and managers and to new employees, the formulation of a company policy on discrimination and the dissemination of equal employment opportunities news to employees through company bulletin boards and publications. Thus, legislation is an important stimulus for the development of policies seeking to create equal employment opportunities.

7 Resistance to the creation of equal employment opportunities

The development of equal employment opportunities is a process of organizational change which involves the potential for a redistribution of a variety of benefits and rewards between individuals within the workplace. In addition it challenges many individuals' beliefs and values. Consequently, attempts to implement policies which create equal employment opportunities are often resisted by managers and employees.

This resistance can take a number of forms. The most basic form of resistance is disbelief in the need for change either because the human resource management policies are not thought to discriminate or because the parties are satisfied with the existing arrangements. Disbelief is sometimes the result of ignorance about the nature of discrimination.

Other forms of resistance involve attempts to undermine support for the creation of equal employment opportunities. These include misrepresentation of the nature of affirmative action; active and passive obstructionism which prevents the implementation of affirmative action measures; and the generation of fear about the consequences of affirmative action and apparent compliance with the formal requirements, such as appointing a manager with responsibilities for equal employment opportunities but circumventing the spirit of the requirement by giving the manager responsibilities for a number of other matters such as retirement benefits and training.

There are a number of reasons employees, policy makers and managers resist equal employment opportunity measures. A major reason is the desire of those who benefit from existing employment arrangements to maintain these in order to protect their position. A further reason involves apathy resulting from individuals distancing themselves from the issue. This distancing can arise either because equal employment opportunities are not regarded as legitimate or serious or, alternatively, because they are not perceived as having any application at the personal level.

Thus, the effective implementation of measures designed to create equal employment opportunities requires the identification of possible forms and sources of resistance within an organization.

8 Managing diversity

One of the expected outcomes of a situation of equal employment opportunities is that the organization would have a pluralist workforce. In a pluralist workforce employees would come from a variety of backgrounds and ideally would be represented at all levels of the organization. The concept of managing a pluralist workforce has been labelled 'managing diversity' and refers to a way of managing which recognizes that competitive advantage can be developed by explicitly acknowledging and using the mix of talent, values and points of view in the workforce (Shipper and Shipper 1987).

A management approach which seeks to manage effectively a pluralist workforce adopts a broad approach to equal employment opportunities. In such a situation of equal employment opportunities each individual is explicitly recognized as being different and having different needs at different times of their working life. Difference, however, is not used as a reason to disadvantage or unlawfully discriminate against individuals. Instead, it is used as the basis for policies to improve the productivity of employees.

Managing diversity differs from affirmative action because it focuses on the need to change the culture and employment systems in an organization in such a way that employee performance is enhanced. It is a comprehensive management process used to develop an environment which works for all employees. Consequently, different employees will need different policies to improve their performance. Such an approach to equal employment opportunities requires long-term commitment by all managers, mutual

adaptation by the organization and the individual and revised definitions of leadership and management.

It is expected that managing diversity will become a more prominent management issue in the future, particularly in organizations and countries where the composition of the workforce is diverse. Increasing international competition and the emphasis on improving productivity, the anticipated increase in the representation of women and a variety of ethnic groups in the workforce, the expected shortage of 'skilled' labour and the growing desire for individuals to acknowledge their special characteristics is expected to encourage a change in the way equal employment opportunities are sought in some organizations.

ROBIN J. KRAMAR
MACQUARIE UNIVERSITY

Further reading

(References cited in the text marked *)

Adler, N.J. and Izraeli D.N. (eds) (1994) *Competitive Frontiers: Women Managers in a Global Economy*, London: Blackwell. (Examines the changing role of women managers in twenty-one countries across Asia, Africa, Europe and North America.)

Australian Bureau of Statistics (1993) *Women in Australia*, Canberra: Australian Bureau of Statistics. (A comprehensive collection of statistics on women in Australia. Simple and easy to read. Useful source on Australian employment data.)

Burton, C. (1991) *The Promise and the Price: The Struggle for Equal Opportunity in Women's Employment*, Sydney: Allen & Unwin. (A collection of eleven readings about the structural inequalities in organizations which prevent the creation of equal employment opportunities.)

Dex, S. and Shaw, L. (1986) *British and American Women at Work: Do Equal Opportunity Policies Matter?*, London: Macmillan. (An examination of women in paid employment in the UK and the USA.)

Dickens, L. (1994) 'The business case for women's equality: is the carrot better than the stick?' *Employee Relations*, 16 (8): 5–18. (Examines the continuing need for initiatives to promote women's equality in the UK and assesses the business case for equal employment.)

* *European Industrial Relations Review* (1995) 252 (January). (A monthly publication examining developments in European labour markets and legislation. This issue includes an article on legal provisions protecting disabled people in seventeen European countries.)

* ILO (1987) *Equal Opportunities: Trends and Perspectives. Women at Work*, no. 2, Geneva: ILO. (This book describes the development in policies to promote equal opportunity in the ILO and member states. Useful source of statistics and easy to read.)

* Jewson, N. and Mason, D. (1986) 'The theory and practice of equal opportunities policies: liberal and radical approaches', *Sociological Review* 34 (2): 43–63. (An analysis of different ways of conceptualizing equal employment opportunity and the implication of this for the types of policies used.)

* Johns, H.E. and Moser, H.R. (1989) 'Where has EEO taken personnel policies?', *Personnel* September: 63–6. (A short, easy to read report of a research study in Tennessee which discusses the way equal employment opportunity legislation has influenced a number of personnel policies.)

Kanter, R.M. (1977) *Men and Women of the Corporation*, New York: Basic Books. (A thorough analysis of the dynamics of the way structures and behaviour within one organization shape and restrict the opportunities for women. Excellent references.)

* Ledwith, S. and Colgan, F. (eds.) (1996) *Women in Organizations: Challenging Gender Politics*. London: Macmillan. (A collection of ten chapters on the role of women in the process of change in organizations. Includes eight research based case studies.)

McCrudden, C. (1986) 'Rethinking positive action', *Industrial Law Journal* 15 (219): 230–42. (An analysis of the nature of positive action to create equal employment opportunities.)

* Poiner, G. and Wills, S. (1991) *The Gifthorse: A Critical Look at Equal Employment Opportunity in Australia*, Sydney: Allen & Unwin. (A thorough analysis of the extent to which formal legislative attempts to achieve equal employment opportunity will be successful in Australia and the USA. Clearly written.)

* Shaeffer, R.G. and Lynton, E.F. (1979) *Corporate Experiences in Improving Women's Job Opportunities*, New York: The Conference Board Inc. (A concise report of a survey of personnel officers in the USA examining factors which contribute to the success of equal employment opportunity policies.)

* Shipper, F.C. and Shipper, F.M. (1987) 'Beyond EEO: towards pluralism', *Business Horizons*, May–June: 53–61. (An easy to read article about the benefits to organizational performance of managing a pluralist workforce. Provides techniques for managing such a workforce.)

See also: HUMAN RESOURCE DEVELOPMENT; HUMAN RESOURCE MANAGEMENT; JOB EVALUATION; PAYMENT SYSTEMS; WOMEN MANAGERS IN ORGANIZATIONS

Related topics in the IEBM: GENDER AND ACCOUNTING; MANAGEMENT IN EUROPE; MANAGEMENT IN JAPAN; MANAGEMENT IN NORTH AMERICA

Flexibility

Overview

In the study of employment, work and organization, the issue of flexibility has come to represent a key focus for discussion. Analysis of changes taking place at several levels, from work practices, production strategies and employee relations arrangements to broader industrial and labour market structures, and even the organizing and control principles of capitalism itself, have drawn on the notion of flexibility to summarize both a series of developments and a key managerial objective behind those developments.

The notion of flexibility denotes pliability, adaptability and a responsiveness to change. In principle, flexibility relates equally to the structure and processes of organizations. To date, however, most attention has been concentrated on aspects of workforce flexibility (and at the macro level, labour market flexibility). In turn this reflects a greater attention paid to flexibility on both sides of the Atlantic by industrial relations and labour market specialists than by those with an organizational behaviour perspective (Atkinson 1984; Blyton and Morris 1991 and 1992; Laflamme *et al.* 1989; Pollert 1991). In practice, however, many of the changes introduced to extend workforce flexibility go hand in hand with other changes designed to bring about greater organizational responsiveness, such as decentralization and the utilization of more adaptive technologies.

Several factors are widely associated with giving added significance to organizational flexibility – in particular, greater market uncertainty and changes in technology and production processes. These factors are reviewed below, prior to examining the potential sources of workforce flexibility in more detail, particularly those relating to tasks undertaken, numbers employed, working time structures and wage payment systems. In considering the future of flexibility, it is evident from the study that various difficulties and unanswered questions remain. Examination of some of the most important of these highlights areas which require closer attention if a more objective understanding and evaluation of flexibility is to be realized. The final section underlines the need to consider flexibility more in conjunction with other managerial approaches to organization and also in the light of employee interests towards flexibility.

1 The search for flexibility

Contrary to impressions which may be given by the recent literature on the topic, flexibility has in fact long been accorded significance by both employers and employees. Indeed, its place as a principle of organization and employment throughout the development of industrialism is evident in employer arrangements such as the putting-out system, subcontracting, seasonal and overtime working, and in employee practices such as working fast to create 'banks' of work which can then be used as a cushion to compensate less productive work periods.

In latter years, however, flexibility has been accorded a greater significance in management and academic discussions. Several factors have been associated with this. These include the growth in international trade and competition, stemming not only from the increased activity of Japan and various newly industrializing countries, but also from the expansion of multinational corporations and the increase in cross-border trade due to liberalizations such as those embodied in the European Community (EC) single market, the collapse of the east–west divide in Europe and the North American Free Trade Agreement (see INDUSTRIAL RELATIONS IN EUROPE). This growth in competition and expansion of multinational activity into a wider range of markets is widely seen to have made those markets more volatile and less dependable for individual companies. This uncertainty is seen in turn to have heightened the need for organizations to increase their responsiveness to market changes and fluctuations: that is, to develop greater flexibility.

This search for greater flexibility has become a major theme at both organizational and macro levels. At the organizational level this has entailed seeking greater flexibility in organizational structures (through, for example, decentralization and the creation of strategic business units) as well as operational aspects (notably the use of technology and labour). At the macro level a major theme (particularly in countries with conservative governments) has been the necessity of removing 'rigidities' in the labour market to allow the forces of supply and demand to operate in an unfettered way between individual buyers and sellers of labour, thereby achieving a 'freer' or more 'flexible' labour market (see LABOUR MARKETS). Such rigidities are judged to include various social protections such as minimum wage agreements, statutory employment protection and trade union bargaining power.

In addition, developments in technology have both facilitated greater flexibility in production and at the same time required greater workforce flexibility to effect their full utilization. The power and versatility of microelectronic technology in process innovations has fundamentally altered traditional engineering and economic principles relating to the organization of production (see WORK AND ORGANIZATION SYSTEMS). The ability to drive equipment by computer and thereby programme (and re-programme) that equipment to conduct a series, rather than a single task, has enabled manufacturers to gain various efficiencies, not least those arising from shorter batch runs. As a result, economies of scale can be reached earlier and economies of scope can be obtained from the capability to market a variety of products rather than a single specification. At the same time, by combining formerly discrete tasks into single functions, various applications of new technology have simultaneously undermined previous job and skill boundaries and necessitated the re-shaping of jobs to match the different aptitudes and skills required to operate the new equipment. Thus, new technology has brought about a greater fluidity in job boundaries, giving further impetus to management preferences to operate with a workforce whose deployment is unconstrained by multiple job grades, skill demarcation lines and traditional work patterns.

The levels of productivity achieved by Japanese companies have also been widely perceived as an advertisement for the benefits to employers of labour flexibility. Interpretations of labour use in Japanese companies have emphasized both the deployment of temporary workers as a buffer against demand fluctuations and the maintenance of permanent employment relationships among other groups, based on a reciprocal exchange of job security for acceptance of internal mobility. For Japan-watchers such as Dore (1986) the Japanese system of lifetime employment, while appearing on the surface to be a source of rigidity, in practice yields high levels of flexibility, due to employees' acceptance of internal transfer and mobility. At the same time the large numbers of Japanese workers on temporary contracts provides companies with a flexible buffer against market fluctuations.

In most Western countries over the last decade labour market conditions have also facilitated management's securing of greater workforce flexibility. Unemployment, job insecurity and the resulting weakening of organized labour have reduced effective resistance to changes in employment and work practices which, in earlier periods, and in some industry and national settings, had met with opposition from trade unions – for example, the removal of demarcations and the extensive use of temporary workers and subcontracting (see TRADE UNIONS). Unemployment, together with the growth in female participation in the labour market, has also allowed employers to expand their use of non-permanent and non full-time labour. Deregulation and other state policies in several countries have further reinforced the extent of employer freedom by reducing the degree of protection afforded to employees through legislation or trade union influence.

Several issues remain problematic in all this, however. Most notable is the question of how much employers actually require more flexibility than they have hitherto enjoyed and what forms this added flexibility needs to take. On the face of it the general argument is persuasive: more players in the market-place = less market certainty for each player = more need for an organizational capability to alter course. In practice, however, less is known about the relationship between market uncertainty and workforce flexibility than might be supposed. Studies of industries such as clothing, for example, have indicated that the degree of workforce flexibility tends to be of secondary importance compared to the responsiveness of design to changes in taste and fashion (Rubery *et al.* 1987). In other industries, however, where competition has also been intense (for example, in the steel industry), workforce flexibility has been a prominent issue in recent years (Blyton 1993). Similarly, on the form of flexibility stimulated by product market characteristics, there is clearly a marked difference between the short-term flexibility in response to temporary fluctuations and the longer term flexibility to adapt to changes in demand. In turn, the type of flexibility stimulated by market characteristics will have very different implications regarding the organizational changes which are introduced to effect the necessary flexibility.

2 The concept of flexibility

Flexibility is generally taken to denote a responsiveness to change. It is typically contrasted with inflexibility and rigidity. In this way flexibility has almost invariably been accorded a positive value. This is particularly evident in Atkinson's (1984) early discussion of flexibility, in which he put forward a model of the 'flexible firm'. At the centre of this model is a core workforce possessing skills critical to the operation of the business. Reflecting this, the core workforce is accorded high status, with its members employed on a permanent, full-time basis with job security and prospects for advancement. Supporting this core workforce are periphery groups, generally engaged in unskilled and semi-skilled work, and occupying positions where job security is lower and opportunities for advancement far less evident. While the core workforce is viewed by Atkinson as a key source of long-term, 'functional' flexibility with employees trained to perform tasks in several skill areas, the periphery is perceived as an important source of shorter term 'numerical' flexibility. These forms of workforce flexibility are examined in more detail in the following section, which considers four main types: *functional, numerical, temporal* and *financial flexibility* (see WORK AND ORGANIZATION SYSTEMS).

Functional or task flexibility

Functional flexibility refers to the mobility and versatility of employees to fulfil a broader range of tasks. This can entail a horizontal integration of tasks (those formerly undertaken by other employees at the same level), a vertical integration (tasks formerly undertaken by employees at higher or lower levels) or a mixture of the two. To date much of the discussion on functional flexibility has concentrated on skilled manual work and the development (or otherwise) of multi-skilling by which former lines of demarcation between one craft and another are eroded. In general, while in certain countries, such as Germany and Sweden, a significant degree of multi-skilling has been achieved, in other countries, such as the UK, multi-skilling developments have been more limited. This broad difference reflects significant variations in institutional structures, regulatory conditions and managerial attitudes towards training in different countries. In Sweden and Germany tighter labour market conditions (in Sweden), relatively strong statutory job protection, the prior development of extensive vocational training and greater support among trade unions for retraining and changes in work practices have helped bring about a more concerted pursuit of functional flexibility by employers. In the UK on the other hand, the widely acknowledged inadequacy of its training infrastructure, coupled with a continuing tendency for managers to regard training primarily as a cost than as an investment, and for trade unions to vigorously defend existing skill boundaries, has tended to restrict the degree of multi-skilling. Certainly, general surveys such as by Cross (1988) have concluded that any multi-skilling which has taken place in the UK has affected the margins rather than the core activities within skill areas. At the same time, the importance of this activity at the margin should not be dismissed as insignificant. In the steel industry, for example, where substantial emphasis has been placed on the restructuring of craft maintenance work, while there has been only very limited cross-skilling between mechanical and electrical trades (the main distinction among maintenance craftsmen), the demarcations within these two areas (particularly on the mechanical side, such as between fitter, welder and boilermaker) are being progressively removed via retraining (Blyton 1993). This pattern is also evident in other industries: while radical cross-trade working may be hard to find, significant multi-skilling within more narrowly defined limits appears increasingly widespread, even in countries such as the UK.

Task flexibility is not just an issue confined to skilled workers, however. Indeed, probably more common are developments taking place within semi-skilled groups. These relate both to operatives undertaking a wider range of production tasks and to assuming greater responsibility for minor maintenance tasks. Developments such as reductions in job classifications, increased responsibility for self-inspection of work, and teamworking are indicative of more general moves towards enlarged job responsibilities and greater mobility between tasks, developments which are equally evident in Europe and North America (see, for example, Belanger 1989). Parts of the automobile industry have been prominent exponents of these forms of work organization in recent years, with Japanese employers such

as Nissan in the vanguard of advocating greater job mobility in contrast to the traditional organization of vehicle assembly lines (Wickens 1987). This task flexibility reflects a managerial desire to operate with lower manning levels, by enlarging individual jobs to cover the range of jobs and with task mobility developed to allow cover for absence, as well as maintaining performance by attempting to reduce monotony.

Numerical flexibility

Numerical flexibility is generally used to refer to management's capability to vary the amount of labour in response to changing levels of output demand. This may be achieved by such means as hiring workers on temporary contracts or relying on 'hire and fire' practices. Numerical flexibility can also be obtained via so-called 'distancing' strategies, by which firms establish (and terminate) agreements with sub-contractors, partly as a response to demand fluctuations. In the UK and elsewhere there is evidence of an increased use of sub-contracting over the recent period. However, while sub-contracting can be (and often is) used for ancillary activities, such as catering and cleaning, its use more clearly reflects a flexibility strategy where elements of production or core service provisions are put out to sub-contractors.

The trend in other aspects of numerical flexibility is less well defined. On the use of temporary workers in the UK, for instance, Casey (1991) has shown that there is no overall significant growth, but that their use tends to fluctuate with stages in the economic cycle. As Casey points out, however, the short time-period over which data has been collected on temporary workers hinders evaluation of recent trends and fluctuations. Whereas in some countries (again, Sweden and Germany are examples) the use of temporary contracts is restricted by law, in other countries (the UK for example) employers are free to offer temporary and fixed-term contracts. In Spain the use of fixed-term contracts as a source of employer flexibility has become particularly prominent. Following changes in labour market regulations in 1984 the number of workers on fixed-term contracts by 1990 had reached 30 per cent of the labour force (up from 16 per cent in 1987); women and new entrants to the labour force comprise the main components of this temporary workforce (Martinez Lucio 1992).

On other aspects of numerical flexibility, such as the operation of hire and fire practices, even less systematic information is available, although there are indications of its continuing and possibly growing importance in several countries. In the UK, for example, it is evident that a significant number of employees have their contracts terminated at the point at which they reach eligibility for employment protection (two years for full-time workers, five years for part-timers); the extension of the qualifying periods (for example from six months to two years for full-time workers) has effectively increased the scope of employers to use the qualifying periods as a *de facto* period for temporary employment. In general the comparatively low level of statutory employment protection in the UK, compared to several of its European counterparts, has made hire and fire a more feasible flexibility option in the UK.

It has been common for part-time working to be discussed under the heading of numerical flexibility, with observers commenting on, for example, the growth of diverse part-time schedules reflecting a managerial desire to concentrate labour input within periods of greatest work pressure. Strictly speaking, however, it is only those working practices which evidence *variability* which are relevant to the issue of flexibility. Thus, part-time working *per se* is not directly germane to the discussion; only where part-time schedules are deployed in a variable way do they represent a source of flexibility. This tendency to conflate flexibility with any change in working patterns is an issue returned to below.

Temporal flexibility

Temporal or working-time flexibility is currently used primarily to refer to management's use of variable working hours to match demand fluctuations. The term can equally apply, however, to employees' discretion over their working schedules, as embodied in 'flexitime' arrangements (whereby employees have some choice over their start and finish times provided that a certain core period is worked by everyone and that contractually agreed working hours are attained over an agreed settlement period). Employers have long relied on modifications to working time to reflect fluctuations in demand, as evidenced by the use of overtime and short-time working. In the recent period, however, somewhat greater attention has been paid to ways of introducing more variability into working-time patterns. Signs of this are evident in several countries. In a series of working-time settlements covering the German engineering industry, for example, employers agreed to cuts in the working week (to 35 hours by 1995) providing that various elements of temporal flexibility were acceded to by the trade union IG Metall (such as an individual settlement period of up to six months to achieve the contractually agreed level of working hours). In the UK temporal flexibility has been a prominent issue in the railway industry, stemming from the introduction of flexible rostering in the early 1980s. This entailed the abandoning of a standard eight-hour working day in favour of variable shifts of between seven and nine hours. This variability was designed to improve the match between employee shift lengths and train running times, thereby increasing the utilization of working time. Having led initially to a strike (in 1982), the issue of flexible rostering has continued to be a significant issue within the industry, as has the calculation of working hours over periods of up to ten weeks, with management attempting to reduce the high number of hours paid as overtime among groups such as signalmen. Outside Europe, flexibility of working time has become a more prominent issue in Japan in recent years. Since the late 1980s the Japanese government has sought to promote temporal flexibility as a means by which employers can maintain plant utilization in the context of reductions in weekly working hours (Sasajima 1993).

More recently, temporal flexibility has also figured in 'annual hours' agreements.

Under such arrangements employees are contracted to work an agreed number of hours per year, with working-time schedules determined at the beginning of 12 month cycles. In the UK such agreements are most commonly found in continuous process industries such as chemicals, cement and paper manufacture, although examples can also be found in various manufacturing and service activities. In many annual hours contracts variability is introduced in one of two ways. First, variability of weekly hours may be specified in agreements such that work periods are longer at specified (busy) times and shorter during slacker periods. Second, the number of shifts rostered in the annual hours schedule may be less than the agreed annual working time. The difference comprises non-rostered working time during which employees are effectively 'on call' and can be brought into work at short notice.

An extreme version of temporal flexibility attracting some attention recently (for example, in the retail sector in the UK) is the concept of 'zero-hours' contracts, under which no formal agreement is made concerning the number of hours the contract holder will work. Instead the employee is on-call, working only those periods which the employer calls for at short notice, for example to cover absence. While such arrangements provide a very high level of flexibility for the employer, they offer little by way of continuity or predictability for the employee.

Financial or wage flexibility

To date, financial flexibility has been discussed mainly in terms of moves away from uniform pay structures towards more variable payment arrangements, more reflective of individual and business performance (see FINANCIAL INCENTIVES; PAYMENT SYSTEMS). Like other forms of flexibility the practice of wage flexibility is long established. Indeed, perhaps the clearest embodiment of relating pay to performance is the use of piece-rate systems, a method of wage payments more common a generation ago than today. Also quite widely used in the past (for example, in the coal and steel industries) has been a sliding

scale based on the selling price of the commodity. By this means wages were directly linked to prices and profit rather than just to output. More generally, output bonuses and other formal and informal incentive schemes have long been used to forge a closer relationship between earnings and output.

More recent manifestations of wage flexibility include performance-related pay (PRP), profit-sharing schemes and fee-for-service payments which, in different ways, all seek to establish a closer relationship between output and reward (see PAYMENT SYSTEMS; PROFIT-SHARING AND EMPLOYEE SHAREHOLDING SCHEMES). Decentralization of collective bargaining within industries and organizations may further stimulate wage flexibility as managers of individual business units seek pay settlements which reflect the particular circumstances of the unit rather than that of the company or industry as a whole. At the macro level conservative governments such as those in the UK have argued that rigidities in wage structures are damaging to competitiveness and job creation. To this end various former protections have been removed or weakened, including the role of wages councils (for example, no longer covering the wages rates of young people), the removal of Fair Wages Resolutions (formerly requiring those undertaking government contracts to pay wages similar to the going rate in the government service) and the withdrawal of collective bargaining machinery for certain groups in public employment (for example, teachers).

While elements in all four forms of flexibility are evident in many countries, there are obvious differences in emphasis in different national approaches, as already indicated in the varying importance attached to functional flexibility in countries such as Germany and the UK. The main variation in national approaches has been captured in a number of bipolar categorizations of flexibility, most notably in the contrast between 'defensive' and 'offensive' forms of flexibility. Defensive flexibility strategies are characterized primarily as short-term, *ad hoc*, low labour cost responses to fluctuations in demand. Offensive forms of flexibility on the other hand are characterized as longer term, more strategic and more pro-active human resource measures in which emphasis is placed on achieving an adaptable, rather than a low-cost response. While numerical flexibility is particularly associated with the short-term, defensive approach, functional flexibility is central to the concept of longer term flexibility. The short-term response which many have noted is more characteristic of the UK may be seen as primarily a cost-minimization approach, while the functional flexibility route, more evident in Germany and Sweden, appears to be based more on a principle of productivity enhancement.

3 Future issues

Despite the differentiation and categorization of forms of flexibility various unresolved issues surrounding the notion still remain. There is space only to note some of the more important ones here. First, the breadth of usage of flexibility has led to it becoming an umbrella term, under which shelter a diverse range of individual elements of work organization and employment. It is questionable whether a single concept can adequately encompass developments ranging from multi-skilling to PRP and annual hours systems to sub-contracting. These problems are visible enough when related only to workforce flexibility; they are magnified when other types of organizational flexibility are introduced. Furthermore, following writers such as Elger (1991) there is questionable value in subsuming aspects of work such as job enlargement under the heading of flexibility, which is as likely to obscure as to illuminate the nature of the work process and work organization (see JOB DESIGN). Also, as noted above in relation to part-time working, the diverse usage of flexibility has been further stretched by the tendency to interpret any new departure in working practices as an example of flexibility. This tendency to conflate flexibility with any change in working patterns has continued to blunt the former's conceptual accuracy.

Second, the tone of many discussions on flexibility has been set by the tendency to juxtapose flexibility only with rigidity, attributing positive attributes to the former and negative ones to the latter. Yet by failing to go beyond this single comparator, and by placing such strong emphasis on the importance of responsiveness to change, this can act to undervalue other important organizational characteristics such as stability and continuity (Standing 1986). While flexibility is not inherently at odds with these latter characteristics, the tenor of much of the discussion has been to champion change above continuity. In the same way, by emphasizing the value of employee mobility and their capability of performing several different tasks, this may potentially act to undervalue specialization and the gaining of job-specific knowledge over time (Blyton and Morris 1992).

Third, the fact that none of the individual practices subsumed under workforce flexibility (temporary working, overtime, subcontracting, etc.) is unique to the recent period, coupled with the evidence that at least some of these aspects are registering limited (if any) change, casts doubt on the validity of ring-fencing these different elements and claiming that they demonstrate a pursuit of flexibility. The additional finding that in the UK few organizations are strategically pursuing a flexible firm model adds further doubt to how much firms are primarily seeking flexibility rather than, say, following a more *ad hoc* pursuit of lower labour costs. Further consideration is needed of the importance of flexibility to organizations, their existing sources of flexibility and the relative importance of workforce flexibility compared to other sources of organizational flexibility.

Fourth, the conceptual integrity of flexibility has been jeopardized by too ready a willingness to accept managerial definitions of what constitutes sources (and objectives) of flexibility rather than examine the issue from the viewpoint of the different parties involved. What a more rounded approach might contribute includes a clearer picture of how much and what forms of flexibility already exist within individual work contexts. Studies of employees' actual working-time patterns, for example, indicate comparatively high levels of flexibility already existing, much of it informal (Marsh 1991). Also, increased attention to employee and trade union attitudes could indicate how their views on more flexible working compare with employer objectives. Some indications of employee views can be gleaned from research findings which reveal, for example, support for flexitime arrangements, willingness to undertake further training and a widespread desire for greater variety at work. Overall, however, employee response to flexibility requires more systematic investigation.

A fuller understanding of flexibility will also be gained from a closer review of how it is actually implemented: how the practice of flexibility compares with the theory. One example from the author's own recent research in the steel industry, for example, indicated how management's securing of a craft restructuring agreement, relating to greater multi-skilled working, in some contexts brought little change to the pattern of task allocation yet had the effect of diminishing informal task flexibility arrangements that had existed prior to the formal agreement (Blyton 1993).

Finally, several issues concerning the relationship between flexibility and other management approaches to increasing competitiveness require closer consideration in the future. As Blyton and Morris have discussed elsewhere in more detail (1992), prominent areas of tension include the use of numerical flexibility (sought, for example, through short-term contracts) and the achievement of increased levels of employee commitment and high-quality output. Similarly, the use of multiple forms of employee contract for different types of temporary and sub-contracted groups could act to undermine other attempts to build unitary and strong organizational cultures. To a lesser extent, potential tensions are also evident in relation to longer term forms of flexibility: for example, the potential problems of maintaining adequate quality levels where workers are undertaking tasks (albeit after training) which lie outside their traditional areas of experience and competence.

4 Conclusion

Although several of the individual components of workforce flexibility have developed at a more modest rate than some predicted, in combination and over time, the changes instigated appear significant and, in some cases, substantial. Various national and cross-national studies also reveal that flexibility has gained a general significance, although the actual form it takes varies significantly from country to country, reflecting different statutory, labour market, industrial relations and other conditions. Furthermore, the factors recognized as fuelling the search for greater flexibility show little sign of abating. If anything, forces such as the intensity of market competition and the diffusion of technological innovations are likely to accelerate in coming years. Similarly, in the EC and elsewhere, levels of unemployment are projected to remain high for several years to come, thereby strengthening management's (and the state's) hand *vis-à-vis* employees and trade unions in introducing new employment conditions and work arrangements.

The issue of flexibility is thus likely to remain an important one within work organizations. In the future, however, it will be crucial for managers, researchers and others not to assume that the subject matter of flexibility is non-problematic. On the contrary, further questioning and clarification is required concerning the nature of flexibility and the way the components of flexibility interact with one another and with other features of the organization. It will be important also to counteract the overly prescriptive and value-laden nature of much of the debate and to give more recognition to the different interests at stake in the search for greater flexibility (see INDUSTRIAL AND LABOUR RELATIONS).

It is also apparent that if management is serious about goals such as building greater employee commitment, sustaining high quality output, etc., it must look more concertedly than hitherto at the scope for reciprocity over flexibility. Over the recent past factors such as cost pressures, weakened labour markets and state policies have led management to define the flexibility agenda. Flexibility, however, is a state of mind and a key feature of informal organizational processes, as well as something which can be contained in a collective agreement or an employment contract. In the longer term, flexibility is only likely to be sustained where management have sought to take account of employee interests as well as their own objectives.

PAUL BLYTON
CARDIFF BUSINESS SCHOOL

Further reading

(References cited in the text marked *)

* Atkinson, J. (1984) 'Manpower strategies for flexible organizations', *Personnel Management* (August): 28–31. (This short article describes the model of the flexible firm, comprising core and periphery groups.)
* Belanger, J. (1989) 'Management strategies and workers' knowledge: the case of the North American automobile industry', in G. Laflamme, G. Murray, J. Belanger and G. Ferland (eds), *Flexibility and Labour Markets in Canada and the United States*, Geneva: International Institute for Labour Studies. (This chapter examines innovations in work organization in the North American automobile sector.)
* Blyton, P. (1993) 'Steel', in A. Pendleton and J. Winterton (eds), *Public Enterprise in Transition*, London: Routledge. (This chapter refers to several workforce flexibility changes in the steel industry, including the introduction of multi-skilling and teamworking.)
* Blyton, P. and Morris, J. (eds) (1991) *A Flexible Future? Prospects for Employment and Organization*, Berlin: Walter de Gruyter. (An international collection, including several empirical studies of flexibility in manufacturing and service organizations.)
* Blyton, P. and Morris, J. (1992) 'HRM and the limits of flexibility', in P. Blyton and P. Turnbull (eds), *Reassessing Human Resource Management*, London: Sage Publications. (This chapter examines several tensions and potential contradictions between flexibility and HRM.)
* Casey, B. (1991) 'Survey evidence on trends in 'non-standard' employment', in A. Pollert (ed.), *Farewell to Flexibility?*, Oxford: Blackwell. (Casey examines British survey data on trends in part-time working, self-employment and temporary workers.)
* Cross, M. (1988) 'Changes to working practices in UK manufacturing 1981–88', *Industrial Relations Review and Report* 415 (May): 2–10. (Examines the extent of the growth of flexible practices during the 1980s.)
* Dore, R. (1986) *Flexible Rigidities*, London: Athlone. (Analyses the Japanese employment system, highlighting the flexibility deriving from lifetime employment systems.)
* Elger, T. (1991) 'Task flexibility and the intensification of labour in UK manufacturing in the 1980s', in A. Pollert (ed.), *Farewell to Flexibility?*, Oxford: Blackwell. (This chapter examines survey evidence on task flexibility and its implications for job enlargement and work intensification.)
* Laflamme, G., Murray, G., Belanger, J. and Ferland, G. (1989) *Flexibility and Labour Markets in Canada and the United States*, Geneva: International Institute for Labour Studies. (This collection of readings examines various aspects of the development of labour flexibility in Canada and the USA.)
* Marsh, C. (1991) *Hours of Work and Men and Women in Britain*, London: HMSO. (This report presents the findings of a survey of working time patterns of over 1,400 employees in the UK.)
* Martinez Lucio, M. (1992) 'Spain', in A. Ferner and R. Hyman (eds), *Industrial Relations in the New Europe*, Oxford: Blackwell. (This chapter contains information on the growth of fixed-term contracts in Spain and their prominence as a source of numerical flexibility.)
* Pollert, A. (ed.) (1991) *Farewell to Flexibility?*, Oxford: Blackwell. (This collection of readings offers a critique of the flexibility concept and the flexible specialization thesis.)
* Rubery, J., Tarling, R. and Wilkinson, F. (1987) 'Flexibility, marketing and the organisation of production', *Labour and Society* 12 (1): 131–51. (Rubery and her colleagues examine the significance of workforce flexibility in comparison to other sources of flexibility in the clothing industry.)
* Sasajima, Y. (1993) 'Japan: the case of the metal manufacturing industry', paper presented at an OECD conference on Flexible Working Time Arrangements, Paris, OECD. (This paper discusses the role of temporal flexibility in facilitating reductions in working hours in Japan.)
* Standing, G. (1986) *Unemployment and Labour Market Flexibility: The United Kingdom*, Geneva: International Labour Organization. (This study of the relationship between labour market flexibility and employment also identifies the possible drawbacks of pursuing flexibility at

the possible expense of organizational stability and continuity.)

* Wickens, P. (1987) *The Road to Nissan*, London: Macmillan. (Describes flexibility, quality and teamwork as core elements in the Nissan production philosophy.)

See also: COMMITMENT; EQUAL EMPLOYMENT OPPORTUNITIES; FINANCIAL INCENTIVES; INDUSTRIAL AND LABOUR RELATIONS; INDUSTRIAL RELATIONS IN EUROPE; INDUSTRIAL RELATIONS IN JAPAN; JOB DESIGN; ORGANIZATION BEHAVIOUR; PAYMENT SYSTEMS; PROFIT SHARING AND EMPLOYEE SHAREHOLDING SCHEMES; TRADE UNIONS; WORK AND ORGANIZATION SYSTEMS

Related topics in the IEBM: ECONOMIC INTEGRATION, INTERNATIONAL; LABOUR MARKETS; MANAGEMENT IN JAPAN; NORTH AMERICAN FREE TRADE AGREEMENT (NAFTA)

Industrial conflict

Overview

Conflict is widely seen as one of the central principles of organizational life. Interpretations of its origin, nature and effects vary substantially, however. In particular, beginning in the 1980s, accounts associated with human resource management and Japanese management often argued that conflict was being eliminated, or at least being made into a minor feature of organizations. This developing orthodoxy contrasts with an earlier one, that conflict was inevitable and even desirable: the issue was not its elimination but its management. The focus of this entry is how such different perspectives conceptualize and analyse what seems to be the same phenomenon. Four main areas are addressed: (1) differing perspectives on conflict; (2) the place of conflict within the organization; (3) variations in the extent of overt conflict over time and between countries; and (4) the future of conflict.

The continuing centrality of conflict is indicated by, first, the conceptual argument that conflict is a central principle of any organization in which workers labour under the authority of management. Second, levels of overt dispute in the Western world have not declined by as much as is sometimes thought, and such declines have been balanced by increases in overt conflict in the Third World. Third, studies in organizations where conflict may appear to have been eliminated, notably Japanese firms and 'high-tech' companies, show high levels of work pressure and a tendency for conflict and tensions to be internalized within employees, rather than being expressed as open disputes between management and worker. Claims that conflict can be eliminated misunderstand how organizations work. It is not a question of its elimination, but of the changing ways in which it is organized and expressed.

1 The nature of conflict

Conflict in organizations includes interdepartmental rivalries, disputes between managers and interpersonal tensions. Industrial conflict refers to those aspects connected with the employment relationship: the employment of one person by another for the production of a defined product or service. It thus excludes purely interpersonal conflicts, although it would include activities where there is no legal employment relationship. For example, a firm may use home workers or agency staff who are not formally employed but, to the extent that such workers come under the authority of the firm, conflict between them and the firm would be included.

The term 'industrial conflict' is used in three main senses:

1 the use of overt sanctions, as when it is said that conflict erupts when workers go on strike;
2 a continuing sense of discord ('there was conflict over the new work rotas');
3 an underlying conflict of interest between worker and manager that need receive no overt expression.

A further complexity is that manifestations are not limited to strikes or organized disagreements. Means of expressing conflict include absenteeism, quitting and sabotage. Yet such activities also reflect many things other than conflict: respectively, genuine sickness, the attractions of a better-paid job and simple mistakes. Not surprisingly these issues, together with the difficulty of measuring something like sabotage, have meant that much research has focused on the strike as the most obvious indicator of conflict. Studies of other topics are rarer, and efforts to indicate how indeed they reflect conflict are rarer still.

A simple distinction provides a starting point. *Industrial conflict* can be defined as behaviour which involves a clear dispute between manager and worker. The strike is the most extreme manifestation, but collective bargaining over a wage demand is also plainly a form of conflict in this sense; the strike is the continuance of bargaining by other means (see PAYMENT SYSTEMS). Such conflict is generally organized in that it involves groups of workers. But the filing of a formal grievance by an individual worker or individual efforts to bargain about wages would also qualify. What matters is the clear recognition of a difference of interest between employer and employee.

Conflict at work refers to the wider principles of antagonism between employer and employee. Its origin lies in the fact that workers work under the authority of managers. Even where there is no open industrial conflict there can still be a division of interest between the two parties. Consider authoritarian regimes: it may be possible for open discontent to be suppressed but the independent observer would not wish to conclude that no conflict existed. The idea of conflict at work is directed at exploring how the conflictual elements of work are expressed, and, if they are not, what mechanisms contain their expression.

2 Perspectives on conflict

Five main theoretical approaches set out to define the origins of conflict. Their specific contexts are Anglo-American. This reflects the fact that the distinct scholarly discipline of industrial relations is more developed here than elsewhere, with the result that formal efforts to conceptualize conflict within the employment relationship have been more complete than in countries where analysis is divided between sociologists, economists, legal specialists and so on. But the approaches have a universal relevance; for example, as shown below several studies of the Third World draw on models of conflict similar to those discussed here, even if they do not use quite the same language. The main features of the first four approaches are given in Table 1. The fifth aims to integrate the strengths of each of these and is not, therefore, separately listed.

Unitary perspectives, analysed in detail by Fox (1974), are so-called because they assume a fundamental unity of interest among members of an organization and thus deny that conflict has any necessary existence. Where it arises it is explained as the outcome

Table 1 Perspectives on industrial conflict

	Unitary	Industrial relations pluralists	Political exchange pluralists	Radical	Transaction cost economics
Basis of conflict	None	Division between organized interests		Exploitation	Gaps in labour contract
Reason for open conflict	Mistakes, poor communication	Disputes of interest or right		Recognition of opposed interests	Opportunism
Form of conflict	Occasional outburst	Collective bargaining	Political exchange	Any levels	Shirking
Focus of analysis	Workplace	Bargaining contract	Political centre	All levels	Workplace
Means to minimize conflict	Communication	Better procedures	Strong corporatism	None	Monitoring
Unresolved problems	Division between two sides	Shop-floor level, limits of institutions, role of state	Shop-floor level, tensions within corporatism	Limits to managerial power, cooperation	Politics of workplace, cooperation

of mistakes or the presence of 'troublema-kers'. Mistakes would include poor communi-cation; dissent might arise because a management failed to explain its goals ade-quately. The troublemaker view is commonly used to explain strikes, particularly where these break out among formerly quiescent workers: outside agitators are claimed to have provoked discontent for their own purposes (see EMPLOYEE RELATIONS, MANAGEMENT OF).

The view that conflict is accidental or pathological is very common. In its simplest guise it occurs in places as different as pater-nalist firms, whose owners cannot conceive of their workers having any real source of griev-ance, and the former Soviet system, whose ideology claimed that workers owned the means of production, that they could not be in conflict with themselves and that strikes were the result of ignorance or agitation. A more sophisticated version informs the human rela-tions tradition, which argues that workers have certain human needs which manage-ments must recognize and that if they behave in this enlightened way, conflict is unneces-sary. It is more sophisticated because it ac-cepts that firms may not be enlightened because of laziness or incompetence: there is always the possibility in any organization that errors will creep in, but these are not seen as fundamental to the operation of the enterprise.

Up until the early 1980s unitary theories were generally dismissed in the scholarly community. At one level the criticism was well founded. The idea that conflict is simply pathological is evidently an unsatisfactory and partial view of organizational life. Yet unitary perspectives remain perhaps the most common popular approaches. Most managers have been found to adhere to broadly unitary beliefs. The theories received new life with the development of human resource manage-ment, which argues that organizations which develop an integrated approach to their hu-man resources can establish a deep sense of commitment. Proponents as well as critics place human resource management firmly among unitary theories.

Why, then, have unitary perspectives re-mained common? One reason is that they address phenomena that can be managed: poor communications can obviously be im-proved. They also see issues in ways which do not fundamentally challenge accepted ways of thinking: all that needs to be done is to alter a specific arrangement Other perspectives have much more unsettling policy implica-tions for managers, as will be seen. Finally, they capture an important truth, namely, that cooperation is an important feature of any work organization and that employer and em-ployee are not in a state of total opposition. For many managements for quite long periods of time it is possible to behave as though the enterprise is unitary in nature.

Pluralist theories address situations when this assumption breaks down. They observe that workers and managers have divergent in-terests (for example, over the level of wages) as well as common ones. In capitalist societies this divergence of interests has led to the for-mation of trade unions (see TRADE UNIONS). Unions and managements offer different sources of identity and have different bases of authority, and when these different sources come into dispute conflict will arise. Al-though individual forms of conflict are recog-nized by pluralists, most attention is given to organized disputes.

An important distinction is made between disputes of interest and disputes of right. The former covers issues such as wages and bene-fits, when there is a potential conflict over the level of remuneration. Disputes of right relate to the application of an existing agreement. For example, an agreement may specify that certain rates will be paid for overtime or that the allocation of new work will be on the basis of seniority; issues of right concern the appli-cation of such conditions. The distinction is particularly clear cut in North America, where the periodic negotiation of collective con-tracts handles issues of interest and where grievance procedures determine issues of right during the term of a contract. It is less clear cut in some other countries but is ana-lytically useful in defining the nature of a dispute.

Pluralism has two main forms. *Industrial relations pluralists* (see Fox 1974; Hyman 1989: 54–95) focus on the immediate relationship between management and unions. The policy implication is that managements need to recognize the divergence of interests, not only by grudgingly accepting the inevitability of unions but also by actively working with them to negotiate structures to manage conflict. Pluralism gives particular weight to structures including the collective bargaining of terms and conditions of employment and formal procedures for discipline and the handling of grievances. The basic assumption is that such arrangements can contain conflict within acceptable boundaries. This message is much more fundamental than the unitary one, for it calls on managements to accept that certain key issues, like hiring and firing, are no longer under their own authority.

Political exchange pluralists broaden the approach in two ways: they examine the effects of relations outside the enterprise on conflict; and they aim to explain patterns across the developed capitalist economies. Their key observation is that certain countries, notably Sweden and Austria, were able to reduce strikes and overt industrial action to minimal levels whereas in countries like the USA, the UK and Australia strike activity remained highly significant (Korpi and Shalev 1979). The explanation was that the focus of contention had been shifted from the industrial to the political arena. Instead of each employer negotiating with a union, bargaining took place between unified bodies representing the two sides; moreover, the state was involved in the bargain, with key issues for workers such as unemployment insurance being handled through political exchange and not direct bargaining with the employer. The term corporatism was applied to cases of this kind, with a distinction between this strong corporatism and weaker efforts to develop corporatist institutions in countries such as Italy and the UK.

Pluralism was the orthodoxy of industrial relations academics in the UK, the USA and other countries up until the 1970s. It was challenged intellectually by the *radical perspective*. This argued that pluralism's diagnosis and prescription were faulty. The diagnosis suggested that conflict occurred only when

there was a collective dispute between a firm and a union. This neglected individual forms of conflict and the fact that the sources of conflict ran much deeper than pluralism acknowledged. There was a permanent battle inside the work process as managements aimed to control and direct workers who resisted the regulation. The pluralist prescription failed to tackle this basic reality: reforming collective bargaining might deal with certain symptoms but could not solve underlying cases. Indeed, conflict was inevitable in any capitalist enterprise. The policy prescription of the radicals themselves was, implicitly if not explicitly, that workers and managers should simply recognize the conflictual relationships in which they were engaged.

Radicalism was a product of a particular period, in particular of the late 1960s and early 1970s when worker militancy was at its height. Its critique of other approaches was important, as were some analytical themes, notably the stress on the place of conflict within the organization of work. But this stark image of the enterprise as a place of unremitting conflict was unduly simple and some writers developed a more subtle view, albeit one still contained within the radical approach. In particular, Fox (1974) developed the concept of trust: although conflict is endemic, there are various ways in which it can be managed and under some circumstances mutual trust can develop. This view was later taken up within the final approach considered below.

The fourth approach derives from *transaction cost economics* (see Edwards 1992). This school argues that 'indeterminacy' is inevitable in any contract: it is impossible to specify in advance exactly all the conditions necessary for complete compliance with a contract. Attempting to monitor contract compliance is costly. In the world of work workers exploit gaps in the labour contract by 'shirking' on their obligations, for example by lowering their work effort. Solutions include improved monitoring; the growth of the large enterprise has been seen as a means to monitor workers more effectively. The limitation of this theory is its assumption that shirking dominates everyone's thoughts; that any opportunity to evade an obligation will be sought out and acted upon. Whereas unitarists assume harmony, with conflict being an accident, theorists of shirking see cooperation as no more than the outcome of a cost–benefit calculation that the risks of shirking, such as disciplinary penalties, outweigh the benefits (Edwards 1992).

The final approach, which may be termed the *theory of labour regulation*, agrees with belief of radicals and economists that conflict is inherent in the organization of work (Edwards 1986). Workers bring to work their capacity to work, their labour power, and this is transformed into actual labour within the production process. There is conflict here because the process is organized not by workers but by managers. Managers need to control the ways in which workers' capacities are used in order to ensure that the enterprise continues to function profitably. The fact that workers are subordinate to managers indicates the conflictual basis of the organization of production.

An important part of this perspective concerns the role of management. In the unitary view managers represent the interests of the whole organization and can in principle operate it smoothly. For pluralists it is possible to minimize if not eliminate conflict through appropriate representational structures. For radicals managers are simply interested in maximizing the exploitation of workers which, save for workers' resistance, they are felt to be able to accomplish. For theorists of shirking management is again a rational activity, aiming to minimize shirking and run the organization in the pursuit of efficiency.

Labour regulation theories, in contrast, focus on the uncertainties and contradictions of management. By 'contradiction' is meant the presence of two or more principles, each of which is central to the functioning of the enterprise but which generates tensions with the other principles. The key contradiction in the management of labour is that between controlling and disciplining workers and developing their creative capacities. This is not, moreover, a matter of balancing equivalents. The basic need is to organize workers under the authority of managers, meaning that there is a permanent underlying antagonism. The role of management is to manage this antagonism, but it cannot remove it. The same argument is made in relation to the state: in contrast to political exchange pluralism, which sees the state as a neutral arbiter (see CORPORATISM), labour regulation theory sees the state as a manager of conflict (Fulcher 1991). States may be unsuccessful in this endeavour as political exchange is a way of handling tensions not eliminating them. Attention to the political centre also means that the bases of conflict at shop-floor level receive no consideration within this approach.

As for the shop floor, managers cannot rely on coercion alone (as the unitary view correctly recognizes) for this is a weak basis on which to persuade workers to provide their capacity to labour. As for workers, there are several aspects to their cooperation with management. These include: the economic, notably their dependence on employers for their livelihood; the power of firms, for example to use discipline for poor performance; and social and cultural factors such as the preference for doing a thorough job rather than a skimped one. The last set of factors is important. In contrast to the view that workers naturally shirk, in any workplace there develops a set of customs or understandings as to what is reasonable behaviour. Detailed examples are given below.

Some aspects of other perspectives are seen as potentially misleading. Most importantly, the claim within human resource management that commitment can replace conflict is seen as no more than a long line of unitarist efforts to downplay the significance of conflict. The relevant techniques are ways not of dissolving conflict but of managing it. They may be able to overcome some manifestations of it but this may be because it has been externalized (that is, pushed out of one organization and into another) or there remain important elements of conflict even though they do not appear in overt forms. Again, examples are given below.

There is no specific policy implication, for example improved communication or better bargaining procedures, with the labour theory approach. Instead it highlights a set of issues which need to be addressed. First, what is appropriate in some cases will not work elsewhere. For example, a small firm in a highly competitive market could not afford human resource management techniques. Changes might also disrupt existing understandings within the workforce: many small firms thrive even though the technical organization of work is apparently irrational – the system is necessary because a 'rational' organization would cut across workers' friendship ties and it works because built into the culture of the organization is a flexibility based on shared understandings (see FLEXIBILITY). Second, management is the management of contradictory forces. A new communication system may bring benefits from the managerial point of view but only if managers explain its purpose and recognize that it may conflict with other aspects of the organization that its benefits may decay. Managing the conflictual aspects of work is a constant activity and cannot be eliminated by new techniques in and of themselves.

A related implication concerns the relationship between the generation and resolution of conflict. It is tempting to make a clear distinction between them, as pluralist theory does most extensively. For labour regulation any organization of work involves the simultaneous production of conflict and cooperation. Means of managing conflict are built into this organization. Workers come to accept certain ways of behaving. It is not a matter of conflict arising and then being managed; the two aspects are part of the same process.

Finally, the applicability of such an approach should be stressed. As noted above, theories of industrial conflict have developed from an Anglo-American base. The relevance of models which take formal collective bargaining as the natural order of things can readily be questioned when other industrialized nations are considered, not least the Third World. As shown below, the organization of conflict in, for instance, Japan, reflects more than formal bargaining structures, also including a set of obligations which go deeper than a calculus of obedience or shirking can recognize. Analyses using ideas of labour

regulation have, in contrast, explored the dynamics of conflict in a wide range of countries.

3 Conflict at work

The methods by which analysis is conducted warrant emphasis. Much pluralist research examines institutions or readily accessible information such as strike statistics. Yet understanding the dynamics of conflict and consent requires a much deeper study of actual processes. In some studies this involves detailed ethnography wherein the researcher enters a workplace for a period of time, usually as a low-level employee. Burawoy (1985) has conducted important work in Zambia, the USA and Hungary (and more recently, Russia). Other studies involve long periods of observation and interviewing. Such work is time-consuming and demanding, and it remains relatively rare in the social sciences.

How, then, does conflict in the sense of conflict at work manifest itself? This issue is addressed in three parts: (1) the inevitability of negotiation; (2) variations in the meanings of apparently similar phenomena; and (3) one concrete example.

There is in any work situation a *negotiation of order*, that is, a process wherein superiors and subordinates work out the balance of their mutual obligations. Conflict is interwoven with other processes. The importance of this negotiation can be seen by considering extreme cases in which subordinates are apparently powerless. Two such cases are slave plantations in the southern USA and peasants in contemporary Asian countries. The common image is one of dictatorial rules and coercive discipline. Conflict in this view either would be suppressed or find expression in occasional outbursts of collective action (slave revolts or peasant rebellions) or in individual escape (running away). Studies (Genovese 1976; Scott 1985) in fact show that such overt protest is only part of the story. It is rare and it reflects exceptional conditions such as a particularly authoritarian style of operation. For the most part it is not a matter of coercion but of negotiated understandings. On slave plantations, for example, there were norms as to how much food slaves deserved at holiday times. Slaves expressed conflict with the owners through tacit means such as feigning illness or pilfering food and other desirable items. Slave owners could not secure their own goals through coercion: slaves had to be persuaded to work and relying solely on coercion was not an effective way of doing so. Peasants likewise managed their lives by engaging in theft and sabotage. Such activity sets some limits to the power of landowners, who have to respect certain established customs. At the same time, however, such behaviour changes the balance of power only at the margins and is covert and unstructured. Accommodation to and resistance against domination develop simultaneously. Slaves 'had an interest, however psychologically antagonistic, in the smooth running of the plantation' (Genovese 1976: 16), but they could also engage in day-to-day resistance.

This negotiation of order within structural conditions is not captured by concepts such as opportunism, which tend to reduce worker behaviour to the narrow pursuit of individual advantage. Understood rules, which are often hidden, are generated within the process of production. As Mars puts it, managements need to 'listen to the music behind the words' (Mars 1982: 204); unknowingly they can disrupt expectations and set off a spiral of discontent. Discontent with management is often driven less by the formal issues in dispute than by the fact that certain informal practices are challenged. What goes on in the sphere of industrial conflict as defined above can depend on the expectations rooted in the negotiation of order.

There is a tendency in writings on organizational behaviour to stop at this point. They tend to treat all organizational life as of a piece, with the negotiation of order being presented as a universal truth. But the ways in which conflict is organized vary substantially. There are some commonalities between slave plantations and modern organizations, but equally significant differences. Consider how the 'same' phenomenon, sabotage, exhibits quite different underlying processes.

The image of *sabotage* is one of the powerless and frustrated individual destroying products or equipment in a mindless fury. Such actions certainly do occur but behaviour that qualifies for the label of sabotage, that is the conscious destruction of goods or the lowering of their quality, displays various dynamics. Studies (reviewed by Edwards 1986) qualify this picture. One celebrated case concerned the manufacture of aeroplane fuselages in the USA in the 1940s. Workers used a device known as the 'tap' to force in bolts, thereby substantially weakening the air frame. Use of the tap was forbidden and ownership of one could lead to dismissal. However, its use was widely accepted. The reason was that it eased the work process: it was the only way to perform a difficult task to tight deadlines. Supervisors were not only aware of the tap's use, they also instructed workers with regard to the appropriate circumstances in which to use it. There developed a set of understandings as to the conditions calling for its use and who was allowed to use it, with only those workers who were sufficiently experienced and responsible being taught its mysteries.

This case offers the following lessons: (1) in contrast to unitary theory, sabotage was not accidental but was integral to the negotiation of order; (2) in contrast to pluralism's expectations, the action received no organized expression and could not be handled through formal devices such as grievance procedures; (3) sabotage was not, contrary to radical theory and to models of shirking, a straight act of worker resistance, for it was regulated by powerful social norms and was as much about accommodation to a system of work organization as about protest against it; (4) the role of management was crucial in two respects: supervisors were active in regulating use of the tap and its use was connected with the wider contradictions of management, which sought a high level of production as well as high quality and which allowed continued production to depend on workers' informal skills. The workers' breaking of the rules actually helped in the achievement of managerial goals. Sabotage was a particular reflection of the organization of conflict and consent.

In other workplaces the situation will be different, the possibilities of sabotage being organized out of the system. Sabotage is most likely where workers are paid by results, and where they have an incentive to cut corners so as to increase earnings. But its occurrence also depends on the technical organization of work (some work processes are more prone to uncertainty and are more easily monitored than others) and on its social organization (if management can require workers to correct mistakes for no extra payment and can prevent collective challenges to this rule then cutting corners becomes less attractive). Sabotage thus is far from universal (Edwards 1986).

A second example is *pilfering* (Mars 1982). In some workplaces, such as supermarkets, the activity is highly individualized. It is always possible in principle to pilfer goods or 'fiddle' money, but whether an individual worker engages in the activity depends on his or her personal skills and attitudes. Anyone caught is likely to be dismissed. At the other extreme there are organized work groups, such as teams of dockers or dustbin men (garbage collectors in North American terms). These have strong norms governing pilfering, making it a socially regulated activity. Anyone disciplined by management will be supported by workmates. Between these extremes are other cases where norms have varying degrees of force (see EMPLOYEE DEVIANCE).

The lessons of this study include the following. Workers generally try to create some space for themselves, but they do so in various ways and are not simply resisting managerial authority. Managers also have an interest in fiddles. These include helping to keep wages low (as workers use perks to increase their actual earnings), giving workers some purpose in boring jobs, thus increasing morale and possibly reducing overt protest, and allowing managers to distance themselves from fiddling even when they know that it is going on. Attempts to regulate fiddles may be short-lived if they replace one such prone workforce with another or counterproductive if they lead to explicit and organized protest.

These examples come from Western companies. Research in the Third World reveals an even wider array of means by which workers resist managerial domination. Cohen (1991), reviewing evidence from Africa, describes the use of tribal songs as a mode of escape from authority, as well as more familiar practices such as absenteeism. Ong (1987), using case material from Malaysia, shows how female workers responded to the demands of industrialism by turning to the traditional practice of possession by spirits in order to retain some space for themselves. This was not, however, simply a matter of a psychic return to a pre-industrial state. It was a device used constructively to make sense of the tension between old and new. Thus, within the workplace workers insisted on their legal right to pray at least five times per day. They were also able to gain autonomy by pretending ignorance of the technical details of production. The implications of such cases include the need for managers to 'listen to the music' through sensitivity to the distinctive cultural language within which workers' demands may be expressed; ignorance of this language may lead to a misreading of the signals which workers are sending, which could in turn lead to a worsening atmosphere and a cycle of mistrust.

Although there is substantial evidence of different ways of expressing conflict in different parts of the world, detailed comparative analyses are rare. One study compared electronics workers in Korea and the USA (Cho 1985). In contrast to expectations that Korean workers would be subordinate and powerless, the study found that in many ways they were more able than their US counterparts to sustain a collective organization against management, a key reason being their community solidarity which contrasted with the individualism of the US workers. Further studies in this area explore international variations and relate them to differences in employer and state policy in the regulation of labour (Burawoy 1985; Fulcher 1991).

These points may be illustrated by the case of Japan. This is particularly relevant as the country often is seen as an illustration of the successful elimination of conflict. In fact studies show that it is organized in distinct ways. First, as discussed in the following section, strikes remained quite common up until the

1980s. They have been, however, a means of ritual demonstration rather than the trials of strength familiar in other countries. Second, the image of harmony in large firms turns on the ability of these firms to insulate workers from insecurity. Although Japan is famed for lifetime employment, this system in fact covers only one-third of the workforce. The costs of adjustment are borne by the small-firm sector, where demands on workers are often intense (Kondo 1990). Third, even within the large-firm sector conflict is not absent. Some studies suggest that control is achieved not by consent but by a drive system in which workers are under great pressure to conform (Kamata 1983). There is also evidence of pressure on managers as well as workers, for example in growing press reports of overwork and strains between the all-embracing requirements of the job and family obligations.

A picture of complete autocracy would be, however, as one-sided as one of harmony. Alongside the pressures there are several ways in which workers are persuaded to work hard. They are of two main types. First there is a set of employment practices including: the job security of large firms (which encourages cooperation with change, a feature also shared with Germany); promotion based on seniority; and a well-organized system of career planning (see CAREERS). Such features encourage a sense of commitment to the organization. Second, there is the technical organization of production: the system of 'lean production' involves the minimization of waste (*muda*), close attention to detail and the search for *kaizen* (continuous improvement). This reduces some of the disorganization of the management process which is marked in countries like the USA and the UK. But it also reinforces pressures towards overwork and stress. A complex web of factors produces acceptance of a system while also revealing significant points of tension, with 'management by stress' being an important underlying dimension (Berggren 1993).

The universal possibility of conflict is thus expressed in particular ways in particular workplaces. The negotiation of order shapes the meaning of behaviour, which cannot simply be categorized as 'conflict' or 'obedience'.

4 Strikes and overt conflict

The importance of conflict at work notwithstanding, strike patterns say something significant about forms of conflict. Measuring strike rates is far from easy since different countries use different criteria, for example on what strikes to include and on where one strike stops and the next one starts. But it is possible to compare overall levels of working days lost in strikes and to examine trends on other dimensions: although strike numbers are counted differently in different countries, it is possible to compare whether the indices are moving in similar directions (see INDUSTRIAL AND LABOUR RELATIONS).

Strikes have been widely studied from a range of perspectives. Five may be highlighted:

1 the trend of conflict over the process of industrialization;
2 differences in level between (a) countries and (b) industries;
3 shorter-term trends over time;
4 the negotiation and management of conflict;
5 outcomes.

An influential early theory was that levels of organized conflict peak during early industrialization and decline thereafter. The reason was that industrialization poses new strains on workers, thus promoting a high sense of grievance, and that mechanisms to contain conflict were underdeveloped, thus meaning that the grievances found vent in overt action. Much later work has questioned the causal model of this analysis, and in particular the view that conflict was an irrational response to social disorganization; on the contrary, it was a forward-looking and organized activity. As discussed below, it also showed that conflict levels under mature industrialization vary substantially over time and place, thus refuting a theory of unilinear development towards harmony. With regard to the basic facts on the level of conflict, reliable data on strikes do not go far enough back for a decisive answer. It is likely, however, that strikes were relatively rare in early industrialization because enterprises were small and workers lacked the organizations to sustain a strike. Certainly they became common with the growth of large-scale enterprises and trade unions. Efforts have been made to fill this gap by examining newspaper records of all forms of open disputation, the evidence suggesting a high rate of food riots and public disturbances. However, this does not mean that conflict has necessarily been replaced by harmony: the language of dispute has changed and the particular form of the food riot disappeared in most Western countries during the latter half of the nineteenth century, but the presence of conflict has been manifest not only in the strike but also in the newer forms of conflict at work discussed above.

For most of the post-war period the most strike-prone Western countries (measured as days lost per 1,000 employees) were Italy, Canada and the USA. The lowest levels were recorded in Sweden and Austria. Data on an array of nine countries are given in Tables 2 and 3. The countries are chosen from around the globe and for their ability to illustrate different strike patterns. The obvious absentee is

the USA, where data recording changed dramatically in 1981; Canada is thus taken as representative of North America.

Table 2 shows overall averages on the main dimensions of strikes. Other measures may be derived from these; for example, the mean size of strikes is given by dividing workers involved by the number of stoppages, and an indication of length by dividing days lost by workers involved. The data need treating with caution, particularly in the case of the Third World countries where data recording may not be as precise as it is in the West. Germany and Sweden were marked by few but quite large strikes, producing low levels of total days lost. Disputes occurred occasionally at the end of bargaining impasses and were serious pitched battles often involving unified action by employers. Italy's strikes were frequent, large and short; they were often brief protests aimed at the political as much as the economic sphere. Strikes in the UK were on average rather smaller and longer and less frequent, but in this country averages are particularly misleading for they mask two distinct patterns: small and short workplace actions and a few large national disputes, particularly in the public sector. In India strikes were large

Table 2 Overall shape of strikes, 1960–89

	GER	ITA	SWE	UK	IND	JAP	KOR	CAN	MEX
Frequency	(11)	148	19	66	35	30	29	80	33
Size	(500)	2190	521	754	649	669	220	517	83
Duration	5.0	1.6	7.9	5.2	16.5	2.8	9.6	14.8	n.a.
Volume	27	528	78	258	373	57	66	609	n.a.

Note: Strike data for the UK exclude the coal industry. For Germany, data on the frequency of strikes are not available. The mean size of strikes has been estimated as similar to that in Sweden, and the figures for frequency calculated accordingly.

'Frequency' is the frequency of strikes: the number per million members of the workforce. For all countries apart from Mexico and India, 'workforce' is the civilian labour force; for India and Mexico it is the estimated non-agricultural economically active population

'Size' is mean size: the number of workers involved divided by the number of strikes.

'Duration' is the number of days lost in strikes divided by the number of workers involved. It measures how long the 'average' striker was on strike, not the length of the average strike

'Volume' is the number of working days lost per 1,000 employees.

If S is number of strikes, W workers involved, D days lost and E number of employees, then:

$$\text{Freq} = S/E; \quad \text{Size} = W/S; \quad \text{Duration} = D/W; \quad \text{and Volume} = D/E$$

Source: Calculated from International Labour Office *Yearbook* statistics

and particularly long in contrast to many Third World countries where, as in Italy, strikes are used as brief political protests. Strikes were more common in Japan than is often thought, being used as ritual protests at the time of the annual wage offensive, as reflected by their brief duration. In Korea and Mexico disputes were at some periods very rare, reflecting strong political repression (Deyo 1989). However, when they did occur they were small but quite long.

For industrial relations pluralists the reasons lay in the level and scope of collective bargaining. For example, there were many strikes in North America because bargaining was decentralized: strikes were long because they were major battles about substantive terms and conditions of employment. In Sweden and Germany centralized bargaining combined with effective dispute procedures reduced the number of strikes, although when disputes did occur they tended to be long. Political exchange pluralists (Korpi and Shalev 1979) argue that strikes were rare in the latter group of countries because key issues were settled in the political arena.

Both theories have difficulties. The first describes an existing structure of bargaining but does not explain where it came from; in particular the roles of employers and the state in choosing a specific way of managing the labour problem are not explored. The second has difficulties in explaining developments in countries like Japan and Germany, where there has been labour peace but no strong corporatism involving labour representation at state level. They share the problem of treating countries as static entities. Work extending these theories offers a more dynamic approach (Fulcher 1991). It shows, for example, that labour peace in Sweden was not the direct product of labour's accession to political power but was the outcome of state and employer policies of containment.

Within countries industries vary dramatically in their strike rates. Some facts are common to most countries; for example, white-collar workers strike rarely. A contrasting observation is that certain groups, notably coal miners and dockers, are more highly strike-prone in most countries. This promoted

the famous thesis of the 'isolated mass' (Kerr and Siegel 1954), which stated that two conditions promoted strikes: isolation from others and agglomeration into an undifferentiated mass. Isolation alone is insufficient (witness agricultural workers), but when combined with the conditions of 'massness' it divorces workers from the limitations on conflict that exist where workers are open to pressures from other social groups.

As a complete theory this thesis is incorrect (Edwards 1992). Some isolated groups such as steelworkers have low strike rates. Coal miners' strike rates vary widely within countries and over time in ways which the static conditions of massness cannot explain. Dockers do not display all the conditions of isolation and social distance yet do have high strike rates. At most massness is one background condition which may in combination with other forces encourage strikes. Its relevance is less in the frequency of strikes than in the solidarity with which they are pursued. The cohesiveness of coal miners in particular enables them to support long and bitter strikes. But many other factors need to be taken into account when explaining the nature of their strike activity.

A similar point applies to other theories. For example, technology has been widely seen as a factor: in particular, car plants, because of their size and the drudgery of the assembly line, were felt to generate boredom and discontent, and hence strikes. However, the plants often have low levels of other possible correlates of discontent such as labour turnover. There is also a marked variation not only between countries but within them. The role of technology cannot be entirely discounted however. Certain technologies tend to bring workers together in large numbers; some call on a gang system of work, like the docks, which promotes a group solidarity and permits not only strikes but also the pilfering discussed above. Technology is among the conditions for strike action even though its role is not as a direct determinant of behaviour (see WORK AND ORGANIZATION SYSTEMS).

There is no simple, unified explanation of inter-industry differences in strike rates. Single-factor explanations rapidly break down but there is no list of all the factors which might be relevant, not least of their relative importance. This is not a failure of research, although it is true that variations between industries have attracted little attention (Edwards 1992). Instead it reflects the complexity of the strike, a point taken up below.

Turning to trends, Table 3 shows increases during the 1960s and 1970s in many countries; in Italy for example there was the famous 'hot autumn' of 1969. Many of these strikes reflected shop-floor discontents and concerns about the quality of working life as well as purely economic issues. During the 1980s rates fell fast in some cases, notably the UK and Japan (and also France and the USA). These trends have led some observers to

identify a re-emergence of labour peace (Shalev 1992). This interpretation has to be qualified in a number of ways: the increases in countries like Sweden, reflecting the breakdown of the 'Swedish model' of social consensus (Fulcher 1991); the fact that rates of action in many countries returned to levels similar to those of the immediate post-war period (the UK being an exception, with particularly steep reductions); and the growth of strikes in the Third World, where they had previously been rare, so that, on a global scale, overt conflict has remained at a more or less constant level (Silver 1991). This trend was far from uniform however. In Korea the late 1980s saw a major explosion of labour unrest (Deyo 1989). Rates also rose in

Table 3 Strike trends: annual averages, 1960–91

	GER	ITA	SWE	UK	IND	JAP	KOR	CAN	MEX
Frequency									
1960–4		175	5.3	52.5	30.7	27.2	15.8	51.8	n.a.
1965–9		162	4.3	79.2	48.7	30.9	1.5	82.1	16.2
1970–4		251	19.3	112	59.0	62.2	1.4	92.8	39.7
1975–9		150	24.6	84.3	38.7	40.2	6.2	109	39.7
1980–4		92.6	29.5	42.4	29.8	16.3	10.1	76.9	58.2
1985–9		67.2	27.4	27.8	18.1	8.9	103.3	60.8	8.9
1990–1		50.9*	16.5	16.5	15.6	4.5*	15.4	41.2	5.4
Workers involved									
1960–4	3.4	148	0.6	55.6	14.3	28.5	2.8	13.6	n.a.
1965–9	2.8	198	2.1	46.1	28.5	25.8	2.0	39.8	0.6
1970–4	9.0	278	6.1	58.7	41.1	43.2	0.5	54.3	1.3
1975–9	6.2	591	4.2	66.1	26.3	22.6	0.8	67.5	1.1
1980–4	7.2	452	42.0	45.3	19.9	5.1	1.8	32.5	2.6
1985–9	3.2	190	15.3	28.4	13.7	1.7	22.8	33.6	5.2
1990–1	7.9	76*	8.4	8.5	11.1	1.3*	8.6	20.6	2.1
Volume									
1960–4	18.6	625	4.9	117	109	101	n.a.	201	n.a.
1965–9	5.5	812	19.7	145	285	70.4	7.0	710	n.a.
1970–4	47.8	1049	55.8	441	460	115	0.7	817	n.a.
1975–9	43.4	1140	26.8	477	401	57.8	1.1	877	n.a.
1980–4	43.6	633	225	244	562	10.7	1.9	597	n.a.
1985–9	1.8	183	112	123	331	4.0	251	404	77.9
1990–1	8.8	211*	87.8	48.2	191	2.3*	215	304	20.3

Note: *1990 only involved.
'Workers involved' is the number of workers involved per 1,000 employees.
'Frequency' and 'Volume' are as for Table 2.

Source: Calculated from International Labour Office *Yearbook* statistics

Mexico, where, like Korea, there was a great deal of volatility.

Reasons for the decline in strikes include the following (Edwards 1992). First, changes in the structure of the economy have shifted employment away from sectors such as coal mining and large-scale manufacturing where organized industrial action was most common. The growth of service sector jobs and part-time work has eroded traditional bases of solidarity. Second, economic trends have been unfavourable. There is a long-established tendency in many countries for strikes to decline with business cycle recessions. This is, however, far from universal: in countries like Denmark strikes are relatively common in recessions. This reflects the structure of bargaining, for in the USA or the UK strikes occur when workers can exploit their bargaining power, whereas in Sweden or Denmark this power is contained by national systems of concertation. This short-term trend may have been overlaid by a long-term one. Some scholars identify 'long waves' of economic activity, each lasting around fifty years, and see strike trends as following them (Silver 1991); given past trends such a wave would have reached its low point in 1990. Third, in many countries employers have re-organized industrial relations. This has included direct attacks on trade unions, and as unions have been weakened it has been more difficult to sustain strikes; France, the USA and the UK all exhibit this phenomenon. There have also been efforts to 'individualize' the employment relationship, for example through merit pay and teamworking (see FINANCIAL INCENTIVES; PAYMENT SYSTEMS). Such developments may have eroded some of the traditional sources of dispute between employer and worker. Such an effect is most likely in countries like the USA and the UK, where the developments are most pronounced and where shop-floor bargaining has been most important. They are less likely to have made an impact in a country like Germany.

Turning to the organization of conflict, there are many case studies of individual disputes. Meredeen (1988) outlines some of the general lessons from these one-off studies. First, disputes go through distinct stages of identification of an issue in dispute; a failure to negotiate an agreement, a strike, a climax which leads to an eventual resolution, and an aftermath. Second, bargaining does not conform to a neat model of estimated costs and benefits. This is partly because the parties cannot accurately estimate the risks of a strike and also because strikes involve issues of power as well as a purely economic calculation. Workers may strike despite being fairly sure that they cannot win because they feel that they have to make a stand. In other cases managers may use a strike to deliver much wider lessons about the need to reorganize the production system. In yet others unions can succeed in their goals even though a cost–benefit calculation at the outset would suggest otherwise, certain public sector disputes in the UK again being good examples. The strike is part of a much wider political process, and once parties enter into a dispute it can develop a logic of its own which is far deeper than economic issues. Third, Meredeen outlines a set of more specific lessons, notably that disputes may be managed more or less effectively, together with detailed tactical advice to the parties involved in disputes. Other lessons include the point that prior to a strike there need be no overt indicators of discontent but overt conflict can rapidly explode when, as discussed above, workers' established expectations are disrupted.

The ways in which disputes are managed are important for whether strikes occur and how long they last. This reflects the fact that the strike is a social phenomenon, there being no such thing as the typical or average strike. This in turn helps to explain the difficulty of causal analysis. It is possible to indicate the forces which tend to encourage strikes: over time strikes correlate with the business cycle; at industry level certain technologies or payment systems may promote discontents; and so on. But these forces do not have determinate effects; as noted above, business cycle effects vary between countries. A variety of explanatory approaches is needed to reflect the range of the phenomenon. Thus countries differ in specific ways in their strike experience, and this can be explained in terms of their labour regulation structures. To explain inter-industry variation calls for a different approach, while to explain a specific dispute requires an approach stressing the dynamics of negotiation within structural constraints.

Finally, this leads to the results of strikes. Some strikes can have effects well beyond the immediate issues, for example waves of strikes in 1968 in France which encouraged a reform of the whole industrial relations system, and the dispute in the German engineering industry over working hours in 1984 which led to a widespread reduction in working hours across the economy. Heavy defeats also have major long-term consequences, for example the defeat of the air traffic controllers' strike in the USA in 1981. The wider economic effects of strikes are relatively small. Although there is some evidence in the USA that strikes reduce the equity value of companies affected, there is little evidence of effects on productivity or on long-term economic performance.

5 Current trends and future prospects

The future of conflict is particularly dangerous to predict. In 1960 two US scholars announced the withering away of the strike in the Western world just before a decade of industrial militancy. With this warning in mind, some trends based on existing tendencies may be identified.

In relation to strikes, forces common to Western economies suggest that low levels will continue here. These include the decline in manufacturing employment and the reduction in the size of establishments. Such forces are complemented in some countries, such as the USA, the UK and New Zealand, by the weakness of trade unions and by the efforts by employers and governments to move against collective bargaining (see COLLECTIVE BARGAINING). Such an individualization of the employment relationship is less noticeable in countries such as Germany and Sweden.

In some countries there are suggestions that conflict may take a new 'micro' form. This refers to a focus by workers on the immediate workplace level and a move away from traditional expressions such as large-scale strikes towards smaller actions. More generally, there is the possibility that workers will find new ways of resisting managerial actions, although what these are is as yet unclear.

Outside the West trends are even more difficult to predict. The 'marketization' of the former Soviet system plainly makes strikes more possible than was the case when any industrial action was defined as illegitimate. In the early 1990s Russia saw several bitter strikes among groups such as coal miners. In contrast, high unemployment and an absence of bargaining traditions may contain the use of the strike as a means to express grievances. The rapid industrialization of other countries, such as Korea and Mexico, suggests that they may see more strikes than in the past, although much depends on how far governments are able to suppress trade unions.

Turning to conflict at work, several developments suggest that overt attempts by workers to control the pace and timing of work and to sustain informal rules governing workplace discipline may become less prominent. First there are structural changes. The decline of sectors like the docks where organized pilfering was common suggests that the scope for such activity will decline. Other developments curb opportunities to carry out fiddles. New technology such as Electronic Point of Sale systems in supermarkets makes some traditional fiddles, such as entering the wrong price on a till, more difficult. Similar trends may exist in manufacturing. New production processes that are less dependent than old ones on the skills of workers may make certain forms of adjustment, such as the use of the 'tap' discussed above, less necessary. Technology can also contain the means to monitor worker performance. Some case studies indicate the systematic use of monitoring, although how extensive this development is and, as suggested below, how far workers may find alternative means of resistance, is not yet clear.

Most controversial is the effect of human resource management practices (see HUMAN RESOURCE MANAGEMENT). Are these promoting commitment and satisfaction, thereby reducing the role of conflict, as their proponents claim? There have been very few detailed studies of the impact of human resource management at shop-floor level but existing reviews make several suggestive points. First, as noted above, the 'lean production' associated with Japanese firms often involves very demanding work schedules and intense pressure on workers; there is some evidence that this promotes high accident rates as well as stress (Berggren 1993) (see WORK AND ORGANIZATION SYSTEMS). The spread of Japanese firms to other countries thus may result not in a lack of conflict but in a new form of the organization of conflict, with formal collective disputes being replaced with enterprise-based systems that remove some of the old sources of division between manager and worker but which also increase the pressures on both parties. The implication is that conflict remains a central principle in the organization of work: it is a matter of how workers are controlled and regulated, not the willing production of commitment. Second, there is little evidence that human resource management has penetrated very deeply into actual practice, even in the countries where it has been most proclaimed, namely the USA and the UK. It is certainly important as a set of managerial beliefs, and there has been a growth in the use of specific techniques such as briefing groups. But such techniques still remain quite rare, and even where they are used they may not form part of a programme based on commitment. They may be isolated initiatives and may go alongside the use of traditional modes of labour discipline.

A variety of effects of human resource management has been noted. First there is the *externalization of conflict*. This occurs when a firm aims to recruit a particularly pliant workforce or sub-contracts its operations so as to maintain employment in the core. The former of these is widely noted in studies of new facilities using human resource management techniques: large numbers of applicants are screened and only those who are seen as cooperative are recruited. One key feature is being relatively young and healthy. 'Problem cases' are thus excluded from the organization. The second form of externalization helps a firm to insulate itself from market uncertainties. This is particularly developed in Japan, where large firms have been able to avoid redundancies by practices including: sub-contracting to smaller firms; planning work schedules to include overtime; putting pressure on older workers to leave; and reducing bonus payments. The avoidance of open conflict is predicated upon the large firms' ability to push market uncertainties onto other firms.

Second, there is the *promotion of unitary beliefs*. Systems such as teamworking are presented as promoting a genuine harmony of interests within an enterprise, often strengthened by competition with other firms or even other parts of the same enterprise: workers and managers within a firm are portrayed as being on the same side. Alongside this is a weakening of the mechanisms of traditional adversarial industrial relations. In many cases new systems operate without trade unions. Where unions are involved, their role is often weakened. It is claimed that strong unions are compatible with, and indeed necessary for, such systems. Yet research in North America indicates that new collective agreements often allow management increased discretion to discipline workers; that unions may be involved initially but find their role being marginalized by the emphasis on jointness; and that experiments in union environments are used to try out ideas subsequently introduced in non-union settings (see TRADE UNIONS).

Third, conflict can be *internalized within individuals*. A study by Kunda (1992) of this process examined a high-tech firm in the USA in which there existed a strong and conscious focus on developing an all-embracing company culture. This cultural control was not an alternative to other systems but merely a change in focus – bureaucratic rules were maintained, but the emphasis shifted 'from the organizational structure to the organizational culture, from the members' behavior to their experience' (Kunda 1992: 220). There were distinct results for three groups of employees. First, temporary workers were subject to traditional coercive control (the fear of dismissal). Second, routine clerical workers experienced utilitarian control (the rewards of pay as long as the job was carried out as required). Third, the more senior employees who were the main target of the culture found that the contradictions of the enterprise were internalized in their own work tasks. The need to plan different activities, which under a bureaucratic system would devolve on management and require the allocation of tasks between workers with defined duties, was left to each worker, for there were no limits to work roles. These workers had several ways of retaining autonomy, for example by keeping a sharp distinction between work and home life and by expressing a certain cynicism about corporate messages but the overall picture is one of a reduction in individuals' personal 'space' and an internalization of work pressures.

Such studies suggest that the nature of conflict may be changing, becoming hidden within the interstices of the organization and even within the behaviour of the individual employee. This takes one stage further the move towards micro-conflicts mentioned above. Overall, therefore, the nature of conflict within the work relationship is going through a number of changes. It may be that collective action such as strikes becomes a less reliable indicator of the ways in which conflict is felt and expressed. Other indices such as absence rates may be of some use, although they need careful interpretation. But to understand properly the forces at work calls for close scrutiny of the ways in which work is actually managed. Such scrutiny is important to analysts in charting the nature of the regime, but also to managers themselves since statistical indicators such as absence rates and the increasingly common attitude surveys do not address the hidden aspects of conflict. Hidden conflicts can surface in overt problems and can also undermine efforts to build consent. In organizations which increasingly stress flexibility and empowerment rather than mere obedience to rules, sensitivity to political processes is increasingly important.

PAUL K. EDWARDS
UNIVERSITY OF WARWICK

Further reading

(References cited in the text marked *)

* Berggren, C. (1993) 'Lean production – the end of history?', *Work, Employment and Society* 7 (2): 163–88. (Synthesis of studies of the Japanese employment system, in Japan and overseas, that stresses hidden pressures on workers.)
* Burawoy, M. (1985) *The Politics of Production*, London: Verso. (Essays on the theory of conflict and differences in patterns between countries and over time.)
* Cho, S.K. (1985) 'The labour process and capital mobility', *Politics and Society* 14 (2): 185–222. (Comparison of assembly workers in the USA and Korea.)
* Cohen, R. (1991) *Contested Domains*, London: Zed Books. (Essays on workers in the Third World, focusing on informal modes of protest and adjustment.)
* Deyo, F.C. (1989) *Beneath the Miracle*, Berkeley, CA: University of California Press. (Labour relations in four newly industrializing countries of southeast Asia.)
* Edwards, P.K. (1986) *Conflict at Work*, Oxford: Blackwell. (Synthesis of workplace-level evidence, plus a history of conflict management in three countries.)
* Edwards, P.K. (1992) 'Industrial conflict: themes and issues in recent research', *British Journal of Industrial Relations* 30 (3): 361–404. (Survey of research findings, including shirking, and long-wave and labour regulation theories.)
* Fox, A. (1974) *Beyond Contract*, London: Faber & Faber. (Unitary and pluralist perspectives subjected to a radical critique, plus examples of how trust can be generated.)
* Fulcher, J. (1991) *Labour Movements, Employers and the State*, Oxford: Clarendon Press. (Historical and comparative study of the UK and Sweden, with important wider methodological lessons.)
* Genovese, E.D. (1976) *Roll, Jordan, Roll*, New York: Vintage. (Celebrated study of life on slave plantations in the USA.)
* Hyman, R. (1989) *The Political Economy of Industrial Relations*, London: Macmillan. (Collection of theoretical essays on conflict and empirical analyses of trade unionism.)
* International Labour Office (1994) *Yearbook of Labour Statistics 1994*, 53rd issue, Geneva: International Labour Office. (Useful annual source of information.)

* Kamata, S. (1983) *Japan in the Passing Lane*, London: Allen & Unwin. (Participant observation of life as a temporary worker in a Toyota plant.)

* Kerr, C. and Siegel, A. (1954) 'The interindustry propensity to strike', in A. Kornhauser, A. Dubin and A.M. Ross (eds), *Industrial Conflict*, New York: McGraw-Hill. (Classic study relating strike patterns to the characteristics of occupations across eleven countries.)

* Kondo, D.K. (1990) *Crafting Selves*, Chicago, IL: University of Chicago Press. (Ethnography of work in the small-firm sector in Japan.)

* Korpi, W. and Shalev, M. (1979) 'Strikes, industrial relations and class conflict in capitalist societies', *British Journal of Sociology* 30 (1): 164–87. (Survey of long-term strike trends in industrialized countries: labour peace results from the political power of workers.)

* Kunda, G. (1992) *Engineering Culture*, Philadelphia, PA: Temple University Press. (Ethnography of a high-tech US company.)

* Mars, G. (1982) *Cheats at Work*, London: Counterpoint. (Entertaining but also deeply analytical account of workplace crime, synthesizing much ethnographic work.)

* Meredeen, S. (1988) *Managing Industrial Disputes*, London: Hutchinson. (Seven case studies of major disputes used to develop general lessons on bargaining conduct.)

* Ong, A. (1987) *Spirits of Resistance and Capitalist Discipline*, Albany, NY: State University of New York Press. (Ethnography of Malaysian factory workers, revealing hidden ways of shaping the workplace order.)

* Scott, J.C. (1985) *Weapons of the Weak*, New Haven, CT: Yale University Press. (Ethnography of peasants in Malaysia, focusing on everyday forms of resistance and its limits.)

* Shalev, M. (1992) 'The resurgence of labour quiescence', in M. Regini (ed.), *The Future of Labour Movements*, London: Sage Publications. (Strike trends for OECD countries suggest a widespread decline in militancy.)

* Silver, B. (1991) 'World-scale patterns of labour–capital conflict', in I. Brandell (ed.), *Workers in Third World Industrialization*, London: Macmillan. (Measures of collective protest across the globe point to rising militancy in much of the Third World.)

See also: CAREERS; COLLECTIVE BARGAINING; CORPORATISM; EMPLOYEE RELATIONS, MANAGEMENT OF; FLEXIBILITY; HUMAN RESOURCE MANAGEMENT; INDUSTRIAL AND LABOUR RELATIONS; OCCUPATIONAL PSYCHOLOGY; ORGANIZATION BEHAVIOUR; PAYMENT SYSTEMS; TRADE UNIONS; WORK AND ORGANIZATION SYSTEMS

Related topics in the IEBM: COMMITMENT IN JAPAN; MANAGEMENT IN DEVELOPING COUNTRY ENVIRONMENTS; MANAGEMENT IN GERMANY; MANAGEMENT IN ITALY; MANAGEMENT IN JAPAN; MANAGEMENT IN NORTH AMERICA; POWER

Industrial and labour relations

Overview

Industrial (or labour) relations encompasses the study of the employment relationship. Ultimately the rationale for the discipline is the continued significance of work for the maintenance and advance of human societies. This necessitates the existence of a vitally consequential labour or employee group, which is involved in a fundamental economic, social and political relationship with employers and management. Moreover, the outcomes of this relationship are so crucial to the long-term survival, let alone continued prosperity of any given country, that it inevitably includes the state or government as well.

To define the subject in these terms is not necessarily contentious but it is an approach which is not universally accepted. Thus US scholars have typically adopted an even broader understanding of the subject, viewing it as an interdisciplinary field which covers all aspects of people at work. For scholars in the Third World, the saliency of the state for employment relationships has been underscored and, hence, the independent role of labour and management is generally considered to be of limited consequence. By contrast, many British definitions have been much more narrow, focusing either on different patterns of job regulation associated with the institutions of collective bargaining or, in more radical accounts, on the 'processes of control over work relations'. But to centre on the employment relationship is sufficiently general to be applicable to all types of industrial and industrializing society; and yet it is sufficiently circumscribed to differentiate the disciplinary boundaries of industrial relations from other cognate social science and management disciplines.

In more detail, industrial relations scholars tend to assume that in every industrial and industrializing country, there are three main 'actors' or parties with partly common and partly divergent interests: employers and managers, employees and labour (and often trade unions), and the state. A degree of conflict between these groups is regarded as inevitable, but there are typically mechanisms to ensure that it is channelled or accommodated, notably: (1) individual resolution (supported by freedom of contract and by the lack of any substantial restrictions to the operation of the labour market); (2) unilateral determination (by employers, managers, the state, trade unions or workers); and (3) plural modes of regulation (typically under collective bargaining and in which differences are 'expressed, articulated and defended' through independent associations of employers and working people and in which joint determination and responsibility for the terms and conditions of employment has been instituted).

It is further assumed that interests may be shared or conflicting in both so-called production and distribution spheres (the first encompasses the actual work process, the second economic rewards which accrue from employment). On the one hand, then, a series of creative or productive activities are defined by the functions of all organizations. But while their performance may be free of conflict (for example, when managerial decision making is legitimated), equally there are often fundamental struggles along the so-called 'frontier of control', between working people who seek 'freedom on the job' and managers and supervisors who endeavour to plan the overall organization and conduct of work. On the other hand, the allocation of rewards from work may also occasion consensus or conflict. The former depends on fairness or justice governing the principles of distribution. However, in its absence, antagonism is likely and is reflected in familiar disputes over pay and income.

1 Historical context

The earliest writings on industrial relations were linked with an analysis of the Labour Movement and with the various assessments of the potential of trade unions for the radical transformation of capitalist societies (see TRADE UNIONS). As it happens neither Marx nor Engels left behind a systematic or coherent analysis of the limits and possibilities of trade union action; but they are broadly linked with the so-called 'optimistic tradition' in which a radical character for trade unions was identified. Essentially, on this view, trade unions were viewed as 'schools of solidarity' and 'schools of socialism' which would play a fundamental role in societal transformation. Nevertheless, even Marx and Engels were aware of the limitations of trade union action and clearly came to view economic crises as having at best the potential for the radicalization of the labour movement. For Lenin, Luxemburg and Trotsky the obstacles to revolutionary consciousness emerging from within trade unions were more strongly crystallized. Lenin in particular articulated the case of the so-called 'pessimistic tradition' which suggests that revolutionary consciousness can never stem from the spontaneous economic struggles of working people; but rather (if it is to occur at all) has to be brought in from 'outside the sphere of production' by intellectuals.

Amongst other of the earliest analysts of industrial relations were Perlman and Commons in the USA and the Webbs in the UK. Perlman was one of the earliest of the critics of Marxist approaches to the study of industrial relations. In a *Theory of the Labor Movement* (1928) he argued against not only the 'orthodox Marxians' but also 'ethical' intellectuals (such as Christian Socialists) and 'social efficiency' intellectuals (the Webbs and the Fabians) on the ground that they viewed 'labour' as an 'abstract mass in the grip of an abstract force' that existed only in the intellectual

imagination and was not based at all on the mentality of manual workers. Perlman went on to emphasize that the home grown ideology of labour is based on 'scarcity consciousness' (namely the perception of limited opportunity). This, in turn, leads to so-called 'communism of opportunity' whereby labour seeks to establish job control, ration the opportunities amongst the group and practice solidarity through trade unionism (the ownership of the production and distribution systems being largely irrelevant from this perspective).

No less pre-eminent amongst the earliest US writers on industrial relations and the founder (along with Perlman) of the Wisconsin School was John R. Commons. Against the view of classical economists that behaviour in the workplace may be explained in terms of individual choices, Commons along with other institutionalists focused on the history, origins and behaviour of trade unions. Moreover, the practical emphasis on protective labour legislation and union organization recognized a clash of interests between employers and workers, but one which was not necessarily the product of capitalism itself. Indeed this assumption was later developed by Barbash who viewed the central labour problem as the conflict between the job security of workers and the organizational efficiency or effectiveness needs of employers (for a review see Kochan 1980).

Earlier, in the UK, the Webbs had laid a further foundation of an analysis of trade unionism and industrial relations in *The History of Trade Unionism* and in *Industrial Democracy*. Above all the most influential definition of a trade union in the entire industrial relations literature as 'a continuous association of wage-earners for the purpose of maintaining or improving the conditions of their employment' is encompassed in the very first sentence of '*The History*'. But the main emphasis of the Webbs' writings was empirical, historical and descriptive. However, they were to contribute monumentally to the study of industrial relations in a number of respects. First of all, they not only classified a series of trade union methods but they were the forerunners of the notion of the 'theory of a labour aristocracy' arguing that the organizing abilities of skilled workers within craft-type trade unions were fundamental in establishing sound principles of organization within other types of trade unions. And, above all, they argued forcefully the merits of collective bargaining (by means of which unions negotiate for improvements in pay and conditions with employers), viewing industrial democracy itself as being ultimately founded on this process (see COLLECTIVE BARGAINING).

Moreover, in the evolving discipline of industrial relations the writings of Hoxie and Tannenbaum from the USA were also influential. Hoxie identified a number of labour union types (business, uplift, revolutionary, predatory and dependent). In particular, business unionism was seen as a bargaining institution and as being essentially trade rather than class conscious. He was also a major critic of Taylor (see TAYLOR, F.W.) and the 'scientific management movement' on the grounds that this approach viewed the worker as 'a mere instrument of production' and that it occasioned 'mutual suspicion and controversy' as a result of its inherently anti-democratic assumptions about the management of work. As such, his writings to some extent mirrored those of Mayo and of other contributors to the human relations movement (see HUMAN RESOURCE MANAGEMENT; PERSONNEL MANAGEMENT). However, there was a subtle but fundamental difference in that Hoxie emphasized the desirability of labour union organizations (rather than the reform of management) as the main checkweight to the advance of Taylorism.

Of all the early to mid-nineteenth century US scholars of industrial relations it was, however, Tannenbaum who came closest to embracing the class-based notions of European theorists. Indeed, he viewed the ultimate goal of labour to be the displacement of the capitalist system by a participative democratic model. And, analytically, his work was important in its understanding of labour unions as a defence against competition (occasioned, not least, by the technology of machine-based production) and their provision for greater security for the individual worker.

Modern systematic analysis

Modern systematic analysis of industrial relations, however, largely began with *systems theory*. The most influential of the attempts to define the field of industrial relations in these terms was by John Dunlop (1956) (see DUNLOP, J.T.). In *Industrial Relations Systems* he argued that, in any given society (or social system), it was possible to identify three interlocking systems (the industrial relations system, the economic system and the political system) which were on the same logical plane and were interrelated. That is to say, developments in the political and economic systems influenced the industrial relations system and vice versa. Within the industrial relations system itself, three groups of actors were identified (workers and their organizations, managers and their organizations and governmental agencies concerned with the workplace and work community).

Furthermore, in Dunlop's view, every industrial relations system creates a complex set of rules to govern the workplace and work community. These rules may take a variety of forms in different systems: agreements, statutes, orders, decrees, regulations, awards, policies, and practices and customs. And these 'actors' in the industrial relations system are regarded as confronting an environmental context at any one time. This is composed of three interrelated contexts:

- technology
- market or budgetary constraints
- the power relations and status of the actors

The function of the industrial relations system was seen to be to establish rules which could encompass substantive rules (for example, remuneration in all its forms) and procedures used for setting and administering the substantive rules. Finally, in Dunlop's view, the system is bound together by an ideology of understandings shared by all the actors.

A variety of refinements of the system model were later to be developed but the systems model itself has not been without its critics. It has been viewed as static and not dynamic or historical in its compass. It has been seen as focusing more on structure than on process. Its emphasis on stability rather than conflict has been a principal source of controversy. And other criticisms include its stress on formal rather than informal relationships, its abstract rather than concrete form, its identification of common rather than diverse or pluralist ideologies and its environmental bias so far as explanations for differences in industrial relations systems are concerned.

The *social action perspective* which is based on Weberian sociology has also emerged as a major strand of modern industrial relations thinking. The fundamental assumption is that the actors' own definitions of the situations in which they are engaged is the fundamental basis of explanation of their behaviour and relationships. Rather than viewing behaviour in industrial relations as a function of the systems in which the actors (labour, managers and the state) are enmeshed, the social action perspective stresses the fundamental importance of freedom of action, the ability of actors to influence events based on distinctive orientations, and the importance of choice. Moreover, given that choices are in practice varied and often in conflict, the importance of power in explaining outcomes is constantly stressed. The social action perspective has thus provided a radically different approach to systems theory. However, it is deficient in respect of the limited emphasis placed on economic, technological and political conditions in shaping rather than determining orientations and choices and an appropriate synthesis does combine the notions of action, power and structure to provide a more encompassing explanation.

This desideratum was partly accomplished by the notion of 'frames of reference' (unitary, pluralist and radical). A frame of reference embodies 'the main selective influences at work as the perceiver supplements, omits and structures' what is noticed. A unitary frame of reference emphasizes common values, the notion of the team and a unitary form of authority in the enterprise. A pluralistic frame of reference emphasizes that the workplace is composed of actors with a variety of different interests, aims and aspirations within diverse and often conflicting organizations and groupings (for example trade unions and management), and with diverse foci of loyalty and allegiance. Finally, a radical perspective entails a focus not only on conflict between industrial relations actors but is based on the assumption that there is structured social inequality and substantial imbalances of power amongst the various parties. Nevertheless, frames of reference are best understood as analytical devices rather than as fully developed explanations for different industrial relations phenomena (Fox 1974).

Comparative and international perspectives

Indeed, the evolving discipline of industrial relations has gradually become more international in its compass. Rather than analysing single countries (or being based on debates in specific national contexts), there have been many attempts to analyse patterns of global uniformity and difference. Comparative industrial relations involves the isolation of environmental and other variables to explain patterns of similarity and diversity in more than one country. International studies are more typically referred to as the focus on supranational phenomena (such as European Community (EC) institutions, international trade union organizations and multinational enterprises (MNEs)), while so-called foreign studies encompass the examination of phenomena in a foreign environment and, for theoretical purposes, do not differ substantially from like cases in a home environment.

There are inevitably very many methodological problems involved in comparative industrial relations. First, there is the level of analysis (for example country or industry) to be selected. There are also problems with actual data, for even when there are reasonable sources of international statistics (as for strikes), there are many pitfalls involved in their use stemming not least from different modes of compilation. There is, then, the choice of countries to compare. Is it better to take matched pairs, groups of countries or to assess phenomena globally? Moreover, phenomena which are superficially common to many countries (for example industrial conflict) may not only have very many different forms from one country to the next but also may be understood and interpreted in radically different ways. And finally there is the problem of the dynamic development of industrial relations and of building models which contain elements of a long-term pattern of movement rather than involving only so-called comparative statics (namely where countries or phenomena are compared at a single point in time). None the less, the richness of insights, the explanatory importance and the practical significance of comparative industrial relations substantially outweigh these disadvantages.

Convergence revisited

The first attempt to formulate a general theory of comparative industrial relations is usually traced to Clark Kerr and his colleagues' (1960) seminal work, *Industrialism and Industrial Man*, though in subsequent discussions, its central arguments have been frequently misinterpreted. Certainly Kerr *et al.* envisaged a convergence to a greater degree of uniformity in the world's industrial relations systems in the future. Moreover, the central logic of industrialism or 'common denominator' was seen to stem from the homogenizing forces of new technology. And a wide variety of sources of uniformity were identified that included history and homogeneity, technology and society, the push of progress, education and equality, government and enterprise, and the 'compulsion of comparisons'. But various potent 'threads of diversity' were also isolated that included the persistence of strategies, the imprint of culture, the hour clock of evolution, the culture of industry, and people and performance. This position was further developed by Kerr in the *Future of Industrial Societies* (1983) where the idea of a relatively wide range of possible industrial relations patterns within pluralistic industrialization was reaffirmed and extended. Indeed, although various elements of 'current comparability' and 'increasing similarity' were noted an extensive range of areas of 'continuing substantial dissimilarity' between the world's economic and industrial relations systems was also observed. This

applied not least in the areas of ideology and patterns of belief.

In the early 1990s, however, there may well have been a new pattern of convergence in industrial relations systems. There is thus a significant dependence on markets and free enterprise, coupled with trade unions and employers relatively free from government intervention, and still extensive (if declining) collective bargaining and tripartite consultation. This is occurring not only in the former communist nations but also in the dynamic Asian economies (such as Korea) and in Africa and South America. There remain substantial differences between the democratic market countries, but globally there have been some far reaching convergent trends in industrial relations systems. The forces behind this movement include: (1) markets and global competition; (2) the internationalization of knowledge; (3) the internationalization of production; and (4) new technology.

Diversity in industrial relations systems

There are, then, several modern forces for convergence in industrial relations systems. But, the forces for dissimilarity are no less insistent. These include cultural values and ideologies, political and economic conditions, the institutional framework for industrial relations, the power of the actors, and various temporal movements. In particular, new nations of the Third World may evolve along different trajectories of development from the West and hence emerge with different industrial relations systems (for instance, in respect to the role of the state and legislature and types of trade union). And this may partly override some other homogenizing forces.

How, then, do we explain diversity in industrial relations systems? The most obvious starting point is a social action perspective and an emphasis on the importance of choice. In most industrial relations systems the three main actors (employers and managers, labour, and the state) thus have some measure of determination over institutional arrangements; and this builds a high degree of potential diversity into industrial relations systems

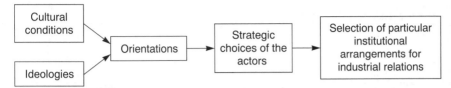

Figure 1 Strategic choice of the actors
Source: Adams and Meltz (1993)

given the differences in objectives and power balances which are in practice feasible. Moreover, strategic choices have a potential significance as potent forces for both stability and change (see Kochan *et al.* 1986).

But if we are to build a satisfactory spatial model of diversity in industrial relations systems, the forces which help to shape strategic choices also require identification. After all, the choices of the actors are focused by orientations which are, in turn, affected by cultural conditions and ideologies (see Figure 1).

It is also vital to note the importance of the distribution of power in the shaping of actual industrial relations outcomes. Whether or not given actors are able to achieve their objectives depends on a process of interaction and struggle and the marshalling of different power resources. These, in turn, are linked with, but not determined by, wider political, economic and technological conditions (see Figure 2).

A temporal model focuses particularly on processes of institutionalization. This implies that industrial relations institutions (for instance, for collective bargaining) can develop in a functionally separate way from wider environmental conditions. Institutions thus

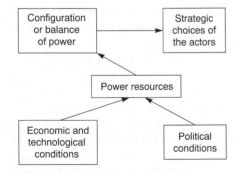

Figure 2 Action, power and structure
Source: Adams and Meltz (1993)

modify the effects of major changes in the environment and ensure a degree of continuity in industrial relations practices over time. They help us to explain the distinctive character of particular industrial relations systems which can continue to differ despite the effects of internationalization.

The way in which diversity continues over time is developed in Figure 3, where the functional separation and autonomy for institutions is shown.

At the point when industrial relations institutions become established (or a major development departs from existing arrangements), the pattern may be understood in terms of the outcome of distinctive strategies of the 'actors' – in specific cultural, ideological, and politico-economic conditions and with a given distribution of power. However, and of great importance, once institutional structures take root they can continue without major change for prolonged periods, despite marked alterations in, say, political and economic conditions. This is partly because of the efforts of those in dominant roles in the institutions concerned who have a clear interest in organizational survival, but also because of processes of socialization (at induction and in committee proceedings and so on) which ensure that new recruits continue to sustain the established machinery. Certainly institutions do change, partly through adaptation to new environmental circumstances, partly through a gradual decline as new arrangements supersede them, and partly through radical transformation in crisis periods. But, over time, they can develop a degree of autonomy from the environmental conditions in which they are situated. Thus, for a long period, the institutions of collective bargaining in the UK appeared to have largely survived the 'Thatcher years', even though the Workplace Industrial

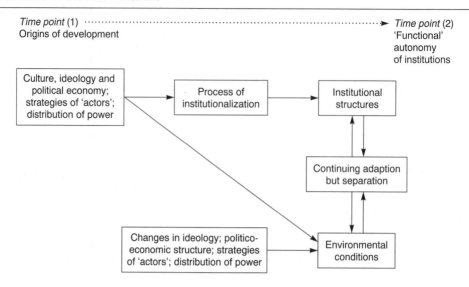

Figure 3 Functional separation

Relations Survey (WIRS 3; Millward *et al.* 1992) does suggest a more substantial decline.

2 The main actors in the industrial relations system

Labour, trade unions and collective bargaining

Turning more specifically, then, to an analysis of the actors in the industrial relations system, in many respects the discipline of industrial relations commenced as we have seen with the study of labour movements (see COLLECTIVE BARGAINING; TRADE UNIONS). The original impetus was an intellectual concern with their radical potential and based on the recognition that labour forms the largest single group in industrial society, the foundation upon which the wealth of nations ultimately rests. More latterly (and linked with the rise of human resource management) has been an understanding of the importance of the motivation and commitment of the workforce for organizational effectiveness and for national competitive advantage (see HUMAN RESOURCE MANAGEMENT).

However, the special focus of industrial relations has been in labour organizations and particularly with trade unions (see TRADE UNIONS). It was once reasonable to classify trade unions from a comparative perspective into:

1 *trade unionism under collective bargaining* (where unions have predominantly instrumental purposes, a high degree of independence from state and management, and largely oppositional functions);

2 *oppositional-type trade unions, with political, religious or nationalist objectives* (political and legislative means predominate in the accomplishment of labour objectives and alignment with political parties is close);

3 *trade unionism under socialism* (predominantly integrative functions and relatively limited independence from the state and management. Given the radical transformation of eastern Europe, however, the last category is no longer so significant.).

Trade unionism under collective bargaining tends to occur in countries with a high degree of industrialization, a strong market economy, a democratic political system and with pluralist rather than corporatist institutions. Collective bargaining involves negotiations between labour organizations (normally trade unions) and either managements or employers' associations and, although a wide range of issues may be encompassed, the typical discussions focus around pay and working conditions (see COLLECTIVE BARGAINING).

The more specific aspects of the analysis of trade unions under collective bargaining cover *density* (namely the percentage of the workforce in trade unions), *structure* and *government*. Clegg (1976) viewed the extent and depth of collective bargaining and support for union density either from employers or from collective bargaining agreements as basic to high levels of union density. In particular, a characteristic of countries with high levels of union density (typically evident in Scandinavian countries) has been the functional separation of political and industrial objectives of labour and the use of Social Democratic parties to ensure a favourable context for trade union recognition. Nevertheless, in the 1990s, the Scandinavian model of industrial relations has been in a process of radical change. Indeed, most (but not all) countries experienced a loss in union membership in the 1980s and early 1990s, a situation which is often attributed to the fulfilment of many labour objectives, as well as to managerial strategies, unfavourable legislation and economic and industrial change (Baglioni and Crouch 1991).

When trade unions use collective bargaining as the foremost means of influencing the terms and conditions of employment, union structure is likely to reflect industrial and occupational divisions and not political or ideological principles. The most common classification of union structures encompasses: craft unions (closed to groups of skilled workers); general unions (open unions prepared in principle to recruit any worker); and industrial unions (linked with specific industries). Later, white-collar and public sector unions emerged and formed independent categories of trade union in countries such as the UK.

How are these variations to be explained? The most detailed and influential thesis is that of Clegg (1976), who focused to begin with on the state of technology and industrial organization at the time of birth and growth of a trade union movement. Although, on his testimony, the new skills of the industrial revolution led

to craft unions; mass production favoured industrial and general unions. Furthermore, as white-collar employees have multiplied, so: 'their unions have grown with the large-scale organizations of the present century' (Clegg 1976: 39). But the methods of trade union regulation are also relevant. Before the advance of collective bargaining unilateral regulation required organization by occupation. But as collective bargaining proliferated, general unions expanded around the previously established crafts which had once relied on unilateral controls. Similarly, if there are no strong occupational unions, industrial unions become pre-eminent. This type of union structure is also strongly favoured on ideological grounds and hence, where unions have been destroyed and when a subsequent reconstruction on a pre-determined pattern is feasible, industrial unionism typically emerges. Finally, white-collar employees: 'tend to perceive their interests as different from those of manual workers and to prefer their own separate occupational unions' (Clegg 1976: 39). Over time, craft unions have tended to decline and a broad evolutionary logic tends to favour either white-collar or general unions. Public sector unions have been affected adversely by trends towards privatization and although industrial unions are preferred on grounds of rationalization, and succeed if they are effectively promoted, they are vulnerable to the fortunes of particular industries.

Trade union *government* involves the internal administrative structures within trade unions and the foremost debates have centred on their democratic potential. The role of the legislature in affecting governmental processes within unions has also been profound. Essentially, environmentalists view the forces affecting democracy or oligarchy in labour unions in terms of external constraints. The political culture (and whether or not it favours pluralism or corporatism) is viewed as of importance here as is the ideological commitment of leaders to democratic principles, environmental uncertainty (which favours oligarchy) or legal provisions. Organizational theorists have examined democratic potential such as participation in elections, divisions of powers and constitutional checks as being salient. In particular, ballots within unions (for the selection of officials) have been seen as fundamental in avoiding oligarchy and these have been supported by the legislature in a variety of countries (for example the USA and the UK).

But trade unions with predominantly instrumental purposes relying on the method of collective bargaining are only one of the main types of labour organization. Indeed, in many instances, a variety of political, religious or nationalist objectives are uppermost and this has pronounced consequences not just for trade union character but also for density, structure and government. Even in the West, many countries in which trade unionism under collective bargaining now predominates once had far more radical labour movements (for example Germany) and important examples remain in which trade unions are dominated by political parties and wider religious affiliations (for example France, Italy). For the bulk of trade unions in the Third World, too, political and legislative channels, rather than collective bargaining, are the foremost means for securing improvements in pay and working conditions.

Globally, then, a second principal type of trade unionism is characterized by: (1) a dominance of political over instrumental purposes; (2) a focus on political or legislative means; (3) a formally oppositional role; and (4) a varied extent of interdependence from state and management.

Most countries with labour organizations of this type have not insignificant private sectors. Above all, however, the strategic choice to establish and to persist with such arrangements rests on: (1) a favourable cultural or ideological background; (2) the stage of industrialism; and (3) a significant state role in industrial and economic activities.

Finally, trade unionism under socialism is characterized by predominantly integrative functions and by a relatively close organic link with state and management. The origins of the main model may be traced to the Leninist conception of democratic centralism which allowed unions some independence but within the strict confines of broader party and government policies. The main break with this model occurred with the rise of Solidarity in Poland that encompassed demands not just for free trade unionism, but also the right to strike, the appointment of managerial staff on the basis of competence, and a range of political demands. Further radical changes in various eastern European countries include: a redefinition of functions including 'pluralization' and 'restructuring' of trade unions; traditional unions having the representation of workers' interests to be their exclusive function, renouncing that of being a 'transmission belt' of party ideology to the workforce; the rise of works collective councils which conflict with traditional trade unions; and a greater independence of trade unions from management and the state generally (Szell 1992).

Managers

Managers are a ubiquitous and expanding group within modern societies and increasingly it has been recognized that their ability to determine many aspects of the employment relationship is of far reaching importance to industry and society (see EMPLOYERS' ASSOCIATIONS; EMPLOYEE RELATIONS, MANAGEMENT OF). To understand the managerial role in industrial relations, the concepts of strategy, style and frame of reference have been fundamental. Strategies are consistent patterns in streams of decisions and actions and are inter-temporal, involving a series of choices taken over a period of time for a given objective. To some extent strategies are linked with market conditions and with the firm's financial performance for, in unfavourable demand conditions, managements are likely to seek greater control over the employment relationship (and not least over pay settlements), whereas organizational slack and local autonomy are more likely where competition in the product market is relatively weak.

Strategies are also linked with preferred styles of industrial relations management. The main styles are authoritarian (directive), paternal (directive but welfare orientated), constitutional (negotiated and based on reaching agreements with organized labour and governments) and participative (involving employees in decisions). The first pair are typically linked with unitary frames of reference and the second pair with more pluralistic notions. Variations of these styles include traditionalism (based on forceful opposition to trade unions), sophisticated paternalism, sophisticated modern and standard modern approaches (see EMPLOYEE RELATIONS, MANAGEMENT OF).

The analysis of the role of manager in industrial relations has also been linked with strategic human resource management (SHRM). Even though many firms still do not practice SHRM, the recognition of the key role of human resources for competitive advantage has occasioned a rich seam of analyses of the importance of employee involvement, human resource flow policies, high commitment work systems and appropriate incentives and rewards of which all managers (and not only those directly involved in personnel or industrial relations) need to have cognizance (see HUMAN RESOURCE MANAGEMENT).

Governments and the role of the state

Despite considerable problems in identifying the personnel, locating its various segments and reaching an acceptable definition, the state is indisputably the third force in the industrial relations system. The state is not easy to define unambiguously, but it is a shorthand expression for a series of institutions encompassing the legislature, the executive, central administration (the civil service), the judiciary, the police and local government. Moreover, all these institutional agents may be involved in industrial relations depending on context and country.

In the West, the main types of state intervention are:

1 *pluralism* (a circumscribed state influence in a fragmented and decentralized political economy such as the USA and the UK);
2 *societal corporatism* of the so-called corporatist democracies (in which centralized or moderately centralized governments reach agreements with strongly organized

and usually centralized interest groups such as Austria and Sweden);
3 *state corporatism* (where strongly interventionist governments are unchecked by independent organizations of labour, for example in Franco's Spain).

The establishment and maintenance of pluralist industrial relations institutions is fostered by: (1) a wider culture in which there is an enduring commitment to 'freedom of association' and a 'moral duty' to seek compromises and concessions; (2) broad ideologies which are in opposition to monist forms of government and in which consensus is seen to rest on deeply rooted political beliefs and not on the performance or output of the system; (3) an economic structure which has evolved from a pronounced *laissez-faire* stage; (4) a democratic political structure comprised of a two- or multi-party system; (5) countervailing powers amongst the other actors in the industrial relations system (the independent strength of labour being vital); and (6) at an institutional level, the durability of collective bargaining institutions and willingness, by managements in particular, to recognize and to bargain in good faith with representatives of labour.

Corporatism in industrial relations is a common form of state role in countries in which governments have always been active in economic planning (see CORPORATISM). It is also nurtured by a commitment to harmony and identity of interests at a cultural or ideological level, reflected in a range of ethical and political philosophies that include Catholicism, Conservatism and Social Democracy. Societal corporatism is the logical outcome of powerful, centrally organized interest groups and of open competitive political systems. By contrast, state corporatism is facilitated by the concentration of powers in government, monopoly forms of capital, the absence of independent association of labour, and political systems with a single party.

In the erstwhile eastern bloc there were once pronounced variations in the state's role in industrial relations, encapsulated in the divergent experiences of command systems and market systems. But in all cases, the patterns of industrial relations were affected by single-party government and by the public ownership of the means of production, ensuring the absence of an independent body of employers and a largely integrative function for trade unions.

In developing societies the role of the state in industrial relations is almost invariably substantial, suggesting that the divergencies amongst nations stem in part from the timing of industrialism. Thus, in the predominantly corporatist countries of the Third World, *laissez-faire* policies in the economy and in industrial relations were seldom considered (as in Latin America). Moreover, in the developing socialist nations (for example China), planning ensures that the state's impact is more substantial than at a comparable stage of industrialism in the west.

It was once assumed that the state would not wither away but would become more important globally as governments intervened both in the economy and in the resolution of labour disputes. But if anything, what appears now to be the case is a trend towards an increasingly legalized form of industrial relations but a diminishing coordinating state role overall. Moreover, privatization has curtailed the state role and diminished the saliency of national-level collective bargaining.

3 Major themes in industrial relations

Industrial conflict

Turning now to examine some of the ascendent themes of industrial relations, conflict in the employment relationship (and attempts to explain its incidence and variations and to develop channels to accommodate it) are basic to the rationale of industrial relations (see INDUSTRIAL CONFLICT). The systems analyst views conflict as ubiquitous, but ultimately as a form of deviant behaviour, and hence focuses upon rule-making processes for tension management and grievance resolution. Pluralists and Marxists see it as endemic in industrial societies with substantial private sectors (the former stress interest-group

divisions and the latter the cleavages based on social class).

Conflict, however, is multidimensional and includes *qualitative* dimensions (for example expressions of hostility) as well as *quantitative* dimensions (for example strike activity). Moreover, strikes themselves are not homogeneous events. They involve a cessation of work, a breakdown in the flow of consent and an open expression of aggression, and remain a social phenomenon of enormous complexity. Indeed, leaving aside problems of validity and reliability of data the experience of particular countries is by no means consistent on every measure of strike activity. The disparate measures of strikes used in comparative analysis yield four main dimensions:

1 *frequency* (the number of work stoppages in a given unit of analysis over a specified time period);
2 *breadth* (the number of workers who participate in work stoppages);
3 *duration* (the length of stoppages, usually in man-days work lost);
4 *impact* (the number of working days lost through stoppages).

Internationally, the following profiles of strikes have been typically identified.

Type 1: Long duration of stoppages is dominant: characteristic of the USA, Canada and Ireland.
Type 2: Considerable breadth of disputes largely determines overall shape, as exemplified by Italy and to a lesser extent Finland, Spain and Israel.
Type 3: The structure of strikes is determined principally by the relatively high frequency figures: the case for Australia and New Zealand and, to a lesser extent, France and Portugal.
Type 4: A similar ranking in terms of frequency, duration and membership involvement produces the characteristic strike 'shape' of the UK and Japan.
Type 5: A typically low incidence of strike activity, but the duration of the few stoppages is not insignificant: characteristic of Belgium,

Denmark, The Netherlands, Norway and Sweden.

Explanations for variations in conflict include culture, political and economic conditions, the strategies of management and industrial relations institutions. Culture, for instance, has been used to explain varied conflict patterns in the Third World with the commitment to harmony in neo-Confucian countries in part accounting for a low incidence of strike activity. Political conditions have usually been linked with the low levels of conflict in the Social Democracies of northern Europe where historical compromises between employers, labour and the state have been isolated as central to relative industrial democracy.

Economic variables such as inflation are seen as enhancing conflict, while high levels of unemployment tend to reduce it. Authoritarian management styles are also seen as likely to enhance conflict. Finally, institutionalists see the level of collective bargaining as crucial with national collective bargaining tending to be associated with low levels of conflict and highly fragmented, decentralized labour-management agreements being viewed as conducive to it. Moreover, for the most part the 1980s and early 1990s witnessed a reduction in the incidence of conflict in most countries of the West (because of changes in legislation, higher levels of unemployment, weakened labour movements and better procedures for resolving disputes).

In the erstwhile eastern bloc, however, strikes were once relatively rare (conflict typically was expressed in terms of protests and high rates of absenteeism and poor workmanship), though this situation has now changed considerably. The Third World revealed (and still reveals) a varied incidence of strike activity (relatively high in India and the Caribbean; very low in east Asia amongst the 'little dragons' such as Taiwan and South Korea), the explanations being linked with culture, the degree of radicalization of labour movements and divergent management styles.

Industrial democracy

During the twentieth century few issues have been more consequential in debates on industrial relations than industrial democracy (see INDUSTRIAL DEMOCRACY). The term usually encapsulates the notion of the exercise of power by workers and their representatives over decisions within their place of employment, coupled with a modification of the distribution of authority within the workplaces. For the Webbs, it will be recalled, it was to be rooted in the institutions and processes of collective bargaining. Increasingly it has proved to be conceptually valuable to distinguish economic and industrial democracy and to attempt a synthesis of the two terms in an inclusive theory of organizational democracy. Economic democracy denotes a variety of forms of employee participation in the ownership enterprises in which they are employed (see PROFIT SHARING AND EMPLOYEE SHAREHOLDING SCHEMES) and in the distribution of economic rewards. Conditions which favour the growth of industrial democracy may also facilitate economic democracy but the two developments are not invariably co-terminous.

A classification of the main types of industrial democracy encompasses:

1 workers' self-management (as in the old Yugoslavia);
2 producer cooperatives (as at Mondragón);
3 co-determination (as in Germany);
4 works councils and similar institutions (as in Germany and The Netherlands);
5 trade union initiatives (as in the UK);
6 shop-floor programmes (as in Sweden and the USA).

Globally, each of these main types has distinctive defining characteristics, internal structural properties and range of incidence.

With respect to the explanations for the development of industrial democracy, however, three main approaches have been dominant based on the notions listed below:

- favourable conjunctures
- evolutionary forces
- cycles.

The favourable conjunctures approach involves the isolation of underlying factors which account for the rise of industrial democracy; but it does not assume the inevitability of either so-called evolutionary or cyclical movements in its development. By contrast, evolutionary thinkers have argued that the state and the legislature have increasingly influenced moves towards organizational democracy. In their view, this has arisen in part because of a determination to regulate industrial relations, but also because of the electoral consequences of governments failing to secure labour peace by means of the active participation of the workforce in ownership and control of the enterprise. It is also argued that modern managers are likely to be well versed in human resourcing techniques that promote employee influence and involvement (see HUMAN RESOURCE MANAGEMENT). However, in the early 1980s, a cyclical interpretation of organizational democracy gained increasing currency. Under this view, the idea that there are long-term movements in modern societies which consistently favour the advance of industrial democracy is disputed. Developments in industrial democracy are viewed as neither radical nor irreversible; and a high failure rate can be explained by the search for consensus coming up against the reality of conflict between the industrial relations parties. Increasingly, there has been the focus on the analysis of micro-situations to highlight the complex patterns which occur in reality and, in the advanced European researches of the Industrial Democracy in Europe International Research Group, on the patterns of influence and power distribution from one country to the next (see industrial democracy).

The distribution of economic rewards

The distribution of economic rewards has always been a major source of conflict within industrial relations and a key theme within the literature itself. Much of *labour* economics has been associated with labour markets and their imperfections and this strand within industrial relations thinking has seen a resurgence associated with the decline of institutional machinery for collective bargaining for reaching agreements on pay and associated issues occurring in many countries in the 1980s and early 1990s (see PAYMENT SYSTEMS).

The theory of human capital has been particularly influential within debates on labour economics and in its contribution to the analysis of industrial relations issues. The basic concept of human capital implies that those who have been trained have incurred a foregone earnings loss. However, their productivity will have increased also which enables them to be paid more assuming that earnings equal marginal product. Moreover, human capital theory implies that rates of return on human and physical capital will be broadly comparable, an argument which is used not only to support increasing investment in education and skills acquisition within industry, but also to persuade governments to invest in their people in this way (see TRAINING). There is a convergence between human capital theory and modern versions of human resource development in these respects (see HUMAN RESOURCE DEVELOPMENT).

Furthermore, there is a long tradition of economic analysis of trade unions viewing these organizations as attempting to maximize a 'utility function', with a focus on wages and employment. However, it should be said that union behaviour is in actuality shaped by a complicated pattern of interdependent relations and unions are clearly not just market bargainers but have a range of political and social objectives.

Typically trade union members do have an income advantage over non-union members and low dispersal of income is generally correlated with trade union density (as in the Scandinavian countries). Furthermore, the power of the state is important. If incomes policies are in operation, typically dispersal of incomes is reduced as a consequence of the narrowing of differentials. But the late 1980s and 1990s have typically seen a spread of differentials in the advanced economies associated with the substantially greater role for markets and the declining power of trade union movements (Baglioni and Crouch 1991).

In so far as comparative analyses of the distribution of economic rewards is concerned a range of cultural, political and economic conditions affect the varying patterns which occur. Broadly speaking, accompanying economic development, income inequality tends first to increase and then substantially to diminish over time. In many Third World countries income dispersal is affected by the penetration of multinational companies and by dualism in labour markets (as in Kenya and Brazil).

4 Emergent issues in industrial relations

So far we have examined various theories of industrial relations (and particularly those focused on comparative analysis) together with the historical origins of the discipline and the main areas of coverage of the subject. At this point some emergent themes are assessed, with the focus on seven areas:

- new technology
- Japanization
- 'new' realism
- human resource management strategies
- privatization and the transformation of eastern Europe
- internationalization
- flexibility.

New technology

Technology has been viewed as a key determinant of industrial relations but for much of the time it has been analysed in a deterministic and ahistorical framework (see WORK AND ORGANIZATION SYSTEMS). But the rise of new technologies (associated with the microelectronics revolution) has in part been the stimulus for new debates on the impact of technology. These have increasingly encompassed the notion of choice and the ways in which technology offers options from which management, trade unions and governments can select. Moreover, technology has been seen to link with broader product and market strategies and not as a force independent of social institutions.

The early debates on new technology have also been enriched by labour process theory. The origins can be traced to Braverman's *Labor and Monopoly Capital* (1974) in which new technologies were seen to be associated with the relentless tightening of managerial control and the consequent 'de-skilling' and 'degradation of work'. However, opponents of this view have focused on its deterministic character, the under-emphasis of worker resistance and the ways in which new skills are constantly thrown up by radical changes in technology. However, from this analysis has arisen a variety of attempts, in both the USA and Europe, to link technology with the organization and control of the labour process that has added an important dimension to earlier analyses.

Japanization

The emergence of Japan as a leading world power in the latter part of the twentieth century has also been accompanied by an increasing focus on the phenomenon of 'Japanization' (see JAPANIZATION). Originally, the analysis tended to focus on industrial relations in Japan itself and typically involved the identification of three main pillars (lifetime employment, enterprise trade unionism and seniority-based payment systems) as crucial. Gradually, however, the tendency not only for Japanese firms operating outside Japan but also for other firms to emulate Japanese practices has stimulated fresh analyses and debates.

The first of these has been associated with the notion of the strategic management of the 'human resource' informed by company and country culture. This, in turn, has been seen to link with a range of more specific practices such as total quality management, quality circles, just-in-time, flexibility, direct employee communications, single status facilities, single union deals and team briefing. Critics of Japanization have argued that these practices are not all easily traceable to Japanese conditions (and that some practices indeed were imported from the USA); that many practices do not easily take root in different cultural and institutional conditions; and that practices in Japan are not static and immutable but are subject to considerable change over time. Indeed, debates have increasingly shifted to encompass east Asian countries (the little dragons) more generally as a consequence of the economic expansion of the whole of this geopolitical region (see INDUSTRIAL RELATIONS IN JAPAN; HUMAN RESOURCE MANAGEMENT IN JAPAN).

'New' realism

In part associated with the phenomenon of Japanization has been the focus on new realism and new strategies for labour movements. Accompanying a significant decline in trade union membership in most advanced western economies there has been a major rethink of labour strategies in many countries. Even so-called traditional unions have turned away from a reliance on voluntarism and collective bargaining and have increasingly sought legal protection. Moreover, unions operating on the basis of a new realism in countries such as the UK have, in return for recognition, accepted 'no strike clauses', single union agreements and compulsory arbitration.

These debates are familiar in North America where the issue of union membership decline has been a preoccupation for a longer period than in western Europe. Here the case has been articulated for 'associational unionism' including a focus on principles (to advance employee rights generally), the support of increased internal education and participation, multiple forms of representation and service, a wider choice of tactics and extended alliances. Certainly a range of contrasting theoretical and empirical issues have emerged as a consequence of debates on the notion of a long-term decline in labour movements, the reduced importance of collective bargaining and collectivism generally and a far less influential role for trade unions in governmental policy at a national level and in the joint regulation of the employment relationship.

Human resource management strategies

The enhanced power of managers at enterprise level has led to a range of industrial relations issues being increasingly subsumed under human resource management. Rather than the joint regulation of the employment relationship by unions and management under collective bargaining, increasingly a resurgent management has sought to determine many aspects of pay and working conditions at enterprise level on a unilateral and unitaristic basis, linked with the overall business strategy of the firm and the striving for competitive advantage in the market place (see HUMAN RESOURCE MANAGEMENT).

Human resource management, which involved more strategic approaches to personnel and was the responsibility of all management (particularly general), originated in the USA and arrived in the mid-1980s in the UK and much of Europe. It was associated with changes in the political climate and a reduced power of labour (see HUMAN RESOURCE MANAGEMENT). Its focus on employee involvement and total quality management, on strategic human resource flow policies (including the maintenance of core labour forces) (see HUMAN RESOURCE FLOWS), on different reward systems (including performance and profit-related pay, and profit sharing) (see FINANCIAL INCENTIVES; PROFIT SHARING AND EMPLOYEE SHAREHOLDING SCHEMES), and new work systems (multi-skilling, multiple roles and job enrichment) (see WORK AND ORGANIZATION SYSTEMS) represented a radical challenge to many aspects of decision making on the employment relationship.

There have been many controversies on the meaning and compass of human resource management, and above all, on whether it is merely a relabelling of practices rather than the harbinger of fundamental changes in the workplace. Moreover, empirically it is often the case that firms with the greatest evidence of having at least traces of human resource management practices are also more likely to have trade unions (albeit with far less influence over decision making in the employment relationship than was once the case). But in most European countries, no issue has been of greater importance to debates in the 1980s and 1990s on the changing nature of industrial relations than the rise of human resource management and the resurgence of managerial power on which this is ultimately based.

Privatization and the transformation of eastern Europe

The global ascendance of markets as a means of resource allocation in the 1980s and 1990s also has had profound consequences for industrial relations. In the West and in many Third World countries there has been extensive privatization and restructuring; a process which has been gaining momentum in a far more fundamental way in eastern Europe.

The advent of privatization (on a large scale) within western Europe has of course ideological roots in political and economic as well as industrial relations assumptions. But in industrial relations terms, in countries such as the UK, the main arguments have been based on the perceived deleterious consequences of the power of unions in the public sector (founded on favourable recognition policies and national collective bargaining agreements), the lack of streamlining of industrial relations, the provision for unilateral arbitration in some procedural agreements, and the lack of responsiveness of pay settlements in the public sector to local, regional and occupational labour markets. Moreover, although the evidence suggests that there have been substantial differences between industries so far as the effects of privatization are concerned, greater flexibility, extensive subcontracting, decentralization of management structures and policies on industrial relations, performance-related pay and profit sharing and employee share ownership have typically emerged from this radical process of change in the ownership of key industries and services (for example in the UK, France and Greece).

But these changes (however dramatic and consequential they may have been) have been dwarfed to some extent by the events in eastern Europe in the 1990s. The upshot of these events is likely to be diverse (although almost inevitably privatization will feature as a major issue). To take some examples: the former German Democratic Republic is likely to witness the extension of West German institutions more or less intact. In that sense, the West German capital labour settlement is likely to be exported and to include works councils, co-determination and a strong legal and institutional basis for trade unionism and collective agreements. On the other hand, the stresses of unification are unlikely to overcome the wider problem of the friction between national modes of regulation and industrial relations and the increasingly internationalized economy which is affecting all European countries. In the various republics which have replaced the old Soviet Union again diversity is to be expected, albeit with greater autonomy for managers at factory level, more independence for trade unions and plant-based organs of worker representation being typical and consequential developments. In Hungary there has been the emergence of independent trade unionism as part of the wider reform process. But, unlike Solidarity in Poland, these are not mass trade union organizations; reform of the existing trade unions has been more typical in countries like Bulgaria and Russia rather than the emergence of radically different trade union movements.

Internationalization

A further dominant tendency in industrial relations in the latter part of the twentieth and into the twenty-first century is the internationalization of markets, production, knowledge and institutions. In respect of industrial relations there have been in any event a series of International Labour Organization (ILO) standards, and indeed its conventions and recommendations are a major source of labour law. Employers' organizations (such as the Union of Industrial and Employers' Confederations of Europe (UNICE)) have developed internationally. And there are three main international federations of trade unions – the International Confederation of Free Trade Unions (ICFTU), the World Federation of Trade Unions (WFTU) and the World Confederation of Labour (WCL). But the modern development of internationalization has not only been enhanced by the spread of knowledge that enables, say, managements to introduce practices developed originally in a different national context (the spread of Japanese practices being an obvious example), but by the growth of geopolitical groupings such as the EC.

In particular, the single European market is likely to impact on industrial relations in member states in a variety of different ways (see INDUSTRIAL RELATIONS IN EUROPE; HUMAN RESOURCE MANAGEMENT IN EUROPE). The development of a single market is linked with the social dimension which covers diverse aspects of the employment relationship such as safety and health, working hours and remuneration. Its effects are likely to be considerable on both institutions and outcomes in member states though harmonization is in practice likely to be uneven. Furthermore, there are the models for the European company and the European works council proposals, even though uneven patterns of development are probable in practice. Centralized pay bargaining is however unlikely and given that the current gender pay differentials appear to depend on the degree of fragmentation of bargaining (being narrower in more centralized bargaining systems) any trend towards decentralization of bargaining (and the erosion of national institutions) may lead to greater convergence but bring about greater rather than lesser inequality.

The rise of the MNE is also of signal importance to industrial relations. Part of this stems from the deployment of common human resource management philosophies and policies in some companies (for example IBM, McDonald's). But, in any event, in their search for productivity and quality improvements, MNEs increasingly seek to win agreements in local bargaining. These operations tend thus to undermine national and regional collective agreements and, in the Third World, to occasion as well as to reinforce segmentation in labour markets. Moreover, and not surprisingly, international union organizations such as the ICFTU have the activities of MNEs high on the agenda of their emerging action strategies.

Flexibility

The ascendance of market over planned systems is intimately linked with the further issue of flexibility (see FLEXIBILITY). This encompasses a number of arrangements such as numerical flexibility (where the peripheral rather than the core labour force adapts to the varying labour requirements of the enterprise); functional flexibility (where the core labour force becomes more flexible, multiskilled and eschews traditional demarcation) and financial flexibility (where the reward and pay systems are flexible, for example by means of profit-related pay or profit sharing). None the less comparative research on these issues suggests a major rethinking of these categories is necessary. Employers in practice develop strategies in an *ad hoc* and incremental fashion and there are configurations rather than either/or choices that are informed by business objectives but which also integrate specific social and national factors.

But the flexibility debate is important in the further respect of highlighting potential future scenarios for industrial relations. First of all, the changing sociopolitical environment which fosters flexibility clearly impacts critically on industrial relations elements such as the influence and role of trade unions and the extent and scope of collective bargaining. Above all, however, it is associated with new (or arguably very old) employment patterns with legislature based on radically overturning bargained job or employment security and protection. The outcomes include short-term contracts, radical alterations to patterns of working time, pay flexibility and job content flexibility. The outcome of this is that in modern discussions, the future often is viewed no longer in terms of an alternative industrial relations system built around human resource management and a heightened managerial prerogative. Rather, what may increasingly emerge are non-union enterprises with very little organized industrial conflict; high labour turnover and industrial injuries; more performance-related and merit pay; little interest in job evaluation; high pay differentials; extensive use of freelance and transitory labour; the resort to compulsory redundancy as a means of reducing a labour force; limited use of formal grievance procedures; limited use of consultative committees or employee health and safety representatives; and limited information for employees (Millward *et al.* 1992). In short, one scenario for the future is the flexible non-union firm and the end of institutional industrial relations as it emerged in the West over a century of struggle. Moreover, although globally the outcomes are unlikely to be quite so stark, it remains a likely outcome of the modern trend towards globalization of production and markets. Nevertheless, divergent as well as convergent forces are unmistakeable in a cross-national context and, for this reason, major transformations in political and economic systems are unlikely to produce an identity of outcomes and will ensure that the considerable variations in industrial relations systems which still characterize global experience are likely to continue well into the twenty-first century.

MICHAEL POOLE
CARDIFF BUSINESS SCHOOL

Further reading

(References cited in the text marked *)

* Adams, R.J. and Meltz, N.H. (eds) (1993) *Industrial Relations Theory: Its Nature, Scope and Pedagogy*, Metuchen, NJ: IMLR Press/Rutgers University and the Scarecrow Press Inc. (An assessment of various approaches to a range of theories of industrial relations. Covers the teaching of industrial relations theory, the nature and scope of the subject.)
* Baglioni, G. and Crouch, C. (eds) (1991) *European Industrial Relations*, London: Sage Publications. (Covers some of the major changes in European industrial relations occasioned by the new political and economic conditions of the 1980s; an important source of analysis and debate.)
* Braverman, H. (1974) *Labor and Monopoly Capital*, New York: Monthly Review Press. (This is a formative work arguing for a de-skilling of work as a result of technological changes and the developments within capitalist society.)
* Clegg, H.A. (1976) *Trade Unionism under Collective Bargaining*, Oxford: Blackwell. (An important comparative work analysing the factors explaining variations in trade unionism and collective bargaining in selected Western industrial societies.)
* Dunlop, J.T. (1956) *Industrial Relations Systems*, New York: Henry Holt & Co. Inc. (A classic theoretical work outlining the systems approach to industrial relations and establishing the 'content' of the discipline.)
  Edwards, P.K. (ed.) (1990) *Industrial Relations: Theory and Practice in Britain*, Oxford: Blackwell. (A valuable, critical and informed overview of the British experience.)
* Fox, A. (1974) *Beyond Contract: Work, Power and Trust Relations*, London: Faber & Faber. (An important and influential work on the evolution of industrial relations thinking in which the notion of 'frames of reference' (unitary, pluralist and radical) are developed.)
* Kerr, C. (1983) *Future of Industrial Societies*, Cambridge, MA: Harvard University Press. (An update of the classic study, *Industrialism and Industrial Man*. Even more diversity in the world's industrial relations systems are identified.)
* Kerr, C., Dunlop, J.T., Harbison, F. and Myers, C.A. (1960) *Industrialism and Industrial Man*, Cambridge, MA: Harvard University Press. (The foundation work for comparative industrial relations outlining the notions of pluralistic industrialism, convergence and the importance of new technology.)
* Kochan, T.A. (1980) *Collective Bargaining and Industrial Relations*, Homewood, IL: Irwin. (An influential study of industrial relations and collective bargaining in the USA. Broadly defined, it sets the historical background within the development of industrial societies.)
* Kochan, T.A., Katz, H.C. and McKersie, R.B. (1986) *The Transformation of American Industrial Relations*, New York: Basic Books. (After a prolonged period of stability, the US's industrial relations underwent a major transformation which is detailed in this major book.)
* Millward, N., Stevens, M., Smart, D. and Hawes, W. (1992) *Workplace Industrial Relations in Transition*, Aldershot: Dartmouth Press. (The third of the influential WIRS in the UK; led to major debates on 'the end of institutional industrial relations' and on the re-emergence of flexible labour markets and employment systems.)
* Perlman, S. (1928) *Theory of the Labor Movement*, New York: Macmillan. (This is a classic of management studies in which the author argues against the Marxist analysis of trade unionism.)
  Poole, M. (1986) *Industrial Relations: Origins and Patterns of National Diversity*, London: Routledge. (Attempts to uncover some of the under-

lying forces (and patterns) of national diversity in industrial relations systems; examples both from the Third World and developed nations.)

Southall, R. (ed.) (1988) *Trade Unions and the New Industrialisation of the Third World*, London: Zed Books. (This is an informed reader covering a variety of aspects of industrial relations in the Third World.)

* Szell, G. (ed.) (1992) *Labour Relations in Transition in Eastern Europe*, Berlin: Walter de Gruyter. (Industrial relations in eastern Europe have been in a state of 'flux' and this is a bold attempt to bring together papers highlighting developments in eastern Europe.)

* Webb, S. and Webb, B. (1902) *The History of Trade Unionism*, London: Longmans Green. (This is a monumental treatise on trade unionism in the UK which is immensely painstaking in its details of the analysis.)

* Webb, S. and Webb, B. (1920) *Industrial Democracy*, London: Longmans Green. (In this classic study the Webbs argue that collective bargaining is the key to industrial democracy.)

See also: COLLECTIVE BARGAINING; COMMITTMENT; CORPORATISM; DUNLOP, J.T.; EMPLOYEE RELATIONS, MANAGEMENT OF; EMPLOYERS' ASSOCIATIONS; FINANCIAL INCENTIVES; FLEXIBILITY; HUMAN RESOURCE FLOWS; HUMAN RESOURCE DEVELOPMENT; HUMAN RESOURCE MANAGEMENT; HUMAN RESOURCE MANAGEMENT IN EUROPE; HUMAN RESOURCE MANAGEMENT IN JAPAN; INDUSTRIAL CONFLICT; INDUSTRIAL DEMOCRACY; INDUSTRIAL RELATIONS IN EUROPE; INDUSTRIAL RELATIONS IN JAPAN; INDUSTRIAL RELATIONS IN THE USA; JAPANIZATION; PAYMENT SYSTEMS; PERSONNEL MANAGEMENT; PROFIT SHARING AND EMPLOYEE SHAREHOLDING SCHEMES; TAYLOR, F.W.; TRADE UNIONS; TRAINING; WOMEN MANAGERS IN ORGANIZATIONS; WORK AND ORGANIZATION SYSTEMS

Related topics in the IEBM: LABOUR MARKETS

Industrial sabotage

Overview

Sabotage or the threat of sabotage is a central determinant of the balance of power in contemporary organizations. Throughout the history of industry and commerce, it has been used as a weapon by those with less formal power and has been practised and refined as an art of resistance. It has been discussed widely, but has been the subject of only a few comprehensive and sustained studies. Loose definitions of the concept predominate. It is defined here as deliberate action or inaction that is intended to damage, destroy or disrupt some aspect of the workplace environment, including the property, product, processes or reputation of the organization.

In contrast to the image of the 'mad saboteur', careful review of existing research leads to the conclusion that most acts of sabotage are highly symbolic, are restrained and selective, are the product of collective or even conspiratorial efforts, and are performed with technical sophistication. They tend to be deliberate and calculated rather than impulsive and careless.

Some level of workplace sabotage corresponds to the class-based organization of society and its associated distribution of advantages and disadvantages. This is compounded in effect due to issues of gender, race and ethnicity and other social barriers that exist. However, these macro conditions for sabotage do not fully explain its occurrence. It is also necessary to consider micro factors that manifest themselves in organizational and occupational settings, such as lack of control and exposure to systematic injustices. Simple desires for fun are sometimes considered as motives for destructive behaviour but such acts are not properly defined as sabotage.

The contemporary and future importance of sabotage are hard to deny. It is therefore time for theorists of organizational behaviour and management to make a sustained effort to understand it.

1 Introduction

Most experienced workers and managers know something crucial about industrial conflict and relations of power in the workplace that has not been discussed very often by academic researchers and writers (see INDUSTRIAL CONFLICT). They know that sabotage at work is the ultimate weapon of resistance (Pouget 1913). Sabotage or the threat of sabotage can empower even the most seemingly powerless individuals and groups in organizations, ensuring that domination is never total. It can serve as a check on the abuse of power and as one explanation of how the exploited and relatively weak manage to survive and even retain a sense of dignity.

Academic writers have used the concept of sabotage to represent a wide variety of employee behaviours (see EMPLOYEE RELATIONS, MANAGEMENT OF). For example, Brown (1977) used the label to refer to any employee actions that restrict output. Similarly, Dubois (1979) viewed activities such as strikes, go-slows, absenteeism, working without enthusiasm and damage that reduces the quality or quantity of goods produced as forms of sabotage. The trouble with such broad definitions is that they do little to separate sabotage from other forms of resistance and industrial conflict. A more focused definition is needed. Building on Taylor and Walton (1971), sabotage may be better conceptualized as deliberate action or inaction that is intended to damage, destroy or disrupt some aspect of the workplace environment, including the property, product, processes or reputation of the organization, with the net effect of undermining the goals and power of the organization's elite (Jermier 1988).

The purpose of this entry is to provide background information about sabotage at work. Some incidents of sabotage are described to illustrate its historical roots and contemporary significance and to illuminate its typical characteristics. The possible motives of saboteurs are reviewed and the current state of the topic is evaluated.

2 Sabotage incidents at work

The uprisings of the Luddites in England during the early-nineteenth century remain the best-known sabotage incidents in industrial history. In March 1811, under cover of night, a band of distressed and enraged workers smashed over sixty stocking frames in the village of Arnold, Nottinghamshire (Hobsbawm 1964). By December 1811, the stocking frame breakers were operating in several other British counties and were signing the name 'Ned Ludd' to threatening letters they wrote to employers. This was adapted from the name of a Leicestershire youth, Ned Ludlam, who, when commanded by his father to square up the needles on his frame, took a hammer and smashed it into a heap.

Soon after the initial raids, planning and stealth replaced riotousness as the Luddites methodically pursued their aims. Luddism became a well-drilled and regimented operation, fine-tuned to destroy only those machines that reduced the price of labourers' wages or produced unemployment. A typical Luddite attack involved a well-coordinated contingent of saboteurs armed with pistols, pikes, hatchets and enormous iron sledges for breaking open doors and smashing frames (Jermier 1988).

In the nearly two centuries that have passed since the Luddite uprisings, sabotage has remained an integral part of capital-labour struggles in Britain, France and the USA and has been, at times, an explicit component in labour's pursuit of workplace justice and independence (Brown 1977; Dubois 1979; Yellen 1980). Moreover, its practice is not limited to the Western industrial democracies (Quataert 1986; Wasserstrom 1987).

Most contemporary sabotage incidents lack the high profile and notoriety of Luddism but share other characteristics. For example, Taylor and Walton (1971: 219) reported a sabotage incident that had as much symbolic effect as it did substantive destructiveness. This was the case of a worker in a sweet factory who, annoyed at being dismissed, ruined a large batch of Blackpool rock by substituting an expletive for the message that usually ran through it.

In discussing the spread of sabotage, Dubois (1979) cited numerous instances that challenge the idea that the destruction of machinery and goods is no longer practised. His review illustrates how widespread sabotage has been in modern France. It also illustrates how selective and restrained sabotage against machines usually is. Dubois argued that sabotage, rather than just being a wanton attack on the machine as such, is often targeted at key points in the production process so as to cause more extended disruption. The actual damage, too, can be very specific: 'just as the sabotaging of one key machine can cause general disruption, so the sabotaging of one key component of a machine can cause it to come to a standstill' (Dubois 1979: 25). For example, a nineteenth-century railwaymen's union boasted that it could prevent a locomotive from running by the judicious placing of two small coins.

Another important feature of industrial sabotage is pictured in Fennell's study of an electronic components factory in the midwestern USA (Fennell 1976). She shows how workers bypass their union and rely on 'informal resistance networks' to combat a variety of problems. Sabotage (in the form of routinely 'losing' parts, materials and equipment and breaking tools and machinery) is clearly illustrated. Fennell's analysis emphasizes the level of socializing and solidarity evidenced among the workers, both on the job and off, and the highly collective nature of sabotage.

Technical sophistication is another feature of sabotage. Sprouse's extensive anthology of acts of sabotage in the contemporary US workplace (Sprouse 1992: 24), gives the example of a technician who worked on the Bank of America's computer system. Resentful of criticism from bosses, the technician introduced a 'logic bomb' into the system, which deleted the payroll programme along with many others. In the age of smart machines and highly advanced technology, sabotage can be especially pernicious because often only a few experts really understand the systems with which they work.

These examples have been selected from among many available because they indicate that sabotage remains a vital force in the politics of organizational behaviour (see ORGANIZATION BEHAVIOUR). In fact, despite the dearth of academic articles and research reports on workplace sabotage, it remains a frequently practised but usually unpublicized activity (Jermier 1988; LaNuez and Jermier 1994; Domagalski and Jermier 1995). Indeed, managerial and labour groups are often ambitious to cover up sabotage when it occurs because the negative publicity it can generate can cause further damage to the organization.

These examples also highlight some of the key characteristics of sabotage. First, contrary to popular conceptions, sabotage is not merely an act or process intended to destroy an immediate material object. It usually has a powerful symbolic quality to it and is intended to send a clear message. Second, sabotage is usually very selective and restrained. Saboteurs do not usually intend to create effects on an enormous scale, but instead seem to take pride in the clever art of understatement. When workers in the building trade throw mustard seed into a sand pile that will be used for construction, they are thinking ahead to the time, shortly after the edifice is erected, when a crop of mustard that no one can remove will grow out of the wall. Third, although many acts of sabotage are committed by individuals, there is usually a social network of fellow conspirators and silent collaborators involved who provide at least tacit endorsement. More often, sabotage acts are committed by groups in the tradition of Luddism: they are prefaced by detailed planning and are well orchestrated (Jermier 1988). Fourth, the method of sabotage can involve merely a swift kick into the panel of a car or the throwing of a brick

through a pane of glass, but more and more it involves the application of detailed and sophisticated technical knowledge. An important feature of contemporary sabotage is that technical expertise is often necessary in order to produce symbolic impressions as well as substantive impacts.

3 Motives underlying industrial sabotage

Popular images of sabotage tend to be pejorative. Frequently they include negative judgements and even condemnation. This is especially the case when material destruction appears random and when it threatens humans with injury or death (Jermier 1988).

According to Wasserstrom (1987), the transformation of Luddism in the public's mind (from heroic movement to dangerous mob activity) was due to the way journalists, novelists and other social commentators portrayed the saboteurs. The result of these interpretations was that machine-breaking and Luddism in general came to be seen as synonymous with backward fanaticism, irrational violence, senseless destruction and a desperate, self-defeating mob mentality. Radical historians and labour leaders have attempted to refashion Luddism into a positive symbol (which apparently has worked better in Australia than elsewhere), but the term is still routinely used disparagingly.

There is a long history of viewing most forms of industrial unrest and dissent as the result of the irrational impulses of isolated misfits. Acts of sabotage tend to be portrayed by top managers and managerial partisans as extremist and are easily cast as the result of psychological imbalance. The image of the 'mad saboteur' who, overwhelmed by the trials and tribulations of everyday organizational life, explodes in a self-indulgent moment of destruction seems to be deeply ingrained in the popular mind.

Historical studies and reports of empirical research challenge the myth of the mad saboteur (Jermier 1988) but often the first popular explanation for acts of sabotage centres on the supposedly unbalanced minds of the actors.

However, the causes of sabotage are often more complex than the image of the mad saboteur allows and some alternative explanations are outlined in the paragraphs below. Sabotage can be seen as a rational response to patterns of exploitation, lack of control and systematic injustices.

At this point in the development of advanced capitalism, it is well accepted by social theorists and analysts that the advantages and disadvantages derived from the operation of the system are not evenly distributed but cohere within social classes (see LABOUR PROCESS). Income and wealth, physical health and longevity, exposure to environmental and technological risks, educational opportunities, patterns of consumption, leisure activities and most other indicators of quality of life vary widely depending on social class location. These differences are amplified when other social factors are included in the equation. Gender, race, ethnicity and religious preference, for example, can compound the reality and experience of deprivation (Mills and Simmons 1995).

Inequality and limited opportunity across life domains, especially to the point where poverty, hunger, disease and hazards co-exist with affluence and safety for elites, create the basic conditions for alienation and withdrawal, but also for resistance and sabotage. In other words, the deprivations associated with working-class living, compounded by patterns of discrimination and blocked opportunity, create the macro conditions for sabotage. Some amount of sabotage is the result of the hardships associated with socio-economic location. Learning to labour in most working-class jobs, for example, involves learning the skills and social rules of sabotage because these methods have been practised strategically for centuries to contain exploitation (Jermier 1988). Thus, some amount of sabotage is to be expected in class society and is the direct result of working for wages and experiencing life from the underprivileged layers of an affluent nation-state.

But sabotage incidents are not totally the result of socio-economic factors. Managerial and technocratic sabotage is also quite common (LaNuez and Jermier 1994), despite the apparent advantages associated with such positions. And sabotage appears to vary in occurrence even among workers, depending on local organizational and occupational conditions.

The primary micro cause of sabotage seems to be associated with struggles for workplace control (see BRAVERMAN, H.). In a comprehensive review of sabotage research, Jermier (1988) identified 18 separate causes. The specific factor most frequently associated with product and machine sabotage was boring, monotonous and tedious work. A majority of the researchers made reference to this factor or to the desire to seize control of time in explaining why sabotage arose. Increases in the rate of work or other changes in work practices were mentioned next most frequently. In addition, researchers associated sabotage with: refusals to build poorly planned, shoddy products; degraded occupational status; assignment to hazardous work; excessive disciplining; slowly processed or denied grievances; conflicts with supervisors; low wages; and sex discrimination. LaNuez and Jermier (1994) also concluded that workers resort to sabotage as a way to increase control over a wide spectrum of work issues, including control over the pace of production as well as rest periods and breaks. In related studies, Hodson (1991, 1995) developed support for the argument that sabotage can be a direct act of resistance to managerial coercion and part of the struggle for control at the workplace. The basic point is that across numerous investigations, researchers associate sabotage incidents with diminished or low control. Thus, sabotage is practised routinely as a way to counteract oppressive conditions of employment and feelings of powerlessness, giving it a tactical and strategic quality incompatible with the sweeping image of the mad saboteur.

A brief case has been made for the idea that sabotage is closely associated with class exploitation and with organizational and occupational factors such as lack of workplace control and systematic injustices. However, not all destructive events can be shown to be measured responses to exploitation and oppression. In some research, it has been suggested that forms of artful sabotage are practised to have fun. For example, Thompson (1983) claimed that workers on a disassembly line in the slaughter division of a major beef processing plant in the midwestern USA commonly cut chunks out of pieces of meat for no reason or merely to throw at co-workers. Molstad (1986) contended that some of his co-workers in the brewery where he conducted participant observation lobbed bottles full of beer into the air to see them crash and explode on the shop floor and surreptitiously used a glue-gun and other equipment in the inspection area to create artistic designs. While these actions may be tied to struggles for control, it is also clear that some destruction is spontaneous and does not have the defining features of sabotage mentioned above, such as symbolism, restraint, collaboration and technical sophistication. It is practised sometimes with no bigger purpose than to experience what it is like to damage or destroy products or machines. However, this is not the motive pattern behind sabotage incidents (see MOTIVATION AND SATISFACTION). Such acts cannot be seen as examples of sabotage as defined above.

4 The current state of the topic

Today, sabotage is a prominent part of public discourse and rhetoric. For example, in an article in the *Washington Post* on 12 October 1995, 'Railroad layoffs raised as possible motive for Amtrak sabotage', it is suggested that the derailment of an Amtrak passenger train, killing or seriously injuring at least seventy-eight passengers, was an act of sabotage committed by railway workers angry over expected layoffs. It is central to the backstage lexicon of the workplace and can shape the balance of power in organizations. But it is still not very well understood. Most academic discussions of organizational life allude to workplace sabotage, but there are few sustained analyses of it. Scientific analysis of the topic is surprisingly scarce. The research that does exist is interesting and suggestive but it is hard to deny that the evidence concerning this phenomenon is meagre, especially in contrast with how important sabotage is in the

contemporary workplace. The studies that have been published vary widely in rigour. Creative interviewing, participant observation and other qualitative methodologies are probably best able to reveal the meaning and significance of workplace sabotage, but most of the research that is available on this topic lacks a complete description of the methods employed. It is possible to derive some preliminary conclusions concerning sabotage and to paint a picture of a rational, deliberate, restrained, conspiratorial and technically sophisticated agent, but this is an extremely under-researched and under-theorized phenomenon. Few deny the contemporary importance of the topic and fewer still deny its future importance. It is time to bring the best and most appropriate social science methods and theoretical inspirations to bear on this problem in order to mount a sustained effort to understand it.

JOHN M. JERMIER
WALTER NORD
UNIVERSITY OF SOUTH FLORIDA

Further reading

(References cited in the text marked *)

* Brown, G. (1977) *Sabotage: A Study in Industrial Conflict*, Nottingham: Spokesman. (A large, comprehensive book on industrial conflict and sabotage.)
* Domagalski, T. and Jermier, J. (1995) 'Sabotage', in N. Nicholson (ed.), *Dictionary of Organizational Behaviour*, Oxford: Blackwell. (A short definitional entry which covers the meaning, forms and causes of workplace sabotage.)
* Dubois, P. (1979) *Sabotage in Industry*, Harmondsworth: Penguin. (A superb work on French industrial relations that focuses on general forms of sabotage, but which has especially valuable material on machine destruction.)
* Fennell, D. (1976) 'Beneath the surface: the life of a factory', *Radical America* 10 (5): 15–29. (A rich ethnographic study of informal resistance networks and the underside of a factory.)
* Hobsbawm, E.J. (1964) 'The machine breakers', in E.J. Hobsbawm (ed.), *Labouring Men: Studies in the History of Labour*, London: Weidenfeld & Nicolson. (One of the best historical studies of Luddism, presenting machine breaking in a sympathetic light.)

* Hodson, R. (1991) 'Workplace behaviors: good soldiers, smooth operators, and saboteurs', *Work and Occupations* 18 (3): 271–90. (A critique of concepts of job satisfaction and the development of a framework for focusing on worker behaviour, including sabotage.)

* Hodson, R. (1995) 'The worker as active subject', in D.B. Bills (ed.), *Factors Reshaping the World of Work*, Albany, NY: State University of New York Press. (An interesting essay discussing implications of conceptualizing workers as free and active agents.)

* Jermier, J.M. (1988) 'Sabotage at work: the rational view', *Research in the Sociology of Organizations* 6: 101–34. (A comprehensive review of research on industrial sabotage and a reconceptualization of the meaning of sabotage incidents.)

* LaNuez, D. and Jermier, J.M. (1994) 'Sabotage by managers and technocrats: neglected patterns of resistance at work', in J.M. Jermier, D. Knights and W.R. Nord (eds), *Resistance and Power in Organizations*, London: Routledge. (An argument, using theory and illustrative examples, in favour of the thesis that managers and technocrats can fit the motive profile of saboteurs.)

* Mills, A.J. and Simmons, T. (1995) *Reading Organization Theory: A Critical Approach*, Toronto: Garamond Press. (A groundbreaking presentation of radical theories of organization for a wider readership. Includes good discussions of class, race and gender.)

* Molstad, C. (1986) 'Choosing and coping with boring work', *Urban Life* 15 (2): 215–36. (An intensive study of patterns of work in a brewery, including interesting content on sabotage episodes.)

* Pouget, E. (1913) *Sabotage*, Chicago, IL: Charles H. Kerr & Company. (An excellent historical piece which takes seriously the idea that sabotage might be used as a weapon of the working class.)

* Quataert, D. (1986) 'Machine breaking and the changing carpet industry of western Anatolia', *Journal of Social History* 19: 473–90. (A detailed account of industrial unrest and sabotage in the Ottoman carpet-making centres.)

* Sprouse, M. (ed.) (1992) *Sabotage in the American Workplace*, San Francisco, CA: Pressure Drop Press. (An interesting book, with over 130 anecdotes about sabotage in a wide variety of occupational and organizational settings.)

* Taylor, L. and Walton, P. (1971) 'Industrial sabotage: motives and meanings', in S. Cohen (ed.), *Images of Deviance*, Harmondsworth: Penguin. (The classic study of industrial sabotage, which provides a compelling rationale for further research.)

* Thompson, W.E. (1983) 'Hanging tongues: a sociological encounter with the assembly line', *Qualitative Sociology* 6 (3): 215–37. (An engaging report of participant observation research in a meat processing plant which proposes some ignoble motives for sabotage.)

* *Washington Post*, (1995) 'Railroad layoffs raised as possible motive for Amtrak sabotage', 12 October. (Discusses the possibility that a fatal derailment may have been caused by an act of sabotage.)

* Wasserstrom, J. (1987) ' "Civilization" and its discontents: the Boxers and Luddites as heroes and villains', *Theory and Society* 16: 675–707. (A sympathetic exploration of the shifting meanings of two of history's best-known sabotage movements that challenges the idea that technological change is always progress.)

* Yellen, S. (1980) *American Labor Struggles, 1877–1934*, New York: Pathfinder Press. (A labour history classic about confrontations between working people and the owners of the USA's mines, mills and railroads.)

See also: HUMAN RESOURCE MANAGEMENT; INDUSTRIAL AND LABOUR RELATIONS; ORGANIZATION BEHAVIOUR; TRADE UNIONS

Related topics in the IEBM: CONFLICT AND POLITICS; INDUSTRIAL REVOLUTION; POWER

Mondragón

Overview

Mondragón is an exception to the commonly held belief that worker cooperatives can only survive in special niches, sheltered from the competition of large private enterprises. The Mondragón cooperative complex has survived and grown from its start in 1956 to become one of the main elements in the regional economy of the Pais Basque country of Spain. Its success is rooted in visionary leadership and social invention.

This entry outlines the establishment and development of the Mondragón cooperatives before going on to discuss the man behind their creation. It then examines the reasons behind the success of Mondragón in the light of the arguments for its failure. Finally, there is discussion of the lessons that may be learned from studying such a model and whether these are applicable to other parts of the world.

1 Historical background

In 1941 a Catholic priest named José María Arizmendiarrieta came to the town of Mondragón. Working in particular with the blue collar youth and their parents, he started a two-year industrial arts school for boys aged fourteen to sixteen. Over the years this expanded into a two-year college programme in engineering and, in the 1990s, the educational programme was extended to a four-year college programme with graduate studies.

In 1956 Don José María worked with the first graduates of the industrial arts programme to found the first worker cooperative, Ulgor. In 1959 he persuaded the leaders of Ulgor to establish the Caja Laboral Popular, a savings bank whose principal mission was to help in the creation and support of cooperatives. More cooperatives were formed. Then, in 1965 ULARCO, the first group of cooperatives, was formed, taking over among other things the management of personnel, accounting and legal services for the member cooperatives. In the 1980s ULARCO was renamed FAGOR, after the logo on its major products. FAGOR has since become Spain's leading producer of white goods, particularly refrigerators, stoves and washing machines.

When the Caja Laboral Popular was created in 1959 the government ruled that Spain's social security system would not cover members of cooperatives. The Caja Laboral Popular then established its own system of worker protection and support. This later became Lagun-Aro, which now provides industrial medicine (studying the health effects of working conditions) and a voluntary life insurance programme alongside a contributory programme supporting cooperative members who become unemployed.

In 1966, in an attempt to combine education and work experience as part of the teaching process at the Escuela Politécnica, Alecop, a student cooperative was established. In two shifts, students worked in Alecop for four hours and in the Escuela for four hours. Alecop operated with a core staff of regular workers but the students participated fully in its governance. Alecop now produces components for the other cooperatives and has developed its own line of experimental equipment for schools.

Another cooperative, Otalora (originally called Ikasbide), was also established, this time to provide a training centre for all of the cooperatives. In the 1980s it began to develop its own management research and development (R&D) programme.

The cooperative complex expanded rapidly into the early 1970s, with new cooperatives and cooperative groups in industry, in machine tools, electronics, construction and heavy machinery. It also expanded via the inclusion of consumer–worker and farmer–worker cooperatives. However, the successive oil shocks of 1973 and 1975 meant that growth and profitability suffered and the leaders of the complex had to reduce their pay scales temporarily to meet their ability to pay.

Mondragón continued to develop none the less. In 1975 the leaders of the cooperatives invested $2 million to create Ikerlan, an R&D cooperative charged with the responsibility for studying and creating new technologies for ten years into the future. (This was independent of those R&D departments already established, which concentrated on more short-term needs.) In 1990 the cooperative group which concentrated on the design and production of machine tools invested $4 million to create Ideko, an R&D cooperative serving cooperatives in that industry as well as private machine-tools firms. (Ikerlan also has contracts for R&D with private firms.)

Until the 1980s the only linkage that held the cooperative complex together was the Caja Laboral Popular, which had a contract of association with all the cooperatives. The Caja provided financial support and services and also oversaw that each cooperative was organized along the lines first established by Ulgor. That contract provided that, before paying its members, each cooperative must set aside at least 30 per cent of its profits into a reserve fund. In times when profits have been difficult to achieve, many cooperatives have been setting aside 50 per cent.

Separate sections of the Caja also had specific roles. The Caja's Entrepreneurial Division worked with groups of individuals to establish new cooperatives and also provided consulting services to the cooperatives and emergency loans to tide individual cooperatives through times of financial losses. The Caja's Economic Studies section provided economic information for the cooperatives as well as making an annual study of the state of the Basque economy. In the 1980s the Caja organized a series of studies for preparing the cooperatives for Spain's expected entry into the European Common Market in 1990. To carry on this transition the cooperatives

banded together to form the Cooperative Congress, which meets every two years and has an executive committee to act between Congress meetings (see DECISION MAKING).

The cooperative groups had originally been formed around sharing a common locality. The studies indicated that greater economic efficiency could be achieved by banding the cooperatives together around common technologies or markets. By 1989 this had led to the creation of the Mondragón Cooperative Corporation, with a president and nine vice-presidents for each division. Javier Mongelos, General Manager of FAGOR, the oldest and most profitable group, was elected President. These changes were worked out in several steps and always approved by the vote of a large majority in the Cooperative Congress.

Growth up to the 1970s was primarily in the creation and expansion of manufacturing cooperatives. After this growth in the manufacturing field slowed down. By the mid-1980s no new manufacturing firms were being created and the cooperatives were hard pressed to preserve some of the existing firms. Nevertheless, in the 1990s there were manufacturing cooperatives exporting 50 to 70 per cent of their production. Growth had also resumed in service cooperatives by this time, particularly within the the consumer–worker cooperative, Eroski, and the Caja. With Eroski expanding into the Basque area of France via the new enlarged supermarkets and the Caja setting up offices in Spain outside of the Pais Basque, in 1994 cooperative membership reached a record high of over 26,000.

2 Arizmendiarrieta's vision

Mondragón's development arose in response to the vision of Don José María Arizmendiarrieta. His leadership consisted of a strong commitment to the idea of Mondragón coupled with a strong sense of current realities and probable future trends. His commitment was shared by his first supporters, with whose help he went on to create the first worker cooperative, the cooperative groups and the Caja Laboral Popular. Working with a small group that he had orientated through years of discussion, he designed the organizational structure of Ulgor (which became the structure of all other manufacturing cooperatives). When he was unable to persuade Ulgor's leaders to establish a bank, he acted alone, signing the names of two Ulgor leaders to the government-required document establishing the Caja. In all other cases he acted as an advisor and only took action after persuading the other members to join him. He designed the structure and social processes of cooperative groups and of consumer–worker and farmer–worker cooperatives. When the others thought Mondragón was not ready to create an R&D cooperative, it was Don José María who persuaded them to make the commitment which was essential to future progress.

Don José María's vision was of a peaceful revolution through which the various social classes could work together to secure mutual gains towards a more just society. This called for social solidarity among all cooperative members and a limited range between the bottom and top of the pay scale. This ratio was originally 3:1, but time and the pressures of competition with private firms means it has risen in stages from 3:1 to 4.5:1 to 6:1.

For Mondragón in its early stages, Don José María's leadership was indispensable. He has since died (in 1976), but the cooperative system he designed has survived and continued to adapt and grow in the following decades.

3 Social invention

The creation of the Caja Laboral Popular was an important social invention. Credit unions were already well known at the time, but they served primarily to supply small credits to consumers. The Caja was created primarily to finance the establishment and support of worker cooperatives (although it has always supplied consumer credit and now has grown so large and prosperous that it must also provide credit for non-cooperative enterprises). By financing the building of educational, manufacturing and service cooperatives, an R&D cooperative and housing cooperatives as well as other types, the Caja has helped to provide an integrated financing and supporting

system which is the basis of Mondragón's success (see FINANCIAL INCENTIVES).

4 The key to success

Many critics have argued that worker cooperatives cannot succeed because they possess a number of in-built weaknesses that prevent them from becoming important factors in modern industrial competition. These include:

1 cooperatives do not have the human, financial or technical resources to compete with large multinational private firms, except in small niches not of interest to those firms;
2 since worker-owners favour immediate income over reinvestment of profits, worker cooperatives tend to lack the funds necessary for research and development and for survival in recessionary periods;
3 worker cooperatives break up if they fail financially, just like a private firm.

However, the latter also occurs if they become highly successful over a period of years. In this case, as the cooperative expands, and as some of the older members retire, the controlling members decide to protect their equity by taking on new people as hired labour. When most of the workers retire they want to sell their ownership shares, but by this time their value has multiplied and the employees cannot afford to buy them. The cooperative is then forced to find a market among outsiders and converts to a private company.

Despite such predictions, Mondragón has been a definite success. The key to its continued prosperity lies with its system of financing and control. Mondragón creates no stock. It is financed using credit from the initial contributions of the members and from the future earnings of the firm. The members receive interest on their contribution and annual shares in profits, deposited to their capital accounts. This means that the cooperative can never revert to private ownership unless a majority of the members vote to sell – which has happened only in the cases of two struggling small firms.

The system also has great advantages in the conservation of employment and human resources (see INDUSTRIAL AND LABOUR RELATIONS). When a Mondragón cooperative becomes insolvent it does not always shut down, as often happens with a private firm, nor are its top executives necessarily fired. The Governing Council of the insolvent cooperative calls upon the Caja Laboral Popular for rescue and reorganization. With the approval of the cooperative's Governing Council, management is reorganized, new credits are extended and the cooperative members agree to cut their pay to 80 per cent of the previous figure during the intervention and also to draw on their individual capital accounts to meet the deficit. In effect, the members use some of their personal savings to preserve their jobs. The reorganization may also involve some changes in the product mix, dropping some products and concentrating on others.

Several of the cooperatives that earlier faced insolvency have recovered sufficiently to be among the most successful in 1994. Furthermore, some managers who were thought to have failed have not been fired but rather shifted to other positions where they have been successful. In one case the managers of a failing cooperative asked to be relieved of their positions. In a private firm they would have been struggling to avoid discharge, but in the Mondragón system they knew that every effort would be made to transfer them to positions where they could succeed.

Another factor of importance in explaining the success of Mondragón is its organizational structure. Consumer cooperatives and farmer cooperatives are conventionally organized, with exclusive control in the hands of consumers or farmers. Mondragón has also worked out a system of governance in which consumers and farmers share control equally with workers in the marketing organizations. The constitution of Eroski provides that its president must always be a consumer member, but otherwise representation in the Governing Council is shared equally between consumer and worker members (see INDUSTRIAL DEMOCRACY).

Mondragón has a dual structure of consultation and control: the Governing Council and the Social Council. The Governing Council is elected by the members-at-large while the Social Council is elected by workers in the sections where they work. Given that the same people are voting in each case, one may question the need for two representative bodies. In effect the Governing Council is the primary governing body (choosing the management) while the Social Council has come to represent the interests of the workers at their workplaces. This has meant trying to find a balance between social interests and technological and economic requirements. If members had to choose between the two interests, it would put them in an ambivalent position – and ambivalence is a poor basis for decision making. The interaction of the Governing Council and the Social Council provides for a full airing of the various interests of ownership and working conditions and terms. Study of decision making within FAGOR, the oldest and largest cooperative group, indicates that the discussants are constantly trying to find the balance between the long-term interests of worker-owners and the interests of worker-members (Greenwood *et al.* 1993).

5 Learning from Mondragón

There is now common agreement that a single worker cooperative, surrounded by a sea of private enterprises, has very poor prospects for long-term survival. Given this, does Mondragón offer any lessons that can be followed by others or is it a peculiar phenomenon of Basque culture? One factor to consider is that the Basques may well be more inclined to work in groups than other cultures. Although in the 1980s there were more worker cooperatives outside the Mondragón system than within it, these cooperatives were all isolated and small – none of them had built up the integrated supporting system of Mondragón.

The best evidence of more general lessons can be found in southern Spain with El Grup Cooperatiu de Valencia (Martinez 1991). When the leaders of the Valencia cooperatives in southern Spain first learned of Mondragón they visited the city and established close consultative relations with the leaders of the Mondragón cooperatives. They then went on to establish a cooperative development bank and an R&D cooperative as well as housing and other cooperatives. Although the group began work in the early 1970s, a much less favourable time to start new enterprises than the 1956 start of Mondragón, it has survived and in 1994, with 4,500 members, is continuing to expand rapidly.

Other organizing groups may not need to follow the Mondragón model so closely. The model involves particular structures and social processes which many supporters have successfully adapted and adopted for their work in other parts of the world. Robert Oakeshott (1973), who introduced Mondragón to the English-speaking world, has been active in promoting employee ownership and Mondragón-type structures and processes in the UK and in eastern Europe. David Ellerman of the Industrial Cooperative Association in Boston has persuaded several US states to adopt legislation supporting several aspects of the Mondragón model and has also been working towards this in eastern Europe. Also in the USA, Joseph Blasi, formerly of Harvard University, persuaded sponsors of employee ownership in Congress to include worker cooperatives in aspects of employee ownership legislation. He has also been working as a consultant to the Russian government on employee ownership (SEE PROFIT SHARING).

As a result of foreign interest in Mondragón the leaders of Otalora, the management research and training institute, have established a research programme. Otalora now holds group study seminars which attract visitors from all over the world.

WILLIAM FOOTE WHYTE
CORNELL UNIVERSITY

Further reading

(References cited in the text marked *)

* Greenwood, D.J. *et al.* (1993) *Industrial Democracy as Process: Participatory Action Research in the Fagor Cooperative Group of Mon-*
dragón, Stockholm: Van Gorcum, Assen/Maastricht. (Report from a participatory action research group study guided by Greenwood and written with five members of the personnel departments of the FAGOR cooperative group.)

* Martinez, A. (1991) *El Grup Cooperatiu de Valencia*, Valencia: Caixa Popular. (Report in Spanish on the Valencia group of cooperatives.)

Morison, R. (1991) *We Build the Road as We Travel*, Philadelphia, PA: New Society Publishers. (Summary of the history of the Mondragón cooperatives, with emphasis on economic data. Views the adaptation of the Mondragón idea as a means to overcome some of the in-built defects of industrial capitalism and socialism.)

* Oakeshott, R. (1973) 'Mondragón: Spain's oasis of democracy', *Observer* 21 January. (First report on Mondragón in English.)

Thomas, H. and Logan, C. (1982) 'The performance of the Mondragón cooperatives in Spain', in D.C. Jones and J. Svejnar (eds), *Participatory and Self-managed Firms*, Lexington, MA: Lexington Books. (Continues the analysis of Mondragón's economic success beyond the 1970s.)

Whyte, W.F. and Whyte, K.K. (1989; 2nd edn 1991) *Making Mondragón: The Growth and Dynamics of the Worker Cooperative Complex*, Ithaca, NY: ILR Press. (A study of the history of the Mondragón cooperatives as they evolved from the 1940s into the 1990s. Based on field studies in 1975, 1983, 1985 and 1990, with the substantial assistance of cooperative members.)

See also: DECISION MAKING; FINANCIAL INCENTIVES; INDUSTRIAL DEMOCRACY; INDUSTRIAL AND LABOUR RELATIONS; PROFIT-SHARING AND EMPLOYEE SHAREHOLDING SCHEMES

Related topics in the IEBM: BUSINESS ETHICS; BUSINESS AND SOCIETY; MANAGEMENT IN SPAIN; ORGANIZATIONAL PERFORMANCE; ORGANIZATION STRUCTURE

Negotiation skills

Overview

Negotiation is a process of joint decision making between people with different preferences. It has been studied by game theorists using an abstract mathematical approach and by other social scientists using a more real-life-oriented approach. The findings of both research streams have contributed to current knowledge about negotiation skills. Each stage of the negotiation process – exploration, bidding and bargaining, and settling – calls for a distinct set of skills. The exploration stage calls for information-gathering and planning skills. Bidding and bargaining call for using either competitive tactics or collaborative tactics, depending on the negotiation game plan. Key skills in the settling stage include recognizing when it is time to move towards agreement and controlling the drafting of negotiation documents. Future work on the topic of negotiation skills is likely to include further investigation of how negotiation expertise is gained, how information processing influences negotiations, and how the effectiveness of various negotiation skills differs across cultures.

1 Background on the topic of negotiation skills

Neale and Bazerman (1992: 42) define negotiation as: 'a decision-making process among interdependent parties who do not share identical preferences' (see DECISION MAKING). Hayes (1991) offers a similar definition, describing negotiation as a joint decision-making process in which people with different preferences attempt to resolve their differences. Negotiation skills are the approaches or tactics that people use in the process of negotiation. An understanding of such skills is important because it can help people achieve desired outcomes in their business transactions.

Historical context

The study of negotiation began largely as a subset of game theory research. As Northcraft and Neale (1991) point out, game theorists made – and still do make – assumptions about human nature and then mathematically deduced outcomes of negotiators' choices. The outcomes deduced by negotiators were/are presumed to be inevitable. One popular topic of early game theoretical research on negotiation was the 'prisoner's dilemma', which was named by A.W. Tucker and described in detail by Rapoport and Chammah (1965). In this dilemma, a reward structure confronts each of two parties with a difficult decision. Figure 1 shows a diagram of the prisoner's dilemma.

The first entry in each cell of this matrix is the payoff (reward) for Party 1 if he or she chooses that cell, and the second entry is the payoff for Party 2 for choosing that cell. The label 'C' refers to the cooperative choice because when one party makes that choice the other party is better off. The label 'D' refers to the defecting (non-cooperative) choice because the other party fares worse when that choice is made. The dilemma facing each party is whether to choose C or D.

The prisoner's dilemma is inherently a negotiation situation for several reasons. First, it involves two self-interested parties making a decision. Second, the parties are interdependent, for it is the *combination* of the two decisions that determines the payoff for each party. Among the issues that game theorists have investigated (with respect to the

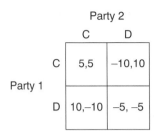

	Party 2 C	Party 2 D
Party 1 C	5,5	−10,10
Party 1 D	10,−10	−5, −5

Figure 1 The prisoner's dilemma
Source: Rapoport and Chammah (1965)

prisoner's dilemma) is the effectiveness of different strategies for eliciting cooperation. A number of researchers, including Oskamp (1971) and Wrightsman *et al.* (1972), found that a matching or tit-for-tat strategy (cooperating when the other party cooperates and not cooperating when the other party does not cooperate) is most effective.

Not long after game theorists began studying negotiation, other social scientists became interested in the topic as well. According to Gulliver (1979), these social scientists took a more real-life approach to the study of negotiation. Specifically, they considered the roles of factors such as uncertainties of information, players' cognitive biases and players' manipulations of each other's perceptions. They examined negotiation tactics from a less abstract perspective than game theorists used. For example, Bartos (1974) found that if one party makes a very low initial demand or a fast concession, then agreement tends to take longer to reach, for the other party expects additional concessions and therefore becomes less willing to make reciprocal concessions. Another example is the research of Lewis and Fry (1977), who found that integrative agreements ('win–win' solutions that satisfy both parties' needs) were more likely when negotiators refrained from using insults and threats. Modern writings on business negotiation skills have built upon lessons learned from both the abstract and real-life-oriented negotiation research streams described above.

2 Current knowledge about negotiation skills

Ramundo (1992) states that the three main stages of negotiation are preparation, presentation and reaching agreement. These stages are, respectively, equivalent to the exploration, bidding and bargaining, and settling stages that Scott (1981) describes. In the exploration stage, negotiating parties analyse the situation (what is wanted and what needs to be negotiated) and decide on negotiation game plans. In the bidding and bargaining stages, parties take their places at the 'negotiating table' and conduct the formal dialogue (exchanging offers, counter-offers and concessions). In the settling stage, parties recognize that each is ready to end negotiations and an agreement is reached. Each of these three negotiation stages calls for a distinct set of skills.

Tactics in the exploration stage of negotiation

Ramundo (1992) suggests that during the exploration stage it is important to do thorough research. This involves carefully investigating the nature of the matter being negotiated and the individuals involved in the negotiation. Such investigation may include having a chat with the other party, making phone-calls to those familiar with the other party, and/or having professional personnel conduct an in-depth investigation of the other party. This gathering of information helps the negotiator develop a game plan, for it enables the negotiator to identify aspects of the situation that can be exploited to gain advantage during bidding and bargaining. Developing a game plan involves choosing between a competitive and a collaborative strategy. According to Hayes (1991), a competitive strategy entails concealment and demanding concessions, while a cooperative strategy entails: (1) offering concessions in the hopes that reciprocation will occur; and (2) disclosing information about goals, priorities and limits. These two strategies are sometimes referred to as the 'hard' approach and the 'soft' approach. Hayes (1991) suggests that a collaborative

strategy is more appropriate when one negotiator trusts the other to some extent and when
the reward structure suggests that a mutually
beneficial exchange – a win–win outcome – is
possible. Conversely, a competitive strategy
is more appropriate when a negotiator
believes that his or her opponent will exploit
him or her. In addition to choosing a strategy,
developing a game plan involves the more
specific task of determining the minimum and
maximum negotiation outcomes that are
acceptable and that are realistic based on the
knowledge of the situation. Identifying leverage possibilities is also a part of game-plan
development.

According to Scott (1981), physical preparation – specifically, planning the layout of
the negotiation room – is necessary as well.
Most negotiators find a round table more comfortable and constructive than a rectangular
one, and Scott emphasizes that the table must
be large enough for parties to sit a moderate
distance from each other. He also recommends that the host make provisions to ensure
the comfort of the other party, including food
and facilities such as a telephone and telex.

Tactics in the bidding and bargaining stage of negotiation

Both Hayes (1991) and Scott (1981) recommend that when choosing an opening bid, a
seller should start with the highest defensible
bid. (Conversely, a buying negotiator should
start with the lowest defensible bid.) Along
the same lines, Northcraft and Neale (1991)
conclude, based on a review of research findings, that extreme initial offers are effective
provided that the party receiving the offer
does not have access to information suggesting the offer is inappropriately extreme. A
high opening bid by the seller is important
because a higher bid cannot normally be made
at a later point in time. Also, if an opening bid
is too low, the opponent will not appreciate
the sacrifice being made; the offer will not
seem as valuable as it would if it came after a
longer period of time. While the bid should be
high, it should not be *too* high. It must be
defensible, or realistic. If a negotiator makes a
bid that cannot be defended when challenged,

credibility will be lost and there is also the risk
of offending the other party.

Following bidding, either competitive or
cooperative bargaining tactics may be employed, based on the negotiation strategy.
Pruitt (1981) and Hayes (1991) summarize
common competitive and collaborative tactics identified by negotiation researchers and
practitioners. Competitive tactics include imposing time pressure, appearing firm, reducing the other's resistance and improving one's
relationship with – or the mood of – the other
party. One party can impose a time pressure
by setting a negotiation deadline, raising the
cost of negotiation (for example, unions encouraging a worker slowdown or strike), or
dragging out the negotiation so that the other
party can no longer afford to spend additional
time in negotiation (see COLLECTIVE BAR-
GAINING; INDUSTRIAL AND LABOUR RELA-
TIONS; TRADE UNIONS). The tactic of
appearing firm may consist of conceding
slowly, indicating that there is no additional
room to concede, and explicitly stating that
any concession is a one-time gesture. Reducing the other's resistance includes the use of
threats of punishment if concessions are not
made, promises of rewards if concessions are
made, and persuasive arguments about why
concessions should be made. *Feints* are a special case of persuasive argument (Hayes
1991). A feint is an effort by one party to focus
attention on an unimportant issue and make
the other party believe it is critical; then, when
the first party concedes on the issue, the second party may be persuaded to reciprocate
with a valuable concession, thinking (mistakenly) that the first party has made a large sacrifice. Efforts to improve the relationship with
the other party or to improve the mood of the
other party include being warm and friendly,
behaving in accordance with the other party's
values, and sending a representative who is
similar to the other party. These efforts may
encourage concessions because people tend
to cooperate more when they like someone or
when they are in a good mood (see OCCUPA-
TIONAL PSYCHOLOGY).

Collaborative tactics summarized by Pruitt
(1981) and Hayes (1991) consist of high-risk
and low-risk approaches. High-risk

collaborative tactics include offering large concessions in the hopes that reciprocation will occur and disclosing values, priorities and limits in order to help the other party search for a mutually acceptable agreement. Offering large concessions is high-risk because it may be seen as a sign of weakness and because it is difficult to return to a previous position after making a concession. Disclosing values, priorities and limits is high-risk because the other party can use such information as a basis for formulating threats or planning another competitive action. Low-risk collaborative tactics include indirect communication (for example, signals, hints, or messages transmitted through intermediaries), informal problem-solving discussions held outside of formal bargaining meetings (such as meeting at a bar or other relaxed setting so that both parties are less defensive), or offering a small concession and following it with a larger one if the other party reciprocates. Such tactics are low-risk because they can be easily disavowed and because they minimize image, position and information losses.

Tactics in the settling stage of negotiation

Both Ramundo (1992) and Hayes (1991) caution that it is critical for a negotiator to recognize when a final agreement is close at hand, for bargaining beyond that point (the point that Ramundo refers to as the 'crunch') becomes counter-productive and may push the other party into abruptly breaking off the negotiation. A negotiator can sense the arrival of the crunch by noticing a narrowing of differences between the sides or signals from the other party indicating that a last offer is being made.

Ramundo (1992) also advises that during this stage it is important to make efforts to control the drafting of negotiation documents; a wise tactic is for the negotiator to offer to prepare the draft. Then, if allowed to prepare it, the negotiator should carefully word its text so that the document is slanted in favour of his/her side while still reflecting the essence of the agreement that was reached.

3 Future outlook for the study of negotiation skills

Carroll and Payne (1991) have noted several opportunities for future research on the topic of negotiation skills. One such opportunity is to determine how negotiation novices become negotiation experts – specifically, what is learned through experience and what types of feedback are valuable to such learning. Another opportunity that Carroll and Payne identified is to obtain a greater understanding of information processing that leads to favourable and unfavourable negotiation outcomes. With the growing presence of multinational corporations and international business transactions, there is also an opportunity for additional research on the topic of cross-cultural negotiation skills.

LISA HOPE PELLED
UNIVERSITY OF SOUTHERN CALIFORNIA
MARSHALL SCHOOL OF BUSINESS

Further reading

(References cited in the text marked *)

Acuff, F.L. (1993) *How to Negotiate Anything with Anyone Anywhere Around the World*, New York: American Management Association. (General guide to negotiation skills.)

* Bartos, O.J. (1974) *Process and Outcome in Negotiation*, New York: Columbia University Press. (A more academic text on negotiation skills.)

* Carroll, J.S. and Payne, J.W. (1991) 'An information processing approach to two-party negotiations', in M.H. Bazerman, R.J. Lewicki and B.H. Sheppard (eds), *Research on Negotiation in Organizations*, vol. 3, Greenwich, CT: JAI Press Inc. (Specialist article on an information processing approach.)

Fisher, R. and Ury, W. (1981) *Getting to Yes: Negotiating Agreement without Giving In*, Boston, MA: Houghton Mifflin. (Popular management guide to negotiation.)

* Gulliver, P.H. (1979) *Disputes and Negotiations: A Cross-Cultural Perspective*, New York: Academic Press. (Excellent book on cross-cultural negotiation.)

* Hayes, J. (1991) *Interpersonal Skills: Goal-directed Behaviour at Work*, London: Routledge. (Very good introduction to interpersonal aspects of negotiation.)

Johnson, R.A. (1993) *Negotiation Basics: Concepts, Skills, and Exercises*, Newbury Park, CA: Sage Publications. (Basic text.)

* Lewis, S.A. and Fry, W.R. (1977) 'Effects of visual access and orientation on the performance of integrative bargaining alternatives', *Organizational Behavior and Human Performance* 20: 75–92. (Specialist article on bargaining alternatives.)

* Neale, M.A. and Bazerman, M.H. (1992) 'Negotiating rationally: the power and impact of the negotiator's frame', *Academy of Management Executive* 6 (3): 42–51. (Specialist article on power and impact.)

* Northcraft, G.B. and Neale, M.A. (1991) 'Dyadic negotiation', in M.H. Bazerman, R.J. Lewicki and B.H. Sheppard (eds), *Research on Negotiation in Organizations*, vol. 3, Greenwich, CT: JAI Press Inc. (Discussion of the use of assumption in predicting choices of decision.)

* Oskamp, S. (1971) 'Effects of programmed strategies on cooperation in the prisoner's dilemma and other mixed-motive games', *Journal of Conflict Resolution* 15: 225–59. (Article on 'tit--for-tat' strategies in negotiation.)

* Pruitt, D.G. (1981) *Negotiation Behavior*, New York: Academic Press. (Useful text.)

Ramundo, B.A. (1992) *Effective Negotiation: A Guide to Dialogue Management and Control*, New York: Quorum Books. (Recent guide to negotiation.)

* Rapoport, A. and Chammah, A.M. (1965) *Prisoner's Dilemma: A Study of Conflict and Cooperation*, Ann Arbor, MI: University of Michigan Press. (The classic text of the prisoner's dilemma.)

Scott, B. (1988) *Negotiating*, London: Paradigm. (General book.)

* Scott, W.P. (1981) *The Skills of Negotiating*, New York: Wiley. (Useful text about negotiation processes and skills.)

* Wrightsman, L.S., Jr, O'Connor, J. and Baker, N.J. (eds) (1972) *Cooperation and Competition: Readings in Mixed-motive Games*, Belmont, CA: Brooks/Cole. (Useful collection of essays on cooperation and competition.)

See also: COLLECTIVE BARGAINING; DECISION MAKING; ORGANIZATION BEHAVIOUR

Related topics in the IEBM: BUSINESS ECONOMICS; GAME THEORY AND GAMING; INTERNATIONAL BUSINESS NEGOTIATIONS; KNIGHT, F.H.; MARCH, J.G. AND CYERT, R.M.; SIMON, H.A.; STRATEGIC CHOICE; STRATEGY, CONCEPT OF

Third party intervention

Overview

Any process of bargaining between parties with different interests in its outcomes creates some risk that they will not be able to agree and, accordingly, that they will break off negotiations. Where the parties are able to select other bargaining partners with whom they can reach agreement, failure to agree presents no problem. Where, as in the case of bargaining between employers and workers, this option either is not open or open only at considerable cost to both parties, it is generally considered that some alternative course of action which avoids breakoff or breakdown needs to be available to the parties. This mechanism may take one of three forms, which differ in the amount of discretion assigned to the third party.

Conciliation is a method of resolving differences by involving an impartial third party in the actual negotiating process, the objective being to assist the parties in exploring other methods of resolving their differences and to arrive at an agreement which accords with their values and interests. Of the three methods, this allows the parties the most discretion to decide the issue for themselves on their own terms.

Mediation is a method of achieving the same result but where an independent third party is either required by law or requested by the parties to make one or more recommendations on the way in which the difference might

be resolved, leaving the parties some discretion to decide the form that any resolution should take.

Arbitration is a method of resolving differences or disputes between two (or more) parties over the establishment, interpretation or application of the terms and conditions of a contract. It involves an independent third party who is either required by law or requested by the parties to make an award on the disputed issue(s) after considering the parties' evidence and arguments.

These mechanisms are often seen to provide an alternative method of resolving disputes to those found in the courts of law, where similar processes are often followed. Mediation and arbitration, for example, are being adopted increasingly either to settle disputes which do not lend themselves to resolution in terms of right and wrong (in which area the courts are well-equipped) or to take advantage of their greater informality and lower cost (Mackie 1991). All three mechanisms offer distinct advantages for cases where disputes are concerned with the interests of the contending parties and where the constraining framework of law is at best replaced by a framework of convention developed largely by the parties themselves.

This entry identifies the main mechanisms which exist to avoid or repair breakdowns (usually in the form of either strikes by workers or lockouts by employers) in the areas of labour and industrial relations. These are typically either judicial (involving the court system and the application of legal principles to determine who is right and who is wrong) or quasi-judicial (involving processes of conciliation, mediation and arbitration and the application of principles derived mainly from customary values and conventions in an attempt to solve a problem in ongoing employment relationships).

1 Context

Most industrial relations differences and disputes are resolved by the parties themselves in negotiations, but there is always a risk that they will not be able to reach agreement on the issues. Most countries which rely on collective bargaining as a way of reaching agreements rely on some form of third party intervention to prevent or repair breakdowns in bargaining (see COLLECTIVE BARGAINING).

This mechanism may involve either the official court system or the quasi-judicial system identified with conciliation, mediation and arbitration. Resolution by reference to the courts is by the far the most frequently used mode of resolving differences concerning questions of individual 'right', regardless of whether these are established by statutes or by contracts. Conciliators, mediators or arbitrators, who may have no connection at all with the judicial system, are more often used to resolve differences and disputes over collective rights and 'interests'. In most countries conciliation is invoked more frequently in collective disputes than either mediation or arbitration, although these do form important fall-back mechanisms for use in the event of failure in conciliation. In some countries, Japan and those of eastern Europe for example, arbitration is generally considered less appropriate than either of the other two mechanisms.

Typically, individuals who consider that their rights have been infringed by another are at liberty to seek redress before a court but sometimes have the option of going down the alternative route to arbitration. Collectivities or classes of people who seek to negotiate a new right into existence or to protect one already established in this way are sometimes encouraged and sometimes legally required to make use of third party assistance before embarking upon collective action which might disrupt commercial relations or result in possible social disorder.

The reasons for relying on alternative methods of collective dispute resolution are that both the principal parties and society in general regard any breakdown in contractual relations as costly and without benefit or advantage to anyone, that resolution by means of court litigation is becoming increasingly time-consuming and costly and that the courts may not be the best forums for resolving disputes which are not concerned simply with questions of right.

The use of either mechanism to avoid a breakdown, therefore, may be made mandatory or may be left to the decisions of the parties themselves. Practice in this respect varies from country to country, usually reflecting cultural attitudes towards the use of industrial action as a means of coercing the other party to agree to terms. Where their use is mandatory the legality of industrial action is often made conditional upon their use and the processes of conciliation, mediation and arbitration then tend to be tied more closely into the judicial system.

Where, on the other hand, the parties are left to decide voluntarily whether they will make use of any of them, the legality of industrial action usually does not depend on their prior use (although it may be defined in other ways). In this context, conciliation, mediation and arbitration will often be undertaken by persons who have no necessary connection with the judicial system. The parties retain greater freedom to select the third party and to define the terms of reference.

2 Historical evolution

Although there is a trend towards adopting non-judicial methods of resolving differences in individual rights cases, their historical development has been associated with and largely dependent upon the growth of collective bargaining over workers' interests and rights. Whenever collective bargaining becomes established the parties quickly recognize that a third party might be able to help them to reduce their differences and allow them to reach agreements without relying on strikes or lockouts to coerce the other party (see COLLECTIVE BARGAINING).

They may then voluntarily agree in advance of any breakdown in negotiations to the appointment of conciliators, mediators or arbitrators to assist them, should the need arise: in Japan this is referred to as 'leaving the dispute with someone' not connected with it. Governments may recognize the virtue of encouraging or mandating the parties to use these mechanisms to avoid open conflicts by: enacting legislation which prescribes (as in some eastern European countries) the use of a form of third party intervention whenever a dispute threatens disruption; and/or creating a public service of conciliation, mediation and arbitration which the collective bargaining partners are free to use if they so wish (as in the UK or Japan).

Legislative prescription usually reflects a belief that disruption is normally more damaging to the worker than to the employers' interests. Legislation takes the form of giving each party to a difference or dispute the right unilaterally to refer the issue to a third party and disallows any veto by the other party on this course of action. Many countries have adopted this approach during emergency conditions (Lockyer 1979) but others, such as Australia and New Zealand in the past (Hanami and Blanpain 1989) and the liberalizing economies of eastern Europe currently, see advantages in generally prescribing third party intervention by law (Organization for Economic Cooperation and Development 1993), although arbitration may be involved only to a limited extent (Hanami and Blanpain 1989).

Where such legal prescription does not occur these modes of dispute resolution remain part of the voluntary collective bargaining process. Even when the State organizes a public facility or agency for the purpose without prescribing its use, the parties are left to decide whether to include any form of third party intervention as part of the final stages of their negotiating or dispute procedures (that is, the procedures they agree to follow in order to reach agreement). This clause may provide for unilateral reference to the third party but more commonly both parties have to agree to refer an issue to a third party and (in the case of arbitration) to be bound by any award made.

Nevertheless, even where voluntary collective bargaining persists, legislation has been used extensively in recent years to prescribe basic or minimum rights for individuals in employment. The tendency is for these issues to be resolved by reference to judicial tribunals or the ordinary courts. Where, in 'voluntary' collective bargaining systems, alternative mechanisms are voluntarily retained for the purpose, two parallel systems of resolving differences over rights may run side by side.

3 Disputes over rights

Where the rights accorded to individuals by law are ones which reciprocate in another's duty, the courts are normally charged with the duty of hearing claims or complaints referred to them unilaterally by any aggrieved party for redress. Similarly, where they are established by contract a claim by one party that the other has breached its terms can also be pursued through the courts under contract law. Legislation usually then proscribes the use of any device which would deny a complainant access to the courts (see INDUSTRIAL CONFLICT).

However, the increasing volume and growing costs of litigation in the area of employment law are fostering the growth of alternative or supplementary methods for resolving even this type of dispute. For these reasons it has been deemed prudent in some countries like the UK to interpose 'individual' conciliation between the stages of initial application and tribunal hearing, although the conciliator has no power to prevent the complainant from pursuing the complaint to a hearing.

Where rights accorded by law to collectivities, or where controversial or complex industrial relations questions are involved, it is often thought that the resolution of differences and disputes might require something more than reference to a simple judicial process. It is sometimes deemed expedient to use a form of arbitration, backed by judicial authority, for the purpose. For example, when for a time legislation accorded British trade unions conditional recognition rights against the employer, the task of resolving claims and complaints in these cases was allocated to the Central Arbitration Committee (CAC), whose function was both judicial and arbitral. Thus, the distinction between the alternative mechanisms becomes blurred, reflecting the diverse nature of the issues and of the outcomes sought.

Nevertheless, where the union seeks redress of complaints about the application of terms which have been agreed in collective bargaining, it usually prefers to use conciliation, mediation and arbitration processes rather than court procedures because it retains more 'control' over the criteria that will be relied upon when making judgements. This is the practice in many countries, including those like the USA where the collective agreement is itself a legally enforceable contract (see COLLECTIVE BARGAINING).

Where there is no legislative prescription of this course of action, a decision to seek the help of conciliators or to refer an issue to mediation or arbitration normally depends on the prior agreement of both parties; without it the disagreeing party can thwart any attempt to achieve resolution. Unilateral references to arbitration are unusual but may be provided for in a collective agreement: usually they occur only where legislation gives one or other party this 'right'. In many cultures, however, unilateral references would be regarded as inhibiting the reaching of a preferred end-state of an agreement which the parties would accept as morally binding (Bamber and Lansbury 1987).

4 Disputes of interest

It is common to deny the competence of a court to resolve disputes of interest, although it is increasingly difficult to identify with precision the dividing line between rights and interests issues (Weiss 1987). Many individual employers and some governments avoid referring interest claims to arbitration, although they may be less averse to proceeding to conciliation to facilitate a settlement. This reluctance stems from the belief that although it is proper to allow external adjudication of claims relating to established rights, it is either improper or inappropriate to allow a third party to establish them when the parties themselves cannot agree on their form.

It is, for example, widely considered that, if the law does not prescribe this course of action, it is inappropriate to place decisions about whether an employer should recognize a union as a bargaining agent for some of the workers, or about the levels of wages or the nature of other conditions, in the hands of a third party. Under the circumstances these issues are for the parties themselves to resolve by bargaining, even if this risks the withdrawal of either party from the relationship as each seeks to compel agreement to its terms.

The number and types of issues referred to conciliation, mediation and arbitration are usually more limited than those involved in collective bargaining, for two main reasons. (1) The parties are often able to resolve some issues in negotiations and only those upon which they fail to agree are referred for conciliation, mediation or arbitration. This is a consequence of the way in which bargaining over complex claims is conducted, although keeping all decisions open until the final package can be identified often helps to facilitate settlement.

(2) The parties, and particularly the employers, are less disposed (in the absence of mandatory legislation) to permit some claims to be determined by a third party over whom they cannot exercise a close control. This influences the types of third party intervention which may be adopted: it leads some to avoid arbitration entirely (as being less amenable to control) and others to accept only those 'awards' (usually in respect of 'rights') which are handed down by courts or tribunals.

'Pendulum arbitration' (in which the arbitrator is presented with a forced choice of the union's last claim or the employer's last offer) has been devised as a way of restricting the scope of the arbitrator and of retaining more control of the award in the hands of the parties (Burrows 1986). The arbitrator cannot then devise an award which accords with neither party's preferred position. It is not widely used (although it is more prevalent in North American countries than in others) because it requires the parties to be more precise in their bargaining behaviours.

5 Private and public interventions

The involvement of third parties in dispute resolution may occur in one of three main ways. They may be appointed privately under existing collective agreements to avoid open disputes with the aim of assuring the parties complete control of the intervention process. Alternatively, the parties may make voluntary use of any available public facility of this kind (that is, of the Labour Relations Commission in Japan or the Advisory Conciliation and Arbitration Service in the UK). In other cases it may be mandatory for the parties (or for one of them) to use some form of third party intervention before they can take lawful industrial action.

Private arrangements are often the first form of third party intervention to be adopted. They still occur under collective agreements made at local or sectoral levels, although, being private, information on their extent is not readily available. The parties appoint persons whom they agree should act as conciliators, mediators or arbitrators, either from within the industry or from outside. The test applied is whether they are sufficiently knowledgeable about the issues involved and sufficiently independent and impartial to be trusted not to favour one party to the detriment of the other.

A public service of conciliation, mediation or arbitration need not be based on principles different from those applying to private arrangements. Tripartite control (by representatives of the State, the employers and the unions) may be adopted, as in the Japanese Labour Relations Commission, to give an indication of the intention to be impartial. Under actual dispute conditions steps are usually taken to ensure that the full consent of all parties is forthcoming before an intervention is made. Care is normally taken to ensure that the parties retain control over the processes involved – for example, in selecting the third party or in supplying the information that the third party will rely on.

In most cases public service does not involve an injection of any greater third party interest than occurs with private arrangements (although the Australian award system did specifically provide for the State to address the Arbitration Court or Commission when issues of public interest were under consideration).

Where the State sets up a public service of conciliation, mediation and/or arbitration on which the parties must or can call as necessary, the conciliators may be drawn from the ranks of the agency's full-time staff and the mediators and arbitrators from a retained panel of 'outsiders' – as in the case of the British Advisory, Conciliation and Arbitration Service (ACAS). The problem faced by a State-provided facility is whether the parties will regard it as sufficiently distanced from the regulatory arms of government to convince them of its impartiality.

It is now common to find the people who are able and willing to act as third parties forming a distinct (if also small) cadre within the society. In some cases, as in Germany or the USA, they may form a professional body or institute from which the parties either must (in prescriptive systems) or may (in voluntary systems) select competent independents to meet the legal requirements or to meet their particular need for assistance.

6 The conciliation process

The procedures followed in third party intervention respond to the objective sought in each case, but also reflect conventions which are designed to leave as much control with the parties as possible.

Collective conciliation is designed to help the parties to reach agreement on their own terms and in accord with their own values. In some systems (such as that adopted in Westphalia in Germany) the conciliator who may eventually be called upon to help may sit in on the negotiations from their inception; thus he or she will be fully conversant with the arguments if called upon to act. In the more common system is that the conciliator who is asked to help when an impasse has already been reached, has to be briefed on the background and arguments before starting.

The conciliator will first acquaint him- or herself with the background and nature of the difference(s) by discussing them with the parties separately, that is, using investigative methods. The conciliator may either visit the site where the negotiations normally take place (for example, the employer's premises) or more commonly bring the parties together in separate rooms on neutral premises. The aim is to discover what the issues are, what value the parties place upon the various facets of the disputed issue, what they seek to achieve and what ideas they have for resolving them. The information can then be used to modify the parties' perceptions of their problem and the possible solutions to it.

The outcome of this phase is usually a knowledge not only of the context, but an appreciation of what parts of the claim/offer are of particular significance to each party (or of what each expects to get out of the exercise). This enables the conciliator to act as an intelligent interpreter of their positions and problems in the interests of removing barriers to their agreement. He or she can explain to each party the nature of the other's objectives and difficulties and, by developing a greater awareness of them, possibly bring the parties to a settlement.

Conciliators usually have to try to get the parties to modify their positions in order to narrow the outstanding differences between them. This is because the lack of awareness of the other's problems is not always the only barrier to agreement. Since disputed claims are often either composed of a number of separate elements, or capable of being resolved in a number of different ways, the conciliator can explore whether the parties might find it easier to settle if the 'package' were composed differently. The conciliator's task of re-packaging complex claims and offers is facilitated if the parties have withheld agreement to parts of a package until all of them have been fully considered in relation to each other, thus allowing for the possibility of trade-offs.

In conciliation the third party thus assumes the role of the intelligent messenger who attempts to narrow the differences between the parties. If successful the conciliator will invite them to reach their own agreement, although he or she may help them to formulate the terms to be used in it.

7 The mediation process

In its 'pure' form mediation often appeals to the parties, and particularly the employer, because it is a pro-active intervention which still avoids giving the third party an irretrievable power to resolve the issue in terms which might not be congenial to them.

The mediator has to be more pro-active than the conciliator in suggesting (or recommending) one or more possible solutions until one is found that the parties can accept. The dividing line between the two processes is thin: although the conciliator formally does not have this pro-active role, many of the conciliator's suggestions are likely to be very similar to those of the mediator although they will not be presented as 'recommendations', nor are they as likely to be given in writing.

The mediator, in order to reach a position from which a recommendation can be made, may hear the parties together or separately, and may rely on either adversarial or investigative methods. Like the conciliator, he or she may suggest to the parties separately a succession of possible recommendations until one that is likely to be acceptable is found. Alternatively, he or she may simply hear the separate arguments and by dint of questioning them in the course of the hearing arrive at a conclusion as to which of a number of alternatives might be acceptable to the parties. Recommendations are then made.

Mediation is more interventionist than conciliation, but it does not permit the imposition of a resolution of an issue. Both are essentially non-dictatorial and are often preferred to arbitration for this reason. They involve different ways of packaging the 'suggestions' made to the parties, but in both cases there is an aim of finding some solution to which the parties can agree. In Japanese culture this aim is elevated to the level where the settlement is made to depend on the parties accepting their moral obligations and displaying goodwill towards the other party. In Western industrialized countries a similar outcome is intended, although it is less often expressed in terms of morality.

Countries display different preferences for mediation and arbitration in dispute settlement. In the past mediation was used relatively little in the UK, although its use as an alternative to arbitration is now increasing. In contrast, France tends to rely more upon mediation than arbitration. Practice thus tends to reflect cultural preferences for adversarial or investigatory methods of establishing the nature of reality.

Although the Japanese attempt to avoid using arbitration to impose a settlement on the parties, in other countries conciliation and mediation may be linked in series with arbitration. A conciliator may attempt to bring the parties together, and if this does not succeed a mediator may be appointed to suggest a solution. But if this fails to produce a settlement the mediator may proceed to arbitrate on the matter and make an award.

8 Arbitration processes

Arbitration is carried out either by a single arbitrator or by a board of arbitration, dependent on any requirements of law or the preferences of the parties. In cases which involve complex technical issues, arbitrators may be assisted by 'assessors' (or technical experts nominated by the parties) who are able to offer information or advice.

The single arbitrator is normally capable of reaching a decision in straightforward cases but the parties may feel more secure if the decision is in the hands of a board, usually tripartite. This allows more minds to be brought to bear on the issues, and where the side-members are separately nominated by the parties themselves, these minds can be counted on to ensure that the parties' distinct values will be brought to bear on the issues.

Before any hearing takes place the parties normally agree the terms of reference which set the limits to the arbitrator's discretion in reaching an award. In framing them the parties may have assistance from conciliators who have previously been involved. The terms usually identify the parties, indicate what the difference between them is about (for example, wages, dismissal) and indicate what issue the parties want the arbitrator to resolve. Because of the formality, however, the terms may not indicate the full extent of what the parties really want to see resolved. Thus the arbitrator may uncover further complexities during the hearing.

The parties then produce written statements of argument or evidence for consideration by the arbitrator prior to the hearing. These usually include any detailed technical or statistical material about which it would be difficult to be eloquent, the parties' definitions of the issue and their views of its provenance. These may be long or short documents, dependent upon either the kind of issue involved or the importance which the parties attach to it.

At the hearing the parties expand on and amplify the information which they consider necessary for reaching a decision and articulate the values which, jointly or severally, they consider relevant to the assessment that the arbitrator has to make (Lockyer 1979). The parties usually appear together in the hearing so that they may hear everything said to the arbitrator, but because it is the arbitrator who has to be persuaded, all arguments are addressed to him or her, not to the other side.

The arbitrator is usually given a great deal of factual information (statistical data in the case of, for example, pay claims; the sequence of events leading up to a disputed decision). This is intended to support the arguments and inform the arbitrator's mind. The parties explain why they have not been able to reach their own agreement. They also place emphasis on the factors they consider to be important and indicate what each considers to be a fair or sensible solution.

The arbitrator is sometimes told much more than this, even if 'not in so many words'. There are occasions where what is said leads the arbitrator inexorably to a particular resolution which it appears that both parties recognize as the sensible one, even though their formal arguments may be at variance with it. This is the basis for regarding some references to arbitration as a process of finding a scapegoat to blame for a settlement.

On other occasions the parties may be very far apart and no clues given as to the settlement that both parties might find acceptable, even if it is not their preferred one. Arbitrators must then reach a judgement as best they can.

However, their task is made easier if there is a multi-faceted claim and offer situation which allows them to advance some benefit, however small, to both sides. This feature allows arbitration to be branded as a process of 'splitting the difference'.

However much or little 'help' the arbitrator gets from the parties, he or she must still reach a decision on the evidence and arguments presented, and not import into the process other values to which the parties might not subscribe. This is fundamental to voluntary arbitration because it provides the only guarantee that the process remains voluntary – and, in particular, immune to influence by the State. Where this principle is adhered to the apparently interventionist process of arbitration remains consistent with a normatively controlled system of bipartite regulation.

9 The conventions of arbitration

The procedures followed in arbitration (and, *mutatis mutandis*, in other modes of third party intervention not associated with the courts) are governed by conventions which allow the parties to retain control of the process and to avoid interference by the State with what is regarded as a private, voluntary process. Although particular parties may not subscribe wholeheartedly to these conventions (listed below) in every instance, they may be regarded as a kind of 'common law' of third party interventions.

1 Arbitration is embarked upon only with the consent of the parties to a dispute, and neither party can impose arbitration upon the other.
2 The parties will, in agreeing to put an issue to arbitration, also agree to accept the award of the arbitrator as binding (in honour or in law).
3 The parties may still continue negotiations on an issue after it has been referred to an arbitrator but will suspend any industrial action which might have the aim of coercing the other party to settle.
4 The parties will, through their own chosen representatives, present the arbitrator(s)

with whatever information is needed to enable a decision to be reached.
5 Arbitration will be carried out by one or more competent persons who are independent (both of the immediate parties and of the State) and impartial.
6 Arbitrators will reach their decisions exclusively on the basis of what is contained in the written and oral materials submitted by the parties and will respect the limits of decision indicated by the parties.
7 Arbitrators will reach their decisions on the basis of two main, broad criteria. These are, given the evidence and defined by the values of the parties: that which is likely to resolve the immediate problem effectively; and that which is likely to resolve the issue fairly or equitably.
8 Arbitrators will serve the parties to the dispute and no other interest in reaching their decisions and, as a servant of the parties, treat anything said by them as confidential.

It is not uncommon to find that, even when the State becomes more directly involved in these processes, the approach follows these same conventions.

10 Conclusion

Third party intervention in whatever form provides an alternative to overt industrial action as a way of compelling the other party in collective bargaining to agree the terms of a settlement, although it is not used only for this purpose. Its origins lie in convention-driven practices developed by collective bargaining parties over time, but governments subsequently gave it some degree of statutory support in order to reduce the incidence of industrial action.

Although practically all industrialized nations have institutionalized arrangements for conciliation, different countries reveal preferences for mediation or arbitration, with more relying on mediation than arbitration. Some countries require reference to one or more forms of intervention to be made before industrial action can acquire legality (particularly in respect of the public sector or 'essential services') whilst others leave the decision to the parties themselves. Some provide a public service of conciliation while others leave the arrangements to be made by the parties on an *ad hoc* basis.

The success of the mechanism appears to depend on the parties retaining or being allowed what, within that particular culture, they consider to be adequate control over the processes involved. This in itself for most countries tends to make conciliation a more acceptable process of third party intervention than mediation or arbitration. A good deal of evidence suggests that while compulsion is unlikely to produce more peaceful industrial relations a mechanism of this kind which can facilitate settlements of differences can help to reduce the incidence of breakdown in formal industrial relationships.

GEORGE F. THOMASON
UNIVERSITY OF WALES, CARDIFF

Further reading

(References cited in the text marked *)

* Bamber, G.J. and Lansbury, R.D. (1987) *International and Comparative Industrial Relations*, London: Allen & Unwin. (A description of the main features of industrial relations systems in a number of countries, with brief descriptions of the modes of third party intervention adopted in them.)
* Burrows G. (1986) *No-strike Agreements and Pendulum Arbitration*, London: Institute of Personnel Management. (A description of no-strike and pendulum arbitration clauses in collective agreements and an account and evaluation of the experience of their use and effects in North America.)
  Clark, J. and Lewis, R. (1992) 'Arbitration as an option for unfair dismissal claimants', *Personnel Management* June: 36–9. (Explores the feasibility of using arbitration as an alternative to industrial tribunals in resolving unfair dismissal claims.)
* Hanami, T. and Blanpain, R. (eds) (1989) *Industrial Conflict Resolution in Market Economies*, Deventer: Kluwer. (A review, in the form of contributed chapters and which includes case studies, of the systems in use in Australia, the Federal Republic of Germany, Italy, Japan and the USA.)
* Lockyer, J. (1979) *Industrial Arbitration in Great Britain*, London: Institute of Personnel Management. (A description of the history and procedures of industrial relation arbitration in the UK compiled by a senior officer of ACAS.)
* Mackie, K.J. (ed.) (1991) *A Handbook of Dispute Resolution*, London: Routledge. (A series of papers on the many varieties of difference or dispute, including those of industrial relations, commercial contracts, families and communities, that have attracted methods of resolution which do not involve the courts of law in various countries.)
* Organization for Economic Cooperation and Development (1993) *Preventing and Resolving Industrial Conflict*, final report of a seminar on industrial conflict settlement in OECD countries and in central and eastern European economies in transition, Paris: OECD. (A summary record of the issues raised and conclusions reached in discussions on dispute resolution in the Warsaw Seminar, supported by appended papers on the systems of dispute resolution in Poland, Hungary, the Czech Republic and Slovakia.)
  Owen Smith, E., Frick, B. and Griffiths, T. (1989) *Third Party Involvement in Industrial Disputes: A Comparative Study of West Germany and Britain*, Aldershot: Avebury. (A review of the history and structure of third party intervention in the UK and Germany, with a comparative and theoretical analysis, supported by eight case studies of particular interventions in the two countries.)
  Rojot, J. (1989) 'The role of neutrals in the resolution of interest disputes in France', *Comparative Law Journal* 10 (3): 324–38. (A description of the conciliation, mediation and arbitration provisions in law and practice in France, set against a background of the relevant aspects of the legal system and the practice of collective bargaining, and demonstrating the considerable reluctance of the collective bargaining parties to involve third parties in dispute settlement.)
* Weiss, M. (1987) *Labour Law and Industrial Relations in the Federal Republic of Germany*, Deventer: Kluwer. (A general description and discussion of the law and collective bargaining practice in the Federal Republic, which contains specific statements on the structure of the labour courts and their roles in the resolution of individual (pp. 96–103) and collective (pp. 184–6) labour disputes.)

See also: COLLECTIVE BARGAINING; DISCIPLINE AND DISMISSALS; EMPLOYERS' ASSOCIATIONS; EQUAL EMPLOYMENT OPPORTUNITIES; HUMAN RESOURCE

MANAGEMENT; HUMAN RESOURCE MAN-
AGEMENT, INTERNATIONAL; HUMAN RE-
SOURCE MANAGEMENT IN EUROPE;
INDUSTRIAL CONFLICT; INDUSTRIAL AND
LABOUR RELATIONS; INDUSTRIAL RELA-
TIONS IN EUROPE; INDUSTRIAL RELATIONS
IN JAPAN; INDUSTRIAL RELATIONS IN
NORTH AMERICA

Trade unions

Overview

Trade unions are associations established for the purpose of maintaining or improving the conditions of the working lives of wage earners. Although some contemporary unions may trace their origins to the medieval guilds, the present day form of trade unions primarily is the result of the industrial revolution and the large wage-earning class which it created. Unions exist in almost every contemporary nation-state, where they are typically considered to be a principal representative of the interests of employees.

1 Historical background

The first modern trade unions began to appear in the UK in the eighteenth century when medieval institutions collapsed, leaving the wage earner without protection from the vagaries of the labour market. The first unions were formed by craftsmen and drew upon craft guild traditions (Slomp 1990). Most of the early unions were confined to specific cities, although contact with organizations in other towns quickly led to informal arrangements to aid itinerant workers. The policies and objectives of the early unions were eclectic. They provided a forum whereby workers in the same trade could socialize with like-minded individuals and they helped members in time of need. Many of the early unions assumed the functions of friendly societies and provided financial assistance to sick or unemployed members. One early service was the provision of insurance so that a deceased

'brother' or 'sister' would be able to have a proper burial.

In difficult times it was natural that these organizations would petition employers to uphold or improve terms and conditions of employment. During the 1800s some of the early worker associations lobbied the government to enforce protective regulations. Where they were strong, the early craft unionists would often agree among themselves not to work for less than a basic 'trade rate' and only for those employers who respected union rules.

The early unions were fragile. They proliferated in prosperous periods and disappeared when times were hard. Employers were generally opposed to the unions because they challenged long-established authority relations, attempted to impose work rules considered to be confining and pushed for higher wages. The state was also wary of unions because they were believed to interfere with efficient market operations and posed the threat of becoming a political power base for the working class. After the French Revolution of 1789 European states generally attempted to discourage the formation of working class organizations. In most countries, unions were banned for at least some time (Adams 1993).

2 Ideology

Despite the opposition of both employers and governments, the 'labour movement' slowly grew in size and strength throughout the first half of the nineteenth century. Isolated local unions consolidated into national unions and in the second half of the nineteenth century national unions in many countries formed national federations of unions. The most pressing concerns of the early unions were survival and the solution of specific problems as they arose. From the mid-nineteenth century, however, labour leaders began to think more consciously about ideology and long-term objectives. Although a wide variety of ideological perspectives competed for the allegiance of working-class organizations, four types emerged as dominant: revolutionary, reform, Christian and business (Larson and Nissen 1987) (see INDUSTRIAL AND LABOUR RELATIONS).

The revolutionary perspective and Marxism

The revolutionary perspective was put forth most vigorously by Karl Marx, who argued that the industrial revolution had ushered in an era of 'capitalism' in which two major social classes clashed. Capitalists, the owners of the means of production, were pulled by the desire for profits and pushed by competition to 'exploit' workers by making those dependent on the sale of their labour work long hours for low pay. According to Marx, these systemic forces were so strong that efforts by individuals, unions or companies to stand against them would be futile. The working class could improve its conditions only by rebelling against capitalism and establishing socialism, a system in which the means of production were owned in common and rational decisions could be made about the distribution of goods, services and purchasing power.

The Marxist prescription for improving the working lives of wage earners called for the formation of both unions and labour political parties. The unions would be responsible for organizing the working class and educating workers about the nature of the capitalist system. They would also defend and improve working conditions within that system. The communist party would have the task of developing working-class strategy for bringing about the transition from capitalism to socialism. According to Marx, the party should be accorded primacy within the labour movement.

The appeal of Marxism

The Marxist analysis and prescription had immense appeal to labour leaders in the second half of the nineteenth century. Working people had few rights and labour leaders within civil society were considered only slightly more legitimate than criminals. In most European countries as well as the USA, trade unions were outlawed for some time. In France, the Loi le Chapelier forbade all associations intermediary between the individual and the State. In the UK, the Combination Acts of 1799–1800 branded all associations of working people as 'conspiracies' in constraint of trade and thus illegal (Hepple 1986). The same doctrine became law in the USA after a court case in 1806. By the mid-nineteenth century these laws were being revised, but the stigma of unionism as a less than proper activity continued for many decades. Marxist philosophy glorified the working class and labour leadership. It insisted that the working class was a force of history that would inevitably lead to the destruction of the capitalist system and the establishment of a more just and perfect society.

Revolutionary syndicalism

The ideology of revolution attracted a wide following among trade unionists in the second half of the nineteenth century. It became the dominant philosophy of labour on continental Europe either in its Marxist form or in its variant, revolutionary syndicalism (van der Linden 1990). The syndicalists shared the Marxist analysis of capitalist society but were very distrustful of political parties and government bureaucracies, instead calling for direct worker action to bring about the revolution through the general strike. Whereas Marxists would initially replace the capitalist state with a strong socialist state the syndicalists demanded the destruction of the state and its replacement with voluntary arrangements between worker-controlled production organizations. Syndicalism became the dominant labour movement philosophy in France where the 1789 revolution and several others in the name of the common people had failed to bring about significant change in the conditions of the working class.

'Productionist unionism'

When the revolution actually occurred in Russia in 1917 the new rulers had to consider the proper role of unions in socialist as opposed to capitalist society. It was decided that the unions would be given the tasks of managing social programmes, negotiating the implementation of the central plan and statutory labour standards in specific enterprises, representing worker grievances to management and, unlike most unions under capitalism, assisting in the mobilization of workers to achieve high productivity. This type of unionism became known as 'productionist', in opposition to the union focus on consumption in capitalist countries (Grancelli 1988). When communism spread from its Russian core to the USSR and later to eastern Europe, Asia and some African nations, this was the trade union model generally adopted. Within the communist world neither free collective bargaining, nor the right to strike, nor union independence of the party and the State was seen as appropriate.

The reform philosophy

In western Europe the ideology of revolution began to be challenged in the late nineteenth century. Reformers agreed with the Marxist proposition that society needed to be changed so that the conditions of work and life were made more comfortable for the many. They argued, however, that change could be brought about through reform rather than revolution. By this time labour/socialist parties had been established in many countries, regulations protecting the safety of workers in mines and factories had been introduced and the right to vote was being extended to a larger part of the adult population. These developments encouraged the reformers to believe that capitalist society could be changed gradually through the extension of democratic institutions. Particularly active in developing the philosophy of reform socialism were Eduard Bernstein in Germany and the British Fabian Society (Landauer 1959).

This philosophy had considerable appeal among trade union leaders whose rank and file members were more interested in their daily conditions of work than they were in macro sociopolitical change. It also won increasingly large numbers of adherents from labour/socialist party leaders after those parties began to win political power. By the 1920s reform socialism had become the dominant philosophy of European unions (Kassalow 1969).

Christian unionism

A third labour philosophy that began to appear in the latter part of the nineteenth century was Christian unionism. Marxist ideology held that the capitalist state was supported by many institutions including Christianity. Christian doctrine held that, even though the lot of the working person might be difficult on earth, if workers led sin-free lives they could expect a better existence in heaven. Marx argued that this helped to perpetuate capitalism by diverting workers' attention from their mundane problems to their potential reward in heaven. They were led to focus on 'pie in the sky' rather than the achievement of change on earth. Thus, Christianity acted as a bulwark for capitalism against working-class aspirations.

Christian unionism and the Church

As swelling numbers of workers were recruited to organizations that officially embraced Marxist ideology, the Christian churches became increasingly alarmed. Church leaders in many European towns encouraged Christian workers to form their own unions. In 1891 Pope Leo XIII issued the encyclical Rerum Novarum which encouraged the formation of Christian unions (Fogarty 1957). During the first two decades of the twentieth century Christian unionism spread significantly across not only Europe but also notably South America. It became a significant force too in the Canadian province of Quebec.

Initially the Christian unions were dominated by the Church which discouraged conflict and cajoled Christian workers and employers to reconcile their differences. The Church held that workers had a duty to do a fair day's work and that employers had a responsibility to treat their employees reasonably and with dignity. Church leaders often offered their services as mediators and conciliators when disputes occurred. From the 1930s onwards the influence of church leaders on these unions began to wane along with the general decline of religious influence on civil society. After the Second World War most Christian union movements became entirely independent of the church hierarchy although in many countries they continued to be guided by Christian principles. In some countries, France being a good example, there was a transition away from Christianity to an entirely independent stance. Never as important globally as socialist unionism, Christian unionism has declined in strength since the Second World War.

Business unionism, pure and simple

The fourth important labour philosophy is that of business or 'pure and simple' unionism. This philosophy holds that the purpose of unions is to win the best conditions of employment for their members within liberal democratic society. It also insists that it is improper for unions to become involved in partisan politics. Union members have many different political interests and thus should be free to join and support the political party of their choice. The proper interest of the union in politics is to ensure that the State allows the labour movement to negotiate effectively with employers over conditions of work and that it adopts legislation in the interests of union members.

Generally, business unionism does not affirm the Marxist analysis of modern society as being split into two antagonistic classes. Instead it tends to accept the theory of the pluralist state as an arena of myriad interest groups, none of which is strong enough to dominate. Unlike Marxism this philosophy does not hold that the labour movement has any long-term mission. Its sole purpose is continually to improve the conditions of its members (Perlman 1928).

The appeal of business unionism

By the end of the nineteenth century business unionism had become the dominant philosophy in the USA and this continued throughout the twentieth century. Because some variant of socialism is dominant in the labour movements of most other modern nations, the US

situation is regarded as extraordinary and 'American labor exceptionalism' has been a major topic of scholarly inquiry (Adams 1995). The philosophy has also been of importance in many other countries where it has competed with socialism and Christian unionism. Whereas the labour movements of northern Europe arrived at reform socialism from the doctrine of revolution, the British and Canadian labour movements arrived from the opposite end of the ideological spectrum. During the nineteenth and the early part of the twentieth century they had been more businesslike and only slowly moved towards an increasingly political strategy.

Business unionism was of considerable appeal to unions of white-collar employees. In many countries white-collar workers during the nineteenth and into the twentieth century had privileges not enjoyed by blue-collar workers and thus found revolution and reform less attractive. White-collar unionism first appeared as an important force during the First World War. In many countries white-collar unions have seen fit to remain independent of the mainstream movement, usually because of ideological differences.

3 The international labour movement

Although autonomous power within labour movements resides primarily at the level of the nation-state, trade unions have established important international organizations.

International trade secretariats

In the 1880s and 1890s international trade secretariats (ITSs) began to be formed. These were organizations composed of national unions in particular crafts or industries. Among the first to appear were those for boot and shoe workers, miners, printers, metalworkers and clothing and textile workers. By the second decade of the twentieth century there were nearly thirty such organizations but, primarily as the result of mergers, the number has declined over the years. By the 1990s there were fewer than twenty (Windmuller 1990).

ITSs carry out research and disseminate information on subjects such as terms and conditions of employment. They also act as vehicles for coordinating the efforts of their members with respect to strikes and boycotts. Most provide assistance to unions in less developed countries.

International trade secretariats and other international organizations

The ITSs also lobby international organizations such as the International Labour Office (ILO) and the United Nations on their members' behalf. In the post-war era a principal concern has been the activities of multinational corporations. Several ITSs have thus set up committees to exchange information and coordinate the activities of trade unionists working for the same company in different countries. For several companies international councils have been established which confer with the management about a range of issues of mutual concern. Pressure exerted by international labour organizations has resulted in bodies such as the Organization for Economic Cooperation and Development (OECD), the ILO and the European Economic Community developing acceptable standards of behaviour for multinational companies in their dealings with employees and their representatives.

Central trade union federations

A second type of international trade union organization is composed of central trade union federations. Conferences of such organizations (in some cases in conjunction with political parties) were held from the late nineteenth century. Out of these meetings emerged a secretariat which, from 1913, was known as the International Federation of Trade Unions. Through this body ideological splits within the labour movements of particular countries were eventually reflected in the international arena.

After the Second World War, three major international union federations of worldwide scope came into existence. The International Confederation of Free Trade Unions (ICFTU) attempted to group together all social democratic and business union federations. The World Federation of Trade Unions (WFTU) brought together all of the union organizations in the communist world as well as those federations in the West who affirmed communist ideology, most notably in France and Italy. The third organization was the International Federation of Christian Trade Unions. In 1968 this latter organization changed its name to World Confederation of Labour (WCL) to reflect the more independent and secular programme that its member federations had adopted by that time.

The International Confederation of Free Trade Unions

The most representative of the three global internationals is the ICFTU. It includes union federations from all of the most developed countries but also has many affiliates in Asia and Latin America. Since the collapse of communism in 1989, many of the new union federations in central and eastern Europe have also affiliated. The ICFTU represents general labour interests to international organizations, assists labour movements in the less developed world and carries out research and educational work.

The World Confederation of Labour

Since moving away from its Christian identity, the WCL has had a difficult time defining its unique reason for existing. Several of its important affiliates have abandoned it for the ICFTU. Its major supporters come from Belgium, The Netherlands, Quebec and Latin America. Its programme of action is similar to that of the ICFTU.

The World Federation of Trade Unions and other federations

Since the collapse of communism many of the previous constituents of the WFTU have disbanded or completely changed their programmes. The previous singular government-supported union federation that existed in most communist nations has been superseded in most east and central European nations by several federations with philosophies ranging from businesslike through various versions of democratic socialism. Although many individuals active in the unions under communism continue to be active in the post-communist era, totalitarian communism as a working philosophy has all but disappeared. Many of the new federations have joined the ICFTU. By the early 1990s the future existence of the WFTU appeared to be in great doubt.

In addition to the ITSs and the international union confederations, there are also independent regional groupings of trade union federations.

4 Union objectives and methods

With the changes noted above there are today two dominant union types in the global arena: social democratic (or reform socialist) and business (pure and simple). Business unions take as their major objective the representation of the interests of their own members while social democratic unions have the wider aspiration of representing the interests of all working people whether or not they are members of a trade union.

Social democratic unions

Typically, social democratic unions are closely associated with a labour or socialist party and political strategies for improving the conditions of the working class are coordinated with the party. Not uncommonly, union leaders simultaneously hold party office, and in many countries unionists also hold political office (von Beyme 1980). In countries where such unions and parties are strong, social and welfare legislation tends to be more highly elaborated than in nations where these organizations are weak.

Business unions

Business or pure and simple unions by definition are not officially associated with any one political party although they may support specific candidates and particular parties in specific circumstances. A major activity of both sorts of unions today is the influencing of legislation of particular interest to their constituents. In addition, in order to avoid economic disruption and price instability, in many

countries unions have been invited to cooperate with employer organizations and the State in the formation of overall socio-economic policy (Williamson 1989). This phenomenon has become known as 'neo-corporatism' or 'tripartism'.

Collective bargaining

An important task of both business and social democratic unions today is collective bargaining with employers over terms and conditions of employment (see COLLECTIVE BARGAINING). In all industrialized, market economy countries, collective bargaining is a dominant method of trade unions (Clegg 1976; Windmuller *et al.* 1987). In western Europe, due to the prevalence of multi-employer bargaining and the extension of agreements to non-associated employers, collective bargaining is the predominant method for the establishment of wage levels, hours of work and other general conditions of employment. Collective bargaining is also a primary activity of unions in North America. However, since unions represent only a minority of the labour force, and because of decentralized bargaining and the absence of agreement extensions, most North American employees have their basic conditions of work established unilaterally by employers. Collective bargaining is also in evidence throughout most of the developing world. Unfortunately, owing to union weakness basic conditions of employment are frequently established unilaterally by employers or specified by the State.

The right to strike

The primary basis of union power is the right to strike (see INDUSTRIAL CONFLICT). The strike or the strike threat plays a critical role in collective bargaining in most countries. Unions generally insist on the general acceptance of the right to strike and in certain countries (for example Italy, France) this right has been embedded in the national constitution. Because it is disruptive of economic activity and the stable delivery of critical services, some countries have outlawed the strike for particular employees such as police and fire-fighters. Certain nations have attempted to convince unions to accept arbitration in lieu of the right to strike. The most extensive experiment with arbitration as a substitute for the right to strike was undertaken in Australia and New Zealand. In neither country did the availability of arbitration and the forbidding of strikes actually result in the absence of strike activity.

Unions administering social and economic policies

In addition to co-determining socio-economic policy and terms and conditions of employment, unions in many nations serve on agencies established to administer social and economic policies. For example, trade unionists serve on bodies designed to oversee labour market policy, training, health and safety, pensions, workers' compensation for industrial accidents and human rights. In some countries (such as Sweden and Belgium) unions have been given primary responsibility for managing the unemployment insurance system. Unions also provide assistance to individuals who believe that their rights under collective agreements or social legislation have been violated. In some countries (for example, the USA and Canada) unions have been instrumental in the development of 'grievance procedures' ending in binding arbitration for the settlement of collective agreement disputes. In other nations (Germany and France) unions are active in representing their constituents before tribunals such as labour courts.

5 Union structure and government

Within any country unions today are typically organized at three levels: local, industry or occupation, and national (Bean 1994; Bamber and Lansbury 1993).

Local level organization

At the local level there are three major types of organizational format. In many countries industrial (for example, the chemical industry) or occupational (nurses) unions are organized locally on a geographic basis. All members within a given city or district belong to the local union. Some unions in some countries prefer, however, to organize on a plant basis. This union form groups all employees who work in a particular plant or location in the same union. This set-up is common among industrial unions in North America. A third local form is the enterprise union. It differs from the plant union type in that all members of a single company (for example Toyota) belong to a single union. Enterprise unionism was pioneered in Japan and has been spreading to other countries in recent decades.

Industrial or craft unions

Local unions are typically grouped in national unions. Initially there were two major types of national union: the industrial union and the craft union. However, over the years, as a result of amalgamations and mergers, these two types have become increasingly intertwined. Thus, a common form of union today is referred to simply as the general union.

Craft unions were the first unions everywhere, but when unskilled and semi-skilled workers began to organize *en masse* around the turn of the twentieth century industrial unions began to become more prevalent.

Socialist movements generally prefer the industrial union form because it is more consistent with their egalitarian principles. By the mid-twentieth century industrial unionism dominated throughout the world, but craft unionism continued to be important in a few countries, notably the UK and others strongly influenced by British traditions such as the USA, Canada and Australasia. In continental Europe craft unionism continued to be important only in Denmark.

National-level organization

At the national level one finds union federations divided by ideology (social democratic versus Christian or formerly Christian versus business). One also finds divisions based on occupational identity. In several countries (France, Sweden, Germany) there are separate central organizations for white-collar workers.

Union governance

In Europe trade unions were major elements in the struggle for democracy, and everywhere unions are formally organized on democratic principles. At each level union officers are elected. Before entering negotiations, unions typically survey members to ensure that their concerns are represented: most commonly, before an official strike takes place, union members must vote in favour of such action. In many nations, tentative collective agreements must be approved by union members before they go into effect.

Often there is tension within union organizations between the democratic imperative and the need for leaders to possess the authority to take quick and decisive action. The latter consideration has led many north European unions to give their negotiators the right to enter into collective agreements on their own initiative without the need to subject the tentative agreement to a member vote.

Most union organizations schedule frequent local union meetings but often these meetings are poorly attended and thus draw criticism from adherents to democracy. To quell such criticisms some union movements go as far as to fine members who do not attend such meetings.

6 Contemporary issues and challenges

The 1960s and 1970s was a period of rapid economic growth, generally low unemployment and price instability. In that milieu union membership generally grew, strike activity was high and union economic and political influence was considerable. Wages, benefits and social programmes expanded considerably. In many countries governments offered unions political concessions in return for their pledge to moderate wage demands and forgo strikes. The period came to an end as a result of the deep recession of the early 1980s.

Unemployment in many European countries reached levels unknown since the worldwide depression of the 1930s. Economic growth in South America and Africa came to a halt and real wages fell. In Asia, however, Japan and the economies of the newly industrializing countries of Hong Kong, South Korea, Taiwan and Singapore continued to expand and prosper, providing enhanced worldwide competition. With the exception of Asia these developments undermined union strength. Membership generally decreased and unions were unable to organize effective strike activity (Adams 1991).

During the 1980s employers in many nations seized the initiative in labour relations and successfully demanded economic concessions, freedom from union and government-imposed constraints and more flexibility. They also took the initiative to reorganize production in order to make better use of employee skill and creativity. These developments led to more bargaining at enterprise level. The general trend by states to involve unions in socio-economic decision making came to a halt. However, in several countries where tripartite consultation had become firmly embedded (Germany, Japan and Austria) effectively it still continued. Against the tide, certain countries (such as Australia) moved in the direction of more tripartite cooperation.

Independent trade unions appeared in all of the ex-communist countries and, during the 1990s, institutions similar to those common in the West were being constructed.

7 Conclusion

Although the contemporary era has been difficult for the trade unions, they continue to be an important feature of most nations of the world. They are generally considered to be a fundamental pillar of democracy, and as long as political democracy continues to be a dominant global force, trade unions should continue to play a significant role in society.

ROY ADAMS
MCMASTER UNIVERSITY

Further reading

(References cited in the text marked *)

* Adams, R.J. (ed.) (1991) *Comparative Industrial Relations, Contemporary Research and Theory*, London: HarperCollins. (A review of industrial relations developments from the 1960s in industrialized, developing and communist countries.)

* Adams, R.J. (1993) 'Regulating unions and collective bargaining: a global, historical analysis of determinants and consequences', *Comparative Labor Law Journal* 14 (3): 272–301. (Global review of government policy towards unions and collective bargaining over the past two centuries.)

* Adams, R.J. (1995) *Industrial Relations under Liberal Democracy, North America in Comparative Perspective*, Columbia, SC: University of South Carolina Press. (The development and implications of North American exceptionalism.)

* Bamber, G. and Lansbury, R. (eds) (1993) *International and Comparative Industrial Relations*, 2nd edn, London: Allen & Unwin. (Chapters on industrial relations in the major industrialized market countries.)

* Bean, R. (1994) *Comparative Industrial Relations*, 2nd edn, London: Croom Helm. (The most widely used textbook. Includes a chapter on trade unions.)

* Beyme, K. von (1980) *Challenge to Power, Trade Unions and Industrial Relations in Capitalist Countries*, London: Sage Publications. (An international comparison by a prominent German political scientist.)

* Clegg, H. (1976) *Trade Unions under Collective Bargaining: A Theory Based on Comparisons of Six Countries*, Oxford: Blackwell. (A major effort at cross-national theorizing.)

* Fogarty, M. (1957) *Christian Democracy in Western Europe, 1820–1953*, London: Routledge & Kegan Paul. (The most comprehensive treatment of the development of Christian trade unionism.)

* Grancelli, B. (1988) *Soviet Management and Labor Relations*, Boston, MA: Allen & Unwin. (Discussion of the practice of industrial relations under communism.)

* Hepple, B. (ed.) (1986) *The Making of Labour Law in Europe: A Comparative Study of Nine Countries Up to 1945*, London: Mansell. (The most comprehensive treatment of this subject.)

* Kassalow, E. (1969) *Trade Unions and Collective Bargaining*, New York: Random House. (History and development of industrial relations with a focus on Europe and the USA.)

* Landauer, C. (1959) *European Socialism*, Berkeley, CA: University of California Press. (The most comprehensive treatment of this subject.)

* Larson, S. and Nissen, B. (eds) (1987) *Theories of the Labor Movement*, Detroit, MI: Wayne State University Press. (Multiple perspectives on the nature and purpose of trade unions. Excerpts from basic sources.)

* Linden, M. van der (1990) *Revolutionary Syndicalism: An International Perspective*, Brookfield, VT: Gower. (Widely referenced treatment of this subject.)

* Perlman, S. (1928) *A Theory of the Labor Movement*, New York: Macmillan. (Most widely referenced statement on business unionism. Also an apologetic for American exceptionalism.)

* Slomp, H. (1990) *Labor Relations in Europe*, New York: Greenwood Press. (The history of labour relations in Europe.)

Webb, S. and Webb, B. (1894) *History of Trade Unionism*, New York: Longmans Green. (The first major study of trade unions.)

* Williamson, P.J. (1989) *Corporatism in Perspective*, London: Sage Publications. (Overview of the phenomenon of corporatism.)

* Windmuller, J.P. (1993) 'The international trade union movement', in R. Blanpain and C. Engels (eds), *Comparative Labour Law and Industrial Relations in Industrialised Market Economies*, 5th rev. edn, Deventer: Kluwer. (Development and contemporary status of the concept by the subject's foremost expert.)

* Windmuller, J.P. *et al.* (1987) *Collective Bargaining in Industrialised Market Economies: A Reappraisal*, Geneva: ILO. (Comparative overview and review of bargaining in several specific countries.)

See also: COLLECTIVE BARGAINING; CORPORATISM; EMPLOYEE RELATIONS, MANAGEMENT OF; EMPLOYERS' ASSOCIATIONS; EMPLOYMENT AND UNEMPLOYMENT, ECONOMICS OF; FLEXIBILITY; INDUSTRIAL CONFLICT; INDUSTRIAL DEMOCRACY; INDUSTRIAL AND LABOUR RELATIONS; THIRD PARTY INTERVENTION; TRAINING, ECONOMICS OF

Related topics in the IEBM: MARX, K.H.

Biographies

Argyris, Chris (1923–)

Personal background

- born 16 July 1923 in Newark, New Jersey
- graduated from Clark University in 1947, completed Master of Science degree at Kansas University in 1949 and received his PhD from Cornell University in 1951
- married Renee Brocoum, two children
- develops what is termed a 'theory of action'
- formative influence on organizational behaviour, intervention theory, organizational learning and competence-enhancing methods of inquiry
- appointed James Bryant Conant Professor of Education and Organizational Behaviour at Harvard University

Major works

Personality and Organization (1957)
Intervention Theory and Method (1970)
Organizational Learning (with Donald Schon) (1978)
Inner Contradictions of Rigorous Research (1980)
Reasoning, Learning and Action: Individual and Organizational (1982)
Overcoming Organizational Defenses (1990)
Knowledge For Action (1993)

Summary

Chris Argyris (1923–) initiated a theory, strategy of inquiry and learning methodology known as *action science*. His approach, which is applicable to persons and organizations, enables human beings and social systems to change. Action science liberates both practitioners and researchers from the often dysfunctional grip of the status quo by generating a valid and useful knowledge of actions.

Argyris argues that people and organizations need to confront the contradictions between intentions and actual behaviours, expose the values and assumptions that govern patterned behaviours, and develop and test alternative behaviours and value systems. His ideas and methods have been applied to repetitive problems, puzzles and paradoxes in a wide range of contexts, including education, organizational development, social theorizing and management development. While his approach has often sparked controversy among conventional scholars and traditional managers, his work has been a major influence on the humanization of management and the development of grounded theories of organizational behaviour, development and social inquiry.

1 Introduction

Argyris has always been concerned with the health and effectiveness of individuals, organizations and institutions (see ORGANIZATION BEHAVIOUR). His early research documented the ways in which budget and accounting procedures, personnel practices, executive development programmes, management style and traditional organizational structures constrain individual performance, personal growth and innovation. He demonstrated repeatedly how low-skilled, fractionated jobs carried out within pyramidal organizational structures retard individual maturity and thwart the satisfaction of higher order human needs. Argyris also showed how such effects are replicated in traditional research methods, which place subjects in top-down, unilaterally controlled situations. Both managers and researchers, he admonished, seemed to be colluding in perpetuating explanations of processes that mitigated against effectiveness and truthfulness in the organization.

As his inquiries progressed, Argyris became increasingly fascinated with what people took for granted and how unaware they seemed to be when acting upon what they took for granted. This led to a line of research which suggested that behind what is taken for granted is highly skilful behaviour, and behind this skilful behaviour is the acculturation of social virtues that foster a lack of awareness. Argyris's focus has led to a mode of inquiry involving intervention in the workplace; such interventions produce directly observable data that demonstrate how the status quo reacts when threatened.

Interventionist research methods require subjects to become 'clients' who participate in defining jointly the aims and methods of the research itself. Moreover, such methods demand that researchers have both the skill to deal with defences at several levels of analysis and the determination to explore what are often considered to be taboo subjects. In one sense, such inquiries represent a violation of culturally sanctioned avoidance strategies.

2 Biographical data

Argyris was the third son born into a middle-class family on 16 July 1923 in Newark, New Jersey, USA. Soon after his birth, his family moved to Greece for several years, returning to Irvington, New Jersey, in time for him to begin his schooling. Argyris experienced difficulty early in school because he could not speak English very well, and rejection as a minority member in the neighbourhood. His early upbringing and his experience of the disapproval of others instilled in him two enduring characteristics: a propensity to examine himself carefully to discover his deficiencies and a desire to work hard to change himself.

Towards the end of the Second World War, Argyris served as an officer in the US Signal Corps. He won awards for technical performance and efficiency while in charge of several depots in Chicago, but also discovered that his subordinates held doubts about his 'human skills'. In keeping with his early upbringing, Argyris's reaction was to endeavour to learn

more about himself. Following his discharge, he continued his university education, studying psychology, business and economics, and pursuing an academic career in organizational studies.

At an early stage in his academic career, he was influenced by the work of Roger Barker, Fritz Heider and Kurt Lewin, each of whom was revolutionizing psychology. Argyris then went to the School of Industrial and Labor Relations (ILR) at Cornell University to complete his PhD. ILR was a new, problem-centred school that encouraged students to question the limits of traditional disciplines. At Cornell, under the guidance of William Foote Whyte, Argyris began the value-based practices which continue to characterize his work in the 1990s: the study of everyday life as the arena in which to discover problems and from which to infer theory; the questioning of the status quo, especially with regard to the way in which it helps to perpetuate problems; making problem solving the test of any discipline; and carrying out research that is guided by concerns for external and internal validity, competence enhancement and justice.

3 Main contributions

The many significant contributions Argyris made to management thinking and practice are his responses to a number of fundamental questions. What is the impact of organizations on their members? How can organizational research be made to produce knowledge that leads to enhanced managerial practices? How can one intervene in organizations in such a way that they become more competent and effective? What inhibits individual and organizational learning and how might it be overcome?

Organizations and individuals

Early in his career, Argyris showed how traditional managers based their structures, systems and practices on inaccurate assumptions about human nature and interpersonal relationships (Argyris 1957, 1964) (see OCCUPATIONAL PSYCHOLOGY). He noted that managers appeared to hold values such as: people are most effective when they are rational, significant human relationships have to do with the achievement of organizational objectives and human relationships are most effectively influenced through unilateral direction, coercion and control. In accordance with these values, organizations are designed using principles of task specialization, unity of direction and a clear-cut unity of command. In addition, management retains the sole right to plan work, evaluate performance and determine what information is important and may be shared, and also the right to construct reward and punishment systems that sanction its values and practices.

Argyris also summarized what is known about healthy, mature human beings in western culture. From infancy to adulthood, persons tend to demonstrate the following kinds of development: from passivity to increasing activity; from dependence on others to relative independence; from being capable of behaving in only a few ways to behaving in many different ways; from having a few, casual, short-lived interests to having many different interests; from having a short-time perspective to having a longer time perspective; from being in a subordinate position to being in an equal and/or superordinate position; and from having little self-awareness to having greater awareness of, and control over, the self (see FREUD, S.). Argyris concluded that formal organizations create in healthy, mature individuals a short-time perspective and feelings of frustration, failure and conflict. Employees consequently express such feelings through such activities as absenteeism, high staff turnover, 'gold-bricking' (output restriction), psychological withdrawal, emphasizing material rewards and, in some cases, by forming trade unions. A majority of managers and organizational researchers are pessimistic, agreeing that trust and loyalty are hard to find in organizations, while conflict is common. These unintended features of organizational life are assumed somehow to be natural, rather than outcomes of the dominant but inadmissible self-fulfilling ideology of control.

At the core of Argyris's analysis of the interface between the individual and the stultifying organization is his identification of unexamined assumptions and values, including those which prohibit making implicitly held values and assumptions explicit (Argyris 1971). Faced with such prohibitions, management has a tendency to solve only symptoms and devise 'quick fix' solutions to complex problems.

Argyris makes the point that when the crucial and inadmissible are viewed simply as hypotheses and hence open to debate, new resolutions for integrating the individual and the organization will be found. In the 1960s, his own suggestions for the organization of the future – enlarged jobs, greater use of self-managed teams, leaner managerial hierarchies, feedback for learning as well as for system correction, and leadership instead of managership – clearly presaged many of the management innovations which have become popular in the 1980s and 1990s.

The collusive effect of research

Paralleling the foregoing discussion, Argyris (1982) argues that social scientists design and conduct research that colludes unwittingly with the beliefs and practices that dominate human activity. Rigorous research methods place subjects in a top-down situation that is consistent with the psychosocial structure of pyramidal organizations. To achieve internal validity, all control lies with the researchers, who make all the decisions. As a consequence, subjects become dependent and conformist. Tasks are stated explicitly and defined rigidly and norms of objectivity and rationality predominate. However, as Argyris has shown, unintended consequences result, ranging from marginal subject participation to covert hostility, from physical withdrawal to trivial responses. In other words, what people say their behaviour is seldom corresponds to their actual behaviour. Discovering valid and useful knowledge through the use of conventional scientific methods thus becomes highly problematic.

To overcome the dysfunctionality and questionable ethics of conventional, rigorous research, Argyris advocates viewing the research relationship primarily as a helping relationship in which subjects are encouraged to act naturally and be fully themselves, and where accurate feedback increases the meaningfulness of the activity for subjects. Field interventions are his mode of inquiry, where subjects become clients who participate in defining jointly the research goals, methods, participation, and research costs and rewards. For Argyris, research produces knowledge that enhances client competence first and change secondarily, as well as aiding the development of theory (see ORGANIZATION BEHAVIOUR). He prefers, and has pioneered, rigorous theories about the way the world is, the way it should be and how to get from the one way of being to the other. He favours knowledge that is understandable, storable and retrievable under the conditions of everyday life.

Obstacles to organizational change

The work summarized above led Argyris to focus on processes of change and renewal. In his writings about management and organizational development, innovation and consultancy, he addressed the question of how an organization might move from traditional values and practices favoured by the status quo to methods that are more conducive to organizational competence and individual growth.

By the late 1960s, conditions creating the need for strategies of organizational change were increasingly in evidence. For example, rapid and unexpected environmental changes were occurring, new management knowledge and techniques were being practised and there was increasing diversity and organizational growth. At the same time, alternative management approaches based on new and very different conceptions of persons (for example, McGregor 1960) and organizations (for example, Likert 1967) were gaining widespread acceptance (see HUMAN RELATIONS). Taken together, these changing practices became known as organizational development. However, the new field greatly resembled prior managerial thinking in so far as it emphasized planned change, management from the top

down and the application of behavioural science. Significantly, all these aspects were rooted in unexamined ideologies of power and control. Without having developed an overall theory, organizational development has, since its inception, elaborated continuously its diagnostic models and interventional technologies and pursued system efficiency and effectiveness.

Argyris's conception of renewal differs from all other organizational development theories in two fundamental ways. One difference is his development of a generic theory of intervention that applies across all levels of social systems and in all contexts. The other is his focus on increasing competency rather than change in the interests of improving effectiveness. On the one hand, Argyris emphasizes moving attention to the values that shape problem-solving routines. On the other, he argues that real and lasting changes in organizations require more trust, more openness, more concern with feelings and greater commitment to experimenting with new ideas than is normally the case. Significantly, these are properties of interpersonal relationships, not of persons or systems. It is especially important that people in positions of authority display a high level of interpersonal competence.

According to Argyris (1970), effective interventions depend upon three centrally important processes: helping to generate valid information in order that situations and problems may be understood accurately; creating opportunities for free choice in the search for solutions; and creating conditions for internal commitment to choices and continual monitoring of actions taken. These processes require that persons, groups and organizations focus not on change but on learning (Argyris 1992). Under such conditions, attention may shift from feedback that alters actions (single-loop learning) to questioning the values that govern conventional problem-solving routines (double-loop learning). This shift is very difficult to make because organizations, and many people who work within them, develop certain deeply ingrained habits. For example, they may have a tendency to attribute blame or disguise inconsistencies in their performance. When questioned about such habits, employees often feel embarrassed or threatened and adopt defensive behaviour which prohibits double-loop learning. Both persons and organizations have theories about how to act effectively, which blind them to opportunities for real learning.

If double-loop learning leads to the competence which leads, in turn, to health, effectiveness and renewal, but defensive routines block such learning, then explaining why defensive routines persist becomes critical if one is to understand and improve management education, organizational development, social inquiry and much else. Argyris (1980) explains the persistence of defensive routines at two levels. What is easy to observe is the collusion of persons in accepting but not confronting the differences between how they justify their behaviour (their espoused theories) and how they actually behave (their theories in use). This collusion, says Argyris, is supported by culturally sanctioned, widely held positive social virtues or values, such as caring and support, respect for others, honesty, strength, integrity and so on. Implicit in such virtues, however, are rules that actually say things like: be rational and minimize emotionality; refrain from being honest with somebody if your honesty is likely to hurt his or her feelings; don't challenge the reasoning or actions of others when you disagree with them; stick to your principles at all costs; feeling vulnerable is a sign of weakness; and achieve your goals in whatever way you see fit. Overlaying these virtues is a double-bind logic, which again is widespread and culturally sanctioned and which says, in effect: act as if there are no ambiguous or inconsistent messages and act as if these are not open to discussion.

Given the existence of defensive routines, measures intended to enhance competence place considerable demands upon persons and organizations. The task of introducing into the workplace a new organizational culture – which involves learning-orientated norms, bilateral protection of others, minimal personal defensiveness, clear acceptance of responsibility for individual action and trust in processes that cannot be confirmed – is fraught with difficulties (see ORGANIZATION

CULTURE). However, such an exercise is more likely to succeed when it is based on the values which govern effective intervention, that is, valid information, free and informal choice, internal commitment to choice and constant monitoring of the effects of initiatives.

Action science

The value-based, double-loop learning cycle outlined above constitutes action science (Argyris 1982), a programme of research and intervention that is designed to understand and alter the reasoning and learning processes of individuals and organizations by exposing and examining the inner contradictions of action. Action science places considerable demands upon the intervener/researcher, who must have the necessary determination and interpersonal skill to deal with organizational and individual defensive routines (the natural response of self-sealing value systems is to reject that which threatens). In contrast to other theories of organizational behaviour and managerial thinking, perhaps the most distinctive feature of action science is that it has the potential to uncover its own contradictions and alter its own learning processes accordingly.

4 Evaluation

Argyris, in a truly large and consistent body of work, has promoted a problem-centred, value-centred approach to a valid and practical theory that examines the unintended consequences of behaviour with the aim of enhancing interpersonal competence. Action science, therefore, is a non-disciplinary theory of action in which persons and organizations are encouraged to identify and examine the values governing their problem-solving routines. At the core of the interventions which promote this kind of learning are a set of values about valid information, experimentation, choice and learning from experience. For Argyris, enhanced competence leads to the sort of change that leads, in turn, to individual and organizational health.

Action science, as strategy for both social-scientific inquiry and organizational improvement, questions conventional approaches to research and problem-solving. As Argyris's own theory predicts, his work threatens the scientific and managerial status quo and he has been criticized by scholars and managers alike. Interestingly, however, both social-scientific inquiry and management thinking is starting to reflect the principles and findings of action science – for example, various forms of collaborative inquiry are being utilized.

CRAIG LUNDBERG
SCHOOL OF HOTEL ADMINISTRATION
CORNELL UNIVERSITY

Further reading

(References cited in the text marked *)

* Argyris, C. (1957) *Personality and Organization*, New York: Harper & Row. (This book first detailed the incompatibility between mature individuals and hierarchical, mechanistic organizations.)
* Argyris, C. (1964) *Integrating the Individual and the Organization*, New York: Wiley. (An examination of ways in which organizations and managerial practices can be redesigned to provide conditions conducive to individual growth and health.)
* Argyris, C. (1970) *Intervention Theory and Method*, Reading, MA: Addison-Wesley. (A classic of organizational development which presents a normative approach to organizational change based on competency enhancement.)
* Argyris, C. (1971) *Management and Organizational Development*, New York: McGraw-Hill. (An outline of person-organization incongruency and how change agents may alter it.)
* Argyris, C. (1980) *Inner Contradictions of Rigorous Research*, New York: Academic Press. (An explanation of defensive routines and how these can serve to block double-loop learning by preventing feedback loops from functioning.)

* Argyris, C. (1982) *Reasoning, Learning and Action*, San Francisco, CA: Jossey Bass. (A description of ten years of research into the possibilities for increasing the capacity of individuals and organizations to solve difficult underlying problems by means of action science.)
Argyris, C. (1990) *Overcoming Organizational Defenses*, Needham, MA: Allyn & Bacon. (A description of the basis for, and maintenance of, designed-in, second-order error and methods of overcoming the resulting defensive routines.)
* Argyris, C. (1992) *On Organizational Learning*, Oxford: Blackwell. (A collection of twenty-one previously published articles and chapters based on the premiss that organizational learning is an ability that organizations should develop.)
Argyris, C. (1993) 'Looking backward and inward in order to contribute to the future', in A. Bedian (ed.), *Leaders in Management Theory and Practice*, vol. 1, Greenwich, CT: JAI Press Inc. (An autobiographical essay in which Argyris describes how themes from his personal life are reflected in his scholarly work.)
Argyris, C. and Schon, D. (1978) *Organizational Learning*, Reading, MA: Addison-Wesley. (An early work on organizational learning that suggests ways in which thinking and feeling can be integrated by studying them as they exist in action.)
* Likert, R. (1967) *The Human Organization*, New York: McGraw-Hill. (Stressing process over structure, four organizational systems are described using an authoritarian-to-participative continuum.)
* McGregor, D. (1960) *The Human Side of Enterprise*, New York: McGraw-Hill. (A human relations classic that outlines contrasting sets of management assumptions and their consequences.)

See also: HUMAN RELATIONS; OCCUPATIONAL PSYCHOLOGY; ORGANIZATION BEHAVIOUR; ORGANIZATION CULTURE

Related topics in the IEBM: LEWIN, K.; ORGANIZATION DEVELOPMENT; SCHON, D.

Bedaux, Charles E. (1886–1944)

Personal background

- born 11 October 1886 in Paris, France
- emigrated to the USA, 1906
- worked for a furniture company in Grand Rapids, Michigan
- founded first Bedaux consultancy firm in Cleveland, 1918
- returned to France, 1927
- became advisor to the Nazis and the Vichy government after the fall of France in 1940
- captured in the Allied invasion of North Africa, 1942
- committed suicide, 18 February 1944

Major works

The Bedaux Efficiency Course for Industrial Application (1917)
Code of Standard Policy (1928, unpublished)
Code of Application Principles (undated, c.1930, unpublished)
Training Course for Field Engineers (undated, c.1930, unpublished)
Vade Mecum (1930, unpublished)

Summary

Charles E. Bedaux claimed to have found a scientific relationship between work and fatigue. This represented an important extension of the systems developed by F.W. Taylor which had failed to satisfactorily deal with the impact of strain and tiredness on performance. Bedaux's approach provided the basis for a universal measure of all work – the Bedaux or 'B' unit. This unit was used as the basis for a time-and-effort-related piecework pay system. The system spread quickly and extensively across Europe and the USA during the 1930s. However, research into the Bedaux system found that it was resisted by middle and supervisory management and it was poorly understood by many workers.

1 Introduction

Charles E. Bedaux led a bizarre life. Born in Paris, France in 1886, he emigrated to the USA at the age of 20 and had a variety of jobs, from selling life insurance to selling toothpaste which removed ink spots. Finally, he was employed by a furniture company in Grand Rapids where he developed a system for measuring worker performance which took account of fatigue. This system was the source of his fame and of a considerable fortune. He developed networks of consultancies in the USA and internationally to apply his ideas.

On returning to France in 1927 he gravitated towards fascist politics and thirteen years later when the country fell he became industrial advisor to the Nazis and the Vichy Government. Bedaux's technocratic views of society held a strong appeal to the Nazis. He had a strong sense of mission, believing that poverty could be eradicated if production was organized on his methods and that an efficient society could be created if led by engineers and technocrats. In 1942 he was captured during the Allied invasion of North Africa where he was directing a scheme to build a 2,000-mile peanut-oil pipeline across the Sahara Desert. Before standing trial, he committed suicide in 1944 (Littler 1982).

This unusual life should not detract from Bedaux's significance to management thinking and practice. His system dealt with a major limitation in Taylor's work (see TAYLOR, F.W.) and as Littler states:

> Overall, it is evident that Bedaux was one of the most important figures in the international spread of scientific management

in the inter-war years and crucial to the diffusion of Taylorian workshop practices in Britain.

Littler 1982: 108)

2 Main contribution

This review of Bedaux's main contribution focuses first on the central features of his system, then on how his system compares with other schemes of work measurement and payment, and finally on its diffusion.

Layton notes that 'Bedaux claimed to have solved the problem which had eluded Taylor, namely discovering the precise scientific relationship between work and fatigue' (quoted in Littler 1982: 108). Taylor had not adequately dealt with fatigue and was criticized for being unable to scientifically ground his notion of 'proper tasks'. Combining studies of fatigue and Taylorism, Bedaux sought to establish the link between elementary work motions and necessary rest periods. In so doing, Bedaux developed a 'relaxation curve' which identified the rest times necessary to offset working time with the total system based on the length of the work cycle. However, as Layton notes, there is nothing to suggest that Bedaux undertook any scientific or experimental investigations, with the result that his rest allowances were simply *ad hoc* 'guesstimates and assessments of what the local market would bear' (quoted in Littler 1982: 109).

The time taken to perform a task modified by relaxation and rest was formulated into a universal unit, the Bedaux or 'B' unit equal to 60 of these modified seconds. This has sometimes been termed the Normal Minute, the Allowed Minute or the Work Unit (Shimmin 1959: 17). It was this formulation of a universal unit which allowed for the system to be applied across very different jobs within the same factory and in so doing to create a single measuring grid, facilitating management monitoring and control.

The timing of jobs was generally based upon an organizations-and-methods procedure by which attempts were made to ensure the best layout and structure for the job. The job was broken down into component parts with each element timed by a stop watch, a simultaneous rating of the worker's speed and effort being made against the standard 60 work units an hour. For example, an employee judged to be working at 25 per cent above normal speed would be rated 75 (60 + 15). A series of studies produced the average times and ratings for each element which were then converted into standard times – the times taken if working at the normal speed of 60 work units per hour. The total then gave the standard time for the whole operation, to which a fixed percentage was added for relaxation (Shimmin 1959).

This measure was primarily used as the basis of a reward system. The wage rate set for a '60B' performance was seen as a minimum wage whatever the actual performance: in other words, the day wage was guaranteed and formed a safety net. Any output above 60B attracted a bonus or 'premium'. Generally, the bonus calculation meant that each B point earned one-sixtieth of the base pay, but this did not produce a proportionate rate of increase in pay. This was because, Bedaux also suggested, the worker could only perform above 60B with the assistance of indirect workers. Thus, the production workers only received 75 per cent of the available bonus, the other 25 per cent going into a reserve fund for indirect staff.

In placing the Bedaux system in the context of other types of bonus scheme it is helpful to use the fourfold classification of schemes set out by Marriot (1957). First, in terms of the basic structure schemes, the Bedaux system, based upon units of output measured in time, can be contrasted with those piecework schemes which pay a price or rate per piece or unit of work. Second, with reference to the primary purpose of schemes, Marriot sees Bedaux's system as an 'inter-departmental plan', one providing equitable treatment for the frequent inter-departmental transfers occasioned by work requirements. This contrasts with systems designed to save time and 'selective plans' seeking to attract efficient workers to the plant and discourage those unable to meet work and performance targets. Third, in relation to the sharing of the bonus, Bedaux clearly shares the increase between employee and employer as well as between direct and indirect workers: this is unlike other systems where employer and employee gain or lose all and the indirect employee receives nothing. Finally, in connection with the relationship between earnings, labour costs and output, workers' earnings under Bedaux vary proportionally less than output. In other schemes, variation is in the same proportion as output or is more than output.

The Bedaux system spread rapidly and extensively across the USA and Europe during the 1930s. The impact of Taylorism on the different countries of Europe had been variable, Italy and Germany being more receptive than Britain. However, stimulated by the establishment of a permanent consultancy office in Britain, Bedaux's ideas appear to have had a broader appeal. While it is difficult to gauge the proportion of national workforces covered by the Bedaux system, Table 1 indicates that a large number of companies adopted the system, especially in the USA, France and Britain.

Table 1 Number of firms using the Bedaux system (1930–8)

USA	500
Canada	28
Britain	225
France	144
Italy	49
Belgium	22
Germany	25
Holland	39
Austria	5
Switzerland	4
Spain	2
Scandinavian countries	24
East European countries	25
Australia	17
Other countries	17
Total	1,126

Source: Littler (1982: 113)

3 Evaluation

Bedaux's contribution to management thinking and practice can be evaluated in a number of different ways. First, it can be assessed from a normative perspective. Thus the managerial advantages of the Bedaux system include the scope it provides for production planning, control and costing, and the 'points' or standard unit system reduces the various types of labour to a common denominator. The managerial disadvantages relate to the costs and complications of installing and maintaining the scheme (Marriot 1957). Moreover, these very complications make it difficult for workers to understand, which detracts from its incentive value. In a study of six factories using Bedaux, Shimmin concluded: 'Most operatives knew little of the formal structure of the scheme, nor were they familiar with the principles of time study and the calculations made by the wage office' (1959: 136). Moreover, De Man (1929) in a study of German workers concluded that one of the main factors making for dissatisfaction with Bedaux-based schemes was the workers' inability to keep track of output and wage calculations.

Second, Bedaux's contribution can be placed in the context of certain scholarly, theoretical debates. For example, it is of value to consider whether the application of the Bedaux system contributed to the craft job simplification and de-skilling central to Braverman's theories on the labour process (see BRAVERMAN, H.). On the basis of a number of factory cases from the inter-war period, Littler (1982) concludes that structural pressures exerted by Bedaux engineers did result in a divorce of 'direct' and 'indirect' labour and job simplification, as well as reducing worker autonomy initiative. However, Bedaux was not used as a direct confrontational means of *craft* de-skilling but instead was used in industries with pre-planned or semi-planned production processes, with low dependence on craft skill and knowledge.

Finally, an evaluation can made by looking at the more practically orientated studies on the operational difficulties arising with the Bedaux system. Research in the 1920s at

W&T Avery in Birmingham revealed considerable resistance to Bedaux from supervisors who opposed the centralizing tendency involved, particularly as exercised through the central time study office. In addition, Bedaux appeared to produce considerable unrest on the shop floor, with a number of strikes in the 1920s and 1930s in such companies as ICI Metal, Joseph Lucas, and Amalgamated Carburettors (Littler 1982). These strikes were related to fears of unemployment, given the goal of the Bedaux system to increase output at a reduced cost, and were also linked to concerns about de-skilling and workers being spied upon by time study engineers.

4 Conclusions

Bedaux made a major contribution to management thinking and practice through addressing a major limitation in the works of F.W.Taylor. By accounting for employee fatigue and strain, he developed a standard unit of time measurement which could be used as the basis for an incentive pay scheme. The resultant system could be applied to very different groups within the same factory, and provided a means of monitoring and controlling the labour force and related costs. The significance of the Bedaux system was reflected in its diffusion within the USA and Europe in the 1930s. Research suggests, however, that its incentive effect was weakened by the difficulties workers had in understanding the mechanics, while it also gave rise to supervisor and employee resistance.

IAN KESSLER
TEMPLETON COLLEGE
UNIVERSITY OF OXFORD

Further reading

(References cited in the text marked *)

Bedaux, C.E. (1917) *The Bedaux Efficiency Course for Industrial Application*, Bedaux Industrial Institute. (Setting out in detail the mechanics of the Bedaux system, this was used as a training manual by Bedaux consultants; only one copy publicly available.)

* Braverman, H. (1974) *Labor and Monopoly Capital*, New York: Monthly Review Press. (Classic work on labour process theory looking at de-skilling as a means of asserting managerial control.)

* De Man, H. (1929) *Joy in Work*, London: Allen & Unwin. (Of historical interest, providing ethnographic insights into factory work in Germany in the early twentieth century.)

* Layton, E. (1974) 'The diffusion of scientific management and mass production from the US in the twentieth century', *Proceedings of the XIVth International Congress in the History of Science, Tokyo*, 4: 377–86. (Short conference paper on the spread of Taylorism from the USA to Europe.)

* Littler, C. (1982) *The Development of the Labour Process in Capitalist Societies*, London: Heinemann Educational Books. (The most comprehensive discussion available of Bedaux's ideas, placed in strong analytical context.)

* Marriot, R. (1957) *Incentive Payment Systems*, London: Staples Press. (Dated but still useful textbook on incentive, combining prescription with some analysis.)

* Shimmin, S. (1959) *Payment by Results*, London: Staples Press. (Rare and enlightening attempt to provide empirical data on operation of bonus schemes in a number of factories.)

See also: INDUSTRIAL AND LABOUR RELATIONS; LABOUR PROCESS; PRODUCTIVITY; TRADE UNIONS

Braverman, Harry (1922–76)

Personal background

- born Brooklyn, New York, 9 December 1922, of Polish–Jewish parents
- attended City College, New York, in 1937 but left after one year without taking a degree
- married Miriam Gutman, 25 December 1941
- started apprenticeship as coppersmith in Brooklyn Navy Yard in 1938 and worked in different skilled manual occupations between 1938 and 1951
- after working as a socialist journalist and book reviewer, entered publishing, becoming in turn editor, general manager and vice president of Grove Press, 1960–7
- director of Monthly Review Press, 1967–76
- died of lymphoma, 2 August 1976

Major works

The Future of Russia (1963)
Labor and Monopoly Capital: The Degradation of Work in the Twentieth Century (1974)

Summary

Harry Braverman (1922–76) is widely regarded as developing what became known as the 'de-skilling thesis' in his classic work *Labor and Monopoly Capital* (1974). Building on Marx's writing on the 'labour process', Braverman set out to analyse critically the degrading effects of technology and scientific management on the nature of work in the twentieth century. Principally, he suggested that the drive for efficient production is also a drive for the control of workers by management. Managerial control is achieved through monopolizing judgement, knowledge and the conceptual side of work, and concomitantly excluding workers from the control and ownership of knowledge and skill acquisition. The history of work in the twentieth century is one of work degradation, as knowledge is systematically removed from direct producers and concentrated in the hands of management and their agents. This leads to the impoverishment and debasement of the quality and experience of labour for both manual and mental workers, who are condemned to execute only the routine and conceptually depleted tasks in the service of capital.

1 Introduction

Braverman's name is associated with:

1 revitalizing and expanding the Marxist analysis of work;
2 the 'degradation' or 'de-skilling' thesis which suggests that there is an underlying tendency within capitalism to substitute less or unskilled labour for skilled;
3 the representation of management as a 'control' function, legitimized by governing and excluding workers from the conceptual part of the labour process (see LABOUR PROCESS);
4 the idea that efficiency is saturated with the ideology and interests of management and is not a neutral goal.

2 Biographical data

Harry Braverman was born in Brooklyn, New York, in 1922 of Polish–Jewish parents. In 1937 he attended City College, New York, but had to leave after a year in order to find work. He later graduated in 1963 from the New

School of Social Research in New York, having studied under Robert Heilbroner.

His working life falls in two parts: as a skilled manual worker (1938–51), and as journalist and publisher (from 1952 until his death in 1976). Most of his working life was spent in white-collar work, and not, as is popularly assumed, as a manual craftsman. Braverman's account of his employment history in the introduction to *Labor and Monopoly Capital* (1974) gives more weight to his early career, which may have perpetuated the idea of his writing being overly concerned with the decline in manual craftsmanship.

From 1938 to 1942 he served a four year apprenticeship as a coppersmith in the Brooklyn navy shipyard and worked there as a coppersmith for a further three years, supervising from eighteen to twenty men. He was drafted into military service in 1945 and sent to Cheyenne, Wyoming, where he worked repairing locomotives for the Union Pacific railway. After his discharge, he moved to Youngstown, Ohio, and worked in steel fabrication. He spent seven years at various trades other than that of coppersmith, including pipe fitting, sheet metal work and layout.

During this period he defined himself as 'always a moderniser' (Braverman 1974a: 6) rather than an opponent of technical change, but also as an observer of the rationalization and erosion of craft work. He also noted that 'throughout these years' he was 'an activist in the socialist movement' and a Marxist (Braverman 1974a: 6). In fact, he joined the Trokskyist Socialist Workers' Party in the 1930s, leaving with a group of other people in 1954 when he helped set up the magazine *The American Socialist*, which he edited between 1954 and 1960 when the magazine closed.

During the 1950s, in addition to socialist journalism, Braverman produced book reviews and summaries for the Book Find Club. According to his son's recollections, Braverman spent considerable time on each review, polishing his style and treating each in a 'craft' manner. The quality of his reviews stood out and attracted the attention of a New York publisher, who recruited him in 1960. Between 1960 and 1967 he worked for Grove Press as an editor. While not in any way a

socialist publishing house, Grove Press had published the unexpurgated version of *Lady Chatterley's Lover* in 1959, a year before Penguin, and while at Grove Braverman was the editor in charge of *The Autobiography of Malcolm X*, which first appeared in 1964. According to his son he was a very conscientious and competent editor, manager and publisher, with considerable business acumen. When he left Grove he was a general manager and vice president, evidence of his business and managerial flair.

Between 1967 and 1976 he worked as a director at Monthly Review Press (MRP). Despite taking a considerable drop in salary to join MRP, Braverman, according to his son, moved because he wanted to 'follow the music of my youth'. The move was in fact a return to socialist publishing, and he was clearly sympathetic with the political orientation of the publishing house. It was while at MRP that Braverman wrote *Labor and Monopoly Capital*. Although he wrote another book and numerous book reviews and short articles, he is best known for that one work.

3 Main contribution

Labor and Monopoly Capital

Braverman began work on *Labor and Monopoly Capital* in the late 1960s, working in the evenings and without sabbatical leave from his job at MRP. Since its appearance the book has not been out of print and has sold over 120,000 copies in English, with the bulk of sales occurring between 1976 and 1980; average sales in English remain around 2,000 per annum. The book has been translated into Italian, Spanish, Japanese, Portuguese, French, Swedish, German, Dutch, Greek, Norwegian and Serbo-Croat, and remains in print in all these languages. It has been MRP's best-selling title.

Fame came posthumously to Braverman, as the debate on the labour process initiated by *Labor and Monopoly Capital* occurred after his death. Apart from a short reply (Braverman 1976) he was unable to respond to his numerous critics, and his premature death gave these critics a free reign in interpretation.

While critical of the political and practical disengagement of university academics, ironically, *Labor and Monopoly Capital* has helped make many academic careers.

Main themes of the book

Labor and Monopoly Capital is 465 pages long, elegantly written, theoretically integrated and carefully crafted. Despite its length, the view it presents of work becoming degraded by capitalism provides a dynamic which animates the text. This view comes from Braverman's own employment experience, keen observation, research training and political outlook, informed by the conviction that:

> The ideal organization toward which the capitalist strives is one in which the worker possesses no basic skill upon which the enterprise is dependent and no historical knowledge of the past of the enterprise to serve as a fund from which to draw on in daily work, but rather where everything is codified in rules of performance or laid down in lists that may be consulted (by machines or computers, for instance), so that the worker really becomes an interchangeable part and may be exchanged for another worker with little disruption.
>
> (Braverman 1994: 24–5)

There are five parts and twenty chapters in the book, covering labour and management, science and mechanization, monopoly capital, the growth of working-class occupations and the working class itself. The substantial parts of the book concern the role and nature of the labour process in capitalism, the role of science and mechanization, the growth and effect of scientific management on the worker and the changing class structure of the USA (see LABOUR PROCESS).

A major theme of the book concerns the debunking of official statistics and quantitative US sociological classification of jobs, skills, occupations and social class. Braverman attacks the view that skills have been 'upgraded' in the twentieth century, that extended time in education equates with more skilled or knowledgeable work and that formal designations of skill equate with actual skill. Skill receives varying definitions in the book, but best equates with the idea of worker-engaged, practical–theoretical workplace systems of learning most associated with craft apprenticeships. Movement away from 'craftsmanship' generally signals skill degradation. More generally, Braverman follows Marx's view of labour as the primary attribute of human beings; as he says in his final interview in December 1975: 'What is work but the central purpose of human existence as a species, the central drive, [and] motivation of the individual as well?' (Braverman 1980: 36).

Management is considered in a primarily negative light, as an agent for controlling the worker, and the growth of management has accompanied the expansion of the workplace or detailed division of labour and dissociation of the worker from authority exercised through command of craft and technical knowledge over the labour process. Efficiency theorists such as Frederick Taylor are represented as the ideologues for management control, flourishing because they provide capital with solutions and ideas for commanding the unruly and unpredictable element of production, namely, living labour (see TAYLOR, F.W.). Scientific management as a theory is equated with capitalism as a *system*, not with the occupational aspirations of engineers or a particular moment in the industrial development of the US workplace.

Discussion of changes in the US class structure take up one-third of *Labor and Monopoly Capital*, yet these ideas have tended to get uncoupled from deliberations on 'skill' which critics have highlighted and abstracted from it. Braverman seeks to show how the US transformed itself from a population of self-employed into one of waged employees, and how these employees have been divided subsequently between manufacturing and service industries and blue-collar and white-collar occupations, engaged in officially skilled but substantially skill-deficient activities and tasks. A recently transcribed lecture given by Braverman in 1975 reinforces his primary concern with what he calls the 'making of the U.S. working class' (Braverman 1994). In both *Labor and Monopoly Capital* and this talk, 'making' is used in the structural rather than cultural sense, through the involuntary movements of Latin American and European peasant and artisan populations into waged employment in US capitalism and through the destruction of US farmers and their transformation into waged workers. Classes in this sense are made and remade through 'the powerful tendency of the capitalist mode of production to convert every form of independent work into hired or wage labour' (Braverman 1994: 19). He also documents the shrinking of employment in agriculture, and subsequently in manufacturing, as the scale and concentration of ownership leads to technical resources intensifying the labour of those that remain. Displaced workers move into the service industry as this becomes a new growth point for capital accumulation. The chapters on clerical and service occupations highlight the spread of scientific management techniques with the growth in scale of service provision.

Other class themes are Braverman's discussion of the dramatic growth of the 'new middle class' of 'intermediate employees' who stand between owners/senior managers and workers. The sexual as well as the social division of labour features in *Labor and Monopoly Capitalism*, and the work was initially praised by feminists for its treatment of female labour (see EQUAL EMPLOYMENT OPPORTUNITIES). However, the book's focus on waged employment downplays the role of the 'household economy' or domestic labour in capitalism, a shortcoming acknowledged by Braverman (1976). Subsequent feminist research on the workplace has also highlighted the male exclusivity of craft and skilled work which distorts the way it is produced and reproduced in capitalism (Cockburn 1983).

An important implicit theme is Braverman's methodology, which elevates the critical role of work experience in forming theory. Braverman's own employment history as craftsman, supervisor, journalist, editor, publisher and manager informs the texture of his approach to work, and he contrasts the poor quality and inaccuracies of academic and official descriptions of work with the value of reflection on lived experience by the politically

engaged (Braverman 1974a). Through numerous observations on the 'de-skilling' of all forms of work, from bread-making to printing, Braverman's confident statements on the actuality of work, on the destruction of craft skills and controls, on the inhumane reduction of people to performers of the most mindless activities, spring from his working knowledge as well as his political outlook and reading. Braverman's critical comment on the ignorance of manual work on the part of the influential sociologist Daniel Bell (Braverman 1974a) is illustrative of his lifelong hostility towards ivory-tower scholasticism and politically and practically disengaged academic commentators on the world of work. Braverman was a lifelong Marxist socialist, and his working experience and writing reflects his political convictions.

4 Evaluation

Labor and Monopoly Capital continues to cast a long shadow over debates on the nature of work in the late twentieth century. From the late 1970s, a debate around the issue of the 'labour process' in capitalist society developed in all countries, especially in English-speaking countries. The labour process perspective on the ordering of work suggests that managerial action is chiefly motivated by capital–labour relations, by the strategies of employers and their agents to try to control and stabilize the 'unruly' element or factor of production, namely, living labour. Labour process analysis carries through inequality from market relations into capital–labour relations in the workplace, and suggests that the dynamics of this unequal social relationship both limit, condition and drive the structuring work. The evolution of management thought, especially around the arrangements of production, is said to follow the evolution of labour organization, with increasing sophistication, unionization, education and expectations of work challenging employers to develop ever more sophisticated control techniques and practices to maintain their power in the employment relationship (see INDUSTRIAL AND LABOUR RELATIONS; TRADE UNIONS).

Reactions to *Labor and Monopoly Capital* passed through different phases, from political commentary by Marxist writers to academic engagement by those both sympathetic to Braverman's Marxist epistemology and those hostile to it, who were concerned with narrowing the focus of debate to limited areas such as the nature of skill acquisition and disposal. Continued treatment of the book as a 'text' – frozen by Braverman's premature death and consequent inability to respond to critics and develop his argument through debate – was only heightened when labour process analysis in some countries (notably the UK) came under the sway of Foucauldian analysis and produced highly abstract and rarefied commentaries far removed from Braverman's desire to link the practical experience of those working for capitalism with a grounded political theory of the dynamics of the system. The 'text' has been de-politicized because the author was removed from the field of debate and response, and *Labor and Monopoly Capital* became simultaneously an icon for the faithful to seize upon and for critics to deprecate. Constructive developments within a labour process tradition, which acknowledge Braverman's contribution and seek to develop the methodology or theory, are more than outnumbered by those which pay lip service to situating the text, codify it into a few clichés and use Braverman as a straw figure who cannot answer back.

Within academic circles *Labor and Monopoly Capital* has influenced a great variety of disciplines such as labour history, labour economics, economic history, industrial relations, industrial sociology, industrial geography and organizational theory. In the USA, initial evaluation was carried out by historians and labour economists (Zimbalist 1979; Edwards 1979). These writers sought to recast the evolution of management thought through the prism of labour–capital conflict over control of the labour process. In the UK, industrial sociologists (Nichols and Beynon 1977; Nichols 1980; Thompson 1989; Littler 1982) found theoretical coherence through the work, while industrial relations writers (Kelly 1982; Wood 1982, 1989; Edwards 1986) recast the nature of conflict, the role of skilled labour

and other themes through reaction and response to *Labor and Monopoly Capital*. Economists in the UK (for example, Friedman 1977) made connections between labour market, product market and labour process restructuring, which in other countries (notably France) produced theories of capitalist 'regulation' informed by crisis and transition between different labour process 'regimes'. Later, organizational theorists entered and almost monopolized ownership of the labour process debate through the annual Aston–UMIST Labour Process Conferences, which produced a stream of edited volumes on different aspects of the labour process (see LABOUR PROCESS) including job design, management strategies, gender, technology, white-collar work, skill, quality and theory.

In Japan, *Labor and Monopoly Capital* fed critical debates on the nature of work which tended to expose the US basis of Braverman's assumptions and the very different reactions to and construction of scientific management and workplace struggles in Japan. In continental Europe, German engagement with the work in the early 1980s also quickly amplified its US stereotypes on skill destruction, which made little sense in the strongly institutionalized craft apprenticeship system in German manufacturing (Lane 1989).

Braverman's message of 'work degradation' therefore fitted some societies better than others. However, even in countries with intrinsic craft apprenticeship systems and an abundance of skilled labour, such as German-speaking countries, writers have confirmed parts of Braverman's thesis of 'skill polarization' or bifurcation, and have uncovered within the firm managers committed to rationalizing work through skill substitution as well as skill upgrading (Altmann *et al.* 1992).

Nevertheless, the lack of a general fit between the degradation of work thesis and particular societies reveals one important limitation of the thesis, namely, coupling to *capitalism* a universal division of labour which is more properly anchored to particular occupational and training systems. More generally, it can be said that *Labor and Monopoly Capital* undervalued the way the labour process is embedded within sociocultural contexts which lays out differing ways of putting together the employment relationship. There is just one footnote concerning Japan in the work, and writing at a time of unquestioned hegemony of US capitalism, it is not surprising that Braverman did not give sufficient attention to different national ways of putting the labour process together.

In addition to ignoring the variety between capitalist societies in the formal systems of skill acquisition and discharge, Braverman also understated the role played by 'tacit' skills, which can be necessary for the most formally unskilled activities and which provide workers with some basis of resistance to or non-compliance with the control demands of management. Skills can also be tied to workers' gender or personality in the form of 'emotional labour' – ways of looking, feeling or servicing capital in particular ways which are not necessarily part of a formalized training structure. Writers such as Hochschild (1983) developed labour process analysis by focusing on the negative consequences for workers' mental health and sense of self in servicing employers in ways which compromise their identity as individuals. Braverman anticipated much of this development in his discussion of the shift towards mass service industries, where household and other activities become subject to disciplinary and rationalizing pressures of scientific management and involve subjecting the identity of the worker to prescribed ways of being and performing.

Another theme of criticism relates to Braverman's treatment of scientific management and Taylorism as though they were the last word in management theories of work organization. Debates on the nature of work from the early 1980s are particularly associated with the rise of the Japanese economy on a international scale (together with powerful continental European economies such as Germany), and deal in post-Taylorist neologisms such as 'flexible specialization', 'innovation-mediated production' or 'lean production', where old craft or new skill structures are forged. Ideologically, these ideas suggest a break from 'de-skilling', although empirical

evidence of such a move remains less convincing (Thompson 1989). Part of a labour process perspective directly offered by Braverman's methodology is that of looking 'behind' the claims of formal classifications and management paradigms, and this still informs contemporary debates about a supposed break from Taylorism.

A major attack on *Labor and Monopoly Capital* relates to the focus in the book on the 'objective' features of skill, class and occupational structures, which neglect the theme the consciousness. Braverman justified this in terms of priorities: in his view, we need an understanding of the structural operations of the labour market and labour process prior to understanding collective or class perceptions. His view of 'subjectivity' is through the idea of class consciousness, a historical class acting for itself. Two points of criticism occur: (1) attacking this orthodox Marxist view of class structure preceding class consciousness; and (2) rejecting limiting consciousness to class: what about gender, race, occupation or identity as significant bases of action? Burawoy (1979) developed a critique of the first by demonstrating how workers use work as a space for ingenuity, games, forms of resistance which, while not challenging capitalism as a class, do offer ways of mediating and modifying managerial controls while simultaneously reproducing capitalist production values. Inserting social action into labour process would arguably have been welcomed by Braverman, who sought not to belittle or play down workers' capacity for struggle over their economic returns and for dignity in the labour process, but rather highlighted the limited effect such struggles have in preventing capitalism transforming jobs into routine activities.

5 Conclusions

The rise of the labour process perspective on management and the organization of work, particularly in English-speaking countries, owes a considerable debt to Harry Braverman. His premature death distorted development of the various hypotheses on the direction of his work as, quite simply, the prime mover of the approach was not around to debate and progress his arguments through the normal avenues of active political and intellectual discourse. Too much time was wasted in second guessing, speaking for and against *Labor and Monopoly Capital*, and too little was spent on building upon and moving on from the text. Debate moved on through a process of distortion and simplistic codification of *Labor and Monopoly Capital* into clichéd debates, such as the de-skilling thesis, often to the neglect of other major themes of the book, subtleties of disposition and argument.

CHRIS SMITH
ROYAL HOLLOWAY COLLEGE
UNIVERSITY OF LONDON

Further reading

(References cited in the text marked *)

* Altmann, N., Kohler, C. and Meil, P. (eds) (1992) *Technology and Work in German Industry*, London: Routledge. (A useful account of the theoretical and practical critique of Taylorism from one branch of German industrial sociology.)

Braverman, H. (1960) 'The momentum of history: review of Heilbroner', *Monthly Review* (April): 433–9. (One of Braverman's early published reviews.)

Braverman, H. (1963) *The Future of Russia*, London: Collier Macmillan. (Early book examining the future of Russia and the Soviet Union.)

Braverman, H. (1967) 'Controls and socialism', *Monthly Review* (January): 33–9. (Article which looks at the important issue of control over the workforce.)

Braverman, H. (1967) 'The successes, the failures and the prospects', *Monthly Review* (November): 22–8. (Another of Braverman's early review articles.)

Braverman, H. (1968) 'Labor and politics', *Monthly Review* (July–August): 134–45. (Another of Braverman's early review articles.)

Braverman, H. (1969) 'Lenin and Stalin: review of Lewin', *Monthly Review* (June): 45–55. (Review article of a prominent work on the Soviet Union.)

* Braverman, H. (1974a) *Labor and Monopoly Capital: The Degradation of Work in the Twentieth Century*, New York: Monthly Review Press. (The main reference for contemporary debates on the labour process. Although heavily criticized and limited by its reliance on US capitalism, the breadth and quality of the writing and analysis make the work a modern classic.)

Braverman, H. (1974b) 'Looking backward and forward', *Monthly Review* (June): 40–8. (Review article.)

Braverman, H. (1975) 'Work and unemployment', *Monthly Review* (June): 18–31. (Often cited article on unemployment.)

* Braverman, H. (1976) 'Two comments', *Monthly Review* (September): 119–24. (Response to articles provoked by *Labor and Monopoly Capital*.)

* Braverman, H. (1980) 'The last interview', *Monthly Review* (March): 34–6. (Transcript of an interview given in Toronto, in which Braverman defends *Labor and Monopoly Capital* and argues for a viable craft system of production.)

* Braverman, H. (1994) 'The making of the U.S. working class', *Monthly Review* (November): 14–35. (A transcribed lecture in which Braverman discusses the growth of waged labour in the USA, its expansion in manufacturing and services and the creation of divided occupations; one of his clearest statements on class and the labour process.)

* Burawoy, M. (1979) *Manufacturing Consent*, Chicago, IL: University of Chicago Press. (Participant observation study on piece-working on the shop floor, building on classical studies of piece-working culture and patterns of managerial indulgence towards workplace informality.)

* Cockburn, C. (1983) *Brothers: Male Dominance and Technological Change*. London: Pluto. (Shows the way men monopolize skilled work in the printing industry.)

* Edwards, R. (1979) *Contested Terrain: The Transformation of the Workplace in the Twentieth Century*, London: Heinemann. (A useful integration of labour process and labour market theory, which overviews the evolution of different management control techniques – personal, bureaucratic and technical – in US industry in the twentieth century.)

* Edwards, P. (1986) *Conflict at Work*, Oxford: Blackwell. (Develops a materialist non-Marxist interpretation of conflict within the workplace, with interesting discussion on the institutional structuring of work and the comparative formation of work cultures and their impact on labour process struggles.)

* Friedman, A.F. (1977) *Industry and Labour*, London: Macmillan. (Early and influential elaboration of labour process theory based on

economic histories of two industrial sectors in the UK, hosiery and cars.)

* Hochschild, A.R. (1983) *The Managed Heart: Commercialization of Human Feeling*, Berkeley, CA: University of California Press. (A ground-breaking account of the development and consequence of the intervention of systematic management for the prescription of workers' behaviour and action in service sector employment.)

* Kelly, J. (1982) *Scientific Management, Job Design and Work Performance*, London: Academic Press. (A sophisticated analysis of the influences of product and labour markets on the redesign of work, suggesting that the labour process should not be privileged as an explanatory force, rather, changes in production reflect the diverse effects of the interaction of products markets, labour markets and production processes.)

* Lane, C. (1989) *Management and Labour in Europe*, Aldershot: Edward Elgar. (A useful overview of the different employment and training systems in the UK, France and Germany, and how these mediate and differentiate the nature and experience of capitalist rationalization.)

* Littler, C.R. (1982) *The Development of the Labour Process in Capitalist Societies*, London: Heinemann. (Useful for advancing labour process theory, especially by separating the procedures and processes around the systematization of the recruitment and selection of labour and its bureaucratic organization in production; and in highlighting the national peculiarities to the evolution of managerial regimes in the USA, the UK and Japan.)

* Nichols, T. (ed.) (1980) *Capital and Labour: Studies in the Capitalist Labour Process*, London: Fontana. (A largely pessimistic collection of essays on the oppression of workers under different forms of capitalism from the first wave of reaction to Braverman's work in the UK, linked by excellent introductions from the editor.)

* Nichols, T. and Benyon, H. (1977) *Living with Capitalism*, London: Routledge. (A Marxist account of work relations and experience inside a

chemical company which drew considerable inspiration from *Labor and Monopoly Capitalism*.)

* Thompson, P. (1989) *The Nature of Work: An Introduction to Debates on the Labour Process*, 2nd edn, London: Macmillan. (Examines key themes which Braverman neglected or understated, such as resistance at work, consent in the employment relationship and gender relations. The second edition also evaluates post-Taylorist debates which hinges on the idea of flexible manufacturing and working.)

* Wood, S. (ed.) (1982) *The Degradation of Work? Skill, Deskilling and the Labour Process*, London: Hutchinson. (An early British critical reaction to Braverman, with useful chapters on gender, consent, skill (several) and managerial strategies.)

* Wood, S. (ed.) (1989) *The Transformation of Work? Skill, Flexibility and the Labour Process*, London: Unwin Hyman. (Ostensibly an new edition of Wood's earlier collection, this reader indicates the pace of change within the debate, revealing more attention to diverse internationalization projects, through attention to Japan and Sweden, and the new theme of flexibility which emerged in the mid-1980s.)

* Zimbalist, A. (ed.) (1979) *Case Studies on the Labor Process*, New York: Monthly Review Press. (An early American example of a case study reader, with a strong labour history bent. Worth reading for the seminal chapter by David Noble, which argues the case for managerial control rather than cost or efficiency as the motive force behind technological innovation.)

See also: HUMAN RESOURCE MANAGEMENT; LABOUR PROCESS; TAYLOR, F.W.; TRAINING; TRAINING, ECONOMICS OF

Related topics in the IEBM: MANAGEMENT IN GERMANY; MANAGEMENT IN JAPAN; MARX, K.H.; ORGANIZATION BEHAVIOUR, HISTORY OF; SMITH, A.; TECHNOLOGY AND ORGANIZATIONS

Clegg, Hugh Armstrong (1920–1995)

Career summary

- born 22 May 1920
- educated at Kingswood School, Bath and then Magdalen College, University of Oxford
- Fellow of Nuffield College, University of Oxford (1949–66)
- member of Royal Commission on Trade Unions and Employers' Associations (1965–68)
- member of National Board for Prices and Incomes (1966–68)
- Professor of Industrial Relations, University of Warwick (1967–79)
- member of Council of Advisory, Conciliation and Arbitration Service (1974–79)
- Director of the Industrial Relations Research Unit of the Social Science Research Council (1970–74)
- Chairman of the Standing Commission on Pay Comparability (1979–80)
- died 9 December 1995

Major works

The System of Industrial Relations in Great Britain (1954), (edited with A. Flanders)

General Union (1954)

A New Approach to Industrial Democracy (1960)

A History of British Trade Unions Vol 1 (1964) (with A. Fox and A. F. Thompson); *Vol 2* (1985), *Vol 3* (1994)

The System of Industrial Relations in Great Britain (1970)

Trade Unionism under Collective Bargaining (1976)

The Changing System of Industrial Relations in Great Britain (1976)

Overview

Hugh Clegg was the most influential British scholar of industrial relations in the latter half of the twentieth century. At a time when the subject dominated economic and political life he was also centrally involved in public policy formulation. He wrote the definitive history of British trade unionism as well as contemporary studies of, *inter alia*, industrial democracy, incomes policy, trade union government and collective bargaining. He established a tradition of empirical research, and also an internationally distinguished centre of industrial relations research and teaching, at Warwick University, which were to continue to flourish after his death.

1 Biography

The son of a Methodist minister, Hugh Clegg demonstrated a rebellious spirit from an early age, joining the Communist Party while head boy of his school. He went to Oxford for one year before the Second World War began and then served five years in the ranks as a telephone engineer. Having battled across Europe with the liberating forces, he returned to Oxford where in due course he took the best degree of his year. It was the labour scholar G.D.H.Cole who there introduced him to the study of industrial relations, which appealed to Clegg's egalitarian and insubordinate instincts. He joined the newly founded Nuffield College and worked on a history of the General and Municipal Workers' Union as a doctoral student. Although he never submitted his thesis for examination, it was to be published as *General Union* in 1954, and he was elected a Fellow of Nuffield College in 1949.

At Oxford Clegg started a twenty-year partnership with Allan Flanders (see FLANDERS, A.D.), a pre-War trade union activist who had played a central role in the recreation of the German trade union movement under the Allied Control Commission. Leaving the Communist Party, Clegg committed his remarkable intelligence to the factual analysis of organized labour, leaving the more theoretical aspects to Flanders in a close division of effort which, after Flanders' death in 1973, he was to have difficulty shaking off. They started a weekly seminar series which provided an unparalleled stimulus to British industrial relations scholarship and gave rise to what was retrospectively to be called the 'Oxford School' of research (Bugler 1968). They edited, and took the major part in writing, the first edition of *The System of Industrial Relations in Great Britain* which, when published in 1954, broke new ground as a research-based, multi-disciplinary analysis of the subject (see INDUSTRIAL AND LABOUR RELATIONS). During his time at Oxford, Clegg was to publish authoritative studies on a wide range of hitherto largely neglected subjects, including industrial relations in the newly nationalized industries and in public transport, employer organization, trade union administration and industrial democracy (see INDUSTRIAL DEMOCRACY; TRADE UNIONS). He also wrote, with Alan Fox and A. F. Thompson, the first volume of the definitive *History of British Trade Unions*, the final two volumes of which he was to complete on his own after his retirement.

The growing industrial unrest (see INDUSTRIAL CONFLICT) of the 1960s led to Clegg increasingly being called to serve on the many official enquiries and arbitrations which were then the favoured means of resolving disputes. His involvement in conflicts in railways, docks, shipping and the car industry revealed unusually subtle political judgement which made him a natural candidate when in 1965 a Labour government set up both a Royal Commission on Trade Unions and Employers' Associations concerned with industrial relations reform, and a National Board for Prices and Incomes, concerned with managing an incomes policy. His contribution to both was substantial, partly because he had considerable drafting skills, and partly because he insisted that both bodies should have very substantial research backing. He initiated unprecedented programmes of surveys and case studies whereby both Commission and Board broke from the traditional mould of passively receiving evidence, adopting instead a far more proactive and investigative form of enquiry.

He built on this appetite for empirical fieldwork when he moved to the newly founded University of Warwick in 1967, winning in 1970 a substantial research unit funded by the (then) Social Science Research Council, which was to provide a financially secure basis for industrial relations research for the next 30 years. At the same time he established a multi-disciplinary post-graduate course in industrial relations which has remained internationally outstanding and a fertile source of doctoral students and industrial relations academics. His own research while at Warwick resulted in books on incomes policy, trade union government, and the international comparative study *Trade Unionism under Collective Bargaining*. He also produced two complete rewrites of *The System of Industrial Relations in Great Britain* which drew on his encyclopaedic knowledge and became the widely accepted textbook on the then politically controversial subject. Clegg took early retirement in 1979 to return to his *History*. In that year, in the wake of substantial disputes in the public services, he was persuaded to become chair of a Standing Commission on Pay Comparability, which was successful in establishing a public service pay policy until wound up by the new government of Margaret Thatcher in the following year. Clegg thus ended his active involvement with both the analysis and the practice of contemporary trade unionism just as it was about to suffer the ignominy of its long retreat.

2 Philosophical underpinnings

A view once expressed by Clegg was that 'an ounce of fact is worth a pound of theory', and there can be no doubting that his published life's work amounted to a great weight of books containing little discussion of theory and a vast amount of sparely expressed fact. It was not, as we shall see, that he was unaware of the theoretical underpinnings of his work; it was rather that he was painfully aware that the study of organized labour has long been awash with, in varying degrees, plausible and optimistic theories, which have usually been sustained by little more than myth and ignorance. His primary purpose in both his historical and contemporary research was therefore to get as close as possible to establishing the facts of what happened when, and to understanding the perceptions and motives of the men and women involved. For some readers this made his writing dull, with too much description and not enough story. But that would not have bothered Clegg. As both a teacher and as a manager of research he was unusually open minded about how others interpreted the facts. His prime concern was that they did so with comprehensive knowledge and complete honesty.

Here we shall not discuss Clegg's historical work, nor his monographs on particular events and industries. Instead we shall focus on those studies in which, as a somewhat reluctant theorist, he distilled out of his empirical broth those particular understandings of industrial relations which have altered the course of subsequent thinking. As a preliminary, however, it is instructive to outline the philosophical and ideological positions that underpinned this work.

Perhaps as a result of his rebellion against both Christianity and Marxism, Clegg exhibited both an antipathy to dogma and a strong sense of morality. It was a feature of most of those scholars who were in at the start of the Oxford School, doubtless reinforced by their bitter youthful experience of fighting against or fleeing from totalitarianism. Forty years later, in a retrospective essay, Clegg was to spell out very clearly what he thought was common to the Oxford School:

we were pluralists, believing that a free society consists of a large number of overlapping groups, each with its own interests and objectives which its members are entitled to pursue so long as they do so with reasonable regard to the rights and interests of others. But that did not distinguish us

from most other social and political theorists of that time, except Marxists, and today only from Marxists and Thatcherites. We were also egalitarians, wishing to see a shift in the distribution of wealth towards those with lower incomes, and a shift of power over the conduct of their working lives and environment towards working men and women; and, for both these reasons, emphasising the importance of trade unions in industry, in the economy, and in society. We therefore attached special importance to collective bargaining as the means whereby trade unions pursue their objectives.

(Clegg 1990)

This commitment to collective bargaining as, if not the only valid means of industrial governance, at least the optimal one, was a recurring theme in Clegg's work. This was reflected in the ringing and unanimous endorsement (which he had himself drafted) of the Report of the Royal Commission:

Properly conducted, collective bargaining is the most effective means of giving workers the right to representation in decisions affecting their working lives, a right which is or should be the prerogative of every worker in a democratic society. While therefore the first task in the reform of British industrial relations is to bring greater order into collective bargaining in the company or plant, the second is to extend the coverage of collective bargaining and the organization of workers on which it depends.

(Donovan 1968: para 212)

Seven years after that Report, Clegg felt obliged to defend this position and its commitment to pluralism against the attacks of Marxist critics who argued that reformism served managerial interests (Clegg 1975). His defence made plain his view that pluralism was a normative philosophy rather than a simple description of a political process. But the climate of criticism was to change. Another seven years later, it was a sign of how sharply the direction of attack had shifted that Clegg was obliged to defend himself against charges of political bias from the then Conservative government. A year-long official inquiry, initiated by the Secretary of State in 1982, was held into the charges that the Industrial Relations Research Unit which he had created was biased because it 'was dominated by a particular philosophy of collective bargaining, favoured by the 1968 Royal Commission, which played down the potential use of legal regulation and led to undue emphasis on trade unions'(Brown 1998). Although his Unit was exonerated of all the charges of bias, a succession of hostile new laws over the next decade was to make plain just how far official opinion had swung against collective bargaining.

3 The emerging themes

If any book was the founding text of the Oxford School it was Flanders and Clegg's *The System of Industrial Relations in Great Britain* (1954). Written at what in retrospect can be seen to have been the high tide of consensus over the British 'system' of industry-based collective bargaining, it far excelled other contemporary texts in its analysis of the contextual circumstances and informal characteristics (Brown 1997). There was a heavy emphasis on the historical origins of institutions, and a sensitivity to economic influences, but a neglect of explicitly sociological analyses, and a frank disdain of personnel management. The legal chapter by Otto Kahn-Freund, arguably the most sophisticated analysis of British labour law that had yet been written was, however, rich in sociological insight.

The System was to influence a generation of British industrial relations scholars, including those involved in a most active period of public policy concern with the subject. But it was also seminal for much of the subsequent work of both Clegg and Flanders. For Clegg, three strands deserve to be followed. The first is the issue of industrial democracy. The second is the optimal level of collective bargaining. The third strand is that of the determinants of collective bargaining structures.

A target of Clegg's criticism in *The System* was the practice of joint consultation, which had blossomed during the War and the immediate post-War years. Having scoured the empirical evidence he asked why it should be that a 'device' which was given almost universal public approval should appear to have such limited success. He concluded that it is because it is based upon the mistaken belief of an identity of interest between employers and employees – what later would be called by Fox a 'unitary' view (Fox 1966) – and that employers only resorted to it when full employment placed them on the defensive. He argued that 'the need to establish channels of communication in large-scale enterprises is not dependent on the state of employment; and the desire for greater industrial democracy has not been completely destroyed even during slumps. . . . Joint consultation may help to reduce antagonism, and to solve difficulties before they become disputes; but antagonisms and difficulties will remain. They are inherent in a free society' (Flanders and Clegg 1954: 364).

This argument was developed in *A New Approach to Industrial Democracy* (1960), which he described in the preface as a 'rather hasty' essay provoked by his being rapporteur at a conference in 1958 in Vienna on 'Workers' Participation in Management'. More than anything else that Clegg wrote, this was an exercise in political science, reviewing the history and theory of industrial democracy, surveying contemporary international experience and, with hitherto uncharacteristic panache, arguing out his 'new theory'. It is surely of significance that his most fulsome thanks in the preface went to Tony Crosland MP 'who has given me more help with this book than I have received before in any book that I have written. I can only hope that it is worthy of him'. Crosland's influential *The Future of Socialism* (Crosland 1956) had argued a non-Marxist, egalitarian and strongly pluralist political philosophy. When in 1977 Crosland, who was by then Foreign Secretary, died unexpectedly at the age of only 59, Clegg was to confess to being dismayed by the scale of his sense of personal loss. Certainly the similarity in their personal philosophy was very evident in *A New Approach*, with its une-quivocal conclusion that strong trade unions, independent of and capable of bargaining with management, were the best vehicle for the furtherance of the democratic rights of employees. It was a view which, as we have seen, was to reappear in the words of the Royal Commission in 1968 and, though barely challenged at the time, was subsequently to fall sharply from favour and be officially repudiated after 1979.

Paradoxically, a second strand of Clegg's thinking, which surfaced clearly for the first time with the Royal Commission's report, was controversial at the time but has subsequently been rendered indisputable by the course of events. This concerns the optimal level of bargaining, and in particular, the necessity for what would now be called 'enterprise bargaining' to replace industrial agreements for much of the private sector (see COLLECTIVE BARGAINING). There had been a general expectation that the Royal Commission would propose new legislative measures which would curb the capacity of shop stewards, bargaining at the workplace, to subvert industry-wide collective bargaining. Supported by the legal analysis of his fellow commissioner Kahn-Freund, and the written evidence of Flanders, Clegg succeeded in winning the Commission over to a contrary view. This was that the central malaise was one of bargaining structure, with a formal system of industrial agreements in conflict with an informal system of workplace bargaining in which employers were heavily implicated. The law could play little part in the procedural reform that was necessary. It was up to employers to decide which system they could best work with and, if it was one of enterprise-based bargaining, to provide the appropriate union representatives with uncompromised authority to conclude agreements. Over the following quarter century, enterprise-based bargaining was largely to displace industrial bargaining in a conclusive vindication of this argument.

The third strand of Clegg's theoretical innovation built on the primacy he gave to employers in determining collective bargaining structures. In *Trade Unionism under Collective Bargaining* he developed a general theory of trade union behaviour on the basis of a comparison of six different countries. His preface made clear the extent to which he felt he was building on the work of Flanders. 'That does not mean he would have agreed with what I have written, had he been able to see it. For, although we usually came to the same conclusion during the twenty-odd years we worked together, more often than not it was by very different routes. The architecture of his theory would have been nobler and more substantial' (Clegg 1976). This was a short and vigorously argued book, deliberately stripped of references and what he called 'the apparatus of scholarship'. It sketched out an overview of union behaviour in the different countries and accounted for variations in terms of a number of distinct dimensions of national bargaining structure. It then explained variations in bargaining structure in terms of employer strategy and the role of legal intervention at particular critical political junctures. Despite twenty intervening years which have seen many trade union movements in severe decline, the theory stands up surprisingly well, still having considerable explanatory power with regard to, among other things, strike behaviour, industrial democracy and wage determination. The major loose end to which Clegg confessed, his inability to deal with trade unions' political role, has been effectively tackled by subsequent scholars. (Martin 1989; Crouch 1993).

4 Conclusion

This brief account of Hugh Clegg's scholarly contribution has deliberately emphasized its strong theoretical content. At a time when industrial relations was at the centre of public concern his work had a major influence on policy formulation. By his emphasis upon the empirical analysis of all aspects of the subject both in what he wrote and in what he caused others to write, he placed it on a firm academic foundation. As a result he sidelined or defused many traditional areas of theoretical debate. But in their place he provided an alternative theoretical approach to the analysis of collective bargaining, organized labour, and the role of management which shows every sign of dominating the study of industrial relations, at least in Britain, for the foreseeable future.

WILLIAM BROWN
UNIVERSITY OF CAMBRIDGE

Further reading

(References cited in the text marked *)

* Bugler, J. (1968) 'The New Oxford Group', *New Society*, 15 February. (A contemporary account of the Oxford School of industrial relations.)
* Brown, W. A.(1997) 'The High Tide of Consensus', *Historical Studies in Industrial Relations*, No 4. (A retrospective review of the first edition of The System.)
* Brown, W. A. (1998) Funders and Research: the Vulnerability of the Subject, in G. Strauss and K. Whitfield (eds.) *Researching the World of Work*, ILR Press, Cornell: Cornell University Press. (An account of the official enquiry into allegations that the work of the research Unit that Clegg founded was 'politically biased'.)
  Clegg, H. A. (1954) *General Union*, Oxford: Blackwell. (Clegg's unsubmitted doctoral thesis.)
* Clegg, H. A. (1960) *A New Approach to Industrial Democracy*, Oxford: Blackwell. (A major essay in political science analysis.)
* Clegg, H. A. (1964) *A History of British Trade Unions Vol 1* (with A. Fox and A. F. Thompson); *Vol 2* (1985); *Vol 3* (1994). Oxford: Oxford University Press. (The definitive study of the subject.)
* Clegg, H. A. (1970) *The System of Industrial Relations in Great Britain*. Oxford: Blackwell. (Clegg's first comprehensive textbook; having no text in common with its predecessor of the same name.)
* Clegg, H. A. (1975) 'Pluralism in Industrial Relations', *British Journal of Industrial Relations*, 13 (3). (A defence of the philosophy of pluralism in industrial relations.)
* Clegg, H. A. (1976) *Trade Unionism under Collective Bargaining*. Oxford: Blackwell. (A theory of trade union behaviour derived from international comparison.)
  Clegg, H. A. (1976) *The Changing System of Industrial Relations in Great Britain*. Oxford: Blackwell. (A complete rewrite of the 1970 textbook at a time of rapid institutional change.)
* Clegg, H. A.(1990) 'The Oxford School of Industrial Relations', Warwick Papers in Industrial Relations, No. 31, IRRU, University of Warwick, Coventry. (A reflective retrospective essay on the rise and dispersal of the Oxford School.)
* Crosland, C. A. R. (1956) *The Future of Socialism*. London: Jonathan Cape. (An influential account of non-marxian Fabian socialist thinking.)
* Crouch, C. (1993) *Industrial Relations and European State Traditions*. Oxford: Clarendon Press. (An ambitious attempt to explain international institutional differences in terms of historical and sociological development.)
* Donovan (1968) *Report of the Royal Commission on Trade Unions and Employers' Associations 1965–1968*. Cmnd 3623, London: HMSO. (An important analysis of contemporary industrial relations, heavily influenced by the Oxford School.)
* Flanders, A. and Clegg, H. A. (1954) *The System of Industrial Relations in Great Britain*. Oxford: Blackwell. (The founding publication of the Oxford School.)
* Fox, A. (1966) *Industrial Sociology and Industrial Relations*. Royal Commission Research Paper No 3, London: HMSO. (A particularly influential contribution to Donovan and subsequent analysis.)
* Martin, R.M. (1989) *Trade Unionism: Purposes and Forms*. Oxford: Clarendon Press. (An attempt to explain the political behaviour of trade union by one of Clegg's close colleagues.)

See also: COLLECTIVE BARGAINING; FLANDERS, A.D.; INDUSTRIAL AND LABOUR RELATIONS; INDUSTRIAL CONFLICT; INDUSTRIAL DEMOCRACY; TRADE UNIONS

Dunlop, John Thomas (1914–)

Personal background

- born 15 July 1914, Placerville, California, USA
- early academic career, University of California at Berkeley; also at Stanford University, USA, and Cambridge, UK
- main academic career spent at Cambridge, Massachusetts (Harvard University)
- extensive practical experience starting with War Labor Board (1943–5)
- Chairman of Construction Industry Stabilization Commission (1971–4); also served on stabilization agencies with informal dispute settlement procedures, boards of inquiry, disputes at critical installations with a special focus on railways, airlines and construction; extensive arbitration experience
- helped greatly to establish industrial relations as a distinctive academic discipline
- focal contribution in the areas of wage determination, industrial relations systems and dispute settlement

Major works

Wage Determination Under Trade Unions (1944)
Industrial Relations Systems (1958)
Dispute Resolution: Negotiation and Consensus Building (1984)

Summary

J.T. Dunlop (1914–) substantially shaped the development of industrial relations as an academic discipline and in a way which was interlinked with his own extensive practical experiences. His *Industrial Relations Systems* helped to isolate the main contours of a subject area. He has also contributed significantly to the study of wage determination under trade unionism; to the theory of practice of dispute settlement; and to the identification of the significance of human resource development for international competitive advantage.

1 Introduction

John Dunlop has exerted a significant influence on theory, policy and practice in the sphere of industrial relations. The analysis which follows addresses five themes: (1) the establishment of the elements in the discipline of industrial relations; (2) the theory and analysis of wage determination (with a focus on the impact of trade unionism); (3) the contribution to the area of dispute resolution; (4) the later focus on human resource development; and (5) the practical aspects of Dunlop's contribution.

So far as his academic career is concerned, Dunlop has set this out in an autobiographical note (Kaufman 1988). The earliest point in his career was spent at the University of California in Berkeley (1933–6) where he was taught by, among others, Charles A. Gulick, Jr. In his second graduate year (1936–7) he moved to Stanford University, followed by a period at Cambridge University, UK (1937–8). In 1938, following the suggestion of John Kenneth Galbraith, he arrived at Cambridge, Massachusetts, as a teaching fellow and Harvard became his main base thereafter.

2 The discipline of industrial relations

Arguably the most important legacy of John Dunlop (at least in the assessment of the worldwide academic community) has been in his contribution to the establishment of a distinctive discipline of industrial relations. Prior to the publication of *Industrial Relations Systems* in 1958 there had of course been very many analyses of labour theory and practice (see INDUSTRIAL AND LABOUR RELATIONS). But critical to John Dunlop's contribution was the establishment of the core elements of a subject area and the attempt to argue that the discipline was fundamentally different from, say, economics or politics.

At the time of writing *Industrial Relations Systems* Dunlop was influenced by the work of Talcott Parsons. Dunlop did not seek a general theory of all social action (as had been the objective of Parsons), but he did attempt to provide an analysis of social action in industrial societies that applied to its industrial relations aspects and which possessed a level of generality greater than that for particular industries or countries. Above all, the need for a far greater 'theoretical structure and orientation' to industrial relations was recognized and as Dunlop (1958: vi) in a famous passage argued: 'Facts have outrun ideas. Integrating theory has lagged far behind expanding experience. The many worlds of industrial relations have been changing more rapidly than the ideas to interpret, to explain, and to relate to them.'

In *Industrial Relations Systems*, Dunlop thus sought to establish a general theory of industrial relations that would: (1) enable analysis and interpretation of the 'widest possible range of industrial relations facts and practices'; (2) facilitate comparative studies of industrial relations among different countries and industries; and (3) link direct experience with the realm of ideas. In every industrial society, Dunlop argued that distinctive groups of workers and managers were created and an industrial relations system could thus be identified in all such countries. Six main propositions were central to Dunlop's formulation:

1 the industrial relations system is an analytical subsystem of industrial society and is on the *same* logical plane as the economic system;
2 the industrial relations system is a separate and distinctive subsystem of society;
3 there are relationships and boundary lines between a society and the industrial relations system;
4 the industrial relations system is logically an abstraction;
5 there is a distinctive analytical and theoretical subject matter to industrial relations;
6 three separate analytical problems include the relation of the industrial relations system to the society as a whole, the relation to the economic system and the inner structure and characteristics of the industrial relations system itself.

This forms the basis of Dunlop's more detailed specification of the structure of the industrial relations system itself (see INDUSTRIAL AND LABOUR RELATIONS). As he argued, 'an industrial relations system at any one time in its development is regarded as comprised of certain actors, certain contexts, an ideology which binds the industrial relations system together, and a body of rules created to govern the actors at the workplace and work community' (Dunlop 1958: 7).

The 'actors' (note again the effect of the language of Talcott Parsons) comprised: (1) a hierarchy of managers and their representatives in supervision; (2) a hierarchy of workers (non-managerial) and any spokesmen; and (3) specialized governmental agencies (and specialized private agencies created by the first two actors) concerned with workers, enterprises and their relationships. The contexts comprised significant aspects of the environment and encompassed: (1) the technological characteristics of the workplace and work community; (2) the market or budgetary constraints which impinge on the actors; and (3) the locus and distribution of power in the wider society. The 'actors' were seen as establishing rules for the workplace and work community (these cover procedures for establishing rules, substantive rules and the procedures for deciding their application to particular situations). And finally, the ideology of the industrial relations system is 'a set of ideas and beliefs commonly held by the actors that helps to bind or to integrate the system together as an entity' (Dunlop 1958: 26).

In terms of mapping the field of industrial relations, much of what was set out by Dunlop is still broadly accepted. However, there have been several improvements to the original conception. This has applied particularly to the development of environmental contexts to include legal and cultural elements. Moreover, the processes of industrial relations have been subsequently refined.

The substantial corpus of critical writings which have also emerged have been testimony to the vigour and relevance of the original Dunlopian conception. The main criticisms have been the absence of testable theories (indeed the industrial relations system conception is a model rather than a theory), the focus on comparative *statics* not dynamics, the consensual nature of the formulation (ideologies are *not* necessary shared) and the absence of a proper treatment of conflict and power (within the industrial relations system) in the original formulation (see IN-DUSTRIAL AND LABOUR RELATIONS). But none of this diminishes the vital importance of Dunlop's conception in establishing the central constituents of the discipline of industrial relations itself.

3 The theory of wage determination under trade unions

Dunlop's (1944) early work (and for which he is most noted in the USA) was linked with an analysis of wage determination under trade unions (see TRADE UNIONS). In his classic book with this title, he articulated the central views that: (1) wage determination under collective bargaining was indeed different from wage fixing under non-economic conditions, but the differences were not as great as had sometimes been supposed; and (2) although trade unions were not solely concerned with the maximization of income of their members,

they certainly could not be construed as essentially political agents.

In *Wage Determination Under Trade Unions*, then, a variety of themes were covered, including: the development of an economic model of a trade union; wage policies of trade unions, 'bargaining power' and inter-market relations; trade unions' interest in related markets; cyclical patterns of industrial wage variation; cyclical variation in labour's share in the national income; labour's return as a cost and the price mechanism and collective bargaining (see COLLECTIVE BARGAINING).

Two particularly lasting themes were the analysis of the wage policies of trade unions and the analysis of 'bargaining power'. In the first place, then, a number of non-income objectives of wage policy were identified that encompassed: (1) the promotion of union membership; (2) work allocation; (3) leisure; (4) controlling the rate of introduction of technical innovations; (5) improvements in working conditions; and (6) control of entry to the trade. But even the income objectives of wage policies were viewed as complex. There could be the national pronouncements of national organization, justification within a bargaining unit and the elements of a wages policy (including differentials, product market conditions, employment effects and method of wage payment). Above all, from an analytical point of view, specific wage policies included: (1) a more cyclical relationship between wage rates and employment; and (2) cyclical fluctuations in wage structure. Finally, wage differentials among enterprises and wage differentials among local unions were assessed.

The interpretation of 'bargaining power' was firmly grounded in the recognition of inequalities between 'buyers' and 'sellers' in the marketplace and was rooted in economic analysis. The factors influencing bargaining power included the tastes of workers and employees, market conditions and so-called 'pure bargaining power' (or the ability to get favourable bargains apart from market conditions). Bargaining power consists of the relative abilities of the two contracting parties to influence the wage; that can be analysed in terms of various types of competition.

Part of Dunlop's heritage has been that he stimulated a great deal of further analysis and debate on trade union wage policies and collective bargaining. In particular, the 'political school' took him to task for his one-sided economic interpretation and preferred a conception of trade unions as political agencies. But against his critics, in the preface to the 1950 edition, Dunlop argued:

1 political wage setting is most likely to occur in newer unions experiencing acute factional struggles but not in mature collective bargaining relations;
2 the political focus tends to apply best to the short run; the longer the time scale the less valuable the emphasis on political considerations;
3 labour leaders are acutely aware of economic and technological considerations and these temper any effects of union politics;
4 the 'stubborn facts' of the external world are avoided even though in reality changes in prices, profits and employment in related markets all affect wage rates and wages rate movements.

4 Dispute resolution

No analysis of John Dunlop would be complete without reference to his work on dispute resolution. Indeed, he has had a long-standing theoretical and practical focus on labour peace and a strong preference for regulations in industrial relations to be jointly negotiated between labour and management. This is a perennial theme in a spectrum of Dunlop's work, including not least his *Industrial Relations Systems*, where the network or 'web of rules' was seen as the primary 'centre of attention' of the industrial relations system.

Throughout his career, Dunlop has been concerned to establish a negotiations alternative in dispute resolution. Broadly speaking, as he argued, it is possible in western societies to discern two major approaches to the resolution of conflicts; 'the give and take' of the market place and governmental regulations.

What he preferred, however, was negotiation coupled with a variety of specialized mediation and arbitration services for securing labour peace. Indeed, quoting George Simmel (1955: 115) he noted that 'on the whole, compromise, especially that brought about through exchange, no matter how much we think it is an everyday technique we take for granted, is one of mankind's greatest inventions'.

This focus of interest led John Dunlop to develop abstract as well as practical approaches to negotiations. He thus noted at least four approaches to negotiation: (1) formal models linked with the notion of bargaining power; (2) the use of experimental or simulated bargaining games; (3) the deployment of econometric methods to measure aspects of arbitration or collective bargaining; and (4) verbatim accounts of exchanges from the earliest stages of negotiations to the achievement of a settlement. Dunlop preferred a somewhat different approach: 'to limit' the types of negotiations considered and then to outline a number of key principles central to an understanding of the negotiation 'process' (Dunlop 1984: 9).

Labour–management negotiations thus had certain interesting characteristics: (1) the parties and organizations expect to continue to be engaged to interact over a future period; (2) the parties to the negotiations are not monolithic; and (3) the negotiators are concerned with more than one single issue. The development of a framework for analysing negotiations thus requires the analyst first to account for diverse internal interests. Acknowledgement then must be made of the initial proposals for agreement, the changing positions in negotiations, the role of a deadline, end-play, a judgement, overt conflict, going public, implementing the settlement and the personal ingredient.

In the event of problems in this process, the role of mediation was seen as fundamental. Moreover, the mediation process was itself capable of analytical interpretation. First, mediation relates fundamentally to the communications flow. Second, the mediator function often involves the development of mutually acceptable factual data. Third, the mediator serves as a private, informal adviser to both sides. Fourth, the mediator can formulate a distinctive and imaginative package. Fifth, the mediator has a special opportunity in the 'end game' of negotiations. Sixth, a critical factor affecting the role of the mediator is the circumstances at the point of entry into a dispute. Seventh, the mediator may be asked to serve as an arbitrator. And finally, mediators may play a role in settlement of some disputes by asserting a moral authority or assuming a role in the public interest.

Overall, too, Dunlop envisaged substantial advantages of the negotiation process, including the likelihood of a successful enforcement of any agreement, the level of detail facilitated, the 'basic' superiority of a genuinely settled controversy and the creative, problem solving nature of negotiations as opposed to litigation or governmental fiat. Moreover, he argued that negotiation would play an increasingly important role in conflict resolution.

An extension of Dunlop's interest in negotiation was obviously, too, a general endorsement of trade unions and a long-standing interest in labour issues. This spanned a variety of contributions (including wage determination). But his contribution here is particularly linked with his work with Derek Bok entitled *Labour and the American Community* (1970). This covered such issues as trade unions and public opinion, a profile of the labour movement, democracy and union government, the protection of minority interests, the administration of unions and collective bargaining. But despite the interest in unions and collective bargaining, Bok and Dunlop had a deep-seated concern for the future of these organizations and their activities which broadly proved to be accurate at least in the USA:

The dangers for the labor movement lie in very different fields. Unions face evident risks that they will be taken more and more for granted by their members, that they will function at a growing disadvantage in dealing with institutions possessing greater knowledge and superior techniques, and that their social role will be preempted increasingly by other groups. Should these

risks materialize, the prospects are that unions will become progressively duller bureaucracies, more fractious at times to arouse an indifferent membership, but largely ignored in the major developments of the society and rather widely disliked as a necessary evil and a source of periodic inconvenience.

(Bok and Dunlop 1970: 486)

5 The challenge of human resource development

A latter-day concern of John Dunlop has been with the emergent issue of human resource development. There has been globally an increasing awareness of these matters (see HUMAN RESOURCE DEVELOPMENT; HUMAN RESOURCE MANAGEMENT). Indeed, alongside technology and knowledge, it is recognized that a key resource in the competitive advantage of nations has become the quality of workforces (their abilities, skills, motivation and education levels).

The backcloth for John Dunlop's interest has been the relatively poor performance of countries like the USA in terms of productivity. For Dunlop economic growth and productivity advance depend on four basic factors: research and development, investment in plant and equipment, investment in infrastructure and investment in human resource development. Furthermore, on his testimony, the 'creation of a more productive, skilled and adaptable workforce in turn depends on: (1) the educational system; (2) health care; (3) training and retraining; (4) family policy; (5) labour–management policies at the workplace; and (6) the general growth of public services' (Dunlop 1992: 52).

The more detailed case of John Dunlop is as follows. Despite a growing educational attainment of the workforce in the USA there are significant educational problems for a substantial percentage of the population. This is compounded by high absenteeism and school dropout rates. Healthcare and housing are also a problem for significant numbers of the American population. There is a bias in US national labour policy towards conflict and against cooperation. And finally, morale in the public service sector is at a low ebb. In essence, then, as he offered the following argument:

> It is my sincere conviction that it is the failure to develop appropriate institutions to educate, to train and retrain to maintain health, to manage and elicit productive and cooperative services from its workforce that is our country's most critical failure. Our poor performance with human resources cannot in the longterm be offset or compensated for the test of international competition by location, national resources, history, capital structure or our political democracy.
>
> (Dunlop 1992: 53)

Fundamentally, John Dunlop has articulated a series of issues of vital consequence for the human resources of modern nations. Above all, he has added weight to the conviction that the development of trained, productive and adaptable human resources is at the very heart of competitive advantage and not simply a desirable but non-essential goal of labour, government and business alike.

6 Practical activities

Another important aspect of John Dunlop's contribution to the field of industrial relations has been his major practical activities. He has been particularly noted for his work on arbitration. For years he chaired the National Joint Board for Jurisdictional Disputes, a construction panel. He was dean of faculty at Harvard University and served on many joint union–management commissions. He has also been chair of the commissions on the Future of Worker–Management Relations (which is primarily concerned with making suggestions for labour law reform). He was a Secretary of Labor in the Ford Administration and had a drive to simplify the number of industrial relations related regulations which, in his view, overburdened the parties. But, dramatically, in an effort to check a wage–price spiral in the construction industry he worked out a deal to centralize bargaining

(the impending bill was vetoed and John Dunlop, in consequence, resigned).

More systematically, his enormous breadth of experience and accomplishment in dispute resolution and problem solving in industrial relations may be set out under the following nine heads: (1) stabilization agencies concerned with dispute settlement; (2) stabilization agencies concerned with informal dispute settlement; (3) Boards of Inquiry under the Taft–Hartley Act; (4) disputes at critical installations; (5) railways and airlines; (6) construction; (7) private umpire arbitration; (8) private labour–management committees: neutral member or umpire; and (9) public sector committees.

In more detail, his work with dispute settlement commenced with the War Labor Board (1943–5). He was also a public member of the Wage Stabilization Board (1950–3) and Chairman of the Construction Industry Stabilization Commission (1971–4). Informal Dispute Settlement Bodies included the Cost of Living Council (1973–4) and the Tripartite Pay Advisory Committee (1979–80) of which he was Chairman. Under the provisions of the Taft–Hartley Act, he was a member of the boards of inquiry into, for example, the General Electric Company (1966).

So far as disputes at critical installations are concerned, these included the President's Commission on Labour Relations in the Atomic Energy Installations (1948–9), the Missile Sites Labour Commissions (1961–7) and the Nevada Test Site Committee (1965–7). But he is particularly noted for his work in the main industrial groupings of railways and airlines, and construction. For instance, he was a member of the Presidential Railroad Commission (1960–2) and Chairman of Emergency Board 167 American Airlines and Transport workers Union of America. But above all, he is noted for his close attention to the construction industry and its various labour problems. These activities are too extensive to develop in detail but include the Wage Adjustment Board (1943–7), the Construction Industry Joint Conference (1959–68), the Appeals Board (Jurisdictional Disputes) (1965–8) and being arbitrator on jurisdictional issues (1981–)

(Alaskan Oilfields Construction Agreements).

Other industries were also covered in his role as private umpire in arbitration including the Pittsburgh Plate Glass Company and Eastern Airlines. In private labour management committees he was a neutral member or umpire in groups that included the Kaiser Steel Company (1959–67), the Tailored Clothing companies (1977–) and the *ad hoc* maritime committee (1977–80).

Finally, his activities in public sector committees included: the Governors' Committee on Public Employee Relations, New York State (1965–9); the Joint Labour Management Committee for Municipal Police and Fire, Commonwealth of Massachusetts (1977–); and the Task Force in Public Pensions and Disability, Commonwealth of Massachusetts (1982).

7 Conclusions

John Dunlop has thus contributed in a major way to the theory and practice of industrial relations. He was substantially responsible for establishing one of the key theoretical contributions to the discipline. He charted a major theory of wage determination under trade unions. He theoretically developed the area of negotiations and collective bargaining behaviour and had a long-standing interest in trade unions. Latterly he has been concerned with the importance of human resource development. And he has had a most impressive and influential public role in arbitration and dispute settlement and in his work for the Dunlop Commission. His contribution to theory and practice in a key area of business and management has thus been impressive, comprehensive and long-lasting.

MICHAEL POOLE
CARDIFF BUSINESS SCHOOL

Note

The author is grateful to Professor George Strauss for his valuable help in preparing this entry.

Further reading

(References cited in the text marked *)

* Bok, D. and Dunlop, J.T. (1970) *Labor and the American Community*, New York: Simon & Schuster. (Develops a detailed account of labour in US society, its public image, practices and future role.)
* Dunlop, J.T. (1944) *Wage Determination under Trade Unions*, New York: Macmillan. (An early classic setting out Dunlop's influential theories on wage determination.)
* Dunlop, J.T. (1958) *Industrial Relations Systems*, New York: Holt, Rinehart and Winston. (Dunlop's classic theoretical work outlining the systems approach to industrial relations and establishing the 'contours' of the discipline).
* Dunlop, J.T. (1984) *Dispute Resolution: Negotiation and Consensus Building*, Dover, MA: Auburn House. (Details Dunlop's theory of negotiation and outlines the importance he attaches to negotiation and mediation as means of dispute settlement rather than markets or governmental fiat.)
* Dunlop, J.T. (1992) 'The challenge of human resources development', *Industrial Relations* 31 (1): 50–5. (Sets out the importance of human resources development for the competitive advantage of nations and the problems faced by the USA in these respects.)
* Kaufman, B. (ed.) (1988) *How Labor Markets Work*, Lexington, MA: D.C. Heath & Co. (Incorporates an autobiographical account and is a vital source for understanding the extent of Dunlop's overall contribution to the theory and practice of industrial relations.)
Kochan, T.A. (1995) 'Using the Dunlop report to achieve mutual gains', Industrial Relations 34 (3): 350–66. (Summarizes the major conclusions and recommendations of the Dunlop Commission report and analyses the potential benefits.)
* Simmel, G. (1955) *Conflict and the Web of Group Affiliations*, Glencoe, IL: The Free Press. (Sets out the theory of groups and the importance of processes of negotiation in reaching successful outcomes.)

See also: COLLECTIVE BARGAINING; HUMAN RESOURCE DEVELOPMENT; HUMAN RESOURCE MANAGEMENT; HUMAN RESOURCE MANAGEMENT, INTERNATIONAL; INDUSTRIAL AND LABOUR RELATIONS; TRADE UNIONS

Flanders, Allan David (1910–1973)

Personal Background

- born 27 July 1910
- educated at Latymer Upper School; Landerziehungsheim Walkemuhle, Germany
- various jobs, including draughtsman
- research Assistant, TUC (1943–46)
- head of Political Branch, British Control Commission, Germany (1946–47)
- senior Lecturer in Industrial Relations, University of Oxford (1949–69; MA 1950)
- faculty Fellow, Nuffield College Oxford (1964–69)
- member, Secretary of State's Colonial Advisory Committee (1954–62)
- industrial Relations Advisor, National Board for Prices and Incomes (1965–68)
- full time member, Commission on Industrial Relations (1969–71)
- reader in Industrial Relations, University of Warwick (1971–73; CBE 1971)
- early writer and theorist of industrial relations, a key member of the influential 'Oxford School of Industrial Relations' and also involved in policy
- died 29 September 1973

Major works

The Fawley Productivity Agreements (1964)
Management and Unions (1970)

Summary

Allan Flanders was an inquiring, inspirational and influential theorist of industrial relations, a subject hitherto renowned for its empiricism and focus on 'facts' and practical problems.

He was also the principal theoretical architect of an important group of academics whose reformist pluralism became so influential in the UK in the 1960s and 1970s. Flanders wrote general and specialized texts and chapters on various aspects of industrial relations, including some early comparative analysis. He continually expounded the panacea of social partnership (as via collective bargaining), which underpinned much of his work. Furthermore, Flanders' relatively late starting and short academic career was interspersed (and perhaps distracted to some extent) with involvement in political and active policy debates when industrial relations was the focus of heated controversy and analysis mixed with prescription, administration and reform. His untimely death robbed the academic community of a perceptive thinker on management with work experience and diverse policy involvement. In short, Flanders was a 'guru' of the 'Oxford School' and industrial relations of the 1960s and 1970s, and one who, unlike contemporary versions, had the ear of politicians and policy makers.

1 Introduction

The coverage of the broad canvas on which such a multi-faceted thinker as Flanders worked is constrained given the nature of this publication. Therefore, his more obviously political work, sympathy for social democracy and hostility of the Marxist and communist left, are not detailed. Flanders' unusual personal background (see Clegg 1990) included an education in Germany at the adult school run by the International Socialist Kampfbund, founded by the socialist philosopher Leonard Nelson. After Hitler came to power, he returned to Britain and sustained ideas of ethical socialism via the Socialist Vanguard/Union group and its *Socialist Commentary*. During the Second World War Flanders joined the TUC to help prepare its

'Report on Postwar Reconstruction' and returned to Germany with the British Control Commission in 1946. He played a key part in setting up the structure of industrial unionism (see TRADE UNIONS), which many saw as a central feature of the political economy of post-war Germany. In 1949 he took up a lectureship at Oxford, where he spent virtually his entire academic career (with a stint at the same college as Clegg and Fox) (see CLEGG, H.A.), while also serving on several important government committees. These diverse experiences helped fertilize, incubate and mature Flanders' thoughts and ideas.

Flanders produced early texts on industrial relations matters, those of major importance being, for example, Flanders (1952) and Flanders and Clegg (1954). Many industrial relations scholars were brought up on, and influenced by, this work. He wrote on a range of topics, such as incomes policy, wages, pay systems, conflict and 'normative systems', and union–state relations (Flanders 1970, 1974). Importantly, Flanders was the first British industrial relations scholar since the Webbs to endeavour to write about theory.

2 Main contribution

A single volume of the more important of Flanders' work exists (Flanders 1970). This collection displays both the evolution and unity of his thought on the changing roles and responsibilities of unions, management and government, and at a theoretical level reflects his concern to analyse industrial relations and the institution of collective bargaining in terms of job regulation and his belief in social partnership. His other seminal work (Flanders 1964) includes many of these themes within a case study of an oil refinery, and which contained lessons of wider application. Flanders' main contributions will be analysed via: his definition of industrial relations; trade unions; management; collective bargaining and productivity bargaining; and the influential 'Oxford School of Industrial Relations' and the public bodies it swayed, although all these are often interlinked (see COLLECTIVE BARGAINING; EMPLOYEE RELATIONS; INDUSTRIAL AND LABOUR RELATIONS).

First, industrial relations was famously defined by Flanders as 'a system of rules' and the 'study of the institutions of job regulation'. Even his critics registered that this was of great significance and an influential pioneering attempt to give theoretical unity, precision and meaning to the notion of industrial relations and its study (Hyman 1975). Its centrality was that it helped give some substance to what industrial relations actually 'was', what to research (and reform), and had some universal applicability.

Second, Flanders wrote about trade unions. Unions had 'two faces' ('sword of justice' and 'vested interest'), and gave priority to their industrial over political methods, which had lower and upper limits. The purpose of unions was participation in job regulation as a means for worker development. Unions were involved in the 'force of tradition' and attachment to 'voluntarism'. However, precisely formulated models of trade union action and behaviour seldom appeared in his writings, although Poole (1981) outlines Flanders' principal explanatory dimensions.

Third, management often felt Flanders' ire. For instance, under-employment, overtime and restrictive labour practices were the 'sign of managerial lethargy and incompetence' (Flanders 1964: 235). The roots of such 'irresponsibility' were within management itself and its frame of mind – to have as little to do with industrial relations as possible, to default to personnel and unions, and to give nothing away unless pressured. Such attitudes prevailed as management had neither the knowledge nor confidence to act differently due to a lack of training and the inherent uncertainties of industrial relations matters. Also, for Flanders (1964: 255) treating management as a 'profession' was invalid 'as long as it has no accepted standards of conduct which fully define its moral responsibilities'. Similar ideas flowed through Flanders' (1970: 147) work on industry's 'social responsibilities', which were based on the 'simple yet overriding consideration' of workers' dignity and respect for the intrinsic worth of the human personality.

Fourth, Flanders developed an influential understanding of collective bargaining. This is an explicitly collective way of managing employment with a role for unions. A spectrum of outcomes result, from collective agreements through to common understandings of varying degrees of formality and precision and levels, from national to factory. Originating in his criticism of the Webbs' classical conception, for Flanders collective bargaining had less economic significance, as simply a device for gaining 'rewards', and was more a political process giving workers 'voice', a participative form of decision making, enhancing self-respect and dignity, and an expression of industrial and pluralist democracy. Workers needed opportunities for making their own choices and decisions, not autocratic nor even paternalistic management. Such notions appear in his interest in industrial democracy, as in the John Lewis Partnership study (Flanders *et al.* 1968).

Similar views appear in Flanders' (1964) seminal work on productivity bargaining (see PRODUCTIVITY). Acceptance of Esso's suggestion to study their Fawley refinery experiment was crucial as the task refreshed and stimulated Flanders and the book established his reputation at home and abroad (Clegg 1990). Flanders believed productivity bargaining could revise 'inefficient' work practices. Importantly, it would reconstruct and democratize workplace relations by negotiation and joint agreement and responsibility, extend collective bargaining and integrate trade union shop stewards into the heart of management decision making processes, while marching management to a 'higher ground' and new 'moral order' as the process produced regard and respect for workplace democracy (Ahlstrand 1990). Flanders' work struck a 'chord' at the time and continued to reverberate. For instance, 'Industrial Relations: What is Wrong with the System?' drew on Fawley's general conclusions and posed questions for the bright new hope for reforming industrial relations – the governmental enquiry into trade unions and employers' associations. Flanders' evidence to the Donovan Commission was revised for publication as 'Collective Bargaining: Prescription for Change', indicating where reform must begin to improve industrial relations. In particular, he criticized the 'drift' and 'chaotic state' of relations between management and trade union shop stewards, with largely informal, fragmented and autonomous collective bargaining resulting in a litany of problems: unofficial strikes; earnings drift; labour under-utilization and resistance to change; overtime and demoralization of incentive pay schemes; inequitable and unstable pay structures; decline in industrial discipline; undermining of external regulation by industry-wide and other agreements; and weakening of membership control by trade unions and employers' associations (see TRADE UNIONS; EMPLOYERS' ASSOCIATIONS). This led to Flanders' (1970: 172) famous dictum that management 'can only regain control by sharing it'.

Fifth, Flanders was a key member of the 'Oxford School of Industrial Relations', whose impact was enhanced by governmental interventions. The group, whose composition and unity are contested, assumed 'progressive' employers and 'pragmatic' governments would cooperate under the influence of 'reason' and 'goodwill', and mixed systems theory (i.e. concern for rule making), with epistemological and theoretical origins grounded in the historiographical researches and substantive theories of the Webbs coupled with Durkheimian sociological precepts (Poole 1981). The group's influence flowed powerfully not only to governmental levels, but also through institutional (e.g. with members serving as arbitrators and on pay boards) and academic (e.g the moulding of students and researchers and development of the Industrial Relations Research Unit) waters. The methods, analysis and prescriptions of this group continued to echo down the years, acting almost as a touchstone for much subsequent thought and work.

3 Evaluation

There can be two views of Flanders' work. First, Flanders was far too narrow, naive, simplistic and overly-focused on collectives, institutions and formality. Yet, industrial relations developed along a more individual-istic, unregulated trajectory, with the erosion of collective bargaining and spread of non-collective pay and employment. These developments were not foreseen. Flanders' work was criticized. This included his industrial relations definition (see Hyman 1975, 1989) due to its perceived interest in 'order' and how patterns of social relations are stabilized rather than in the significance of challenges to prevailing structures. This 'conservative' tendency appeared in the words he used: 'institutions', directing attention to formal, rather than informal, organizations, the more likely sources of challenges; 'regulation', which is too restrictive, focusing on how conflict is controlled rather than on processes through which disputes are generated; and 'system' as a Dunlopian set of rules, putting undue emphasis on stability maintenance. Indeed, pluralism was criticized for accepting 'the master institutions, principles and assumptions of the *status quo* as non-problematical' (Fox 1973: 219), thus reinforcing views that these are legitimate, inevitable and unchangeable. The Flanderite underpinnings of Donovan were also attacked for over-emphasis on collective bargaining and methodological and theoretical paucity and even 'total ignorance' of collective bargaining history in those industries where it first extensively developed and for following the 'Oxford Line's' 'short-term rule of thumb over the broader generalization, a rather low awareness of those disciplines . . . which illuminate the field with normative observations, and a variety of propagandist mini-reformism which consists partly in leading people boldly in the direction they appear to be going anyway' (Turner 1968: 358).

There were also critiques of Flanders' conception of, and belief in, collective bargaining, often incorrectly seen as almost a magic elixir for workplace ills. This contained a 'basic error at the heart' (Fox 1975: 154) because its anti-Webbsian foundations and distinctions – as between individual and collective bargaining and its implications and results – were flawed. Flanders' evaluation of productivity bargaining was blurred by his vision of what 'ought' to be and his own personal philosophy and ideological beliefs (Ahlstrand 1990). Tellingly, productivity bargaining even failed in its Fawley heartland, being used to minimize rather than enhance the collective role of unions, with remaining hostility to union participation as management operated in a unitarist manner and even withdrew collective bargaining (Ahlstrand 1990)(see MANAGERIAL BEHAVIOUR). In short, pluralist, reformist ideas were not really useful for the realities of workplace employment relations and became even less so over time – as seen when the unitarist assumptions of human resource management gathered pace and penetrated businesses. Thus, at first glance, Flanders has seemingly not 'weathered well' and while of historical significance, his work is of less contemporary relevance.

On the other hand, Flanders was in many ways a path-breaking and far-sighted thinker and despite operating within a particular socio-economic and political milieux, has retained his importance and relevance and has stood the test of time. For instance, Flanders' industrial relations definition was acceptable as, for example, 'institutions' covers both formal and informal organizations, as used in his Fawley study (Clegg 1979). Criticisms of the pluralist Donovanites were unfair given their diversity and that many later produced theoretical work (Poole 1981). Indeed, Flanders' thoughts contributed to more systematic explanations for union growth and the nature of trade unionism under collective bargaining (Clegg 1976), the notable analytical advances of the 1970s. Flanders' research on productivity bargaining was important as it was a managerial attempt to seize the initiative and sent widespread shock waves as it opened lengthy debate about endemic problems and solutions and it also contained antecedence for 'strategy', often seen as an almost paradigmatic development in industrial relations (Ahlstrand 1990). It explored the world of informal bargaining and how it might be contained by formal structures, emphasized the central priority of management initiative and control systems and was the first academic study to argue for the replacement of multi- by single-employer bargaining.

Other precursors of debates of contemporary relevance can be seen. Flanders (1964: 247) noted management's use of 'every method available for the direct communication of information', all too often mistakenly presented as a panacea for creating co-operation and resolving problems. Indeed, as Flanders' (1970: 172) warned, co-operation could not be fostered by 'propaganda and exhortation, by preaching its benefits', nor communication, which was often 'auxiliary to the system of control'. Debates on differences between human resource management and personnel management were previewed when Flanders (1964: 255) argued that 'the success of personnel management as a specialized function has to be judged by the extent to which the need for it declines, and that there is a need to integrate into line management decisions on labour relations'. Flanders' robust and visionary views on management's failings and weaknesses have remained poignant.

Nevertheless, Flanders' clarion calls were often ignored. We must not overlook his over-optimism concerning reform and behavioural change. Rapacious management, the collapse of the public sector and the state as the model 'good employer' and the increasing fragmentation and diversity of the workforce in a world of increasingly marginalized and flexible labour, are difficult terrain for Flanderite analysis and solutions. He seemed to focus less on the messy, murky world of individual employment relations which are less receptive to universal panaceas. To be sure some of these caveats are based on hindsight, and apply to many of his contemporaries, but they temper any wholly positive evaluation of Flanders' work.

4 Conclusions

Flanders' writings have had a mixed history but his place in management thought is secure. His often carefully crafted work contains important perceptions which often emerge on re-reading. While it is true that Flanders' policy prescriptions and his theory of collective bargaining were partial and are now somewhat dated; he still advanced this theory further than anyone else at the time;

and his sharp observations about managerial failings are as pertinent as they ever were. The pluralist ideal of collective bargaining, which looked moribund by the 1980s, is re-emerging in a different (European and Blairite) guise. Flanders' analysis of collective bargaining as a political process and the non-economic objectives of trade unionists still holds. Also, pluralism seemed conservative to the 1970s radicals, but in the light of contemporary managerial unitarism and beliefs in new nostrums, a Flanders who warned about managers believing their own rhetorics and who demonstrated the values of sharing control could play a major role. Current interests in social partnership are definitely Flanders' style. In sum, Flanders made key contributions to many areas of industrial relations and initiated and encouraged important debates and advances. He was also a 'guru' in his day with public influence. Flanders' work was of significance for its relatively rare comparative analysis and theoretical unity, and has continued to have resonance down the years.

CHRIS ROWLEY
ROYAL HOLLOWAY COLLEGE
UNIVERSITY OF LONDON

Note

My thanks to Nuffield College's peerless library and librarians, Arthur Marsh, Malcolm Warner and especially Pat McGovern, Rod Martin, Willy Brown, Paul Edwards and John Kelly for insightful comments and suggestions on an earlier draft. The normal disclaimers apply.

Further Reading

(References cited in the text marked *)

* Ahlstrand, B. (1990) *The Quest for Productivity: A Case Study of Fawley after Flanders*. Cambridge: Cambridge University Press. (An interesting follow-up analysis of Flanders' key work.)
* Clegg, H. (1976) *Trade Unionism under Collective Bargaining: A Theory Based on Comparisons of Six Countries*. Oxford: Blackwell. (Acknowledges the importance and influence of Flanders' ideas.)

* Clegg, H. (1979) *The Changing System of Industrial Relations in Great Britain.* Oxford: Blackwell. (Standard text whose antecedence was Flanders and Clegg 1954.)
* Clegg, (1990) 'The Oxford School of Industrial Relations', *Warwick Papers in Industrial Relations*, IRRU, University of Warwick No.31 January. (Fascinating outline of origins, membership, role and characteristics of the Oxford School.)
* Flanders, A. (1952) *Trade Unions.* London: Hutchinson's University Library. (Standard text on trade unions which had gone through seven editions by 1968.)
* Flanders, A. (1964) *The Fawley Productivity Agreements: A Case Study of Management and Collective Bargaining.* London: Faber and Faber. (Seminal work on productivity bargaining and seen as one of his key contributions.)
* Flanders, A. (1970) *Management and Unions: The Theory and Reform of Industrial Relations.* London: Faber and Faber. (The key collection of much of his most important work.)
* Flanders, A. (1974) 'The Tradition of Voluntarism', *British Journal of Industrial Relations* xii (3): 352–370. (Appearing after his death, displays his increasing interest in the role of the state.)
* Flanders, A. and Clegg, H. (eds) (1954) *The System of Industrial Relations in Great Britain: Its History, Law and Institutions.* Oxford: Blackwell. (A path-breaking, but almost exclusively institutional, formative text.)
* Flanders, A.; Pomeranz, R. and Woodward, J. (1968) *Experiment in Industrial Democracy: A Study of the John Lewis Partnership.* London: Faber and Faber. (An analysis of industrial democracy in the major retailer and its wider implications.)
* Fox, A. (1973) 'Industrial Relations: A Social Critique of Pluralist Ideology' in J. Child (ed) *Man and Organization: The Search for Explanation and Social Relevance.* (pp.185–231). London: Allen and Unwin. (An influential critique of pluralism and its proponents.)
* Fox, A. (1975) 'Collective Bargaining, Flanders and the Webbs', *British Journal of Industrial Relations* xiii (2): 151–174. (An important attack on Flanders' analysis and work on collective bargaining.)
* Hyman, R. (1975) *Industrial Relations: A Marxist Introduction.* London: Macmillan. (An alternative theoretical view of industrial relations.)
* Hyman, R. (1989) *The Political Economy of Industrial Relations: Theory and Practice in a Cold Climate.* London: Macmillan. (A useful collection providing different perspectives to Flanders.)
* Poole, M. (1981) *Theories of Trade Unionism: A Sociology of Industrial Relations.* London: Routledge and Keegan Paul. (A comprehensive study of trade unionism, with an excellent section on Flanders.)
* Turner, H.A. (1968) 'The Royal Commission's Research Papers', *British Journal of Industrial Relations* vi (3): 346–359. (A withering attack on Donovan and its contributors, including Flanders.)

See also: CLEGG, H.A.; COLLECTIVE BARGAINING; EMPLOYEE RELATIONS, MANAGEMENT OF; EMPLOYERS' ASSOCIATIONS; HUMAN RESOURCE MANAGEMENT; INDUSTRIAL AND LABOUR RELATIONS; MANAGERIAL BEHAVIOUR; PRODUCTIVITY; TRADE UNIONS

Related topics in the IEBM: GURU CONCEPT; MANAGEMENT DEVELOPMENT

Follett, Mary Parker (1868–1933)

Personal background

- born 3 September 1868 in Quincy, near Boston, Massachusetts
- graduated *summa cum laude* from Radcliffe College, Cambridge, Massachusetts, in economics, government, law and philosophy in 1898
- introduced the concept of the business as a social agency and economic unit; advocated group-work and democratic governance in the workplace for most effective performance
- died Boston, 18 December 1933

Major works

The Speaker of the House of Representatives (1896)

The New State–Group Organization: The Solution for Popular Government (1918)

Creative Experience (1924)

Summary

Mary Parker Follett (1868–1933) was primarily a political scientist who advocated the establishment of neighbourhood groups as primary units of self-governance and as the most effective means of achieving true citizenship and the fairer and more productive society. She was also active, and an innovator, in the field of social work. She brought to business organization and management her knowledge and experience from these other fields. As in government and in social work, so in the business: group-work and self-governance through the group would ensure most satisfying and productive results.

Follett dealt with the basic questions which underlie all relations: conflict, power, authority, leadership, control. She applied the findings of both the physical and social sciences to the business organization and demonstrated the need to create unity of action out of diversity of interests and to foster good human relations in the workplace. Her teachings, widely acclaimed in her lifetime, lost favour after her death. However, their underlying importance and value have been gaining ground and, at the onset of the twenty-first century, Follett is coming into her own: she is now considered to be the 'Prophet of Management' (Graham 1995a).

1 Introduction

Follett brought to the study of business organization and management the concepts she had developed as a political scientist and the hands-on experience she acquired as a manager in the social work field. She held that the unit of society was not the individual in isolation but the 'group-individual' (Child 1969). It is through the groups to which they belong that individuals derive their identity and fulfil their potential (see ORGANIZATION BEHAVIOUR).

Managers and managed are basically of the same ilk. For Follett, thinking and doing are not separate activities, but parts of the same process, in which either part may precede and have greater weight than the other. To structure the work organization on a strict hierarchical order does not reflect the realities and the needs of everyday life, and to resolve conflict constructively, domination and compromise do not work in the long run. The parties in conflict must themselves find their own solution, the solution that meets their mutual, underlying real demands.

As against the concept of 'power-over' which is reductionist and wasteful of resources, Follett introduced the concept of 'power-with', also found in nature, which is co-active and increases the total power of the group. Follett demonstrated that there is no need for personal order-giving or order-taking. Each situation has its own law and it is this law which dictates the order, to be obeyed by both manager and managed. Within the group, Follett held that the followers' responsibility is to keep their leader in full charge by actively participating in the ongoing decision-making process, and not merely complying with direction.

It is difficult to encapsulate Follett's teaching but the following two quotations give an idea of the comprehensiveness and the modernity of her thought: 'The form of [business] organization should be such as to allow or induce the continuous coordination of the experience of men' (Metcalf and Urwick 1941: 121); 'If we want harmony between labor and capital, we must make labor and capital into one group: we must have an integration of interests and motives, of standards and ideals of justice' (Follett 1918: 117).

Follett's teachings failed to make headway after her death. In the USA, the difficult social conditions of the Depression years in the 1930s and the ensuing conflicting relations between labour and capital meant that her concepts of partnership and participation in the workplace went against the grain of the ideology of the times. Further, she had come to management late in life and *Dynamic Administration*, the collection of her lectures on business organization, was not published until 1941, some years after her death. However, her philosophy started to gain ground in the 1950s and gathered momentum by the 1990s. Follett's ideas, based on connecting, coordinating and integrating, are better attuned to the latest open systems thinking.

2 Biographical data

Mary Parker Follett was born in Quincy, near Boston, Massachusetts, in September 1868. Her parents came from old-established Quincy stock. Her mother was an invalid and her father died when she was in her teens. The domestic manager from very early on, Follett, on her father's death, had also to take charge

of the family's financial affairs. Money, on her mother's side, in due course made her financially independent.

Follett was a brilliant scholar, first at the Thayer Academy in Braintree, then at the Society for the College Instruction of Women (now Radcliffe College), with a year spent at Newnham College, Cambridge, England, and finally returning to Radcliffe College to graduate from there in 1898 *summa cum laude* in economics, government, law and philosophy. She was fluent in French and German and kept herself informed in her fields of interest of what was new on both sides of the Atlantic.

Even before her graduation, Follett gained recognition as an original and serious historian with her book *The Speaker of the House of Representatives* which was published in 1896. Here, she detailed the intricate workings of the legislative process and pioneered the twin-pronged approach she would later use in all her work: studying meticulously the records and, in addition, interviewing the people involved to get directly from them their views and reactions.

Follett was 32 years old when she completed her formal studies. In 1891 she had met a Miss Isobel Briggs, an Englishwoman some twenty years her senior and, by 1896, they had set up house together; theirs was 'one of the closest, most fertile and noble friendships I have known' a friend wrote. Through Miss Briggs and her own connections and interests, Follett became an integral part of the sparkling intellectual and social Boston/Harvard milieu of those days.

After her studies, Follett went into social work. She started in a men's club, in a very rough district of Boston. With her cast of mind, it was perhaps inevitable that she would be an innovator. Very quickly, recognizing the environment as of the essence, she visualized that the local schoolhouse, if used in the evenings as a club, would be more congenial than the institutional settlement house.

Under her leadership and with her unremitting attention to detail, evening centres in the schools were started and soon prospered. Recreation was important, but even more so was work. 'Why not use the evening centres additionally as placement bureaux?' she asked herself. The Boston centres in due course became models for other cities to copy. In 1917, they were incorporated into Boston's public school system and, a tribute to Follett's organizing ability, continued to be run for many years on the same structures she had set up.

During those years in social work, Follett was learning at first-hand the workings and the potential of the group-process: how people working together could evolve, develop and carry out their own plans. She saw the local group as the political base for self-government. Always the scholar, she recorded her experiences and crystallized her new thinking in her next book: *The New State–Group Organization: The Solution for Popular Government* (1918).

This book had a favourable reception, nationally and internationally, and established her as a public figure on both sides of the Atlantic. At home in Massachusetts, she began to represent the public on arbitration boards, minimum wage boards and public tribunals. As a member of these committees, Follett now experienced at first hand the politics of industrial relations (see INDUSTRIAL AND LABOUR RELATIONS). Many of the examples in her next book *Creative Experience* (1924) came from these new activities and situations.

Creative Experience brought her a new career and a different audience: businessmen, many of whom asked for her help with their management problems. She investigated specific situations in their factories, studied their organizations and suggested improvements. The Bureau of Personnel Administration, in New York, which held annual conferences for business executives and invited prestigious speakers for these occasions set the seal of approval upon Follett as a front-rank management thinker. Its director, Henry C. Metcalf, who had worked with her in the early 1900s and knew the range of her interests, invited her to give a series of lectures on 'The psychological foundations of business administration' at the 1925 conference and continued to ask her to lecture at this annual event over the years.

In England, Seebohm Rowntree, both a businessman and a management pioneer, asked her, first in 1926 and then in later years, to address his annual conferences on management themes at Balliol College, Oxford. It was here that she met Lyndall Urwick, who became her greatest admirer and worked unremittingly to spread her teaching. From her Newnham College days, Follett had developed close ties with England. Her books and activities now connected her with the top academics, politicians and businessmen in England. After Miss Briggs's death, Follett came in 1928 to live in England and shared a house with Dame Katharine Furse in Chelsea, London.

In early 1933, Follett was invited to give the inaugural lectures at the Department of Business Administration (later to become the Department of Industrial Relations) of the London School of Economics – a distinct honour. Lyndall Urwick later collected and published them, under the title of *Freedom and Coordination*. In December 1933, Follett went to Boston to sort out her financial affairs. While there, she was taken ill and died on 18 December 1933.

3 Main contribution

Follett's work, especially in the field of management, was in many ways seminal. She came to the subject when American industrial expansion was proceeding at a phenomenal rate, with an inevitable impact on social conditions. The problems of management were of course growing in parallel. Frederick W. Taylor (see TAYLOR, F.W.) had established the *rationale* of management. Follett came on the scene to establish its *philosophy*, although this role has not escaped criticism (for example, Pugh *et al.* 1975).

Not engaged in business management herself, she was frequently taxed by industrialists about their growing problems. To these, she brought the insights and the disciplines of the social scientist she was. Each problem, she held, was *sui generis* and had to be examined in its component parts and also as a whole. The relevant technology, the complexities of human nature and the demand of the market had to be understood in their dynamic interaction. It was from this analysis as a whole that the solution had to be propounded and then tested against the realities of life in the workplace.

It follows that Follett could be no believer in set systems, for she knew that no system could encompass all the richness and contingency of life. One of the foundations of Follett's philosophy was her belief in the unity of knowledge. She once said:

> I do wish that, when a principle has been worked out, say in ethics, it did not have to be discovered all over again in psychology, in economics, in government, in business, in biology and in sociology. It's such a waste of time.

In expanding this view and seeing clearly the interconnectedness of things, she wrote:

> I think we should undepartmentalize our thinking in regard to every problem that comes to us. I do not think that we have psychological and ethical and economic problems. We have human problems, with psychological, ethical and economic aspects, and as many others as you like.
> (Metcalf and Urwick 1941: 184)

As a dedicated social scientist, Follett was no sentimentalist. She appealed not to men's better nature but to their common sense and their long-term interest.

No small part of Follett's main contribution was in her laying down the four fundamental principles of organization:

1 coordination as the reciprocal relating of all the factors in a situation;
2 coordination by direct contact of the responsible persons concerned;
3 coordinating in the early stages;
4 coordination as a continuing process.

These principles for effective organization, she held, can be applied to any set-up, not merely to those in commerce or industry.

4 Evaluation

Apart from her work as a political scientist and innovator in the social work field, Mary Parker Follett is chiefly remembered for her contribution to management thinking. She has not been uniformly appreciated since her death in 1933, as her teachings lost favour in the struggling Depression years. In her day, she was in considerable demand as a lecturer and counsellor on management, but she died before she could consolidate and publish her lectures. So, she left no definitive account of her work in the management field. It was Lyndall Urwick and Henry C. Metcalf who rescued it for posterity and published her lectures in 1941 in *Dynamic Administration: The Collected Papers of Mary Parker Follett*. It was Lyndall Urwick who, in 1949, published under the title of *Freedom and Coordination* the lectures she had given at the London School of Economics. And it is from these two works that the generations since her death have gradually come to value her teachings in administration and management.

Follett's strength derives from the combination of three factors. The first is the knowledge and skills she brought from her mastery of much of the social science field – she had studied deeply across the whole gamut from economics to psychology to jurisprudence; the second was her profound empathy with people; and the third was her own practical experience and her shrewd assessment of the ways of the world. It was thus that she brought a new look at the problems of society in general and those of industry in particular. This new look is now becoming established practice in forward-looking management thinking and practice.

5 Conclusion

Follett made a major contribution to the management thinking of her day, emphasizing good human relations in the workplace. She added a new dimension to the study of management by applying to it the findings of the social sciences, in particular of psychology. Her teaching is as valid today as it was when she was developing it in the mid-1920s. Her work will be further developed with the changing social, economic and technological scene but it is unlikely to be superseded.

PAULINE GRAHAM
UNIVERSITY OF BRADFORD

Further reading

(References cited in the text marked *)

* Child, J. (1969) *British Management Thought*, London: Allen & Unwin. (A review and a critical analysis of British management thought.)
* Follett, M.P. (1896) *The Speaker of the House of Representatives*, New York: Longmans Green. (Gives a detailed analysis of the legislative process involved in the work of the Speaker of the House of Representatives.)
* Follett, M.P. (1918) *The New State–Group Organization: The Solution for Popular Government*, New York: Longmans Green. (Gives Follett's basic tenets on the place of the individual in society and the importance of the group for effective self-governance and democracy.)
* Follett, M.P. (1924) *Creative Experience*, New York: Longmans Green. (Uses Gestalt psychology to explain relationships and to show how shared experience can be used to bring about democratic governance.)
  Fox, E.M and Urwick, L.F (eds) (1973) *Dynamic Administration: The Collected Papers of Mary Parker Follett*, London: Pitman. (Gives the most comprehensive collection of Follett's lectures and an up-to-date assessment of Follett's work.)
  Graham, P. (1987) *Dynamic Managing – The Follett Way*, London: Professional Publishing and British Institute of Management. (Looks at the value of Follett's concepts for effective management.)
  Graham, P. (1991) *Integrative Management: Creating Unity from Diversity*, Oxford: Blackwell. (Uses Follett's concepts to ensure that a business is recognized both as a social agency and an economic unit.)
* Graham, P. (ed.) (1995a) *Mary Parker Follett: Prophet of Management*, Boston, MA: Harvard Business School Press. (Offers Follett's writings on key concepts with commentaries on them by experts.)
  Graham, P. (1995b) 'The mother of management', *European Quality Journal* 2 (4): 21–3. (Gives an overview of some of Follett's concepts.)
* Metcalf, H.C. and Urwick, L.F. (eds) (1941) *Dynamic Administration: The Collected Papers of Mary Parker Follett*, Bath: Management Publications Trust. (The first edition of Follett's collection of lectures, bringing Follett's teachings to the attention of the discerning reader of management literature.)
* Pugh, D., Mansfield, R. and Warner, M. (1975) *Research in Organizational Behaviour*, London: Heinemann. (Gives a short summary of organizational behaviour as a subject.)
  Shadovitz, D. (1995) 'Back to the present', *Human Resource Executive Journal* (June): 71–3. (Quotes Follett on authority, partnership, collective bargaining, etc.)
* Urwick, L.F. (ed.) (1949) *Freedom and Coordination*, London: Management Publications Trust. (A collection of Follett's lectures given in early 1933 at the London School of Economics.)
  Urwick, L. and Brech, E.F.L. (1945) *The Making of Scientific Management: Thirteen Pioneers*, London: Management Publications Trust. (Covers studies of thirteen pioneers in management and includes a chapter on Follett.)
  Wood, S. (1995) 'Ideas with a contemporary ring', *European Quality Journal* 2 (4): 23–4. (Shows the relevance of Follett's insights on total quality management.)

See also: HUMAN RELATIONS; HUMAN RESOURCE MANAGEMENT; INDUSTRIAL AND LABOUR RELATIONS; ORGANIZATION BEHAVIOUR; TAYLOR, F.W.

Related topics in the IEBM: BUSINESS SCHOOLS; MANAGEMENT IN NORTH AMERICA; ORGANIZATION BEHAVIOUR, HISTORY OF; POWER

Ford, Henry (1863–1947)

Personal background

- born of Irish immigrant farmers near Dearborn, Michigan, on 30 July 1863
- attended school intermittently for eight years
- trained as machinist in Detroit, and built first experimental car in 1896
- married Clara Bryant, 1888
- built up Ford Motor Company from 1903
- successfully pursued vision of motoring for the masses, rather than as a hobby for the rich
- main single architect of high-volume, highly efficient assembly-line production
- died Dearborn, Michigan, on 7 April 1947

Major works

My Life and Work (1922)*
Today and Tomorrow (1926)*
My Philosophy of Industry (1929)
Moving Forward (1931)*

* Ford was the nominal co-author of these, with Samuel Crowther

Summary

Henry Ford (1863–1947) was a major creative force behind the twentieth-century growth of very large-scale assembly-line production in general, and of the car industry and motoring for the masses in particular. He helped to free the nascent motor industry in the USA from Eastern financial interests, and combined highly efficient, high-volume and vertically integrated production with high wages and low pricing. These innovations were copied widely in many industries and countries, although Ford cars were rarely famous for being technically advanced. Ford's achievements helped to stimulate urbanization, large-scale road building and important developments in agriculture and services, as well as in manufacturing. Ford was an eccentric philanthropist and a not always benevolent autocrat. He and his work are still controversial.

1 Introduction

Ford is generally regarded as the prime mover of the twentieth century's 'industry of industries', and as having brought the industrial revolution to its culmination. His company combined the manufacture and assembly of virtually all of the parts that went into making a car, using perpetual directed motion in the form of the moving assembly line with numerous moving subassembly lines feeding into the main one, and applying the principle of vertical integration through a complex of interdependent units. Money and human effort were expended in ways designed to sustain high levels of output: Ford workers were paid, from 1914, exceptionally high wages; prices were kept low; sales were maintained at a high level; and company expansion was internally financed.

Although Ford is often credited with inventing the assembly line and highly efficient high-volume mass production, most of the inventions and ideas that enabled him to become successful and famous had existed for decades, or in some cases for centuries. Apart from the internal combustion engine and the motor car itself, such inventions and ideas included scientific management, with its development of time study, motion study and the planned use of pay as an incentive; interchangeable parts; the use of planning and standardized procedures in stock control, production, accounting and so on; assembly lines and production lines; and even continuously moving assembly-line production (see TAYLOR,F.W.).

However, Ford did develop a system of production, assembly and transport which was unprecedented in its mobility and extent, and which anticipated late twentieth-century just-in-time practice. Ford's main ambition, to bring motoring to the masses, was quintessentially American, with his belief in equality, movement, change, realism, straightforwardness and simplicity. The way in which Ford's genius for self-publicity dramatized and facilitated his achievement, his neglect of organization for the long term, and the weaknesses in the Ford company's management after its early success were also very American. Ford is now often associated with rigid patterns of production and with exploitation of employees (Galbraith 1960; Beynon 1973), but there are grounds, too, for calling him a remarkable innovator and philanthropist (Ford 1991) (see LABOUR PROCESS).

2 Biographical data

Henry Ford was born on his father's farm near Dearborn, Michigan, eight miles west of Detroit, on 30 July 1863. He was one of eight children of William and Mary Ford. He attended a one-room rural school when not helping on the family farm or tinkering with watches and farm machinery. He learned some basic arithmetic and reading and writing and was barely literate.

For three years from the age of 16 Ford served an apprenticeship as a machinist in James Flower's Machine Shop in Detroit. He learned about the internal combustion engine, and he supplemented his income by repairing watches, toying with the idea of mass-producing them. He worked as a qualified machinist at the Detroit Drydock Company, but soon returned to the family farm, where he set up a small machine shop and worked part-time for the Westinghouse Engine Company. He built a tractor with a home-made steam engine and an old mowing machine chassis.

Ford returned to Detroit to become an engineer for the Edison Illuminating Company and became its chief engineer in 1893. He had married Clara Bryant in 1888, and in 1893 she gave birth to Ford's only son, Edsel. As chief engineer with the Edison Company, Ford was responsible for maintaining electrical services in Detroit and on call for twenty-four hours a day. Without regular hours, he could experiment at length with his ideas of making a petrol-powered vehicle. He had made his first internal combustion engine in 1893. He finished the 'quadricycle', his first car, in 1896. The lightest of the pioneer cars, with a buggy frame mounted on four bicycle wheels, it possibly foreshadowed Ford's later emphasis on low price. He sold it to help finance the building of his second car, which he also sold in due course to finance the third. In this way he was also different from many other pioneer car inventors, who kept their creations, and he was foreshadowing his later strong reliance on expansion through growth of sales to a mass market, as opposed to reliance on external finance of sales to the wealthy.

Between 1896 and 1903 Ford built several new cars and had various backers, including those who, in 1899, formed the Detroit Automobile Company. This had Ford as its superintendent and failed mainly because of his inexperience in organizing production. It was dissolved after just over a year and replaced by the Henry Ford Company with the same main financial backer, William Murphy, a Detroit lumber dealer. During these years Ford enhanced his reputation by building and driving several successful racing cars, and he also acquired Childe Harold Wills, a brilliant engineer who was to be crucial in developing Ford cars.

At this time, however, Ford felt that his passenger cars were not yet ready for customers and insisted on improving whatever car he was working on, whereas his backers wanted more, and more profitable, cars to put on the market. In 1902 he left the Henry Ford Company, which was later to become the Cadillac Motor Car Company. Although he had offended many of Detroit's wealthiest citizens by his dealings with his former backers, Ford found other partners in a group headed by Alexander Malcomson, a Detroit coal dealer, and the Ford Motor Company was founded in June 1903 with Ford and Malcomson as the main stockholders. Others included John and Horace Dodge, who made the chassis, engines and transmissions for Ford's cars, and James Couzens, who was to become Ford's business agent. In 1905 Ford bought Malcomson out after a quarrel, which Ford won, over whether to build high-priced cars or cars for the masses. Thus, by 1905 Ford was in almost complete financial and operational control of his own company.

In the first decade of the twentieth century the American car industry became independent, no longer an experimental sideline of companies with other interests, but one made up of companies solely dedicated to making cars. It was relatively easy to sell cars, but production methods were still in their infancy. However, cars were beginning to drop their buggy and bicycle ancestry, with steering wheels replacing tillers, engines moving from under the driver's seat to the front, and metal starting to replace wood in construction. Ford was pursuing his aim of making a car that was tough, cheap and easy to run. By the time that Ford's Model T appeared in 1908, the Ford Motor Company was already established as a leader in the industry.

The years from 1908 to 1914 saw Ford start to establish himself as a popular hero through the production of the Model T, the successful fight against the Selden patent, and through the development by 1914 of the most advanced and widely publicized system of production yet devised. The Model T, 'Tin Lizzie', was made for 19 years from October 1908, and nearly 17,000,000 were sold, as many as all other cars made worldwide in that period, mainly in the USA but with 250,000 going to the UK and nearly 1,000,000 to Canada. The Model T was a major force for change in the USA, stimulating large-scale highway building, urbanization and the growth of suburbs, ending the physical isolation of many farmers and the reign of the horse in farm transport, and enabling millions of people to travel widely and independently for the first time.

Ford's fight against the Selden patent, which covered the production of all petrol-powered cars and supposedly reserved it for members of the Association of Licensed Automobile Manufacturers (ALAM), lasted six years. The victory apparently set the industry free from Eastern financial power and industrial combinations and added to Ford's burgeoning status as a popular hero. However, the ALAM did not in fact operate as a monopoly; it was mainly the fact that the suit against the ALAM was mounted at the height of the campaign against trusts in the USA that allowed Ford to derive so much favourable publicity from it.

The construction of Ford's new plant at Highland Park, Detroit, with the constantly moving chassis assembly line installed in January 1914, made possible the delivery of parts, assemblies and subassemblies to the main line at precise times. Where it had previously taken over twelve hours to produce a complete chassis, it now took only a fraction over one and one-half. This was one part of a series of developments which made Ford world famous. In 1914 the average daily wage in the US car industry was $2.34. In that year Ford decided to pay eligible workers at least $5 per day and to cut the working day by one hour to eight hours, enabling a three-shift system to be worked. Ford was portrayed as either a naive socialist or great humanitarian. Most firms tried to pay the lowest wages and to seek the highest prices that they could get away with. However, Ford priced the Model T as low as possible (over its lifetime, its price went down from $950 in 1908 to $290 by 1927) so as to sell as many as he could, meeting the price by efficiency and volume. He foresaw that if this philosophy were applied extensively, workers would be able to buy things which had hitherto been luxuries, such as cars, in ways which would profit everyone, not least employers, leading to the mass US affluence of the 1950s.

Ford relied on several strong personalities to help him realize his ambitions. His business genius was James Couzens, and William Knudsen and Charles Sorensen were his production ones, and the industrial architect Albert Kahn designed the epoch-making Highland Park plant. John Lee was his industrial and human relations expert and the creator of the company's sociological department, which made the first attempt, a little eccentric and crude like its ultimate author, at a systematic personnel and industrial relations policy in the motor industry. Between 1903 and 1913 Couzens was a major force in the company, organizing its sales and controlling its spending while driving it to expand and develop its production.

In the decade spanning 1920 Henry Ford's career was at its height. For the company it was an era of financially secure expansion. Until the USA entered the First World War in 1917 its motor industry did little to gear itself up for war. Ford had made a naive effort to get the combatants to stop fighting in 1915. In 1917 he announced that his company would be at the US Government's disposal and that he would return all profits on war contracts to it. This was merely a publicity stunt but the company did make many aeroplane engines, military vehicles and a number of submarine chasers. During the same period the enormous new River Rouge plant began to be built in Detroit and Ford's production of cars reached its highest level. In 1919 the Ford family became the sole owners of the Ford Motor Company, buying the shares held by others. By 1920 several other companies were starting to compete in the mass car market, mainly by trying to build a slightly better car than the Model T for an only marginally higher price.

When, in 1920, the Ford Motor Company was reorganized under Ford and his family co-owners, no single person had ever controlled so enormous an enterprise so completely. In 1927 the company moved its main centre from the Highland Park to the River Rouge plant. The latter finally embodied all of Ford's ideas about self-sufficiency, with its supplies coming from Ford-owned ore and coal mines, timberland, rubber plantations, a sawmill, a glassworks, foundries and steelworks, on Ford-owned railways and ships. All this was done with profits from the Model T, without a cent being borrowed.

The Ford Motor Company diversified in 1922 when it acquired the up-market Lincoln car company. It ventured quite promisingly into aviation for a few years from 1926 and later, during the Second World War, produced large numbers of bomber aircraft and tanks, and aircraft and tank engines.

The very scale of Ford's domination of both his own business and the car industry in general, combined with the growth of competitor companies, products and industries, and Ford's own slowly diminishing energy pointed the way towards relative decline. His famous statement about customers being able to buy any car 'as long as it is black' is illustrative of Ford's mixture of democratic and creative, and autocratic and egotistical, impulses.

Ford, having achieved by 1920 most of what he had originally set out to do, became increasingly complacent and erratic. He manipulated his managers, often ruthlessly, and fired or otherwise drove out many of the best ones. His cars were increasingly technically conservative, with their brakes, four-cylinder engines and transmissions often conspicuously dated in the 1920s and 1930s. The company lost its industry leadership, coming third in the US motor industry in terms of sales in 1936, behind General Motors and Chrysler, although a V-8 engine was introduced in 1932. The Model A, which had at last replaced the popular but obsolete Model T in 1927, was a reasonable success, but it was only made for four years. Ford resisted trade union organization by using worker spies, company police and violence, and cut wages to below the industry norms (to $4 a day) in 1932. He first signed a union contract in 1941, several years after GM and Chrysler had first recognized the Union of Automobile Workers (see TRADE UNIONS).

In the Second World War the company was largely devoted to war production. Henry Ford had a stroke and his son Edsel became fatally ill, worn down by the intrigues which his father had fostered. Indeed from around 1925 onwards Henry Ford had lost much of his interest in the details of the Ford Motor Company's affairs, and Edsel was largely an administrator. 'Cast Iron Charlie' Sorensen ran the plant and was increasingly responsible for maintaining the company as an organization until his retirement early in 1944. Ford's grandson, Henry II, became a director in 1943, Executive Vice-President in 1944, and President in September 1945, two years before his grandfather died. At the age of 27,

Henry Ford II began converting the company from wartime to peacetime production.

Under the terms of Henry Ford's will 95 per cent of the company's common stock went to the Ford Foundation. This philanthropic trust had been set up in 1936 as a way of keeping family control of the company. In 1956 most of its securities were sold to the public and the Ford Motor Company became much more like a typical large American corporation. The Ford Foundation became the wealthiest private foundation in the world.

As an engineer and manager of a kind, Ford was untutored, often highly original, and above all an enthusiast, an experimenter and an empiricist. His often highly naive and idealistic enthusiasms exposed him to ridicule from time to time, as when he chartered an ocean liner in 1915, the 'Peace Ship', to take himself and a number of pacifists to Europe to try to end the First World War by persuasion. In 1918 he was almost elected to the US Senate, and in the same year he began publicizing a number of anti-Semitic views (eventually withdrawn) in a newspaper that he had bought. He established schools, a mainly rural museum, a restored rural town and village factories. He socialized publicly with fellow innovators like Thomas Edison and through the old-fashioned dances which he had organized in opposition to jazz. In much of what Ford did in his later years there was a strong element of didacticism concerned with teaching people about that which, for Ford, was worth retaining from the slower-moving world which his efforts had done and were doing so much, so dramatically, to transform.

3 Main contribution

According to Chandler (1990), Ford's key strength as the 'first mover' of the US motor industry was his understanding of 'throughput'. One key aspect of this was Ford's desire for his company to be as self-contained as possible. Another was his belief in 'plenty for all', as expressed in his slogan 'high wages to create large markets'. He did not invent (although he certainly did symbolize) mass production, just-in-time inventory control, vertical integration, a slightly crude but quite

effective version of the marketing concept, the large motor company as a multinational, human resource management or corporate philanthropy, but he brought several of these to fruition, added significantly to the development of others, and integrated most of them with considerable effectiveness (see HUMAN RESOURCE MANAGEMENT). His major achievements were, however, to bring motoring to the US masses and, in the process, to help generate mass affluence and to liberate millions of people from hard physical labour. He was also ahead of his time when he put the needs of customers and workers before those of shareholders.

In spite of all these achievements, Ford had a markedly happy-go-lucky attitude towards the development of techniques and theories of management and organization. He was prejudiced against college-trained engineers and his company organized and ran in a very haphazard way what would now be called research and development activities. Little if anything was done to organize accounting along systematic lines, advertising was also badly neglected, and his approach to personnel management oscillated between advanced forms of empowerment and enlightened paternalism on the one hand and the large-scale mobilization of paranoia on the other (see PERSONNEL MANAGEMENT).

Although he has often been associated with scientific management, there is little if any evidence to show that Ford was directly affected by any of the advanced management thinking of the eras that he lived and worked through. While he did develop a highly rational and organized system of production before 1920 his personal control of it from then into the 1940s was more or less disastrous. From the early 1930s to the death of his son Edsel in 1943, the management of the Ford Motor Company was split inefficiently between Ford himself, a fading autocrat whose occasional interventions usually came through Harry Bennett, the near-criminal boss of the 'Service Department', which was responsible for 'personnel', and Charlie Sorensen, who managed production and who tried to hold the company together with the administrative help of Edsel, its president since 1919, who was able and popular but much abused by his father.

Ford's philosophy and attitudes were moulded by the tension between the simplicities of his early life and the complexities of his business in the USA in the late nineteenth and early twentieth century. Very American, a pure Yankee with a strong belief in equality and an acceptance of social flux built into him, he attracted adjectives like homely, original, pragmatic, optimistic, unconventional, democratic and empirical. He was certainly a simplifier of issues and tasks whose love of efficiency came from his austere rural background. Such qualities hardened as he did, with age, into stubbornness and authoritarianism. The strength of his approach to management was his tough-minded 'can-do' innovativeness, but its corresponding weakness was a lack of respect for orderly planning and rational ways of dividing labour. Ford largely achieved his aim of using machinery to make jobs easy and to create new ones on a very large scale, developing a system of employment, production and marketing which brought mass affluence into being because the strengths outweighed the weaknesses for most of his career.

A utilitarian belief in the greatest good for the greatest number and a deep sense of responsibility clearly underpinned much of what Ford did. He valued affluence and mobility, and his attitude towards his workers, a combination of *laissez-faire* and paternalism, and his very American aim of turning luxuries into necessities, were all associated with his faith in the notion that moral development is most likely to follow material progress.

Typically of the Midwest farm boys of his generation, who had left the land to seek work in the rapidly growing US cities, Ford believed that the country was natural and good, and the city artificial and evil. He also felt that industrialization was destroying cities and making it possible for everyone to live in the country. Like Frederick Taylor of the scientific management movement, and Thorstein Veblen, the Norwegian-US economist and sociologist, Ford thought that industrialization would help replace corrupt and parasitical Eastern aristocrats and finance capitalists

with a new class of producers (see TAYLOR, F. W.). All three were typical of the Progressive thinkers of the USA between the late nineteenth and early twentieth centuries. The Progressive movement acquired an ideal of a community which was mobile and continually expanding, although in the same era the term 'backwash' was being used to describe how the US dream of infinite land and the continually moving frontier had ended, with people more concerned with settling down than before.

Like many outstandingly successful individuals, Ford is more easily understood when a few important facts about him are remembered. One is his unsophisticated background and lack of formal education, another is the context of extraordinary change and opportunity through which he grew from youth to middle-aged success, and a third is his considerable age and reduced physical and mental capacities in the last fifteen or so often erratic and sad years of his life. Both at and away from the Ford Motor Company his life and behaviour were often dramatically complex and contradictory. As an employer, for example, he was highly enlightened and progressive in some ways and at some times, and a repressive and capricious autocrat in and at others. However, there is evidence of a pattern of a lengthy struggle to succeed, followed by dramatic success, followed by long and only partially concealed decline, all interwoven with and influencing many aspects of his life.

Ford's anti-Semitism was an unfortunate product of his strong penchant for self-publicity and his often startling parochialism and ignorance. More loutish than malicious, it was common among his generation, before the Second World War, and foolishly misdepicted Jews as international capitalists, overly commercial and decadent. Ford also believed, benevolently in this case, in rural production, in bringing factories and farming close together, rather than in having them located apart and in mutual opposition. His many contradictions were exemplified further by his apparent belief, in late middle age, that people were happier when deprived of choice.

4 Evaluation

The essence of Ford's work and of his vision was to define mass production and to bring the industrialization process to a kind of maturity. Mechanization, moving inventories and vertical integration were central to the achievement of his vision. So, too, was Ford's use of his power, material and personal, to inspire. He defined morality as 'the law of right action', as more than just trying to be good, as the exercise of will in order to accelerate the inevitable and the positive. He advocated money-making as a service to others, not as exploitation. To 'find a way or to make one' of liberating people from back-breaking toil was another major strand of his ideal.

One of the main criticisms of Ford was that of inadequate organization. It was a justified criticism. Thus, as Ford himself wrote in 1926:

> a business, in my way of thinking, is not a machine. It is a collection of people who are brought together to do work and not to write letters to one another. It is not necessary for any one department to know what any other department is doing . . . It is not necessary to have meetings to establish good feelings between individuals or departments. It is not necessary for people to love each other in order to work together.
> (Ford and Crowther 1926: 91–2)

There is a lot that is didactic and written for effect in this brief quotation from Ford's book with Samuel Crowther, *My Life and Work*, but it certainly reflects much of Ford's way of working. There is no doubt that Ford was far better at building a team in 1910 than in 1925, that he had become an autocrat unable to relinquish power, an omnipotent, selfish dictator professing humanitarian objectives. In the 1930s the weaknesses of his methods were being highlighted by hard times. Thus, the very integrated nature of the Ford Motor Company's production in the USA became overly expensive because as demand and output decreased, unit costs rose much faster for Ford than for other companies.

Also, as Ford grew older and more inflexible the weaknesses of his management of people, always apparent, became dramatically obvious. Increasingly after the 1910s he drove the most able people away and half-destroyed his organization in the process. He had always treated some of his managers badly but in the 1930s especially, such treatment became the norm. His erratic judgements of people were also more obvious. His tendency to work by hunch, his impulsiveness and lack of thoroughness were central both to his success and his decline.

At least from the standpoint of the late twentieth century, Ford was no very great engineer or business person, and much more of a coordinator, exploiter and publicity-seeking impresario of a number of powerful existing trends. He was someone whose flaws were increasingly apparent, both in his generally deteriorating attitudes and behaviour, and more specifically in the growing commercial and technical conservatism of his last twenty-five years. Much of his early success, up to 1915, has also been attributed, with considerable justification, to his early business genius James Couzens.

Ford's lack of system and his prejudices, his often small-minded, suspicious, jealous, opinionated, malicious and insincere behaviour were widely documented, even by those who praised him the most. Yet so, too, were his many often major innovations, his flexibility when seriously challenged, as by trade unions in his later years, and the fact that he was a pioneer and major achiever.

From a reading of Ford's life and of the work of many critics of assembly-line mass production, it is clear that while popular portrayals of Ford as a high priest of modernism and of rationalist exploitation of employees contain important grains of truth, the real picture is more complicated. It is clear that a great deal of very flexible thinking went into the creation of 'inflexible' Fordist methods of production, and into the partly self-regarding publicizing of them and of their wider ramifications. Also, Ford himself was plainly a very idiosyncratic person and not merely understandable as a farm boy made good. Thus, although his methods were central to a great many of the changes of his life and times, they were often unique to him and his company and not always typical of the motor industry in particular or to mass production in general. Much of what Ford did was strictly technology- and/or market-driven, and unconnected in any direct way with scientific management.

His paternalism was much more inspired by commercial foresight and self-interest and by vanity than by human relations-style thinking, which it largely pre-dated, in any case. Perhaps the two main effects of Ford's work on subsequent management thinking were through the conflation and stereotyping of his treatment of workers and of the supposedly 'alienating' character of assembly-line mass production, which fuelled negative perceptions and portrayals of manufacturing; and the awful example of mismanagement and disorganization that the Ford Motor Company presented in the last quarter century of his life, which almost certainly helped to stimulate creative and rational forms of work organization into being at General Motors and elsewhere.

In spite of all of his errors, Ford's life offers a very great example of bold and broadly positive change. He was admired more in developing, or in what were then developing countries, than in those with abundant supplies of mechanical skill, such as Germany and the UK. There was much that was courageous as well as much that was venal in his use of publicity. His practice of working and innovating by hunch, widely criticized in the years after his death, has increasingly been recognized as an integral feature of effective behaviour by management researchers. Nevins and Hill (1962: 269–70) regarded his career as 'perhaps the most impressive and certainly the most spectacular of American industrial history', and wrote of Ford as being 'before 1915...on the whole an attractive figure', whose early idealism and ignorance caused him to suffer, harden and then inflict suffering in later life and in the face of powerfully changing times and cynical, spiteful and hurtful attacks and distortions from lesser people. It was only as a schoolboy that he thought that 'history is bunk'. As a mature man he expressed considerable respect for and interest in it, because he had grown to be so keen to retain and cherish what had been positive in his past.

5 Conclusion

The main elements of Ford's work were: (1) large-scale mechanization of a major, epoch-defining, industry; (2) large-scale vertical integration; (3) continually moving inventory; and (4) the worker as consumer, developing mass markets through mass production and high wages. Ford's work included the temporary culmination of many technical and commercial trends. The reactions to it that it provoked, in the form of more varied and more rational divisions of labour and forms of human resource management, in many organizations and sectors, were probably just as important as its direct ones of bringing motoring to the multitude and of developing mass affluence.

IAN GLOVER
UNIVERSITY OF STIRLING

Further reading

(References in the text marked*)

* Beynon, H. (1973) *Working for Ford*, London: Allen Lane. (A very critical account of assembly line work for Ford UK *c*.1970.)

Burlingame, R. (1949) *Backgrounds of Power: the Human Story of Mass Production*, London and New York: Charles Scribner's Sons. (Very wide-ranging and readable history of mass production which contains an invaluable account of what was original in Ford's achievements, and what was not.)

Burlingame, R. (1954) *Henry Ford*, New York: Knopf. (An excellent short biography.)

Chandler, A.D., Jr (1964) *Giant Enterprise: Ford, General Motors and the Automobile Industry*, New York: Harcourt, Brace and World. (A very useful collection of edited readings covering most aspects of Ford's history until the 1960s.)

* Chandler, A.D., Jr (1990) *Scale and Scope: The Dynamics of Industrial Capitalism*, Cambridge, MA: Belknap Press, Harvard University Press. (General account of growth of large-scale industry in the twentieth century with many useful references to Ford, including ones about Ford's activities in Germany and the UK.)

Dale, E. (1960) *The Great Organizers*, New York: McGraw-Hill. (On the development of systematic organization in American management, with useful references to the apparent lack of it at Ford.)

Ford, H. (1929) *My Philosophy of Industry*, London: Harrap. (Ninety short pages of often homespun, often original thoughts which need to be appraised with historical empathy. Foreword by Ronnie Lessem emphasizes Ford's visionary qualities.)

* Ford, H. (1991) *Ford on Management*, Oxford: Blackwell. (Contains material from Ford's *My Life and Work* and *My Philosophy of Industry*.)

* Ford, H. and Crowther, S. (1926) *My Life and Work*, New York: Doubleday. (Reprint of the 1922 work. Lively account, written by Crowther but relies on material from Ford and is widely regarded as authoritative.)

Ford, H. and Crowther, S. (1926) *Today and Tomorrow*, New York: Garden City. (Second of three accounts, written by Crowther but based on material from and inspired by Ford, on Ford's work and philosophy, which sold all over the world.)

Ford, H. and Crowther, S. (1931) *Moving Forward*, New York: Garden City. (Covers production, technology, management, wages and other issues, offering constructive and imaginative advice to business around the beginning of the inter-war Depression.)

* Galbraith, J.K. (1960) *The Liberal Hour*, New York: Hamish Hamilton. (Contains a coherent but not altogether convincing attack on 'the Ford myth', and other related essays.)

Gelderman, C.W. (1989) *Henry Ford: The Wayward Capitalist*, New York: St Martin's Press. (Comprehensive, respected biography.)

McKinlay, A. and Starkey, K. (1994) 'After Henry: continuity and change in the Ford Motor Company', *Business History* 36 (1): 184–206. (Briefly builds on and continues the story of Ford after the first Henry Ford and his grandson, the Henry in the title.)

Nevins, A. and Hill, F.E. (1954) *Ford: The Times, The Man, The Company*, New York: Charles Scribner's Sons. (Very detailed, authoritative overview.)

Nevins, A. and Hill, F.E. (1957) *Ford: Expansion and Challenge, 1925–1933*, New York: Charles Scribner's Sons. (Heavyweight, very detailed and wide-ranging, very well written, balanced classic account of Ford's heyday, expansion and first serious problems.)

*Nevins, A. and Hill, F.E. (1962) *Ford: Decline and Rebirth, 1933–1962*, New York: Charles Scribner's Sons. (Takes the story of Henry Ford and the Ford Motor Company from the 1930's Depression through the Second World War, Ford's death, and post-war recovery and expansion.)

Noble, D.W. (1981) *The Progressive Mind: 1890–1917*, Minneapolis, MN: Burgess. (Deals with the collective identity of middle class Americans in the years when Ford was establishing himself, paying specific attention to his values and influence.)

Rae, J.B. (1959) *American Automobile Manufacturers: The First Forty Years*, Philadelphia, PA: Chilton. (Covers the history of the industry's companies until the mid-1930s; contains a history of Ford and his company up until then, and includes many helpful comparisons with competitors.)

Rae, J.B. (1965) *The American Automobile: A Brief History*, Chicago, IL: University of Chicago Press. (Covers the industry from the 1890s to the 1960s; includes a balanced account of Ford's role.)

Sorensen, C.E. (1957) *Forty years with Ford*, London: Jonathan Cape. (Ford's tough production boss's vivid and ultimately sympathetic (and unwittingly self-revealing) account of 'What . . .Henry Ford [was] really like'.)

Starkey K. and McKinlay, A. (1990) 'Managing for Ford', *Sociology* 28 (4): 975–90. (How management in Ford became very autocratic around 1920, its history since then, and how it has recently been changing under pressure from foreign competition.)

Sward, K. (1948) *The Legend of Henry Ford*, New York: Rinehart. (Hostile account by a former Union of Automobile Workers organizer; a useful antidote to the hero-worship of Ford.)

Wik, R.M. (1972) *Henry Ford and Grass-Roots America*, Ann Arbor, MI: University of Michigan Press. (A catalogue of the fan letters sent to Ford, mainly by the US public.)

See also: HUMAN RESOURCE MANAGEMENT; OHNO, T.; PERSONNEL MANAGEMENT; TAYLOR F.W.

Related topics in the IEBM: ADVERTISING CAMPAIGNS; BIG BUSINESS AND CORPORATE CONTROL; BUSINESS HISTORY; CHANDLER, A. D.; JUST-IN-TIME PHILOSOPHIES; MANAGEMENT IN NORTH AMERICA; MANAGEMENT SCIENCE; MANUFACTURING SYSTEMS, DESIGN OF; MULTINATIONAL CORPORATIONS; SLOAN, A. P.; TOYODA FAMILY; VEBLEN, T. B.

Gilbreth, Frank Bunker (1868–1924) and Gilbreth, Lillian Evelyn Moller (1878–1972)

Gilbreth, Frank Bunker

Personal background

- born 7 July 1868 in Fairfield, Maine, USA
- family background of New England settlers, with strong Puritan and Pilgrim traditions
- on leaving school worked as a bricklayer's apprentice, learning the building industry trade, and set about devising means of saving wasteful labour; became a highly successful building contractor
- married Lillian Evelyn Moller in 1904
- from 1907 to 1913, collaborated with Taylor and Gantt in the development of 'scientific management', his contribution being in 'motion study'
- in 1912, opened his own consultancy business to concentrate on 'management engineering'
- died suddenly on 14 June 1924

Major works

Bricklaying System (1909)
Motion Study (1911)
Primer of Scientific Management (1912)
Fatigue Study (with Lillian M. Gilbreth) (1916)
Applied Motion Study (with Lillian M. Gilbreth) (1917)
Motion Study for the Handicapped (with Lillian M. Gilbreth) (1920)

Gilbreth, Lillian Evelyn Moller

Personal background

- born 24 May 1878 in Oakland, California, USA into a prosperous family of German extraction
- studied at the University of California
- married Frank Bunker Gilbreth in 1904
- completed doctoral thesis on *The Psychology of Management* in 1911
- joined her husband's management consultancy business in 1912, becoming a fully-fledged partner in the quest for 'the one best way to do work'
- on Frank Gilbreth's sudden death in June 1924, went in his place to the First International Management Congress in Prague
- continued running the business, extended her writing and lecturing and did volunteer work for various organizations
- received more than twenty honorary degrees and special commendations from universities and professional societies
- died 2 February 1972 at the age of ninety-three

Major works

The Psychology of Management (1914)
The Quest of the One Best Way: A Sketch of the Life of Frank Bunker Gilbreth (1924)
The Home-Maker and Her Job (1927)
Normal Lives for the Disabled (with Edna Yost) (1944)
Management in the Home: Happier Living through Saving Time and Energy (1954)

Summary

Frank Bunker Gilbreth (1868–1924) pioneered the field of 'motion study' and is recognized as one of the founders of 'scientific management'. His constant quest, and on marriage in partnership with his wife, was to eliminate waste by finding the 'one best way to do work'. Lillian M. Gilbreth (1878–1972), a teacher and industrial psychologist, was among the first to appreciate the need of good human relations in the workplace. She had a profound influence on her husband in alerting him to the dynamic aspects of management.

Together, they formed a most successful partnership, each complementing the other's abilities and experience. In their quest for the 'one best way', they studied task, worker, tools and working environment in 'scientific detail' to adjust and integrate them for highest productivity. The process charts and other techniques they devised remain essentially unchanged in modern systems analysis. They were also interested in the human aspect of industry and emphasized the need for training and worker involvement.

Lillian Gilbreth, after her husband's death in 1924, continued to run the business, lectured on management and on home economics at different universities and worked on applying motion study principles to help the handicapped. She also made time for voluntary work with local and national organizations. She has been called the 'First Lady of Management'.

1 Early lives

Frank Bunker Gilbreth

Gilbreth was born on 7 July 1868 in Fairfield, Maine, into a family deeply rooted in the strong Puritan and Pilgrim traditions of the New England settler. This background greatly influenced his character and outlook. His father died when he was 3 years old, but his mother spared no effort to give the children a good education and the best training available. Frank Gilbreth was educated at Phillips Academy, Andover, where his feeling for mechanics first appeared; and at the Rice Grammar School, Boston, where this developed into an interest in mathematics and

mechanical drawing. He succeeded in qualifying for entry to the Massachusetts Institute of Technology but decided instead to start work immediately after school.

At 17, he became a bricklayer's apprentice. His progress was rapid. He went, with great success, through trade after trade of the construction company in which he worked and took evening classes to complement his knowledge of the building industry. By the age of 27, he was chief superintendent of his employing company.

From the beginning, Gilbreth was struck by the waste involved in the methods and practices existing in the construction industry and he set out to eliminate or at least reduce it. He developed 'the best ways' of laying bricks and handling materials; of rigging scaffolding and training apprentices: generally improving methods, while lowering costs and paying higher wages.

In April 1895, Gilbreth decided to open his own contracting business in Boston, Massachusetts. Working on the basic principles of good workmanship and sound materials, he was successful from the start. His business quickly grew. Always a keen observer, he learnt a great deal from his client firms. His business journeys abroad kept him abreast of what was new outside the USA. He gradually moved from being the contractor carrying out the full job with his own plant and men to the construction consultant, advising the client on all aspects of the work required. As the business grew, he was able to run not only a busy New York office with branches throughout the USA but also a London office with contracts for the Admiralty and the War Office.

In October 1904, he married Lillian Evelyn Moller. Together, they became 'partners for life' in marriage and in a most successful working partnership, in which each was able to complement the other's knowledge, abilities and experience.

Lillian Evelyn Moller

Lillian Moller was born in Oakland, California on 24 May 1878, to one of the leading families in the town. After being tutored at home and attending public elementary and high schools in Oakland, she studied at the University of California, where she received a B.Litt. degree in 1900 and, later, a Master's degree in English, on a thesis on Ben Jonson's *Bartholomew Fair*. Studying for a doctorate, she took leave in 1903 to tour Europe. In Boston, prior to her departure, she met Frank Gilbreth, a cousin of her chaperon. They married in 1904.

2 Frank and Lillian Gilbreth: the partnership

From the outset, they were determined to work together but with a growing family (there were to be twelve children, six boys and six girls), Lillian's contribution to the joint enterprise was somewhat restricted in the early days. However, she worked at home in editing her husband's many publications and on her own researches where, the better to complement his field of knowledge, she took up the subject of industrial psychology.

Gilbreth became closely associated with Frederick W. Taylor (see TAYLOR, F.W.) in 1907. They admired each other's work and became firm allies in the development of scientific management. In *Primer of Scientific Management* (1912), Gilbreth answered some of the questions in the hundreds of letters Taylor was receiving from all over the world. The answers ranged from definition of terms to the laws of scientific management and their application; from the effect on the worker of scientific management to its relation to other lines of activity; and always extolled the virtues of 'scientific management' as a 'square deal' for both worker and employer (see ORGANIZATION BEHAVIOUR).

Taylor, on his side, admired Gilbreth's work, constantly quoting his work on bricklaying as an outstanding example of the principles he was seeking to popularize. Together, they came to England in 1910 on a formal visit to the Institution of Mechanical Engineers to put before them the concepts developed through 'scientific management'. However, the happy relationship ended, somewhat abruptly, in 1913. By then, the Gilbreths were established as management consultants. This development brought them into direct competition not with Taylor himself but with the circle of men round Taylor whom he assigned to firms who asked for his help. Taylor recommended one of these friends to a firm while Gilbreth was still there acting as a consultant. The Gilbreths were incensed. Relations between the two men cooled considerably and Lillian Gilbreth was to hold thereafter that Taylor 'was not a nice person'.

In his 'management engineering' consultancy, Gilbreth extended the application of motion study to the general field of manufacturing and turned his focus to the study of fatigue. He isolated 42 variables causing fatigue, 15 relating to the worker himself, fourteen to the surroundings and thirteen to the motions required for the job itself. He developed two techniques to study a movement in the required precision. He subdivided it into basic motions – such as search, select, lift, load, position and so on – which he called 'therbligs' (a variation on the spelling of Gilbreth) and he placed a large-faced clock calibrated in fractions of minutes in the field of vision of the camera as it filmed the worker. These two innovations enabled him to catch and time the smallest motion and was the beginning of his micromotion study.

Gilbreth also developed the 'cyclegraphic' technique by attaching small electric light bulbs to the hands or other moving parts of the worker. As the worker moved, the paths of lights appeared, giving the direction of all the movements made. The cyclegraph grew into the 'chronocyclegraph', where a flashing bulb showed acceleration and deceleration of movements by appearing on the screen as a series of dots and dashes.

As a major in the US Army in 1917, Gilbreth successfully applied his motion study methods to the training of recruits. He also applied them in work for the rehabilitation of the injured. In the article he wrote in December 1915 for the *Journal of the American Society of Mechanical Engineers* entitled 'Motion study for the crippled soldier', he explained how motion study could help the handicapped.

The Gilbreths knew that he had developed a heart condition during the War but this did not make him reduce his activities in any way.

He continued his very busy professional life. He went from factory to factory, installing time-saving systems; he wrote; he spoke at conferences and seminars; he worked in his laboratories at his home. The strain would have been tremendous. The end came suddenly. He died on 14 June 1924, just before he was due to sail for Europe.

Lillian Gilbreth was his active partner in all this work and together they published *Fatigue Study* (1916), *Applied Motion Study* (1917) and *Motion Study for the Handicapped* (1920). On marriage, she had changed the focus of her studies to psychology, the better to complement his work. In 1911, she produced a doctoral thesis on *The Psychology of Management* which was serialized in *The Industrial Engineering Magazine* in 1912–13 and published in book-form in 1914. The publishers, reflecting the times, insisted that she be listed by her initials only, to avoid indicating the author was a woman.

She lectured at the private laboratory in their home and at schools of engineering and business. She became a full working partner in the consultancy business. It was her special contribution to insist on the importance of good human relations and training in the workplace and she did much to humanize her husband's views and widen the outlook of their clients.

In her letter of 10 April 1925 to the Editor of *The National Cyclopedia of American Biography*, Lillian Gilbreth wrote about their work on motion study:

> When we started this work, we had at our command Mr Gilbreth's technical training, and his many years' experience through every stage from apprentice to contracting engineer in erecting buildings, dams and so forth, my own theoretical training in education and psychology and some practical experience in teaching. It is really impossible and it seems to me unnecessary, and I am sure that you will agree with this, to try to separate our work. If it is worth anything, it is as a demonstration of what can be done by a cooperation founded on mutual interests and desires, and a training on the one hand for leadership, in the case of

Mr Gilbreth, and on the other hand for 'tending' in my own case.
>
> (Urwick and Brech 1945: 126–7)

3 Lillian Gilbreth

The partnership ended dramatically. In June 1924, three days before he was due to leave for conferences in England and Czechoslovakia, Frank Gilbreth died in a telephone booth as he was calling Lillian to tell her of 'an idea I had about saving motions on packing those soapflakes for Lever Brothers' (Gilbreth and Carey 1949: 137).

On his death, she was left with eleven children (one had died) ranging in age from 2 to 19. Showing her indomitable spirit, she called a family conference and told them:

> I am going on that boat tomorrow, the one your father planned to take. He had the tickets. I am going to give those speeches for him in London and Prague, by jingo. I think that's the way your father wants it.
>
> (Gilbreth and Carey 1949: 236)

She was not long in redirecting her energies. Purdue University, where her husband had been a visiting lecturer, asked her on his death to take his place. This she did until 1935 when she was appointed Professor of Management, a chair she continued to occupy until 1948.

This pursuit was not her only activity. She started to use motion study to analyse work in the home, studies which she continued, on and off, for some twenty years. The results appeared from time to time in popular periodicals like *Good Housekeeping* and *Better Homes and Gardens* and in two major publications, *The Home-Maker and Her Job* (1927) and *Management in the Home* (1954). Apart from her work at Purdue University, she also acted as consultant to university departments on home economics, and here she exercised considerable influence on the development of home management courses throughout the country.

As an extension of her husband's work for disabled soldiers, Lillian Gilbreth used the techniques of motion study analysis to design special equipment and routines to make housework possible for handicapped people.

She reported this in *Normal Lives for the Disabled* (1944), co-authored by Edna Yost.

Lillian Gilbreth was extraordinarily energetic and public-spirited and responded wholeheartedly to all the calls that were made upon her. She became a member of the President's Emergency Committee for Unemployment Relief in 1930, an educational adviser during the Second World War and joined the Civil Defense Advisory Commission in 1951. She also found time to do volunteer work for the Girl Scouts of America, for various organizations helping the handicapped and for churches and libraries in her community.

Lillian Gilbreth continued her research work beyond the age of 70 and was in fact still lecturing and writing in her eighties. Honours were showered on her. In all, she received more than twenty honorary degrees and special commendations from professional societies. She has been called 'The First Lady of Management'. She died in 1972.

4 Contributions

Gilbreth's early work in the construction industry was original. He pioneered what became known as the 'Science of Motion Study'. He simplified the work of bricklaying so well that the eighteen motions thought necessary to place a brick were reduced to at most five, thus increasing the daily output per man, after some training and without additional strain, from 1,000 to 2,700 bricks. Through detailed analysis and study of the movements involved in the performance of operations and of the environment in which they were taking place, he laid the foundations of effective production management.

In due course, the Gilbreths also devised process charts to map out the flow of work as it moved through the shop. This technique and the various symbols used to show the various stages of the task remain essentially the same in modern systems analysis. The Gilbreths were as interested in understanding the psychological bases of organized human activity as they were in developing the physical 'one best way' to do a task.

To begin with, they enthusiastically promoted scientific management. In the *Primer of Scientific Management* (1912) Frank Gilbreth explains it in detail and supports it unreservedly. In *The Psychology of Management* (1914) Lillian Gilbreth distinguishes three types of management: traditional, transitory and scientific, this last type being 'a science, i.e., which operates according to known, formulated, and applied laws' (Gilbreth 1914: 8), this last being the one to aim for (see OCCUPATIONAL PSYCHOLOGY).

However, they had a more *inclusive* view of management than Taylor. Over time, they began to disagree with some of his methods, as for example that of secretly recording the workers' activities. They wanted to show the workers how to improve productivity not by working *faster*, but by working *better*; to show them not only *how* to change or improve their methods of work but also *why*.

Their interest in scientific management was but a part of their overall social vision to help individuals lead a fuller life. In *Cheaper by the Dozen* (the best-selling non-fiction book in 1949, later made into a film) his children, reminiscing about their home life, recorded that:

> Someone once asked Dad: 'But what do you want to save time *for*? What are you going to do with it?' 'For work, if you love that best,' said Dad. 'For education, for beauty, for art, for pleasure.' He looked over the top of his pince-nez. 'For mumblety-peg, if that's where your heart lies.'
> (Gilbreth and Carey 1949: 237)

5 Critique

'Motion study' has not been used in production management as much as the Gilbreths would have wished. Misunderstood, it has been suspected of being a means of controlling workers in their every movement. The battle lines between capital and labour were drawn in the decades (the 1920s to the 1940s) following the introduction of 'scientific management' and attempts to measure and standardize the workers' productivity brought trade union accusations of 'unfair labor practices' and of dehumanizing the workers (see TRADE UNIONS; INDUSTRIAL AND LABOUR RELATIONS). For this, perhaps the Gilbreths were partly responsible. By defining their search for 'the one best way', their work could be interpreted as seeking to robotize workers by limiting them to a strict sequence of steps in carrying out their tasks.

It cannot be denied, also, that specialization and shorter job cycles de-skill the worker. To some extent, Gilbreth himself in part recognized this by saying that, in any case, it should not cause the worker any unhappiness. More liberal than Taylor in his views, Gilbreth nevertheless, in his writings, treats the worker in the main as a fairly *static* factor.

Lillian Gilbreth, writing some fifty years later, could see the limitations of the early work of the pioneers:

> The people who started the scientific management movement did not have the advantage of an arts and letters background or training in philosophy, and they did not read or speak other languages fluently or travel a great deal. They were mechanical engineers, trained in the fashion of their time. They went into industry and devoted their lives to making the best use of their own and other people's time, energy and money. They did not realize that management was something that had come down through the ages and was being practiced in some form or other in every country in the world.

She was also able to recognize that her husband's work was not as unique as they had thought:

> As it turned out, many things which were done quite independently in the United States proved to have been done previously in other countries. For example, my husband found, after he spent a long time developing the cyclegraph method, that Marey had done it in France
>
> (Gilbreth 1963: 119)

Lillian Gilbreth herself, by inclination and training, understood the dynamic of relationships and the contribution that the workers could make, if involved and committed to the common task (see HUMAN RELATIONS). After her husband's death, and over time, she worked hard to promote the use of 'motion study'; and she also worked hard to bring about effective cooperation in the workplace.

PAULINE GRAHAM
UNIVERSITY OF BRADFORD

Further reading

(References cited in the text marked *)

Gilbreth, F.B. (1908) *Concrete System*, New York: Engineering News Publishing. (Detailed advice to concrete contractors on how best to direct the workers.)

Gilbreth, F.B. (1908) *Field System*, New York: Myron C. Clark Publishing. (An accounting system, without a set of books, for construction contractors to see weekly the total cost of the job.)

Gilbreth, F.B. (1909) *Bricklaying System*, New York: Myron C. Clark Publishing. (Technical book showing the best way of laying bricks through motion study.)

Gilbreth, F.B. (1911) *Motion Study*, New York: D. van Nostrand. (Shows how the efficiency of the worker can be improved using illustrations of motion study in bricklaying.)

* Gilbreth, F.B. (1912) *Primer of Scientific Management*, New York: D. van Nostrand. (Explains scientific management by means of questions and answers, with a foreword by Louis D. Brandeis.)

* Gilbreth, F.B. (1915) 'Motion study for the crippled soldier', *Journal of the American Society of Mechanical Engineers* 37: 669. (Shows how motion study can help the crippled soldier.)

* Gilbreth, F.B. and Gilbreth, L.M. (1916) *Fatigue Study*, New York: Sturgis & Walton. (A meticulous analysis of the variables that cause fatigue and the means to be used to avoid or reduce it.)

* Gilbreth, F.B. and Gilbreth, L.M. (1917) *Applied Motion Study*, New York: Sturgis & Walton. (Covers applications of motion study analysis.)

* Gilbreth, F.B. and Gilbreth, L.M. (1920) *Motion Study for the Handicapped*, New York: Macmillan. (Explains how motion study can be used to help the handicapped.)

Gilbreth, F.B., Jr (1970) *Time out for Happiness*, New York: Thomas Y. Crowell. (The third sequel of the Gilbreth story, this time written by F.B. Gilbreth on his own.)

* Gilbreth, F.B., Jr and Carey, E.G. (1949) *Cheaper by the Dozen*, New York: Thomas Y. Crowell. (Written by two of the Gilbreth children, this is an affectionate memoir of life in the Gilbreth household.)

Gilbreth, F.B., Jr and Carey, E.G. (1950) *Belles on Their Toes*, New York: Thomas Y. Crowell. (The sequel to *Cheaper by the Dozen*.)

* Gilbreth, L.M. (1914) *The Psychology of Management*, New York: Sturgis & Walton. (Analyses the different typologies of management.)

Gilbreth, L.M. (1924) *The Quest of the One Best Way: A Sketch of the Life of Frank Bunker Gilbreth*, Chicago, IL: Society of Industrial Engineers. (A reprint of Lillian Gilbreth's biography of her husband, republished in 1973 by Hive Publishing, Easton, PA.)

* Gilbreth, L.M. (1927) *The Home-Maker and Her Job*, New York: D. Appleton. (Shows how motion study can be used in the home for the highest efficiency.)

* Gilbreth, L.M. (1954) *Management in the Home: Happier Living through Saving Time and Energy*, New York: Dodd, Mead. (Applies scientific management principles and techniques to home management.)

* Gilbreth, L.M. (1963) 'Work and management', *Advanced Management Journal* September: 119. (Gilbreth's later reflections on the topic.)

* Gilbreth, L.M. and Yost, E. (1944) *Normal Lives for the Disabled*, NY: Appleton & Co. (Shows how, using motion study analysis, special equipment can be designed to help the disabled lead normal lives.)

Spriegel, W.R. and Meyers, C.E. (eds) (1953) *The Writings of the Gilbreths*, Homewood, IL: Irwin. (Comprehensive coverage of the writings of the Gilbreths.)

* Urwick L. and Brech, E.F.L. (1945) *The Making of Scientific Management: Thirteen Pioneers*, London: Management Publications Trust. (An overview of the early European and US pioneers in management thinking.)

Yost, E. (1949) *Frank and Lillian Gilbreth: Partners for Life*, New Brunswick, NJ: Rutgers University Press. (An affectionate biography of the Gilbreths, by a close friend of Lillian Gilbreth.)

See also: ORGANIZATION BEHAVIOUR; HUMAN RELATIONS; INDUSTRIAL AND LABOUR RELATIONS; OCCUPATIONAL PSYCHOLOGY; TAYLOR, F.W.; TRADE UNIONS

Related topics in the IEBM: ORGANIZATION BEHAVIOUR, HISTORY OF; SYSTEMS ANALYSIS AND DESIGN

Gouldner, Alvin W. (1920–80)

1 Gouldner's contribution to industrial sociology
2 Gouldner's approach to critical theory

Personal background

- born in New York City, 29 July 1920
- studied sociology at the University of Columbia, New York, 1943–7
- taught sociology at the University of Buffalo, New York, 1947–52
- obtained a doctorate from Columbia, 1952
- taught at the University of Antioch, Ohio, 1952–4
- Associate Professor in the Department of Sociology, University of Illinois, 1954–9
- appointed Max Weber Research Professor in Social Theory at Washington University, St Louis, 1959
- spent a year at the Center for Advanced Studies in the Behavioural Sciences, Palo Alto, 1961–2
- served as President of the Society for the Study of Social Problems, 1962
- received the Russell Sage Foundation Research Award, 1965–6
- appointed Professor of Sociology at the University of Amsterdam, 1969
- while in Europe, founded and edited the journal *Theory and Society*
- died 15 December 1980 in Madrid, aged 60

Major works

Studies in Leadership (ed.) (1950)
Patterns of Industrial Bureaucracy (1954a)
Wildcat Strike (1954b)
Applied Sociology: Opportunities and Problems (edited with S.M. Miller) (1965)
Enter Plato: Classical Greece and the Origins of Social Theory (1965)

The Coming Crisis of Western Sociology (1971)
For Sociology. Renewal and Critique in Sociology Today (1975)
The Dialectic of Ideology and Technology (1976)
The Future of Intellectuals and the Rise of the New Class (1979)
The Two Marxisms: Contradictions and Anomalies in the Development of Theory (1980)
Against Fragmentation. The Origins of Marxism and the Sociology of Intellectuals (1985)

Summary

Gouldner's formative training in the discipline of sociology took place at the University of Columbia, New York, where he came into contact with a teaching staff of the highest calibre including Robert Lynd, Robert MacIver, Charles Page, Paul Lazarsfeld and Robert Merton. With Merton he sustained a lifelong intellectual friendship. Before leaving Columbia he was to have research experience with members of the Frankfurt School in exile. He worked under the direction of Marie Jahoda, who was collaborating with Max Horkheimer and others on the Studies in Prejudice project, which was to develop the concept of 'the authoritarian personality'. He taught sociology for five years at the University of Buffalo and conducted fieldwork in the gypsum plant near by, work which formed the basis of his doctorate, which the examiners saw as a piece of original research and scholarship. It led to the publication of two books, *Patterns of Industrial Bureaucracy* and *Wildcat Strike*. Later, teaching at Illinois, he had special responsibility for the teaching of social theory thus, in effect, succeeding the great cultural theorist, Florian Znaniecki. *Theory and Society*, the journal he founded and edited while living in Europe, quickly and deservedly established an international reputation for the high quality of its contributions to social theory.

1 Gouldner's contribution to industrial sociology

Alvin Gouldner was a US sociologist in the radical tradition of Thorstein Veblen, Robert Lynd and C. Wright Mills. His political radicalism expressed itself in membership of the Communist Party in the USA for a short time in the 1940s but he was scarcely cut out to be a Party man. By the end of his life he called himself an Marxist outlaw. His early contacts with members of the Frankfurt School were important. As late as 1976, in *The Dialectic of Ideology and Technology*, he was giving serious but not uncritical attention to the work of the School, especially their treatment of the mass media and the cultural apparatus in capitalist societies. Even so, his own intellectual orientation was shaped by significant non-Marxist sources. Mannheim's influence is plain and acknowledged and has to be negotiated in any discussion of the role of the intelligentsia. Weber is there and announced from the beginning of his work in industrial sociology. Merton, although it was not always realized at the time, was there as guide, mentor and friendly critic and the lifelong correspondence that took place between them is both moving and revealing. Merton thought very highly of Gouldner's 1959 essay 'Reciprocity and autonomy in functional theory' (reproduced in *For Sociology* 1975). Although not persuaded by it, Gouldner also found the work of Talcott Parsons a challenge. Thus it was that a great part of *The Coming Crisis of Western Sociology* (1971) involved a critical exposition of Parsons' work since its functionalism represented the dominant sociological paradigm of the 1950s and 1960s in the USA.

2 Gouldner's approach to critical theory

Patterns of Industrial Bureaucracy, published in 1954, is widely recognized as a classic of industrial sociology. Gouldner used Weber's ideal type approach to the study of bureaucracy whilst showing originality in reformulating the typology in the light of his research experience. Thus he distinguishes between punishment-centred, representative and 'mock' bureaucracy as he seeks to show how and why rules are sometimes obeyed and sometimes not. He shows how the succession from one plant manager to another, in the context of wider changes in the market, led to changes in the nature of rule making and enforcement from an indulgency to a stringency pattern. This allowed him to give central consideration to the ways in which the legitimacy of managerial behaviour in relation to employees came to be seriously questioned and of the ways in which this was reinforced by the nature of the local community. The changing expectations and conflicts to which this gave rise were further explored in *Wildcat Strike* (1954b), a subject which he sought to elucidate within a general theory of group tensions (see INDUSTRIAL CONFLICT). This kind of theorizing he saw as a strategic bridge between 'pure' and 'applied' sociology. If the first was concerned with prediction and understanding the second was seen as a guide for action in time of trouble. There is, in *Patterns of Industrial Bureaucracy* a valuable appendix on fieldwork procedures which gives us a clue to the exercise of the sociological imagination in ways in which Wright Mills would most certainly have approved. It shows how theory and method can come together in research practice. There was a value concern written in to this work, namely, how far can we move to more representative forms of bureaucracy in modern industry, and thus to industrial democracy. In this Gouldner was resisting what he was to term 'metaphysical pathos' in Weber's treatment of bureaucracy and Michel's 'iron law of oligarchy' (see ORGANIZATION BEHAVIOUR).

Gouldner returned to the relation between pure and applied sociology in the course of a very different study, *Enter Plato*, published in 1965. There he explored different kinds of knowledge – knowledge for its own sake contrasted with technical knowledge – and the significance of the dialectical method in approaching and critiquing truth claims. In particular, he examined the adequacy of Plato's approach to planned social change. Gouldner argued that sociologists today have to balance optimism and pessimism within themselves when approaching social problems. They should be aware of their own limitations while doing all they can to relieve human suffering, without glossing over the difficulties. Sociologists should, nevertheless, play with, formulate and entertain various solutions to social problems rather than simply describe and explain them:

> They need a constructive quality of the imagination which can sense what might be. If some of their proposals turn out to be extravagant, needless, wasteful, outrageous, or even utopian, no one needs to buy them: but let them be freely available on the market place of ideas – rather than be self-inhibited – where they can be compared with the shopworn social worlds that are presently up for sale.
>
> (Gouldner 1965: 295–6)

Gouldner saw sociology as having both a repressive and a liberating potential. *The Coming Crisis of Western Sociology*, published in 1971, was a fierce attack on the practice of sociology in the USA and the former Soviet Union, which, in both cases, albeit for different reasons and in different ways, had become repressive. But there was one similarity: they were both grounded in functionalist theories of the social system. Sociologists became integrated into the liberal establishment of US welfarism or into the state Marxism of the Soviet Union and in each case lost their critical independence. Appearing to be neutral, they were in practice acting in ways which were supportive of the status quo. Gouldner argued for the development of what he termed a reflexive sociology. This involved examining the domain assumptions and sentiments on which theories are grounded, including our own, and being seriously prepared to amend work in the face of hostile information (rather than ignore or smother it). Such an emancipatory sociology could not just return to 'pure' sociology since it was now 'in' the world and not 'above' it, but it had to be historically sensitive. We have to be prepared to see the ways in which

yesterday's good news, say of Freudianism, the scientific revolution or Marxism, can become part of today's bad news, the dark side of the dialectic. This study, reminiscent in some ways of Wright Mills' *The Power Elite* (1956) and *The Sociological Imagination* (1959), attracted a barrage of criticism from some of his US colleagues.

Gouldner did not flinch from contest and controversy. This is memorably captured in the book of essays *For Sociology* (1975). The advocacy of the title was itself a side-swipe at Althusser's *For Marx* (1969). Unlike Althusser, who dealt in ahistorical analysis with no place for agency, Gouldner was preoccupied with the relationship between agency and structure, constraint and human action, and sought to apprehend ways in which human beings could recover their own society and culture (see CULTURE). In this collection are included an extended reply to critics of *The Coming Crisis*; 'The politics of the mind', a much published and cited essay on value-freedom; 'Anti-minotaur: the myth of a value-free sociology'; and 'The sociologist as partisan: sociology and the welfare state'. This last was a response to Howard Becker's Presidential Address to the Society for the Study of Social Problems, 'Whose side are we on?'. First published in 1968 it can be seen as a forerunner to *The Coming Crisis*. His interest in the relationship between sociology and Marxism is evident in part three of the book. In particular, 'The two Marxisms' gives us a sense of the argument to be taken up in great detail in the book of that title. He is concerned to distinguish between scientific and critical Marxism and is unconvinced by the first and not finally satisfied by the second (Gouldner 1980).

It is significant that the book ends with a chapter entitled 'Nightmare Marxism'. Every theoretical system, he argued, has another system inside struggling to get out. The nightmare is that the caged system will break out. In the case of Marxism the nightmare is that it is just another religion of the oppressed:

> In the nightmare, socialism does not mean that the proletariat becomes the ruling class, but that the state becomes the dominant force; this new collectivist state

brings a new stagnation to the economy, rather than a new productivity; . . . the expropriation of the bourgeoisie is not the basis of a new emancipation, but of a new, many times worse domination.

(Gouldner 1980: 382)

Since the nightmare had become reality in some forms of existing socialism, and especially Stalinism, Gouldner recognized that Marxism itself not only had to be seen as a critique of bourgeois societies but itself had to be open to critique. It also had to be demystified by showing the limits of Marxist consciousness. This, after all, is part of the practice of the dialectic and the exercise of reflexivity. It helps to explain why he advocated the development of a culture of critical discourse in which there is nothing in principle that speakers will permanently refuse to discuss or make problematic. This is treated extensively in *The Dialectic of Ideology and Technology* (1976) and *The Future of Intellectuals and the Rise of the New Class* (1979). No system can capture this kind of critical thinking as it seeks, in an open-ended way, to understand itself and the world.

JOHN ELDRIDGE
UNIVERSITY OF GLASGOW

Further reading

(References cited in the text marked *)

* Althusser, L. (1969) *For Marx*, London: Allen Lane. (Offers a version of Marxist structuralism that severely plays down the role of agency in social explanation.)

Burawoy, M. (1982) 'The written and the repressed in Gouldner's industrial sociology', *Theory and Society* 11: 831–51. (Excellent overview of Gouldner's sociology; crisp and true.)

Gouldner, A.W. (ed.) (1950) *Studies in Leadership*, New York: Harper & Row. (One of the first, and still best, studies of leadership.)

* Gouldner, A.W. (1954a) *Patterns of Industrial Bureaucracy*, Glencoe, IL: The Free Press. (Groundbreaking study of the ways in which a US gypsum mine changed its social organization and the consequences for social relations in the plant and community.)

* Gouldner, A.W. (1954b) *Wildcat Strike*, New York: Antioch Press. (Much-cited case study of

a US gypsum mine. A companion volume to *Patterns of Industrial Bureaucracy*.)

* Gouldner, A.W. (1965) *Enter Plato: Classical Greece and the Origins of Social Theory*, London: Routledge & Kegan Paul. (Study offering a sociological account of the structure and culture of ancient Greece. Covers the continuing significance of the Socratic method for critical theory.)

* Gouldner, A.W. (1971) *The Coming Crisis of Western Sociology*, London: Routledge & Kegan Paul. (Account of the state of sociology in the USA and former Soviet Union. Critiques the functionalist orientation and advocates a reflexive sociology.)

* Gouldner, A.W. (1975) *For Sociology. Renewal and Critique in Sociology Today*, Harmondsworth: Penguin. (A collection of essays on themes related to sociological and Marxist theory, with contributions to the value debate in sociology.)

* Gouldner, A.W. (1976) *The Dialectic of Ideology and Technology*, London: Macmillan. (A study about ideology as a form of discourse, with a valuable discussion on the communications revolution.)

* Gouldner, A.W. (1979) *The Future of Intellectuals and the Rise of the New Class*, London: Macmillan. (Discussion of the role of intellectuals and technical intelligentsia in the modern world, and in what sense they constitute a new class.)

* Gouldner, A.W. (1980) *The Two Marxisms: Contradictions and Anomalies in the Development of Theory*, London: Macmillan. (Review of the varieties of Marxism and their role in the development of social theory. Pivots on the distinction between 'scientific' and 'critical' Marxism.)

Gouldner, A.W. (1985) *Against Fragmentation. The Origins of Marxism and the Sociology of Intellectuals*, Oxford: Oxford University Press. (Posthumous publication developing themes discussed in *The Future of Intellectuals* and *The Two Marxisms*.)

Gouldner, A.W. and Miller, S.M. (1965) *Applied Sociology: Opportunities and Problems*, New York: The Free Press. (Basic textbook covering the fundamentals of sociology.)

Jay, M. (1982) 'For Gouldner: reflections on an outlaw Marxist', *Theory and Society* 11: 759–78. (Sophisticated discussion of Gouldner's critical theory.)

Lemert, C. and Piccone, P. (1982) 'Gouldner's theoretical method and reflexive sociology', *Theory and Society* 11: 733–57 (Thoughtful account of Gouldner's approach to the relationship between theory and method in sociology.)

Merton, R.K. (1982) 'Alvin W. Gouldner: genesis and growth of a friendship', *Theory and Society* 11: 915–38. (Account of his lifelong intellectual debates and correspondence with his former student.)

* Wright Mills, C. (1956) *The Power Elite*, New York: Oxford University Press. (A study of the role of elites, especially political, military and economic, in the mid-twentieth century, within the framework of mass society theory.)

* Wright Mills, C. (1959) *The Sociological Imagination*, New York: Oxford University Press. (A critical discussion of the state of US sociology in the mid-twentieth century and a claim that sociology should be grounded in historical and comparative study.)

See also: CULTURE; INDUSTRIAL CONFLICT; ORGANIZATION BEHAVIOUR

Related topics in the IEBM: MARX, K.H.; MICHELS, R.; ORGANIZATION PARADIGMS; ORGANIZATION TYPES; VEBLEN, T.B.; WEBER, M.

Herzberg, Frederick (1923–)

Personal background

- born 18 April 1923, USA
- trained first in psychology, he studied mental health in the industrial world
- his research focused on human motivation in the work situation, its effects on the individual's satisfaction at work and on mental health
- extremely influenced by his Judaeo-Christian roots, which explains his frequent and lengthy references to the Bible
- Professor of Management at a Utah University
- gained an international reputation and was a well-known consultant in the 1960s and 1970s

Major works

The Motivation to Work (with B. Mausner and B. Snyderman) (1959)
Work and the Nature of Man (1966)

Summary

Frederick Herzberg, psychologist by training and a university professor, studied motivation at work in companies where he was also involved as a consultant. His theory of motivation at work, also called 'actualization–atmosphere' factors, is based on the hierarchical human needs approach, as well as on the study of the great biblical myths of Adam and Abraham. The actualization factors are work and all forms of gratitude achieved through work. Acting upon these factors allows one to modify individual behaviour at work in a deep and long-lasting manner. The atmosphere factors are remuneration, job security, management policy in the company and relations between colleagues. Acting on these factors only gives temporary satisfaction and does not modify behaviour on a long-term basis. The implicit hypothesis in Herzberg's work – that a person should grow through their work – and its applications in the organization of companies had considerable success in the 1970s. The management of companies puts in place policies of job enrichment and enlargement of tasks, polyvalency and job rotation, of which he was the instigator. He criticized the idea of the individual at work, central to Taylorism. Today, society has considerably evolved, and his arguments seem very far from contemporary preoccupations, which underlines even more the theoretical weaknesses in his hypothesis.

1 Theoretical foundations

Frederick Herzberg is a social psychologist who deals specifically with the field of work and the company (see OCCUPATIONAL PSYCHOLOGY; ORGANIZATION BEHAVIOUR). His work is inspired by the theory of human needs: he finds the source both in psychology and Darwinism, and also in great Christian myths. Psychology and the comparison of humans with animals taught him that the human organism is comparable to the animal's in so far as they must both submit to their needs. For humans, however, the needs are in hierarchical order: at the top lies the need of self-accomplishment which can be achieved through work. On the other hand, the study of certain great Judaeo-Christian myths shows that they express motivations common to all humanity.

The myth of Adam tells us that the first man was created with all the attributes of perfection, but that God chased him from

Paradise on Earth when he ate the fruit from the tree of knowledge:

> Two thousand years of teaching convinced multitudes that when Adam was thrown out of Paradise, humanity was condemned, perverted, chained to a life of suffering. From that notion of human guilt, life has to be expiated by the suffering of the fall of Adam. His first aim is, therefore, to escape the multiple situations which generate pain, which he encounters in his new world of alienation.
>
> (Herzberg 1966: chapter 2)

There is, therefore, in every human an aspiration to flee the pains of this world. One can see it in the world of work, when the individual seeks to improve their work conditions. But this improvement does not correspond to the dynamic approach of the individual at work and does not satisfy the need for fulfilment and self-realization.

The second myth, expressing a universal vision of man, is that of Abraham. This perspective is radically different. Herzberg recalls the passage from the Bible in which God promises Abraham descendants as innumerable as the grains of sand by the sea, as long as Adam obeys Him, and rises and travels to the Promised Land. Herzberg's lesson: 'The second definition of man, as explained by Abraham, is that man is a resourceful being, has received inborn virtualities, such that God has chosen him to be His emissary here on earth' (Herzberg 1966: chapter 2). This is a dynamic and positive perspective, where man is considered a being full of potential who needs help in accomplishing his goal.

The biblical myth teaches us that two co-existing natures in man correspond to two outlooks on humanity. The first one is the pessimistic tradition of human nature, eighteenth century Jansenism, where man is first and foremost subjected to the consequences of his original sin. He needs to be supervised and guided, he seeks protection from the pain caused by the environment he has been in since his fall – 'you'll earn your bread with the sweat of your brow', the valley of tears where the man's days drift away awaiting death. The other outlook, an optimistic one, is where man, having been created in the image of God, is a being full of virtue and resources, so long as he is given the power to exercise them.

2 The application in the world of work

These myths, transposed into the world of work, are interpreted as an escape from the suffering and the aspiration to grow. The motivation at work must rely on the second tendency (see MOTIVATION AND SATISFACTION; WORK ETHIC). Herzberg finds confirmation of the second theory of motivation in several empirical inquiries that he directed. These allowed him to discover and define the factors of satisfaction or discontent at work. The first ones – the satisfaction factors – correspond to Abraham's nature and are called actualization factors. The second ones – the factors of discontent – are called atmosphere or 'hygiene' factors and correspond to Adam's nature. There are five actualization factors: achievement, recognition for achievement, work itself, responsibility, and the possibility of development or growth. Atmosphere factors are more numerous: management policy in the company, management (its qualities and defects), remuneration, work conditions, relations between people (management, employees, equals), prestige, job security, factors from personal life (when work affects one's personal life, like a transfer to a new place.)

Actualization factors provide individuals with a sense of long-term satisfaction. Carrying out tasks which lead to accomplishment at work (and not to humdrum and uninteresting work), recognizing the work accomplished, changing the job itself, being given responsibility at work – all these actions lead to long-term and positive changes in attitude because they rely on Abraham's nature, the only one capable of encouraging motivation. Atmosphere factors such as rising salaries, changing management, altering the management of personnel, improving work conditions, job guarantee, acting upon relations between people, however, all tend towards a decline in tension, which may be significant but their influence is only temporary and does not modify in-depth behaviour.

In order to confirm the theoretical foundations and generalize the applications of such factors, Herzberg relies on the results of his empirical enquiries, carried out in companies around the world (the USA; industrial, rural, and hospital environments; all professional categories in Europe, Finland and Hungary). When he asks individuals to recall their best and worst memories, they always remember positively actions concerning actualization factors ('I had a more interesting job', or 'My boss congratulated me on this job') and remember negatively actions concerning atmosphere factors ('I had a rise in salary, it's better, but it does not correspond at all to what the company could have done', etc).

Two of Herzberg's examples remain famous. The first concerns the work organization of secretaries at the Bell Telephone Company. These secretaries had to answer the letters from the shareholders of the company. The results were programmed according to pre-established formulas and verified twice by supervisors. The morale of the secretaries was low, absenteeism high and errors numerous. Several atmosphere factors (rise in salary, changes and development of hierarchies, planning of the work environment) failed to change anything. The organization of work was changed. Each secretary was put in charge of a specific area, where they became an expert, and in which they advised their colleagues. Supervision was reduced. Each wrote and signed the letters themselves. Among themselves they organized the workload for the day. After a decline in productivity in the first weeks, there was a considerable rise in productivity and a level of response quality never reached before.

The other example is the installation of telephone lines at the same Bell Telephone Company. As before, work for the same client was divided between several departments: departments for orders, connection and installation, and of verification. The overall outfit did not work well, with delays and mediocre quality. All tasks were then merged, one person being in charge of the ordering, connection, verification and ultimate contacts with the client. The results were phenomenal in terms of productivity, quality and employee satisfaction.

3 Changes introduced in the company

In terms of personnel management policies in companies, the influence of Frederick Herzberg's theories was important and was followed by immediate effects, although these differed from country to country (see HUMAN RESOURCE MANAGEMENT; HUMAN RESOURCE MANAGEMENT, INTERNATIONAL).

There is no doubt that managerial policies on task enrichment and enlargement, as well as policies on job rotation which expanded rapidly in the 1960s and 1970s, owe much to Herzberg. The ideas which had prevailed until then on human nature and human needs at work were those of Taylorism and Fordism, where individuals at work demanded high salaries that ensured them a standard of living which previous generations could not even have imagined (see FORD, H.; TAYLOR, F.W.). Following that idea, the nature of work took second place to the preoccupations of managers. The fact that workers asked for a high salary so that their essential needs were more or less met acknowledged the assumption that they could work without being interested in the work itself – which is what Taylorism results in when the workload is organized by the manager and not by the workers. The disastrous consequences of this vision of the organization of work came at the time Herzberg was carrying out his research. After the boom of the post-war years, the period between the second half of the 1960s and the beginning of the 1980s was the time when disaffection with work and the rejection of unskilled work appeared to be important developments in the world of work. In a number of large companies in all the industrialized countries, the results were the same: the absenteeism rate among unskilled workers reached an all-time high, a lack of concern for quality sometimes stretched as far as sabotage, and there was a rejection of work due to lack of interest. All these factors became important concerns for managers and politicians. Movements like those of the hippies of the West Coast of the USA, or those of 1968 in Europe, appeared to threaten the society built on industrial order. Métro, boulot, dodo (tube, work, sleep) the famous French slogan of the student revolution of 1968, illustrates the rejection of a society which is supposed to confer well-being but which alienates those who serve it.

Several explanations for this crisis seem plausible. For instance, the absence of any consideration of the fundamental needs of human nature, the dislike of hard working conditions, the rejection of constraints linked to industrial production, are all explanations given in Herzberg's works. Many managers, political figures and trade union officials accepted this explanation and sought remedies at this level, introducing changes in the policies of government in industrialized countries to improve work conditions. Meanwhile many companies instigated concrete reforms, especially for unskilled or semi-skilled workers in large firms.

Two theoretical movements guided these changes. The first one can be directly linked to the works of Herzberg, as mentioned above – and is concerned with task enrichment and enlargement, and with job rotation. If the rejection of work comes from the fact that the job is not interesting, all possible measures must be taken to change the situation. Increasing the responsibility of those who supervise machinery, allowing them to carry out extra tasks, such as minor adjustments, maintenance, cleaning or customer despatch – by identifying the team or the worker in charge of that task – implementing job rotation between workers instead of the same people always doing the same job, all are designed to make work more attractive and to motivate the workers. This can be carried over to office work. The main point is to re-examine work stations and work content in order to give employees responsibilities, which Taylor's over-emphasized division of work removed.

The success of the application of Herzberg's theory of motivation cannot be understood without considering the contribution from another theoretical movement,

which consolidates these principles and adds nuances. This is the sociocultural movement which was based on the pioneer works of the Tavistock Institute of London. These had started before the Second World War and were orientated towards psychology and psychoanalysis. The main idea developed in this group was that, in order to modify individual behaviour, one must act on the group (see GROUPS AND TEAMS). Members of a small work group, when given autonomy and confidence in its own organization, will behave more productively than under the old system. Work in small self-organized groups is much superior to the traditional model of work organized and run by a hierarchy. This idea is translated into practice by the introduction of semi-autonomous groups.

In 1950, a famous experiment on work organization in coal mines was interpreted as the demonstration of the importance of the connection between the type of work and the organization of that work (Trist and Bamforth 1951). In certain technical conditions, the organization of specialized tasks discouraged people. Morale and collective output were considerably improved by giving teams of miners more autonomy in the organization of their work, by creating semi-autonomous groups. Spectacular results were obtained in connection with clocking-in, absenteeism and work accidents. Other experiments confirm these results. The idea of the semi-autonomous group was very successful, at a time when the influence of Herzberg's ideas was expanding. The influence of these two currents became conjoined.

The two theories have in common the principle of behaviour dictated by the individual – either the individual themselves, as in Herzberg, or the influence of the group on the individual, as in the movements that have grown from the work of the Tavistock Institute. The reforms introduced into companies as a result of these movements almost always combine work enrichment and enlargement with autonomous or semi-autonomous groups.

4 The great reforms

In line with Herzberg and the Tavistock group, a certain number of steps were taken following the difficulties experienced by companies and industrial society. Some of the most famous cases are discussed below.

First are the changes introduced by the Volvo factories in Kalmar, Sweden, at the beginning of the 1970s. Following the development of a bad social climate, which translated into a very high absenteeism rate in the assembly workshop and a lack of quality that damaged Volvo's brand image and thus the sales of its cars, the management decided to remove the assembly line for cars and to replace it with production organized by units. Car parts were brought to the reduced workshops, where a team of workers was in charge of the assembly. This team (the same size as the old one) organized itself to share out the work, carry it out in the given time and control the quality. The job was thus expanded and enriched, and the workers gained versatility. They received extra training for their new maintenance and control tasks, as well as gaining the experience of teamwork. The results were extremely positive according to those involved – employees, management and trade unions. There was a better social climate, a significant fall in absenteeism, and a spectacular rise in quality. Its success attracted observers from around the world.

Many other measures were taken at the same time in other European countries, often by governmental and official bodies. In Germany, the *Humanisierung der Arbeit* programme, launched at the beginning of the 1970s by the Social Democratic government, carried out important research and encouraged changes in German factories similar to those at Volvo. These changes centred on the reorganization of the job, in accord with Herzberg's theories mentioned above. In France, in 1974, the government created *l'Agence Nationale pour l'Amélioration des Conditions de Travail* to encourage social innovations and to launch research programmes. Many innovations aimed at improvement of the conditions and organization of work in companies were encouraged, followed through and later given as examples in publications circulated by the agency.

It seems that the movement was less important in the UK, for reasons such as the long history of industrialization, the absence of sociopolitical upheaval which was important in countries like Germany and France, and especially the emphasis given to professional abilities and skilled workers. The result was the constant presence of a high degree of autonomy and control within workshops. Nevertheless, many new forms of work organization were introduced in UK companies, in the shape of enriched and enlarged work and autonomous groups. Traces of this are found in two reports: the Donovan Report, *Report of the Royal Commission on Trade Unions and Employers' Associations* (1968), which centred especially on changes in professional relations; and the Bullock Report, *Report of the Committee of Inquiry on Industrial Democracy* (1977), which was orientated more towards the idea of industrial democracy (see INDUSTRIAL AND LABOUR RELATIONS; INDUSTRIAL DEMOCRACY).

In the USA it seems the movement was slowed down because of the tradition of collective bargaining, in which trade union officials and management negotiate on a basis of rules which are supposed to be unchangeable, or very difficult to alter (such as the seniority rule and job descriptions) and which make the workers feel they own their work rights, so to speak (see COLLECTIVE BARGAINING). New reforms in the organization of work were introduced by management, not without great resistance from trade unions. Quantitative evaluation is difficult, but Herzberg's homeland did not value his ideas as highly as did other nations.

In sum, Herzberg's ideas contributed to the launch of an important movement in favour of work reorganization and changes within companies and in industrial relations in most of the industrialized countries which operated on the Taylor/Ford system of the division of labour and offered a limited outlook on the idea of people at work, their motivations and their expectations.

5 Twenty years later

Re-reading Herzberg's written work 20 years on and re-evaluating the impact of the reforms initiated by his theories, one is struck by the gap between the problems of that period and the problems today, and by the fate of the changes he promulgated. What is also striking is the compartmentalization of the world of ideas. At a time when Herzberg's ideas were triumphing in the world of management and industrial relations, the great theoretical movements which were to impose themselves in later years (the analysis of organizations in particular) were entirely ignored by supporters of Herzberg's theories.

The undoubted contribution of Herzberg is his rejection of the basic ideas of Taylor and Ford on human nature, ideas which had previously prevailed. 'Good' salaries, given by the management to workers, seemed to be a sufficient reason to make them accept the job, and the work conditions, and to sufficiently motivate them to work. Against that, Herzberg reminded us strongly that the worker is motivated by his interest in what he does and by his involvement in work, that he is not a machine, and that he tolerates with great difficulty an organization which distances itself from his work. Herzberg made possible a new way of thinking about the work itself and the organization of that work as a function of the interest workers or employees have in what they do – and not as a function of the salary alone. He reminded managers that the worker and the employee can be interested in their work. A late piece of evidence, perhaps, but an important one.

Another contribution made by Herzberg is in the modification of the division of labour and the omnipotent power of overall command management. Autonomy was given back to specialized and less-qualified workers. So, beyond work conditions as such, the organization of work itself was rethought. Giving the workers more room to organize, through machine control and maintenance, was a way of weakening the traditional division of labour, of ending the slogan 'work and shut up' of Taylor – and of rethinking the radical division of labour which prevailed until then. In this sense, Herzberg was the instigator of more flexible, supple organizations, and of network companies as we know them today.

Despite all this, Herzberg's theories appear very remote from today's analysis of work behaviour. There are several reasons for this. The first is the theoretical weakness in his argument – especially in his theory about needs. That the individual has needs is a way of presenting human nature in an acceptable form. What is not acceptable is the hierarchy of these needs, regardless of the work situation and discussion of the actual individual. Herzberg introduces a behavioural determination which removes all freedom from the individual. In order to achieve this, he adopts an implicit hypothesis whereby man must fulfil himself through work – his book could have been entitled 'Work is the nature of man', replacing 'and' by 'is'. This implicit assumption was never demonstrated or proved by him, and neither has anybody subsequently managed to offer sufficient proof that fulfilment through work is a universal and permanent motivation. Every individual chooses their own path to self-fulfilment, but that path can change course throughout a lifetime and nobody but the person involved is able to know how. Furthermore, there are a thousand forms of fulfilment at work: for example, strikes, sabotage and industrial action. Absenteeism is another form of behaviour where the individual prefers other options to work, even if it is interesting. The theory of needs has limits in its universal claim to explain human behaviour beyond specific situations and individual judgements.

When one analyses Herzberg's experiments closely, one can see that he essentially concentrated on the reorganization of work. His advice was to propose a better organization, a simplification of the communication structure. A good consultant in an organization would have probably come to the same conclusions. That the new form of organization makes some individuals momentarily 'happier' in their work, and shows an improvement in productivity, does not demonstrate the validity of the theory of needs. All organizational changes seen as managerial action in favour of the employees are always greeted well by them. Fulfilment of oneself is not the point. But this is what Herzberg tried to demonstrate, with his biblical references. Man is fulfilled by developing his creative abilities and work is the ideal place for human fulfilment, according to Herzberg. This argument, central to Herzberg's theory, is what makes it weak.

Unemployment and the precarious situation of today's industrial world has radically changed things since Herzberg's time. This makes his arguments remote from today's problems and renders his work obsolete. The outdated character of his argument does not come from the socio-economic context, but from the weaknesses in his theoretical foundations. Nobody, today, supports seriously his theory of needs. A theory which lasts is a theory whose basic elements are solid enough to acknowledge reality, even years after it was formulated.

Since Frederick Herzberg, theories on work motivation have leant more towards the idea of work satisfaction rather than company incentives, where motivations seem to be linked to organizational structure rather than to human nature. The most progressive work has been that of March and Simon (1958) and after that the work of Aoki (1984), or with a more managerial perspective, the works of Mintzberg, especially his *The Structuring of Organizations*.

PHILIPPE BERNOUX
UNIVERSITÉ LUMIÈRE LYON II

Further reading

(References cited in the text marked *)

* Aoki, M. (1984) *The Co-operative Game Theory of the Firm*. Oxford: Clarendon Press.

* Bullock Committee (1977) *Report of the Committee of Inquiry on Industrial Democracy*, London: HMSO.
* Donovan Commission (1968) *Report of the Royal Commission on Trade Unions and Employers' Associations*, London: HMSO.
  Herzberg, F. (1959) *Managerial Choice: To Be Efficient and To Be Human*, New York: Dow-Jones Irwin.
* Herzberg, F. (1966) *Work and the Nature of Man*, Cleveland, OH: The World Publishing Company. (Herzberg's main work in which he exposes his theory of needs and the biblical roots in his 'actualization–atmosphere' theory.)
  Herzberg, F., Mausner, B. and Snyderman, B. (1959) *The Motivation to Work* New York: Wiley. (Presentation of his enquiry into the feelings humans have towards their work. This enquiry led to his theory put forward in *Work and the Nature of Man*.)
  Grootings, P., Gustavsen, B. and Hethy, L. (eds) (1989) *New Forms of Work Organization in Europe*, New Brunswick, NJ, and Oxford: Transaction Publishers. (Presentation and critical analysis of the main changes in the organization of work in European countries, whether influenced by Herzberg or not.)
* March, J.G. and Simon, R.M. (1958) *Organizations*. New York: Wiley.
* Mintzberg, H. (1979) *The Structuring of Organizations*. Englewood Cliffs, NJ: Prentice-Hall. (The first, now famous, book by Mintzberg.)
  Paul, W.J., Jr, Robertson, K.B. and Herzberg, F. (1969) 'Job enrichment pays off', *Harvard Business Review* 47: 61–78.
* Trist, E.L. and Bamforth, K.W. (1951) 'Some social and psychological consequences of the longwall method of coal-getting', *Human Relations* 4 (1): 6–24, 37–8. (Report of the famous 1950 experiment, demonstrating the connection between the type of work and the organization of that work.)

See also: HUMAN RELATIONS; MAYO, G.E.; MOTIVATION AND SATISFACTION; TAYLOR, F.W.

Related topics in the IEBM: ORGANIZATION BEHAVIOUR, HISTORY OF

Ishikawa, Kaoru (1915–89)

Personal background

- born in 1915 into a family of prominent industrialists
- graduated in applied chemistry from University of Tokyo (1939)
- technical officer in the Japanese Navy (1939–41)
- worked in industry until 1947 when he joined the University of Tokyo, developing a keen interest in the study of statistical techniques
- developed the Ishikawa diagram in 1943
- invited by the Japanese Union of Scientists and Engineers (JUSE) in 1949 to join the QC Research Group
- became Director of the Chemical Society in Japan (1952), promoting quality control
- a member of the International Standards Organization (ISO) from 1969, becoming its chairman in 1977 and encouraging standardization of quality
- became a member of the ISO's executive committee in 1981
- was constantly in demand worldwide to give seminars and advice on Japanese quality control techniques until his death in 1989

Major works

Introduction to Quality Control (1954)
What is Total Quality Control? The Japanese Way (1985)

Summary

Kaoru Ishikawa will always be recognized as a major contributor to the concept of total quality control or the management of quality. He maintained that the management of quality necessitates the company-wide involvement of employees and managers through quality circles, a focus on the process rather than the individual when a problem is investigated through the use of the Ishikawa diagram, and a reliance on statistical techniques for company-wide quality control. Ishikawa believed that Japanese success in dominating world markets comes from their dedication and belief in the power of quality control.

1 Biographical data

Kaoru Ishikawa was born in 1915 in Japan. On graduating from the Department of Applied Chemistry at the University of Tokyo in March 1939, he took up employment with a company in the utilities sector. A few months later he had to join the Japanese Navy where he spent two years as a technical officer and was involved in education and training. After that he returned to work in industry.

In 1947 he joined the University of Tokyo to carry out research. As a scientist he realized the difficulties in analysing scattered data and being able to interpret it. This drove him to take a keen interest in statistics and in the study of statistical techniques. In 1949 he was invited by the Japanese Union of Scientists and Engineers (JUSE) to join a task force called QC Research Group to conduct pioneering work in the area of quality control (QC) and the use of statistical methods. For the next forty years or so Ishikawa dedicated himself entirely to this field and tried to help professional associations, academic institutions and industrial organizations worldwide in the application of QC principles.

Ishikawa promoted the slogan 'The next process is your customer' in the 1950s to resolve conflict between departments and to encourage teamwork between the various functions. In 1952 he became Director of the

Chemical Society in Japan and encouraged networks and joint projects with academic institutions in the field of QC and the co-sponsorship of annual conferences on QC activities. These annual conferences started to focus on the needs of various groups in employment, including managers, supervisors and workers. This led to the birth of quality circles in 1962 and the acknowledgement that QC has to involve everyone in the organization and that it should focus on the process and the end customer.

This great period of QC revolution in Japan was marked by intensive programmes of education and training on QC and quality circles, the publication of various journals on the subject and the development of case studies about the application of these concepts and their related benefits. Ishikawa was heavily involved in the setting up of quality standards and was closely involved in the Japanese Industrial Standards body (JIS) and the International Standards Organization (ISO). In 1969 he became a member of the ISO chapter in Japan and its chairman in 1977. He became a member of the ISO's executive committee in 1981 and this gave him the opportunity to influence international cooperation through standardization of quality. Although Ishikawa believed that standards were essential in determining minimum and acceptable levels of quality, he did not consider they were enough in themselves or that their implementation would necessarily lead to customer satisfaction. He believed that while taking into account standards, the challenge for QC was also to set higher goals and avoid complacency through continuous improvement and a commitment to satisfying customer requirements time and time again.

Until his death in 1989, Ishikawa travelled extensively and was constantly in demand by governments, universities and industrial organizations to give seminars and advice on Japanese QC techniques. He worked closely with the other gurus of quality including Deming and Juran whom he met in the 1950s when they were invited to give seminars on QC to Japanese managers (see DEMING, W.E.; JURAN, J.M.). He served as president of the Musashi

Institute of Technology and in great demand as a consultant in Japan and other countries.

2 Main contribution

Ishikawa's major contribution can perhaps be highlighted by focusing on his role in the development of the Japanese total quality control (TQC) approach, the introduction of the Ishikawa diagram (cause-and-effect analysis) and the promotion of QC circles. These are now examined in turn.

Total quality control in Japan

Japan's post-war economic success is often regarded as being mainly due to the way that the Japanese have recognized human potential. This is shown in a commitment to harnessing employees' creativity and a determination to optimize quality and eliminate waste. Ishikawa and others are recognized for their efforts in bringing about this so-called 'miracle' by insisting that QC becomes everybody's responsibility. During his worldwide travels Ishikawa urged his audiences to purchase Japanese products and services because the quality would be guaranteed.

Controlling quality effectively involves, argued Ishikawa, integrating various elements:

1 the control of the quality of the product/service *per se*;
2 the integrated control of cost, price and profit;
3 the control of a reliable supply chain and delivery system.

Ishikawa stated that 'to practice quality control is to develop, design, produce and service a quality product which is most economical, most useful, and always satisfactory to the consumer' (Ishikawa 1985).

Ishikawa strongly believed that organizations had no choice but to control quality for as long as they had a desire to compete in the marketplace with products and services. He often warned that 'total quality control consists of doing what should be done as a matter of course' (Ishikawa 1989a). Ishikawa also maintained that TQC is not a fast-acting drug like penicillin, but a slow-acting herbal remedy that will gradually improve a company's constitution if taken over a long period (Ishikawa 1989a). The evolution process of TQC in Japan was recognized as being successful due to ten critical factors:

1 QC activities that represent a company-wide approach with the full participation and involvement of everyone;
2 a senior management commitment not to compromise on quality and a belief in the quality-first principle;
3 the development and sharing of a company vision and achieving desired objectives by implementing a quality policy;
4 QC audits through self-assessment using the Deming prize framework, first introduced in 1951;
5 quality assurance and process management using facts and a continuous improvement approach in all the various functions;
6 the positive encouragement of teamwork and quality circles throughout the organization;
7 insistence on QC training and education on a regular basis;
8 the use of statistical techniques at elementary and advanced levels;
9 appreciation of the relevance of QC at all levels and in all industrial sectors and the need for it to be spread throughout Japanese industry and commerce;
10 governmental support and national QC promotion through such means as Quality Month, various QC symposia and the establishment of QC circle headquarters.

The Ishikawa diagram

Ishikawa advocated the use of statistical techniques in company-wide quality control (CWQC). He classified them into three categories (elemental, intermediate and advanced) and argued that 90 to 95 per cent of all problems can be solved using the elemental statistical techniques, which do not require specialist knowledge.

The Ishikawa diagram, also referred to as cause-and-effect (C&E) analysis or the fishbone diagram, is one of the most basic and important tools of quality improvement. It was introduced by Ishikawa in 1943 and represents a structured approach to problem solving (see PROBLEM SOLVING). It is used to organize the information generated by brainstorming sessions in order to consider potential causes of problems. All possibilities are scrutinized until a cause-and-effect relationship is established.

The diagram provides a comprehensive view of the quality process and its surrounding environment. Ishikawa developed this technique (not a truly statistical technique) to help Japanese managers analyse problems associated with the processes that they were responsible for. He believed that causes can be associated with any of the following factors in a manufacturing/service environment: (1) methods; (2) materials; (3) manpower; (4) machines; and (5) environment. In addition to determining the impact of individual causes, the Ishikawa diagram can establish the interrelationships between various causes. It is highly compatible with brainstorming techniques and encourages the involvement of different people, all of whom are encouraged to participate in isolating key sources of problems.

The following steps should be observed when using cause-and-effect diagrams:

1 identify the is;
2 build major causes around the problem structure;
3 use team effort to brainstorm sub-causes under each cause;
4 allow for an incubation period before revisiting and re-examining these sub-causes;
5 highlight the vital few/most likely causes;
6 check the most likely causes through data collection and analysis to determine the level of impact on the problem under study.

Quality control circles

During the early stages of promoting TQC in Japan it became very clear to Ishikawa and others that education and training on QC principles should not simply be limited to management and engineering levels, but had to be spread downwards to all other employees too. It was therefore considered very important to involve both shop-floor supervisors and employees in QC activities since they are more closely associated with the various processes than anyone else. They possess all the facts and information needed by senior managers in order to make the right decision. The effectiveness of senior managers can only be measured by their success in involving all employees.

A journal, referred to as *Gemba-to-QC*, was issued for the first time in April 1962 and marked the big launch of the quality circles movement. The QC circle headquarters was established in 1963, with nine QC circle regional chapters in 1964 and others after that. Quality circles are promoted through journals, books, videos, case studies, conferences, seminars and courses.

The notion of voluntarism is at the heart of QC circles. Unlike project teams, people decide whether they want to join without any coercion from senior managers. The following points compare quality circles with other teamwork approaches for tackling improvement projects:

1 QC circles deal with local issues only, while other teamwork deals with problem solving and the control of organizational problems;

2 a bottom-up approach is used for QC circles and a top-down, project-based approach for other teamwork;

3 quality circles allow free choice to determine areas for improvement, whereas project teams are specifically allocated tasks from the top;

4 quality circles constitute a continuous process while project teams are dismantled once the project is finished;

5 quality circles do not have to formally report to senior managers while project teams have to keep senior managers informed on a regular basis.

The major premise behind the role of quality circles, according to Ishikawa, is encouraging all employees to contribute to the value-added process for the benefit of the end customer. He also realized the need to show respect for people by allowing employees to decide on the setting up and management of their work environment. More importantly, he allowed individual employees to contribute to their best ability in terms of creativity and innovation and encouraged the harnessing of their ideas.

3 Evaluation

The concept of TQC was first introduced by Armand V. Feigenbaum in his book entitled *Total Quality Control: Engineering and Management*, in 1961. His definition of TQC is functionally based since he recommends that one specific function should have the task of controlling quality. This suggests specialism rather than encouraging company-wide involvement.

The benefits of involving all employees

In contrast to Feigenbaum, Ishikawa argued that TQC had to depend on contributions from all employees and that individuals alone would be unable to deliver quality to the end customers. He believed that TQC was not just a mere set of tools or specialist skills, but that it was also about education, training and altering employees' behaviour so that they would continuously strive to improve quality and eliminate waste. He considered it to be about respect for others and appreciating the valuable contributions of everyone concerned. TQC, in Japanese terms, is about pursuing one process where particular goals and the means to achieve them cannot be separated. Performance management and measurement are thus heavily dependant on the ability of senior managers to deploy organizational objectives effectively at all levels.

Total quality control compared with the zero defects movement

Ishikawa believed that TQC 'starts and finishes with education'. He criticized the zero defects (ZD) movement which was introduced in the West and which was considered to have failed for the following reasons:

1 The emphasis of the ZD movement was on encouraging people to do their best and to work harder rather than teaching them to work in a more intelligent way.
2 People were not educated or trained to use tools and techniques for controlling quality. The ZD principle was not regarded as a scientific approach to the management of quality.
3 In the ZD approach people were strongly encouraged to comply with the standard and to observe the written rules. This contrasts with Ishikawa's approach where people are strongly encouraged to challenge existing standards and continuously improve on them so that quality is optimized and performance greatly enhanced. Quality circles are, according to Ishikawa, the ideal tool for enhancing quality since they are created with a long-term objective in mind and are based on 'voluntarism'. Quality is likely to be sustainable since people's attitudes and behaviour are geared towards improving quality.
4 Taylorism and scientific management principles inherent in many organizations in the West are thought to be more detrimental to human potential since creativity and innovation are suppressed and human dignity can often be disregarded (see TAYLOR, F.W.).
5 Participation and close involvement were not included in the zero defects movement. People were asked to agree to initiatives often instigated by senior managers.
6 Employees were often held responsible for mistakes, since the ZD movement focuses on the individual and the task rather than the process and its immediate environment.

The so-called Japanese 'miracle'

Many people, including gurus such as Deming and Juran, have questioned whether there is 'a Japanese miracle'. QC ideas were introduced in several countries, but none of these attained the quality improvement results achieved by the Japanese. Juran, like Deming, blames this failure on attitudes and a lack of commitment from management (Lake 1988; Wild 1985). The core of the Japanese miracle is perhaps the ability to recognize the power of the human potential. It is people who control and manage processes and their continuous creativity and innovation will determine the standards of quality, and not the other way round. The contribution of Ishikawa was to highlight the following features:

1 All work is a process and therefore it is important to understand who the customers and suppliers are and determine their true requirements.
2 The management of quality requires an integrated approach, taking into consideration cost, quality *per se*, productivity and reliable delivery.
3 Work is a horizontal process which involves all the key functions; quality improvements therefore can only happen if all key areas are involved using both a team-based approach and quality circles.
4 QC is very much about behaviour and attitude rather than a set of tools and techniques: continuous education and training is essential for effective QC and management.
5 Quality circles are the real way to improve quality and they are a means of establishing respect for people and harnessing their creative and innovative potential.

4 Conclusion

Ishikawa's legacy is apparent in the many organizations around the world that are now using the principles of CWQC and total quality management. Worldwide, thousands of quality circles strive for continuous improvement and help enhance the degree of competitiveness of their organizations. Newly emerging industrial nations and global companies are using the TQC approach based on Japanese principles. South Korea, Singapore, Malaysia and the Republic of China make extensive use of quality circles and have benefited from the early teachings of Ishikawa.

In the West, in addition to a fresh approach which focuses more on people and human dignity at work, other principles have now evolved which have been used in Japan for many years. For instance, the use of auditing systems of QC and its management through self-assessment is an important development. In the USA the Malcolm Baldrige National Quality Award (MBNQA), introduced in 1987, is a framework for auditing quality which is extensively used in American firms. In Europe the European Foundation for Quality Management, created in 1988, introduced the European Quality Award (EQA) which is increasingly used in European organizations.

Ishikawa always believed that if other nations had the courage to imitate the Japanese and look at the 'soft issues' of people and how they work, they could also perform miracles. This has already started to happen: many non-Japanese competitors are now achieving superiority in the marketplace and have even superseded the standards of Japan.

MOHAMED ZAIRI
UNIVERSITY OF BRADFORD

Further reading

(References cited in the text marked *)

Cocheu, T. (1992) 'Training with quality', *Training and Development* 46 (5): 22–32. (Details a quality improvement strategy and a training strategy for organizations.)

Gitlow, H., Gitlow, S. and Oppenheim, A. (1989) *Tools and Methods for the Improvement of Quality*, Boston, MA: Irwin. (A reference for process improvement techniques which covers the fishbone diagram technique.)

Ishikawa, K. (1985) *What is Total Quality Control?: The Japanese Way* Englewood Cliffs, NJ: Prentice Hall. (A complete reference guide to the introduction of TQC.)

Ishikawa, K. (1988) 'Group wide quality control', *Journal for Quality and Participation*, 11 (March): 4–6. (Describes how the concept of group wide QC, an extension of CWQC, is used in Japan.)

* Ishikawa, K. (1989a) *Introduction to Quality Control*, 3rd edn, Tokyo: Chapman and Hall. (Covers basic principles of QC as well as TQC and its implementation; first edition in 1954)

Ishikawa, K. (1989b) 'How to apply company-wide quality control in foreign countries', *Quality Progress*, 12 (September): 70–4. (Discusses the problems encountered in countries that have attempted to introduce the Japanese approach to total quality management.)

* Lake, M. (1988) 'Re-examining the role for industrial engineering', proceedings of IIE Integrated Systems Conference, 30 October–2 November, St Louis, MO.

* Wild, R. (1985) 'The education and training of engineers and managers for manufacture', *Industrial and Commercial Training* (September–October): 17–19.

Zairi, M. (1991) *Total Quality Management for Engineers*, Cambridge: Woodhead Publishing. (Covers the evolution of the quality philosophy and describes the work of all the gurus including Ishikawa.)

See also: PROBLEM SOLVING; TAYLOR, F.W.; TOTAL QUALITY MANAGEMENT

Related topics in the IEBM: COMMITMENT IN JAPAN; DEMING, W.E.; JURAN, J.M.; MANAGEMENT IN JAPAN; TEAMS IN MANUFACTURING

Mayo, George Elton (1880–1949)

1 Main contribution
2 Evaluation
3 Conclusion

Personal background

- born 26 December 1880, Adelaide, Australia
- studied philosophy and psychology at the University of Adelaide
- lecturer and later professor of philosophy and psychology, University of Queensland, Australia, 1911–23
- married Dorothea McConnel, 1913
- conducted research programme in industrial psychiatry at the University of Pennsylvania, 1923–6
- appointed to a research position at Harvard Business School, 1926
- commenced involvement in Hawthorne experiments, 1928
- developed human relations theory of management
- conducted research on human relations in wartime industries during the Second World War
- retired and moved to England to write and continue consulting work, 1947
- died 1 September 1949, Guildford, England

Major works

The Human Problems of an Industrial Civilization (1933)
The Social Problems of an Industrial Civilization (1945)

Summary

Elton Mayo sought to apply the insights of psychiatry and the social sciences to the organization of work and to management practice. He criticized engineers and management theorists, such as F.W. Taylor, for focusing solely on the technical organization of work and for believing that workers were solely motivated by economic incentives. Using the findings of the Hawthorne experiments, in which he was the pivotal figure, Mayo argued that managers needed to take account of the social organization of the workplace and the human needs of the workers. The writings of Mayo and his colleagues at the Harvard Business School formed the basis of human relations theory and had a significant impact on management theory and practice in the 1940s and 1950s.

1 Main contribution

Research at Hawthorne

In 1928, Mayo was invited by the Western Electric Company to inspect some experiments being undertaken at the company's Hawthorne Works on the outskirts of Chicago. Mayo's name has since become synonymous with the Hawthorne experiments, both because of his influence on the experiments and because the Hawthorne experiments dominated and defined his career (see TAYLOR, F.W.).

The Western Electric factory was a prime example of the principles of scientific management espoused by Frederick Winslow Taylor and of the mass production techniques of Henry Ford. When Mayo first visited, it was a huge factory of almost 25,000 workers, the main manufacturing plant for the Bell telephone system in the USA. Engineers controlled every stage of the production process, time and motion studies were made of every task and, wherever possible, work was fragmented into simple tasks performed by machine operatives and assemblers. But the company was also a leader in the implementation of personnel management. Its senior managers constantly emphasized the importance of gaining the enthusiasm and loyalty of the workers, not just their obedience.

Two sets of experiments had already been undertaken. Tests on the effects of lighting on worker productivity had been conducted from 1924–7, as part of a national research programme instigated by the electrical industry. The study at Hawthorne involved measuring the impact of different levels of lighting on the output of several groups of workers. From the start, the engineers in charge of the study recognised that it would be difficult to control other factors such as changes in supervision associated with the tests and the workers' knowledge that lighting levels were being changed, and indeed the results seemed to show that these factors were more important than changes in lighting levels. Hawthorne's senior managers decided to use similar techniques to explore the effects of personnel practices such as the level of supervision and wage payment systems.

Relay assembly test room

Using the test room built for the lighting experiments, production engineers instigated a new experiment to test the effect of rest periods and changes in the hours of work on production and on workers' attitudes. The five workers in the 'relay assembly test room' were engaged in the assembly of small electrical relays, a repetitive task requiring speed and manual dexterity. Detailed records were compiled of individual production rates, temperature and humidity in the test room, workers' family lives and medical conditions and even the conversations that the workers had among themselves.

Conditions in the test room were then systematically altered, primarily by introducing a separate group payment scheme for the test-room workers and then by introducing various combinations of rest periods and shortened working hours. The output of the workers climbed steadily, and climbed even higher when two of the workers were replaced because they were restricting their production and encouraging the others to do the same. When the rest periods were removed and

hours of work returned to the normal 48 hours per week, production remained some 20 per cent higher than at the start of the test over a year earlier.

Later, writers on the experiments have referred to this marked increase in production despite the return to the original test-room conditions as the Hawthorne Effect; arguments have raged ever since as to how to explain it. At the time, the company researchers were unsure whether it was due to fewer relay types, changes in supervision, economic incentives due to the small group payment scheme or psychological factors triggered by the special attention received by the workers.

Interpreting the relay assembly test

Mayo initially looked at the relay assembly test room as the opportunity to continue the research he had pursued in textile mills in Philadelphia and factories in Boston. He had left Australia for the USA in order to pursue his interest in explaining and preventing industrial unrest by applying theories and techniques drawn from psychiatry and physiology. His thesis was that poor working conditions, long hours and awkward postures led to industrial fatigue and, most importantly, to mild psychiatric disturbances, which in turn could collectively lead to industrial unrest (see OCCUPATIONAL PSYCHOLOGY). He was convinced that the relay test showed that rest periods would reduce fatigue and result in increased production. Mayo's interpretations added further layers of explanation rather than simplifying the explanations of the data. But he reconciled the Hawthorne engineers to the fact that they would not find easy answers and encouraged them to use the experiments to explore deeper into the complex question of worker motivation and productivity (see MOTIVATION AND SATISFACTION; PRODUCTIVITY).

Although the relay test continued for another four years, the focus of the industrial research at Hawthorne shifted to other projects. Mayo played a central role in all of these as advisor and interpreter, although the company researchers did not always agree with his views or follow his advice. Equally

important, Mayo gave his academic imprima-
tur to the experiments, ensured that senior
company executives understood and supported the work and kept social scientists in
North America and the UK fully informed of
the latest developments.

In the next stage of the experiments, the
company researchers commenced a massive
programme of interviewing all the workers at
the plant, with the intention of providing an
insight into the workers' likes and dislikes, attitudes and morale. Under Mayo's guidance,
the interviewers were trained in clinical techniques borrowed from psychiatry; he suggested that the interviews should be seen as a
way for the workers to 'let off steam' rather
than a mechanism for identifying legitimate
grievances. In practice, the company researchers used the interviews in both ways.
The interviews also became the basis for a
new supervisory training programme, which
stressed the need for supervisors to understand the personal needs of their subordinates.

Bank wiring test

In the final major study, the bank wiring test,
the focus shifted to a study of the social structures and social relationships among a group
of male workers and their influence on production (see GROUPS AND TEAMS). It was
quickly recognized that the workers were
restricting their output, with the knowledge
and tacit agreement of their immediate supervisor. Explanations for this differed. The
company researchers and Mayo's student,
Fritz Roethlisberger, were initially inclined to
see the workers' behaviour as a rational, economic response, for the workers anticipated
that if they worked consistently faster, their
payment rate would be cut. Mayo firmly
rejected such an interpretation, arguing
instead that the restriction of output was an
unconscious reaction by the workers to a system that did not provide them with an incentive to work harder. The workers' desire to be
part of a group, in this case based around the
restriction of output, was overwhelming the
technical and managerial organization of the
workplace, in which workers were meant to
produce as much as possible.

Human relations in industry

The research at the Hawthorne Works ceased
in 1932, a victim of the Depression, but the
Hawthorne experiments entered a new phase
at the Harvard Business School, where under
Mayo's direction they were written up for
publication in three books and numerous articles. At Harvard, many of the differences in
interpretation that had been evident during the
experiments themselves were ironed out and
the major work, Roethlisberger and Dickson's *Management and the Worker* (1939),
provided a definitive official account that
accorded closely with Mayo's theoretical perspectives. A less significant work, *The Industrial Worker* by Mayo's colleague Thomas
North Whitehead (1938), provided an
exhaustive statistical analysis of the relay
assembly test room data.

Mayo much preferred giving informal
talks about the experiments and his publications on them consisted of short essays and a
collection of lectures published as *The Human Problems of an Industrial Civilization*
(1933). This book captures neatly Mayo's
strengths and weaknesses and gives a flavour
of the informal communication style that the
Western Electric managers, corporate executives and Rockefeller Foundation officials
found so refreshing. (Between 1923 and
1943, Mayo and his colleagues received
grants totalling $1,520,000 from the Rocke-
feller Foundation – a huge sum even by
Rockefeller standards.) The breadth of
Mayo's interests and reading leaps off the
page: the theories and research findings of
psychiatry, psychology, physiology, political
theory, social anthropology, biochemistry,
economics and sociology surround the three
central chapters on the Hawthorne
experiments.

Mayo argued that the social collaboration
found in traditional societies and small communities was due to the individual's unconscious adherence to social codes. Modern
society had broken down traditional social
codes and collaboration, resulting in a mass
society of maladjusted individuals. The solution lay not in mass democracy, unions or industrial democracy, but in the emergence of a

properly trained administrative elite that would develop techniques to promote social collaboration. He pursued this argument further in *The Social Problems of an Industrial Civilization* (1945), suggesting that the real threat to civilization was not the atomic bomb, but business and political leaders' lack of skill in managing human relations.

Mayo thus saw the relay assembly and bank wiring test rooms as exemplars of the choices that lay before society. The relay test room was an industrial utopia, in which the workers were content and well adapted and production rose, because managers had inadvertently created a positive environment that forged a social group. The bank wiring test room, by contrast, was an industrial dystopia, its workers discontented and maladjusted and restriction of output the result. For the remainder of his career, Mayo would seek ways to encourage industrial managers to understand the human dimensions and needs of the people in their organization, although always within a framework that emphasized the irrationality and emotionalism of workers (see HAWTHORNE EXPERIMENTS; HUMAN RELATIONS).

2 Evaluation

The work of Mayo and his colleagues had a significant impact on management theory and practice from the late 1930s into the 1950s, especially in North America. *Management and the Worker* was widely quoted and summarized, while Fritz Roethlisberger published a large number of articles that popularized the new human relations approach. Mayo had visited Britain every year during the summer, keeping researchers there informed of his work, and worked there briefly as a consultant after his retirement from Harvard. In post-war Europe, information about human relations and the Hawthorne experiments was widely disseminated through productivity councils and training programmes sponsored by the US Marshall Plan.

The term 'human relations' quickly came to embrace a diversity of views and practices, many of them far removed from Mayo's conservative ideas. Thus, while Mayo opposed the emergence of powerful industrial unions

in the USA in the late 1930s, Roethlisberger and other human relations researchers readily accepted the new system of collective bargaining (see COLLECTIVE BARGAINING; TRADE UNIONS). Indeed, they argued that the presence of organized labour made it all the more important that managers and supervisors should understand the human dynamics of the shop floor. As other centres of research into human relations were established, Mayo's theoretical approach was set aside. For example, research at the Tavistock Institute of Human Relations in Britain emphasized the impact of technology on the organization of work and on worker satisfaction.

Human relations became so successful that by the late 1940s it was starting to attract a steady stream of criticism. Sociologist Daniel Bell criticized Mayo and his associates for psychologizing the worker while ignoring the institutional and power relationships of industry and for seeing industrial relations as a problem of communication and leadership rather than the accommodation of conflicting interests.

Many commentators have subsequently dismissed Mayo and his colleagues as being simply servants of powerful corporate interests, creating an ideology of human relations that dismissed workers' views and providing new manipulative techniques for managers. Certainly Mayo can be criticized on these grounds: thus he readily used increases in production as a measure of worker contentment with working conditions and management. But he saw himself as a reformer setting out to reduce the conflict of industrial capitalism by changing the attitude of workers and employers alike and reshaping the workplace culture.

3 Conclusion

Elton Mayo can be credited with two major achievements. First, he stressed that managers had to take into account the human and social dimensions of the workplace, not simply maintain their obsession with the technical organization of work. Mayo was not alone in making this point in the 1920s and 1930s, but in the Hawthorne experiments he was able to link his arguments to a large-scale research project that seemed to provide scientific proof.

Second, Mayo showed the benefits of being able to undertake long-term research in the workplace. In contrast to the frustrating experiences of many other researchers, Mayo was able to persuade Western Electric to continue to expand its research programme at Hawthorne without the company becoming overly concerned about immediate benefits or that the research would show up deficiencies in the organization. Mayo and the Hawthorne researchers opened up a space for research in the workplace that many other social scientists later explored. Ever since Mayo, managers and social scientists have been trying to find new ways of creating Hawthorne Effects.

RICHARD GILLESPIE
MUSEUM OF VICTORIA

Further Reading

(References cited in the text marked *)

Baritz, L. (1960) *The Servants of Power: A History of the Use of Social Sciences in American Industry*, Middletown, CT: Wesleyan University Press. (An early and influential radical history of industrial psychology and sociology in America.)

Bourke, H. (1982) 'Industrial unrest as social pathology: the Australian writings of Elton Mayo', *Historical Studies* 20 (79): 217–33. (An analysis of Mayo's early social and political views.)

Carey, A. (1967) 'The Hawthorne studies: a radical criticism', *American Sociological Review* 32 (3): 403–16. (The first major critical analysis of the Hawthorne experiments, based simply on a rereading of the official accounts.)

Franke, R.H. (1980) 'Worker productivity at Hawthorne', *American Sociological Review* 45 (6): 1006–27. (An example of one of the many statistical reworkings of the relay assembly test room data.)

Gillespie, R. (1991) *Manufacturing Knowledge: A History of the Hawthorne Experiments*, Cambridge: Cambridge University Press. (A detailed account of the Hawthorne experiments based on a close analysis of the original records of the experiments.)

* Mayo, G.E. (1933) *The Human Problems of an Industrial Civilization*, New York: Macmillan. (A collection of lectures that interprets the Hawthorne experiments in the context of Mayo's broader psychological theories and social thought.)

Mayo, G.E. (1945) *The Social Problems of an Industrial Civilization*, Boston, MA: Graduate School of Business Administration, Harvard University. (Mayo argues that the future of civilization depends on managers and social administrators acquiring human relations skills.)

Roethlisberger, F.J. (1977) *The Elusive Phenomena*, Boston, MA: Harvard Business School Press. (Includes chapters on Mayo and the Hawthorne experiments, written by Mayo's closest colleague.)

* Roethlisberger, F.J. and Dickson, W.J. (1939) *Management and the Worker*, Cambridge, MA: Harvard University Press. (The official account of the Hawthorne experiments, written under Mayo's supervision.)

Rose, M. (1978) *Industrial Behaviour: Theoretical Development Since Taylor*, Harmondsworth: Penguin. (Analyses Mayo's thought and the Hawthorne experiments in the context of subsequent research on industrial behaviour in Britain and the USA.)

Smith, J.H. (1975) 'The significance of Elton Mayo', in G.E. Mayo, *The Social Problems of an Industrial Civilization*, London: Routledge & Kegan Paul: ix–xiii. (A spirited defence of the value of Mayo's work for contemporary industrial sociology.)

Trahair, R.C.S. (1984) *The Humanist Temper: The Life and Work of Elton Mayo*, New Brunswick, NJ: Transaction Publishers. (The most detailed account of Mayo's career, based on his personal papers.)

* Whitehead, T.N. (1938) *The Industrial Worker*, Cambridge, MA: Harvard University Press. (A statistical analysis of the data by one of Mayo's colleagues, seeking to prove the role of personal and social relationships in the relay assembly room).

See also: FOLLETT, M.P.; HAWTHORNE EXPERIMENTS; HUMAN RELATIONS; HUMAN RESOURCE MANAGEMENT; MOTIVATION AND SATISFACTION

Related topics in the IEBM: LEWIN, K.; ORGANIZATION BEHAVIOUR, HISTORY OF; ORGANIZATION STRUCTURE; TRIST, E.L.

Ohno, Taiichi (1912–1990)

Personal background

- born at Port Arthur, Manchuria, China, in February 1912
- graduated from Department of Mechanical Engineering of Nagoya Technical High School in Nagoya, Japan in 1932
- joined Toyoda Spinning and Weaving Company in 1932
- transferred to Toyota Motor Company 1942
- named machine shop manager 1949
- appointed managing director of Toyota Motor Company in 1964
- promoted to executive vice president in 1975
- retired from Toyota Motor Company in 1978
- became chairman of Toyoda Gosei, a Toyota Motor Company supplier, in 1978
- resided in Toyota-shi, Aichi-ken, until his death in 1990

Major works

Toyota Production System: Beyond Large-Scale Production (1988)
Just-in-Time For Today and Tomorrow (1988)

Summary

Taiichi Ohno is generally regarded as the 'father' of the Toyota Production System (TPS). This innovative approach to production can simultaneously reduce costs, improve quality, and reduce lead times. It played a major role in the growth of the Toyota Motor Company, and has spread throughout the world as 'just-in-time' (JIT) manufacturing.

Ohno combined missionary zeal with engineering pragmatism in developing the Toyota System. He had an idealized, Platonic vision of manufacturing, with products flowing continuously through the factory, from work station to work station, eliminating completely what he called 'waste'. He considered all activities that did not add value to the product a form of waste. Non-value activities include product moves, inspections, and, particularly, the accumulation of inventory. For a period of thirty years, from 1945 to 1975, Ohno systematically pursued the elimination of production 'waste'. The collection of techniques that he used evolved into an effective and integrated system – the TPS.

1 Introduction

Taiichi Ohno's transfer to the Toyota Motor Company in 1942 was a fortuitous move. He was the right man, in the right place, at the right time. In post-war Japan automobile demand was low, raw material costs were high, and productivity was very low. In 1945, Toyota's President, Kiichiro Toyoda, launched a bold 'Catch Up With America' campaign. This was a formidable challenge, since the productivity of the US car manufacturers was ten times that of Japanese producers like Toyota (see PRODUCTIVITY). Ohno realized that this productivity gap could not be explained by differences in physical effort. He concluded that the reason had to be wasteful practices in Japanese manufacturing and for him, the elimination of this waste at Toyota became an obsession.

2 Biographical data

Taiichi Ohno was born in 1912 in Manchuria, China. He attended school in Japan, graduating from the mechanical engineering department of Nagoya Technical High School in the spring of 1932. Jobs were scarce, but fortunately Ohno's father was an acquaintance of Kiichiro Toyoda, President of the Toyoda Spinning and Weaving Company. Ohno joined Toyoda shortly after graduation. He worked as a textile engineer for ten years, gaining valuable experience during a period in which the Japanese textile industry made great strides in global competitiveness by improving production methods and reducing costs. In 1942 Ohno moved to another part of the Toyoda organization, the Toyota Motor Company – a marketing consultant had recommended that the family name be modified.

Ohno's textile experience proved to be a valuable asset, since the automotive industry, including Toyota, was lagging behind the textile industry in manufacturing effectiveness. Ohno started developing the Toyota System while he was foreman of the machine shop. He was greatly influenced by what he considered two 'pillars of wisdom', developed by Kiichiro Toyoda as part of his 'Catch Up With America' campaign. First, just-in-time production flow: parts should arrive at each work station at the exact time and in the exact quantity needed. Second, 'autonomation', or automation with a human touch: machines should be equipped with an automatic checking device to ensure that every piece produced is acceptable. If not, the machine should shut itself off and activate a trouble signal.

Toyoda's 'pillars of wisdom' meshed well with Ohno's desire to eliminate waste, and they became cornerstones of his production system. His success in dramatically increasing Toyota's productivity gained him a series of promotions. He became a director in 1954, managing director in 1964 and executive vice president in 1975. He retired from Toyota in 1978 and assumed the chairmanship of a member of the Toyota *keiretsu* (family of suppliers), Toyoda Gosei. He resided in Toyota-shi, Aichi-ken until his death, 28 May 1990.

3 Main contributions

Ohno 'stood on Henry Ford's shoulders' (see FORD, H.). The Ford system of mass production, developed in the early 1900s, was a dramatic break with the prevailing craft-based production. Ford eliminated the need for craft skills by the use of interchangeable parts. He capitalized on this advantage by linking together an army of unskilled workers, each performing a short, standardized portion of the total process. The emphasis on flow was enhanced by the development of the moving assembly line.

The Ford system was the standard of competitiveness in the post-war auto industry, but it had to be modified to suit the conditions at Toyota. The need for long production runs of a single model at Ford was incompatible with the low volume of the Japanese automobile market and the severe shortage of resources in Japan made it impractical to adopt the Ford system of using large inventories of parts. The Toyota Production System (TPS) evolved out of the need to adapt Ford mass production to the economic realities of post-war Japan.

The challenge facing Ohno was to overcome Ford's economies of scale with greater flexibility, or 'economies of scope'. This had to be done without the large buffer inventories needed by Ford to keep the assembly line going in the face of problems such as late part deliveries, machine breakdowns and defective parts. Ohno's major contribution is the manner in which he met this challenge.

By dramatically reducing machine and assembly set-up times, it became feasible for Toyota to produce a continuous stream of small quantities of a variety of models. This 'mixed model production' decreased inventories, increased model flexibility and shortened delivery times. To ensure continuity of product flow without large buffers, support programmes were developed to eliminate production problems systematically. These programmes included 'Total Preventative Maintenance', 'Total Quality Management', 'Continuous Improvement', 'Autonomation', and 'Just-in-Time supplier deliveries'.

Ohno's innovative solution improved the Ford system for mass production by making it more efficient and more flexible. But it also improved the low volume production of repetitively built products. Because the TPS reduces inventories, and because it does not require major capital investment, it can be implemented by smaller producers to realize the benefits of continuous flow production. This is a major contribution, since about 75 per cent of manufacturing companies have insufficient volume to qualify as mass producers.

Ohno's philosophy in developing the TPS has changed the way in which production system designers approach their task. His relentless pursuit of perfection, striving for the 'wasteless' manufacturing of 'zero defect' products, is a powerful model for improving established manufacturing practices (see ISHIKAWA, K.). There inevitably are obstacles to attaining perfection. Ohno's philosophy is to systematically remove as many of these obstacles as possible, by identifying and eliminating their root causes:

> Underneath the 'cause' of a problem, the *real cause* is hidden. In every case, we must dig up the real cause by asking *why, why, why, why, why?*. Otherwise countermeasures cannot be taken and the problems will not be truly solved.
>
> (Ohno 1988b: 126)

In Ohno's view, asking the five 'whys' leads to the 'how' of the real cause. His emphasis on finding fundamental solutions contrasted with the prevailing notion of providing short term relief for symptoms – to 'keep the line going'. It resulted in one of his most famous contributions – giving workers the authority to shut down production in the face of a problem, until the cause is identified and corrected. Ohno recognized that keeping the line going by the use of contingency resources removed much of the incentive for management to address the root causes of problems. Shutting down production is a very effective way to attract management's attention and gain their commitment to finding long-term solutions.

4 Evaluation

The TPS has spread throughout the industrialized world, setting new standards of product quality and cost, benefiting consumers and contributing to higher living standards. The TPS sharply reduces inventories in the production process. This has dampened the impact of inventory swings on the amplitude of business cycles, promoting economic stability. Ohno's innovative thinking has influenced a generation of manufacturing theorists and practitioners, providing them with both an effective method of organizing production and a proved philosophy for continual improvement.

For the workers, the TPS provides an orderly and organized workplace, relative freedom from frustrating production problems, and the opportunity to participate in continuous improvement efforts. There is, however, a negative side. There is considerable anecdotal evidence of high stress levels among just-in-time (JIT) workers, especially in automotive plants. The use of stressful practices in the design and operation of JIT appears to run counter to Ohno's stated philosophy. For example, he questioned the practice of 'speeding up' a production line: 'Ford never intended to cause workers to work harder and harder, to feel driven by their machines, and alienated from their work . . . however, an idea does not always evolve in a direction hoped for by its creator' (Ohno 1988b: 100).

Ironically, there is evidence of a conflict between Ohno's enlightened human resource philosophy and his passion for eliminating waste. Horseley and Buckley claim that at Toyota 'the workers lived in fear of Taiichi Ohno. . . . He seemed to his juniors like a man with a special mission' (1990: 156). Apparently, that mission caused him to engage in stressful practices such as removing some of the workers from a smoothly operating line, to force further improvements. The potential for stressful practices in JIT appears to be high. However, managers implementing JIT according to Ohno's stated philosophy should reject the use of stressful tactics that yield marginal returns at the expense of worker safety and well-being.

5 Conclusion

It is likely that Taiichi Ohno will have a place in manufacturing history alongside giants like Henry Ford and Frederick Taylor (see TAYLOR, F.W.). Like Ford's 'mass production' and Taylor's 'scientific management', Ohno's

Toyota Production System is a significant break with prevailing manufacturing practice. In Thomas Kuhn's terms, Ohno's work represents a 'paradigm shift' – a new standard for the organization of production that makes it possible to achieve dramatic increases in productivity and quality (Kuhn 1970).

Like the systems of Ford and Taylor, however, Ohno's TPS also has the potential for a negative effect on workers. Managers, trade unions and workers should be collectively concerned that Ohno's innovative approach to producing high quality, low cost products be implemented with due concern for the welfare of the work force.

ROBERT F. CONTI
BRYANT COLLEGE
SMITHFIELD

Further reading

(References cited in the text marked *)

* Horsley, W. and Buckley, R. (1990) *Nippon, New Superpower*, London: BBC Books. (Places the TPS in the context of the history of Japan's emergence as a post-Second World War economic superpower.)

Klein, J. (1989) 'The human costs of manufacturing reform', *Harvard Business Review* March–April: 60–6. (Excellent coverage of the causes of JIT worker stress, with some practical prescriptions for minimizing the problem.)

* Kuhn, T.S. (1970) *The Structure of Scientific Revolutions*, Chicago, IL: Chicago University Press. (The classic treatment of scientific revolution as a process of change in the accepted 'paradigm', or conceptual foundation, in a given discipline.)

Monden, Y. (1993) *Toyota Management System, Linking the Seven Key Functional Areas*, Portland, OR: Productivity Press. (Description of how the TPS is integrated into a total management system that links the major functional areas at Toyota.)

Ohno, T. (1988a) *Just-in-Time For Today and Tomorrow*, Cambridge, MA: Productivity Press. (Development of the theme that the biggest waste is a product that doesn't sell. Emphasizes the use of market information to avoid speculative production.)

* Ohno, T. (1988b) *Toyota Production System, Beyond Large-Scale Production*, Cambridge, MA: Productivity Press. (Discussion of the evolution and operation of the Toyota Production System by the person most responsible for its success.)

Shingo, S. (1989) *A Study of the Toyota Production System From an Industrial Engineering Viewpoint*, Cambridge, MA: Productivity Press. (Excellent technical coverage of the details of the Toyota System by an associate of Ohno.)

Shonberger, R. (1982) *Japanese Manufacturing Techniques*, New York: The Free Press. (Very readable introduction to the concepts and techniques of JIT manufacturing.)

Toyoda, E. and Toyoda, S. (1988) *Toyota – A History of the First 50 Years*, Toyota City: Toyota Motor Corporation. (Fascinating history of the growth of Toyota, beginning with the decision to build cars in 1933. Excellent coverage of the role of the Toyota Production System in the company's success.)

Whitehall, A. (1991) *Japanese Management, Tradition and Transition, London: Routledge.* (Comprehensive coverage of aspects of the management process unique to the Japanese. Discusses the Toyota System in the context of a national focus on 'getting the most from the least' in manufacturing.)

Womack, J.P., Jones, D.T., and Roos, D. (1990) *The Machine That Changed the World*, New York: Rawson/Macmillan. (Major worldwide study of the automobile industry which concludes that the use of 'lean production' – a generic version of the Toyota Production System – is a competitive necessity for car manufacturers.)

See also: FORD, H.; ISHIKAWA, K.; PRODUCTIVITY; TAYLOR, F.W.; TOTAL QUALITY MANAGEMENT

Related topics in the IEBM: INVENTORY AND JUST-IN-TIME MODELS; JUST-IN-TIME PHILOSOPHIES; MANAGEMENT IN JAPAN; MANUFACTURING SYSTEMS, DESIGN OF; TEAMS IN MANUFACTURING; TOYODA FAMILY

Peters, Thomas J. (1942–)

1 Introduction
2 Biographical data
3 Main contribution
4 Evaluation
5 Conclusions

Personal background

- born Baltimore, Maryland, 7 November 1942
- served in the US Navy, 1966–70
- BCE, MCE Cornell University, MBA Stanford University (1972), PhD (1977)
- consultant with Peate Marwick Mitchell in Washington, DC, 1970–3
- worked for the US government in Washington, 1973–4
- joined McKinsey & Co. in San Francisco, 1974, becoming principal practice leader on organizational effectiveness, 1976
- left McKinsey & Co. in 1981 to set up his own firm, the Tom Peters Group, based in Palo Alto, California
- widely quoted and cited commentator on business in the USA, appearing frequently in US newspapers and on television
- married with family, lives in California and Vermont

Major works

In Search of Excellence: Lessons from America's Best-run Companies (with Robert H. Waterman, Jr) (1982)

A Passion for Excellence: The Leadership Difference (with Nancy Austin) (1985)

Thriving on Chaos: Handbook for a Management Revolution (1987)

Liberation Management: Necessary Disorganization for the Nanosecond Nineties (1992)

Summary

Tom Peters (1942–) is possibly the most popular and widely read management 'guru' of the 1980s and 1990s. Unlike contemporaries such as Michael Porter, Peter Drucker and Charles Handy, Peters does not have a strongly academic background; his theories on management are derived from his own personal experiences as a consultant. Peters has come to believe that many of the fundamental principles on which management in the USA is based are wrong, and he speaks increasingly of the need for 'revolution' and 'liberation' from old, outmoded management techniques and styles. He has been criticized for an allegedly superficial approach in his writings, but many of the concepts he has called for, such as looser structures, broader perspectives and the ability to manage ambiguity, are now part of the accepted canon of management thinking.

1 Introduction

Peters entered the world of management consultancy in the 1970s at a time when business in the USA was increasingly being seen (not least by himself) as moribund, lacking in imagination and suffering more and more from foreign competition. His work with the consulting firm McKinsey & Co. led him to believe that some US companies could be described as 'excellent', and further, that there were certain identifiable features which all these companies had in common. His determination to identify those features led to his first and best-known book, *In Search of Excellence* (1982), co-written with Richard H. Waterman.

Peters' later books, as well as his articles, television appearances and consulting work, have expanded on these earlier themes. He continues to believe that excellence is both possible and achievable, and he continues to advocate, more strongly than ever, the need for a fundamentally new approach to business and management, based on organizational culture, quality, customer focus and – perhaps most controversially – decentralized organizations with strongly empowered employees (see HUMAN RESOURCE DEVELOPMENT; ORGANIZATION BEHAVIOUR; ORGANIZATION CULTURE). In Peters' view, management should be about decentralization and deliberate lack of focus and control, fostering an atmosphere of 'intentional chaos' where creativity and dynamism can be nurtured. His books are phenomenally popular, especially with younger and middle managers, and many of his ideas are now part of modern management thinking (see MANAGERIAL BEHAVIOUR).

2 Biographical data

Tom Peters was born in 1942. After attending university he served for four years in the US Navy, from 1966 to 1970 at the height of the Vietnam War. He refers to the war later in *In Search of Excellence*, where he is highly critical of the 'rationalist' approach of US military leaders during the war.

Leaving the navy, he first joined the consulting firm Peate Marwick Mitchell in Washington, DC. In 1973, he joined the US Government Office of Management and Budget, also in Washington, first as director of a cabinet committee on international narcotics control and then as assistant to the director for federal drug abuse policy. Leaving government service in 1974, he moved to San Francisco where he became an associate with the international management consulting firm McKinsey & Co.

It was at McKinsey that Peters began to develop his concepts of organizational effectiveness and excellence. In 1976, he became the firm's principal practice leader on organizational effectiveness, and also began to become known as a writer and speaker. His team at McKinsey began investigating the nature of organizational and business excellence, ultimately conducting a survey of leading US businesses and creating the frameworks which were later distilled into *In Search of Excellence*.

In Search of Excellence sold over one million copies around the world and became one of the most popular management books of all time. It also made Peters himself a highly visible figure. He became known as a pundit; his media credits include a weekly column syndicated in US newspapers and a television series on the PBS network. In 1981, he left McKinsey to set up his own firm, the Tom Peters Group, through which he manages his media work and also seminars and consulting sessions for a variety of clients. Few other figures in management have reached such a wide audience.

Peters continues to write and develop his theories, paying particular attention to changes in the business environment. In *Thriving on Chaos* (1987), he warned that the recommendations spelled out in *In Search of Excellence* were no longer 'nice-to-do' but 'must-do' concepts. In *Liberation Management* (1992), he described his own view of a management revolution, the principles of which were a complete rethinking of organizational scale and control with a greater emphasis on decentralized units and flexibility. The concept of managing ambiguity, which he discussed as a key feature of managerial excellence in *In Search of Excellence*, is now a major theme running through all his work.

3 Main contribution

In *In Search of Excellence*, Peters asked what it is that companies can do to achieve excellence. He chose to examine the subject not by using academic models, but by using his own experiences and those of his colleagues, selecting real-life examples of companies which had achieved excellence and then seeking common factors.

Peters' '7–S' model consists of seven organizational variables: structure, strategy, systems, skills, staff, style and shared values. The latter is at the centre of the model and is obviously most important. In Peters' view, excellence is a cultural factor, with companies working hard to make sure employees buy into that culture; he quotes psychologist Ernest Becker to the effect that people are driven by a dualism: a need to conform and a simultaneous need to be seen as individuals. Companies which achieve excellence will meet both these needs on the part of their employees. Peters accepts that this is a paradox, and continues: 'If there is one striking feature of the excellent companies, it is this ability to manage ambiguity and paradox. What our rational economist friends tell us ought not to be possible the excellent companies do routinely' (1982: xxiv).

Quality and customer orientation are also important hallmarks, but Peters' other strongest emphases are on streamlining and simplifying organizations. *In Search of Excellence* claimed that excellent companies were those which were 'brilliant on basics': 'Tools didn't substitute for thinking... those companies worked hard to keep things simple in a complex world' (Peters and Waterman 1982: 13). His later books attack this theme more strongly. In *Thriving on Chaos*, he attacks the cult of 'giantism' and, by implication, Taylorism and the whole concept of specialized labour, calling for greater empowerment of employees and fewer controls (Peters 1987: 13 ff.) (see TAYLOR, F.W.). In *Liberation Management*, he cites the German *mittelstand* system which encourages many small to medium enterprises to establish themselves in niche markets, limiting growth but managing innovation and customer service through small, focused units (Peters 1992). He has consistently attacked large, inflexible organizations and in 1992 claimed that: 'Middle management, as we have known it since the railroads invented it right after the Civil War, is dead' (Peters 1992: 758).

Most of all, however, Peters has argued for a revolution in outlook on the part of management. He believes that the notion of management as a science has come close to eclipsing the notion of management as an art and:

Professionalism in management is regularly equated with hard-headed rationality.... The numerative, rationalist approach to management dominates the business schools. It teaches us that well-trained professional managers can manage anything. It seeks detached, analytical justification for all decisions. It is right enough to be

dangerously wrong, and it has arguably led us seriously astray.
(Peters and Waterman 1982: 29)

He attacks concepts such as economy of scale and low-cost production which are often believed to be the only ways to success: 'The numerative, analytical component has an in-built conservative bias. Cost reduction becomes priority number one and revenue enhancement takes a back seat' (Peters and Waterman 1982: 44). He encourages 'overspending' on product development and quality control, and customer service, arguing that even if these do not yield value for money in the classical sense, encouraging innovation and focusing on customers are powerful marketing tools and will help the company achieve excellence.

His commitment to the need for a management revolution is as strong as Taylor's and, like Taylor, Peters believes that success depends on people. Unlike Taylor, however, he believes that successful management of people depends on removing controls, encouraging individuality and promoting 'stars'. In the Peters revolution, small, responsive, flexible management units which stay close to both their customers and their employees represent the way of the future.

4 Evaluation

It is difficult to evaluate the impact which Peters' work has had on management in the USA. His books are read around the world, and many of his themes have universal applicability, but there is a strong cultural bias throughout on US management and its environment (see CULTURE, CROSS-NATIONAL). Within that parameter, it can be seen that a number of US companies and organizations have been adapting themselves and their operations along the lines Peters suggests; but whether they did so as a result of reading his work cannot be proven. Nor should it be ignored that not all of the companies that Peters cites as examples of excellence have been successful over the long term; IBM, for example, has run into repeated problems since the publication of *In Search of Excellence*.

In Search of Excellence drew favourable attention from business schools and business leaders, and many of the former put it on their reading syllabus for students. The later works have sometimes been criticized but have more often been ignored by academics. The increasingly radical tone of the books may have offended many scholars, and his criticisms of business schools and their apparent dedication to excessive rationality has also won him few friends. One criticism of Peters' work is that it is too superficial, concentrating on a handful of examples and lacking academic rigour. However, Peters himself is strongly influenced by academic thinking; his comment that 'organization falls out of strategy' is drawn from Chandler, and his theories on organizational culture owe something to the work of Mayo and Barnard at Harvard Business School in the 1930s (see MAYO, G.E.). In *Liberation Management*, Peters acknowledges the influence of Charles Handy.

Peters has made a considerable contribution to the debate about the future of management, especially in the USA but elsewhere in the world as well. He has sometimes been criticized for too prescriptive an approach, offering a 'cookbook' of 'recipes' for success; yet those same recipes have proven to be popular and enduring. Phrases like 'managing ambiguity' have now passed into the management lexicon, and his call for a more holistic view of management with less specialization and more attention to general themes has been widely taken up by business schools, especially in Europe.

The influence of his ideas can be seen indirectly in academic thinking as well. Service industries, with their special operations and marketing problems of managing a product which is consumed at the same time as it is produced, were quick to see the applicability of Peters' theories. Textbooks on services marketing such as Bateson (1988) speak of empowering employees and promoting 'stars' as one of the key aspects of a successful service organization. Production industries were perhaps slower to come to the same view, but Hill (1989) has pushed the idea that manufacturing companies needed to pay more

attention to the marketing–operations interface, get closer to their customers and look to smaller, more focused units as ways of improving profitability. The view that cost control is the bottom line is no longer as prevalent as it once was.

What Peters has undeniably done is make a contribution to the debate about how companies should be run and open it up to a broad audience. This was not necessarily his primary or his only goal:

> Am I a middle management basher? Yes. Are most of the people who come to my seminars middle managers? Yes. Why do they come? Beats me.
>
> (Peters 1992: 715)

In fact, middle managers follow Peters because, in an era when the role and value of the middle manager are increasingly uncertain, he offers them a chance to at least discuss how they might make a greater contribution. His books, which have now sold over four million copies, and his other writings have given many managers greater enthusiasm for and interest in the complexities and ambiguities of their jobs; in the revolution, he himself has been a catalyst in bringing managers closer to the fundamentals of excellence.

5 Conclusion

In *In Search of Excellence* (1982: 13–16), Peters defined eight attributes as distinctive of the excellent company:

1. a bias for action (taking the initiative);
2. close to the customer;
3. autonomy and entrepreneurship;
4. productivity through people;
5. hands-on, value-driven leadership;
6. stick to the knitting (stay close to the business you know);
7. simple form, lean staff;
8. simultaneous tight-loose properties (central core values combined with decentralized organization).

His arguments for simplicity, meaning and action are powerful ones, and have struck a chord with many managers around the world; he is one of the most popular management gurus of his generation precisely because he offers managers and companies the prospect of hope and an exciting future. While many of his prescriptions are radical and his work contains a strong cultural bias towards the USA, the fundamentals about which Peters writes have universal applicabiLITY.

MORGEN WITZEL

LONDON BUSINESS SCHOOL

DURHAM UNIVERSITY BUSINESS SCHOOL

Further reading

(References cited in the text marked *)

Barnard, C.I. (1968) *The Functions of the Executive*, Cambridge, MA: Harvard University Press. (Summary of Barnard's theories, including the experimental work referred to in the text.)

* Bateson, J.E.G. (1988) *Managing Services Marketing*, Chicago, IL: Dryden. (A standard textbook on services marketing.)

Chandler, A.D., Jr (1962) *Strategy and Structure: Chapters in the History of American Industrial Enterprise*, Cambridge, MA: MIT Press. (Classic work of business history, which tries to make past business practices appear relevant to modern conditions.)

* Hill, T. (1989) *Manufacturing Strategy: Text and Cases*, Homewood, IL: Irwin. (A standard textbook on operations strategy.)

* Peters, T.J. (1987) *Thriving on Chaos: Handbook for a Management Revolution*, New York: Knopf. (Urges companies to adopt a more radical approach to management, with five key strategic focal points.)

Peters, T.J. (1991) *Beyond Hierarchy: Organizations in the 1990s*, New York: Knopf. (Study of organizations and how breaking down hierarchies can lead to competitive freedom.)

* Peters, T.J. (1992) *Liberation Management: Necessary Disorganization for the Nanosecond Nineties*, New York: Knopf. (Peters' most recent and most radical work, calling for greater decentralization and freedom.)

* Peters, T.J. (1994) *The Pursuit of Wow! Every Person's Guide to Topsy Turvy-Times*. New York: Vintage. (Urges managers to pursue what Peters calls the 'wow market' when everything comes together and true excellence is achieved; chaotic and impressionistic, with no systematic approach.)

Peters, T.J. and Austin, N. (1985) *A Passion for Excellence: The Leadership Difference*, New York: Random House. (Largely a follow-up to *In Search of Excellence*.)

Peters, T.J. and Townsend, R. (1988) *Excellence in the Organization*, New York: Nightingale-Conant. (A further dissertation on the factors necessary for excellence.)

* Peters, T.J. and Waterman, R.H., Jr (1982) *In Search of Excellence: Lessons from America's Best-run Companies*, New York: Harper & Row. (The classic Peters, probably his best and certainly his best-known book.)

See also: LEADERSHIP; ORGANIZATION BEHAVIOUR

Related topics in the IEBM: BARNARD, C.I.; CHANDLER, A.D.; ENTREPRENEURSHIP; GURU CONCEPT; MANAGEMENT IN GERMANY; ORGANIZATION BEHAVIOUR, HISTORY OF; ORGANIZATION STRUCTURE; ORGANIZATIONAL PERFORMANCE; STRATEGIC COMPETENCE

Reich, Robert M. (1946–)

Personal background

- born Scranton, Pennsylvania, 24 June 1946
- studied economics: BA Dartmouth College (1968) and MA Oxford (1970, Rhodes Scholar)
- received doctorate in law from Yale (1973)
- Assistant Solicitor-General, US Justice Department (1974–6)
- Director of Policy Planning, Federal Trade Commission (1976–81)
- joined the faculty of the John F. Kennedy School of Government at Harvard University, 1981
- appointed Secretary of Labor in the Clinton administration, 1993

Major works

Minding America's Business (with Ira C. Magaziner) (1982)
The Next American Frontier (1983)
New Deals: The Chrysler Revival and the American System (with John D. Donahue) (1985)
Tales of a New America (1987)
The Work of Nations (1991)

Summary

Reich regards strategy as the re-enactment of core beliefs and stories which exist in society. He uses this analysis to attempt to understand the fundamental nature of the US economy and, more importantly, the reasons for its steady decline since the 1960s. An economist and lawyer by training, he has attempted to synthesize a variety of disciplines including history and anthropology to arrive at a holistic view of attitudes in the USA to business, government, and the relations between them. During the 1980s his ideas gained broad acceptance among Democratic politicians in the USA, notably Michael Dukakis, the 1988 presidential candidate, and Bill Clinton (elected President in 1992). His analysis is broad-reaching and rich, but he has so far been less specific on solutions, concentrating on the need for a more cooperative, integrated business culture.

1 Introduction

Robert Reich makes a joke about his small physical stature: 'When I first began worrying about the American economy, I was over 6 feet tall'. Yet he has worried to considerable effect, and his intellectual stature is formidable. Educated in economics and the law, he has serious misgivings about the value of both disciplines and writes more in the style of a popular social anthropologist and political essayist. His writing shows a formidable grasp of the structure of polemic, ideology and myth, along with an extraordinary gift for the exposition of beliefs with which he profoundly disagrees, but which he describes with a marvellous coherence and inner consistency.

Like John Kenneth Galbraith, a colleague at Harvard, Reich is a critic of 'conventional wisdom'. His lectures on business and politics at the Kennedy School of Government are so popular that students enter lotteries to take his classes. Reich's chief contribution to our understanding of strategy lies in his grasp of the fact that the US experience is organized by the dominant culture stories people tell themselves and by the abiding myths by which they live.

2 Biographical data

After taking degrees in economics, Robert Reich studied law at Yale Law School under Professor Robert Bork, and later worked for Bork when the latter was Solicitor-General in the Nixon administration. However, increasingly finding that law was an abstraction removed from real life, he began searching for a synthesis between law and economics, and to this end accepted a job with the Federal Trade Commission.

His experience with the Commission taught him that economics, too, was something removed from the real life of businesses, which tended to be separated and divided into different mental and disciplinary departments. His conversations with more than a thousand business leaders convinced him that something had to be done to revitalize the economic future of the USA, and that some form of partnership between business and government was needed. With business consultant Ira Magaziner, Reich produced his first book, *Minding America's Business* (1982).

Minding America's Business was a grim catalogue of the USA's declining share of world trade and was the first book on the subject to recommend that the USA adopt a formal industrial policy. To Reich's surprise, the book provoked vigorous reaction from both opponents and supporters. There were similar reactions to his next book, *The Next American Frontier* (1983), in which Reich combined history and anthropology with economics to propose that the next challenge facing the USA was to build a strong economic future, securing jobs and prosperity for its citizens. Published as it was in 1983, when a Republican administration was in power and Reaganomics was the prevailing economic orthodoxy, the book became seen in strongly political terms; among the exponents of *The Next American Frontier* were leading Democrat politicians. Michael Dukakis, who was for a time a colleague of Reich at the Kennedy School of Government at Harvard, referred explicitly to 'the next American frontier' in his speech accepting the Democratic presidential nomination in 1988. In 1993, Reich was appointed US Secretary of Labor by the newly elected Democratic President, Bill Clinton.

Fearing that he was becoming too abstract, Reich descended into concrete case history for his next book, *New Deals* (1985), an account of how the US government rescued the Chrysler corporation. The book, based on extensive interviews with all involved, maintained that the so-called 'miracle' at Chrysler had been wrought not by the corporation's president, Lee Iacocca, but by the government, which changed the competitive ground rules. Reich felt that the Chrysler case illustrated the way by which change was bound to come in the USA; not through national debate on industrial policy but through small, often local *ad hoc* adjustments.

Delving still deeper into how people in the USA perceive business and society, Reich set out to write a book which would explain how Americans think and the questions they ask (as well as those they do not ask). The result was *Tales of a New America* (1987b), which analyses the mythological structure of US socio-political thinking and the 'cycles of righteous fulmination' directed by turns at 'big business' and then at 'big government'. In this book, Reich was able to tap into the folklore and mythology which the USA and its people have built up around themselves to expose some of the fundamental concepts which affect thinking about and by businesses.

3 Main contribution

Reich sees strategy as the re-enactment of core beliefs and stories within each society. Americans, he believes, tell themselves stories and re-enact folklore about themselves; no matter how diverse and new their experiences, they continue to fit politics and business into received narrative moulds. Reich gives names to some of these stories or moulds: 'The Rot at the Top', 'The Mob at the Gates', 'The Benevolent Community', 'The Triumphant Individual', 'The Scientific Manager'. In his view, these basic themes intertwine to create some of the major blind spots and distortions from which the US economy has been suffering since the 1960s.

Reich starts from the premise that in the USA, as well as in Britain and Canada, there has been a fundamental split between business values and civic or political values. Instead of economic evolution and development constituting one process in which civic and liberal values play a major part and in which government has a vital role, the two sets of values are seen as being in opposition. The wealth created by business culture is taxed and redistributed by the political culture, an arrangement that reduces the influence of civic values on what is deemed affordable while narrowing business values to a mixture of scientism and philistinism. Americans, says Reich, have a long history of running away from government and civic issues, first by immigration and later simply by moving on to new frontiers. In the 'next frontier', they are going to have to confront decades of social issues left behind, but not as some unresolved residue; social, human and civic issues are the heart of the USA's economic malaise and are an inseparable part of creating wealth in knowledge-intense economy.

In order to succeed, therefore, the USA needs to adapt its organizations in order to help it confront new economic realities. Doing so will require not only the participation of government in business, but also a re-evaluation and reassessment of some of the prevailing myths.

One of the myths Reich attacks most strongly is that of the 'Scientific Manager' (see TAYLOR, F.W.). The scientific principles developed by Taylor in the early part of the twentieth century undoubtedly played a role in creating the wealth of the USA and developing its manufacturing base. Yet, as in a Greek tragedy, the very values that facilitated the hegemony of the USA from the 1920s to the 1960s are now contributing to the country's failure. In 1965 the USA's share of world trade was 26 per cent; by 1980 it had fallen to below 17 per cent.

Efficiency, specialization and the separation of planning from action were not enough to protect US industry from foreign competition, which could use these same virtues to produce goods at lower wages and sell them in the USA more cheaply than domestically produced goods. But scientific management did not die; on the contrary, according to Reich, it evolved into what he calls 'paper entrepreneurship', where the principles of scientific management are applied not to the making and selling of goods, but the making and selling of companies. The old scientific disciplines such as engineering were supplemented by new ones such as finance, accounting and law.

Individual fortunes continue to be made by the buying and selling of companies and the assembling of vast conglomerates such as Gulf and Western and ITT. Most of these companies have, however, failed to perform up to expectation. This is because, according to Reich, paper entrepreneurship does not create; it merely rearranges industrial assets. Managers preside over a symbolic economy where assets are rearranged on paper, and where the resources needed for research and development and for long-term product strategies are instead tied up in acquisitions and mergers. Paper entrepreneurism is a giant distraction from the genuine tasks of the company: creating, making and supplying.

The consequences of this syndrome are enormous. Employee turnover is increasing rapidly, particularly in firms which are taken over (see INDUSTRIAL AND LABOUR RELATIONS; HUMAN RESOURCE MANAGEMENT). This in turn has knock-on effects for innovation. Competitive advantage lies in accumulating and synthesizing experience, and there are few ways in which an organization can learn how to create and produce more effectively if more than 90 per cent of its employees depart within a three-year period. Another consequence is increasing tariff protection as companies, unable to compete with the flood of foreign imports, press government to discriminate against foreign competition.

In his article on US–Japanese joint ventures (Reich and Markin 1986), Reich contrasts the US approach to that of Japanese firms. In most of the joint ventures studied, the basic research behind new products was carried out in the US (usually at universities), but the commercial development and manufacture of the new products was carried out in Japan; US companies participate in the assembly and marketing stages. The latter make good short-term profits, but the long-term strategic consequences, Reich believes, are ominous; Japanese companies are ending up with a coherent body of integratable experience and learning which extends from development through to manufacture and includes the major portion of high value-added skills. When the joint venture comes to an end, the Japanese partners walk away with these skills; US corporations are left at the top and bottom of a sandwich without the meat. Corporations are left with an elaborate satire on scientific management in which a remote controller in the USA apparently 'calls the shots' in Japan but is in truth only the front man for a business whose essentials have moved across the Pacific. The distance between planning and action has reached its logical culmination.

Reich then asks, why is the USA so blind to these dynamics? The answer is, because it cannot see the wood for the trees or, more precisely, it cannot see the community for the individuals, the self-interests of whom are paramount in its mythology. It is here, Reich believes, that the heart of the problems lies. The myth of the 'Triumphant Individual' has been passed on in the USA from Benjamin Franklin to Horatio Alger to modern television. This spirit is still celebrated today, by authors such as George Gilder who lauds 'fighters, fanatics, men with a lust for contest, a gleam of creation and a drive to justify their break from the mother company' (Gilder 1992).

Reich attacks this point of view. For him, individualism ends not in triumph, but in traffic jams; this is what Thurow (1981) calls 'the zero-sum society'. Individualism, he says, begets rules, which begets lawyers to undo the rules, which begets more lawyers to tighten them, while everyone hates the government and regulations which are made necessary by these struggles to resist. The paradox is that, in a society which values free enterprise and choice, the USA is one of the most over-regulated economies in the world. It is this deadlock that Reich is convinced the USA must break if it is to halt its inevitable decline.

4 Evaluation

Reich is at his best attacking the prevailing myths in US business and society and identifying the sources of problems. Looking at the question of why the USA and the UK have consistently lost ground, particularly in the high value-added, knowledge-intense and complex-product sectors, Reich deduces five reasons:

1 because few business leaders have been trained or selected for the role of guiding product and process innovation;
2 because flexible system production requires for its success a radical reorganization of corporate hierarchies, and would require collaborative and power-sharing arrangements with workers and trade unions;
3 because the ability to upgrade human skills rapidly is well beyond the capacity of any one corporation (which would in any case hesitate to train employees who might move on to its competitors);
4 because scientific management sees quantities but misses qualities;
5 because US culture subscribes to the myth of 'entrepreneurs and drones', where brilliant 'Triumphant Individuals' create big ideas which are then implemented by drone workers, whose sole function is to operationalize genius as quickly and cheaply as possible.

Reich attacks this last view as fundamentally flawed. In the first place, genuine new ideas are quite few, and stem from the experience of complex development and manufacture; innovation is thus a group or collective skill, not an individual one. Attacking the 'drones', breaking their unions, putting pressure on their wages and endlessly exalting the individual above the common herd is a kind of national 'ghost dance' by which the USA will hasten its own decline.

He is perhaps less specific on solutions. Going back to the narrative stories in US folklore, Reich believes that the USA needs to choose the model of 'The Benevolent Community' to mould its future strategies. At the same time, however, he is highly critical of the liberal system of social benevolence of the 1960s and 1970s, arguing instead for a social system based on reciprocal obligation. Government should give incentives to business to train and develop human capital; market forces alone, he believes, will not achieve this aim.

It is this notion that market forces can be understood and aided, rather than opposed, that distinguished Reich from welfare liberalism and socialism. The market is not 'it', it is 'we'; it is for us to choose how we develop ourselves and adjust to the constantly shifting demands of the international market. Above all, he says, we have to grasp that the logic of economic development and complex creation is a cooperative one. In the world of information, it is the 'Triumphant Team', rather than the individual, which is best able to grasp the knowledge overload and create complexity. Collective entrepreneurialism is best suited to those seamless webs of information in which products are embedded. Integrated product systems are best created by integrated human systems, with the makers mimicking the structure of what is made. There are isomorphic patterns between the knowers and the known, who are joined by the same patterns.

Reich is oddly dismissive of all the embryonic idealism in US business, such as McGregor's views on managers' capacity to develop the growth of subordinates, and Mayo and Roethlisberger and the human relations movement. He appears only to regard such sentiments as genuine if they come from Japan. While it is true that these approaches have been largely coopted by the much stronger tide of Taylorism, they are not without significance or genuine insight. Nor is it the fault of the individuals concerned that their concepts were reduced to calculated techniques by the prevailing mind-set.

5 Conclusion

Society advances politically and socially by making creative syntheses between bodies of knowledge usually regarded as remote. Reich has reached out to the falsely dichotomized cultures of business and government, right and left, economics and humanity, West and East, hard and soft, competing and cooperative, and has created a skein of ideas of extraordinary promise and power. By analysing the myths of US culture, he has gone some way towards exposing the roots of that culture and has shown at least in outline one possible way in which the culture and the US economy can adapt and prosper.

CHARLES HAMPDEN-TURNER
JUDGE INSTITUTE OF MANAGEMENT STUDIES,
UNIVERSITY OF CAMBRIDGE

Further reading

(References cited in the text marked *)

* Gilder, G. (1992) *Recapturing the Spirit of Enterprise*, San Francisco, CA: ICS Press. (A study of the personal dynamics of enterprise.)
* Reich, R.B. (1983) *The Next American Frontier*, New York: Times Books. (Famous work in which Reich discusses the economic challenge facing the USA.)
  Reich, R.B. (1987a) 'Entrepreneurship reconsidered: the team as hero', *Harvard Business Review* May–June. (Argues for more team building at top level.)
* Reich, R.B. (1987b) *Tales of a New America*, New York: Times Books. (Describes how Americans see themselves and their organizations.)
  Reich, R.B. (ed.) (1988) *The Power of Public Ideas*, Cambridge, MA: Harvard University Press. (Argues for more debate in public on the future of the USA.)
  Reich, R.B. (1991) *The Work of Nations: Preparing Ourselves for Twenty-first Century Capitalism*, London: Simon & Schuster. (Lays out a blueprint for the USA in the future. This is the book which won Reich his post as US Secretary of Labor.)
* Reich, R.B. and Donahue, J.D. (1985) *New Deals: The Chrysler Revival and the American System*, New York: Times Books. (An incisive and challenging look at industry–government relations in the USA.)
* Reich, R.B. and Magaziner, I.C. (1982) *Minding America's Business*, New York: Harcourt Brace Jovanovich. (Reich's first book, arguing the need for an industrial policy in the USA.)
* Reich, R.B. and Markin, E.D. (1986) 'Joint ventures with Japan give away our future', *Harvard Business Review* March–April. (Contrasts US and Japanese approaches to joint ventures and innovation, reporting on twenty-two cases studies.)

* Thurow, L. (1981) *The Zero-Sum Society*, New York: Viking Press. (Sociological critique of Western society by a noted writer in the field.)

See also: INDUSTRIAL AND LABOUR RELATIONS; HUMAN RESOURCE MANAGEMENT; TAYLOR, F.W.

Related topics in the IEBM: BUSINESS ETHICS; BUSINESS AND SOCIETY; ENVIRONMENTAL MANAGEMENT; GALBRAITH, J.K.; INNOVATION AND CHANGE; MANAGEMENT IN JAPAN; MANAGEMENT IN NORTH AMERICA; STRATEGY, CONCEPT OF

Schuler, Randall S. (1945–)

1 Introduction
2 Main contributions
3 Evaluation

Journal of Management 19 (2) 419–459 (1993)

Personal background

- born 29 April 1945 in Michigan, USA
- graduated with his Masters in Industrial Relations and his Ph.D. in Management from Michigan State University
- held faculty positions at Cleveland State University, Penn State University, the Ohio State University, the University of Michigan, the University of Maryland and New York University
- during this time he was also a Faculty Fellow at the US Office of Personnel Management in Washington, DC
- interests include strategic human resource management, global human resource management, organizational behaviour, and management consulting. His current interests focus on defining the human resource implications of critical business issues, and investigating the cultural imperative on human resource practices of multinational firms

Major works

'Linking competitive strategies with human resource management practices', (with Susan Jackson) *The Academy of Management Executive*, No. 2 (1987)

Human Resource Management: Positioning for the 21st Century, 6th edn. (1996)

'Technical and strategic human resource management effectiveness as determinants of firm performance', (with Mark Huselid and Susan Jackson) *Academy of Management Journal*, (1997)

'An integrative framework of strategic international human resource management', (with Peter Dowling and Helen Decieri)

1 Introduction

Randall Schuler is one of the most prominent American scholars in the area of human resource management. Since 1986 he has been Professor of Human Resource Management at the Stern School of Business, New York University. His main contributions have been in the areas of strategic human resource management; human resource management as a specialism, and international human resource management. He has authored or edited over thirty books including, most notably, *Human Resource Management: Positioning for the 21st Century*, and *Managing Human Resources*, and published over one hundred articles. He is Editor of the *Journal of World Business* and is on the Editorial Boards of some dozen other major journals including the *Academy of Management Review* and *Academy of Management Executive*.

2 Main contributions

Randall Schuler has made a significant contribution in three main areas of human resources: (1) strategic human resource management and its linkage with business strategy, (2) human resource management as a field and profession (3) international human resource management (see HUMAN RESOURCE MANAGEMENT; HUMAN RESOURCE MANAGEMENT, INTERNATIONAL). His most sustained and significant contribution has been in the first of these and so this is where we will start and where also we will place the most emphasis. His work in the other two areas to a large extent flows out of his stance on the first.

Strategic human resource management and the link with business strategy

Schuler has explicated the linkages between HRM and organizational strategy choices in a number of different publications. His most well-known article on this theme was published (jointly with Susan Jackson) in the *Academy of Management Executive* in 1987 and was entitled 'Linking competitive strategies with human resource management practices'. This article is notable in that it makes a persuasive case for shaping HRM practices to fit the requirements of different business strategies. Randall Schuler thus firmly rejects the idea of universal best practice in HRM and opts instead for a best-fit approach. His analysis is built on Michael Porter's conceptual framework. For instance, the fundamental starting point is the idea that a firm's ability to grow or even survive is dependent upon gaining and maintaining some kind of 'competitive advantage'. Moreover, following Porter, it is suggested that there are three main forms of such advantage: innovation, low cost or superior quality.

Schuler's contribution is to show a theoretical linkage (what he terms a 'rationale') between competitive strategy and HRM practices. The basis of this rationale is the idea of focusing on what behaviours are required from employees under different competitive conditions. In other words, the attention is shifted from job specific technical skills and towards the idea of what he terms 'needed role behaviours' (that is, needed under specific circumstances). The rationale for these derives from Schuler's seminal research in the area of role conflict and role ambiguity (Jackson and Schuler 1985). These role behaviours relate to dimensions such as risk taking, creativity, concern for quality, tolerance of ambiguity and so on. Each one ranges across a continuum – for some situations one end of the continuum is more preferable whereas in other situations the opposite end is more appropriate (or some point elsewhere on the continuum).

For example, within a business strategy based on innovation, the role behaviours which are at a premium include a high degree of creativity, long- rather than short-term focus, relatively high levels of cooperative, interdependent behaviour and high tolerance of ambiguity. The implication for people management strategy are that recruitment and selection may have to target highly skilled individuals, job design would have to be such that employees are given considerable autonomy and discretion, appraisal would be geared to long-term rather than short-term performance. 'Rather than managing people so that they work harder (cost reduction strategy) or smarter (quality strategy) on the same products or services, the innovation strategy requires people to work differently. This then is the necessary ingredient' (Schuler and Jackson 1987: 210).

A quality enhancement strategy requires a different set of needed role behaviours and by extension, a different set of HRM practices. The required behaviours include relatively repetitive and predictable performance, intermediate time focus, a modest concern for output, a high concern for process, low risk taking and a high commitment to the goals of the organization. The package of HRM policies associated with these requirements include the selection of employees comfortable with this profile, communication lines which allow employees to shape the process, wider job roles so that employees can use greater skills, and investment in training so that employees can learn the wider set of skills. Job redesign and compensation policies should underpin these practices.

A cost reduction strategy requires employee behaviour which is marked by focused application, tolerance of repetitive and predictable routines, short term focus, low risk taking and high concern for quantity of output. The HRM practices associated with this set of needs include stretching targets, tight controls, a focus on headcount reduction, low wage levels (possibly entailing relocation of plants to low-wage areas), increased use of contingent workers, and tight work rules.

There are a whole plethora of HRM tools or practices which can be deployed in pursuit of the required role behaviours. These 'practice choices' (Schuler 1987) are set out as a 'menu' as if one were choosing a starter and a main course and so on. In reality they are clusters of choices about pay, planning, staffing, evaluating and appraising, training and developing. As Schuler is at pains to point out, there is no one set of best practices here, rather these choices again should be viewed as constituting a continuum – for example, decisions about pay can be seen to comprise a whole set of choices including whether to offer few perks or many, a standard fixed package or a flexible one, short-term incentives or long-term, whether to focus on internal equity or external and so on (see PAYMENT SYSTEMS). The central point is that different choices stimulate and reinforce different role behaviours.

Which is the best strategy will depend upon market conditions. Thus, if a product or service is relatively undifferentiated, such as overnight parcel delivery services, then a cost reduction strategy may be the way to gain competitive advantage: the HRM policies would then need to follow from that choice. However, if customers are demanding high quality then an emphasis on cost reduction may lead to a loss of market share and a quality enhancement strategy may be required.

This work is often criticized on the grounds that in practice firms often pursue more than one of these competitive strategies. They may pursue high quality and low costs. Schuler is not unaware of this. On the contrary, he explicitly points out examples of firms with these multiple strategies and contends that 'perhaps the top managers job is facilitated by separate business units or functional areas that have different competitive strategies'. And that managing the tensions 'may be the very essence of the top manager's job' (1987: 216).

Moreover, as competitive conditions change, so too there will be a need for an ever-changing employment relationship; employees may face different demands at different times. The key point is that managers need to make choices across the practice menu which reinforce the necessary employee behaviours. Thus, internal fit is just as vital as securing external fit.

Human resource management as a field and as a professional specialism

Schuler has made the case for the critical importance of HRM in corporate positioning for the twenty-first Century (Schuler and Jackson 1996). This case is based in part on the idea that the new growth industries (such as biotechnology) are knowledge based industries but it is based also on the premise that sustained competitive advantage rests on resources not easily imitated – such as the skill to make better use of people. Using a multiple stakeholder framework, Schuler and Jackson garner evidence from a wide range of studies in order to demonstrate that good human resource management practice can pay in a whole range of ways (:financial bottom line, employee and customer satisfaction, union relations and suppliers. They emphasize that managing human resources effectively is important and is likely to become even more so in future years; that managing human resources effectively means responding to many stakeholders. Additionally, effective human resource management under contemporary conditions demands more than simple technical expertise in compensation management or selection. It requires a systematic and thoughtful approach which integrates sets of policies. Consistency and clarity are emphasized. Systematic management of human resources, Schuler maintains, means fitting HRM practices to the situation of particular companies. In this sense there is no one best way. 'In firms that manage their employees systematically, managers know why they manage their people the way they do: their entire set of HR practices has been explicitly developed to match the needs of their constituencies, their employees and their customers, and the strategies of the business. In this way they all fit each other and fit the qualities of the company' (Schuler and Jackson 1996). There is thus no one best way; some trial and error is inevitable and the practices must fit the changing circumstances. The contrast between this stance and the citation of Huselid's work which is used to emphasize the power of best practice is not however discussed – although it is just possible that a meaningful distinction could be drawn between general policies and specific practices, and that while Huselid addresses the former, Schuler has paid more attention to the latter.

The point is emphasized even more fully in Jackson and Schuler (1995). In that article they construct an integrated framework for understanding HRM in context (see ORGANIZATION BEHAVIOUR). This seeks to take into account the external context such as laws and regulations, culture, politics, labour markets and the like as well as internal contextual features such as technology, organization structure, size, life cycle and business strategy. Above all however, the main message of Schuler's writing is that *human resource management matters*. Used wisely, he argues, HRM can transform a lacklustre company into a star performer; used unwisely it can create havoc.

This same upbeat message is echoed in a review of the place of world class HRM departments (Schuler 1994). In this piece Schuler locates the HRM department firmly in the top strategic team – world class organizations will need, he maintains, world class HRM departments. Schuler recognizes the role of line mangers in HRM but at the same time his analysis leads to the conclusion that HRM departments in effective organizations will become more important than ever in the future.

International HRM

Schuler has recently sought to extend his work into the international arena (see HUMAN RESOURCE MANAGEMENT, INTERNATIONAL). The starting point is the increasing globalization of business and the need to operate across the world as one vast market while simultaneously being attentive to local conditions. An integrated framework of strategic international human resource management (SIHRM) is offered in Schuler et al. (1993). SIHRM is defined as 'human resource management issues, functions and policies and practices that result from the strategic activities of multinational enterprises and that impact the international concerns and goals of those enterprises' (1993:422). Schuler emphasizes the point that while many of the attributes of

conventional human resource management are relevant to a study of multinational enterprises there are also some distinctive elements in the latter which call for special study.

The essential aspects of the integrated framework are the identification of the interplay between the key issues, the resulting functions and the required policies in HR which pertain to SIHRM conditions. The main SIHRM *issues* are identified as inter-unit linkages (control and variety) and internal operations (remaining alert to local sensitivities and ensuring strategic fit). The main SHIRM *functions* revolve around the resources devoted to HRM and the location of these resources. The SIHRM *policies and practices* relate to questions of staffing, appraising, compensating and developing. A series of testable propositions are put forward which hypothesize the likely choices which different MNEs will make when balancing competing imperatives under different conditions.

This work is taken a stage further by Sparrow *et al.* (1994). Drawing upon an international survey by IBM and Towers Perrin they identify emerging trends across a number of country clusters. These include a predicted far greater emphasis on seeking competitive advantage through people and, most notably, in a drive for empowerment, equality, diversity management, flatter organizational structures, customer-based measures of performance and related remuneration, more training and development and greater communication of goals and objectives (see JOB DESIGN; MOTIVATION AND SATISFACTION; TRAINING). In other words, a reaffirmation of the optimistic high commitment version of the HRM model. Thus, while cultural differences were certainly identified the most notable conclusion from this work is the idea that there are certain HRM policies and practices which are expected to travel well in future years. In the words of the authors: 'organisations seeking to have a truly global operation are likely to pursue the above stated key themes in the workplace with human resource practices that have some cross-cultural variation but that can all be fitted under a common policy umbrella' (1994: 296).

3 Evaluation

Schuler is evidently an articulate champion of the idea of the vital importance of HRM. He is most often cited for his work on making a connection between strategy and HRM. This work has been criticized on a number of fronts. The main criticism has been that the hypothesized connections between competitive strategies and HRM practices remain highly speculative and hypothetical. The connections have not been rigorously tested by Schuler though there was a fairly large-scale test of the link between innovation strategy and personnel practices and this did lend support to the hypotheses (Jackson *et al.* 1989). Much of his other work rests on the selective use of high profile cases which illustrate the argument rather than test it. More recent studies have moved towards the use of statistical tests of large data sets. While the links sound plausible it has proved to be very difficult to substantiate the propositions when they are subjected to statistical tests. Contemporary work has shifted to the exploration of the 'bundles' of HRM practices which are so mutually reinforcing that they provide true competitive advantage (Huselid 1995; MacDuffie 1995; Youndt *et al.* 1996). Some of these studies could be interpreted as supportive of Schuler's position, but the diversity of findings, the differences in the compositions of the bundles, the methodological problems associated with single respondent answers to tick-box questionnaires, and the tension between best practice versus best fit (to name just a few of the problems) suggest that the jury is still out.

Exploration of the link between HRM and business strategy was not of course confined to the work of Schuler. A number of other American scholars had sought to map the contours of the 'match' between them. Fombrun *et al.* (1984) published the best known version and this linked HRM with strategy and structure of businesses. Thus single product companies with functional structures were shown to require a different suite of selection, appraisal, rewards and development practices than, for example, companies in multiproduct divisionalized corporations. The added contribution of Schuler was the focus on the intermediate constructs of 'needed role behaviours' and an explicated 'menu' of human resource options: these provide a much needed *theoretical linkage* between HRM practices and business priorities under different strategic options.

There might also be some criticism that the analysis neglects the core–periphery characteristics of so much modern employment. The optimism reflected in the work on strategic HRM in large leading American corporations (and echoed in the international study which reflects on the data from IBM/Towers Perrin) tends to neglect the evidence which points towards the growing insecurity of employment, failure to invest more in training and declining scores on employee attitude surveys. The fact is that in large measure the expected diffusion of best practice in HRM has been notoriously slow to materialize. Some balanced attention to these practices is, hence, also required.

Although it is never made sufficiently explicit, there is a sense that strategy is a rational top-down process. It is implied that business strategy is reached in a rational, planned way and that with access to this strategy, the HR specialist can design a matching HRM strategy by selecting from the practice 'menu'. This view of strategy has been challenged by those who see strategy as an emergent process. It is also surprising perhaps that Schuler takes as a given that HR policies will necessarily be downstream of business strategy. Given the emphasis upon core competencies by the resource based view of the firm there could be scope for an alternative line of analysis which starts with comparative advantage based on competence and works backwards to the choice of markets and hence to the kind of business strategy. This dimension at least deserves some consideration.

Relatedly, it is not made entirely clear whether the analysis running through Schuler's work on strategy is descriptive or prescriptive. There is a sense that leading companies are already pursuing activities of this kind and that the author has educed the essence of these for others to emulate. But the evidence for this is rather thin. Detailed case-study work by Storey (1992) revealed that even in the leading blue-chip corporations where sophisticated HRM policies might have been most expected, there was evidence of the running being made by manufacturing directors and other non-HR players; of lack of integration between policies; of failure to sustain the implementation of new initiatives; and of a rather insecure place for HRM in the wider corporate agenda – despite an ability of the senior team to recite the HRM rhetoric.

Despite such criticisms, the significance of Schuler's contribution in this area should not be underestimated. Schuler clarifies the linkages set out in more general terms in the model offered by Beer *et al.* (1982). While research has progressed in different directions there has been little evidence of major advances of a theoretical kind beyond that which has been achieved by Schuler. The need to build systematic theory and explanation concerning HRM and business strategy remains. His considerable reputation in this area is well deserved.

JOHN STOREY
THE OPEN UNIVERSITY

Further reading

(References cited in the text marked *)

* Beer, M., Spector, B., Lawrence,. P., Mills, D. and Walton, R. (1985) *Human Resource Management: A General Manager's Perspective.* New York: Free Press.
* Fombrun, C. J., Tichy, N.M., and Devanna, M.A. (1984) *Strategic Human Resource Management.* New York: Wiley.
* Huselid, M.A. (1995) 'The impact of human resource management practices on turnover, productivity and corporate financial performance', *Academy of Management Journal*, 38: 635–70.
* Jackson, S. and Schuler, R. S. (1985) 'A meta-analysis and conceptual critique of research on role ambiguity and role conflict in work settings', *Organizational Behavior and Human Decision Processes*, 36: 16–78.
* Jackson, S. and Schuler, R. S. (1995) 'Understanding human resource management in the context of organisations and their environments', *Annual Review of Psychology*, 46: 237–64.
* Jackson, S., Schuler, R.S., and Carlos Rivero, J. (1989) 'Organizational characteristics as predictors of personnel policies', *Personnel Psychology*, 42: 727–85.
* MacDuffie, J.P. (1995) 'Human resource bundles and manufacturing performance: organisational logic and flexible production systems in the world auto industry', *Industrial & Labor Relations Review*, 48 (2): 197–221
* Schuler, R.S. (1986) 'Fostering and facilitating entrepreneurship in organisations: implications for organisation structure and human resource management practices', *Human Resource Management*, 25: 607–29.
* Schuler, R.S. (1987) 'Human resource management choices and organisational strategy', *Human Resource Planning*, March: 1–19.
* Schuler, R.S. and Jackson, S.E. (1987) 'Linking competitive strategies with human resource management practices', *Academy of Management Executive*, 1 (3): 207–19
* Schuler, R.S.and Jackson, S. (1996) *Human Resource Management: Positioning for the 21st Century*, St Paul: West Publishing Co.
* Storey, J. (1992) *Management of Human Resources: An Analytical Review*, Oxford: Blackwell.

See also: HUMAN RESOURCE MANAGEMENT; HUMAN RESOURCE MANAGEMENT, INTERNATIONAL; JOB DESIGN; MOTIVATION AND SATISFACTION;ORGANIZATION BEHAVIOUR; PAYMENT SYSTEMS; TRAINING

Related topics in the IEBM: APPRAISAL METHODS; COMPETITIVE STRATEGY, DEVELOPMENT OF; CREATIVITY MANAGEMENT; INNOVATION AND CHANGE; PORTER, M.E.; SHORT-TERMISM; STRATEGY, CONCEPT OF

Taylor, Frederick Winslow (1856–1915)

Personal background

- born 28 March 1856 in Philadelphia, Pennsylvania, into a middle-class Quaker family, but did not go to college
- trained as an apprentice and eventually studied at night school
- married Louise M. Spooner, 1884
- developed what he called the 'scientific' study of work
- formative influence on work-study and industrial engineering
- early death in Philadelphia on 21 March 1915 from pneumonia

Major works

Shop Management (1903)
The Principles of Scientific Management (1911)
Two Papers on Scientific Management (1919)

Summary

F.W. Taylor (1856–1915) was the initiator of scientific management and a major influence on the development of production management as a subject. He set out to systematize the study of workflow organization by breaking tasks into minute detail and devising ways to speed up their accomplishment. Taylor aimed at a 'mental revolution' in order to break down the barriers to good labour relations between workers and management. His ideas on efficiency were propagated by his disciples after his death through an international movement to promote such management techniques. While he was a controversial figure in his time, Taylor's contribution still continues to provoke lively debate in many management texts.

1 Introduction

Taylor is widely seen as the initiator of the scientific management movement, although his work has also been described as a synthesis of already existing notions. He has become one of, if not the, best known 'management guru' of all time. His contribution to the study of organizations has been described as original in that he set out to study jobs scientifically and to measure workflows in order to achieve higher productivity (see ORGANIZATION BEHAVIOUR). He believed that management normally tried to push workers to achieve output, without an objective yardstick to measure a proper day's work. He therefore tried to devise a science of work to resolve this problem. Taylor thought that he was transforming what had previously been a crude art form into a firm body of knowledge.

Taylor set out to analyse tasks into their smallest details, diagnose the abilities of workers and then fit the two together to achieve greater efficiency. Job techniques would be redesigned to make maximum use of operatives' skills. In proposing these notions, he combined an engineer's outlook with an obsession for control. The main concept in Taylor's work was the 'task-idea', based on the principle that management should specify what must be done in the minutest detail and how it could be done. If these instructions were followed, industry would become more productive and trouble-free. While many writers have positively recognized Taylor's contribution (Merkle 1980; Kelly 1982), others have negatively referred to it as 'the degradation of work' (Braverman 1974).

2 Biographical data

Taylor was born into a Quaker, middle-class family on 20 March 1856, just outside the city of Philadelphia. Having completed his apprenticeship during the Depression in the 1870s, he went on to perform labouring work at the Midvale Steel Company in Philadelphia. In order to get out of this low-level employment, he decided to study engineering at the Stevens Institute's evening classes, eventually receiving his Master's Degree in Mechanical Engineering in 1883. Once qualified, he began a set of time studies at Midvale Steel in the early 1880s, out of which grew what was later called the Taylor System of Scientific Management. He started with the analysis of machine speeds in metal cutting in order to achieve greater efficiency.

In 1895, he gave a paper to the American Society of Mechanical Engineers entitled 'A piece-rate system: a step toward partial solution of the labor problem'. It was not the first paper on incentives, but it contained the basis of the distinctly Taylorist system and was founded on twelve years' experience at Midvale Steel, by which time he was chief engineer. It combined technical and organizational expertise, synthesizing several currents of efficiency management at hand. Taylor aimed to subdivide tasks, time them and find a way to speed them up. To prevent fatigue, carefully timed rest periods were to be built into the system. He continued his work in a new post at Bethlehem Steel, where he was made their management consultant in 1898, until 1901 when he lost his job on the sale of the company (Kanigel 1997).

After *Shop Management* was published in 1903, he became a well-known writer and lecturer and was elected President of the American Society of Mechanical Engineers. By this time, he had acquired several disciples, including C.G. Barth, H. Emerson and F.B. Gilbreth (see GILBRETH, F.B. AND GILBRETH, L.E.M.). An important implementation of his new methods of standardizing tools and tasks was later tried out between 1909 and 1912 at the Watertown Arsenal in Cambridge, Massachusetts (Aitken 1960). It led to the adoption of similar practices in arsenals all over the USA. In 1911, he published his *Principles of Scientific Management* and became an increasingly public and controversial figure giving talks to top industrialists among others. He was invited as a visiting lecturer to the newly formed Harvard Business School and taught there once a year from 1909 until his death.

After organized labour tried to block rationalization techniques in industry influenced by Taylor's ideas in 1910–11, Taylor was confronted with Congressional investigation (Nelson 1980). A special House Committee summoned him as a leading witness in 1912. While the Committee conceded that Taylorism offered advantages to industry, it still believed Taylorism gave employers too much power. In the years following his death in 1915, Taylor's followers were to improve their relations with organized labour by recognizing the role of the unions in negotiating the introduction of new working methods, but still Taylor had gained a reputation as 'the enemy of the working man' (Morgan 1997: 22) (see TRADE UNIONS).

3 Main contribution

Taylor saw 'slacking' by workers as the main source of inefficiency in industry. The labourer, he reasoned, would not exert himself; the manager would use guesswork. Both had to be guided towards rational behaviour. To this end, he invented what he called a 'science of shovelling' while working in the steel industry in the early 1880s. To illustrate his notion of a fair day's work, he trained a labourer called Schmidt to increase by four times his workload of loading mouldings called 'pigs': the latter gained a bonus of 50 per cent as a result of the rationalization of his job. Piecework rates were devised to boost motivation, with what Taylor liked to call 'first-class men' setting the pace (see PAYMENT SYSTEMS). He believed his system was more than a mere efficiency device: it involved a complete 'mental revolution' on the part of management as well as workers, and involved a coming together of capital and labour, a delusion according to his critics.

Taylor also tried to extend the division of labour to management, believing that there should be no fewer than eight kinds of functional foremen, dealing with work speed and repairs. He believed that 'a good organization with a poor plant will give better results than the best plant with poor organization' (Taylor 1903: 65). The planning department was to play a pivotal role in Taylor's schema, as it would work out the detailed work schedules for the employees to follow in order to increase output.

At the Congressional inquiry, Taylor argued that better production methods were not only in the interests of management but also of the workers. He believed that:

> The new way is to teach and help your men as you would a brother; to try to teach him the best way and show him the easiest way to do his work. This is the new mental attitude of the management toward the men, and that is the reason I have taken so much of your time in describing this cheap work of shovelling. It may seem to you of very little consequence, but I want you to see, if I can, that this new mental attitude is the very essence of scientific management; that the mechanism is nothing if you have not got the right sentiment, the right attitude in the minds of the men, both on the management's side and on the workman's side. Because this helps to explain the fact that until this summer, there has never been a strike under scientific management.
>
> (cited in Pugh 1991: 139)

Against the notion of the survival of the fittest which was prominent at the time, Taylor offered a strategy of collaboration. He argued that wasteful conflict was inefficient and therefore wrong (see INDUSTRIAL CONFLICT). It was this moral element in his thought that inspired his disciples and generated a crusade for scientific management according to his defenders (Merkle 1980).

4 Evaluation

F.W. Taylor promoted not only systematic time-and-motion study, production control methods and incentive pay, but a wider philosophy and methodology of work organization (see WORK AND ORGANIZATION SYSTEMS). Scientific management would create an atmosphere of trust in industry based on a value-neutral approach, probably a dubious notion from the start. He always stressed the word scientific: he thought it would increase his credibility with managers and engineers and even ordinary workers who were sceptical about the impersonal forces of the market. Science, he thought, would create both high wages and high profits.

Taylorism has been criticized by many writers on organizational behaviour for its individualist assumptions that gave priority to distinctly individual motivation, rewards and controls in order to break the collective power of work groups (see MOTIVATION AND SATISFACTION; GROUPS AND TEAMS). Furthermore, time-and-motion study techniques and financial incentives were seen as part of management's definition of what were appropriate workloads and work methods in order to increase managerial control. Other critics of Taylor's theories have argued that his work did not deserve the term scientific and that Taylorism took too narrow a view of work:

> Time-study; the confusion of human labour with the play of inanimate mechanisms; the ignorance of the physical and mental functioning of the organism and its own demands; the procedure adopted to stimulate and reward effort; the place of vocational guidance; the selection by output, and finally the empiricism of generalizations elevated to the status of 'laws' – everything proves that we have here a system created by a man who was doubtless a great technician but who could not see beyond the confines of his engineer's universe.
>
> (Friedmann 1955: 64–5)

None the less, Taylor carried out several important field experiments at both the Midvale Steel works and Bethlehem Steel, and later as an industrial consultant at Watertown Arsenal, for example, passing on his findings to meetings of bodies such as the American Society of Mechanical Engineers, although not without criticism and even Congressional scrutiny. The later phase of Taylor's work was, however, more linked with what were to become mainstream developments. For example, there was a considerable continuity between late Taylorism and early industrial psychology (Kelly 1982) (see OCCUPATIONAL PSYCHOLOGY). During and after the First World War, industrial psychologists started to investigate the conditions for industrial cooperation. Union–management cooperation was encouraged as part of the war effort as were joint consultation mechanisms (see INDUSTRIAL AND LABOUR RELATIONS). In spite of proposing greater managerial control and increased specialization of tasks, Taylor emphasized many features of what later became subsumed under the human relations heading, including motivational factors, such as promotional prospects, friendly supervisors, positive work rhythms and clear working goals, which remain important concerns of managerial practice (see HUMAN RELATIONS).

Taylorism evolved into an experimental approach which was to persist long after its founder's death in most capitalist economies. Japanese management was appreciably influenced by Taylorism in the inter-war years and in much of its post-1945 development (Warner 1994)(see UENO, Y.). Even in the Soviet Union, Taylorism was encouraged as part of an ambitious programme of social engineering as carried out by the Russian efficiency expert Gastev in the early 1920s. Taylor's name was openly used along with studies of work physiology, labour fatigue and selection methods. After initial opposition to such ideas, Lenin observed that 'Socialism plus Taylorism would equal Communism' because of businesslike methods and one-man management. Soviet and later Chinese industry continued to be influenced by scientific management as adapted to their respective systems (Kaple 1994).

5 Conclusions

Taylor's four Principles of Scientific Management (1911) are: (1) to establish a science of production; (2) to select and train workers to achieve this; (3) to apply such a science to operatives' tasks; and (4) to build cooperation

between the workers and management to achieve common goals. Its impact on contemporary society and its so-called 'McDonaldization' (see Ritzer 1996) has been considerable. Taylorism was not a single innovation, but a series of notions and practices elaborated by the initiator and his collaborators. The movement promoted an international crusade for efficiency in the 1920s and 1930s with its effect being felt long after. Taylor's epitaph in Philadelphia reads: 'Father of Scientific Management' (Kakar 1970: 1). Without his innovations (and later those of Henry Ford), assembly-line mass production as we know it today would not have been possible (see FORD, H.). In anticipating the routinization of everyday life, 'History may judge that Taylor came before his time' (Morgan 1997: 26).

MALCOLM WARNER
JUDGE INSTITUTE OF MANAGEMENT STUDIES,
UNIVERSITY OF CAMBRIDGE

Further reading

(References cited in the text marked *)

* Aitken, G.H. (1960) *Taylorism at the Watertown Arsenal: Scientific Management in Action, 1908–1915*, Cambridge, MA: Harvard University Press. (A detailed monograph on a specific application of Taylor's work in arms manufacture, which is probably of interest mostly to specialists.)

* Braverman, H. (1974) *Labor and Monopoly Capital: The Degradation of Work in the Twentieth Century*, New York: Monthly Review Press. (A controversial work based on a critique of Taylorism from a Marxist perspective, which has played an important role in generating the de-skilling debate.)

Copley, F.B. (1923) *Frederick W. Taylor: Father of Scientific Management*, 2 vols, New York: Harper & Co. (A definitive, extended biography of Taylor, published not long after his death, which is dated but contains useful detail.)

* Friedmann, G. (1955) *Industrial Society: The Emergence of the Human Problems of Automation*, Glencoe, IL: The Free Press. (A well-known work on automation by a renowned French industrial sociologist who was a critic of Taylorism.)

* Kakar, S. (1970) *Frederick Taylor: A Study in Personality and Innovation*, Cambridge, MA: MIT Press. (A psychoanalytic biography of Taylor, which concisely examines the personal factors in his life that influenced his behaviour and the specific direction of his work.)

* Kanigel, R. (1997) *The One Best Way: Frederick Winslow Taylor and the Enigma of Efficiency*. New York: Viking. (A new insightful, up-to-date biography of Taylor and his work which argues that his techniques owe more to 'guesswork' than to 'science'.)

* Kaple, D.A. (1994) *Dream of a Red Factory: The Legacy of High Stalinism in China*. Oxford: Oxford University Press. (An account of Taylorist influence on both Soviet and Chinese communist industrial practice.)

* Kelly, J. (1982) *Scientific Management, Job Design and Work Performance*, London: Academic Press. (This book constitutes an excellent critique of Taylor's work, which is distinctive in that it sees the later development of his thought as overlapping with the human relations school.)

* Merkle, J.A. (1980) *Management and Ideology: The Legacy of the International Scientific Management Movement*, Berkeley and Los Angeles, CA: University of California Press. (The author has written an interesting monograph on Taylorism as a social movement with reference to its influence on the UK, France, Germany and the Soviet Union.)

* Morgan, G. (1997) *Images of Organization*. Thousand Oaks, CA: Sage. (A provocative textbook which has attempted to re-write modern organizational theory.)

* Nelson, D. (1980) *Frederick Taylor and the Rise of Scientific Management*, Madison, WI: University of Wisconsin Press. (A more recent account of Taylor's life and work placing it in the context of US economic history.)

Pruijt, H.D. (1997) *Job Design and Technology: Taylorism-vs-Anti-Taylorism*. London: Routledge. (A timely account of anti-Taylorist innovations in European firms.)

* Pugh, D.S. (ed.) (1991) *Organization Theory: Selected Readings*, Harmondsworth: Penguin. (This is a set of useful readings covering more of the field and including detail on Taylor's evidence to the Congressional investigation.)

* Ritzer, G. (1996) *The McDonaldization of Society*. Newbury Park, CA: Sage. (An imaginative attempt to link Taylorism and later phenomena like McDonald's and Disney.)

Shingo, S. (1981) *The Toyota Production System*. Tokyo: Japanese Management Association. (Shingo describes the links between Taylorism and the Toyota system.)

* Taylor, F.W. (1903; 1919) *Shop Management*, New York: Harper Brothers. (Taylor's first major publication on work-study which made his reputation as a thinker and practitioner in the field.)

* Taylor, F.W. (1911) *The Principles of Scientific Management*, New York: W.W. Norton & Co. Inc. (Taylor's classic exposition of his views which has become internationally known as one of the classics of management theory.)

Taylor, F.W. (1919) *Two Papers on Scientific Management*, London: Routledge. (This book constitutes the late work of Taylor, which was published posthumously.)

* Warner, M. (1994) 'Japanese culture, Western management: Taylorism and Human Resources in Japan', *Organization Studies* 15: 509–533. (This paper explicitly points to the role of Taylorism in the development of the Japanese employment system.)

See also: BEDAUX, C.E.; COLLECTIVE BARGAINING; FOLLETT, M.P.; FORD, H.; GILBRETH, F.B. AND GILBRETH, L.E.; FINANCIAL INCENTIVES; HUMAN RELATIONS; HUMAN RESOURCE MANAGEMENT; INDUSTRIAL AND LABOUR RELATIONS; INDUSTRIAL CONFLICT; JOB DESIGN; JOB EVALUATION; LABOUR PROCESS; MAYO, G.E.; MOTIVATION AND SATISFACTION; OCCUPATIONAL PSYCHOLOGY; ORGANIZATION BEHAVIOUR; PAYMENT SYSTEMS; PRODUCTIVITY; RECRUITMENT AND SELECTION; TRADE UNIONS; UENO, Y.; WORK AND ORGANIZATION SYSTEMS

Related topics in the IEBM: GURU CONCEPT; MANAGEMENT IN JAPAN; ORGANIZATION BEHAVIOUR, HISTORY OF; SMITH, A.

Ueno, Yôichi (1883–1957)

Personal background

- born Shiba, Tokyo, 28 October 1883, into a middle-class family; his father died when he was twelve years old
- gained a BA degree in psychology at the Tokyo Imperial University, 1908
- married Teruko Miimi, 1910; following her death in 1922, he married Shige Kochi
- promoted industrial efficiency movement, based on F.W. Taylor's notion of scientific management, in pre-war Japan
- established a school for industrial efficiency in 1942
- died at home of heart failure, 15 October 1957, aged 73

Major works

Shinrigaku tsûgi (Introduction to Psychology) (1914)

Hito oyobi jigyô nôritsu no shinri (Psychology of Efficiency of People and Business) (1919)

Jigyô tôseiron (Control of Enterprise) (1928)

Sangyô nôritsu-ron (Industrial Management) (1929)

Nôritsu gairon (An Introduction to Management) (1938)

Nôritsu handobukku (Management Handbook) (1939–41)

Nôritsu-gaku genron (Principles of Management) (1948)

Summary

Trained as a psychologist, Yôichi Ueno (1883–1957) was a pioneer in many fields in pre-war Japan. He is best remembered as the promoter in Japan of the notion of production efficiency based on the theory of scientific management devised by F.W. Taylor and developed by Taylor's followers. Ueno firmly believed in Taylor's idea that efficient work organization, informed by 'mental revolution', would reduce conflict and thereby lead to better relations between workers and management. Through consultancy, writing, lecturing and teaching, Ueno worked tirelessly to introduce the practice of industrial efficiency into the Japanese workplace. The philosophy of efficiency he developed was deeply influenced by the spiritual discipline of Zen Buddhist thought and could be extended to apply to life itself. Through pioneers like Ueno, Taylorism influenced Japanese management before the Second World War and provided the basis for further development in post-war Japan.

1 Introduction

Yôichi Ueno's professional life divides into four major phases. After his graduation in 1908 and until 1919, he worked to establish himself as a psychologist. Towards the end of this phase he became interested in industrial efficiency, introducing the works of F.W. Taylor and others to Japan (see TAYLOR, F.W.). From 1919 to 1925, he practised as an industrial efficiency consultant and visited the USA, where he contacted Taylor's followers. During the period 1925 to 1942, he established the Japanese chapter of the Taylor Society of America, participated in international activities and published Taylor's works. Later, when the official economic and industrial organizations became dominated by the military, Ueno concentrated on private consultancy work. During the final period of his life, he devoted himself to the development of his own school of industrial efficiency while continuing his writing and consultancy work.

2 Biographical data and main contributions

Ueno's family originated in Nagasaki, where his grandfather, Shunnojô Ueno (1791–1852), had been a scientist and industrialist. Shunnojô introduced the first camera into Japan and is today regarded as Japan's 'father of photography' (Misawa 1967). Ueno's father, a skilful photographic technician, left Nagasaki for Tokyo to establish himself as a professional photographer. However, this venture did not succeed and he changed jobs several times. He died in the year Ueno completed the eight years of his elementary education. The family returned to Nagasaki to live under the protection of Ueno's uncle, Hikoma, a successful photographer.

Ueno went to a missionary school where all the textbooks, except those used for Japanese and Chinese language studies, were in English. This early exposure to English was to serve him well. At the age of seventeen, he returned to Tokyo with a strong desire to study at Tokyo Imperial University, which was then the foremost educational establishment in Japan. Working as a live-in English language assistant to an eminent educationist, he also taught English in the evening to finance his admission to the university as an auditing student in 1903. Continuing to work throughout his years at university, he first acquired full student status and, finally, in 1908 gained a degree in psychology.

Psychology and industrial efficiency

The experience Ueno gained in his first job as an editor at Dôbunkan, a major publisher, was important for his subsequent activities. While he was with Dôbunkan, he began lecturing, writing, editing and publishing in psychology-based disciplines. Psychology was established as an academic subject in Japan by Ueno's teacher, Yûjirô Motora, a professor at the Tokyo Imperial University. Between 1909 and 1921, Motora and his graduates gave monthly public lectures to popularize psychology. The lectures, edited by Ueno and published by Dôbunkan, proved to be popular. The success of the venture led to the launch of a monthly psychological journal, *Shinri kenkyû* (The Study of Psychology) in 1912, with Ueno as its chief editor. In 1926, it amalgamated with another journal to become *Shinri-gaku kenkyû* (Journal of Psychological Studies), the journal of the Japan Psychological Society.

Ueno's comprehensive psychology textbook, published in 1914 for student teachers, became both the best seller among his early publications and a long-selling book. The first revision in 1926 incorporated new psychological developments, including Sigmund Freud's psychoanalytic theory (see FREUD, S.), and by 1942 it had run to sixty-five editions. This success established Ueno's reputation as a psychologist and brought him financial independence (Saito 1983).

Turning his attention to the study of industrial efficiency, Ueno found the practical application of psychology to industry fascinating. At university he had read a journal from the USA in which Gilbreth, one of Taylor's followers, demonstrated the use of photography in the motion study (see GILBRETH, F.B. AND GILBRETH, L.E.M.). Ueno wrote to ask Gilbreth for further explanation and thus made contact with a leading exponent of scientific management. In 1912, he was asked to contribute to a special edition of the journal *Jitsugyôkai* (Business World), centred on scientific management. In writing this article, he studied the work of H. Münsterberg to establish a connection between psychology and scientific management and came to see Gilbreth's work in this light. To *Shinri-gaku kenkyû*, he contributed papers describing the accomplishments of Taylor, Gilbreth and Thompson and translated the work of Münsterberg. In 1919, using the material Gilbreth had sent, Ueno wrote and published his book *Hito oyobi jigyô nôritsu no shinri* (Psychology of Efficiency of People and Business). This achievement marked the end of the period when his study of industrial efficiency largely involved introducing the works of western scholars.

937

Industrial consultancy

From 1916, Ueno taught the psychology of advertising at Waseda University. In 1919, while working in this capacity, he came into contact with the director of marketing at the Kobayashi Company, the maker of Lion Brand tooth powder. The company wanted to improve its existing packing process, giving Ueno the opportunity to work on the practical application of theories of industrial efficiency to production. Using the time-and-motion technique, he introduced a change in the flow of work and a team-based work group and achieved a 20 per cent increase in output, a saving of 30 per cent in space, a reduction of waste and a decrease in the working hours. His success at Kobayashi established him as the first industrial consultant in Japan. The success of other assignments such as those at Nakayama Taiyôdô, a cosmetic firm, and Fukusuke Tabi Company, the maker of Japanese-style socks, helped to popularize the practical application of scientific management and brought Ueno a stream of speaking engagements and consultancy contracts.

In 1921, Ueno became the head of the *Sangyô Nôritsu Kenkyûsho* (Efficiency Research Institute), an arm of *Kyôchôkai*, a body established in 1919 to promote cooperation and adjustment between capital and labour through improvements in production efficiency. Ueno's achievements in industrial efficiency convinced the members of *Kyôchôkai* that there was a scientific basis to the notion of cooperation between capital and labour (see INDUSTRIAL RELATIONS IN JAPAN).

Before starting work at the institute, Ueno was sent to the USA and Europe on a ten-month fact-finding tour. The tour turned out to be immensely significant for the subsequent development of his career. Helped by Gilbreth, he visited many universities, businesses, governmental offices and private associations, mainly in the USA. He met many people, including F.W. Taylor's widow, the known followers of Taylor and many other exponents of scientific management. At the spring conference of the Taylor Society held in Philadelphia, Ueno gave an impressive speech to an audience of 500 people (Misawa 1967). The contacts he made with the members of the Taylor Society led to many lasting friendships. In Europe, he visited London, Paris, Munich and Berlin. He wrote *Nôritsu gakusha no tabinikki* (The Travel Diary of the Efficiency Management Scholar), describing his visits.

In the first part of the 1920s, Japan was ready to embrace the idea of industrial efficiency and Ueno was extremely busy running the institute, working as a consultant and writing. One of the institute's major achievements was its programme for training efficiency experts. Four courses held in 1923 qualified 450 people as efficiency supervisors, who became the backbone of the efficiency movement in subsequent decades (Misawa 1967). However, the institute was closed in March 1925, due mainly to lack of funds.

Keen to continue the institute's work, Ueno took it over as his personal consultancy business, with the same aims and staff, under the name of *Nihon Sangyô Nôritsu Kenkyûsho*, (Japan Institute of Industrial Efficiency). His activity extended to Manchuria, China, when it came under Japanese control. The institute's office moved, in 1933, to Ueno's home. In 1927, *Nihon Nôritsu Rengôkai*, (National Management Association of Japan), was formed as an amalgam of six existing regional efficiency institutes, with Ueno as one of its committee members and later as its director-general. He also edited the association's house journal, *Sangyô Nôritsu*. (In pre-war Japan, the term *nôritsu*, or 'efficiency', which was employed by Harrington Emerson, was more commonly used in Japanese industrial circles than the term *keikei*, or 'management'.)

Furthering the aims of scientific management

In 1925, Ueno established the Japan chapter of the Taylor Society, the first outside the USA. In the following five years, many leading US experts in scientific management came to Japan, and most of them were at the World Engineering Congress held in Tokyo in the autumn of 1929.

In the spring of 1929, Ueno attended the fourth *Comité International de l'Organisation Scientifique* (CIOS) congress in Paris, both as director-general of the National Management Association of Japan and as a representative of the Japan Branch of the Taylor Society. One item of interest at the congress was an historical map submitted by Ueno which showed the development of scientific management (*L'histoire graphique de l'organisation scientifique du travail, 1856–1929*). This map charted the four stages of the movement's development, the names of its major proponents, their publications and their contacts (Saito 1986).

A year later, the Taylor Society of America invited Ueno to lead a party of sixteen Japanese industrialists on a very successful tour of US factories. His next project was the publication of a three-volume comprehensive collection of works by Taylor and on Taylor. Only two volumes were published, however. The third volume, a projected biography of Taylor, was abandoned for financial reasons.

In 1934, Ueno extended his work to include the promotion of efficiency in the distribution/retail sector. Keen to introduce the idea of efficiency into people's lives, both at home and at school, he joined *Kanamoji-kai* (Phonetic Scripts Society), a society aimed at popularizing a simplified version of written Japanese which uses fewer Chinese script symbols. Aware of the implications for clerical and personal efficiency, Ueno also introduced the practice of writing Japanese from left to right.

In 1935, having received a grant from *Nihon Gakujutsu Shinkôkai* (the Japan Society for the Promotion of Learning), Ueno and the staff of the efficiency institute began the task of compiling a management handbook. Ueno wanted to produce a book on scientific management, framed within the Japanese concept, for the Japanese. The whole work was published in three volumes between 1939 and 1941.

Although Ueno enjoyed passing his knowledge and experience in management on to students, he remained largely outside mainstream management education at a higher education level in pre-war Japan, which was heavily influenced by the German tradition based on management economics. He taught at Waseda and Nihon Universities as a part-time lecturer, although from 1943 to 1945 he was professor in charge of the departments of Economics and Management at St Paul's University, Tokyo (now more commonly known as Rikkyô University). Of greater significance was his time at the Yokohama Polytechnical School (today's Kanagawa University), where he became the director of a newly inaugurated department of industrial management in 1939, after some years spent teaching the history of scientific management. The satisfaction Ueno got from contact with students there was an important factor in his decision to establish his own school of efficiency, *Nihon Nôritsu Gakkô*, in 1942.

Ueno's school of industrial efficiency

Ueno first discussed the idea of establishing a school of industrial efficiency in his book *Nôritsu gairon* (An Introduction to Management), published in 1938. In this text, he outlined the basic principles of efficiency as applied to the entire way people live and learn: 'The principle of efficiency is not just the method and technique but it is a philosophy and the way, and beyond learning one must act to disseminate the philosophy' (Saito 1983: 104).

In addition to being a writer and consultant, Ueno became directly involved in establishing his own teaching organization. The first stage of this development was the establishment of *Nôritsu dôjô* (the Efficiency Training Centre). This was underpinned by Ueno's emerging 'philosophy of efficiency', which rested on the five elements of: the right food, the right posture, learning without prejudice, the right belief and the right use of language. Followers of Ueno's efficiency activities in the Kyoto/Osaka region started several study circles called *Ochibo-kai* (the Society of Fallen Ears of Rice). The movement spread to Tokyo and Hakata in 1941. Based on this experience, Ueno opened a school in 1942, but it had to be closed the following year because of the Second World War.

In 1947, the Allied Occupation Force invited Ueno to serve on the *ad hoc* personnel committee for the creation of *Jinjiin* (the National Personnel Agency) and the civil service personnel structure. His post was equivalent to that of a cabinet minister, an unusual appointment for a person not connected with the government. During his four years in this post, he introduced the '*Jinjiin* Supervisory Training' (JST), a training programme for clerical supervisors. It was the 'first training programme made by the Japanese and for the Japanese' (Saito 1983: 124).

In 1948, Ueno published *Nôritsu-gaku genron* (Principles of Management), an original work on his philosophy which brings together the results of his life's work in management. In this book, the notion of three '*mu*', namely *muda* (waste), *muri* (inappropriateness) and *mura* (unevenness) – the avoidance of which is central to efficiency – is presented as an integral part of his philosophy.

While working for the occupation force, Ueno was elected chairman of the All-Japan Federation of Management Associations, which replaced the war-time association. He also played an important role in establishing the Japan Association of Management Consultants, which gave official recognition to management consultants' professional status in 1951.

Ueno's school, when it reopened in 1947, became a vocational school catering for the needs of adults through evening classes. In 1950, it obtained two-year junior college status, offering production and clerical efficiency programmes. In 1953, it introduced correspondence courses in four subjects, becoming Japan's only higher education institution providing working adults with part-time management education. After completing his tenure as a bureaucrat, Ueno devoted his remaining years to the development of the college *Sangyô Nôritsu Tanki Daigaku* (the Industrial Efficiency Junior College).

Ueno published over 100 books, particularly in the area of scientific management. Another area of publishing that was important to him as a communicator was his editorship of a succession of journals and the numerous articles he contributed to those publications. Starting with *Shinri kenkyû* (The Study of Psychology), he went on to become involved in the publication of *Nôritsu Kenkyû* (Efficiency Review) by the Japan Efficiency Study Group from 1923 to 1927, followed by *Sangyô Nôritsu* (Industrial Efficiency), published by the National Management Association from 1927 onwards. These journals had a more public character than his previous work. In 1935, Ueno began publishing his own house journal, *Ochibo* (The Fallen Ears of Rice), which was renamed *Nôritsudô* (The Way of Efficiency) in 1942 and ran until his death. Through these journals, he communicated his experiences in consultancy work, introduced works of efficiency scholars from the USA and elsewhere and propounded his own philosophical views and educational ideas for the furtherance of scientific management.

Ueno's enthusiasm for the promotion of industrial efficiency never waned. He represented Japan at the tenth CIOS congress in São Paulo, Brazil, in 1954. A year later, he travelled to India and Thailand as adviser on flood prevention and other matters for the Economic Commission for Asia and the Far East. Towards the end of his life, he worked on a book about creativity, which was published a month after his death. The evening before his death from heart failure, Ueno was teaching at his college (see MANAGEMENT EDUCATION IN JAPAN).

3 Evaluation

Although he was not the first person to introduce Taylor's theories of scientific management to Japan (Greenwood and Ross 1982), within his own country, Ueno was probably the person who best understood what Taylorism truly stood for. Certainly, he worked steadfastly and passionately throughout his life to promote scientific management, which was encapsulated in the notion and practice of industrial efficiency. While mainstream Japanese management academics were concerned essentially with the textual interpretation of the German school of management economics represented by Nicklisch (Saito 1986), Ueno played a leading role in spreading the American concept of 'efficiency' by applying at a practical level.

Perhaps, because it was in the pioneering stage, Ueno's work, although highly successful, began with small companies and did not involve large and heavy engineering concerns. Large companies tended to introduce 'Taylorist' practices through the mediation of their own trained industrial engineers, often in piecemeal fashion, with the result that their understanding of the principles of scientific management was often incomplete. Large companies were also suspicious of consultants such as Ueno, outsiders who offered their 'advisory' services for a pecuniary return, as it was customary for such 'non-concrete' expertise to be offered free of charge in Japan in the 1920s and 1930s (Saito 1983). Nevertheless, Ueno contributed enormously to raising the business community's concern for efficiency, by organizing the fragmented regional societies for the promotion of efficiency into a national-level organization.

A considerable part of Ueno's contribution to Japanese management was in the area of international exchange. Through the establishment of the Japan branch of the Taylor Society of the USA, he was able to organize an industrial mission to the USA and invite prominent disciples of Taylor (who were also Ueno's personal friends) to Japan to give talks to Japanese businessmen. Ueno was an active participant in international conferences on scientific management, raising the profile of Japanese management internationally.

Ueno's influence on efficiency activities at a national level waned from the early 1930s, when Japan was dominated increasingly by the military. This loss of influence was occasioned probably by his close association with the USA as well as by his lack of political adroitness (Saito 1983). However, the fertility of Ueno's mind was such that he continued to extend the notion of efficiency beyond the manufacturing sector, to advertizing, retailing, the service industry and clerical work, promoting it through his writing and consultancy. There is no doubt that his work

prepared Japanese businesses for the promotion of productivity in the early 1950s.

Ueno's death in 1957 occurred just as enthusiasm for new management techniques gripped Japanese managers (Okazaki-Ward 1993). Industry was in the process of large-scale capital investment into new technology imported mainly from the USA. A flood of new American management ideas and techniques was to enter Japan, to be seized upon by managers and management academics. Many American management experts were invited to Japan to give lectures, and hundreds of industrial missions were sent to the USA. It is hard to ignore the role played by the tradition of the Taylorist management practices, established in the prewar Japan by people like Ueno, in providing a receptive climate for new American management ideas after the Second World War. However, because Ueno's work was concerned with the practical aspects of industrial management, his pioneering contribution to management in Japan is not properly appreciated by the academic community (Saito 1983).

Ueno never was a mere mouthpiece for Taylor's theory, nor was he a simple follower of the practitioners of scientific management in the USA. He stood equal to them in stature, and continued to evolve the practice of scientific management by incorporating the Japanese approach, not only to work but to the way of living, to create a unique synthesis. Once, he debated the possibility of such an approach to management being exported back to the USA (Saito 1983), presaging the worldwide interest which the so-called Japanese-style of management created in the 1980s.

4 Conclusion

As an early advocate and interpreter of American scientific management, Ueno worked tirelessly for its adoption into Japanese industrial culture. It was in recognition of this fact that he was given the title 'the Father of Industrial Efficiency' in Japan and also called 'Benefactor to the Efficiency Movement'. His work is carried on by his son, Ichirô Ueno, through the Sannô Institute of

Business Administration, a unique educational organization that integrates undergraduate education in management, business education for adults and consultancy and research.

L.I. OKAZAKI-WARD
CRANFIELD SCHOOL OF MANAGEMENT

Further reading

(References cited in the text marked *)

Araki, T. (1955) *Nôritsu Ichidaiki – Keieikomon 30nen* (Record of a Life in the Efficiency Profession – Thirty Years as a Management Consultant), Tokyo: Nihon Keiei Nôritsu Kenkyûsho. (An account written by one of Ueno's junior colleagues.)

* Greenwood R.G. and Ross, R.H. (1982) 'Early American influence on Japanese management philosophy: the scientific management movement in Japan', in S.M Lee and G. Schwendiman (eds), *Management by Japanese Systems*, New York: Praeger. (Describes the early scientific management movement in Japan, in which Ueno figured prominently.)

* Misawa H. (ed.) (1967) *Ueno Yôichi-den* (Yôichi Ueno, a Biography), Tokyo: Sangyô Nôritsu Junior College Press. (A short biography/autobiography of Ueno, the first half of which is written by him.)

Nihon Nôritsu Kyôkai (ed.) (1982) *Nihon Nôritsu Kyôkai Konsarutingu 40 nen-shi* (The Forty-Year History of Consulting Activities at the Japan Management Association), Tokyo: JMA. (A collection of writings about the JMA's consultancy work, covering the period *c.*1940 to *c.*1980.)

* Okazaki-Ward, L.I. (1993) *Management Education and Training in Japan*, London: Graham and Trotman. (A comprehensive study of how managers are developed in Japan today, with some historical overview.)

Okuda, K. (1985) *Hito to keiei – Nihon keiei kanri-shi kenkyû* (Men and Management – Research into the History of the Development of Scientific Management in Japan), Tokyo: Manejimento-sha. (A detailed history of the development of scientific management in Japan before the Second World War.)

* Saito, T. (1983) *Ueno Yôichi – Hito to gyôseki* (Yôichi Ueno – The Man and his Achievements), Tokyo: Sangyô Nôritsu University Press. (A work published to commemorate the centenary of Ueno's birth; includes full biographical details.)

* Saito T. (1986) *Ueno Yôichi to keieigaku no paionia* (Yôichi Ueno and the Pioneers of Management), Tokyo: Sangyô Nôritsu University Press. (A collection of documents and correspondence relating to Ueno and his colleagues in the scientific management movement, interspersed with the author's comments.)

* Taylor. F.W. (1911) *The Principles of Scientific Management*, New York: W.W. Norton & Co. Inc. (Taylor's exposition of his views which is widely regarded as a classic of management theory.)

Ueno, Y. (1914) *Shinrigaku tsûgi* (Introduction to Psychology), Tokyo: Dainihon Tokyo. (Comprehensive textbook written for students of teacher training. First to apply psychology to education.)

* Ueno, Y. (1919) *Hito oyobi jigyô nôritsu no shinri* (Psychology of Efficiency of People and Business), Tokyo: Dôbunkan. (The first half covers the effect of an individual's personal characteristics upon efficiency, while the second deals with topics such as scientific management.)

Ueno, Y. (1928) *Jigyô tôseiron* (Control of Enterprise), Tokyo: Dôbunkan. (Ueno advocates the practical application to Japanese business of the concept of planning and control which lies at the root of scientific management.)

Ueno, Y. (1929) *Sangyô nôritsu-ron* (Industrial Management), Tokyo: Chikura Shobô. (Comprehensive work on the theory and practice of management which incorporates practical wisdom distilled from Ueno's consultancy work.)

* Ueno, Y. (1938) *Nôritsu gairon* (An Introduction to Management), Tokyo: Dôbunkan. (Argues that the principle of efficiency must extend to all areas of human life, not simply factories and other organizations. Advocates the need to view efficiency as a philosophical principle which offers guiding precepts for behaviour.)

Ueno, Y. (1939–41) *Nôritsu handobukku* (Management Handbook), Tokyo: Dôbunkan. (Three-volume text designed to fulfil the need for a comprehensive handbook on scientific management written in Japanese, for the Japanese, based on the actual situation in Japan.)

* Ueno, Y. (1948) *Nôritsu-gaku genron* (Principles of Management), Tokyo: Nihon Nôritsu Gakkô. (Summarizing Ueno's life works on efficiency, this comes in two parts: the first dealing with the theory of management and the second with the history of industrial development and that of scientific management.)

Urwick, L.F. (1984) 'Yoichi Ueno', in L.F. Urwick and W.B. Wolf (eds), *The Golden Book of Management*, New York: American Management Association. (A collection of short biographies of 106 major international figures in management; Ueno is one of seven Japanese pioneers in management included in the collection.)

See also: HUMAN RELATIONS; JAPANIZATION; ORGANIZATION BEHAVIOUR; TAYLOR, F.W.; TOTAL QUALITY MANAGEMENT

Related topics in the IEBM: BUSINESS HISTORY, JAPANESE; ECONOMY OF JAPAN; FUKUZAWA, Y.; JUST-IN-TIME PHILOSOPHIES; MANAGEMENT EDUCATION IN JAPAN; MANAGEMENT IN JAPAN; MANAGEMENT IN PACIFIC ASIA; ORGANIZATION BEHAVIOUR, HISTORY OF

Index